# MILLER AND LEA'S GUIDE TO THE COASTAL MARINE FISHES OF CALIFORNIA

## SECOND EDITION

Revised and edited by
MILTON S. LOVE
JULIANNE KALMAN PASSARELLI

Cabrillo Marine Aquarium

UNIVERSITY OF CALIFORNIA
Agriculture and Natural Resources

PUBLICATION 3556

This printing is made possible by a collaboration between the Cabrillo Marine Aquarium and University of California Agriculture and Natural Resources.

To order or obtain UC ANR publications and other products, visit the UC ANR catalog at anrcatalog.ucanr.edu or call 1-800-994-8849. Direct inquiries to:

UC Agriculture and Natural Resources
Publications
2801 Second Street
Davis, CA 95618
Telephone 1-800-994-8849
E-mail: anrcatalog@ucanr.edu



Second edition, 2020. First edition, 1976, was published as Publication 4065.

**Publication 3556**
ISBN-13: 978-1-62711-125-6

**Library of Congress Cataloging-in-Publication Data**

Names: Miller, Daniel J., author. | Love, Milton S., editor. | Passarelli, Julianne Kalman, 1973- editor.
Title: Miller and Lea's guide to the coastal marine fishes of California / revised and edited by Milton S. Love, Julianne Kalman Passarelli.
Other titles: Guide to the coastal marine fishes of California
Description: Second edition. | Davis, CA : University of California Agriculture and Natural Resources, 2020. | Series: Publication ; 3556 | First edition, 1976, was published as Publication 4065. | Includes bibliographical references and index. |
Identifiers: LCCN 2019046833 | ISBN 9781627111256 (paperback)
Subjects: LCSH: Marine fishes--California--Identification.
Classification: LCC QL628.C2 M53 2020 | DDC 597.17709794--dc23
LC record available at https://lccn.loc.gov/2019046833



1.5m-reprint 4-23-LR/WS

Citation for this publication:
Love, M. S., and J. K. Passarelli. 2020. Miller and Lea's guide to the coastal marine fishes of California, 2nd ed. Davis: UC Agriculture and Natural Resources Publication 3556.

# TABLE OF CONTENTS

# ABSTRACT

This is a comprehensive identification guide encompassing all shallow water marine fishes within California waters. The goal of this second edition remains the same as that of the first: to assist in the identification of the nearshore marine fishes of California. To that end, this new version has a similar layout, typeface, and font and virtually all of the species found in the first edition are present here.

Since 1972, there has been a vast expansion of both fish collections and observations off California by both fishermen (of all kinds) and by researchers. Thus, the number of fish species that are now somewhat routinely encountered has grown substantially. In response, and to help ensure that this edition is useful to as wide a range of potential users as possible, we have taken some liberties with the term "nearshore." In this instance, the universe that we have created contains the following parameters: 1) the fish has been taken or observed either in California waters or very near to them; 2) benthic-oriented species must come into waters as shallow as 500 m (1,640 ft); and 3) a species must dwell within 40 km (25 mi) of the California coastline.

In all, 753 species are described. A few of these have not been recorded or confirmed as occurring in California waters but are included since they are apt to appear in the waters in the future. A dichotomous key to 195 families includes an outline figure of a representative of each family. Keys are presented for all families with four or more species. Diagnostic features are pointed out on most of the figures. Illustrations are presented for all but a few species.

If available, geographic range limits, maximum size, depth range, a brief color description, and some meristic counts are given. Body proportions and shapes are used in the keys and a statement concerning the rarity or commonness in California is given for each species. An illustrated glossary is included to facilitate use of the identification keys and species descriptions.

# MILLER AND LEA'S GUIDE TO THE COASTAL MARINE FISHES OF CALIFORNIA

## PREFACE AND SOMETHING OF A CANDID ADMISSION

It is difficult to remember what California marine fish field biology was like before the 1972 *Guide to the Coastal Marine Fishes of California*, Fish Bulletin Number 157, was published by the California Department of Fish and Game (now Wildlife). A biologist attempting to determine what fish species was at hand had some resources, of course, with books including D. S. Jordan and B. Evermann's (1896–1900) *The Fishes of North and Middle America*, P. Barnhart's (1936) *Marine Fishes of Southern California*, L. Walford's (1937) *Marine Game Fishes of the Pacific Coast from Alaska to the Equator*, and P. Roedel's (1953) *Common Ocean Fishes of the California Coast*. However, even taken in the aggregate, all of these publications were dated, incomplete, or difficult to use. This was particularly true because none contained keys, that most efficient way of determining the identity of an organism. Publications that did include keys, such as J. B. Phillips' (1957) *A Review of the Rockfishes of California*, tended to focus on one group of fishes, thus necessitating that a researcher create a whole notebook of almost random fish keys of greater or lesser efficacy.

Thus, the first edition of Dan Miller and Bob Lea's field guide was an inspiration to several generations of both working and aspiring California fish biologists. It was the reference turned to when a trawl haul yielded something unexpected. It was the reference kept close to hand by decades of students in ichthyology classes. And it was the reference used in hundreds of research papers by those wanting to establish a certain street cred regarding their knowledge of the basic facts about a fish species. No fish biologist worthy of the name had an unmarked copy. In fact, one might say it was a badge of honor to have the most beaten up, pulped, and horribly defaced copy — by implication the result of endless thumbing by slime-covered fingers.

But science marches on and, inevitably, our copies became crowded with a venation of spider web-like notes — updates necessitated by new records of range, depth, or size or improved ways of identifying a species. And, indeed, there reached a point when "Miller and Lea" became sufficiently dated that it often sat on bookcase shelves rather than out on the deck of a heaving research vessel.

And thus was born the decision to create a new edition, although we are the first to admit that this effort feels to us somewhat like tampering with holy writ. We did not reach this decision quickly or lightly, as we wished to produce a work that, while updated, of course, kept intact the flavor, intent, and integrity of the original. We apologize in advance if your favorite drawing has been replaced by a newer version, and we feel your pain when you search in vain for that page you always liked that illustrated your five favorite jacks. Please know that our goal was not to add discomfiture to your lives, but rather to burnish the luster that is Fish Bulletin Number 157.

A word about this edition's new title. We made the decision to change the name of this guide to more accurately and permanently reflect the great contributions Dan Miller and Bob Lea made to this field. We believe that over the years the authorship of new editions may change but that the role that Dan Miller and Bob Lea played in creating this most useful field guide will not.

Milton S. Love, Ph.D.
University of California, Santa Barbara

Julianne Kalman Passarelli, Ph.D.
Cabrillo Marine Aquarium

# DAN MILLER REFLECTS

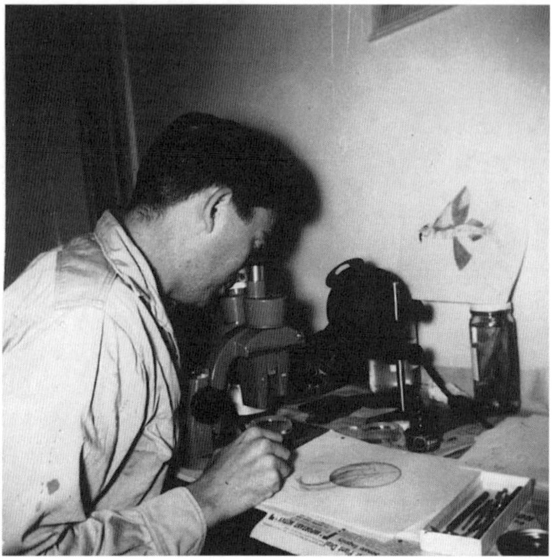

1925–2012

*"The photo at the table is Dan drawing the fish for his book. That was pretty much where he was every evening for about a year and a half. I was a teenager, so he occasionally glanced up to greet one or more of my teenage friends, who were typically in various states of altered consciousness. For most of them, all they remember of my Dad was him drawing fish. The only thing missing from that picture is our cat, who needed to sit on every new drawing that Dan started."*

*–Scott Miller*

*Shortly before he died in 2012, we asked Dan Miller to tell us how the first edition came to be.*

The genesis of the first edition of *Guide to the Coastal Marine Fishes of California* (referred to herein as the *Guide*) had several roots.

I was a biologist for the State Department of Fish and Game [now the California Department of Fish and Wildlife] for 34 years. With my training in Wildlife Conservation under Dr. Aldo Starker Leopold at UC Berkeley, I became highly knowledgeable of the coastal marine fishes and mammals from Washington into Baja California. In any new study, the first thing to do is to research the scientific literature on the many species living in the animal and plant communities in the study area.

Another element was the struggle to set up and maintain needed research on the funding available from both the state and federal governments. Dr. Leopold gave me a hint of how life was when in 1943 he asked his students in pre-course interviews "Do you want to get rich?" My answer was "no," knowing it was rare to do so in that kind of work in those days. Later on, like most other state employees, I often voluntarily continued work for short periods on a day's work without pay. This was to play a role in the completion of the *Guide*.

The lack of a comprehensive field guide to California marine fishes was immediately apparent when I (along with Dan Gotshall) started the work that became *Ocean Sportfish Catch and Effort* from Oregon to Point Arguello, California, July 1, 1957 – June 30, 1961 (California Department of Fish and Game, Fish Bulletin 130, 1965). When we started that work, most of the identification of marine fishes of California were not in guides but scattered in various publications or made by instructors for their college classes. It was very difficult to train new samplers to cover increasing fishing effort and new technology. In many projects a fisheries guide was becoming necessary.

I suggested to the officials [at the California Department of Fish and Game (eds.)] that myself and my new project partner, taxonomist Robert N. Lea, write an identification guide for the known coastal marine fishes in California. When asked what the price would be, I could not relate that until I had an estimate of what the drawings would cost. Many of the drawings had to show ratios of parts of a species' body and accurate drawings of morphological characters had to be made from photographs. Getting the pictures of the fishes was possible by us, but not the drawings.

To determine the cost of producing the *Guide*, I asked an artist who drew such figures to draw three fishes and found that the cost of such drawings would not be possible with our funding. Using those examples and getting more information of drawing techniques, I decided to do them myself, if I could, but without pay. I am a Great Depression child (born 1925) who stood in lines for food and clothes and highly respected the U.S. government under Roosevelt, and ever since I have felt that it was a privilege to do such voluntary work for the state or the U.S. government. I was very pleased how my life evolved because of that feeling.

I had enough funds in the project to pay several temporary workers to make pictures of the fish to be the size for my original drawings that would then be reduced to the size for the *Guide*. I made the drawings in my home during many evenings for a year and a half. I then sent the text and figure notations to the state printer, who sent them back on sticky notes for me to cut and make the final layout ready for printing. My associate Bob Lea and I also had funding to visit the major fish collections through the state for range extensions and other features we ran into. We had the full cooperation of the collection taxonomists. The DF&G Chief Editor was Herbert W. Frey, with DF&G Associate Editors' Librarian Patricia Powell and Marine Resources head Doyle E. Gates.

The first printing of the *Guide* was in 1972 by the State Department of Fish and Game as Fish Bulletin 157, and in 1976 it was printed by the Division of Agricultural Sciences of the University of California, with an addendum.

Daniel J. Miller

Daniel J. Miller
July 16, 2012

## SUMMARY FROM BOB LEA

My involvement with the *Guide to the Coastal Marine Fishes of California* dates from approximately 1969, when Dan Miller asked if I would like to join him in producing a field guide to all nearshore fishes known to occur in the marine waters of California. Prior to joining the Department of Fish and Game in 1967, I had just finished a semester at sea with Stanford University on the research schooner Te Vega, with Drs. Rolf L. Bolin and N. B. Marshall. My project was to assess the meso- and bathypelagic fishes that were collected by opening–closing midwater trawl. Prior to the Te Vega experience, as a graduate student at University of California, Berkeley, I worked as a research assistant at the California Academy of Sciences, Department of Ichthyology. Dan saw this background as a means to fulfilling his primary mission.

What do I remember regarding our experiences in the preparation of the *Guide*? Much of that early work is a faded memory, but what I recall most faithfully are the trips to the various California fish collections: California Academy of Sciences, University of California at Los Angeles, Los Angeles County Museum of Natural History, and Scripps Institution of Oceanography. Although both Dan and I considered ourselves as field biologists, much of our work relating to the completion of the *Guide* was museum based.

Museum collections have changed dramatically since our work in the 1970s, but the one aspect that has remained constant are the specimens and associated collection data. Unusual specimens and records require confirmation. Incorrect identifications are not uncommon in many collections and, if questionable, validation is required. This consideration is occasionally overlooked, and erroneous information once imbedded in the literature can easily be perpetuated and is often extremely difficult to correct. Correspondence with colleagues and other researchers was by normal mail (considerably before email), and data bases were not online at that time, so all specimens needed to be checked. For species that were on shelves, this was tedious but not impossible. At that time the Department had files with good basic information on many of California's game fishes. We corresponded frequently with co-workers John E. Fitch and Julius B. Phillips; Fitch was an authority on eastern North Pacific fishes and Phillips was renowned for his work on the family Scorpaenidae, principally rockfishes. Digital photography and videography were not yet in use and have since proven to be of tremendous value in documenting species identification and aspects of behavior.

An additional aspect of our research was the relationships that were developed with colleagues during our visits to the natural history museums, a number of which have continued to this day. The professional relationships we fostered following the publication of Fish Bulletin 157 are far too numerous to list. However, those realized during the years of production I discuss below. We worked quite closely with associates at the California Academy of Sciences, Department of Ichthyology, and considered the Academy as our home institution since it was by far the nearest to our offices in Monterey. William Eschmeyer had just filled the position of Curator of Fishes and was occupied with the incorporation of the Stanford University fish collection to the Academy. Tomio Iwamoto and Pearl Sonoda were soon to join the Department of Ichthyology. I had worked there as a research assistant while at UC Berkeley under the direction of William I. Follett and Lillian J. Dempster, so those friendships were very meaningful. The above associates were extremely helpful in our quests regarding California fishes and in the location of specimens and related collection information. At that time, the old Academy was still intact, a beautiful building of classic architecture, and the fish collection was immediately accessible from the offices and general work area. That structure is now replaced by a new "green building" of sustainable architecture containing the Steinhart Aquarium, planetarium, rainforest, natural history displays, and modern department working areas and preparation facilities.

We made several trips to the three major collections in southern California: the University of California at Los Angeles collection, and the Los Angeles County Museum of Natural History (LACM), and Scripps Institution of Oceanography (SIO) in La Jolla. The UCLA collection was overseen by Dr. Boyd Walker with assistance from John Bleck and was primarily represented by specimens collected by Walker's ichthyology classes, mainly from southern and central California and the Sea of Cortez. This collection is now in part at LACM, with the majority recently incorporated into the SIO Marine Vertebrates Collection.

My memories are somewhat vague regarding our time at UCLA, other than the collection being extremely well organized and divided into a main research-teaching collection and a selected number of specimens that Walker set aside for his ongoing research that were not fully available. Our visits to the Los Angeles County Museum of Natural History paralleled our association at the California Academy. I had worked in Sea Survey at the Department's Marine headquarters in Terminal Island and Long Beach in my first years with DF&G prior to moving to Monterey. Sea surveys' coverage was from the Oregon-California border to Magdalena Bay in southern Baja California, and during that 2-year period I had made numerous collections, which were deposited at LACM. In addition, I participated in a LACM collecting trip to Cocos Island and had been appointed as a Research Associate in the Section of Fishes. We had excellent working relationships with Robert Lavenberg and Camm Swift, the curators of fishes at that time, and essentially complete access to the facilities and collection. The LACM collection was extensive in terms of world representation with southern California fishes and eastern Pacific fishes, including mesopelagic collections, being especially well represented.

Our visits to Scripps Institution of Oceanography were especially informative, as much for the association we developed with Drs. Carl L. Hubbs and Richard H. Rosenblatt. The collection was in large part a reflection of Hubb's penchant for collecting and was especially well represented by California, outer Baja California, and Sea of Cortez fishes. The SIO collection in the early 1970s was in Ritter Hall and extremely crowded; however, it now resides in Vaughn Hall with adequate space and excellent research facilities. These three major institutions (CAS, LACM, and SIO) are all considered as world-class natural history resources.

Fish Bulletin 157 has provided students, marine biologists, and ecologists a means for identifying California marine fishes since 1972, with a revised version in 1976. The contents, although valuable, are badly outdated and in need of new records since 1976, as well as current information on size, distribution, and meristic values. There has been a wealth of new information since, which is mainly a reflection of the increase in activity in college and university ichthyology and marine ecology classes. Changes in oceanographic conditions since the 1980s have also contributed to a number of new records to California's ichthyofauna.

I have received several of the family and species accounts for perusal and comment; what I have seen has been impressive. It is my feeling the new contribution will be well received by the current generation of users. I look forward to seeing it in publication and having a copy for my personal library.

Robert N. Lea

Robert N. Lea
June 7, 2018

## ACKNOWLEDGMENTS TO THE SECOND EDITION

This book would not have been possible without the enormous support of Mike Schaadt, director emeritus of the Cabrillo Marine Aquarium (CMA). In addition, Leonardo Alannis, CMA, and Rick Feeney, Natural History Museum of Los Angeles County (LACM), were crucial to the successful completion of this revision. Many thanks to Danny Tang, Orange County Sanitation District (OCSD), for his valuable feedback. Special thanks to Dan Miller and Bob Lea for their support of this revision.

Editing: The Southern California Association of Ichthyological Taxonomists and Ecologists (SCAITE) was essential in the testing of the dichotomous keys and editing of the book. Specifically, Craig Campbell, City of Los Angeles, LA Sanitation & Environment (CLA, LASAN); Dario W. Diehl, Southern California Coastal Water Research Project (SCCWRP); Rick Feeney, LACM; Robin Gartman, City of San Diego (CSD); Pete Major, Major Management; Jim Mann, Aquatic Bioassay and Consulting Laboratories, Inc.; Michael J. Mengel OCSD, retired; Terra Petry, Los Angeles County Sanitation Districts (LACSD); Bill Power, LACSD; James M. Rounds, CLA, LASAN, retired; Fred Stern, LACSD, retired; and Jonathan P. Williams, Vantuna Research Group, Occidental College. Thanks to M. James Allen for the inspiration that is now SCAITE.

Drawings and layout: New drawings were made mostly by Leonardo Alannis, Laurel Mundy, and Atsuhiro Kubo. Peter Moyle, Chris Van Dyck, Camm Swift, and Paul Vecsi agreed to the use of images from Moyle (2002). Leonardo Alannis did the final layout of the revision.

Keys: Credit for each key is designated within the text according to the changes made compared to the first edition. Designations include: "Edited by" (the author changed existing key text, but no species were added or removed); "Revised by" (the author added or removed one or more species to the existing key); "Created by" (the author contributed a new key, not occurring in M&L (1972)); and "Translated by" (the author translated a key from the literature).

Authors of the dichotomous keys:
Eric Anderson, South African Institute for Aquatic Biodiversity
Donald G. Buth, University of California, Los Angeles
Peter Davison, Scripps Institution of Oceanography
Dario W. Diehl, Southern California Coastal Water Research Project
David Ebert, Moss Landing Marine Laboratories
Rick Feeney, Natural History Museum of Los Angeles County
Kristy Forsgren, California State University, Fullerton
F. Javier Gago, Glendale Community College
Kathy Hieb, California Department of Fish and Wildlife
Tomio Iwamoto, California Academy of Sciences
Daniel J. Kamikawa, National Oceanic and Atmospheric Administration
Cynthia Klepadlo, Scripps Institution of Oceanography
Milton S. Love, University of California, Santa Barbara
James W. Orr, National Oceanic and Atmospheric Administration
Bruno Passarelli, Saddleback College
Julianne Kalman Passarelli, Cabrillo Marine Aquarium
Terra Petry, Los Angeles County Sanitation Districts
Theodore W. Pietsch, University of Washington
Daniel J. Pondella II, Vantuna Research Group, Occidental College
Bill Power, Los Angeles County Sanitation Districts
Kurt Schaefer, Inter-American Tropical Tuna Commission
Fred Stern, Los Angeles County Sanitation Districts, retired
Camm C. Swift, Natural History Museum of Los Angeles County, retired
H.J. Walker Jr., Scripps Institution of Oceanography, retired
Jonathan P. Williams, Vantuna Research Group, Occidental College

## ACKNOWLEDGMENTS TO THE SECOND EDITION (continued)

Funding: Thanks to Friends of Cabrillo Marine Aquarium. Contributions were from Orange County Sanitation District; Pete Major; Port of Los Angeles; American Institute of Fishery Research Biologists–Northern and Southern; CSU Council on Ocean Affairs, Science & Technology; American Fisheries Society, California-Nevada Chapter; The Bay Foundation; Los Angeles County Sanitation Districts; Ecomarine Consulting LLC; ECORP Consulting, Inc.; City of Los Angeles, Environmental Monitoring Division; Merkel and Associates; Tenera Environmental; Mike Horn, California State University, Fullerton; Ed Mastro; Ann Scarborough Bull; Robin Gartman; and Bill Power.

FRIENDS OF CABRILLO MARINE AQUARIUM

In-kind donations:

## ACKNOWLEDGMENTS TO THE SECOND EDITION (continued)

Other contributions: The following were also involved in testing of the dichotomous keys and final edits, Donald G. Buth, UCLA; Wayne Dossett, MBC Aquatic Sciences (MBC); Bill Furlong, LACSD; Danny Heilprin, ManTech International, formerly with Tenera Environmental; Erica Jarvis Mason, Scripps Institution of Oceanography (SIO), formerly with California Department of Fish and Wildlife (CDFW); Brianna Jones, Aquatic Bioassay and Consulting Laboratories, Inc.; Cody Larsen, CLA, LASAN; Karen Martin, Pepperdine University; Eric Miller, formerly with MBC; Gabriel Rodriguez, CSD; Milinda Thompson, CMA; Brian White, Department of Water and Power, retired; Alfonso Montiel, CMA; Calvin Won, CMA; Larry Allen, California State University, Northridge (CSUN); Delci Primous, CSD; and Chris Lowe, California State University, Long Beach (CSULB).

In addition, Ed Mastro, CMA, began the layout specifications. We thank Katie Perry and Paul Hamdorf, CDFW, for their support. Also, thanks to Jeff Armstrong, OCSD, for his contribution and Bruno Passarelli for his support. Jeff Landesman, CMA, provided comments and edited keys. Shelly Moore, SCCWRP, helped with database content and quality control. Thanks to Margaret Neighbors, LACM, for editing and reviewing keys. Katherine Maslenikov, Burke Museum, provided specimens, data, and took photographs. Also James W. Orr, NOAA, Jerry Hoff, NOAA, and Morgan Busby, NOAA, went through the snailfish key. John Snow and Schoen Acheson provided a number of images and lots of data. Krista Fahy, SBMNH, supplied specimens for verification. Dave Ebert, Moss Landing Marine Laboratories, provided skate information. Robert Humphreys provided armorhead information. Daniel Gharrett provided an image of *Inopsetta*. Rick Feeney, LACM, Christine Thacker, LACM, retired, Dave Catania, CAS, Peter Moyle, UC Davis, Ted Pietsch, University of Washington, and Chris Van Dyck provided many images and valuable information. Dave Catania, CAS, checked specimens and helped with scans of figures. We thank Catherine Mecklenburg for providing us with data on Arctic fishes. James Fong, CAS, scanned images from Follett and Anderson (1990). Linda Kuntz, MBARI, helped with the range and depths extension data for a number of species. Ken Jones provided photos. Lonny Lundsten, MBARI, helped with range extensions. Ralph Lampman helped with lamprey differentiation. Daniel Garrett provided a photograph of the hybrid sole, *Inopsetta ischrya*. Thanks to Matthew Knope, University of Hawai'i, Hilo, Eli Cytrynbaum, Steve Moffit, Alaska Department of Fish and Game (ADFG), Leon Shaul, ADFG, Pat Malecha, NOAA Alaska Fisheries Science Center, and Joe Orsi, NOAA Fisheries Auke Bay Laboratories. Carlos Bustamante Diaz supplied photographs of *Hydrolagus melanophasma*. Daniel Conley, SIO, took pictures of clingfishes. We thank Ramona Swenson, AFS, for her partnership and support. Thanks to Paula Moore for her support during the initial stages of the revision. James Gawley, formerly with CMA, scanned images. Thanks to Laura Tocki-Toggenburger, Monterey Bay Aquarium. Joe Bizzarro, NOAA, reviewed the elasmobranch section and also provided substantial insights regarding the depth and geographic ranges of Pacific Coast groundfishes. We thank Curtis Cash, CLA, LASAN, for his support. Thanks to H. J. Walker, Jr., SIO, for supplying specimens and his feedback. Also, thanks to Ben Frable, SIO, for his valuable insight.

Thank you to M. James Allen for his tremendous contribution to the field of Ichthyology. He will be sorely missed.

# ACKNOWLEDGMENTS TO THE FIRST EDITION

This guide has been made possible through the works and studies of hundreds of fishery researchers and taxonomists, past and present. We cannot thank those of the past whose immortality lies in libraries, but we can credit most of those who have personally aided us. Unfortunately, space does not permit us to fully credit all that has been received from each contributor or to mention all who have helped us.

First, we extend credit to fellow Department colleagues. The meticulously recorded data on range limits, depth, and sizes of California marine fishes offered to us by John Fitch has been of primary importance. John also gave taxonomic advice, offered information on identification, and stimulated us to conduct the museum search for geographic and depth range limit extensions. Dan Gotshall and John Geibel had originally planned to collaborate on this publication but their heavy work loads precluded full collaboration. Dan Gotshall was able to assist in preparing the sections on the eelpouts, poachers, and pricklebacks; and John Geibel assisted in preparing the section on scombrids and printing photographs of some of the fish drawings. Dick Nitsos and Dick Parrish supplied data on depth of bottomfishes, and Paul Gregory and Jack Schott supplied pictures on which some of the fish drawings are based. Dan Collier and his wife Cynthia made photographic prints of most of the fish drawings. Jim Houk spent many hours in the museums searching bottles for pertinent data and helped in the literature search. Bill Craig and Dick Burge supplied information on ranges, and Pat Powell and the library staff aided in supplying literature and editing the reference section. Nancy Durell and Margaret Hughes typed the manuscript. Herb Frey edited the entire manuscript, and Harold Orcutt offered encouragement and suggestions to undertake this project.

Many fish researchers and taxonomists have given us aid. Geographically, from north to south, we wish to extend our thanks to the following for their suggestions and information so generously offered: Jay C. Quast, National Marine Fish. Service, Auke Bay, Alaska; Sigmund J. Westrheim, Fisheries Research Board of Canada, Nanaimo, B.C.; John L. Hart, Fisheries Research Board of Canada, St. Andrews, N.B.; Alex E. Peden, British Columbia Provincial Museum, Victoria, B.C.; William G. Pearcy, Oregon State University, Corvallis, Ore.; W. I. Follett and Earl S. Herald, California Academy of Sciences, San Francisco; Leonard J. V. Compagno, Systematic Zoology Dept., Stanford University; John S. Stephens, Occidental College, Los Angeles; Boyd W. Walker, University of California at Los Angeles; Robert J. Lavenberg and Camm Swift, Los Angeles County Museum of Natural History; Shelly R. Johnson, University of Southern California; Elbert H. Ahlstrom, National Marine Fisheries Service, La Jolla; Carl L. Hubbs, Laura Hubbs, Richard H. Rosenblatt, Robert L. Wisner, and Layton P. Taylor, Jr., Scripps Institution of Oceanography; and Lo-Chai Chen, California State University at San Diego.

Museum staff members and curators were most cooperative and helpful. Special thanks must be extended to the sage of reference, grammar, and literature, Lillian J. Dempster, California Academy of Sciences, for her enthusiastic search for descriptions and references. The entire staff of the California Academy of Sciences Ichthyology Department, especially Pearl M. Sonoda and William N. Eschmeyer, made it possible to conduct primary museum work in development and testing identification keys. John Bleck, University of California at Los Angeles, and Joe Copp and Donald Dockins, Scripps Institution of Oceanography, gave us much aid in the museum search for range and size extensions.

To all the above and to those not listed, we offer our sincere gratitude for all the help you have given us.

Daniel J. Miller
Robert N. Lea

# INTRODUCTION TO THE SECOND EDITION

## ABOUT THIS GUIDE

The goal of this second edition remains the same as that of the first: to assist in the identification of the nearshore marine fishes of California. To that end, this new version has a similar layout, typeface, and font, and virtually all of the species found in the first edition are present here. Please note all the information in this guide is current as of May 31, 2019.

Inevitably, of course, there are differences — useful ones we hope. Since 1972, there has been a vast expansion of both fish collections and observations off California's coast by fishermen, divers, and researchers. Thus, the number of fish species that are now somewhat routinely encountered has grown substantially. In response, and to help ensure that this edition is useful to as wide a range of potential users as possible, we have taken some liberties with the term "nearshore." In this instance, the universe that we have created contains the following parameters, with a few exceptions: 1) the fish has been taken or observed either in California waters or very near to them; 2) benthic-oriented species must come into waters as shallow as 500 m (1,640 ft); and 3) a species must dwell within 40 km (25 mi) of the California coastline. This, of course, begs the question of what to do with the myriad of deeper-dwelling midwater fishes, the lanternfishes and dragonfishes for instance, that are found further than 40 km (25 mi) off the coast and live (particularly in their larval stages) at least part time in waters less than 500 m (1,640 ft) deep at night. If all of these were included, this volume would be substantially larger and would be primarily a guide to seldom-seen species. Thus, we have more or less punted on the issue of mesopelagic and bathypelagic species and have opted to include species that we (with help from a range of individuals more expert than us) view as "typical" off California's coast. This will, of course, not please those aficionados of things flabby and bioluminescent who will decry the arbitrariness of it all, but please chalk it up to the exigencies of the situation. Given these parameters, this new edition contains 195 families (up from 144) and 753 species (as compared to 554 species in the first edition); over 200 of these species are new to this edition. Some species, such as the WHITESPOTTED GREENLING, *Hexagrammos stelleri*, DUSKY ROCKFISH, *Sebastes variabilis*, and HARLEQUIN ROCKFISH, *Sebastes variegatus*, have not been reported from California waters. We include these species, however, because they were either included in the first edition and/or occur so close to the border that they will likely be reported in California in the near future. Some of the species in this edition are introduced to California. Fishes are arranged roughly in phylogenetic order. However, due to space limitations, some groups may be out of place.

What else is different? First, many of the original keys have been revised or edited, and for groups lacking keys, new ones were created. When this has occurred, we have given credit to those who have done the revisions or new constructions. In addition, the species accounts tend to be somewhat more detailed in this edition, as we have added more material concerning, 1) a species' geographic range and where it is abundant; 2) body and fin coloration and patterning; and 3) meristics. Please note that, as in the first edition, diagnostic characters are denoted in the illustrations. In practice, this means that any *subtle* differences in the illustrations of similar species that are not indicated in some way *do not* represent diagnostic characters but rather the vagaries of art.

We remind the reader that, first and foremost, this is a *field* guide that is designed to be primarily used on living or freshly dead specimens. It is clear that this was the intent of the original authors, as many critical characters in their keys (the one for rockfishes is a good example) are based on color of freshly captured specimens, a character lost in preserved specimens and often not representative of a species' appearance underwater.

Lastly, we note that some of the fish illustrations in this guide appeared in the first edition. However, a substantial number are new to this version and were created especially for this edition or reprinted from other published sources. Most of the unique illustrations are the work of Leonardo Alannis, Laurel Mundy, and Atsuhiro Kubo and were either drawn from fresh or preserved specimens or were redrawn from previously published works. The credits for every illustration are listed under Drawing Citations (page 373).

# HOW TO USE THE GUIDE

## THE KEYS

A substantial portion of this guide is an accumulation of artificial diagnostic keys based on such features as body shape, proportion, and color, and such "countable" characters as numbers of fin spines, fin soft-rays, gill rakers, lateral line pores, and scales. The term "artificial" refers to a key based on characters not necessarily indicative of taxonomic or phylogenetic relationships. However, many taxonomic characters are skeletal and internal, and depict evolutionary trends from primitive to more specialized or advanced forms. Even though the keys are not based necessarily on evolutionary criteria, the sequence of families is generally in phylogenetic order; i.e., from the primitive hagfishes to highly specialized molas.

The keys work on the principle of an either/or choice using "a" and "b" alternatives. If a fish does not fit the description of "a," go on to "b," etc. In each case where there is a jump to another section of the key, there is a citation of the section from which you were referred, facilitating backtracking through the key. The key to the families is primarily the same as in the first edition, with a few additional families. The original family key was based on information and keys in Jordan and Evermann (1896–1900), Roedel (1953), Schultz (1936), Wilimovsky (1958), and Clemens and Wilby (1961), with additional characters from Berg (1940). Terminology of key characters is given in the glossary and illustrated glossary.

In general, most of the characters in the keys are external, except for such characters as gill rakers and teeth that can be examined without dissection. At times we have included characters that require length measurements and ratio calculations. For example, a measurable distance (such as BD, body depth) "into" another measurable distance (such as TL, total length) is calculated as TL/BD.

With a few notable exceptions, these are keys to adult individuals. However, in those instances where a juvenile looks very different from the adult, we have included these in the keys along with an illustration (for example WRASSES and PARROTFISH, Family Labridae).

As with the first edition, we have decided to combine relevant and logical families in a single key. For instance, all of the flatfishes, regardless of what family they are in, reside in one key.

Lastly, this is a field guide–we expect you to be staring at a fish that is either alive or at least a reasonable facsimile (i.e., a well-preserved individual) thereof. In practice this means that characters designed to differentiate preserved fishes (e.g., tiny things that need a microscope, intense dissections, and an almost saintly level of patience to observe) are either not included or, on occasion, are relegated to secondary status.

Want to know more about these fine, fine fishes? Of course you do. Check out (or better still, buy) Kells et al. (2016) *A Field Guide to Coastal Fishes from Alaska to California*; Love (2012) *Certainly More Than You Want to Know About the Fishes of the Pacific Coast*; Lamb and Edgell (2010) *Coastal Fishes of the Pacific Northwest*; Allen et al. (2006) *The Ecology of Marine Fishes: California and Adjacent Waters*; and Leet (2001) *California's Living Marine Resources: A Status Report*.

# HOW TO USE THE GUIDE (continued)

## THE SPECIES ACCOUNTS

Along with keys to each species, we also provide a summary of each species' geographic and depth range and maximum length, as well as a brief description of its color and body pattern, and some details of its meristic (countable) characters. Below we give an example of a species account.

**PACIFIC CHUB MACKEREL, *Scomber japonicus* Houttuyn, 1782.** Pacific and Indian Oceans; in western Pacific as far north as Japan, southern Kuril Islands, and southeastern Kamchatka; western Gulf of Alaska to Gulf of California and to Chile, including Islas Galápagos. In western Pacific common from northern Japan to at least Kuril Islands and to the east common as far northward as Vancouver Island (periodically) and common southward into Gulf of California. Length to nearly 63.5 cm (25 in) TL. Coastal pelagic to epi- or mesopelagic; depth: surface and surf zone to about 300 m (984 ft). Head dark blue or green, back green with dark wavy lines, silver-green below. D VIII–XIII + 10–15 + 4–6 finlets; A I–II,10–15 + 4–6 finlets; Pect. 19–22; GR 10–14 + 26–34; Vert. 30–32. (Formerly PACIFIC MACKEREL: M&L) (Alternative name CHUB MACKEREL).

### Names

Each species account begins with common name and scientific name (including describer name(s)) in bold. Note that in circumstances where the genus name has been changed since the original desciption, the describer name(s) will be in parentheses. In most (but not quite all) instances, common and scientific names follow Page et al. (2013).

### Geographic Range

We present the geographic range in the following sequence: 1) general range worldwide (if applicable) and 2) more specific ranges in the western and eastern Pacific, beginning with the western Pacific (if applicable) and running eastwards. Following this is our assessment of the abundance of the species in the western and eastern Pacific based on the categories *common*, *uncommon*, and *rare*. This assessment is somewhat qualitative as it is based not only on how often the species has been taken by recreational and commercial fishermen and by researchers within a geographic region, but also how often it has been observed underwater by scuba divers and by remotely operated vehicles and manned research submersibles. The term "at least" is used for areas with insufficient data.

Geographic range limits not accompanied by a museum number are derived from the literature but are not cited. Institutional acronyms are CAS (California Academy of Sciences); CMA (Cabrillo Marine Aquarium); LACM (Natural History Museum of Los Angeles County); SBMNH (Santa Barbara Museum of Natural History); SIO (Scripps Institution of Oceanography); UAM (University of Alaska Museum of the North); UCLA (University of California, Los Angeles); UW (University of Washington); and VRG (Vantuna Research Group).

### Size

Almost all sizes are given as total length (abbreviated as TL). There are a few exceptions to this rule: 1) We list fork length (FL) or standard length (SL) where published maximum lengths use only these measurements and when we do not have conversion factors allowing these lengths to be converted to total length and 2) we give disc width measurements (DW) for the measurement of rays. Measurements of length and width are given first in metric units and then (in parentheses) in English units.

### Depth Range

We first list the area or zone followed by "depth," which includes the minimum and maximum depth range in meters followed by (feet). Within the depth category there is a difference between "surface" and "0" m. Surface refers to the sea surface, regardless of the depth of the bottom below that surface; 0 m refers to bottom depth and is equivalent to intertidal. Terminology of the pelagic realm is from the first edition and based on Hedgpeth (1957):

| Realm | Meters (m) | Feet (ft) |
|---|---|---|
| Epipelagic | 0–200 | 0–656 |
| Mesopelagic | 200–1,000 | 656–3,280 |
| Bathypelagic | 1,000–4,000 | 3,280–13,120 |

## THE SPECIES ACCOUNTS (continued)

### Description

The description focuses mainly on body color and markings. Many other diagnostic characters are both illustrated and noted in the keys and thus are not repeated in this section. The color description of "mouth cavity" or "gill cavity" refers to the lining of the cavity.

### Counts

Primary sources for counts include the first edition of this guide, along with Moser (1996), Mecklenburg et al. (2002), Nakabo (2002), Ebert (2003), Butler et al. (2012), and the Ichthyoplankton Information System (see References). Counts may include minimum and maximum values for a number of structures including:

### Fin Elements

Fin spines are represented by Roman numerals and fin soft-rays are in Arabic numerals. When there are 2 or 3 dorsal fins, counts are given for each, separated by the + sign. Fin symbols are: D = dorsal fin; A = anal fin; Pect. = pectoral fin; Pelvic = pelvic fin. In the example given in this section, the species has between 8–13 spines in the 1st dorsal fin, and 10–15 soft-rays in the 2nd dorsal fin, followed by 4– 6 finlets. Similarly, the anal fin has 1 or 2 spines and between 10–15 soft-rays followed by 4–6 finlets.

### Lateral Line

Scales on the lateral line are referred to as LLs and pores along the lateral line as LLp. If the lateral line pores continue onto the caudal fin, the count will be divided into those on the body and those on the tail whenever these are differentiated in the literature. For example, KELP PERCH lateral line scales (page 267) are 37–44 on the body and 4–6 on the tail. In certain instances, we have also included a count of scales in midbody along the sides, referred to as midlateral scales.

### Gill Rakers

Abbreviated as GR, counts are always of the anterior rakers on the 1st gill arch. A gill arch is composed of an upper and lower limb. A raker (or rakers) in the junction of these limbs is counted either separately or with the lower limb. When counts of the upper and lower limb are presented separately, the count is given as GR. When only total gill rakers are given (upper and lower limbs combined) the count is given as GRt. Rudimentary rakers are included in all counts to the extent that we were able to determine this from the literature. In the example given in this section, there are 10–14 rakers on the upper limb and 26–34 rakers on the lower limb. Note that in some instances, due to individual variability, the range of total gill rakers will not be equal to the sum of the upper and lower gill rakers. As an example, BIGEYE TUNA raker numbers (page 335) are (upper) 7–13 and (lower) 18–25. However, gill raker total numbers range from 23–31. In addition, members of the family Macrouridae have both inner and outer gill rakers on each gill arch and we present counts from the inner set of the 1st gill arch.

### Vertebrae

Abbreviated as Vert., counts are of all vertebrae including the hypural.

### Former and Alternative Names

The end of the species account may have a former or an alternative common name, one used in the first edition or one still in use. In the example used in this section, the first edition of this guide (in the text we abbreviate it as M&L) used PACIFIC MACKEREL. In some instances, the scientific species, genus, or family name is different from that of the first edition; we have also placed these former names at the end of the account. These names appear in the index.

### Conversions

Feet (ft) = meters (m) × 3.28
Inches (in) = centimeters (cm) ÷ 2.54
Miles (mi) = kilometers (km) × 1.61
Feet (ft) = fathoms × 6
Pounds (lb) = kilograms (kg) × 2.205

# GLOSSARY AND INDEX TO ILLUSTRATED GLOSSARY

NOTE: Figure page numbers on page xix.

ABDOMEN: belly. Figure 1.
ABDOMINAL: (pelvic fin placement). Figure 6a.
ACCESSORY DORSAL BRANCH: ADB, additional branch from lateral line, e.g., flatfishes.
ADB: accessory dorsal branch of lateral line, e.g., flatfishes.
ADHERENT: (scales) not easily shed or rubbed off.
ADIPOSE: soft, fleshy fin. Figure 9l.
ALAR: (thorns). Figure 17.
ANADROMOUS: fishes that spawn in freshwater and spend at least some time in marine systems, e.g., salmon and smelt.
ANAL FIN: Figures 1, 2.
ANTERIOR: toward the head.
ANUS: vent. Figure 1.
ATTENUATED: (body form) eel-like or elongated. Figure 12a.
AXIL, AXILLA: area behind or under fin base. Figure 5.
AXILLARY PROCESS: spear-like protrusion at base of pelvic fin, e.g., trout and salmon.
BAR: (body markings) vertical band. Figure 15a.
BARBEL: an elongate, fleshy appendage on chin. Figures 7b, 16.
BASE: (of fin). Figures 1, 2.
BASIBRANCHIAL: (teeth) hyoid. Figure 11b.
BASIPTERYGIUM: (bone). Figure 6.
BASS-LIKE: (body form). Figure 12b.
BATHYPELAGIC: part of the pelagic zone extending from a depth of 1,000–4,000 m (3,280–13,120 ft) below the ocean surface.
BD: body depth, (body form). Figures 3, 12d.
BEAK: bill, spear. Figure 13d. (teeth). Figure 11d.
BELLY: area covering viscera. Figure 1.
BENTHIC: living at the sea floor.
BENTHOPELAGIC: living near the bottom but spending some time in the water column.
BIFID: with two points.
BILL: beak, spear. Figure 13d.
BL: body length. Figure 2.
BLOTCH: (body markings). Figure 15d.
BODY DEPTH: BD, (body form). Figures 3, 12d.
BODY LENGTH: BL. Figure 2.
BODY PLATES: modified scales, e.g., poachers.
BRANCHIAL: (length) relating to the gills. Figure 16.
BRANCHIOSTEGALS: Figure 5.
BREAST: Figure 8a.
BUCCAL: (mouth cavity). Figure 11.
CANINE: (teeth). Figure 11c.
CARUNCLE: spherical light organ associated with dorsal fin, e.g., anglerfishes.
CATADROMOUS: fishes that spawn in saltwater and spend some time in freshwater, e.g., some eels.
CAUDAL FIN: (tail). Figures 1, 2, 9.
CAUDAL PEDUNCLE: Figures 1, 2.
CHIN: Figure 1.
CIRRUS (*pl.* CIRRI): thin, usually fringed flap. Figure 5.
CLASPER: male reproductive organ in cartilaginous fishes. Figure 17.
CLAVUS: modified caudal fin, e.g., molas.
CLEFT: a split.
CLEITHRUM: large bone that extends upwards from base of pectoral fin. Figure 6c.
CLUB-LIKE: Figure 7c.
COMPRESSED: (body form). Figure 12d.
CONCAVE: depressed inward. Figure 12f.
CONE-LIKE: Figure 7f.
CONTIGUOUS: (fins) adjoining. Figure 9j.
CONTINUOUS: (fins). Figure 9i.
CONVEX: bulging outward. Figure 12d.
CORSELET: densely scaled area usually behind pectoral fins in certain tuna-like fishes.
CTENOID: (scale types). Figure 14d.
CYCLOID: (scale types). Figure 14c.
DECIDUOUS: (scales) easily shed or rubbed off.
DEEP, DEPTH: (body form). Figures 3, 12d.
DENTIGEROUS: with small teeth. Figure 20.
DEPRESSED: held down, pressed onto body. (body form). Figure 12e.
DISC: modified pelvic fins. Figure 7. Modified dorsal fin, e.g., remoras.
DISC LENGTH: DL, in skates and rays, from tip of snout to insertion of pectoral fin. Figure 17.
DISC WIDTH: DW, (wingspan), in skates and rays, widest point between pectoral fins. Figure 17.
DISTAL: situated away from the body.
DL: disc length, in skates and rays, from tip of snout to insertion of pectoral fin. Figure 17.
DORSAL: upper surface (fin). Figures 1, 9i, 9j.
DORSAL FIN: Figures 1, 9i, 9j.
DUSKY: darkish in color.
DW: disc width (wingspan), in skates and rays, widest point between pectoral fins. Figure 17.
EEL-LIKE: (body form). Figure 12a.
ELEVATED: (spine) above. Figure 5.
ELONGATE: (spine). Figure 5. (body form). Figures 12a, 12b.
EPIPELAGIC: part of the pelagic zone extending from a depth of 0–200 m (0–656 ft) below the ocean surface.
ESCA: luminescent organ at tip of modified 1st dorsal fin spine, e.g., anglerfishes.
EYE: (orbit). Figures 1, 4, 17.
EXTENDED: (spine). Figure 5. (mouth form). Figure 13f.
FANG: (teeth). Figure 11g.
FILAMENTOUS: (spine) thread-like. Figure 5.
FIN: (shapes). Figures 1, 5, 6, 7, 9.

# GLOSSARY AND INDEX TO ILLUSTRATED GLOSSARY (continued)

FINFOLD: median body wall folds, e.g., hagfishes. Figure 16.
FINLET: series of separate, small fins posterior to dorsal and anal fins, e.g., tunas. Figure 9k.
FL: fork length. Figure 2.
FLAP: a thick extension of skin. Figure 5.
FLATTENED: (body form). Figure 12e.
FORK LENGTH: FL. Figure 2.
FORKED: (tail shape). Figure 9e.
FOSSA: shallow pit, e.g., grenadiers, grunts.
FRENUM: connecting or restraining membrane.
FRONTAL RIDGE: raised bony area on head. Figure 20.
FUSIFORM: (body form). Figure 12b.
GANOID: (scale types). Figure 14b.
GAS BLADDER: (swim bladder) internal gas-filled organ.
GAS GLAND: structure that adds gas to swim bladder.
GILL: cavity, arch, rakers (GR), filaments. Figures 10, 11. membrane. Figures 5, 8.
GILL COVER: Figures 1, 5, 8a, 10a, 20.
GILL OPENING: e.g., hagfish. Figure 16.
GILL SLIT: e.g., sharks.
HAEMAL: (bone) ventral spine on caudal vertebrae.
HEAD: Figures 3, 4, 5.
HEAD LENGTH: HL. Figures 3, 4a.
HEAD WIDTH: HW. Figures 4b, 12d.
HEMISPHERICAL: (body form). Figure 12f.
HETEROCERCAL: (tail form). Figure 9m.
HL: head length. Figures 3, 4a.
HW: head width. Figure 4b, 12d.
HYOID: (teeth) basibranchial. Figure 11b.
HYPURAL: modified bones that support caudal fin soft-rays. Figures 2, 3, 9k.
ILLICIUM: modified 1st dorsal fin spine that bears the fleshy "bait," the esca, e.g., anglerfishes.
INCISED: (teeth or fins) notched. Figure 5.
INCISOR: (teeth). Figure 11f.
INCLUDED: (mouth form). Figure 13f.
INDENTED: (tail form). Figure 9a.
INFERIOR: (mouth form). Figures 13c, 13f.
INSERTION: posterior attachment of a fin to body. Figure 1.
INTERDORSAL: (ridge) elevated area between 1st and 2nd dorsal fins, e.g., sharks. (thorn), e.g., skates. Figure 17.
INTERORBITAL: space between the eyes, width. Figures 4b, 20.
INTROMITTENT ORGAN: male copulatory structure, e.g., sculpins.
IRIDESCENT: refraction of light waves causing luminous coloration.
ISOLATED: not connected by a membrane.
ISTHMUS: Figure 8.
JAWS: (upper and lower). Figures 11, 13.
KEEL: narrow ridge or projection along ventral midline, caudal peduncle, or top of head, e.g., tunas, sharks. Figure 9k.
LABIAL FURROWS: (upper and lower) grooves located at corner of mouth, e.g., sharks.
LACHRYMAL: (bone) spines, width. Figures 4a, 20.
LATERAL LINE: LL. Figure 1.
LENGTH: Figures 2, 3, 4.
LEPTOCEPHALUS: ribbon-like pelagic larva of eels and some ancestral fishes, e.g., bonefishes.
LIPS: Figures 5, 13e, 13f.
LONGITUDINAL: lengthwise, horizontal.
MALAR: (thorns). Figure 17.
MANDIBLE: lower jaw. Figures 11b, 20.
MAXILLA: (bone) upper jaw. Figures 5, 11a, 20.
MEDIAN: (thorn). Figure 17.
MEDIAN FIN: unpaired fins (dorsal, anal, caudal).
MEMBRANE: thin connective tissue.
MESOPELAGIC: part of pelagic zone extending from a depth of 200–1000 m (656–3,280 ft) below ocean surface.
MIDLATERAL SCALE: longitudinal series of scales from upper edge of operculum to caudal peduncle.
MOLAR: (teeth). Figure 11e.
MOTTLING: (body markings). Figure 15f.
MOUTH: Figures 1, 11, 13.
MULTIFID: with many points.
NAKED: (tail form) without scales or soft-rays. Figure 9h.
NAPE: region posterior to eyes, e.g., rockfishes.
NOSTRIL: Figures 5, 20.
NUB-LIKE: Figure 7c.
NUCHAL: (thorn). Figure 17.
OBLIQUE: slanted.
OBSOLETE: nearly absent or missing.
OCELLUS (*pl.* OCELLI): eyespot, dark spot bordered by a ring. Figure 15e.
OPERCULUM: gill cover. Figures 1, 4a, 5, 10a, 20.
ORBIT, ORBITAL: Figures 4, 20.
ORIGIN: anterior attachment of fin to body. Figure 1.
OVATE: (body form). Figure 12c.
OVERHANGING: (snout form). Figure 13c.
PALATINE: (bone and teeth). Figure 11a.
PAPILLAE: short, broad-based fleshy protuberances.
PARIETAL RIDGE: raised bony area on head. Figure 20.
PARR MARKS: bars and spots along the sides of juvenile salmon.
PECTORAL FIN: Figures 1, 6c. wings, e.g., skates. Figure 17.
PECTORAL GIRDLE: Figure 6c.
PELAGIC: open water, generally away from coast.
PELVIC FIN: Figures 1, 5, 6, 7, 17.
PELVIC GIRDLE: Figure 6c.
PERCH-LIKE: (body form). Figures 12d, 14d.
PERITONEUM: membrane lining abdominal cavity.

# GLOSSARY AND INDEX TO ILLUSTRATED GLOSSARY (continued)

PHOTOPHORE: light-emitting organ that appears as luminous spot, e.g., bristlemouths. Figure 18. e.g., lanternfishes. Figure 19.
PLACOID: (scale types). Figure 14a.
POINTED: (tail form). Figures 9f, 9g.
PORE: sensory organ in skin or scales.
POSTERIOR: toward the tail.
PREBRANCHIAL: (length) area anterior to gills. Figure 16.
PRECAUDAL VERTEBRAE: vertebrae from most anterior to the last one before the 1st vertebrae with a haemal spine.
PREDORSAL BLADE: fused pterygiophore(s) anterior to dorsal fin, e.g., hatchetfishes.
PREDORSAL SCALES: row of scales along midline between dorsal fin and back of skull.
PREDORSAL VERTEBRAE: vertebrae from most anterior to the 1st dorsal fin, but not including those vertebrae below that fin.
PREMAXILLA: (bone) upper jaw. Figures 5, 11a, 20.
PREOPERCLE: Figures 1, 5.
PRICKLES: small dermal denticles on the body.
PROCURRENT CAUDAL RAYS: small dorsal and ventral rays of the caudal fin located anterior to principal soft-rays, not supported by hypural elements. Figure 3.
PROJECTING: ahead of. Figures 13a, 13c.
PROLONGED: (spine). Figure 5. (snout form). Figure 13d.
PROTRACTILE: protrude or extend mouth.
PROXIMAL: situated close to the body.
PSEUDOBRANCHIA: (pseudobranch) small, gill-like organ on inner surface of operculum, e.g., snailfishes.
PTERYGIOPHORE: bone or cartilage that supports the base of a fin element, e.g., hatchetfishes.
PTERYGOID: (bone). Figure 11a.
PUPIL: Figure 4.
PYLORIC CAECA: fleshy appendages attached to posterior end of stomach.
RAKER: (gill). GR. Figures 10b, 10c.
RAYS: (in fins). Figures 2, 9k.
ROSTRUM: projecting snout or beak. Figure 13d.
ROUNDED: (tail form). Figure 9b.
RUDIMENTARY: (gill raker) small. Figure 10b.
SADDLES: (body markings). Figure 15g.
SAGITTAL: (crest) elevated bone running along midline of head, e.g., cutlassfishes.
SCALE POCKET: area where a scale has detached.
SCAPULAR: (thorn). Figure 17.
SCUTE: (scale types) thickened, hardened scale. Figure 14e.
SERRATED: saw-like edge.
SHIELD: thickened, hardened scale on lateral line or sides.
SHOULDER: (girdle) pectoral. Figure 6c.
SIMPLE: not divided.
SL: standard length. Figures 2, 3.
SLIME PORE: e.g., hagfishes. Figure 16.
SNOUT: Figures 3, 4, 13, 17.
SNOUT LENGTH: Figures 3, 4, 20.
SOFT-RAY: (fin). Figures 1, 2, 6c.
SPEAR: beak, bill. Figure 13d.
SPINE: (fin). Figures 2, 5, 6c. (head spines), e.g., rockfishes. Figure 20.
SPINULATED: with minute spines or hooks.
SPIRACLE: opening behind the eye that leads to the gill chamber in cartilaginous fishes. Figure 17.
SPOT: (body markings). Figure 15c.
SQUARE: (tail form) straight. Figure 9d.
STANDARD LENGTH: SL. Figures 2, 3.
STRIATED: with close-set lines or grooves.
STRIPE: (body markings) lengthwise or horizontal line. Figure 15b.
SUBCIRCULAR: (body form). Figure 12f.
SUBEQUAL: (jaws) nearly equal or about the same.
SUBORBITAL SERIES: thin bones below eye, e.g., manefishes.
SUBORBITAL STAY: Figure 5.
SUBTERMINAL: (mouth form). Figure 13c.
SUCKING DISC: (modified pelvic fins). Figure 7.
SUPRAMAXILLA: (bone). Figure 5.
SUPRAORBITAL: region above eye.
SWIM BLADDER: (gas bladder) internal gas-filled organ.
SWORD-LIKE: (snout form). Figure 13d.
SYMPHYSEAL KNOB: Figure 20.
TAIL: (caudal fin). Figures 1, 2, 9. (length). Figure 16.
TERMINAL: (mouth) at the end. Figure 13e.
THORACIC: (pelvic fin placement). Figures 6b, 6c.
THREAD-LIKE: Figure 7a.
TL: total length. Figures 2, 3.
TONGUE: Figure 11b.
TOTAL LENGTH: TL. Figures 2, 3.
TRANSLUCENT: transparent.
TRUNCATE: (tail form). Figures 9c, 9d. (body form). Figure 12c.
TRUNK: body region between head and anus.
TUBULAR: (snout form). Figure 13b.
TUBULAR PAPILLA: conspicuous opening immediately below lateral line, e.g., tubeshoulders.
UNITED: (gill membranes) joined. Figure 8b.
VENT: anus. Figure 1.
VENTRAL: lower surface.
VERTICAL: upright, as bar or band on sides.
VOMER: (bone, teeth). Figure 11a.
WINGS: pectoral fins, e.g., skates. Figure 17.
YOUNG-OF-THE-YEAR: less than 1-year-old.

# FIGURES

The following figures show various morphological characters, common measurements, and fin shapes and placements on exemplar fishes (Figures 1–15, pages xix–xxvii). Composite figures of the following families are placed within their respective key: HAGFISHES, Family Myxinidae (Figure 16, page 23); SKATES, Order Rajiformes (Figure 17, page 45); BRISTLEMOUTHS, Family Gonostomatidae (Figure 18, page 85); LANTERNFISHES, Family Myctophidae (Figure 19, page 98); ROCKFISHES, SCORPIONFISHES, and THORNYHEADS, Family Scorpaenidae (Figure 20, page 142).

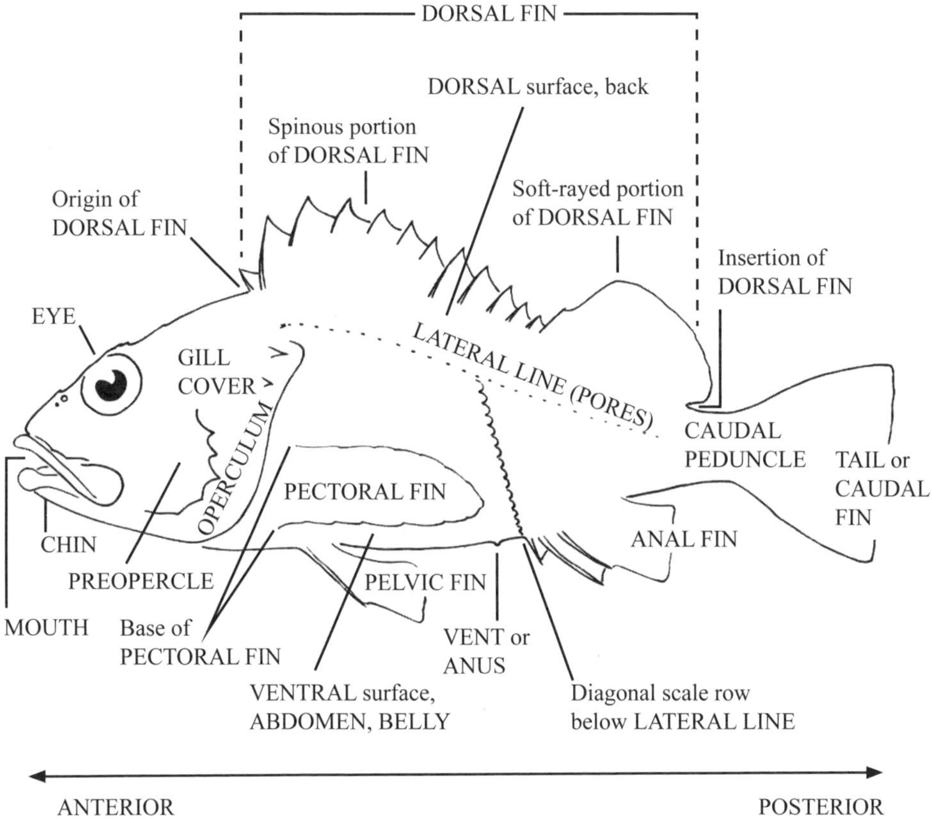


**FIGURE 1. Fins and general body areas of a bony fish.**

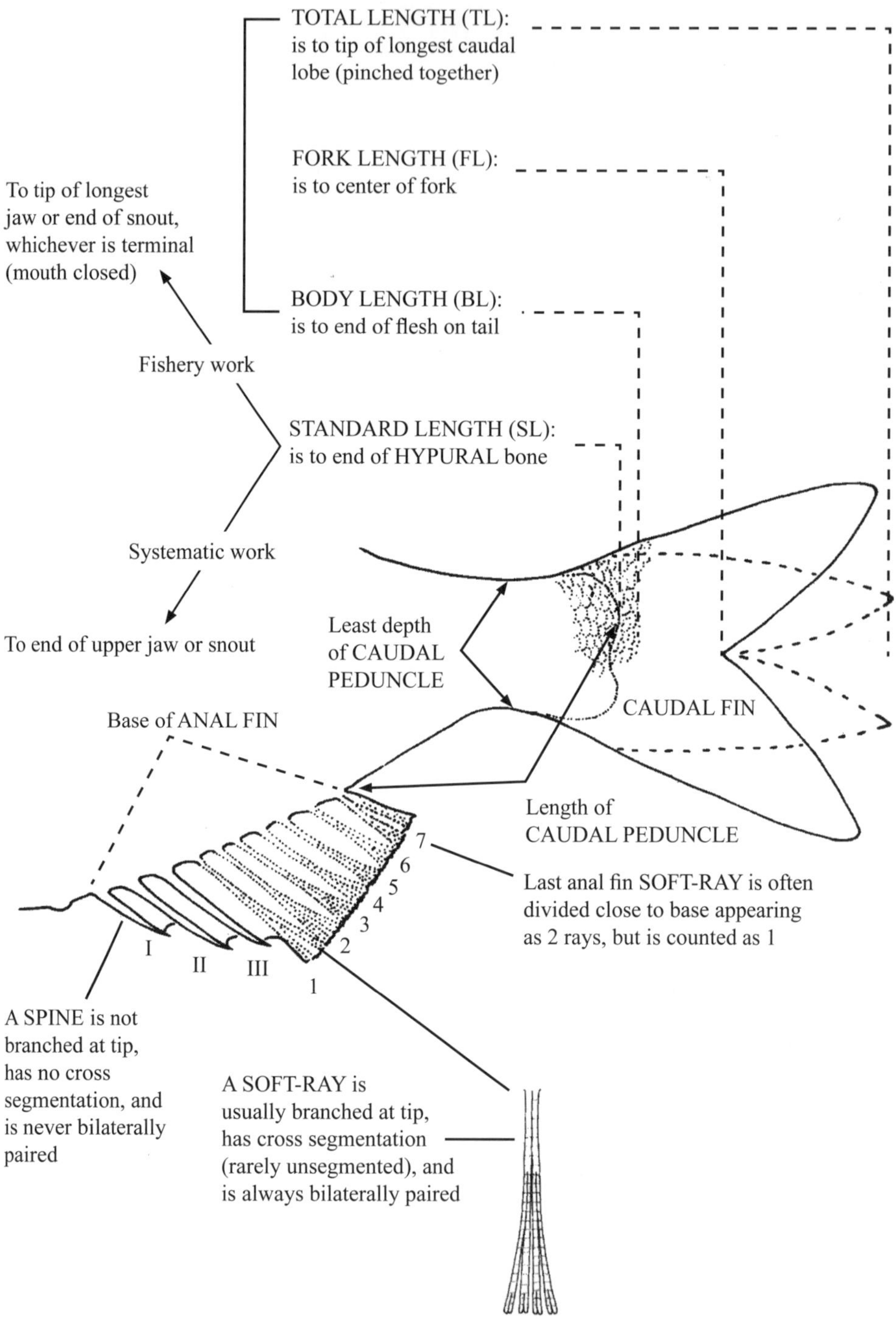


**FIGURE 2. Tail area showing lengths, fin element construction, and other structures.**

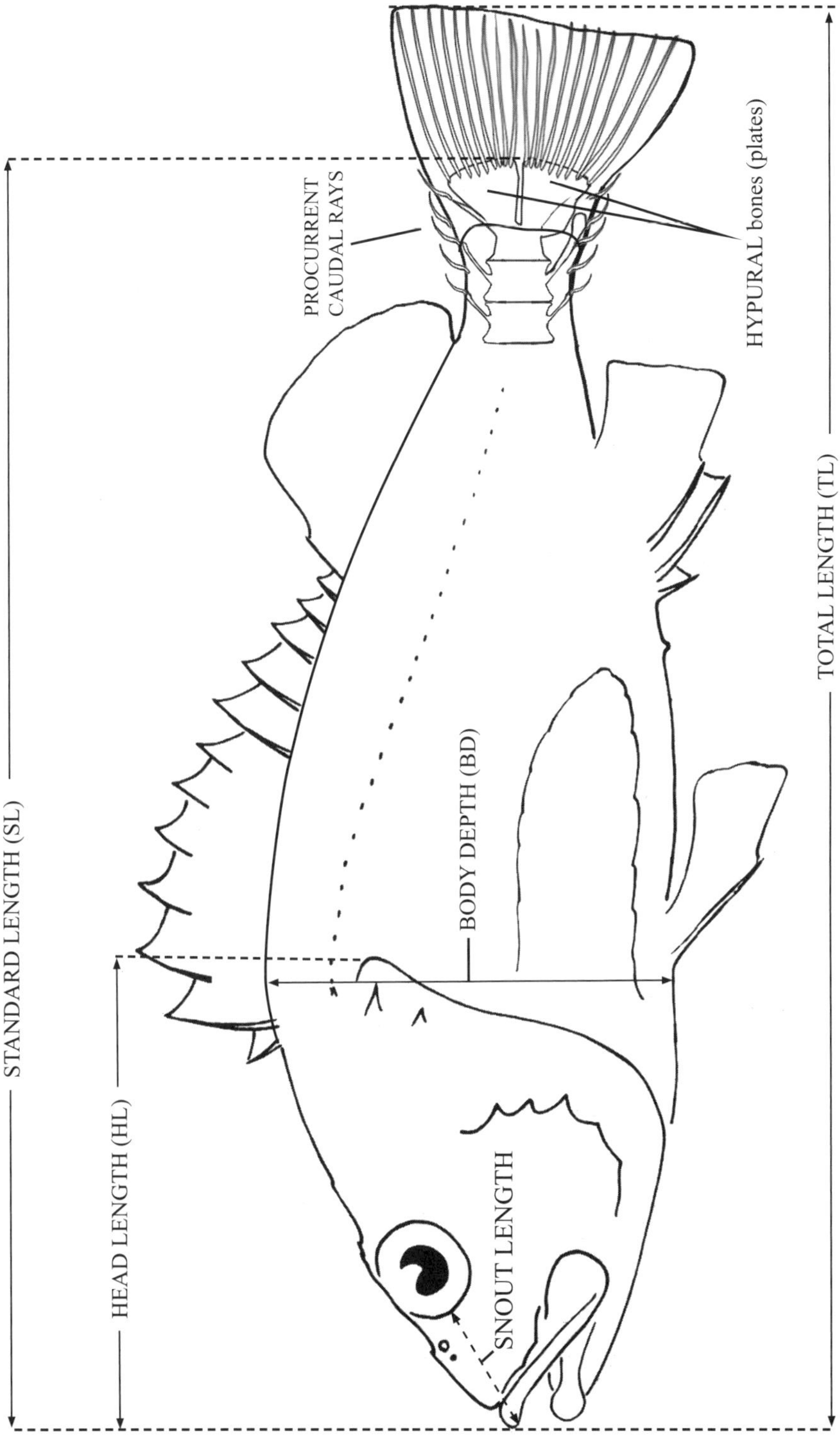


**FIGURE 3. Common length and depth measurements.**

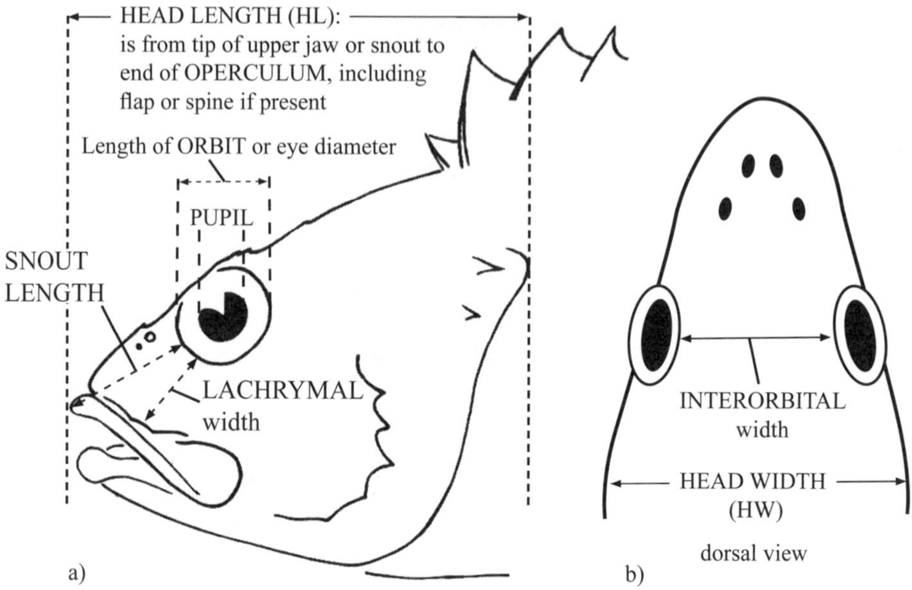


**FIGURE 4. Head measurements.**

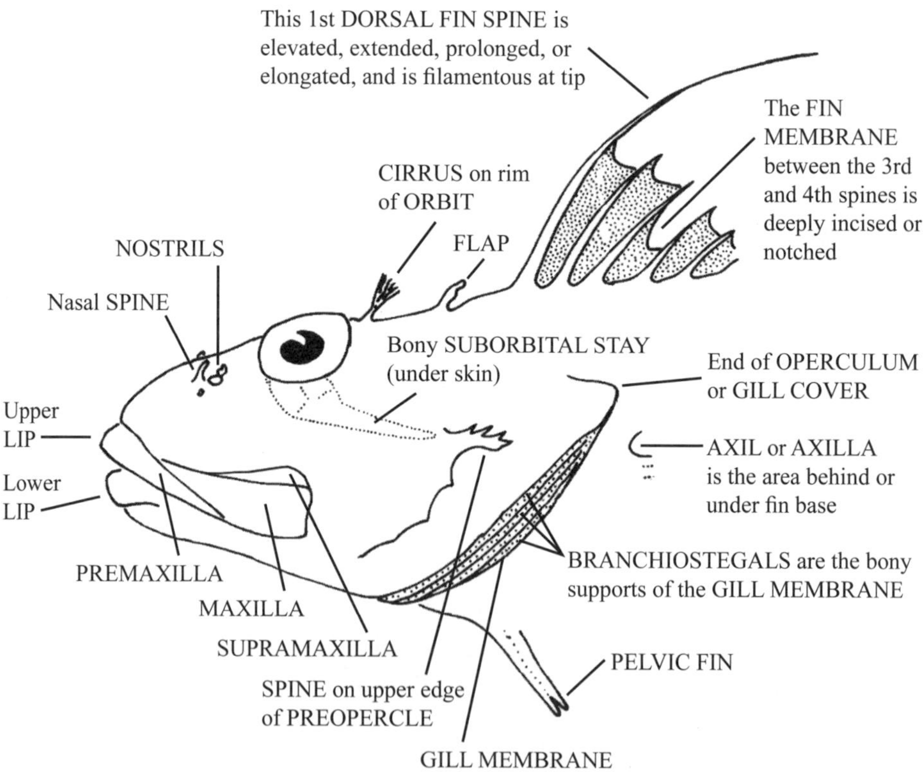


**FIGURE 5. Head and fin structures.**

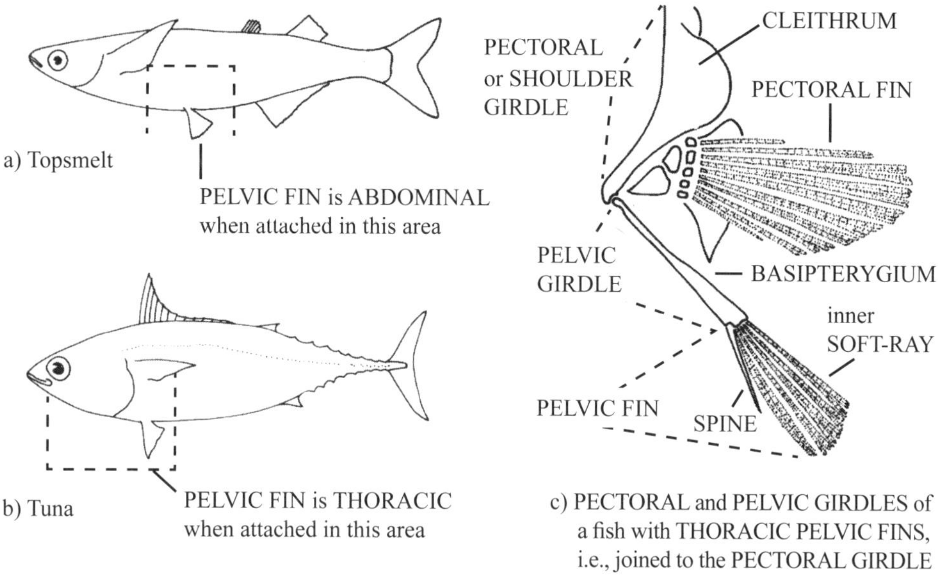


**FIGURE 6. Abdominal and thoracic fin placement and construction.**

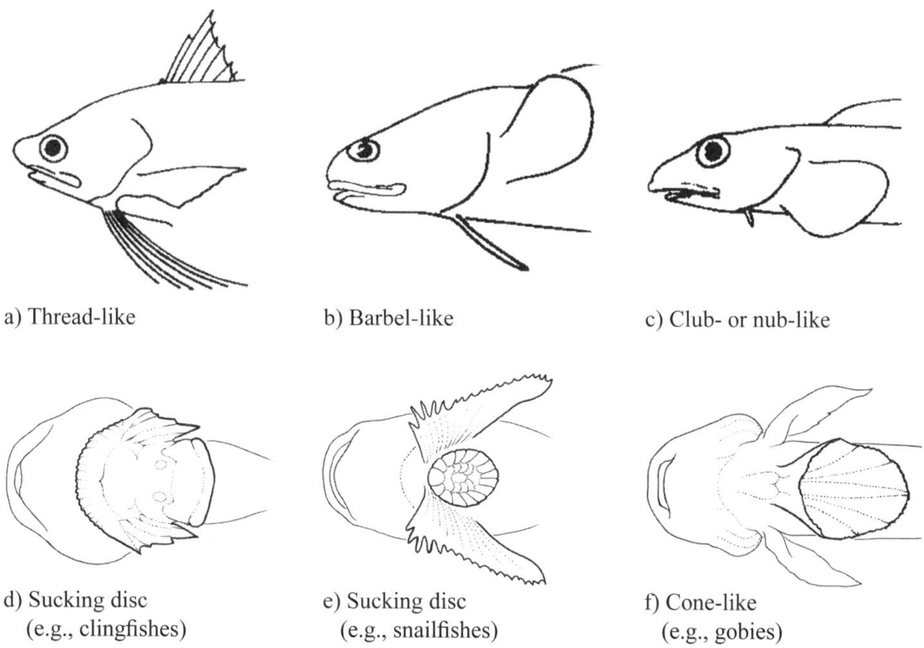


**FIGURE 7. Modified pelvic fins.**

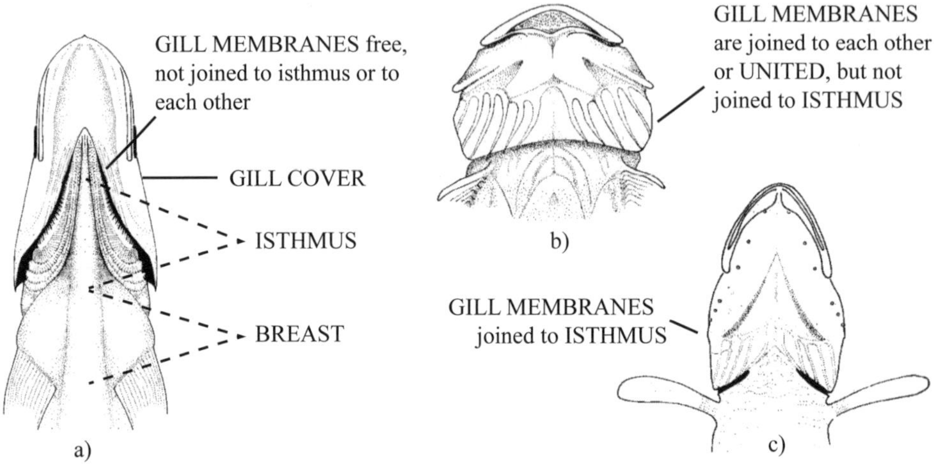


**FIGURE 8. Gill membranes and their attachment. Ventral view of: a) *Spirinchus starksii*; b) *Clinocottus globiceps*; c) *Anoplarchus purpurescens*.**

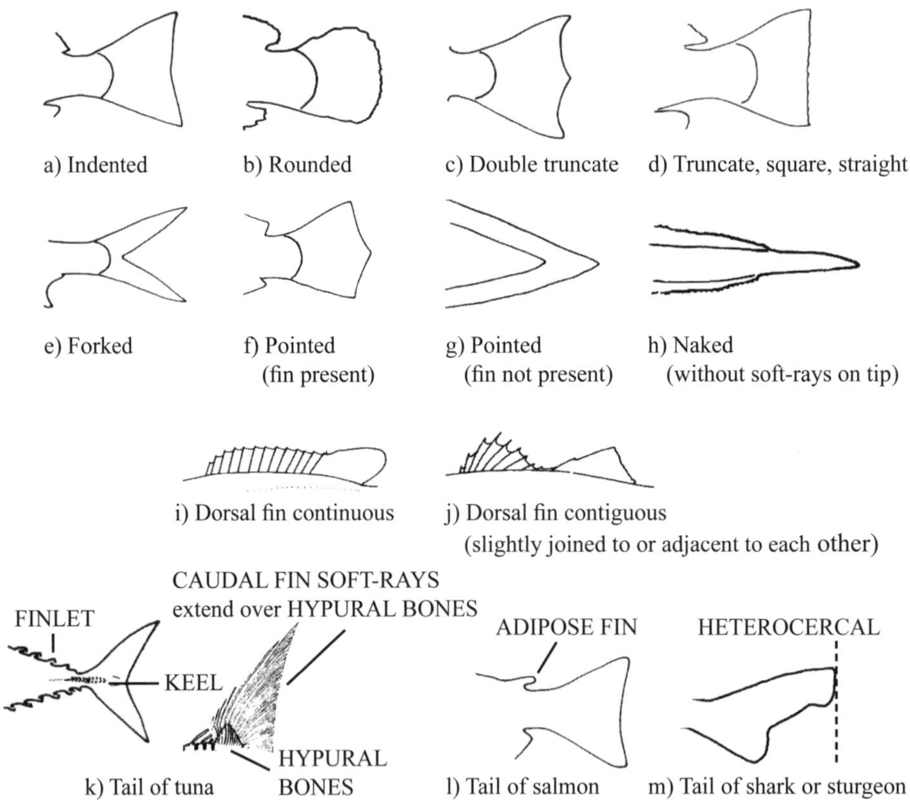


**FIGURE 9. Tail and dorsal fin shapes and construction.**

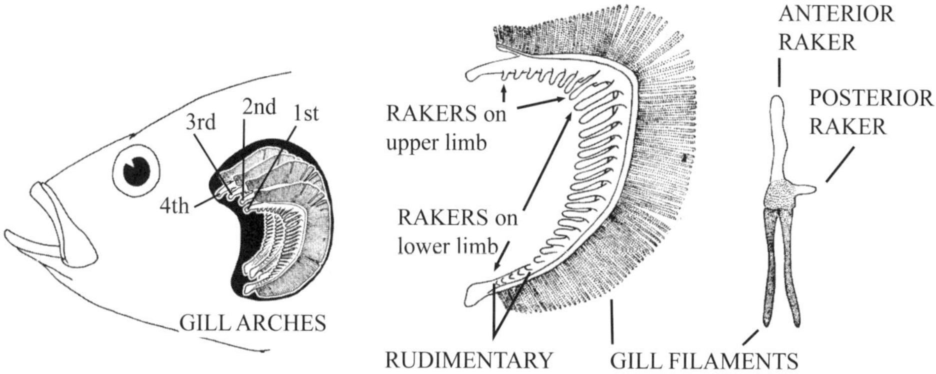


a) Position of GILL ARCHES inside GILL CAVITY of a bony fish (GILL COVER or OPERCULUM removed)

b) Side view of 1st GILL ARCH (A raker in the angle between the upper and lower limbs is counted with the lower rakers)

c) Top view of cross-section of 1st GILL ARCH

**FIGURE 10. Gill rakers and gill arches of a bony fish.**

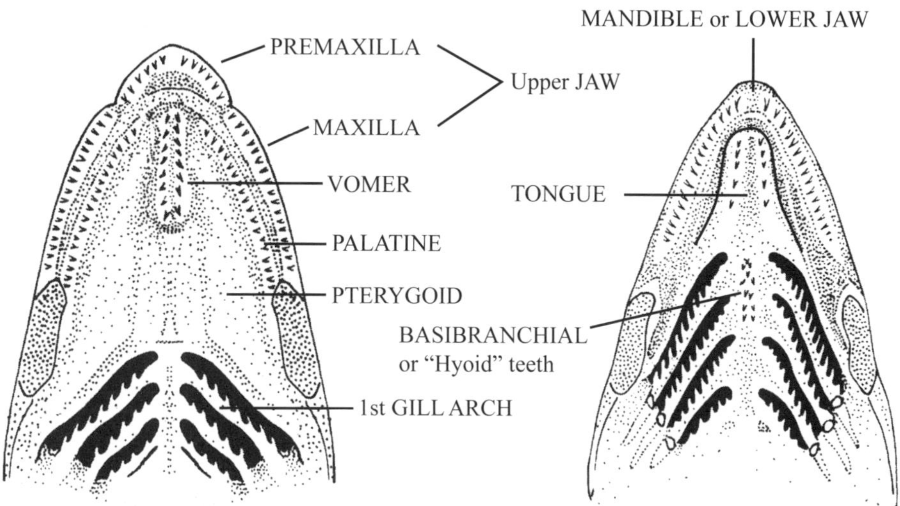


a) Roof of mouth showing bones and teeth of upper jaw.

b) Floor of mouth showing bones, teeth, and tongue of lower jaw.

c) Canine teeth (caniniform) d) Beak-like e) Molar-like g) Fang-like

**FIGURE 11. Bones and teeth inside mouth or buccal cavity.**

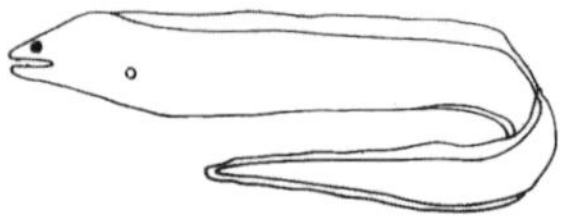

a) Eel-like, greatly elongated, attenuated

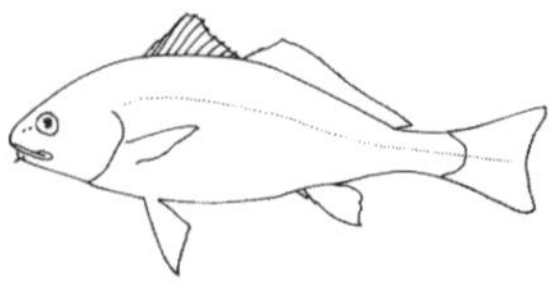

b) Elongate, fusiform, bass-like

c) Ovate, truncated

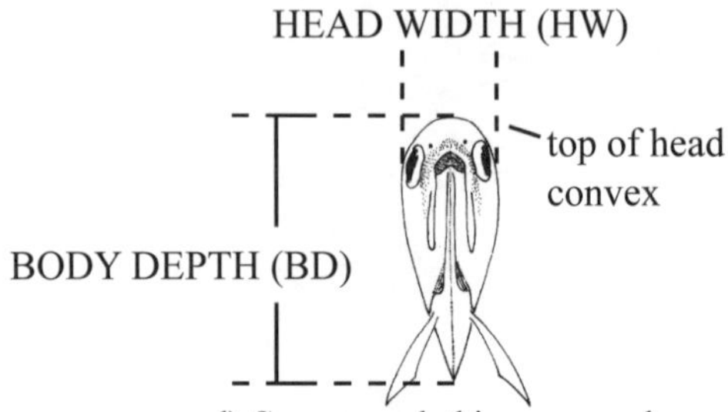


d) Compressed, thin, narrow, deep, or perch-like

e) Body depressed, flattened

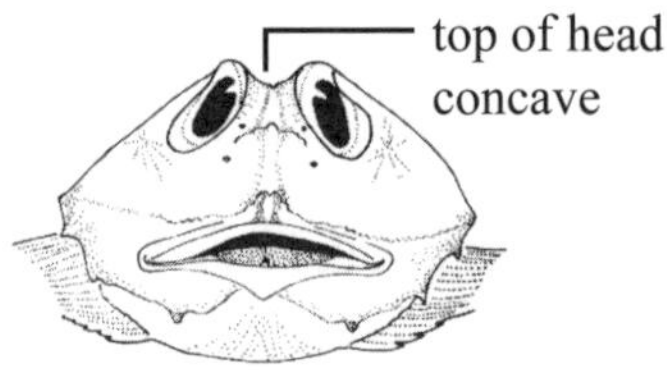


f) Body subcircular, hemispherical

**FIGURE 12. Some body forms of fishes.**

a) Lower jaw projecting beyond upper jaw

b) Snout tubular with jaws at tip

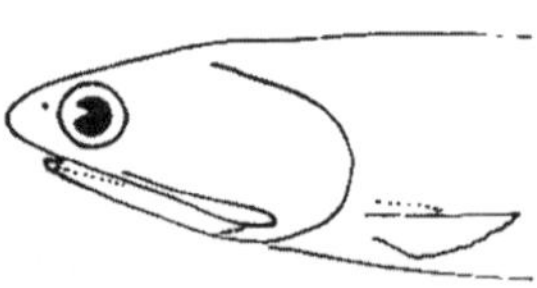

c) Snout overhanging or projecting beyond mouth; the mouth is thus inferior or subterminal

d) Upper jaw is prolonged into a sword-like beak (bill, spear, rostrum)

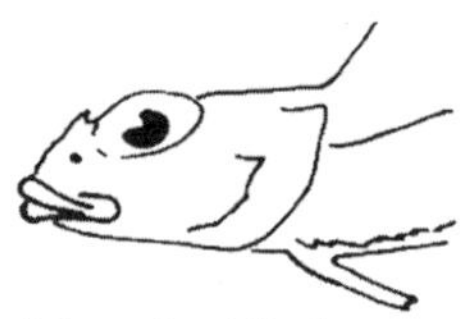

e) Jaws (and lips) are terminal, i.e., at front end of body

f) The upper jaw is extended, and the lower lip is inferior or included

**FIGURE 13. Terminology of mouth and snout forms.**

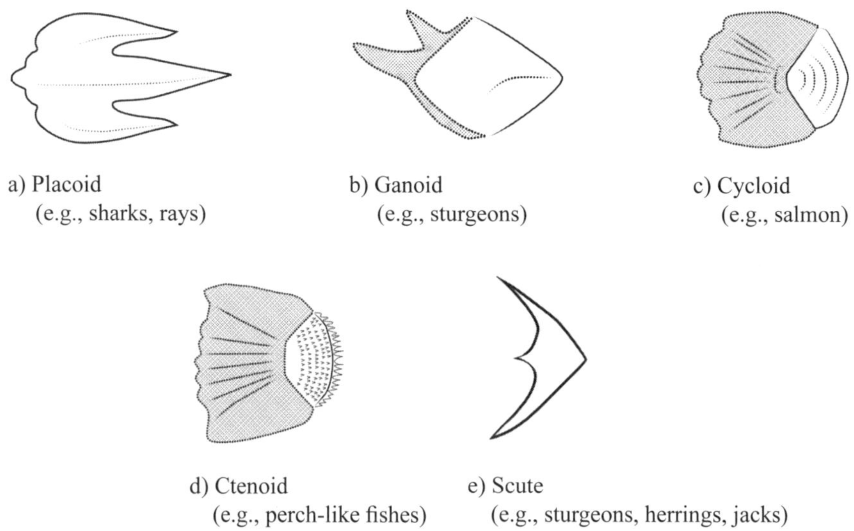


**FIGURE 14. Scale types (embedded part of scale is shaded).**

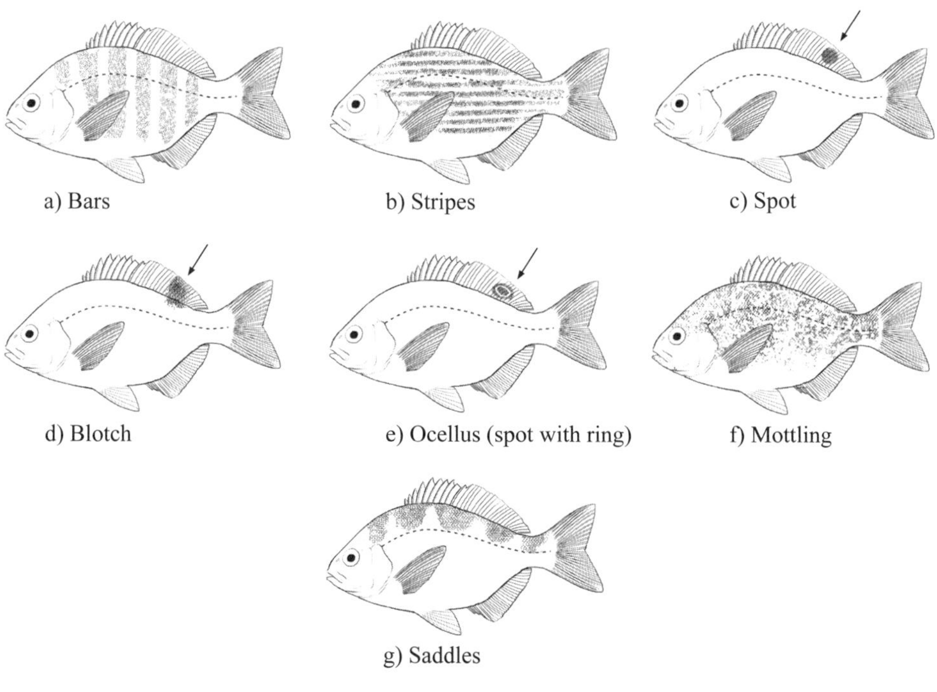


**FIGURE 15. Various types of body markings.**

# KEY TO THE FAMILIES

Revised by Rick Feeney, Julianne Kalman Passarelli, and Milton S. Love

## Section A

1a No jaws, mouth circular or disc-like.................... **HAGFISHES, LAMPREYS** Pages 23, 24

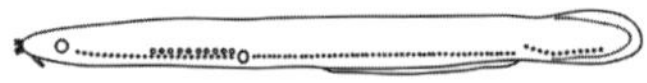

1b Jaws present...................................................... 2

2a Five to 7 paired gill openings............................... **CARTILAGINOUS FISHES (SHARKS, SKATES, RAYS)** (except CHIMAERAS) Page 25

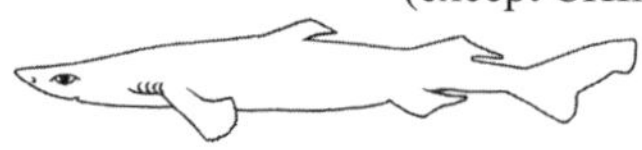

2b One paired gill opening...................................... 3

3a Eyes on same side of head................................... **FLATFISHES** Page 343

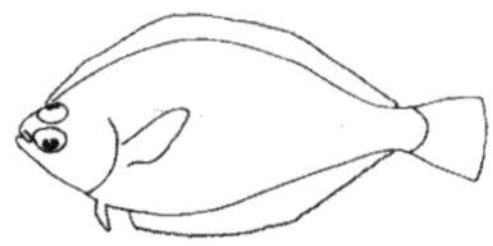

3b One eye on each side of head............................. 4

4a Pelvic fins absent or highly reduced
(may be rudimentary scale-like spine)........................................................................ **SECTION B** Page 2

4b Pelvic fins present............................................... 5

5a Pelvic fins thoracic.............................................. 8

5b Pelvic fins abdominal.......................................... 6

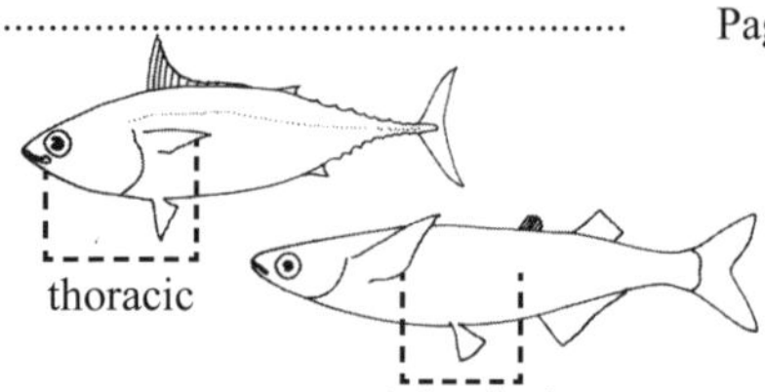


6a Single fin on back........................................................................................................ **SECTION C** Page 6

6b Two or more fins on back................................... 7

7a First dorsal fin with spines and/or soft-rays,
2nd fin adipose (no soft-rays)....................................................................................... **SECTION D** Page 8

7b Both dorsal fins with spines and/or soft-rays............................................................ **SECTION E** Page 10

8a *From 5a: pelvic fins thoracic*
Pelvic fins fused, strongly modified, most forming
sucking disc or cone on belly............................... **SECTION F** Page 11

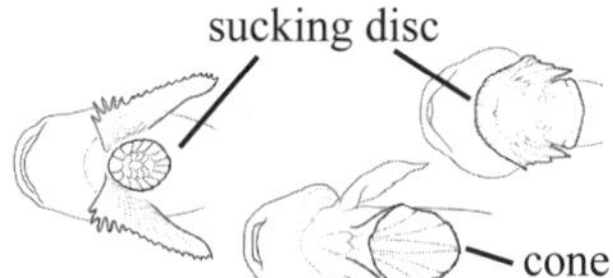


8b Pelvic fins paired, not as sucking disc or cone,
normal (soft-rays and membranes obvious) or
barbel-like or club-like....................................... 9

9a Pelvic fins with 1 spine and 5 soft-rays
(often appears as less) ................................................................................................. **SECTION G** Page 12

9b Pelvic fins with fewer than 5 soft-rays,
often barbel-like, club- or nub-like structures or
sometimes normal................................................ **SECTION H** Page 20

9c Pelvic fins with more than 5 soft-rays (some WALLEYE POLLOCK may have 5)...... **SECTION I** Page 22

## Section B: Pelvic Fins Absent or Highly Reduced

1a Body elongate, but coiled with prehensile tail........................

**SYNGNATHIDAE (PACIFIC SEAHORSE)** Page 139

1b Body elongate, eel-like (BD into SL usually more than 5)...................................................... 12 (next page)

1c Body not elongate or eel-like (BD into SL usually less than 5)........................................................ 2

2a Upper jaw flattened, sword-like............................

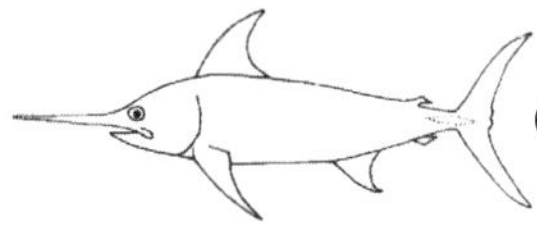

**XIPHIIDAE (SWORDFISH)** Page 337

2b Upper jaw not flattened...................................... 3

3a Caudal fin modified into clavus; body deeply compressed....................................................

**MOLIDAE (OCEAN SUNFISHES)** Page 359

3b Caudal fin not as above; body not as above........ 4

4a Large keel on caudal peduncle followed by pair of smaller keels...............................................

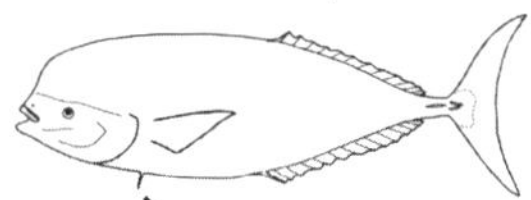

juveniles with pelvic fins

**LUVARIDAE (LOUVAR)** Page 340

4b No keel on caudal peduncle............................... 5

5a Dorsal fin with spines in anterior portion.......... 10 (next page)

5b Dorsal fin wholly of soft-rays (some PUFFERS may have 1 spine).................. 6

6a Dorsal fin short, in posterior portion of back...... 8

6b Dorsal fin covering more than half of dorsal surface..................................................... 7

7a Lower pectoral fin soft-rays partially free, extending anteriorly beneath head........................

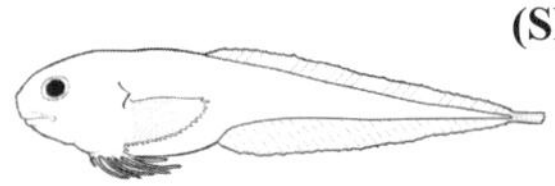

**LIPARIDAE (SNAILFISHES)** Page 211

7b Pectoral fin soft-rays not as above.........................

juveniles with pelvic fins

**ICOSTEIDAE (RAGFISH)** Page 303

8a *From 6a: dorsal fin short*
Teeth confluent into 1 or 2....................................

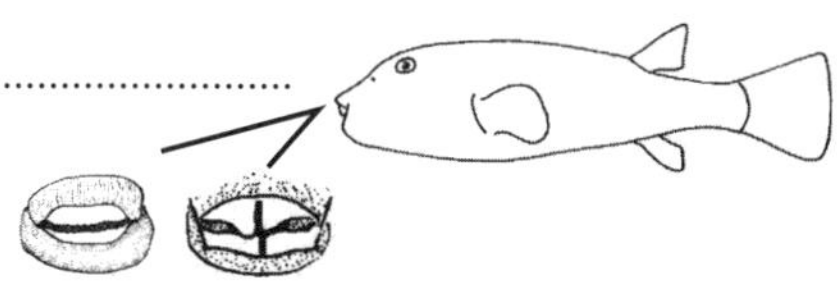

**TETRAODONTIDAE, DIODONTIDAE (PUFFERS, PORCUPINEFISHES)** Page 359

8b Teeth separate, many.......................................... 9

9a Body encased in bony box; no fleshy growth on head.......................................

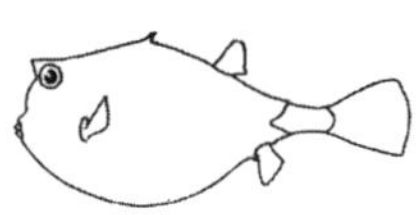

**OSTRACIIDAE (SPINY BOXFISH)** Page 359

9b (next page)

## Section B: Pelvic Fins Absent or Highly Reduced (continued)

9b Body not encased in bony box;
fleshy growth on head (illicium and esca).............

CERATIIDAE, HIMANTOLOPHIDAE, ONEIRODIDAE, MELANOCETIDAE
**(ANGLERFISHES)**
Page 127

10a *From 5a: dorsal fin with spines in anterior portion*
Dorsal fin spines more than 50............................

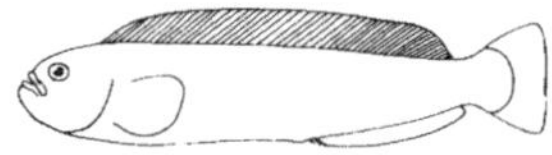

ZAPRORIDAE
**(PROWFISH)**
Page 301

10b Dorsal fin spines 7–10 (single species here, all other SCULPINS have pelvic fins).....................

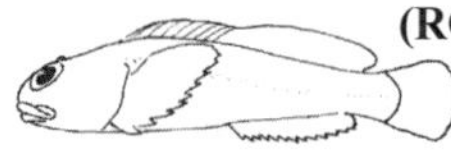

PSYCHROLUTIDAE
**(ROSYLIP SCULPIN)**
Page 179

10c Dorsal fin spines 4 or fewer........................... 11

11a Dorsal fin spines forming an interlocking mechanism, separated from soft-rays.................

BALISTIDAE
**(TRIGGERFISHES)**
Page 361

11b Dorsal fin spines connected to soft-rayed portion of dorsal fin.........................................................

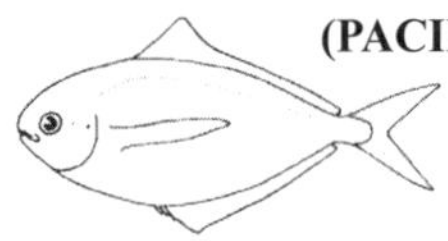

STROMATEIDAE
**(PACIFIC BUTTERFISH)**
Page 341

12a *From 1b: body elongate, eel-like*
Caudal fin present, which may or may not be joined to dorsal and anal fins........................... 24 (next page)

12b Caudal fin soft-rays not forming distinct fin, or tip of tail without soft-rays.......................... 13

13a Pectoral fins present....................................... 16

13b Pectoral fins absent......................................... 14

14a Jaws not needle-like............................................

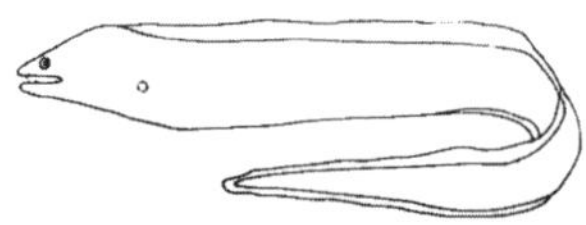

MURAENIDAE
**(MORAYS)**
Page 57

14b Jaws needle-like and elongated....................... 15

15a Dorsal fin origin anterior to anal fin origin..........

NETTASTOMATIDAE
**(DOGFACE WITCH EEL)**
Page 59

15b Dorsal fin origin posterior to anal fin origin........

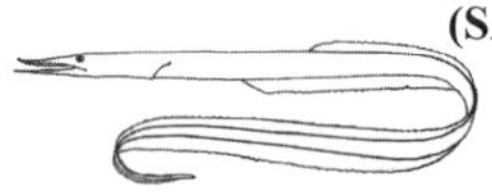

SERRIVOMERIDAE
**(SAWTOOTH EEL)**
Page 57

16a *From 13a: pectoral fins present*
Jaws needle-like, greatly elongated and curved outward.............................................

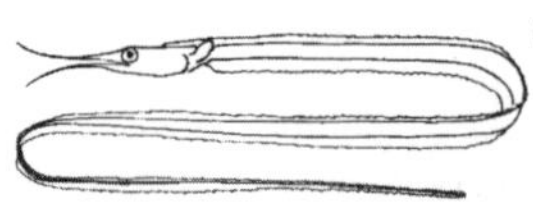

NEMICHTHYIDAE
**(THREADTAIL SNIPE EELS)**
Page 61

16b (next page)

## Section B: Pelvic Fins Absent or Highly Reduced (continued)

16b Jaws not needle-like....................................... 17

17a No spines in dorsal fin (PACIFIC CUTLASSFISH has 3 spines but are difficult to see).................. 19

17b Dorsal fin with spines..................................... 18

18a Body large and robust.........................................

**ANARHICHADIDAE (WOLF-EEL)** Page 299

18b Body thin and slender..........................................

**PTILICHTHYIDAE (QUILLFISH)** Page 301

19a *From 17a: no spines in dorsal fin*
Tip of tail without soft-rays............................. 23

19b Tip of tail with soft-rays................................. 20

20a Origin of dorsal fin posterior to pectoral fin.........

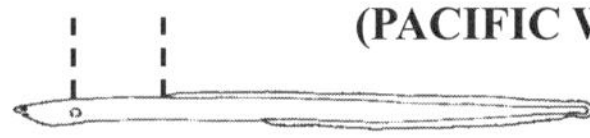

**OPHICHTHIDAE (PACIFIC WORM EEL)** Page 59

20b Origin of dorsal fin anterior to or above pectoral fin...................................................... 21

21a Lateral line with enlarged scales.........................

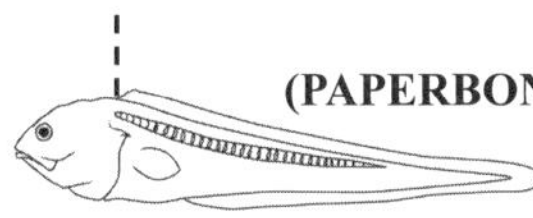

**OPHIDIIDAE (PAPERBONE CUSK-EEL)** Page 104

21b Lateral line without enlarged scales................ 22

22a Anterior nostril tubular.........................................

**CONGRIDAE (CONGER EELS)** Page 57

22b Anterior nostril not tubular..................................

**ZOARCIDAE (EELPOUTS)** Page 283

23a *From 19a: tip of tail without soft-rays*
Lower jaw longer than upper (pelvic fins are present on some CUTLASSFISHES as spine or scale-like structure; caudal fin also present on some)...........................................................

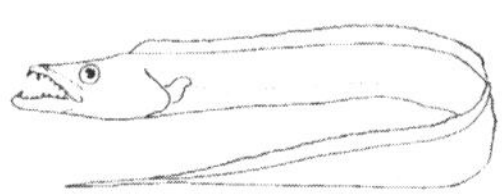

**TRICHIURIDAE (PACIFIC CUTLASSFISH)** Page 323

23b Lower jaw shorter than upper.............................

**OPHICHTHIDAE (SNAKE EELS)** Page 59

24a *From 12a: caudal fin present*
Body encased in bony plates..............................

**SYNGNATHIDAE (PIPEFISHES)** Page 139

24b Body not encased in bony plates.................... 25

25a Anal fin lacking (juveniles of this family have pelvic fins, see SECTION I, 4a); caudal fin lobes uneven, upper lobe enlarged, fan-shaped...........

**TRACHIPTERIDAE (RIBBONFISHES)** Page 135

25b Anal fin present; caudal fin lobes evenly forked, rounded, or tapering....................................... 26 (next page)

## Section B: Pelvic Fins Absent or Highly Reduced (continued)

26a Caudal fin rounded or tapering........................ 28

26b Caudal fin forked............................................ 27

27a Midventral sides with oblique folds of skin;
lateral line along dorsal fin; teeth small..............

AMMODYTIDAE
**(PACIFIC SAND LANCE)**
Page 301

27b Folds of skin on midventral sides lacking;
lateral line not as above;
teeth large, fang-like..........................................

GEMPYLIDAE, TRICHIURIDAE
**(SNAKE MACKERELS, CUTLASSFISHES)**
Page 323

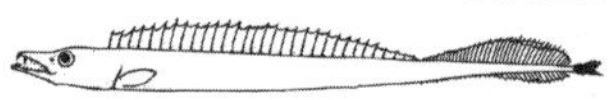

28a *From 26a: caudal fin rounded or tapering*
Dorsal fin with spines.................................... 30

28b Dorsal fin without spines............................... 29

29a Body deeper before anus; high crest over eyes
(deep water species)............................................

LOPHOTIDAE
**(NORTH PACIFIC CRESTFISH)**
Page 133

29b Body deeper behind anus; high crest over eyes
lacking (tide pool species).................................

SCYTALINIDAE
**(GRAVELDIVER)**
Page 301

30a *From 28a: dorsal fin with spines*
Dorsal fin with spines anteriorly and soft-rays
posteriorly.........................................................

STICHAEIDAE
**(PRICKLEBACKS)**
Page 289

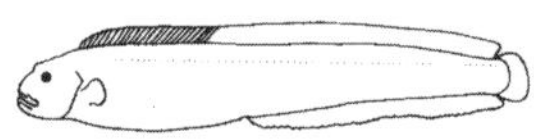

30b Dorsal fin wholly of spines............................. 31

31a Distance from snout to anal fin origin greater
than distance from anal fin origin to
base of caudal fin...............................................

PHOLIDAE
**(GUNNELS)**
Page 296

31b Distance from snout to anal fin origin equal to
or less than distance from anal fin origin to
base of caudal fin.......................................... 32

32a Mouth horizontal to oblique, not vertical...........

STICHAEIDAE
**(PRICKLEBACKS)**
Page 289

32b Mouth strongly oblique to nearly vertical...........

CRYPTACANTHODIDAE
**(WRYMOUTHS)**
Page 299

## Section C: Pelvic Fins Abdominal; One Dorsal FIn

1a Dorsal fin with isolated spines and no conspicuous soft-rays............................................ **NOTACANTHIDAE (SNUBNOSED SPINY EEL)** Page 55

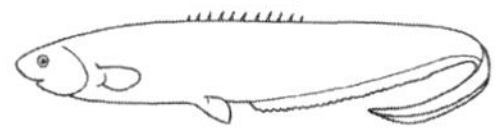

1b Dorsal fin not as above....................................... 2

2a Eyes directed upward, tubular............................... **OPISTHOPROCTIDAE (BROWNSNOUT SPOOKFISH)** Page 77

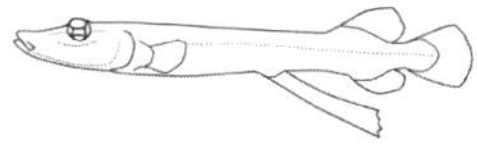

2b Eyes not as above................................................ 3

3a Photophores absent.............................................. 6

3b Photophores present............................................ 4

4a Barbel under chin (rudimentary in LONGFIN DRAGONFISH).................................................. **STOMIIDAE, IDIACANTHIDAE, MALACOSTEIDAE, MELANOSTOMIIDAE (DRAGONFISHES)** Page 90

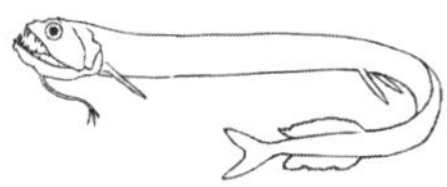

4b Barbel under chin lacking.................................. 5

5a Tubular papilla present just below lateral line......... **PLATYTROCTIDAE (TUBESHOULDERS)** Page 79

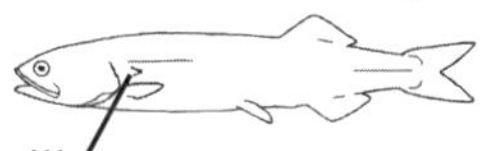

tubular papilla

5b Tubular papilla and lateral line absent.................. **GONOSTOMATIDAE (BRISTLEMOUTHS)** Page 85

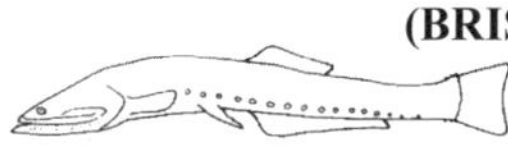

6a *From 3a: photophores absent*
Fin on dorsal surface adipose (no soft-rays and flabby)....................................... **PARALEPIDIDAE (NORTH PACIFIC DAGGERTOOTH)** Page 93

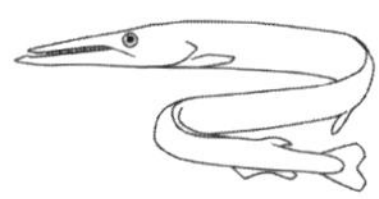

6b Dorsal fin with soft-rays...................................... 7

7a Caudal fin broadly rounded or truncated............... **POECILIIDAE, FUNDULIDAE (LIVEBEARERS, TOPMINNOWS)** Page 120

7b Caudal fin pointed or forked.............................. 8

8a Tail heterocercal (upper lobe extended); body with rows of bony plates (scutes)................. **ACIPENSERIDAE (STURGEONS)** Page 55

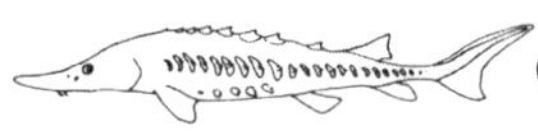

8b Caudal fin evenly forked or lower lobe elongated; no bony plates (scutes) on body.......................... 9

9a Dorsal fin about midbody.................................. 11

9b Dorsal fin attached posteriorly, much closer to tail than to head....................................................... 10

10a Dorsal fin origin well in advance of anal fin origin...................................................... **MICROSTOMATIDAE (DUSKY PENCILSMELT)** Page 81

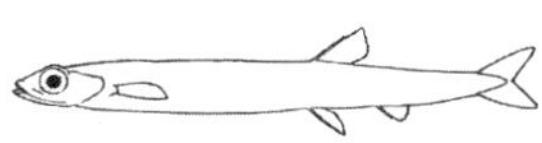

10b Dorsal fin origin not well in advance of anal fin origin.................................................. 15 (next page)

11a *From 9a: dorsal fin about midbody*
Lateral line present.......................................... 13 (next page)

11b (next page)

## Section C: Pelvic Fins Abdominal; One Dorsal FIn (continued)

11b Lateral line absent........................................... 12

12a Jaws terminal, even, or lower jaw projecting slightly beyond upper jaw...................................

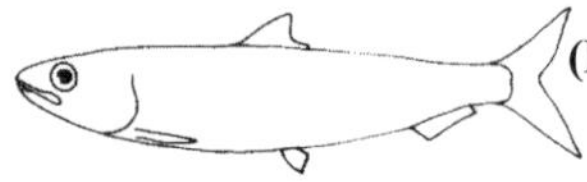

**CLUPEIDAE (HERRINGS)** Page 63

12b Snout overhanging lower jaw..............................

**ENGRAULIDAE (ANCHOVIES)** Page 67

13a *From 11a: lateral line present*
Mouth oblique, extending behind eye.................

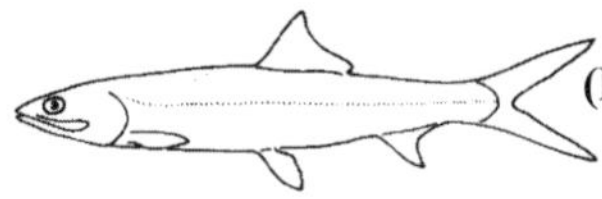

**ELOPIDAE (MACHETE)** Page 55

13b Mouth horizontal, not extending to eye.......... 14

14a Upper jaw overhanging lower jaw......................

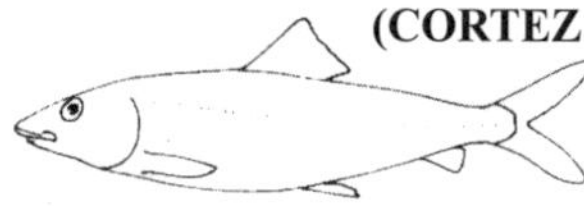

**ALBULIDAE (CORTEZ BONEFISH)** Page 55

14b Jaws about equal.................................................

**CHANIDAE (MILKFISH)** Page 116

15a *From 10b: dorsal fin origin not well in advance of anal fin origin*
Dorsal and anal fins followed by 5–7 finlets........

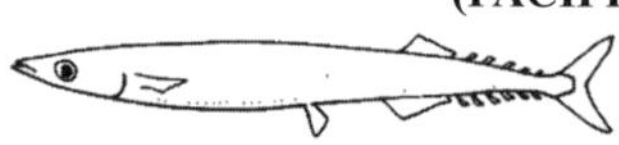

**SCOMBERESOCIDAE (PACIFIC SAURY)** Page 116

15b No finlets after dorsal and anal fins................ 16

16a Body and fins bright red or reddish-orange.........

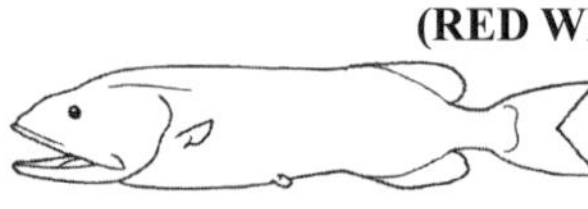

**BARBOURISIIDAE (RED WHALEFISH)** Page 131

16b Body not as above........................................... 17

17a No scales on head; body brown or black.............

**ALEPOCEPHALIDAE (CALIFORNIA SLICKHEAD)** Page 79

17b Head with scales; body silvery........................ 18

18a Jaws separate, normal, lower longer, or beak-like; caudal filament absent...................

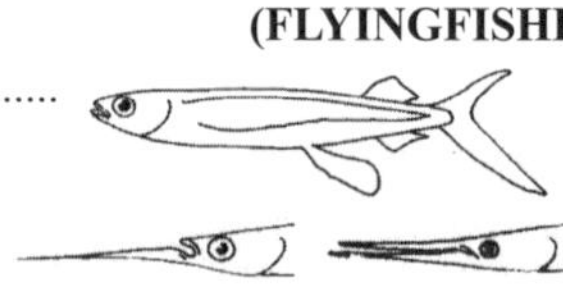

**EXOCOETIDAE, BELONIDAE, HEMIRAMPHIDAE (FLYINGFISHES, NEEDLEFISH, HALFBEAKS)** Page 117

18b Mouth small at end of tube-shaped snout; caudal filament present......................................

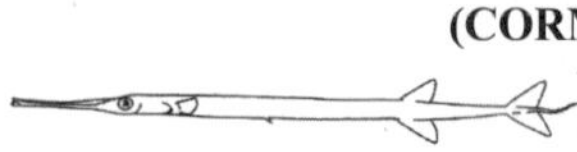

**FISTULARIIDAE (CORNETFISHES)** Page 137

## Section D: Pelvic Fins Abdominal; Two Fins on Back (One with Fin Elements, Other Adipose)

1a Photophores present.......................................... 11 (next page)

1b Photophores absent........................................... 2

2a Dorsal fin base longer than HL.............................

**ALEPISAURIDAE**
**(LONGNOSE LANCETFISH)**
Page 95

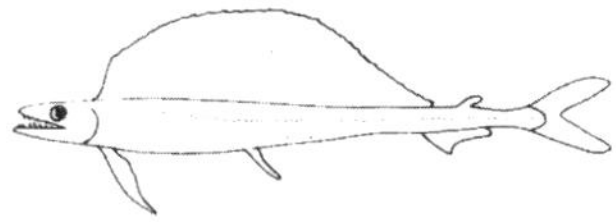

2b Dorsal fin base shorter than HL......................... 3

3a Single strong spine at origin of dorsal fin; barbels under chin...............................................

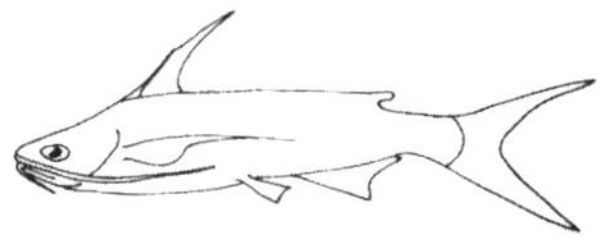

**ARIIDAE**
**(CHIHUIL)**
Page 116

3b Dorsal fin without single strong spine; barbels under chin lacking................................. 4

4a Eyes directed upwards, tubular, or with secondary eyes.....................................................

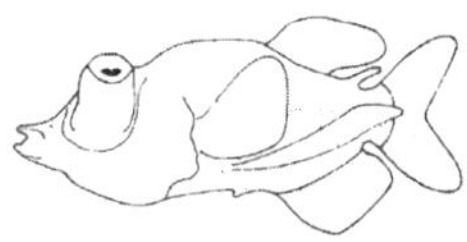

**OPISTHOPROCTIDAE**
**(SPOOKFISHES)**
Page 77

4b Eyes not as above............................................... 5

5a Axillary process at base of pelvic fin.....................

**SALMONIDAE**
**(TROUT, SALMON)**
Page 69

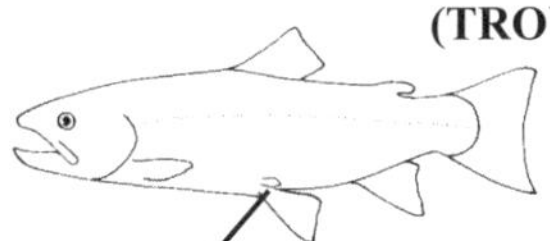


5b No axillary process at base of pelvic fin............. 6

6a Jaws extend well beyond eye (at least an eye diameter).......................................

**SYNODONTIDAE**
**(LIZARDFISHES)**
Page 95

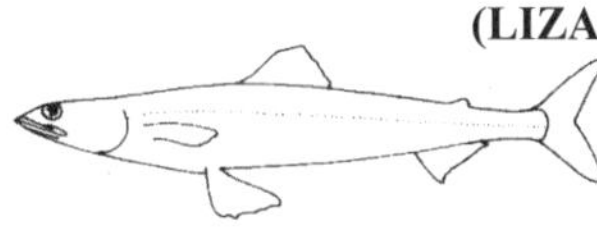

6b Jaws extend before, under, or slightly beyond eye.......................................................... 7

7a Jaw length equal to or shorter than eye diameter...................................................... 10

7b Jaw length longer than eye diameter................... 8

8a No teeth on tongue; body sides not silvery............

**NOTOSUDIDAE**
**(SCALY WARYFISH)**
Page 95

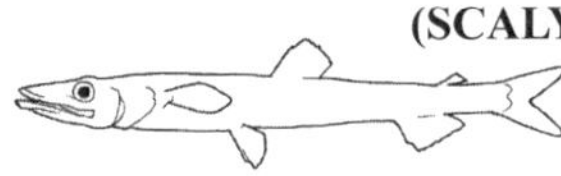

8b Teeth on tongue; body sides silvery.................... 9

9a Snout length at least 2 times longer than eye diameter.........................................................

**PARALEPIDIDAE**
**(BARRACUDINAS)**
Page 93

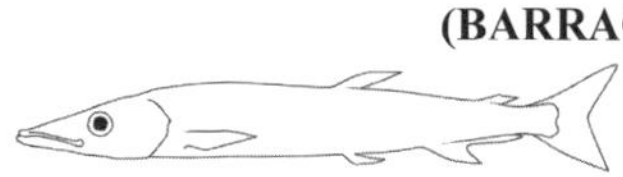

9b Snout length not as above....................................

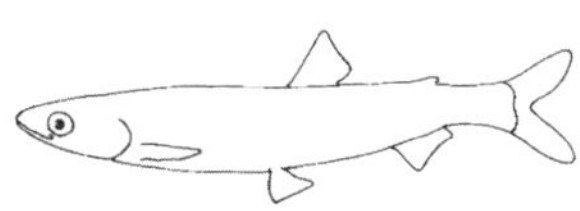

**OSMERIDAE**
**(SMELTS)**
Page 74

10a *From 7a: jaw length equal to or shorter than eye diameter*
Branchiostegals 5; scales persistent; jaws reaching ⅔ distance or less from snout to eye......................

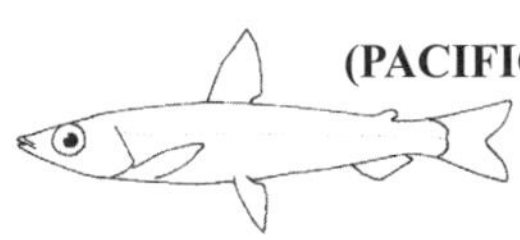

**ARGENTINIDAE**
**(PACIFIC ARGENTINE)**
Page 79

10b (next page)

## Section D: Pelvic Fins Abdominal; Two Fins on Back (One with Fin Elements, Other Adipose) (continued)

10b Branchiostegals 2–4; scales easily rubbed off; jaws reaching to or nearly to anterior edge of eye............................................ **MICROSTOMATIDAE (PENCILSMELTS)** Page 81

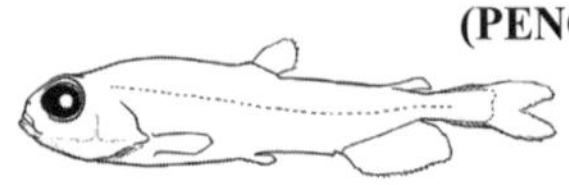

11a *From 1a: photophores present*
Photophores in duct between lower jaw and pelvic fins; scales fan-like, forming tube along lateral line, otherwise scaleless.......................... **PARALEPIDIDAE (SLENDER BARRACUDINA)** Page 93

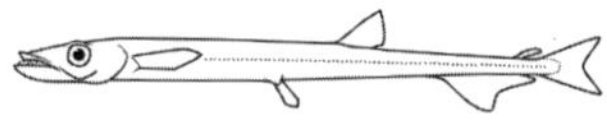

11b Photophores on side of head or on body; scales not as above.......................................... 12

12a Photophores only present as small silver patch on side of eye................................... **SCOPELARCHIDAE (NORTHERN PEARLEYE)** Page 95

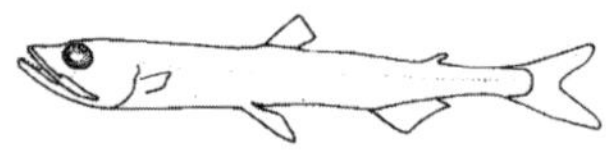

12b Photophores on body...................................... 13

13a Photophores not arranged in parallel rows........... **MYCTOPHIDAE (LANTERNFISHES)** Page 98

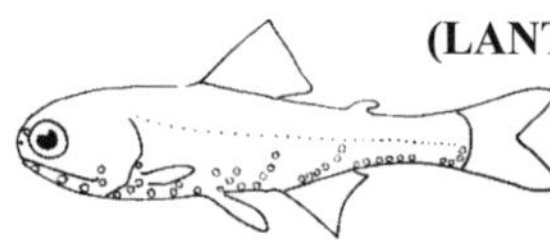

13b Photophores arranged in parallel rows............ 14

14a Teeth fang-like................................................... **CHAULIODONTIDAE (PACIFIC VIPERFISH)** Page 90

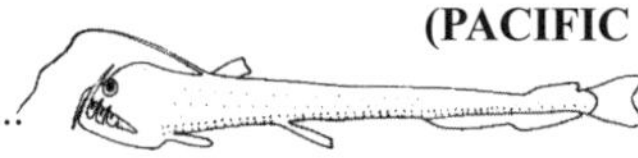

14b Teeth not fang-like.......................................... 15

15a Body deep and extremely compressed (except BOTTLELIGHT); dorsal fin soft-rays 6–11.................................... **STERNOPTYCHIDAE (HACHETFISHES)** Page 87

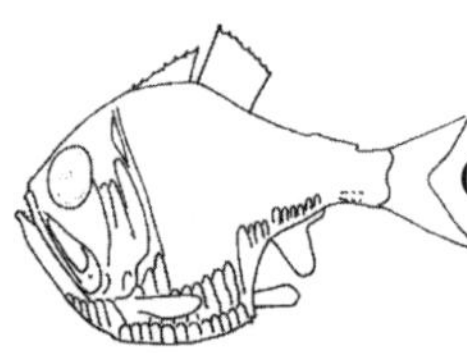

15b Body elongate; dorsal fin soft-rays 11–16................................... **PHOSICHTHYIDAE (LIGHTFISHES)** Page 84

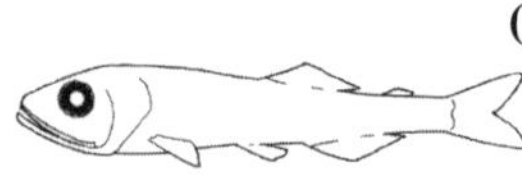

## Section E: Pelvic Fins Abdominal; Two Fins on Back (Both with Fin Elements)

1a First dorsal fin with single strong (venomous) spine at origin; gill cover weak and pliable............

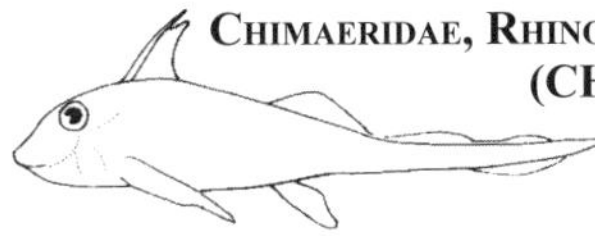

**CHIMAERIDAE, RHINOCHIMAERIDAE**
**(CHIMAERAS)**
Page 27

1b First dorsal fin with more than 1 spine; gill cover bony...................................................... 2

2a Snout elongated, tubular, with small jaws at tip.............................................

**MACRORAMPHOSIDAE**
**(LONGSPINE SNIPEFISH)**
Page 137

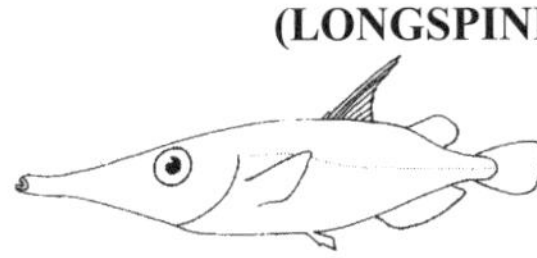

2b Snout not tubular.................................................. 3

3a Lower jaw projecting beyond upper jaw; teeth large, canine-like...........................................

**SPHYRAENIDAE**
**(BARRACUDAS)**
Page 340

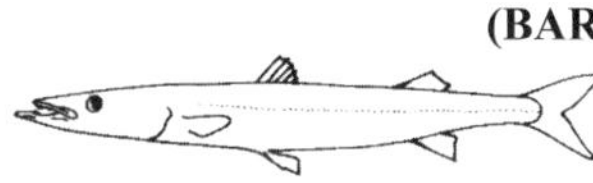

3b Jaws about equal; teeth small or absent.............. 4

4a Anal fin spine 1; distinct translucent band along midbody.......................................................

**ATHERINOPSIDAE**
**(NEW WORLD SILVERSIDES)**
Page 123

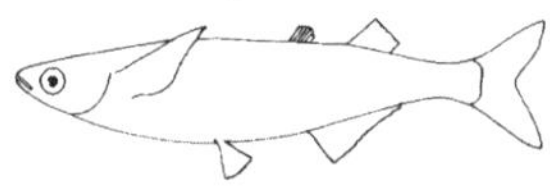

4b Anal fin spines 3 (sometimes 2 in juveniles); distinct translucent band along midbody lacking.....................................................

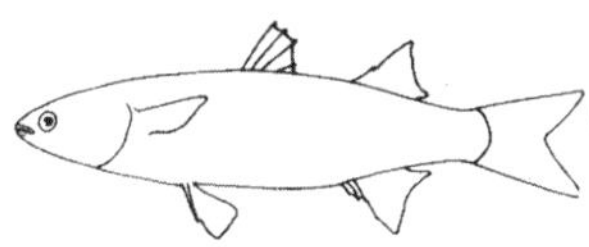

**MUGILIDAE**
**(MULLETS)**
Page 122

## Section F: Pelvic Fins Thoracic, Strongly Modified into Cone or Sucking Disc on Belly

1a Pelvics united into cone; 2 dorsal fins.................... **GOBIIDAE (GOBIES)** Page 315

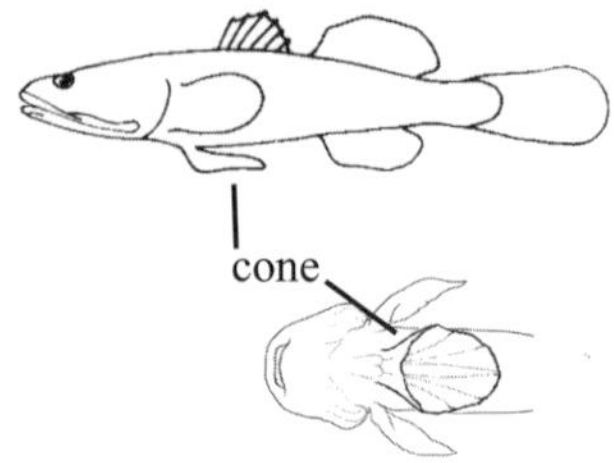


1b Pelvics forming sucking disc; 1 dorsal fin.......... 2

2a Gill membranes united but free from isthmus; dorsal fin origin far back on body, covering less than ½ of dorsal surface......................................... **GOBIESOCIDAE (CLINGFISHES)** Page 312

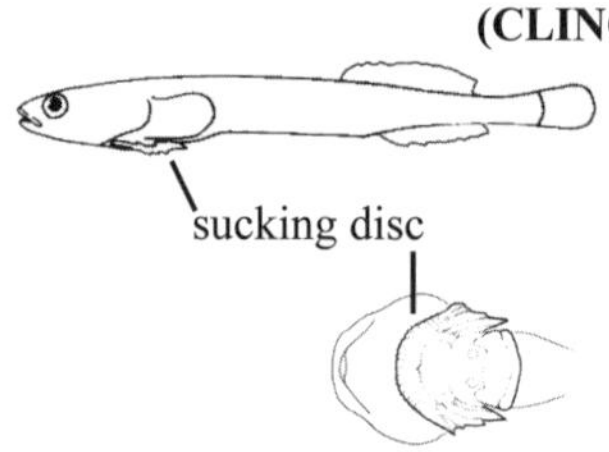


2b Gill membranes joined to isthmus; dorsal fin origin more anterior and elongated, covering over ½ of dorsal surface.......................... **LIPARIDAE (SNAILFISHES)** Page 211

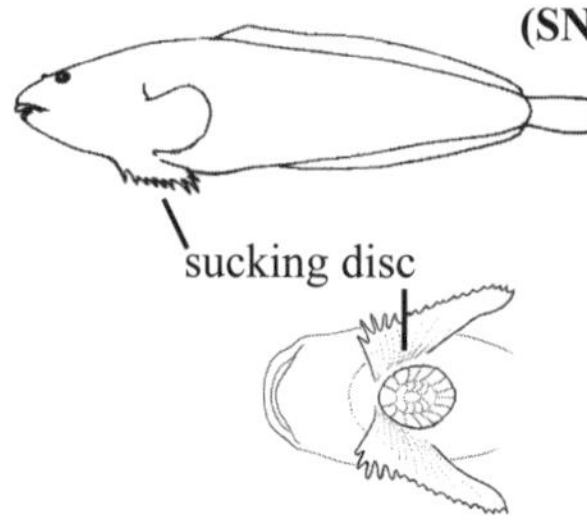

## Section G: Pelvic Fins Thoracic with Exactly One Spine and Five Soft-Rays

1a Gill openings in front of pectoral fins................. 4

1b Gill openings small, behind, above, or below pectoral fins............................................ 2

2a Body ovate, not flattened or depressed..................

**ANTENNARIIDAE (ROUGHJAW FROGFISH)** Page 125

2b Body relatively flattened or depressed................ 3

3a Mouth small............................................................

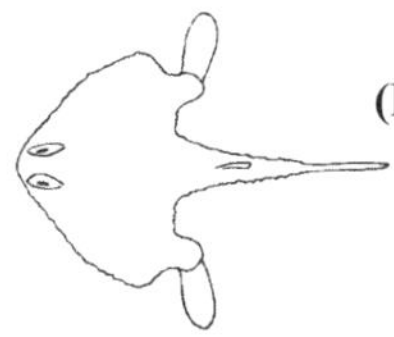

**OGCOCEPHALIDAE (ROUNDEL BATFISH)** Page 125

3b Mouth large...........................................................

**LOPHIIDAE (GOOSEFISHES)** Page 125

4a *From 1a: gill openings in front of pectoral fins* Depressible sharp spine at base of caudal fin...............................................................

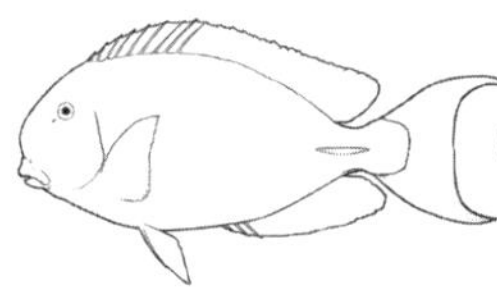

**ACANTHURIDAE (YELLOWFIN SURGEONFISH)** Page 300

4b Depressible sharp spine at base of caudal fin lacking................................................ 5

5a First dorsal fin modified into sucking disc on top of head..............................................................

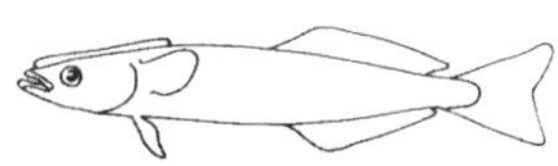

**ECHENEIDAE (REMORAS)** Page 230

5b First dorsal fin not as above................................ 6

6a Body with bony shields along base of dorsal and anal fins..........................................................

**ZEIDAE (MIRROR DORY)** Page 130

6b Body without bony shields along base of dorsal and anal fins........................................ 7

7a Dorsal fin(s) followed by 1 or no finlet.............. 9

7b Dorsal fin(s) followed by 2 or more finlets.......... 8

8a Keels present on caudal peduncle; anterior dorsal fin spines elevated (except WAHOO); scales small or lacking........................

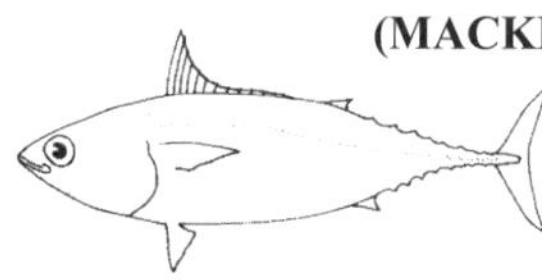

**SCOMBRIDAE (MACKEREL, TUNAS)** Page 329

8b No keels on caudal peduncle (except ESCOLAR); anterior dorsal fin spines not elevated; scales modified...............................

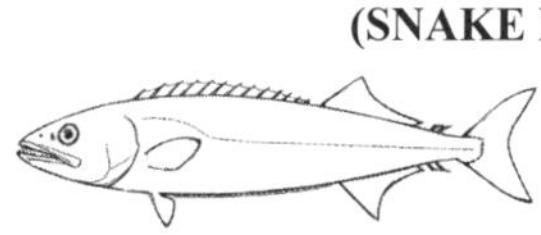

**GEMPYLIDAE (SNAKE MACKERELS)** Page 323

9a *From 7a: dorsal fin(s) followed by 1 or no finlet* Single or 1st dorsal fin with spines and soft-rays, or wholly of spines.............................................. 15 (next page)

9b (next page)

## Section G: Pelvic Fins Thoracic with Exactly One Spine and Five Soft-Rays (continued)

9b Dorsal fin wholly of soft-rays (anterior dorsal fin soft-rays may appear to be spines in some POMFRETS)....................................................... 10

10a Large spine above pectoral fin; eyes on top of head............................................ 

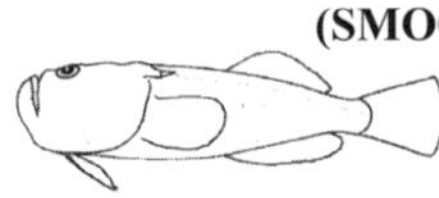

**URANOSCOPIDAE (SMOOTH STARGAZER)** Page 303

10b No large spine above pectoral fin; eyes not as above............................................... 11

11a Tail forked........................................................ 14

11b Tail rounded....................................................... 12

12a Body elongate......................................................

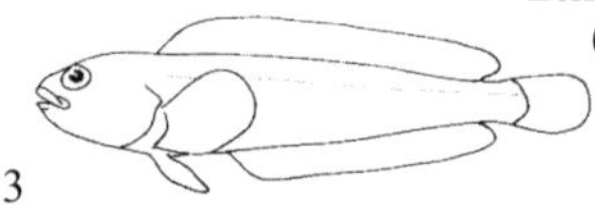

**BATHYMASTERIDAE (RONQUILS)** Page 278

12b Body ovate........................................................ 13

13a Dorsal fin broadly expanded; pelvic fins elongate............................................

**CARISTIIDAE (MANEFISHES)** Page 244

13b Dorsal fin not as above; pelvic fins short...................................................

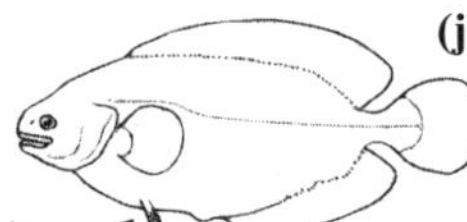

pelvic fins absent in adults

**ICOSTEIDAE (juvenile RAGFISH)** Page 303

14a *From 11a: tail forked* Body blue-green and yellow; anal fin base about ½ length of dorsal fin base.................................

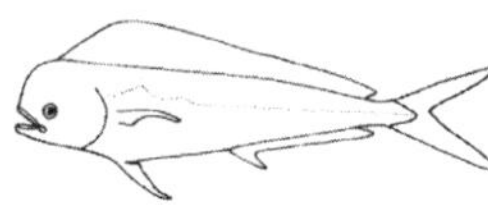

**CORYPHAENIDAE (DOLPHINFISH)** Page 243

14b Body not as above; anal fin base about equal to dorsal fin base....................................................

**BRAMIDAE (POMFRETS)** Page 245

15a *From 9a: dorsal fin with spines* Large spine above pectoral fin; mouth vertical.....................................................

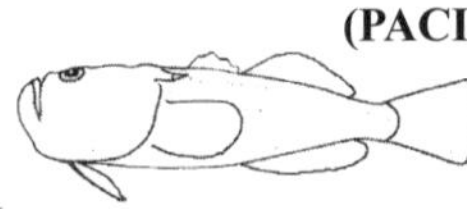

**URANOSCOPIDAE (PACIFIC STARGAZER)** Page 303

15b No large spine above pectoral fin; mouth less than vertical.................................... 16

16a Usually 5 or more spines on single or 1st dorsal fin (some JACKS may have fewer)............................................................... 18 (next page)

16b Usually 4 or fewer spines on single or 1st dorsal fin....................................................... 17

17a Two dorsal fins....................................................

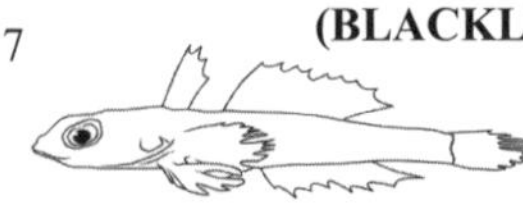

**CALLIONYMIDAE (BLACKLIP DRAGONET)** Page 303

17b (next page)

## Section G: Pelvic Fins Thoracic with Exactly One Spine and Five Soft-Rays (continued)

17b Single dorsal fin................................................  **CENTROLOPHIDAE (MEDUSAFISH)** Page 341

18a *From 16a: five or more spines on single or 1st dorsal fin*
Lowermost soft-rays of pectoral fin not detached from fin........................................ 20

18b Lowermost soft-rays of pectoral fin detached and thread-like or barbel-like............................ 19

19a Three lowermost pectoral fin soft-rays detached.............................................................. 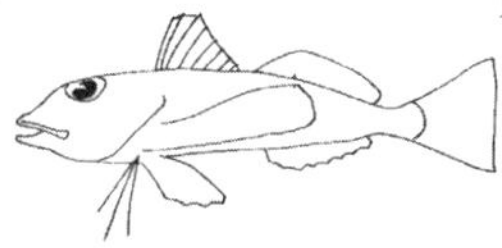 **TRIGLIDAE (SEAROBINS)** Page 173

19b Five to 9 lowermost pectoral fin soft-rays detached.............................................................. 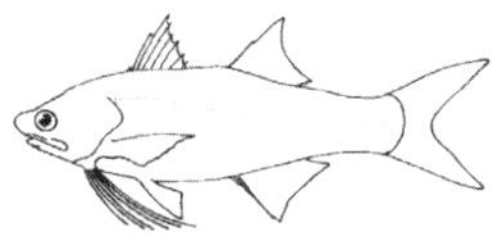 **POLYNEMIDAE (BOBOS)** Page 253

20a *From 18a: lowermost soft-rays of pectoral fin not detached*
Suborbital stay absent....................................... 25 (next page)

20b Suborbital stay present...................................... 21

21a Two or more anal fin spines............................... 23

21b Anal fin spines 0–1 or buried (not obvious)..................................................... 22

22a Dorsal fin with 20 or more spines........................ 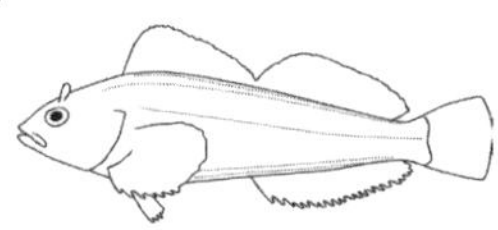 **ZANIOLEPIDIDAE, HEXAGRAMMIDAE (COMBFISHES, GREENLINGS)** Page 175

22b Dorsal fin with 19 or fewer spines....................... 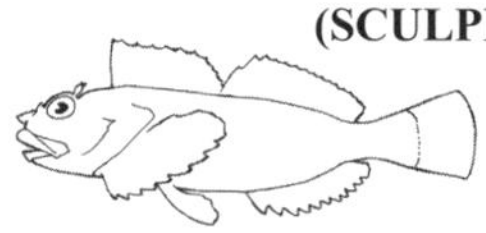 **SCORPAENICHTHYIDAE, JORDANIIDAE, COTTIDAE (SCULPINS, POACHERS)** Page 179

23a *From 21a: two or more anal fin spines*
Preopercle with 5 spines; anal fin soft-rays 4–11........................................ 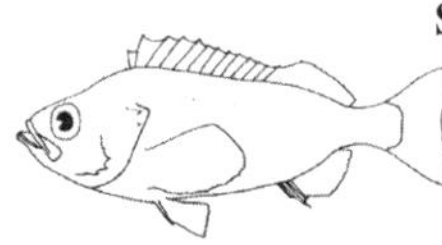 **SCORPAENIDAE (ROCKFISHES, SCORPIONFISHES, THORNYHEADS)** Page 142

23b Preopercle with fewer than 5 spines; anal fin soft-rays 11 or more............................ 24

24a Dorsal fins separated; 2 well-developed nostrils on each side of head............................................. 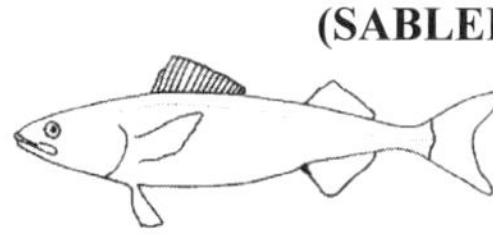 **ANOPLOPOMATIDAE (SABLEFISH, SKILFISH)** Page 173

24b Dorsal fin continuous (may be deeply notched); only anterior nostril well developed................... 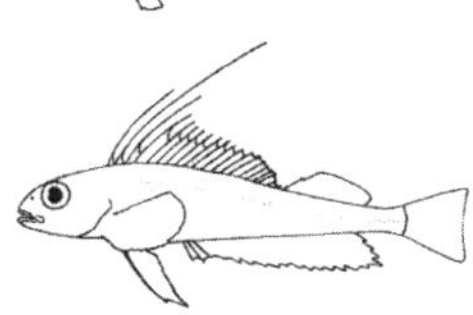 **ZANIOLEPIDIDAE, HEXAGRAMMIDAE (COMBFISHES, GREENLINGS)** Page 175

25a (next page)

## Section G: Pelvic Fins Thoracic with Exactly One Spine and Five Soft-Rays (continued)

TRICHODONTIDAE
**(PACIFIC SANDFISH)**
Page 300

25a *From 20a: suborbital stay absent*
Anal fin without spines; lips fringed....................

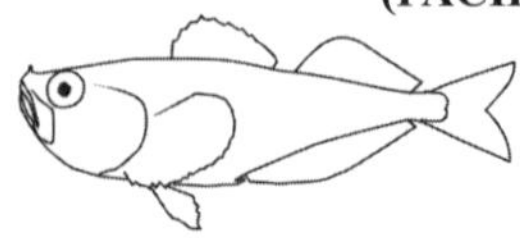

25b Anal fin with spine(s) (some SMALLEYE SQUARETAIL may lack anal fin spines); lips not fringed ................................................. 26

MULLIDAE
**(BIGSCALE GOATFISH)**
Page 274

26a Chin with 2 long barbels.....................................

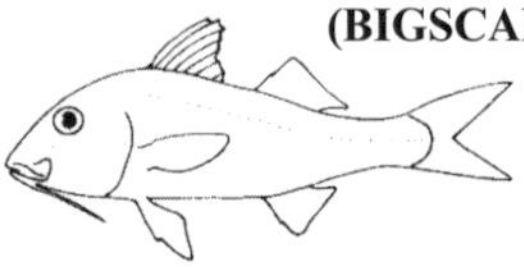

26b Chin without barbels.......................................... 27

27a Anal fin usually with 3 or more spines (many juveniles and larvae only have 2 spines; some MOZAMBIQUE TILAPIA may only have 2 spines).................................................... 37 (next page)

27b Anal fin usually with 1 or 2 spine(s) (rarely 3 spines in ROOSTERFISH; in some families these anal spines are very weak and may be mistaken for soft-rays)...................................... 28

28a One or 2 anal fin spine(s) isolated from soft-rays (all carangids have 3 anal fin spines except some very old adults with 1 or 2 spines).................... 39 (page 17)

28b Anal fin spine(s) connected to soft-rays by membranes................................................... 29

29a First 7 dorsal fin spines greatly elongated; pelvic fins appear to have 6 soft-rays, 5th being divided deeply at base of fin................................

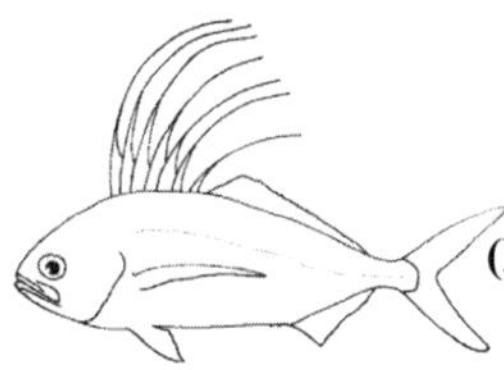

NEMATISTIIDAE
**(ROOSTERFISH)**
Page 243

29b Anterior dorsal fin spines not elongated; pelvic fins not as above..................................... 30

TETRAGONURIDAE
**(SMALLEYE SQUARETAIL)**
Page 341

30a Caudal peduncle with 2 keels; body covered with hard-grooved scales....................................

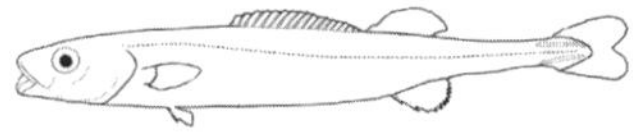

30b Caudal peduncle without keels; body not covered with hard-grooved scales..................... 31

31a Double nostril pores on each side of head......... 33 (next page)

31b Single nostril pore on each side of head............ 32

CICHLIDAE
**(MOZAMBIQUE TILAPIA)**
Page 263

32a Lateral line interrupted, lower line extending to caudal fin........................................

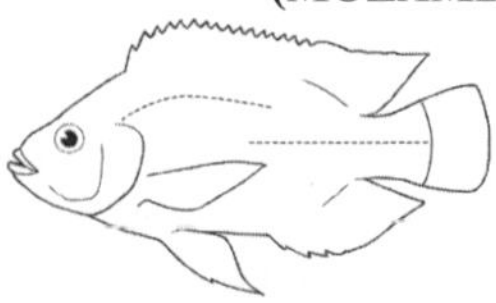

32b (next page)

## Section G: Pelvic Fins Thoracic with Exactly One Spine and Five Soft-Rays (continued)

32b Lateral line uninterrupted and not extending to caudal fin..................................

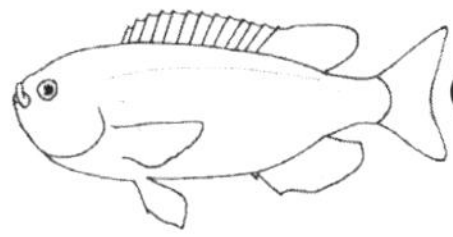

**Pomacentridae (DAMSELFISHES)**
Page 275

33a *From 31a: double nostril pores*
Two dorsal fins, separated or nearly so............. 35

33b Dorsal fin continuous, nearly same height throughout............................................. 34

34a Maxilla ends anterior to or below eye.................

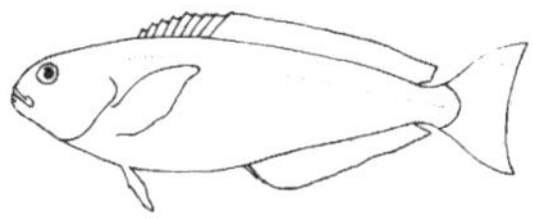

**Malacanthidae (TILEFISHES)**
Page 229

34b Maxilla extends well beyond eye.........................

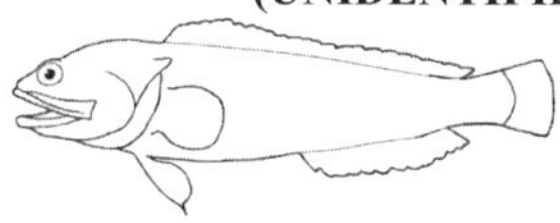

**Opistognathidae (UNIDENTIFIED JAWFISH)**
Page 227

35a *From 33a: two dorsal fins, separated*
Caudal peduncle depth about same length as distance from origin of 1st dorsal fin to insertion of 2nd dorsal fin; single strong spine at origin of 2nd dorsal fin...................................................

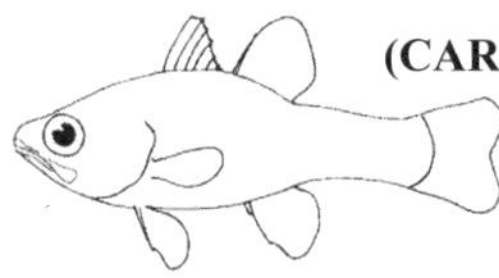

**Apogonidae (CARDINALFISHES)**
Page 233

35b Caudal peduncle depth much shorter than distance from origin of 1st dorsal fin to insertion of 2nd dorsal fin; spine(s) at origin of 2nd dorsal fin weak, pliable.......................... 36

36a Lateral line extending onto middle soft-rays of caudal fin; tail slightly forked or pointed, not broadly rounded..................................................

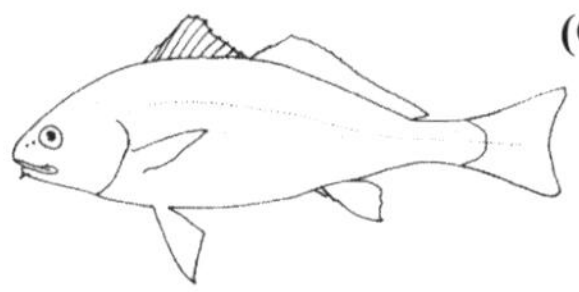

**Sciaenidae (CROAKERS)**
Page 255

36b Lateral line not extending onto middle soft-rays of caudal fin; tail broadly rounded......................

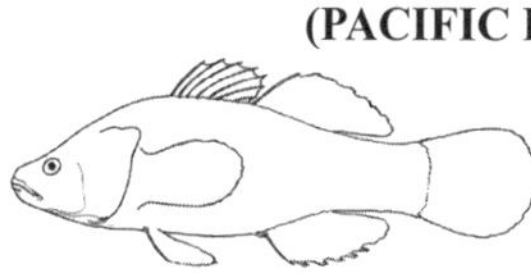

**Eleotridae (PACIFIC FAT SLEEPER)**
Page 301

37a *From 27a: three or more anal fin spines*
Single nostril pore on each side of head.............

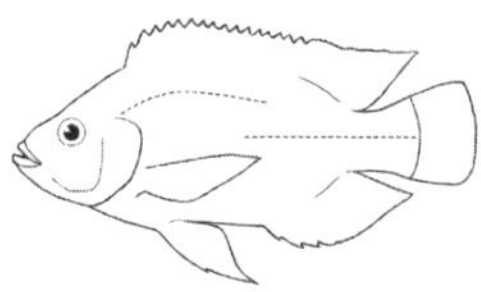

**Cichlidae (TILAPIAS)**
Page 263

37b Double nostril pores on each side of head........ 38

38a Anal fin usually with 4 spines (SURFPERCHES rarely have 4; ARMORHEAD may have 3 or 5).......................

**Pentacerotidae (NORTH PACIFIC ARMORHEAD)**
Page 263

38b Anal fin usually with 3 spines (many juveniles and larvae only have 2 spines).......................... 39 (next page)

## Section G: Pelvic Fins Thoracic with Exactly One Spine and Five Soft-Rays (continued)

39a *From 28a: one or 2 anal fin spines isolated from soft-rays and 38b: anal fin spines 3*
Anal fin spines isolated from fin, retractable (may be small or embedded in adults); length of caudal lobes more than 4 times depth of caudal peduncle.................................................

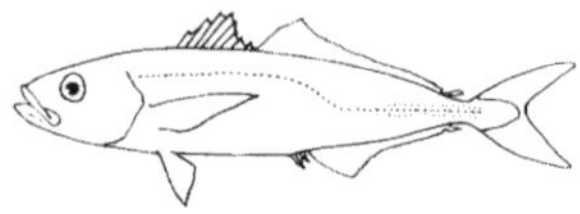

**CARANGIDAE (JACKS)** Page 235

39b Anal fin spines connected to soft-rayed portion; length of caudal lobe(s) less than 4 times depth of caudal peduncle............................................ 40

40a Strong spine on preopercle............................... 46

40b Strong spine on preopercle lacking.................. 41

41a Snout pointed and elongated...............................

**CHAETODONTIDAE (BUTTERFLYFISHES)** Page 260

41b Snout not pointed and elongated....................... 42

42a No sheath of scales extending onto dorsal fin.................................................... 51 (next page)

42b Sheath of scales extending onto dorsal fin........ 43

43a Tip of soft dorsal fin extends over caudal fin; caudal fin rounded.............................

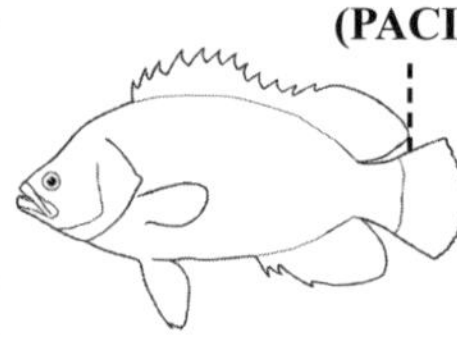

**LOBOTIDAE (PACIFIC TRIPLETAIL)** Page 274

43b Dorsal fin not as above; caudal fin not rounded...................................................... 44

44a Teeth on jaws fused, forming beak.....................

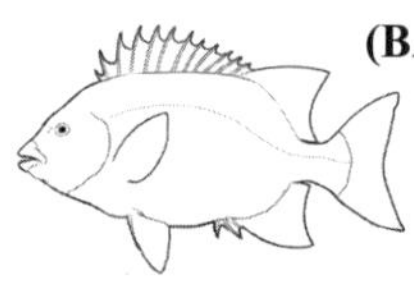

**OPLEGNATHIDAE (BARRED KNIFEJAW)** Page 253

44b Teeth on jaws not fused or forming beak.................................................... 45

45a Anal fin soft-rays 10 or more (rarely 9 in ZEBRAPERCH).............................................. 48 (next page)

45b Anal fin soft-rays 9 or fewer............................. 47

46a *From 40a: strong spine on preopercle*
Body elongate....................................................

**HAEMULIDAE (ARMED GRUNT)** Page 249

46b Body ovate.........................................................

**POMACANTHIDAE (CORTEZ ANGELFISH)** Page 263

47a *From 45b: anal fin soft-rays 9 or fewer*
Large solitary canines in mouth (except some PACIFIC RED SNAPPER); teeth on vomer present; small pores but no enlarged pores or fossa on chin......................................................

**LUTJANIDAE (SNAPPERS)** Page 247

47b (next page)

## Section G: Pelvic Fins Thoracic with Exactly One Spine and Five Soft-Rays (continued)

47b No large solitary canine teeth; teeth on vomer absent; enlarged pores and/or fossa on chin......................................................

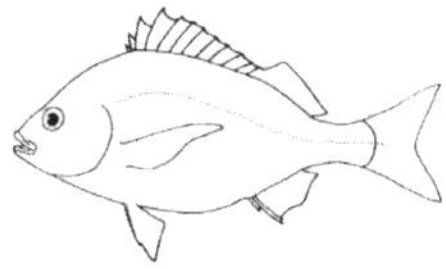

**Haemulidae**
**(GRUNTS)**
Page 249

48a *From 45a: anal fin soft-rays 10 or more*
Anal fin soft-rays more than 14........................ 50

48b Anal fin soft-rays 14 or fewer........................... 49

49a Top of head with oblique profile..........................

**Embiotocidae**
**(DWARF PERCH)**
Page 265

49b Top of head with rounded profile.........................

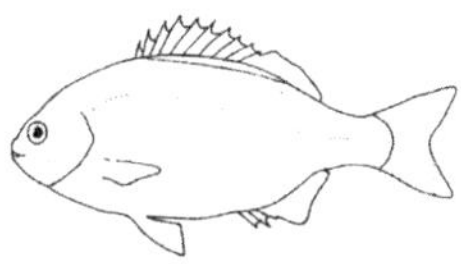

**Kyphosidae**
**(SEA CHUBS)**
Page 261

50a *From 48a: anal fin soft-rays more than 14*
Pectoral fin short, reaching only about halfway to tip of pelvic fin when depressed......................

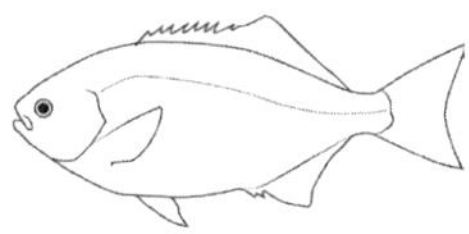

**Kyphosidae**
**(HALFMOON)**
Page 261

50b Pectoral fin long, nearly reaching to or extending beyond tip of pelvic fin when depressed.............

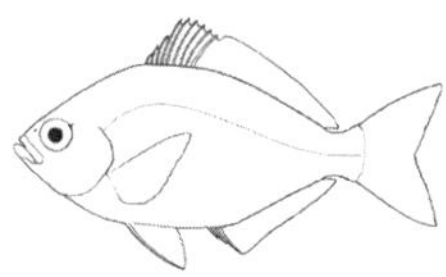

**Embiotocidae**
**(SURFPERCHES)**
Page 265

51a *From 42a: no sheath of scales extending onto dorsal fin*
Maxilla fully exposed or slightly covered by edge of bone above when mouth is closed........ 56 (next page)

51b Maxilla mostly hidden by sliding under bone above when mouth is closed............................ 52

52a Anal fin soft-rays 19 or more..............................

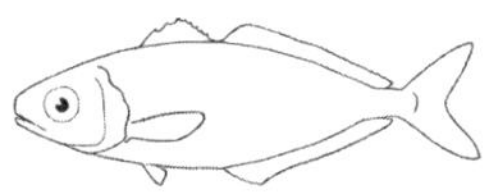

**Nomeidae**
**(DRIFTFISHES)**
Page 342

52b Anal fin soft-rays 14 or fewer........................... 53

53a Anterior teeth minute and numerous; lateral line extends onto caudal fin.......................................

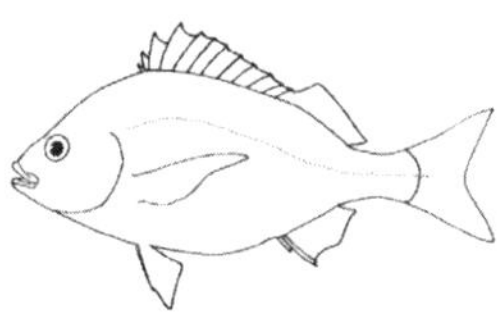

**Haemulidae**
**(GRUNTS)**
Page 249

53b Anterior teeth either canine-like, conical, incisor-like, or beak-like; lateral line not extending onto caudal fin............................ 54

54a Anterior teeth canine-like or beak-like................

**Labridae**
**(WRASSES, PARROTFISH)**
Page 279

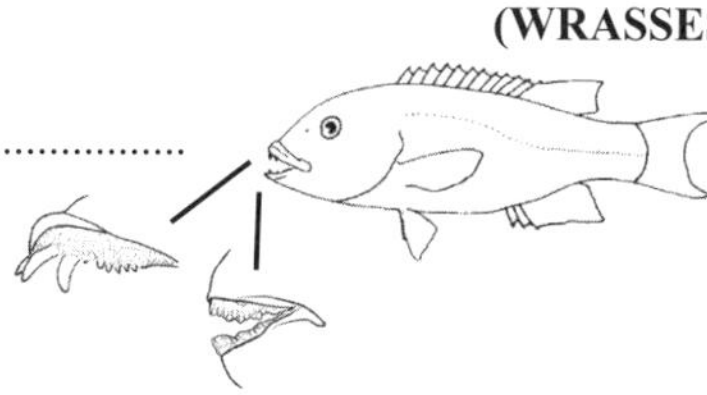

54b Anterior teeth conical or incisor-like............... 55 (next page)

## Section G: Pelvic Fins Thoracic with Exactly One Spine and Five Soft-Rays (continued)

55a Dorsal fin spines longer than soft-rays; rear teeth molar-like............................................

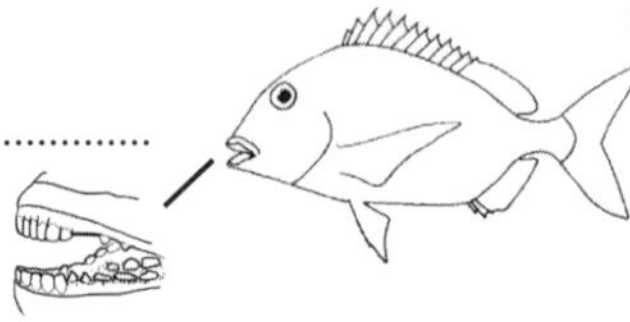

**SPARIDAE**
**(PACIFIC PORGY)**
Page 253

55b Dorsal fin spines about equal to or shorter than soft-rays; rear teeth not molar-like......................

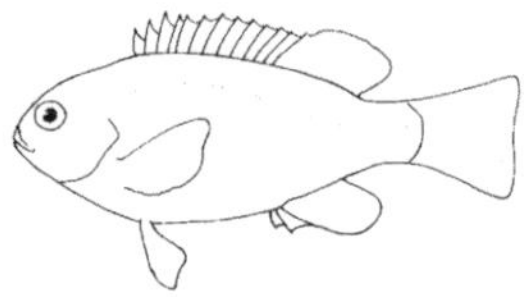

**KYPHOSIDAE**
**(OPALEYE)**
Page 261

56a *From 51a: maxilla exposed when mouth closed* Gill membranes broadly united to isthmus..........

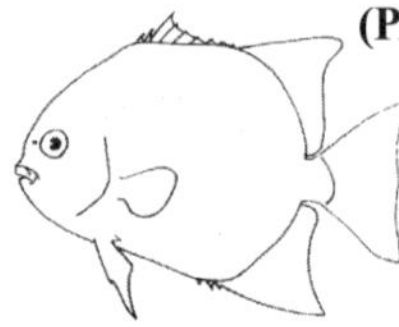

**EPHIPPIDAE**
**(PACIFIC SPADEFISH)**
Page 253

56b Gill membranes free or narrowly united to isthmus......................................................... 57

57a Premaxilla excessively protractile, with basal processes long, folding into groove at top of cranium...........................................................

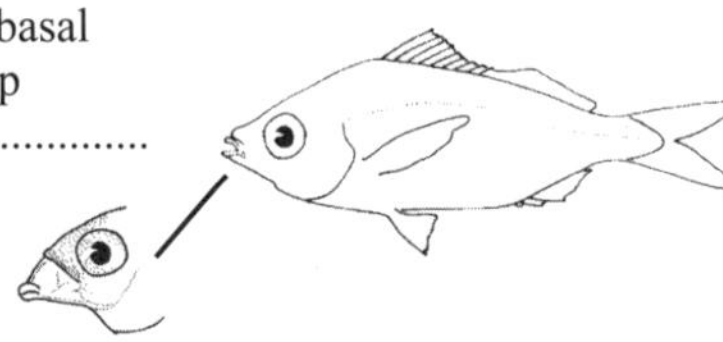

**GERREIDAE**
**(MOJARRAS)**
Page 252

57b Premaxilla not as above.................................... 58

58a Two dorsal fins.....................................................

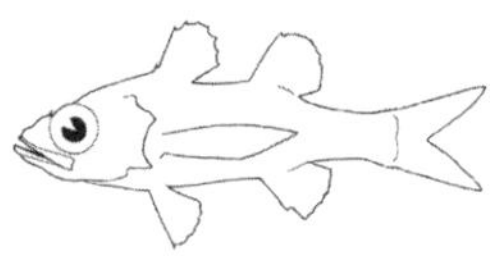

**ACROPOMATIDAE**
**(BASSLETS)**
Page 227

58b Single dorsal fin................................................ 59

59a Base of soft anal fin equal to or longer than base of soft dorsal fin..................................................

**PRIACANTHIDAE**
**(BIGEYES)**
Page 227

59b Base of soft anal fin shorter than base of soft dorsal fin......................................................

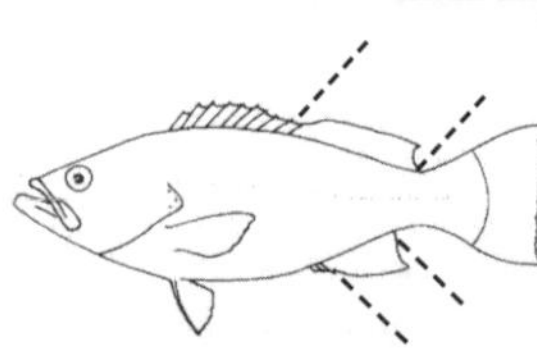

**SERRANIDAE, EPINEPHELIDAE, MORONIDAE, POLYPRIONIDAE**
**(SEA BASSES, GROUPERS, TEMPERATE BASSES, WRECKFISH)**
Page 218

## Section H: Pelvic Fins Thoracic with Fewer Than Five Soft-Rays (Either Normal or Modified into Barbel-like or Club-like Structures)

1a Upper jaw forming spear;
keel(s) on caudal peduncle....................................

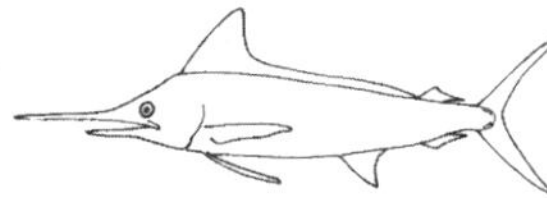

**ISTIOPHORIDAE (BILLFISHES)** Page 337

1b Upper jaw not as spear; keel(s) lacking............. 2

2a Pelvic fins short................................................ 4

2b Pelvic fins long, at least ½ BL........................... 3

3a Anterior dorsal fin soft-rays greatly elongated.......

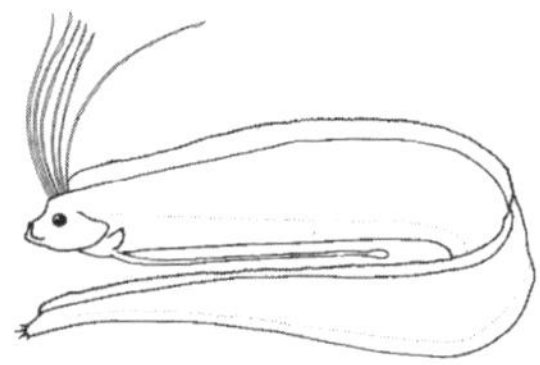

**REGALECIDAE (OARFISH)** Page 133

3a Anterior dorsal fin soft-rays not as above.............

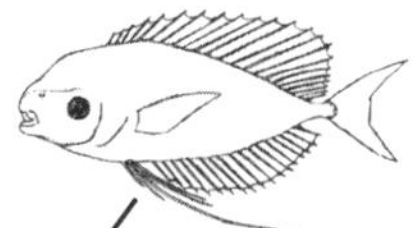

pelvic fins reduced in adults

**LUVARIDAE (juvenile LOUVAR)** Page 340

4a *From 2a: pelvic fins short*
Photophores present.............................................

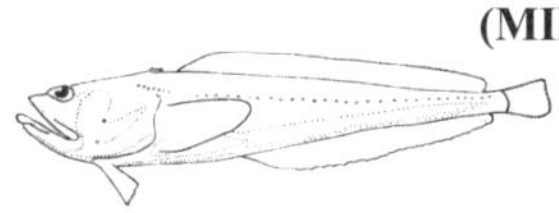

**BATRACHOIDIDAE (MIDSHIPMANS)** Page 97

4b No photophores on body.................................... 5

5a Body encased in bony plates.................................

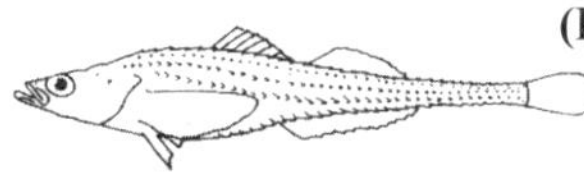

**AGONIDAE (POACHERS)** Page 179

5b Body not encased in bony plates........................ 6

6a No isolated spines in dorsal fin........................... 8

6b Dorsal fin preceded by isolated spines............... 7

7a Isolated spines on back 23–26..............................

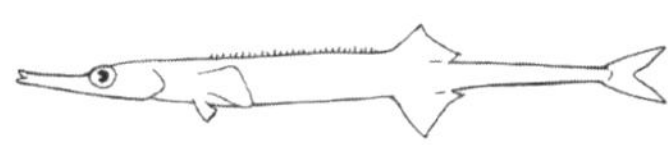

**AULORHYNCHIDAE (TUBESNOUT)** Page 137

7b Isolated spines on back 2–3.................................

**GASTEROSTEIDAE (THREESPINE STICKLEBACK)** Page 137

8a *From 6a: no isolated spines in dorsal fin*
Dorsal fin wholly of soft-rays............................. 15 (next page)

8b Dorsal fin entirely of spines or of spines
and soft-rays....................................................... 9

9a Dorsal fin with both spines and soft-rays........... 12 (next page)

9b Dorsal fin wholly of spines................................ 10

10a Body not elongate or eel-like; anterior
dorsal fin spines elevated...................................

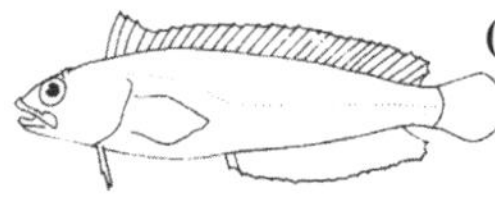

**LABRISOMIDAE (REEF FINSPOT)** Page 307

10b Body elongate or eel-like; dorsal fin spines
about same height............................................ 11 (next page)

## Section H: Pelvic Fins Thoracic with Fewer Than Five Soft-Rays (Either Normal or Modified into Barbel-like or Club-like Structures) (continued)

11a Distance from snout to anal fin origin equal to or less than distance from anal fin origin to base of caudal fin.................................................

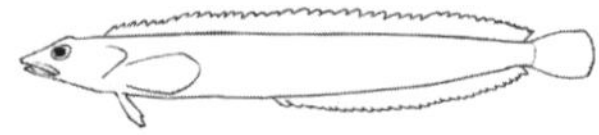

**STICHAEIDAE (PRICKLEBACKS)** Page 289

11b Distance from snout to anal fin origin greater than distance from anal fin origin to base of caudal fin (except LONGFIN GUNNEL)............

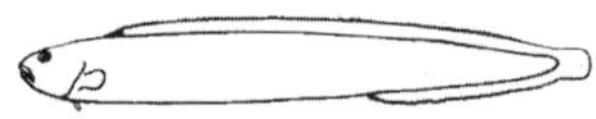

**PHOLIDAE (GUNNELS)** Page 296

12a *From 9a: dorsal fin with both spines and soft-rays* No anal fin spines.................................................

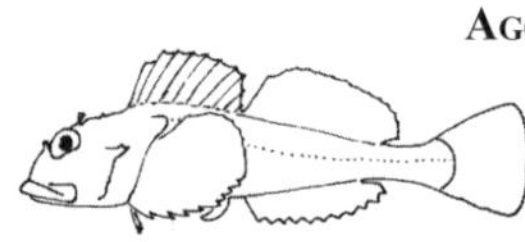

**RHAMPHOCOTTIDAE, PSYCHROLUTIDAE, SCORPAENICHTHYIDAE, JORDANIIDAE, AGONIDAE, COTTIDAE (SCULPINS, POACHERS)** Page 179

12b Anal fin with spines........................................... 13

13a Finlets present......................................................

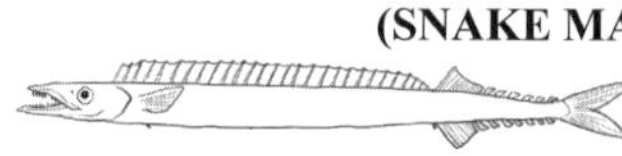

**GEMPYLIDAE (SNAKE MACKEREL)** Page 323

13b Finlets lacking.................................................... 14

14a Gill membranes free from isthmus; more spines than soft-rays in dorsal fin (except ORANGETHROAT PIKEBLENNY)...................................................

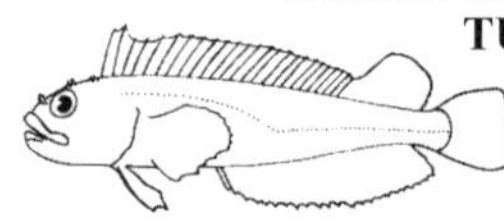

**CLINIDAE, LABRISOMIDAE, CHAENOPSIDAE (KELP BLENNIES, LABRISOMID BLENNIES, TUBE BLENNIES)** Page 307

14b Gill membranes attached to isthmus; more soft-rays than spines in dorsal fin..............

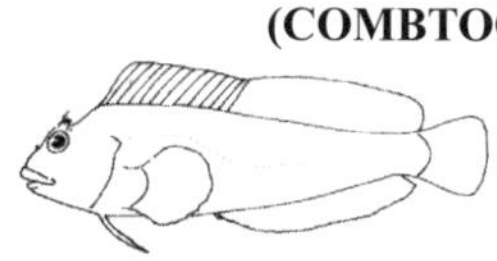

**BLENNIIDAE (COMBTOOTH BLENNIES)** Page 305

15a *From 8a: dorsal fin wholly of soft-rays* Gill membranes joined to isthmus.......................

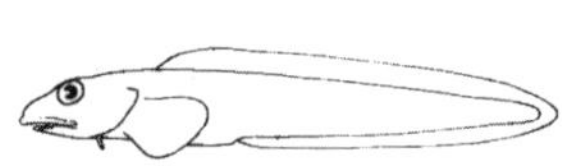

**ZOARCIDAE (EELPOUTS)** Page 283

15b Gill membranes free from isthmus (or slightly joined to isthmus in BROTULAS).................... 16

16a Body oblong; dorsal fin soft-rays fewer than 60.....................................................

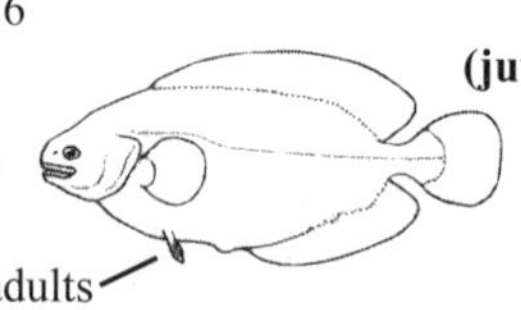


**ICOSTEIDAE (juvenile RAGFISH)** Page 303

16b Body elongate; dorsal fin soft-rays more than 60.......................................................

**OPHIDIIDAE, BYTHITIDAE (CUSK-EELS, BROTULAS)** Page 104

## Section I: Pelvic Fins Thoracic with More Than Five Soft-Rays

1a Body elongate, much longer than deep.............. 4

1b Body ovate, compressed.................................... 2

2a Teeth large, fang-like.............................................

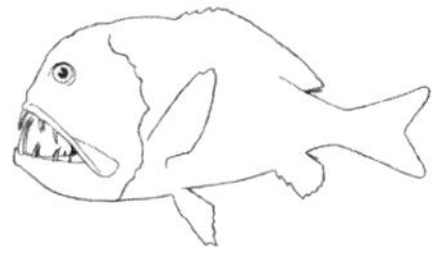

**ANOPLOGASTRIDAE (LONGHORN FANGTOOTH)** Page 130

2b Teeth not large and fang-like............................ 3

3a No spines in anal fin; tail strongly forked.............

**LAMPRIDAE (OPAHS)** Page 133

3b Strong spines in anal fin; tail rounded..................

**OREOSOMATIDAE (OXEYE OREO)** Page 130

4a *From 1a: body elongate*
Anal fin absent.......................................................

**TRACHIPTERIDAE (juvenile RIBBONFISHES)** Page 135

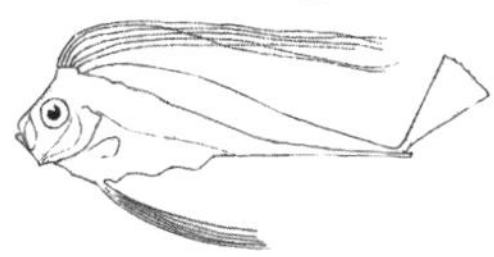

pelvic fins absent in adults

4b Anal fin present................................................. 5

5a No spines in anal fin..... ..................................... 7

5b One or 2 spines in anal fin................................. 6

6a One dorsal fin .......................................................

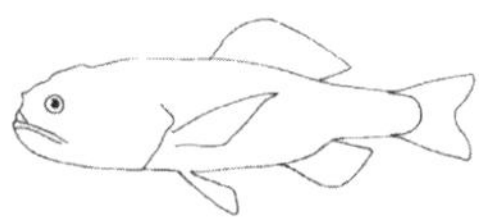

**MELAMPHAIDAE (BIGSCALES)** Page 131

6b Two dorsal fins (See Nematistiidae, ROOSTERFISH, Section G: 30a, page 15)

7a *From 5a: no spines in anal fin*
Caudal fin absent, tail pointed..............................

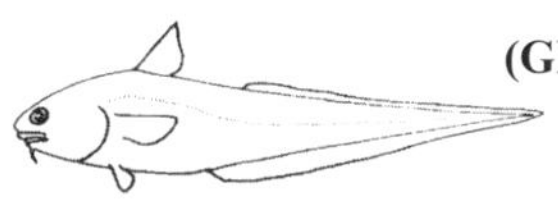

**MACROURIDAE (GRENADIERS)** Page 111

7b Caudal fin present.... ......................................... 8

8a Two anal fins; 3 dorsal fins ..................................

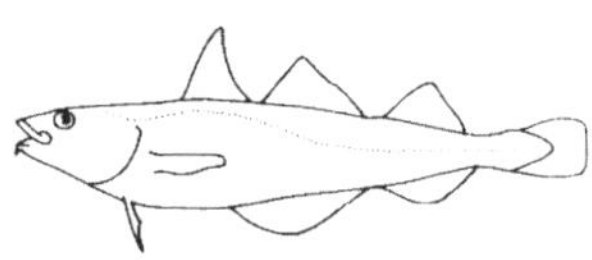

**GADIDAE (CODS)** Page 109

8b One anal fin (may be deeply notched); 2 dorsal fins (ARROWTAIL may only have 1)....................... 9

9a Barbel on lower jaw; pelvic fins filamentous.........

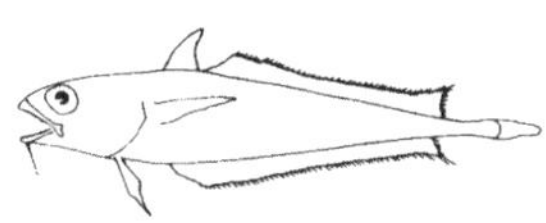

**MORIDAE (CODLINGS)** Page 107

9b No barbels under chin; pelvic fins normal.......... 10

10a Deep notch in 2nd dorsal and anal fins................

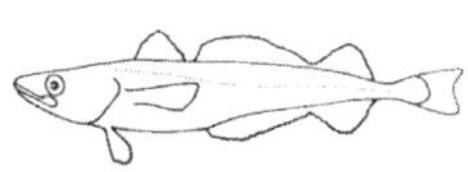

**MERLUCCIIDAE (PACIFIC HAKE)** Page 107

10b No deep notch in 2nd dorsal and anal fins..............................................................

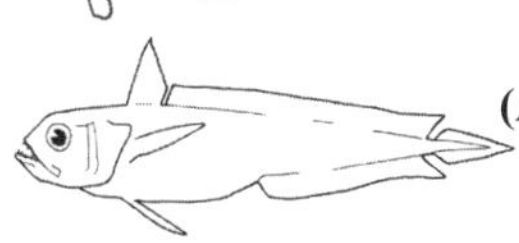

**MELANONIDAE (ARROWTAIL)** Page 107

# SPECIES PRESENTATION: JAWLESS FISHES, Class Myxini and Class Petromyzontida

## HAGFISHES, Family Myxinidae

**WHITEFACE HAGFISH, *Myxine circifrons* Garman, 1899.** San Francisco, northern California to north-central Chile. The Islas Galápagos record listed in M&L appears to be in error. Length to 52.6 cm (20.7 in) TL. Depth: about 700–1,860 m (2,297–6,102 ft). Body uniform black, head lighter near mouth. Separated from other hagfishes by having only 1 gill opening on each side.

**SHORTHEAD HAGFISH, *Eptatretus mcconnaugheyi* Wisner & McMillan, 1990.** Two populations: 1 from Santa Monica Bay, southern California to Islas Cedros and San Benito, central Baja California; and 1 in the lower portion of the Gulf of California. Apparently rare off southern California. Length to 48.2 cm (19 in) TL. Depth: 42–415 m (138–1,362 ft). Reddish-brown without pale spots or areas; barbels pale on distal thirds.

**BLACK HAGFISH, *Eptatretus deani* (Evermann & Goldsborough, 1907).** Southeastern Alaska to Islas San Benito, central Baja California. Common at least from Oregon to northern Baja California. Length to 62.2 cm (26 in) TL. Depth: 52–2,743 m (171–8,997 ft). Uniform purplish-black or very dark brown, with occasional pale spots and areas; anterior of head often pale; ventral and caudal finfolds usually without pale margin.

**PACIFIC HAGFISH, *Eptatretus stoutii* (Lockington, 1878).** Hecate Strait (52°38'N, 130°00'W), British Columbia to southern Baja California (26°37'N). Common from about Vancouver Island southward to at least Islas San Benito, central Baja California. Reported but not confirmed from southeastern Alaska. Length to 82 cm (32.3 in) TL. Depth: 16–1,155 m (53–3,788 ft). Purplish-gray to light brown, with occasional pinkish overtones, commonly with pale spots and blotches.

## KEY TO THE HAGFISHES:

Created by Julianne Kalman Passarelli
(Principal sources: Miller & Lea, 1972; Wisner & McMillan, 1990; Mecklenburg et al., 2002)

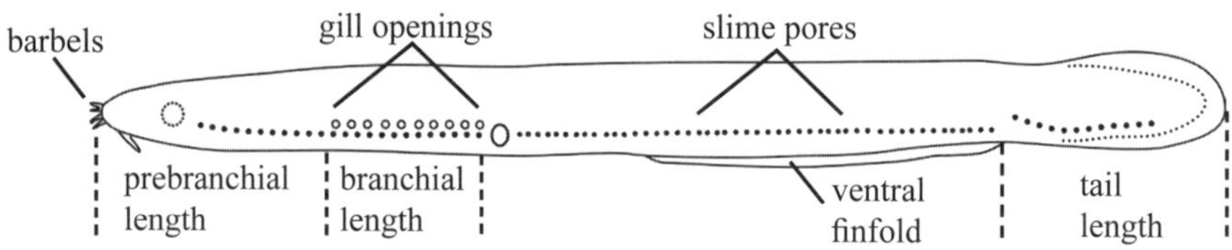


**FIGURE 16. HAGFISH composite.**

1a Single gill opening: **WHITEFACE HAGFISH**

1b Multiple gill openings….. 2

2a Prebranchial length equal to or shorter than branchial length; tail length shorter than branchial length:
**SHORTHEAD HAGFISH**

2b Prebranchial and tail lengths longer than branchial length….. 3

3a TL at least 5 times prebranchial length; prebranchial slime pores 4–10; body dark, uniform purplish-black or very dark brown; ventral finfold weakly developed, often vestigial or absent:
**BLACK HAGFISH**

3b TL less than 5 times prebranchial length; prebranchial slime pores 12–17; body light, purplish-gray to light brown; ventral finfold prominent, with wide pale margin:
**PACIFIC HAGFISH**

# LAMPREYS, Family Petromyzontidae

**PACIFIC LAMPREY, *Entosphenus tridentatus* (Richardson, 1837).** Honshu, Hokkaido, Japan; eastern Chukchi Sea; Bering Sea to Punta Canoas, northern Baja California and likely to Isla Clarión, Revillagigedo Archipelago, Mexico. Southernmost freshwater occurrence is currently in the Big Sur River, central California. In ocean, common from Kamchatka, Russia to eastern Bering Sea and to at least northern Baja California (30°43'N, 116°02'W). Length to 85 cm (33.5 in) TL. Anadromous, may be found at sea, often far offshore. At sea, depth: near surface to 1,508 m (4,946 ft). At sea, slate-gray or bluish-gray; spawning adults brown, red, or gray. Author of the species description sometimes incorrectly given as Gairdner, 1837, or Gairdner in Richardson, 1837. (Formerly *Lampetra tridentata*: M&L).

**WESTERN RIVER LAMPREY, *Lampetra ayresii* (Günther, 1870).** Tee Harbor, southeastern Alaska to San Francisco Bay, northern California. Apparently found in widely scattered populations. Common in the Sacramento-San Joaquin River system. Length to 33.5 cm (13.2 in) TL. Anadromous, found in estuaries and coastal marine waters for a few months in summer. Dark blue above, silvery below.

**PACIFIC LAMPREY**

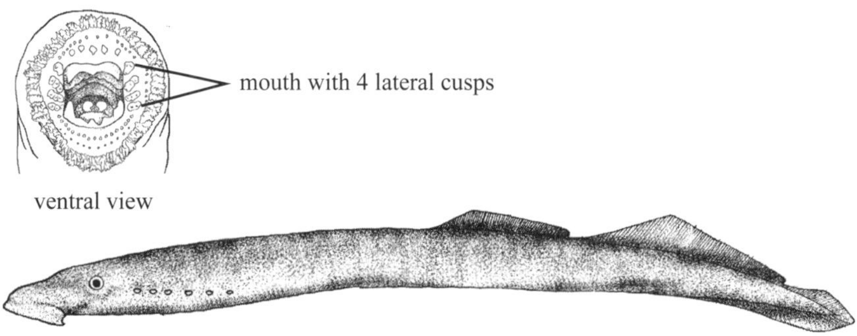


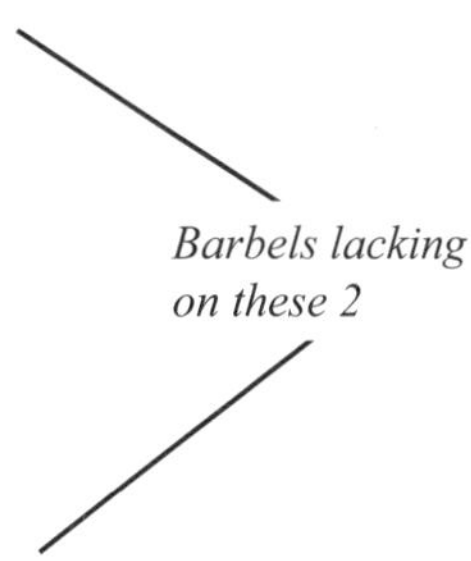


**WESTERN RIVER LAMPREY**

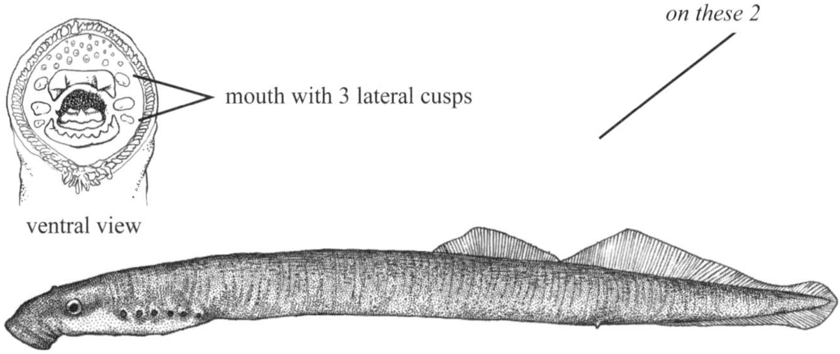

# SPECIES PRESENTATION: CARTILAGINOUS FISHES, Class Chondrichthyes

## Order Heterodontiformes, Order Orectolobiformes, Order Squatiniformes, and Order Torpediniformes
## HORN SHARK, Family Heterodontidae, WHALE SHARK, Family Rhincodontidae, ANGEL SHARK, Family Squatinidae, and ELECTRIC RAY, Family Torpedinidae

**HORN SHARK, *Heterodontus francisci* (Girard, 1855).** Order Heterodontiformes, Family Heterodontidae
Bolinas, northern California to Gulf of California and Colombia to Peru. Common from southern California southward into tropics. Length to at least 96 cm (37.8 in) TL, possibly to 122 cm (48 in) TL; at birth 15–17 cm (5.9–6.7 in) TL. Depth: intertidal to 200 m (656 ft). Brown or gray on back and sides with dark spotting on body; yellowish belly. Juveniles sometimes with white spots. Vert. 112.

**WHALE SHARK, *Rhincodon typus* Smith, 1828.** Order Orectolobiformes, Family Rhincodontidae
Circumtropical; just north of Hokkaido Island, Japan; Patrick's Point (41°10'N, 124°15'W), northern California to northern Chile and Islas Galápagos. Rare off California; common in tropical waters. Length to at least 18.8 m (61.7 ft) TL, possibly 21.4 m (70.6 ft) TL; at birth 55–64 cm (21.7–25.2 in) TL. Pelagic; depth: surface to in excess of 1,700 m (5,576 ft). Black, brown, or blue above, with white spots. Vert. 153.

**PACIFIC ANGEL SHARK, *Squatina californica* Ayres, 1859.** Order Squatiniformes, Family Squatinidae
Clover Point (48°24'N, 123°21'W), Vancouver Island to southern Baja California and Gulf of California and Peru. Unverifiable records from southeastern Alaska and Chile. Common from Tomales Bay, northern California southward. Length to 175 cm (68.9 in) TL; at birth about 25 cm (9.8 in) TL. Depth: surf zone to 205 m (672 ft). Gray to dusky above with dark spotting, white below. Vert. 140–141.

**PACIFIC ELECTRIC RAY, *Tetronarce californica* (Ayres, 1855).** Order Torpediniformes, Family Torpedinidae
Japan, south Kuril Islands, and Kinmei Seamount; Wiah Point, Graham Island, northern British Columbia to Todos Santos (23°25'N, 110°14'W), southern Baja California, including Isla Guadalupe, central Baja California, and Peru. One record from the Gulf of California. Common from about San Francisco Bay southward into southern Baja California. Length to more than 140 cm (55.1 in) TL; at birth 18–23 cm (7.1–9.1 in) TL. Depth: surf zone to 1,079 m (3,539 ft), usually shallower than 300 m (984 ft). Blue-black to dark gray above, slate-gray below, often with black spotting. Vert. 95–105. (Formerly *Torpedo californica* Ayres, 1855: M&L) (Alternative name PACIFIC TORPEDO RAY).

## KEY TO THE ORDERS OF CARTILAGINOUS FISHES:
Created by David Ebert
(Principal sources: Ebert, 2003; Ebert et al., 2013)

1a One paired gill opening: CHIMAERIFORMES (page 27)

1b Five to 7 paired gill openings….. 2

2a Body flat, ray-like….. 8 (next page)

2b Body not ray-like….. 3

3a Anal fin absent: ECHINORHINIFORMES and SQUALIFORMES (page 28)

3b Anal fin present….. 4

4a One dorsal fin; 6 or 7 paired gill openings: HEXANCHIFORMES (page 31)

4b Two dorsal fins; 5 paired gill openings….. 5 (next page)

5a Dorsal fin spines present:
HETERODONTIFORMES (HETERODONTIDAE)

**HORN SHARK**

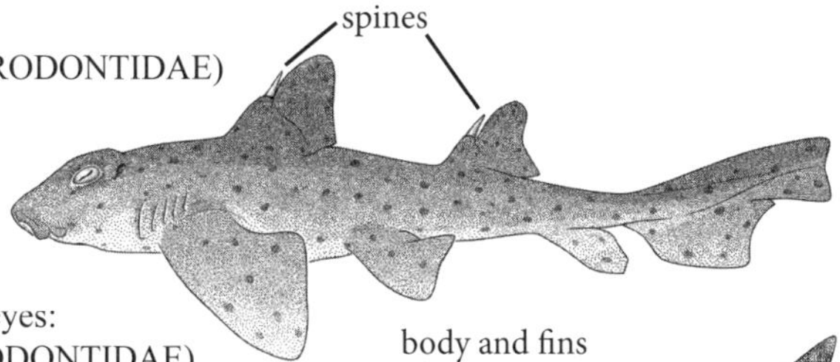


5b Dorsal fin spines absent….. 6

6a Mouth terminal, located in front of eyes:
ORECTOLOBIFORMES (RHINCODONTIDAE)

**WHALE SHARK**

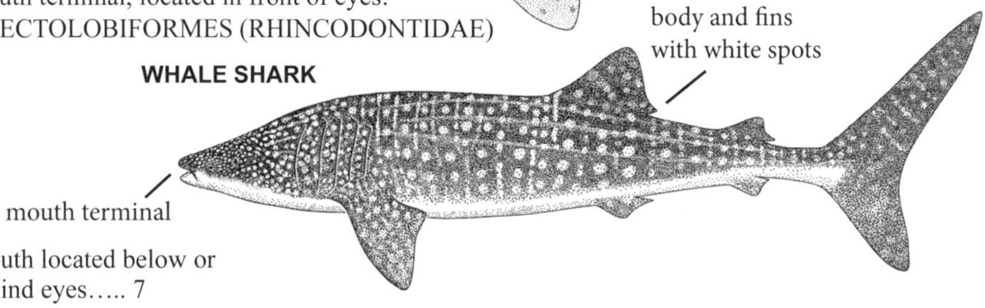


6b Mouth located below or
behind eyes….. 7

7a Nictitating eyelids absent; caudal keel present (lacking in GOBLIN SHARK, MEGAMOUTH SHARK, RAGGED-TOOTH SHARK, and THRESHER SHARKS):
LAMNIFORMES (page 32)

7b Nictitating eyelids present; caudal keel absent:
CARCHARHINIFORMES (page 37)

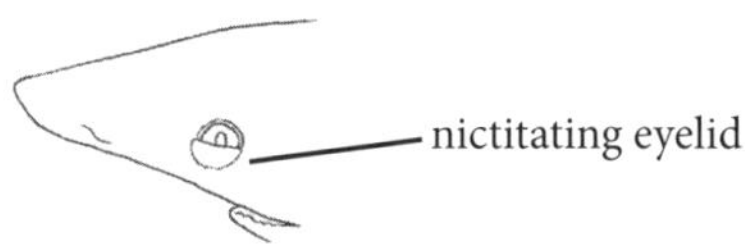


8a *From 2a: body flat, ray-like*
Mouth terminal; gills lateral on head; pectoral fins not attached to head:
SQUATINIFORMES (SQUATINIDAE)

**PACIFIC ANGEL SHARK**

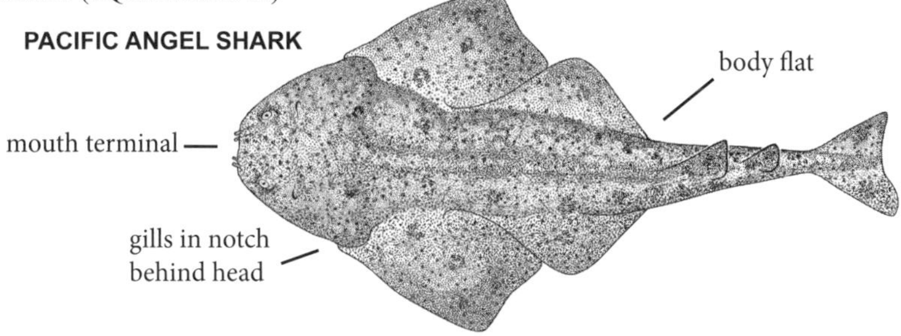


8b Mouth and gills ventral (mouth terminal in MANTA); pectoral fins attached to head….. 9

9a Spine or thorns lacking; pectoral fins rounded;
disc with electric organs:
TORPEDINIFORMES (TORPEDINIDAE)

**PACIFIC ELECTRIC RAY**

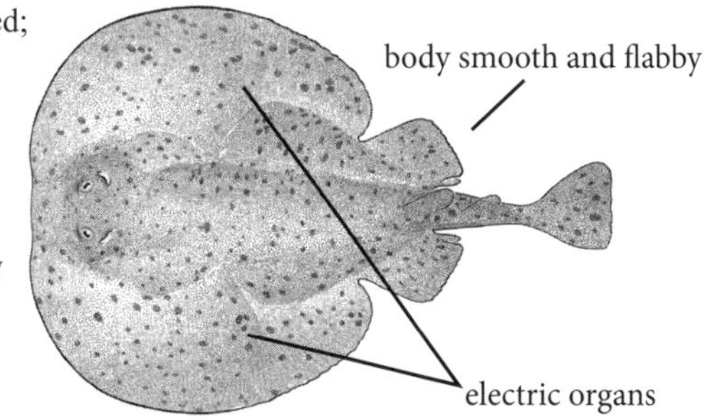


9b Spine or thorns present on body (spine vestigial in MANTA); pectoral fins typically pointed (if rounded, then spine present); disc without electric organs….. 10

10a Tail base or body with no stinging spine (prominent row of thorns may be present); with 2 dorsal fins: RHINOPRISTIFORMES and RAJIFORMES (page 45)

10b Tail base with stinging spine (vestigial in MANTA); single or no dorsal fin:
MYLIOBATIFORMES (page 51)

# Order Chimaeriformes
# CHIMAERAS,
## Family Rhinochimaeridae and Family Chimaeridae

**LONGNOSE CHIMAERA, *Harriotta raleighana* Goode & Bean, 1895.** Family RHINOCHIMAERIDAE
Circumglobal; Japan; southern California (CAS 235591) to Peru. Rare in southern California. Length to 120 cm (47.2 in) TL. Depth: 350–2,603 m (1,148–8,538 ft). Uniform chocolate brown, fin edge darker. (Alternative name PACIFIC LONGNOSE CHIMAERA).

**SPOTTED RATFISH, *Hydrolagus colliei* (Lay & Bennett, 1839).** Family CHIMAERIDAE
Western Gulf of Alaska to Cabo Blanco (9°26'N, 85°30'W), Costa Rica and northern Gulf of California. Two isolated populations in the Gulf of California: 1 at Isla Tiburon, the other in the Bahía de La Paz-Cabo San Lucas region. Common at least from Cape Fairweather, southeast Alaska to at least as far south as Punta Canoas, central Baja California. Length to 100 cm (39.3 in) TL. Depth: surface and intertidal to 1,463 m (4,799 ft). Uniformly dark brown to reddish-brown, lighter gray ventrally with numerous white spots on head, back, and trunk. (Formerly RATFISH: M&L) (Alternative name WHITESPOTTED RATFISH).

**EASTERN PACIFIC BLACK GHOSTSHARK, *Hydrolagus melanophasma* James, Ebert, Long & Didier, 2009.** Family CHIMAERIDAE
Monterey, central California to Gulf of California and to Valdivia, Chile. Common off California. Length to 128 cm (50.4 in) TL. Depth: 31–1,720 m (102–5,642 ft). Uniform black; sometimes lighter band over snout between eye and snout tip.

NOTE: This group also known as RATFISHES. Venomous dorsal fin spine on these 3.

## KEY TO THE CHIMAERIFORMES:
Created by David Ebert
(Principal source: Ebert, 2003)

1a Snout more than 50% of HL:

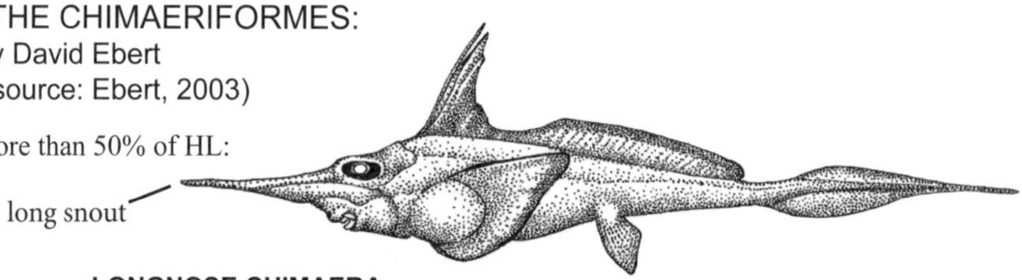


**LONGNOSE CHIMAERA**

1b Snout less than 50% of HL….. 2

2a Body surface with numerous, scattered white spots; 2nd dorsal fin with deep notch, appearing as 2 fins:

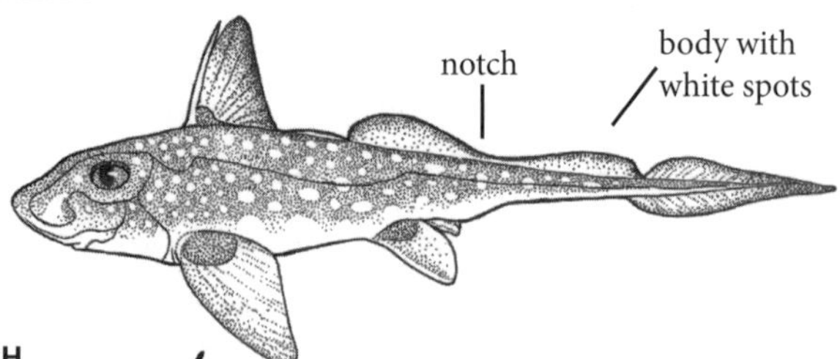


**SPOTTED RATFISH**

2b Body surface without spots or other markings; 2nd dorsal fin continuous, without notch:

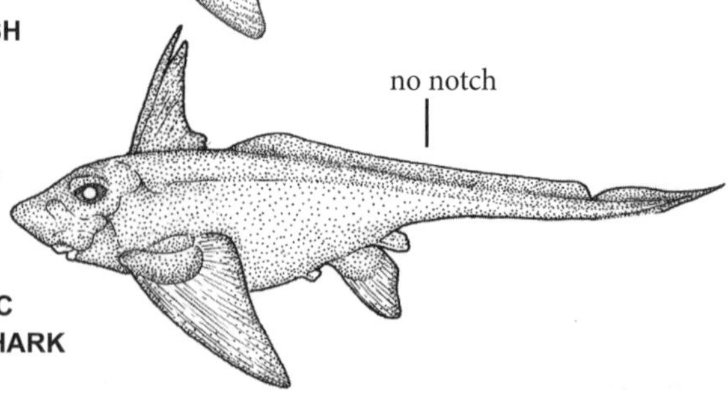


**EASTERN PACIFIC BLACK GHOSTSHARK**

## Order Echinorhiniformes and Order Squaliformes
## PRICKLY SHARK, Family Echinorhinidae, DOGFISHES, Family Squalidae and Family Etmopteridae, KITEFIN SHARKS, Family Dalatiidae, and SLEEPER SHARKS, Family Somniosidae

**PRICKLY SHARK, *Echinorhinus cookei* Pietschmann, 1928.** Order ECHINORHINIFORMES, Family ECHINORHINIDAE
Moolach Beach, Oregon to barely into Gulf of California to Chile, including Islas Galápagos and Hawai'i. Common in discrete locations off California (such as in Monterey Submarine Canyon). Length to 4.5 m (14.8 ft) TL; at birth 35–45 cm (13.8–17.7 in) TL. Depth: 4–1,100 m (13–3,608 ft). Brown, black, or gray; mouth and under snout white; trailing edge of fins blackish; very large denticles irregularly scattered over body and fins. Vert. 88–92.

**PACIFIC SPINY DOGFISH, *Squalus suckleyi* (Girard, 1855).** Order SQUALIFORMES, Family SQUALIDAE
Korea northward to Russia and to Bering Sea and southeastern Chukchi Sea (near Kotzebue), Alaska to southern Baja California. Common from Sea of Japan and Gulf of Alaska (and perhaps Bering Sea) to Bahía San Quintin, northern Baja California and perhaps somewhat further southward. Length to at least 140 cm (55.1 in) TL and possibly to 160 cm (63 in) TL; at birth 22–33 cm (8.7–13 in) TL. Coastal, inshore, and offshore; depth: intertidal to 1,460 m (4,789 ft). Dark gray to brown on back; often with white spotting on sides. Vert. 97–106. (Formerly SPINY DOGFISH, *Squalus acanthias* Linnaeus, 1758: M&L).

## KEY TO THE ECHINORHINIFORMES and SQUALIFORMES:
Created by David Ebert
(Principal sources: Ebert, 2003; Ebert et al., 2013)

NOTE: These 7 sharks all lack an anal fin.

1a Dorsal fins with prominent anterior spine….. 3

1b Dorsal fins with inconspicuous, small spines or without spines….. 2

2a Origin of 1st dorsal fin posterior to pelvic fin origin; strong denticles on dorsal body:

**PRICKLY SHARK**

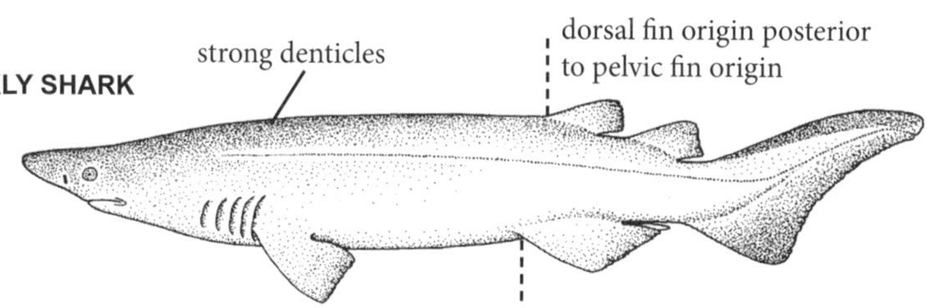


2b Origin of 1st dorsal fin anterior to pelvic fin origin; strong denticles on dorsal body lacking….. 4 (page 30)

3a *From 1a: dorsal fins with prominent anterior spine*
Teeth similar in both jaws:

**PACIFIC SPINY DOGFISH**

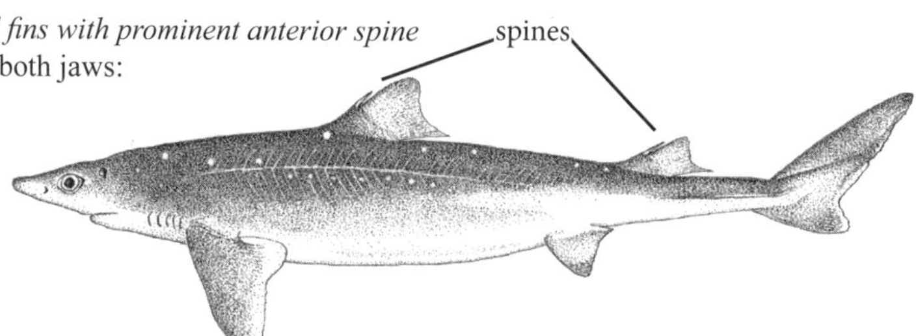


3b (next page)

## Order Echinorhiniformes and Order Squaliformes (continued)

**COMBTOOTH DOGFISH, *Centroscyllium nigrum* Garman, 1899.** Order SQUALIFORMES, Family ETMOPTERIDAE
Southern California and northern Baja California to Chile, Cocos Island, Islas Galápagos, and Hawai'i. Common off southern California. Length to about 52 cm (20.4 in) TL; at birth 11–13 cm (4.3–5.1 in) TL. Depth: 269–1,212 m (883–3,975 ft). What was likely a COMBTOOTH DOGFISH was photographed off La Jolla, southern California, at a depth of 32 m (105 ft). Dark brown or black; dorsal, pectoral, and anal fins often lighter-tipped. Vert. 81–85. (Alternative name PACIFIC BLACK DOGFISH).

**PYGMY SHARK, *Euprotomicrus bispinatus* (Quoy & Gaimard, 1824).** Order SQUALIFORMES, Family DALATIIDAE
Circumglobal; a few caught 805 km (500 mi) off southern California (LACM 6989-1); Peru through Chile and Easter Island. Length to 30.5 cm (12 in) TL; at birth 6–10 cm (2.4–3.9 in) TL. Depth: surface at night to perhaps 1,800 m (5,904 ft). Uniform brown or black; ventral area bioluminescent. Vert. 60–70. This species might more properly be placed in the genus *Squaliolus* (Naylor et al., 2012).

**COOKIECUTTER SHARK, *Isistius brasiliensis* (Quoy & Gaimard, 1824).** Order SQUALIFORMES, Family DALATIIDAE
Circumglobal; as far as Hokkaido, Japan and San Nicolas Island, southern California to Peru (13°46'S) and Islas Galápagos. Common in tropical waters worldwide. Freshly wounded pinnipeds found off Año Nuevo, central California imply this species lives even further north. Length to 56 cm (22 in) TL. Depth: surface to 3,700 m (12,136 ft). Uniform brown or gray on back, lighter below; dark band around gill slits; dorsal and anal fins with light margin; caudal fin lobes dark. Vert. 81–89.

**PACIFIC SLEEPER SHARK, *Somniosus pacificus* Bigelow & Schroeder, 1944.** Order SQUALIFORMES, Family SOMNIOSIDAE
Taiwan to Bering Sea and to southeastern Chukchi Sea (66°20'N, 165°47'W) and on Russian side of southern Chukchi Sea to Pacific Ocean off southern Baja California. Reports from as far south as Pisco, Peru and Bahía de San Antonio (33°35'S), Chile are questionable and may represent the SOUTHERN SLEEPER SHARK, *Somniosus antarcticus* Whitley, 1939. Abundance pattern is poorly known; likely common western and eastern Bering Sea and along Aleutian Islands, but also likely common off central California. Length to at least 4.4 m (14.4 ft) TL and possibly larger. Depth: surface to about 2,205 m (7,232 ft); at the greatest depths in the southern part of the range. Light gray, brown, or black above. Vert. 39–43.

**VELVET DOGFISH, *Zameus squamulosus* (Gunther, 1877).** Order SQUALIFORMES, Family SOMNIOSIDAE
Circumglobal; in western Pacific as far north as off southern Kuril Islands, Russia; 1 fish taken from southern California (33°43'N, 118°32'W); Peru through Chile. Length to 84 cm (33 in) TL or perhaps to 105 cm (41.3 in) TL. Depth: 0–2,000 m (6,560 ft). Dark brown to black.

3b Teeth dissimilar on upper and lower jaws:

**COMBTOOTH DOGFISH**

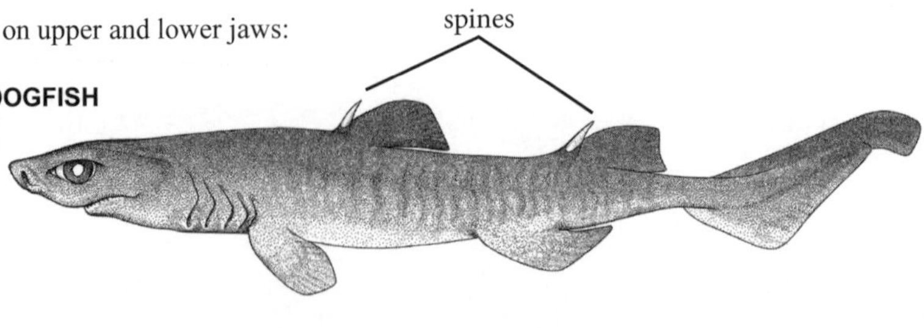


4a (next page)

4a *From 2b: origin of 1st dorsal fin anterior to pelvic fin origin*
First dorsal fin originating closer to pectoral fins….. 6

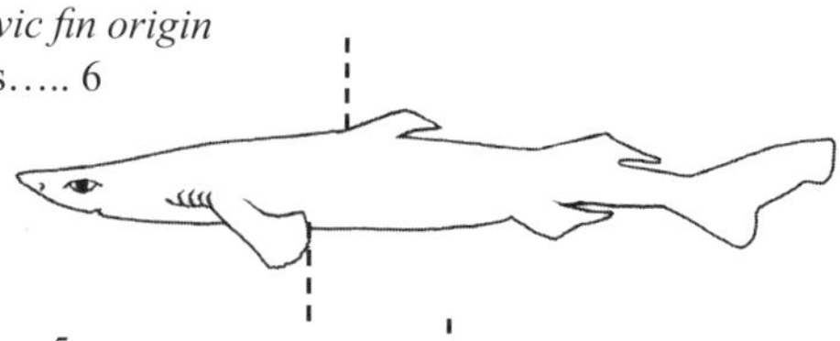

4b First dorsal fin originating closer to pelvic fins….. 5

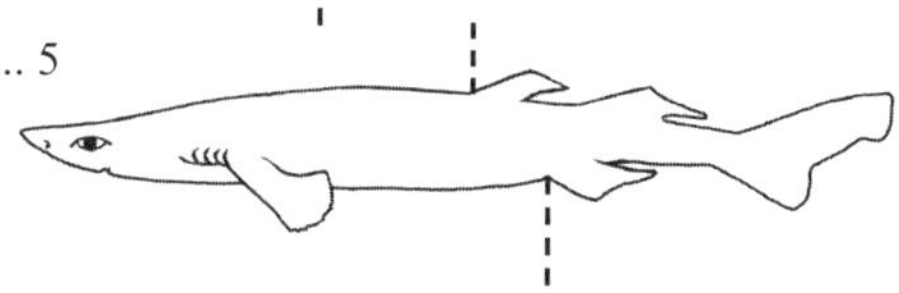

5a Insertion of 1st dorsal fin well anterior to pelvic fin origin; 2nd dorsal fin about 4 times length of 1st dorsal fin:

**PYGMY SHARK**

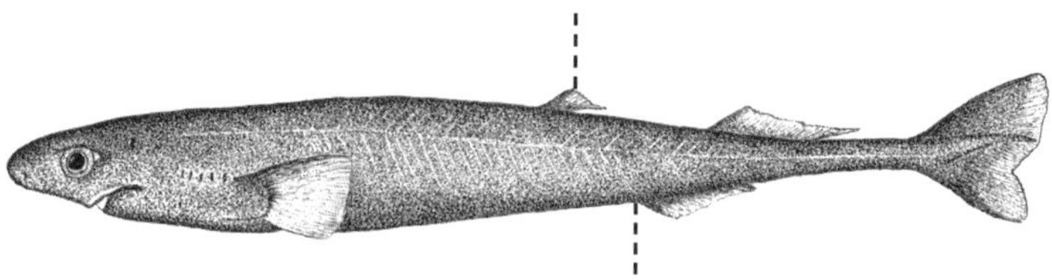

5b Insertion of 1st dorsal fin over pelvic fin origin; dorsal fins similar in size:

**COOKIECUTTER SHARK**

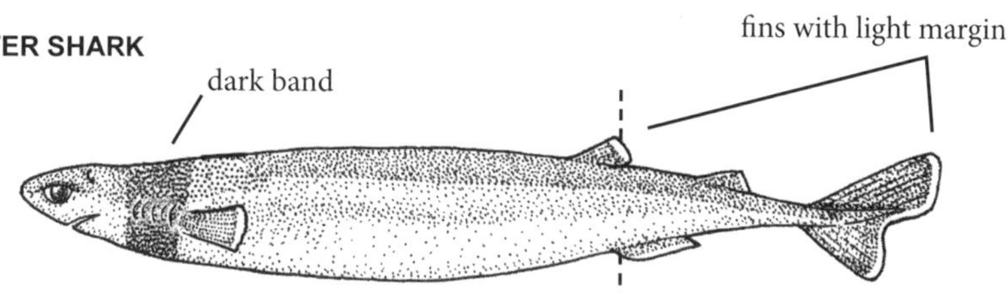


6a *From 4a: first dorsal fin originating closer to pectoral fins*
Dorsal fin spines absent; snout blunt:

**PACIFIC SLEEPER SHARK**

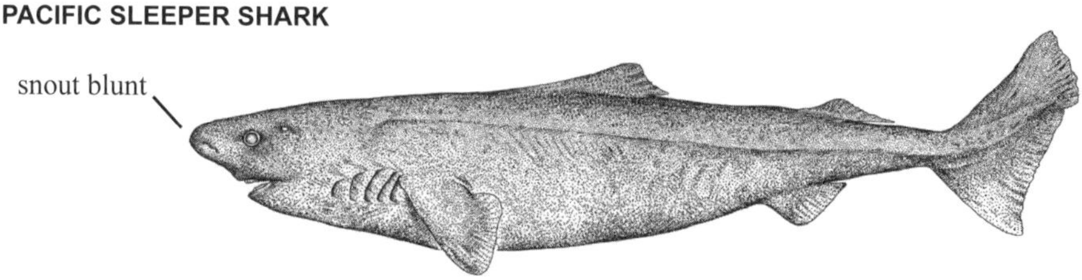


6b Dorsal fin spines present, though short and partly covered by skin; snout pointed:

**VELVET DOGFISH**

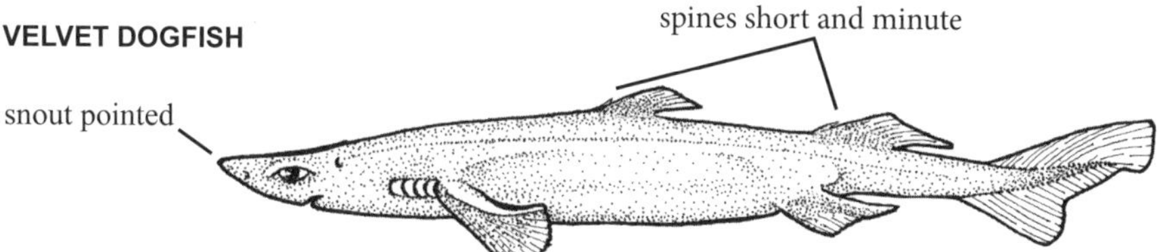

# Order Hexanchiformes
# FRILL SHARK, Family Chlamydoselachidae and COW SHARKS, Family Hexanchidae

**FRILL SHARK, *Chlamydoselachus anguineus* Garman, 1884.** Family CHLAMYDOSELACHIDAE
Circumglobal; Japan (LACM 43793-1); one record from off Point Arguello, central California, and one off Chile. Rare off California. Length to at least 1.96 m (6.4 ft) TL. Depth: surface to 1,570 m (5,150 ft). Dark brown, brown-gray, or blackish. Vert. 146–171. (Formerly FRILLED SHARK: M&L).

**BLUNTNOSE SIXGILL SHARK, *Hexanchus griseus* (Bonnaterre, 1788).** Family HEXANCHIDAE
Circumglobal in temperate and tropical waters; southern Japan; eastern North Pacific south of Aleutian Islands to Gulf of California to Chile. Common from at least Washington to southern California. Length to 6 m (19.7 ft) TL. Depth: surface to at least 2,500 m (8,200 ft) or perhaps to 3,000 m (9,840 ft); adults usually below 91 m (298 ft). Dark gray, brown, or black; light streak along side and margin of fins; sometimes with dark spots. Vert. 128–145. (Formerly SIXGILL SHARK: M&L) (Alternative name MUD SHARK).

**BROADNOSE SEVENGILL SHARK, *Notorynchus cepedianus* (Péron, 1807).** Family HEXANCHIDAE
Circumglobal in temperate waters; China and Japan; southeastern Alaska to southern Baja California and Colombia to Chile. Common at least from Washington to southern California. Length to at least 2.96 m (9.7 ft) TL. Depth: less than 1 m (3 ft) to 570 m (1,870 ft). Reddish-brown, olive-brown to gray; usually dark spotting on back and fins. Some very dark fish lack spots. Newborns with black-tipped dorsal fin and upper lobe of caudal fin. Vert. 123–130. (Formerly SEVENGILL SHARK, *Notorynchus maculatus* Ayres, 1856: M&L).

## KEY TO THE HEXANCHIFORMES:
Created by David Ebert
(Principal sources: Ebert, 2003; Ebert et al., 2013)

NOTE: These 3 are the only sharks with 1 dorsal fin and more than 5 gill slits.

1a Six paired gill slits, 1st extending across throat; tip of lower jaw near end of snout:

**FRILL SHARK**

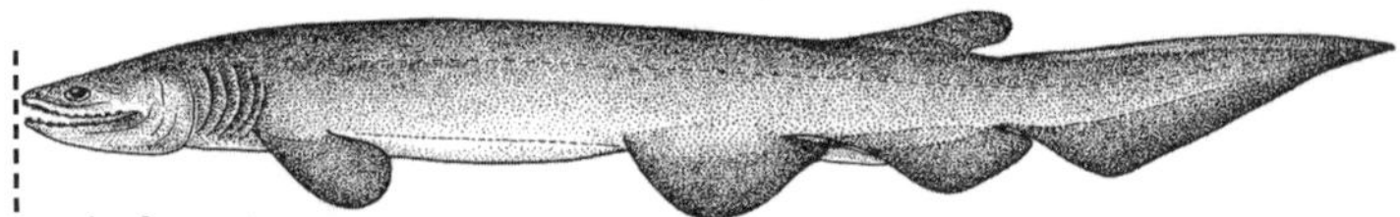

tip of lower jaw near end of snout

1b Six or 7 paired gill slits, without 1st extending across throat; tip of lower jaw under eye..... 2

2a Six paired gill slits:

**BLUNTNOSE SIXGILL SHARK**

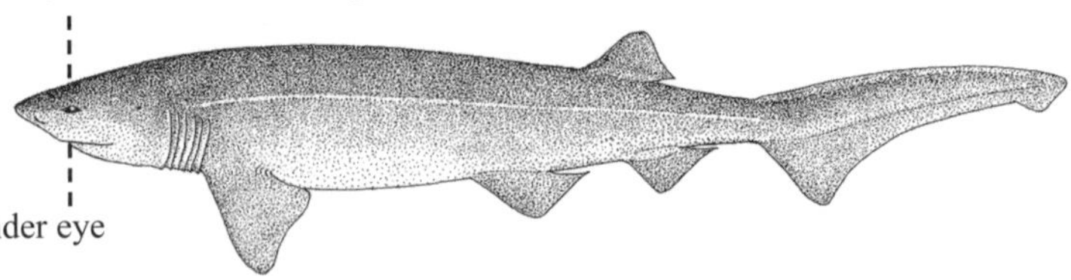

tip of lower jaw under eye

2b Seven paired gill slits:

**BROADNOSE SEVENGILL SHARK**

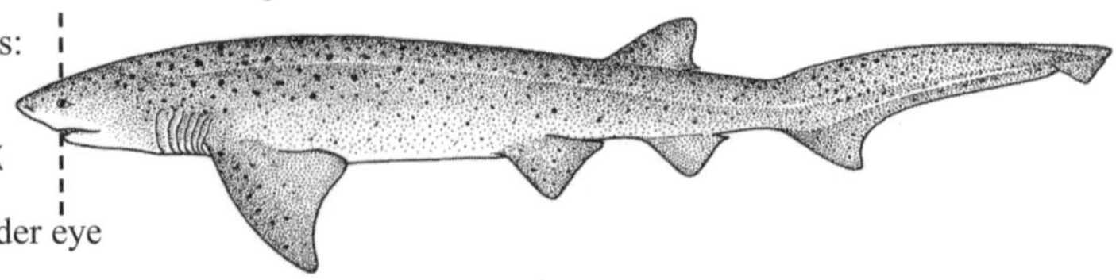

tip of lower jaw under eye

# Order Lamniformes
## GOBLIN SHARK, Family Mitsukurinidae, MEGAMOUTH SHARK, Family Megachasmidae, RAGGED-TOOTH SHARK, Family Odontaspididae, BASKING SHARK, Family Cetorhinidae, THRESHER SHARKS, Family Alopiidae, and MACKEREL SHARKS, Family Lamnidae

**GOBLIN SHARK, *Mitsukurina owstoni* Jordan, 1898.** Family Mitsukurinidae

Circumglobal; San Clemente Island, southern California (LACM 47362-1). Rare off southern California. Length to 5.4 m (17.7 ft) TL or perhaps to 7.6 m (24.9 ft) TL; at birth around 100 cm (39.4 in) TL. Depth: surface to 1,300 m (4,264 ft). Pinkish-white, pink, pink-brown, or white; bluish fins. Vert. 122–124.

**MEGAMOUTH SHARK, *Megachasma pelagios* Taylor, Compagno & Struhsaker, 1983.** Family Megachasmidae

Circumglobal; as far northward as northern Japan; southern California (LACM 43745-1) and near Punta Eugenia, Baja California; Hawai'i. Occasional off California. Length to at least 5.76 m (18.9 ft) TL. Depth: surface to 1,000 m (3,280 ft). Dark blue, brownish-black, or gray above, lighter below; white band along upper jaw; posterior margin of fins white. Vert. 139–151.

## KEY TO THE LAMNIFORMES:
Created by David Ebert
(Principal sources: Ebert, 2003; Ebert et al., 2013)

1a Snout extremely elongated, flat, and blade-like:

**GOBLIN SHARK**

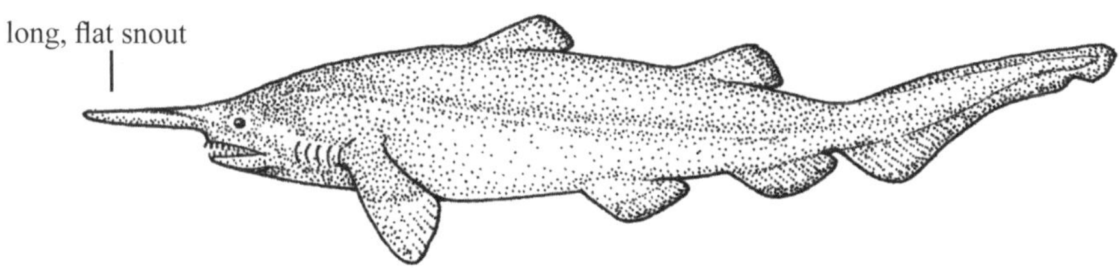


1b Snout short to moderate, not greatly elongated or blade-like, and broadly rounded….. 2

2a Caudal fin about as long as trunk of body….. 6 (page 34)

2b Caudal fin much shorter than trunk of body….. 3

3a Mouth terminal, lower jaw extending to snout tip:

**MEGAMOUTH SHARK**

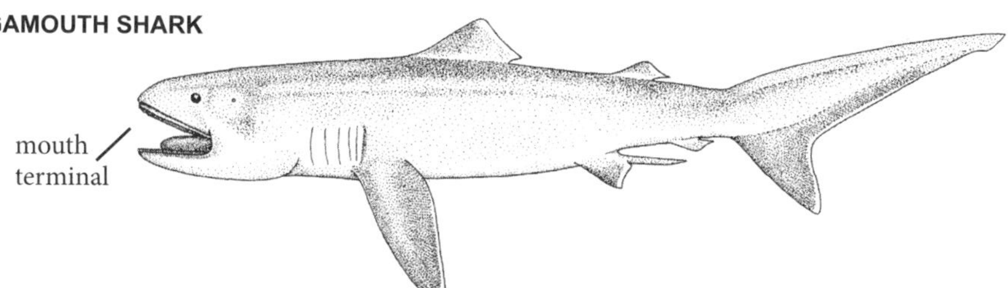


3b Mouth subterminal, lower jaw not extending to snout tip….. 4 (next page)

## Order Lamniformes (continued)

**RAGGED-TOOTH SHARK, *Odontaspis ferox* (Risso, 1810).** Family Odontaspididae
Circumglobal in temperate waters; Newport Beach and Santa Barbara Island, southern California to Gulf of California and Colombia to Chile. Rare off southern California. Length to about 4.5 m (14.8 ft) TL; at birth about 100 cm (39.5 in) TL. Depth: 10–1,015 m (33–3,329 ft) and possibly at surface. Brown, olive, or dark gray above, white below. Vert. 177–183. (Alternative name SMALLTOOTH SANDTIGER SHARK).

**BASKING SHARK, *Cetorhinus maximus* (Gunnerus, 1765).** Family Cetorhinidae
Circumglobal in temperate waters; Yellow Sea, Sea of Japan, Sea of Okhotsk, and western North Pacific Ocean to eastern North Pacific south of Aleutian Islands and in Gulf of Alaska to at least Punta Abreojos (26°42'N, 113°35'W), central Baja California; Colombia to Chile. Records from further south and in Gulf of California are poorly documented. Historically, patchily common from Vancouver Island southward to perhaps northern Baja California; Vancouver Island population appears to have been completely, or nearly completely, killed off. Length well documented to 12.2 m (40 ft) FL; at birth perhaps 150–200 cm (59.1–78.7 in) TL. Coastal pelagic; depth: surface to 1,264 m (4,146 ft). Brown, lead-gray, gray-brown, or black with lighter patches, pale below. Vert. 110.

**BIGEYE THRESHER, *Alopias superciliosus* (Lowe, 1841).** Family Alopiidae
Circumglobal; Cape Mendocino, northern California to Gulf of California and Islas Galápagos; Colombia to Chile. Common as far northward as southern California, particularly during warm-water periods. Length to 4.84 m (15.9 ft) TL; unsubstantiated reports to 5.5 m (18 ft) TL; at birth 130–140 cm (51.2–55.1 in) TL. Depth: surface to 955 m (3,132 ft). Purple, purple-brown, or almost black. Vert. 301–304.

**PELAGIC THRESHER, *Alopias pelagicus* Nakamura, 1935.** Family Alopiidae
Circumtropical; southern California to Panama, including southern tip of Baja California, Colombia to Peru, and Islas Galápagos. Common off southern California during some El Niños; common at least in the Gulf of California. Length to 3.65 m (12 ft) TL; at birth 158–190 cm (62.2–74.8 in) TL. Oceanic; depth: surface to at least 700 m (2,296 ft). In life, dark blue to purple-black on back ranging to white below. Vert. 453–477. (Alternative names THINTAIL THRESHER SHARK, SMALLTOOTH THRESHER).

**COMMON THRESHER SHARK, *Alopias vulpinus* (Bonnaterre, 1788).** Family Alopiidae
Circumglobal in warm waters; in the western Pacific at least as far northward as Hokkaido Island, Japan; west of Yakobi Island, southeastern Alaska and Goose Bay, British Columbia to Chile including Gulf of California. During the summer, common as far north as Vancouver Island; common throughout the year from about southern California to about Punta Eugenia, Baja California. Length to at least 5.73 m (18.8 ft) and possibly to 6.36 m (20.9 ft) TL; at birth 120–150 cm (47.2–59 in) TL. Coastal and oceanic epipelagic; depth: surface to 650 m (2,132 ft). In life, purple, brown, or gray. Vert. 359–362.

4a Lower precaudal pit absent; caudal keel absent; caudal fin not crescent-shaped:

**RAGGED-TOOTH SHARK**

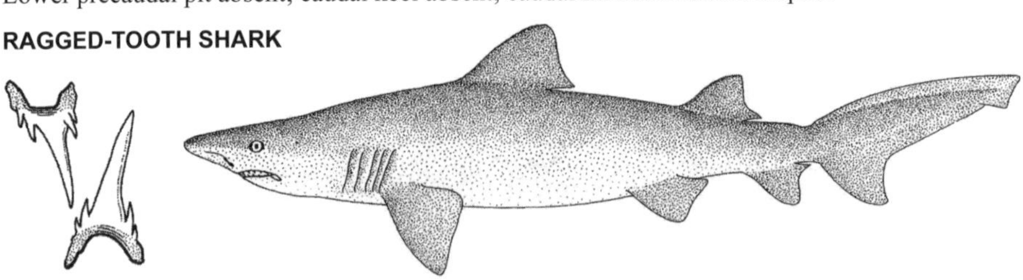

4b Lower precaudal pits present; strong caudal keel present; caudal fin crescent-shaped….. 5 (next page)

5a Teeth minute, hook-shaped, but not blade-like; gill slits extremely long, extending onto dorsal surface of head with 1st slit nearly extending across throat; gill rakers present:

**BASKING SHARK**

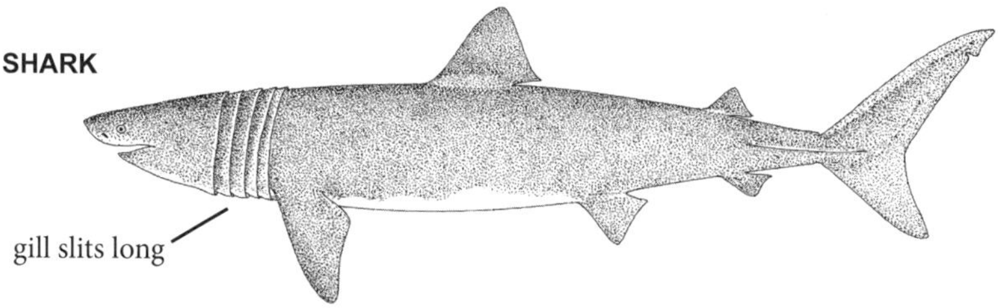


5b Teeth large, triangular, and blade-like; gill slits long, but not extending onto dorsal surface of head or across throat; gill rakers absent….. 8 (next page)

6a *From 2a: caudal fin about as long as trunk of body*
Head with deep horizontal groove extending around each side; eyes very large, expanded onto dorsal head surface:

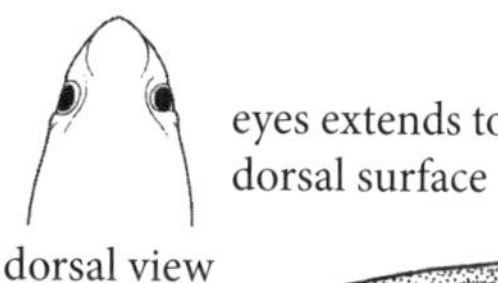


**BIGEYE THRESHER**

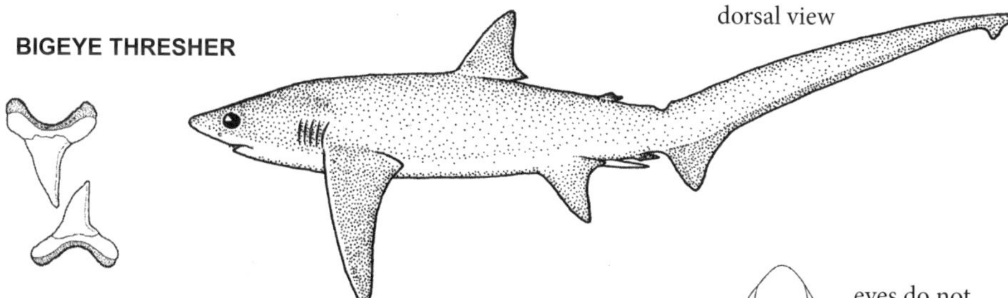

6b Head without deep horizontal groove extending around each side; eyes small, not expanded onto dorsal head surface….. 7

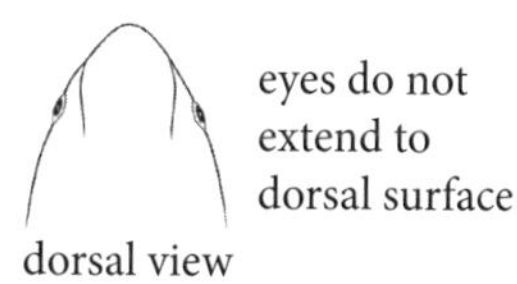


7a Flanks above pectoral and pelvic fins dark; labial furrows absent:

**PELAGIC THRESHER**

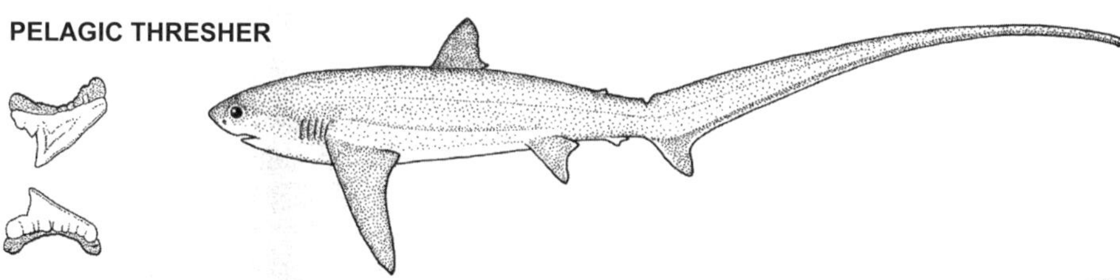

7b Flanks above pectoral and pelvic fins white; labial furrows present:

**COMMON THRESHER SHARK**

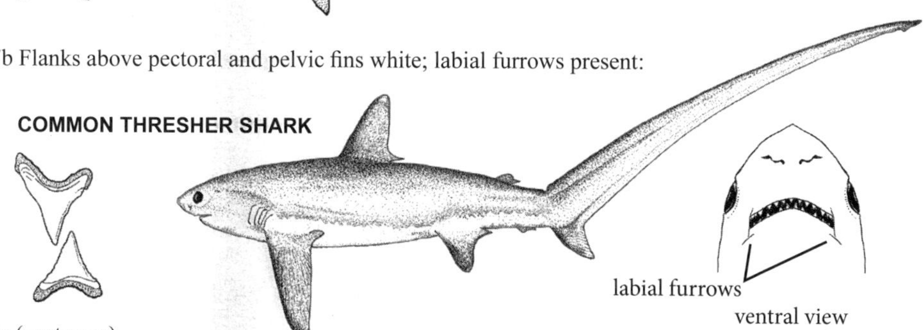


8a (next page)

## Order Lamniformes (continued)

**WHITE SHARK, *Carcharodon carcharias* (Linnaeus, 1758).** Family LAMNIDAE
Circumglobal, mostly in temperate waters; in western Pacific as far northward as Sea of Japan and northwest Bering Sea (59°56'N, 178°56'W) and Gulf of Alaska (60°17'N, 145°35'W) to Gulf of California and to Nayarit, Mexican Pacific; Panama to Chile and Islas Galápagos. Common from southeast Alaska to central Baja California, particularly from northern to southern California, and at Isla Guadalupe, central Baja California. Length to about 6 m (19.5 ft) TL, possibly to 6.4 m (21.1 ft) TL; at birth 120–150 cm (47.2–59.1 in) TL. Pelagic, coastal, and offshore over island and continental shelves; depth: surf zone to 1,280 m (4,198 ft). Slate-gray, blue-gray, or brown above, white below. Vert. 172–185. (Alternative name GREAT WHITE SHARK).

**SALMON SHARK, *Lamna ditropis* Hubbs & Follett, 1947.** Family LAMNIDAE
Korea and Japan to Okhotsk and Bering Seas to Bering Strait and Gulf of Alaska to central Baja California, including Isla Guadalupe (although the latter without documentation). Common from the Sea of Japan to the south Kuril Islands, Russia and from the Bering Sea to (at pupping season) off northern Baja California. Length to 3.05 m (10 ft) TL; at birth 65–80 cm (25.6–31.5 in) TL. Coastal and oceanic pelagic; depth: surface to 1,864 m (6,114 ft). Cobalt blue or blue-black; gill slits white; large individuals with black blotches ventrally. Vert. 170–181.

**SHORTFIN MAKO, *Isurus oxyrinchus* Rafinesque, 1810.** Family LAMNIDAE
Circumglobal in warm waters; British Columbia to Chile and Islas Galápagos. Common from off Oregon southward into tropics. Length to 5.85 m (19.2 ft) TL; at birth about 70 cm (27.6 in) TL. Coastal and oceanic pelagic; depth: surface to 750 m (2,460 ft). Cobalt blue. Vert. 183–196. (Formerly BONITO SHARK: M&L).

**LONGFIN MAKO, *Isurus paucus* Guitart Manday, 1966.** Family LAMNIDAE
Circumglobal; 2 records from southern California and 1 from well off Cabo San Lucas, Baja California. Likely rare or uncommon off southern California. Length to 4.27 m (14 ft) TL; at birth 92–97 cm (36.2–38.2 in) TL. Pelagic; depth: surface to 1,767 m (5,796 ft). Grayish-black on back, white below; dusky around mouth and on underside of snout; dorsal and caudal fins dusky black. Vert. 195–197.

8a *From 5a: teeth large, triangular, and blade-like*
Teeth serrated and broadly triangular in adults approximately 3 m (10 ft) and longer (juveniles with narrow teeth):

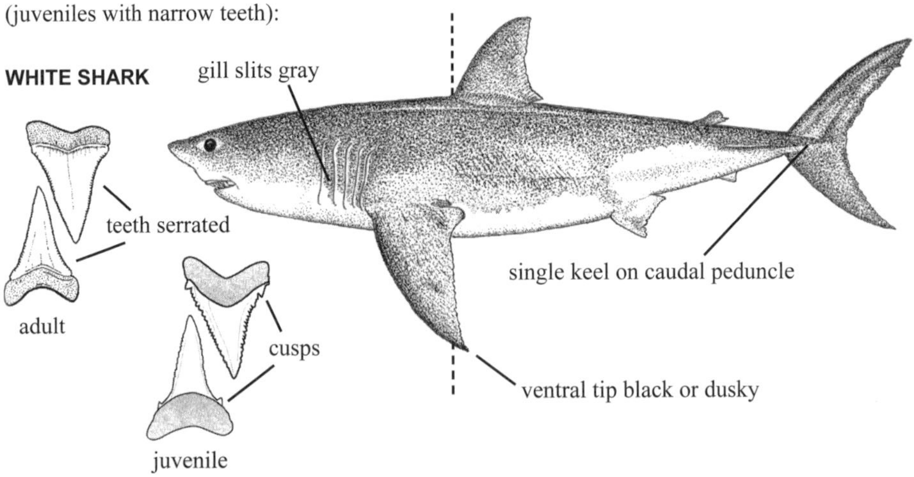


8b Teeth without serrations, long and narrow….. 9 (next page)

9a Teeth with small lateral cusplets; origin of 1st dorsal fin over pectoral fin; secondary keel on caudal peduncle:

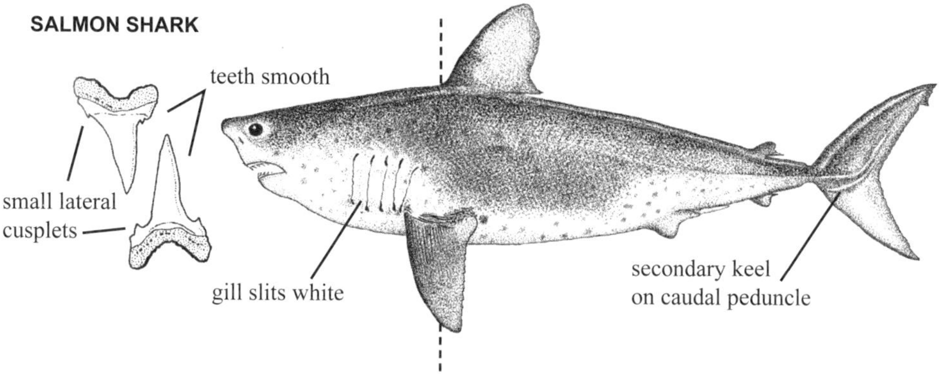


9b Teeth without small lateral cusplets; origin of 1st dorsal fin posterior to pectoral fin; secondary keel on caudal peduncle lacking….. 10

10a Underside of snout and mouth area white; cusps of anterior teeth recurved forward; pectoral fins much shorter than HL:

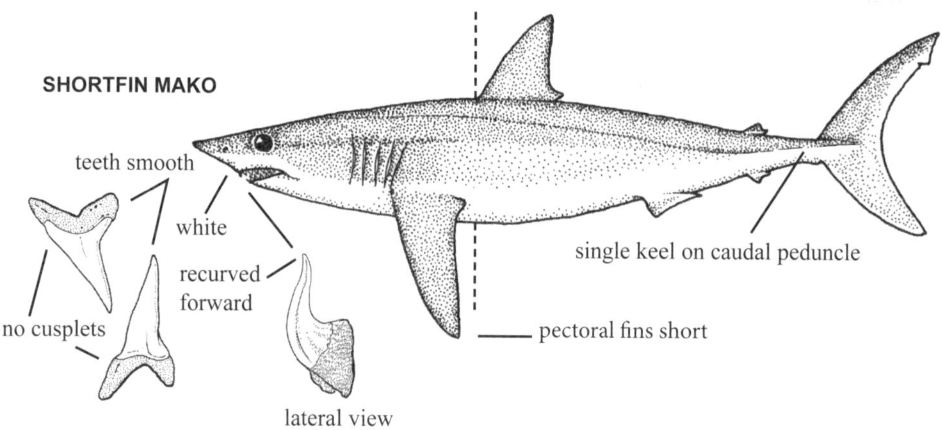


10b Underside of snout and mouth area dusky; cusps of anterior teeth straight; pectoral fins about equal to HL:

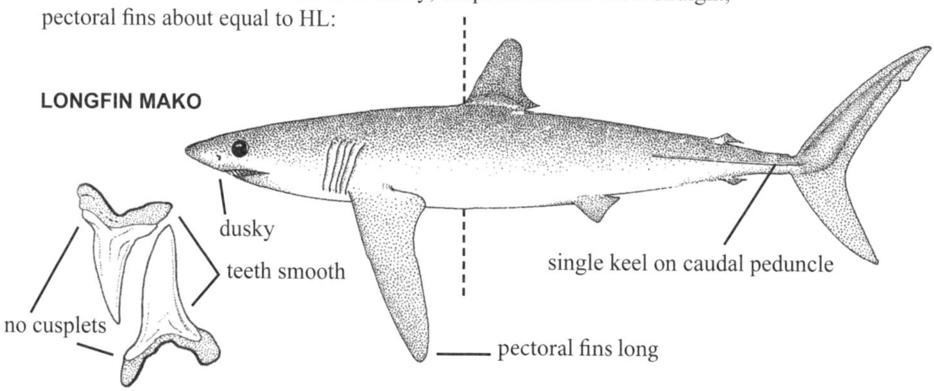

## Order Carcharhiniformes
## HAMMERHEAD SHARKS, Family Sphyrnidae, CAT SHARKS, Family Scyliorhinidae, HOUND SHARKS, Family Triakidae, and REQUIEM SHARKS, Family Carcharhinidae

**BONNETHEAD, *Sphyrna tiburo* (Linnaeus, 1758).** Family SPHYRNIDAE
Historically, San Diego, southern California to Paita, Peru, including Gulf of California; also western Atlantic. Perhaps extirpated from Gulf of California. Rare in southern California; common in tropics. Length to about 1.5 m (4.9 ft) TL, possibly to 1.8 m (6 ft) TL; at birth 24–30 cm (9.4–11.8 in) TL. Depth: intertidal to 90 m (295 ft). Brown or gray above, white below. Vert. 163–173. This species, at least in the western Atlantic, is likely a species complex. (Alternative name BONNETHEAD SHARK).

**SCALLOPED HAMMERHEAD, *Sphyrna lewini* (Griffith & Smith, 1834).** Family SPHYRNIDAE
Circumtropical; Santa Barbara, southern California and south to Puerto Pizarro, Peru, including Islas Galápagos. Rare in southern California; common as far northward as at least Bahía Magdalena, southern Baja California and into tropics. Length to 4.3 m (14.1 ft) TL; at birth 38–56 cm (15–22 in) TL. Depth: surface to 1,043 m (3,421 ft), comes into shallow bays and estuaries. Brown, gray, bronze, or black above, light below. Vert. 174–206. *Sphyrna lewini* may be a species complex and the species in the eastern Pacific may be different at least from that in the Atlantic and Gulf of Mexico (Naylor et al., 2012).

**SMOOTH HAMMERHEAD, *Sphyrna zygaena* (Linnaeus, 1758).** Family SPHYRNIDAE
Circumglobal; in the western Pacific at least as far northward as Hokkaido Island, Japan; central California to Gulf of California and to Bahía de San Antonio (33°35'S), Chile, including Islas Galápagos. Usually rare in southern California (but most commonly seen species here); can be common during warm-water periods; historically common from central Baja California into tropics. Length to 4 m (13.1 ft) TL; at birth 50–61 cm (19.7–24 in) TL. Depth: surface to 200 m (656 ft), possibly deeper. Gray, brown, or olive above, light below. Vert. 93–206.

**SWELL SHARK, *Cephaloscyllium ventriosum* (Garman, 1880).** Family SCYLIORHINIDAE
Monterey Bay, central California to Acapulco, Mexico, including Gulf of California and Ecuador to Chile. Common from Morro Bay southward to at least Bahía de Sebastián Vizcaíno, central Baja California and in Gulf of California. Length to at least 110 cm (43.3 in) TL; at birth 14–15 cm (5.5–5.9 in) TL. Depth: 5–457 m (15–1,500 ft). Brownish or yellow-brown with dark blotches and spotting. Vert. 109–112.

## KEY TO THE CARCHARHINIFORMES:
Created by David Ebert
(Principal sources: Ebert, 2003; Ebert et al., 2013)

1a Head with lateral, blade-like expansions….. 4 (next page)

1b Head normal, without lateral expansions….. 2

2a First dorsal fin above or posterior to pelvic fins….. 6 (next page)

2b First dorsal fin anterior to pelvic fins….. 3

3a Precaudal pits present; spiracles absent (except TIGER SHARK)….. 13 (page 42)

3b Precaudal pits absent; spiracles present posterior to eye….. 9 (page 40)

4a *From 1a: head with lateral, blade-like expansions*
Head expanded into distinctive bonnet shape:

**BONNETHEAD**

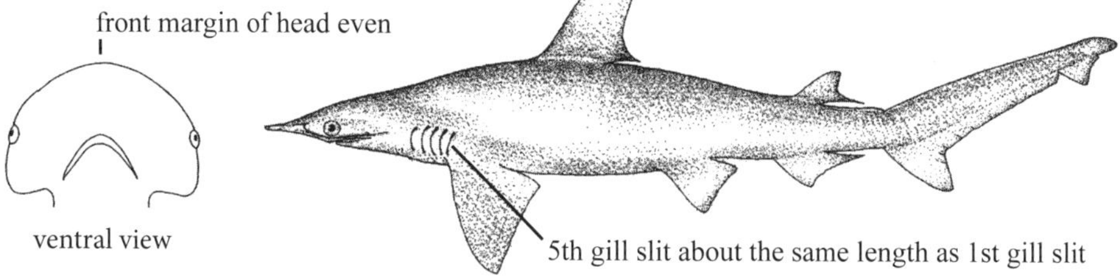


4b Head expanded into distinctive hammer shape….. 5

5a Anterior margin of head with 4 lobes and prominent central indentation:

**SCALLOPED HAMMERHEAD**

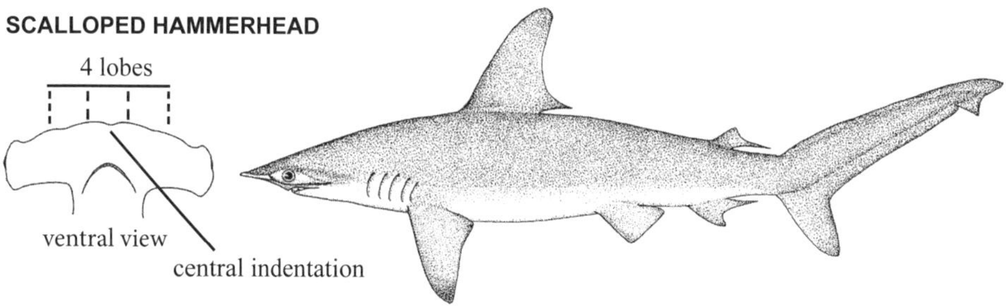


5b Anterior margin of head with 3 lobes and without prominent central indentation:

**SMOOTH HAMMERHEAD**

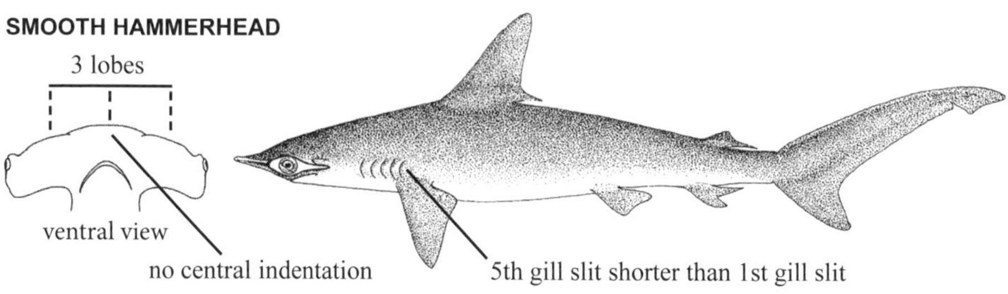


6a *From 2a: first dorsal fin above or posterior to pelvic fins*
Supraorbital crests present on head, above eyes; ability to swell body trunk into nearly spherical shape by swallowing water or air:

**SWELL SHARK**

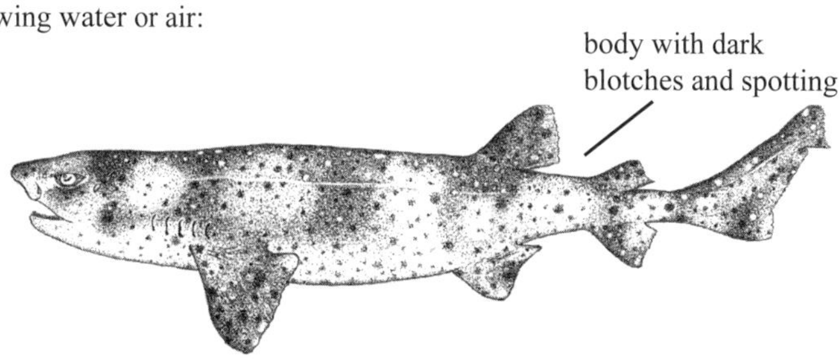


6b Supraorbital crests absent from head; lacks ability to swell body trunk into spherical shape by swallowing water or air….. 7 (next page)

## Order Carcharhiniformes (continued)

**FILETAIL CAT SHARK, *Parmaturus xaniurus* (Gilbert, 1892).** Family Scyliorhinidae
Cape Foulweather (44°07'N), Oregon to Baja California and Gulf of California. Common at least off central and southern California. Length to at least 61 cm (24 in) TL, but perhaps to 71 cm (28 in) TL; at birth 7–9 cm (2.8–3.5 in) TL. Depth: 88–1,519 m (290–4,982 ft). Dark gray, brownish, or black with white-edged fins. Vert. 109–131.

**BROWN CAT SHARK, *Apristurus brunneus* (Gilbert, 1892).** Family Scyliorhinidae
Icy Point (58°00'N), southeastern Alaska to central Baja California (28°48'N); Ecuador to Chile. Common at least from Vancouver Island to southern California. Length to 71 cm (28 in) TL; at birth 7–9 cm (2.8–3.5 in) TL. Depth: 24–1,341 m (79–4,398 ft). Uniform brown or black; margin of fins black. Vert. 116–122.

**LONGNOSE CAT SHARK, *Apristurus kampae* Taylor, 1972.** Family Scyliorhinidae
Washington (47°36'N) to Gulf of California and Peru. Individuals reported from Islas Galápagos may be an undescribed species. Common at least from northern to southern California. Length to 64.7 cm (25.5 in) TL; at birth about 14 cm (5.5 in) TL. Depth: 65–1,888 m (213–6,193 ft). Uniform black or dark brown; white-edged fin margin. Vert. 104–111.

**LEOPARD SHARK, *Triakis semifasciata* Girard, 1855.** Family Triakidae
Samish Bay (48°37'N, 122°28'W), Washington to Mazatlán, Mexico, including Gulf of California and Isla Guadalupe, central Baja California. Common from perhaps Coos Bay, Oregon southward into Gulf of California. Length to 2.13 m (7 ft) TL; at birth about 20 cm (7.9 in) TL. Depth: surf zone to 156 m (515 ft). Gray with black crossbars and spots, occasionally with dark streaks. Vert. 129–150.

**SOUPFIN SHARK, *Galeorhinus galeus* (Linnaeus, 1758).** Family Triakidae
Temperate waters, nearly worldwide; northern British Columbia to Gulf of California; Ecuador to Chile. Common from at least Hecate Strait, British Columbia to at least central Baja California. Length to about 2 m (6.5 ft) TL; at birth 30–40 cm (11.8–15.7 in) TL. Coastal pelagic; depth: surf zone to 1,100 m (3,608 ft). Dark gray or brown above, white below; juveniles black on forward edge of dorsal and pectoral fins. Vert. 123–146. Although we treat the eastern Pacific population of this species as part of a worldwide population, Chabot and Allen (2009) and Naylor et al. (2012) found evidence that it may merit status as a separate species, *Galeorhinus zyopterus* Jordan & Gilbert, 1883. (Formerly *Galeorhinus zyopterus*: M&L) (Alternative name TOPE).

7a Anterior margin of upper caudal fin with prominent row of enlarged dermal denticles:

**FILETAIL CAT SHARK**

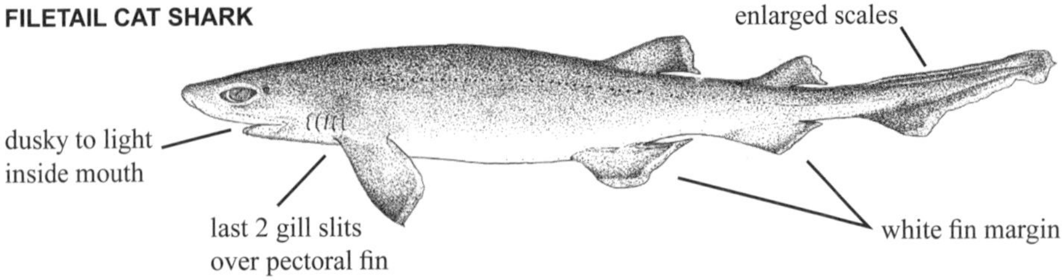


7b Anterior margin of upper caudal fin without prominent row of enlarged dermal denticles….. 8 (next page)

8a Upper labial furrows longer than lower; posterior fin margin black; anal fin long and low, nearly reaching base of caudal fin:

**BROWN CAT SHARK**

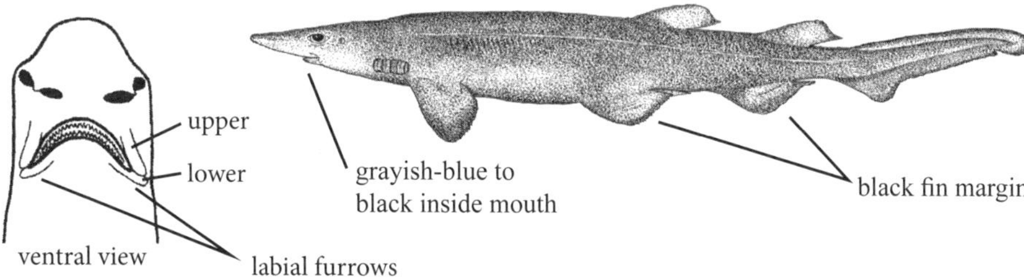


8b Upper labial furrows not longer than lower; posterior fin margin white; anal fin short and high, not reaching base of caudal fin:

**LONGNOSE CAT SHARK**

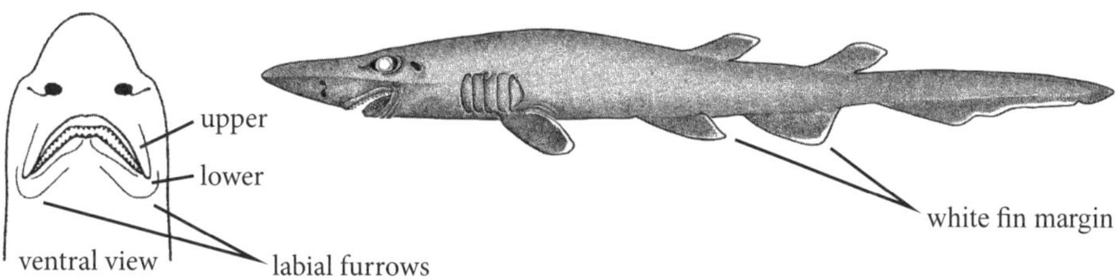


9a *From 3b: precaudal pits absent; spiracles present posterior to eye*
Well-defined, bold, black saddles and dark spots on dorsal surface:

**LEOPARD SHARK**

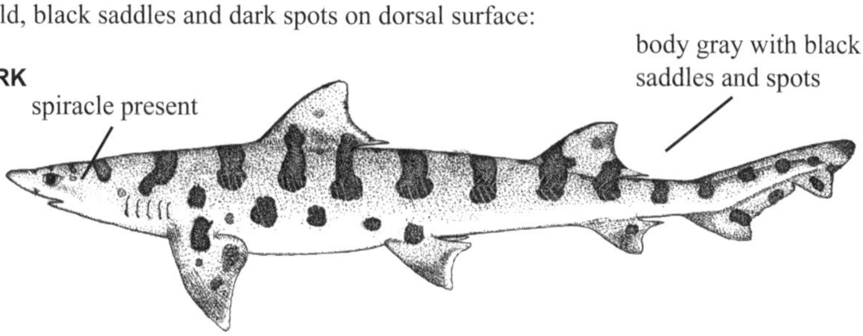


9b No saddles, dark spots, or other prominent markings on dorsal surface…. 10

10a Second dorsal fin much smaller than 1st dorsal fin, about as large as anal fin; terminal lobe of caudal fin about half the length of dorsal caudal fin margin:

**SOUPFIN SHARK**

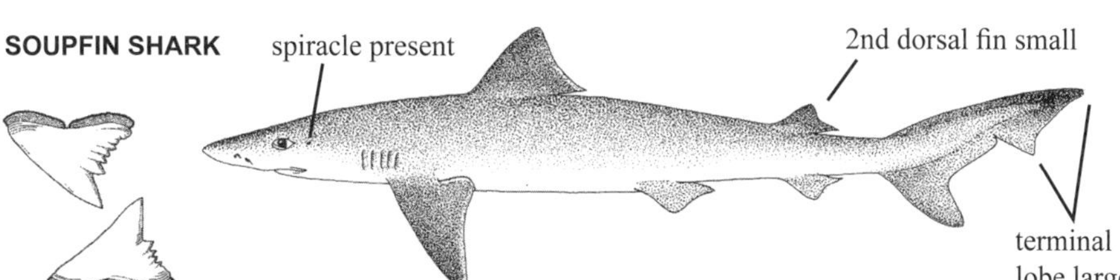


10b Second dorsal fin nearly as large as 1st dorsal fin, much larger than anal fin; terminal lobe of caudal fin less than half the length of dorsal caudal fin margin….. 11 (next page)

## Order Carcharhiniformes (continued)

**BROWN SMOOTHHOUND, *Mustelus henlei* (Gill, 1863).** Family TRIAKIDAE
Northern Washington to Gulf of California and Costa Rica to Peru. Common from Humboldt Bay southward to tropics. Length to 153 cm (60 in) TL; at birth 19–30 cm (7.5–11.8 in) TL. Depth: surf zone to 296 m (971 ft). Red-brown or bronze above, silvery below. Vert. 152–160.

**GRAY SMOOTHHOUND, *Mustelus californicus* Gill, 1864.** Family TRIAKIDAE
Cape Mendocino, northern California to Mazatlán, Mexico, including Gulf of California and Isla Guadalupe, central Baja California and Peru. Common from central California southward into Gulf of California. Length to 1.42 m (4.7 ft) TL, possibly to 1.6 m (5.2 ft) TL; at birth 23–30 cm (9.1–11.8 in) TL. Depth: surf zone to 265 m (869 ft). Brown to dark gray above, whitish below. An albino individual has been noted. Vert. 145–157.

**SICKLEFIN SMOOTHHOUND, *Mustelus lunulatus* Jordan & Gilbert, 1882.** Family TRIAKIDAE
San Diego, southern California to at least Panama and perhaps to Talara, Peru, including Gulf of California. Rare in southern California; common from northern Baja California southward into tropics. Length to 175 cm (68.9 in) TL; at birth 32–35 cm (12.6–13.8 in) TL. Depth: inshore to 200 m (656 ft). Plain brown or gray. Vert. 133–154.

**TIGER SHARK, *Galeocerdo cuvier* (Péron & Lesueur, 1822).** Family CARCHARHINIDAE
Circumglobal in tropical waters; sighting (unverifiable) at Prince William Sound, Gulf of Alaska to southern California to Peru, including Islas Galápagos and Gulf of California. Rare along the U.S. Pacific Coast; common in tropics. Length to 7.4 m (24.4 ft) TL; at birth 51–76 cm (20–29.9 in) TL. Coastal pelagic; depth: surface and intertidal to 1,112 m (3,647 ft). Color variable: brown, black, gray, or bluish above, gray to yellow below; dark bars and blotches. Vert. 216–234. TIGER SHARKS living in the Atlantic may represent a separate species (Naylor et al., 2012).

**BLUE SHARK, *Prionace glauca* (Linnaeus, 1758).** Family CARCHARHINIDAE
Circumglobal in temperate and tropical waters; in western Pacific as far north as southern Kuril Islands, Russia; Kodiak Island, western Gulf of Alaska and near Seward, Alaska to Chile, including Gulf of California and Islas Galápagos. Migrates northward during spring and summer. Overall, common from southeast Alaska southward to tropics. Length to 3.83 m (12.6 ft) TL, possibly to 4.8–6.5 m (15.7–21.3 ft) TL but without documentation; at birth 34–53 cm (13.4–20.9 in) TL. Oceanic pelagic; typically over water depths greater than 183 m (600 ft) but often venturing near shore; depth: surface to about 1,000 m (3,280 ft). Dark blue above, white below. Vert. 239–252. This species may more properly be placed in the genus *Carcharhinus* (Naylor et al., 2012).

11a Posterior margin of dorsal fins frayed:

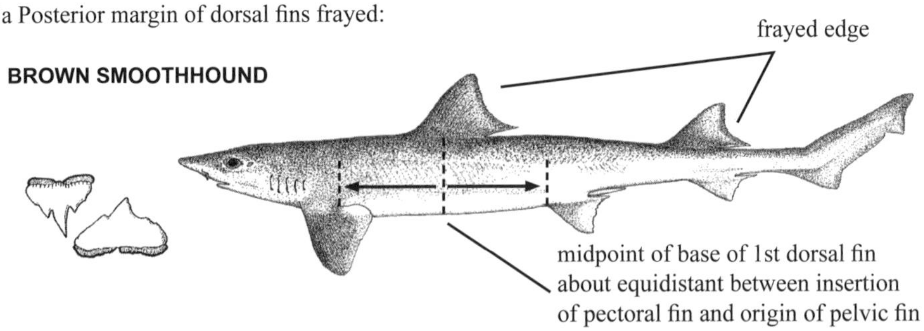


11b Posterior margin of dorsal fins not frayed….. 12 (next page)

12a First dorsal fin originating posterior to rear tip of pectoral fin; posterior margin of 1st dorsal fin slightly curved; lower lobe of caudal fin not elongated:

**GRAY SMOOTHHOUND**

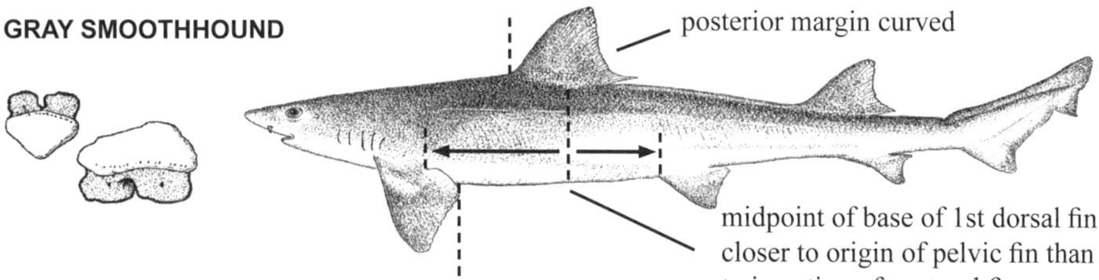


12b First dorsal fin originating over rear tip of pectoral fin; posterior margin of 1st dorsal fin vertical; lower lobe of caudal fin elongated and pointed in adults:

**SICKLEFIN SMOOTHHOUND**

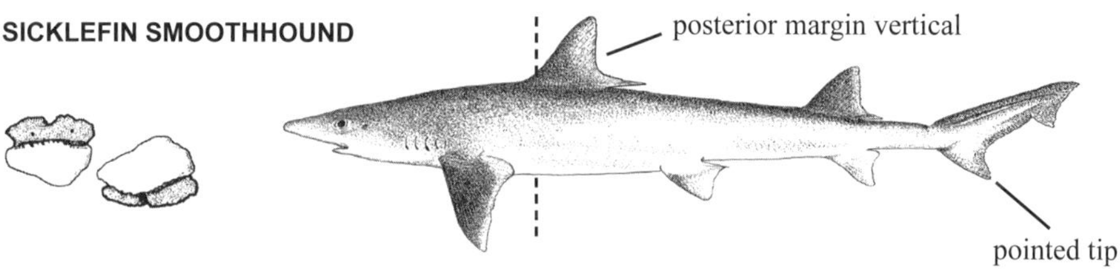


13a *From 3a: precaudal pits present; spiracles absent* (*except TIGER SHARK)*
Spiracles present; upper labial furrows elongate, extending to front of eyes; prominent lateral ridges on caudal peduncle:

**TIGER SHARK**

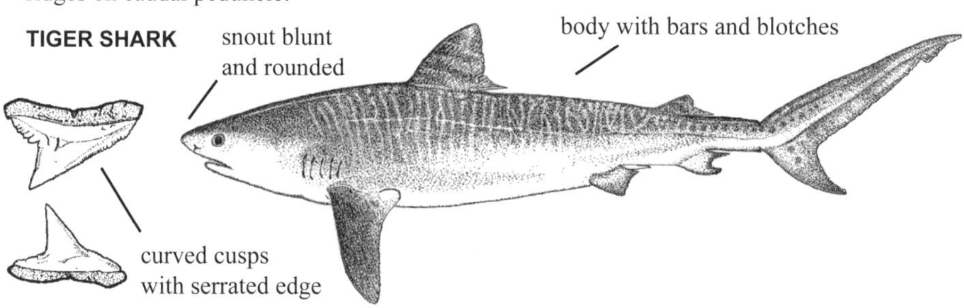


13b Spiracles absent; upper labial furrows not elongate, or extending to front of eyes; lateral ridges on caudal peduncle not prominent….. 14

14a Midpoint of 1st dorsal fin base closer to pelvic fin origin than to pectoral fin insertion; color bright blue in life:

**BLUE SHARK**

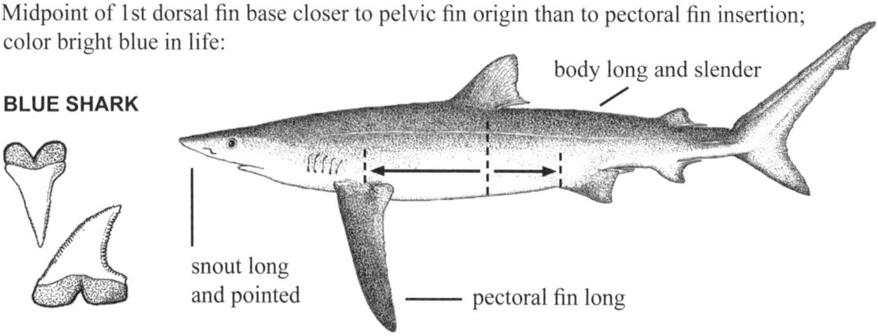


14b Midpoint of 1st dorsal fin base closer to pectoral fin insertion than to pelvic fin origin; color gray to bronze in life….. 15 (next page)

## Order Carcharhiniformes (continued)

**PACIFIC SHARPNOSE SHARK, *Rhizoprionodon longurio* (Jordan & Gilbert, 1882).** Family Carcharhinidae
Southern California to Paita, Peru, including Gulf of California. Rare in southern California; common in tropics. Length to at least 1.54 m (5.1 ft) TL; at birth 30–34 cm (11.8–13.4 in) TL. Depth: intertidal to 100 m (328 ft). Brown or gray above, light below. Vert. 146–167.

**NARROWTOOTH SHARK, *Carcharhinus brachyurus* (Günther, 1870).** Family Carcharhinidae
Circumglobal; Santa Cruz Island, southern California (LACM 44909-1) to central Mexico and Colombia to Peru, including Gulf of California and Islas Galápagos. Apparently occasional in southern California, visiting during warm-water periods; common in tropics. Length to about 3.25 m (10.7 ft) TL; at birth 59–70 cm (23.2–27.6 in) TL. Depth: surf line to 360 m (1,181 ft). Bronze to brownish-gray above, white below; light streak along sides from above pectoral fin to caudal fin. Vert. 196–203. Naylor et al. (2012) suggest that *Carcharhinus brachyurus* may be comprised of at least two species; 1 from the Indo-Pacific and 1 from the Atlantic and South Africa. (Formerly *Carcharhinus remotus* Duméril, 1865: M&L) (Alternative names COPPER SHARK, BRONZE WHALER).

**BULL SHARK, *Carcharhinus leucas* (Müller & Henle, 1839).** Family Carcharhinidae
Circumglobal in warm waters; possibly southern California; Isla Guadalupe, central Baja California and southern Baja California to Paita, Peru, including Gulf of California. Common in tropics. Marine and fresh water. Length to 3.4 m (11.1 ft) TL or perhaps to 3.66 m (12 ft) TL; at birth 55–81 cm (21.7–31.8 in) TL. Depth: surface to 164 m (538 ft) or perhaps to 500 m (1,640 ft). Brown or gray above, yellow-white or white on sides and belly. Vert. 206–215. Naylor et al. (2012) suggest that *C. leucas* may be a species complex.

**OCEANIC WHITETIP SHARK, *Carcharhinus longimanus* (Poey, 1861).** Family Carcharhinidae
Circumtropical; unconfirmed reports from central California; perhaps Gaviota, southern California and Cortes Bank, southern California, to Puerto Pizarro, Peru, including Gulf of California and Islas Galápagos. Rare off California; common in tropics. Maximum length variously listed as between 3.5 and 3.95 m (11.5 and 13 ft) TL; at birth 55–77 cm (21.7–30.3 in) TL. Depth: surface to 1,190 m (3,903 ft). Gray, with tip of 1st dorsal, caudal, pelvic, and pectoral fins white. Underside of pectoral and pelvic fins often brown mottled. Vert. 232–244. (Formerly PELAGIC WHITETIPPED SHARK: M&L).

**DUSKY SHARK, *Carcharhinus obscurus* (Lesueur, 1818).** Family Carcharhinidae
Circumglobal; Redondo Beach, southern California to Gulf of California and to Ecuador. Rare off southern California; common in tropics. Length to at least 3.6 m (11.8 ft) TL, possibly to 4.2 m (13.8 ft) TL; at birth 70–100 cm (27.6–39.3 in) TL. Depth: surf zone to 573 m (1,879 ft). Gray or beige. Vert. 173–184.

15a Anal fin origin well in front of 2nd dorsal fin origin:

**PACIFIC SHARPNOSE SHARK**

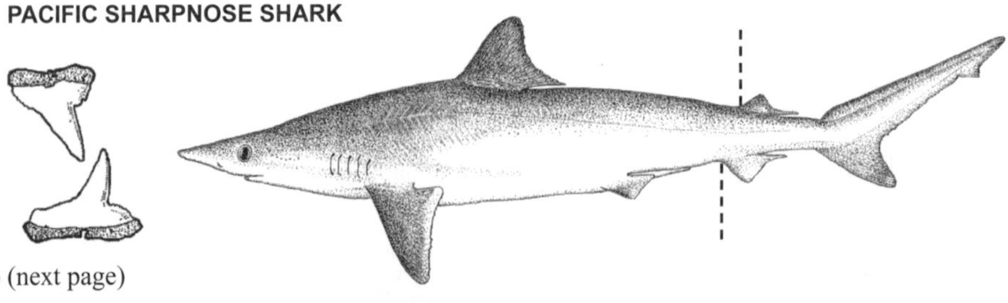

15b (next page)

15b Anal fin origin under or behind 2nd dorsal fin origin….. 16

16a Interdorsal ridge present….. 18

16b Interdorsal ridge absent….. 17

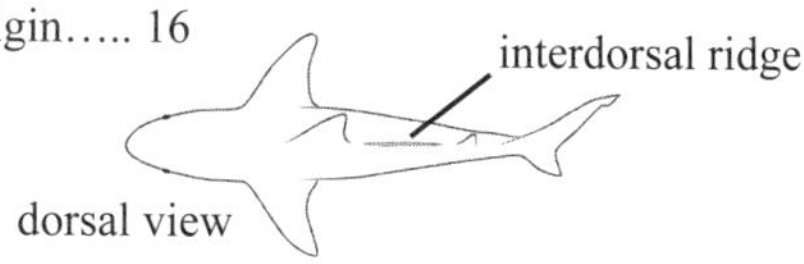


17a Body slender; snout about as long as mouth width:

**NARROWTOOTH SHARK**

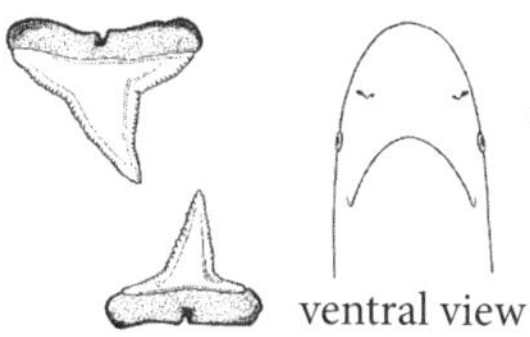


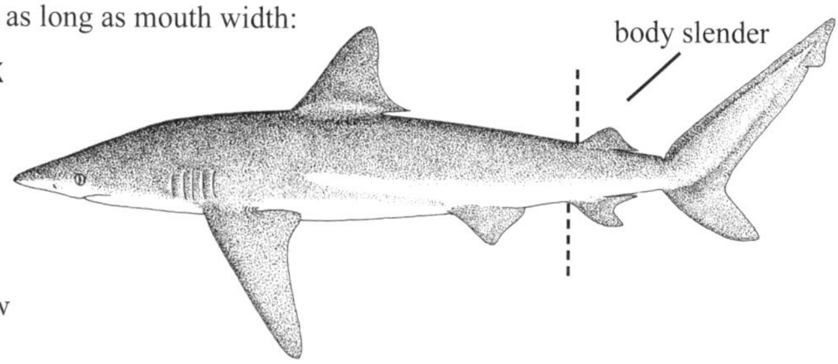


17b Body deep and robust; snout shorter than mouth width:

**BULL SHARK**

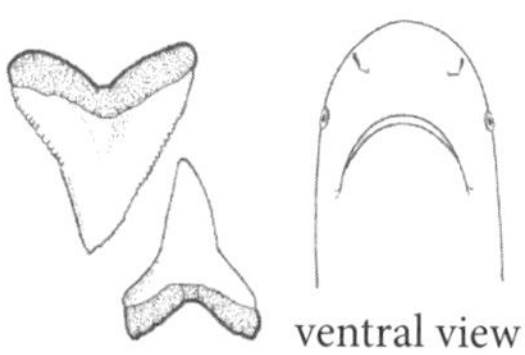


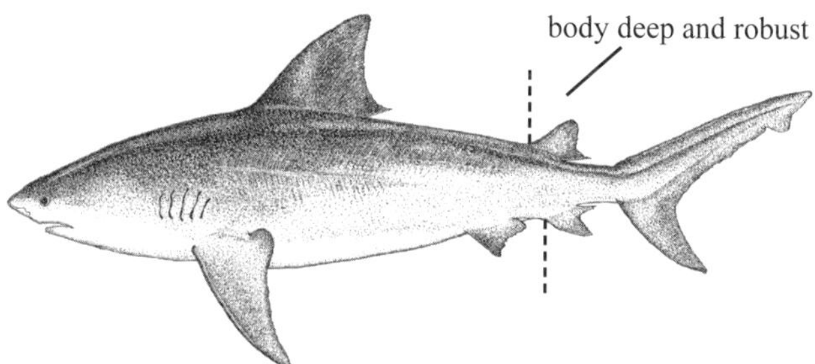


18a *From 16a: interdorsal ridge present*
Dorsal and pectoral fins broadly rounded; tip of fins mottled or with some black markings (mostly prominent in juveniles):

**OCEANIC WHITETIP SHARK**

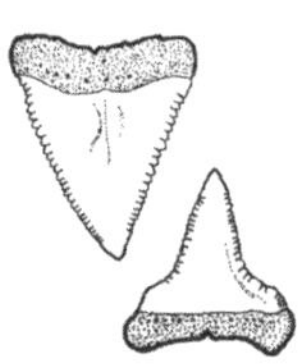

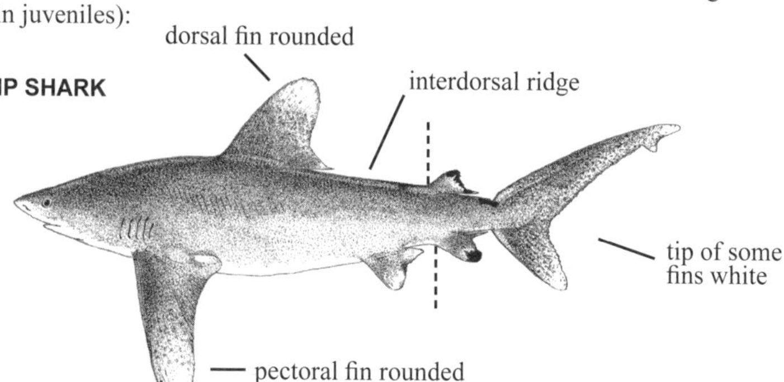


18b Dorsal and pectoral fins not broadly rounded; tip of fins not as above:

**DUSKY SHARK**

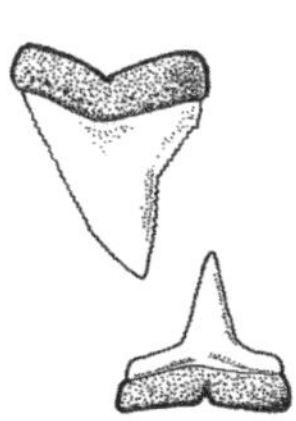

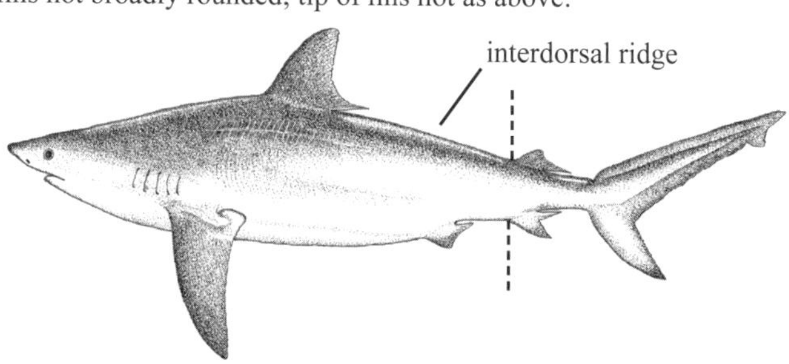

# Order Rhinopristiformes and Order Rajiformes THORNBACK, Family Platyrhinidae, GUITARFISHES, Family Rhinobatidae and Family Trygonorrhinidae, SKATES, Family Arhynchobatidae and Family Rajidae

**THORNBACK, *Platyrhinoidis triseriata* (Jordan & Gilbert, 1880).** Order Rhinopristiformes, Family Platyrhynidae

Tomales Bay, northern California to Gulf of California; also reported from Ecuador. Common from about Monterey Bay southward to at least central Baja California. Length to 91 cm (35.8 in) TL; at birth about 11 cm (4.3 in) TL. Depth: surf zone to 137 m (449 ft). Brown or gray on back, white or cream-colored below. Vert. 130–133. (Alternative name THORNBACK FANRAY).

**SHOVELNOSE GUITARFISH, *Pseudobatos productus* (Ayres, 1854).** Order Rhinopristiformes, Family Rhinobatidae

San Francisco, northern California to southern Mexico, including Gulf of California. Common from about Monterey Bay, central California southward into Gulf of California. Length to 156 cm (61.5 in) TL; at birth 15–23 cm (5.9–9.1 in) TL. Depth: 1–91 m (3–298 ft). Brownish-gray above, lighter below. Vert. 171–179. (Formerly *Rhinobatos productus* Ayres, 1854: M&L).

**BANDED GUITARFISH, *Zapteryx exasperata* (Jordan & Gilbert, 1880).** Order Rhinopristiformes, Family Trygonorrhiidae

Jalama Beach, central California (LACM 44302-1) to Gulf of California to Oaxaca, Mexico; Peru. Common from about La Jolla, California southward into Gulf of California. Ebert (2003) questions captures south of Mazatlán, Mexico, noting possible confusion with *Zapteryx xyster* Jordan & Evermann, 1896, a more southerly species. Length to 125 cm (49.2 in) TL; at birth 15–22 cm (5.9–8.7 in) TL. Depth: intertidal to 200 m (656 ft). Brown on back, lighter below with blackish transverse bands. Vert. 149–150. (Formerly Rhinobatidae: M&L). Taxonomic revision is required on eastern Pacific *Zapteryx*.

## KEY TO THE RHINOPRISTIFORMES and RAJIFORMES:

Created by David Ebert

(Principal source: Ebert, 2003; Last et al., 2016)

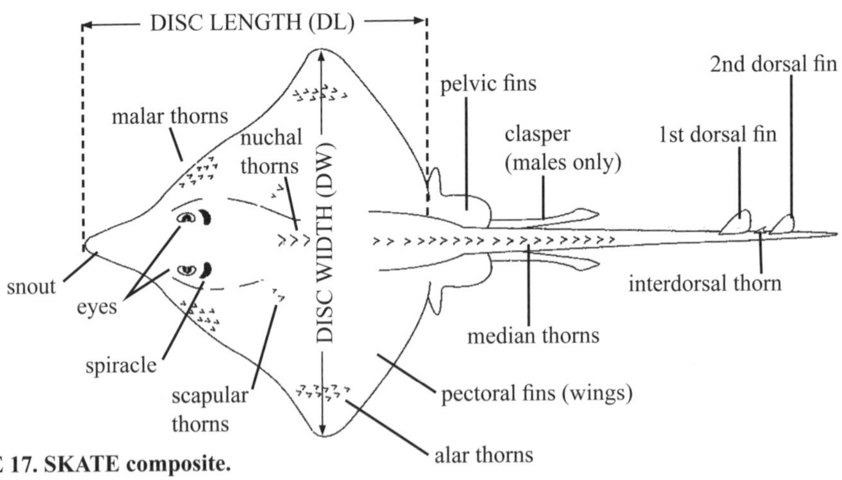


**FIGURE 17. SKATE composite.**

1a Caudal fin small or absent..... 4 (next page)

1b Caudal fin prominent..... 2 (next page)

2a Three rows of prominent thorns on back; snout rounded:

**THORNBACK**

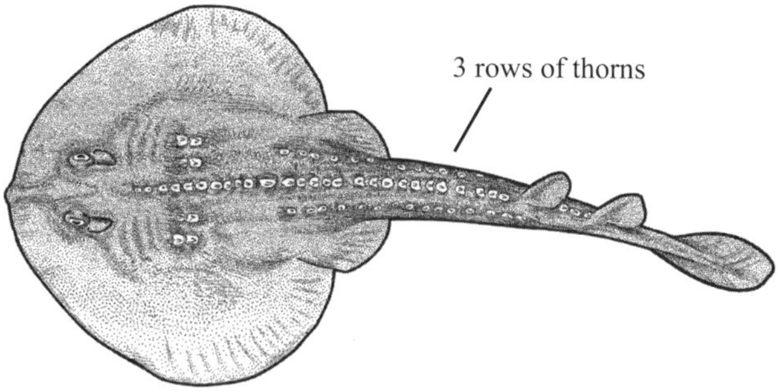


2b Fewer than 3 rows of prominent thorns on back; snout pointed….. 3

3a DL greater than DW; dorsal surface usually plain, occasionally with dark spots, but without prominent dark bands:

**SHOVELNOSE GUITARFISH**

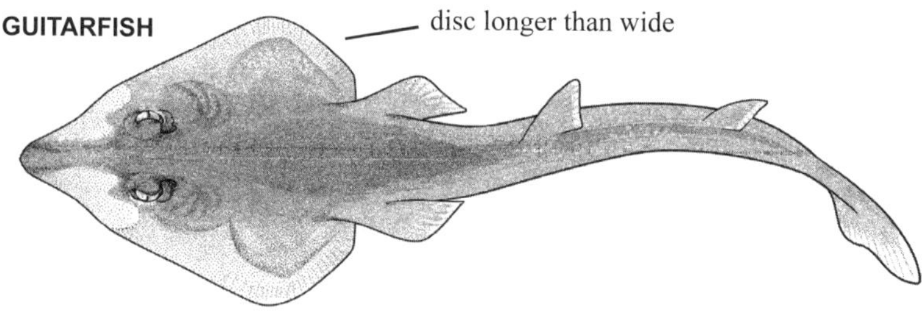


3b DL about equal to DW; dorsal surface with several prominent dark bands:

**BANDED GUITARFISH**

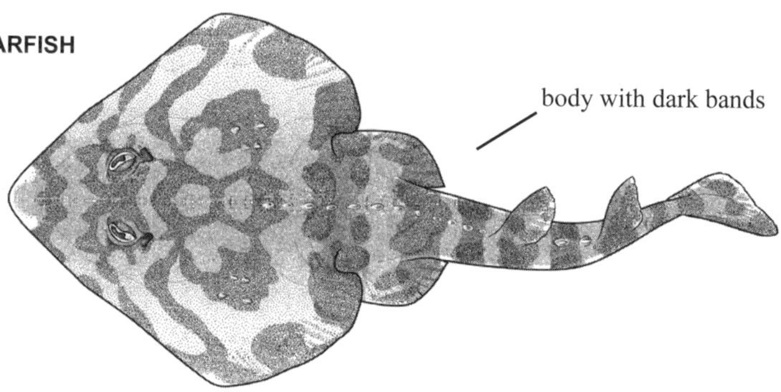


4a *From 1a: caudal fin small or absent*
Snout rigid and stiff….. 9 (page 49)

4b Snout soft and flexible….. 5

5a Scapular thorns absent….. 7 (page 48)

5b Scapular thorns present….. 6

6a (next page)

## Order Rhinopristiformes and Order Rajiformes (continued)

NOTE: Family Arhynchobatidae is considered a subfamily of Rajidae by some researchers.

**ALEUTIAN SKATE, *Bathyraja aleutica* (Gilbert, 1896).** Order Rajiformes, Family Arhynchobatidae
Northern Japan to Bering Sea to southeastern Alaska and northern British Columbia to central California (36°12'N). Common from at least the Kamchatka-Kuril Islands, Russia, to the Gulf of Alaska and probably common as far south as northern California. Length to about 161 cm (63.4 in) TL; at birth 12–15 cm (4.7–5.9 in) TL. Depth: 15–1,602 m (49–5,256 ft). Dorsal side dark brown, olive, or gray; vague dark ocelli on pectoral fins sometimes present; underside with gray margin. Predorsal vert. 67–90.

**SANDPAPER SKATE, *Bathyraja kincaidii* (Garman, 1908).** Order Rajiformes, Family Arhynchobatidae
Southeastern Alaska to northern Baja California. Length to 63.5 cm (25 in) TL. Depth: about 18–1,370 m (59–4,494 ft). Dorsal brownish-gray, often with dark spots, especially in juveniles; ventral dirty-white to white. (Formerly *Raja kincaidii* Garman, 1908: M&L). Until recently considered a synonym of *Bathyraja interrupta* (Gill & Townsend, 1897).

**DEEPSEA SKATE, *Bathyraja abyssicola* (Gilbert, 1896).** Order Rajiformes, Family Arhynchobatidae
Southern Japan to Sea of Okhotsk and Bering Sea and Aleutian Islands south of Tanaga Island and north of Unalaska Island (UW 45833) to Islas Coronados, northern Baja California; Gulf of California; Isla Galápagos. Common at least from Sea of Okhotsk to central California. Length to 157 cm (63 in) TL; at birth perhaps 34–36 cm (13.4–14.2 in) TL. Depth: 362–2,904 m (1,187–9,525 ft). Dorsal side variably colored: black, brown, or purple, sometimes with small dark spots; anterior tip of pectoral fins sometimes light or whitish; large males with whitish blotches and dark spots. Predorsal vert. 70–78. (Formerly *Raja abyssicola* Gilbert, 1896: M&L).

**ROUGHTAIL SKATE, *Bathyraja trachura* (Gilbert, 1892).** Order Rajiformes, Family Arhynchobatidae
Sea of Okhotsk and northern Kuril Islands, Russia, to Cape Navarin, western Bering Sea, Commander-Aleutian Islands Chain, and eastern Bering Sea and Gulf of Alaska to Ensenada, northern Baja California, including north of Isla Guadalupe, central Baja California and mid-Gulf of California. Common from at least the Sea of Okhotsk and eastern Bering Sea and Gulf of Alaska to southern California. Length to 94 cm (37 in) TL. Minimum depth at least as shallow as about 400 m (1,312 ft) and perhaps as shallow as 76 m (249 ft) to 2,900 m (9,512 ft). Black, brown, or dark gray on both surfaces; mouth and cloaca white. One albino individual has been documented. Predorsal vert. 62–66. (Formerly BLACK SKATE, *Raja trachura* (Gilbert, 1892): M&L).

**PACIFIC WHITE SKATE, *Bathyraja spinosissima* (Beebe & Tee-Van, 1941).** Order Rajiformes, Family Arhynchobatidae
Waldport, Oregon to Isla Cocos, Costa Rica, including Gulf of California, Mexican mainland at Sinaloa, and Islas Galápagos. Length to 208 cm (81.9 in) TL; at birth about 25 cm (9.8 in) TL. Depth: 800–2,938 m (2,624–9,637 ft). Uniform gray-white to gray on both sides, outer disc dusky. Skin surface rough to touch due to fine denticulation on both sides (absent in embryo) forming shark-like skin texture. Predorsal vert. 82. (Formerly WHITE SKATE: M&L).

6a Dorsal surface with continuous row of similar-sized median thorns; ventral surface white (except snout, posterior disc margin, pelvic fins, anal area, and underside of tail, prominently dark brown or gray):

**ALEUTIAN SKATE**

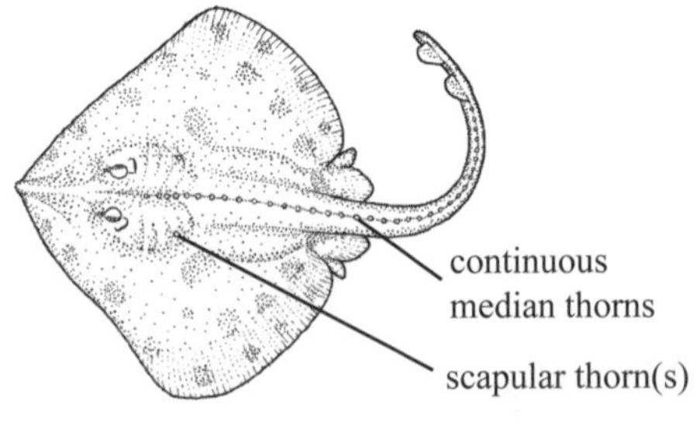


6b (next page)

6b Dorsal surface with discontinuous row of similar-sized median thorns; ventral surface, including tail, white without dark mottling:

**SANDPAPER SKATE**

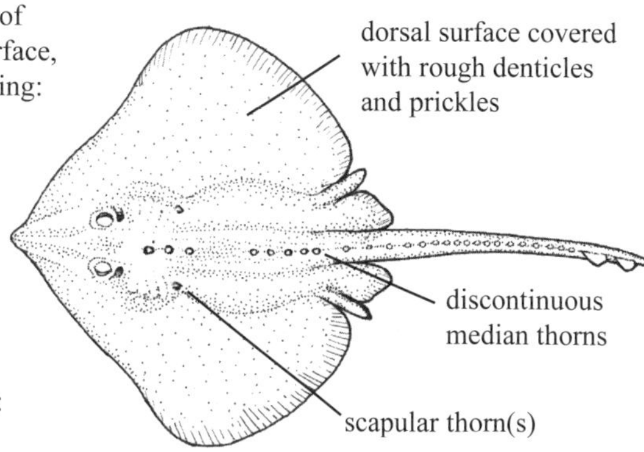


7a *From 5a: scapular thorns absent*
Disc with 1–5 prominent nuchal thorns:

**DEEPSEA SKATE**

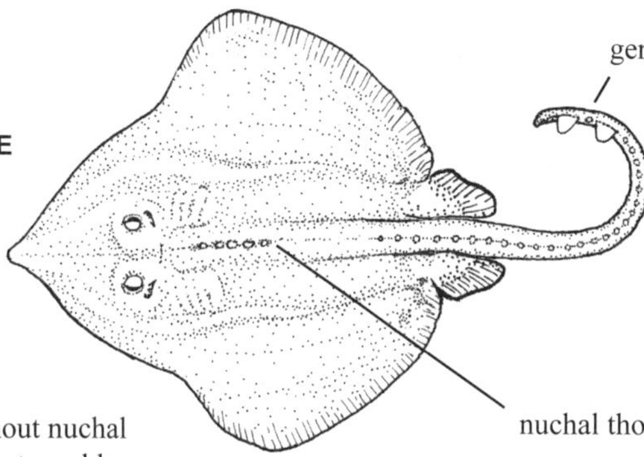


7b Disc usually without nuchal thorns, or if present weakly developed and fewer than 3….. 8

8a Dorsal surface covered with prominent thorns and prickles:

**ROUGHTAIL SKATE**

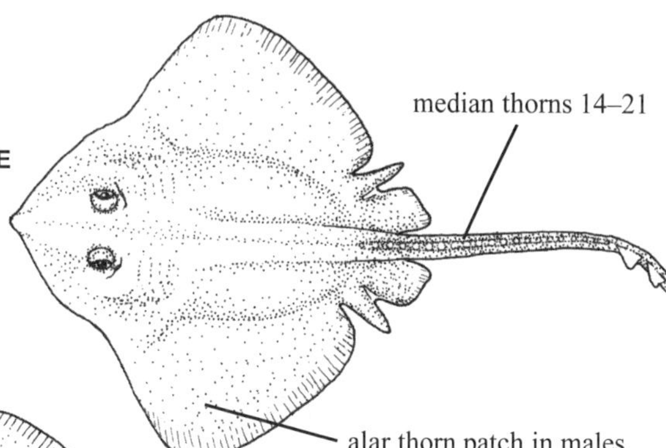


8b Dorsal surface covered with fine, minute prickles:

**PACIFIC WHITE SKATE**

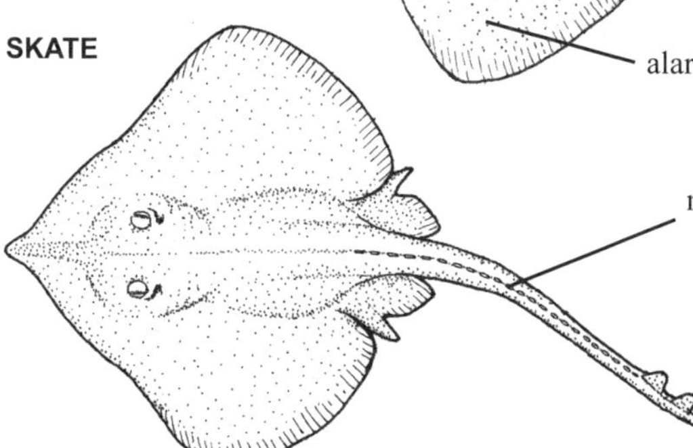


9a (next page)

## Order Rhinopristiformes and Order Rajiformes (continued)

**BIG SKATE, *Beringraja binoculata* (Girard, 1855).** Order Rajiformes, Family Rajidae
Bering Sea and Aleutian Islands, at least as far west as Unalaska Island, to eastern Gulf of Alaska to Cabo Falsa (22°54'N, 110°02'W), southern Baja California and Gulf of California. Common at least from the Gulf of Alaska to southern California. Length to 244 cm (96 in) TL; at birth 18–23 cm (7.1–9.1 in) TL. Depth: 2 m (7 ft) or less to more than 500 m (1,640 ft) and perhaps to 800 m (2,624 ft). Dorsal side variously brown, reddish-brown, or gray with white spots and dark mottling; dark spot on center of wing ringed with small, white spots. Predorsal vert. 96. (Formerly *Raja binoculata* Girard, 1855: M&L).

**STARRY SKATE, *Beringraja stellulata* (Jordan & Gilbert, 1880).** Order Rajiformes, Family Rajidae
Vancouver Island to Isla Cedros and Bahía de Sebastián Vizcaíno, central Baja California and northern Gulf of California. Bering Sea and Gulf of Alaska records of this species are incorrect (Mecklenburg et al., 2002) and perhaps reflect catches of *Bathyraja parmifera* (Ebert, 2003). Common at least off central and southern California. Length to 79 cm (31.1 in) TL; at birth 12–16 cm (4.7–6.3 in) TL. Depth: 2 m (7 ft) or less to at least 730 m (2,394 ft). Dorsal side light brown or gray-brown above with lighter spotting; often with larger white or yellowish spot ringed with brown at base of each pectoral fin. Predorsal vert. 119. (Formerly *Raja stellulata* Jordan & Gilbert, 1880: M&L).

**LONGNOSE SKATE, *Beringraja rhina* (Jordan & Gilbert, 1880).** Order Rajiformes, Family Rajidae
Southeastern Bering Sea to just below Punta San Juanico (25°59'N, 113°17'W), southern Baja California, and Gulf of California. Common from the Alaska Peninsula to at least southern California. Length to at least 204 cm (80.3 in) TL; at birth 12–17 cm (4.7–6.7 in) TL. Depth: 9 m (30 ft) to at least 1,294 m (4,244 ft). Dorsal side dark brown or gray above, light brown, black, or purple-gray with darker blotches below; ventral side black-blue to purple-gray. Predorsal vert. 47–53. (Formerly *Raja rhina* Jordan & Gilbert, 1880: M&L).

**CALIFORNIA SKATE, *Beringraja inornata* (Jordan & Gilbert, 1881).** Order Rajiformes, Family Rajidae
Strait of Juan de Fuca to southern Baja California and Gulf of California. Common at least from northern California to southern Baja California and in Gulf of California. Length to 79 cm (31.1 in) TL; at birth 15–23 cm (5.9–9.1 in) TL. Depth: 5–792 m (16–2,598 ft). Olive-brown above, tan below, sometimes with dark rings on pectoral fins; group of ventral pores anterior to pelvic fins form "V" or "U" shape. Predorsal vert. 42–46. (Formerly *Raja inornata* Jordan & Gilbert, 1881: M&L).

9a *From 4a: snout rigid and stiff*
Pelvic fins shallowly notched:

**BIG SKATE**

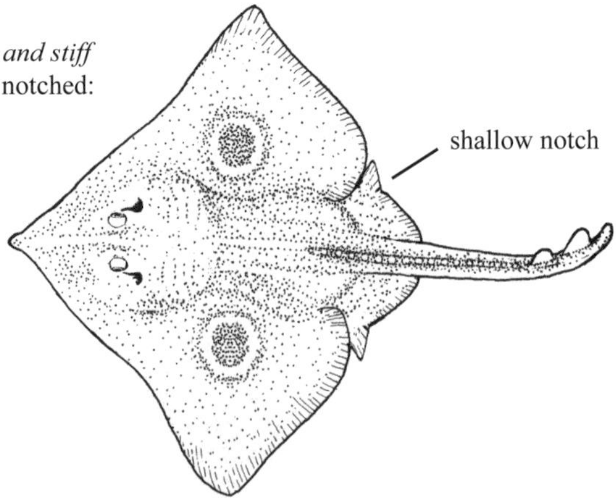


9b Pelvic fins deeply notched….. 10 (next page)

10a Snout very short, bluntly pointed:

**STARRY SKATE**

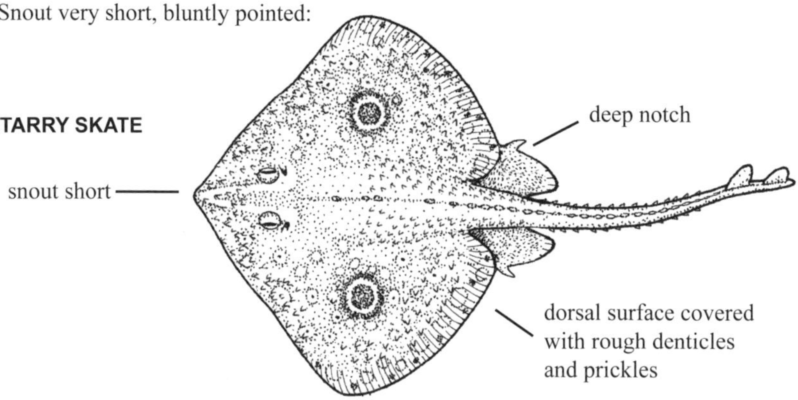


10b Snout long, acutely pointed….. 11

11a Snout extremely long, tapering to acute point; straight line from snout to tip of pectoral fin touches 2 times; ventral surface mottled light to dark gray:

**LONGNOSE SKATE**

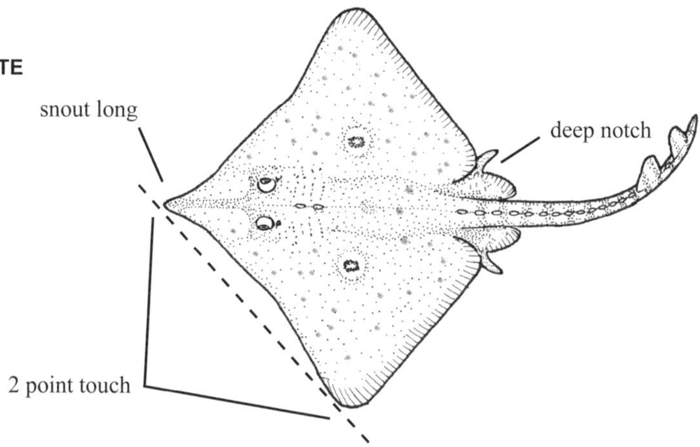


11b Snout moderately long, acutely pointed; straight line from snout to tip of pectoral fin touches 3 times; ventral surface white to pale tan:

**CALIFORNIA SKATE**

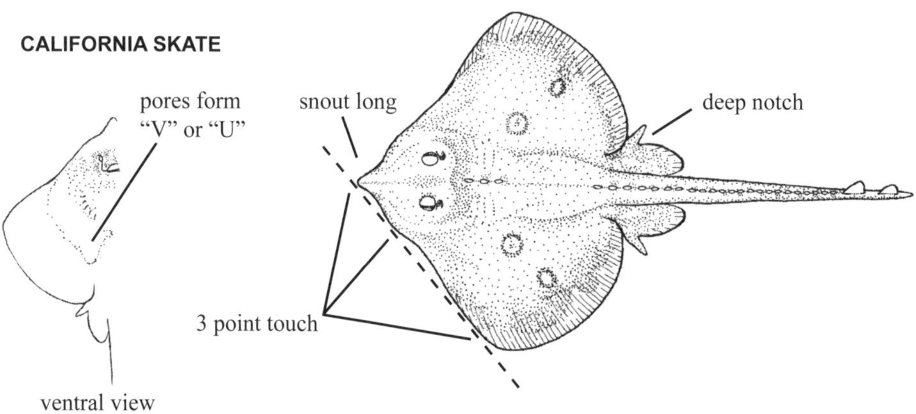

## Order Myliobatiformes
## ROUND STINGRAY, Family Urotrygonidae, BAT RAY, Family Myliobatidae, BUTTERFLY RAY, Family Gymnuridae, DEVILRAYS, Family Mobulidae, and WHIPTAIL STINGRAYS, Family Dasyatidae

**ROUND STINGRAY, *Urobatis halleri* (Cooper, 1863).** Family UROTRYGONIDAE
Humboldt Bay, northern California to Peru, including Gulf of California. Uncommon in central California, common from Santa Barbara, southern California southward into tropics. Historically, may also have been common in Morro Bay, central California. Length to 58 cm (22 in) TL, width to 31 cm (12.1 in) DW; at birth 6–8 cm (2.4–3.1 in) DW. Depth: 0.3–21 m (1–70 ft), but possibly to at least 91 m (298 ft). Brownish, grayish, or almost black above with dark or light diffuse spotting and cross hatching, yellowish below. Vert. 86. (Formerly *Urolophus halleri* Cooper, 1863: M&L) (Alternative name ROUND RAY).

**BAT RAY, *Myliobatis californica* Gill, 1865.** Family MYLIOBATIDAE
Yaquina Bay, Oregon to Gulf of California, including Islas Galápagos. Common from Arcata Bay, northern California to Bahía Magdalena, southern Baja California and in Gulf of California. Width to 1.8 m (6 ft) DW; at birth 20–31 cm (7.9–12.2 in) DW. Depth: intertidal to 176 m (577 ft). Dark brown to olive or black above, white below. An albino fish was taken near Bahía Magdalena, southern Baja California. Vert. 82.

**CALIFORNIA BUTTERFLY RAY, *Gymnura marmorata* (Cooper, 1864).** Family GYMNURIDAE
Point Conception, California to Mazatlán, Mexico, including Gulf of California. Records from south of Gulf of California may be *Gymnura crebripunctata* (Peters, 1869) or *Gymnura afuera* Hildebrand, 1946. Common as far north as the southern part of southern California and southward into tropics. Width to 157 cm (61.8 in) DW; at birth 14–26 cm (5.5–10.2 in) DW. Depth: surf zone to 94 m (308 ft). Brown to gray above with darker and lighter mottling. Vert. 129.

## KEY TO THE MYLIOBATIFORMES:
Created by David Ebert
(Principal sources: Ebert, 2003; Last et al., 2016)

1a Caudal fin well developed:

**ROUND STINGRAY**

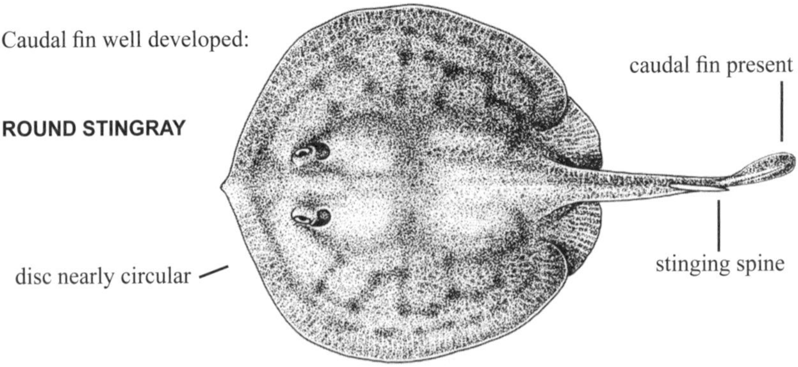


1b Caudal fin absent….. 2 (next page)

2a Head not elevated above disc; eyes and spiracles on top of head….. 4

2b Head elevated above disc; eyes and spiracles on sides of head….. 3

3a Head without paired horn-like flaps:

**BAT RAY**

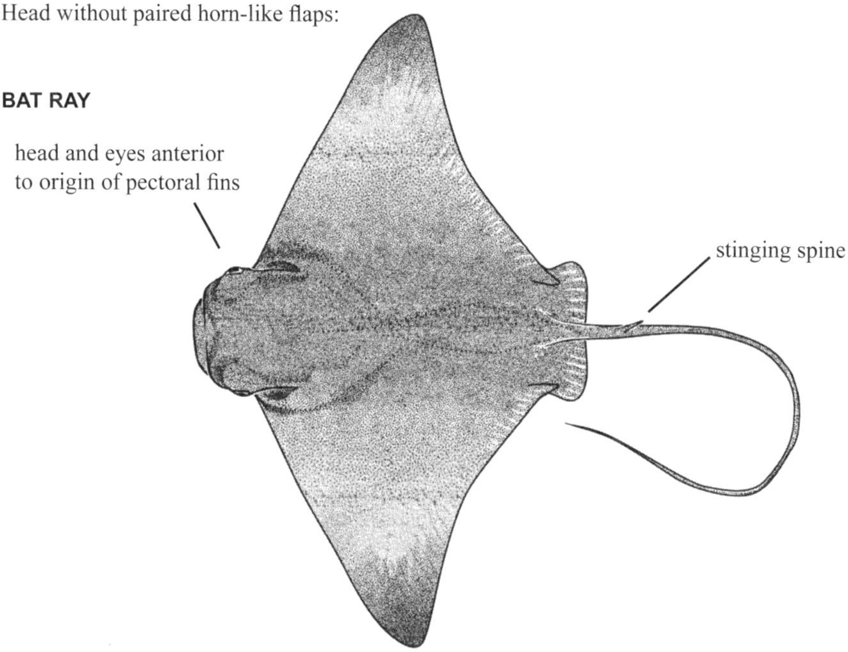


3b Head with paired horn-like flaps….. 5 (next page)

4a *From 2a: head not elevated above disc; eyes and spiracles on top of head*
DW nearly twice DL; tail short and slender, shorter than DL; stinging spine short:

**CALIFORNIA BUTTERFLY RAY**

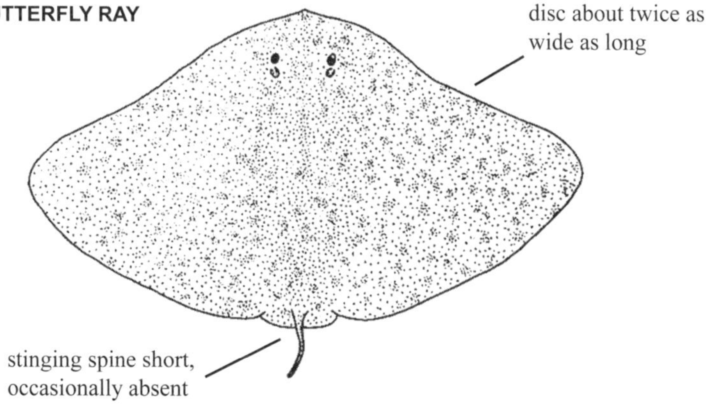


4b DW only slightly longer than DL; tail long and whip-like, longer than DL;
stinging spine long….. 6 (page 54)

## Order Myliobatiformes (continued)

**MANTA, *Mobula birostris* (Walbaum, 1792).** FAMILY MOBULIDAE

Circumglobal in warm waters; Santa Barbara, southern California to Peru (12°00'S), including Gulf of California and Islas Galápagos; sighting (unverifiable) reported from Prince William Sound, Alaska. Rare in southern California; common in tropical waters. Width to at least 9 m (29.5 ft) DW; at birth 110–130 cm (43.3–51.2 in) DW. Pelagic; depth: surface to 217 m (712 ft). Black to dark brown above, sometimes with white shoulder patches. Stinging spine vestigial. (Formerly PACIFIC MANTA, *Manta hamiltoni* Hamilton & Newman in Newman, 1849: M&L) (Alternative name GIANT MANTA).

**GIANT DEVILRAY, *Mobula mobular* (Bonnaterre, 1788).** Family MOBULIDAE

Circumglobal; central California to Peru, including Gulf of California. Rare in California; common in tropical waters. Width to at least 5.2 m (17.1 ft) DW; at birth 70–85 cm (27.6–33.5 in) DW. Depth: surface to 649 m (2,129 ft). Black or blue above; adults white below with dark blotches; juveniles with white crescent-shaped shoulder bars. The *Mobula thurstoni* (Lloyd, 1908) reported by MacGinitie (1947) from Laguna Beach, southern California is likely this species. (Formerly *Mobula lucasana* Beebe & Tee-Van, 1938: M&L). *Mobula japonica* (Müller & Henle, 1841) is a synonym.

**DIAMOND STINGRAY, *Hypanus dipterurus* (Jordan & Gilbert, 1880).** Family DASYATIDAE

At least Malibu, southern California to northern Chile and Islas Galápagos, including Gulf of California. Unverified captures in both British Columbia and central California. In the 19th century, common as far northward as San Diego Bay. Today, occasional off southern California; common at least as far northward as Bahía Magdalena, southern Baja California and into tropics. Length to 200 cm (78.7 in) TL, width to 122 cm (48 in) DW; at birth 19–23 cm (7.5–9.1 in) DW. Depth: surf zone to 355 m (1,164 ft). Blackish, brown, or orangish above, white below. Vert. 105–124. (Formerly *Dasyatis dipterura* Jordan & Gilbert, 1880: M&L).

**PELAGIC STINGRAY, *Pteroplatytrygon violacea* (Bonaparte, 1832).** Family DASYATIDAE

Circumglobal; in the western Pacific as far north as the southern Kuril Islands, Russia; British Columbia to Baja California and to central Chile and Islas Galápagos. Common northward in offshore waters at least as far north as southern California and into tropics. Length to 163 cm (64.2 in) TL, width to 80 cm (32 in) DW and possibly to 96 cm (37.8 in) DW; at birth 15–25 cm (5.9–9.8 in) DW. Pelagic; depth: surface to 381 m (1,250 ft). Dark black or purplish above, purplish, brown, or gray below. Vert. 94–99. (Formerly *Dasyatis violacea* (Bonaparte, 1832): M&L).

5a *From 3b: head with paired horn-like flaps*
Mouth on front of head; small teeth arranged in tooth-like plate on lower jaw only:

**MANTA**

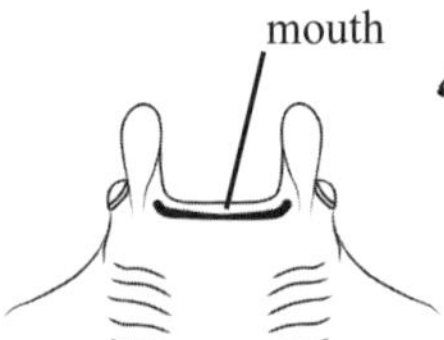


ventral view

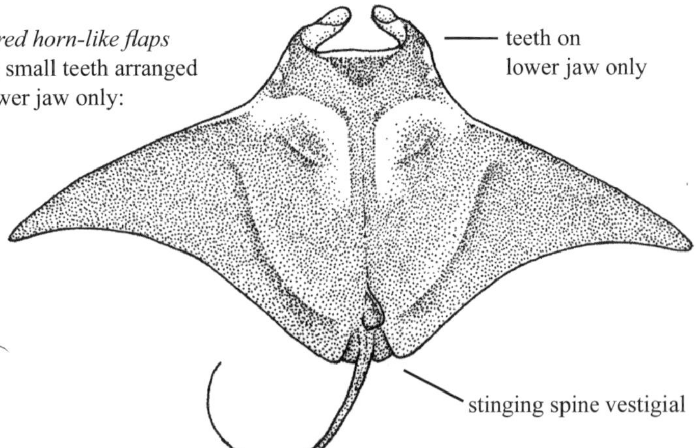


5b (next page)

5b Mouth on underside of head; small teeth arranged in tooth-like plate on both jaws:

**GIANT DEVILRAY**

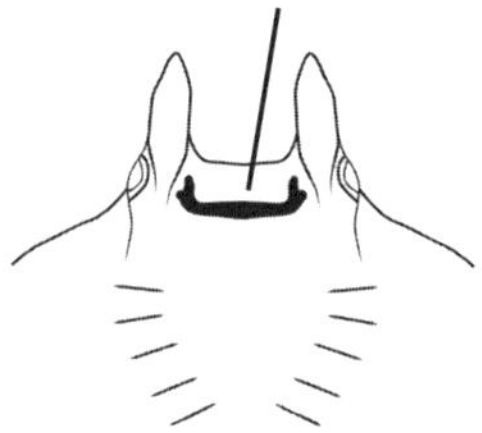


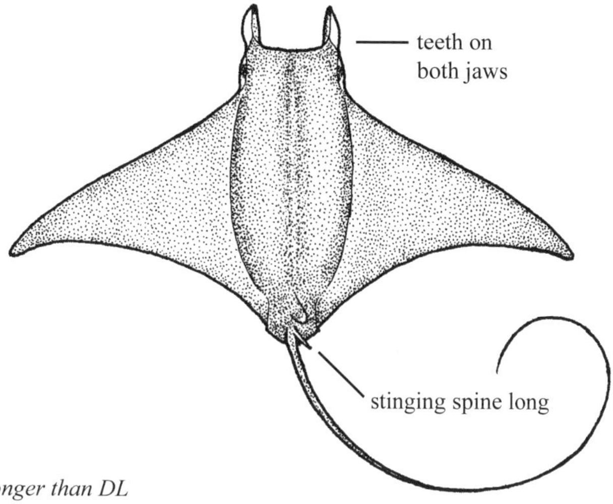


6a *From 4b: DW only slightly longer than DL*
Snout pointed; brown to grayish or blackish above, white below:

**DIAMOND STINGRAY**

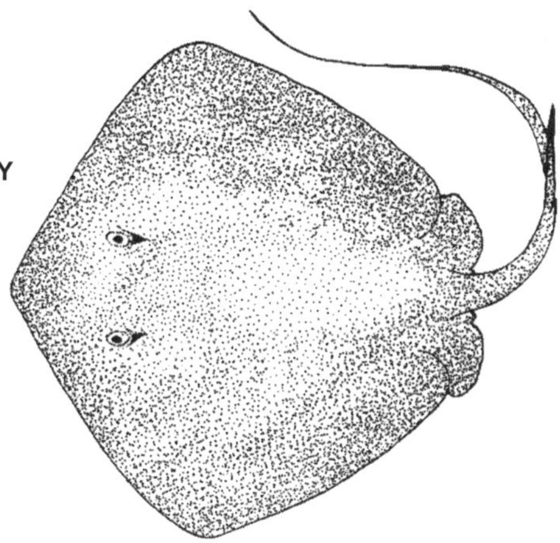


6b Snout rounded; uniformly dark purple above and below:

**PELAGIC STINGRAY**

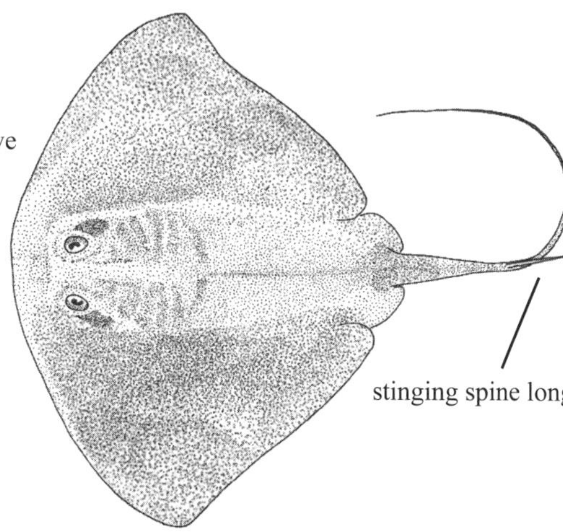

# SPECIES PRESENTATION: RAY-FINNED FISHES, Class Actinopterygii

## STURGEONS, Family Acipenseridae, MACHETE, Family Elopidae, BONEFISH, Family Albulidae, and SPINY EEL, Family Notacanthidae

**GREEN STURGEON, *Acipenser medirostris* Ayres, 1854.** Family Acipenseridae
Peter the Great Bay, Sea of Japan and Tohoku, Japan to Pacific coast of Kamchatka, eastern Bering Sea (perhaps as far north as about Norton Sound), and Gulf of Alaska to just south of Bahía de San Quintin, northern Baja California. Common from British Columbia to San Francisco Bay. Length to 270 cm (108 in) TL. Anadromous; depth: to 110 m (361 ft) at sea. Olive-green or gray above, white below; olive stripes on sides. D 29–42; A 18–30; Plates (scutes): midlateral 23–30, dorsal 7–12, ventral 7–11.

**WHITE STURGEON, *Acipenser transmontanus* Richardson, 1837.** Family Acipenseridae
Northern Gulf of Alaska to Ensenada, northern Baja California. Common from the Fraser River area, British Columbia to San Francisco Bay. Length to perhaps 6 m (20 ft) TL. Moyle (2002) noted that the largest length records for this species were made before 1900 and "were subject to inaccurate measurements and exaggerated reporting." Largest recent record, from Oregon, was 3.2 m (10.5 ft) long. Anadromous; depth: to 122 m (400 ft) at sea. Uniform gray. D 44–48; A 28–31; Plates (scutes): midlateral 38–48, dorsal 11–14, ventral 9–12; GRt 24–36.

**MACHETE, *Elops affinis* Regan, 1909.** Family Elopidae
Mandalay Beach, southern California (LACM 35515-1) to Talara, Peru, including Gulf of California. Rare in California. Length to 91.4 cm (36 in) TL. Depth: 1–10 m (4–33 ft), frequently enters fresh water. Silvery. D 20–27; A 13–17; Pect. 16–17; LLs 100–120; GR 10–12 + 12–20 = 22–32; Vert. 79–82. (Alternative names PACIFIC LADYFISH, TENPOUNDER).

**CORTEZ BONEFISH, *Albula gilberti* Pfeiler & van der Heiden, 2011.** Family Albulidae
San Francisco, northern California, southward along west coast of Baja California and into the Gulf of California to Acapulco, Mexico. Common as far north as Marina del Rey, California. Length to about 41.2 cm (16.2 in) TL. Depth: nearshore waters. Gray above, silvery below; base of fins yellowish. D 17–18; A 8–9; Pect. 18–20; Pelvic 9–12; LLs 68–73; GR 4–10 + 10–12 = 15–21; Vert. 70–74. (Formerly BONEFISH, *Albula vulpes* Linnaeus, 1758: M&L).

**SNUBNOSED SPINY EEL, *Notacanthus chemnitzii* Bloch, 1788.** Family Notacanthidae
Probably circumglobal; Greenland; Japan; Sea of Okhotsk; northern Bering Sea to edge of Monterey Submarine Canyon, central California; Chile. Likely rare in California. Length to more than 135 cm (54 in) TL. Benthopelagic; depth: 128–3,285 m (420–10,775 ft). Uniform gray or brown; margin of opercular flap and fins blackish. D V–XII,2; A XIII–XXI,110–130; Pect. 12–17; Pelvic III–IV,6–7; GRt 12–17; Pyloric caeca 4; Vert. 225–234. Perhaps a species complex.

NOTE: Fishes in Elopidae, Albulidae, and Notacanthidae have a leptocephalus larval stage.

**GREEN STURGEON**

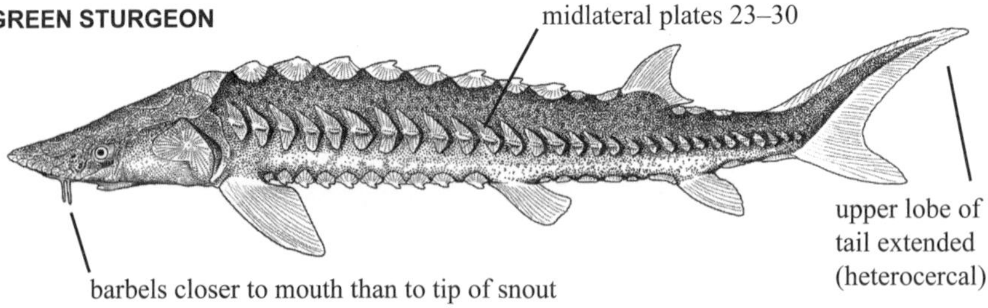

**WHITE STURGEON**

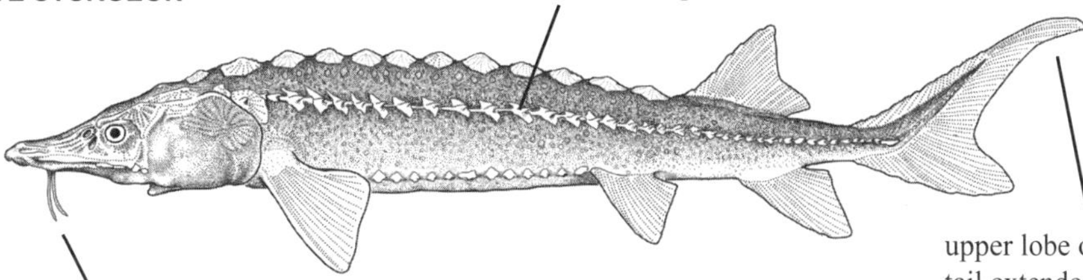


**MACHETE**

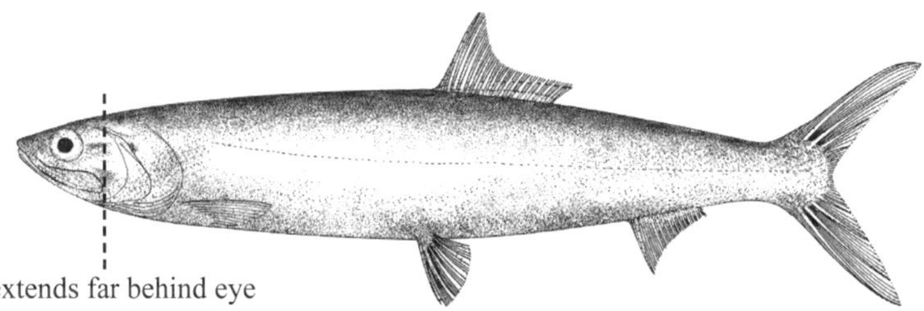


**CORTEZ BONEFISH**

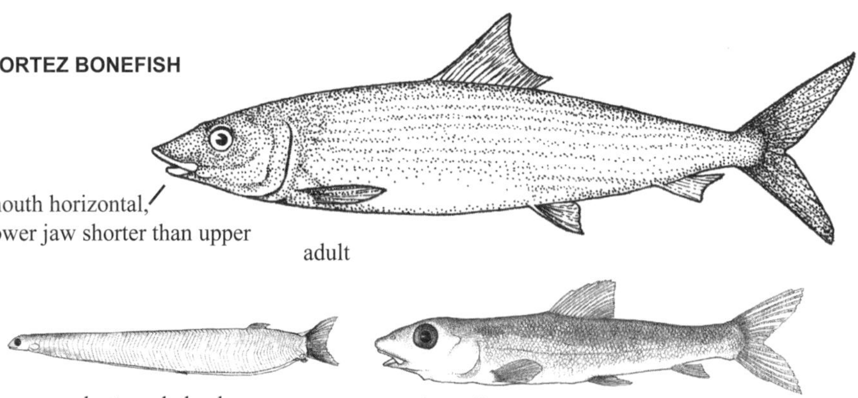


**SNUBNOSED SPINY EEL**

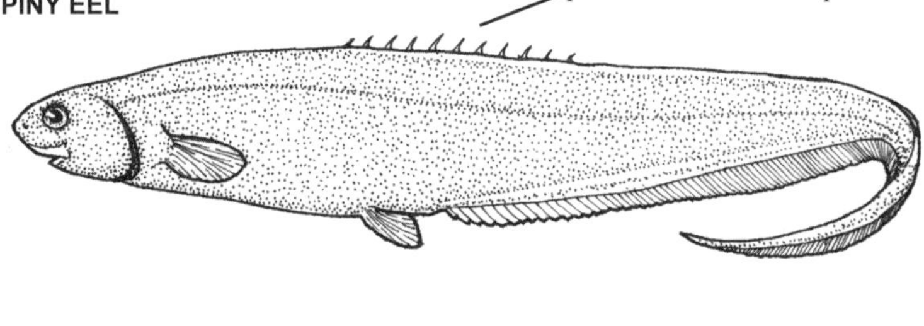

# SAWTOOTH EEL, Family Serrivomeridae, MORAYS, Family Muraenidae, and CONGER EELS, Family Congridae

**SAWTOOTH EEL, *Serrivomer sector* Garman, 1899.** Family Serrivomeridae

Pacific and Indian Oceans; Japan; Washington (47°12'N) to northern Chile. Common from southern California southward. Possibly to 76 cm (30 in) TL. Depth: 0–4,268 m (13,999 ft). Dusky-brown to dark gray-black; mouth, peritoneum, and gill cavities black. D 145–148; A 143–152; Pect. absent; Pelvic reduced; Vert. 151–153.

**CALIFORNIA MORAY, *Gymnothorax mordax* (Ayres, 1859).** Family Muraenidae

Point Conception, California to Todos Santos (23°25'N, 110°14'W), southern Baja California, including Isla Guadalupe, central Baja California and Rocas Alijos, southern Baja California (SIO 90-135). However, early stage larvae have been taken around Cabo San Lucas, in the lowermost part of the Gulf of California (on both sides), and down the Mexican mainland as far south as Mazatlan. Larvae tentatively identified as this species have also been captured off Colombia. Common as far north as about Santa Catalina Island, southern California and southward to about Bahía Tortugas, southern Baja California. Length to 152 cm (60 in) TL. Depth: lower intertidal to 40 m (131 ft). Dark brown to greenish, often with dark mottling. D 367; A 226; Vert. 143–154.

**ARGUS MORAY, *Muraena argus* (Steindachner, 1870).** Family Muraenidae

Santa Catalina Island and Redondo Beach, southern California and Bahía Magdalena (SIO 62-131), southern Baja California and Gulf of California to Islas Lobos de Afuera, Peru, including Islas Galápagos and other offshore islands. Rare in southern California. Length to 120 cm (47.2 in) TL. Depth: 5–120 m (17–394 ft). Brown, with 2–3 rows of large irregular yellow-brown or brown blotches and many small white spots; black spot covering gill opening. (Alternative name WHITE-SPOTTED MORAY).

**HARDTAIL CONGER, *Gnathophis cinctus* (Garman, 1899).** Family Congridae

Santa Rosa Island, southern California to Peru, including Gulf of California and Islas Galápagos. Uncommon off southern California; common from central Baja California southward into tropics. Length to 41.9 cm (16.5 in) TL. Depth: 9–366 m (30–1,200 ft). Brownish-gray. LLp 132. (Formerly CATALINA CONGER, *Gnathophis catalinenis* (Wade, 1946): M&L).

**DEEPWATER CONGER, *Xenomystax atrarius* Gilbert, 1891.** Family Congridae

Vancouver Island, British Columbia; Newport Beach, southern California (LACM 44131-1) to central Chile (37°31'S), including Gulf of California and Islas Galápagos. One California record. Length to 100 cm (39.3 in) TL. Depth: 116–1,050 m (380–3,444 ft). Black or brown; few black spots on sides may be present; lateral line and head pores white; tip of pectoral fin white; sometimes lighter areas on head and caudal region. Pect. 11–14; Vert. 159–177. (Alternative name TWINPORED EEL).

NOTE: Fishes in Serrivomeridae, Muraenidae, and Congridae have a leptocephalus larval stage.

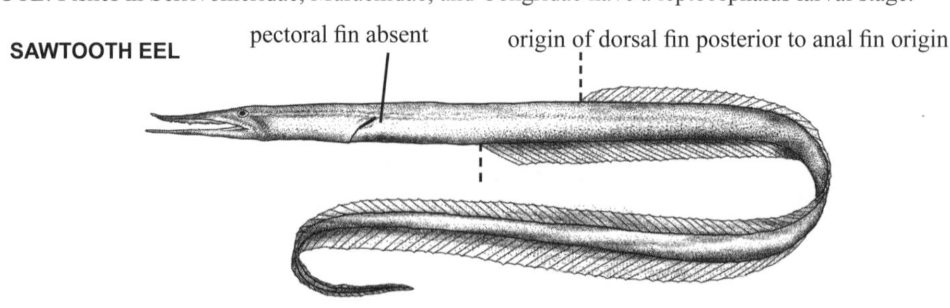

**CALIFORNIA MORAY**

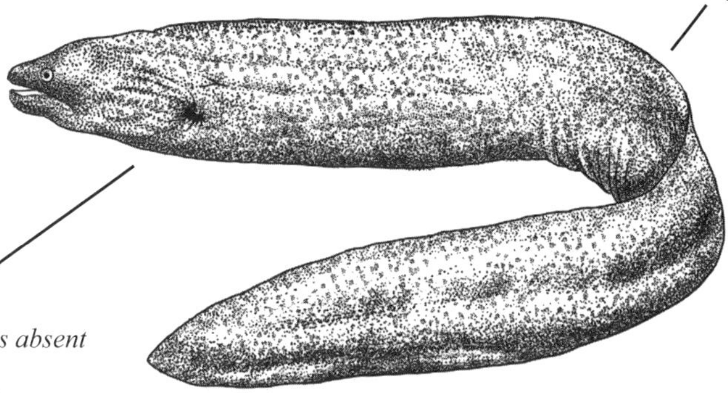


**ARGUS MORAY**

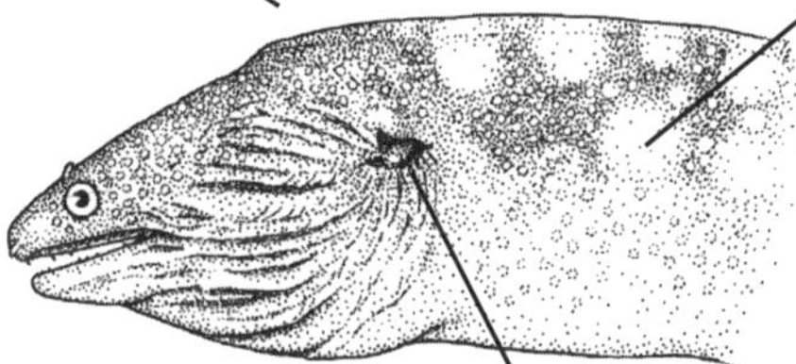


**HARDTAIL CONGER**

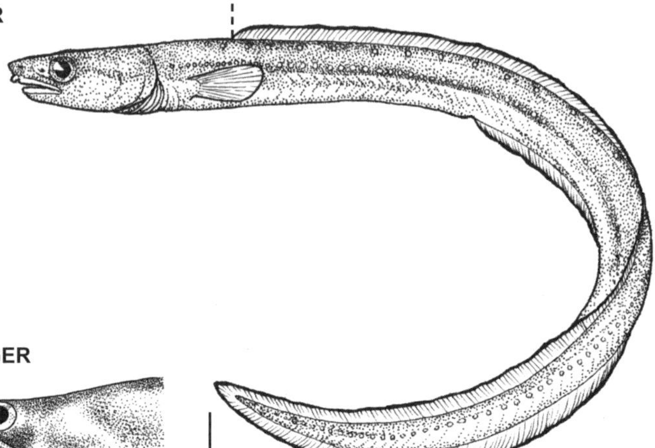


**DEEPWATER CONGER**

## WITCH EEL, Family Nettastomatidae and SNAKE EELS, Family Ophichthidae

**DOGFACE WITCH EEL, *Facciolella equatorialis* (Gilbert, 1891).** Family Nettastomatidae
Point Conception, California to Peru, including Islas Galápagos. Common from southern California southward. Length to 90 cm (35.4 in) TL. Depth: 64–1,000 m (210–3,280 ft). Uniformly brown. D 370; A 283. *Facciolella gilberti* (Garman, 1899) is a junior synonym.

**PACIFIC WORM EEL, *Myrophis vafer* Jordan & Gilbert, 1883.** Family Ophichthidae
San Pedro, southern California to Punta Aguja, Peru, including Gulf of California. Rare in southern California; common from Bahía Magdalena, southern Baja California, into tropics. Length to 47 cm (18.5 in) TL. Depth: intertidal to 15 m (49 ft). Whitish-gray. D 344; A 256; Vert. 146–155.

**PACIFIC SNAKE EEL, *Ophichthus triserialis* (Kaup, 1856).** Family Ophichthidae
Off Lincoln City (44°59'N, 124°09'W), Oregon to Peru, including Gulf of California and Islas Galápagos. Common from southern California southward into tropics. Length to 121.5 cm (47.8 in) TL. Depth: surface and intertidal to 155 m (508 ft). Tan, with large black spots. D 296; A 197; Vert. 144–160. The *O. triserialis* mentioned as living around the Islas Galápagos in Eschmeyer and Herald (1983) is another island endemic species. (Formerly SPOTTED SNAKE EEL: M&L).

**YELLOW SNAKE EEL, *Ophichthus zophochir* (Jordan & Gilbert, 1882).** Family Ophichthidae
Humboldt Bay, northern California to Arica, northern Chile, including Gulf of California. Common as far north as about Santa Monica Bay, southern California and southward into tropics. Length to 98 cm (38.6 in) TL. Depth: intertidal to 110 m (361 ft). Brownish or purple-brown above, yellowish or pale below. D 258; A 190; Vert. 144–162.

NOTE: Fishes in Nettastomatidae and Ophichthidae have a leptocephalus larval stage.

**DOGFACE WITCH EEL**

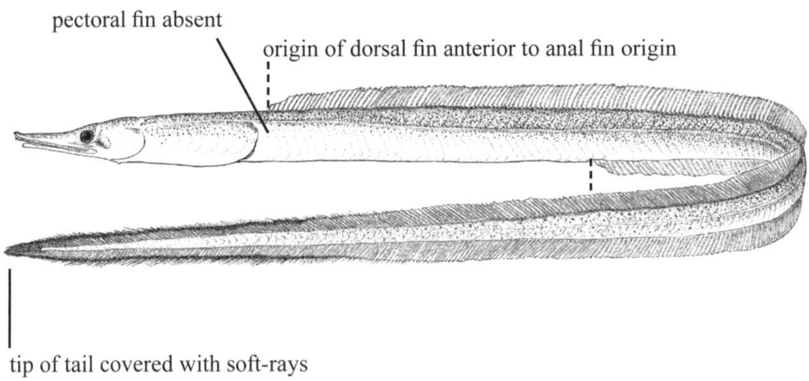

PACIFIC WORM EEL

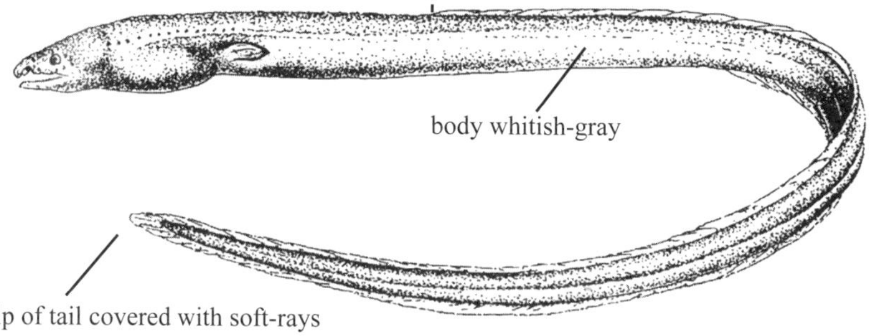


PACIFIC SNAKE EEL

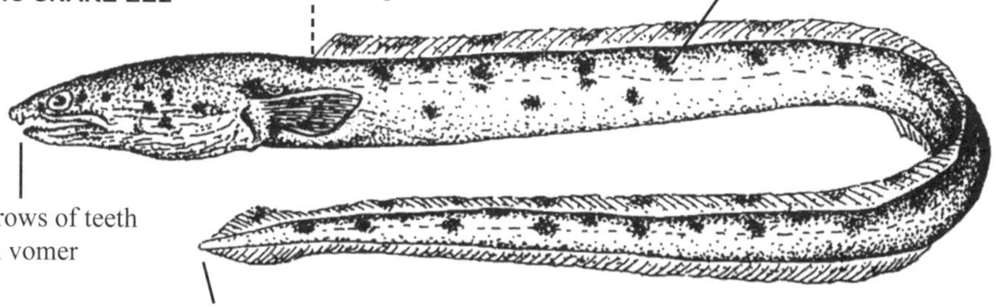


YELLOW SNAKE EEL

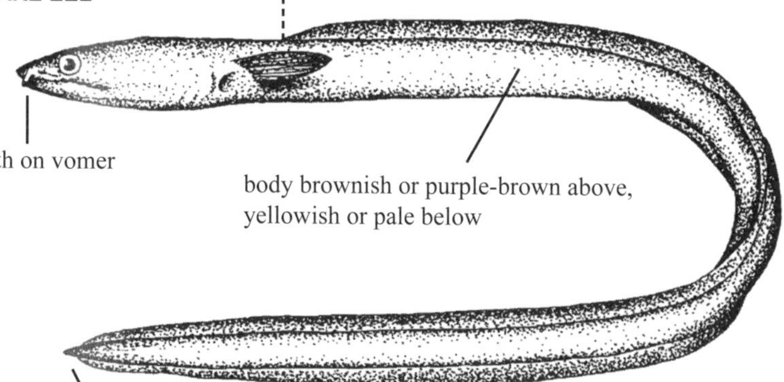

## THREADTAIL SNIPE EELS, Family Nemichthyidae

**PALE SNIPE EEL, *Nemichthys larseni* Nielsen & Smith, 1978.** Eastern North Pacific from between Springfield and Warwick Seamounts (47°56'N, 131°26'W), British Columbia to central Mexico, including Gulf of California. Common at least from central California southward (usually well offshore). Length to about 161 cm (63.4 in) TL. Primarily mesopelagic; depth: 170–2,439 m (558–8,000 ft). Young pale cream or tan; adults light gray to tan, darker ventrally. D and A more than 300 each; Pect. 10–12; Pelvic absent; Vert. 400 or more.

**SLENDER SNIPE EEL, *Nemichthys scolopaceus* Richardson, 1848.** Circumglobal in temperate and tropical waters; Japan; Gulf of Alaska to southern Chile (52°00'S), including Gulf of California. Common at least off Japan and in the eastern Pacific from at least as far northward as Oregon to southern Baja California. Length to 200 cm (78.7 in) TL. Primarily meso- and bathypelagic, sometimes over continental shelf; depth: surface to 4,337 m (14,225 ft). Uniform blackish, dark or light brown. D variously reported as 170–253, 279–432, 300+; A variously reported as 186–273, 240–372, 300+; Pect. 10–14; Pelvic absent; Precaudal vert. 77–105.

**BLACKLINE SNIPE EEL, *Avocettina infans* (Günther, 1878).** Circumglobal; Japan; Commander-Aleutian Islands Chain and northern Bering Sea to central Mexico, including Gulf of California. Common at least off Japan and from Gulf of Alaska southward to Chile (primarily well offshore) and in Gulf of California. Length to 80 cm (31.5 in) TL. Pelagic; meso- and bathypelagic and far from shore, rarely over continental shelf; depth: surface to 4,571 m (14,993 ft). Dusky brown to black, most heavily pigmented along lateral line. D 279–432; A 240–372; Pect. 14–18; Pelvic absent; LLp 181–201; Vert. 187–202.

**SMALLEYE SNIPE EEL, *Avocettina bowersii* Garman, 1899.** Eastern and central Pacific; Patton Seamount, Gulf of Alaska (UW 042773); San Francisco, northern California to northern Chile (19°44'S). Common at least as far northward as southern California. Length to 67.5 cm (26.8 in) SL. Mesopelagic; depth: 0–4,000 m (13,120 ft). D 233–333; A 208–297; Pect. 15–19; Pelvic absent; Vert. 177–195.

NOTE: Fishes in Nemichthyidae have a leptocephalus larval stage.

## KEY TO THE THREADTAIL SNIPE EELS:

Created by Cynthia Klepadlo
(Principal source: Nielsen & Smith, 1978)

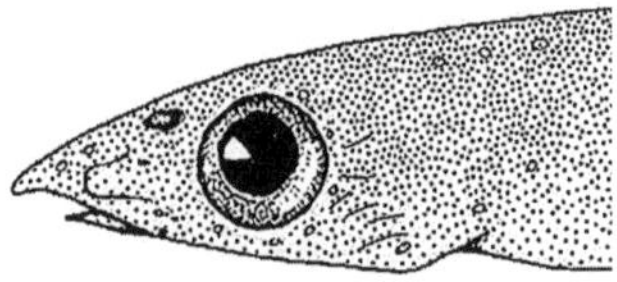

all males lack elongated jaws

1a Anal fin origin well behind pectoral fin; dorsal fin origin posterior to or above pectoral fin; lateral line pores in 1 row; caudal filament absent….. 3 (next page)

1b Anal fin origin under pectoral fin; dorsal fin origin anterior to pectoral fin; lateral line pores in 3 rows; caudal filament present….. 2 (next page)

2a Lateral line pores form a rectangle shorter than high; color pale:

**PALE SNIPE EEL**

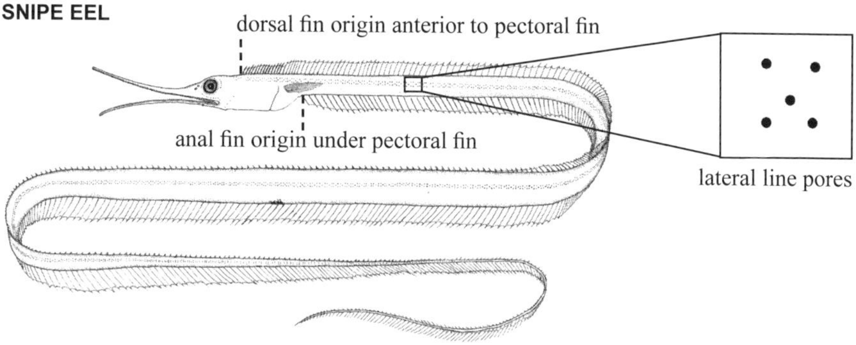


2b Lateral line pores form a rectangle longer than high; color dark:

**SLENDER SNIPE EEL**

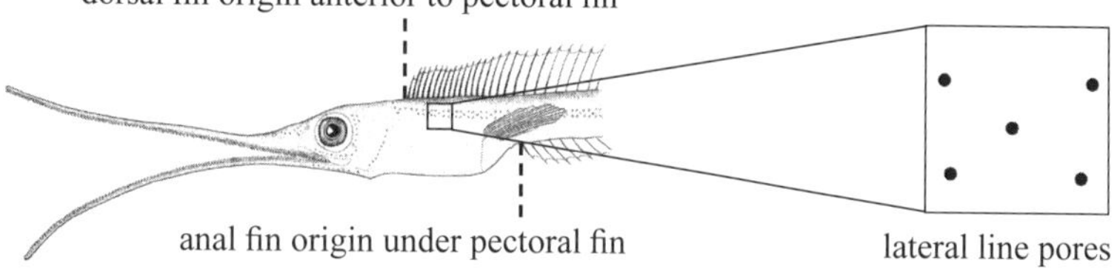


3a *From 1a: anal fin origin well behind pectoral fin*
Dorsal fin origin above pectoral fin; body not uniformly brown; first 6–16 (mean 11–12) dorsal fin soft-rays closely spaced:

**BLACKLINE SNIPE EEL**

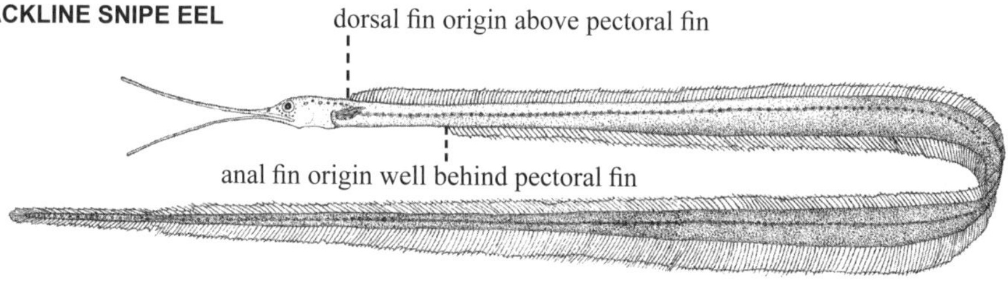


3b Dorsal fin origin posterior to tip of pectoral fin; body uniform brown; first 4–10 (mean 6) dorsal fin soft-rays closely spaced:

**SMALLEYE SNIPE EEL**

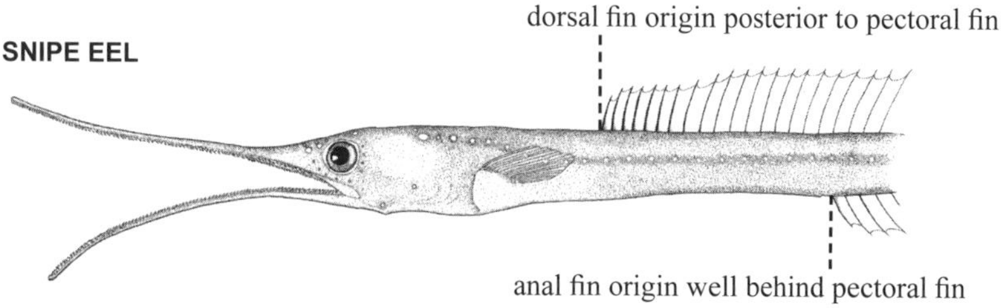

## HERRINGS, Family Clupeidae

**THREADFIN SHAD, *Dorosoma petenense* (Günther, 1867).** Native to the southeastern United States and south to Belize. Introduced to West Coast. Off Oregon to San Diego Bay, southern California and Gulf of California. Common in Sacramento-San Joaquin River system and in a few southern California embayments. Length to 33 cm (13 in) TL. Shallow fresh, brackish, and marine waters; depth: not reported. Silvery with single black spot near operculum. D 11–17; A 17–27; Pect. 12–17; Midlateral scales 40–48; Ventral scutes 15–18 anterior and 8–12 posterior to pelvic base; Vert. 40–45.

**DEEPBODY THREAD HERRING, *Opisthonema libertate* (Günther, 1867).** Port Hueneme, southern California to Chile, including Gulf of California and Islas Galápagos. Rare in southern California; common at least from Bahía San Juanico, southern Baja California to tropics. Length to about 30 cm (11.8 in) TL. Nearshore; depth: 1–70 m (3–230 ft). Blue on back, silvery white sides and belly; often narrow dark stripes and scattered dark spots on upper part of body and scattered black spots on sides; usually black mark behind upper rear corner of gill cover; base of dorsal and caudal fins yellow. D 17–20; A 19–22; Pect. 15–18; Pelvic 8–9; GR 110–149 + 161–224; Vert. 44–48. (Alternative name PACIFIC THREAD HERRING).

**MIDDLING THREAD HERRING, *Opisthonema medirastre* Berry & Barrett, 1963.** Redondo Beach, southern California to Huacho, Peru, including Gulf of California. Rare in southern California. Length to 30 cm (11.8 in) TL. Depth: surface to perhaps 10 m (33 ft). Blue back, silver sides and belly. D 17–20; A 19–22; Pect. 15–18; Pelvic 8–9; GR 110–149 + 161–224; Midlateral scales 48–50; Ventral scutes 17–18 anterior and 14–15 posterior to pelvic base; Vert. 44–48.

**ROUND HERRING, *Etrumeus acuminatus* Gilbert, 1890.** Circumglobal; Japan; Monterey Bay, central California to Chile, including Gulf of California and Islas Galápagos. Common in southern California during some El Niño years, otherwise uncommon off California; common in Bahía Magdalena and into tropics. Length to 30.5 cm (12 in) TL. Pelagic; depth: surf zone to 200 m (656 ft). Dark blue above, white below. D 16–22; A 9–19; Pect. 14–17; Pelvic 8–9; GR 12–15 + 28–35; Midlateral scales 48–55; Vert. 48–55. (Formerly *Etrumeus teres* (DeKay, 1842): M&L).

## KEY TO THE HERRINGS:

Revised by Julianne Kalman Passarelli

(Principal sources: Miller & Lea, 1972; Fischer et al., 1995)

1a Last dorsal fin soft-ray shorter than 1st dorsal fin soft-ray….. 4 (next page)

1b Last dorsal fin soft-ray greatly elongated, thread-like….. 2

2a No scales on dorsal midline anterior to dorsal fin; 8–12 ventral scutes posterior to pelvic base; origin of pelvic fin about under origin of dorsal fin:

THREADFIN SHAD

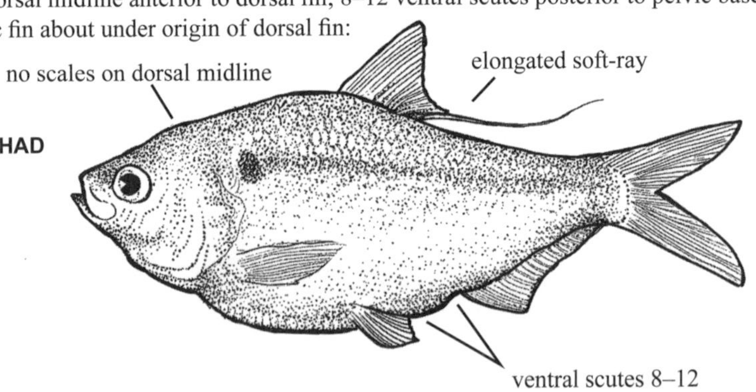


2b (next page)

2b Scales present on dorsal midline anterior to dorsal fin; 14–15 ventral scutes posterior to pelvic base; origin of pelvic fin about midpoint to base of dorsal fin….. 3

3a Black mark behind upper rear corner of gill cover; may have narrow dark stripes on upper part of body:

**DEEPBODY THREAD HERRING**

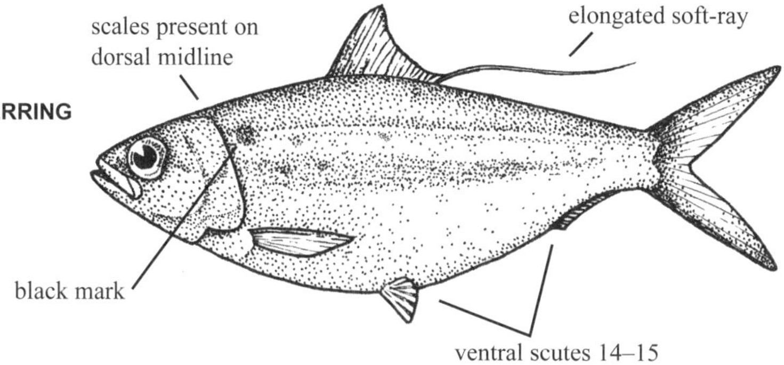


3b Black mark behind upper rear corner of gill cover lacking; dark stripes on upper part of body lacking:

**MIDDLING THREAD HERRING**

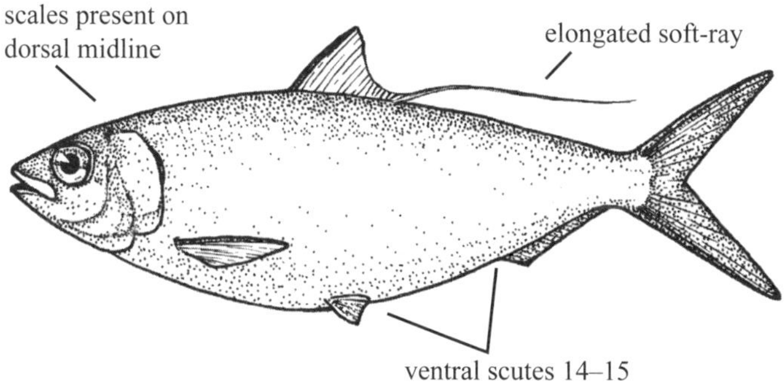


4a *From 1a: last dorsal fin soft-ray shorter than 1st dorsal fin soft-ray*
Pelvic fin origin posterior to, or even with, insertion of dorsal fin:

**ROUND HERRING**

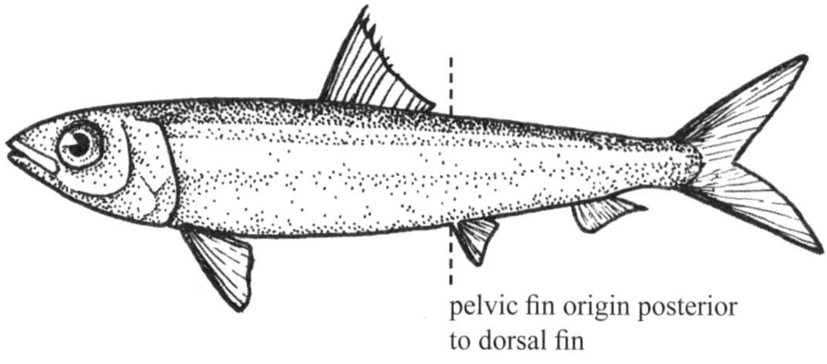


4b Pelvic fin origin under dorsal fin….. 5 (next page)

## HERRINGS (continued)

**PACIFIC HERRING, *Clupea pallasii* Valenciennes, 1847.** Korea and Japan to Arctic Ocean off Alaska and south to northern Baja California; Arctic Canada as far northeast as Melville Sound and southeast as far as Bathurst Inlet, Coronation Gulf. Scattered populations in Norwegian Barents Sea and Russian White and Pechora Seas. Common from Sea of Japan north throughout western and southern Alaska and southward to central California. Small pockets of them may still exist in a few southern California estuaries. Length to 46 cm (18 in) TL. Marine and brackish waters; depth: surface to 250 m (820 ft), or perhaps as deep as 723 m (2,371 ft), almost always captured above 150 m (492 ft). Dark green above, white below. D 15–21; A 13–20; Pect. 15–20; Pelvic 9; Midlateral scales 38–54; GR 20–23 + 41–50; Vert. 46–58. (Formerly *Clupea harengus pallasii*: M&L).

**PACIFIC SARDINE, *Sardinops sagax* (Jenyns, 1842).** North Pacific from south of Japan to southern Kamchatka and Commander Islands, Russia, and Cross Sound, southeastern Alaska to Gulf of California and Islas Galápagos; other populations in western and eastern South Pacific, and off southern Africa. In some years, common as far north as British Columbia. During the cold-water part of the Pacific Decadal Oscillation, fish tend to retreat southward into Mexico. Length to 41 cm (16.1 in) TL. Depth: surface and surf zone to 383 m (1,256 ft) or perhaps to 982 m (3,221 ft). Blue-green above, white below; series of black spots on back (occasionally absent). D 17–20; A 17–20; Pect. 16–19; Pelvic 8–9; Midlateral scales 52–60; GRt varies with length, about 90–145; Vert. 48–54. (Formerly *Sardinops sagax caeruleus*: M&L).

**AMERICAN SHAD, *Alosa sapidissima* (Wilson, 1811).** Native to Atlantic; intentionally introduced to Pacific, spread to Kamchatka, Russia to southeastern Bering Sea and Gulf of Alaska to Bahía de Todos Santos, northern Baja California. In marine waters, common from Vancouver Island to off San Francisco Bay. Length to 76 cm (30 in) TL. Anadromous; depth at sea: surface to 250 m (820 ft), possibly to 440 m (1,443 ft). Dark blue above, white below; black spots on back. D 15–19; A 18–24; Midlateral scales about 60; Ventral scutes 19–23 anterior and 12–19 posterior to pelvic base; GR 59–73 lower limb (59–76 in Atlantic); Vert. 55–58 (53–59 in Atlantic).

**FLATIRON HERRING, *Harengula thrissina* (Jordan & Gilbert, 1882).** La Jolla, southern California to Callao, Peru, including Gulf of California. Rare off southern California; common in Gulf of California and other tropical waters. Length to 18.4 cm (7.3 in) TL. Inshore; depth: surface to at least 7 m (23 ft). Bluish above, silver below. D 16–20; A 14–17; Pect. 15–16; Pelvic 8–9; Midlateral scales 37–42; Ventral scutes 16–17 anterior and 12–14 posterior to pelvic base; GR 9–18 + 24–34; Vert. 40–43.

5a No black spotting on back or sides; ventral scutes without bony keel; teeth present on vomer:

PACIFIC HERRING

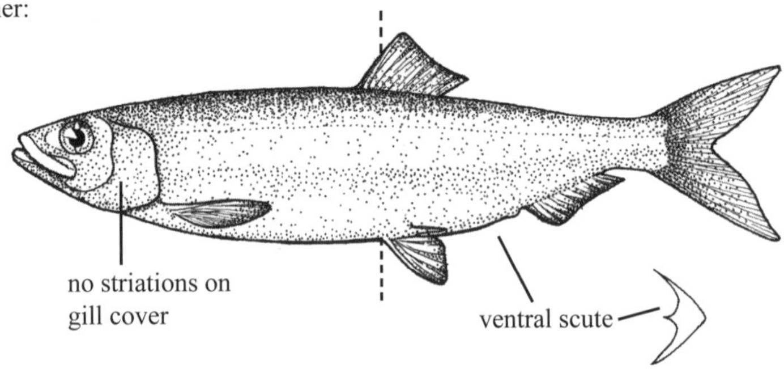


5b Black spots or spot present (rarely absent) on sides; ventral scutes with bony keels or points; no teeth on vomer….. 6 (next page)

6a Ventral scutes with fine points, barely protruding beyond scales; last anal fin soft-ray elongated:

**PACIFIC SARDINE**

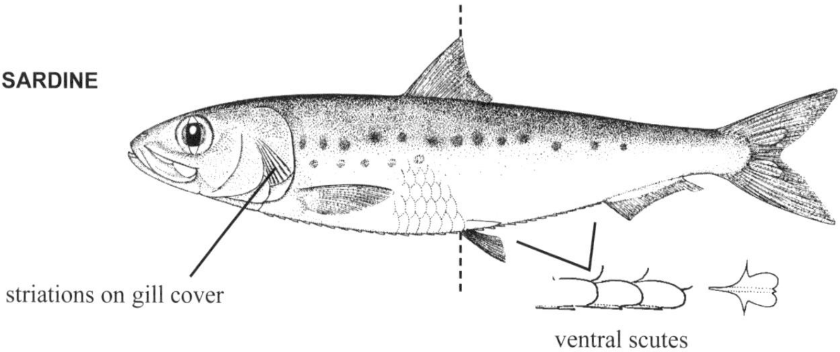


6b Ventral scutes with strong bony keel, appearing saw-toothed between pelvic and anal fins; last anal fin soft-ray not elongated….. 7

7a Anal fin soft-rays 18–24; row of black spots above lateral line:

**AMERICAN SHAD**

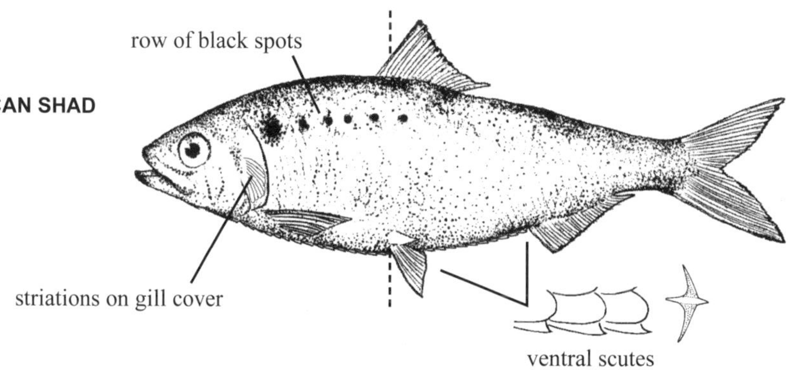


7b Anal fin soft-rays 14–17; may have 1 black spot behind operculum:

**FLATIRON HERRING**

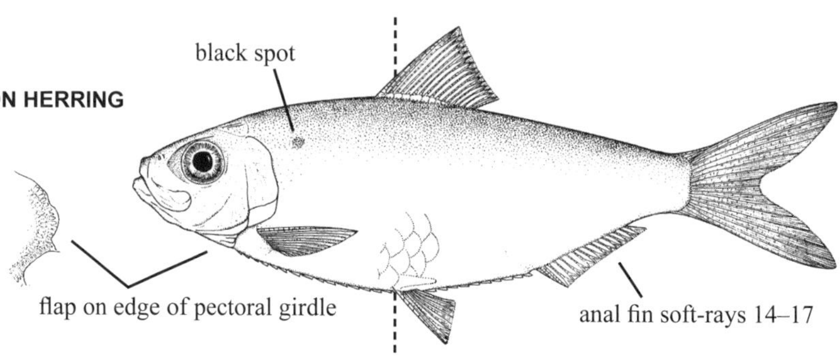

# ANCHOVIES, Family Engraulidae

NOTE: *Anchoviella miarcha*, listed in M&L, is now thought to be an invalid species (Whitehead et al., 1988).

**ANCHOVETA, *Cetengraulis mysticetus* (Günther, 1867).** Los Angeles, southern California to Callao, Peru, including Gulf of California and Islas Galápagos. Rare in southern California; common from Laguna San Ignacio, southern Baja California into tropics. Length to about 22 cm (8.7 in) TL. Depth: surface to 38 m (125 ft). The maximum depth of capture was made by bottom trawl and it is possible this species was captured in midwater. Greenish above, silvery below. D 13–17; A 18–27; Pect. 15–17; Pelvic 6–7; Midlateral scales 42–52; GRt 63–145 (number increasing with size); Vert. 39–43. M&L note that "its occurrence off California may be the result of inadvertent introductions by American tuna boat seiners returning from tropical waters." Since the demise of the tropical tuna seining industry (in the early 1980s) in southern California, there have been no reports of this species from southern California waters.

**NORTHERN ANCHOVY, *Engraulis mordax* Girard, 1854.** One record off Yakutat, eastern Gulf of Alaska; Haida Gwaii, British Columbia to Cabo San Lucas, southern Baja California and Gulf of California. The most abundant anchovy off California; common from southern British Columbia to Bahía Magdalena, southern Baja California. Length to 24.8 cm (9.7 in) TL. Depth: surface and intertidal to 528 m (1,732 ft); occasionally in estuarine waters. Metallic blue to green above, silver below. Body roundish and scales easily rubbed off. D 14–19; A 19–26; Pect. 13–20; Pelvic 6–8; Midlateral scales about 41–50; GR 28–41 + 37–45 (number increasing with size); Vert. 43–47.

**DEEPBODY ANCHOVY, *Anchoa compressa* (Girard, 1858).** Morro Bay, central California to Bahía Magdalena, southern Baja California. Common from about Long Beach, southern California southward. Length to 16.5 cm (6.5 in) TL. Depth: surf zone to perhaps 18.5 m (61 ft). Brownish to green above, silvery below with silvery lateral band; body deep, strongly compressed. D 12–14; A 29–33; Pect. 13–16; Pelvic 7–8; Midlateral scales about 45; GR 19–22 + 24–27 = 43–48; Vert. 39–41.

**SLOUGH ANCHOVY, *Anchoa delicatissima* (Girard, 1854).** Marina del Rey, southern California to Bahía Magdalena, southern Baja California. Common from about Alamitos Bay, southern California southward. Length to 12.9 cm (5.1 in) TL. Mostly in estuaries and backwaters of bays, occasionally near shore outside of bays; depth: intertidal to about 16 m (52 ft). Greenish above, silvery below with bright silvery lateral band. D 13–16; A 23–26; Pect. 12–14; Pelvic 6–8; Midlateral scales about 43; GR 18–21 + 26–32; Vert. 39–41.

## KEY TO THE ANCHOVIES:

Revised by Bill Power
(Principal source: Miller & Lea, 1972)

1a Gill membranes broadly united:

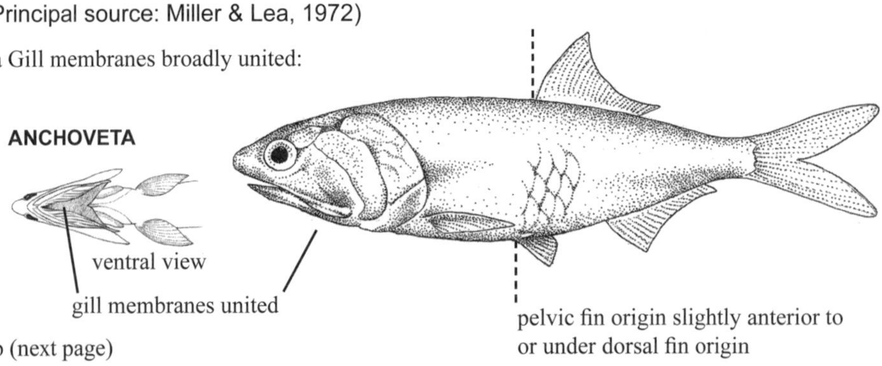


1b (next page)

1b Gill membranes not united….. 2

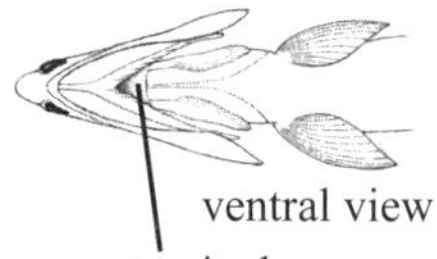


2a Origin of anal fin under or posterior to last few soft-rays of dorsal fin; body relatively round in cross section:

**NORTHERN ANCHOVY**

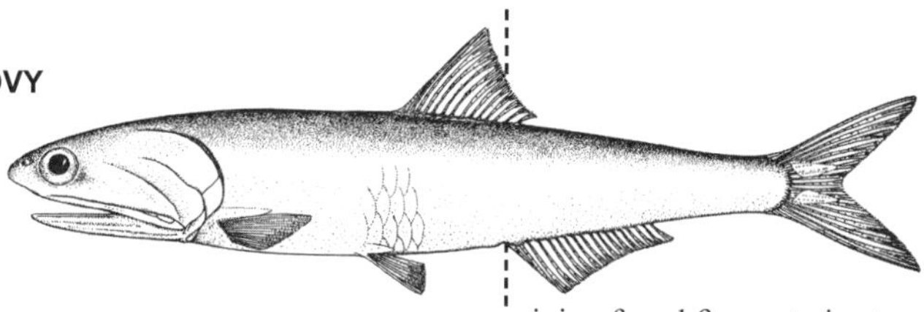


2b Origin of anal fin anterior to middle of dorsal fin base; body relatively oval in cross section….. 3

3a Anal fin base more than 2 times length of dorsal fin base; anal fin soft-rays 29–33; inside of mouth light in color:

**DEEPBODY ANCHOVY**

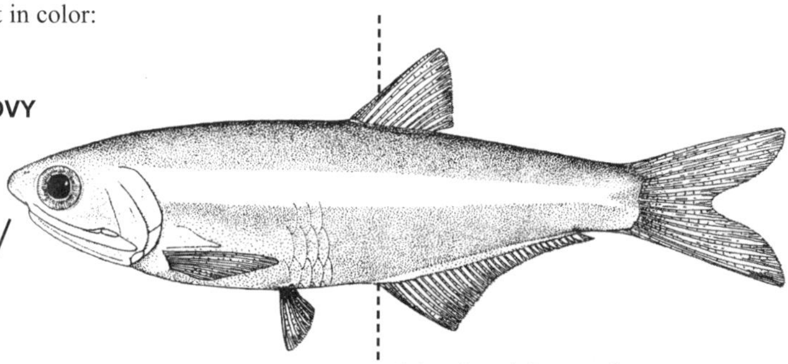


3b Anal fin base less than 2 times length of dorsal fin base; anal fin soft-rays 23–26; inside of mouth dark:

**SLOUGH ANCHOVY**

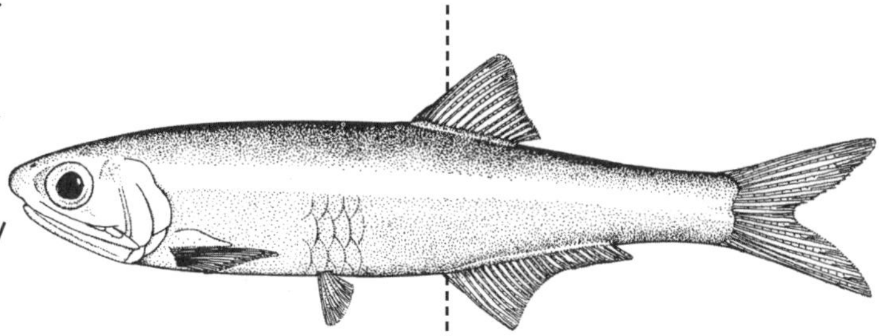

# TROUT and SALMON, Family Salmonidae

NOTE: Various alternatives for salmonid classification are in use, such as classifying the Pacific trouts in the genus *Parasalmo* as preferred by some Russian taxonomists. The various proposals were summarized and referenced by Mecklenburg et al. (2002).

**STEELHEAD, *Oncorhynchus mykiss* (Walbaum, 1792).** Pacific off Kuril Islands, Sea of Okhotsk, and Kamchatka, Russia, to Kuskokwim Bay and Port Moller, southeastern Bering Sea to northern Baja California near Cuidad Durango. At least small runs to as far south as San Luis Rey River, near Oceanside, southern California. Length to 122 cm (48 in) TL. Anadromous and freshwater populations; depth: not reported. The anadromous form is typically called STEELHEAD, while freshwater populations are called RAINBOW TROUT. At sea, bluish back with small black spots on back, dorsal, and anal fins. Spawning males with small red or pink stripe along sides. D 12–15; A 13–16; Pect. 11–17; Pelvic 9–10; LLs 110–160; scale in row above LL 100–164; GRt 15–24; Vert. 60–66. (Formerly RAINBOW TROUT, *Salmo gairdneri* Richardson, 1836: M&L).

**CUTTHROAT TROUT, *Oncorhynchus clarkii* (Richardson, 1837).** Outer coast of Kenai Peninsula, northern Gulf of Alaska to Eel River, northern California. Length to 99.1 cm (39 in) TL. Freshwater and anadromous; depth: not reported. Dark olive above, with red stripe on sides in adult; black spotting on upper part of body and fins. D 10–13; A 8–13; Pect. 12–15; Pelvic 9–10; scales in row above LL 116–230; GRt 14–28; Vert. 59–64. (Formerly *Salmo clarkii* Richardson, 1837: M&L).

**CHUM SALMON, *Oncorhynchus keta* (Walbaum, 1792).** Arctic coasts of Siberia west to Laptev Sea and east across Alaskan and Canadian Arctic to Kugluktuk, Nunavut; Korea and southern Japan to Beaufort Sea, Alaska and to Del Mar, southern California. Common from the Chukchi Sea to about Oregon. Historic run in Sacramento River probably no longer exists. Length to 109 cm (42.9 in) TL. Anadromous; depth at sea: surface to 253 m (830 ft) and perhaps to 400 m (1,312 ft). At sea, metallic blue above, silvery below; white tip on fins of mature fish; occasional fine black speckling on back but no dark spots. D 13–16; A 16–20; Pect. 14–16; Pelvic 10–11; LLs 124–153; scales in row above LL 124–153; GRt 18–26; Pyloric caeca 140–186; Vert. 59–71. (Alternative names CALICO SALMON, DOG SALMON).

## KEY TO THE ADULT TROUT and SALMON:
Edited by Julianne Kalman Passarelli
(Principal source: Miller & Lea, 1972)

NOTE: All drawings in spawning phase. See page 73 for juveniles.

1a Inside of mouth black or with black blotches; anal fin soft-rays 11–26….. 3 (next page)

1b Inside of mouth bright white; anal fin soft-rays 8–16….. 2 (next page)

2a Dorsal fin soft-rays 12–15; anal fin soft-rays 13–16; basibranchial (hyoid) teeth usually absent; no red mark on mandible:

**STEELHEAD**

2b Dorsal fin soft-rays 11–13; anal fin soft-rays 8–13; basibranchial (hyoid) teeth usually present; red mark on mandible in adults (occasionally absent in sea-run fish):

**CUTTHROAT TROUT**
(not illustrated; body shape as in 2a)

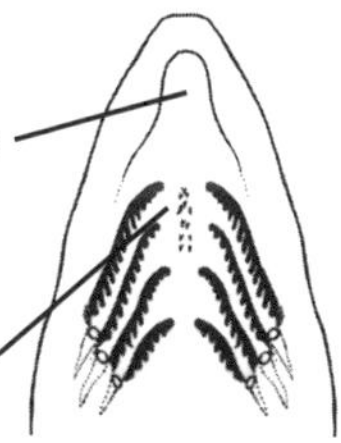


3a *From 1a: inside of mouth black*
Black spots on back and tail….. 5 (page 72)

3b No black spots on back and tail (some fine speckling may be present)….. 4

4a Gill rakers short, total count 18–26; anal and pelvic fins with white tip in adults:

**CHUM SALMON**

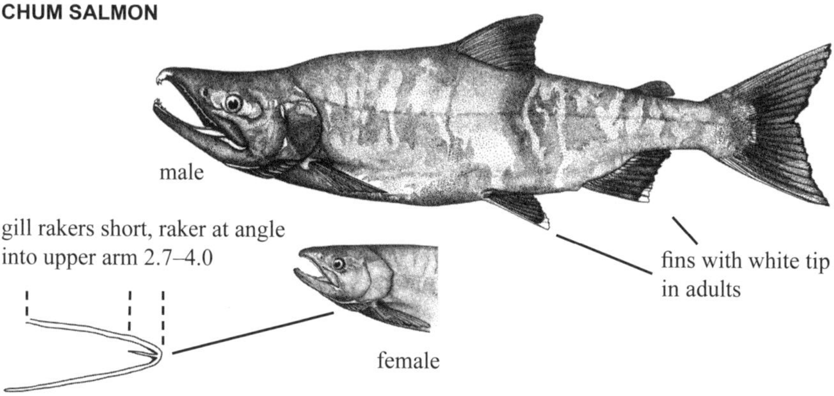


4b (next page)

## TROUT and SALMON (continued)

**SOCKEYE SALMON, *Oncorhynchus nerka* (Walbaum, 1792).** Northern Japan and Sea of Okhotsk to Point Hope, Chukchi Sea, Alaska and to Klamath River, northern California, with strays along Arctic Alaska and Canada coasts to Bathurst Inlet and northward to Sachs Harbour, Banks Island; across Pacific Ocean north of about 40°00'N. Spawns in watersheds entering Chukchi Sea south to Klamath River, northern California. Range of the nonanadromous (freshwater) form, called Kokanee, not included here. Length to 84 cm (33.1 in) TL. Anadromous and freshwater populations; depth at sea: surface to 83 m (272 ft). At sea, bluish-green above, silvery below; no spots on back. D 12–18; A 11–26; Pect. 11–21; Pelvic 9–11; LLs 122–150; scales in row above LL 120–150; GRt 28–40; Pyloric caeca 60–115; Vert. 56–67. (Alternative names BLUEBACK, RED SALMON).

**PINK SALMON, *Oncorhynchus gorbuscha* (Walbaum, 1792).** Northern Siberia to western Canada; North Korea and Japan to Beaufort Sea coast of Alaska and Canada (westwards to Sachs Harbor, Banks Island), and south to La Jolla, California; throughout North Pacific and Bering Sea north of about 40°00'N. Common from western Beaufort Sea throughout Alaskan waters and southward to Puget Sound. Historical runs in California rivers such as Russian and Sacramento no longer exist. Length to 76 cm (30 in) TL. Anadromous; depth at sea: surface to 74 m (243 ft) and perhaps to 96 m (315 ft). Dark green or blue above; large black oval spots on back and tail. D 13–16; A 16–20; Pect. 14–18; Pelvic 9–11; LLs 147–205; GRt 24–35; Pyloric caeca 165–196; Vert. 60–72. (Alternative name HUMPBACK SALMON).

**CHINOOK SALMON, *Oncorhynchus tshawytscha* (Walbaum, 1792).** Northern Japan to Point Hope, Chukchi Sea, Alaska with strays across northern Alaska to Coppermine River in Canada, to central Baja California at Bahía de Sebastián Vizcaíno (27°54'N, 114°17'W). Common from Bering Sea to central California; in some years common in southern California. Length to 160 cm (63 in) TL. Anadromous; depth at sea: surface to 538 m (1,765 ft). Dark blue, greenish-blue, purple, or black above, silvery below; irregularly shaped black spots on back. D 13–17; A 16–22; Pect. 14–19; Pelvic 10–11; LLs 130–165; GRt 18–31; Pyloric caeca 140–185; Vert. 64–75. (Formerly KING SALMON: M&L).

**COHO SALMON, *Oncorhynchus kisutch* (Walbaum, 1792).** North Korea and Japan to Point Hope, Chukchi Sea, Alaska and to Monterey Bay, central California, with strays to MacKenzie Delta, Northwest Territories, and to Bahía Camalu, northern Baja California. Common from the Chukchi Sea to about Monterey Bay. Length to 108 cm (42.5 in) TL. Anadromous; depth at sea: surface to 97 m (318 m) and perhaps to 250 m (820 ft). At sea, both sexes blue or blue-green on back and silvery below; ascending streams, males with green back and red sides, sometimes blackish on belly; females bronze to reddish on sides. Black spots on back and upper part of caudal fin (occasionally on lower lobe); gums white at base of teeth. D 12–15; A 15–19; Pect. 13–16; Pelvic 9–11; LLs 121–144; GRt 18–25; Pyloric caeca 45–114; Vert. 61–69. (Formerly SILVER SALMON: M&L).

4b Gill rakers long, total count 28–40; anal and pelvic fins without white tip:

**SOCKEYE SALMON**

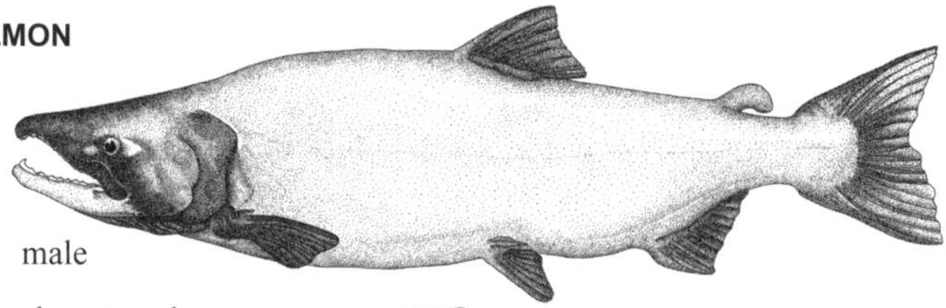


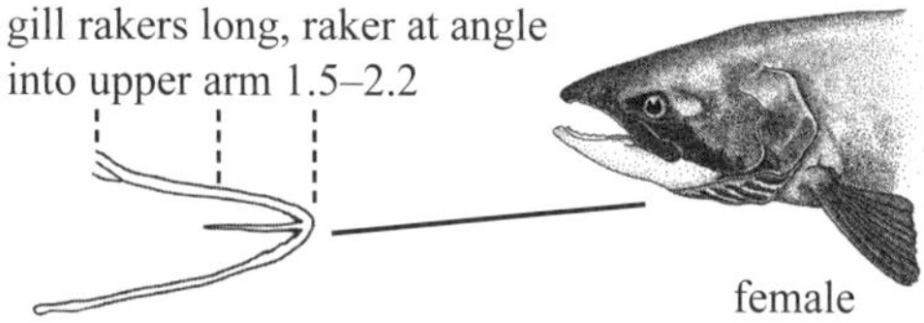


5a *From 3a: black spots on back and tail*
Spots on back large, oval-shaped, many as large or larger than eye diameter; scales small:

**PINK SALMON**

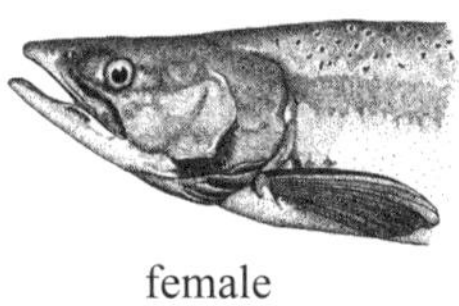

5b Spots on back roundish, mostly smaller than eye diameter; scales large….. 6

6a Gums at base of teeth black:

**CHINOOK SALMON**

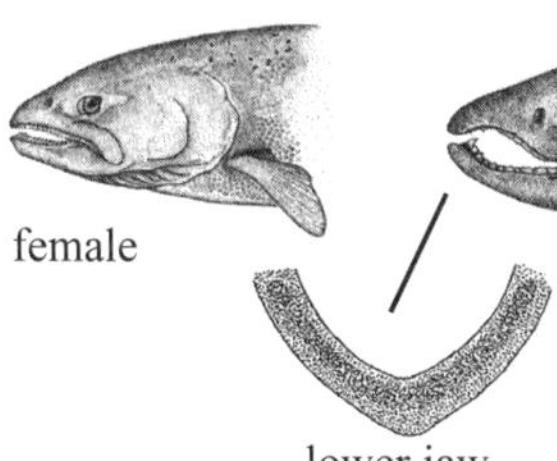

6b Gums at base of teeth white:

**COHO SALMON**

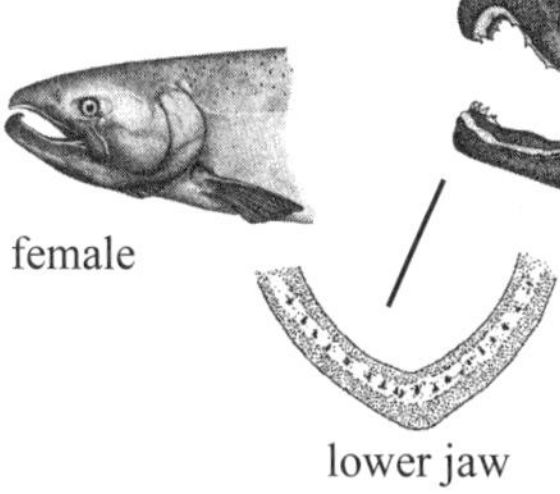


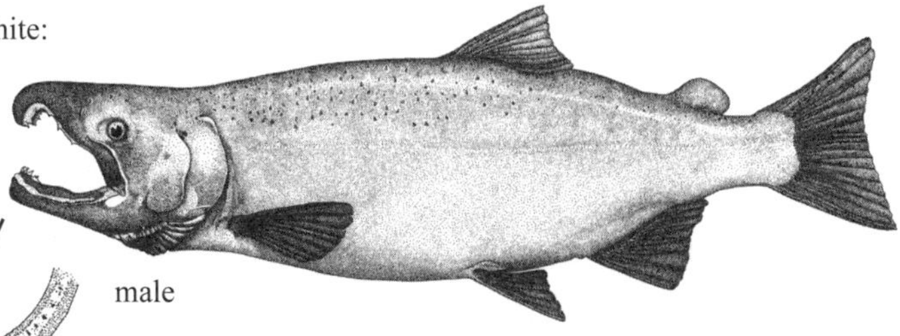

# JUVENILE TROUT and SALMON, Family Salmonidae

**STEELHEAD and CUTTHROAT TROUT**

red stripe along lateral line

spots in fins

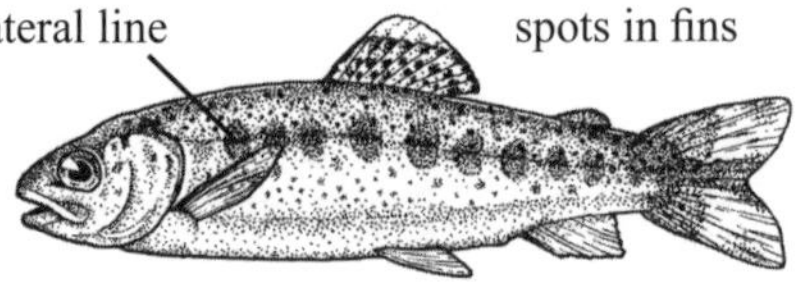

Fry remain in fresh water 2–4 years before entering ocean

*None of the juvenile salmon below have spots in fins*

**CHUM SALMON**

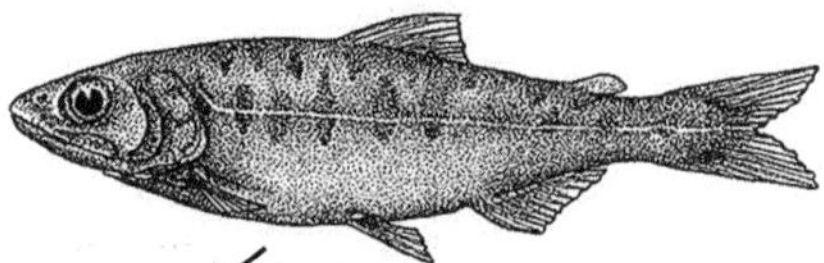

Fry start migration to ocean soon after emerging from gravel

parr marks mostly above lateral line

**SOCKEYE SALMON**

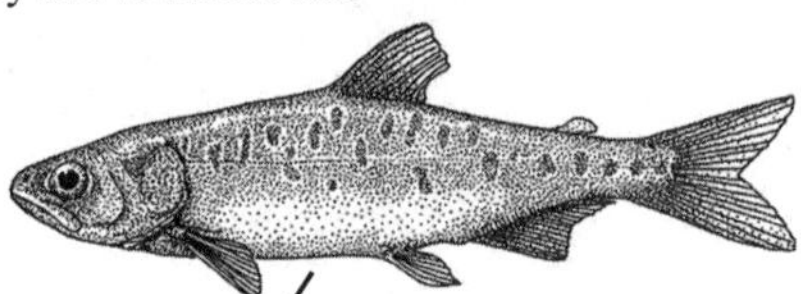

Fry spend 1–3 years in fresh water before migrating to ocean

parr marks variable in size and their relation to lateral line

**PINK SALMON**

Young migrate to sea soon after hatching

no parr marks

**CHINOOK SALMON**

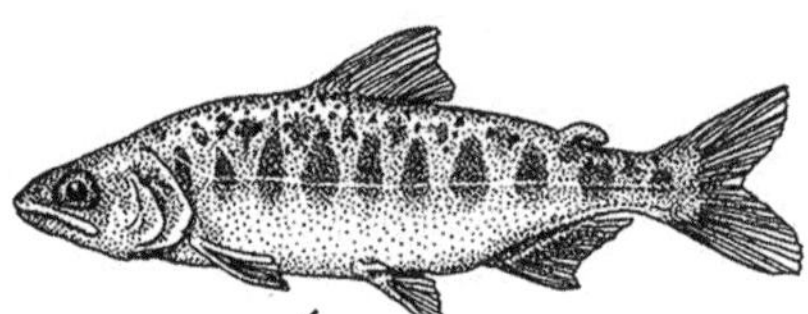

Fry usually start downstream to ocean the same year they hatch

spaces between parr marks narrower than width of marks

**COHO SALMON**

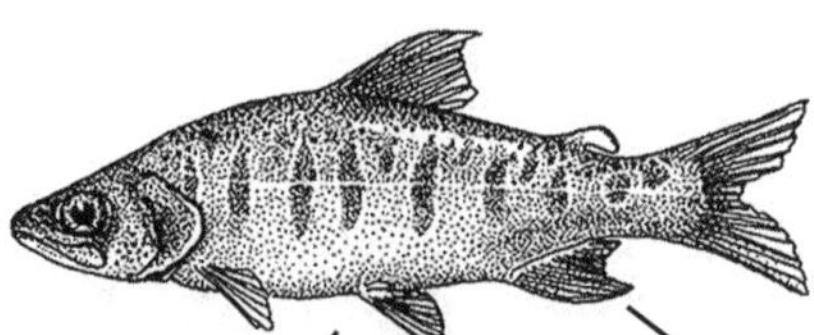

Fry remain in fresh water a year after hatching

spaces between parr marks wider than width of marks

first 3 anal fin soft-rays elongated

# SMELTS, Family Osmeridae

**SURF SMELT, *Hypomesus pretiosus* (Girard, 1854).** North side of Alaska Peninsula at Izembek Bay and Gulf of Alaska to Long Beach, southern California. Common from about Kodiak Island, Gulf of Alaska to Monterey Bay. Length to 30.5 cm (12 in) TL. Near coast, including surf zone (and perhaps to as deep as 130 m, 426 ft), sometimes found in brackish water and rarely in fresh water. Back of males olive-brown, females green; lighter on sides and belly. Breeding males with small bumps on body or fins. D 8–12; A 12–17; Pect. 13–17; Pelvic 8; LLp 4–12; Midlateral scales 66–76; GR 10–13 + 20–25 = 30–36; Vert. 62–70. (Formerly *H. pretiosus pretiosus*).

**DELTA SMELT, *Hypomesus transpacificus* McAllister, 1963.** Brackish and freshwater habitats of the Sacramento and San Joaquin river systems, California. Length to 12 cm (4.8 in) TL. Depth: not reported. Silvery-tan with faintly speckled lateral band. D 8–11; A 15–19; Pect. 10–12; Pelvic 8; LLp 8–9; Midlateral scales 53–60; GR 8–10 + 19–23 = 27–33; Vert. 53–56.

## KEY TO THE SMELTS:

Revised by Milton S. Love

(Principal sources: Miller & Lea, 1972; Moyle, 2002)

1a Maxilla extends beyond middle of eye….. 4 (page 76)

1b Maxilla not extending beyond middle of eye….. 2

2a HL more than 4 times eye diameter and more than 2.5 times longest anal fin soft-ray; midlateral scales 66–76:

**SURF SMELT**

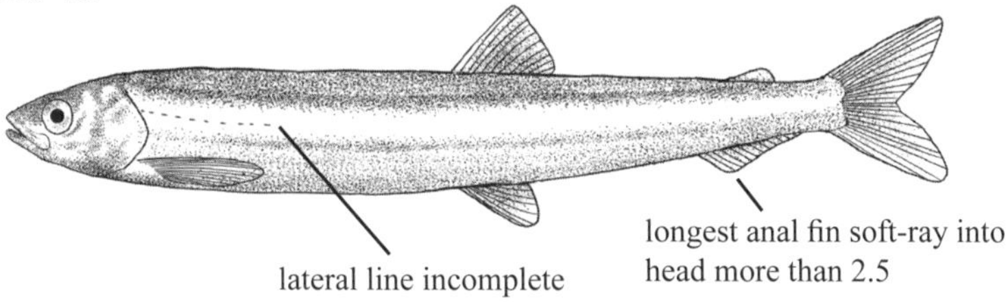


2b HL less than 4 times eye diameter and less than 2.5 times longest anal fin soft-ray; midlateral scales 53–60….. 3

3a One or no dark spots between mandibles (on chin); anal fin soft-rays 15–19:

**DELTA SMELT**

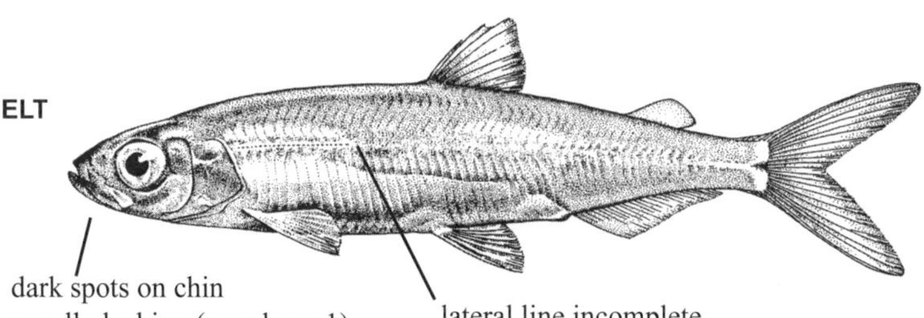


3b (next page)

## SMELTS (continued)

**WAKASAGI, *Hypomesus nipponensis* McAllister, 1963.** Widespread in Japan; introduced to California lakes in 1959, now in Sacramento–San Joaquin Estuary. Length to 19.5 cm (7.8 in) SL. Primarily a brackish-water species; found also in fresh water; depth: not reported. Nearly translucent, sides steely blue. D 8–11; A 14–17; Pect. 11–14; Pelvic 8; GR 9–13 + 20–25 = 29–36.

**EULACHON, *Thaleichthys pacificus* (Richardson, 1837).** Eastern Bering Sea from west of Saint Matthew Island and off Kuskokwim Bay and Nushagak River, also Bowers Bank, central Aleutian Islands to southern California (34°00'N). Common from at least Bristol Bay, Alaska southward to vicinity of Klamath River, northern California. Spawns in rivers from Mad River, northern California northward. Length to 25.4 cm (10 in) TL. Anadromous; depth: near coast, surface to about 150 m (492 ft). Records of much greater depths probably pertain to fish that entered nets near the surface, not near maximum fishing depths. Bluish-brown or bluish-black on back, silvery on sides; fins speckled. At spawning, gray-brown, males with small bumps on head and along lateral line. D 10–13; A 17–23; Pect. 10–12; Pelvic 8–12; LLp 70–78; GR 4–6 + 13–18 = 17–23; Vert. 65–72. (Alternative names CANDLEFISH, HOOLIGAN).

**WHITEBAIT SMELT, *Allosmerus elongatus* (Ayres, 1854).** Vancouver Island, British Columbia to southern California (34°24'N). Eschmeyer and Herald (1983) also list a questionable record from San Pedro, southern California. Common from Washington to, occasionally, San Francisco Bay. Length to 22.9 cm (9 in) TL. Depth: shallow water to at least 130 m (426 ft) and perhaps 170 m (558 ft). Back greenish or brown, sides silvery. D 9–11; A 14–17; Pect. 12–14; Pelvic 8; LLp about 20; Midlateral scales 62–68; GR 10–13 + 23–28 = 33–41; Vert. 65–67.

**NIGHT SMELT, *Spirinchus starksi* (Fisk, 1913).** Shelikof Bay, southeastern Gulf of Alaska to southern California (34°00'N). Common southward to at least Morro Bay. Length to 23 cm (9 in) TL. Depth: surf zone to 128 m (422 ft). Brownish-green or tan-brown on back, sides silver. D 8–11; A 15–21; Pect. 10–11; Pelvic 8; LLp 16–24; Midlateral scales 60–66; GR 8–13 + 22–32 = 32–45; Vert. 60–65.

**LONGFIN SMELT, *Spirinchus thaleichthys* (Ayres, 1860).** Kodiak Island, Gulf of Alaska to Monterey Bay, central California. Common in scattered bays and estuaries from at least Prince William Sound to southern California (33°54'N). Length to 20 cm (8 in) TL. Anadromous; depth: surface and surf zone to about 137 m (452 ft). Brownish dorsally, sides silver. D 6–10; A 15–22; Pect. 8–12; LLp 14–21; Midlateral scales 54–65; GR 10–13 + 26–35 = 36–47; Vert. 54–61.

3b Numerous (5–77) small dark spots between mandibles (on chin); anal fin soft-rays 14–17:

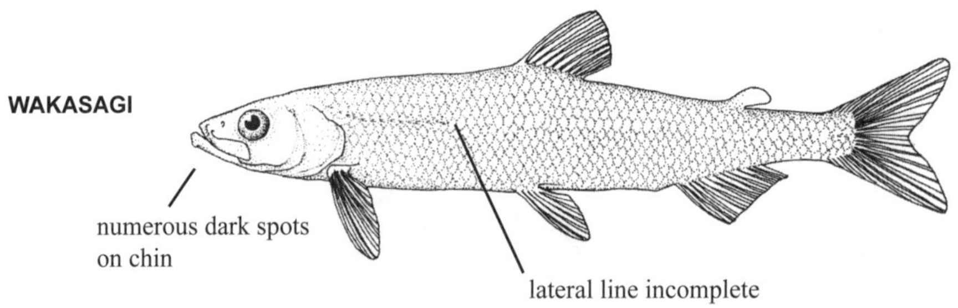


4a (next page)

4a *From 1a: maxilla extends beyond middle of eye*
Striations on gill cover; lateral line complete with 70–78 pores:

**EULACHON**

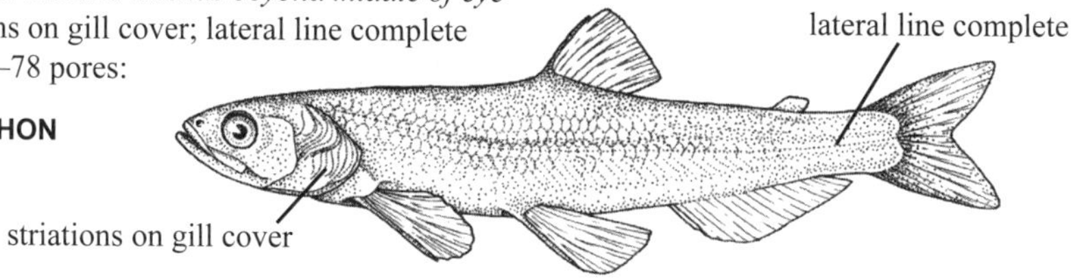


4b No striations on gill cover; lateral line incomplete or absent, if present, with fewer than 25 pores..... 5

5a One to 3 large canine teeth on vomer; pectoral fin soft-rays 12–14; eye diameter ⅘ or more (usually about equal) to depth of caudal peduncle:

**WHITEBAIT SMELT**

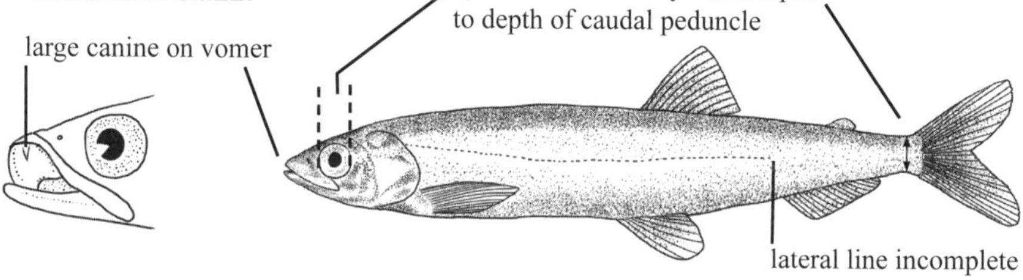


5b No large canines on vomer; pectoral fin soft-rays 8–12; eye diameter ⅘ or less of depth of caudal peduncle..... 6

6a Angle of jaw at 54°–65° to top of snout; midlateral scales 60–66; longest anal fin soft-ray into head 2.2–3.1:

**NIGHT SMELT**

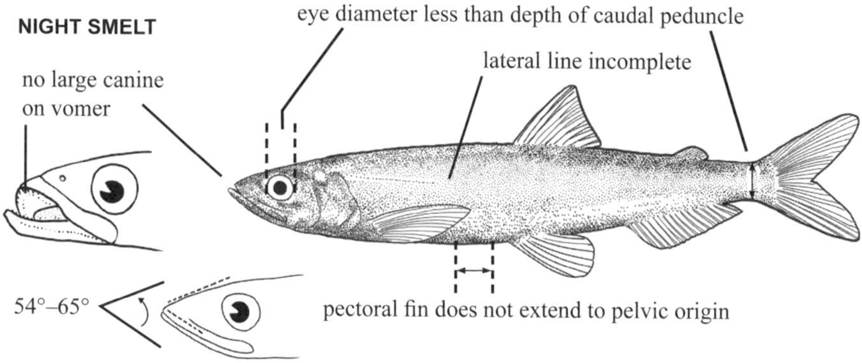


6b Angle of jaw at 68°–90° to top of snout; midlateral scales 54–65; longest anal fin soft-ray into head 1.4–2.2:

**LONGFIN SMELT**

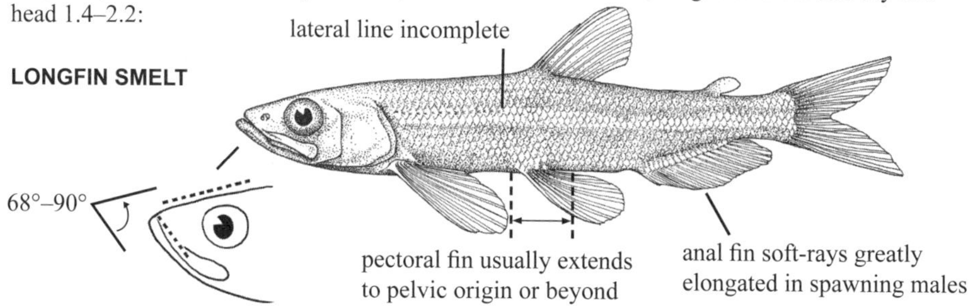

## SPOOKFISHES, Family Opisthoproctidae

**JAVELIN SPOOKFISH, *Bathylychnops exilis* Cohen, 1958.** Circumglobal; Japan to Kuril Islands, Russia, to British Columbia to at least Isla Guadalupe, central Baja California (SIO 67-67); also reported from Chile (21º27'S) (SIO 72-177). Rare off California. Length to 58 cm (22.8 in) SL. Bathypelagic; depth: about 151–3,329 m (495–10,900 ft). Body opaque, dark blotches on back of head through caudal fin; snout dark. D 13–16; A 10–14; Pect. 10–13; Pelvic 7–8; Vert. 78–84.

**BROWNSNOUT SPOOKFISH, *Dolichopteryx longipes* (Vaillant, 1888).** Circumglobal in temperate and tropical waters; central California (36°57'N, 122°13'W) (UW 113807) to Chile. Rare at least off southern California to central Baja California. Length to 18 cm (7.1 in) SL. Pelagic; depth: 152–2,160 m (500–7,085 ft). Body almost transparent; brown streak on snout. D 10–11; A 8–10; Pect. 11–14; Pelvic 8–11; GR 8 + 17; Vert. 40–52.

**BARRELEYE, *Macropinna microstoma* Chapman, 1939.** Western North Pacific off northern Japan and Kuril Islands, Russia to Bering Sea and Gulf of Alaska to eastern South Pacific west of Islas Juan Fernández, Chile. Uncommon from Japan and Kamchatka-Kuril Islands, Russia around to central Baja California. Length to 16 cm (6.3 in) TL. Primarily mesopelagic; depth: 16–2,150 m (53–7,052 ft). Adult dark brown or brown-black; young light brown, with bars on sides. D 11–12; A 10–14; Pect. 17–19; Pelvic 9–10; LLs 23–26; GRt 12; Vert. 34–37. (Formerly PACIFIC BARRELEYE: M&L).

**GLASSHEAD BARRELEYE, *Rhynchohyalus natalensis* (Gilchrist & von Bonde, 1924).** Atlantic and Pacific; off San Clemente Island (LACM 38791-8) and in Catalina Basin (LACM 30524-5), southern California and off northern Baja California (31°00'N) (LACM 30029-18). Scattered catches throughout geographic range. Length to 16 cm (6.3 in) SL. Depth: 0–775 m (2,542 ft). Dorsal area black, ventral area silvery; sides may be pink-red; head transparent; eyes large and upward facing. D 10–12; A 7–10; Pect. 14–17; Pelvic 11–12.

## KEY TO THE SPOOKFISHES:

Created by Rick Feeney
(Principal sources: Cohen, 1964; Robison & Reisenbichler, 2008; Partridge et al., 2014)

1a Body foreshortened and laterally compressed….. 3 (next page)

1b Body elongate and not laterally compressed….. 2

2a Vomerine teeth in 1 row; vertebrae 78–84:

**JAVELIN SPOOKFISH**

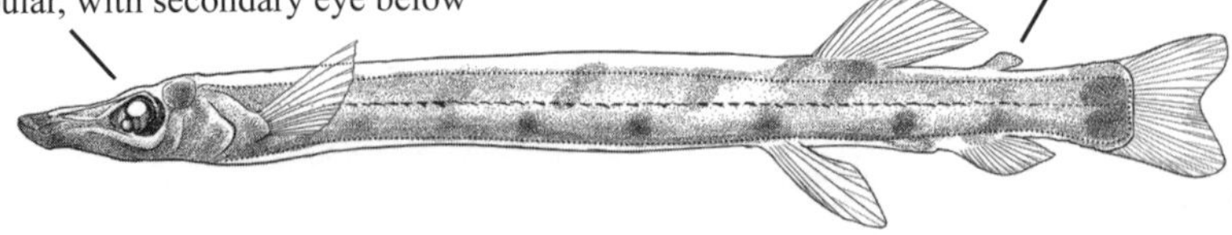


2b (next page)

2b Vomerine teeth in 2 or more rows; vertebrae 40–52:

### BROWNSNOUT SPOOKFISH

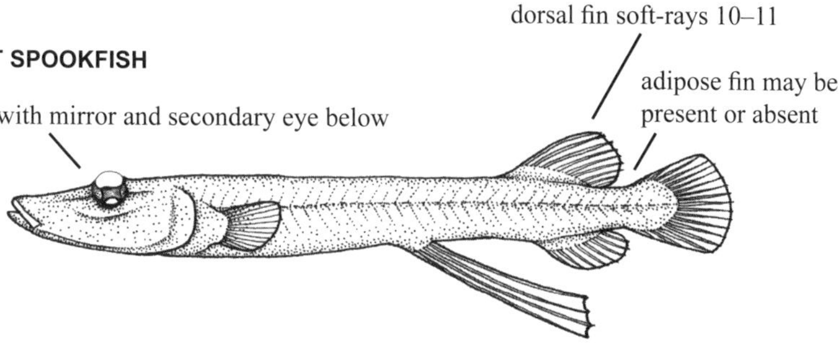


3a Anal fin origin anterior to dorsal fin insertion; branchiostegal rays 3; secondary eye absent:

### BARRELEYE

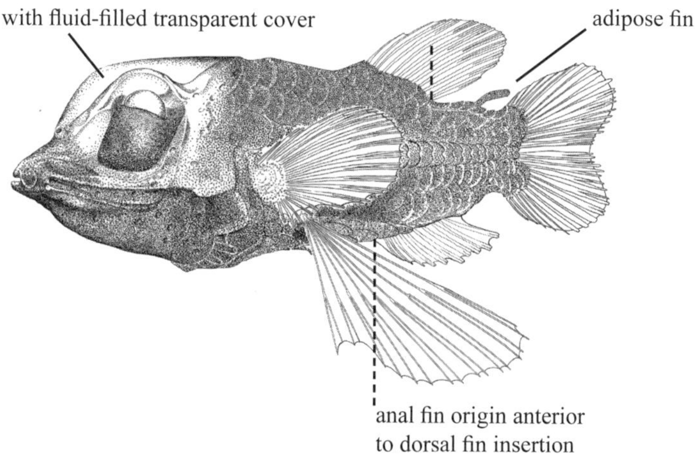


3b Anal fin origin posterior to dorsal fin insertion; branchiostegal rays 4; secondary eye present:

### GLASSHEAD BARRELEYE

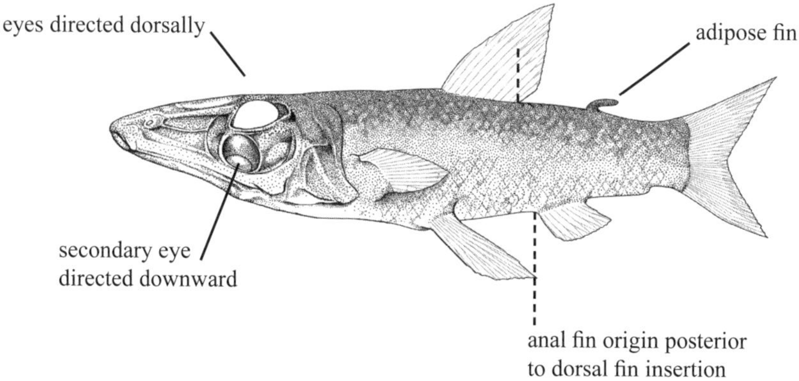

## SLICKHEAD, Family Alepocephalidae, ARGENTINE, Family Argentinidae, and TUBESHOULDERS, Family Platytroctidae

**CALIFORNIA SLICKHEAD, *Alepocephalus tenebrosus* Gilbert, 1892.** Family ALEPOCEPHALIDAE
Eastern Gulf of Alaska to southern Baja California (23°13'N), Central America, and Chile. Reports from eastern Bering Sea not verifiable. Common at least from Oregon to southern California and around Isla Guadalupe. Length to 61 cm (24 in) TL. Benthopelagic; depth: 294–2,040 m (965–6,691 ft) and perhaps to 2,287 m (7,501 ft). Mecklenburg et al. (2002) note that although greater depths have been reported, they are unverifiable. Uniform dark brown or black; head dark; scales absent on head. D 15–18; A 15–18; Pect. 10–12; Pelvic 6–7; lateral line tubes 55; GR 6–7 + 17–18; Vert. 51–55.

**PACIFIC ARGENTINE, *Argentina sialis* Gilbert, 1890.** Family ARGENTINIDAE
West coast of Vancouver Island (49°03'N, 126°23'W), British Columbia to Gulf of California; probably northern Peru. Common from northern California to southern Baja California and in Gulf of California. Length to 22 cm (8.7 in) TL. Depth: 11–907 m (36–2,975 ft). Back tan or tan-brown, silvery on sides; sides with faint dark bars in live specimens; scales large. D 10–13; A 11–15; Pect. 11–19; Pelvic 10–12; LLs 48–51; GR 7–9 + 14–21; Branchiostegals 5; Vert. 47–51.

**STREAKLIGHT TUBESHOULDER, *Holtbyrnia latifrons* Sazonov, 1976.** Family PLATYTROCTIDAE
Western Bering Sea; Gulf of Alaska to Chile. Uncommon off California. Length to 25 cm (9.8 in) SL. Meso- and bathypelagic; depth: 225–1,400 m (738–4,592 ft). Body black; no luminous tissue in eye; photophores present. D 17–20; A 14–16; Pect. 16–20; Pelvic 8–9; GR 7–9 + 18–21; Vert. 46–50.

**SHINING TUBESHOULDER, *Sagamichthys abei* Parr, 1953.** Family PLATYTROCTIDAE
Southern Japan and Sea of Okhotsk to southeastern Bering Sea to southern Chile. Common from at least Oregon southward. Length to 27.2 cm (10.7 in) SL. Primarily mesopelagic; depth: adults at about 200–2,088 m (656–4,849 ft) and perhaps to 4,268 m (13,999 ft). Reported from shallower depths but these records likely represent juveniles. Adults black, juveniles gray-blue; luminous tissue in eye; bar-like photophores on belly; no premaxilla tusks. D 15–18; A 13–16; Pect. 14–18; Pelvic 8–10; LLs 110–125; GR 7–9 + 16–19 = 24–29; Vert. 50–52.

## CALIFORNIA SLICKHEAD

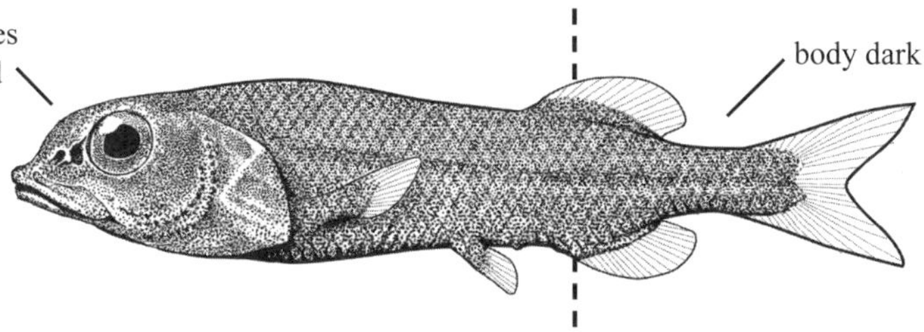


## PACIFIC ARGENTINE

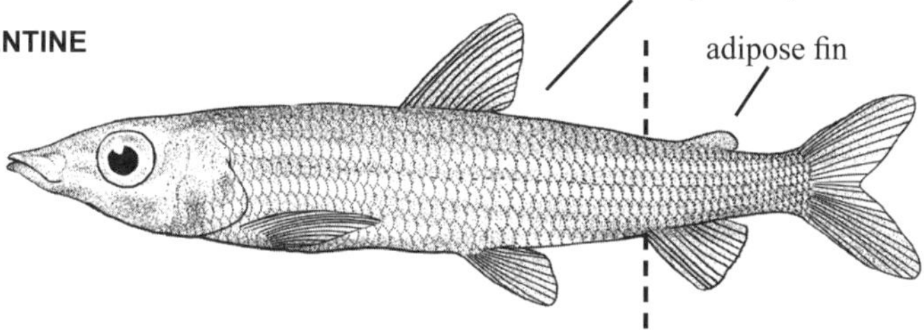


## STREAKLIGHT TUBESHOULDER

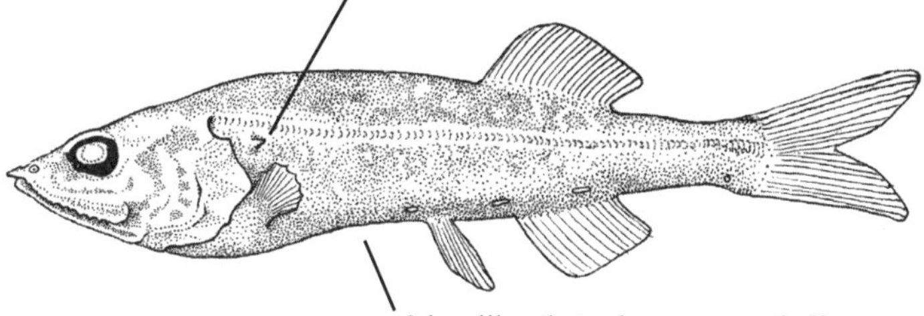


## SHINING TUBESHOULDER

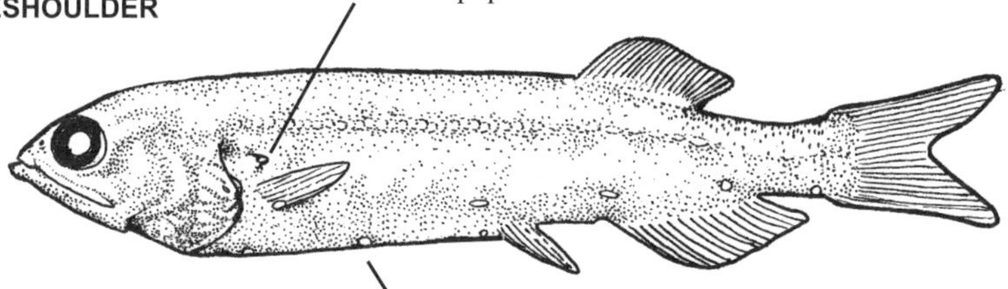

## PENCILSMELTS, Family Microstomatidae

NOTE: Members of the genera *Bathylagoides*, *Bathylagus*, *Leuroglossus*, *Lipolagus*, *Melanolagus*, *Nansenia*, and *Pseudobathylagus* are placed in the family Bathylagidae by some researchers.

**BLUETHROAT ARGENTINE, *Nansenia candida* Cohen, 1958.** Northern Japan and southern Kuril Islands, Russia to southern Bering Sea and Gulf of Alaska to northern Baja California. Common at least from Gulf of Alaska to southern California. Length to 23.9 cm (9.4 in) SL. Primarily epi- to mesopelagic; depth: surface to about 1,500 m (4,921 ft). Back dark, silvery on sides and below; bluish tint on nape, cheek, and throat. D 9–12; A 8–10; Pect. 9–12; Pelvic 9–11; GRt 25–32; Vert. 44–50. (Alternative name WHITE PENCILSMELT).

**DUSKY PENCILSMELT, *Microstoma microstoma* (Risso, 1810).** Circumglobal; in eastern Pacific from Oregon to central Baja California. Common at least off California. Length to 21 cm (8.3 in) TL. Mesopelagic; depth: surface to 4,145 m (13,596 ft). Body silvery, darker near tail; adipose fin absent. D 9–11; A 7–8; Pect. 11; Pelvic 9; GR 9 + 15; Vert. 49–50. Moser and Butler (1996) considered the eastern Pacific form to be an undescribed species. (Alternative name SLENDER ARGENTINE).

**CALIFORNIA SMOOTHTONGUE, *Leuroglossus stilbius* Gilbert, 1890.** Washington to Peru, including Gulf of California. Common from at least as far northward as central California to southern Baja California and in Gulf of California. Length to 20 cm (7.9 in) TL. Epi- to mesopelagic; depth: near surface to perhaps 3,824 m (12,542 ft). Silvery to brassy. D 9–12; A 11–15; Pect. 8–11; Pelvic 8–10; GR 7–9 + 17–20; Branchiostegals 2; Vert. 39–52. (Formerly Bathylagidae: M&L).

**POPEYE BLACKSMELT, *Lipolagus ochotensis* (Schmidt, 1938).** Southern Honshu, Japan and Sea of Okhotsk to Bering Sea to south-central Baja California (about 25°N). Common from Japan and Kamchatka-Kuril Islands, Russia, around to northern Baja California. Length to 19 cm (7.5 in) TL. Depth: near surface to 300 m (984 ft), adults generally within mesopelagic depths. Gray-brown, sometimes with faint dark blotches on back, sides silvery. D 9–13; A 12–17; Pect. 6–12; Pelvic 9–12; Midlateral scales 40; GR 8–9 + 13–20; Vert. 47–49. (Formerly *Bathylagus ochotensis* Schmidt, 1938, Bathylagidae: M&L).

**SNUBNOSE BLACKSMELT, *Bathylagoides wesethi* (Bolin, 1938).** Oregon to southern Baja California. Common from central California to southern Baja California. Length to about 13.5 cm (5.3 in) TL. Pelagic; depth: 25–1,130 m (82–3,706 ft), and perhaps to 4,268 m (13,999 ft). Dark brown above, sides silvery to whitish with black spots. D 10–14; A 13–17; Pect. 9–12; Pelvic 8–11; GR 8–10 + 14–19 = 24–25; Branchiostegals 2; Vert. 43–47. (Formerly *Bathylagus wesethi* Bolin, 1938, Bathylagidae: M&L).

## KEY TO THE PENCILSMELTS:

Revised by Cynthia Klepadlo
(Principal source: Miller & Lea, 1972)

1a Anal fin soft-rays 11 or more; branchiostegal rays usually 2; lateral line does not extend onto caudal fin….. 3 (next page)

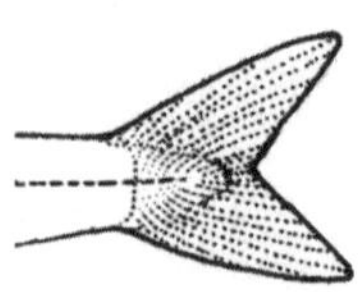

1b Anal fin soft-rays 7–10; branchiostegal rays usually 3–4; lateral line extends onto caudal fin….. 2 (next page)

2a Adipose fin present; dorsal fin origin anterior to pelvic fin origin:

**BLUETHROAT ARGENTINE**

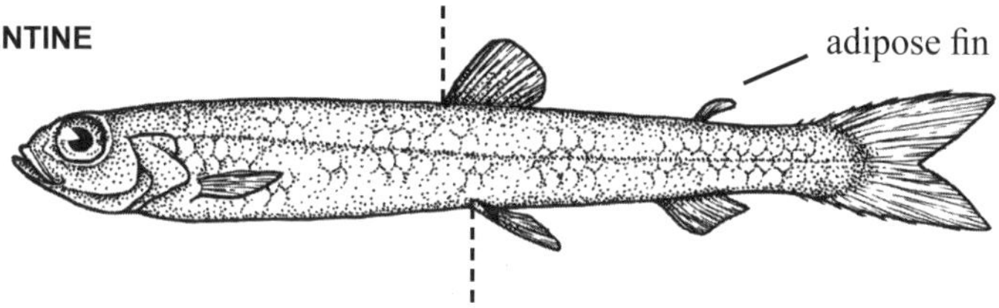


2b Adipose fin absent; dorsal fin origin above pelvic fin origin:

**DUSKY PENCILSMELT**

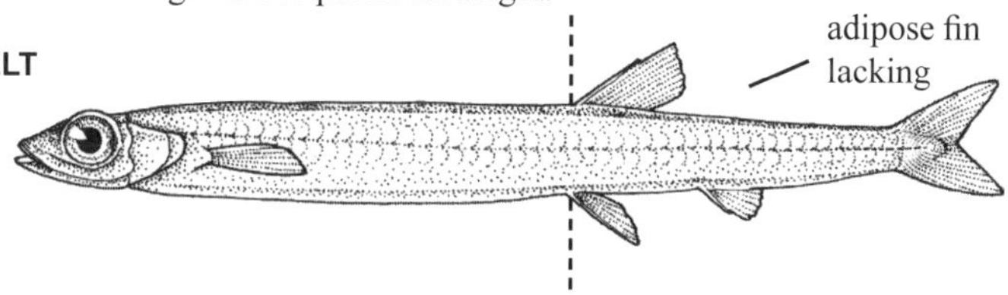


3a *From 1a: anal fin soft-rays 11 or more; branchiostegal rays usually 2*
Snout length greater than eye diameter:

**CALIFORNIA SMOOTHTONGUE**

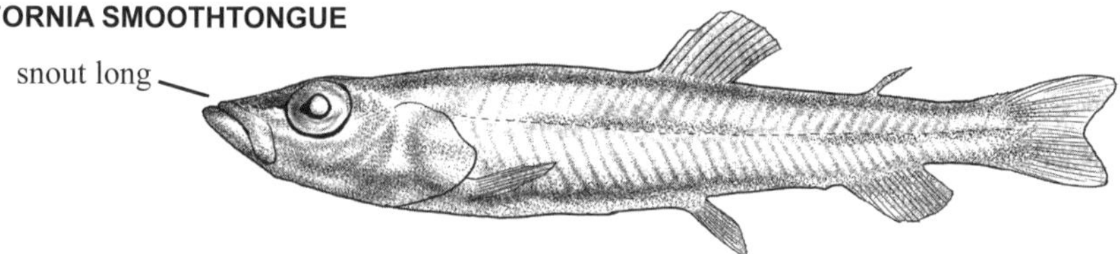


3b Snout length less than or equal to eye diameter….. 4

4a Anal fin base length less than or equal to caudal peduncle length:

**POPEYE BLACKSMELT**

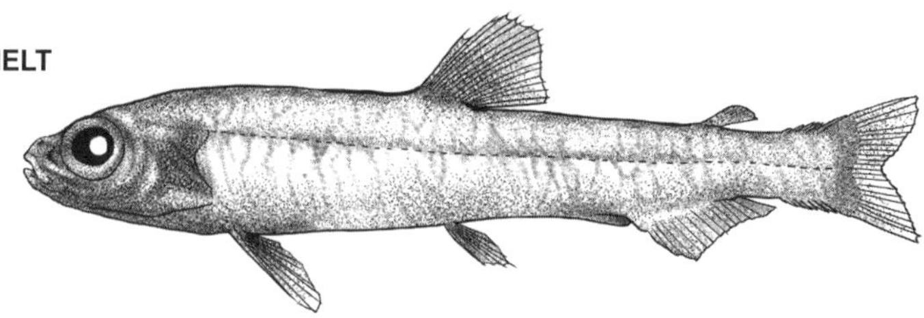

4b Anal fin base length greater than caudal peduncle length….. 5

5a Gill slits not restricted, extending at least halfway up side of body; midlateral scales (or scale pockets) absent:

**SNUBNOSE BLACKSMELT**

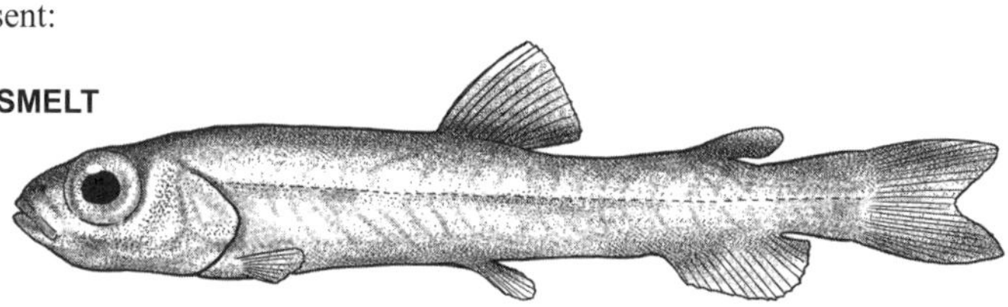

5b Gill slits restricted, not reaching to halfway up side of body; midlateral scales (or scale pockets) obvious….. 6 (next page)

## PENCILSMELTS (continued)

**BIGSCALE DEEPSEA SMELT, *Melanolagus bericoides* (Borodin, 1929).** Circumglobal in warm waters; Japan and Russian western Pacific; and Oregon to central California, and at least off Chile. Common at least off Japan. Length to at least 24.4 cm (9.6 in) TL. Mesopelagic; depth: 100–3,065 m (328–10,053 ft). D 9–11; A 17–22; Pect. 8–12; Pelvic 8–10; Midlateral scales about 50; GR 12–15 + 13–17; Vert. 48–54. Classified as *Bathylagus* by some authors.

**STOUT BLACKSMELT, *Pseudobathylagus milleri* (Jordan & Gilbert, 1898 in Jordan & Evermann, 1898).** Southern Honshu, Japan and southern Sea of Okhotsk to Bering Sea to northern Baja California (31°45'N, 118°30'W) (LACM 9582-5) and Isla Guadalupe, central Baja California. Common from Japan and Kamchatka-Kuril Islands, Russia, around to southern California. Length to 22 cm (8.7 in) TL. Generally meso- and bathypelagic; depth: 60–6,600 m (197–21,648 ft). Uniform black to black-brown; gill membranes blue-black. D 6–9; A 20–28; Pect. 9–16; Pelvic 6–9; Midlateral scales 23–27; GRt 25–27; Vert. 49–55. (Formerly ROBUST BLACKSMELT, *Bathylagus milleri* Jordan & Gilbert, 1898 in Jordan & Evermann, 1898, Bathylagidae: M&L).

**PACIFIC BLACKSMELT, *Bathylagus pacificus* Gilbert, 1890.** Southern Japan and Sea of Okhotsk to southern Bering Sea to off Bahía Magdalena (24°11'N, 113°07'W), southern Baja California (SIO 64-21), including Gulf of California, and well off Ecuador (03°30'S, 112°02'W) (SIO 93-6). Common at least from Japan and Gulf of Alaska southward to southern California. Length to about 25 cm (10 in) TL. Adults generally in lower meso- and bathypelagic and not ascending to epipelagic zone; depth: 150–7,700 m (492–25,256 ft). Uniform black to blackish-brown; head black or blue-black; gill membranes blue-black. D 8–13; A 15–25; Pect. 7–11; Pelvic 7–10; Midlateral scales 37–42; GR 8–12 + 18–20; Vert. 44–51. (Formerly Bathylagidae: M&L) (Alternative name SLENDER BLACKSMELT).

6a Midlateral scales (or scale pockets) about 50:

**BIGSCALE DEEPSEA SMELT**

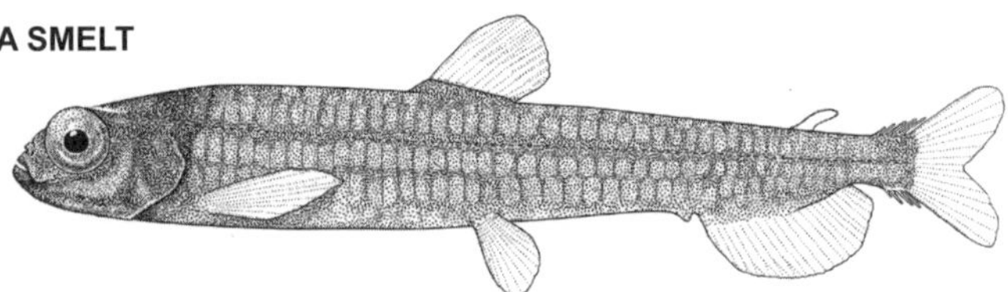

6b Midlateral scales (or scale pockets) 42 or fewer….. 7

7a Midlateral scales (or scale pockets) about 23–27; pectoral fin soft-rays 9–16 (usually 13–14):

**STOUT BLACKSMELT**

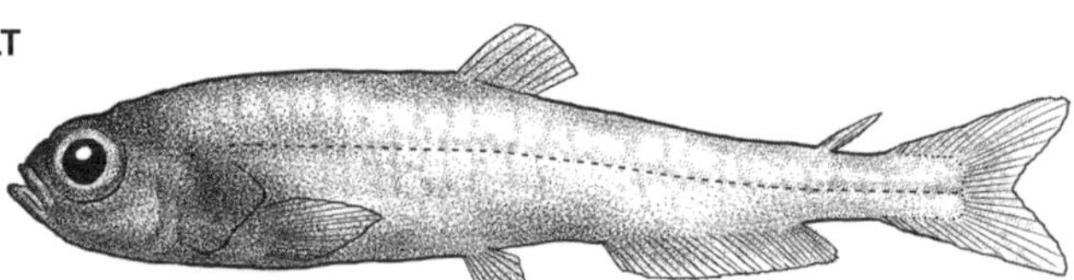

7b Midlateral scales (or scale pockets) about 37–42; pectoral fin soft-rays 7–11:

**PACIFIC BLACKSMELT**

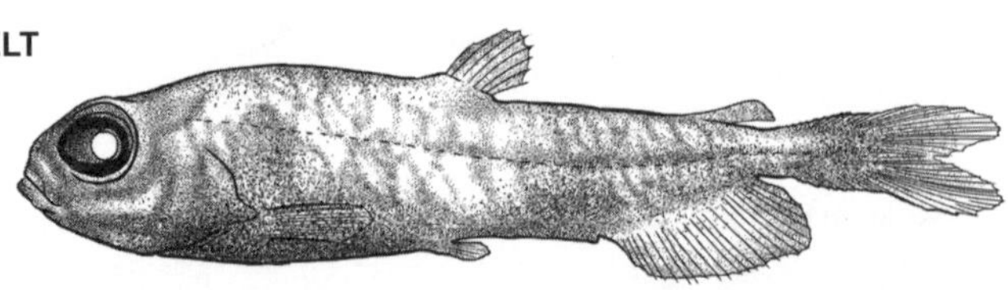

## LIGHTFISHES, Family Phosichthyidae

**BULLDOG LIGHTFISH, *Ichthyococcus irregularis* Rechnitzer & Böhlke, 1958.** Monterey, central California to Peru, including Islas Galápagos. Common from southern California southward. Length to 7.6 cm (3 in) TL. Meso- and bathypelagic; depth: 360–3,658 m (1,180–11,998 ft). Back black, sides black to gray, belly black. D 10–13; A 13–15; Pect. 7–8; Pelvic 7–8; GR 8 + 15–19; Vert. 38–39.

**PANAMA LIGHTFISH, *Vinciguerria lucetia* (Garman, 1899).** Central California (34°54'W) to northern Chile, including Gulf of California; larvae found as far north as San Francisco, northern California. Common from southern California southward. Length to 6 cm (2.4 in) SL. Mesopelagic; depth: surface to 4,268 m (13,999 ft). D 13–16; A 13–17; Pect. 10; Pelvic 7; GR 8–11 + 18–23 = 27–33; Vert. 39–43.

**OCEANIC LIGHTFISH, *Vinciguerria nimbaria* (Jordan & Williams, 1895).** Circumglobal; Japan; off northern California to off La Jolla, southern California to Chile. Common from southern California southward. Length to about 5.1 cm (2 in) TL. Mesopelagic; depth: near surface to 1,255 m (4,116 ft). D 13–15; A 13–16; Pect. 9–11; Pelvic 7; GR 5–7 + 13–17 = 19–21; Vert. 39–44.

NOTE: Adipose fin present on these 3 species; photophores in parallel rows.

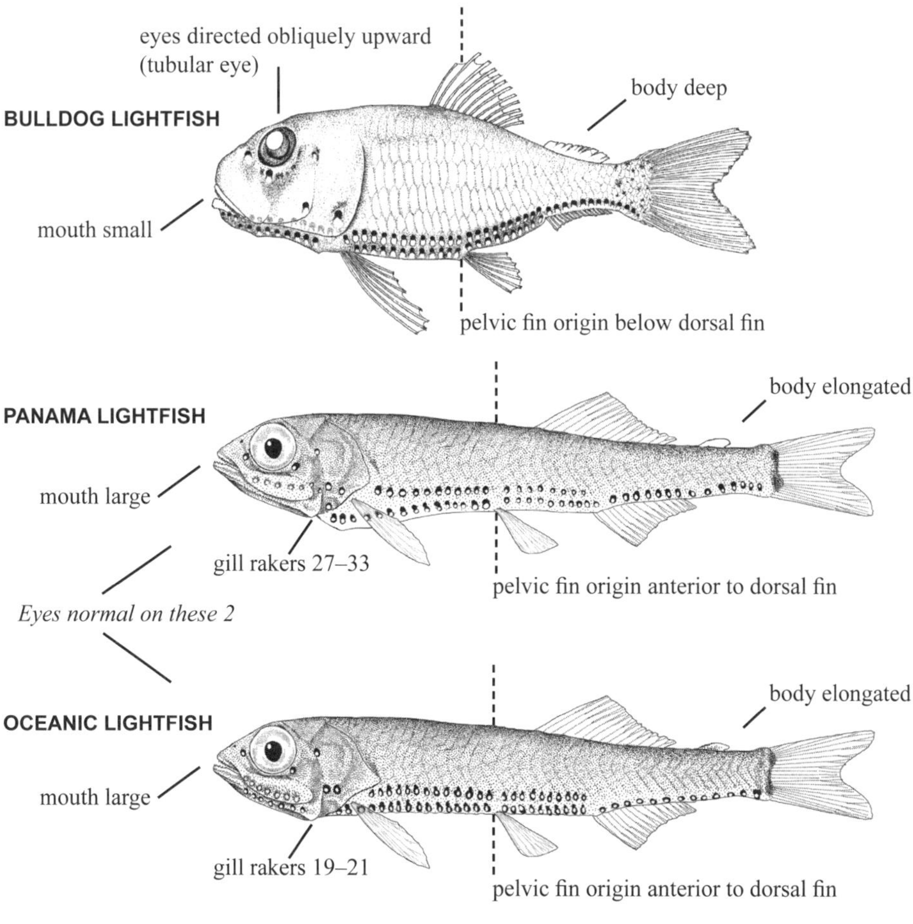

## BRISTLEMOUTHS, Family Gonostomatidae

**ATLANTIC FANGJAW, *Gonostoma atlanticum* Norman, 1930.** Circumglobal; Japan and Oregon to at least Baja California. Uncommon off California. Length to 6.4 cm (2.6 in) SL. Epi- to mesopelagic; depth: 50–2,500 m (164–8,200 ft). Body dark above, sides translucent. D 16–18; A 21–31; Pect. 9–11; GR 6–7 + 11–12; Vert. 38–39.

**SHOWY BRISTLEMOUTH, *Cyclothone signata* Garman, 1899.** Bering Sea to Chile. Common from at least central California to southern Baja California. Length to 4.4 cm (1.7 in) SL. Primarily mesopelagic; depth: surface to 1,854 m (6,081 ft). Body pale with stripes. D 12–14; A 17–20; Pect. 8–10; GR 3–5 + 9–11; Vert. 30–32.

**SLENDER BRISTLEMOUTH, *Cyclothone pseudopallida* Mukhacheva, 1964.** Circumglobal; Japan and Bering Sea to Chile. Common from northern California southward along Baja California coast and into tropics. Length to 7 cm (2.8 in) SL. Primarily mesopelagic; depth: surface to about 3,000 m (9,840 ft). D 12–15; A 17–21; Pect. 9–10; Pelvic 6–7; GR 4–7 + 11–14; Vert. 29–34.

**TAN BRISTLEMOUTH, *Cyclothone pallida* Brauer, 1902.** Circumglobal primarily in warm waters; Japan, Kuril Islands, Russia, and southern Bering Sea to Chile. Common in both western and eastern Pacific, but mostly southward of 40°00'N. Length to 7.5 cm (3 in) SL. Primarily meso- and upper bathypelagic; depth: near surface to 3,000 m (9,840 ft). Snout pigment conspicuous and diffuse throughout region; body dark gray. D 12–15; A 16–19; Pect. 9–11; Pelvic 6–7; GR 7–10 + 13–18; Vert. 30–34.

**BENTTOOTH BRISTLEMOUTH, *Cyclothone acclinidens* Garman, 1899.** Circumglobal; Oregon to central Chile. Common from Oregon southward. Length to 7.1 cm (2.8 in) TL. Depth: 20–2,124 m (66–6,967 ft). Dark gray or black; abdomen black. Photophores small. D 13–15; A 18–20; Pect. 8–10; Pelvic 6–7; GR 6–9 + 12–17 (2 rakers at angle); Vert. 30–32.

**BLACK BRISTLEMOUTH, *Cyclothone atraria* Gilbert, 1905.** Sea of Okhotsk, Bering Sea, and North Pacific to Chile, including Gulf of California. Common at least from Bering Sea to tropics. Length to 7 cm (2.8 in) SL. Primarily lower meso- and bathypelagic; depth: near surface to 3,400 m (11,155 ft). Brownish or black. D 12–15; A 17–21; Pect. 9–11; Pelvic 6–7; GR 7–10 + 13–18; Vert. 31–33.

## KEY TO THE BRISTLEMOUTHS:

Created by Cynthia Klepadlo
(Principal source: Nakabo, 2002)

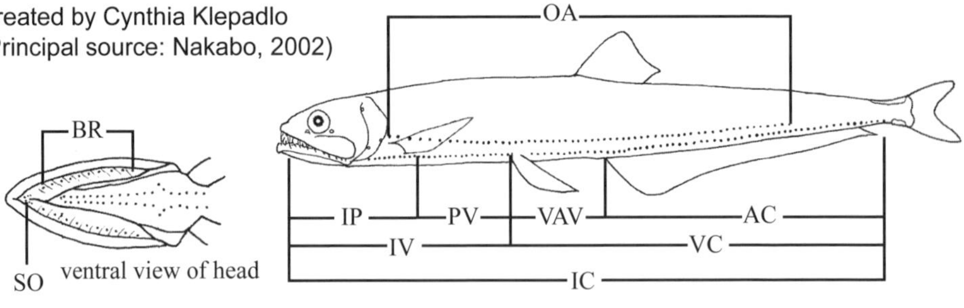


**Figure 18: BRISTLEMOUTH composite.**

NOTE: Photophores (light-producing organs) are present in all California species and are arranged in species-specific patterns. They are concentrated in ventrolateral rows on head and body. Subscript number indicates which photophore, counting from anterior to posterior, e.g., $VAV_2$ refers to 2nd photophore in VAV series. Lateral line lacking.

1a Maxilla with series of well-separated, long, slender teeth, and short teeth between them; palatine teeth in single row; pterygoid bone with large patch of minute teeth anteriorly and few irregular teeth posteriorly (sometimes enlarged); anal fin soft-rays 21–31; OA 11–21; SO present; BR 9:

**ATLANTIC FANGJAW**

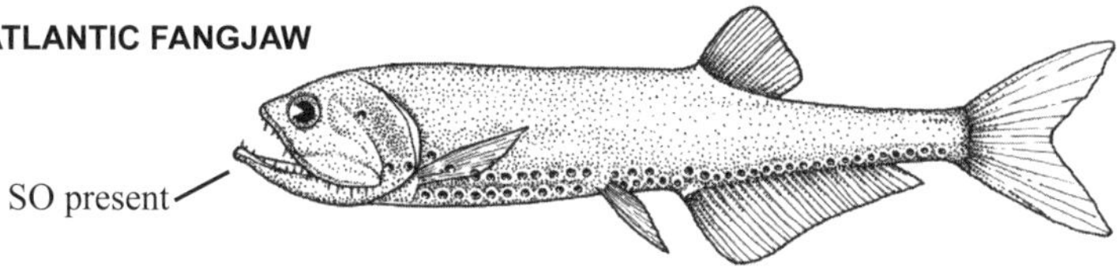


1b Maxilla with series of close-set teeth increasing in size posteriorly, sometimes few moderately enlarged; palatine teeth in small group anteriorly; pterygoid bone usually toothed anteriorly only, with small group of prominent teeth on each side; anal fin soft-rays 16–21; OA 6–10; SO absent; BR 8–11….. 2

2a One gill raker at angle of 1st arch; gill rakers on lower limb 9–11; total gill rakers fewer than 15; vomerine teeth absent; anus forward of $VAV_2$ (rarely at $VAV_2$):

**SHOWY BRISTLEMOUTH** (not illustrated; body shape as in 4a)

2b Two gill rakers at angle of 1st arch; gill rakers on lower limb 11 or more; total gill rakers more than 15; vomerine teeth present; anus at or behind $VAV_2$….. 3

3a Branchiostegal membrane with pigment concentrated over rays and along margin; pigment on 1st gill arch concentrated in dark brown slashes at base of median spines; total gill rakers fewer than 20 (rarely 20):

**SLENDER BRISTLEMOUTH** (not illustrated; body shape as in 4a)

3b Branchiostegal membrane with pigment more or less uniform; pigment on 1st arch mostly uniform dark, no conspicuous slashes; total gill rakers 20 or more….. 4

4a Differences in size of teeth on posterior half of maxilla conspicuous and only moderately inclined forward (less than 50°); OA fewer than 9:

**TAN BRISTLEMOUTH**

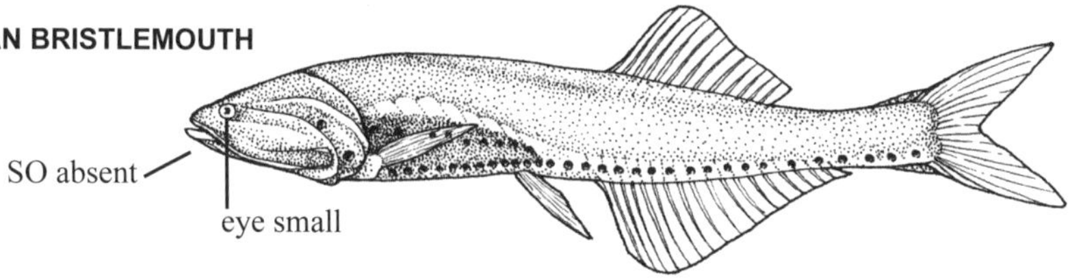


4b Difference in size of teeth on posterior half of maxilla relatively inconspicuous and strongly inclined forward (greater than 45°); OA 9–10 (rarely 8)….. 5

5a Teeth on posterior half of maxilla increase evenly in size; scale pockets inconspicuous; BR 10 or more (seldom 9); VC fewer than 20; IC fewer than 33; branchiostegal rays 14 or more (seldom 13):

**BENTTOOTH BRISTLEMOUTH** (not illustrated; body shape as in 4a)

5b Teeth on posterior half of maxilla generally increase in size (1–4 smaller teeth between each set of 2 larger ones); scale pockets conspicuous; BR fewer than 10; VC 20 or more (seldom 18 or 19); IC 33 or more (seldom 31 or 32); branchiostegal rays fewer than 14:

**BLACK BRISTLEMOUTH** (not illustrated; body shape as in 4a)

## MARINE HATCHETFISHES, Family Sternoptychidae

**BOTTLELIGHT, *Danaphos oculatus* (Garman, 1899).** Pacific and Indian Oceans; off the Brooks Peninsula (50°07'N, 128°18'W), British Columbia to Chile. Common from northern California southward. Length to 5.7 cm (2.3 in) TL. Epi- and mesopelagic; depth: 52–914 m (172–2,998 ft). Whitish; large serial photophores ventrally. D 6; A 23–26; Pelvic 6–7; GR 2 + 11–13 = 11–15; Vert. 38–40. (Formerly BIGEYE LIGHTFISH, Gonostomatidae: M&L).

**SPURRED HATCHETFISH, *Argyropelecus hemigymnus* Cocco, 1829.** Circumglobal; Japan and Russian northwestern Pacific; Washington to Chile. Common from southern California southward. Length to 4.9 cm (1.9 in) TL. Epi- and mesopelagic; depth: 50 to at least 3,065 m (164–10,053 ft). Silvery. D 8–9; A 11–12; Pect. 9–11; Pelvic 6; GRt 18–25; Vert. 35–41.

**SLENDER HATCHETFISH, *Argyropelecus affinis* Garman, 1899.** Circumglobal; Japan; Oregon to northern Chile. Common off Japan and from at least central California southward. Length to 9.4 cm (3.7 in) SL. Epi- and mesopelagic; depth: 100–2,056 m (328–6,744 ft). Silvery, black above. D 8–9; A 11–14; Pect. 10–11; Pelvic 6; GR 7–9 + 9–13; Vert. 35–41.

**LOWCREST HATCHETFISH, *Argyropelecus sladeni* Regan, 1908.** Circumglobal; Japan; western Bering Sea; British Columbia to Chile. Common from northern California southward. May not be found in tropics. Length to 6.7 cm (2.6 in) SL. Primarily mesopelagic; depth: 1,200 m (3,936 ft). Silvery. D 9–10; A 11–13; Pect. 9–11; GR 7–8 + 9–13; Vert. 35–38. (Formerly SILVERY HATCHETFISH: M&L).

**TROPICAL HATCHETFISH, *Argyropelecus lychnus* Garman, 1899.** Eastern Pacific and possibly Indian Oceans; Gulf of Alaska (59°05'N, 147°00'W) to Chile, including Islas Galápagos. Common at least from northern California southward. Length to at least 7.6 cm (3 in) TL. Upper mesopelagic; depth: 198–2,124 m (650–6,967 ft). Dark back, silvery on sides and belly; dark spots along sides. D 9; A 12; Pect. 10–12; Pelvic 6; GR 8–9 + 12–14; Vert. 35–37. Specimens previously reported as *A. lychnus* from British Columbia are *A. sladeni*. (Formerly SILVER HATCHETFISH: M&L).

## KEY TO THE MARINE HATCHETFISHES:

Revised by Cynthia Klepadlo and Peter Davison
(Principal sources: Baird, 1971; Miller & Lea, 1972; Badcock & Baird, 1980)

NOTE: Photophores in parallel rows.

1a Body elongate; no deep abdominal keel anterior to pelvic fin; no postabdominal spines:

**BOTTLELIGHT**

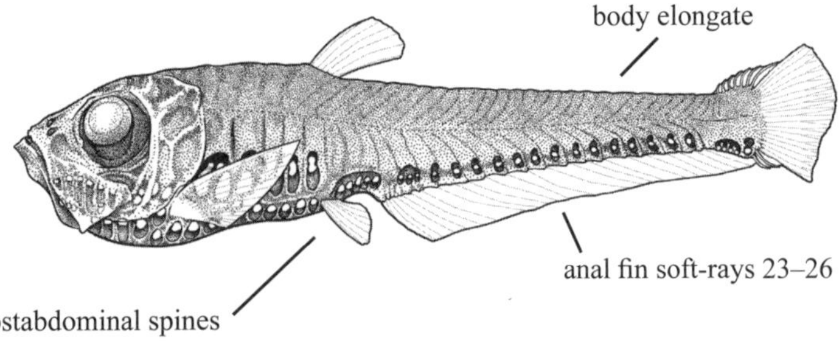


1b Body not elongate; deep abdominal keel extending from below eye to pelvic fin; postabdominal spine(s) present..... 2 (next page)

2a "Normal" eyes directed laterally; predorsal blade with 1 spine-like structure at posterior edge of blade; 1 (complete) row of 10 abdominal photophores….. 6 (next page)

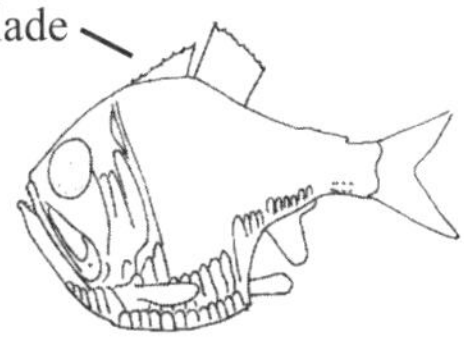


2b Telescopic eyes directed upward; predorsal blade with several spine-like structures; 2 rows of abdominal photophores, lower row with 12….. 3

3a Single postabdominal spine forms long serrated spur directed towards the tail:

**SPURRED HATCHETFISH**

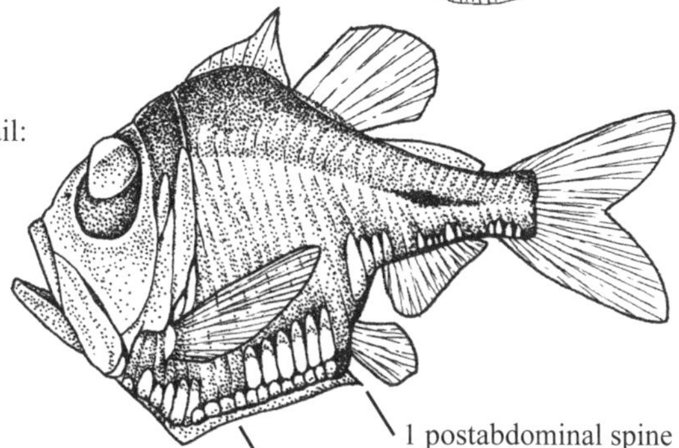


3b Two postabdominal spines roughly equal in size, not serrated, directed ventrally….. 4

4a Space between subcaudal photophores; no pigment on forebrain:

**SLENDER HATCHETFISH**

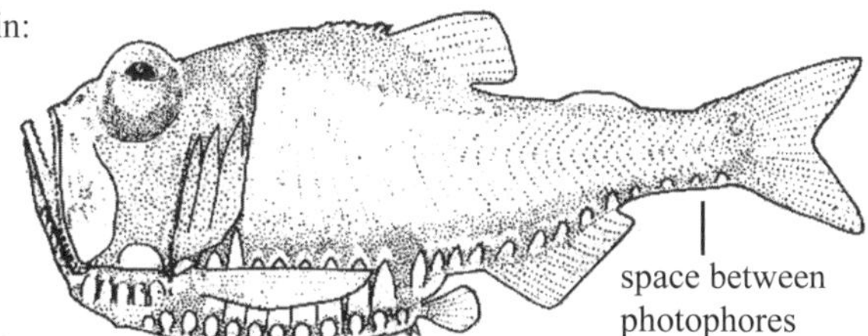


4b No space between subcaudal photophores; pigment on forebrain….. 5

5a Upper preopercular spine curves up; minute spines under caudal photophores lacking:

**LOWCREST HATCHETFISH**

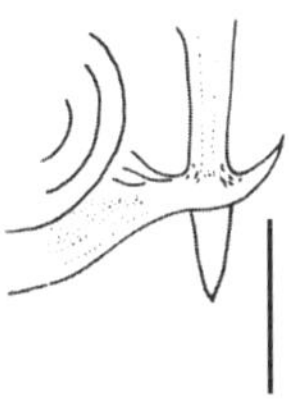

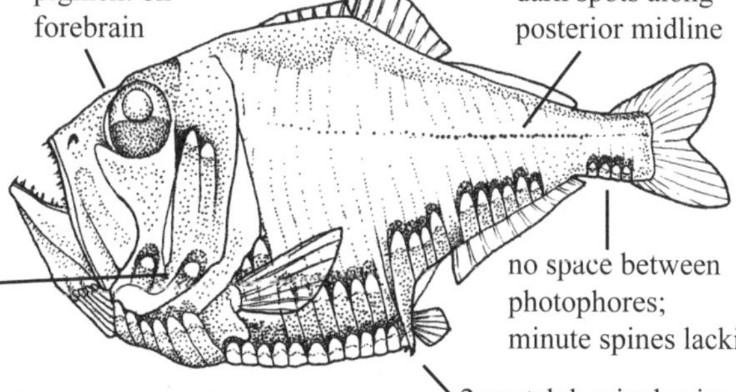


5b Upper preopercular spine curves down; minute spines under caudal photophores present in larger specimens:

**TROPICAL HATCHETFISH**

(not illustrated; more deep-bodied than in 5a)

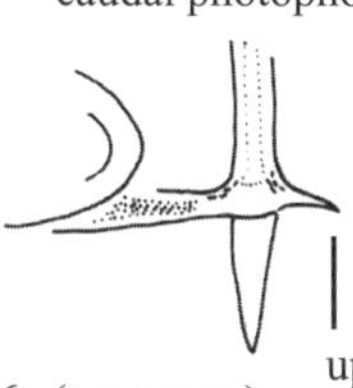


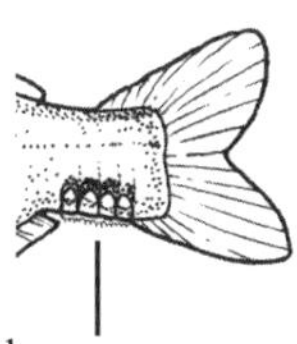


6a (next page)

## MARINE HATCHETFISHES (continued)

**DUSKY HATCHETFISH, *Sternoptyx obscura* Garman, 1899.** Pacific and Indian Oceans; Japan; central California to Peru–Chile border. Common from central California southward. Length to 4.5 cm (1.8 in) SL. Primarily mesopelagic; depth: 190–1,393 m (623–4,569 ft) and perhaps to 4,268 m (13,999 ft). Dark back, silvery sides and belly. D 9–11; A 12–15; Pect. 9–11; Pelvic 5–6; GRt 7–9; Vert. 29–31. (Formerly DOLLAR HATCHETFISHES, *Sternoptyx* spp: M&L).

**HIGHLIGHT HATCHETFISH, *Sternoptyx pseudobscura* Baird, 1971.** Circumglobal; Japan; British Columbia to Chile. Common Japan and at least from southern California southward. Length to 7 cm (2.8 in) SL. Primarily mesopelagic; depth: 156–2,300 m (512–7,544 ft) and perhaps to 3,290 m (10,791 ft). Dark back, silvery sides and belly. D 9–11; A 13–16; Pect. 9–11; Pelvic 5–6; GRt 7–9; Vert. 27–31. (Formerly DOLLAR HATCHETFISHES, *Sternoptyx* spp: M&L).

**LONGSPINE HATCHETFISH, *Sternoptyx diaphana* Hermann, 1781.** Circumglobal; Japan to Kuril Islands, Russia; Oregon to northern Chile (31°55'S). Common from Japan and northern California southward. Length to 6 cm (2.4 in) SL. Mesopelagic; depth: 275–2,374 m (902–7,787 ft) and perhaps to 4,667 m (15,308 ft). Dark back, silvery sides and belly. D 9–11; A 13–16; Pect. 10–11; Pelvic 5–6; GRt 6–9; Vert. 27–30. (Formerly DOLLAR HATCHETFISHES, *Sternoptyx* spp: M&L).

6a *From 2a: "normal" eyes directed laterally*
"Depth" (at insertion of dorsal fin to insertion of anal fin) into SL (snout to farthest extension of lower peduncle) greater than 3:

**DUSKY HATCHETFISH**

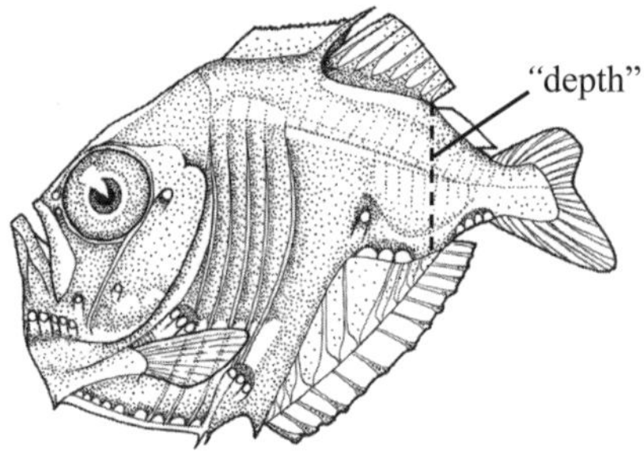


6b "Depth" (at insertion of dorsal fin to insertion of anal fin) into SL (snout to farthest extension of lower peduncle) less than 2.8….. 7

7a Supra-anal photophore "high"; anal pterygiophores posterior to anal photophores long:

**HIGHLIGHT HATCHETFISH**

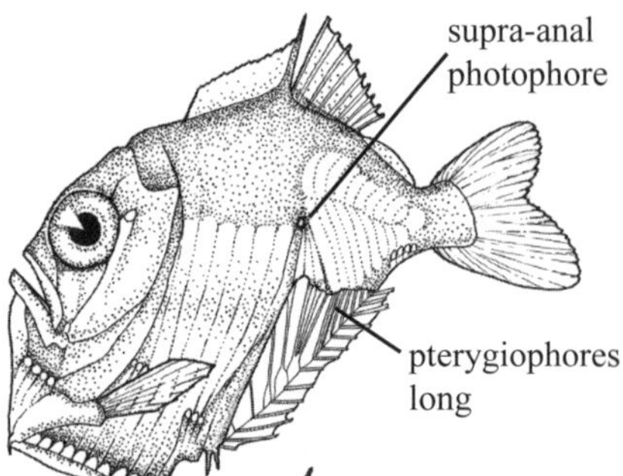


7b Supra-anal photophore "low"; anal pterygiophores posterior to anal photophores short:

**LONGSPINE HATCHETFISH**

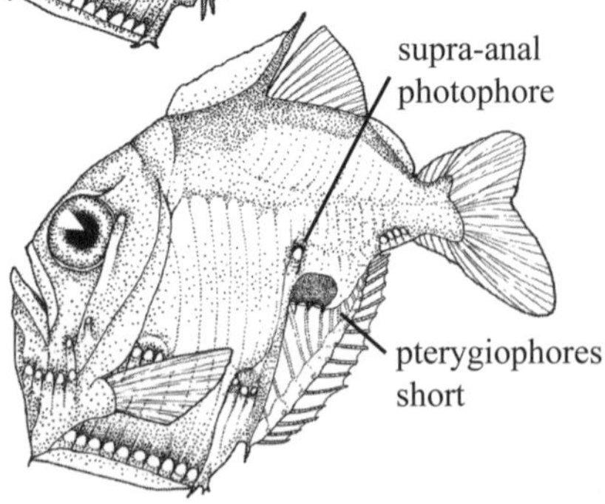

## DRAGONFISHES, Families Stomiidae, Chauliodontidae, Idiacanthidae, Malacosteidae, and Melanostomiidae

NOTE: Sometimes all of these families are placed in the family Stomiidae.

**BLACKBELLY DRAGONFISH, *Stomias atriventer* Garman, 1899.** Family Stomiidae
Washington (48°00'N) to Gulf of California and to northern Chile. Common from southern California southward. Length to 25 cm (10 in) TL. Depth: 52–2,124 m (171–6,967 ft). Dark back and belly, silvery sides with hexagonal patterns. D 16–20; A 16–22; Pect. 6; Pelvic 5; Vert. 69–74.

**PACIFIC VIPERFISH, *Chauliodus macouni* Bean, 1890.** Family Chauliodontidae
North Pacific; southern Japan to Bering Sea to central Baja California and Gulf of California. Larvae have been taken as far south as Cabo San Lucas, southern Baja California. Common from Japan and Sea of Okhotsk to at least southern California. Length to 29.6 cm (11.5 in) TL. Primarily meso- and bathypelagic; depth: 25–4,390 m (82–14,403 ft). Blackish to dark brown; sides spotted with hexagonal patterns. D 5–7; A 9–14; Pect. 9–14; Pelvic 6–10; LL absent; Midlateral scales 56; GRt 11–13; Vert. 56–62.

## KEY TO THE DRAGONFISHES:
Created by Cynthia Klepadlo and Peter Davison
(Principal sources: Grey, 1964; Morrow, 1964; Morrow & Gibbs, 1964)

NOTE: Photophores in parallel rows.

1a Scales absent or body without scale-like patterns….. 3 (next page)

1b Scales present or body marked with longitudinal rows of scale-like patterns….. 2

2a Dorsal fin origin far behind base of pelvic fin;
premaxillaries (upper jaw) capable of moving outward and back:

**BLACKBELLY DRAGONFISH**

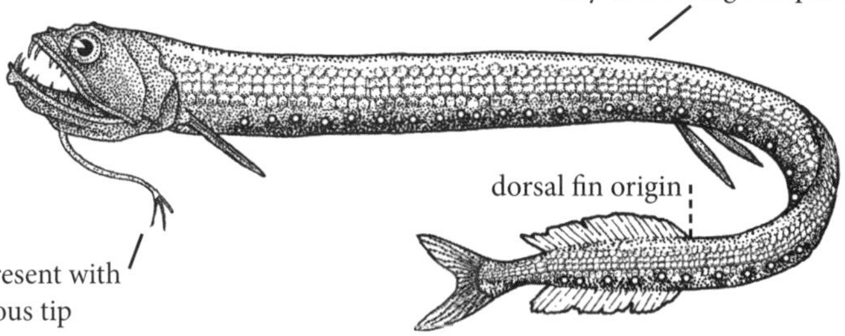


2b Dorsal fin origin well anterior to base of pelvic fin;
premaxillaries (upper jaw) not movable outward and back:

**PACIFIC VIPERFISH**

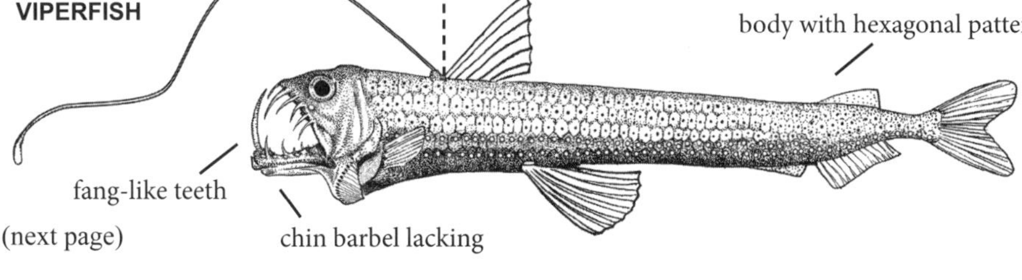


3a (next page)

## DRAGONFISHES (continued)

**PACIFIC BLACKDRAGON, *Idiacanthus antrostomus* Gilbert, 1890.** Family IDIACANTHIDAE
Japan; Triangle Island (50°48'N, 129°06'W), British Columbia to Chile. Common from at least Oregon to southern Baja California. Length: males to 7.6 cm (3 in) TL; females to 42.2 cm (16.6 in) SL. Depth: near surface to 1,830 m (6,002 ft) and perhaps to 4,100 m (13,448 ft). Males dark brown; females black. D 54–66; A 28–43; Pect. absent; Pelvic 6; Vert. 81–85.

**SHINING LOOSEJAW, *Aristostomias scintillans* (Gilbert, 1915).** Family MALACOSTEIDAE
Russian northwestern Pacific; Gulf of Alaska (59°09'N, 146°06'W) to southern Baja California (23°17'N, 120°33'W) (SIO 66-156); also near equator (7°00'N) (SIO 88-170). Report from Bering Sea probably in error. Common at least from northern British Columbia to about central Baja California. Length to 23 cm (9 in) TL. Primarily mesopelagic; depth: 29–1,237 m (95–4,057 ft) and perhaps surface to 2,001 m (6,563 ft). Black; red photophore just below and on front edge of eye. D 21–25; A 25–29; Pect. 4–8; Pelvic 6–7.

**HIGHFIN DRAGONFISH, *Bathophilus flemingi* Aron & McCrery, 1958.** Family MELANOSTOMIIDAE
Gulf of Alaska to southern Baja California (26°19'N, 114°40'W) (LACM 30072-1) and just south of equator well off Ecuador (LACM 36581–3). Common from at least Vancouver Island to central Baja California. Length to 16.5 cm (6.5 in) TL. Primarily meso- and bathypelagic; depth: less than 60 m to 1,372 m (197–4,501 ft), and perhaps to 2,287 m (7,501 ft). Uniform black or very dark brown. D 15–16; A 16–17; Pect. 5–7; Pelvic 15–19; LLs absent; Scales absent; Photophores in ventrolateral row 27–28; Vert. 44–48. (Formerly Melanostomiatidae: M&L).

**SOOTY DRAGONFISH, *Photonectes margarita* (Goode & Bean, 1896).** Family MELANOSTOMIIDAE
Circumglobal; Japan; northern California to northern Baja California and Isla Guadalupe, central Baja California (LACM 30603-1). Rare off California. Length to 39.6 cm (15.6 in) SL. Depth: surface to 3,290 m (10,791 ft). Black. D 15–18; A 19–24; Pect. 2.

**LONGFIN DRAGONFISH, *Tactostoma macropus* Bolin, 1939.** Family MELANOSTOMIIDAE
Japan and Sea of Okhotsk to Bering Sea to Chile. Common at least from Sea of Okhotsk to southern California. Length to 45.5 cm (17.9 in) SL. Primarily meso- and bathypelagic; depth: 25 m or less to 2,200 m (82–7,216 ft). Uniform black or dark brown. D 12–18; A 15–22; Pect. absent; Pelvic 8–10; GR 13–18 + 32–34 = 47–50; Vert. 79–82. (Formerly Melanostomiatidae: M&L).

3a *From 1a: scales absent*
Dorsal fin origin well anterior to anal fin origin:

**PACIFIC BLACKDRAGON**

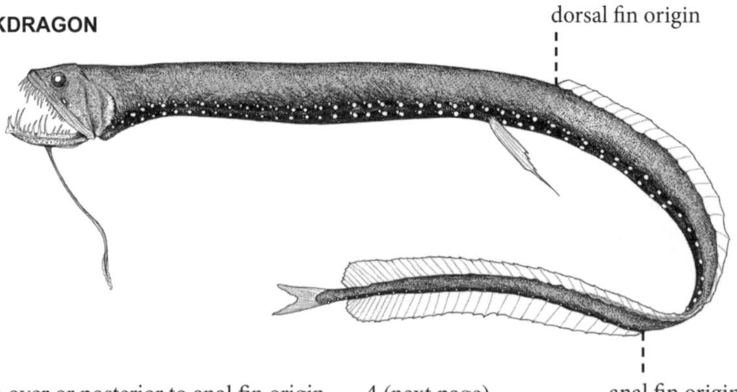


3b Dorsal fin origin over or posterior to anal fin origin..... 4 (next page)

4a Lower jaw connected to body only by single muscular cord from middle of jaw to "chest," no floor in mouth:

**SHINING LOOSEJAW**

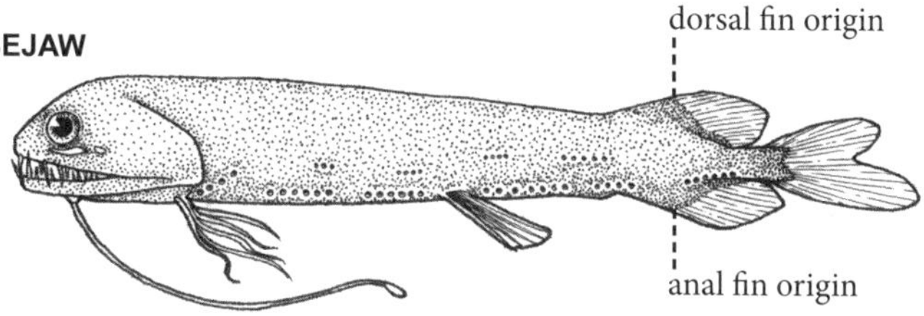


4b Lower jaw connected to body by membrane, thick or thin, forming floor of mouth….. 5

5a Origin of pelvic fins far apart, closer to mid-body than to ventral profile; lower jaw not longer than upper, not strongly curved upward; pectoral fin soft-rays 5–7:

**HIGHFIN DRAGONFISH**

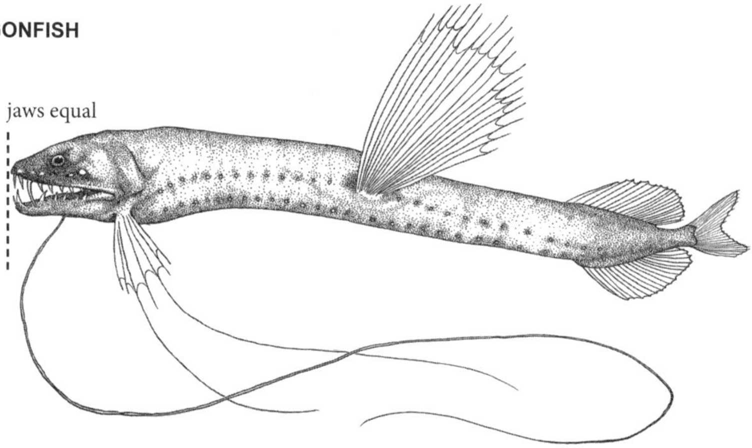


5b Origin of pelvic fins close together at ventral profile; lower jaw longer than upper and strongly curved upward; pectoral fin soft-rays 0–2….. 6

6a Vomer with teeth; barbel well developed, with luminous bulb:

**SOOTY DRAGONFISH**

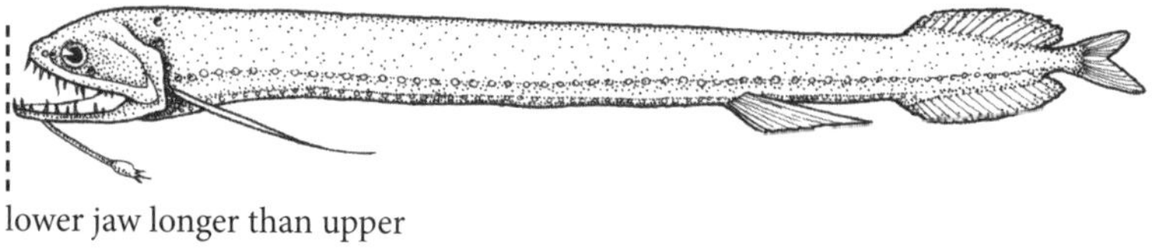


6b Vomer without teeth; barbel rudimentary stub, without luminous bulb:

**LONGFIN DRAGONFISH**

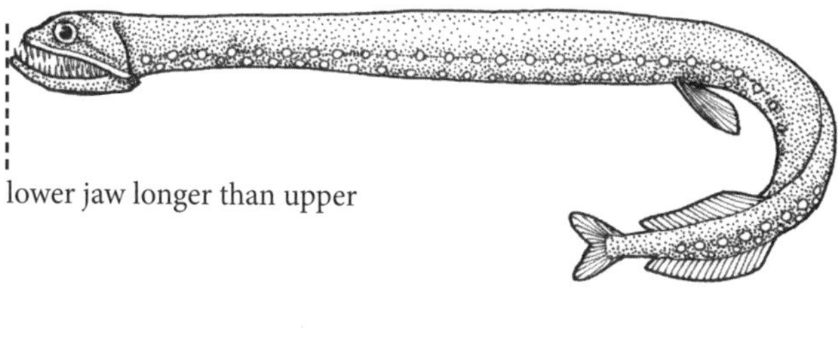

## BARRACUDINAS, Family Paralepididae

**NORTH PACIFIC DAGGERTOOTH, *Anotopterus nikparini* Kukuev, 1998.** North Pacific; south of Japan to southern Bering Sea and Gulf of Alaska to south of Baja California. Likely common from at least Kamchatka-Kuril Islands, Russia to southern California and perhaps further southward, but often well offshore. An *Anotopterus* reported from the Gulf of California is likely this species. Length to 146 cm (57.5 in) TL. Primarily epi- and mesopelagic; depth: surface (at night) to 2,750 m (9,022 ft). Dark on back, silvery sides, caudal fin dark. D absent (adipose fin only); A 14–17; Pect. 12–16; Pelvic 9–11; GR none; Vert. 77–83. Occasionally found lacking teeth. (Formerly DAGGERTOOTH, *Anotopterus pharao* Zugmayer, 1911, Anotopteridae: M&L).

**SLENDER BARRACUDINA, *Lestidiops ringens* (Jordan & Gilbert, 1880).** Northern Japan, Pacific off southern Kuril Islands, Russia to southern Kamchatka; western Bering Sea near Alaska border; Gulf of Alaska (58°21'N, 147°51'W) to southern Baja California (26°38'N, 114°21'W) (SIO 65-213) and Gulf of California. Common at least off Japan and probably from Bering Sea and Gulf of Alaska to central Baja California, however, larvae have been taken in southern Baja California waters as far south as about 25°00'N. Length to 25.2 cm (9.9 in) SL. Primarily mesopelagic; depth: near surface to 3,920 m (12,861 ft). Light olive above, silvery on sides. D 8–13; A 26–33; Pect. 11–12; Pelvic 8–11; Scales absent except along lateral line; GR 3–9 + 221–31; Vert. 82–91. (Formerly *Lestidium ringens* (Jordan & Gilbert, 1880): M&L).

**RIBBON BARRACUDINA, *Arctozenus risso* (Bonaparte, 1840).** Circumglobal; Japan, Sea of Okhotsk, and western Bering Sea to northern Gulf of Alaska to southern Baja California (24°39'N, 121°12'W) (SIO 54-96) and at 0°54'N, 82°00'W (SIO 98-129). Common from central Gulf of Alaska to northern Baja California. Length to 31 cm (12.2 in) SL. Mainly mesopelagic; depth: 0–3,465 m (11,365 ft). Light gray; base of anterior anal fin spines dark. D 8–13; A 28–34; Pect. 10–13; Pelvic 8–12; GRt 46–47; Vert. 75–85.

**DUCKBILL BARRACUDINA, *Magnisudis atlantica* (Krøyer, 1868).** Circumglobal; tropical to polar waters; Japan, Sea of Okhotsk, and western Bering Sea and eastern Bering Sea (to 52°32'N, 179°50'W) to Chile. Uncommon off California. Length to about 50 cm (19.7 in) SL. Epi- to bathypelagic; depth: less than 6 m (19.7 ft) to 2,308 m (7,570 ft). Dark brown or tan on back, lighter sides; fins and base of fins dark. D 9–12; A 20–26; Pect. 15–18; Pelvic 9–10; GR 7–10 + 25–32; Vert. 60–69.

## KEY TO THE BARRACUDINAS:
Created by Milton S. Love
(Principal source: Mecklenburg et al., 2002)

1a Dorsal fin absent (adipose fin only); lower jaw protruding:

**NORTH PACIFIC DAGGERTOOTH**

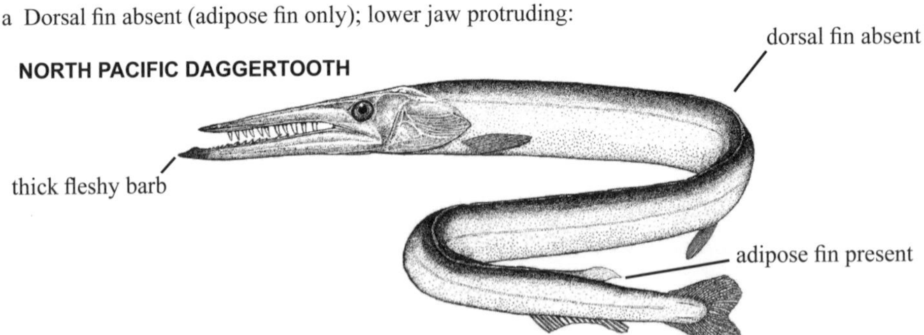


1b Dorsal fin present; jaws equal..... 2 (next page)

2a Pelvic fins well in front of dorsal fin; scales absent except along lateral line:

**SLENDER BARRACUDINA**

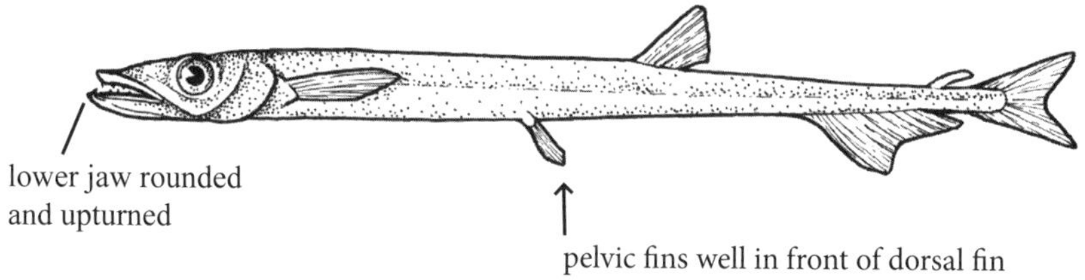


2b Pelvic fins below or behind dorsal fin; body covered with scales….. 3

3a Pelvic fins usually behind dorsal fin insertion; anal fin soft-rays 28 or more; eye diameter into HL less than 5:

**RIBBON BARRACUDINA**

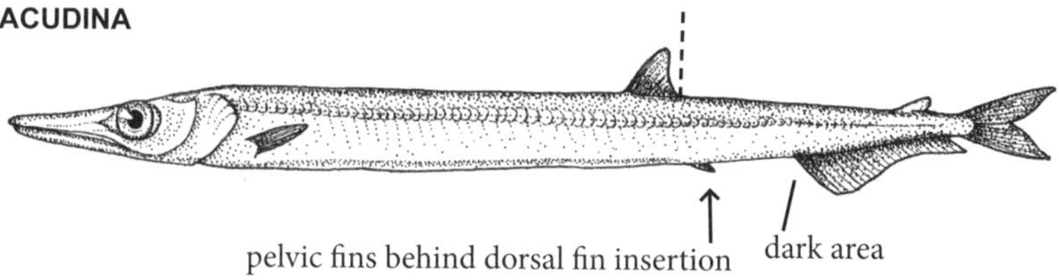


3b Pelvic fins usually below dorsal fin insertion; anal fin soft-rays 26 or fewer; eye diameter into HL greater than 5:

**DUCKBILL BARRACUDINA**

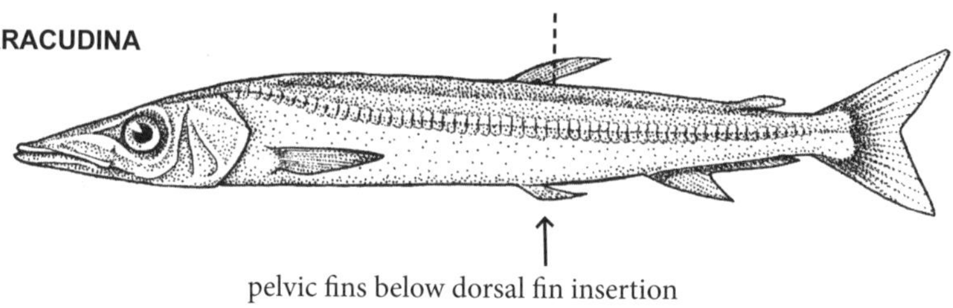

## PEARLEYE, Family Scopelarchidae, WARYFISH, Family Notosudidae, LIZARDFISHES, Family Synodontidae, and LANCETFISH, Family Alepisauridae

**NORTHERN PEARLEYE, *Benthalbella dentata* (Chapman, 1939).** Family SCOPELARCHIDAE

Japan, Sea of Okhotsk and western and eastern Bering Sea (to 58°30'N, 177°52'W) and Gulf of Alaska to Isla Guadalupe, central Baja California, and several locations well off Central America. Common off Japan and at least from Bering Sea and Aleutian Islands to northern Baja California. Length to least 28 cm (11 in) TL. Primarily mesopelagic; depth: 59–1,502 m (196–4,927 ft) and perhaps to 2,083 m (6,832 ft). Silver-black to dark brown above, paler below; bright silvery area on outer margin of eye. D 6–8; A 17–21; Pect. 20–25; Pelvic 9; LLs 54–58; GR none; Vert. 54–55.

**SCALY WARYFISH, *Scopelosaurus harryi* (Mead, 1953).** Family NOTOSUDIDAE

Northern Japan, Sea of Okhotsk, and Bering Sea to southern Baja California (20°00'N). Common from British Columbia to northern Baja California. Length to 32 cm (12.6 in) SL. Primarily mesopelagic; depth: 20–1,310 m (66–4,298 ft) and perhaps to 2,125 m (6,970 ft). Dark overall; inside of mouth black. D 10–12; A 16–19; Pect. 10–14; Pelvic 9–10; GR 0–2 + 17–20; Vert. 58–61. (Alternative name SCALY PAPERBONE). Note, we treat *Scopelosaurus adleri* (Federov, 1967) as a synonym of *S. harryi*.

**CALICO LIZARDFISH, *Synodus lacertinus* Gilbert, 1890.** Family SYNODONTIDAE

From 6 km (4 mi) south of U.S.-Mexican border to Chile, including Gulf of California and Islas Galápagos and other offshore islands. Not yet taken in U.S. waters. Common as far northward as about Bahía Magdalena, southern Baja California and into tropics. Length to 23.9 cm (9.4 in) TL. Depth: 1–156 m (3–512 ft). Color variable: mottled reddish or brown on upper half, white below; back with 5 saddles extending as irregular bars on to sides; lower side with 10–12 red or brown blotches; fins with red or dark banding. D 11–13; A 8–9; Pect. 11–12; LLs 59–63; Vert. 59–61. (Alternative name BANDED LIZARDFISH).

**CALIFORNIA LIZARDFISH, *Synodus lucioceps* (Ayres, 1855).** Family SYNODONTIDAE

Cape Beal, British Columbia to Guaymas, Gulf of California. Common from southern California southward to at least Bahía Magdalena, southern Baja California; in some years common at least as far north as San Francisco area. Length to 63.9 cm (25.2 in) TL. Depth: 1.5–229 m (5–751 ft). Uniform or blotchy brown above, tan to whitish below; gill membranes yellow; fins (particular pelvic) often yellow. D 11–13; A 12–15; Pect. 13–15; Pelvic 8; Vert. 60–63.

**LONGNOSE LANCETFISH, *Alepisaurus ferox* Lowe, 1833.** Family ALEPISAURIDAE

Atlantic and Pacific; Japan and Sea of Okhotsk to Bering Sea (as far northward as 58°21'N, 175°19'W) and Aleutian Islands to Chile. Common from Japan around to northern California. Length to about 231 cm (90.9 in) TL. Epi- to bathypelagic; depth: near surface to 1,830 m (6,004 ft). Uniform blue-black or brown with silvery and brassy overtones. D 30–45; A 13–18; Pect. 12–15; Pelvic 8–10; scales absent; GR 2–6 + 16–24 = 20–30; Vert. 47–52.

**NORTHERN PEARLEYE**

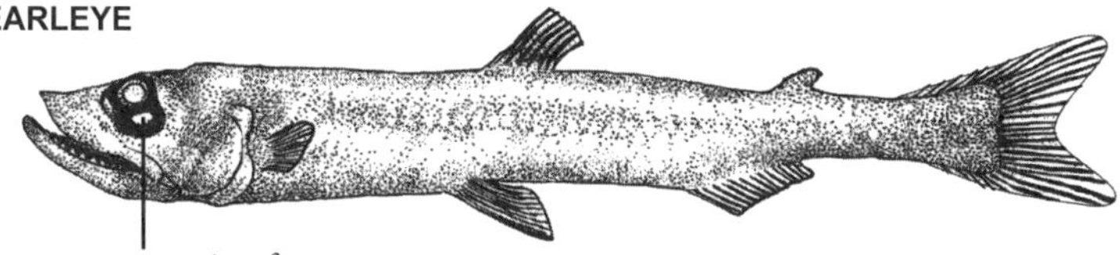


**SCALY WARYFISH**

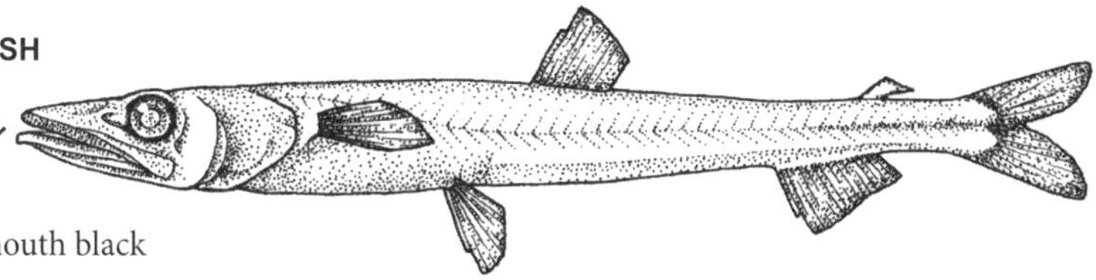


**CALICO LIZARDFISH**

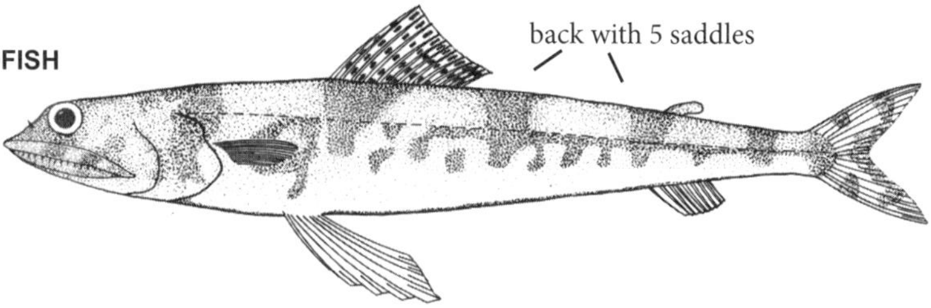


**CALIFORNIA LIZARDFISH**

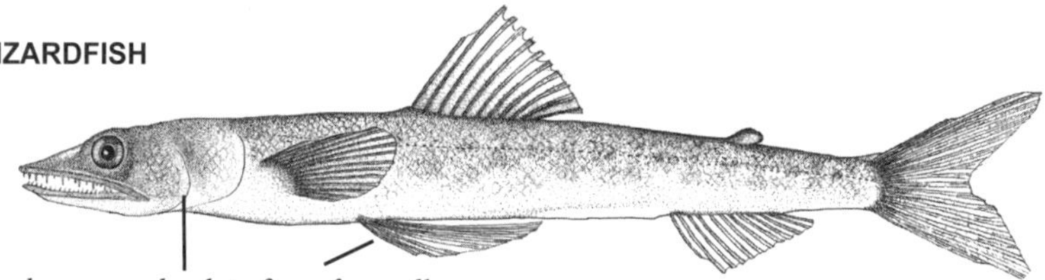


**LONGNOSE LANCETFISH**

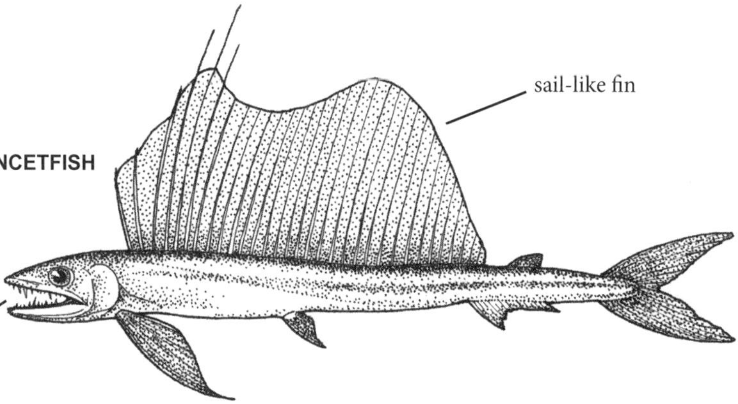

## MIDSHIPMAN, Family Batrachoididae

**SPECKLEFIN MIDSHIPMAN, *Porichthys myriaster* Hubbs & Schultz, 1939.** Near Point Arguello, California to at least Bahía Magdalena, southern Baja California. Also reported in northern Peru. Common from southern California to Bahía Magdalena, southern Baja California. Length to 51 cm (20 in) TL. Depth: intertidal to 126 m (414 ft). Dark gray, brownish, or purple above, pale below; belly yellowish; pectoral fins heavily spotted. D II + 35–40; A 33–39; Pect. 17–20; Pelvic I,2; GR 10–14 (lower limb), usually 12; Vert. 46–49. (Alternative name SPECKLED MIDSHIPMAN).

**PLAINFIN MIDSHIPMAN, *Porichthys notatus* Girard, 1854.** Smith Sound, southern British Columbia to southern Baja California (about 24°12'N, 111°21'W). Records south of Baja California and into the Gulf of California are misidentifications; *P. notatus* is replaced by *Porichthys mimeticus* Walker & Rosenblatt, 1988 in the Gulf of California. A report from Sitka, southeastern Alaska, is unconfirmed. Common from Strait of Georgia and west coast of Vancouver Island to Puget Sound and from Humboldt Bay, northern California to at least Bahía Magdalena, southern Baja California. Length to 46 cm (18.1 in) SL. Depth: intertidal to 464 m (1,522 ft). Dark purple-gray, brown, or olive-green above, yellowish below. D II + 33–38; A 28–35; Pect. 15–20; Pelvic I,2; GR 1 + 8–16 = 9–17; Vert. 42–46.

SPECKLEFIN MIDSHIPMAN

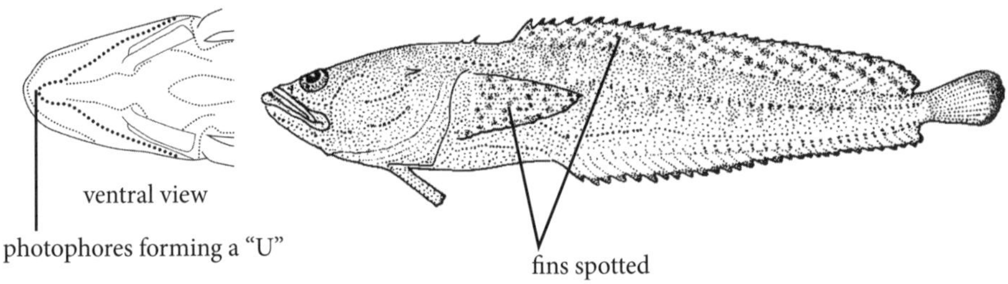


PLAINFIN MIDSHIPMAN

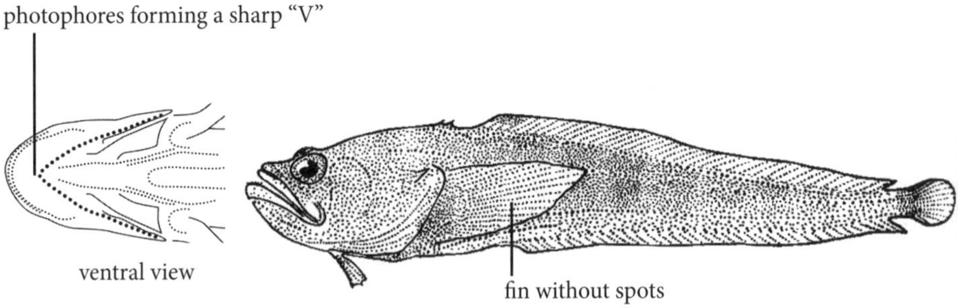

## LANTERNFISHES, Family Myctophidae

**BLUE LANTERNFISH, *Tarletonbeania crenularis* (Jordan & Gilbert, 1880).** South of Commander-Aleutian Islands Chain to Gulf of Alaska to southern Baja California (25°33'N, 115°10'W), perhaps coast of Mexico and Peru; probably also in Bering Sea but voucher specimens are lacking. Reported from Japan, but evidently those records are now considered to belong to *Tarletonbeania taylori* Mead, 1953. Common at least from Bering Sea and Gulf of Alaska southward to southern California. Length to 12.7 cm (5 in) TL. Depth: surface to 1,348 m (4,421 ft). Blue-black to black on back, silvery on sides. D 11–14; A 17–20; Pect. 11–15; Pelvic 7–8; Midlateral scales 45–50; GR 4–7 + 10–13 = 14–18; Photophores: VO 5–7, AO 9–12 + 3–5, Prc 1; Vert. 39–42.

## KEY TO THE LANTERNFISHES:
Revised by Cynthia Klepadlo and Peter Davison
(Principal source: Miller & Lea, 1972; Wisner, 1974)

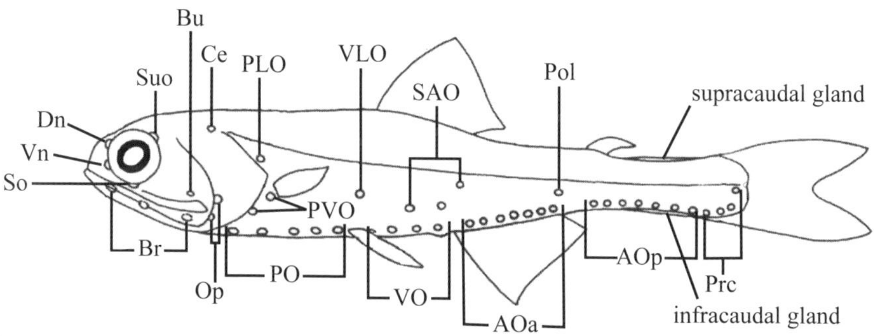


**Figure 19: LANTERNFISH composite.**

NOTE: Photophores (light-producing organs) are present in all California species and are arranged in species-specific patterns. They are concentrated in unparallel, ventrolateral rows on head and body. Subscript number indicates which photophore, counting from anterior to posterior, e.g., $PO_4$ refers to 4th photophore in PO series. AO sometimes separated into AOa and AOp.

1a Three or 4 Prc (1 could be far above or on lateral line); $PO_4$ may or may not be elevated….. 7 (page 101)

1b One or 2 Prc; $PO_4$ not elevated, but $PO_5$ may be elevated….. 2

2a Jaws moderate, extending 0.5 or more eye diameter behind orbit; mouth subterminal, snout projecting:

**BLUE LANTERNFISH**

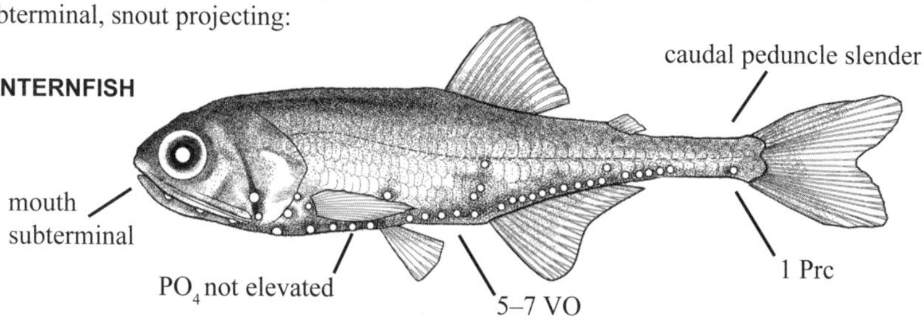


2b Jaws short, extending less than 0.5 eye diameter behind orbit; mouth terminal, snout not projecting….. 3 (next page)

## LANTERNFISHES (continued)

**CHUBBY FLASHLIGHTFISH, *Electrona risso* (Cocco, 1829).** Circumglobal; Japan, southern Kuril Islands, Russia; Oregon to Chile. Rare at least off west coast of U.S. and Mexico. Length to 9 cm (3.5 in) SL. Mesopelagic; depth: 0–2,979 m (9,771 ft). D 13–15; A 18–20; Pect. 13–16; GR 8–9 + 18–21; Photophores: VO 4, AO 10–13, Prc 2; Vert. 32–34.

**CALIFORNIA FLASHLIGHTFISH, *Protomyctophum crockeri* (Bolin, 1939).** Northern Japan to southern British Columbia to Baja California and Chile. Common at least from northern California (and perhaps Oregon) to central Baja California. Length to about 4.6 cm (1.8 in) SL. Depth: surface to 950 m (3,117 ft) and perhaps to 4,268 m (13,999 ft). D 11–13; A 19–24; Pect. 13–17; Pelvic 8; GR 4–6 + 13–20 = 17–24; Photophores: VO 4, AO 13–15, Prc 2; Vert. 36–38.

**LONGFIN LANTERNFISH, *Diogenichthys atlanticus* (Tåning, 1932).** Circumglobal; Japan; northern California to northern Chile. Common from southern California southward. Length to 3.6 cm (1.4 in) SL. Epi- to mesopelagic; depth: surface to 1,720 m (33–5,640 ft). D 10–12; A 14–18; Pect. 12–13; GR 3 + 9–12; Photophores: VO 4, AO 5–7 + 2–4, Prc 2; Vert. 31–35.

**BROADHEAD LANTERNFISH, *Hygophum reinhardtii* (Lütken, 1892).** Circumglobal; Japan; Oregon to Chile. Reported from Gulf of Alaska but documentation evidently lacking. Rare off California. Length 6.1 cm (2.4 in) SL. Epi- to mesopelagic; depth: surface to 3,290 m (10,791 ft). D 13–16; A 21–25; Pect. 13–16; GR 3–5 + 12–16; Photophores: VO 4, AO 5–8 + 6–9, Prc 2; Vert. 38–40.

**BIGFIN LANTERNFISH, *Symbolophorus californiensis* (Eigenmann & Eigenmann, 1889).** Japan to Haida Gwaii, British Columbia to southern Baja California (24°14'N, 114°12'W) (USNM 196570.514893). Not adequately documented for Alaska. Common at least off northern Japan and at least from northern California to southern Baja California. Length to about 12.7 cm (5 in) TL. Depth: surface to 1,514 m (4,966 ft) and perhaps to 3,824 m (12,543 ft). Back black, silvery over dark background on sides. D 13–15; A 19–22; Pect. 15–20; Pelvic 8; LLs 38–42; GR 6–7 + 15–17; Photophores: VO 4, AO 6–7 + 8–10, Prc 2; Vert. 37–40. (Formerly CALIFORNIA LANTERNFISH: M&L).

3a PLO dorsal to pectoral fin origin; AO series (AOa + AOp) separated by gap; 1–2 distinct Pol….. 5 (next page)

3b PLO ventral to pectoral fin origin; AO series usually continuous; Pol lacking….. 4

4a PVO inclined, in line with $PO_1$; SAO series at angle; dorsal fin soft-rays 13–15; anal fin soft-rays 18–20:

**CHUBBY FLASHLIGHTFISH**

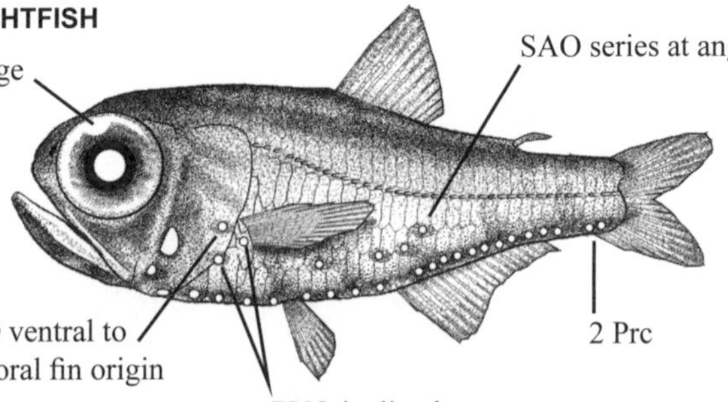


4b (next page)

4b PVO series horizontal; SAO series in straight line; dorsal fin soft-rays 11–13; anal fin soft-rays 19–24 (usually 21–22):

**CALIFORNIA FLASHLIGHTFISH**

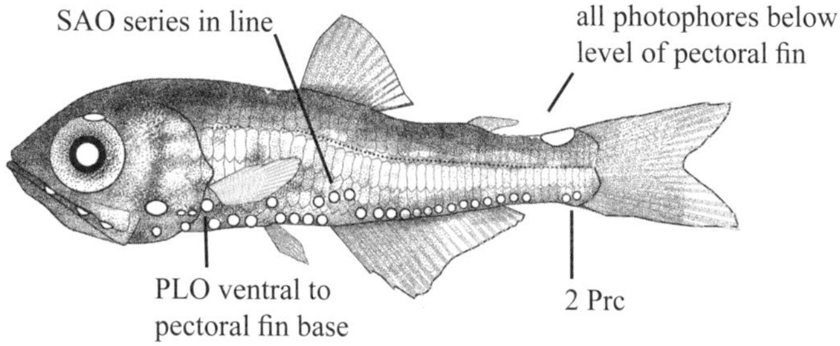


5a *From 3a: PLO dorsal to pectoral fin base*
PVO series nearly horizontal; $VO_2$ elevated; 1 Pol:

**LONGFIN LANTERNFISH**

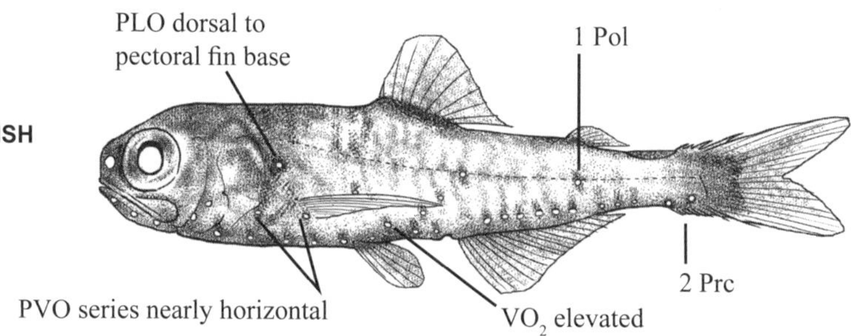


5b PVO series inclined (usually fairly steep); VO series level; 1 or 2 Pol….. 6

6a Two Pol; supracaudal luminous glands of males large, single, and bordered by heavy black pigment:

**BROADHEAD LANTERNFISH**

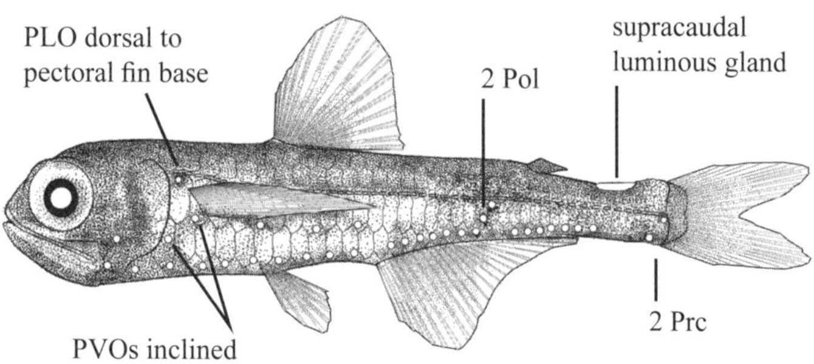


6b One Pol; supracaudal luminous glands variable (in males 5–7 non-overlapping scales) but never as above:

**BIGFIN LANTERNFISH**

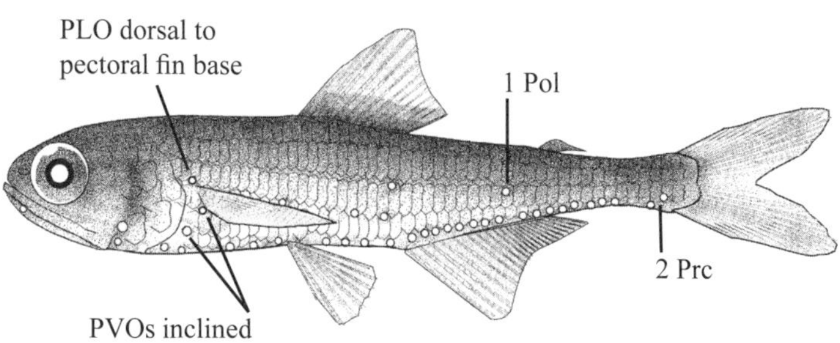


7a (next page)

## LANTERNFISHES (continued)

**CALIFORNIA HEADLIGHTFISH, *Diaphus theta* Eigenmann & Eigenmann, 1890.** Japan and southern Bering Sea to Chile. Common at least off Japan and Kuril Islands, Russia, and at least from western Bering Sea and Gulf of Alaska southward to northern Baja California. Length to 11.7 cm (4.6 in) SL. Depth: surface to 4,100 m (13,448 ft), typically above 800 m (2,624 ft). Black. D 11–15; A 12–14; Pect. 9–12; Pelvic 7–8; LLs 34–38; GR 4–7 + 13–18 = 19–23; Photophores: VO 5 (3 on same level), Prc 4; Vert. 34–36.

**SUNBEAM LAMPFISH, *Lampadena urophaos* Paxton, 1963.** Atlantic and Pacific; Japan and British Columbia to Chile and westward to Hawai'i. Off West Coast of North America, common at least from southern California to southern Baja California. Length to 23.7 cm (9.3 in) SL. Depth: near surface to perhaps 4,268 m (13,999 ft). Black; scales with dark pigment at margin creating honeycomb pattern. D 14–16; A 13–14; Pect. 14–17; Pelvic 8; GR 3–5 + 9–11; Photophores: VO 4–6, AO 5–6 + 2–3, Prc 2 + 1; Vert. 35–38.

**POPEYE LAMPFISH, *Bolinichthys longipes* (Brauer, 1906).** Pacific and Indian Oceans; northern Japan; southern California to Peru. Uncommon off southern California. Length to 6.5 cm (2.6 in) SL. Epi- to mesopelagic; depth: 50–725 m (164–2,379 ft). Black with bluish metallic sheen; fins dusky. D 11–13; A 13–15; Pect. 12–14; GR 4–5 + 12–15; Photophores: VO 5, AO 4–6 + 2–5, Prc 4; Vert. 32–35.

**DOGTOOTH LAMPFISH, *Ceratoscopelus townsendi* (Eigenmann & Eigenmann, 1889).** Circumglobal; Gulf of Alaska (59°15'N, 142°08'W) to southern Baja California. Common from southern California southward. Length to 8.5 cm (3.3 in) SL. Mesopelagic; depth: 100–800 m (328–2,625 ft), possibly to 923 m (3,028 ft). D 13–15; A 13–16; Pect. 10–15; GR 4–8 + 10–16; Photophores: VO 5, AO 4–6 + 5–7, Prc 4; Vert. 35–38.

**NORTHERN LAMPFISH, *Stenobrachius leucopsarus* (Eigenmann & Eigenmann, 1890).** Southern Japan off Honshu to southern Bering Sea and Gulf of Alaska to southern Baja California (26°00'N, 115°00'W) (LACM 30074-11). Length to 12.5 cm (4.9 in) TL. Common at least from Hokkaido, Japan to Sea of Okhotsk and Gulf of Alaska southward to northern Baja California. Depth: 30 m (98 ft) or less to 3,824 m (12,543 ft), but possibly to 2,896 m (9,500 ft). Silvery, gray, to greenish-blue; black on operculum; light gray fins. D 12–15; A 14–16; Pect. 8–11; Pelvic 8–10; LLs 35–38; GR 5–8 + 11–15 = 16–22; Photophores: VO 3–5, AO 5–8 + 6–8, Prc 4; Vert. 35–38.

7a *From 1a: three or 4 Prc*
No supracaudal or infracaudal luminous glands; $PO_1$, $PVO_1$, and $PVO_2$ in straight ascending line; Dn present:

**CALIFORNIA HEADLIGHTFISH**

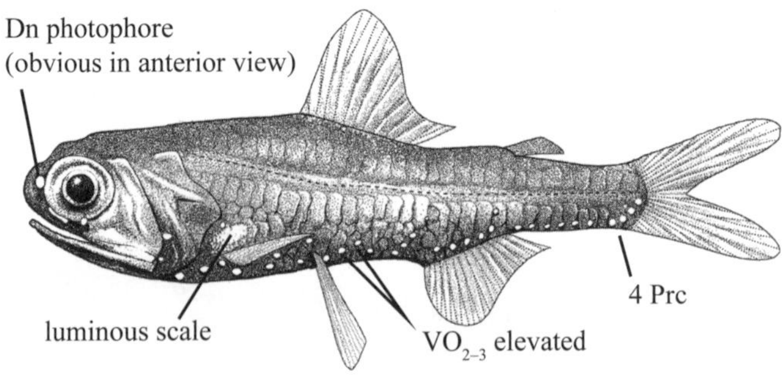


7b Supracaudal or infracaudal glands present; $PO_1$, $PVO_1$, and $PVO_2$ not in straight ascending line; Dn absent….. 8 (next page)

8a Supra- and infracaudal luminous glands large, each as single organ edged in black pigment:

**SUNBEAM LAMPFISH**

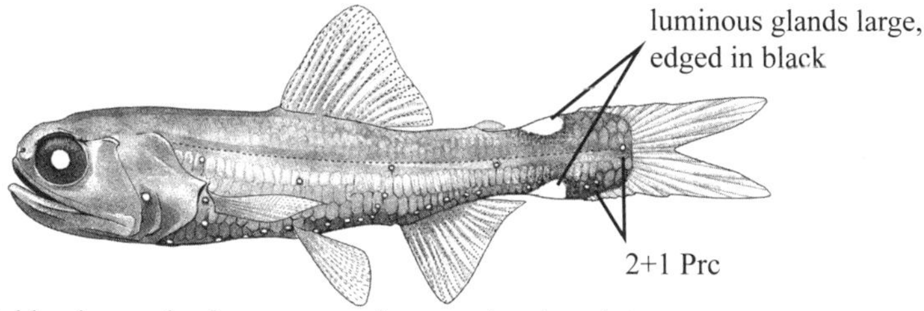


8b Supra- and infracaudal luminous glands narrow, each as overlapping plates with no pigment….. 9

9a Luminous tissue restricted to caudal luminous glands and occasionally at base of adipose fin….. 11

9b Luminous tissue over base of anal fin and on other portions of body, in addition to caudal luminous glands….. 10

10a Crescent-shaped white tissue on posterior half of iris; posterior spines on procurrent caudal rays lacking; moderate luminous tissue patches over eyes; 1 or 2 (rarely 3) luminous tissue patches present at base of dorsal, anal, and pelvic fins:

**POPEYE LAMPFISH**

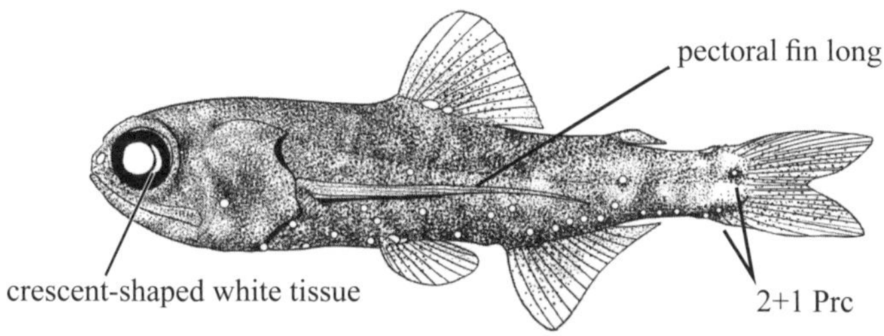


10b Crescent-shaped white tissue on iris lacking; dorsal and ventral series of procurrent caudal rays with posterior spines; prominent luminous tissue patches over eyes, forming "eyebrows"; luminous tissue scattered along dorsal and ventral surfaces, and under PLO photophore:

**DOGTOOTH LAMPFISH**

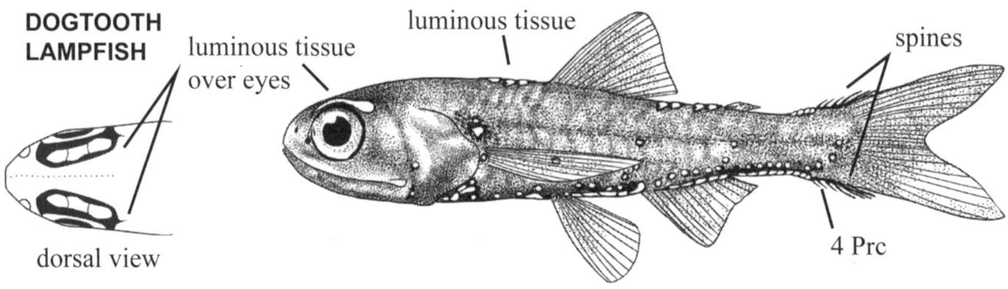


11a *From 9a: luminous tissue restricted to caudal luminous glands and occasionally at base of adipose fin*
One Pol:

**NORTHERN LAMPFISH**

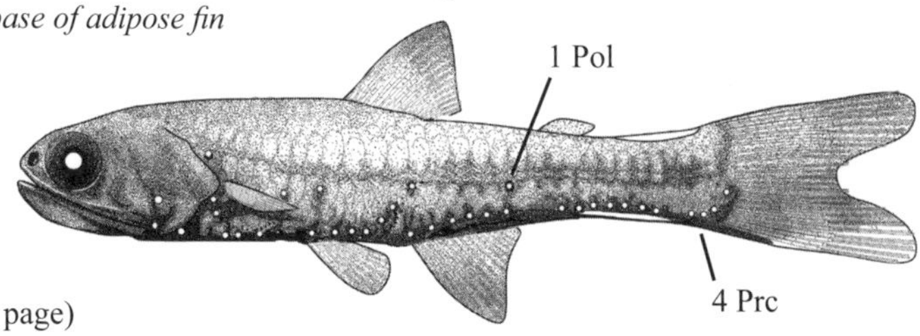


11b Two Pol….. 12 (next page)

## LANTERNFISHES (continued)

**MEXICAN LAMPFISH, *Triphoturus mexicanus* (Gilbert, 1890).** British Columbia to off southern Mexico, including Gulf of California. Common from central California southward into tropics. Length to about 8 cm (3.1 in) SL. Depth: 20–2,882 m (66–9,453 ft). D 13–16; A 14–17; Pect. 8–10; Pelvic 7–9; LLs 35–38; GR 3–5 + 10–14; Photophores: VO 5 ($VO_2$ and $VO_3$ elevated), AO 4–6 + 4–6, Prc 3 (continuous with AO series); Vert. 33–35.

**SLENDER LANTERNFISH, *Lampanyctus tenuiformis* (Brauer, 1906).** Throughout Pacific; Japan and northwestern Pacific; northern California (37°06'N, 122°50'W) (SIO 89-188) to South America. Common at least from southern California southward. Length to 15.6 cm (6.1 in) SL. Mesopelagic; depth: 40–800 m (131–2,624 ft). D 13–14; A 17–18; Pect. 13–15; Pelvic 8; GR 4–5 + 10–12; Photophores: VO 4, AO 6–7 + 6–7, Prc 3+1; Vert. 35–37.

**BROADFIN LAMPFISH, *Nannobrachium ritteri* (Gilbert, 1915).** Eastern North Pacific Ocean south of Aleutian Islands and Gulf of Alaska to southwest of Cabo San Lucas (about 19°00'N, 115°00'W), southern Baja California. Records from Central or South America not verified. Common from about southeastern Alaska to southern Baja California. Length to 13.9 cm (5.5 in) SL. Depth: 8–1,100 m (26–3,609 ft). Blakish to metallic blue on back, light on sides; mouth and gill cavity black; fins with wavy lines. D 12–16; A 16–19; Pect. 10–13; Pelvic 8–9; LLs 37–38; GRt 13–18; Photophores: VO 4, AO 6–8 + 8–9, Prc 4; Vert. 35–38. (Formerly *Lampanyctus ritteri* Gilbert, 1915: M&L).

12a Five VO with $VO_2$ and $VO_3$ elevated:

**MEXICAN LAMPFISH**

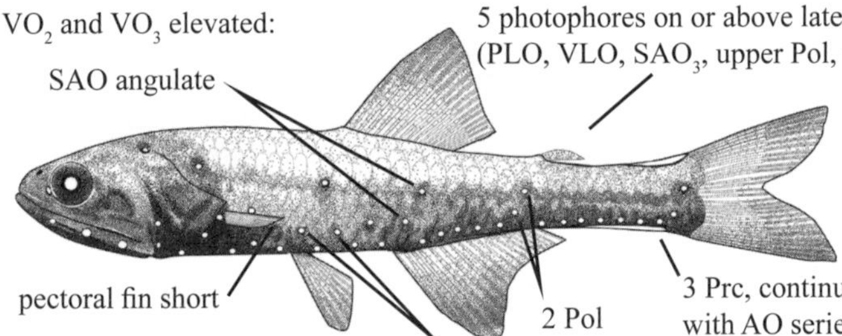


12b Four VO, none elevated….. 13

13a $SAO_3$ usually anterior to or even with origin of anal fin; pectoral fin long:

**SLENDER LANTERNFISH**

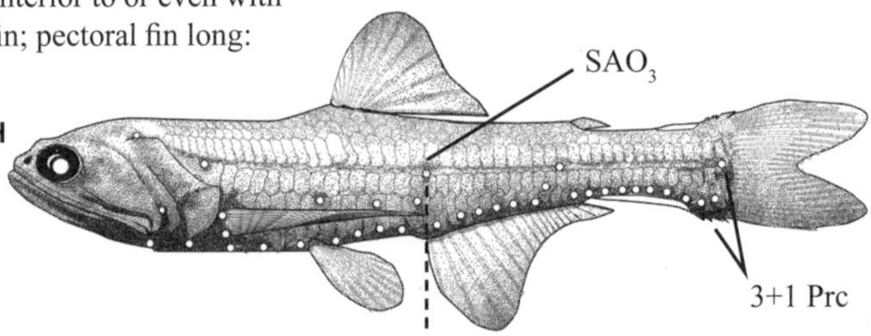


13b $SAO_3$ usually posterior to origin of anal fin; pectoral fin short:

**BROADFIN LAMPFISH**

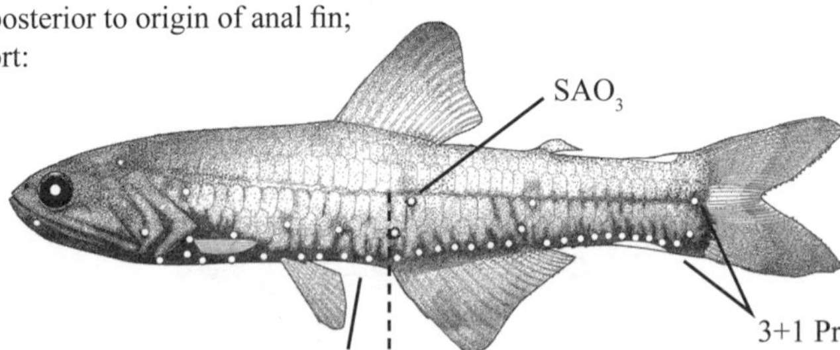

# CUSK-EELS, Family Ophidiidae and BROTULAS, Family Bythitidae

**PACIFIC BEARDED BROTULA, *Brotula clarkae* Hubbs, 1944.** Family OPHIDIIDAE
Palos Verdes Peninsula, southern California (SIO 07-67) to Paita, Peru, including Gulf of California. Rare in California. Length to 115 cm (45.3 in) TL. Adults benthopelagic, juveniles common on reefs; depth: 1–645 m (3–2,116 ft). Reddish-brown; dorsal and anal fins dark brown to blackish; juveniles under 20 cm (8 in) with dark stripe on head behind eye and large, dark spots on body. D about 106–118; A 78–89; Pect. 26–28; Pelvic 1 ray with 2 branches of unequal length; Vert. 55–56.

**PAPERBONE CUSK-EEL, *Lamprogrammus niger* Alcock, 1891.** Family OPHIDIIDAE
Circumglobal; Washington (47°12'N) to northern Peru, also Isla Guadalupe, central Baja California (LACM 9732-3). Uncommon in California. Length to 61 cm (24 in) TL. Adults usually taken near bottom, small specimens occasionally in midwater trawls at mesopelagic depths; depth: 165–2,670 m (541–8,758 ft). Uniform black to blue-black becoming lighter posteriorly. D about 110; A about 90; Pect. 17; Pelvic absent.

## KEY TO THE CUSK-EELS and BROTULAS:
Created by Bill Power
(Principal sources: Miller & Lea, 1972; Nielsen et al., 1999)

1a Barbels on snout and chin:

**PACIFIC BEARDED BROTULA**

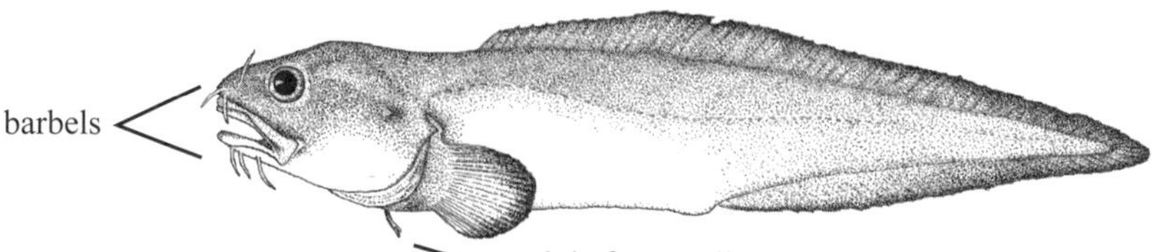


1b No barbels on snout and chin….. 2

2a Pelvic fins under gill opening….. 5 (page 106)

2b Pelvic fins lacking or under eyes if present….. 3

3a Pelvic fins lacking (in adults, unclear for juveniles); uniform black body color; large opercular spine present:

**PAPERBONE CUSK-EEL**

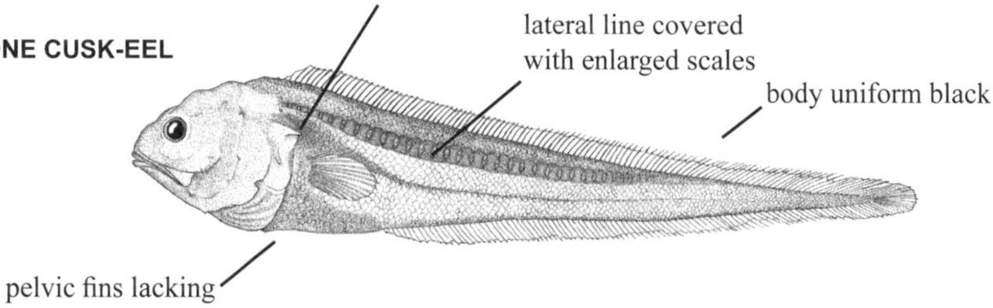


3b Pelvic fins present under eyes; body with numerous spots and blotches or crisscross pattern; large opercular spine absent….. 4 (next page)

## CUSK-EELS and BROTULAS (continued)

**SPOTTED CUSK-EEL, *Chilara taylori* (Girard, 1858).** Family Ophidiidae
Bowen Island (49°23'N, 123°24'W), British Columbia to 23°25'N, 110°14'W, southern Baja California and Ecuador. Common from northern California southward to southern Baja California. Length to 45.2 cm (17.8 in) TL. Depth: intertidal to 731 m (2,398 ft). Light brown to cream-colored; fish over 10 cm (4 in) TL with dark spots and blotches on upper part and sides of body. D 187–229; A 150–181; Pect. 22–29; GR 1–4 + 5–9 = 6–12; Vert. 86–91.

**BASKETWEAVE CUSK-EEL, *Ophidion scrippsae* (Hubbs, 1916).** Family Ophidiidae
Point Arguello, central California to Bahía Santa Maria (24°40'N, 112°10'W), southern Baja California (SIO 62-491). Previous records from further north in central California and in the Gulf of California are in error. Common from southern California to southern Baja California. Length to nearly 28 cm (11 in) TL. Depth: shallow waters to 213 m (699 ft), possibly to 260 m (853 ft). Brownish to olive above, tan below; scales forming a crisscross pattern on sides. D 124–153; A 99–126; Pect. 20–23; GR 2–4 + 4–8 = 6–11; Vert. 65–69. (Formerly *Otophidium scrippsi* Hubbs, 1916: M&L).

**RED BROTULA, *Brosmophycis marginata* (Ayres, 1854).** Family Bythitidae
Petersburg, southeastern Alaska to Ensenada, northern Baja California. However, larvae have been taken along much of the northern and central Baja California coast south to Punta Eugenia, southern Baja California. Common at least from Washington to southern California. Length to 46 cm (18 in) TL, possibly to 50.8 cm (20 in) TL. Depth: 3–256 m (10–840 ft). Dark red or red-brown; bright red fins. D 92–110; A 72–81; Pect. 20–26; Pelvic 2; Scales over LL 170; GR 4–6 + 13–17 = 18–21; Vert. 63–65. (Formerly Brotulidae: M&L).

**PURPLE BROTULA, *Grammonus diagrammus* (Heller & Snodgrass, 1903).** Family Bythitidae
San Clemente Island and Santa Catalina Island, southern California to Ecuador, including Gulf of California, Islas Galápagos, and Islas Revillagigedo. Rare in southern California; common from central Baja California into tropics. Length to 20.3 cm (8 in) TL. Depth: 6–37 m (18–120 ft). Deep purplish-black or slate. D 95–115; A 75–91; Pect. 24–29; Midlateral scales about 100–115; GR 0 + 2–3; Vert. 49–53. (Formerly *Oligopus diagrammus* (Heller & Snodgrass, 1903), Brotulidae: M&L).

**RUBYNOSE BROTULA, *Cataetyx rubrirostris* Gilbert, 1890.** Family Bythitidae
Queen Charlotte Sound, British Columbia to central Baja California (28°48'N) and Gulf of California (SIO 68-90); Punta Coles, Peru to central Chile. Common at least off central and southern California. Specimens from South America may be this or an undescribed species. Length to 15.7 cm (6.2 in) TL. If the South American form is not this species, the maximum length is 13 cm (5.2 in) TL. Juveniles mesopelagic, larger individuals benthic; depth: 212–1,023 m (695–3,355 ft) or perhaps as deep as 3,824 m (12,543 ft). Large individuals brownish-gray with dark fins and brown snout; smaller individuals lighter-colored with red snout. D 100–114; A 76–86; Pect. 25–26; Pelvic 1; GRt 3; Vert. 60–63.

4a Dark blotches (covering more than 1 scale) on dorsal area; crisscross patterns on sides and back lacking; dorsal fin soft-rays 187–229, anal fin soft-rays 150–181:

**SPOTTED CUSK-EEL**

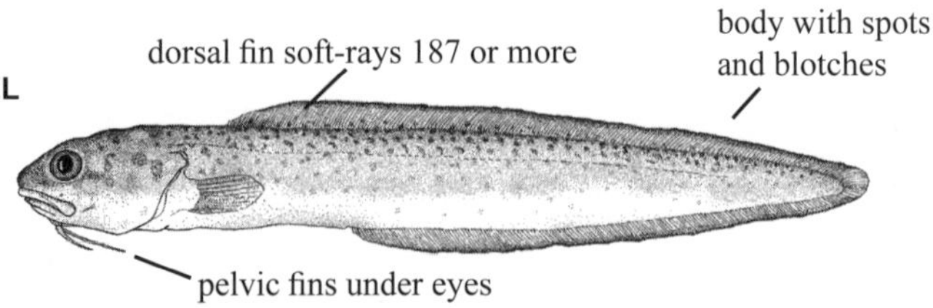


4b (next page)

4b No blotches on dorsal area; crisscross patterns in scales on sides and back (viewable with magnification); dorsal fin soft-rays 124–153, anal fin soft-rays 99–126:

**BASKETWEAVE CUSK-EEL**

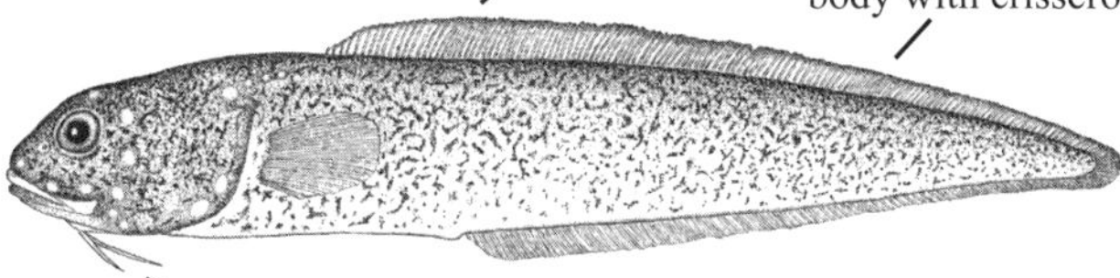


5a *From 2a: pelvic fins under gill opening*
Caudal fin distinct, separate from dorsal and anal fins; pelvic fin soft-rays 2:

**RED BROTULA**

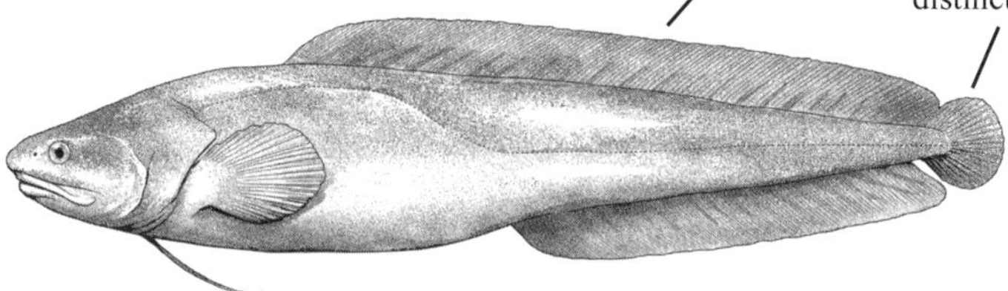


5b Caudal fin not distinct, confluent with dorsal and anal fins; pelvic fin soft-ray 1….. 6

6a Double lateral line present; prominent opercular spine lacking; body purple:

**PURPLE BROTULA**

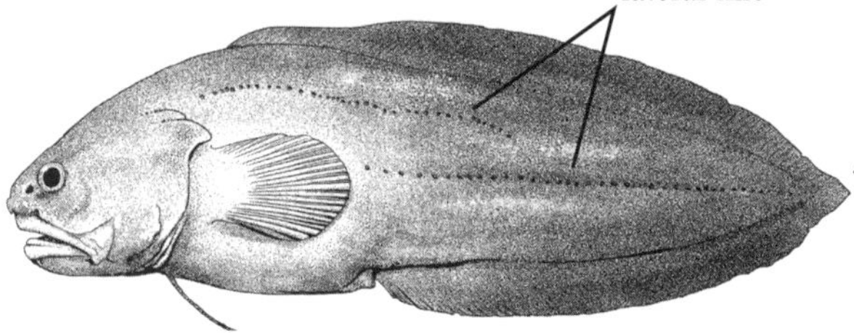


6b Double lateral line lacking; prominent opercular spine present; body lighter than head:

**RUBYNOSE BROTULA**

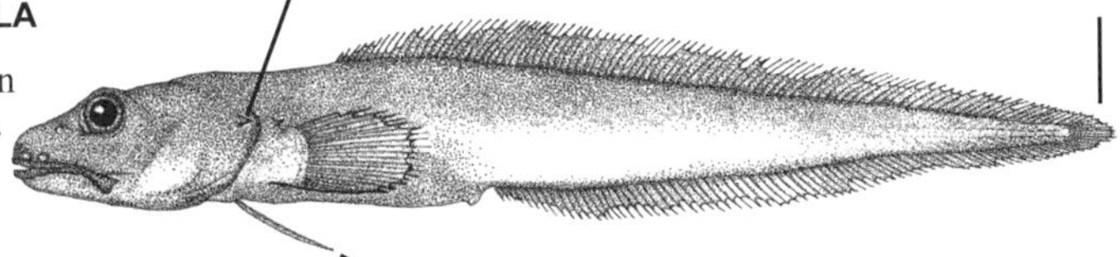

## CODLINGS, Family Moridae, ARROWTAIL, Family Melanonidae, and HAKE, Family Merlucciidae

**HUNDRED-FATHOM CODLING, *Physiculus rastrelliger* Gilbert, 1890.** Family Moridae
Oregon (44°42'N, 124°42'W) (UW 041995) to northern Peru. Common at least from southern California to southern Baja California. Length to 25 cm (9.8 in) TL. Depth: 21–578 m (68–1,896 ft). Uniform dusky. D 8–11 + 52–62; A 56–63; Pect. 24–28; Pelvic 7; LLp 99–105; GR 7–9 + 18–22 = 26–30; Vert. 50–55.

**PACIFIC FLATNOSE, *Antimora microlepis* Bean, 1890.** Family Moridae
North Pacific and tropical mid-North Pacific; Pacific off southern Japan to Sea of Okhotsk to Bering Sea and Gulf of Alaska to Gulf of California. Common from Japan, Sea of Okhotsk, and from Bering Sea to central Baja California. Length to 73.3 cm (28.9 in) TL. Benthopelagic; depth: about 61–3,408 m (200–11,178 ft). Body color variable: gray, blue-gray, or blue-black; pectoral, pelvic, and caudal fins dark. D 4–5 + 50–55; A 36–42; Pect. 18–20; Pelvic 6–7; GRt 15–20; Vert. 57–58. (Formerly FINESCALE CODLING: M&L).

**ARROWTAIL, *Melanonus zugmayeri* Norman, 1930.** Family Melanonidae
Circumglobal; Pacific off Honshu, Japan; Dixon Entrance, northern British Columbia, southern British Columbia, and California to northern Chile (21°05'S, 71°07'W). Uncommon off California. Length to 29.4 cm (11.6 in) TL. Oceanic, mainly meso- and bathypelagic; depth: 0–3,000 m (9,840 ft). Black or gray-black, sometimes with red or pink highlights. D 67–81; A 50–68; Pect. 10–17.

**PACIFIC HAKE, *Merluccius productus* (Ayres, 1855).** Family Merlucciidae
Attu Island, Aleutian Islands (one record), eastern Bering Sea, and Gulf of Alaska to Bahía Magdalena, southern Baja California and Gulf of California to Colombia and Islas Revillagigedos. Reported from continental slope of Bering Sea, but vouchers are needed to confirm continued existence there. Common from southeast Alaska (at least periodically) to southern Baja California. Length to 91.4 cm (36 in) TL. Oceanic and neritic pelagic; depth: 12–1,400 m (39–4,593 ft). Uniform gray to dusky brown with brassy overtones; mouth and gill cavities dark. D I,9–13 + 37–44; A 36–44; Pect. 14–17; Pelvic 6–8; LLs 121–135; GR 3–6 + 13–18 = 18–23; Vert. 52–55. *Merluccius angustimanus* Garman, 1899 is likely a junior synonym.

NOTE: One or 2 dorsal fins and 1 anal fin on these 4 species. The family name for the PACIFIC HAKE, Family Merlucciidae, is correctly spelled with two "i"s, often seen with one "i".

**HUNDRED-FATHOM CODLING**

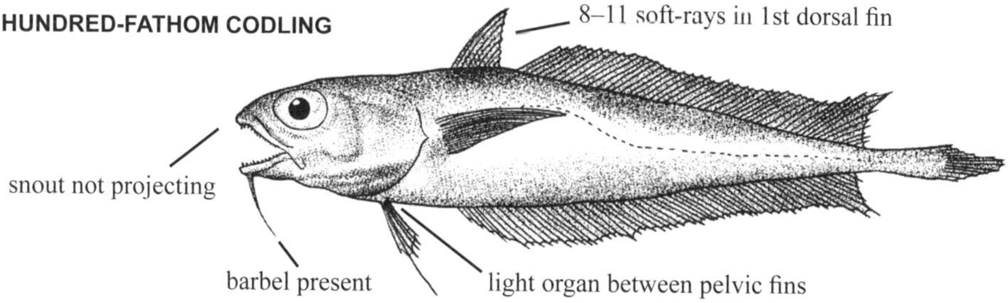


*Pelvic fins filamentous on these 2*

**PACIFIC FLATNOSE**

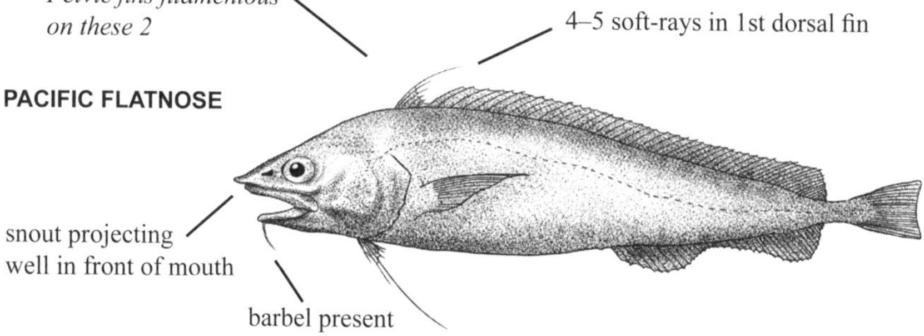


**ARROWTAIL**

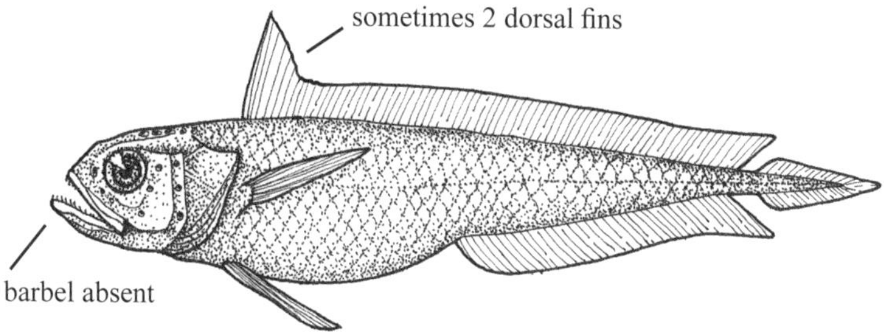


**PACIFIC HAKE**

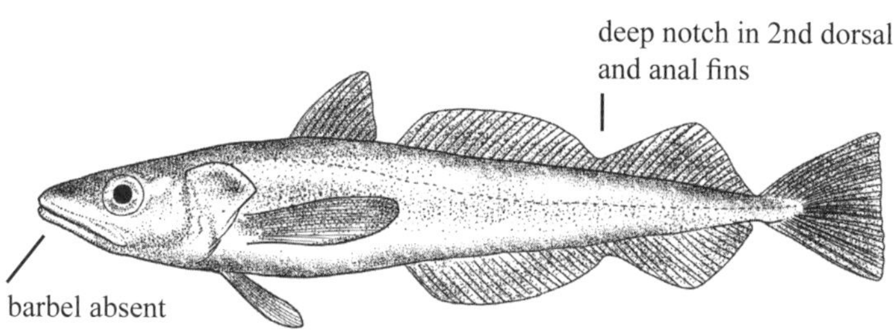

## CODS, Family Gadidae

**WALLEYE POLLOCK, *Gadus chalcogrammus* Pallas, 1814.** Pacific and Atlantic; Seas of Okhotsk and Japan to Bering Sea to off Cape Halkett, Beaufort Sea, and Gulf of Alaska to Carmel, central California. Apparently a separate population off Norway. Common from Sea of Japan north and east to western-most Beaufort Sea and southward to off Washington; rare off California. Length to 95 cm (37.4 in) TL. Generally demersal, also taken pelagically near surface and in midwater; depth: surf zone to 1,280 m (4,198 ft). Gray, yellow, or blue with faint mottling above, gray or white below; brown or yellow spots and blotches on back and sides; dorsal, anal, and caudal fins sometimes white-edged. D 10–13 + 12–18 + 14–25; A 15–24 + 15–23; Pect. 17–22; Pelvic 5–7; GR 5–7 + 28–35 = 33–42; Vert. 48–54. *Theragra finnmarchica* Koefoed, 1956 is a synonym. (Formerly *Theragra chalcogramma* (Pallas, 1814): M&L) (Alternative name PACIFIC POLLOCK).

**PACIFIC COD, *Gadus macrocephalus* Tilesius, 1810.** Arctic-boreal waters of Pacific and Atlantic (Atlantic range now includes the synonymous *Gadus ogac* Richardson, 1837). Isolated population in White Sea. Chukchi Sea across Canada to Gulf of Saint Lawrence. Yellow Sea off Manchuria, China to Bering Sea, Aleutian Islands, and Gulf of Alaska to Carlsbad (33°08'N, 117°35'W), southern California. Common from northern Japan and Sea of Okhotsk to much of Bering Sea to Washington; rare off California. Length to 120 cm (47.2 in) TL. Benthic, also pelagic over deep water; depth: near surface and surf zone to 1,280 m (4,198 ft). Gray to brown above, pale below; greenish to yellow spots and mottling on upper part and sides of body; fins dusky with white edge. D 10–16 + 11–21 + 10–21; A 16–27 + 12–25; Pect. 19–22; Pelvic 6–7; GR 18–23 + 23–24 = 41–43; Vert. 51–56. (Alternative names GRAY COD, TRUE COD).

**PACIFIC TOMCOD, *Microgadus proximus* (Girard, 1854).** Southeastern Bering Sea and eastern Aleutian Islands to Point Sal, central California. Marine and brackish waters. Common from eastern Bering Sea to about Monterey Bay. Length to 37 cm (14.6 in) TL. Depth: near surface (young fish) and surf zone to 275 m (902 ft). Uniform brown, tan, yellow, or olive-green above, white or lightly speckled below; fins brown or gray with dusky tip. D 9–15 + 16–21 + 17–24; A 20–29 + 18–24; Pect. 19; Pelvic 6–7; GR 3–5 + 18–23 = 22–28; Vert. 53–60. (Alternative name TOMCOD).

NOTE: Three dorsal and 2 anal fins on these 3 species.

### WALLEYE POLLOCK

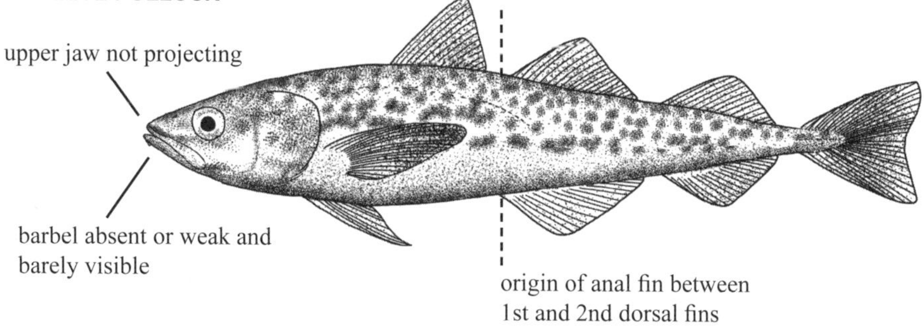


### PACIFIC COD

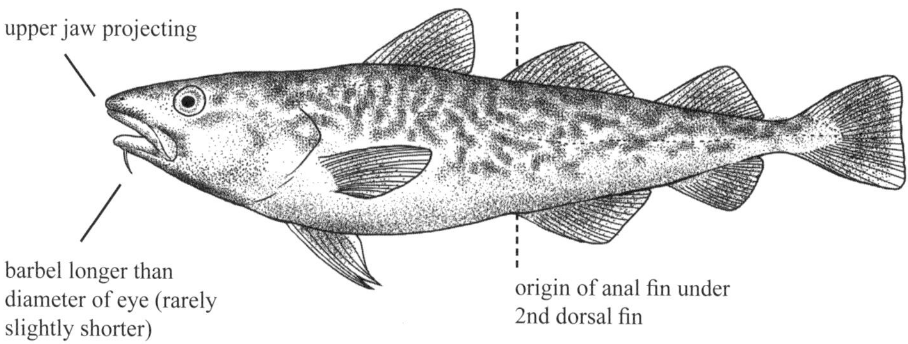


### PACIFIC TOMCOD

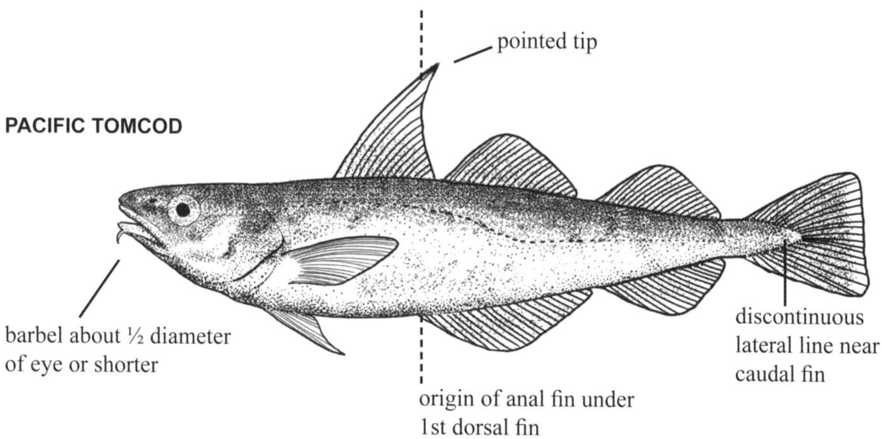

## GRENADIERS, Family Macrouridae

NOTE: Some researchers consider the first 2 elements of the dorsal fin to be spines. However, we assume they are paired elements (like rays) that fuse ontogenetically to form the "spine" and follow Nelson (2006) and assume "no true fin spines." However, despite this we continue the tradition of recording these first 2 elements in Roman numerals. Major source: Iwamoto and Stein (1974). Note that counts of both the 2nd dorsal and the anal fins are rarely of use for species identification because the tip of the tail (and the associated dorsal and anal soft-rays) are often broken off. Also, there are both inner and outer gill rakers on each gill arch; we present counts from the inner set of the 1st gill arch (GR-1 inner), as the outer rakers are difficult to count due to membranous skin folds attaching the upper arm and part of the lower arm to the gill cover. This group also known as RATTAILS.

**SOFTHEAD GRENADIER, *Malacocephalus laevis* (Lowe, 1843).** Circumglobal; Point Sur, central California to Baja California and Chile. Rare off California. Length to 60 cm (23.6 in) TL. Benthopelagic; depth: 140–1,220 m (459–4,003 ft). Maximum depth perhaps of a specimen taken in midwaters over deeper waters. Blue, black, or brown with scales, blue-white without scales; fins dusky. D II,9–13; Pect. 16–22; Pelvic 8–9; GR-1 inner 11–14; Pyloric caeca 50–100+; Gas gland 2. (Alternative name VELVET GRENADIER).

**CALIFORNIA GRENADIER, *Nezumia stelgidolepis* (Gilbert, 1890).** Vancouver Island, British Columbia to northern Chile (26°00'S). Common from northern California to at least through southern California. Length to at least 50 cm (19.7 in) TL. Benthopelagic; depth: 116–1,244 m (380–4,080 ft). Dark brown to black with scales, blue-gray without scales; gill cover, belly, and gill membranes dark; gill and mouth cavities pale with dark areas. D II,9–11 + 138–153; A 123–135; Pect. 20–26; Pelvic 8–11; GR-1 inner 10–11; Pyloric caeca 24–58; Gas gland 2; Vert. 86–90. (Formerly CALIFORNIA RATTAIL: M&L).

**SMOOTH GRENADIER, *Nezumia liolepis* (Gilbert, 1890).** Southern Washington (45°57'N, 124°52'W) to Panama and Gulf of California. Common from about northern California southward through at least southern California and in Gulf of California. Length to about 30 cm (11.8 in) TL. Benthopelagic; depth: 153–1,655 m (502–5,430 ft). Gray-brown with scales, blue-brown to blue without scales; darker blue-black coloration on belly and branchiostegal region. D II,8–11; Pect. 20–25; Pelvic 10–11, rarely 12; GR-1 inner 9–12; Pyloric caeca 24–37; Gas gland 2.

**MIDWATER GRENADIER, *Mesobius berryi* Hubbs & Iwamoto, 1977.** Atlantic, Pacific, and Indian Oceans; eastern North Pacific from southern California to southern Baja California, Hawai'i, and Christmas Island. Rare off southern California. Length to 41 cm (16.1 in) TL. Mainly bathypelagic; depth: surface to 2,700 m (8,858 ft). Head black, midbody black-purple; fins dark. D II,8–10; Pect. 12–14; Pelvic 7–9; GR-1 inner 10–13; Pyloric caeca 12–17; Gas gland 2.

## KEY TO THE GRENADIERS:

Created by Tomio Iwamoto
(Principal source: Iwamoto, 1979)

1a Vent close to anal fin and separated by 0–2 scale rows (or vent surrounded by broad, black, naked ring); branchiostegal rays 6….. 4 (next page)

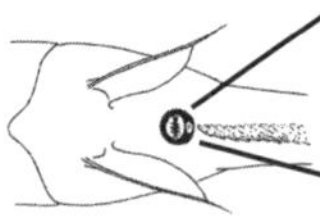


1b Vent separated from anal fin by more than 2 scale rows and usually closer to base of pelvic fins than to anal fin origin; branchiostegal rays 7….. 2 (next page)

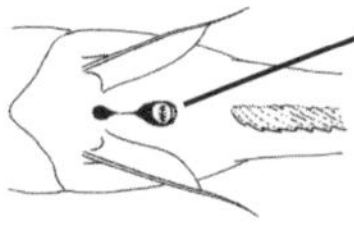

2a Spinous ray of 1st dorsal fin smooth along leading edge; teeth in 2 rows in upper jaw with outer series enlarged; teeth in single row in lower jaw large and spaced; small, finely spined scales cover entire head and body giving velvety feel to skin:

**SOFTHEAD GRENADIER**

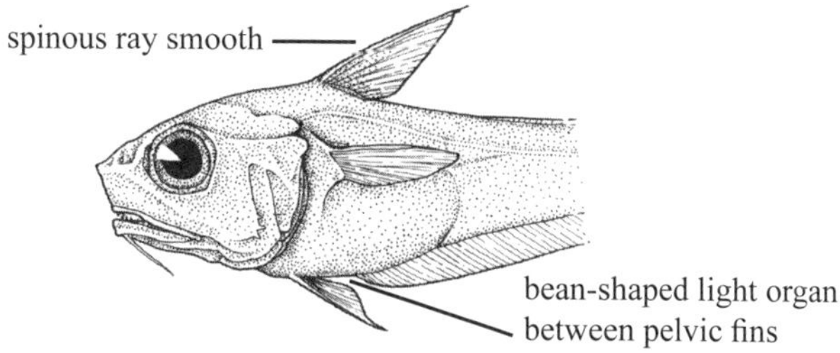


2b Spinous ray of 1st dorsal fin serrated along leading edge (serration lost in some SMOOTH GRENADIER); teeth in wide band in upper jaw with only outer series slightly enlarged; teeth in lower jaw small, in band; broad naked areas lacking scales on underside of snout, scale surface covered with rudimentary to coarse spines or smooth….. 3

3a Spinous ray of 1st dorsal fin strongly serrated; scales adherent, densely covered with sharp, well-developed spines; thick spiny scales forming stout ridge under orbit; terminal and lateral angles of snout tipped with coarse tubercular scales; small but noticeable black naked fossa (shallow pit) between base of pelvic fins:

**CALIFORNIA GRENADIER**

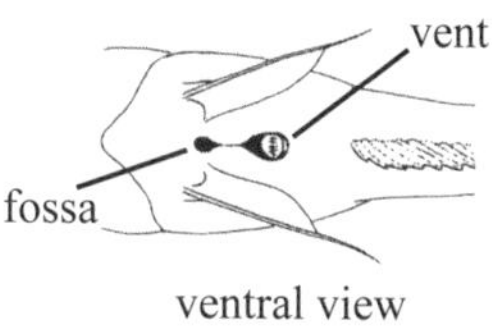


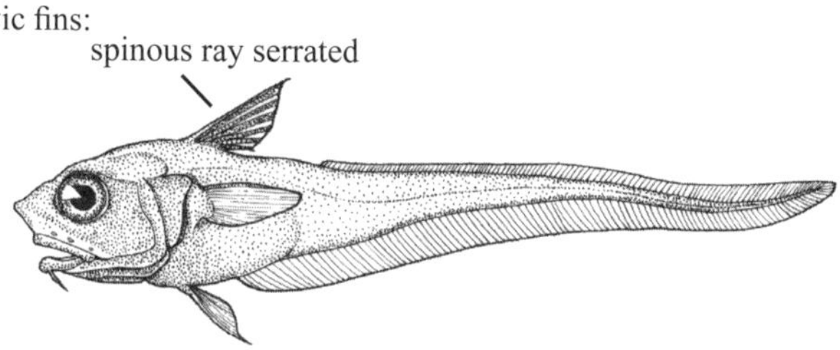


3b Spinous ray of 1st dorsal fin weakly serrated or smooth; scales deciduous, with weak sparse spines or smooth; no stout spiny ridge under orbit, no tubercular scales on snout; no black naked fossa between base of pelvic fins:

**SMOOTH GRENADIER**

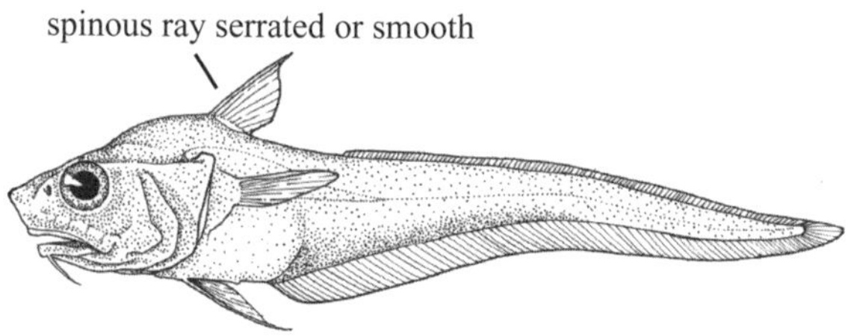


4a *From 1a: vent close to anal fin*
Chin barbel absent; snout smoothly rounded, head without ridges; small scales with longitudinally aligned spines fully cover head, giving striated appearance to surfaces:

**MIDWATER GRENADIER**

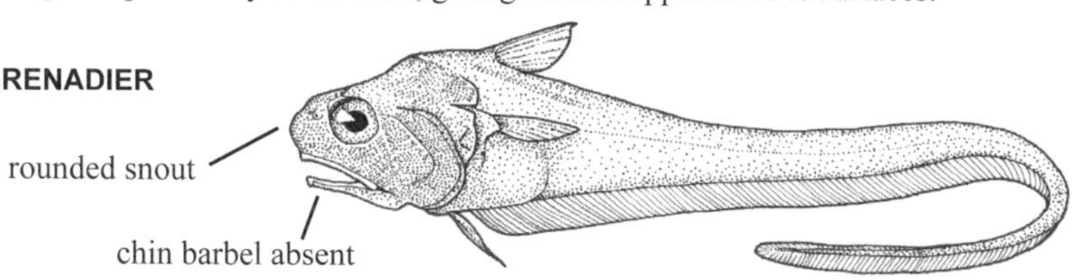


4b Chin barbel present; snout moderately to strongly pointed or blunt, head with weakly to strongly developed ridges; scales variously developed but not giving striated appearance to head surfaces….. 5 (next page)

## GRENADIERS (continued)

**SHOULDERSPOT GRENADIER, *Coelorinchus scaphopsis* (Gilbert, 1890).** Northern California (41°14'N, 124°24'W) to Gulf of California. Common from southern California southward. Length to at least 34 cm (13.4 in) TL. Benthopelagic; depth: 166–414 m (544–1,358 ft). Gray-brown with scales, blue-gray without scales; bluish-black on belly; dark pectoral, pelvic, and dorsal fins and gill cavity. D II,7–9; Pect. 17–20; Pelvic 7; GR-1 inner 1–2 + 8–10 (9–12 total); Pyloric caeca 15–26; Gas gland 4. (Recently and commonly misspelled as *Caelorhynchus* or *Caelorinchus*).

**GIANT GRENADIER, *Coryphaenoides pectoralis* (Gilbert, 1892).** Sea of Okhotsk, northern Honshu, Japan to Kuril Islands, Russia, and Bering Sea to northern Baja California, including Isla Guadalupe (SIO 70-44). Also Falkland Islands, southern Atlantic. Common from Hokkaido to much of Bering Sea and Aleutian Islands and southward to at least northern California. Length to 220 cm (86.6 in) TL. Benthopelagic, young fish bathypelagic; depth: 140–3,500 m (459–11,480 ft). Maximum depth somewhat questionable; most likely deepest-caught fish was taken in midwaters over deeper waters. Freshly caught specimens with intact scales metallic gray to gray-brown (juveniles darker), white to light gray when scales absent; fins, lateral line, lips, and lower surface of snout blackish; swimbladder small. D II (can be extremely small or even buried),7–9 + 121–126; A 131; Pect. 15–21; Pelvic 6–8 (usually 7); GR-1 inner 2 + 10–11, outer 5 + 7 (12–14 total); Pyloric caeca 12–16; Gas gland 2; Precaudal vert. 13–15. (Alternative name SMALL-EYED RATTAIL).

**GHOSTLY GRENADIER, *Coryphaenoides leptolepis* Günther, 1877.** North Atlantic and North Pacific; Japan; west of Prince of Wales Island in Gulf of Alaska to southwest of Cabo San Lucas, southern Baja California. Common at least off Oregon and northern California. Length to 62 cm (24.4 in) TL or more. Benthopelagic; depth: 145–4,138 m (476–13,572 ft). Juveniles (to about 15 cm, 5.9 in) dark brown with lips, head, abdomen, and fins black; adults brown, but denuded specimens whitish overall. D II,8–10; Pect. 18–22; Pelvic 9–11; GR-1 inner 10–13; Pyloric caeca 11; Gas gland 6; Precaudal vert. 12. This account includes *Coryphaenoides* (*Chalinura*) *liocephalus* (Günther, 1887) in the synonymy of *C. leptolepis.* The two forms could be distinct (although currently this is not considered likely), in which case *C. liocephalus* would be the name for the Pacific species; see Mecklenburg et al. (2002).

**POPEYE GRENADIER, *Coryphaenoides cinereus* (Gilbert, 1896).** Northern Japan and southern Sea of Okhotsk to Navarin Canyon, Bering Sea to southern California (33°24'N). Common off Japan, Sea of Okhotsk, Bering Sea, and Gulf of Alaska; rare in California. Length to 68 cm (26.8 in) TL. Benthopelagic; depth: 135–2,832 m (443–9,291 ft). Reported from trawl nets towed as deep as 3,480 m (11,417 ft), but maximum depth may represent midwater catch over deeper bottom. Light grayish-brown (scales easily lost in this species and denuded fish ivory-white); fins blackish to dusky; mouth and gill cavities black. D II,10–12, rarely 14; Pect. 17–23; Pelvic 8–10, usually 9; GR-1 inner 1–2 + 10–13 (12–14 total); Pyloric caeca 5–7; Precaudal vert. 13–14.

5a Long spinous ray of 1st dorsal fin smooth along leading edge; snout strongly pointed; sharp, prominent ridge of modified scales running under orbit from tip of snout to angle of preopercle, ending posteriorly in a sharp point; teardrop-shaped black, naked fossa between and slightly forward of base of pelvic fins:

**SHOULDERSPOT GRENADIER**

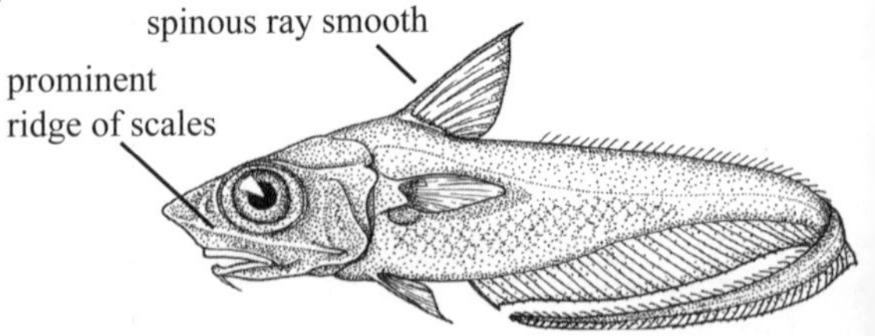


5b (next page)

5b Long spinous ray of 1st dorsal fin serrated along leading edge; snout not strongly pointed; no sharp ridge of scales from snout tip to angle of preopercle; naked fossa lacking….. 6

6a Pelvic fin soft-rays 6–8, usually 7, length less than half of HL; 10–11 scale rows below middle of 1st dorsal fin to, but not including, lateral line scales:

**GIANT GRENADIER**

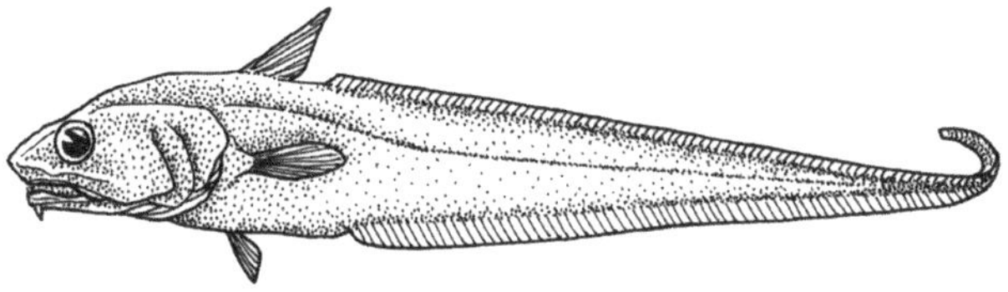

6b Pelvic fin soft-rays 8–11, length more than half of HL; 6–11 scale rows below middle of 1st dorsal fin to, but not including, lateral line scales….. 7

7a Orbits small, 5 or more times into HL; snout low, blunt, scarcely protruding beyond upper jaw; dorsal profile with prominent dip above orbit, then rises steeply to form an arched humpbacked nape; sensory pores on head large and prominent:

**GHOSTLY GRENADIER**

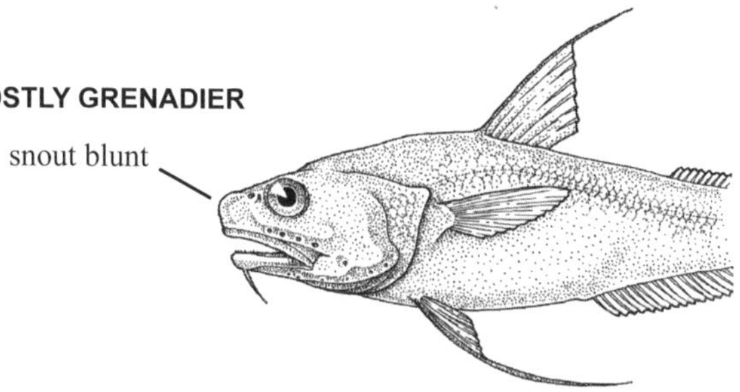


7b Orbits moderate to large, less than 5 times into HL; snout pointed, protruding well beyond upper jaw; no prominent dip in dorsal profile above orbit; head sensory pores small, inconspicuous….. 8

8a Barbel 2–8% of HL; orbit diameter 27–34% of HL; interorbital space 24–30% of HL; scales deciduous:

**POPEYE GRENADIER**

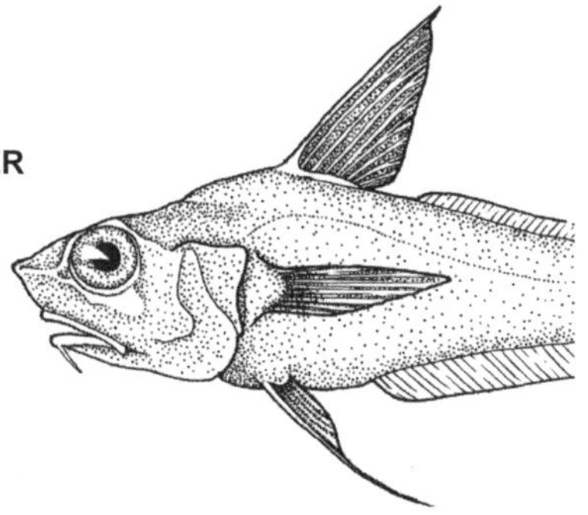

8b Barbel 6–19% of HL; orbit diameter 22–31% of HL; interorbital space 18–27% of HL; scales relatively adherent….. 9 (next page)

## GRENADIERS (continued)

**PACIFIC GRENADIER, *Coryphaenoides acrolepis* (Bean, 1884).** Sea of Okhotsk and Pacific off Japan to southern Bering Sea and Aleutian Islands to Isla Guadalupe, central Baja California; southwest Atlantic near Falkland Islands. Common from Japan and Sea of Okhotsk throughout much of Bering Sea and southward to at least northern Baja California. Length to 154.1 cm (60.7 in) TL. Bentho- and bathypelagic; depth: typically 600–2,500 m (1,968–8,202 ft), possibly as shallow as 31 m (102 ft) and as deep as 3,700 m (12,136 ft). The maximum depth may represent fish taken in midwater over deeper bottom, true maximum depth may be around 1,500 m (4,920 ft). Grayish-brown to dark chocolate with scales, brown-gray without scales; peritoneum, orbit, mouth, and gill cavity black. D II,9–11 + 109–111; A 103–105; Pect. 19–22; Pelvic 8 (rarely 9); GR-1 inner 2 + 10–11; Pyloric caeca 12–14; Gas gland 4. (Formerly PACIFIC RATTAIL: M&L) (Alternative name ROUGHSCALE RATTAIL).

**THREADFIN GRENADIER, *Coryphaenoides filifer* (Gilbert, 1896).** Sea of Okhotsk, off Hokkaido, Japan; Bering Sea and Aleutian Islands to Monterey Bay, central California. Although Ambrose (in Moser, 1996) gives 32°00'N (southern California), this evidently is a generalization from Matarese et al. (1989) and not based on a specific record. Rare off California. Length to 140 cm (55.1 in) TL. Benthopelagic; depth: 374–3,658 m (1,227–11,998 ft). Maximum depth may represent midwater catch over deeper bottom. Body dark brown or light gray with scales, white with blue tint without scales; fins, nostrils, undersides of snout, lips, and gill membranes bluish to black. D II,8–14, usually 12 or 13; Pect. 18–23, usually 19–22; Pelvic 9–10; GR-1 inner 12–14; Pyloric caeca 8–12; Gas gland 4. (Alternative name FILAMENTED RATTAIL).

9a Pelvic fin soft-rays 8, rarely 9; barbel 11–19% of HL; outer pelvic fin soft-ray 50–70% of HL; 1st dorsal fin soft-rays 9–11:

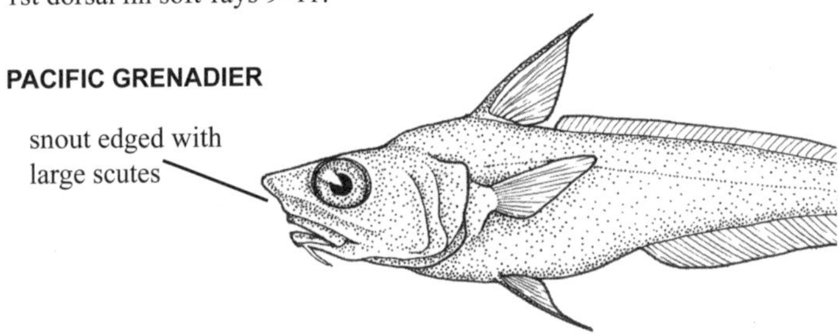


9b Pelvic fin soft-rays 9–10; barbel 6–13% of HL; outer pelvic fin soft-ray 74–135% of HL; 1st dorsal fin soft-rays 11–14:

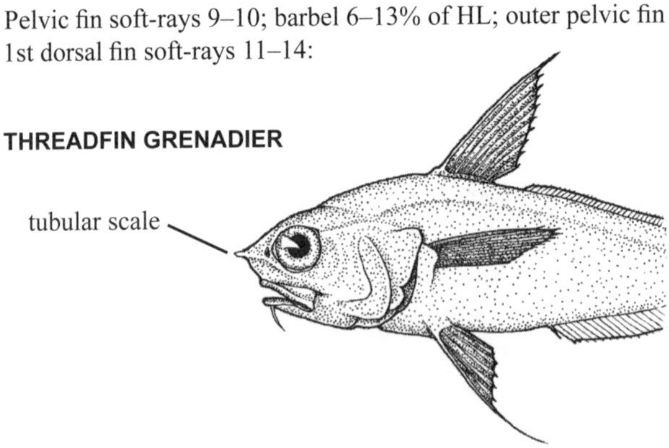

# MILKFISH, Family Chanidae, CHIHUIL, Family Ariidae, and SAURY, Family Scomberesocidae

**MILKFISH, *Chanos chanos* (Forsskål, 1775).** Family Chanidae
Pacific and Indian Oceans; San Pedro, southern California to Callao, Peru, including Islas Galápagos. Rare in southern California. Length to 180 cm (70.9 in) TL. Juveniles estuarine, adults marine; depth: 0–20 m (66 ft). Silvery to silvery blue-green on back; inner surface of pectoral and pelvic fins black; caudal fin dark. D 13–17; A 9–11; Pelvic 9–12; LLs 78–90; GR 147–160 + 107–165.

**CHIHUIL, *Bagre panamensis* (Gill, 1863).** Family Ariidae
Off Santa Ana River, southern California to Isla Lobos de Tierra, Peru, including Gulf of California. Rare in southern California; common from Bahía Magdalena, southern Baja California into tropics. Length to about 57 cm (22.4 in). Depth: 3 m or less to 177 m (10–584 ft). Back blue or gray with brassy sheen, silvery sides and belly. D I,7; A 25–30; Pect. I,12–13; GR 5–7 + 12–14. (Alternative name CHIHUIL SEA CATFISH).

**PACIFIC SAURY, *Cololabis saira* (Brevoort, 1856).** Family Scomberesocidae
Yellow Sea to western Bering Sea; southeastern Bering Sea, Pacific Ocean south of Aleutian Islands, and offshore Gulf of Alaska to Islas Revillagigedo, Mexico, including Gulf of California. Common as far northward as about Kuril Islands, Russia, in the western Pacific and, in eastern Pacific, common from Vancouver Island to at least southern Baja California. Length to about 44 cm (17.3 in) TL. Oceanic and neritic epipelagic; depth: surface and surf zone to 295 m (968 ft). Bright blue or green on back, metallic silver on sides. D 9–12 + 4–6 finlets; A 12–15 + 4–7 finlets; Pect. 12–15; Pelvic 6–7; scales above midline 120–129; GR 8 + 32–43 = 32–51; Vert. 62–69.

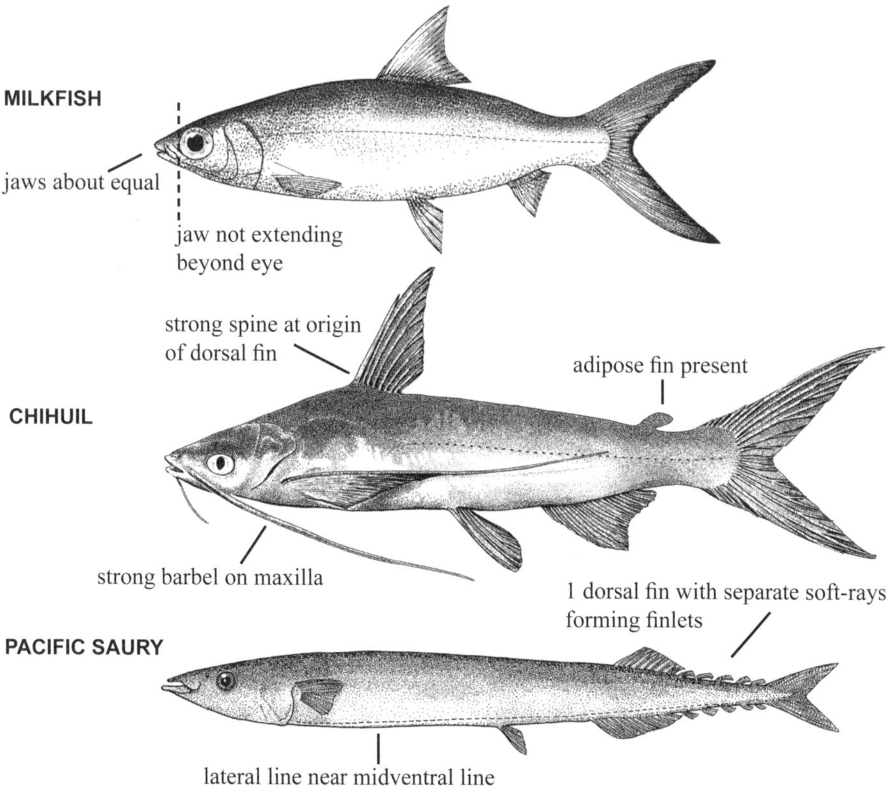

## FLYINGFISHES, Family Exocoetidae, NEEDLEFISH, Family Belonidae, and HALFBEAKS, Family Hemiramphidae

**SHARPCHIN FLYINGFISH, *Fodiator acutus* (Valenciennes, 1847).** Family Exocoetidae
Circumglobal, mostly in tropical waters; off Point Conception (34°12'N, 120°57'W) and Goleta, southern California to Chile, including Gulf of California and Islas Galápagos. Uncommon off southern California; common at least as far northward as southern Baja California. Length to 25 cm (9.8 in) TL. Neritic and oceanic; depth: surface, usually in coastal waters and sometimes in surf zone. Dark blue above, silver below; dorsal fin black; pectoral fins gray and black. D 9–11; A 9–12; Pect. 12–14; Pelvic 6; Predorsal scales 24–26; GR 7–8 + 21–26; Vert. 39–41. (Formerly *Fodiator rostratus* (Günther, 1866)) (Alternative name PACIFIC FLYINGFISH).

**BLACKWING FLYINGFISH, *Hirundichthys rondeletii* (Valenciennes, 1847).** Family Exocoetidae
Circumglobal; northern Baja California ("100–200 miles S of San Diego, found on deck in the morning"; SIO 57-175) to Chile, including Islas Galápagos. Length to about 30 cm (11.8 in) TL. Oceanic and neritic; depth: surface. Body dark blue above, silvery below; dorsal and caudal fins grayish. Paired fins of juveniles black. D 10–12; A 11–12.

**BLOTCHWING FLYINGFISH, *Cheilopogon heterurus* (Rafinesque, 1810).** Family Exocoetidae
Circumglobal in tropical waters; Santa Catalina Island, southern California to Chile. Rare off southern California. Length to 34.8 cm (13.7 in) SL. Oceanic and neritic; depth: surface. Blue back, sides silvery; pectoral fins with light band in center bordered by dusky-gray, black posteriorly. D 12–15; A 8–10; Pect. 16–18; Predorsal scales 28–41; GR 5–7 + 15–17; Vert. 47–49. (*Cypselurus hubbsi* (Parin, 1961) is a junior synonym) (Formerly *Cypselurus heterurus* (Rafinesque, 1810): M&L).

**SMALLHEAD FLYINGFISH, *Cheilopogon pinnatibarbatus* (Bennett, 1831).** Family Exocoetidae
Circumglobal; in western Pacific as far north as southern Kuril Islands, Russia; Astoria, Oregon to southern Baja California and into Gulf of California. Common from southern California southward. Length to 48 cm (18.9 in) TL. Oceanic and nearshore; depth: surface to perhaps 10 m (33 ft). Blue or blue-gray above, silvery on sides and belly; pectorals uniform dusky with clear edge. D 9–13; A 9–12; Pect. 14–15; Pelvic 6; Predorsal scales 47–50; Midlateral scales 64–70; GR 4–8 + 13–16; Vert. 48–51. (Formerly CALIFORNIA FLYINGFISH, *Cypselurus californicus* (Cooper, 1863): M&L).

**CALIFORNIA NEEDLEFISH, *Strongylura exilis* (Girard, 1854).** Family Belonidae
San Francisco, northern California to northern Chile, including Islas Galápagos and Gulf of California. Patchily common as far north as Marina del Rey, southern California, more common in warmer waters to the south. Length to 91.4 cm (36 in) TL. Nearshore; depth: surface and intertidal to 100 m (328 ft). Greenish-blue on back, dark blue stripe on flank, silver on sides and belly; occasionally caudal and dorsal fins red; fins and eye yellowish; teeth green. D 12–17; A 15–20; Pect. 11–13; Pelvic 5–6; GR none; Vert. 67–74.

**RIBBON HALFBEAK, *Euleptorhamphus viridis* (van Hasselt, 1823).** Family Hemiramphidae
Tropical and subtropical waters of Pacific and Indian Oceans; Japan; southern California to Easter Island, including lower Gulf of California and Islas Galápagos. Rare in southern California. Length to 53 cm (20.9 in) TL. Epipelagic; depth: at and near surface. Greenish above, silver below. D 21–25; A 21–23; Pect. 8–9; Pelvic 6–9; Predorsal scales 53–72; GR 9–14 + 23–32; Vert. 70–74. (Formerly *Euleptorhamphus longirostris* Cuvier, 1829: M&L).

# KEY TO THE FLYINGFISHES, NEEDLEFISH, and HALFBEAKS:

Revised by Julianne Kalman Passarelli
(Principal source: Miller & Lea, 1972)

1a Tip of pectoral fins does not reach pelvic fin base….. 5 (Halfbeaks and Needlefish)

1b Tip of pectoral fins extends beyond pelvic fin base….. 2 (Flyingfishes)

juvenile flyingfish may have elongated lower jaw

2a Pectoral fins not extending beyond insertion of dorsal fin; snout longer than eye diameter:

**SHARPCHIN FLYINGFISH**

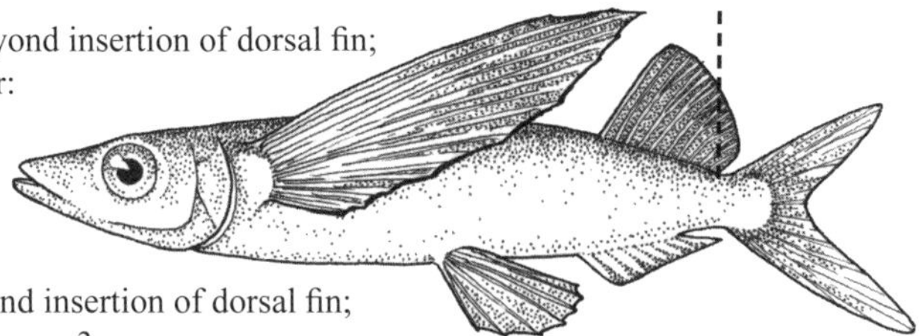

2b Pectoral fins extend well beyond insertion of dorsal fin; snout shorter than eye diameter….. 3

3a Second pectoral fin soft-ray unbranched:

**BLACKWING FLYINGFISH**
(not illustrated; body shape as in 4b)

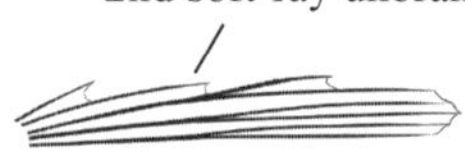


3b Second pectoral fin soft-ray branched….. 4

4a Posterior portion of pectoral fin black; predorsal scales 28–41:

**BLOTCHWING FLYINGFISH**
(same body shape as in 4b)

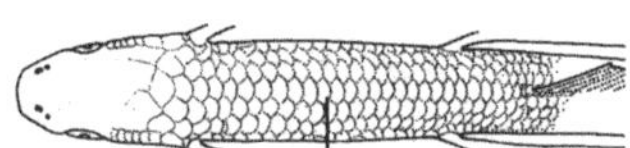


4b Pectoral fin evenly dusky; predorsal scales 47–50:

**SMALLHEAD FLYINGFISH**

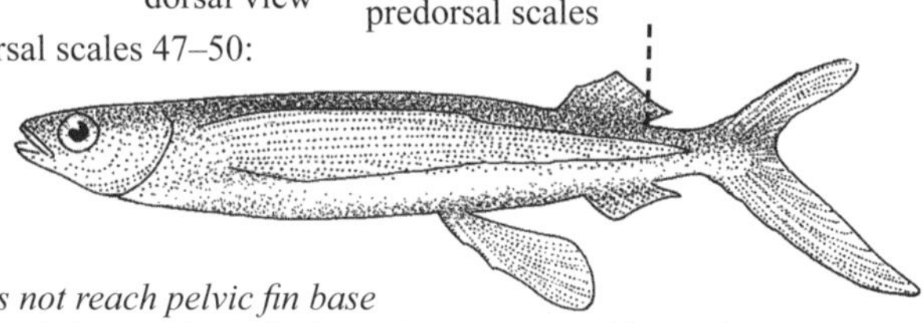

5a *From 1a: tip of pectoral fins does not reach pelvic fin base*
Upper and lower jaw of equal length (except juveniles); teeth on upper and lower jaws:

**CALIFORNIA NEEDLEFISH**

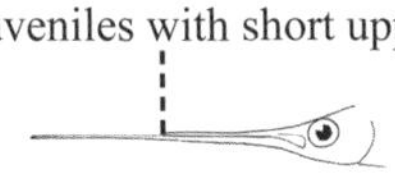


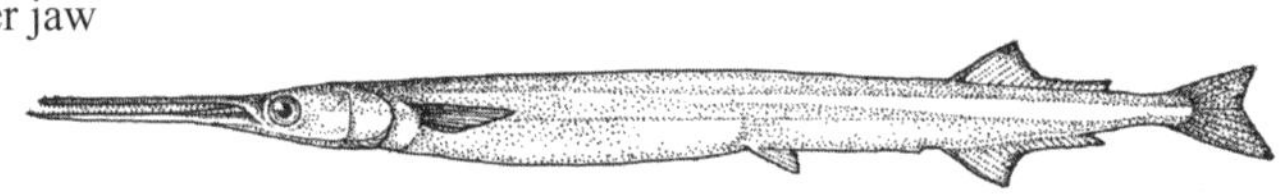

5b Lower jaw extending well beyond upper jaw; no obvious teeth on jaws….. 6

6a Pectoral fins about twice as long as head (excluding jaw); lower jaw more than twice as long as head:

**RIBBON HALFBEAK**

6b Pectoral fins about equal to or shorter than head (excluding jaw); lower jaw less than 2 times HL….. 7 (next page)

## FLYINGFISHES, NEEDLEFISH, and HALFBEAKS (continued)

**LONGFIN HALFBEAK, *Hemiramphus saltator* Gilbert & Starks, 1904.** Family HEMIRAMPHIDAE
Tropical eastern Pacific; Isla Cedros, central Baja California (LACM 32045-12) to northern Chile including Gulf of California and Islas Galápagos. Length to 55 cm (21.7 in) TL. Epipelagic; depth: near surface to 27 m (89 ft). Dusky-brown or blue above, sides silver. D 12–15; A 11–13; Pect. 10–12; Pelvic 6; Midlateral scales 53–61; GR 26–27 (lower limb); Vert. 54–58. M&L reported this species from California. We can find no documentation for this record.

**CALIFORNIA HALFBEAK, *Hyporhamphus rosae* (Jordan & Gilbert, 1880).** Family HEMIRAMPHIDAE
Tropical eastern Pacific; Marina del Rey, southern California to Gulf of California and Bahía Nonura, Peru. Historically, common in San Diego Bay, now less common; common along much of Baja California coast and in Gulf of California. Length to 20 cm (7.9 in) TL. Nearshore; depth: at and near surface, including intertidal; enters fresh water. Greenish back with silvery stripes along sides. D 14; A 14; Pect. 9–11; Pelvic 6; GRt 28–36; Vert. 47–50.

**PACIFIC SILVERSTRIPE HALFBEAK, *Hyporhamphus naos* Banford & Collette, 2001.**
Family HEMIRAMPHIDAE
San Diego, southern California to Paita, Peru, including Islas Galápagos and Gulf of California. The Galápagos fish may be an undescribed species. Rare in southern California; common from central Baja California into tropics. Length to 31 cm (12.2 in) TL. Inshore, coastal, and estuarine waters; depth: near surface to perhaps 30 m (99 ft). Blue-green above, silver below. D 12–16; A 15–17; Predorsal scales 35–39; GRt 26–39; Vert. 51–52. (Formerly SILVERSTRIPE HALFBEAK, *Hyporhamphus unifasciatus* (Ranzani, 1841): M&L).

7a Origin of anal fin behind origin of dorsal fin; anal fin soft-rays 11–13:

**LONGFIN HALFBEAK**

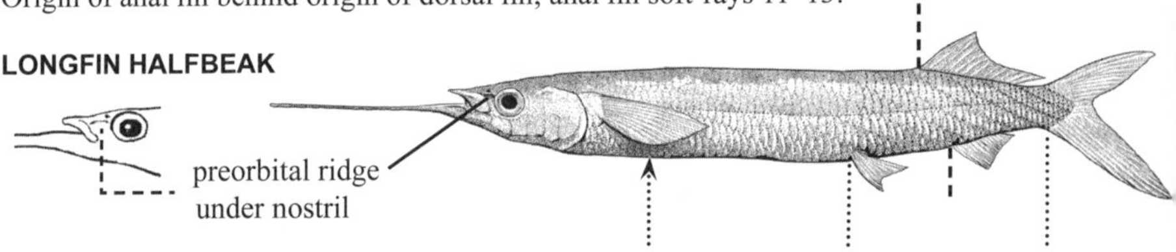


7b Origin of anal fin under origin of dorsal fin;
anal fin soft-rays 14 or more….. 8

8a Length of lower jaw 1.2–1.6 times HL; scales lacking on base of dorsal and anal fins:

**CALIFORNIA HALFBEAK**

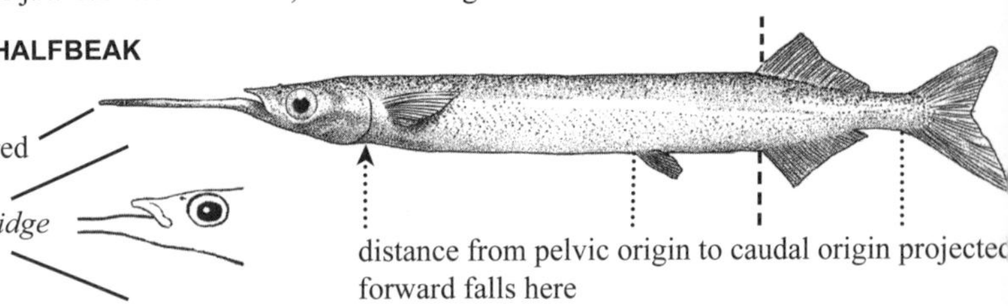


8b Length of lower jaw 0.8–1.3 times HL;
scales present on base of dorsal and anal fins:

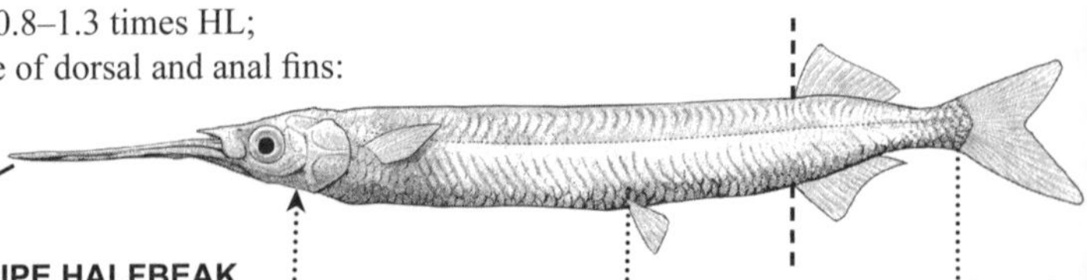


**PACIFIC SILVERSTRIPE HALFBEAK**

# LIVEBEARERS, Family Poeciliidae and TOPMINNOWS, Family Fundulidae

**SAILFIN MOLLY, *Poecilia latipinna* (Lesueur, 1821).** Family POECILIIDAE
Native to southern Atlantic United States and Gulf of Mexico, now introduced into much of warmer Pacific Rim. Along California coast, known from Ballona Marsh (Los Angeles County), intertidal wetlands of San Diego Bay, southern California, and other sloughs and estuaries in Ventura, Los Angeles, and San Diego Counties. Length to 15 cm (5.9 in) TL. Shallow marine waters and fresh waters. Colors highly variable: often brown on back merging to iridescent blue or pink on sides and white belly, with 5–6 horizontal rows of dark spots on sides interspersed with red, blue, or green spots; dorsal fin pale blue, with rows of black spots and yellow border. Females more faintly-colored and marked; some males black or checkered. D 13–16; A 9–10; Pect. 13; Pelvic 6; LLs 23–28.

**WESTERN MOSQUITOFISH, *Gambusia affinis* (Baird & Girard, 1853).** Family POECILIIDAE
Native to tributaries running into Gulf of Mexico from southern Illinois to eastern Mexico, introduced worldwide for mosquito control. Length to 6 cm (2.4 in). Upper and lower salinity and freshwater margins of estuarine areas throughout California. Gray or olive. D 6; A 9; Pect. 12–14; Pelvic 6; Midlateral scales 29–32.

## KEY TO THE LIVEBEARERS and TOPMINNOWS:

Created by Camm C. Swift
(Principal sources: Moyle, 2002; Boschung & Mayden, 2004)

1a Three or more longitudinal rows of dark spots dorsally and laterally on body, occasionally partly or completely black; dorsal fin origin anterior to pelvic fin origin (in males only):

**SAILFIN MOLLY**

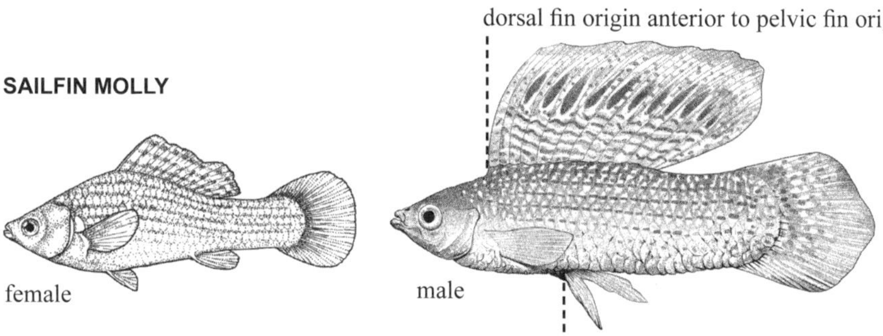


1b Fewer than 3 longitudinal rows of dark spots dorsally and laterally on body; dorsal fin origin posterior to pelvic fin origin….. 2

2a Dorsal fin origin posterior to anal fin origin; 3rd anal fin soft-ray unbranched and modified into enlarged tubular intromittent organ in adult males:

**WESTERN MOSQUITOFISH**

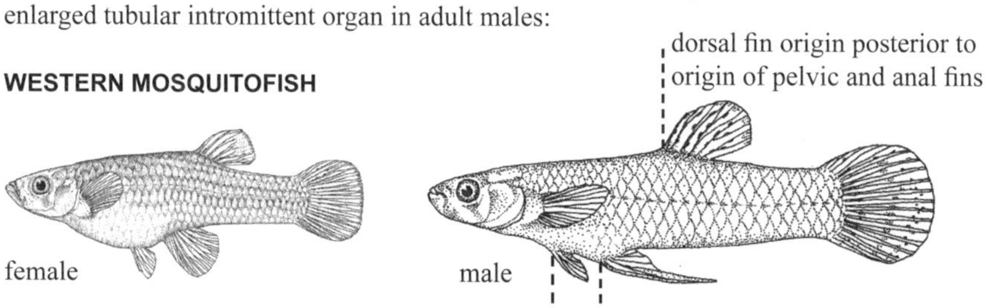


2b Dorsal fin origin anterior to anal fin origin; 3rd anal fin soft-ray branched and unmodified in males (anal fin may be elongated in males but not modified)….. 3 (next page)

# LIVEBEARERS and TOPMINNOWS (continued)

**CALIFORNIA KILLIFISH, *Fundulus parvipinnis* Girard, 1854.** Family FUNDULIDAE

Morro Bay, central California to tip of southern Baja California. Common, at least historically, in Morro Bay; common from southern California to Bahía Magdalena, southern Baja California. Length to 13.3 cm (5.2 in) TL. Inshore in estuaries, coastal lagoons, and shallow bays. Olive-green above, yellowish-brown below; breeding males dark brown on back with yellow belly, pelvic and pectoral fins, and lower part of head. D 10–15; A 11–13; Pect. 16–21; Pelvic 6; Midlateral scales 31–37; GR 0–1 + 7–10 = 7–11; Vert. 34–37. (Formerly Cyprinodontidae: M&L).

**BLUEFIN KILLIFISH, *Lucania goodei* Jordan, 1880.** Family FUNDULIDAE

Native from South Carolina to Alabama, introduced to a few estuarine locations in southern California. Length to 5 cm (2 in) TL. Body green or yellowish on back, light or yellow on belly; black stripe along side from chin to caudal fin base; base of dorsal and anal fins dark; mature males with many bright colors on fins. D 8–11; A 9–11; Pect 12–13; Midlateral scales 25–27 (incompletely pored).

**RAINWATER KILLIFISH, *Lucania parva* (Baird & Girard, 1855).** Family FUNDULIDAE

Native to Atlantic Ocean and Gulf of Mexico, introduced to brackish portions of Yaquina Bay, Oregon; Suisan and San Francisco Bays, northern California; a few estuarine locations in southern California. Length to 6.2 cm (2.3 in) TL. Primarily freshwater, along with brackish bays and estuaries. See key for colors. D 9–14; A 8–13; Pect. 10–15; Pelvic 4–7; Midlateral scales 25–27 (incompletely pored); GRt 4–12. (Formerly Cyprinodontidae: M&L).

3a Body with prominent dark bars against gray or pale background; midlateral scales 31–37; breeding males black over yellow: **CALIFORNIA KILLIFISH**

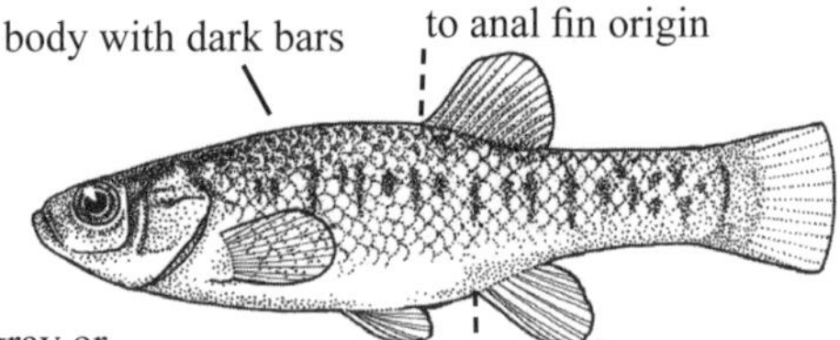


3b Body without prominent dark bars against gray or pale background; midlateral scales 25–27; breeding males blue, red, orange, or yellow….. 4

4a Body with black midlateral stripe; anterior chin black; males with blue dorsal fin; black horizontal band across middle of dorsal fin: **BLUEFIN KILLIFISH**

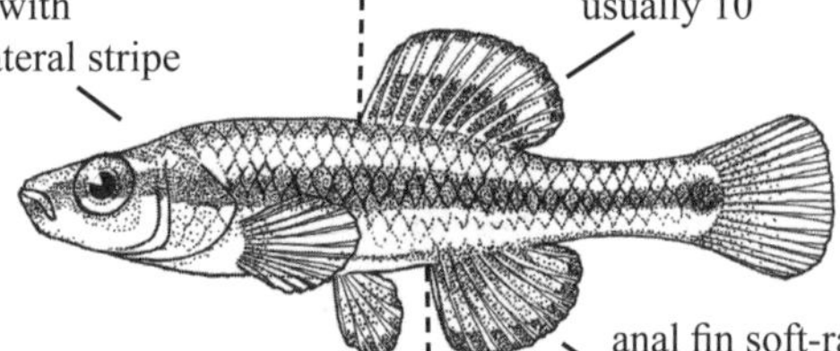


4b Body lacking midlateral stripe; chin not darkened; males with yellow to orange dorsal fin; black horizontal band on dorsal fin lacking: **RAINWATER KILLIFISH**

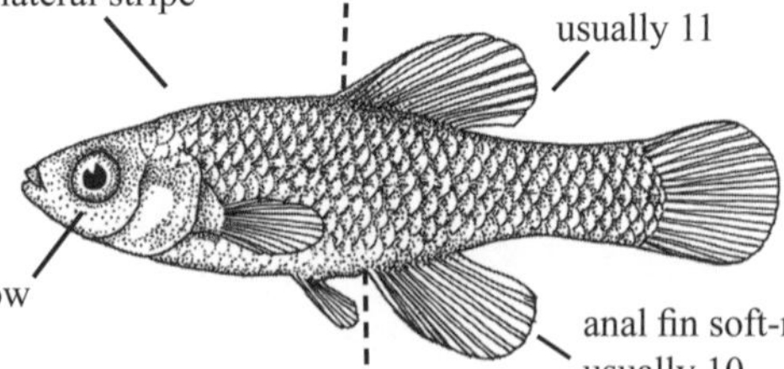

## MULLETS, Family Mugulidae

**STRIPED MULLET, *Mugil cephalus* Linnaeus, 1758.** Circumglobal; Japan, Sea of Okhotsk, and southern Kuril Islands, Russia; Humboldt Bay, northern California to Chile and Islas Galápagos. Common as far north as southern California during all years; during some periods common as far north as San Francisco Bay and Delta region. Length to 135 cm (53.1 in) TL. Coastal, including estuaries and fresh water; depth: in ocean, intertidal to 122 m (400 ft). Gray or olive on back, silvery belly; sides with dark stripes; small black blotch at upper base of pectoral fin. D IV–V + I,6–8; A II–III,7–9; Midlateral scales 37–41; Vert. 24. (Alternative names FLATHEAD MULLET, GREY MULLET).

**WHITE MULLET, *Mugil curema* Valenciennes, 1836.** Atlantic and Pacific Oceans; Mission Creek, Santa Barbara County, southern California (LACM 58223-1) to Chile, including Gulf of California and Islas Galápagos. Occasionally common in some southern California backwaters; common from at least central Baja California into tropics. Length to 91 cm (35.8 in) TL. Shallow marine and brackish waters; depth: intertidal to 25 m (82 ft). Olive to bluish on back, silvery on sides, and white below; body striping none or faint; small black blotch at upper base of pectoral fin; caudal fin yellowish with black posterior margin. D IV + I,8; A II–III,9–10; Pect. 17; LLs 35–40; Vert. 24. We note that Britzke et al., (2019) determined that fish identified as "*Mugil curema*" from the eastern Pacific are, in fact, *Mugil setosus* Gilbert, 1892. Their work, and those of Menezes et al., (2015), limit the geographic range of *M. curema* to the western south Atlantic.

STRIPED MULLET

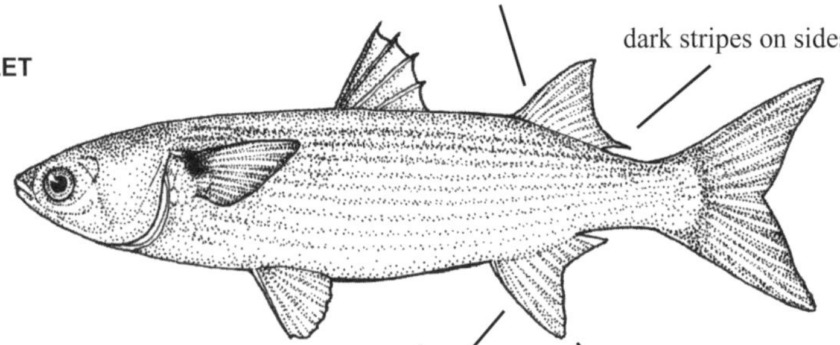


WHITE MULLET

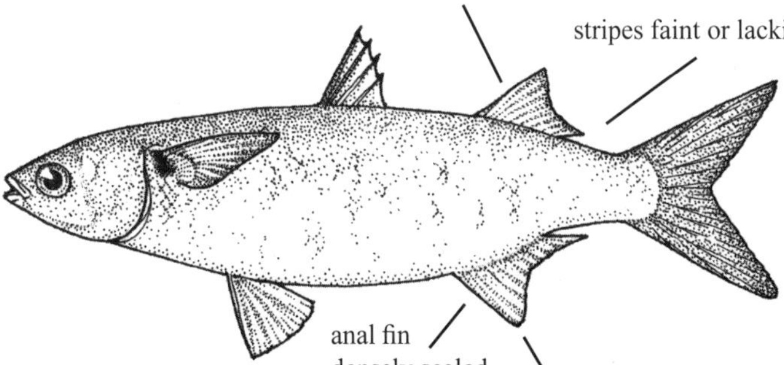

## NEW WORLD SILVERSIDES, Family Atherinopsidae

NOTE: Formerly with Old World silversides in the family Atherinidae, the New World silversides were removed and placed in their own family, Atherinopsidae.

**MISSISSIPPI SILVERSIDE, *Menidia audens* Hay, 1882.** Native from about Maine to Veracruz, Mexico (but there is likely confusion with INLAND SILVERSIDE, *Menidia beryllina* (Cope, 1867)), introduced to Pacific Coast, now widespread in San Francisco Bay and Delta, also in coastal southern California. Length to 15 cm (5.9 in) TL. Pale yellowish or yellow-green above, silver stripe along side. D IV–V + I,8–9; A I,16–18; LLs 35–45. California specimens sometimes referred to as *M. beryllina*.

**JACKSMELT, *Atherinopsis californiensis* Girard, 1854.** Yaquina Bay, Oregon to at least Bahía Magdalena, southern Baja California, including western and northeastern Gulf of California. Common from at least Coos Bay, Oregon to at least Bahía Magdalena, southern Baja California. Length to 48.6 cm (19.1 in) TL. Nearshore; depth: surface (SIO 46-76) and surf zone to at least 29 m (95 ft); also found in hypersaline ponds. Greenish-blue above, silvery on sides with midline stripe. D V–IX + I,11–14; A I,21–26; Pect. 15–17; Pelvic I,5; LLs about 75; GRt 18–44; Vert. 50–54. (Formerly Atherinidae: M&L).

**TOPSMELT, *Atherinops affinis* (Ayres, 1860).** Near Sooke Harbour, Vancouver Island, British Columbia to Gulf of California; not in central or southern Gulf of California. Common at least from northern Oregon to Bahía Magdalena, southern Baja California and in northern Gulf of California. Marine and brackish waters. Length to 38.8 cm (15.3 in) TL. Nearshore; depth: surface and intertidal to 26 m (85 ft). Bright green or blue above, silvery below with midline stripe; often with yellow spots on sides. D V–IX + I,8–14; A I,19–25; Pect. 13–15; Pelvic I,5; LLs 63–65; GR 4–8 + 21–34 = 27–41; Vert. 44–52. (Formerly Atherinidae: M&L).

**CALIFORNIA GRUNION, *Leuresthes tenuis* (Ayres, 1860).** Tomales Bay, northern California to Bahía Magdalena, southern Baja California. Predictably common from southern California to at least Bahía Tortugas, southern Baja California. Periodic runs in Monterey Bay, San Francisco Bay, and Tomales Bay. Length to 19 cm (7.5 in) TL. Depth: surf zone to 18 m (60 ft). Greenish above, silver or silver-blue on sides, with lateral stripe. D III–VII + I,8–10; A I,20–24; Pect. 12–15; Pelvic I,5; LLs 75; GR 5–7 + 23–29 = 30–35; Vert. 47–50. (Formerly Atherinidae: M&L).

## KEY TO THE NEW WORLD SILVERSIDES:
Revised by Camm C. Swift
(Principal sources: Miller & Lea, 1972; Swift et al., 2014)

1a Depressed pelvic fin usually extends 70–90% of distance to vent; pelvic fin length 66% or more of pectoral fin length; dorsolateral scales large and outlined with 1 row of finely divided pigment cells; lateral line scales 35–45:

**MISSISSIPPI SILVERSIDE**

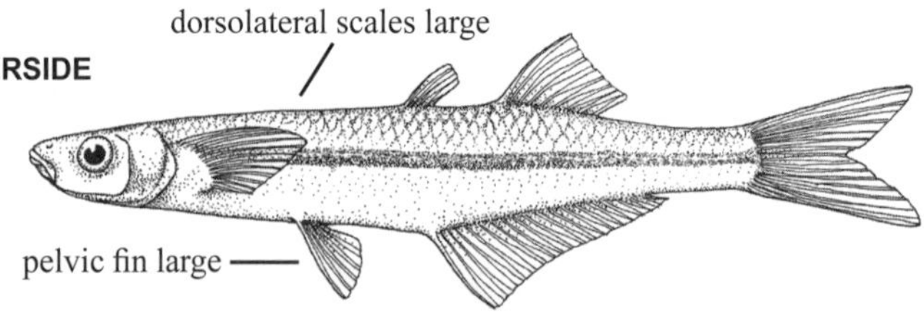


1b Depressed pelvic fin usually extends only 50–70% of distance to vent; pelvic fin length 58% or less of pectoral fin length; dorsolateral scales small with several rows of dark concentrated cells; lateral line scales more than 50….. 2 (next page)

2a Ten to 12 scales between base of dorsal fins; insertion of 1st dorsal fin well in advance of origin of anal fin; teeth in multiple rows and pointed:

**JACKSMELT**

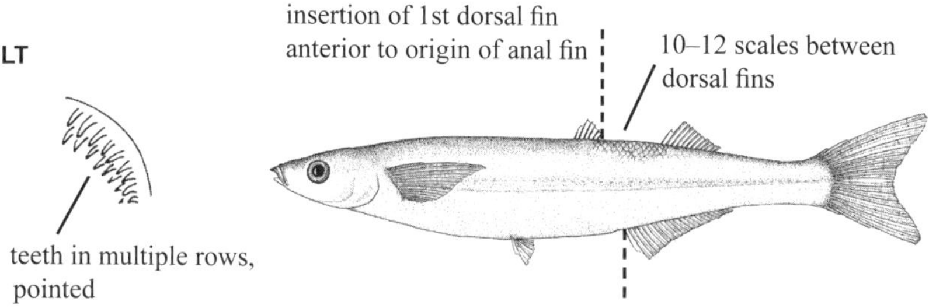


2b Five to 9 scales between base of dorsal fins; insertion of 1st dorsal fin above or posterior to origin of anal fin; teeth absent or in single row and forked in fish over 5 cm (2 in) SL (teeth pointed in smaller fish)….. 3

3a Teeth distinctly developed in fish over 5 cm (2 in) SL; 5–8 scales between base of dorsal fins; protruded upper jaw extends forward, not downward; body relatively deep, BD into SL 4–6:

**TOPSMELT**

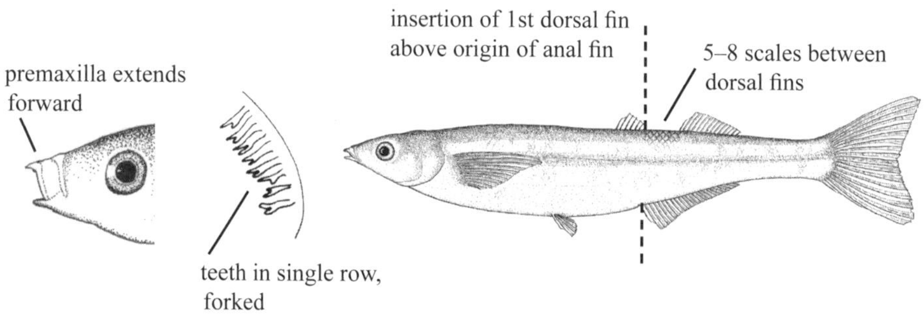


3b Teeth lacking or minute, difficult to detect even in adults; 7–9 scales between base of dorsal fins; protruded upper jaw extends forward and downward; body slender, BD into SL 6–8:

**CALIFORNIA GRUNION**

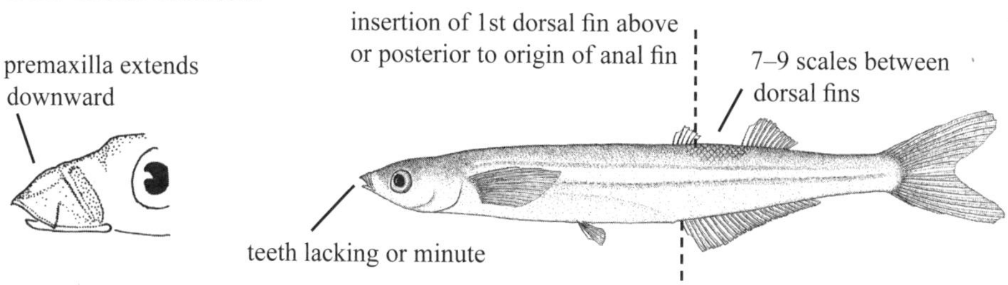

## GOOSEFISHES, Family Lophiidae, FROGFISH, Family Antennariidae, and BATFISH, Family Ogcocephalidae

**SPOTTEDTAIL GOOSEFISH, *Lophiodes caulinaris* (Garman, 1899).** Family Lophiidae
Central California (about 37°00'N, 122°00'W) (SIO 01-122) to Callao, Peru, including Gulf of California and various offshore islands. One record, possibly in error, from Islas Galápagos. Rare off California. Length to 40 cm (15.7 in) TL. Depth: 15–888 m (49–2,913 ft). Mottled brown; outer half of pectoral fins blackish with narrow white margin; caudal fin dark brown or blackish with vertical row of white spots across middle of fin. D III + III–IV,8; A 6–7; Pect. 16–21; Pelvic I,5; GR none; Vert. 19. (Alternative name PACIFIC GOOSEFISH).

**THREADFIN GOOSEFISH, *Lophiodes spilurus* (Garman, 1899).** Family Lophiidae
Off Monterey Bay, central California to northern Peru, including Gulf of California. Rare off California. Length to 35.4 cm (13.9 in) TL. Depth: 80–850 m (262–2,788 ft). Uniform dark to brown; all fins with clear outer edge; caudal fin with small clear spots; 2nd and 3rd dorsal fin spines black. D III + III,7–8; A 6–7; Pect. 15–18; Pelvic I,5; GR none; Vert. 19.

**ROUGHJAW FROGFISH, *Fowlerichthys avalonis* (Jordan & Starks, 1907).** Family Antennariidae
Santa Catalina Island, southern California to Iquique, Chile, including Gulf of California, Islas Galápagos, and Isla Cocos. Rare in southern California; common at least as far northward as Bahía Magdalena, southern Baja California and into tropics. Length to 53 cm (20.9 in) TL. Depth: intertidal to 311 m (1,020 ft). Color variable: brown, black, gray, yellow, orange, and red with dark brown spotting. D III,12–14; A 8–9; Pect. 13; Pelvic I,5; GR rudimentary; Vert. 19. (Formerly *Antennarius avalonis* Jordan & Starks, 1907: M&L).

**ROUNDEL BATFISH, *Zalieutes elater* (Jordan & Gilbert, 1882).** Family Ogcocephalidae
Point Conception, California to Paita, Peru, including Gulf of California, Isla Cocos, and Isla Malpelo. Rare in California. Length to 16.5 cm (6.5 in) TL. Depth: about 10–251 m (33–823 ft). Light olive to tan, with dark brown spotting; two gold spots ringed with black on back. D 4–6; A 4; Pect. 12–14; Pelvic I,5; Vert. 18–19. (Formerly SPOTTED BATFISH: M&L).

**SPOTTEDTAIL GOOSEFISH**

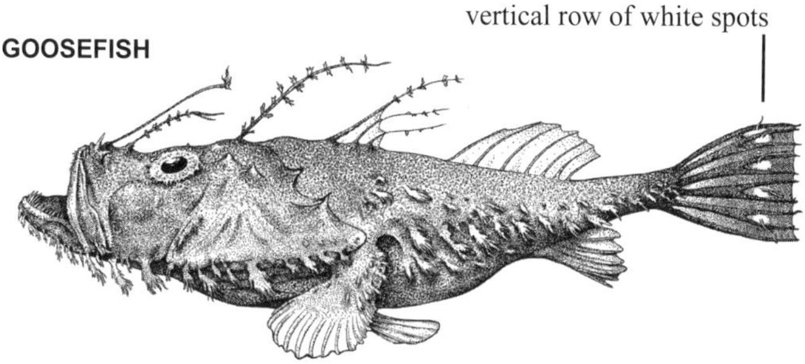


**THREADFIN GOOSEFISH**

(not illustrated; same body shape as SPOTTEDTAIL GOOSEFISH; no white spots on caudal fin)

**ROUGHJAW FROGFISH**

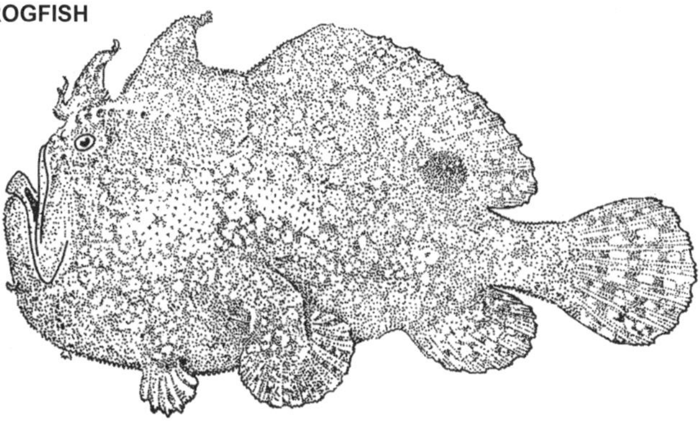

**ROUNDEL BATFISH**

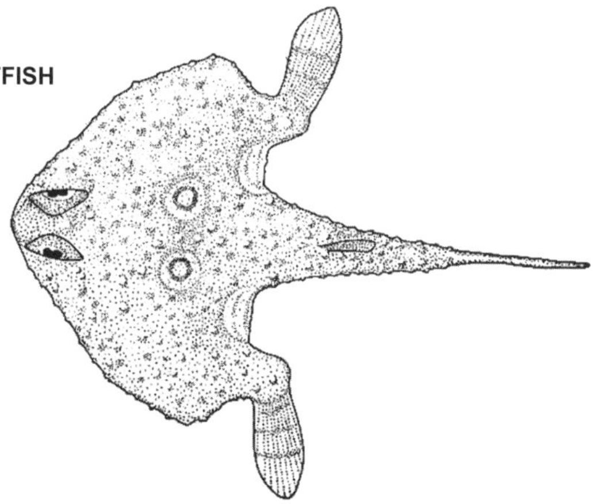

# OCEANIC ANGLERFISHES,
## Families Melanocetidae, Ceratiidae, Oneirodidae, and Himantolophidae

NOTE: The mature males of the family Ceratiidae are sexual parasites of the females and are permanently attached to them.

**BLACKDEVIL, *Melanocetus johnsonii* Günther, 1864.** Family MELANOCETIDAE
Circumglobal; Japan; British Columbia (48°41'N, 126°30'W) to northern Chile (31°14'S). Rare from Washington to at least California. Length to 64 cm (25.2 in) SL; however, this record is much larger than the next largest fish, an 18 cm (7.2 in) SL individual (Pietsch, 1986). Black. Meso- and bathypelagic; depth: about 100–3,603 m (328–11,818 ft), but perhaps as deep as 4,500 m (14,760 ft). D 12–17; A 3–5; Pect. 17–23; Pelvic absent.

**NORTHERN SEADEVIL, *Ceratias holboelli* Krøyer, 1845.** Family CERATIIDAE
Circumglobal; Japan; Hawai'i; Bering Sea, Gulf of Alaska, and off British Columbia and central California. Larvae reported from off Punta Eugenia, southern Baja California. Rare off California. Length to 152.4 cm (60 in) SL. Meso- to bathypelagic; depth: 120–3,400 m (394–11,154 ft). Red-brown to black. D 3–4; A 4; Pect. 15–19; Pelvic absent. (Alternative name NORTHERN GIANT SEADEVIL).

**TRIPLEWART SEADEVIL, *Cryptopsaras couesii* Gill, 1883.** Family CERATIIDAE
Circumglobal, with overall latitudinal range of 63°00'N to 43°00'S; Japan to New Zealand; Hawai'i; British Columbia to Peru. Rare from British Columbia to California. Length to about 44 cm (17.6 in) TL. Meso- to bathypelagic; depth: 75–4,000 m (246–13,123 ft), but mostly taken at 500–1,250 m (1,640–4,101 ft). Dark red-brown to black. D 4–5; A 4; Pect. 14–18; Pelvic absent. (Formerly WARTED SEADEVIL: M&L).

## KEY TO THE FEMALES OF OCEANIC ANGLERFISHES:
Created by Theodore W. Pietsch
(Principal source: Pietsch, 2009)

NOTE: This key pertains to females only. For illustrative purposes we also present drawings of the male of 3 species: BLACKDEVIL, 2.1 cm TL; NORTHERN SEADEVIL, 1.0 cm TL; TRIPLEWART SEADEVIL, 1.1 cm TL (Moser, 1996).

1a Dorsal fin soft-rays 12–17:

**BLACKDEVIL**

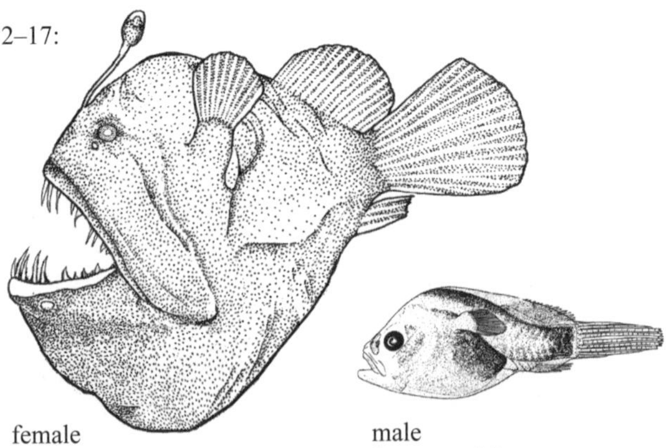

female

male
(not to scale)

1b Dorsal fin soft-rays 3–7….. 2 (next page)

2a Dorsal midline without club-shaped caruncles; cleft of mouth nearly horizontal to weakly oblique….. 4 (next page)

2b Dorsal midline with 2 or 3 club-shaped caruncles just anterior to soft dorsal fin; cleft of mouth vertical to strongly oblique….. 3

3a Illicium (modified 1st dorsal fin spine) long, considerably longer than length of esca; 2 caruncles on dorsal midline of trunk just anterior to origin of soft dorsal fin (minute in specimens longer than ~40 cm TL):

**NORTHERN SEADEVIL**

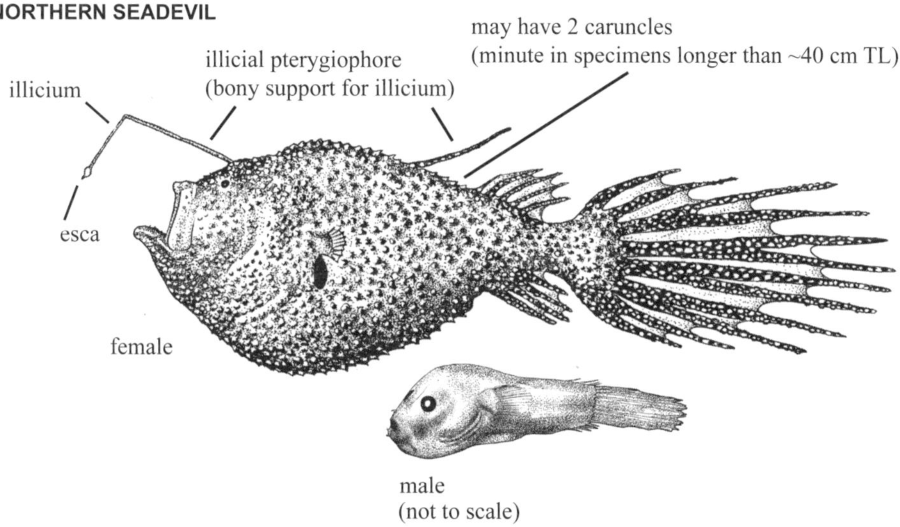


3b Illicium short (nearly completely enveloped by tissue of escal bulb); 3 caruncles on dorsal midline of trunk just anterior to origin of soft dorsal fin:

**TRIPLEWART SEADEVIL**

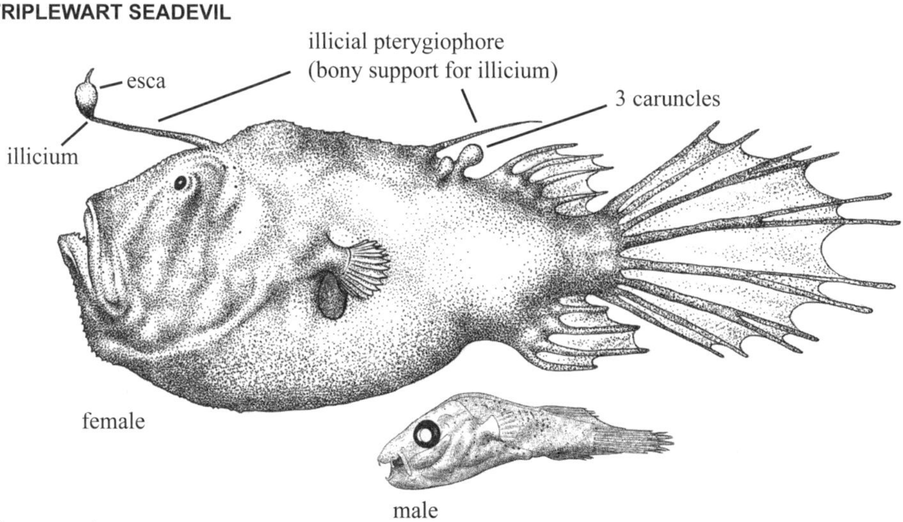


4a (next page)

## OCEANIC ANGLERFISHES (continued)

**COSMOPOLITAN DREAMER, *Oneirodes eschrichtii* Lütken, 1871.** Family ONEIRODIDAE
Circumglobal; Kuril-Kamchatka Trench, Russia; near U.S.-Canada border (48°12'N, 125°59'W) to Chile (34°00'S). Rare off California. Length to 21.3 cm (8.4 in) SL. Meso- to bathypelagic; depth: 150–6,200 m (492–20,336 ft). D 5–7; A 4; Pect. 15–19; Pelvic absent. (Alternative name TWOPOLE DREAMER).

**PACIFIC FOOTBALLFISH, *Himantolophus sagamius* (Tanaka, 1918).** Family HIMANTOLOPHIDAE
Eastern Indian Ocean; Japan; Kamchatka, Russia; northern California to Chile. Rare off California. Length to 38 cm (15 in) SL. Depth: 300–915 m (984–3,001 ft) and perhaps to 1,300 m (4,264 ft). Black or dark brown; southern California specimen had white membranes between dorsal, anal, and caudal soft-rays. D 5; A 4; Pect. 14–18; Pelvic absent. One specimen (SIO 02-2) washed ashore in Del Mar, California. Reported as *Himantolophus* sp. in Lea (1988). Classified by some authors as a synonym of *Himantolophus groenlandicus* Reinhardt, 1837.

**BLACK HORNED FOOTBALLFISH, *Himantolophus nigricornis* Bertelsen & Krefft, 1988.** Family HIMANTOLOPHIDAE
Off Monterey Bay, central California (SIO 94-171); in San Clemente Basin, southern California; and in western tropical Pacific and eastern Indian Oceans. Rare off California. Length to 19.5 cm (7.7 in) SL. Depth: about 219–2,500 m (720–8,200 ft) or more. D 5; A 4; Pelvic absent.

4a *From 2a: dorsal midline without caruncles*
Snout and chin more or less pointed; bones of lower jaw narrow; chin small, more or less equal to anterior extent of snout; skin naked or appearing so, with dermal spinules microscopic or absent:

**COSMOPOLITAN DREAMER**

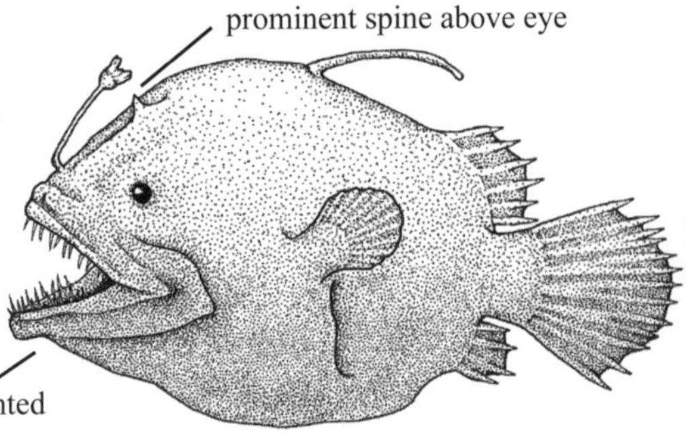


4b Snout and chin rounded and blunt; bones of lower jaw enlarged and expanded ventrally; chin large, protruding anteriorly beyond snout; skin more or less covered with dermal spinules or with some large bony plates, each bearing a median spine….. 5

5a Esca complex, bearing elongate anterior, distal, and posterior appendages:

**PACIFIC FOOTBALLFISH**

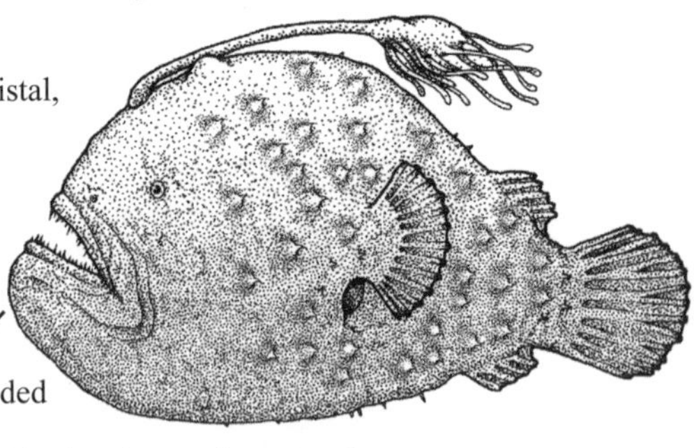

esca complex

5b Esca simple, bearing only short bifurcated distal and posterior appendages:

esca simple

**BLACK HORNED FOOTBALLFISH**
(not illustrated; body shape as in 5a)

# OREO, Family Oreosomatidae, DORY, Family Zeidae, and FANGTOOTH, Family Anoplogastridae

**OXEYE OREO, *Allocyttus folletti* Myers, 1960.** Family OREOSOMATIDAE

Honshu, Japan to Bering Sea and Gulf of Alaska to central California (34°36'N, 120°40'W) (SIO 96-74). Common from Bering Sea to northern California. Length to 47 cm (18.5 in) TL. Depth: surface to 1,800 m (5,905 ft). Most adults caught near bottom at 360–868 m (1,181–2,847 ft); one record from 47–292 m (154–958 ft). Prejuveniles taken near surface offshore and midocean. Adults dark brown to tan; juveniles light with dark spots. D V–VII,30–36; A III,30–33; Pect. 19–21; Pelvic I,6–7; LLs 88–90; GR 3–7 + 15–25; Vert. 39–41. (Formerly *Allocyttus verrucosus* (Myers, 1960): M&L).

**MIRROR DORY, *Zenopsis nebulosa* (Temminck & Schlegel, 1845).** Family ZEIDAE

Widespread in temperate waters of North and South Pacific; Japan; central and southern California to Chile. Rare off California. Length to 70 cm (27.6 in) TL. Depth: 30–800 m (100–2,624 ft). Uniform silvery; smaller juveniles with dark spots on sides. D VIII–X + 25–28; A III,25–27; Pect. 12–13; Pelvic I,5.

**LONGHORN FANGTOOTH, *Anoplogaster cornuta* (Valenciennes, 1833).** Family ANOPLOGASTRIDAE

Nearly circumglobal; northern Japan and Sea of Okhotsk to western Gulf of Alaska to northern Chile (18°26'S). Common at least off Japan and from Oregon or northern California southward to at least central Baja California. Length to 16.4 cm (6.5 in) SL. Meso- to bathypelagic; depth: adults 75–4,992 m (246–16,378 ft); juveniles as shallow as 2 m (7 ft). Adults black or dark brown; juveniles gray to brown, usually with 1 or more black patches on belly. D 17–20; A 7–10; Pect. 13–16; Pelvic I,6; GR 5–11 + 7–13; Vert. 25–29. (Alternative name FANGTOOTH).

**OXEYE OREO**

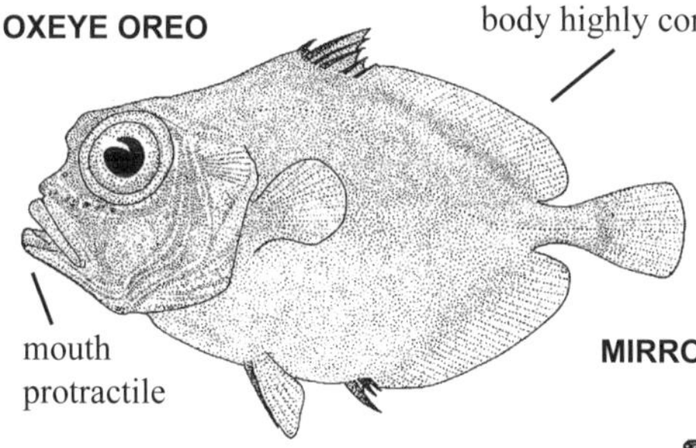


**MIRROR DORY**

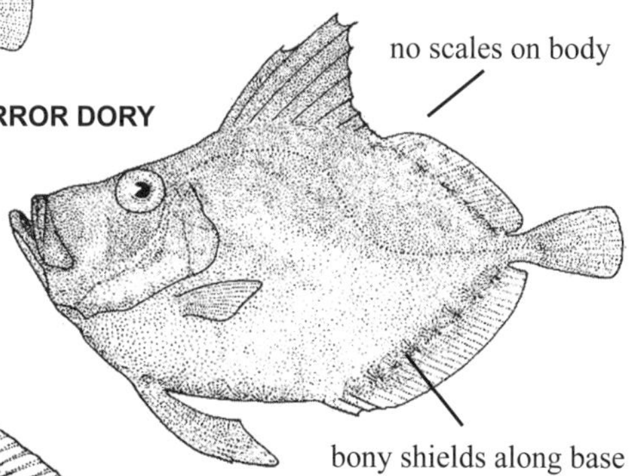


**LONGHORN FANGTOOTH**

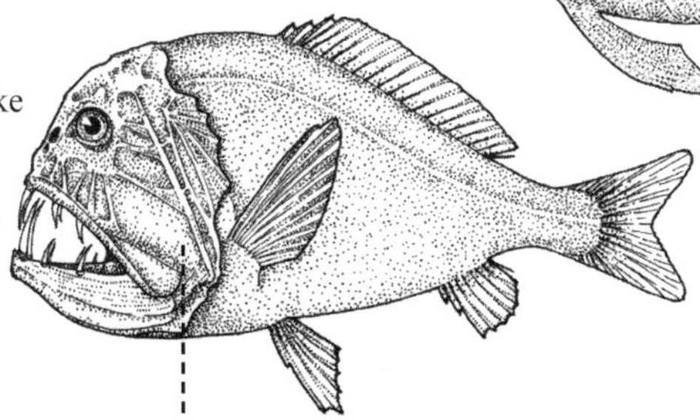

## WHALEFISH, Family Barbourisiidae and BIGSCALES, Family Melamphaidae

**RED WHALEFISH, *Barbourisia rufa* Parr, 1945.** Family BARBOURISIIDAE
Circumglobal at low latitudes; Japan, Emperor Seamounts, Hawai'i; Bering Sea (55°59'N, 168°45'W) and Pacific Ocean south of Amukta Pass, Aleutian Islands to northcentral California to southern Chile. Length to 41 cm (16.1 in) TL. Pelagic and benthopelagic; depth: 120–2,000 m (394–6,562 ft). Body and fins bright red or red-orange. D 20–23; A 14–18; Pect. 12–14; GR 4–6 + 13–16; Vert. 40–44.

**HIGHSNOUT BIGSCALE, *Melamphaes lugubris* Gilbert, 1891.** Family MELAMPHAIDAE
Japan, Sea of Okhotsk and Bering Sea to southern Baja California (25°30'N, 115°17'W) (SIO 51-87). Common from southern Bering Sea to at least central Baja California. Length to 10.9 cm (4.3 in) SL. Meso- to bathypelagic; depths: adults 150–2,287 m (492–7,501 ft), juveniles below 30 m (98 ft). Dark brown or brown-black; black throat and branchiostegals. D III,13–16; A I,7–9; Pect. 15–17; Pelvic I,6–7; Midlateral scales 29–34; GR 4–6 + 13–18; Vert. 28–31.

**CRESTED BIGSCALE, *Poromitra crassiceps* (Günther, 1878).** Family MELAMPHAIDAE
Nearly cosmopolitan, absent only from Arctic Ocean and Mediterranean Sea; Japan to southern Bering Sea and Gulf of Alaska to Chile. Common at least off Japan, from Bering Sea and Aleutian Islands to southern Baja California and in Gulf of California. Length to 19 cm (7.5 in) SL. Adults meso- and bathypelagic; depth: about 0–4,000 m (13,120 ft); juveniles shallower, one record from 150 m (492 ft). Uniform black. D III,11–15; A I–II,8–12; Pect. 13–15; Pelvic I,7–8; Midlateral scales approx. 23–28; GR 8–12 + 18–24; Vert. 26–29. (Alternative name CRESTED RIDGEHEAD). This species split into many by Kotlyar (2009).

**TWOSPINE BIGSCALE, *Scopelogadus bispinosus* (Gilbert, 1915).** Family MELAMPHAIDAE
Southwest of La Perouse Bank (48°08'N, 126°36'W), British Columbia to Chile. Common at least from southern California to Gulf of California. Length to 17.5 cm (6.9 in) SL. Meso- and bathypelagic; depth: 104–4,268 m (343–13,999 ft). Black with lighter scale pockets. D II,10–12; A I,7–9; Pect. 14–15; Pelvic I,7–9; Midlateral scales fewer than 15; GR 6–9 + 15–18; Vert. 24–27. Previously considered the subspecies *Scopelogadus mizolepis bispinosus* (Günther, 1878).

**RED WHALEFISH**

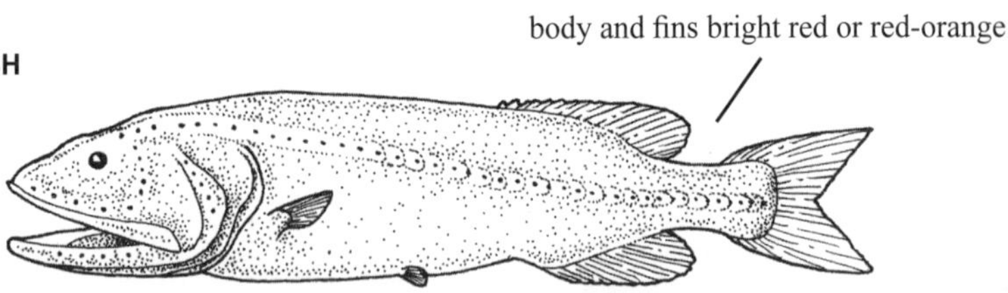

**HIGHSNOUT BIGSCALE**

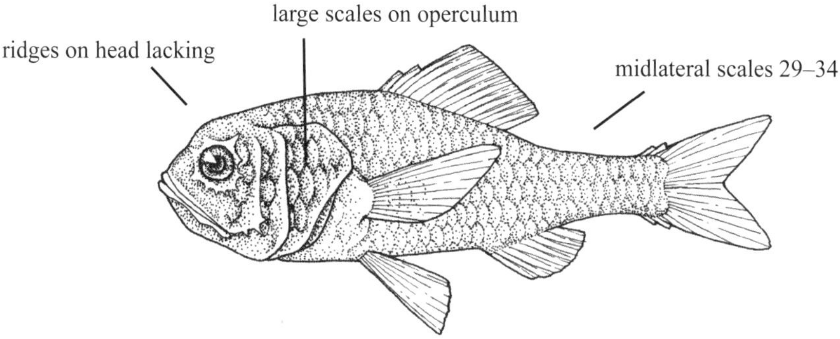


**CRESTED BIGSCALE**

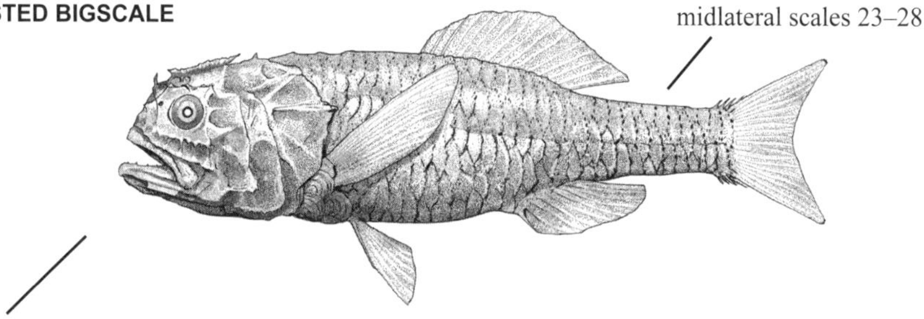


*Crest-like ridges on head,*
*large scales on operculum lacking on these 2*

**TWOSPINE BIGSCALE**

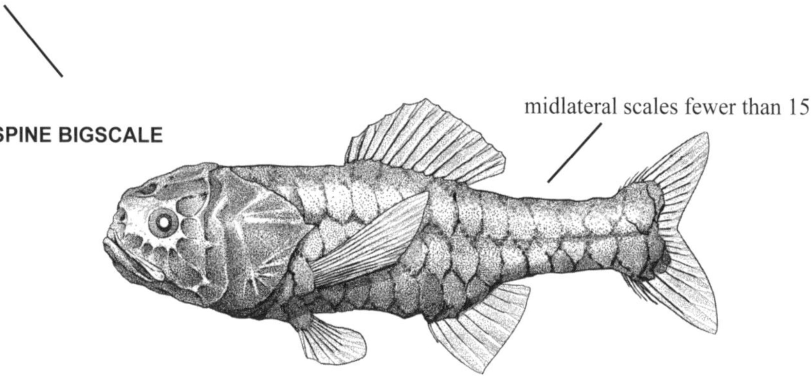

# OPAHS, Family Lampridae, CRESTFISH, Family Lophotidae, and OARFISH, Family Regalecidae

NOTE: We follow Underkoffler et al. (2018) and, off California, separate the previously regarded single circumglobal species SPOTTED OPAH, *Lampris guttatus* (Brünnich, 1788) into two species. Because of this, the data presented below are provisional.

**SMALLEYE PACIFIC OPAH, *Lampris incognitus* Underkoffler, Luers, Hyde & Craig, 2018.**
Family Lampridae
Geographic range unclear, but probably restricted to central and eastern North Pacific from at least Washington to well offshore south and east of Cabo San Lucas, Baja California. Length to at least 123 cm (48.4 in) FL and undocumented to 183 cm (72 in) TL. Pelagic, oceanic; depth: near surface to perhaps 736 m (2,414 ft). Body irridescent blue, gray on back fading to silver ventrally; fins red; dorsal and caudal fins sometimes white-tipped; spots small and circular. D I,49–50; A 40; Pect. 22; Pelvic 15. (Formerly OPAH, *Lampris regius* (Bonnaterre, 1788), Lamprididae: M&L).

**BIGEYE PACIFIC OPAH, *Lampris megalopsis* Underkoffler, Luers, Hyde & Craig, 2018.**
Family Lampridae
Circumglobal; at least California and Chile. Abundance off California unclear. Length to at least 124 cm (48.8 in) FL and undocumented to 183 cm (72 in) TL. Pelagic, oceanic; depth: surface to perhaps 736 m (2,414 ft). Body irridescent blue, gray on back fading to silver ventrally; fins red; spots irregular in shape. D I,50–51; A 38; Pect. 22–23; Pelvic 14–15. (Formerly OPAH, *Lampris regius,* Lamprididae: M&L).

**NORTH PACIFIC CRESTFISH, *Lophotus capellei* Temminck & Schlegel, 1845.** Family Lophotidae
Western and eastern North Pacific; well offshore, to 610 km (379 mi) off Point Arena, northern California and near coast at Morro Bay, central California through San Diego, southern California. Length to at least 100 cm (39.4 in) SL. Depth: surface to at least 92 m (300 ft) and probably to greater depths. Blue back, silver sides; dorsal, anal, and caudal fins red. Discharges ink through cloaca near anus. D 220–240; A 18–20; Pect. 15–19; Pelvic 5–6; Vert. 123–144. Craig et al. (2004) consider CRESTFISH from the western and eastern North Pacific to be a different species than those from South Pacific and Atlantic. We present data only from North Pacific fish. (Formerly HIGHBROW CRESTFISH, *Lophotus cristatus* Johnson, 1863: M&L).

**OARFISH, *Regalecus russelii* Cuvier, 1817.** Family Regalecidae
North Pacific; Japan; Surf (34°41'N, 120°36'W), central California to Panama (records from South America appear to be of *Regalecus glesne* Ascanius, 1772). Uncommon off California. Length to 7–8 m (23–26 ft) TL. Primarily epi- and mesopelagic. Body silver, red, or black with dark or iridescent blue dashes, bars, or spots and variable bluish to violet reflections. Dorsal fin entirely or partly red; pectoral fins colorless or sometimes pink or reddish; pelvic fins elongate, mainly red with ornaments that may be partly black. Anterior dorsal crest 3–6 + 1; D (to end of abdomen directly over vent) 68–80; D (total) 179–371; A none; Pect. 11–15; Pelvic 1; GRt 47–60 (neotype 13+39); Vert. (to end of abdomen directly over vent) 34–37; Vert. (total) 113–122. We follow Roberts (2012) and separate this species from *R. glesne*.

**SMALLEYE PACIFIC OPAH**

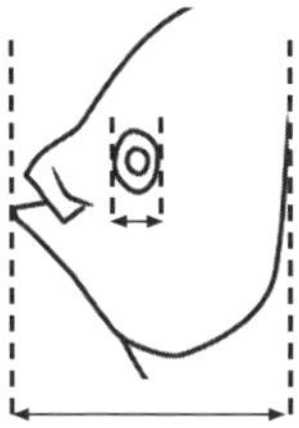


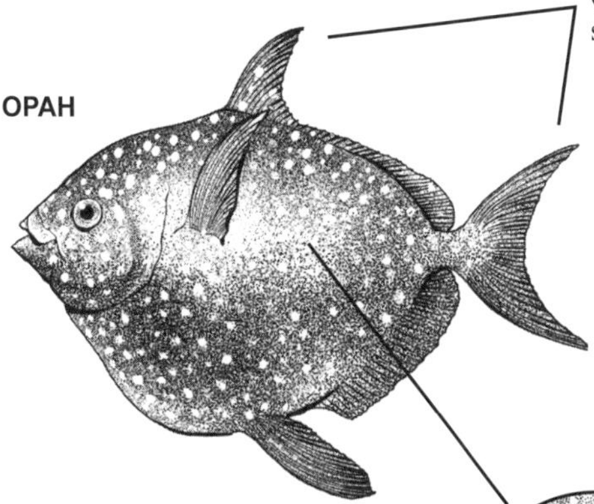


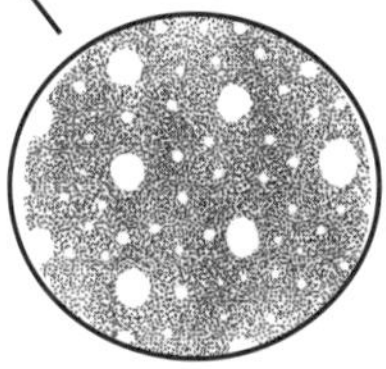

**BIGEYE PACIFIC OPAH**
(same body shape as above)

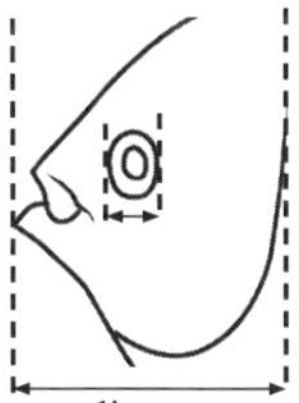


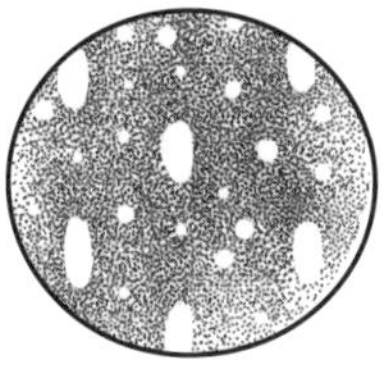


**NORTH PACIFIC CRESTFISH**

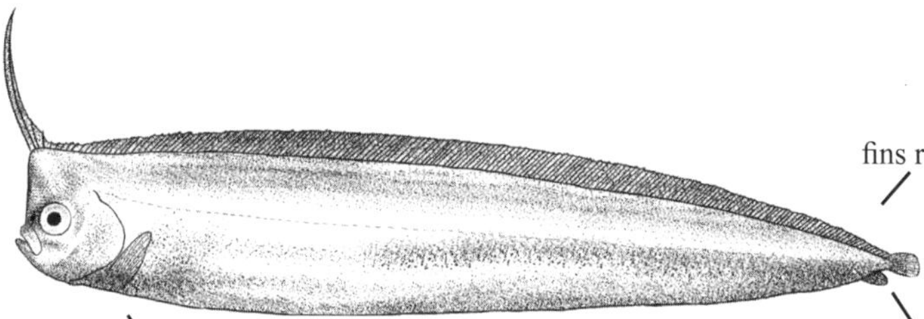


**OARFISH**

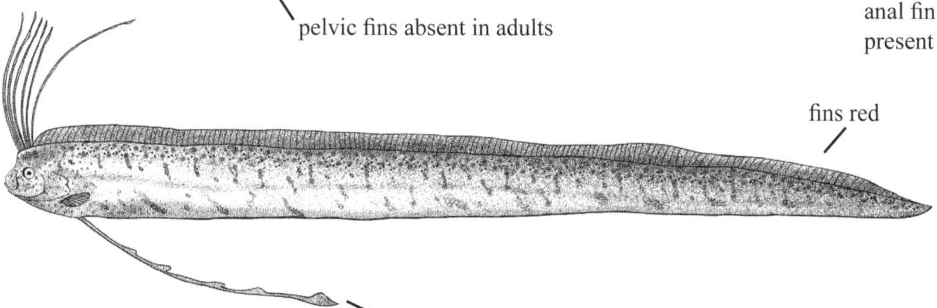

## RIBBONFISHES, Family Trachipteridae

**WHIPTAIL RIBBONFISH, *Desmodema lorum* Rosenblatt & Butler, 1977.** Temperate waters of North Pacific; Japan, southern Kuril Islands, Russia; Southern Oregon (44°26'N, 155°05'W) (UW 021784) to Peru including Gulf of California. Common at least off Japan, probably common at least off southern California. Length to at least 110 cm (43.3 in) SL or perhaps to 114 cm (44.9 in) TL. Epi- to mesopelagic; depth: juveniles can be found in surface waters, adults from a minimum of at least 30 m to at least 902 m (98–2,959 ft) and probably both shallower and deeper. Silvery with dark red tones on back and head; fins red, except dorsal soft-rays along tail extension black. D 197–215; A absent; Pect. 1 + 11–14; Adults without pelvic fins; Vert. 106–111. (Formerly POLKADOT RIBBONFISH, *Desmodema polysticta* (Ogilby, 1898): M&L).

**KING-OF-THE-SALMON, *Trachipterus altivelis* Kner, 1859.** Southeastern Bering Sea and Gulf of Alaska to Chile. Common at least from British Columbia to southern California. Length to 245 cm (96 in) TL. Primarily mesopelagic as adults; juveniles can be found in surface waters; depth: near surface to 1,214 m (3,982 ft). Silvery to dusky; median fins often reddish; some dark spots or blotches may be present particularly in younger fish. D 163–191; A absent; Pect. 9–11; Pelvic (juveniles) 6–7; LLs 106–122; GR 3–5 + 9–11 = 12–16; Vert. 90–94. Considered by some a synonym of the circumglobal species *Trachipterus trachypterus* (Gmelin, 1789).

**TAPERTAIL RIBBONFISH, *Trachipterus fukuzakii* Fitch, 1964.** Just north of San Francisco, northern California to Chile, including Gulf of California. Length to 143 cm (56.3 in) TL. Epi- and mesopelagic; depth: as shallow as 5 m (16 ft). Metallic silver; several dark blotches on sides. D 5–6 + 153–172; A absent; Pect. 10–13; Pelvic (juveniles) 5; LLs 91–105; GR 3–4 + 7–9; Vert. 69–72.

**SCALLOPED RIBBONFISH, *Zu cristatus* (Bonelli, 1819).** Circumglobal in tropical to warm temperate waters; Japan; central California (34°53'N, 124°30'W) to Chile and Islas Galápagos. Apparently rare off California. Length to 118 cm (46.5 in) TL. Epi- to mesopelagic; depth: near surface to about 1,200 m (3,936 ft). Silver with about 6 dark bars (these fade in older individuals); fins red with dark patches; caudal fin edged with black; young with scalloped margin between pelvic and anal fins. D 120–151; A absent; Pect. 10–12; Pelvic (juveniles) 6–7; LLs 114–118; GR 2–3 + 8–9; Vert. 63–69.

NOTE: Pelvic fins absent in adults but present in juveniles.

**WHIPTAIL RIBBONFISH**

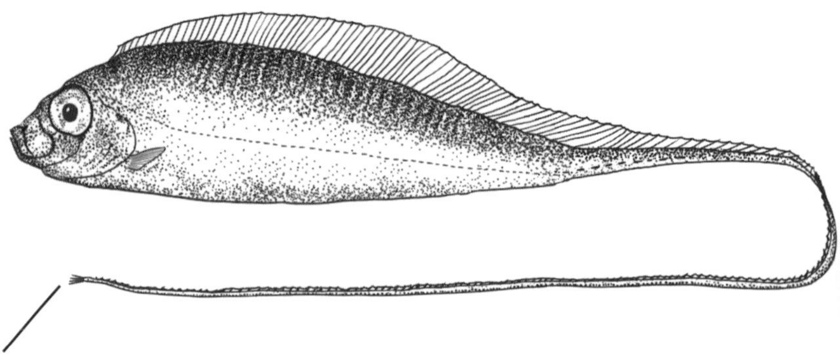

caudal fin soft-rays parallel to body axis

## KING-OF-THE-SALMON

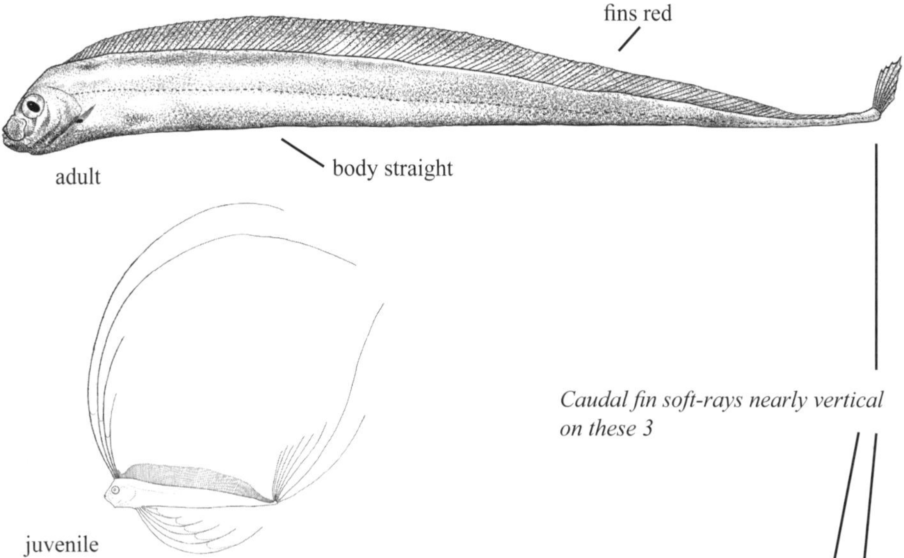


## TAPERTAIL RIBBONFISH

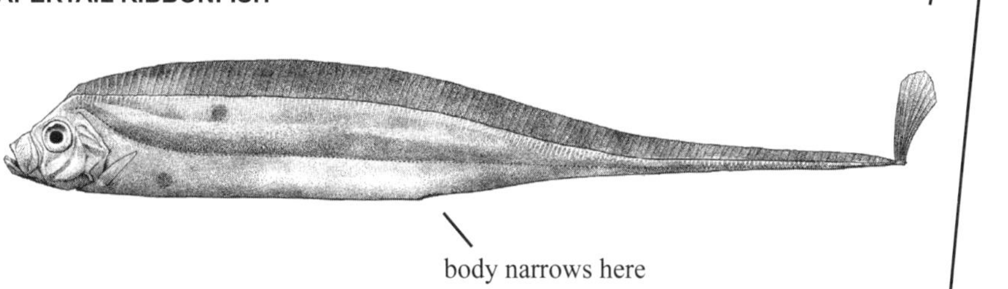


## SCALLOPED RIBBONFISH

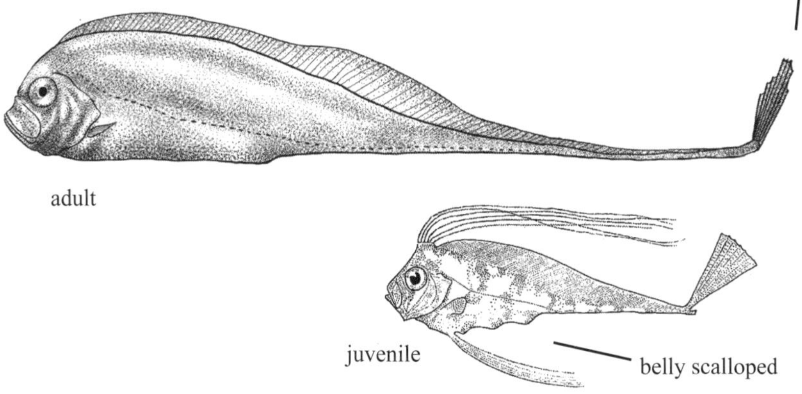

# TUBESNOUT, Family Aulorhynchidae, STICKLEBACK, Family Gasterosteidae, SNIPEFISH, Family Macroramphosidae, and CORNETFISHES, Family Fistulariidae

**TUBESNOUT, *Aulorhynchus flavidus* Gill, 1861.** Family AULORHYNCHIDAE
Pavlof Bay, southwest Alaska Peninsula and Kodiak Island, Gulf of Alaska to Punta Rompiente (27°42'N, 115°W), southern Baja California (LACM 32052-1). Uncertain record from Captains Bay, Unalaska Island. Common at least from Prince William Sound, Gulf of Alaska to Punta Baja, northern Baja California. Mostly marine, but will enter brackish waters. Length to 18.8 cm (7.4 in) TL. Shoreline to well offshore; depth: surface to at least 40 m (130 ft). Brown, green, or bluish on back (sometimes with white flecking and dark barring), silvery sides and belly; courting males with blue snout and blue spots and orange pelvic fins. D XXIII–XXVII free spines + 9–11; A I,9–10; Pect. I,9–10; Pelvic I,4; GR 9–12 + 13–17 = 25–31; Vert. 52–56. (Formerly Gasterosteidae: M&L).

**THREESPINE STICKLEBACK, *Gasterosteus aculeatus* Linnaeus, 1758.** Family GASTEROSTEIDAE
North Atlantic, arctic Europe and Asia, and North Pacific. In marine waters, Korean Peninsula to Seas of Japan and Okhotsk to Bering, Chukchi, and Beaufort Seas, and Gulf of Alaska to Monterey Bay, central California. In fresh waters, as far south as Rio Rosario, northern Baja California. Common from Sea of Japan and Chukchi Sea to northern Baja California. Length to 10.5 cm (4.1 in) TL. Anadromous and resident freshwater forms; depth: shallow waters to about 27 m (90 ft), recorded near surface as far as 805 km (500 mi) offshore of Alaska. See Moyle (2002) for a complete discussion of this species in California. Olive to dusky above, silver below; male blackish with reddish throats, belly, and sometimes flanks in springtime. D II–III isolated spines + I,7–14; A I,6–12; Pect. 9–11; GR 4–9 + 12–18 = 17–27; Vert. 30–34.

**LONGSPINE SNIPEFISH, *Macroramphosus scolopax* (Linnaeus, 1758).** Family MACRORAMPHOSIDAE
Circumglobal in warm waters; Japan; between Santa Rosa and Santa Cruz Islands, southern California to Chile. Common from southern California southward. Length to 22.8 cm (9 in) TL. Depth: surface to 600 m (1,968 ft). Silvery, with reddish or greenish, darker on back. D IV–VIII + 10–13; A 18–19; Pect. 15–17; Pelvic I,4–5; Vert. 23–24. Considered to be *Macroramphosus gracilis* (Lowe, 1839) by some authors. (Formerly SLENDER SNIPEFISH: M&L) (Alternative name LONGNOSED SNIPEFISH). Some authors place this genus in the family Centriscidae.

**REEF CORNETFISH, *Fistularia commersonii* Rüppell, 1838.** Family FISTULARIIDAE
Circumglobal in warm waters; Japan; Laguna Beach and San Clemente Island, southern California and Bahía Magdalena, southern Baja California to Iquique, northern Chile, including Gulf of California and Islas Galápagos. Rare in southern California. Length to 1.6 m (5.2 ft) TL. Depth: surface to 132 m (433 ft). Greenish on back, sides silvery; back with 2 blue stripes or 2 rows of spots; caudal filament light. D 14–17; A 14–16; Pect. 13–15; Vert. 83–86.

**DEEPWATER CORNETFISH, *Fistularia corneta* Gilbert & Starks, 1904.** Family FISTULARIIDAE
Huntington Beach, southern California to Callao, Peru, including Gulf of California and Islas Galápagos. Rare in California. Length to 128 cm (50.4 in) TL. Depth: surface to 50 m (164 ft). Orange to brown on back, sometimes with dark blotches, sides silvery; base of dorsal and anal fins orange; caudal filament dark. D 17–20; A 16–19; Pect. 15–18. Vert. 75–76. (Alternative name PACIFIC CORNETFISH).

**TUBESNOUT**

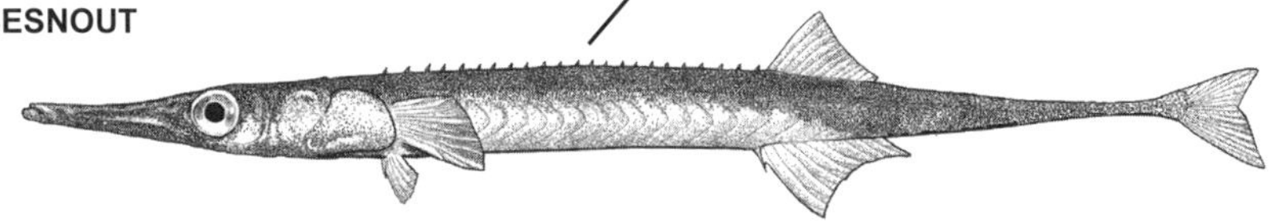


**THREESPINE STICKLEBACK**

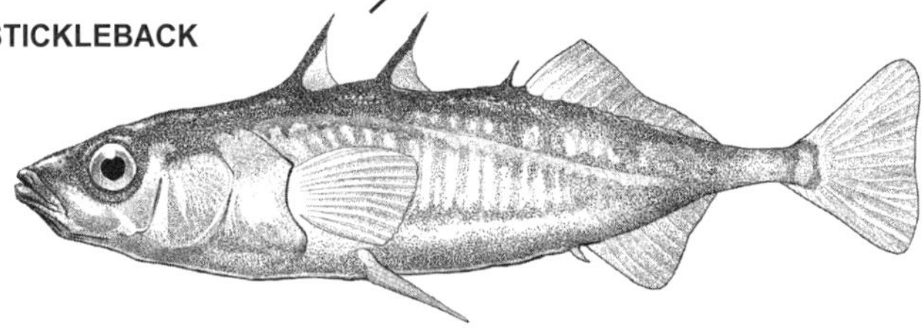


**LONGSPINE SNIPEFISH**

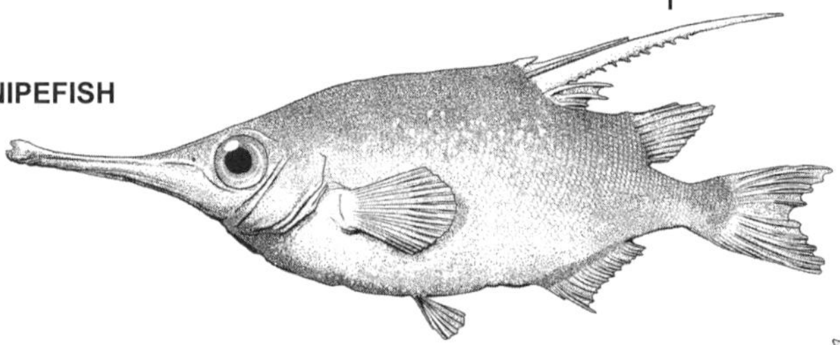


*Snout tubular with jaws at tip on these 3*

**REEF CORNETFISH**

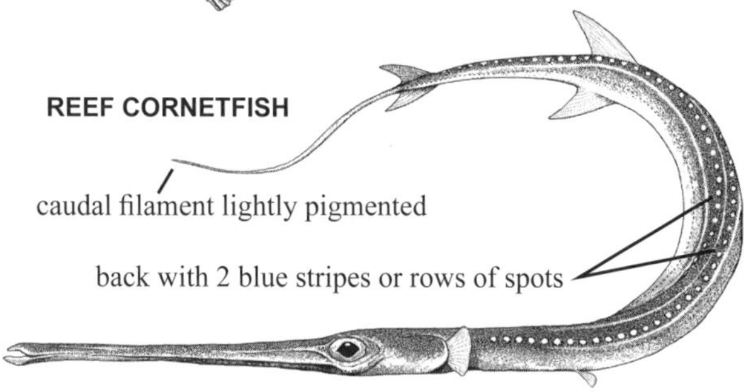


**DEEPWATER CORNETFISH**

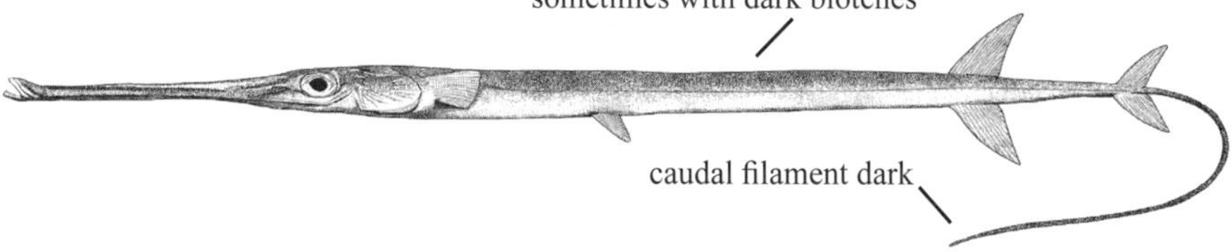

## SEAHORSE and PIPEFISHES, Family Syngnathidae

**PACIFIC SEAHORSE, *Hippocampus ingens* Girard, 1858.** Beached specimen on Pismo Beach (35°08'N, 120°38'W), California to Chile, including Isla Guadalupe, Gulf of California, and Islas Galápagos; old (undocumented) record from San Francisco Bay. A small, and perhaps self-sustaining, population is found in San Diego Bay, otherwise normally rare in California and likely common from about central Baja California southward. However, during some warm-water periods common into southern California. Length to 30.5 cm (12 in) TL. Depth: surface, and bottom at 1–107 m (3–351 ft). Red, yellow, or green with mixture of light and dark mottling and light and dark spots. D 17–22; A 4–5; Pect. 15–17; Trunk rings 11–13; Tail rings 36–41.

**SNUBNOSE PIPEFISH, *Cosmocampus arctus* (Jenkins & Evermann, 1889).** Humboldt Bay, northern California to Chile and throughout Gulf of California. Common from southern California southward. Length to 13 cm (5.1 in) TL. Depth: intertidal to at least 20 m (66 ft). Pale brown; double row of spots on sides. D 18–23; A 5–7; Pect. 9–11; C 5–7; Trunk rings 13–16; Tail rings 22–41; Subdorsal rings 5–6. (Formerly *Syngnathus arctus* (Jenkins & Evermann, 1889): M&L).

**BARRED PIPEFISH, *Syngnathus auliscus* (Swain, 1882).** Santa Barbara Channel, southern California to Puerto Pizarro, Peru, including Gulf of California. Common from about Newport Bay, southern California southward. Length to 19 cm (7.5 in) TL. Shallow inshore waters; depth: intertidal to 20 m (66 ft). Brown to green; light bar every 4–5 body rings along body, may have dark line along sides of body. Snout round, length to 0.6 cm (0.2 in). D 26–37; A 5–9; Pect. 10–14; C 5–9; Trunk rings 13–17; Tail rings 30–39; Subdorsal rings 6–7.

**BAY PIPEFISH, *Syngnathus leptorhynchus* Girard, 1854.** Prince William Sound and eastern Gulf of Alaska to Bahía Santa Maria, southern Baja California and perhaps in northern Gulf of California. Common from Prince William Sound to at least Punta Baja, northern Baja California. Common in eelgrass beds of bays, will enter brackish water. Length to 38.5 cm (15.2 in) TL. Depth: intertidal to 18 m (60 ft). Pale to dark olive-green or brown, may have mottling and spots on body; brown spots may be present on dorsal fin; dark coloration at base of dorsal fin. Snout round, length to 2 cm (0.8 in). D 27–45; A 2–10 (only females have anal fin Wang, 2010); Pect. 11–13; C 5–10; GR 1 + 3–5 = 4–6; Trunk rings 16–21; Tail rings 36–48; Subdorsal rings 8–10.

**CHOCOLATE PIPEFISH, *Syngnathus euchrous* Fritzsche, 1980.** Santa Rosa Island (SIO 51-264) and Redondo Beach, southern California to Bahía Ballenas, southern Baja California. Length to 31.2 cm (12.3 in) TL. Depth: surface and intertidal to 18 m (60 ft). Greenish-brown to reddish-brown. Snout round, length to 1.9 cm (0.7 in). D 28–49; A 3–9: Pect. 11–13; C 7–9; Trunk rings 17–20; Tail rings 34–49; Subdorsal rings 7–11.

## KEY TO THE SEAHORSE and PIPEFISHES:

Revised by Kristy Forsgren

(Principal sources: Miller & Lea, 1972; Fritsche, 1980)

NOTE: Many members of this family are capable of matching their colors and patterns to the surrounding habitat; thus color is a relatively poor diagnostic character. Males have brood pouch on abdomen.

1a Caudal fin absent; head at right angle to main axis of body:

**PACIFIC SEAHORSE**

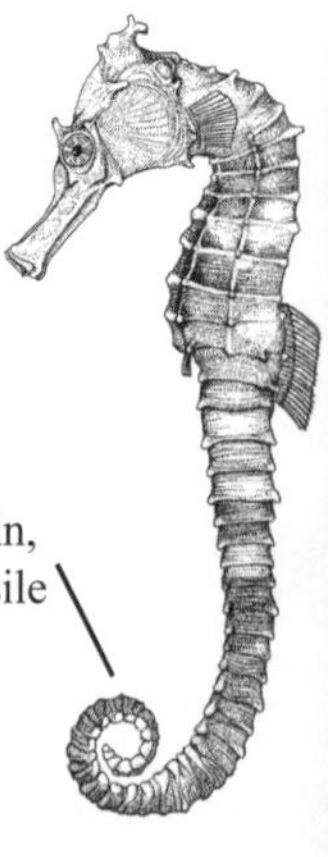


1b Caudal fin present; head on same axis as body….. 2 (next page)

2a Snout length into HL 2.85 or greater; double row of dark spots along sides of body:

**SNUBNOSE PIPEFISH**

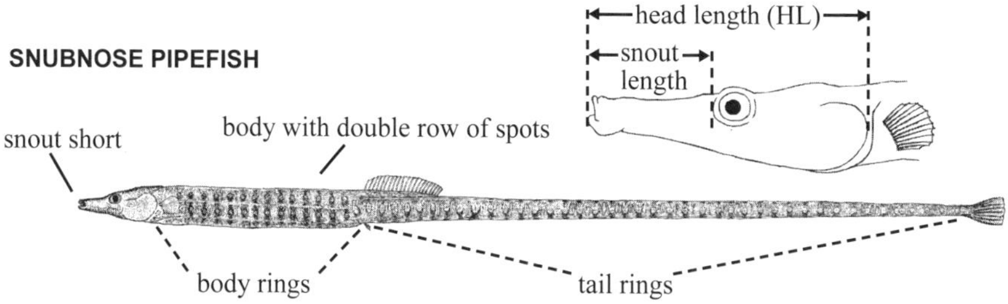


2b Snout length into HL less than 2.85; no rows of dark spots on body….. 3

3a Light bar every 4–5 body rings, may have horizontal dark line along body:

**BARRED PIPEFISH**

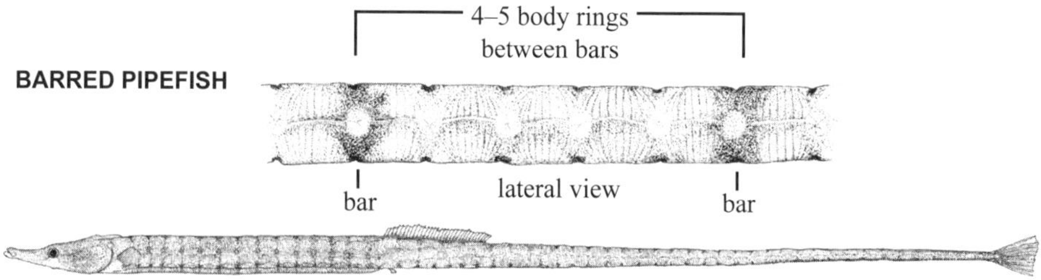


3b Body without barring and no horizontal dark line along body….. 4

4a Snout oval (compressed) in cross section….. 6 (next page) 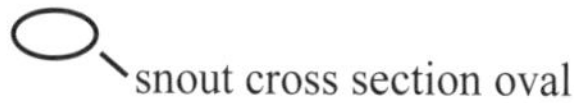


4b Snout round in cross section….. 5 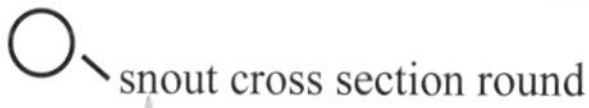


5a Dark coloration at base of dorsal fin, may extend throughout fin; caudal fin soft-rays 5–10 (median 6):

**BAY PIPEFISH**

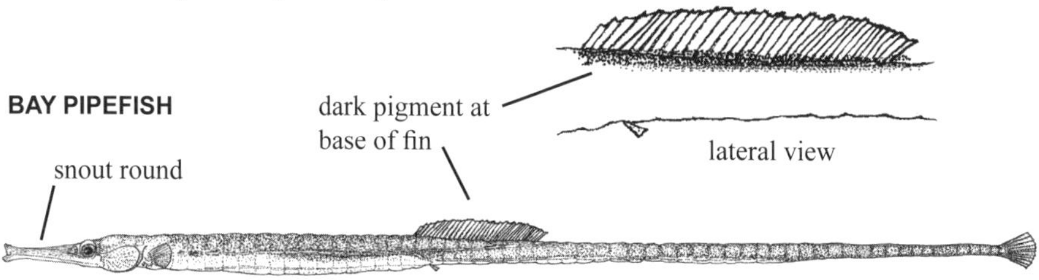


5b No dark coloration at base of dorsal fin; caudal fin soft-rays 7–9 (median 8):

**CHOCOLATE PIPEFISH**

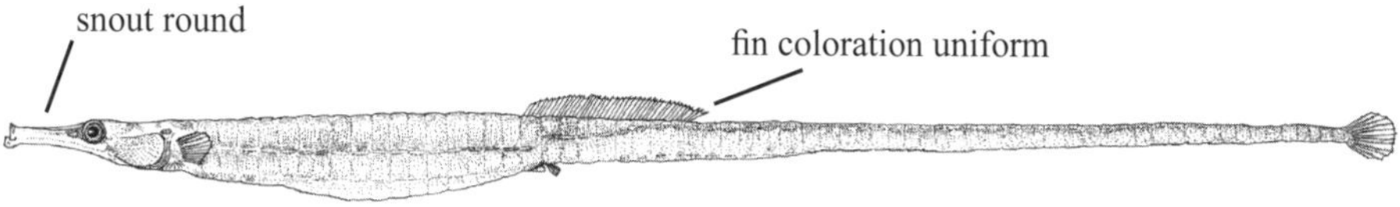


6a (next page)

## SEAHORSE and PIPEFISHES (continued)

**BARCHEEK PIPEFISH, *Syngnathus exilis* (Osburn & Nichols, 1916).** Half Moon Bay, central California to Bahía Magdalena, southern Baja California, including offshore islands. Common from at least Monterey Bay, central California south to Bahía Magdalena. Shallow sandy areas, including bays with eelgrass and algae. Length to 30.2 cm (11.9 in) TL. Depth: surface and intertidal to at least 5 m (17 ft). Green to brown with dark line behind eye extending on to operculum. Snout oval, length to 2.3 cm (0.9 in). D 24–51; A 3–11; Pect. 11–13; C 5–11; Trunk rings 17–21; Tail rings 43–49; Subdorsal rings 7.5–11.

**KELP PIPEFISH, *Syngnathus californiensis* Storer, 1845.** Bodega Bay, northern California to Bahía Santa Maria, southern Baja California. Common from about central California southward to at least Punta Baja, northern Baja California. Inhabits a variety of habitats, including subtidal bays and rocky reefs, eelgrass, kelp beds, and drifting kelp mats. Length to 49.5 cm (19.5 in) TL. Depth: intertidal to 15 m (48 ft). Green to brown with several color variations and patterns. Snout oval, length to 3.3 cm (1.3 in). D 26–52; A 3–10; Pect. 11–14; C 5–10; Trunk rings 16–22; Tail rings 46–52; Subdorsal rings 7.5–11.

6a *From 4a: snout oval (compressed) in cross section*
Dark line extending from eye on to operculum (may be absent); maximum snout length to 2.3 cm:

**BARCHEEK PIPEFISH**

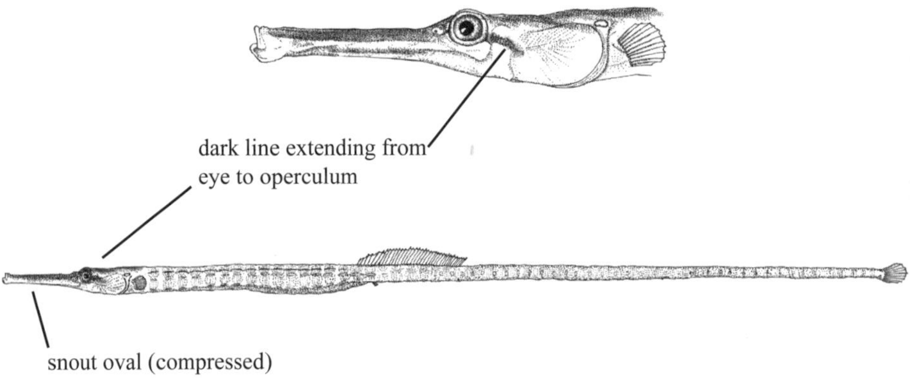


6b No dark line extending from eye; maximum snout length to 3.3 cm:

**KELP PIPEFISH**

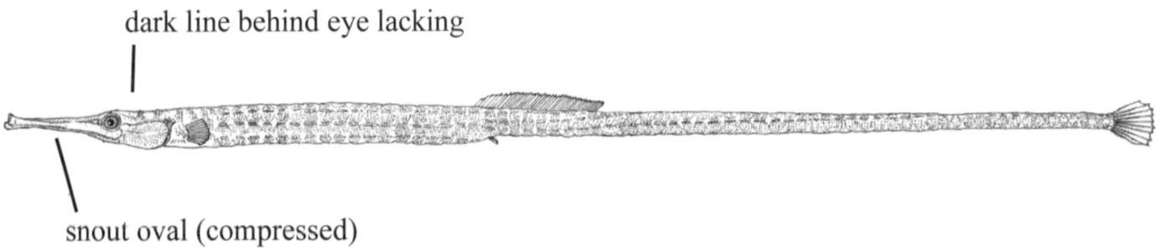

# ROCKFISHES, SCORPIONFISHES, and THORNYHEADS, Family Scorpaenidae

NOTE: We follow Smith et al. (2018) and place the genera *Scorpaena*, *Scorpaenodes*, *Sebastes*, and *Sebastolobus* in the family Scorpaenidae. The family Scorpaenidae contains the largest number of California marine species, comprising four genera and 71 species in this key. These are among the most difficult of our marine fishes to identify. The principal literature sources are Phillips (1957), Barsukov (1964), Chen (1971), Love et al. (2002), and Butler et al. (2012). The key to the rockfishes (genus *Sebastes*) relies heavily on color with additional meristic counts and body proportions given. Because diagnostic color may disappear in preserved material, this key may not be applicable for some museum specimens. As in Phillips' work, this key may not apply to some juvenile forms less than 10–15 cm (4–6 in), since color pattern, shape, number of head spines, and body proportions may change considerably with size. Color images of all of the species found below are available in Butler et al. (2012).

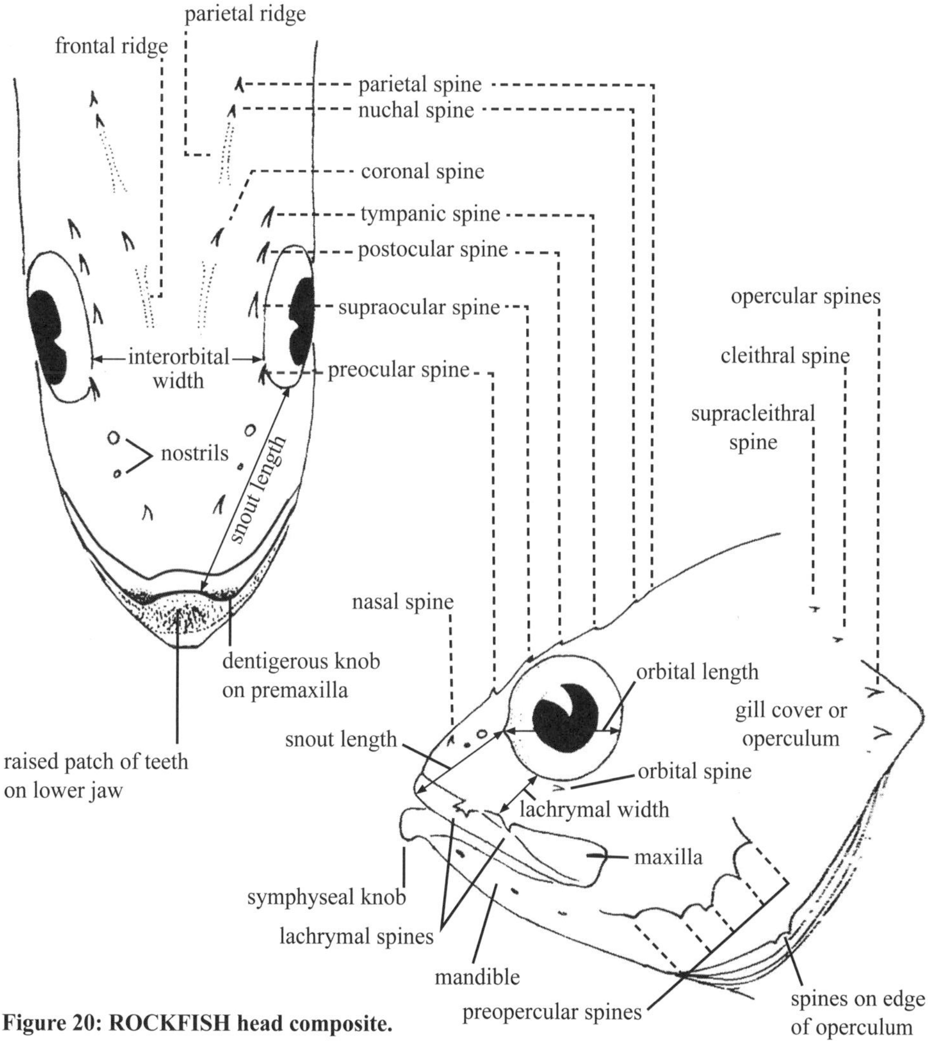


**Figure 20: ROCKFISH head composite.**

## ROCKFISHES, SCORPIONFISHES, and THORNYHEADS (continued)

**LONGSPINE THORNYHEAD, *Sebastolobus altivelis* Gilbert, 1896.** Bering Sea and Shumagin Islands, western Gulf of Alaska to Cabo San Lucas, southern Baja California. Common from western Gulf of Alaska to at least southern California. Length to 39 cm (15.4 in) TL. Depth: 163–1,756 m (535–5,760 ft). Red with dark blotches on body and fins; dark spot on posterior of dorsal fin; gill cavity dark gray or black. Occasionally body entirely dark. Newly settled juveniles with black pectoral fins. D XV–XVII,8–10; A III,4–6; Pect. 22–24; LLp 28–32 + 2 on tail; GR 7–9 + 14–17 = 21–26; Vert. 29.

**SHORTSPINE THORNYHEAD, *Sebastolobus alascanus* Bean, 1890.** Northern Honshu Island, Japan and Seas of Okhotsk and Japan to Pacific Ocean and Bering Sea off Kamchatka to Navarin Canyon and Aleutian Islands to Pacific off Boca de Santo Domingo (25°32'N, 113°04'W), southern Baja California and Costa Rica (09°14.1'N, 85°07.1'W). Common from Sea of Okhotsk and Kuril Islands, Russia to the Bering Sea and southward to at least southern California. Length to 82.6 cm (32.5 in) TL. Depth: 17–1,524 m (56–5,000 ft). Red to pink, sometimes with darker areas on body and fins; sometimes with dark spot on posterior of dorsal fin; gill cavity pale. A darker morph has extensive black on fins, body, and head. Juveniles may have small white spots on pectoral fin soft-rays. D XIV–XVIII,8–11; A III,4–6; Pect. 20–23; LLp 29–33 + 2 on tail; GR 5–8 + 12–17 = 18–24; Vert. 29–31.

**RAINBOW SCORPIONFISH, *Scorpaenodes xyris* (Jordan & Gilbert, 1882).** Anacapa Island and Santa Barbara Island, southern California to Islas Chincha, Peru, including Gulf of California and Islas Galápagos. Generally uncommon off southern California; common beginning about central Baja California and into tropics. Length to 15 cm (6 in) TL. Depth: intertidal to about 50 m (164 ft). Red, dark to light brown, with lighter spotting over body and fins; black spot on operculum; red eyes. D XIII,9–11; A III,4–6; Pect. 6–19; LLs 44–50; GRt 16–19; Vert. 23–25.

**STONE SCORPIONFISH, *Scorpaena mystes* Jordan & Starks, 1895.** Redondo Beach, southern California (LACM 43543-1) to Chile, including Gulf of California, Islas Galápagos, and other offshore islands. Rare in California; common from Bahía Magdalena into tropics. Length to 51 cm (20 in) TL. Depth: intertidal to 100 m (328 ft). Highly variable colors, but often drab grays, greens, blues, reds, and browns; small white spots on inner side of pectoral fin base. Young with dark bars and prominent white caudal peduncle. D XII,9–10; A III,5–6; Pect. 18–21; GR 6 + 8 (including rudiments). (Recently as *Scorpaena plumieri mystes* Jordan & Starks, 1895) (Alternative name PACIFIC SPOTTED SCORPIONFISH).

## KEY TO THE ROCKFISHES, SCORPIONFISHES, and THORNYHEADS:

Revised by Milton S. Love
(Principal sources: Miller & Lea, 1972; Love et al., 2002)

NOTE: See Figure 20 (page 142) for spine configuration.

1a Dorsal fin spines 12–14 (rarely 11 or 15); lateral ridge from preorbital to preopercle under eye absent or with 0–4 spines….. 3 (next page)

1b Dorsal fin spines 14–17; lateral ridge from preorbital to preopercle under eye with 8–10 spines….. 2 (next page)

2a Third dorsal fin spine usually longest (rarely spine 4 slightly longer), following spines considerably shorter; gill cavity dark gray or black:

**LONGSPINE THORNYHEAD**

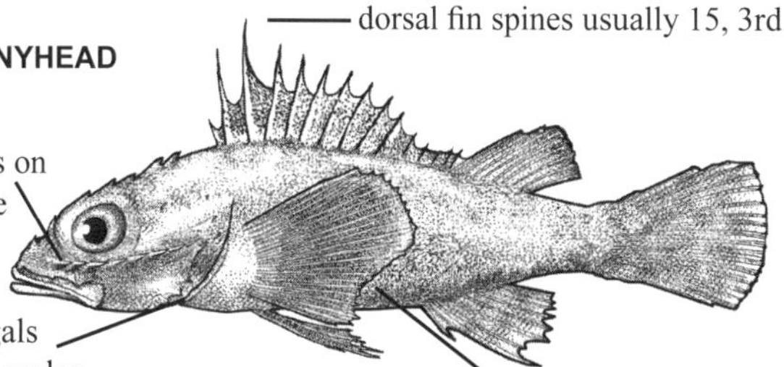


2b Third, 4th, or 5th spine slightly longer than others, following spines gradually shorter; gill cavity pale (often with dusky splotch on inside of operculum):

**SHORTSPINE THORNYHEAD**

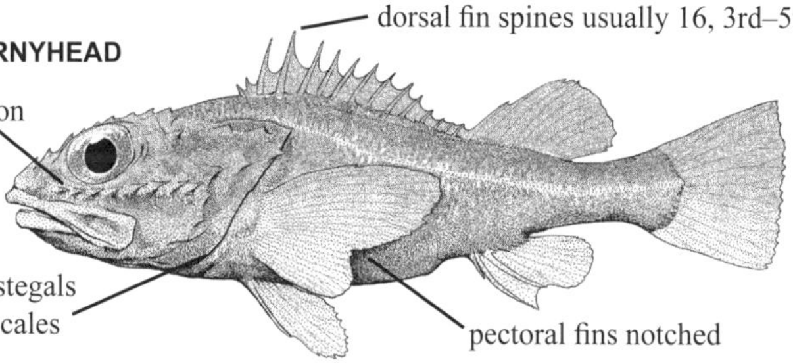


3a *From 1a: dorsal fin spines 12–14 (rarely 11 or 15); lateral ridge absent or with 0–4 spines*
Dorsal fin spines 13 (rarely 11, 12, or 14); lateral ridge under eye absent….. 6 (next page)

3b Dorsal fin spines 12–13; lateral ridge under eye with 0–4 spines….. 4

4a Dorsal fin spines 13; dark spot on lower gill cover:

**RAINBOW SCORPIONFISH**

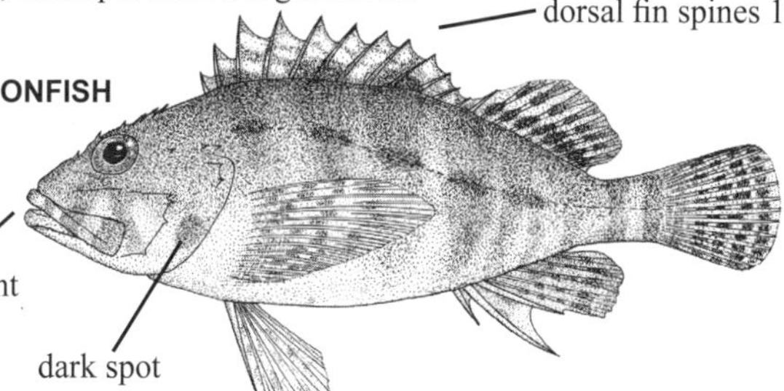


4b Dorsal fin spines 12; no dark spot on lower gill cover…. 5

5a Dense white spots on inner side of pectoral fin:

**STONE SCORPIONFISH**

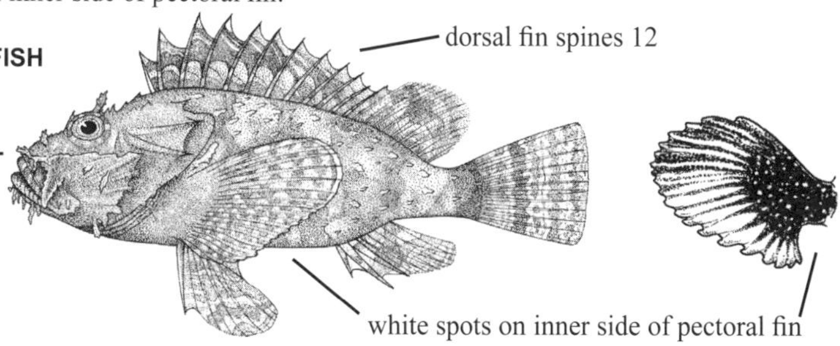


5b (next page)

## ROCKFISHES, SCORPIONFISHES, and THORNYHEADS (continued)

**CALIFORNIA SCORPIONFISH, *Scorpaena guttata* Girard, 1854.** Santa Cruz, central California to Gulf of California. Length to 47 cm (18.5 in) SL, an estimated 57.9 cm (22.3 in) TL. Common from southern California southward into Gulf of California. Depth: intertidal to 191 m (626 ft). Coloration highly variable, including red, lavender, brown, and green; adults with many black or brown spots on body and fins; juveniles occasionally lacking spots. D XII,8–10; A III,5–6; Pect. 17–19; LLp 24–26; LLs 50; GRt 16–19; Vert. 24. (Formerly SPOTTED SCORPIONFISH, SCULPIN: M&L).

**COPPER ROCKFISH, *Sebastes caurinus* Richardson, 1844.** East of Kodiak Island, Western Gulf of Alaska to Islas San Benito, central Baja California. Common from southeastern Alaska to northern Baja California. Length to 66 cm (26 in) TL. Depth: intertidal to 408 m (1,338 ft). Color highly variable: dark brown to almost black, red, yellow-brown to almost white; posterior of lateral line light; 2 or more yellow, copper, or brown bands radiating posteriorly from eye. D XIII,11–14; A III,5–7; Pect. 16–18; LLp 35–45; GR 5–7 + 19–24 = 26–33; Vert. 25–26. (Formerly WHITEBELLY ROCKFISH, *Sebastes vexillaris* (Jordan & Gilbert, 1880): M&L).

**CALICO ROCKFISH, *Sebastes dallii* (Eigenmann & Beeson, 1894).** San Francisco, northern California to Punta Rompiente, southern Baja California (LACM 32056-5). Common from about Monterey Bay, central California to Bahía de Sebastián Vizcaíno, central Baja California. Length to 25.4 cm (10 in) TL. Depth: intertidal to 305 m (1,000 ft). Brown to yellowish-green with irregular red-brown blotches and bars (back-slanting); brown streaks on tail. D XII–XIII,12–14; A III,6–7; Pect. 16–17; LLp 37–51; GRt 30–37; Vert. 27.

**SILVERGRAY ROCKFISH, *Sebastes brevispinis* (Bean, 1884).** Southeastern Bering Sea to Bahía de Sebastián Vizcaíno, central Baja California. Common from the Gulf of Alaska to at least Washington; uncommon off northern California and rare further southward. Documented length to 75 cm (29.5 in) TL. Depth: surface to at least 580 m (1,902 ft). Dark gray, greenish, brown, or black above, silver-gray, pink, or reddish-orange on sides, white below; lower portions of pectoral, anal, and pelvic fins pinkish; lateral line pink. D XIII,13–17; A III,7–8; Pect. 16–18; LLp 43–53; GR 9 + 24–27 = 33–36.

**TREEFISH, *Sebastes serriceps* (Jordan & Gilbert, 1880).** San Francisco, northern California to Isla Cedros, central Baja California. Common from southern California to northern Baja California. Length to 41 cm (16 in) TL. Depth: shallow waters to 103 m (338 ft). Olive to yellowish with 5–6 black, brown, or dark green bars on sides; body often with many light speckles; lips red, orange, or pink. D XIII,13–15; A III,5–7; Pect. 17–19; LLp 44–54; GRt 27–30.

5b No dense white spots on inner side of pectoral fin:

**CALIFORNIA SCORPIONFISH**

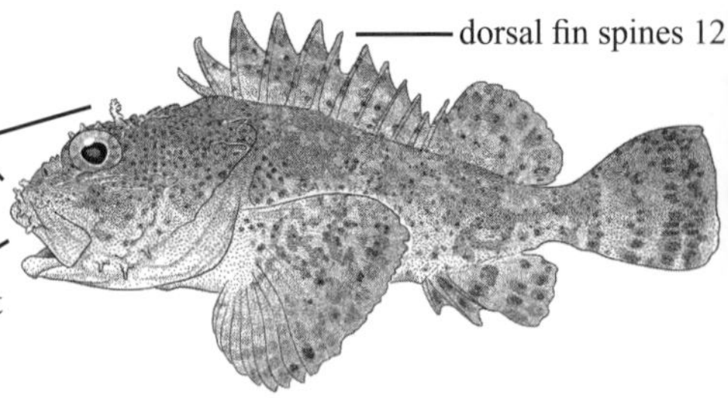


6a *From 3a: dorsal fin spines 13 (rarely 11, 12, or 14); lateral ridge under eye absent*
Body color bright red, pink, or red-orange, often with bars, stripes, blotches, or spotting overlaying basic reddish color….. 28 (page 154)

6b Body color shades of black, blue, dark gray, green, olive, or brown, with no red on body other than small orange spotting and flecking on some individuals, or with occasional reddish flush on belly around base of pectoral or pelvic fins….. 7 (next page)

7a Mandibles covered with scales, rough to touch….. 18 (page 150)

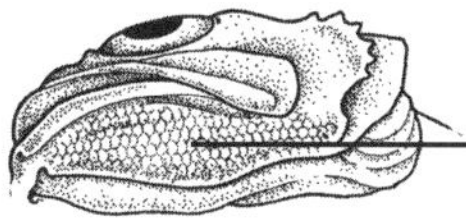


7b Mandibles without scales or with only small patches of fine scales, smooth to touch….. 8

8a Posterior ⅔ of lateral line in whitish or pinkish band:

**COPPER ROCKFISH**

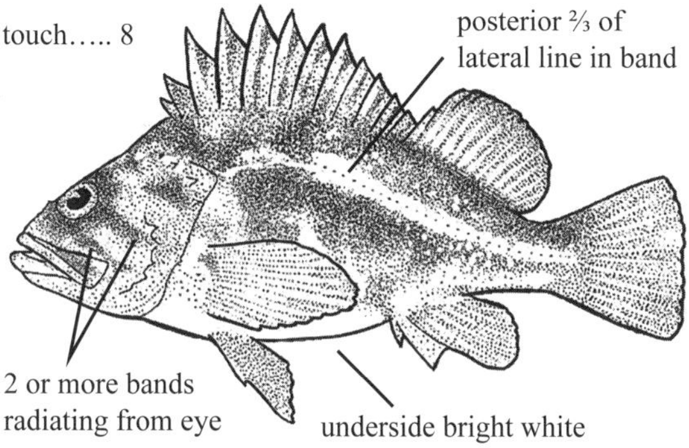


8b Lateral line area not as in 8a….. 9

9a Tail broadly rounded….. 11

9b Tail indented or truncated….. 10

10a Oblique dark bars on sides; back strongly mottled; head spines strong, at least 5 pairs present:

**CALICO ROCKFISH**

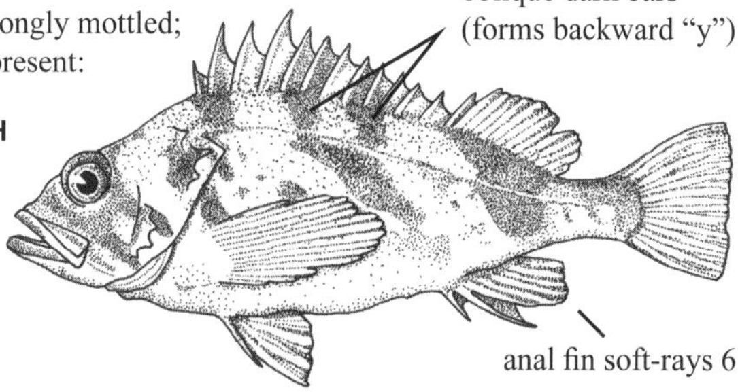


10b Body color uniform greenish, gray, or black on back, silvery below ringed with orange or pink; head spines weak, usually no more than 4 pairs present:

**SILVERGRAY ROCKFISH**

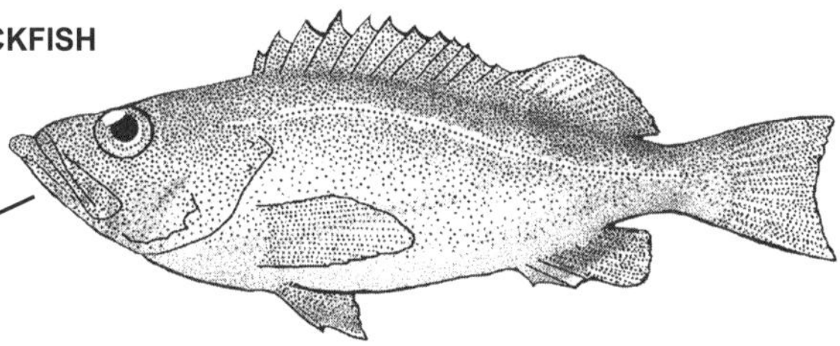


11a *From 9a: tail broadly rounded*
Body yellowish or greenish with dark bars on sides reaching belly; lips reddish or pinkish:

**TREEFISH**

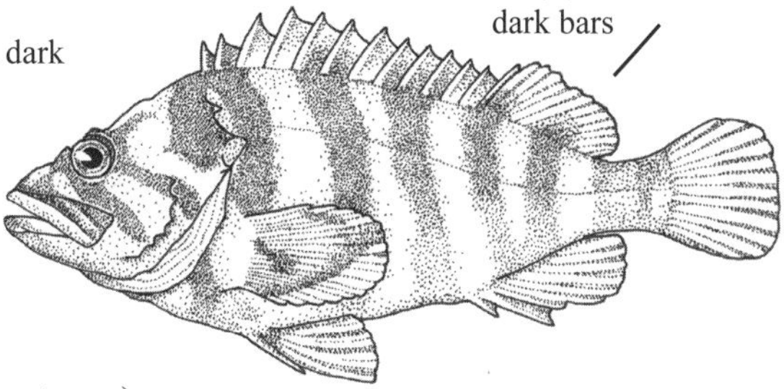


11b No strong bars as in 11a….. 12 (next page)

## ROCKFISHES, SCORPIONFISHES, and THORNYHEADS (continued)

**CHINA ROCKFISH, *Sebastes nebulosus* Ayres, 1854.** Kodiak Island, western Gulf of Alaska to Redondo Beach and San Nicolas Island, southern California. Common from at least British Columbia to central California. Length to 45 cm (17.7 in) TL. Depth: 3–128 m (10–420 ft). Black with yellow and white mottling; broad yellow stripe from about 3rd dorsal fin spine along lateral line to tail. An entirely yellow morph is known. D XIII,12–14; A III,6–8; Pect. 17–19; LLp 37–48; GR 7–9 + 19–22 = 25–31; Vert. 26.

**BLACK-AND-YELLOW ROCKFISH, *Sebastes chrysomelas* (Jordan & Gilbert, 1881).** Cape Blanco, Oregon to Bahía Santa Maria (24°46'N, 112°15'W), southern Baja California. Common from Fort Bragg, northern California to northern Baja California. Length to 38.7 cm (15.3 in) TL. Depth: intertidal to 37 m (120 ft). Black or dark olive with yellow blotches and spotting. D XIII,12–14; A III,5–7; Pect. 17–18; LLp 35–46; GRt 24–31.

**GOPHER ROCKFISH, *Sebastes carnatus* (Jordan & Gilbert, 1880).** Cape Blanco, Oregon to Punta San Roque (27°12'N, 114°26'W), southern Baja California. Common from northern California to northern Baja California. Length to 43 cm (16.9 in) TL. Depth: intertidal to 86 m (282 ft). Olive-brown to reddish-brown with flesh-colored or whitish spotting and blotches; anterior of lower jaw often yellow. D XIII,12–14; A III,5–7; Pect. 16–18; LLp 34–49; GRt 23–32; Vert. 26.

**BROWN ROCKFISH, *Sebastes auriculatus* Girard, 1854.** Prince William Sound, northern Gulf of Alaska to Bahía Magdalena, southern Baja California (LACM 31831-1). Common from southeastern Alaska to Puget Sound and from Bodega Bay, northern California to perhaps Bahía Tortugas, southern Baja California. Length to 56 cm (22 in) TL. Depth: surf zone to 294 m (964 ft). Brown to red-brown with light orange-brown to black mottling; dark brown spot on operculum. D XIII,12–15; A III,5–8; Pect. 15–19; LLp 40–50; LLs 45–52; GR 7–8 + 18–21 = 21–30; Vert. 26.

**QUILLBACK ROCKFISH, *Sebastes maliger* (Jordan & Gilbert, 1880).** West of Shumagin Islands (54°36'N, 161°30'W), Gulf of Alaska to Anacapa Passage, southern California (LACM 47276-1). Common from southeastern Alaska to central California. Length to 63.6 cm (25 in) TL. Depth: intertidal to 274 m (899 ft). Brown or orange-brown with yellow mottling on back and in dorsal fin; orange spotting on underside. D XIII,12–14; A III,6–8; Pect. 16–18; LLp 34–48; GR 8–9 + 21–25 = 29–33.

12a Interorbital space convex, flat, or slightly concave; space between base of preocular spines much wider than space between tip of nasal spines; no yellow band reaching to caudal fin; no large diagonal spots above lateral line….. 15 (next page)

12b Interorbital space strongly concave; space between base of preocular spines usually narrower than or about equal to distance between tip of nasal spines; yellow longitudinal stripe on back or diagonal spots above lateral line….. 13

13a Continuous yellow stripe extending from membranes of 3rd and 4th dorsal fin spines to tail; anal fin soft-rays 7 (rarely 6 or 8); unbranched pectoral fin soft-rays usually 10 (occasionally 9 or 11):

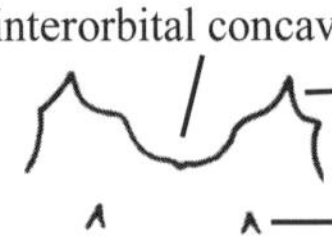


**CHINA ROCKFISH**

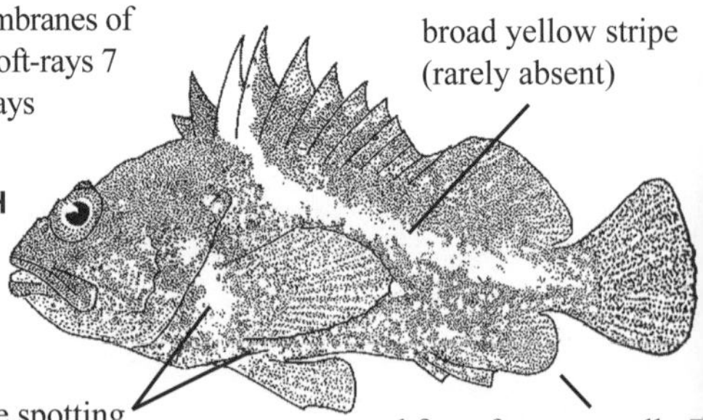


13b (next page)

13b No continuous yellow stripe on body; anal fin soft-rays 6 (rarely 5 or 7); unbranched pectoral fin soft-rays usually 8 or 9 (occasionally 7 or 10) ….. 14

14a Large yellow spots on back; body blackish: **BLACK-AND-YELLOW ROCKFISH** (not illustrated; body shape as in 14b)

14b Large whitish to flesh-colored spots on back; body brown:

**GOPHER ROCKFISH**

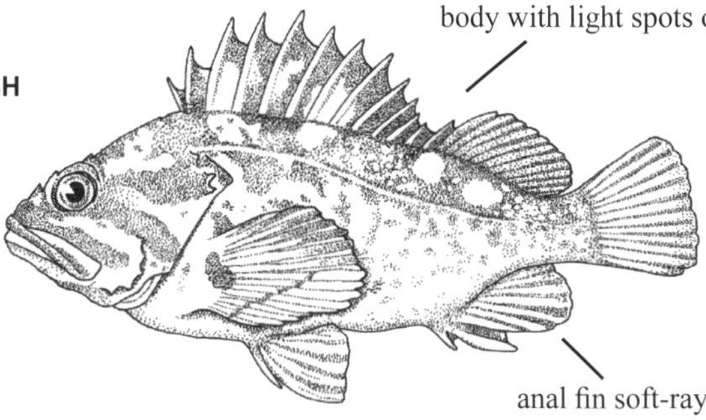


15a *From 12a: interorbital space convex, flat or slightly concave*
Coronal spines present (rarely absent); caudal, pelvic, and pectoral fin membranes may be pinkish:

**BROWN ROCKFISH**

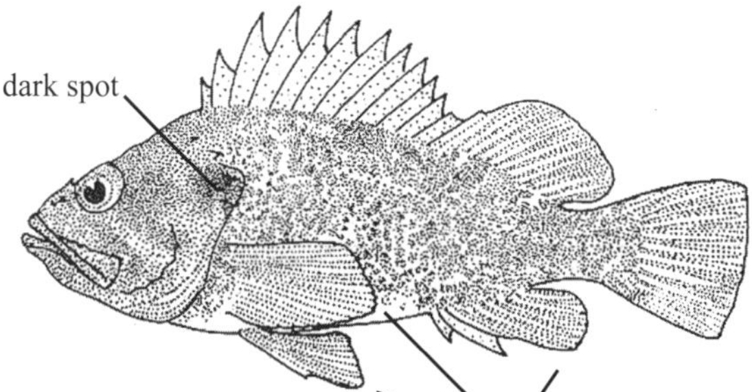


15b Coronal spines absent; caudal, pelvic, and pectoral fins without pink….. 16

16a Orange-yellow area in fin membranes of 2nd to 6th or 8th dorsal fin spines extending part way down back; pectoral and pelvic fins blackish:

**QUILLBACK ROCKFISH**

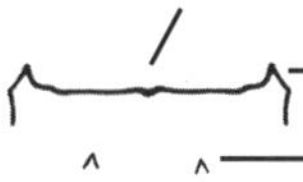


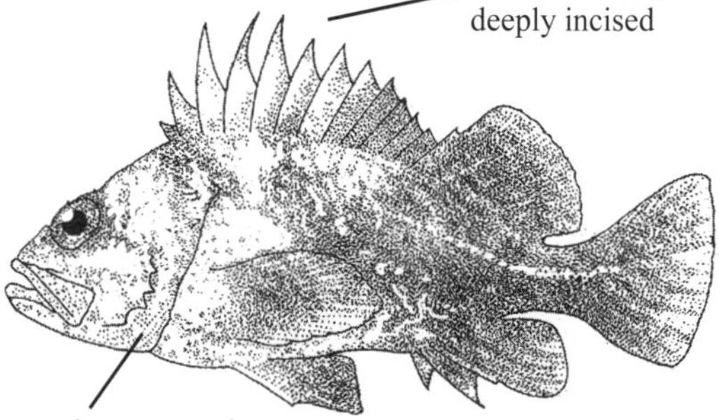


16b No orange-yellow area as in 16a; pectoral and pelvic fins not blackish….. 17 (next page)

## ROCKFISHES, SCORPIONFISHES, and THORNYHEADS (continued)

**GRASS ROCKFISH, *Sebastes rastrelliger* (Jordan & Gilbert, 1880).** Ucluelet, Vancouver Island, British Columbia to Bahía Playa Maria (28°50'N), central Baja California. Common from northern California to central Baja California. Length to 55.9 cm (22 in) TL. Depth: intertidal to 46 m (150 ft). Dark green to almost black above, mottled lighter green and brown below; occasionally with dark blotch on operculum. D XIII,12–14; A III,6; Pect. 18–20; LLp 40–49; GRt 17–26; Vert. 26.

**KELP ROCKFISH, *Sebastes atrovirens* (Jordan & Gilbert, 1880).** Fort Bragg, northern California (SIO 00-54) to Bahía San Carlos (29°36'N, 115°12'W) and Islas Cedros and San Benito, central Baja California. Common from around Point Reyes, northern California to northern Baja California. Length to 42.5 cm (16.8 in) TL. Depth: shallow inshore to 82 m (269 ft). This species was reportedly taken in 190–300 m (623–984 ft) by Snytko (1986). However, this is much deeper than any other record and needs documentation. Color variable: mottled brown, yellowish, pinkish, white, or black with darker flecking; sometimes with vague blotch on operculum; 2 faint bands radiating posteriorly from eye. D XIII,12–15; A III,6–8; Pect. 16–18; LLp 36–50; GRt 28–36; Vert. 26.

**BLACK ROCKFISH, *Sebastes melanops* Girard, 1856.** Southern Bering Sea and Rat Island, Aleutian Islands to northern Baja California. Common from about Kodiak Island, Gulf of Alaska to central California. Length to 69 cm (27.2 in) TL. Depth: surface to 366 m (1,200 ft). Black with gray streak and white mottling on sides. Young-of-the-year with dark spot on rear of spinous dorsal fin. D XII–XIII,13–16; A III,7–10; Pect. 18–20; LLp 45–55; GR 9–10 + 23–29 = 32–40; Vert. 26.

**DARK ROCKFISH, *Sebastes ciliatus* (Tilesius, 1813).** Western Aleutian Islands and eastern Bering Sea to Johnstone Strait, British Columbia and perhaps to Whidbey Island, Washington. Common at least from along Aleutian Islands to southeast Alaska. Length to 47 cm (18.5 in) FL. Depth: 5–160 m (17–528 ft). Often more or less uniformly gray-black to gray, sometimes with black spots and splotches; belly region dark. D XIII (rarely XIV),13–17; A III,7–9; Pect. 16–19; LLp 39–54; GRt 32–37. Although not reported off California, occasionally an individual in California waters may have been misidentified as BLACK ROCKFISH.

**DEACON ROCKFISH, *Sebastes diaconus* Frable, Wagman, Frierson, Aguilar & Sidlauskas, 2015.** At least Vancouver Island, British Columbia to Santa Rosa Island, southern California. Common from Morro Bay, central California, northward. Records of "BLUE ROCKFISH" from Alaska [i.e., Chatham Strait and Kruzof Island, southeastern Alaska and perhaps to Elfin Cove, southeastern Alaska] are likely either this species or DARK ROCKFISH. It is likely that all "BLUE ROCKFISH" from the Bering Sea and the western Gulf of Alaska refer to DARK ROCKFISH. Length to 41 cm (16.1 in) FL. Depth: at least 8–72 m (26–236 ft). Body dark brown to blue-gray, belly white to light gray; small speckles covering sides (not forming blotches as in BLUE ROCKFISH). Young-of-the-year with dark spot on rear of spinous dorsal fin. D XII–XIII,14–17; A III,8–9; Pect. 16–18; LLp 41–51; GR 8–10 + 20–25 = 28–35; Vert. 26–27.

17a Gill rakers 17–26, short and blunt on 1st gill arch (in juveniles up to about 18 cm [7 in], rakers are short only on upper limb); no scales on mandibles:

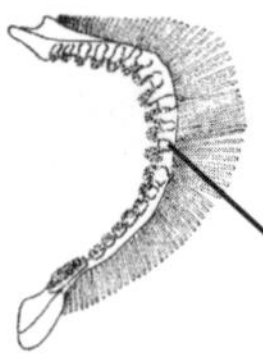

**GRASS ROCKFISH**

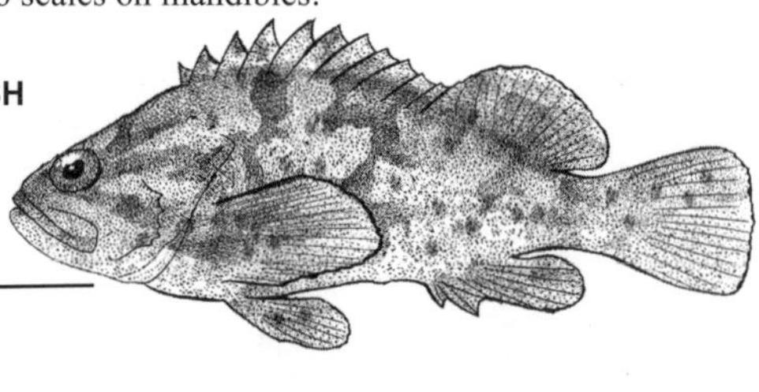

gill rakers short and blunt on 1st arch

17b (next page)

17b Gill rakers 28–36, long and slender in both juveniles and adults; mandibles usually (but not always) without scales: **KELP ROCKFISH** (see 18a)

18a *From 7a: mandibles covered with scales*
Tail rounded; head spines strong, at least 5 pairs present:

**KELP ROCKFISH**

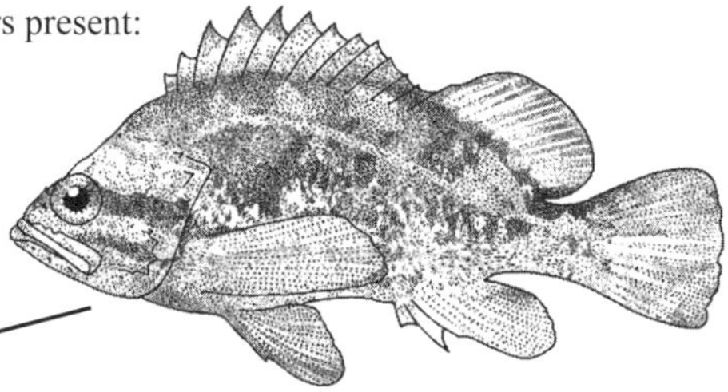


18b Tail indented or deeply forked; head spines weak or obsolete, usually with 4 pairs or fewer….. 19

19a Body color olive, yellow-brown, grayish green/brown, or bronze….. 23 (page 152)

19b Body color black or blue….. 20

20a Spinous dorsal membranes blackish with distinct black spotting; maxilla extends to under rear of orbit or beyond:

**BLACK ROCKFISH**

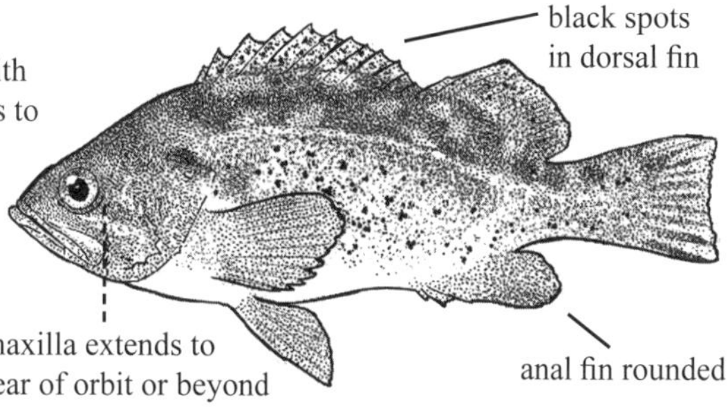


20b Spinous dorsal fin membranes blackish but without distinct spotting; maxilla does not extend beyond rear of orbit….. 21

21a Parietal spine present (occasionally absent); head coloration uniform (occasionally 2 faint bands below eye):

**DARK ROCKFISH**

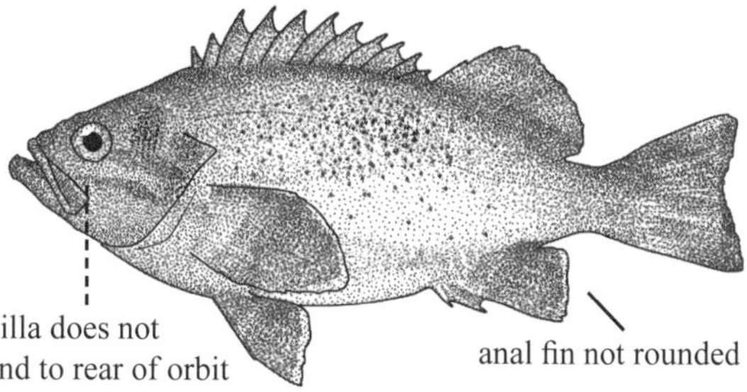


21b Parietal spine absent; 4 dark bands across head and back of neck….. 22

22a Trunk dark brown to blue-gray with small blue-gray speckles (pattern difficult to distinguish from that of BLUE ROCKFISH in specimens less than 10 cm [4 in] TL); symphyseal knob protruding:

**DEACON ROCKFISH**

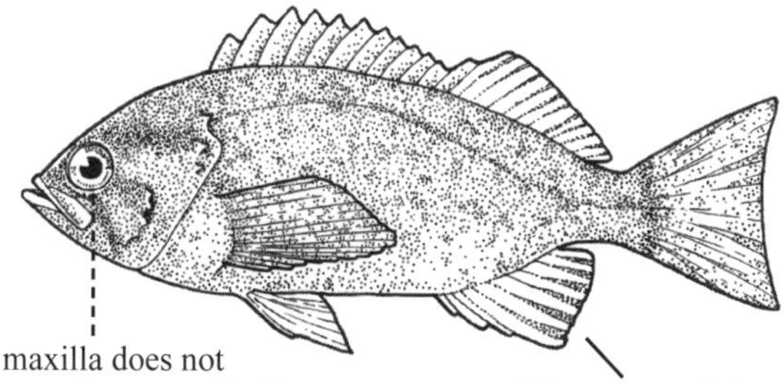


22b (next page)

## ROCKFISHES, SCORPIONFISHES, and THORNYHEADS (continued)

**BLUE ROCKFISH, *Sebastes mystinus* (Jordan & Gilbert, 1881).** At least central Oregon (40°30'N) to northern Baja California (32°30'N) and probably to just south of Punta Baja (29°55'N, 115°49'W), northern Baja California. Common off central and southern California. Records from off Canada and Alaska are either of DEACON ROCKFISH or DARK ROCKFISH. Length to at least 38.5 cm (15.2 in) TL, but perhaps to 53.3 cm (21 in) TL. Depth: surface to at least 156 m (512 ft) and probably including the intertidal zone; a record of about 549 m (1,800 ft) (Eschmeyer and Herald, 1983) is without documentation. Body color variable: steel-blue to greenish-blue; belly white; sides with large, dark, angular blotches and no speckles (blotches absent and speckles present in DEACON ROCKFISH). Young-of-the-year with dark spot on rear of spinous dorsal fin. D XII–XV,13–17; A III,8–10; Pect. 16–19; LLp 42–52; Vert. 26–27. The maximum size, geographic, and depth ranges of this species are unclear due to previous confusion with DEACON ROCKFISH and DARK ROCKFISH.

**SQUARESPOT ROCKFISH, *Sebastes hopkinsi* (Cramer, 1895).** Southern Oregon to Punta Eugenia-Isla Natividad, central Baja California and Isla Guadalupe, central Baja California. Common from at least central California to off Bahía San Quintin, northern Baja California. Length to 29 cm (11.5 in) TL. Depth: 15–305 m (50–1,000 ft). Brown, tan, or yellow-brown with dark brown square-shaped blotches (these may be faint in some individuals); dark bars radiate posteriorly from eye. D XII–XIII,13–17; A III,6–8; Pect. 16–18; LLp 49–58; GRt 35–43.

**SPECKLED ROCKFISH, *Sebastes ovalis* (Ayres, 1862).** Northern Washington (47°38'N) to Arrecife Sacramento (29°40'N, 115°47'W), central Baja California. Common from central California to at least Punta Colnett, northern Baja California. Length to 56 cm (22 in) TL. Depth: 30–366 m (100–1,200 ft). Tan or brown (often with pink or yellow overtones) with dark speckles on body and dorsal fin; vague saddles may be present on back. D XIII,13–17; A III,7–9; Pect. 17–19; LLp 45–55; GRt 29–37.

**WIDOW ROCKFISH, *Sebastes entomelas* (Jordan & Gilbert, 1880).** Albatross Bank, western Gulf of Alaska to Bahía de Todos Santos, northern Baja California. Common from southeastern Alaska to southern California. Length to 62 cm (24.4 in) TL. Depth: near surface (juveniles and adults) to 800 m (2,625 ft). Young-of-the-year rarely in tide pools. Brassy-brown or brown on sides often with reddish flush on belly; often some faint dark blotching on back; pectoral, pelvic, and anal fin membranes dark. Juveniles with dark spot on rear of spinous dorsal fin, light saddles on back and light bars radiating posteriorly from eye. D XII–XIII,14–16; A III,7–10; Pect. 17–19; LLp 50–60; GR 9–10 + 25–28 = 33–39; Vert. 26.

22b Trunk steel-blue to greenish-blue with large, brighter gray-blue blotches (blotches visible in preserved specimens); symphyseal knob weak to absent:

**BLUE ROCKFISH**

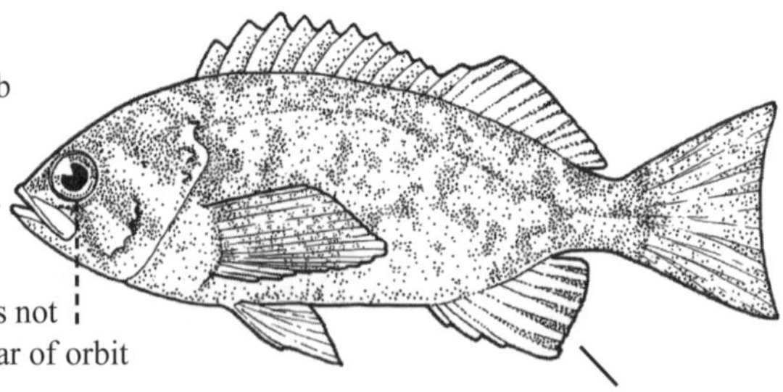


23a (next page)

23a *From 19a: body color olive, yellow-brown, grayish-green/brown, or bronze*
Tip of 2nd anal fin spine extends beyond tip of 3rd anal fin spine; body with angular dark blotches on and above lateral line:

**SQUARESPOT ROCKFISH**

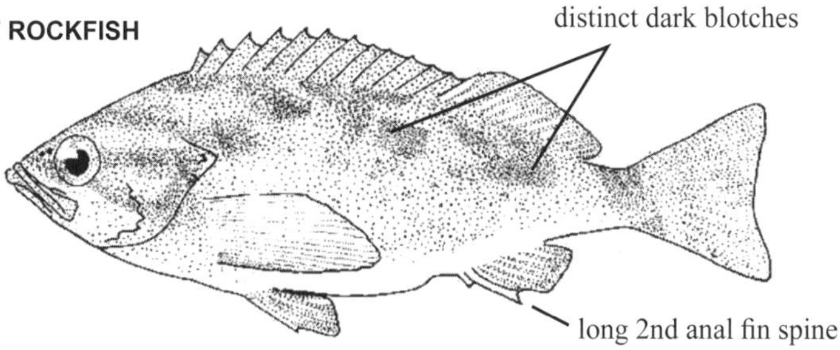


23b Tip of 2nd anal fin spine does not extend beyond tip of 3rd anal fin spine; body without angular dark blotches….. 24

24a Body orange-brown above, yellow-tan below, profusely covered with small jet-black speckles (speckles rarely larger than nostril openings); 2 lachrymal spines pointing directly backward:

**SPECKLED ROCKFISH**

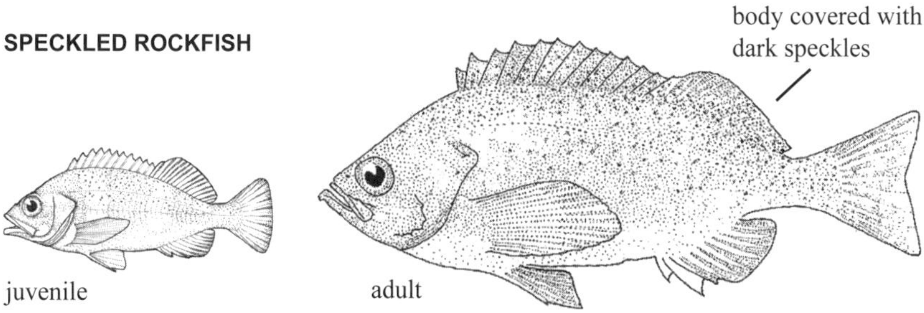


24b Body without black spots; 0–1 lachrymal spine….. 25

25a Fin membranes yellowish or olive….. 27 (page 154)

25b Pectoral, pelvic, and anal fin membranes dark….. 26

26a End of maxilla usually not extending beyond middle of eye; no symphyseal knob:

**WIDOW ROCKFISH**

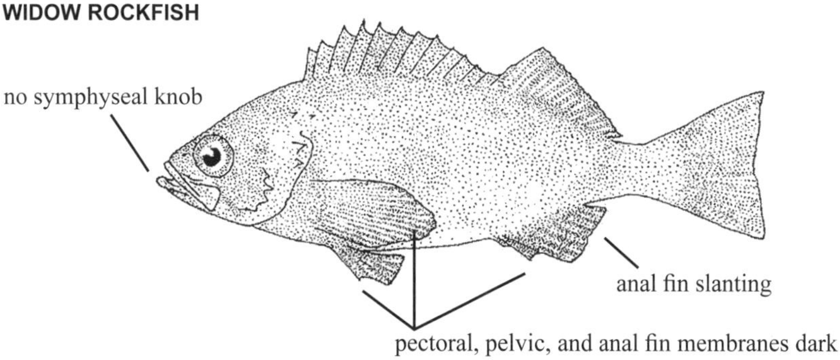


26b (next page)

## ROCKFISHES, SCORPIONFISHES, and THORNYHEADS (continued)

**DUSKY ROCKFISH, *Sebastes variabilis* Pallas, 1814.** Hokkaido, Japan; eastern Kamchatka to about 60°00'N in the Bering Sea and along the Aleutian Islands to Johnstone Strait, British Columbia; one record from Oregon (44°24'N, 124°47'W). Common at least from off Aleutian Islands to southeast Alaska. Length to 59 cm (23.2 in) FL, an estimated 60.9 cm (24 in) TL. Depth: 6–675 m (20–2,214 ft). Golden-yellow to greenish-brown sides; belly pink, white, or red; pectoral, pelvic, and anal fin membranes dark. Juveniles similar, but with reddish-orange flecking on sides. D XIII (rarely XIV),13–16; A III,7–9; Pect. 16–19; LLp 42–54; GRt 32–37. (Alternative name LIGHT DUSKY ROCKFISH).

**YELLOWTAIL ROCKFISH, *Sebastes flavidus* (Ayres, 1862).** Eastern Aleutian Islands south of Unalaska Island to Isla San Martin, northern Baja California. Common from Gulf of Alaska southward to San Miguel Island, southern California. Length to 66 cm (26 in) TL. Depth: surface to 549 m (1,801 ft), including intertidal zone. Brown, brassy, or greenish-brown with yellow fins, light areas under dorsal fin. Young-of-the-year with dark spot on rear of spinous dorsal fin. D XII–XIII,13–16; A III,7–9; Pect. 17–19; LLp 46–60; GR 9–12 + 23–29 = 31–39; Vert. 26.

**OLIVE ROCKFISH, *Sebastes serranoides* (Eigenmann & Eigenmann, 1890).** Southern Oregon to Islas San Benito, central Baja California. Common from northern California to northern Baja California. Length to 61 cm (24 in) TL. Depth: surface and intertidal to 172 m (564 ft). Dark brown or olive-brown on back and lighter greenish-brown, brown, or gray on sides; greenish or light blotches on back. Young-of-the-year with dark spot on rear of spinous dorsal fin. D XII–XIII,15–17; A III,8–10; Pect. 17–19; LLp 50–58; GRt 29–36; Vert. 26.

**STARRY ROCKFISH, *Sebastes constellatus* (Jordan & Gilbert, 1880).** Sea Lion Gulch State Marine Reserve, northern California to off Todos Santos (23°24'N, 110°14'W), southern Baja California. Tentatively identified from photographs taken at Rocas Alijos (about 25°00'N, 115°45'W), southern Baja California. Common from central California to at least off Bahía Tortugas, southern Baja California. Length to 46 cm (18 in) TL. Depth: 15–274 m (50–900 ft). Adults and subadults: body orange, red, or red-brown; body profusely covered in white to blue-white spots; 3–5 white blotches on back. Young lemon-yellow and lack spotting. D XIII–XV,12–14; A III,5–7; Pect. 16–18; LLp 37–47; GRt 24–30; Vert. 25–26.

**GREENSPOTTED ROCKFISH, *Sebastes chlorostictus* (Jordan & Gilbert, 1880).** Vancouver Island (49°04'N, 126°43'W) to at least Isla Cedros (28°23'N, 115°17'W), central Baja California or perhaps to southern Baja California (25°32'N, 113°04'W) but without documentation. Common from central California to at least off Bahía San Quintin, northern Baja California. Length to 53.4 cm (21 in) FL, an estimated 54.2 cm (21.3 in) TL. Depth: 30–379 m (98–1,243 ft). Orange, yellowish, or reddish on back with 3–5 white or pink blotches on back; back and top of head profusely covered in greenish or brownish speckles and vermiculations. D XIII,11–15; A III,5–7; Pect. 16–18; LLp 34–43; GRt 29–36; Vert. 26–27.

26b End of maxilla extends beyond middle of eye; symphyseal knob present:

**DUSKY ROCKFISH**

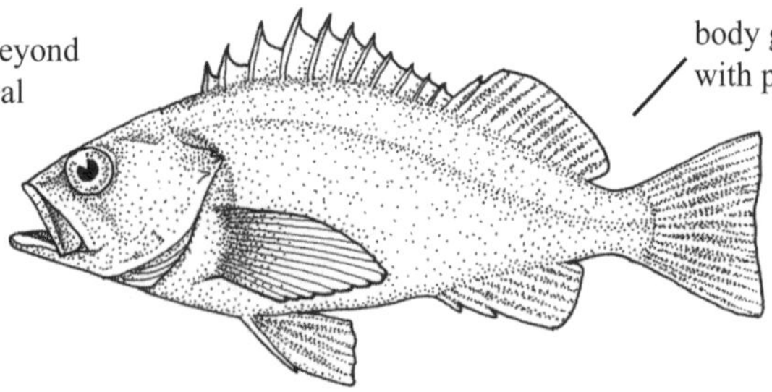


27a (next page)

27a *From 25a: fin membranes yellowish or olive*
Anal fin soft-rays usually 8 (rarely 7 or 9); fine reddish-brown speckling on few to many scales; gill rakers 31–39:

**YELLOWTAIL ROCKFISH**

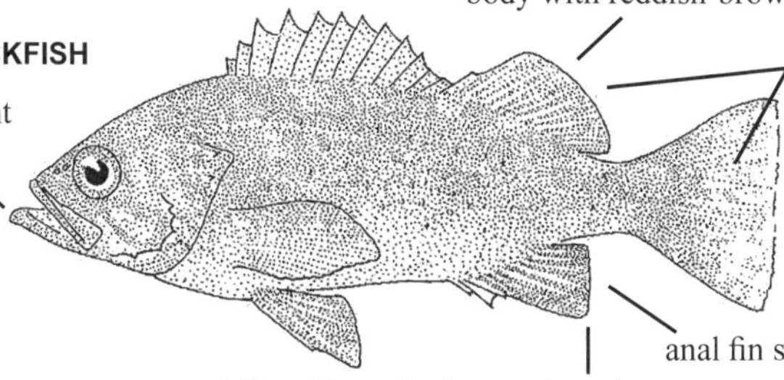


27b Anal fin soft-rays usually 9; no reddish-brown speckling on scales; gill rakers 29–36:

**OLIVE ROCKFISH**

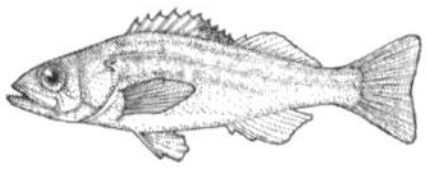


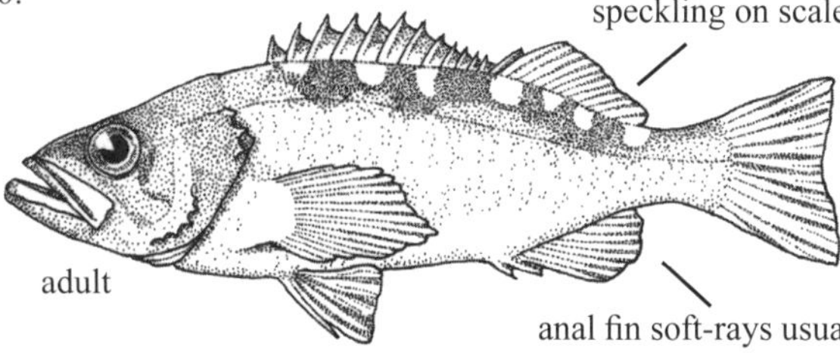


28a *From 6a: body color bright red, pink, or red-orange*
Area between dorsal fin and lateral line without 3–5 irregular whitish blotches; interorbital space convex, flat, or slightly concave (on all but FLAG, REDBANDED, and CHAMELEON ROCKFISHES, which have deeply concave interorbital space)….. 38 (page 158)

28b From 3–5 irregular white blotches (sometimes yellowish or pink) on back; interorbital space moderately to deeply concave….. 29

29a Body red-orange, profusely covered with small, regular white, yellow, or light blue spots:

**STARRY ROCKFISH**

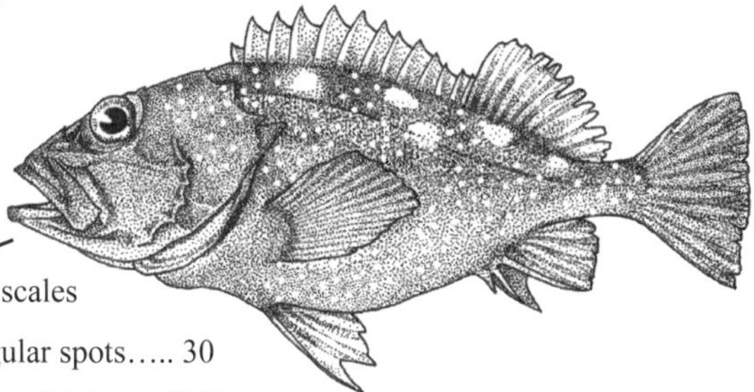


29b Body not profusely covered with regular spots….. 30

30a Mandibles more or less fully scaled….. 34 (page 156)

30b Mandibles without scales or with small patches of fine scales….. 31

31a Body red-orange to pink with sharply defined bright green speckles and vermiculations on back and top of head:

**GREENSPOTTED ROCKFISH**

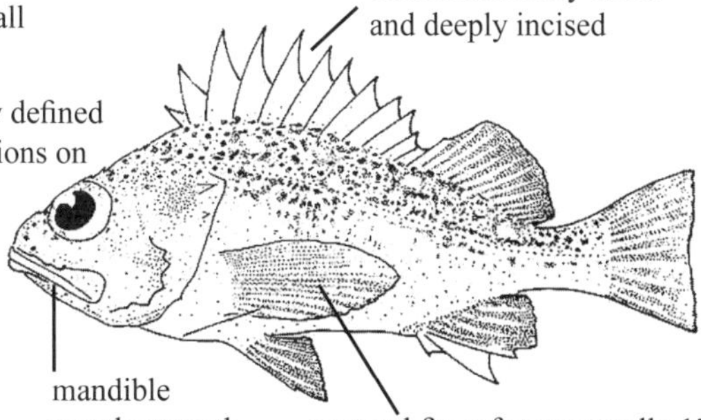


31b No sharply defined bright green speckles as in 31a….. 32 (next page)

## ROCKFISHES, SCORPIONFISHES, and THORNYHEADS (continued)

**ROSY ROCKFISH, *Sebastes rosaceus* Girard, 1854.** Cobb Seamount (46°44'N, 130°47'W) to Bahía Tortugas (27°30'N, 114°50'W), southern Baja California. A report from the Strait of Juan de Fuca, Washington is undocumented. Common from northern California to Punta Colnett, northern Baja California. Length to 35 cm (13.8 in) FL, about 36.9 cm (14.5 in) TL. Depth: 7–328 m (24–1,076 ft). Body often mixture of red-orange, purple, and red; 3–6 white, white-purple, or purple blotches on back (rarely absent); lateral line occasionally purple. D XIII–XIV,11–14; A III,5–7; Pect. 16–18; LLp 36–46; GR 8–11 + 20–24 = 27–34; Vert. 26–27.

**ROSETHORN ROCKFISH, *Sebastes helvomaculatus* Ayres, 1859.** Western Gulf of Alaska east of Sitkinak Island to at least the U.S.-Mexican border (32°26'N, 119°07'W) (SIO 64-988) or perhaps to Banco Ranger (28°33'N, 115°25'W), central Baja California, but without documentation. Common from about Yakutat, Gulf of Alaska to central California. Length to 43 cm (16.9 in) TL. Depth: 16–1,145 m (52–3,756 ft). Body various shades of orange, reds, and yellows (often with greenish tinge on back); dusky blotch on operculum; 4–5 white or pink blotches (if white then lined with pink or orange) on back. D XII–XIV,12–14; A III,5–7; Pect. 15–18; LLp 34–45; GR 8–11 + 20–23 = 28–33; Vert. 26.

**PINKROSE ROCKFISH, *Sebastes simulator* Chen, 1971.** Mattole Canyon State Marine Reserve, northern California to Punta Colnett (30°53'N, 116°30'W), northern Baja California and Isla Guadalupe, central Baja California. Common from central California southward. Documented length to 34.5 cm (13.6 in) TL, undocumented length to 42.1 cm (16.4 in) TL. Depth: 99–450 m (325–1,476 ft). Body red, red-orange, or red-yellow; 4–5 white or pink blotches on back; usually a greenish or brownish blotch on operculum. D XIII,12–14; A III,5–6; Pect. 16–18; LLp 33–40; GR 8–10 + 20–23 = 28–33; Vert. 26.

**FRECKLED ROCKFISH, *Sebastes lentiginosus* Chen, 1971.** Point Conception (34°36'N), central California to southern Baja California (25°37'N, 113°40'W) (LACM 42178-4). Common from Santa Monica Bay, southern California southward to at least Punta San Roque, southern Baja California. Length to about 23 cm (9 in) TL. Depth: 22–168 m (73–551 ft), possibly to 290 m (951 ft). Orange-brown with dark or green freckling. D XIII,12–13; A III,6–7; Pect. 16–18; LLp 33–41; GR 9–12 + 24–27 = 34–39; Vert. 26.

**HONEYCOMB ROCKFISH, *Sebastes umbrosus* (Jordan & Gilbert, 1882).** Point Pinos, central California to Rocas Alijos (24°57'N, 15°44'W), southern Baja California (LACM 37658-2). Common from about Santa Monica Bay, southern California southward to at least central Baja California. Length to 28.5 cm (11.2 in) TL. Depth: 18–270 m (60–886 ft). Body orange-brown, light orange, or pink-yellow; 3–5 whitish, brown, pink, or orange blotches on back; dark edge on scales forming honeycomb pattern. D XII–XIV,11–13; A III,5–7; Pect. 15–18; LLp 33–44; GRt 31–38.

32a White blotches bordered with purple-red; purple bar across nape behind eyes:

**ROSY ROCKFISH**

32b White blotches not bordered by purple-red; no purple bar across nape….. 33 (next page)

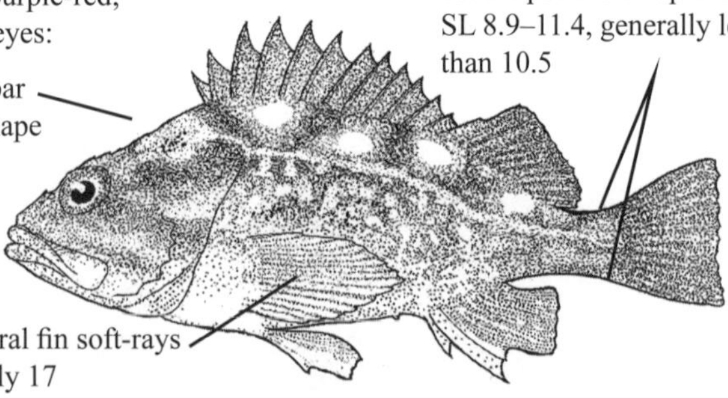

33a Body pinkish-yellow on sides, greenish-yellow on back; pectoral fin soft-rays usually 16 (rarely 15, 17, or 18); lachrymal width into interorbital space 1.3–1.9:

**ROSETHORN ROCKFISH**

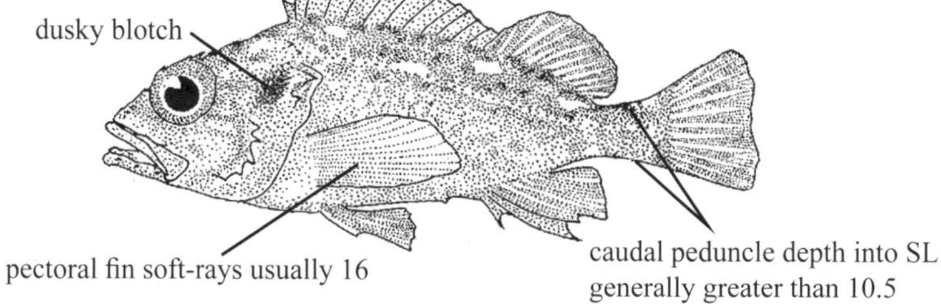


33b Color plain red or red-orange; pectoral fin rays usually 17 (rarely 16 or 18); lachrymal width into interorbital space 1.9–2.5:

**PINKROSE ROCKFISH**

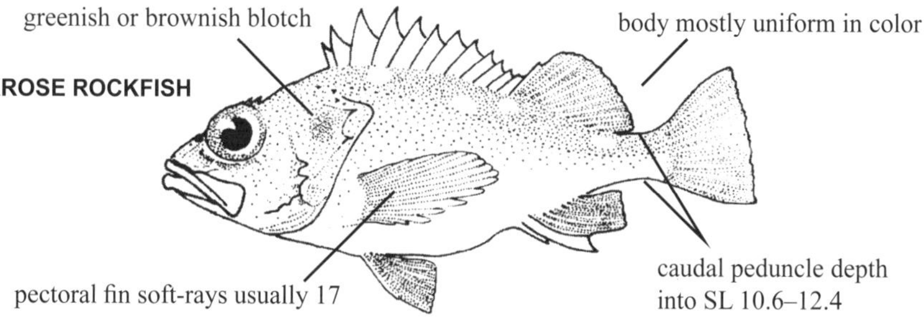


34a *From 30a: mandibles more or less fully scaled*
Premaxillaries extending forward forming dentigerous knobs; body densely freckled with dark green or brown:

**FRECKLED ROCKFISH**

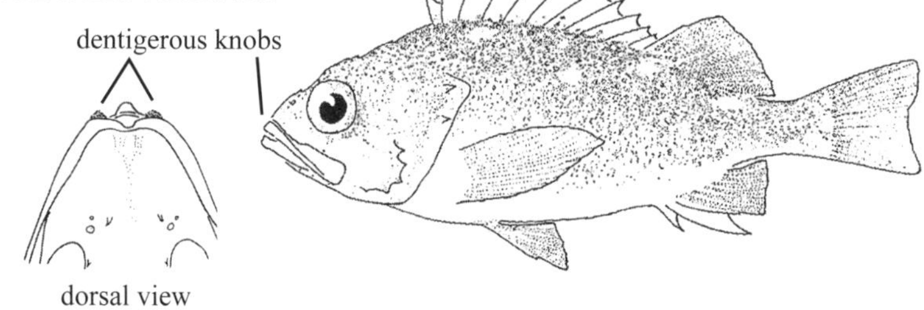


34b No dentigerous knobs extending as in 34a; body without green freckling….. 35

35a Scales along midbody bordered with black forming a honeycomb appearance:

**HONEYCOMB ROCKFISH**

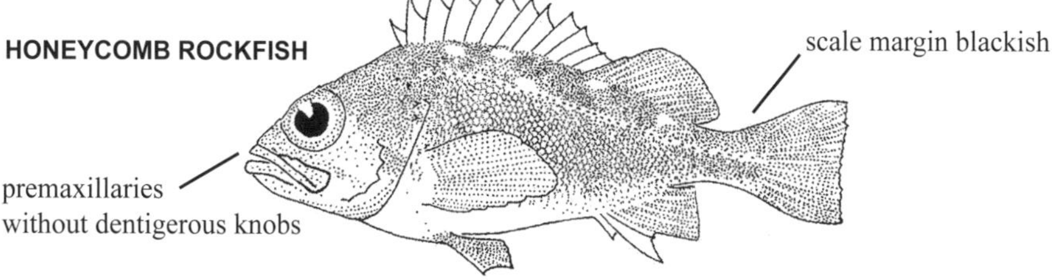


35b Scales without dark margin as in 35a….. 36 (next page)

## ROCKFISHES, SCORPIONFISHES, and THORNYHEADS (continued)

**SWORDSPINE ROCKFISH, *Sebastes ensifer* Chen, 1971.** San Francisco, northern California to Banco Ranger (28°25'N, 115°32'W), central Baja California. Common from Santa Barbara Channel, southern California southward. Length to 30.5 cm (12 in) TL. Depth: 50–433 m (164–1,420 ft). Orange-red, white below often with purplish-red mottling on back; 3–5 white blotches on back sometimes edged in green. D XIII,12–14; A III,5–7; Pect. 16–18; LLp 34–44; GR 10–12 + 24–28 = 34–40; Vert. 26.

**PINK ROCKFISH, *Sebastes eos* (Eigenmann & Eigenmann, 1890).** Central Oregon (44°33'N) to southern Baja California (27°01'N, 114°16'W) (SIO 65-203) or perhaps to 25°24'N, 113°01'W, but without documentation, and Isla Guadalupe, central Baja California. Common from southern California to central Baja California. Length to 56 cm (22 in) TL. Depth: 45–366 m (150–1,200 ft). Pink or orange with olive-green vermiculations on upper part of body (vermiculations "fuzzy" on edge, fading in large individuals); 3–5 white or pink blotches on back. D XIII,11–13; A III,5–7; Pect. 16–18; LLp 34–42; GRt 26–31.

**GREENBLOTCHED ROCKFISH, *Sebastes rosenblatti* Chen, 1971.** Point Delgada (40°04'N), northern California to Banco Ranger, central Baja California. Common from central California to Banco Ranger and Isla Guadalupe, central Baja California. Length to 54 cm (21.3 in) TL. Depth: 55–491 m (180–1,610 ft). Pink, orange, and yellow with green or brownish vermiculations on back and head (vermiculations on large fish difficult to see). D XIII–XIV,11–13; A III,5–6; Pect. 16–18; LLp 34–42; GRt 28–34; Vert. 26.

**SHORTBELLY ROCKFISH, *Sebastes jordani* (Gilbert, 1896).** North of Graham Island (54°23'N, 133°27'W), British Columbia to southern Baja California (23°28'N, 110°43'W). A record from Granite Island, northern Gulf of Alaska is questionable; a number of larvae have been collected from the southeastern Bering Sea. Common from northern California to southern California. During the 1980s, this species was common at least as far southward as Palos Verdes Peninsula, southern California. Length to at least 35 cm (13.8 in) TL. Depth: adults at about 91–491 m (300–1,611 ft); juveniles in quite shallow water. Pink or olive-pink dorsally, light pink on sides; heavy blotching may be present when viewed underwater. D XIII,13–16; A III,8–11; Pect. 18–22; LLp 52–64; GRt 42–47; Vert. 26.

**TIGER ROCKFISH, *Sebastes nigrocinctus* Ayres, 1859.** Off Eider Point, Unalaska Island, Aleutian Islands to Tanner and Cortes Banks, southern California. Common from southeastern Alaska to northern California. Length to 61 cm (24 in) TL. Depth: 2–298 m (7–978 ft). White or pink with black, brown, purple, or red bars. D XII–XIV,12–15; A III,6–7; Pect. 18–20; LLp 36–50; GR 8 + 19–24 = 27–32.

36a Lower jaw slightly projecting, generally with prominent symphyseal knob directed downward and forward; body pink or red-orange mixed with greenish-yellow:

**SWORDSPINE ROCKFISH**

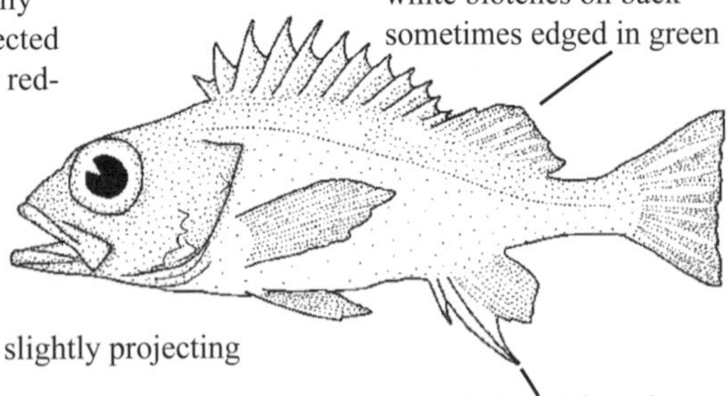


36b Jaws subequal, with symphyseal knob on lower jaw generally round and not projecting much; body color not as in 36a..... 37 (next page)

37a Gill rakers 26–31 with 1st 4–7 gill rakers on 1st gill arch rudimentary and spinulated; usually without spine on lower edge of gill cover:

**PINK ROCKFISH**

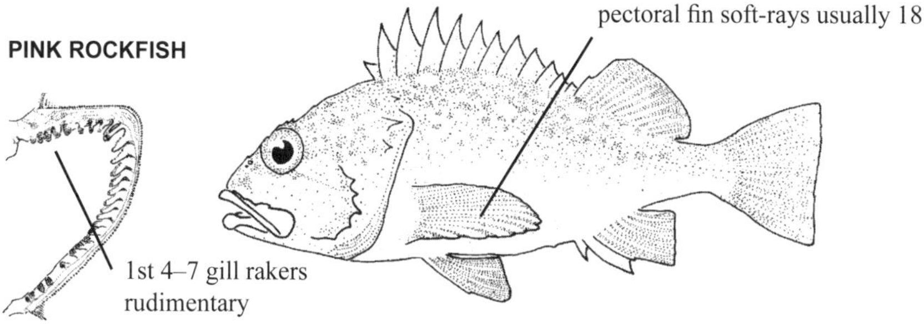


37b Gill rakers 28–34 with 1st 4–7 gill rakers on 1st gill arch not rudimentary and not spinulated; usually with spine on lower edge of gill cover:

**GREENBLOTCHED ROCKFISH**

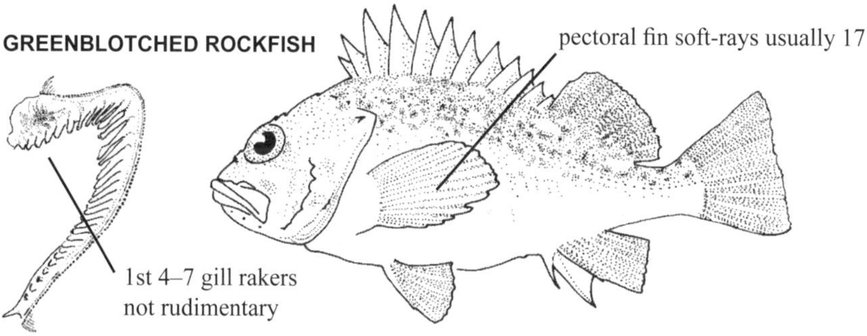


38a *From 28a: area between dorsal fin and lateral line without whitish blotches*
Vent about midway between insertion of pelvic fin base and origin of anal fin:

**SHORTBELLY ROCKFISH**

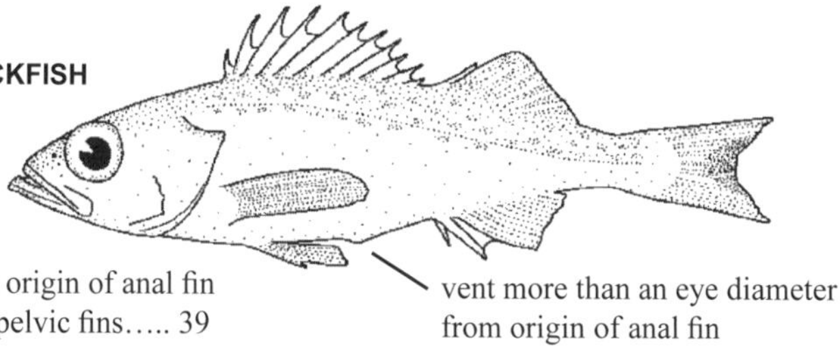


38b Vent much closer to origin of anal fin than to insertion of pelvic fins….. 39

39a Body without bars or, if bars present, those under soft dorsal fin do not extend onto anal fin….. 42 (page 160)

39b Body with 4–6 red to black bars, the bars (or bar) under soft dorsal fin extending onto anal fin….. 40

40a Five black, reddish-black, or red bars on body:

**TIGER ROCKFISH**

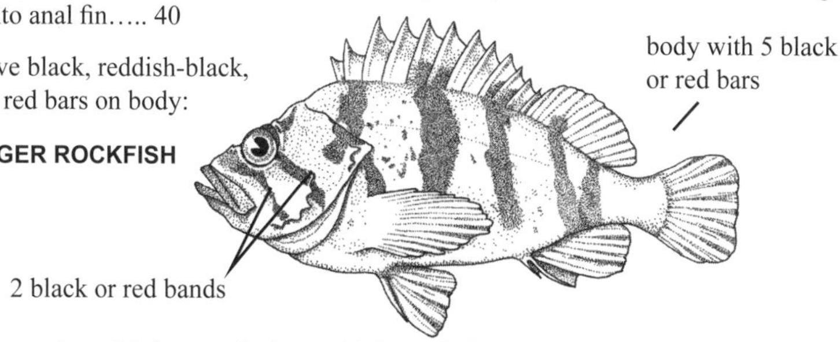


40b Four red or pink bars on body….. 41 (page 160)

## ROCKFISHES, SCORPIONFISHES, and THORNYHEADS (continued)

**FLAG ROCKFISH, *Sebastes rubrivinctus* (Jordan & Gilbert, 1880).** Stonewall Bank (44°31'N, 124°26'W), Oregon to southern Bahía de Sebastián Vizcaíno (28°06'N), central Baja California. Common from central California to at least off Bahía San Quintin, northern Baja California. Length to 44 cm (17.2 in) TL. Depth: 30–431 m (100–1,414 ft). Juveniles often under drifting kelp mats and other debris. Adults white or pinkish with red or orange bars (bars of young juveniles black); caudal fin edged in white. D XIII,12–15; A III,6–8; Pect. 16–18; LLp 39–49; GRt 26–32. Until fairly recently, most researchers considered the REDBANDED ROCKFISH to be synonymous with the FLAG ROCKFISH. It is now assumed that most older records of FLAG ROCKFISH from Oregon to Alaska, along with records of fish deeper than perhaps 431 m and larger than about 45 cm (17.7 in) TL, refer to REDBANDED ROCKFISH.

**REDBANDED ROCKFISH, *Sebastes babcocki* (Thompson, 1915).** Bering Sea at Zhemchug Canyon and Amchitka Island, Aleutian Islands to San Diego, southern California. Common from the Kodiak Island area, Gulf of Alaska to central California. Length to 71 cm (28 in) TL. Depth: 31–1,145 m (102–3,756 ft). White or pale pink with 4 orange or red bars; soft dorsal, anal, and caudal fins often black-streaked. D XIII,12–16; A III,6–9; Pect. 17–20; LLp 41–51; GR 7–10 + 21–25 = 29–33. Until the early 1970s, researchers considered the REDBANDED ROCKFISH to be synonymous with the FLAG ROCKFISH. Rosenblatt and Chen (1972) distinguished these species, and it is now assumed that most or all "FLAG ROCKFISH" previously reported from Oregon to Alaska are REDBANDED ROCKFISH.

**GREENSTRIPED ROCKFISH, *Sebastes elongatus* Ayres, 1859.** Chirikof Island, western Gulf of Alaska to Isla Cedros, central Baja California. Common from about Yakutat, Gulf of Alaska to at least Bahía San Quintin, northern Baja California. Length to about 48.7 cm TL (19.2 in). Depth: 12–1,145 m (39–3,756 ft). Body pink, reddish, or silvery with 4 dark green horizontal stripes (formed by series of blotches); lateral line clear. D XIII,12–14; A III,5–7; Pect. 16–18; LLp 37–47; GR 7–10 + 20–26 = 28–34.

**BOCACCIO, *Sebastes paucispinis* Ayres, 1854.** Western Gulf of Alaska south of Shumagin Islands and Alaska Peninsula to Isla Cedros, central Baja California. Larvae have been taken as far south as about 26°00'N, 115°00'W in southern Baja California. Common off British Columbia, relatively uncommon off Washington and Oregon, and common from northern California to at least off Bahía San Quintin, northern Baja California. Length to at least 98.1 cm (38.6 in) TL. Depth: juveniles near surface and in inshore waters (rarely in tide pools); adults about 20–475 m (66–1,558 ft). Uniform dark or dusky-red on back, pinkish below; young with dark brown spotting on sides. D XII–XV,13–16; A III,8–10; Pect. 14–16; LLp 51–70; GR 8–9 + 19–24 = 26–32; Vert. 26.

**CHILIPEPPER, *Sebastes goodei* (Eigenmann & Eigenmann, 1890).** Pratt and Durgin Seamounts, eastern Gulf of Alaska and northeast of Graham Island (54°37'N, 131°24'W), British Columbia to off Bahía Magdalena, southern Baja California. Common from Cape Mendocino, northern California to at least Punta Colnett, northern Baja California. Length to 59 cm (23.2 in) TL. Depth: near surface to 515 m (1,689 ft). Uniform pink-brown or brown on back and pink on sides; lateral line often bright red. D XIII,13–16; A III,7–10; Pect. 16–19; LLp 48–58; GRt 31–39.

41a *From 40b: four red or pink bars on body*
Mandibles without scales or with an occasional patch; lachrymal width into interorbital space 1.0–1.3:

**FLAG ROCKFISH**

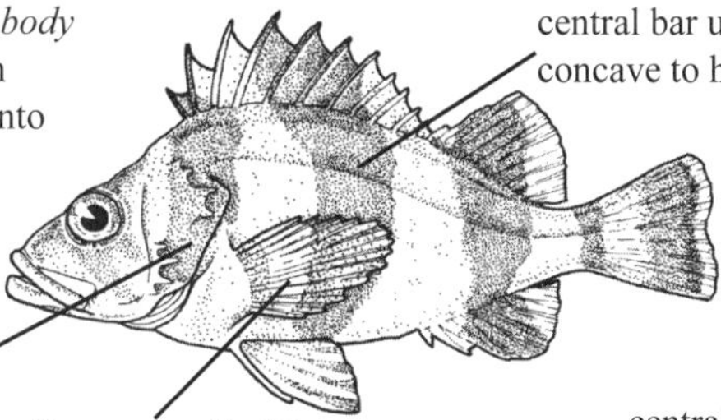


41b Mandibles with scales (in fish over 10 cm [4 in] TL); lachrymal width into interorbital space 1.7–2.2:

**REDBANDED ROCKFISH**

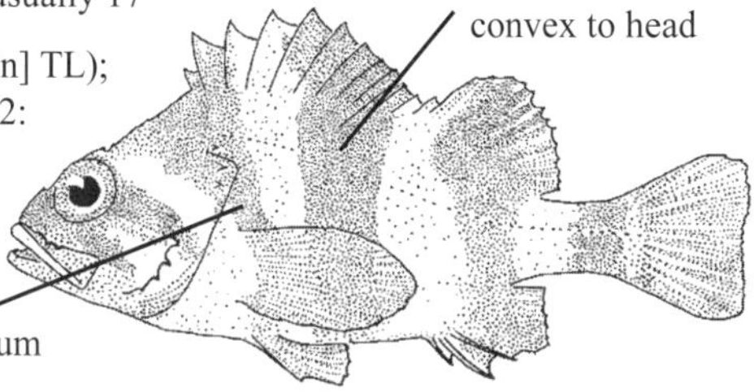


42a *From 39a: body without bars extending onto anal fin*
Body pink with 4 dark green horizontal stripes:

**GREENSTRIPED ROCKFISH**

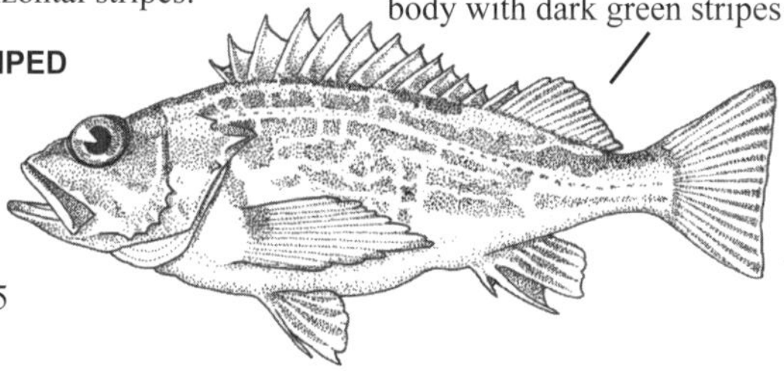


42b Body without green horizontal stripes as above….. 43

43a Head spines visible with at least 5 pairs present….. 45

43b Head spines weak, hard to locate, with 3 or fewer pairs present….. 44

44a Maxilla extends to or beyond rear margin of eye; lateral line in cream-colored or pinkish-red zone; anal fin soft- rays usually 9 (rarely 8 or 10); gill rakers 26–32:

**BOCACCIO**

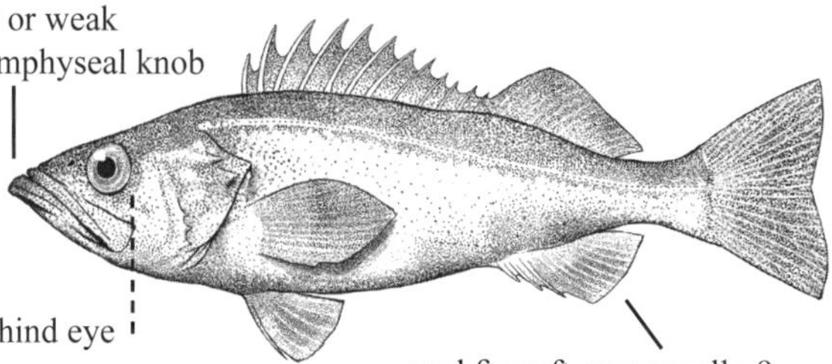


44b Maxilla extends to about middle of eye; lateral line in wide, bright red zone; anal fin soft-rays 8 (rarely 9); gill rakers 31–39:

**CHILIPEPPER**

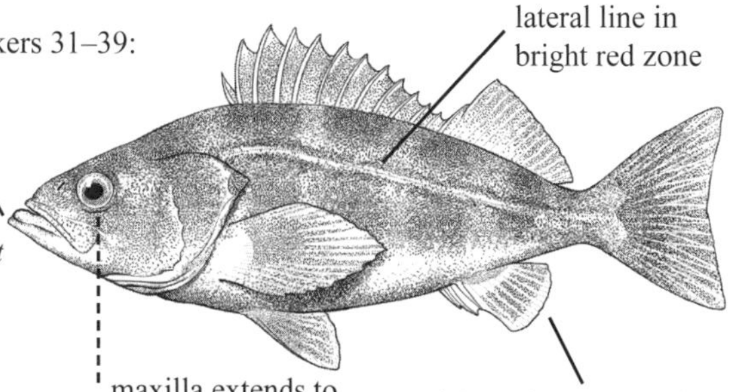


45a *From 43a: head spines visible with at least 5 pairs of head spines present*
Mandibles partially or fully covered with scales….. 50 (page 162)

45b Mandibles without scales….. 46 (next page)

## ROCKFISHES, SCORPIONFISHES, and THORNYHEADS (continued)

**SPLITNOSE ROCKFISH, *Sebastes diploproa* (Gilbert, 1890).** Sanak Islands, western Gulf of Alaska to Isla Cedros, central Baja California. Common from at least British Columbia to at least southern California. Length to 45.7 cm (18 in) TL. Depth: 45–924 m (148–3,031 ft). Young fish often found near surface under drifting kelp. Adults uniform pink-red. Juveniles tan-brown with lighter blotches. D XIII,11–14; A III,5–8; Pect. 17–19; LLp 32–43; GR 8–10 + 22–27 = 32–38.

**BRONZESPOTTED ROCKFISH, *Sebastes gilli* (Eigenmann, 1891).** West coast of Vancouver Island (about 49°N, 127°W), British Columbia to off Punta Colnett (30°53'N, 116°30'W), northern Baja California. Common from southern California southward. Length to at least 85 cm (33.5 in) TL. Depth: 75–413 m (246–1,354 ft). Orange or reddish with brown spots; heavily blotched with copper, brown, or whitish; 3 bands radiating posteriorly from eye; lateral line pink or red. Juveniles whitish with dark spots. D XIII,13–15; A III,6–8; Pect. 18–20; LLp 40–46; GRt 26–30.

**YELLOWEYE ROCKFISH, *Sebastes ruberrimus* (Cramer, 1895).** South of Umnak Island, Aleutian Islands to Ensenada, northern Baja California. Common from the western end of the Alaska Peninsula to central California and San Miguel Island, southern California. Length to 91.4 cm (36 in) TL; perhaps to 103.5 cm (40.8 in) TL. Depth: 11–549 m (36–1,800 ft). Adults orange to red-orange. Early benthic juveniles black, becoming orange-red with 2 white stripes that fade as fish matures. D XIII,13–16; A III,5–8; Pect. 16–20; LLp 39–46; GR 5–6 + 18–24 = 23–31; Vert. 26.

**COWCOD, *Sebastes levis* (Eigenmann & Eigenmann, 1889).** Northern Oregon (45°44'N, 124°40'W) (UW 47548) to Rocas Alijos, southern Baja California and Isla Guadalupe, central Baja California. Common from central California to at least off Bahía San Quintin, northern Baja California. Length to at least 100 cm (39.4 in) TL. Depth: juveniles as shallow as 40 m (132 ft); adults 72–491 m (236–1,610 ft). White, pink, yellow, or yellowish-red with faint bars in adults; white or yellow with dark bars in juveniles. D XIII–XIV,12–14; A III,6–8; Pect. 17–19; LLp 45–53; GRt 29–33; Vert. 26.

**SEMAPHORE ROCKFISH, *Sebastes melanosema* Lea & Fitch, 1979.** Perhaps central Oregon (44°41'N, 124°48'W) but without documentation; documented from Santa Barbara Channel to Punta San Pablo (27°13'N, 114°30'W), central Baja California. Common at least in southern California. Length to 39 cm (15.4 in) TL. Depth: 97–490 m (318–1,607 ft). Reddish with lighter blotching on back; sometimes with dark blotch on underside of operculum; lateral line light red or pink; black or brown dotting on dorsal and anal fin membranes, outer fringe of membrane black. D XIII,11–12; A III,6; Pect. 17–19; LLp 34–43; GRt 34–37.

46a Posterior ⅔ of lateral line in clear zone; body reddish-brown to copper; belly white, often turning pink upon exposure to air: **COPPER ROCKFISH** (see 8a, page 146 for dark color morph)

46b Lateral line not in clear zone as in 46a….. 47

47a Dentigerous knobs prominent; body uniform whitish-pink (this species is both with and without scales on mandibles):

**SPLITNOSE ROCKFISH**

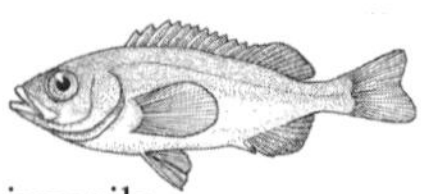

juvenile

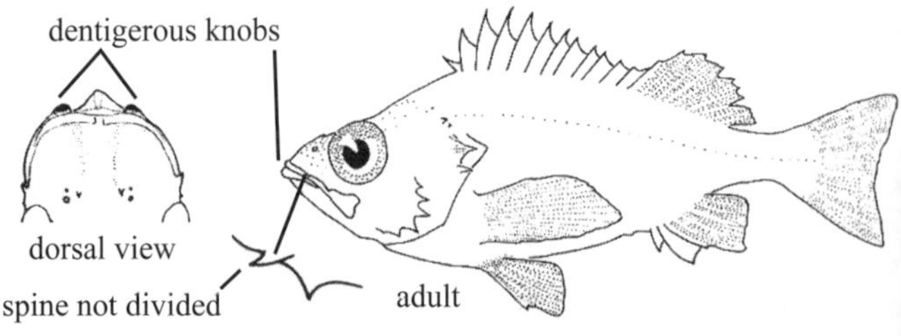


47b (next page)

47b Dentigerous knobs lacking; body red-orange….. 48

48a Back with round brown spots and 2 bright orange areas under soft dorsal fin; mouth oblique, lower jaw curving upward:

**BRONZESPOTTED ROCKFISH**

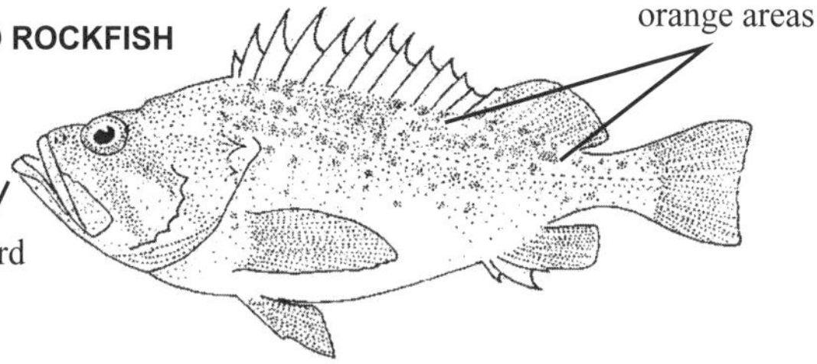


48b Back without brown spots and without 2 orange areas as above; lower jaw nearly horizontal….. 49

49a Ridges on head serrated; head spines numerous but difficult to differentiate in fish over about 28 cm (11 in) TL; 2 bright-white horizontal stripes along side of body in fish under 30 cm (12 in); eyes bright yellow:

**YELLOWEYE ROCKFISH**

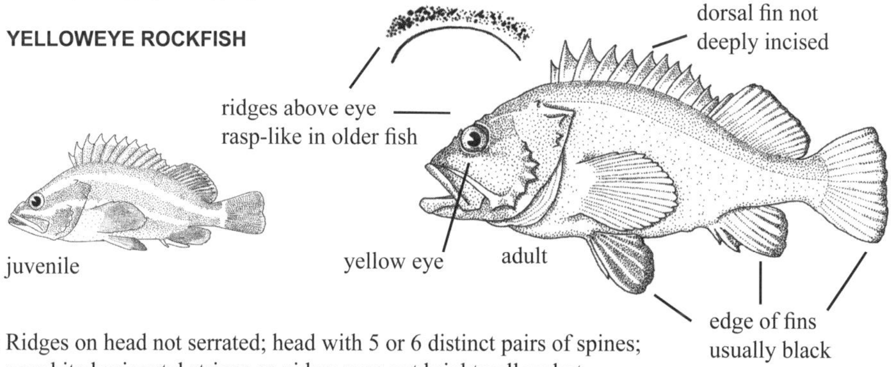


49b Ridges on head not serrated; head with 5 or 6 distinct pairs of spines; no white horizontal stripes on sides; eyes not bright yellow but may be brownish-yellow:

**COWCOD**

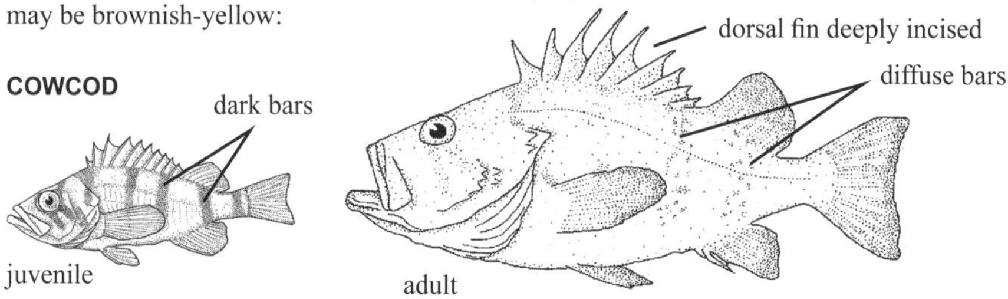


50a *From 45a: mandibles with scales*
Outer (distal) fringe of membranes between dorsal fin spines with conspicuously black, looping pattern [BANK ROCKFISH has black on membranes but not on fringes in looping pattern]:

**SEMAPHORE ROCKFISH**

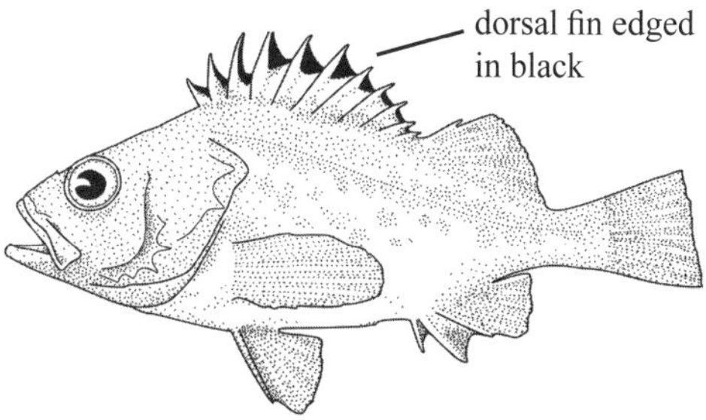


50b No continuous fringe of black on outer membranes between dorsal fin spines (dorsal fin may have black spots or splotches)….. 51 (next page)

## ROCKFISHES, SCORPIONFISHES, and THORNYHEADS (continued)

**WHITESPOTTED ROCKFISH, *Sebastes moseri* Eitner, Kimbrell & Vetter, 1999.** Off Big Creek (36°03'N, 121°37'W), central California to off Punta Colnett (30°53'N, 116°30'W), northern Baja California and Isla Guadalupe, central Baja California. Uncommon in northern part of southern California; common in southern part and likely at least off northern Baja California. Length to 23 cm (9.1 in) FL. Depth: 50–274 m (165–900 ft). Reddish with white or bluish-white flecks on sides, dark brown flecks on gill operculum and below lateral line. D XII,15; A III,9; Pect. 17; GRt 49. (Alternative name WHITESPECKLED ROCKFISH).

**CHAMELEON ROCKFISH, *Sebastes phillipsi* (Fitch, 1964).** Point Saint George (41°34'N), northern California to Nine Mile Bank (32°39'N, 117°28'W), southern California. Common at least from Monterey Bay to southern California. Length to 52 cm (20.3 in) TL. Depth: 174–390 m (570–1,279 ft). Light pink when first caught, turning crimson; often light dusky streaks on back. D XIII–XIV,12–13; A III,5–6; Pect. 18–19; LLp 29–33; GRt 36–40.

**DWARF-RED ROCKFISH, *Sebastes rufinanus* Lea & Fitch, 1972.** San Miguel Island to 60 Mile Bank (32°01'N, 118°13'W), southern California. Common from mid-southern California southward. Length to 17 cm (6.8 in) TL. Depth: 58–220 m (190–722 ft). Dusky-red on back, fading to bright red on belly; fin membranes, except anal, dusky-red; anal fin lighter; lateral line pale. D XIII,14; A III,8; Pect. 17; LLp 30–33; GR 10 + 27–28 = 37–38; Vert. 27. (Formerly *Sebastes* sp.: M&L).

**AURORA ROCKFISH, *Sebastes aurora* (Gilbert, 1890).** Southeast Alaska (about 55°56'N, 135°26'W) to Isla Cedros, central Baja California. Larvae have been taken much further south, off Banco Thetis (24°40'N, 112°18'W), southern Baja California. Common from British Columbia to at least southern California. Length to 41 cm (16 in) TL. Depth: 81–893 m (266–2,930 ft). Uniform pink-red. Underwater with white blotches on head, sides, and back. D XIII,12–14; A III,5–7; Pect. 16–19; LLp 27–31; GRt 24–30.

**BLACKGILL ROCKFISH, *Sebastes melanostomus* (Eigenmann & Eigenmann, 1890).** Off west coast of Haida Gwaii, Northern British Columbia to Isla Cedros, central Baja California. Pelagic juveniles have been taken as far south as Punta Abreojos (26°06'N, 114°05'W), southern Baja California. Common from at least northern California to northern Baja California. Length to 61 cm (24 in) TL. Depth: 88–768 m (289–2,520 ft). Bright red; dark back, occasionally with dusky bars; lateral line lighter; mouth cavity and gill membranes mostly black. Juveniles pink with dark bars extending to below lateral line. D XIII,12–15; A III,6–8; Pect. 17–20; LLp 28–34; GRt 27–35; Vert. 26–27.

51a Body profusely covered with white or bluish-white flecks:

**WHITESPOTTED ROCKFISH**

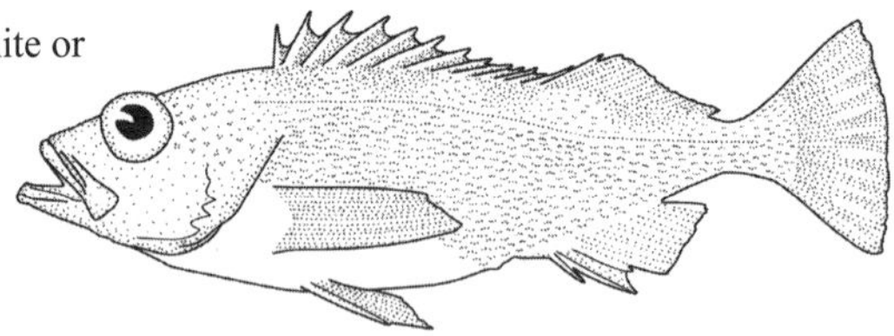

51b Body not as in 51a….. 52

52a Dentigerous knobs absent or weak; anterior lachrymal spine, if present, directed backward (rarely downward)….. 54 (next page)

52b Dentigerous knobs prominent; anterior lachrymal spine projecting forward (sometimes downward in fish under 10 cm [4 in] TL)….. 53

53a Anterior lachrymal spine entire; interorbital space slightly concave to flat; no orbital spines: **SPLITNOSE ROCKFISH** (see 47a, page 161)

53b (next page)

53b Anterior lachrymal spine multifid; top of head strongly concave; orbital spines 2–4:

**CHAMELEON ROCKFISH**

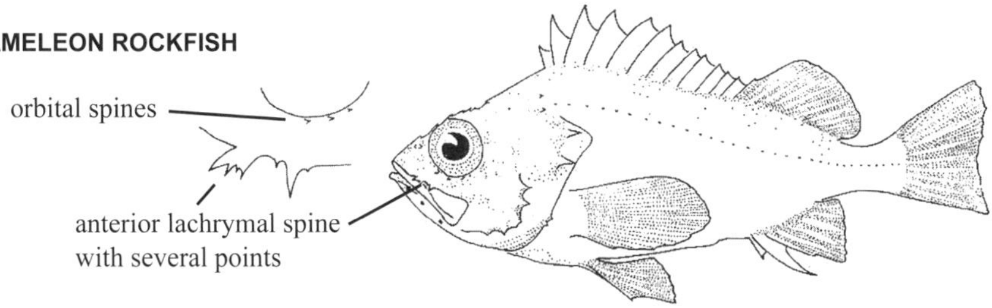


54a *From 52a: dentigerous knobs absent or weak*
Lateral line pores 35 or more..... 60 (page 166)

54b Lateral line pores fewer than 35 (BLACKSPOTTED ROCKFISH rarely has 35 or 36) ..... 55

55a Supraocular spines absent;
gill rakers over 36:

**DWARF-RED ROCKFISH**

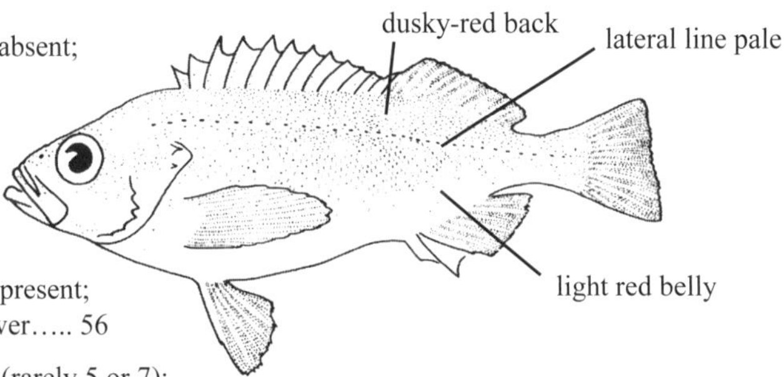


55b Supraocular spines present;
gill rakers 36 or fewer..... 56

56a Anal fin soft-rays 6 (rarely 5 or 7);
gill rakers 24–30; body color pink or
reddish with no markings:

**AURORA ROCKFISH**

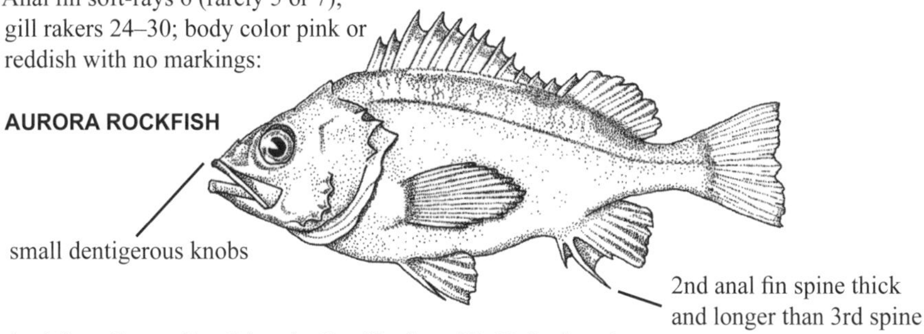


56b Anal fin soft-rays 7 or 8 (rarely 6); gill rakers 27–35; body color
pink, orange-red, or red, with or without markings..... 57

57a Membranes of gill cover (branchiostegals) jet black (at least dorsally of the pectoral fins):

**BLACKGILL ROCKFISH**

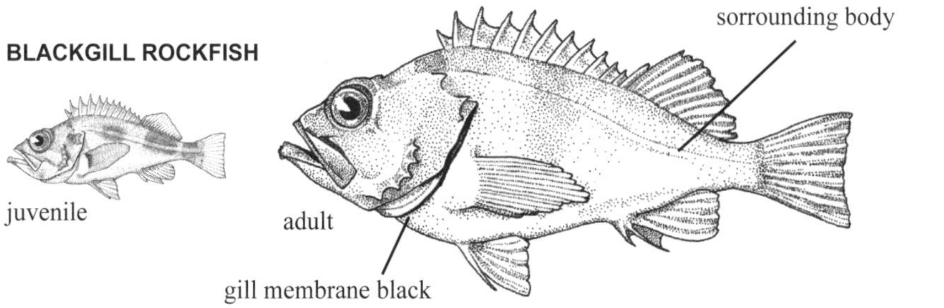


57b (next page)

## ROCKFISHES, SCORPIONFISHES, and THORNYHEADS (continued)

**SHORTRAKER ROCKFISH, *Sebastes borealis* Barsukov, 1970.** Okhotsk Sea, Pacific off northern Hokkaido, Japan to Kamchatka, and western Bering Sea to Navarin Canyon (and perhaps to Bering Strait) and Aleutian Islands to Point Conception, California. Common from Sea of Okhotsk and Bering Sea, Aleutian Islands, and Gulf of Alaska; rare off California. Length to 120 cm (47.2 in) TL. Depth: 25–1,200 m (82–3,937 ft). Orange-pink, reddish-orange, or pink; fins reddish, sometimes black-edged; short, blunt gill rakers. Dusky-red bars sometimes present, particularly on small fish. Underwater with white blotches. D XIII–XIV,12–15; A III,6–8; Pect. 17–20; LLp 28–32; GRt 27–31; Vert. 27.

**ROUGHEYE ROCKFISH, *Sebastes aleutianus* (Jordan & Evermann, 1898).** North Pacific from at least the eastern Aleutian Islands off Unalaska Island, the eastern Bering Sea at Pribilof Canyon at 59°18'N, 177°41'W, south to northern California. Common at least in the Gulf of Alaska. Length to 74 cm (29.1 in) FL, an estimated 76.8 cm (30.2 in) TL. Depth: 45 m to at least 765 m (148–2,509 ft). Pink, red, or reddish-orange with darker brownish-red mottling in faint bands at and above lateral line, often extending onto dorsal fin base; irregular dark blotch at dorsal-posterior corner of head; posterior part of lateral line may be light. Juveniles red with dark blotches and black-edged fins. D XII–XIV,12–15; A III,6–8; Pect. 17–19; LLp 29–34; GR 8–10 + 21–24 = 28–34; Vert. 27. A previous maximum size of 96.5 cm (38 in) TL was based on specimens measured before the distinction between ROUGHEYE ROCKFISH and BLACKSPOTTED ROCKFISH was recognized. Therefore the maximum size, as well as precise geographic and depth ranges, are unclear.

**BLACKSPOTTED ROCKFISH, *Sebastes melanostictus* (Matsubara, 1934).** Pacific coast of Japan (about 35°00'N), north through the Kuril Islands, Russia, Aleutian Islands, and the Bering Sea to 60°30'N, and south to southern California on Coronado Bank (32°36'N). Common at least in the Gulf of Alaska and likely southward to at least British Columbia. Length to at least 78 cm (30.7 in) FL, an estimated 79.9 cm (31.5 in) TL. Depth: at least 25–1,000 m (82–3,280 ft). Body color light or dark. Light fish pink to red with greenish-black spotting on sides or back. Dark fish with black to greenish wash over red or pink with heavy spotting and mottling. D XII–XIV,12–15; A III,6–8; Pect. 17–19; LLp 30–36; GRt 30–36; Vert. 26–27. This species and ROUGHEYE ROCKFISH have only recently been recognized as a distinct species, and thus it is not possible to use older published data on maximum size and geographic and depth ranges.

**REDSTRIPE ROCKFISH, *Sebastes proriger* (Jordan & Gilbert, 1880).** Pribilof Canyon, southeastern Bering Sea and Amchitka Island, Aleutian Islands to southern Baja California (26°46'N, 114°07'W). Common from southeastern Alaska to Oregon. Length to 61 cm (24 in) TL. Depth: 12–511 m (40–1,676 ft) and perhaps to 589 m (1,932 ft). Body reddish, pink, or brown; lateral line reddish, bordered in green. D XIII,13–16; A III,6–7; Pect. 16–18; LLp 44–55; GR 11 + 25–32 = 36–43; Vert. 27.

57b Membranes of branchiostegals not blackened as in 57a (light dusting of dark pigment occ. present)….. 58

58a Body either uniform reddish-pink or with broad red bands (usually fade as the fish dies) and without dark spots or other markings; gill rakers knob-tipped; coronal spine usually absent:

**SHORTRAKER ROCKFISH**

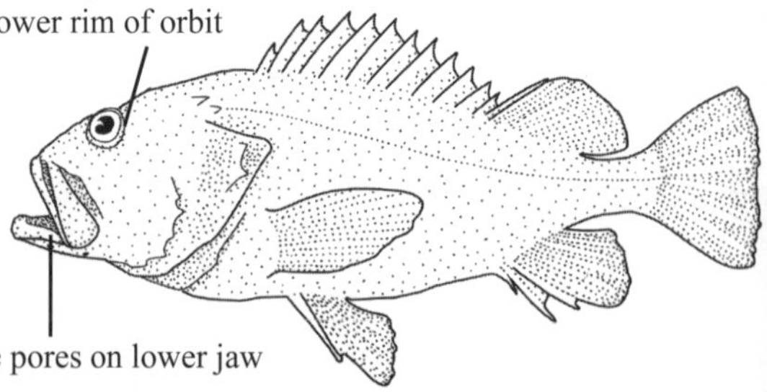


58b (next page)

58b Body color not as above, at least some dark spots or other markings present; gill rakers without knobs; coronal spine usually present….. 59

59a Spinous dorsal fin not discretely spotted, occasionally with diffuse blotches at base of dorsal fin; 1st dorsal fin spine into orbit length 1.5–3.0:

**ROUGHEYE ROCKFISH**

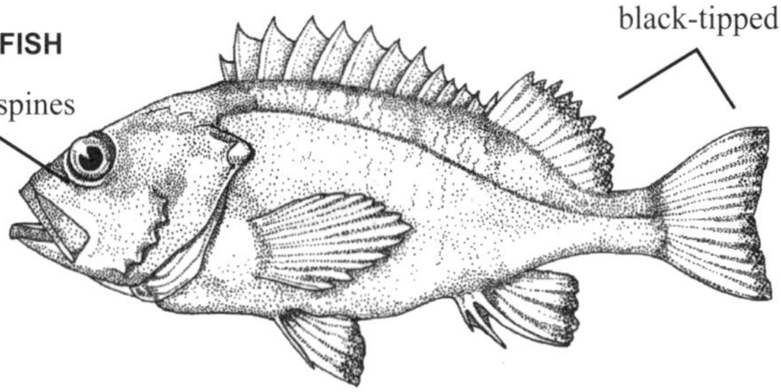


59b Spinous dorsal fin almost always discretely spotted; 1st dorsal fin spine into orbit length 1.0–1.8:

**BLACKSPOTTED ROCKFISH**

(NOTE: in a small number of instances, ROUGHEYE and BLACKSPOTTED ROCKFISHES cannot be identified to species other than using genetic characters)

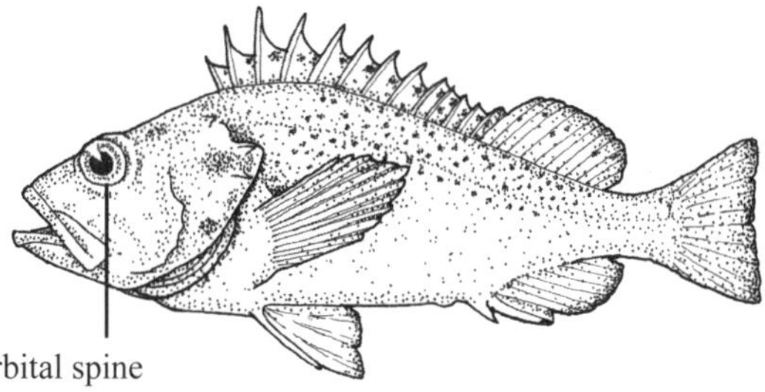


60a *From 54a: lateral line pores 35 or more*
At least 3–5 vertical or oblique bars or blotches on back, with at least 1 bar extending uninterrupted to below lateral line….. 69 (page 170)

60b Either none or up to 5 blotches or bars on back (often faint) above lateral line or interrupted by clear light red or gray lateral line zone….. 61

61a Supraocular spines present (supraocular spines occasionally absent in PACIFIC OCEAN PERCH, see 65a)….. 64 (page 168)

61b Supraocular spines absent….. 62

62a Symphyseal knob strong; pectoral and pelvic fin membranes light red or yellowish:

**REDSTRIPE ROCKFISH**

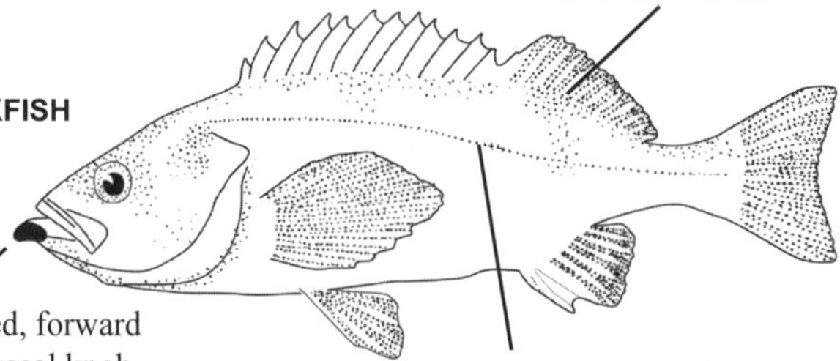


62b Symphyseal knob weak or absent; pectoral and pelvic fin membranes with at least some black or dusky….. 63 (next page)

## ROCKFISHES, SCORPIONFISHES, and THORNYHEADS (continued)

**HARLEQUIN ROCKFISH, *Sebastes variegatus* Quast, 1971.** Bering Sea (to 60°08'N, 178°52'W) and west of Buldir Island, western Aleutian Islands to 95 km (59 mi) southwest of Newport (44°32'N, 124°39'W), Oregon. Length to 38 cm (15 in) TL. Depth: 6–558 m (20–1,831 ft). Note that the 6 m record is from a juvenile; shallowest adult record appears to be 49 m (161 ft). Red, orange, or pink-tan often with dark mottling on sides; fins dark (edge of caudal, soft dorsal, and anal fins orange, red, or clear); lateral line white, pink, or orange; dark forked bar radiates back from eye. D XIII (rarely XIV),13–15; A III,6–7; Pect. 17–19; LLp 37–47; GRt 36–41.

**BANK ROCKFISH, *Sebastes rufus* (Eigenmann & Eigenmann, 1890).** Haida Gwaii, British Columbia to central Baja California (29°02'N, 118°13'W) and Isla Guadalupe. Common from perhaps northern to at least southern California and at Isla Guadalupe, central Baja California. Length to 56 cm (22 in) FL, about 56.9 cm (22.4 in) TL. Depth: 31–512 m (102–1,680 ft). Body brown, black-brown, pink-brown, or nearly white, most often covered with black spots; black fin membranes; lateral line raised and reddish. D XIII,13–16; A III,5–9; Pect. 17–19; LLp 49–56; GRt 31–37; Vert. 27–28.

**MEXICAN ROCKFISH, *Sebastes macdonaldi* (Eigenmann & Beeson, 1893).** Point Sur, central California to southern Baja California (23°24'N, 111°11'W) and central Gulf of California. Uncommon in most of southern California except for the southernmost areas; far more common off Baja California and in Gulf of California. Length to 66 cm (26 in) TL. Depth: 76–350 m (249–1,148 ft). Dorsal area very dark (sometimes with lighter patches), lower sides red; dark bars radiate posteriorly from under eye and from between eye and upper jaw; lateral line in clear red zone; pelvic and anal fins reddish. Juveniles with dark saddles and bands extending from back downwards to belly. D XII–XIV,12–15; A III,7–8; Pect. 18–20; LLp 52–58; GRt 35–42.

**PACIFIC OCEAN PERCH, *Sebastes alutus* (Gilbert, 1890).** Southern Japan and Sea of Okhotsk to Bering Sea at Navarin Canyon, and Commander-Aleutian Islands Chain to Punta Blanca (29°08'N, 115°26'W), central Baja California. Larvae and juveniles may drift into the Chukchi Sea. We note that the southernmost record is hundreds of miles below the previous one (Point Loma, southern California) and is the only record from Baja California and may be in error. Most common from northern Kuril Islands, Russia, to Bering Sea to perhaps Oregon. Relatively uncommon in California and rare in southern California. Length to 78.7 cm (31 in) TL. Depth: near surface (juveniles) to 825 m (2,707 ft). Light red or pink; dark areas under spinous (occasionally) and soft dorsal fin, caudal peduncle, and on gill operculum. D XIII–XIV,13–17; A III,6–9; Pect. 15–19; LLp 44–55; GR 10–13 + 20–28 = 30–40; Vert. 27.

63a Posterior ⅔ of lateral line in light zone; some dark or dusky color on pectoral and pelvic fins; black spots lacking on back and dorsal fin:

**HARLEQUIN ROCKFISH**

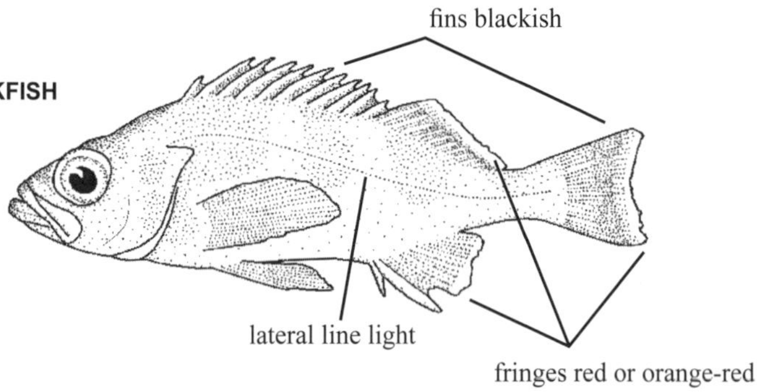


63b (next page)

63b All of lateral line in red or pink zone; pectoral and pelvic fin membranes blackish; black spots, most slightly larger than nostril openings, over back and dorsal fin (by comparison, in SEMAPHORE ROCKFISH edge of membranes between dorsal fin spines have conspicuously black looping pattern):

**BANK ROCKFISH**

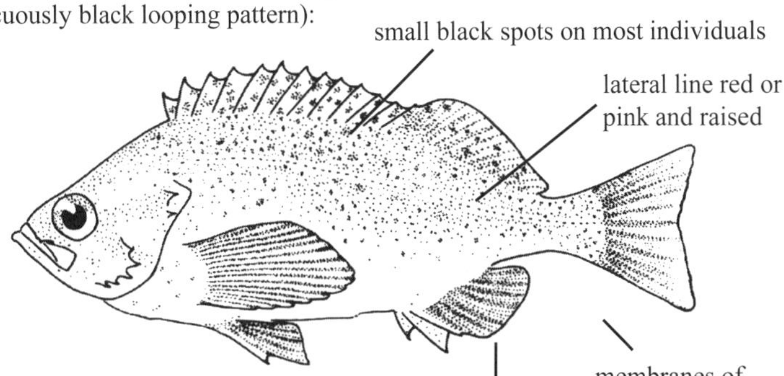


64a *From 61a: supraocular spines present*
Membranes of pectoral fins black; upper portion of body uniform blackish-red with bright red lateral line zone; flat spine present (rarely absent) below anterior margin of eye:

**MEXICAN ROCKFISH**

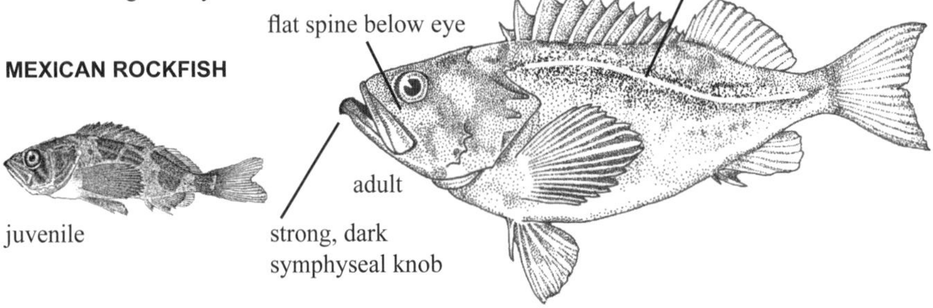


64b Membranes of pectoral fins red, pinkish, or whitish; body color not as above; no flat spine below anterior margin of eye….. 65

65a Symphyseal knob prominent; anal fin soft-rays usually 8 or 9 (rarely 6 or 7); darkened area at base of soft dorsal fin:

**PACIFIC OCEAN PERCH**

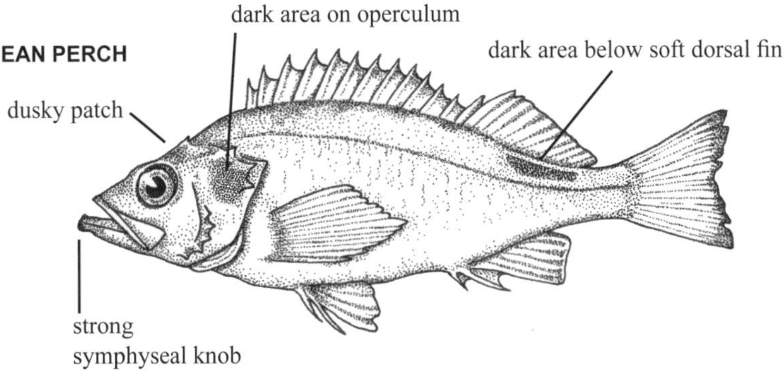


65b Symphyseal knob absent or small; anal fin soft-rays usually 7 (rarely 6 or 8); no darkened area under soft dorsal fin….. 66 (next page)

## ROCKFISHES, SCORPIONFISHES, and THORNYHEADS (continued)

**YELLOWMOUTH ROCKFISH, *Sebastes reedi* (Westrheim & Tsuyuki, 1967).** Aleutian Islands (54°20'N, 165°21'W), Alaska to near San Francisco, northern California (UW 117066). Common at least from the Gulf of Alaska to British Columbia. Length to about 58 cm (23 in) TL. Depth: 70–540 m (230–1,771 ft). Body red and yellow-orange (black in smaller individuals); brown mottlings on back; often with 3 faint dark bands across head; interior of mouth with black, yellow, and red blotches. D XIII,13–15; A III,6–8; Pect. 18–20; LLp 47–55; GRt 30–37.

**CANARY ROCKFISH, *Sebastes pinniger* (Gill, 1864).** Pribilof Islands, Bering Sea and western Gulf of Alaska south of Shelikof Strait to Punta Colnett, northern Baja California. Common from British Columbia to central California. Length to 76 cm (30 in) TL. Depth: young fish in shallow waters; adults about 18–838 m (59–2,749 ft). Orange or yellow-orange with gray or white background; 3 orange stripes across head; pelvic and anal fins with white lead edge; lateral line gray. D XIII,13–16; A III,7–8; Pect. 16–19; LLp 39–44; GR 13–14 + 27–31 = 40–45; Vert. 26.

**VERMILION ROCKFISH, *Sebastes miniatus* (Jordan & Gilbert, 1880).** This taxon is composed of 2 species, VERMILION ROCKFISH (*Sebastes miniatus*) and the tentatively named **SUNSET ROCKFISH *(Sebastes crocotulus)*** (Hyde et al., 2008). Because of previous confusion between the 2 species, precise maximum sizes, and geographic and depth ranges of each species are unknown. Overall geographic range for the 2 species is Zaikof Bay, Montague Island, Prince William Sound, Alaska to Islas San Benito, central Baja California. Overall maximum length is 76 cm (30 in) TL. Depth: overall, juveniles in shallow water, adults 12–478 m (39–1,568 ft). Genetically identified VERMILION ROCKFISH are known from Neah Bay, Washington to Punta Baja, northern Baja California. Common from at least central California to northern Baja California. Adults common only shallower than 100 m (328 ft). Adults brick-red, sometimes with black or gray markings. Likely for both species, newly settled juveniles mottled brown with black patches on dorsal fins and clear tail; somewhat older juveniles mottled orange or red with black-edged fins. D XIII,13–14; A III,6–8; Pect. 17–19; GRt 34–39. Genetically identified SUNSET ROCKFISH from Monterey, central California to Colnett Bank, northern Baja California. Common from southern California to northern Baja California. Adults common only deeper than 100 m (328 ft). Adults yellowish-orange, sometimes with red fins. D XIII,12–15; A III,6–8; Pect. 15–19; GRt 36–43 (rarely 36–38).

**DARKBLOTCHED ROCKFISH, *Sebastes crameri* (Jordan, 1897).** Eastern Bering Sea southeast of Zhemchug Canyon and Aleutian Islands off Tanaga Island to near Santa Catalina Island, southern California and Laguna Beach, southern California (LACM 35710-10). Common from about Yakutat, Gulf of Alaska to southern California. Length to 59.5 cm (23.4 in) TL. Depth: 29–915 m (95–3,001 ft). Pink to orange with 3–5 irregular dark saddles on back crossing below lateral line. There are at least 2 color morphs of this species: 1 has lighter background colors and bars, the other darker ones. D XIII,12–15; A III,5–7; Pect. 18–20; LLp 40–51; GR 8–10 + 21–24 = 28–35.

66a Discrete, often square, blotch on operculum; discrete dark blotch under soft dorsal fin; pectoral fin soft-rays 18–20; scale rows below lateral line 57–67:

**YELLOWMOUTH ROCKFISH**

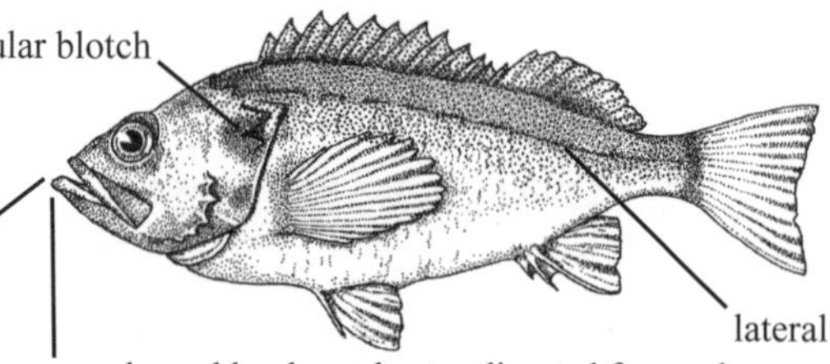


66b (next page)

66b No discrete blotch on operculum or under soft dorsal fin; pectoral fin soft-rays 16–19; scale rows below lateral line 43–50….. 67

67a Underside of mandibles smooth to touch (scales present but mostly embedded); lateral line in gray zone; fish shorter than about 35 cm (14 in) TL with black blotch in posterior portion of spinous dorsal fin:

**CANARY ROCKFISH**

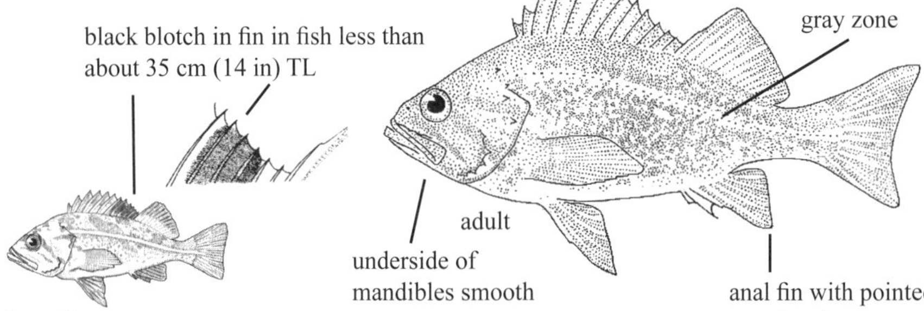


67b Underside of mandibles rough to touch; lateral line not in gray zone; no black blotch in spinous dorsal fin in fish shorter than 35 cm (14 in)….. 68

68a Gill rakers on 1st arch 38 or fewer (make sure to include small nubby ones); adults brick-red, sometimes with black or gray markings:

**VERMILION ROCKFISH**

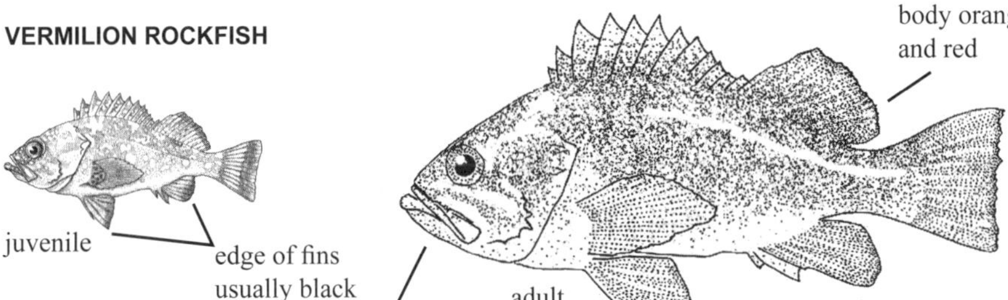


68b Gill rakers on 1st arch 39 or more; adults yellowish-orange, sometimes with red fins: **SUNSET ROCKFISH** (not illustrated; body shape as in 68a)

69a *From 60a: at least 3–5 dark bars or blotches on back*
Supraocular spines present; BD at origin of pelvic fins greater than HL in fish longer than 12.5 cm (5 in) TL:

**DARKBLOTCHED ROCKFISH**

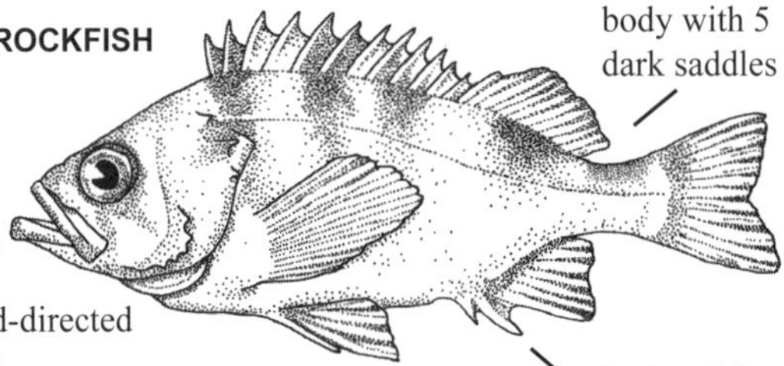


69b (next page)

## ROCKFISHES, SCORPIONFISHES, and THORNYHEADS (continued)

**STRIPETAIL ROCKFISH, *Sebastes saxicola* (Gilbert, 1890).** Yakutat Bay, eastern Gulf of Alaska to Punta Rompiente (27°41'N, 115°01'W), southern Baja California (LACM 32061-6). Common from British Columbia to at least Punta Canoas, central Baja California. Length to 41 cm (16.1 in) TL. Depth: 25–547 m (82–1,795 ft). Pink-red to yellow-pink with dark saddles; caudal fin membrane with green stripes. D XIII,11–14; A III,5–8; Pect. 15–19; LLp 35–43; GRt 29–40. This "species" is likely composed of 2 distinct species (Hyde and Vetter, 2007).

**HALFBANDED ROCKFISH, *Sebastes semicinctus* (Gilbert, 1897).** Strait of Juan de Fuca, Washington (UW 49113) to Bahía Asuncion, southern Baja California. Common from at least northern California to central Baja California. Length to 25 cm (10 in) TL. Depth: 15–402 m (48–1,320 ft). Pinkish-brown to red-brown with 2 dark red-brown blotches on posterior of body; dorsal and caudal fins streaked with brown. D XIII,12–14; A III,6–8; Pect. 16–18; LLp 40–50; GR 10 + 26–32 = 36–42; Vert. 26.

**SHARPCHIN ROCKFISH, *Sebastes zacentrus* (Gilbert, 1890).** Saint George Island, eastern Bering Sea (UAM Fishes 5092) and Attu Island, Aleutian Islands to San Diego, southern California. Common from Kodiak Island, Gulf of Alaska to central California. Length to 49 cm (19.3 in) TL. Depth: 25 m to perhaps 660 m (83–2,164 ft). Blotchy pink-brown or pink, with dark brown blotches on back. D XIII,13–16; A III,6–8; Pect. 16–19; LLp 38–51; GR 9–13 + 22–31 = 31–41; Vert. 27–28.

**PUGET SOUND ROCKFISH, *Sebastes emphaeus* (Starks, 1911).** Outer coast of Kenai Peninsula and Prince William Sound, northern Gulf of Alaska to Point Sur, central California. Common from Gulf of Alaska perhaps to central California (34°24'N). Length to 19 cm (7.5 in) TL. Depth: 3–470 m (10–1,542 ft). Red-brown or copper-red with vague brownish blotches; green bands radiating from eye; spinous dorsal fin with some green, tip of spines may be red; often dark blotch on caudal peduncle; dark streak on lower sides sometimes present. D XIII,13–15; A III,6–8; Pect. 16–18; LLp 39–47; GR 10 + 27–31 = 37–43.

**PYGMY ROCKFISH, *Sebastes wilsoni* (Gilbert, 1915).** Kodiak Island, northern Gulf of Alaska to 60 Mile Bank (32°01'N, 118°13'W), southern California. Common from Gulf of Alaska southward to southern California. Length to 24 cm (9.4 in) TL. Depth: 29–383 m (95–1,256 ft). Tan, pink, orange, or reddish, often with red or brown stripe on sides, sometimes with yellow belly. D XIII–XIV,13–15; A III,5–7; Pect. 16–18; LLp 37–47; GRt 36–43. Butler et al. (2012) note that there are 2 "forms" of this species, perhaps representing 2 species. One form is pinkish-red with white stripe along lower sides. The other form is more variable in color but tends to be blotchy red, often with distinct yellow stripe along lower sides.

69b Supraocular spines absent; BD at origin of pelvic fins less than HL (rarely about the same in SHARPCHIN ROCKFISH)….. 70

70a Tail with green stripes in membranes; dorsal fin soft-rays 12 (occasionally 13 or 14); unbranched pectoral fin soft-rays 6 or 7:

STRIPETAIL ROCKFISH

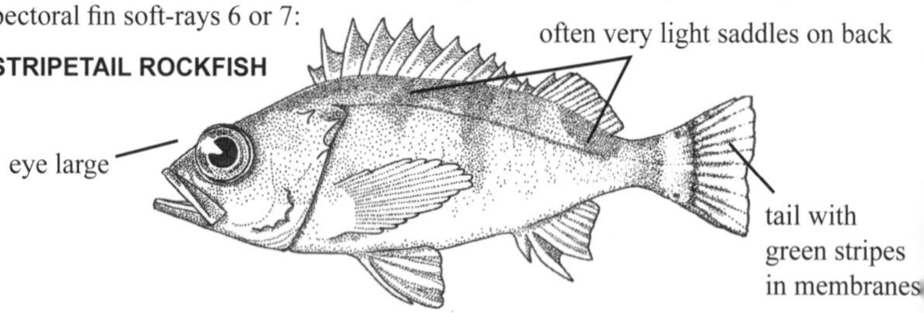


70b Tail without green stripes (brown streaks in HALFBANDED ROCKFISH); dorsal fin soft- rays usually 13–15 (occasionally 12); unbranched pectoral fin soft-rays 7–9….. 71 (next page)

71a Two (occasionally 3) strong, oblique reddish-black blotches between midbody and caudal peduncle; 2 sharp spines on lower edge of gill cover, upper spine twice the size of lower:

**HALFBANDED ROCKFISH**

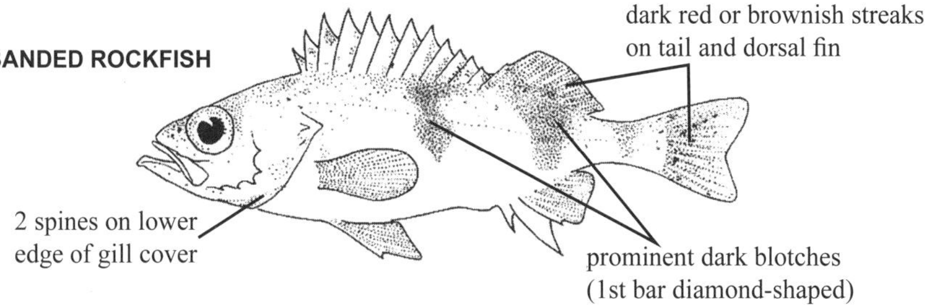


71b No strong oblique bars as above; either none, 1 or 2 small spines on lower edge of gill cover (if 2 present, upper about same size as lower)….. 72

72a Two dark bands radiating from eye to edge of operculum; gill rakers 31–41; symphyseal knob prominent; BD at origin of pelvic fins into SL 2.7–3.2:

**SHARPCHIN ROCKFISH**

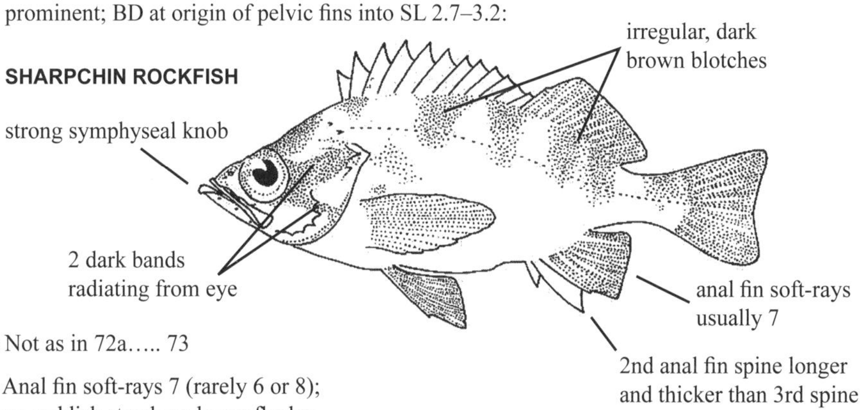


72b Not as in 72a….. 73

73a Anal fin soft-rays 7 (rarely 6 or 8); no reddish streak on lower flanks; distal margin of anal fin rounded:

**PUGET SOUND ROCKFISH**

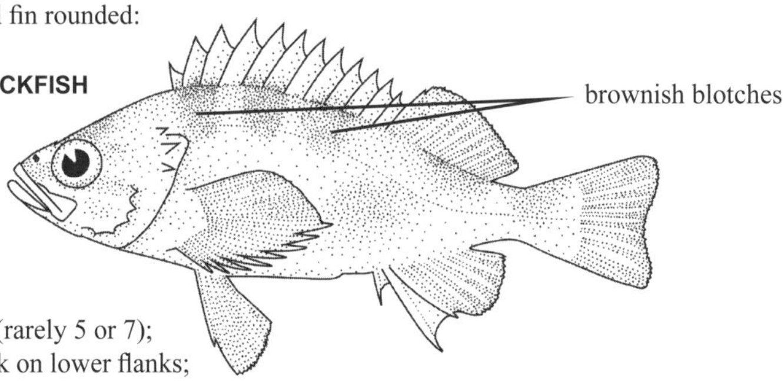


73b Anal fin soft-rays 6 (rarely 5 or 7); reddish-brown streak on lower flanks; distal margin of anal fin almost straight:

**PYGMY ROCKFISH**

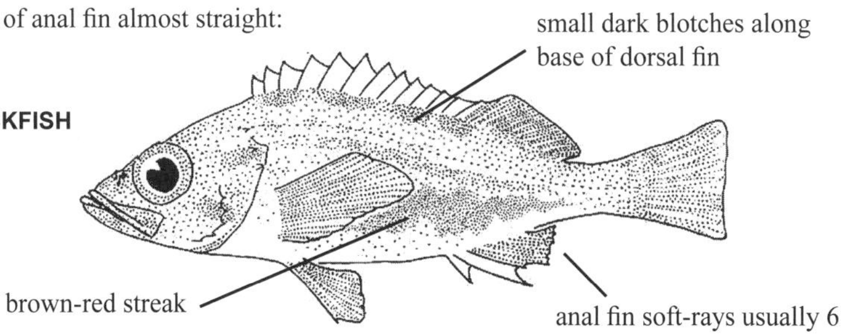

# SEAROBINS, Family Triglidae and SABLEFISH and SKILFISH, Family Anoplopomatidae

**SPLITNOSE SEAROBIN, *Bellator xenisma* (Jordan & Bollman, 1890).** Family Triglidae
Three reported off Santa Barbara, southern California; Todos Santos (23°41'N, 110°23'W) and Gulf of California to northern Peru. Length to 12.5 cm (4.9 in) TL. Depth: 17–200 m (55–656 ft). Light red or brown mottled with darker brown and black; blue or brown ocellus toward rear of 1st dorsal fin. D X–XI,10–11; A I,12; Pect. 11; Pelvic I,5; LLp 35–40; LLs 60–70; GRt 7.

**LUMPTAIL SEAROBIN, *Prionotus stephanophrys* Lockington, 1881.** Family Triglidae
La Perouse Bank, British Columbia to Chile, including Gulf of California. Usually uncommon along U.S. Pacific Coast, but during some El Niño years common in southern California; common from southern Baja California into tropics. Length to 43 cm (16.9 in) TL. Depth: 2–255 m (7–836 ft). Purplish-brown, blackish-brown, brown, or silvery with rust spots and blotches on back, sides, and soft dorsal, caudal, and pectoral fins; pectoral fin mostly dark sometimes edged in white; white belly may have orange or red tinge. D X–XI,11–13; A I,10–12; Pect. 13+3; Pelvic I,5; LLp 51–52; GR 1–3 + 11–12; Vert. 26.

**SABLEFISH, *Anoplopoma fimbria* (Pallas, 1814).** Family Anoplopomatidae
Pacific Ocean off central Honshu, Japan to Aleutian Islands and Bowers Bank to Bering Sea south of Saint Lawrence Island, Alaska to west of Bahía San Bartolome (27°41'N, 115°36'W), southern Baja California (SIO 61-311). Common from the Sea of Okhotsk and Kuril Islands, Russia to Aleutian Islands to Banco Ranger, central Baja California. Length to 116.8 cm (46 in) TL. Depth: adults near bottom to 2,740 m (8,989 ft); juveniles often near surface or shore and shallower in 2 m (7 ft) or less. Color variable: black, blackish-gray or greenish-gray on back and sides, gray to white below; back sometimes with blackish or gray reticulations. D XVII–XXX + 16–21; A II–III,15–23; Pect. 14–17; Pelvic I,5; LLs (oblique rows) about 190; GR 4–5 + 14–20 = 18–25; Vert. 61–66. (Alternative name BLACKCOD).

**SKILFISH, *Erilepis zonifer* (Lockington, 1880).** Family Anoplopomatidae
Sagami Bay, Pacific coast of central Honshu, Japan to south of Commander-Aleutian Islands Chain and southern Gulf of Alaska to Monterey Bay, central California. Common at least along the Hawaiian-Emperor Ridge seamount chain, North Pacific; apparently uncommon in many other places within geographic range; rare in California. Length to 188 cm (74 in) TL. Depth: adults close to bottom 200–1,047 m (656–3,438 ft); juveniles and young adults to about 110 cm (43 in) TL collected near surface. Adults black to dark gray above, whitish below. Juveniles black, gray-blue, or green above with light blotches on head and anterior portion of body. D XI–XIV + I–II,13–17; A II–III,11–19; Pect. 16–19; Pelvic I,5; LLp 133; LLs (oblique rows) 122–124; GR 5–6 + 16 = 21–22; Vert. 45–46.

**SPLITNOSE SEAROBIN**

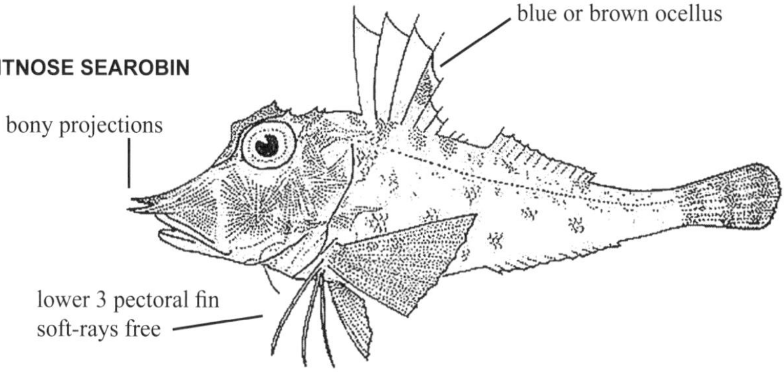


**LUMPTAIL SEAROBIN**

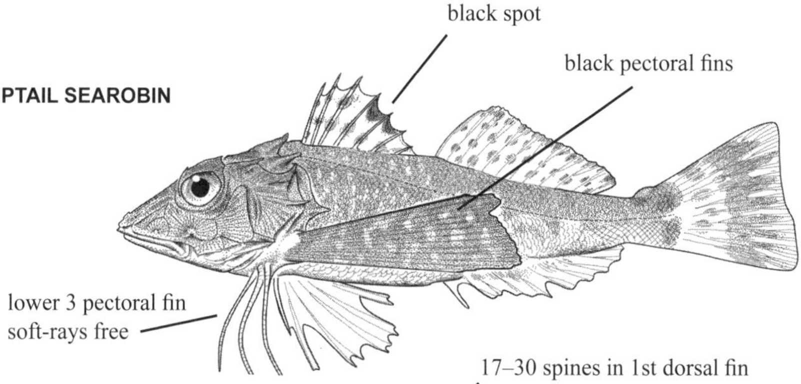


**SABLEFISH**

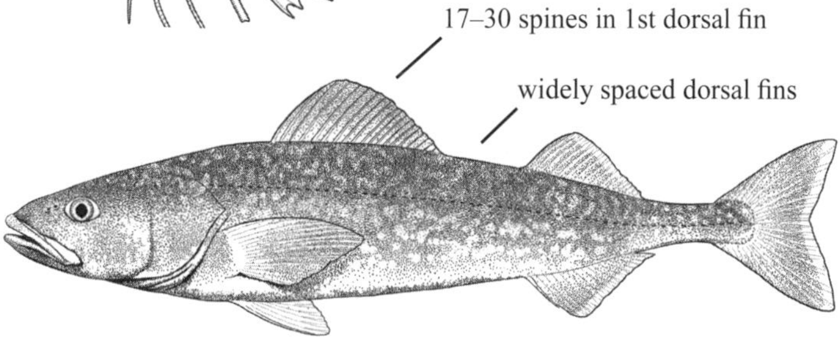


**SKILFISH**

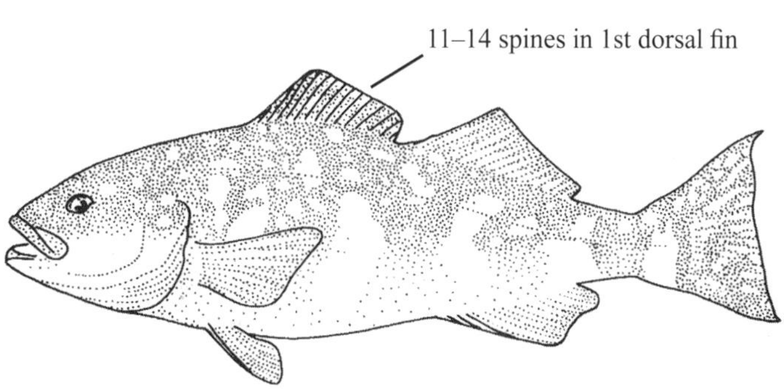

# COMBFISHES, Family Zaniolepididae and GREENLINGS, Family Hexagrammidae

**SHORTSPINE COMBFISH, *Zaniolepis frenata* Eigenmann & Eigenmann, 1889.** Family Zaniolepididae
Southern Oregon to Bahía San Cristobal (27°22'N, 114°37'W), southern Baja California and in Gulf of California. Common at least from central California to central Baja California (about 28°00'N). Length to 25 cm (10 in) TL. Depth: 7–411 m (23–1,348 ft) or perhaps to 450 m (1,476 ft). Light tan, brown, or pink, generally with dark streaks and blotches (occasionally missing); dark oblique bands in dorsal fin. Skin covered with minute rough scales forming shagreen-like surface. D XX–XXIII,11–13; A III,15–17; Pect. 14–15; GR 4 + 9–12 = 13–16; Vert. 40–43.

**LONGSPINE COMBFISH, *Zaniolepis latipinnis* Girard, 1858.** Family Zaniolepididae
Vancouver Island, southern British Columbia to southern Baja California (25°45'N, 112°23'W) (LACM 31762-17). Occasionally in Puget Sound and common from about San Francisco, northern California to Bahía Sebastian Vizcaino, central Baja California. Length to 30.5 cm (12 in) TL. Depth: at least 16–288 m (53–945 ft), or perhaps to 421 m (1,381 ft). Light brown or brown-yellow with dark spots on body and fins; dark streak from tip of snout to eye. D XX–XXIII,11–12; A III,15–17; Pect. 13–15; GR 2–3 + 8–10 = 11–12; Vert. 40–42.

**PAINTED GREENLING, *Oxylebius pictus* Gill, 1862.** Family Zaniolepididae
Kachemak Bay and Prince William Sound, northern Gulf of Alaska to Punta San Pablo (27°14'N, 114°29'W), southern Baja California (LACM 32082-2). Common from at least southeastern Alaska to at least Punta Banda, northern Baja California. Length to 25.4 cm (10 in) TL. Depth: intertidal to 249 m (816 ft). Red or red-brown bars alternating with gray, tan, orange-red, or white; red head flaps; some individuals heavily marked with small white spots and have yellow throats. Spawning males dark with light spots. See DeMartini (1985) for more details. D XIV–XVII,13–17; A III–IV,12–15; Pect. 14–17; GR 2–5 + 6–9 = 9–14; Vert. 36–39. (Formerly Hexagrammidae: M&L).

**LINGCOD, *Ophiodon elongatus* Girard, 1854.** Family Hexagrammidae
Shumagin Islands, south-western Gulf of Alaska to Punta San Carlos and Isla Natividad, central Baja California; perhaps eastern Bering Sea as far north as the Yukon-Kuskokwim Delta. Common from Kodiak Island area, Gulf of Alaska to at least Punta San Antonio, central Baja California. Mostly marine, but juveniles enter brackish waters. Length to 152 cm (60 in) TL. Depth: intertidal to 475 m (1,558 ft). Benthic juveniles and adults gray-brown to green, or bluish with dark, yellow, or orange spotting and mottling. Pelagic and newly settled juveniles brown or greenish on back, silvery sides, sometimes with darker blotches. Small cirrus sits above each eye. D XXII–XXVIII,18–24; A III,18–25 (spines often embedded and not visible); Pect. 16–18; LLp 154–180; GR 5–8 + 16–19 = 21–26; Vert. 55–59.

## KEY TO THE COMBFISHES and GREENLINGS:
Edited by Dario W. Diehl
(Principal sources: Miller & Lea, 1972; Mecklenburg & Eschmeyer, 2003)

1a More than 1 lateral line, usually 5 (some on or near belly)….. 5 (page 178)

1b One lateral line….. 2

2a Second dorsal fin spine not elongated; 1st 4–5 dorsal spinous fin membranes with shallow notching….. 4 (next page)

2b Second dorsal fin spine elongated; 1st 4–5 dorsal spinous fin membranes deeply incised or notched….. 3 (next page)

3a Cirrus present above eye; 2nd dorsal fin spine shorter than HL:

**SHORTSPINE COMBFISH**

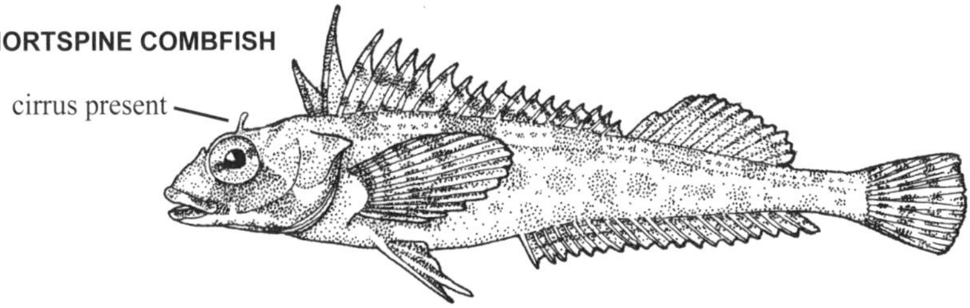


3b No cirrus above eye; 2nd dorsal fin spine longer than HL:

**LONGSPINE COMBFISH**

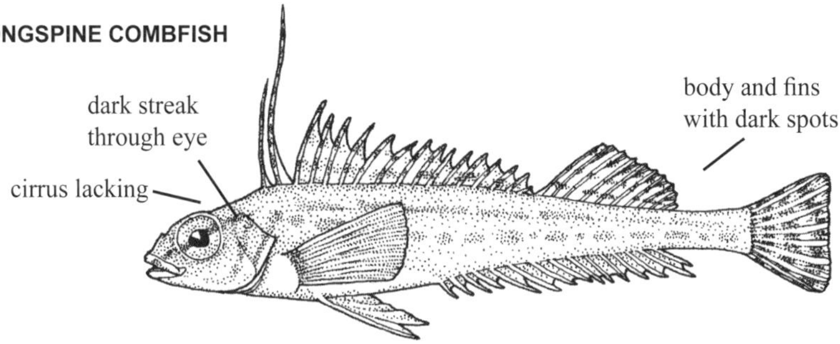


4a *From 2a: second dorsal fin spine not elongated*
Maxilla not reaching or barely reaching anterior margin of eye; anal fin soft-rays 12–14; anal fin spines 3 or 4; body with distinct bars or bands (usually reddish) extending onto fins:

**PAINTED GREENLING**

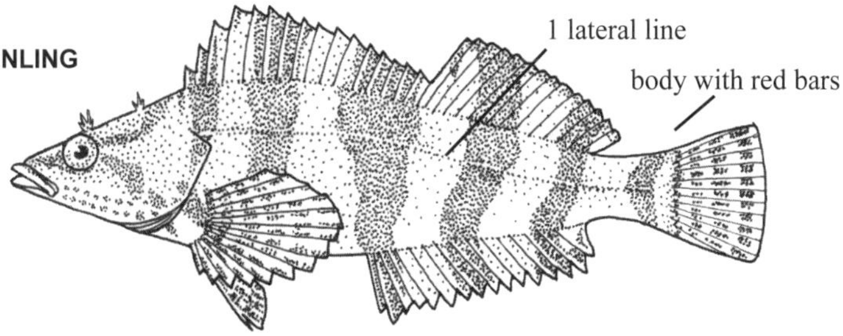


4b Maxilla reaching to or beyond posterior margin of eye; anal fin soft-rays 18 or more; visible anal fin spines 0–2 (some anal spines may be buried and not visible); body without distinct bars or bands:

**LINGCOD**

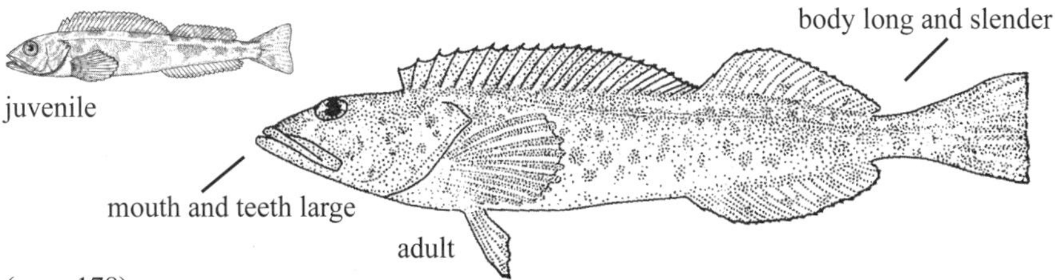


5a (page 178)

## COMBFISHES and GREENLINGS (continued)

**ATKA MACKEREL, *Pleurogrammus monopterygius* (Pallas, 1810).** Family Hexagrammidae
Sea of Japan and Sea of Okhotsk to Commander-Aleutian Islands Chain and northern Bering Sea to Bering Strait to Redondo Beach, southern California. Rare in eastern North Pacific south of Alaska; common from at least off the southern Kuril Islands, Russia to the Bering Sea and east of the Kodiak Island—Prince William Sound area. Length to at least 54 cm (21.3 in) TL. Depth: lower intertidal to 720 m (2,362 ft). However, this deep record was from a trawl-caught fish that might have been taken in midwater. Color highly variable. Females and juveniles mottled gray-blue with white blotches on head and back and dark ventral bars. Territorial males bright yellow or orange with dark bars. Nonterritorial males yellow with dark blotches. D XXI–XXIV,24–30; A 23–28; Pect. 23–28; LLp 139–166; GR 6–8 + 16–19 = 22–26; Vert. 58–63. A branched cirrus (not mentioned in previous texts) sits above each eye (R. Feeney, pers. comm.).

**WHITESPOTTED GREENLING, *Hexagrammos stelleri* Tilesius, 1810.** Family Hexagrammidae
Sea of Japan to Commander-Aleutian Islands Chain and northeast to Simpson Cove (about 70°00'N, 145°00'W), western Beaufort Sea, and Bering Sea to Puget Sound, Washington. Common from Sea of Japan to Bering Sea to Puget Sound. Length to about 48 cm (18.9 in) TL. Depth: intertidal to 275 m (902 ft). Adults light brown to greenish (males golden during spawning season), body and fins often tinged with reddish or yellow; conspicuous white spots on body; prominent black spot on anterior dorsal fin. Newly settled juveniles dark on back, silvery sides, some darker barring. Older juvenile colors variable, often brown or reddish. D XX–XXV,18–24; A 18–25; Pect. 18–20; GR 4–5 + 12–15 = 16–20; Vert. 51–56.

**KELP GREENLING, *Hexagrammos decagrammus* (Pallas, 1810).** Family Hexagrammidae
Bering Sea (56°50'N, 169°54'W) and Attu Island, Aleutian Islands to La Jolla, southern California (SIO 59-33). Common from Kiska Island, Aleutian Islands to Santa Barbara Channel, southern California. Length to 62.9 cm (24.8 in) TL. Depth: intertidal to 149 m (489 ft); possibly to 242 m (794 ft). Females gray-brown with bright golden to light brown spots on body and head; males dark gray, brown-orange, or red-purple with bright blue spots on head and sides; inside of mouth yellowish in both sexes. Individuals occasionally gray with orange and yellow spots. Pelagic and newly settled juveniles dark on back with silvery sides; older benthic juveniles reddish, yellow-brown, or gray, heavily mottled. Color and pattern variations are discussed in DeMartini (1986). D XX–XXIII,22–26; A 0–I,21–26; Pect. 18–20; Midlateral scales 112; GR 3–5 + 9–16 = 13–20; Vert. 52–57.

**ROCK GREENLING, *Hexagrammos lagocephalus* (Pallas, 1810).** Family Hexagrammidae
Yellow, Japan, and Okhotsk Seas to Commander-Aleutian Islands Chain to Point Conception, central California. A few larvae have been collected in southern California as far south as Santa Monica Bay. Common at least from Kuril Islands, Russia, along Aleutian Islands to central California. Length to 61 cm (24 in) TL. Depth: intertidal and shallow waters, recorded to 80 m (262 ft) in eastern Pacific and to 596 m (1,955 ft) in western Pacific. Brown or greenish; males with intense red or orange mottling; females with blue or light spots; dark spot often above base of pectoral fin; inside of mouth usually blue. D XIX–XXIII,20–25; A 0–I,21–25; Pect. 18–22; GR 4–5 + 9–13 = 13–18; Vert. 52–57. (Formerly *Hexagrammos superciliosus* (Pallas, 1810): M&L).

5a *From 1a: more than 1 lateral line*
Dorsal fin not notched or only very slight; caudal fin deeply forked; strongly-developed ridges on upper surface of skull:

**ATKA MACKEREL**

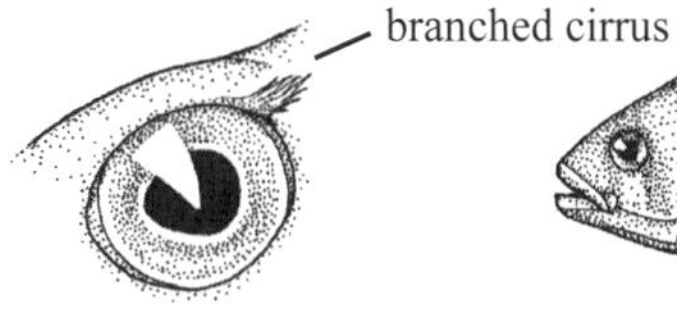


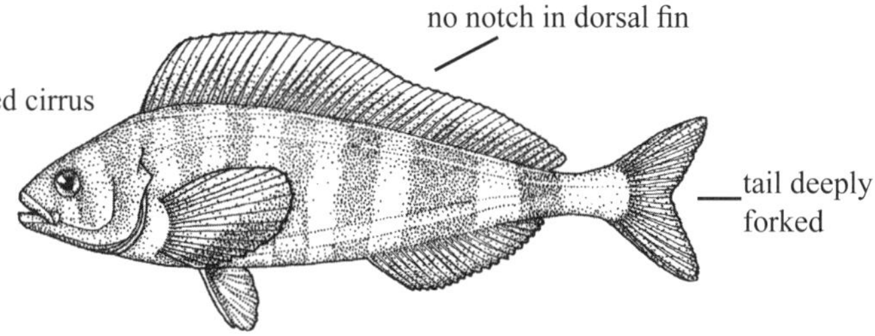


5b Dorsal fin notched about midbody; caudal fin rounded or only slightly indented; no strong ridges on skull….. 6

6a Fourth lateral line not extending beyond origin of anal fin; palatines without teeth; conspicuous white spots on body:

**WHITESPOTTED GREENLING**

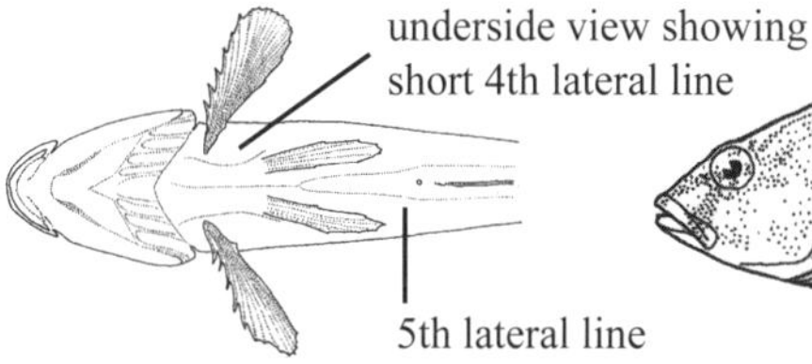


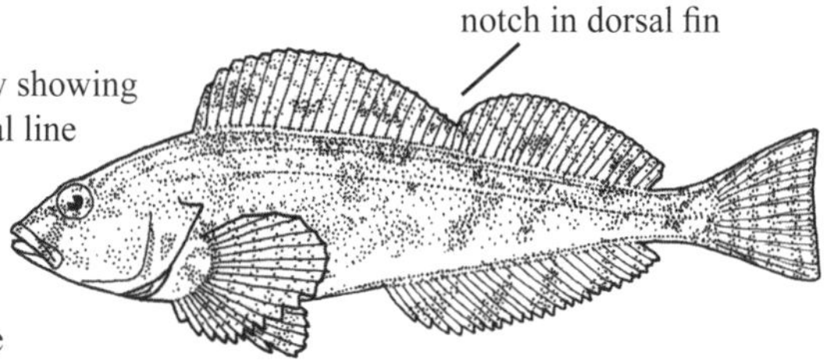


6b Fourth lateral line extends well beyond origin of anal fin; palatine teeth present; bright golden-brown, blue, or red spots on body….. 7

7a Two pairs of cirri on head, 1 above eye and other between eye and dorsal fin origin (2nd pair small, occasionally absent); caudal fin slightly indented; inside of mouth yellowish:

**KELP GREENLING**

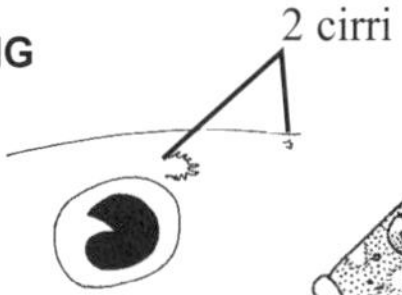


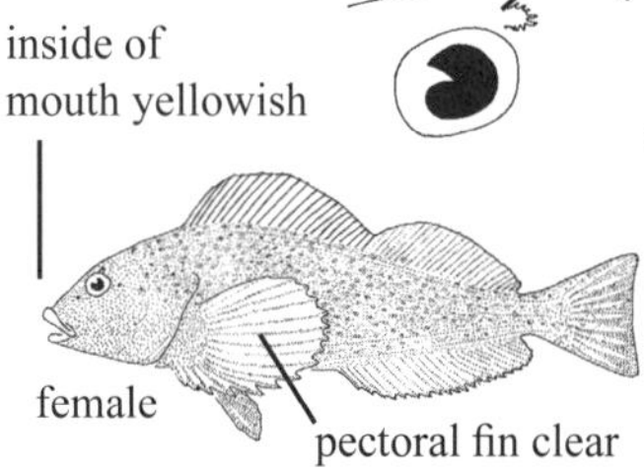


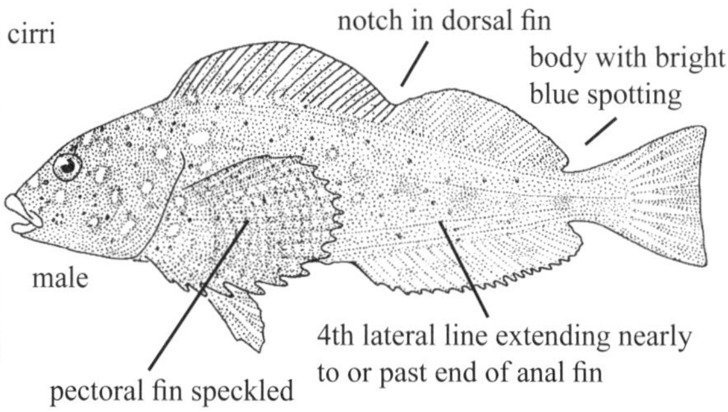


7b One pair of long cirri on head (more than ¾ diameter of eye in large fish); caudal fin rounded; inside of mouth bluish:

**ROCK GREENLING**

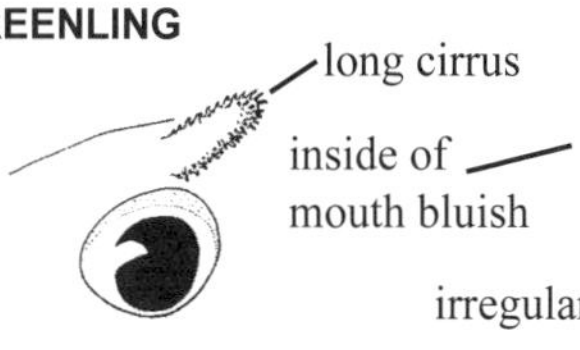


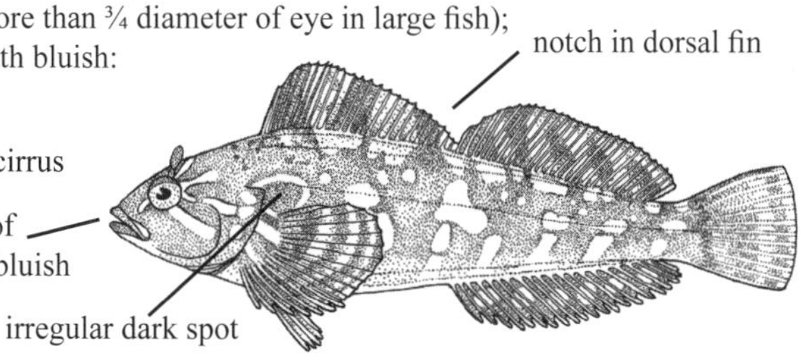

# GRUNT SCULPIN, Family Rhamphocottidae, MARINE SCULPINS,[1] Family Psychrolutidae, CABEZON, Family Scorpaenichthyidae, LONGFIN SCULPINS,[1] Family Jordaniidae, POACHERS, Family Agonidae, and FRESHWATER SCULPINS,[1] Family Cottidae

NOTE: The classification used here follows Sheiko (1993), Sheiko and Mecklenburg (2004), and Smith and Busby (2014). In particular, we follow Smith and Busby (2014) and remove the genera *Blepsias*, *Hemitripterus*, and *Nautichthys* from the family Hemitripteridae and place them in the family Agonidae and remove virtually all of the Pacific Coast marine sculpins from the family Cottidae, placing them instead within the family Psychrolutidae. [1]Name suggested by Leo Smith.

**GRUNT SCULPIN, *Rhamphocottus richardsonii* Günther, 1874.** Family Rhamphocottidae
Japan; western Gulf of Alaska near Unalaska Island to Santa Monica Bay, southern California and Tanner Bank (32°38'N, 119°09'W) (SIO 79-60). Also undocumented report from Bering Sea. Common from at least Alaska Peninsula to Cape Mendocino, northern California. Length to 9.3 cm (3.7 in) TL. Depth: intertidal to 258 m (846 ft), and possibly deeper. Cream, tan, or yellow-orange with brown streaks; fins reddish and orange. D VII–IX + 12–14; A 6–9; Pect. 14–18; Pelvic I,3–4; LLp around 25; GR 1–3 + 5–9 = 6–11; Vert. 24–28. (Formerly Cottidae: M&L).

**ROSYLIP SCULPIN, *Ascelichthys rhodorus* Jordan & Gilbert, 1880.** Family Psychrolutidae
Olsen Bay, Prince William Sound, northern Gulf of Alaska to Pillar Point, central California. Common from Haida Gwaii, British Columbia southward to northern California. Length to 18.8 cm (7.4 in) TL. Depth: intertidal to 15.2 m (50 ft). Black or dark olive-brown on back and lighter below; lips bright red; margin of spinous dorsal fin red. D VII–X,17–20; A 13–16; Pect. 16–18; Pelvic absent; LLp 34–38 on body + 1–2 on tail; GR 1–2 + 3–7 = 3–9; Vert. 32–36. (Formerly Cottidae: M&L).

**MANACLED SCULPIN, *Synchirus gilli* Bean, 1890.** Family Psychrolutidae
Chuginadak Island, Aleutian Islands to San Miguel Island, southern California (SIO 64-637). Common at least from Kenai Peninsula, southeastern Alaska to central California. Length to 6.9 cm (2.7 in) TL. Depth: intertidal to at least 14 m (46 ft). Yellowish or greenish to reddish-brown; male with silvery stripe on sides. D VIII–X,19–21; A 18–21; Pect. 21–24; Pelvic I,3; LLs 38–42; GR 2 + 7 = 9; Vert. 38–39. (Formerly Cottidae: M&L).

**CABEZON, *Scorpaenichthys marmoratus* (Ayres, 1854).** Family Scorpaenichthyidae
Icy Bay, Prince William Sound, Alaska to Punta Abreojos, central Baja California on mainland and Isla Cedros, Islas San Benitos, and Isla Natividad, central Baja California. Larvae have been collected from the western Gulf of Alaska east of Kodiak Island. Common from about Haida Gwaii, British Columbia to Bahía Playa Maria, central Baja California. Length to 99 cm (39 in) TL. Mostly marine but juveniles enter brackish waters. Depth: intertidal to 231 m (758 ft). Color variable: green, blue, red, brown, or whitish with intense dark and light mottling. Juveniles sometimes bright red without mottling. D VIII–XII,15–19; A 11–14; Pect. 14–16; Pelvic I,4–5; LLp 71–88 on body + 4–8 on tail; GR 3–6 + 12–16 = 16–22; Vert. 35–37. (Formerly Cottidae: M&L).

## KEY TO THE SCULPINS and POACHERS:

Revised by Rick Feeney and Milton S. Love
(Principal sources: Bolin, 1944, 1950; Clemens & Wilby, 1961; Miller & Lea, 1972; Mecklenburg et al., 2002; Smith & Busby, 2014)

1a Body encased in bony plates….. 50 (page 203)

1b Body not encased in bony plates….. 2 (next page)

2a HL 50% or more of SL; lowermost pectoral fin soft-rays free, not connected by membranes:

**GRUNT SCULPIN**

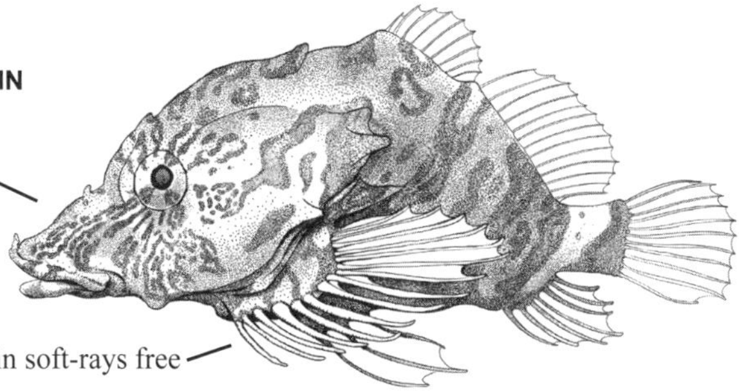


2b HL less than 50% SL; lowermost pectoral fin soft-rays not free of membranes….. 3

3a Pelvic fins absent:

**ROSYLIP SCULPIN**

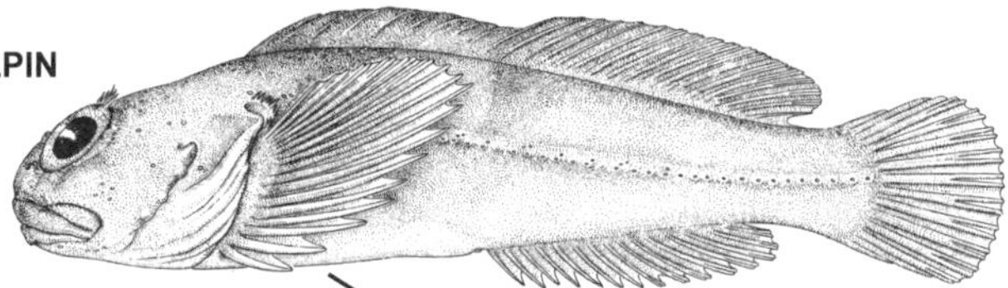


3b Pelvic fins present….. 4

4a Pectoral fins united to each other across belly:

**MANACLED SCULPIN**

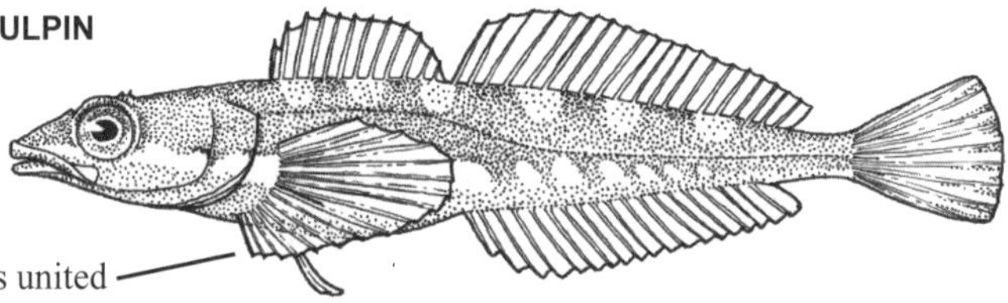


4b Pectoral fins separate….. 5

5a Pelvic fin soft-rays 2–4 (if 4, both fins have 4)….. 8 (page 182)

5b Pelvic fin soft-rays 5 (rarely 1 fin may have 4, the other 5, but never both with 4)….. 6

6a Body without scales; anal fin soft-rays 11–14; large broad-based cirrus extending along midline of snout:

**CABEZON**

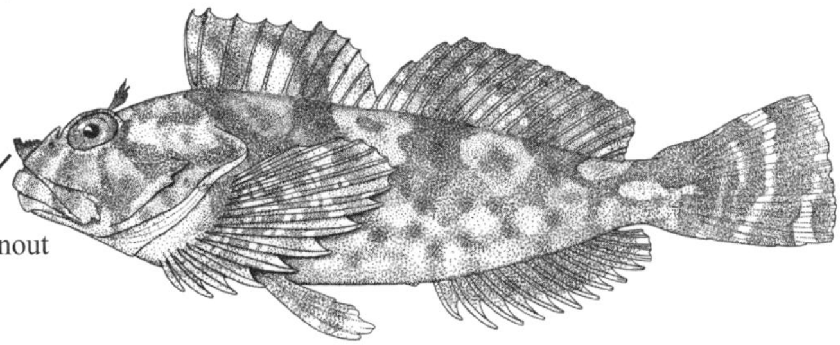


6b Body scaled; anal fin soft-rays 22–24; no cirrus on midline of snout….. 7 (next page)

## SCULPINS and POACHERS (continued)

**LONGFIN SCULPIN, *Jordania zonope* Starks, 1895.** Family JORDANIIDAE
Danger Island, Prince William Sound to Diablo Canyon, central California (LACM 31859-11). Common at least from Vancouver Island, British Columbia southward to Diablo Cove, central California. Length to 15 cm (6 in) TL. Depth: intertidal to at least 497 m (1,630 ft). Red, brown, or greenish; alternating narrow-light and wide-dark bars on cheeks; 6–8 dark saddles on back; dark blotches on sides; caudal fin often orange or yellow; pelvic fins black; anal fin yellow or orange. D XVII–XVIII,15–18; A 22–24; Pect. 13–15; Pelvic I,4–5; LLs 48–50 on body + 2–3 on tail; GR 2 +7 = 9; Vert. 46–48. (Formerly Cottidae: M&L).

**THORNBACK SCULPIN, *Paricelinus hopliticus* Eigenmann & Eigenmann, 1889.** Family JORDANIIDAE
Gulf of Alaska (55°29'N, 134°10'W) and Bering Sea to southern California (32°32'N, 117°22'W) (UCLA W49-416). Common at least as far south as Rittenburg Bank (37°53'N, 123°18'W), central California. Length to about 20 cm (7.9 in) TL. Depth: nearshore to at least 273 m (895 ft), typically deeper than 20 m (66 ft). Olive-green on back; body with bright blue spots; heavily marked with purplish or brown bars and blotches. D XII–XIII,19–20; A 23–24; Pect. 14–15; Pelvic I,5; LLs 43 on body + 1–2 on tail; GRt 9; Vert. 42–43. (Formerly Cottidae: M&L).

**GIANT BLOB SCULPIN, *Psychrolutes phrictus* Stein & Bond, 1978.** Family PSYCHROLUTIDAE
Sea of Okhotsk and Pacific side of Honshu, Japan to Commander Islands and western Bering Sea north to Cape Navarin, to Bering Sea as far northward as 59°20'N, 178°20'W to off San Diego, southern California; one record from off the coast of Guerrero (17°45'N, 101°59'W), Mexico. Common from at least Bering Sea to central California. Length to about 70 cm (27.5 in) TL. Depth: 220–2,800 m (722–9,186 ft). Blackish, grayish, or purple-gray, sometimes with white mottling; face sometimes white. D VII–IX,19–20; A 12–14; Pect. 22–26; Pelvic I,3; LLp 12–14; GRt 9–13; Vert. 33–36. (Alternative name BLOB SCULPIN).

**BIGMOUTH SCULPIN, *Hemitripterus bolini* (Myers, 1934).** Family AGONIDAE
Eastern Sea of Okhotsk and northern Kuril Islands, Russia to Commander-Aleutian Islands Chain, Bering Sea to Cape Navarin, to north side of Alaska Peninsula to Eureka, northern California. Common from Bering Sea and Aleutian Islands southward to southeastern Alaska; rare in northern California. Length to 78 cm (30.7 in) TL. Depth: 25–925 m (82–3,034 ft). Gray or brown mottling on back, lighter belly; 4–5 dark saddles on back; reddish, yellow-brown, and orange patches on much of body. D VIII–XV + 11–12; A 11–14; Pect. 20–23; Pelvic I,3; LLp 40–42; GR 5 + 16 = 21; Vert. 38–40.

7a No enlarged spinuous scales along dorsal fin base; dorsal fin spines 17–18:

**LONGFIN SCULPIN**

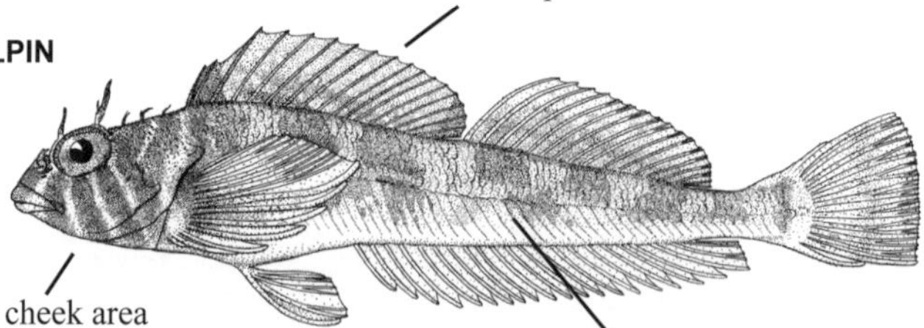


7b (next page)

7b Row of enlarged spinuous scales along dorsal fin base; dorsal fin spines 12–13:

**THORNBACK SCULPIN**

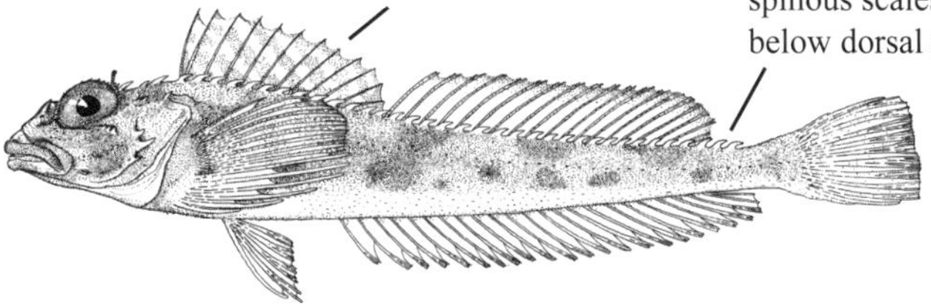


8a *From 5a: pelvic fin soft-rays 2–4*
Dorsal fin spines short, partially buried under flabby skin and continuous with 2nd dorsal fin; interorbital width 2.5 times or more than eye diameter:

**GIANT BLOB SCULPIN**

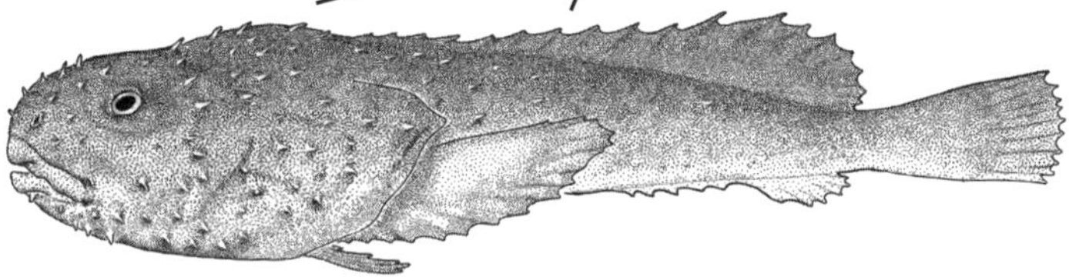


8b Dorsal fin spines neither short nor buried; interorbital width less than 2.5 times eye diameter….. 9

9a First dorsal fin base as long as or longer than 2nd dorsal fin base:

**BIGMOUTH SCULPIN**

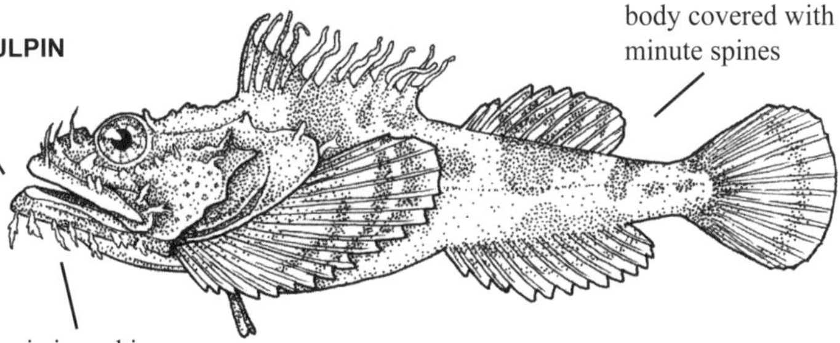


9b First dorsal fin base shorter than 2nd dorsal fin base….. 10

10a Second dorsal fin base less than 2.75 times length of 1st dorsal fin base….. 12 (page 184)

10b Second dorsal fin base more than 2.75 times length of 1st dorsal fin base….. 11 (next page)

## SCULPINS and POACHERS (continued)

**SAILFIN SCULPIN, *Nautichthys oculofasciatus* (Girard, 1858).** Family AGONIDAE
Shumagin Islands, western Gulf of Alaska to San Miguel Island, southern California (SIO 54-191). A specimen was reported in the eastern Bering Sea at about 57°30'N, 169°20'W, but without documentation. Common from at least Cook Inlet, Gulf of Alaska to central California. Length to 20.3 cm (8 in) TL. Depth: intertidal to 208 m (682 ft). Yellowish-brown, orange-brown to gray; black bars on back, fins, and almost vertically through eye. D VIII–IX,27–30; A 16–21; Pect. 13–14; Pelvic I,3; LLs 41–46 on body + 1–2 on tail; GR 0–1 + 6–7 = 6–8; Vert. 40–41. (Formerly Cottidae: M&L) (Alternative name SAILFIN SEA RAVEN).

**SILVERSPOTTED SCULPIN, *Blepsias cirrhosus* (Pallas, 1814).** Family AGONIDAE
Sea of Okhotsk and Sea of Japan to western Bering Sea near Cape Olyutorskiy (59°44'N, 170°20'E) (ZIN 17737) and Commander-Aleutian Islands Chain and Pribilof Islands, Bering Sea, Alaska to San Simeon, central California (SIO 15-2042). Common from Sea of Japan to eastern Bering Sea to central California. Length to 26 cm (10.2 in) TL. Depth: intertidal to 95 m (312 ft), possibly to 150 m (492 ft), but voucher or other documentation not found. Brown to greenish above, reddish, yellow, and white below; dark patches often present on back; row of bright silver spots on body and often on fins and cheeks. D VI–X + 20–25; A 18–22; Pect. 11–14; Pelvic I,3; LLs 43–57 on body + 1–3 on tail; GR 2 + 5–6 = 7–8; Vert. 37–39. (Formerly Cottidae: M&L) (Alternative name SILVERSPOTTED SEA RAVEN).

**PACIFIC STAGHORN SCULPIN, *Leptocottus armatus* Girard, 1854.** Family COTTIDAE
Pribilof Islands and Port Moller, southeastern Bering Sea to Punta Baja, northern Baja California. Common from the Pribilof Islands, Bering Sea to Bahía San Quintin, northern Baja California. Length to 48 cm (18.9 in) TL. Nearshore marine waters, brackish and fresh waters, including lower portions of coastal rivers and streams; depth: intertidal to 335 m (1,099 ft). Greenish-brown or gray above, white to yellow below; dorsal, caudal, and pectoral fins yellow or creamy white with brown or greenish bars. D VI–IX + 15–21; A 14–20; Pect. 17–20; Pelvic I,4; LLp 37–42 on body + 1–3 on tail; GR 1–3 + 8–12 = 10–13; Vert. 35–39. (Formerly STAGHORN SCULPIN: M&L).

**PRICKLY SCULPIN, *Cottus asper* Richardson, 1837.** Family COTTIDAE
Seward, Alaska (coast of northern Gulf of Alaska) to Ventura River, southern California. Common from at least Bristol Bay, Alaska to southern California. Length to 19.2 cm (7.7 in) SL. Usually in fresh water, occasionally in estuaries and nearshore marine waters. Depth: shallow waters to 92 m (300 ft). Dark brown, reddish-brown, greenish, or gray on back, white to yellow ventrally; dark vertical bands on body; orange edge (breeding males and females) and blackish blotches on 1st dorsal fin; breeding males very dark. D VII–XI + 18–23; A 12–19; Pect. 12–19; Pelvic I,4 (rarely 3 or 5); LLp 28–43; GR 0–1 + 5–7 = 5–7; Vert. 34–36.

11a Gill membranes joined to isthmus; pelvic fins extend more than ½ distance to anal fin origin:

**SAILFIN SCULPIN**

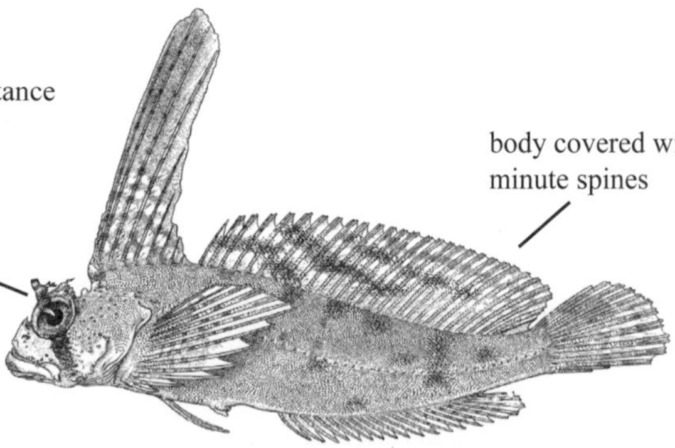


11b (next page)

11b Gill membranes free from isthmus; pelvic fins extend less than ½ way to anal fin origin:

**SILVERSPOTTED SCULPIN**

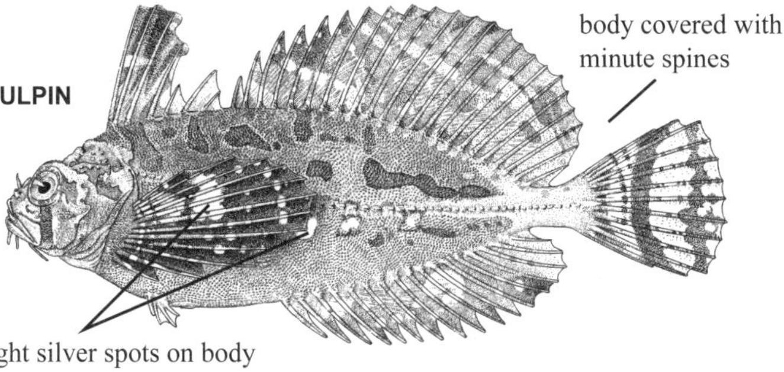


12a *From 10a: 2nd dorsal fin base less than 2.75 times length of 1st dorsal fin base*
Scales below lateral line large, forming well-defined bands extending to about caudal fin base; 1st and 2nd dorsal fins continuous….. 49 (page 202)

12b Scales below lateral line absent, represented by minute prickles, or restricted to area covered by pectoral fins; 1st and 2nd dorsal fins separated or contiguous (barely attached by membrane)….. 13

13a Gill membranes free from isthmus or at least forming distinct free fold across it….. 18 (page 186)

13b Gill membranes completely joined to isthmus (sometimes with shallow groove)….. 14

14a Lateral line scales as conspicuous, heavy bony plates; dorsal fin soft-rays 8–13; anal fin soft-rays 6–10….. 17 (page 186)

14b Lateral line scales not evident; dorsal fin soft-rays 15–23; anal fin soft-rays 12–20….. 15

15a Preopercle spine antler-like with several upward-directed spines:

**PACIFIC STAGHORN SCULPIN**

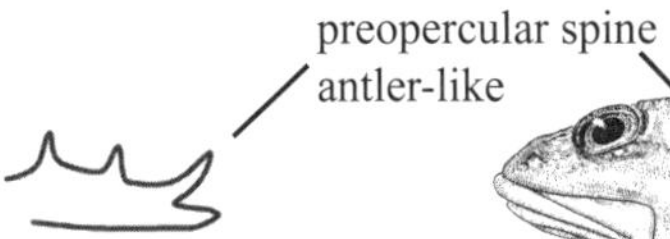


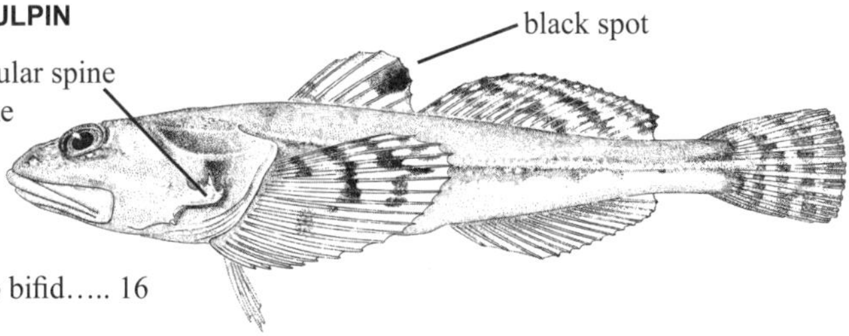


15b Preopercle spine simple to bifid….. 16

16a Anal fin soft-rays usually 16–19; pelvic fins do not reach vent when depressed; posterior nostril small:

**PRICKLY SCULPIN**

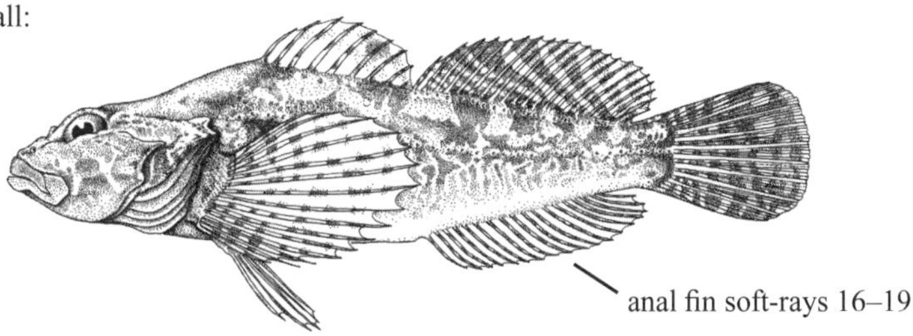


16b (next page)

## SCULPINS and POACHERS (continued)

**COASTRANGE SCULPIN, *Cottus aleuticus* Gilbert, 1896.** Family COTTIDAE
Kobuk River (drains to Kotzebue Sound, eastern Chukchi Sea); Bristol Bay, Alaska Peninsula, and Aleutian Islands drainages to Oso Flaco Creek, Santa Barbara County, central California. Common from Alaska southward to drainages of San Luis Obispo County, central California. Length to 17.2 cm (6.8 in) TL. Fresh waters, estuaries, and nearshore marine waters. Brown, green, or gray mottling on back, white on belly; 2–3 vertical bands below 2nd dorsal fin, 1 on caudal peduncle. Spawning males with orange-edged 1st dorsal fin. D VIII–X + 16–20; A 12–16; Pect. 13–16; Pelvic I,4; LLp 32–44; GRt 4–7; Vert. 34–38.

**BUFFALO SCULPIN, *Enophrys bison* (Girard, 1854).** Family PSYCHROLUTIDAE
Amchitka Island, Aleutian Islands to Monterey Bay, central California. One specimen perhaps taken in southern California (33°18'N). Common from Kodiak Island, Gulf of Alaska to about San Francisco, northern California. Length to 37.1 cm (14.6 in) TL. Marine and brackish waters. Depth: intertidal to 194 m (636 ft). Black, dark gray, green, or brown above; purplish bony plates on head and along lateral line; often with 3 dark saddles across back; dorsal, caudal, and pectoral fins heavily barred and spotted with black; anal, pectoral, and pelvic fin margin orange. D VII–IX + 9–13; A 8–10; Pect. 15–18; Pelvic I,2–3; LLs 29–33 on body + 0–2 on tail; GR 0–1 + 4–6 = 5–7; Vert. 29–31. (Formerly Cottidae: M&L).

**BULL SCULPIN, *Enophrys taurina* Gilbert, 1914.** Family PSYCHROLUTIDAE
Fort Bragg, northern California (LACM 38371-1) to Santa Catalina (LACM 902) and San Nicolas islands, southern California. Apparently common in central California. Length to 17 cm (6.8 in) TL. Depth: 11–256 m (36–840 ft). Dark gray, brown, pink, or white above, whitish below; 3 dark bars on back; brown spots or marbling on dorsal, caudal, and pectoral fins. D VI–VIII + 8–10; A 6–7; Pect. 15–18; Pelvic I,3; LLs 24–29 on body + 0–3 on tail; Vert. 27–29. (Formerly Cottidae: M&L).

**YELLOWCHIN SCULPIN, *Icelinus quadriseriatus* (Lockington, 1880).** Family PSYCHROLUTIDAE
Sonoma County, northern California (CAS 13997) to Cabo San Lucas, southern Baja California. Common from Monterey Bay to Bahía Sebastian de Vizcaino, central Baja California. Length to 11 cm (4.4 in) TL. Depth: intertidal to 201 m (660 ft). Dark brown to gray above, pale below; males with yellow-orange chin, black brachiostegal membranes, and blackish pelvic and anal fins. D VII–X + 12–16; A 10–15; Pect. 15–18; Pelvic I,2; LLs 34–37 on body + 1 on tail; GR 0 + 3–6 = 3–6; Vert. 33–35. (Formerly Cottidae: M&L).

16b Anal fin soft-rays 12–15; pelvic fins usually reach vent when depressed; posterior nostril large:

**COASTRANGE SCULPIN**

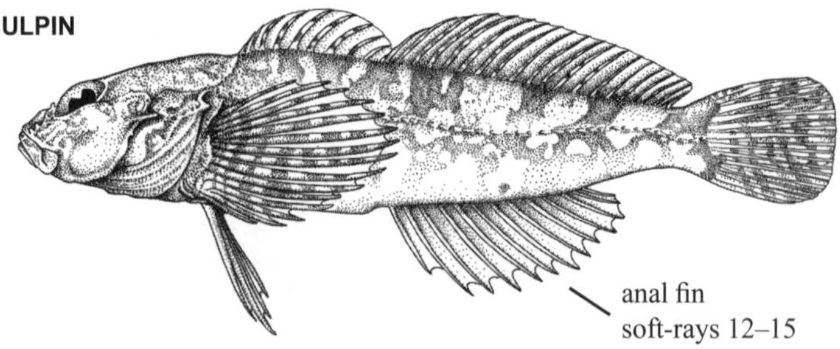


17a (next page)

17a *From 14a: lateral line scales as conspicuous, heavy bony plates*
Anal fin soft-rays 8–10; dorsal fin soft-rays 9–13; orbit into maxilla 1.4–2.4:

**BUFFALO SCULPIN**

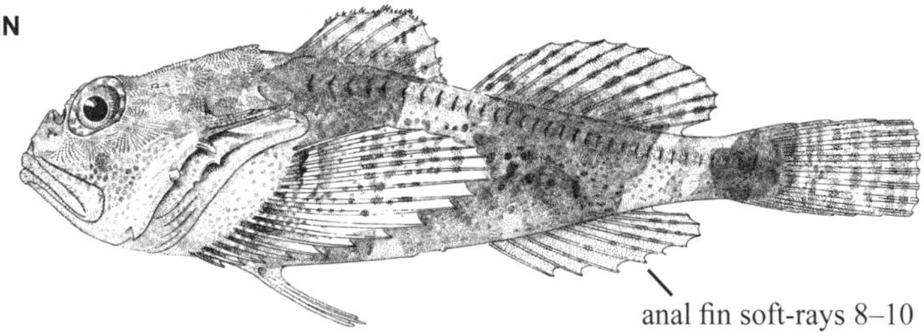


17b Anal fin soft-rays 6–7; dorsal fin soft-rays 8–10; orbit into maxilla 1.1–1.3:

**BULL SCULPIN**

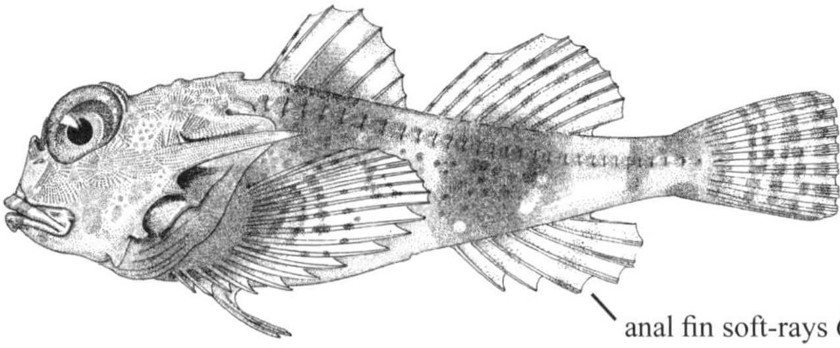


18a *From 13a: gill membranes free from isthmus*
Area between dorsal fins and lateral line entirely without scales or only with minute prickly papillae….. 39 (page 196)

18b Area between dorsal fins and lateral line with well-developed scales covering entire area or in oblique or longitudinal band….. 19

19a Pelvic fins with 1 spine and 3 soft-rays (ROUGHBACK, SNUBNOSE, SMOOTHHEAD, PUGET SOUND, PADDED, and BONYHEAD SCULPINS may rarely have 2 soft-rays); area between dorsal fins and lateral line filled entirely with scales, with dorsal band of more than 2 scale rows, or with scales immediately above lateral line….. 27 (page 190)

19b Pelvic fins with 1 spine and 2 soft-rays; area between dorsal fins and lateral line with dorsal band of 2 scale rows well above lateral line….. 20

20a Dorsal scale band not extending beyond 2nd dorsal fin….. 23 (page 188)

20b Dorsal scale band extends onto dorsal surface of caudal peduncle (may be interrupted)….. 21

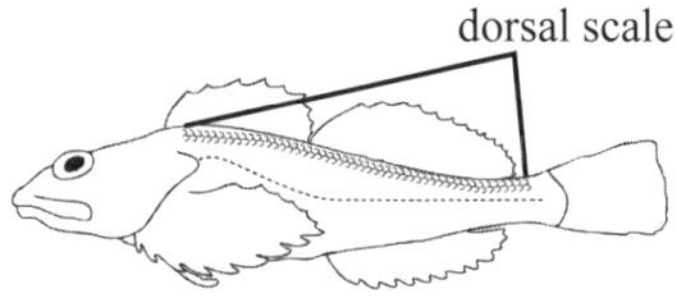


21a Dorsal scale band interrupted for short space under end of 2nd dorsal fin; pelvic fins extend longer than ⅓ of distance to anal origin:

**YELLOWCHIN SCULPIN**

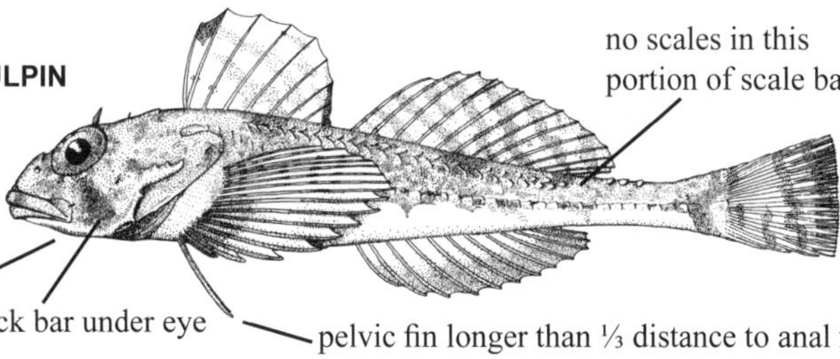


21b (next page)

## SCULPINS and POACHERS (continued)

**FRINGED SCULPIN, *Icelinus fimbriatus* Gilbert, 1890.** Family Psychrolutidae
Pendrell Sound, southern British Columbia to San Diego, California and perhaps to Isla Cedros, central Baja California. Common at least in southern California. Length to 22 cm (8.7 in) TL. Depth: 30–265 m (98–869 ft). Dark gray, brown, or gray above; brown, yellow, or pale ventrally; small, irregular green-yellow spots on sides; dorsal, caudal, and pectoral fins yellow-green with dark bars. D X–XI + 12–17; A 12–13; Pect. 16–18; Pelvic I,2; LLs 36–37 on body + 1 on tail; GR 2 + 6 = 8; Vert. 35–37. (Formerly Cottidae: M&L).

**FROGMOUTH SCULPIN, *Icelinus oculatus* Gilbert, 1890.** Family Psychrolutidae
Oregon (44°53'N, 124°47'W) (UW 047550) to southern California (32°35'N, 117°25'W) (SIO 08-81). Length to 16.6 cm (6.3 in) SL. Depth: 110–350 m (360–1,148 ft). Dark brown above, whitish below. D X–XI,15–17; A 13–14; Pect. 16–18; Pelvic I,2; LLs 37–39 on body + 1 on tail; Vert. 36–37. (Formerly Cottidae: M&L).

**DUSKY SCULPIN, *Icelinus burchami* Evermann & Goldsborough, 1907.** Family Psychrolutidae
Southeastern Alaska (55°56'N, 135°26'W) to La Jolla, southern California (SIO 50-245A). Common from southeastern Alaska to central California. Length to 12.9 cm (5.1 in) TL. Depth: 61–567 m (200–1,860 ft). Dark brown above, grayish below. D VIII–XI + 15–18; A 10–14; Pect. 16–19; Pelvic I,2; LLs 35–38 on body + 1 on tail; GR 1–2 + 7–9 = 8–10; Vert. 33–37. (Formerly Cottidae: M&L).

**THREADFIN SCULPIN, *Icelinus filamentosus* Gilbert, 1890.** Family Psychrolutidae
Near Chirikof Island, western Gulf of Alaska to Cortes Bank (UCLA W54-392) and Point Loma, southern California. Common from at least Vancouver Island, British Columbia to the northern Channel Islands, southern California. Length to 29 cm (11.4 in) TL. Depth: 18–482 m (60–1,581 ft), possibly to 1,145 m (3,756 ft) and 1,201 m (3,940 ft). Brown to green above, tan below; creamy yellow to brown on belly; usually with 4 dark saddles; jet-black cirri on head. D IX–XII + 13–18; A 13–16; Pect. 16–18; Pelvic I,2; LLs 36–39 on body + 1–2 on tail; GR 0–1 + 6–8 = 7–8; Vert. 34–37. (Formerly Cottidae: M&L).

21b Dorsal scale band continuous; pelvic fins not extending to ⅓ of distance to anal fin origin..... 22

22a Fringe of cirri along posterior end of maxilla; cirrus at base of nasal spine with expanded tip; small cirrus between pectoral base and lateral line:

**FRINGED SCULPIN**

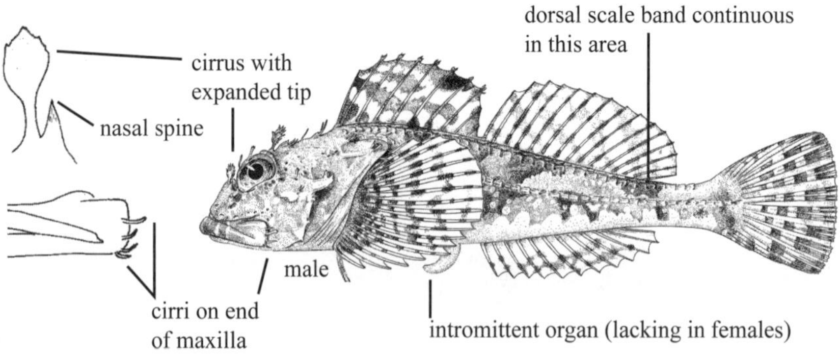


22b (next page)

22b Single cirrus near posterior end of maxilla; cirrus at base of nasal spine long, slender, simple; no cirrus between pectoral base and lateral line:

**FROGMOUTH SCULPIN**

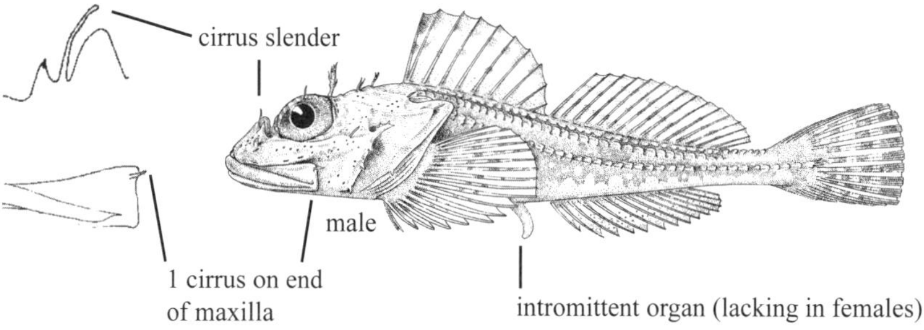


23a *From 20a: dorsal scale band not extending beyond 2nd dorsal fin*
Pelvic fins short, extending less than ¼ of distance to anal fin origin; anal fin origin under 3rd to 4th dorsal fin soft-rays:

**DUSKY SCULPIN**

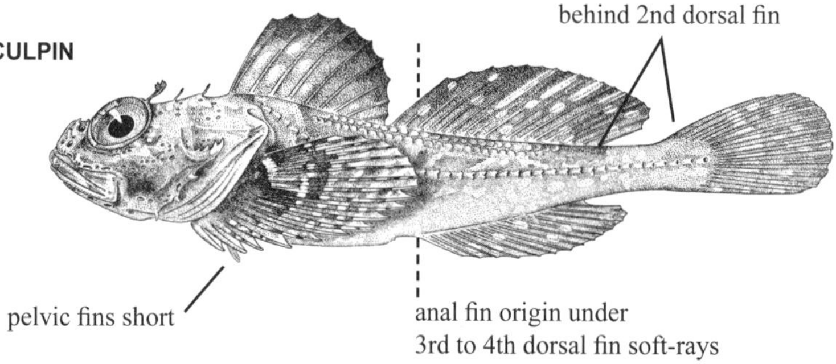


23b Pelvic fins of moderate size, extending more than ¼ of distance to anal fin origin; anal fin origin anterior to or under 1st to 2nd dorsal fin soft-rays….. 24

24a Two distinct spines at upper posterior angle of orbit; dorsal scale band not extending to base of last dorsal fin soft-ray….. 26 (page 190)

24b No distinct spines at upper posterior angle of orbit; dorsal scale band extending to end of last dorsal fin soft-ray….. 25

25a Anal fin soft-rays 13–16; 1st and 2nd dorsal fin spines filamentous, often reaching beyond end of 1st dorsal fin:

**THREADFIN SCULPIN**

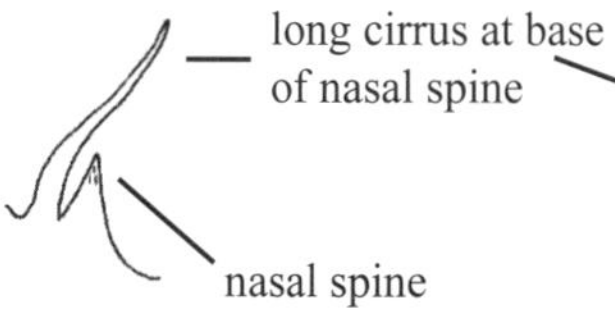


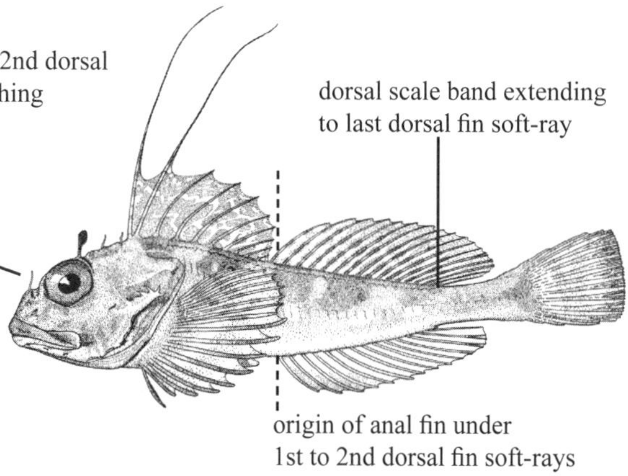


25b (next page)

## SCULPINS and POACHERS (continued)

**CANYON SCULPIN, *Icelinus limbaughi* Rosenblatt & Smith, 2004.** Family PSYCHROLUTIDAE
Anacapa Island area to San Diego and at Cortes Bank, southern California. Likely common in southern California. Length to 8.2 cm (3.2 in) SL. Depth: 16–86 m (52–282 ft). Body heavily marked with bands, bars, spots, and blotches of red-brown, red-orange, olive, purplish-brown, yellow, and black. D IX–X + 13–15; A 8–12; Pect. 15–17; Pelvic I,2; LLs 30–38; Precaudal vert. 9–11; Caudal vert. 22–25. (Formerly Cottidae: M&L).

**SPOTFIN SCULPIN, *Icelinus tenuis* Gilbert, 1890.** Family PSYCHROLUTIDAE
Gulf of Alaska (57°42'N, 136°29'W) (UW 117021) to Islas San Benito, central Baja California. Common from southeastern Alaska southward to northern Baja California. Length to 18 cm (7.1 in) TL. Depth: 7–375 m (23–1,230 ft). Light brown, red, or purple above with dark mottling; often with red or lavender patches on sides; males with dark spot on 1st dorsal fin. D IX–XI + 16–19; A 13–17; Pect. 15–17; Pelvic I,2; LLp 38–42 on body + 1 on tail; GR 0–1 + 6–8 = 6–9; Vert. 37–39. (Formerly Cottidae: M&L).

**PIT-HEAD SCULPIN, *Icelinus cavifrons* Gilbert, 1890.** Family PSYCHROLUTIDAE
Monterey Bay, central California almost to southern tip of Baja California (22°54'N). Common from southern California to central Baja California. Length to 8.9 cm (3.5 in) TL. Depth: 11–110 m (36–361 ft). Light brown with dark mottling on sides. D IX–XII + 12–15; A 11–13; Pect. 14–16; Pelvic I,2; LLp 36–38 on body + 1 on tail; Vert. 34–37. (Formerly Cottidae: M&L).

**ROUGHBACK SCULPIN, *Chitonotus pugetensis* (Steindachner, 1876).** Family PSYCHROLUTIDAE
Mears Pass (55°17'N, 133°11'W) and Coco Harbor (55°03'N, 133°02'W), southeastern Alaska to Isla Cedros and Bahía Santa Maria, southern Baja California. Common from Vancouver Island to northern Baja California (LACM 32050-3). Length to 22.9 cm (9 in) TL. Depth: intertidal to 240 m (787 ft). Brown, red-brown, to green above, white below; dark brown saddles; pectoral fin yellow; breeding males have red areas behind pectoral fin, at base of soft dorsal fin, and on back of head and red, orange, lavender, or white patch above eye. D VIII–XI + 14–17; A 14–17; Pect. 16–18; Pelvic I,2–3; LLs 36–39 on body + 1 on tail; GR 0–2 + 5–9 = 6–10; Vert. 35–36. (Formerly Cottidae: M&L).

25b Anal fin soft-rays 8–12; 1st and 2nd dorsal fin spines not filamentous:

**CANYON SCULPIN**

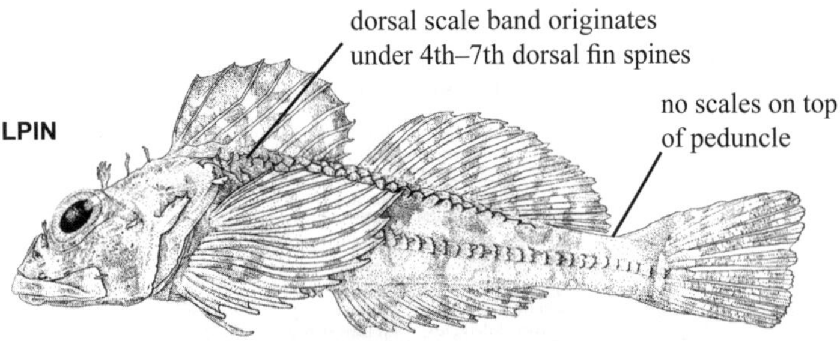


26a (next page)

26a *From 24a: Two distinct spines at upper posterior angle of orbit*
Top of head gently concave; dorsal fin soft-rays 16–19; anal fin soft-rays 13–17; body slender:

**SPOTFIN SCULPIN**

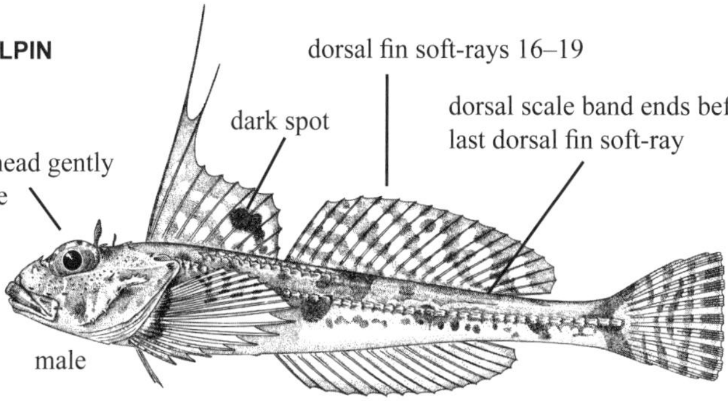


26b Top of head with pit or abrupt depression; dorsal fin soft-rays 12–15;
anal fin soft-rays 11–13; body robust:

**PIT-HEAD SCULPIN**

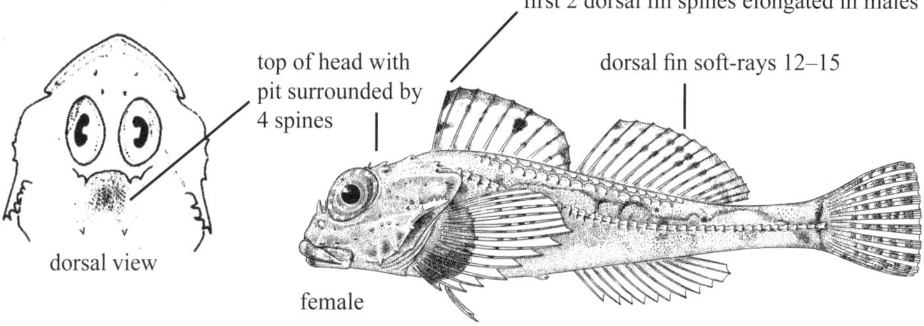


27a *From 19a: pelvic fins with 1 spine and 3 soft-rays*
First dorsal fin spine much longer than 2nd spine; 1st dorsal fin deeply notched between 3rd and 4th spines; upper preopercular spine antler-like:

**ROUGHBACK SCULPIN**

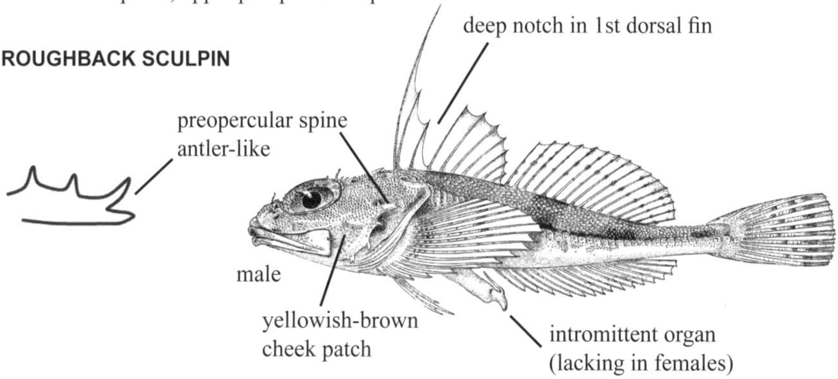


27b First dorsal fin spine not greatly longer than 2nd spine;
1st dorsal fin without pronounced notch; upper preopercular spine simple to multifid (2–4 points at tip)….. 28 (next page)

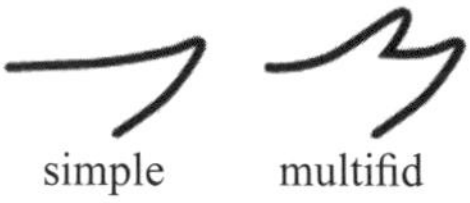

## SCULPINS and POACHERS (continued)

**SNUBNOSE SCULPIN, *Orthonopias triacis* Starks & Mann, 1911.** Family Psychrolutidae
Solander Island (northwest Vancouver Island) to Bahía Tortugas (27°38'N, 114°51'W), central Baja California (SIO 48-52). Apparently common from central California to at least northern Baja California. However, note that many SNUBNOSE were observed at the northernmost, Solander Island, site. Length to 9.6 cm (4 in) TL. Depth: intertidal to 30 m (100 ft). Color variable, often orange, maroon, white, red, and brown; heavily and darkly saddled; 2nd dorsal fin without spotting. D VIII–IX + 15–18; A 11–13; Pect. 13–15; Pelvic I,3 (rarely I,2); LLs 36–38 on body + 1 on tail; GR 1 + 5 = 6; Vert. 33–35. (Formerly Cottidae: M&L).

**CORALLINE SCULPIN, *Artedius corallinus* (Hubbs, 1926).** Family Psychrolutidae
Orcas Island, Washington to Punta Rocosa (28°45'N, 114°24'W), central Baja California (SIO 52-164). Common from about Cape Mendocino, northern California to central Baja California. Length to 14 cm (5.5 in) TL. Depth: lower intertidal to 70 m (230 ft). Dark gray to brown above; purplish-red mottling on head and back. D VII–IX +15–17; A 12–14; Pect. 14–16; Pelvic I,3; LLs 34–35 on body + 1 on tail; Vert. 31–33. (Formerly Cottidae: M&L).

**SMOOTHHEAD SCULPIN, *Artedius lateralis* (Girard, 1854).** Family Psychrolutidae
Sanak Island, western Gulf of Alaska to Bahía Playa Maria (28°52'N, 114°30'W), central Baja California (SIO 52-168). Common from at least southeastern Alaska to central California and about Punta Clara to Punta Baja, northern Baja California. Length to 14 cm (5.5 in) TL. Depth: intertidal to 70 m (228 ft). Dark maroon, brown, or green above, blue-green, red, white, or yellow below; 2 or more dark saddles; light patch frequently on caudal peduncle. D VII–X + 15–17; A 12–14; Pect. 14–16; Pelvic I,3 (rarely I,2); LLs 35–36 on body + 1–2 on tail; GR 1–2 + 5–9 = 7–11; Vert. 32–34. (Formerly Cottidae: M&L).

**PUGET SOUND SCULPIN, *Ruscarius meanyi* Jordan & Starks, 1895.** Family Psychrolutidae
Unimak Pass, western Gulf of Alaska (and perhaps in the Bering Sea) to Cordell Bank, northern California (CAS 51609) . Length to 5.9 cm (2.3 in) TL. Depth: intertidal to 82 m (269 ft). Cream to green; dark saddles on back; dark bars below lateral line. D IX–XI + 14–17; A 10–13; Pect. 14–16; Pelvic I,3 (rarely I,2); LLp 36–39; Vert. 33–35. (Formerly Cottidae: M&L).

28a Vent much closer to pelvic base than to anal fin origin in adults (about midway in juveniles):

**SNUBNOSE SCULPIN**

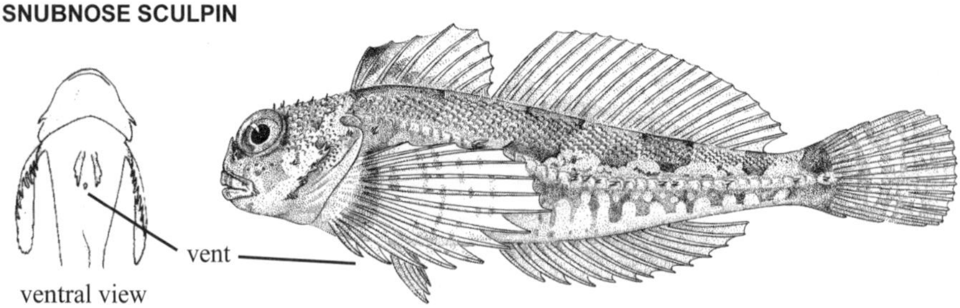


28b Vent closer to anal fin origin….. 29

29a First dorsal fin origin above or behind upper end of gill opening;
no teeth on palatines….. 36 (page 194)

29b First dorsal fin origin anterior to upper end of gill opening;
teeth present on palatines….. 30 (next page)

30a Scales present on head (ctenoid, may be embedded or minute)….. 32

30b No scales on head….. 31

31a Dorsal scale band with 39–49 oblique rows of scales and 10–18 scales in longest row; few small scales present just behind or above opercular flap between pectoral base and lateral line:

**CORALLINE SCULPIN**

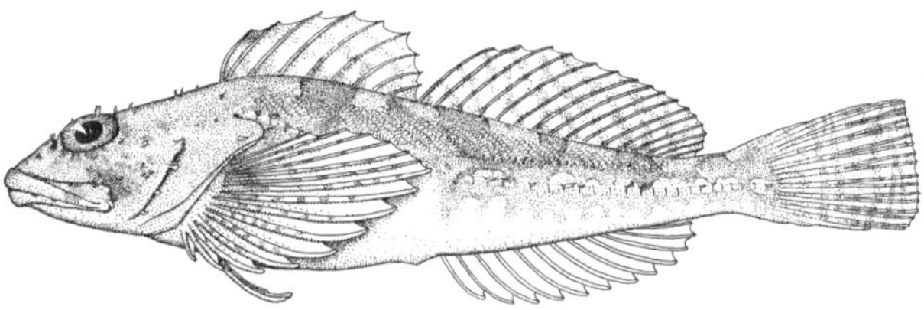

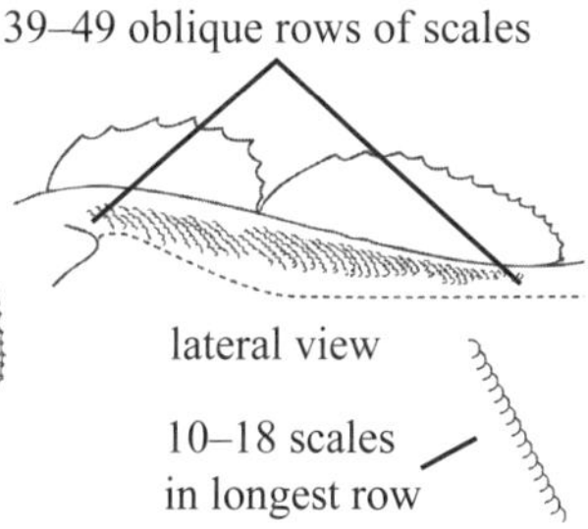


31b Dorsal scale band with 18–29 oblique rows of scales and 3–11 scales in longest row; no scales behind or above opercular flap between pectoral base and lateral line:

**SMOOTHHEAD SCULPIN**

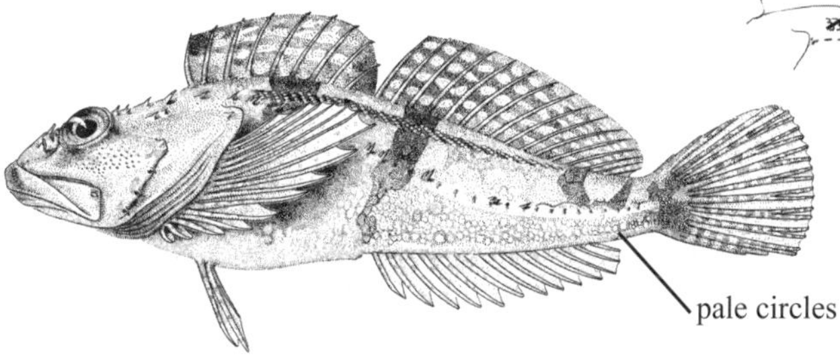


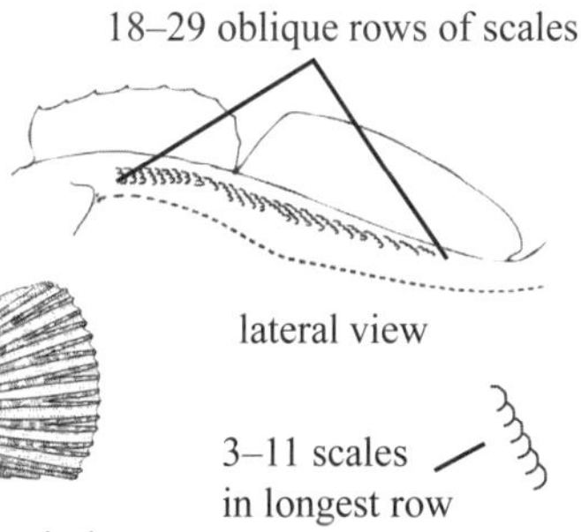


32a *From 30a: scales present on head*
Obvious ctenoid scales present on upper eye, covering upper portion of eye:

**PUGET SOUND SCULPIN**

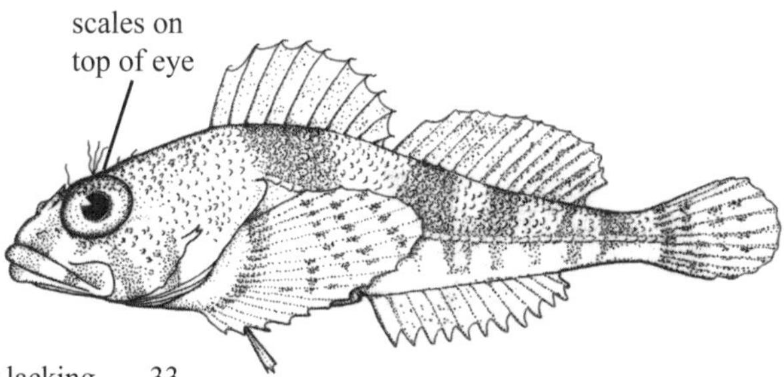


32b Scales on upper eye lacking….. 33

33a Preorbital cirrus present on upper anterior margin of orbit; dorsal scale band more or less merging with head scales….. 35 (page 194)

33b Preorbital cirrus lacking; dorsal scale band originating about under base of 3rd dorsal fin spine, separated from head scales by naked area or preceded by scales so minute and scattered that they do not obscure definite origin of band….. 34 (next page)

## SCULPINS and POACHERS (continued)

**PADDED SCULPIN, *Artedius fenestralis* Jordan & Gilbert, 1883.** Family PSYCHROLUTIDAE
Tanaga Island, Aleutian Islands to north side of Alaska Peninsula at Herendeen Bay (UW 22140) to about San Francisco Bay, northern California. The Diablo Cove, central California record in M&L is in error. Common from about Kodiak Island, Gulf of Alaska to about Sonoma County, northern California. Length to 14 cm (5.5 in) TL. Mostly marine, occasionally enters brackish waters. Depth: intertidal to 122 m (402 ft). Body brownish, yellowish, orangish, or greenish; pale orange to blue-gray ventrally with irregularly-shaped pale circles; dark bars along sides and black spots (sometimes partially rimmed in red-yellow) in spinous dorsal fin. D VIII–X + 14–18; A 11–14; Pect. 14–16; Pelvic I,3 (rarely I,2); LLs 36–37 on body + 1–2 on tail; GR 1–2 + 8–11 = 10–12; Vert. 32–35. (Formerly Cottidae: M&L).

**BONYHEAD SCULPIN, *Artedius notospilotus* Girard, 1856.** Family PSYCHROLUTIDAE
Puget Sound, Washington to Punta Rocosa (28°45'N, 114°24'W), central Baja California (SIO 52-164). Reports of occurrence in Alaska are incorrect. Common from northern California to northern Baja California. Length to 25.4 cm (10 in) TL. Depth: intertidal to 52 m (170 ft). Dark green to gray above with ligher mottling on sides. D IX–X + 14–16; A 11–13; Pect. 14–17; Pelvic I,3 (rarely I,2); LLs 35–37 on body + 1–2 on tail; GR 2 + 8–10 = 10–12; Vert. 32–34. (Formerly Cottidae: M&L) (Alternative name BONEHEAD SCULPIN).

**SCALYHEAD SCULPIN, *Artedius harringtoni* (Starks, 1896).** Family PSYCHROLUTIDAE
Unalaska Island, Aleutian Islands and Kodiak Island, western Gulf of Alaska to San Miguel Island, southern California (SIO 54-91). Common from about Kodiak Island, Gulf of Alaska to as far south as central California. Length to 11.2 cm (4.4 in) TL. Depth: intertidal to 40 m (131 ft). Brown, orange, or white above, sometimes with red or pink; mottled white and tan below; red or brown-black saddles or bars on back; anterior margin of 1st dorsal fin often with red blotch; anal fin of males with conspicuous white hexagon patterns. Breeding males with orange branchiostegal membranes, red-brown spots in mouth, and yellow-white spots on anal fin. D VIII–X + 15–18; A 10–14; Pect. 13–15; Pelvic I,3; LLs 35–38 + 1–2 on tail; GR 1 + 5–7 = 6–8; Vert. 32–34. (Formerly Cottidae: M&L).

**ROUGHCHEEK SCULPIN, *Ruscarius creaseri* (Hubbs, 1926).** Family PSYCHROLUTIDAE
Monterey Bay, central California (CAS 30460) to Punta San Pablo, southern Baja California; Islas San Benito (LACM 37006-11) and Isla Cedros, central Baja California (LACM 32041-9). Common from central California to about Isla San Martin, central Baja California. Length to 7.6 cm (3 in) TL. Depth: intertidal to 27 m (90 ft). Olive-green to light brown; dark bars on back. D IX–XI + 12–14; A 9–11; Pect. 15–17; Pelvic I,3; LLs 33 on body + 1 on tail; Vert. 30–31. (Formerly *Artedius creaseri* (Hubbs, 1926), Cottidae: M&L).

34a Dorsal scale band continues on dorsal surface of caudal peduncle, forming dense patch of scales; scales under orbit; anal fin soft-rays 12–14:

PADDED SCULPIN

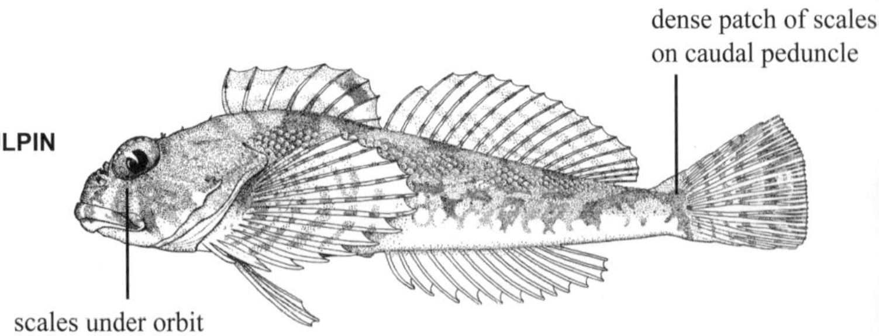


34b (next page)

34b Dorsal scale band extending to end of 2nd dorsal fin, sometimes continued on dorsal surface of caudal peduncle by few widely scattered scales, never forming dense patch; scales usually not under orbit; anal fin soft-rays 11–13:

**BONYHEAD SCULPIN**

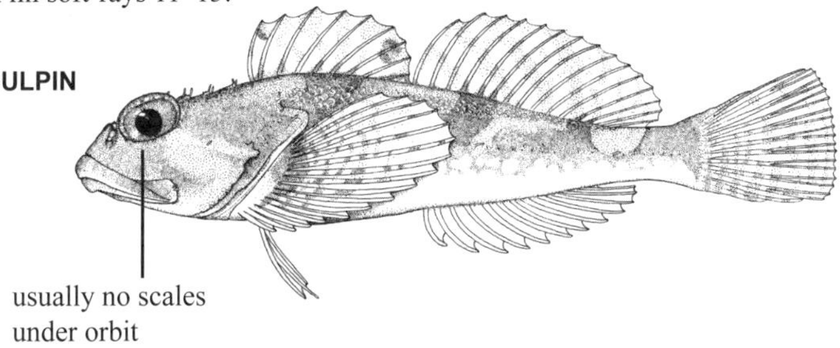


35a *From 33a: cirrus present on upper anterior margin of orbit*
Dorsal fin soft-rays 15–18; scales extending only under posterior part of orbit, if at all, and absent from snout (preorbital cirrus large and profuse in males):

**SCALYHEAD SCULPIN**

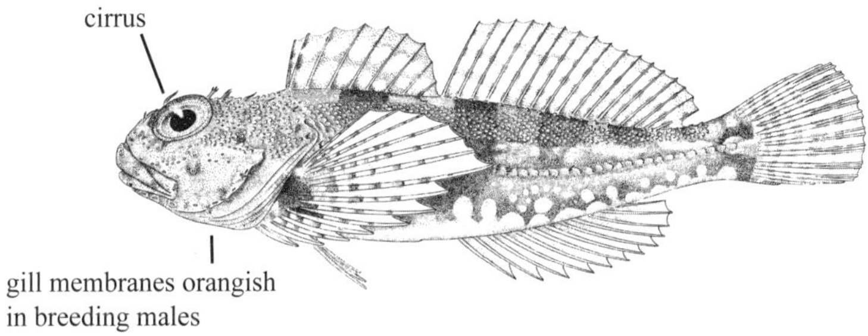


35b Dorsal fin soft-rays 12–14; scales extending under entire orbit and present on snout:

**ROUGHCHEEK SCULPIN**

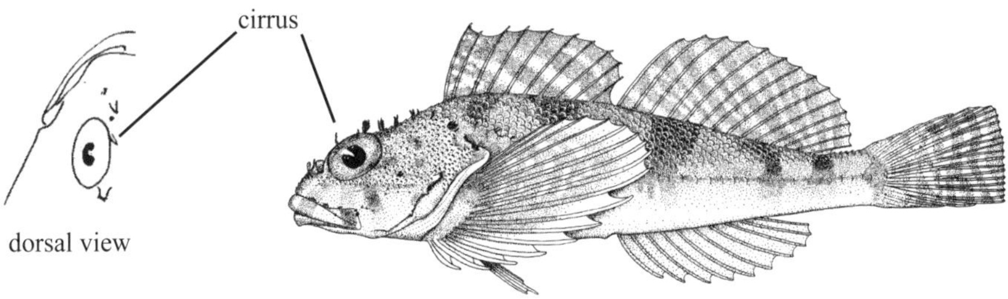


36a *From 29a: first dorsal fin origin above or behind upper end of gill opening*
Dorsal fin soft-rays 17 or fewer; anal fin soft-rays 18 or fewer; cirri may be present slightly below lateral line under origin of 2nd dorsal fin….. 38 (page 196)

36b Dorsal fin soft-rays 20 or more; anal fin soft-rays 21 or more; no cirri present as in 36a….. 37 (next page)

## SCULPINS and POACHERS (continued)

**DARTER SCULPIN, *Radulinus boleoides* Gilbert, in Jordan & Evermann, 1898.** Family PSYCHROLUTIDAE
Gulf of Alaska east of Kodiak Island to Santa Catalina Island and Tanner Bank, southern California (LACM 35687-2). Length to 12.7 cm (5 in) SL or about 14.9 cm (5.9 in) TL. Depth: 15–182 m (50–597 ft). Olive-gray dorsally, silvery white below; 3–4 dark saddles; dark blotches along midflanks; dark bars on dorsal, caudal, and pectoral fins. D X + 20–21; A 21–23; Pect. 18–20; Pelvic I,3; LLs 39–40; GR 0–1 + 9–11 = 9–11; Vert. 39–40. (Formerly Cottidae: M&L).

**SLIM SCULPIN, *Radulinus asprellus* Gilbert, 1890.** Family PSYCHROLUTIDAE
Pribilof Islands (56°40'N, 171°59'W), Bering Sea and Aleutian Islands off Amchitka Island to Islas Coronados, northern Baja California. Common at least from Kodiak Island, Gulf of Alaska to central California. Length to 15.2 cm (6 in) TL. Depth: 9–380 m (30–1,246 ft). Back olive-green or tan with orange-brown mottling; vague dark spots along lateral line; brown bars on dorsal, caudal, and pectoral fins; males with dark spot on posterior of 1st dorsal fin. D VIII–XI + 20–23; A 21–25; Pect. 17–20; Pelvic I,3; LLs 38–41; GR 0–1 + 5–8 = 5–9; Vert. 38–39. (Formerly Cottidae: M&L).

**SMOOTHGUM SCULPIN, *Radulinus vinculus* Bolin, 1950.** Family PSYCHROLUTIDAE
Diablo Cove, central California (LACM 31739-4) to between Santa Cruz and Anacapa Islands, southern California (SIO 15-2150). Length to 10.4 cm (4.1 in) TL. Depth: 21–100 m (70–328 ft). Brown with 3 dark brown crossbars on sides. D IX–X + 17; A 17–18; Pect. 17; Pelvic I,3; Vert. 35. (Formerly Cottidae: M&L).

**SPINYNOSE SCULPIN, *Asemichthys taylori* Gilbert, 1912.** Family PSYCHROLUTIDAE
At junction of Sumner and Clarence Straits off Strait Creek (56°12'N, 133°15'W), southeastern Alaska to Keystone Jetty, Whidbey Island, Puget Sound and Esalen Pinnacle (36°08'N, 121°39'W), central California. Common at least from southeastern Alaska to the Salish Sea. Length to 7.4 cm (2.9 in). Depth: intertidal to 27 m (88 ft), possibly to 49 m (162 ft). Color variable, often olive-brown to brown above (darker brown and reddish blotches may also be present) and lighter below; 4 dark saddles along body; lower part of face dark; light streak often under eye to rear of operculum; amorphous bright blue area often near rear of 1st dorsal fin. D X–XI + 14–17; A 13–17; Pect. 16–19; Pelvic I,3; LLp 34–37; GRt 4–8. (Classified by some authors as *Radulinus taylori* (Gilbert, 1912)).

**FLABBY SCULPIN, *Zesticelus profundorum* (Gilbert, 1896).** Family PSYCHROLUTIDAE
Sea of Okhotsk, northern Kuril Islands, Russia, and Pacific Ocean off southeastern Kamchatka to southeastern Bering Sea and Aleutian Islands to northern Baja California. Common at least in Bering Sea; perhaps rare off California. Length to 6.4 cm (2.5 in) TL. Depth: 587–2,580 m (1,926–8,465 ft). A reported minimum depth of 88 m (289 ft; Eschmeyer and Herald, 1983) is evidently a printer's error. Brown to black with blue overtones; fins blackish; mouth and gill cavity dusky. D V–VII + 10–13; A 8–11; Pect. 19–21; Pelvic I,2–3; LLs 14–17; Vert. 25–26. (Formerly Cottidae: M&L).

37a Nasal spines short, triangular; pelvic fins short, 1.0–1.2 times width of pectoral base; snout longer than eye diameter:

**DARTER SCULPIN**

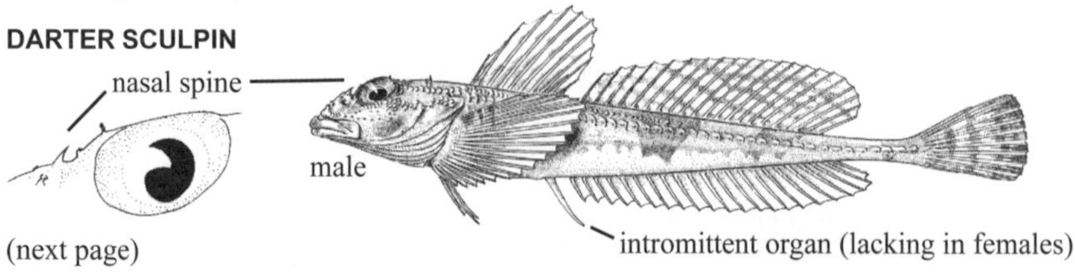


37b (next page)

37b Nasal spines long, needle-like; pelvic fins long, 1.7–2.6 times width of pectoral base; snout equal to or shorter than eye diameter:

**SLIM SCULPIN**

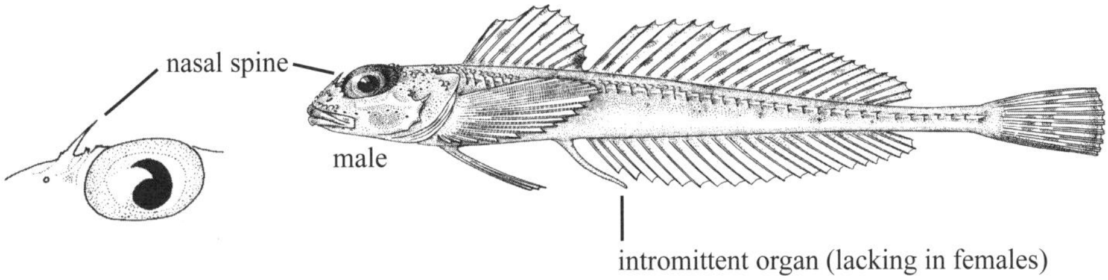


38a *From 36a: dorsal fin soft-rays 17 or fewer*
Body slender, BD into SL more than 6; teeth on vomer lacking:

**SMOOTHGUM SCULPIN**

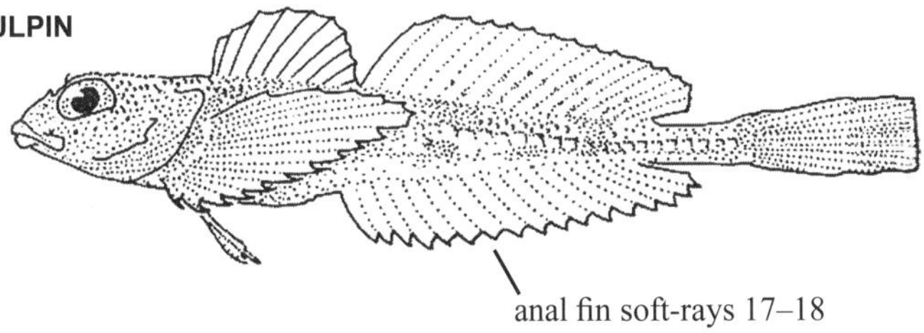


38b Body of medium depth, BD into SL less than 6; teeth on vomer:

**SPINYNOSE SCULPIN**

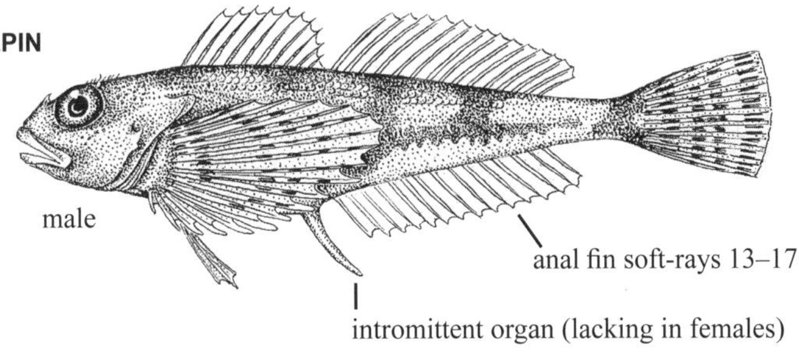


39a *From 18a: back without scales or with minute prickly papillae*
Dorsal fin spines 5–7; dorsal fin soft-rays 10–13; lateral line pores 14–17:

**FLABBY SCULPIN**

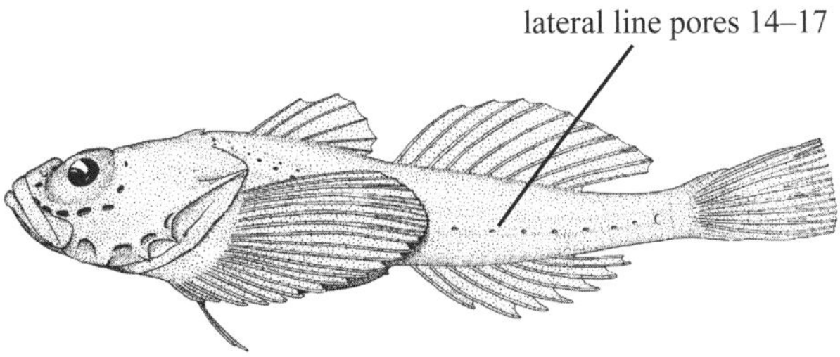


39b Dorsal fin spines 7–10; dorsal fin soft-rays 13–20; lateral line pores 33–43….. 40 (next page)

## SCULPINS and POACHERS (continued)

**SADDLEBACK SCULPIN, *Oligocottus rimensis* (Greeley, 1899).** Family PSYCHROLUTIDAE

Prince William Sound, Gulf of Alaska (UAM Fishes 3505) to northern Baja California. Common at least from Haida Gwaii, British Columbia to central California. Length to 6.5 cm (2.6 in) TL. Depth: intertidal and shallow subtidal to 11 m (36 ft). Heavily mottled on sides; brown, green, purplish to reddish above, light tan to greenish below; 4–5 dark saddles sometimes bordered with blue; 2nd dorsal, anal, and caudal fins with red bars. D VIII–X + 16–19; A 13–15; Pect. 13–15; Pelvic I,3; LLp 35–40 on body + 0–1 on tail; GR 1 + 4–5 = 5–6; Vert. 34–37. (Formerly Cottidae: M&L).

**TIDEPOOL SCULPIN, *Oligocottus maculosus* Girard, 1856.** Family PSYCHROLUTIDAE

Pribilof Islands, southeastern Bering Sea; Shumagin Islands, western Gulf of Alaska to Palos Verdes Peninsula, southern California (LACM 21250). Common from at least Cook Inlet, Gulf of Alaska to the San Francisco area. Length to 13 cm (5.2 in) SL. Marine and brackish waters. Depth: intertidal and shallow intertidal to 9 m (30 ft). Greenish to red above, whitish below; body with speckles and stripes; dark spot sometimes near anterior margin of 1st dorsal fin; dorsal, caudal, and pectoral fins yellowish with greenish or dusky bars; mature females may have red anal fin margin. D VIII–X + 15–18; A 11–14; Pect. 12–15; Pelvic I,3; LLp 34–39 on body + 1–2 on tail; GR 0–2 + 4–5 = 4–6; Vert. 33–34. (Formerly Cottidae: M&L).

**FLUFFY SCULPIN, *Oligocottus snyderi* Greeley, in Jordan & Evermann, 1898.** Family PSYCHROLUTIDAE

Chernabura Island, western Gulf of Alaska to Punta Cono (29°06'N, 114°42'W), central Baja California (SIO 52-201). Common from Vancouver Island to central California. Length to about 9.2 cm (3.6 in) TL. Depth: intertidal to 6 m (20 ft) or perhaps more; typically in 2 m (7 ft) or less. Variably colored: mostly bright green to reddish-brown, also light pink, orange, brown, and gray. D VII–IX + 17–20; A 12–15; Pect. 12–15; Pelvic I,3; LLp 36–39 on body + 1–2 on tail; GRt 4; Vert. 34–37. (Formerly Cottidae: M&L).

**ROSY SCULPIN, *Oligocottus rubellio* (Greeley, 1899).** Family PSYCHROLUTIDAE

Fort Bragg, northern California to Punta Baja, northern Baja California. Length to 10 cm (4 in) TL. Common from northern California to northern Baja California. Depth: lower intertidal zone to 11 m (36 ft). Reddish-brown to red and purplish with white spotting. D VII–IX + 13–17; A 10–14; Pect. 13–15; Pelvic I,3; LLp 34–38 on body + 1–2 on tail; GR 1 + 4–6 = 5–7; Vert. 32–35. (Formerly Cottidae: M&L).

40a Vent midway between pelvic fin base and anal fin origin….. 44 (page 199)

40b Vent immediately in front of anal fin origin….. 41

41a Preopercular spine simple; body with scales as scattered prickly papillae:

**SADDLEBACK SCULPIN**

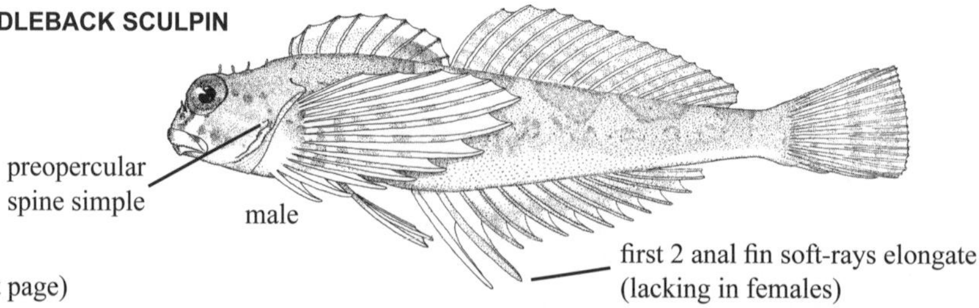


41b (next page)

41b Preopercular spine bifid to 4-pointed (except juveniles); body without visible scales….. 42

42a No cirrus on nasal spine; no tufts of cirri along base of dorsal fins:

**TIDEPOOL SCULPIN**

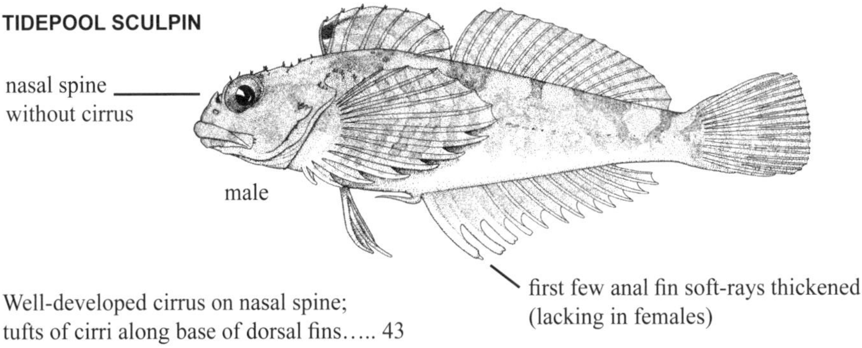


42b Well-developed cirrus on nasal spine;
tufts of cirri along base of dorsal fins….. 43

43a No cirri on maxilla or suborbital stay; preopercular spine usually bifid in adults:

**FLUFFY SCULPIN**

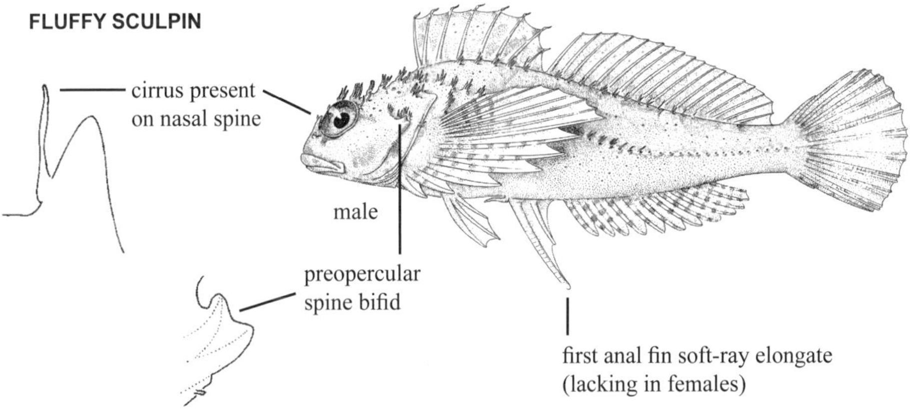


43b One to 4 cirri on end of maxilla and small tuft of cirri on suborbital stay; preopercular spine usually trifid in adults:

**ROSY SCULPIN**

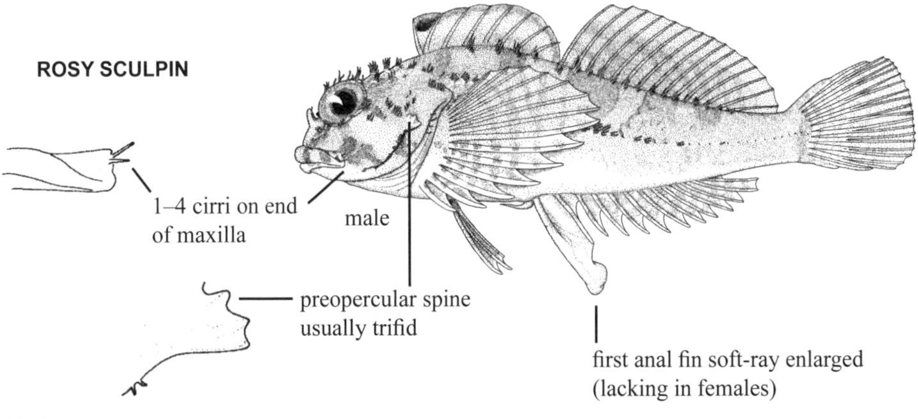


44a (next page)

## SCULPINS and POACHERS (continued)

**LAVENDER SCULPIN, *Leiocottus hirundo* Girard, 1856.** Family Psychrolutidae
Gaviota Pier, southern California (LACM 51395-1) to Punta Banda, northern Baja California. Common from southern California to Punta Banda. Length to 25.4 cm (10 in) TL. Depth: intertidal to 37 m (120 ft). Olive-green, brown, orange-brown, or lavender with 3–4 brown saddles on posterior body and 4 brown bars on lips. D IX–X + 16–17; A 14–16; Pect. 17–18; Pelvic I,3; LLp 38 on body + 1–2 on tail; Vert. 35–36. (Formerly Cottidae: M&L).

**WOOLLY SCULPIN, *Clinocottus analis* (Girard, 1858).** Family Psychrolutidae
Cape Mendocino, northern California (CAS 20074) to Punta Abreojos, southern Baja California and Isla Cedros, central Baja California (LACM 32014-13). Common from northern California to Bahía Tortugas, southern Baja California. Length to 17.8 cm (7 in) TL. Depth: intertidal to 18 m (60 ft). Color variable: reddish to green with heavy mottling. D VIII–X + 14–18; A 11–15; Pect. 14–17; Pelvic I,3; LLp 35–36 on body + 1 on tail; GR 0–1 + 5–6 = 6–7; Vert. 31–35. This species is likely not in the genus *Clinocottus* (Knope, 2012). (Formerly WOOLY SCULPIN, Cottidae: M&L).

**SHARPNOSE SCULPIN, *Clinocottus acuticeps* (Gilbert, 1896).** Family Psychrolutidae
Attu Island, Aleutian Islands to Big Sur River, central California (CAS 13613). Common from Amchitka Island, Aleutian Islands to northern California. Length to 6.4 cm (2.5 in) TL. Depth: intertidal to 20 m (66 ft). Mostly in marine and brackish water, occasionally in fresh water. Mottled brownish-green, green, pinkish, or dark above; white, green, or tan below; anterior of 1st dorsal fin dark. D VII–IX + 13–17; A 9–13; Pect. 13–15; Pelvic I,3; LLp 33–36 on body + 1–2 on tail; GRt 1; Vert. 31–33. Perhaps more properly in the genus *Artedius* (Knope, 2012). (Formerly Cottidae: M&L).

**CALICO SCULPIN, *Clinocottus embryum* (Jordan & Starks, 1895).** Family Psychrolutidae
Attu Island, Aleutian Islands to Punta Banda, northern Baja California. Common at least from Gulf of Alaska to central California. Length to 7 cm (2.8 in) TL. Depth: intertidal and shallow subtidal to at least 2m (5 ft). Mottled olive-green to deep red or pink above, gray or greenish below. D VIII–X + 14–17; A 9–12; Pect. 12–15; Pelvic I,3; LLp 34–38 on body + 1–2 on rail; GR 1 + 5–6 = 6–7; Vert. 33–35. (Formerly Cottidae: M&L).

44a *From 40a: vent midway between pelvic and anal fins*
First dorsal fin spine about twice as long as 3rd spine; no postorbital cirrus and no cirri on opercular flap:

LAVENDER SCULPIN

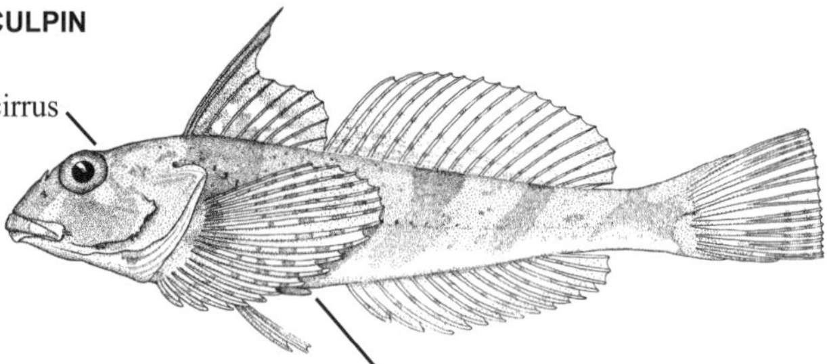


44b First dorsal fin spine about equal to or shorter than 3rd spine; large postorbital cirrus and 1 or more cirri on opercular flap..... 45 (next page)

45a Preopercular spine bifid or trifid; cirri and minute prickly papillae present between dorsal fins and lateral line:

**WOOLLY SCULPIN**

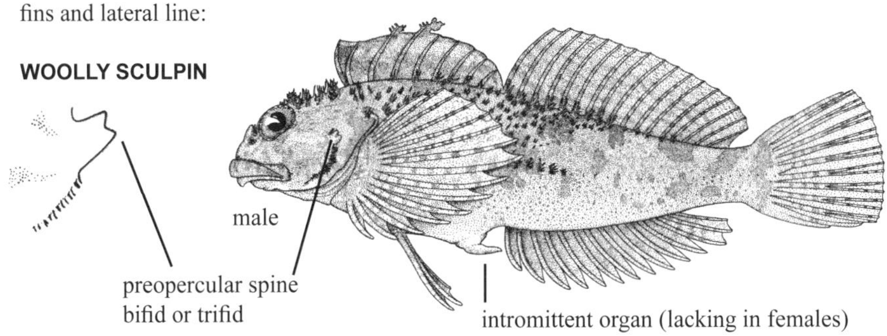


45b Preopercular spine simple; neither cirri nor scales present between dorsal fins and lateral line (cirri may be present along lateral line)….. 46

46a One to 2 cirri on end of maxilla; inner pelvic fin soft-ray strongly attached to belly by membrane:

**SHARPNOSE SCULPIN**

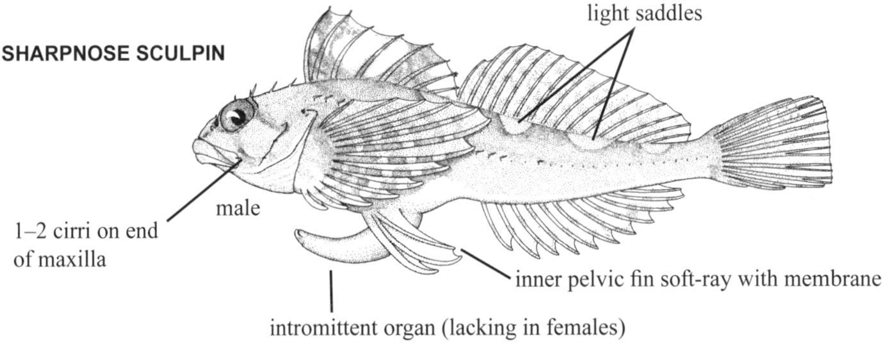


46b No cirri on maxilla; inner pelvic fin soft-ray not attached to belly by membrane….. 47

47a Head moderately pointed and angular, not hemispherical (in dorsal view); upper lip terminal; small fleshy tubercle in median line of lip groove, which limits upper lip dorsally; no cirri between pectoral base and lateral line:

**CALICO SCULPIN**

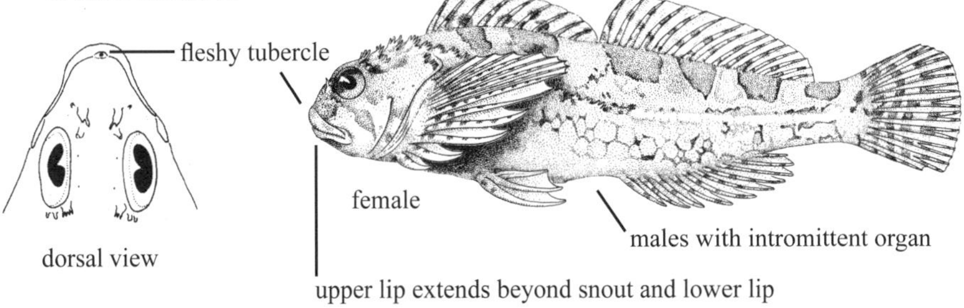


47b Head very bluntly rounded, hemispherical (in dorsal view); upper lip inferior to snout (except juveniles); fleshy tubercle in lip groove lacking; patch of cirri between pectoral base and lateral line….. 48 (next page)

## SCULPINS and POACHERS (continued)

**MOSSHEAD SCULPIN, *Clinocottus globiceps* (Girard, 1858).** Family PSYCHROLUTIDAE
Chernabura and Kodiak islands, western Gulf of Alaska to Gaviota, southern California. Common at least from southeastern Alaska to central California. Length to 19 cm (7.5 in) TL. Depth: intertidal and shallow subtidal to 44 m (144 ft). Reddish-brown, gray, black, or olive on back, yellow or brown below; heavy mottling on sides; fins barred. D VIII–X + 13–17; A 10–12; Pect. 13–15; Pelvic I,3; LLp 34–37 on body + 1–2 on tail; GR 1 + 4–5 = 5–6; Vert. 32–34. (Formerly Cottidae: M&L).

**BALD SCULPIN, *Clinocottus recalvus* (Greeley, 1899).** Family PSYCHROLUTIDAE
Shelter Cove, northern California to Punta Rompiente, southern Baja California. Common from northern California to northern Baja California. Length to 13 cm (5.1 in) TL. Depth: intertidal and shallow subtidal to 2 m (6 ft). Light to dark brown, with lighter reddish and white mottling. D VIII–IX + 14–17; A 9–13; Pect. 13–15; Pelvic I,3; LLp 33–37 on body + 1–2 on tail; GR 1 + 4–7 = 5–8; Vert. 32–33. (Formerly Cottidae: M&L).

**BROWN IRISH LORD, *Hemilepidotus spinosus* Ayres, 1854.** Family PSYCHROLUTIDAE
Southern Bering Sea and northern Gulf of Alaska to Santa Barbara Island, southern California; on mainland to Ventura, southern California (SIO 15-311). Common from about Kodiak Island, Gulf of Alaska southward to central California. Length to 33 cm (13 in) TL. Depth: intertidal to 131 m (430 ft) and perhaps to 151 m (495 ft). Light to dark brown with dark mottling; top of head often red; dark saddles; blackish or reddish mottling on fins. D X–XI,18–20; A 14–16; Pect. 14–16; Pelvic I,4; LLs 57–66 on body + 3–6 on tail; GR 0–2 + 5–8 = 5–10; Vert. 35–37. (Formerly Cottidae: M&L).

**RED IRISH LORD, *Hemilepidotus hemilepidotus* (Tilesius, 1811).** Family PSYCHROLUTIDAE
Commander-Aleutian Islands Chain and southeastern Bering Sea to Mussel Point, Monterey Bay, central California. Common from the Pribilof Islands, Bering Sea and along much of the Aleutian Islands to northern California. A Diablo Cove, central California observation (Burge and Schultz, 1973) predates the revision of this group by Peden (1978) and cannot be confirmed. Length to 50.8 cm (20 in) TL. Mostly marine, occasionally enters brackish water. Depth: intertidal to 235 m (771 ft). Color variable: red, orange-brown, orange, or pink; white, brown, and black mottling; 4 dark saddles on back. D X–XIII,17–20; A 13–16; Pect. 15–17; Pelvic I,4; LLs 59–69 on body + 2–5 on tail; Vert. 35–37. (Formerly Cottidae: M&L).

48a Cirri in anterior half of interorbital space in specimens over 35 mm SL:

**MOSSHEAD SCULPIN**

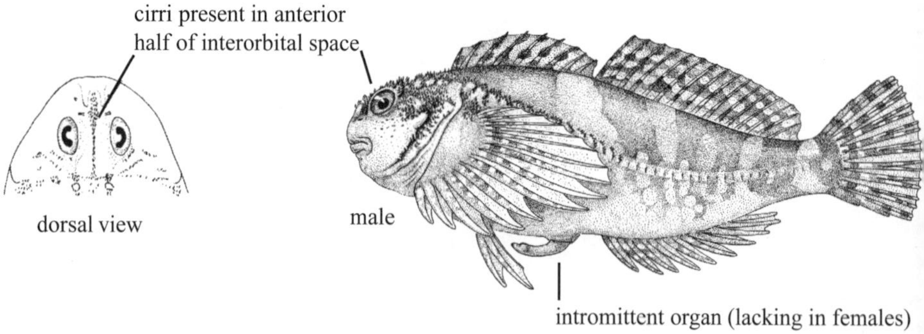


48b (next page)

48b No cirri in anterior half of interorbital space:

**BALD SCULPIN**

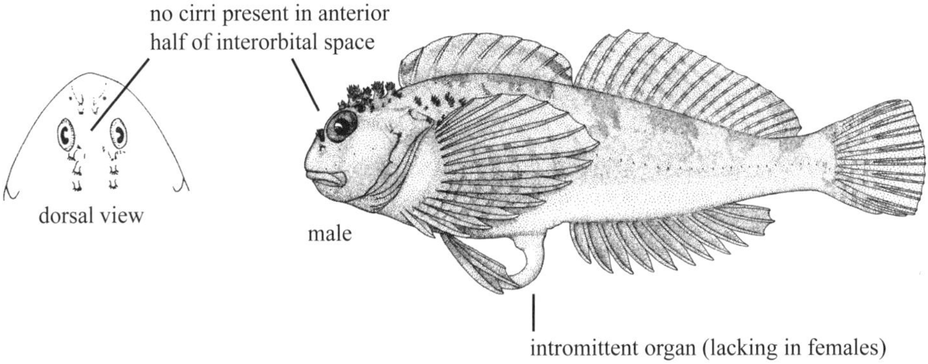


49a *From 12a: scales below lateral line large*
Rows of scales under dorsal fin 7–8; gill membranes completely joined to isthmus or with free fold narrower than pupil diameter:

**BROWN IRISH LORD**

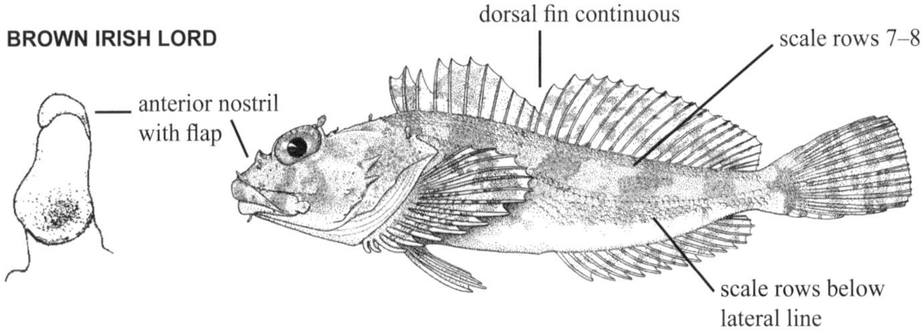


49b Rows of scales under dorsal fin 4–5; gill membranes attached to isthmus but with free fold wider than pupil diameter:

**RED IRISH LORD**

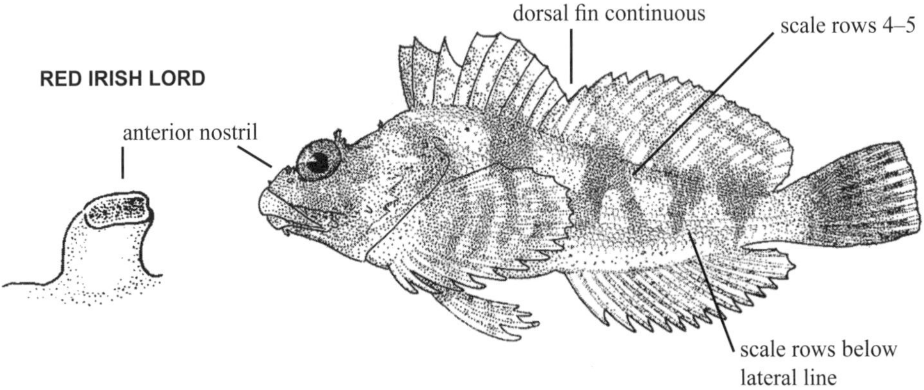


50a (next page)

## SCULPINS and POACHERS (continued)

**SMOOTH ALLIGATORFISH, *Anoplagonus inermis* (Günther, 1860).** Family AGONIDAE
Aleutian Islands at Petrel Bank to Point Arena, northern California. Common from at least Gulf of Alaska to as far southward as Yaquina Bay, Oregon; rare in northern California. Length to 15 cm (6 in) TL. Mostly marine, but occasionally in slightly estuarine waters. Depth: 2–139 m (7–456 ft), possibly to 458 m (1,502 ft). Dark brown or gray with dark bands on body and caudal fin. D 4–6; A 4–5; Pect. 8–11; Pelvic I,2; LLp 38–43; Vert. 41–45.

**ROCKHEAD, *Bothragonus swanii* (Steindachner, 1876).** Family AGONIDAE
Kodiak Island, Gulf of Alaska to Santa Monica Bay (33°56'N, 118°27'W), southern California (SBMNH FH 886). Common at least from as far northward as British Columbia southward to perhaps central California. Length to 8.9 cm (3.5 in) TL. Depth: intertidal to 21 m (70 ft). Brown, red, and white with brown, orange, and red mottling. D II–V + 4–6; A 4–5; Pect. 10–12; Pelvic I,2; LLp 32; GRt 6; Vert. 29–32.

**TUBENOSE POACHER, *Pallasina barbata* (Steindachner, 1876).** Family AGONIDAE
Seas of Japan and Okhotsk and Kuril Islands, Russia to eastern Chukchi (as far northward as Point Barrow) and Bering Sea and Aleutian Islands to Bodega Bay, central California. Common from Sea of Japan to eastern Bering Sea and to Puget Sound. Length to 20.8 cm (8.2 in) TL. Depth: intertidal to 128 m (420 ft). Gray to brown above, paler or sometimes yellow below. D IV–IX + 6–9; A 8–14; Pect. 10–13; Pelvic I,2; LLp 45–46; GR 1 + 10–13 = 11–14; Vert. 42–52.

**KELP POACHER *Agonomalus mozinoi* Willimovsky & Wilson, 1979.** Family AGONIDAE
Sitka, Alaska to San Simeon, central California; one unconfirmed report from Sitka, southeastern Alaska. Apparently uncommon in California. Length to 8.9 cm (3.5 in) TL. Depth: intertidal to 15 m (50 ft). Body mottled with black, white, orange, red, and brown; orange-red flap on snout. D VII–IX + 6–8; A 10–12; Pect. 11–12; Pelvic I,2; GR 1–2 + 5–6 = 7–8. Classified in *Hypsagonus* by some authors. (Formerly *Agonomalus* sp.: M&L).

50a *From 1a: body encased in bony plates*
One dorsal fin:

**SMOOTH ALLIGATORFISH**

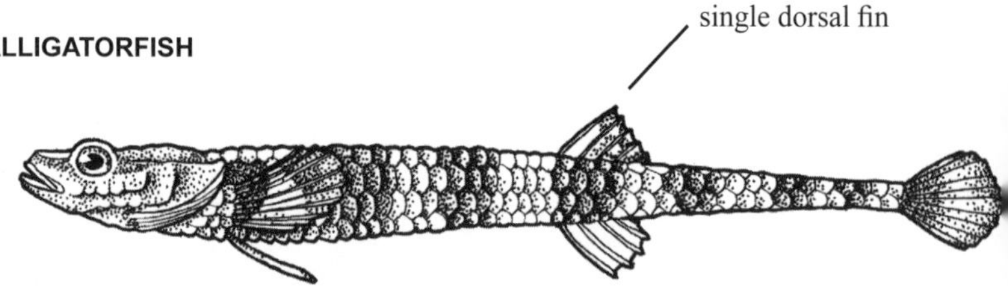


50b Two dorsal fins….. 51

51a Body plates spiny….. 53 (next page)

51b Body plates not spiny….. 52 (next page)

52a Deep pit in top of head; body deep and wide:

**ROCKHEAD**

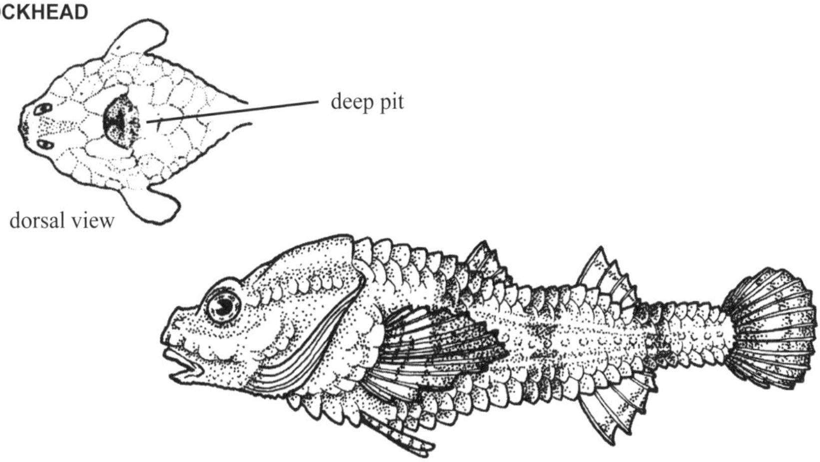


52b Deep pit in top of head lacking; body greatly elongated:

**TUBENOSE POACHER**

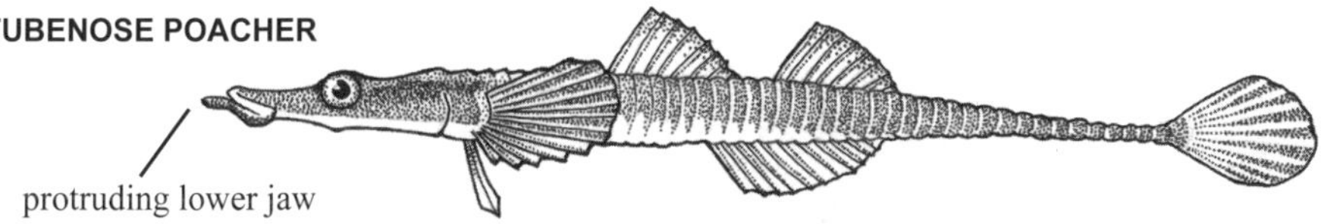


53a *From 51a: body plates spiny*
Gill membranes attached to isthmus….. 56 (page 206)

53b Gill membranes free from isthmus, or if joined, with free fold across isthmus longer than eye diameter….. 54

54a Large flap on snout:

**KELP POACHER**

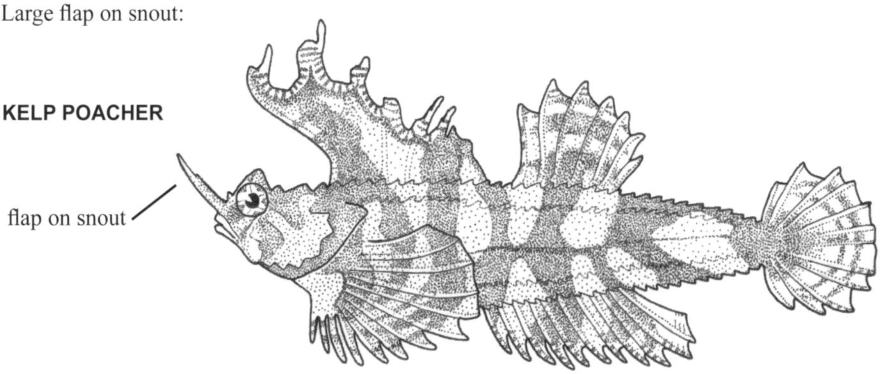


54b Large flap on snout lacking….. 55 (next page)

## SCULPINS and POACHERS (continued)

**WARTY POACHER, *Chesnonia verrucosa* (Lockington, 1880).** Family AGONIDAE
Bristol Bay, southeastern Bering Sea and Shelikof Bay, eastern Gulf of Alaska to Purisima Point (34°45'N, 120°42'W), central California (SBMNH FH 1653). Common perhaps from Bering Sea southward to northern California. Length to 20 cm (8 in) TL. Depth: 18–289 m (59–948 ft). Dark gray or brown above, paler below; dark bands on body; males with orange, black, and yellow pelvic region, black and orange pelvic fins, and longer pelvic fins (reaching anal fin) than females. D VII–X + 6–9; A 7–13; Pect. 13–15; Pelvic I,2; LLp 36–38; GR 1–2 + 8–12 = 10–14; Vert. 34–38. (Formerly *Occella verrucosa* (Lockington, 1880): M&L).

**PRICKLEBREAST POACHER, *Stellerina xyosterna* (Jordan & Gilbert, 1880).** Family AGONIDAE
Icy Bay, northern Gulf of Alaska to Bahía Magdalena, southern Baja California (SIO 50-237). Common at least in northern and central California. Length to 16.5 cm (6.5 in) TL. Depth: 2 m (7 ft) to at least 100 m (328 ft). Light olive-brown above, pale below; spotting on dorsal surface; rear half of pectoral fin with dark band and clear edge; dorsal fins with black edge; black mark on rear of anal fin; caudal fin black; prickles on breast. D VI–VIII + 5–7; A 7–9; Pect. 16–19; Pelvic I,2; GR 1–3 + 8–16 = 16–19; Vert. 34–37.

**STURGEON POACHER, *Podothecus accipenserinus* (Tilesius, 1813).** Family AGONIDAE
Pacific coast of Hokkaido, Kuril Islands, Russia, southeastern Kamchatka, Commander-Aleutian Islands Chain to northern Bering Sea, Alaska near Saint Lawrence Island to Point Reyes, northern California. Common from Sea of Okhotsk to eastern Bering Sea to at least Washington. Length to 38 cm (15 in) TL. Depth: intertidal to 570 m (1,870 ft) or perhaps to 710 m (2,329 ft) (an unverified record). Various shades of brown, yellowish-brown, to gray above, yellowish to orange below; dorsal and caudal fins with dark edge; anal fin with dark blotch on rear edge; cirri under chin yellow; barbels around mouth white. D VIII–X + 6–9; A 6–9; Pect. 16–19; Pelvic I,2; LLp 37–40; GR 2–3 + 9–12 = 11–15; Vert. 39–42. (Formerly *Agonus acipenserinus* Tilesius, 1813: M&L).

**NORTHERN SPEARNOSE POACHER, *Agonopsis vulsa* (Jordan & Gilbert, 1880).** Family AGONIDAE
Kachemak Bay, northern Gulf of Alaska to Point Loma, southern California. Common from Vancouver Island, British Columbia to perhaps northern California. Length to 20.3 cm (8 in) TL. Depth: intertidal to 393 m (1,289 ft). Various shades of brown above, white below; 6 or more dark bars on sides; pelvic fins white-tipped. D VIII–XI + 7–9; A 10–12; Pect. 13–15; Pelvic I,2; LLp 38–42; GRt 13–15. (Formerly NORTHERN SPEARNOSE, *Agonopsis emmelane* (Jordan & Starks, 1895) and BEARDLESS SPEARNOSE, *Ganoideus vulsus* (Jordan & Gilbert, 1880): M&L).

55a Breast with large bony plates; pectoral fin soft-rays 13–15:

**WARTY POACHER**

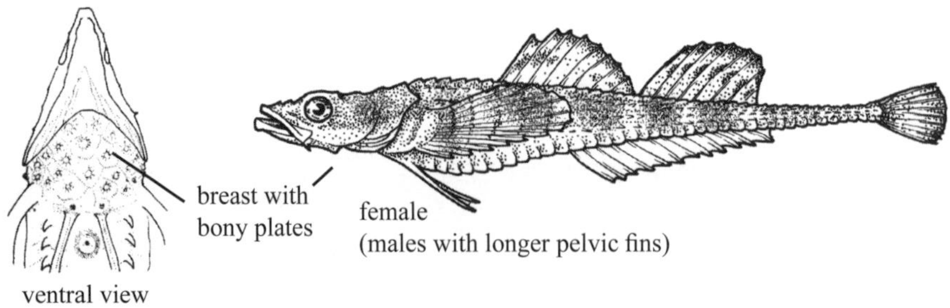


55b (next page)

55b Breast covered with even felt of minute prickles; pectoral fin soft-rays 17–19:

**PRICKLEBREAST POACHER**

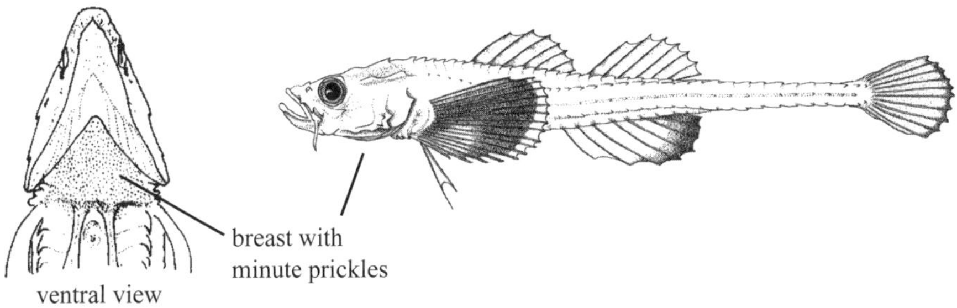


56a *From 53a: gill membranes attached to isthmus*
Rostral plate at tip of snout with 1–3 upright spines….. 59 (page 208)

56b Rostral plate at tip of snout with 2 forward-projecting spines….. 57

57a Snout long, about 2 times greater than eye diameter; dense clusters of cirri or small barbels under snout and at corners of mouth:

**STURGEON POACHER**

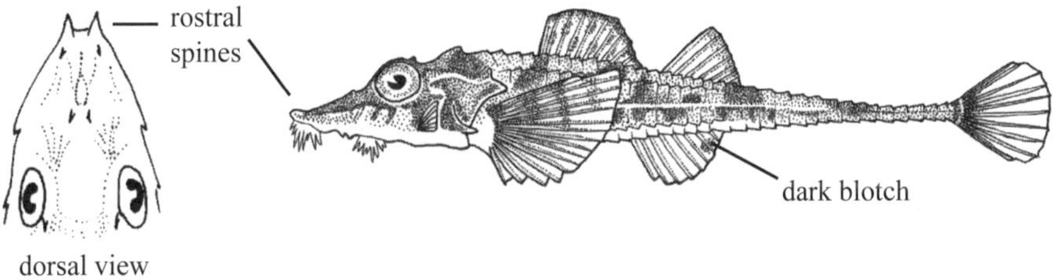


57b Snout length about same as eye diameter; single cirrus under snout and corners of mouth but no dense clusters of cirri or barbels as above….. 58

58a Pelvic fins dark brown with white tip; cirri present below rostral spines:

**NORTHERN SPEARNOSE POACHER**

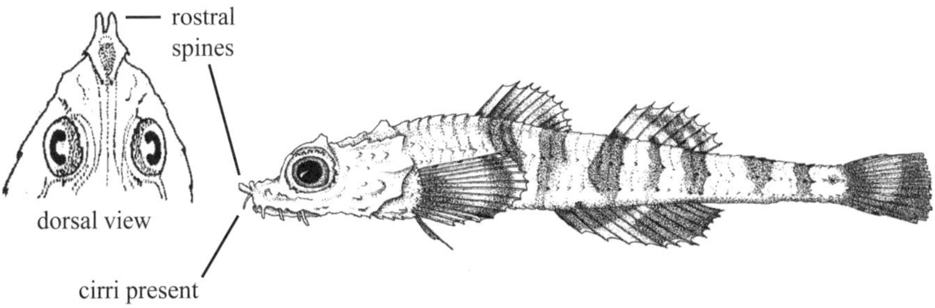


58b (next page)

## SCULPINS and POACHERS (continued)

**SOUTHERN SPEARNOSE POACHER, *Agonopsis sterletus* (Gilbert, 1898).** Family AGONIDAE
San Simeon Point, central California (UCLA W66-67) to near southern tip of Baja California (22°54'N). Common from southern California to at least central Baja California. Length to 15.1 cm (5.9 in) SL. Depth: 3–119 m (10–390 ft). Dark brown or black above, white below; usually 7 dark bars; pelvic fins white. D VI–VIII + 7–8; A 8–9; Pect. 12–13; Pelvic I,2; GR 0–1 + 7–8; Vert. 38–39. (Formerly SOUTHERN SPEARNOSE: M&L).

**PYGMY POACHER, *Odontopyxis trispinosa* Lockington, 1880.** Family AGONIDAE
Prince William Sound, northern Gulf of Alaska to Isla Cedros, central Baja California. One possible record from southeastern Bering Sea, but voucher specimen has been lost. Common from Prince William Sound to at least northern Baja California. Length to 13 cm (5.1 in) TL. Depth: 5–373 m (16–1,224 ft). Olive-brown to gray; 6–7 blotches or bands on body. D III–VI + 5–7; A 5–7; Pect. 13–15; Pelvic I,2; LLp 35–38; GR 0–2 + 7–10 = 8–12; Vert. 37–42.

**BLACKFIN POACHER, *Bathyagonus nigripinnis* Gilbert, 1890.** Family AGONIDAE
Pacific coast of northern Japan, northern Kuril Islands, Russia, and southeastern Kamchatka to Commander-Aleutian Islands Chain and northern Bering Sea near Cape Navarin to Point Arguello (34°34'N), California. Common from Japan and Kamchatka-Kuril Islands, Russia to Oregon or perhaps northern California. Length to 29 cm (11.4 in) TL. Depth: 18–1,248 m (59–4,094 ft). Uniform brown; fins entirely black (but pectoral fins may have blue tint); underside of head blue. D IV–VIII + 5–8; A 6–10; Pect. 14–17; Pelvic I,2; LLp 40–44; GR 0–2 + 11–18 = 12–18; Vert. 43–46. (Formerly BLACKFIN STARNOSE: M&L).

**BIGEYE POACHER, *Bathyagonus pentacanthus* (Gilbert, 1890).** Family AGONIDAE
Near Islands (52°23'N, 174°19'W), Aleutian Islands to Cortes Bank and off Point Loma, southern California (SIO 79-85). Common from Gulf of Alaska to southern California. Length to 26.2 cm (10.3 in) TL. Depth: 50–1,145 m (164–3,756 ft). Olive-brown above, paler below; caudal fin dark; 4–6 vague saddles on back and sides; posterior edge of dorsal fin sometimes dark. D V–VIII + 5–8; A 6–9; Pect. 14–16; Pelvic I,2; LLp 39–42; GR 1 + 8–10 = 9–11; Vert. 40–46. (Formerly BIGEYE STARNOSE, *Asterotheca pentacantha* (Gibert, 1890): M&L).

**GRAY STARSNOUT, *Bathyagonus alascanus* (Gilbert, 1896).** Family AGONIDAE
Bering Sea northwest of Saint Matthew Island and Adreanof Islands, Aleutian Islands to northern California. Common from Bering Sea to Washington; rare in California. Length to 14.1 cm (5.6 in) TL. Depth: 18–297 m (60–974 ft). Greenish-gray to brown on back, lighter below; 4–6 dark bands and blotches on body; bars on dorsal, pectoral, and caudal fins; fins pale. D V–VIII + 5–8; A 6–8; Pect. 14–16; Pelvic I,2; LLp 39–41; GR 1–2 + 6–11 = 7–13; Vert. 39–42.

58b Pelvic fins white; cirri below rostral spines lacking:

**SOUTHERN SPEARNOSE POACHER**

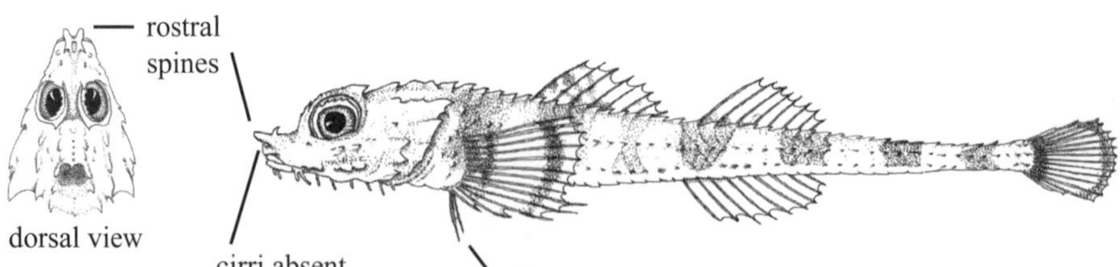


59a (next page)

59a *From 56a: rostral plate at tip of snout with 1–3 upright spines*
Posterior top of head with deep divided pit:

**PYGMY POACHER**

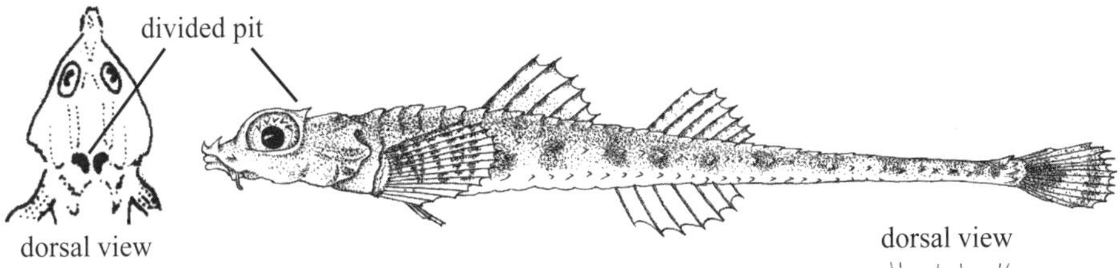


59b Posterior top of head with depression but no deep divided pit….. 60

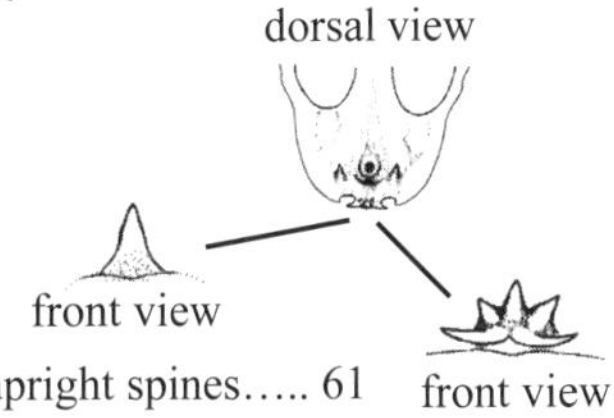


60a One simple upright spine on rostral plate….. 64 (page 210)

60b Spines on rostral plate star-like with 5 or more points and 3 upright spines….. 61

61a All fins blue-black (pectoral fin may have blue tint); lower jaw projecting beyond upper:

**BLACKFIN POACHER**

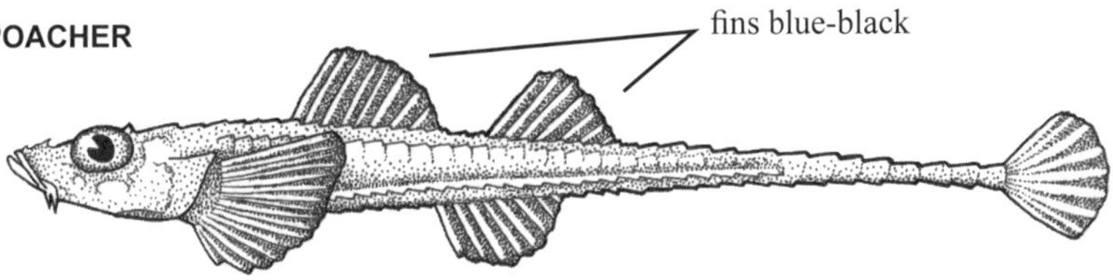


61b Fins not blue-black; jaws nearly even….. 62

62a Two pairs of plates immediately in front of pelvic fins:

**BIGEYE POACHER**

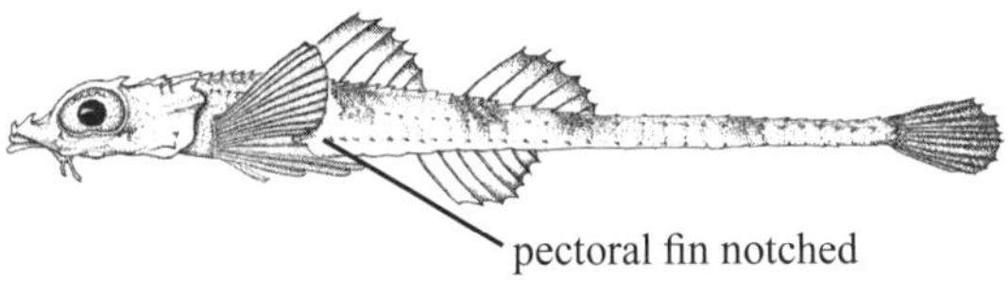


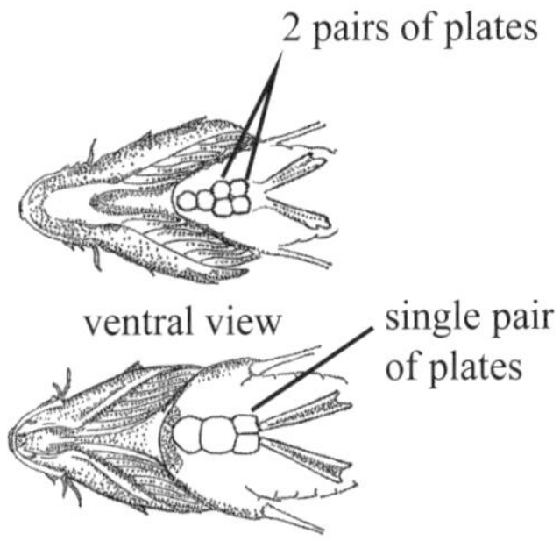


62b Single pair of plates or single plate immediately in front of pelvic fins….. 63

63a Lachrymal without forward projecting spines; anal fin origin below 1st dorsal fin insertion or between dorsal fin interspace:

**GRAY STARSNOUT**

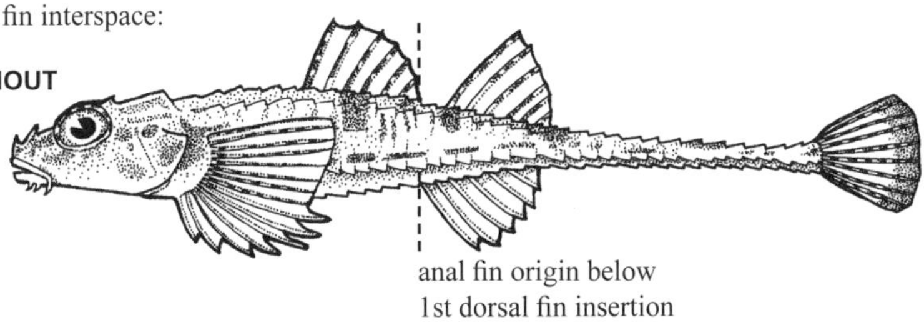


63b (next page)

## SCULPINS and POACHERS (continued)

**SPINYCHEEK STARSNOUT, *Bathyagonus infraspinatus* (Gilbert, 1904).** Family AGONIDAE
Southeastern Bering Sea from vicinity of Pribilof Islands, Islands of Four Mountains, and Aleutian Islands to northern California near Eureka. Common about Gulf of Alaska to Washington; uncommon in northern California. Length to 14.3 cm (5.6 in) TL. Depth: 6–183 m (20–600 ft). Light olive-green to brown above, white below; 5–6 dark bars or blotches on body. D V–VIII + 5–8; A 5–8; Pect. 14–16; Pelvic I,2; LLp 37–39; GR 0–1 + 6–10 = 7–10; Vert. 38–41. (Formerly SPINYCHEEK STARNOSE, *Asterotheca infraspinata* (Gilbert, 1904): M&L).

**STRIPEFIN POACHER, *Xeneretmus ritteri* Gilbert, 1915.** Family AGONIDAE
Malibu, southern California to Isla Cedros, central Baja California; isolated population in northern Gulf of California. Length to 15.9 cm (6.3 in) TL. Depth: 105–366 m (344–1,200 ft). Dark brown above, pale below; faint blotches on side. Dorsal fins usually dark-edged, 1st dorsal fin with black band on base and margin. D V–VII + 6–7; A 6–7; Pect. 16–17; Pelvic I,2; LLp 40–41; Vert. 40–41. (Formerly FLAGFIN POACHER: M&L).

**BLUESPOTTED POACHER, *Xeneretmus triacanthus* (Gilbert, 1890).** Family AGONIDAE
Near Haida Gwaii (54°18'N, 132°38'W), British Columbia to Punta Baja, northern Baja California. Common from Washington to at least southern California. Length to 20 cm (7.9 in) TL. Depth: 15–429 m (49–1,407 ft). Olive-brown; blue spots on and near head; fins dusky. D V–VII + 6–7; A 5–7; Pect. 12–14; Pelvic I,2; GR 1 + 8–14 = 9–15; Vert. 41–42.

**BLACKTIP POACHER, *Xeneretmus latifrons* (Gilbert, 1890).** Family AGONIDAE
Near Haida Gwaii (54°16'N, 133°17'W), British Columbia to Punta Colnett, northern Baja California. The presence of larvae in the northern Gulf of Alaska indicates adults are also present there. Common from at least Washington or British Columbia southward to at least southern California. Length to 19 cm (7.5 in) TL. Depth: 2 m (7 ft) or less to 1,291 m (4,235 ft). Light brown or olive above, white or yellow belly; 5–8 dark blotches on side usually present; dorsal fins edged in black; caudal fin dark often with dark posterior margin. D VI–VIII + 6–8; A 6–9; Pect.13–15; Pelvic I,2; LLp 39–41; GR 0–2 + 10–16 = 12–17; Vert. 39–43. (Formerly BLACKEDGE POACHER: M&L).

**SMOOTHEYE POACHER, *Xeneretmus leiops* Gilbert, 1915.** Family AGONIDAE
Northern Gulf of Alaska (59°16'N, 141°07'W) to Santa Catalina Island, southern California. Length to 27 cm (10.8 in) TL. Depth: 37–470 m (122–1,542 ft). Dusky-olive above, whitish below; 6 or more dark blotches on sides; tip of snout black; margin of 1st dorsal fin black. D VI–VII + 6–8; A 5–8; Pect. 13–15; Pelvic I,2; LLp 43; GR 1 + 10 = 11; Vert. 39–45.

63b Lachrymal serrated with forward projecting spines; anal fin origin anterior to 1st dorsal fin insertion:

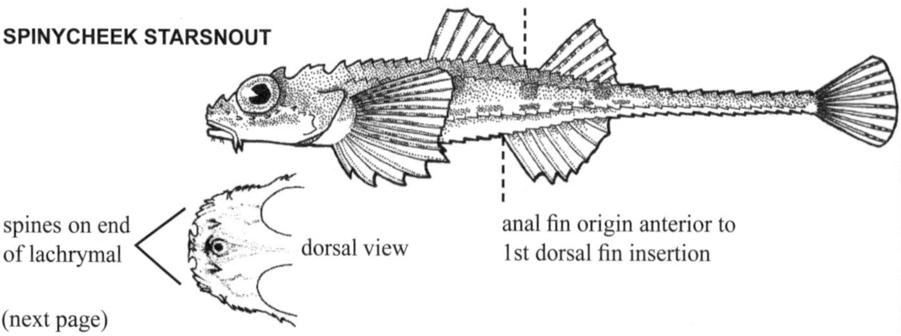


64a (next page)

64a *From 60a: one upright spine on rostral plate*
Pectoral fin soft-rays 16–17; black band on base and margin of 1st dorsal fin present:

**STRIPEFIN POACHER**

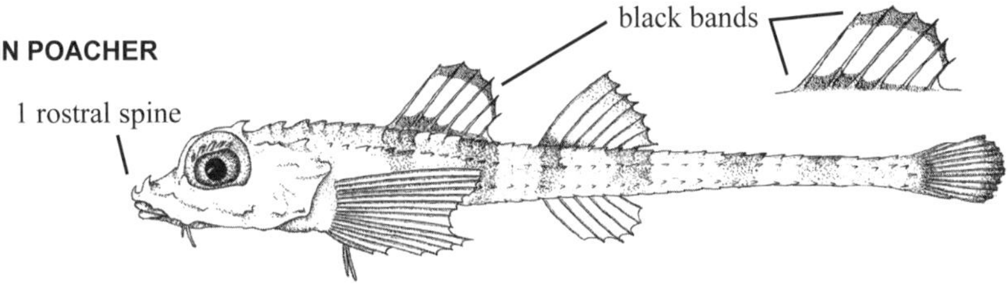


64b Pectoral fin soft-rays 13–15; black band on base of 1st dorsal fin lacking (dorsal fin margin may have black band or blotch)….. 65

65a Margin of 1st dorsal fin clear (some fine speckling may be present); bright blue spots on head and body near head:

**BLUESPOTTED POACHER**

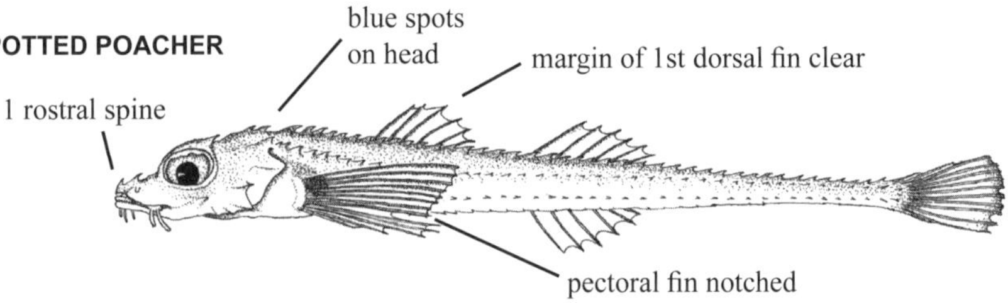


65b Margin of 1st dorsal fin black; no bright blue spots as above….. 66

66a Spinous scales present on eye; 1st dorsal fin with even black margin:

**BLACKTIP POACHER**

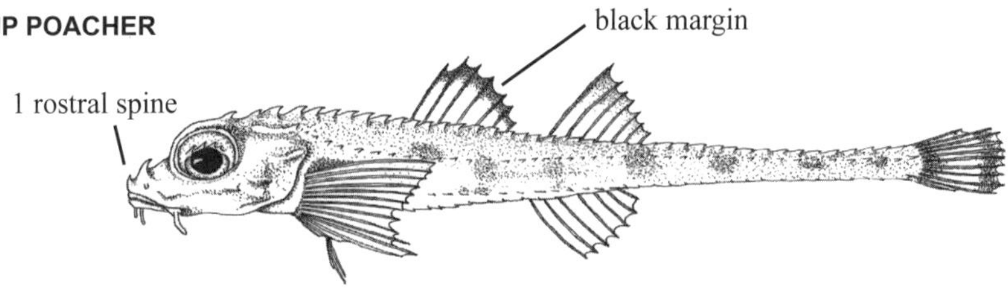


66b Spinous scales on eye lacking; margin of 1st dorsal fin with enlarged black blotch anteriorly and often with narrower black margin posteriorly:

**SMOOTHEYE POACHER**

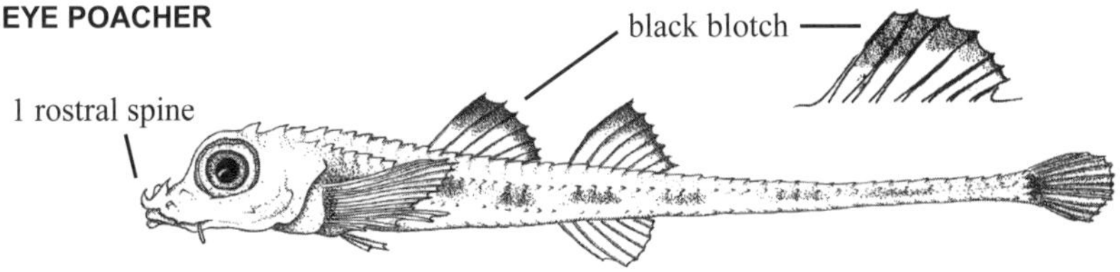

## SNAILFISHES, Family Liparidae

**BLACKTAIL SNAILFISH, *Careproctus melanurus* Gilbert, 1892.** British Columbia to at least Isla Guadalupe, central Baja California (LACM 30840-1). Apparently common throughout range. Length to 54 cm (21.3 in) TL. Depth: 70–1,600 m (230–5,248 ft) and perhaps to 2,453 m (8,046 ft). Whitish, pink, or rose-red; black caudal and posterior portions of dorsal and anal fins; dusky on belly; lips, snout, and chin sometimes dark. D 52–66; A 46–55; Pect. 27–34; LL absent; GRt 10–12; Pyloric caeca 20–31; Vert. 56–63. "*Careproctus melanurus*" from north of British Columbia is an undescribed species; all data above comes from specimens captured from British Columbia southwards.

**SMALLDISK SNAILFISH, *Careproctus gilberti* Burke, 1912.** Western Aleutian Islands and eastern Bering Sea to central California at about 35°10'N and perhaps to southern California (33°44.9'N, 120°12'W). Common from Bering Sea to about Oregon. Length to 12.7 cm (5 in) TL. Depth: 55–2,040 m (180–6,691 ft). Pink or pink-orange, slightly darker posteriorly; stomach black; mouth reddish. D 45–55; A 41–48; Pect. 30–33; Scales absent; LL absent.

**ALASKA SNAILFISH, *Careproctus colletti* Gilbert, 1896.** Seas of Japan and Okhotsk to Bering Sea and Gulf of Alaska to northern California (39°32'N, 124°13'W) (UW 152457) and perhaps central California (35°37'N, 121°46'W). Common at least from Sea of Okhotsk and Kamchatka-Kuril Islands, Russia to Oregon. Length to 44 cm (17.3 in) SL. Depth: 64–1,556 m (210–5,105 ft). Reddish-black with many small black dots; pelvic fins and rear of dorsal and anal fins black; caudal fin and peritoneum black. D 51–58; A 47–52; Pect. 25–31; Scales absent; LL absent; Pyloric caeca 10–18; Vert. 58–65.

**FALCATE SNAILFISH, *Careproctus cypselurus* (Jordan & Gilbert, 1898).** Pacific Ocean off Honshu, Japan to Kuril Islands, Russia and Sea of Okhotsk to Bering Sea; northern Haida Gwaii, British Columbia to northern California (35°27'N, 121°44'W) (UW 153142); also reported further south in southern California (33°24'N) without documentation. Common at least from Sea of Okhotsk and Kamchatka-Kuril Islands, Russia to Oregon. Length to 54 cm (21.3 in) TL. Depth: 35–1,993 m (115–6,539 ft). Body color variable: dusky pink to dark purple-pink with red highlights; posterior black; dorsal, caudal, and anal fins and gill cavity black. D 58–64; A 52–58; Pect. 32–40; Scales absent; LL absent; Pyloric caeca 29–49; Vert. 63–70.

## KEY TO THE SNAILFISHES:
Revised by James W. Orr
(Principal sources: Miller & Lea, 1972; Hart, 1973; Stein, 1978; Mecklenburg et al., 2002)

1a Pelvic disc absent, or barely discernible, reduced to tiny lobes..... 10 (page 215)

1b Pelvic disc (sucking disc) present..... 2

2a Two nostrils on each side of snout; pseudobranchia present; pelvic disc usually large, 30% or greater of HL; head and body coloration variable from green, brown to pale, often with mottling, stripes, or spots..... 6 (page 213)

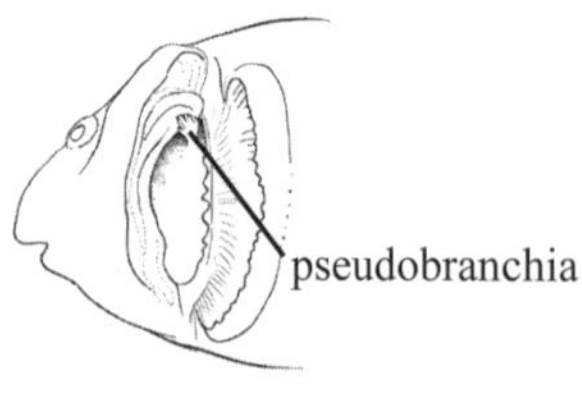


2b Single nostril on each side of snout; pseudobranchia absent; pelvic disc small, less than 30% of HL; head and body uniformly pink to purple, most with posterior fins dark..... 3 (next page)

3a Pelvic disc triangular; head and body coloration purple to gray….. 5

3b Pelvic disc oval or round; head and body uniformly pink, red, to orange….. 4

4a Gill slit extending ventrally to no farther than 1st pectoral fin soft-ray; pelvic disc oval, 13–16% of HL; peritoneum pale with pale stomach; median fins dark posteriorly:

**BLACKTAIL SNAILFISH**

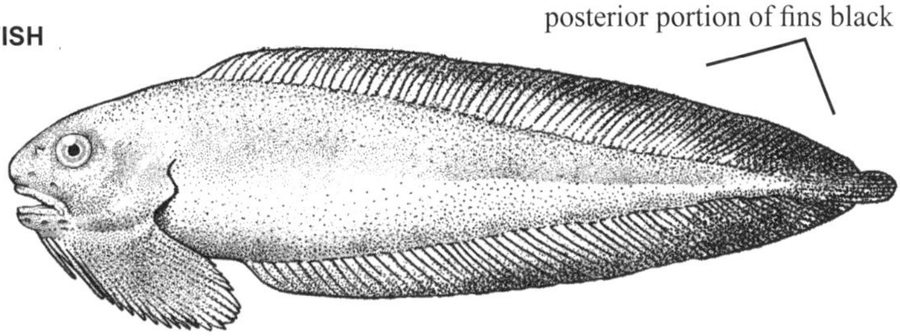


4b Gill slit extending ventrally to about 14th pectoral fin soft-ray; pelvic disc round, very small, 8–11% of HL; peritoneum pale with black stomach; median fins light for entire length:

**SMALLDISK SNAILFISH**

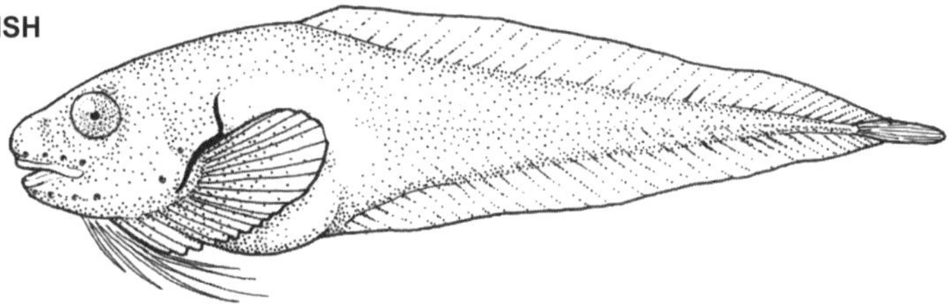

5a *From 3a: pelvic disc triangular*
Lower soft-rays of pectoral fin elongate, often as long filaments, some longer than HL; pectoral fin soft-rays 25–31; caudal fin emarginated:

**ALASKA SNAILFISH**

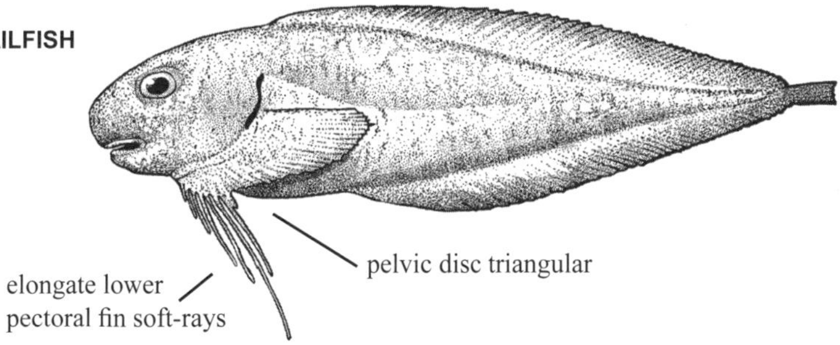


5b Lower soft-rays of pectoral fin shorter than HL; pectoral fin soft-rays 32–40; caudal fin deeply forked:

**FALCATE SNAILFISH**

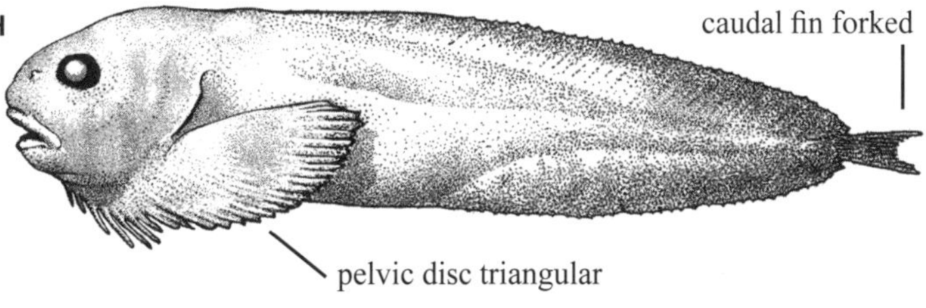


6a (next page)

## SNAILFISHES (continued)

**SHOWY SNAILFISH, *Liparis pulchellus* Ayres, 1855.** Southeastern Bering Sea and Aleutian Islands to Monterey Bay, central California (CAS 16021). Common from Semidi Islands, Gulf of Alaska to northern California. Length to 25.4 cm (10 in) TL. Depth: intertidal to 183 m (600 ft). Body color variable, often uniform light to dark brown above, paler below; occasionally with wavy lines or spots on sides. D 47–53; A 39–42; Pect. 36–37; Scales absent; LL absent; GR 0 + 6–9; Pyloric caeca 25–35; Vert. 50–55.

**TIDEPOOL SNAILFISH, *Liparis florae* (Jordan & Starks, 1895).** Kodiak Island, western Gulf of Alaska to King Harbor, southern California. Common from Kenai Peninsula, Alaska to central California. Length to 18.3 cm (7.2 in) TL. Depth: intertidal to 15 m (50 ft). Uniform brown, green-brown, yellow-brown, to olive-brown and purplish. D 30–35; A 21–27; Pect. 29–33; Scales absent; LL absent; GRt 3–5; Vert. 39–40.

**SLIPSKIN SNAILFISH, *Liparis fucensis* Gilbert, 1896.** Southeastern Bering Sea and Unimak Pass, eastern Aleutian Islands to near San Simeon, central California (SIO 15-2016). Common from western Gulf of Alaska southward to northern California. Length to 17.8 cm (7 in) TL. Depth: 4–388 m (13–1,272 ft). Olive-brown to dark brown with faint mottling; light oblique bar in caudal fin. D 30–35; A 26–29; Pect. 34–43; Scales absent; LL absent; GR 0 + 7–9; Vert. 39–43.

**ROSYBROWN SNAILFISH, *Liparis adiastolus* Stein, Bond & Misitano, 2003.** Washington to northern California; probably British Columbia but not confirmed. Length to 16.7 cm (6.6 in) SL. Depth: intertidal to 10 m (33 ft). Maroon, pinkish-lavender, or purple; white patches on body; pale band around caudal peduncle. D 35–37; A 25–26; Pect. 32–36; Scales absent; LL absent; Vert. 35–37. (Formerly RINGTAIL SNAILFISH and previously part of *Liparis rutteri* (Gilbert & Snyder in Jordan & Evermann, 1898): M&L).

**SLIMY SNAILFISH, *Liparis mucosus* Ayres, 1855.** Samsing Cove, southeastern Alaska to Bahía San Carlos (29°36'N, 115°12'W), central Baja California (SIO 52-212). Common at least from outer coast of Vancouver Island to northern Baja California. Length to about 12.7 cm (5 in) TL. Depth: intertidal to 15 m (50 ft). Uniform gray, brown, pink, red, or purple, often with wavy lines on body. D 28–33; A 22–27; Pect. 27–32; Scales absent; LL absent; GR 0 + 8–9; Vert. 36–38.

6a *From 2a: two nostrils on each side of snout; pseudobranchia present*
Caudal fin small, indistinct, and nearly confluent with dorsal and anal fins; dorsal fin not notched:

**SHOWY SNAILFISH**

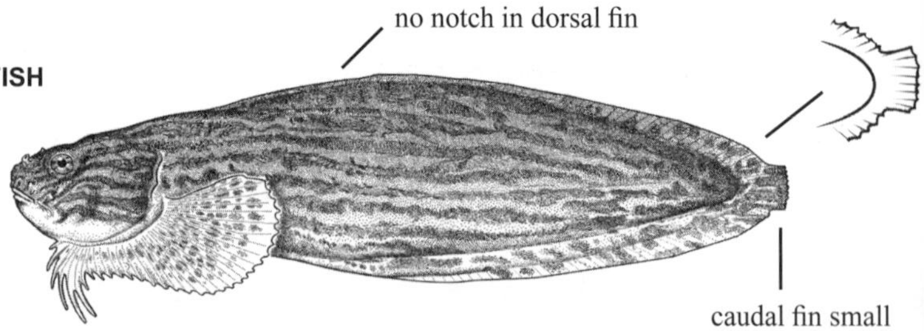


6b Caudal fin large, distinct, and not confluent with dorsal and anal fins; dorsal fin notched, ranging from deep, appearing as an anterior lobe, to shallow (notch may be lacking in SLIPSKIN SNAILFISH)….. 7 (next page)

7a Dorsal fin deeply notched with distinct anterior lobe:

**TIDEPOOL SNAILFISH**

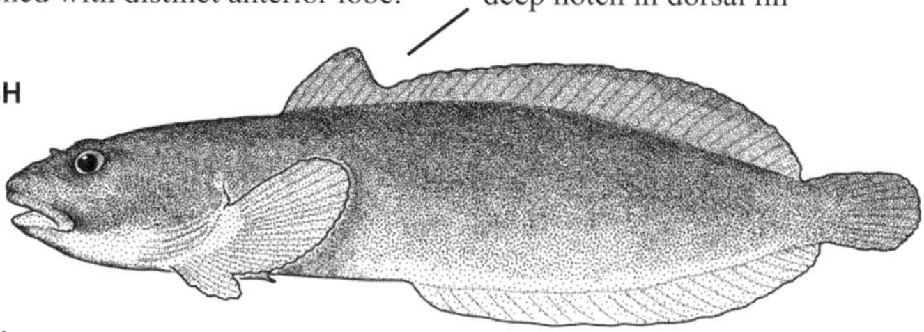


7b Dorsal fin entire, notch moderate to shallow….. 8

8a Gill slit large, extending ventrally to or beyond 6th pectoral fin soft-ray; pelvic disc relatively small, less than half of HL:

**SLIPSKIN SNAILFISH**

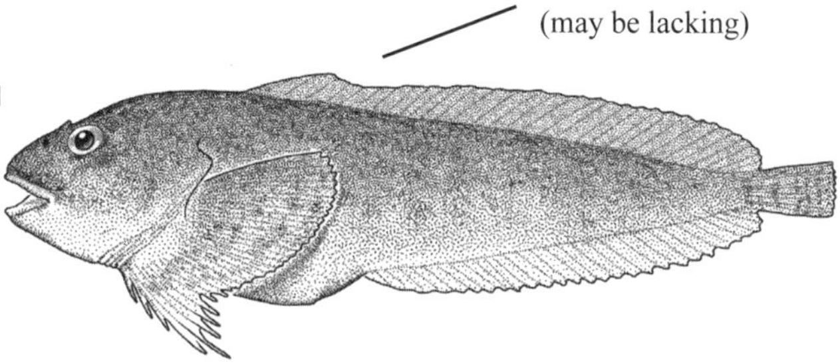


8b Gill slit small, extending ventrally to at most 6th pectoral fin soft-ray; pelvic disc relatively large, greater than half of HL….. 9

9a Gill slit extending ventrally to only 1st pectoral fin soft-ray; pectoral fin soft-rays 32–36; dorsal fin notch long and shallow to moderately deep; peritoneum pale:

**ROSYBROWN SNAILFISH**

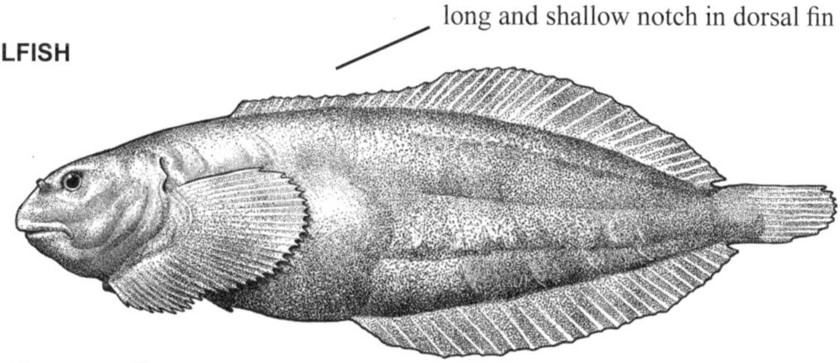


9b Gill slit usually extending ventrally to 3rd–6th pectoral fin soft-rays, sometimes less; pectoral fin soft-rays 27–32; dorsal fin notch short and shallow; peritoneum black:

**SLIMY SNAILFISH**

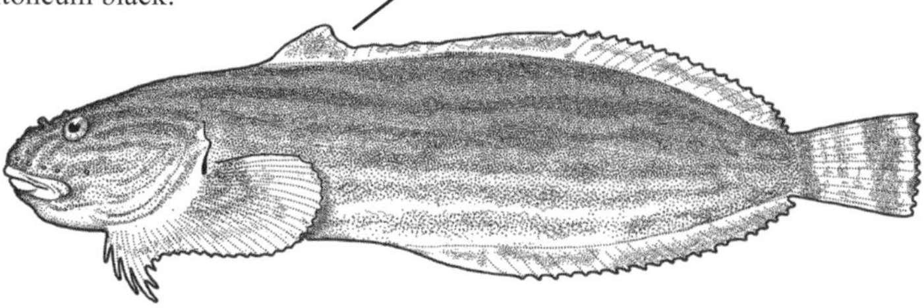


10a (next page)

## SNAILFISHES (continued)

**PRICKLY SNAILFISH, *Paraliparis deani* Burke, 1912.** Shelikof Strait, western Gulf of Alaska to northern California. Rare in northern California. Length to less than 10 cm (3.9 in) TL. Depth: 18–1,008 m (59–3,306 ft). Translucent pale brown, ventral silvery with black specks; lips and fins pinkish; stomach black. D 56–59; A 44–49; Pect. 18–22; Scales absent; LL absent; GRt 11; Pyloric caeca 9; Vert. 54–58.

**PHANTOM SNAILFISH, *Paraliparis albescens* Gilbert, 1915.** Monterey, central California to Point Conception, California. Length to 6.1 cm (2.4 in) SL. Perhaps benthopelagic; depth: about 192–500 m (630–1,640 ft). Light pink. D 49–57; A 44–53; Pect. 17–18; Pelvic absent; Scales absent; LL absent; Vert. 54–61. Anderson et al. (1979) gives descriptive detail.

**TADPOLE SNAILFISH, *Nectoliparis pelagicus* Gilbert & Burke, 1912.** Hokkaido, Japan and Sea of Okhotsk to Bering Sea to San Diego (32°32'N, 117°24'W), southern California (SIO 63-870). Common from Aleutian Islands and eastern Bering Sea to southern California. Length to 6.5 cm (2.5 in) TL. Pelagic, usually taken in midwater; depth: 2 m (7 ft) or less to at least 541 m (1,775 ft). A reported maximum depth of 3,383 m (11,096 ft) is likely in error. Body tan; head and abdomen shiny silver; body covered with small black dots; skin transparent; mouth, gill cavity, and peritoneum black. D 44–58; A 40–53; Pect. 19–25; Scales absent; LL absent; GRt 1–4; Vert. 63–66.

**SWELLHEAD SNAILFISH, *Paraliparis cephalus* Gilbert, 1892.** Vicinity of Commander Islands; northern Bering Sea (to 59°25'N, 178°07'W) and western Aleutian Islands near Buldir Island (52°22'N, 175°36'E) to northern Baja California (32°40'N, 117°35'W) (SIO 54-126). Common from northern British Columbia to southern California. Length to 8.2 cm (3.2 in) SL. Depth: 294–1,799 m (965–5,902 ft). Light red to pink-orange; abdomen blue-black; mouth and gill cavity white to dusky. D 50–57; A 44–51; Pect. 14–16; Scales absent; LL absent; Pyloric caeca 6–10; Vert. 57–63.

**HUMPBACK SNAILFISH, *Elassodiscus caudatus* (Gilbert, 1915).** Eastern Bering Sea, southeastern Alaska to southern California (34°07'N, 120°20'W) (LACM 57821-2). Common from Bering Sea to northern California. Length to 19.9 cm (7.8 in) TL. Depth: 241–1,556 m (791–5,105 ft). Light rose-red, translucent; caudal fin and rear of dorsal and anal fins black; mouth pale; gill cavity, peritoneum, and stomach black. D 50–69; A 41–63; Pect. 25–36; Scales absent; LL absent; Pyloric caeca 10–20; Vert. 54–74. Anderson et al. (1979) provided meristics that were somewhat outside values in other publications but are included here.

10a *From 1a: pelvic disc absent, or barely discernible*
Gill slit small, length about size of orbit, opening either above pectoral fin and extending ventrally to no more than 5th pectoral fin soft-ray or opening entirely in front of pectoral fin….. 12 (next page)

10b Gill slit large, length much larger than orbit, opening extending from well above 1st pectoral fin soft-ray ventrally to about 12th pectoral fin soft-ray….. 11

11a Peritoneum pale with black stomach; pectoral fin soft-rays 18–22:

**PRICKLY SNAILFISH**

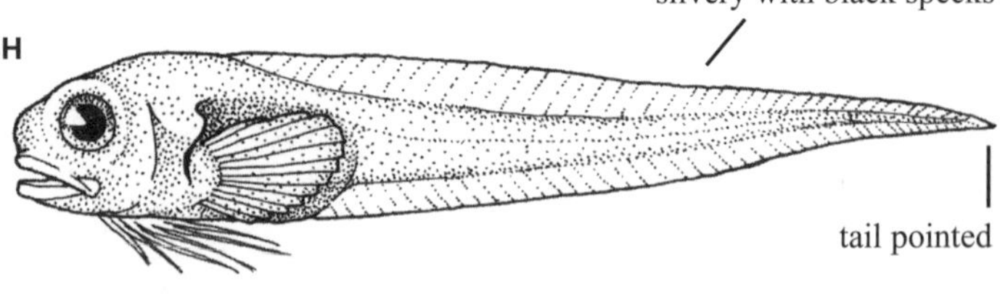


11b (next page)

11b Peritoneum dark with dusky stomach; pectoral fin soft-rays 17–18:

**PHANTOM SNAILFISH**

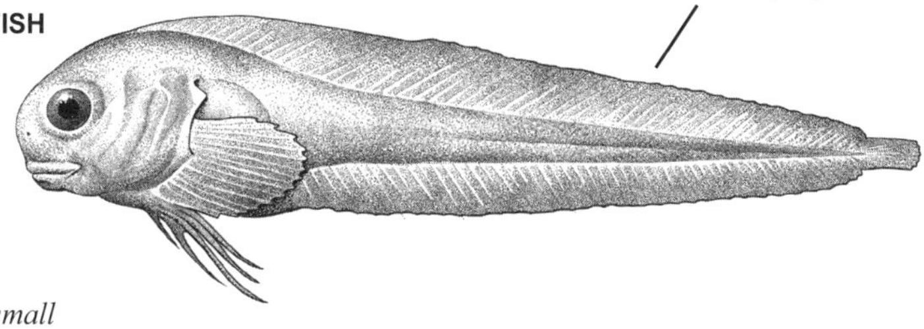


12a *From 10a: gill slit small*
Gill slit entirely in front of pectoral fin; anus anterior, below posterior rim of orbit in adults:

**TADPOLE SNAILFISH**

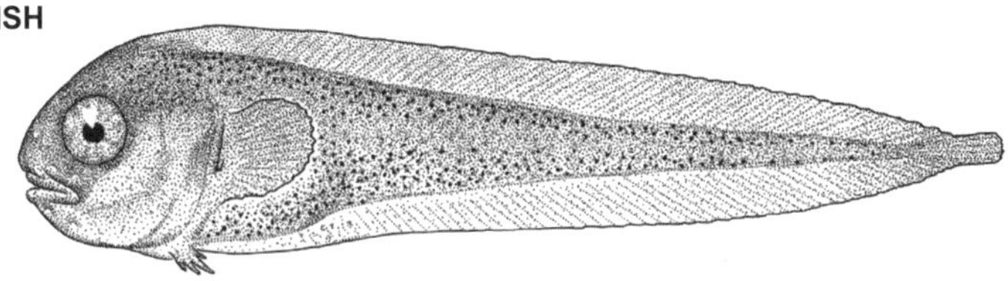

12b Gill slit above pectoral fin, extending ventrally no farther than 5th pectoral fin soft-ray; anus posterior, below gill slit….. 13

13a Snout barbels present, darkly pigmented or translucent….. 16 (next page)

13b Snout barbels absent….. 14

14a Pectoral fin soft-rays 14–16; teeth simple:

**SWELLHEAD SNAILFISH**

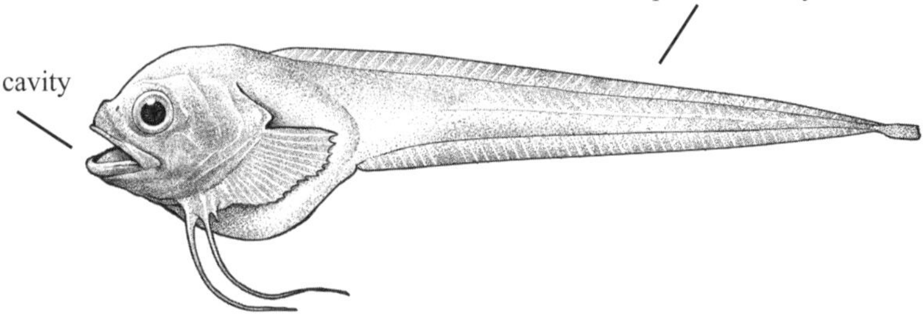


14b Pectoral fin soft-rays 25 or more; teeth strongly trilobed….. 15

15a Pelvic disc present as reduced tiny lobes; peritoneum black with black stomach:

**HUMPBACK SNAILFISH**

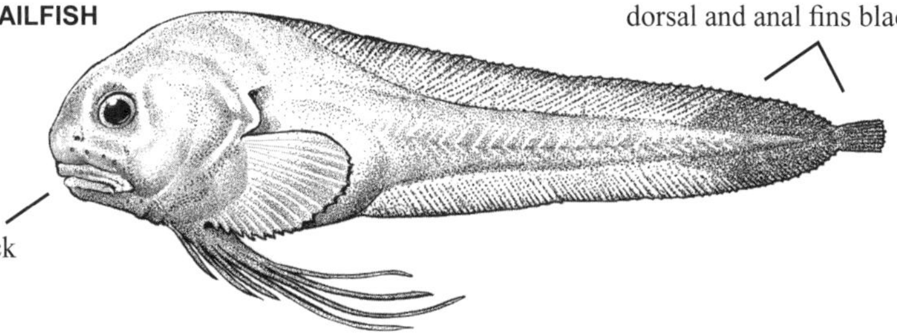


15b (next page)

## SNAILFISHES (continued)

**RED SNAILFISH, *Paraliparis dactylosus* Gilbert, 1896.** Commander Islands and eastern Bering Sea to off Point Arguello, central California (UW 117540) or perhaps to southern California (but without documentation). Common at least from the Bering Sea to central California. Length to 12.1 cm (4.7 in) SL. Depth: 309–1,062 m (1,014–3,483 ft). Body pink to red; mouth, gill cavity, peritoneum, and posterior part of dorsal and anal fins and caudal fin black. D 54–61; A 49–55; Pect. 28–30; Scales absent; LL absent; Pyloric caeca 17–23; Vert. 59–67.

**SLIM SNAILFISH, *Rhinoliparis attenuatus* Burke, 1912.** Northern Kuril Islands and southeastern Kamchatka, Russia; eastern Bering Sea and Gulf of Alaska to somewhat south of Morro Bay, central California and perhaps to southern California (32°48'N). Common at least from eastern Bering Sea to Monterey Bay, central California. Length to 14.5 cm (5.7 in) SL. Pelagic; depth: 362–2,189 m (1,188–7,182 ft). Skin transparent, but rear portion of body dusky; mouth, gill cavity, and peritoneum black. D 68–78; A 60–73; Pect. 21–25; Scales absent; LL absent; Pyloric caeca 9–10; Vert. 80–83. (Sometimes classified in *Paraliparis*.)

**LONGNOSE SNAILFISH, *Rhinoliparis barbulifer* Gilbert, 1896.** Sea of Okhotsk; Pacific off northern Honshu and Hokkaido; Commander Islands; Umnak Pass and vicinity of Unalaska Island to southern California. Rare off California. Length to 11 cm (4.3 in) TL. Benthopelagic; depth: 252–1,500 m (827–4,921 ft). Transparent; mouth, gill cavity, and peritoneum black. D 63–68; A 57–59; Pect. 18–21; Scales absent; LL absent; Pyloric caeca 7–9; Vert. 68. (Sometimes classified in *Paraliparis*.)

15b Pelvic disc absent; peritoneum black with pale stomach:

**RED SNAILFISH**

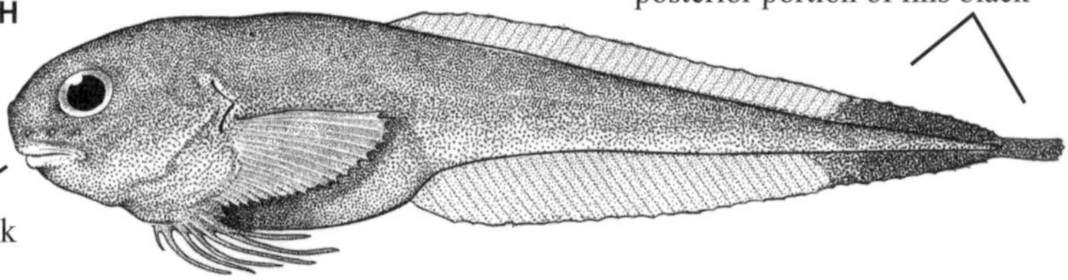


16a *From 13a: snout barbels present*
Snout barbels 9, darkly pigmented; pectoral fin soft-rays 21–25:

**SLIM SNAILFISH**

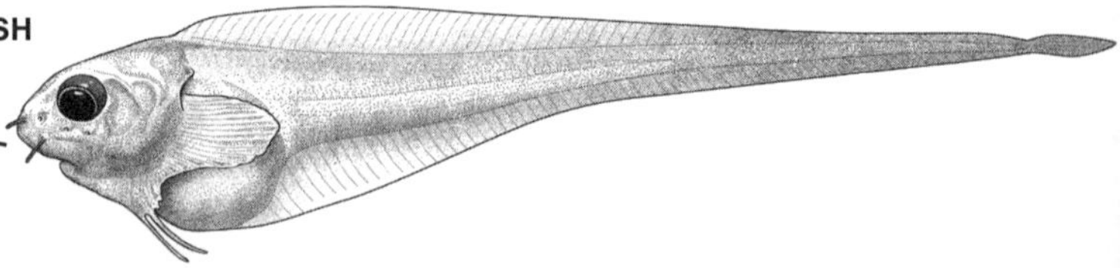


16b Snout barbels 2, translucent; pectoral fin soft-rays 18–21:

**LONGNOSE SNAILFISH**

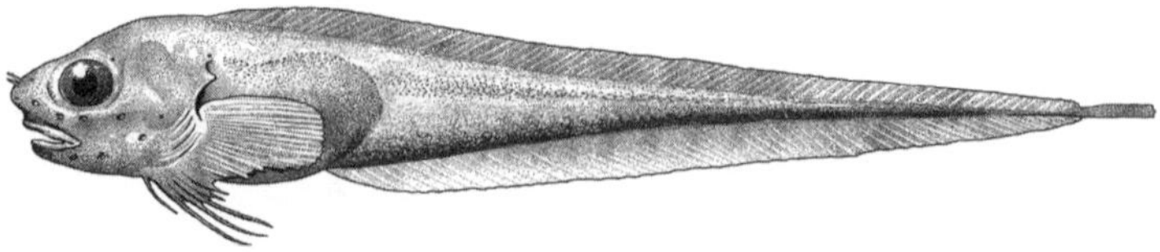

# SEA BASSES, Family Serranidae, GROUPERS, Family Epinephelidae, TEMPERATE BASSES, Family Moronidae, and WRECKFISHES, Family Polyprionidae

NOTE: The Serranidae, formerly encompassing both sea basses and groupers, are now limited to sea basses and their allies. The subfamily Epinephelinae was raised to family status (Craig and Hastings, 2007; Smith and Craig, 2007).

**STRIPED BASS, *Morone saxatilis* (Walbaum, 1792).** Family Moronidae

Atlantic and Pacific; Barkley Sound, British Columbia to just south of U.S.-Mexican border. Introduced to West Coast. Common in San Francisco Bay, northern California and central California. Small breeding population in Coos Bay, Oregon. Length to about 122 cm (48 in) TL in eastern Pacific; 183 cm (72 in) TL in Atlantic. Anadromous; depth: when in ocean, in nearshore waters. Greenish on back, silvery on sides, with black stripes. D VII–XII + I–II,8–14; A III,7–12; Pect. 13–19; LLs 53–65; GR 8–11 + 14–17 = 22–28; Vert. 25. (Formerly *Roccus saxatilis* (Walbaum, 1792), Serranidae: M&L).

**GIANT SEA BASS, *Stereolepis gigas* Ayres, 1859.** Family Polyprionidae

Humboldt Bay, northern California to Oaxaca, southern Mexico, including Gulf of California. Common from southern California southward along Baja California and into Gulf of California (however, population along Baja California and in Gulf of California likely severely reduced). Length to 2.7 m (8.9 ft) TL. Depth: 5–55 m (18–180 ft). Older juveniles and adults dark gray, often with dark spots on sides. Newly settled juveniles black with white caudal fin; somewhat older juveniles bright red or orange, with black spots. D XI–XII,9–10; A III,8–9; Pect. 18–19; Pelvic I,5; GR 2 + 7–8 = 9–10; Vert. 25–26. (Formerly Serranidae: M&L) (Alternative name BLACK SEA BASS).

## KEY TO THE SEA BASSES, GROUPERS, TEMPERATE BASSES, and WRECKFISHES:

Revised by Daniel J. Pondella II and Jonathan P. Williams
(Principal sources: Rosenblatt & Johnson, 1974; Heemstra & Randall, 1993; Pondella, 1999, 2001)

1a Posterior margin of operculum with 3 spines….. 3 (next page)

1b Posterior margin of operculum with 2 spines….. 2

2a Body with 6–9 black stripes; dorsal fin soft-rays 11–12:

**STRIPED BASS**

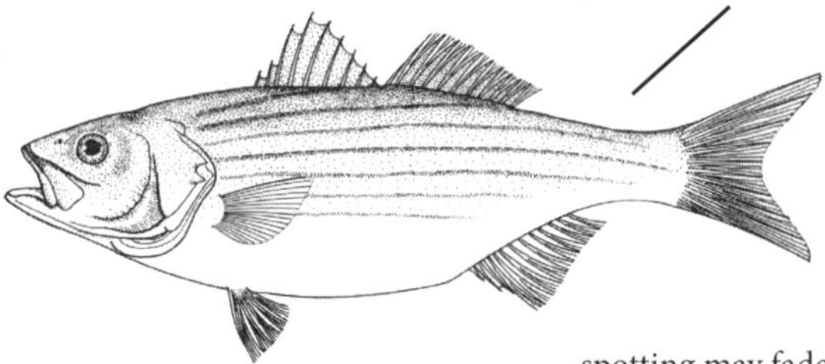


2b Body without stripes; dorsal fin soft-rays 9–10:

**GIANT SEA BASS**

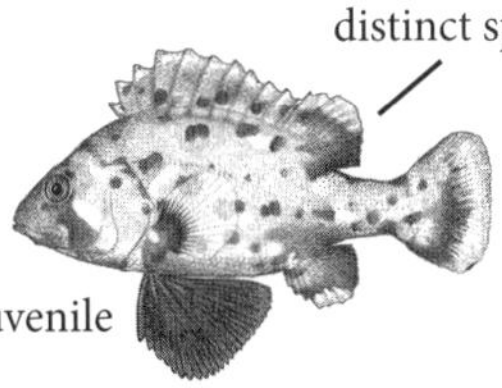


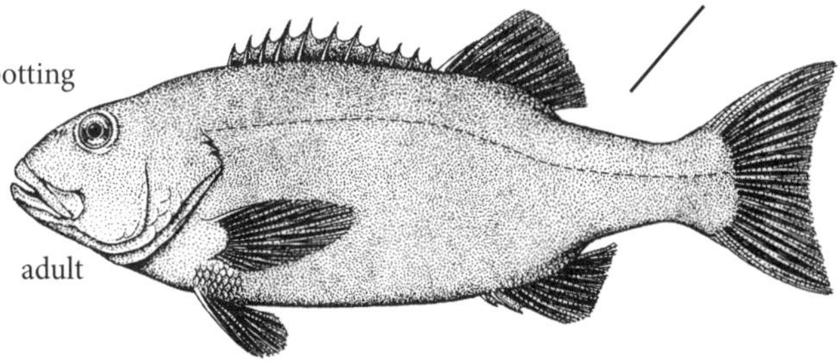


3a (next page)

# SEA BASSES, GROUPERS, TEMPERATE BASSES, and WRECKFISHES (continued)

**PACIFIC CREOLEFISH, *Cephalopholis colonus* (Valenciennes, 1846).** Family EPINEPHELIDAE
San Diego, southern California to Islas Lobos de Afuera, Peru, including Gulf of California and such offshore islands as Islas Galápagos. Rare in southern California; common in tropical waters. Length to 43 cm (16.9 in) TL. Depth: surface to 120 m (394 ft). After death, dark red on back and fins, lighter red on sides; 4–5 white, light-blue, or dark spots on back. Young juveniles bright yellow to pink-yellow with blue or dark spots; red spot on pectoral fin. Older juveniles salmon-colored and similarly spotted. Underwater, back and sides of adults olive. D IX,18–21; A III,9–11; Pect. 19–23; GR 12–15 + 24–29; Vert. 24. (Recently as *Paranthias colonus* Valenciennes, 1846).

**GULF CONEY, *Hyporthodus acanthistius* (Gilbert, 1892).** Family EPINEPHELIDAE
El Capitan (north of Santa Barbara), southern California to Isla Lobos de Tierra, Peru, including Gulf of California. Rare in southern California; common in tropical waters. Length to 130 cm (51 in) TL. Depth: 12–256 m (40–840 ft). Red, rosy-red or brown body and fins (fins sometimes dark); body sometimes with white blotches. D IX,17; A III,9; Pect. 18–19; GR 10–11 + 14–17 = 25–27. (Formerly *Epinephelus acanthistius* (Gilbert, 1892)) (Alternative names ROOSTER HIND, ROSE CONEY).

**THREADFIN BASS, *Pronotogrammus multifasciatus* Gill, 1863.** Family SERRANIDAE
Off east end of Anacapa Island, southern California and south of Point Mugu (34°00'N, 119°00'W), southern California to Talara, Peru, including Gulf of California and Islas Galápagos. Usually uncommon in southern California (catches increase after some El Niños); common from southern Baja California into tropics. Length to 35.9 cm (14.1 in) TL. Depth: 14–300 m (45–984 ft). Red or red-pink, with dark mottling or crosshatching on upper body; yellow striping on head; some or all (but particularly caudal) fin membranes yellow; chin and ventral areas often yellow. D X–XI,14–15; A III,6–8; Pect. 16–20; Pelvic I,5; GR 10–12 + 25–30; Vert. 26.

**LEATHER BASS, *Dermatolepis dermatolepis* (Boulenger, 1895).** Family EPINEPHELIDAE
El Segundo, southern California to northern Peru and such offshore islands as Islas Galápagos. Rare in southern California; common in tropical waters. Length to 100 cm (39.4 in) TL. Depth: 2–82 m (8–269 ft). Adults with alternating dark-gray to black and light-gray to white bars with many light blotches and sometimes dark spots; margin of fins yellow. A specimen off southern California was light brown with only very faint bars (Moore, 1991). Juveniles white with numerous dark bars on body and fins. D XI,18–20; A III,9–10; Pect. 19–20; GRt 21–24; Vert. 24.

3a *From 1a: operculum with 3 spines*
Dorsal fin with 10–11 spines….. 5 (next page)

3b Dorsal fin with 9 spines….. 4

4a Head small, HL into SL 3.3–4.0; caudal fin lunate; 2nd–4th dorsal fin spines similar in size; dark moustache streak above maxilla absent:

**PACIFIC CREOLEFISH**

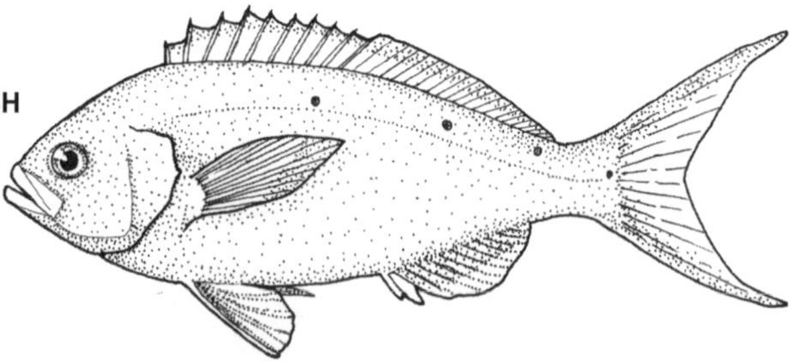

4b (next page)

4b Head large, HL into SL less than 3; caudal fin slightly rounded; 2nd–4th dorsal fin spines elongated (adults only); prominent dark moustache streak above maxilla (not in juveniles):

**GULF CONEY**

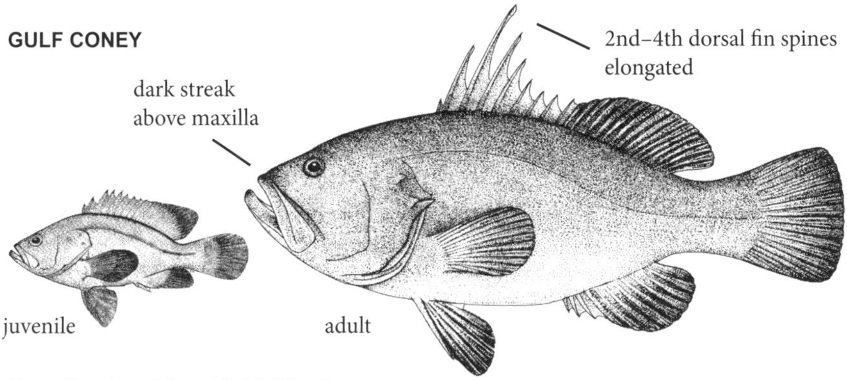


5a *From 3a: dorsal fin with 10–11 spines*
Long filamentous pelvic fin:

**THREADFIN BASS**

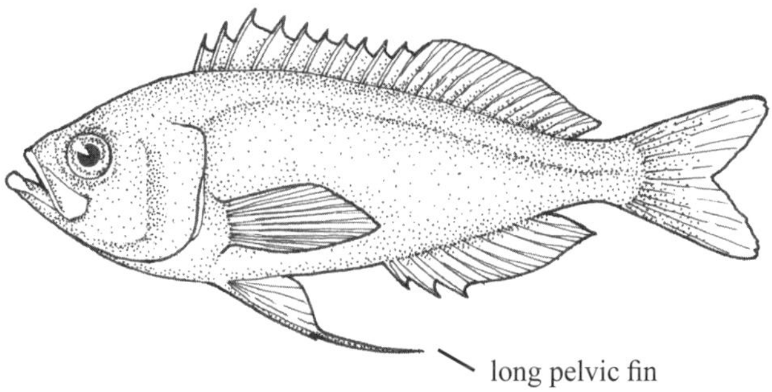


5b Pelvic fin normal….. 6

6a Dorsal fin with 10 spines….. 12 (page 224)

6b Dorsal fin with 11 spines….. 7

7a Body deep and compressed, BD distinctly greater than HL and into SL 2.1–2.7; dorsal fin soft-rays 18–20; body scales smooth and covered by skin:

**LEATHER BASS**

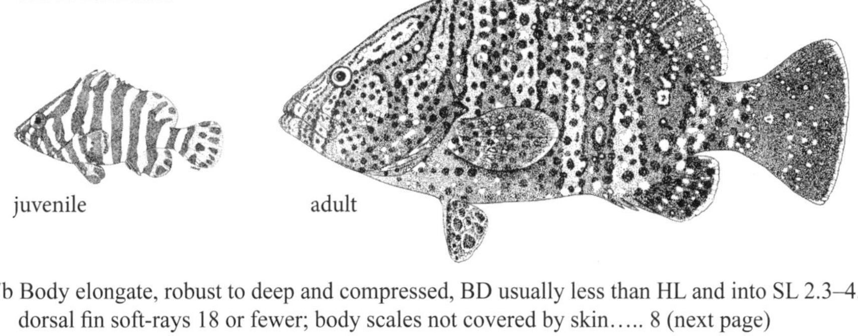


7b Body elongate, robust to deep and compressed, BD usually less than HL and into SL 2.3–4.1; dorsal fin soft-rays 18 or fewer; body scales not covered by skin….. 8 (next page)

## SEA BASSES, GROUPERS, TEMPERATE BASSES, and WRECKFISHES (continued)

**FLAG CABRILLA, *Epinephelus labriformis* (Jenyns, 1840).** Family EPINEPHELIDAE
Mission Bay, southern California to Paita, Peru, including upper Gulf of California and Islas Galápagos. Rare in southern California; common from Bahía Magdalena, southern Baja California into tropics. Length to 60 cm (23.6 in) TL. Depth: intertidal to at least 50 m (164 ft). Olive-green to reddish-brown with white spots and blotches; soft dorsal, anal, and caudal fins reddish, greenish, or brownish, sometimes with red margin; black saddle on caudal peduncle. D XI,16–18; A III,8; Pect. 18–19; GR 7–9 + 15–17; Vert. 24. (Alternative name STARRY GROUPER).

**STAR-STUDDED GROUPER, *Hyporthodus niphobles* (Gilbert & Starks, 1897).** Family EPINEPHELIDAE
Central California (36°21'N, 121°40'W) (SIO 95-24) to Islas Lobos de Afuera, Peru, including Gulf of California and Islas Galápagos. Uncommon off California; common in tropical waters. Length to 121 cm (47.6 in) TL. Depth: 1–450 m (3–1,476 ft). Reddish-brown sometimes with white spotting; white spotting may fade after death. D XI,13–15; A III,8–9; Pect. 17–21; GR 8–9 + 15–17 = 22–27. (Formerly SNOWY GROUPER, *Epinephelus niveatus* (Valenciennes, 1828), Serranidae: M&L; also previously as *Epinephelus niphobles* (Gilbert & Starks, 1897)).

**LEOPARD GROUPER, *Mycteroperca rosacea* (Streets, 1877).** Family EPINEPHELIDAE
Islas Coronados, northern Baja California to Bahía Banderas, Jalisco, Mexico, including Gulf of California and Isla Guadalupe, central Baja California (LACM 44237-1). Common in Bahía Magdalena and in the Gulf of California. Length to 100 cm (39.4 in) TL. Depth: 1–100 m (4–328 ft). Adults greenish to gray-brown, covered in brown spots with series of dark saddles (edged in white) on back; juveniles tan to whitish with more widely spaced small brown or reddish-brown spots. Few individuals golden. D XI,16–18; A III,10–11; Pect. 15–17; GRt 37–43.

**GULF GROUPER, *Mycteroperca jordani* (Jenkins & Evermann, 1889).** Family EPINEPHELIDAE
La Jolla, southern California to Mazatlán, Mexico, including Gulf of California. Currently rare in California, but likely more common before overfishing. Common off southern Baja California and into tropics. Length to 198 cm (78 in) TL. Depth: 2–50 m (5–164 ft). Brown or gray-brown, often with dark blotches on body and dark streaks under eye; margin of some fins may be white. D XI,16–17; A III,10–11; Pect. 16–18; GRt 21–26; Vert 24. (Formerly Serranidae: M&L).

8a Anal fin soft-rays 10–11….. 10 (next page)

8b Anal fin soft-rays 9 or fewer….. 9

9a Anal fin soft-rays 8; dorsal fin soft-rays 16–18; body reddish-brown with irregular white spots or blotches (juveniles with pale reticulations); 3rd or 4th dorsal fin spines longest; lateral line scales 84–100:

**FLAG CABRILLA**

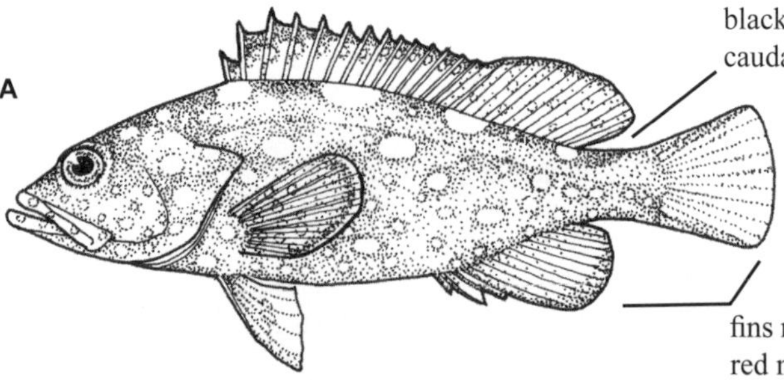


9b (next page)

9b Anal fin soft-rays 9; dorsal fin soft-rays 13–15; body reddish-brown usually without spots (juveniles with white spots in vertical series and horizontal rows); 2nd dorsal fin spine longest; lateral line scales 100–106:

**STAR-STUDDED GROUPER**

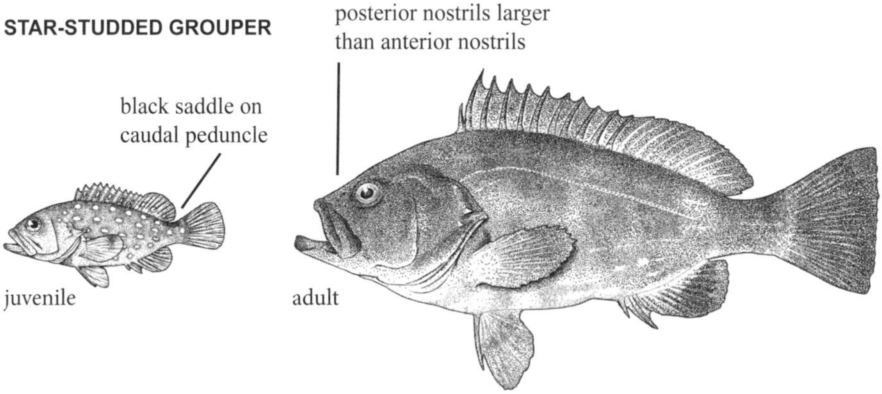


10a *From 8a: anal fin soft-rays 10–11*
Body with small brown spots and dark saddles; total gill rakers 37–43:

**LEOPARD GROUPER**

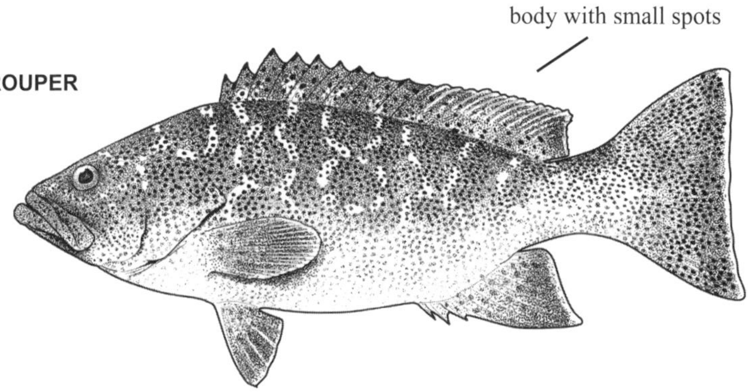


10b Body with large blotches or vermiculations; total gill rakers fewer than 33….. 11

11a Caudal fin soft-rays not exserted (not protruding); total gill rakers 21–26; soft dorsal fin rounded; anal fin margin angular (pointed in large adults, rounded in small juveniles):

**GULF GROUPER**

11b (next page)

## SEA BASSES, GROUPERS, TEMPERATE BASSES, and WRECKFISHES (continued)

**BROOMTAIL GROUPER, *Mycteroperca xenarcha* Jordan, 1888.** Family EPINEPHELIDAE
San Francisco, northern California to Callao, Peru, including Gulf of California and Islas Galápagos. Currently rare in California, but likely more common before overfishing. Common off southern Baja California and into tropics. Length to 150 cm (59 in) TL. Depth: intertidal to 70 m (230 ft). Brown, gray, or greenish, often with dark brown or gray-green vermiculations or blotches; often dark lines radiating from eye. Juveniles with dark saddle on top of caudal peduncle. D XI,15–16; A III,10–11; Pect. 16–18; GR 9–12 + 18–23 = 29–33; Vert. 24. (Formerly Serranidae: M&L).

**SPOTTED CABRILLA, *Epinephelus analogus* Gill, 1863.** Family EPINEPHELIDAE
San Pedro, southern California to Pucusana, Peru, including Gulf of California and Islas Galápagos. Rare in southern California; historically common from southern Baja California southward. Length to 114 cm (44.9 in) TL. Depth: less than 1 m (3 ft) to 107 m (353 ft). Reddish-brown with dark brown spots over body. D X,16–18; A III,8; Pect. 19–20; GR 8–10 + 15–18 = 26–28; Vert. 24. (Formerly Serranidae: M&L).

**HOOKTHROAT BASS, *Hemanthias signifer* (Garman, 1899).** Family SERRANIDAE
Playa del Rey, southern California to Talara, Peru, including Gulf of California. Rare in southern California. Length to 42 cm (16.5 in) TL. Depth: 23–305 m (75–1,000 ft). Red-orange with yellowish and dark speckling; fins tipped in orange-red or yellow. D X,13–14; A III,7–9; Pect. 18–21; Pelvic I,5; LLs 56–58; GR 9–11 + 23–27. (Formerly SPLITTAIL BASS, *Hemanthias peruanus* (Steindachner, 1875): M&L).

**GREATER SAND PERCH, *Diplectrum maximum* Hildebrand, 1946.** Family SERRANIDAE
Newport Beach, southern California to northern Peru, including Gulf of California. Rare in southern California; common from about Bahía Magdalena, southern Baja California to tropics. Length to 45 cm (17.7 in) TL. Depth: 1–130 m (3–426 ft). Back and upper sides dark gray-brown, white below; dark blue-gray blotch on upper operculum; dorsal fin with 3 bands: lowermost blue-gray, middle red-brown, upper blue-gray, with red-brown margin. D X,12; A III,7; Pect. 17; GR 6–6 + 13–14; LLs 48–50. (Alternative name TORPEDO SAND PERCH).

**DEEPWATER SERRANO, *Serranus aequidens* Gilbert, 1890.** Family SERRANIDAE
White Point, southern California to western Gulf of California; central Mexico to western Panama, including Isla Galápagos. Rare in southern California; common at least in the southern Gulf of California. Length to 24.5 cm (9.6 in) TL. Depth: 75–486 m (246–1,594 ft). Back and sides dusky-brown, tan, or gray, white below; operculum with dusky or dark blotch; 6–7 irregular dusky or dark saddles on body (last 1 on base of tail); spinous dorsal fin with yellowish margin, center of membrane between spines blackish; soft dorsal fin with blackish margin and blackish stripe along its base. D X,11–12; A III,7; Pect. 17–18; GR 16–17 (lower limb).

11b Caudal fin soft-rays exserted (protruding); total gill rakers 29–33; soft dorsal fin pointed; anal fin margin pointed (rounded in small juveniles):

**BROOMTAIL GROUPER**

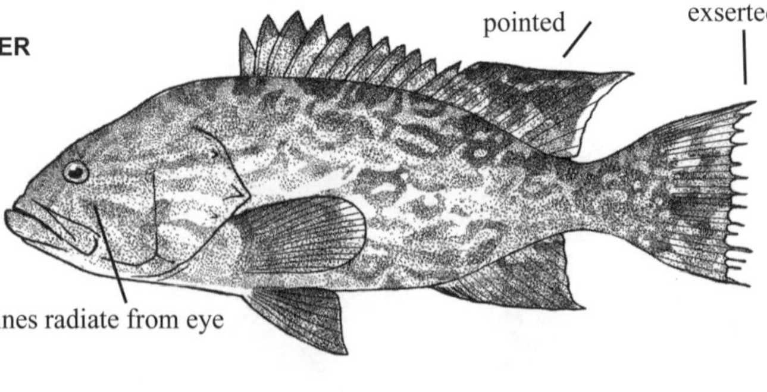


12a (next page)

12a *From 6a: dorsal fin with 10 spines*
Dorsal fin soft-rays 16–18; body covered with numerous dark spots:

**SPOTTED CABRILLA**

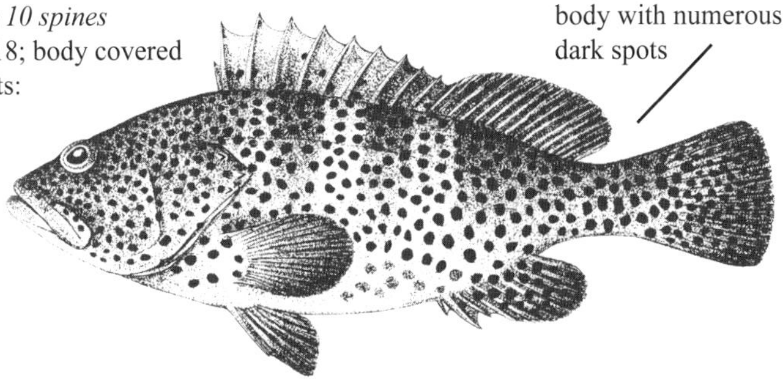


12b Dorsal fin soft-rays 15 or fewer; body not covered with numerous dark spots (except SPOTTED SAND BASS has black spots and GOLDSPOTTED SAND BASS has orange spots)….. 13

13a Third dorsal fin spine thread-like, over twice as long as other dorsal fin spines:

**HOOKTHROAT BASS**

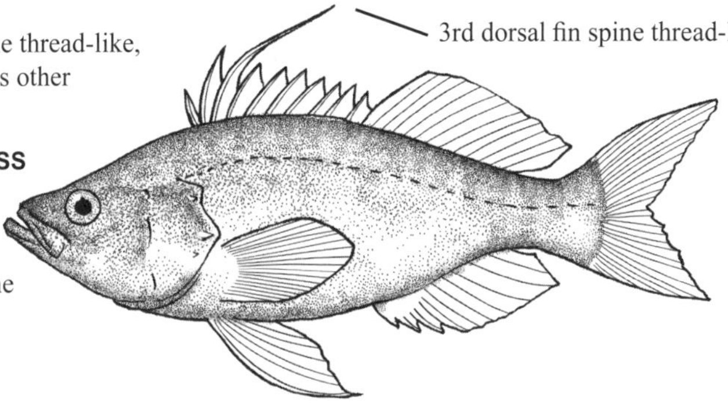


13b Third dorsal fin spine not as in 13a….. 14

14a Preopercle with bony flap armed with strong cluster of divergent spines:

**GREATER SAND PERCH**

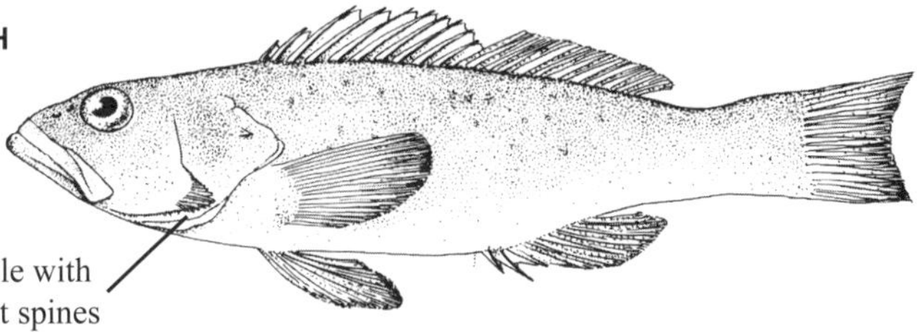


14b Preopercle without strong cluster of divergent spines….. 15

15a Operculum with dusky or dark blotch; spinous dorsal fin with yellowish margin, centers of membranes between spines blackish; soft dorsal fin with blackish margin and blackish stripe along base:

**DEEPWATER SERRANO**

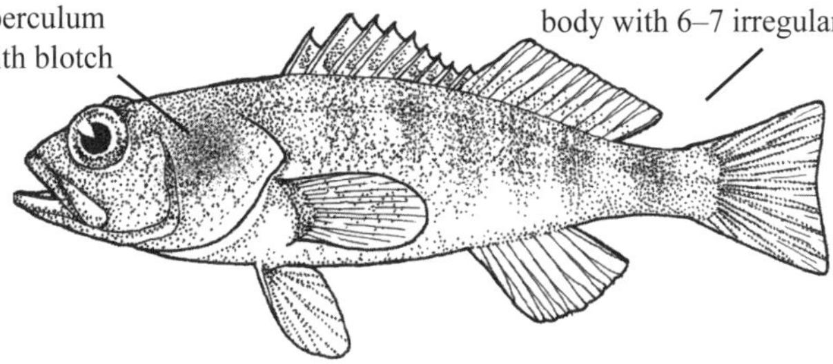


15b Operculum without dusky or dark blotch; dorsal fin not as in 15a….. 16 (next page)

# SEA BASSES, GROUPERS, TEMPERATE BASSES, and WRECKFISHES (continued)

**KELP BASS, *Paralabrax clathratus* (Girard, 1854).** Family SERRANIDAE
Columbia River, Washington to Todos Santos (23°25'N, 110°14'W), southern Baja California and Rocas Alijos, southern Baja California. Historically, common from Point Conception, California to at least Isla Asuncion, southern Baja California; common into central California during some warm-water intrusions. Length to 72.1 cm (28.4 in) TL. Depth: surface and surf zone to 61 m (200 ft); juveniles occasionally intertidal. Dark brown, gray-brown, green, or olive on back and sides; whitish angular blotches and spotting on back; ripe males with orange snouts. D X,13–14; A III,7–9; Pect. 14–16; Pelvic I,5; LLp 64–74; GR 11–13 + 20–24 = 32–36; Vert. 24–25. (Alternative name CALICO BASS).

**GOLDSPOTTED SAND BASS, *Paralabrax auroguttatus* Walford, 1936.** Family SERRANIDAE
One record from off Santa Barbara (34°21'N, 119°37'W), southern California; Islas Guadalupe (SIO 71-107) and just north of Punta Rosalia (28°40'N, 114°16'W) and Isla Cedros, central Baja California to Gulf of California and to central Mexico. Common from southern Baja California into Gulf of California. Length to 71 cm (28 in) TL. Depth: 2–183 m (5–600 ft). Body of adults profusely covered in large orange, red, or brown spots; head covered in smaller orange spots; back with 2–3 thin, light, yellow, or greenish stripes, with brightest stripe along lateral line; gill cavity orange. Juveniles light with 2–3 dark brown stripes and series of large brown or dark spots between stripes. D X,13–14; A III,7; Pect. 14–16; GR 6 + 17 (1st 3 on lower arch may be rudimentary); LLs 71–81. (Alternative name GOLDEN SPOTTED ROCK BASS).

**SPOTTED SAND BASS, *Paralabrax maculatofasciatus* (Steindachner, 1868).** Family SERRANIDAE
Monterey, central California to Acapulco, Mexico, including Gulf of California. Reported from San Francisco Bay in late 1800s. Common from Newport Bay, southern California to Gulf of California. Length to 38.1 cm (15 in) TL. Depth: surface and intertidal to 90 m (295 ft). Brown, green, olive, or white body with black spots and bars. Females often yellow-flushed, males often whiter. Juveniles with several dark stripes on sides and row of dots near belly. D X,13–15; A III,6–8; Pect. 14–17; Pelvic I,5; LLp 58–64; LLs 92–120; GR 6 + 13; Vert. 24.

**BARRED SAND BASS, *Paralabrax nebulifer* (Girard, 1854).** Family SERRANIDAE
Santa Cruz, central California to Todos Santos (23°23'N, 110°12'W), southern Baja California (SIO 08-11) and perhaps in La Paz area in Gulf of California and southern Mexico in region around Acapulco. Common from the Santa Barbara Channel, southern California to Bahía Magdalena, southern Baja California. Length to 65 cm (25.6 in) TL. Depth: surf zone to 183 m (600 ft). Dark gray and greenish; faint crossbars on sides, bars fading after death; freckles on snout. D X,13–15; A III,7–9; Pect. 17–18; Pelvic I,5; LLs 71–76; GR 8–9 + 14–18 = 22–27; Vert. 24.

NOTE: We suggest that the common name "SAND BASS" for 3 of the *Paralabrax* species is a misnomer as all of these species, to a greater or lesser degree, inhabit rocky sea floors. More appropriate would be the name "ROCK BASS" along with modifiers.

16a Third dorsal fin spine about same length as 4th and 5th dorsal fin spines:

**KELP BASS**

juvenile

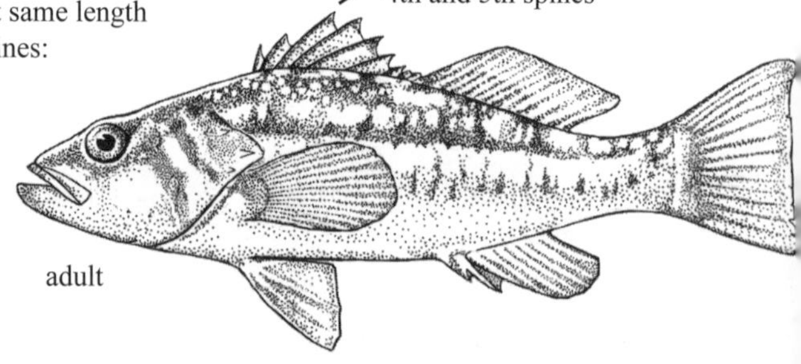


adult

16b (next page)

16b Third dorsal fin spine much longer than 4th and 5th dorsal fin spines….. 17

17a Distinctive orange spots on body and head; 2–3 white stripes on back:

**GOLDSPOTTED SAND BASS**

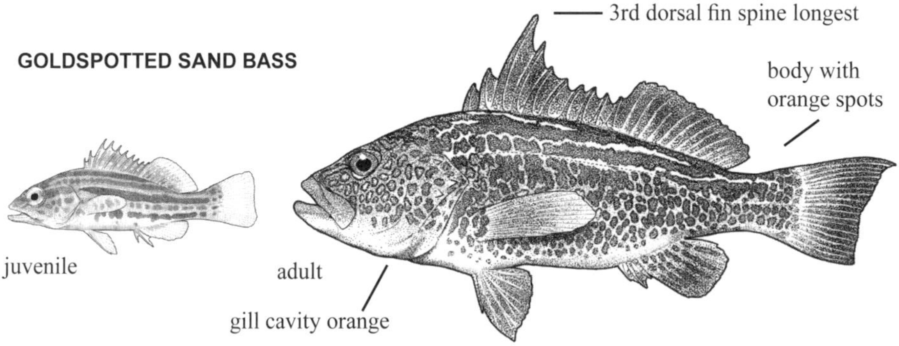


17b Black spots on body or head; no white stripes on back….. 18

18a Body covered with black spotting, especially around base of pectoral fin; distinct uniform bars on body; in juveniles and young adults, stripe from orbit to isthmus often diffuse, broken or absent:

**SPOTTED SAND BASS**

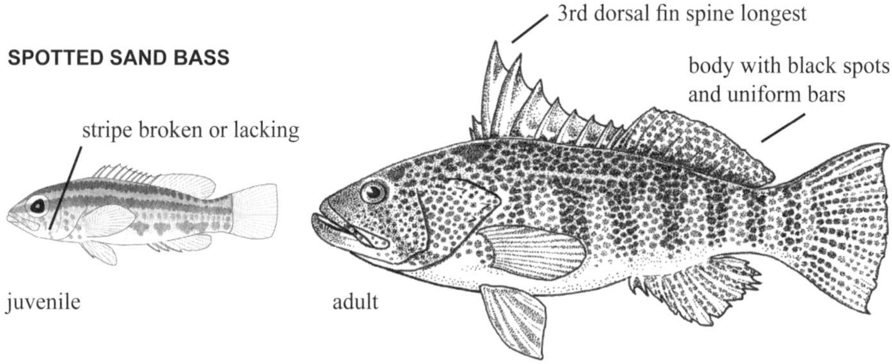


18b Body with minimal black spotting; irregular bars on body; in juveniles and young adults, stripe from orbit to isthmus solid:

**BARRED SAND BASS**

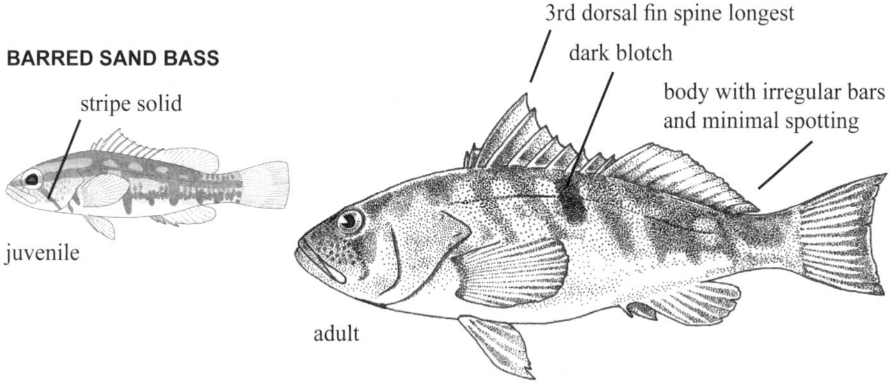

## BASSLETS, Family Acropomatidae, BIGEYES, Family Priacanthidae, and JAWFISH, Family Opistognathidae

NOTE: Prokofiev (2007) proposed placing the genus *Howella* in the family Howellidae. As noted by Busby and Orr (1999), the taxonomy of the two eastern Pacific species of BASSLET, *Howella sherboni* and *Howella brodiei*, is confused and needs further investigation.

**SHORTSPINE BASSLET, *Howella sherborni* (Norman, 1930).** Family ACROPOMATIDAE
Circumglobal; North Pacific Ocean south of Krenitzin Islands, Aleutian Islands to Chile. Common at least well off southern California. Length to 11 cm (4.3 in) SL. Pelagic; depth: surface to about 2,700 m (8,858 ft). Dark brown or black. D VII–VIII + I,8–10; A III,7–8; Pect. 14–17; Pelvic I,5; LLs 35–41; GR 7–9 + 19–23 = 28–33; Vert. 25–26.

**PELAGIC BASSLET, *Howella brodiei* Ogilby, 1899.** Family ACROPOMATIDAE
Pacific and Atlantic Oceans; Oregon (44°04'N, 124°57'W) (UW 41683) to Chile. Length to 10.2 cm (4 in) SL. Mesopelagic; depth: 30–1,829 m (100–6,000 ft) or more. Black. D VI–VIII + I,9; A III,6–7; Pect. 14–15; Pelvic I,5; GR 4–8 + 14–22.

**PACIFIC GLASSEYE, *Heteropriacanthus carolinus* (Cuvier, 1829).** Family PRIACANTHIDAE
Indo-Pacific; Santa Catalina Island; Isla Guadalupe, central Baja California to perhaps Chile, and at least around Isla Cerralvo, Gulf of California and Islas Galápagos. Rare off California; common in tropics. Length to 51 cm (20 in) TL. Depth: 5–300 m (16–984 ft). Body bright red; black dots on posterior of dorsal, anal, and caudal fins. After capture, some specimens with light and dark blotches on sides. D X,13; A III,13–14; Pect. 17–19; Pelvic I,5; GRt 21–25; Vert. 23. Previously *Heteropriacanthus cruentatus* (Lacepède, 1801).

**POPEYE CATALUFA, *Pristigenys serrula* (Gilbert, 1891).** Family PRIACANTHIDAE
Newport, central Oregon to Chile, including Gulf of California and Islas Galápagos. Occasional off southern California, rare further north; apparently common in tropical waters. Length to 35 cm (13.8 in) TL. Depth: less than 3 m to more than 250 m (10–820 ft). Body uniform crimson-red to orange; soft-dorsal, caudal, and anal fins sometimes bordered in black. D X,10–12; A III,10–11; Pect. 17–18; Pelvic I,5; LLp 36; LLs 37; GR 6–8 + 15–18; Vert. 23. (Formerly *Pseudopriacanthus serrula* (Gilbert, 1891): M&L).

**UNIDENTIFIED JAWFISH.** Family OPISTOGNATHIDAE
Lissner and Dorsey (1986) observed an unidentified jawfish at Cortes or Tanner Bank, southern California, from a manned submersible. Based on geographic ranges of eastern Pacific jawfishes, the species was most likely the GIANT JAWFISH, *Opistognathus rhomaleus* Jordan & Gilbert, 1882. Here we present relevant data from the GIANT JAWFISH: Bahía Ballenas, southern Baja California into northern Gulf of California to west Panama and Islas Revillagigedo. Length to more than 50.8 cm (20.3 in) TL. Depth: 3–61 m (10–200 ft). Gray with many small black spots on head and upper back. Juveniles with 5–6 large dark blotches at base of dorsal fin and along sides. D XI,12–14; A II,13; Pect. 20–21.

**SHORTSPINE BASSLET**

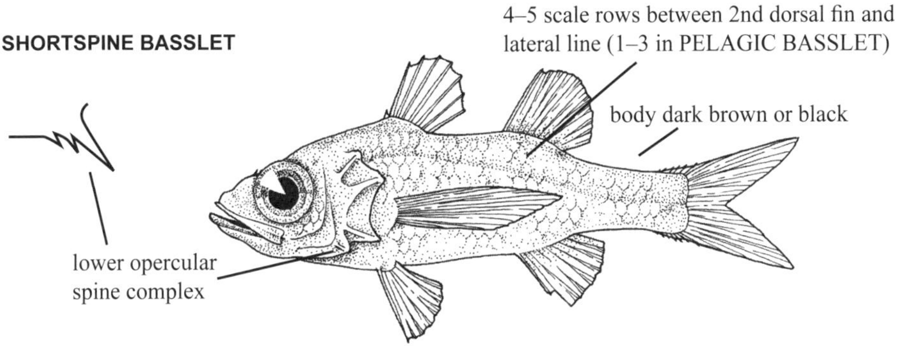


**PELAGIC BASSLET**
(same body form as above)

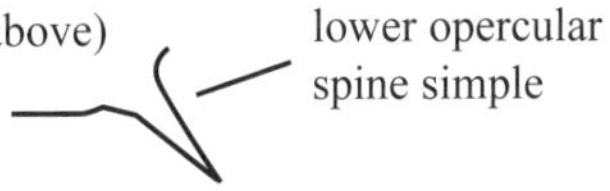


**PACIFIC GLASSEYE**

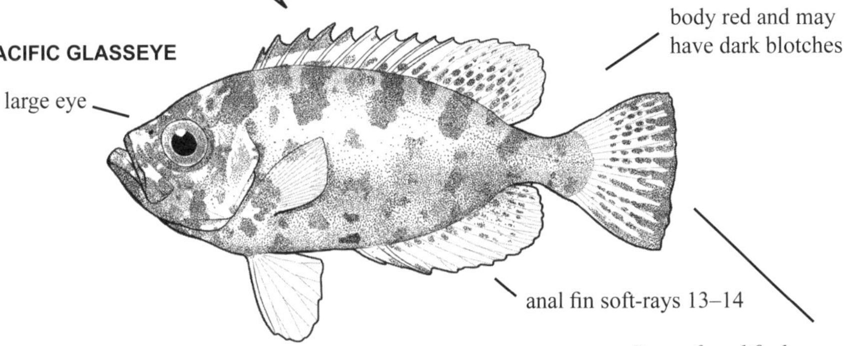


*Base of anal fin longer than base of soft dorsal fin on these 2*

**POPEYE CATALUFA**

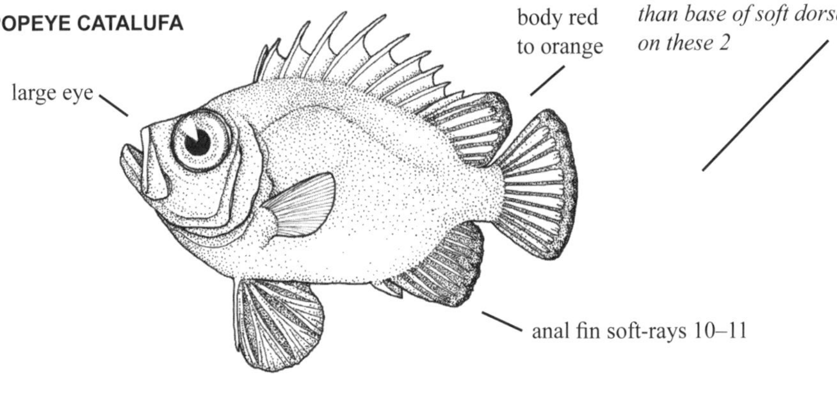


**UNIDENTIFIED JAWFISH**
(based on GIANT JAWFISH)

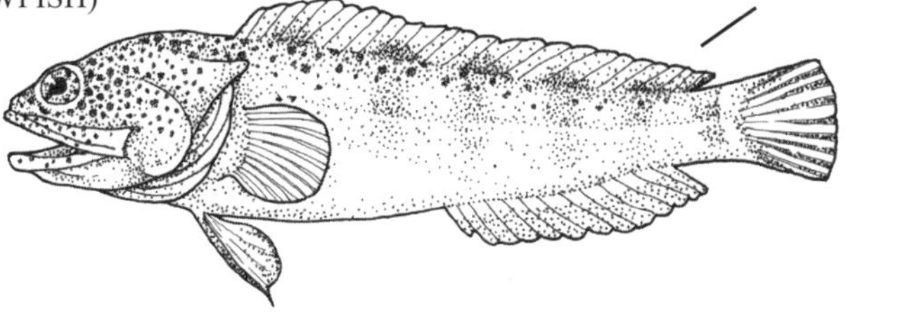

## TILEFISHES, Family Malacanthidae

**PACIFIC GOLDEN-EYED TILEFISH, *Caulolatilus affinis* Gill, 1865.** Off Mussel Shoals (34°21'N, 119°27'W) and Anacapa Island, southern California to Isla Guadalupe (SIO 84-241) and southern tip of Baja California to Isla Lobos de Tierra, Peru, including Islas Galápagos and Gulf of California. While usually rare in southern California waters, Walker et al. (2002) report that over 100 of these fish were taken by sport fishermen off Point Loma, southern California, during the winter of 2000–2001; common in tropics. Length to 60 cm (23.6 in) TL. Depth: 30–230 m (98–756 ft). Blue-gray to olive-green on back, silver sides, and belly; newly captured fish have lavender scale margin; yellow stripe below and in front of eye; dark patch at top of pectoral fin insertion. D VII–IX,22–25; A I–II,21–24; Pect. 18–19; LLs 80–91; GRt 22. (Alternative name BIGHEAD TILEFISH).

**OCEAN WHITEFISH, *Caulolatilus princeps* (Jenyns, 1840).** Vancouver Island, British Columbia to Chile, including Gulf of California and Islas Galápagos. Uncommon off central California; common from southern California southward into tropics. Length to 102 cm (40 in) TL. Depth: surface and 3–189 m (10–620 ft). Yellowish-brown above, sometimes with blue overtones, paler below; fins often yellow, often with blue striping. DVII–X,23–27; A I–II,20–26; Pect. 18–20; Pelvic I,5; LLs 116–134; GR 6–10 + 12–15; Vert. 27. *Caulolatilus hubbsi* Dooley, 1978 is a junior synonym. (Formerly Branchiostegidae: M&L).

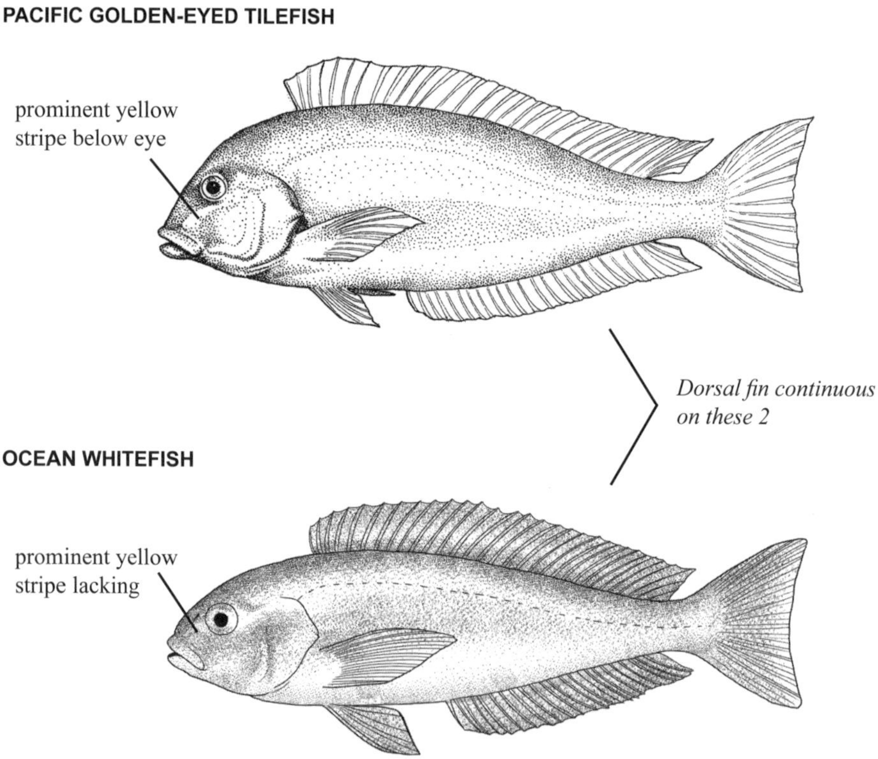

# REMORAS, Family Echeneidae

**SLENDER SUCKERFISH, *Phtheirichthys lineatus* (Menzies, 1791).** Circumglobal; southern California to northern Peru, including Gulf of California and Islas Galápagos. Rare off southern California; common in tropics. Length to 76 cm (29.9 in) TL. Oceanic, pelagic; depth: surface to perhaps 100 m (328 ft). May be free living or attached to turtles and fishes. Blackish with 2 white lateral bands; all fins with white margin. D laminae 9–11, soft-rays 26–40; A 29–38; Pect. 17–21; GR 1 + 10–11; Vert. 39–41.

**SHARKSUCKER, *Echeneis naucrates* Linnaeus, 1758.** Circumglobal; Sea of Japan, off northern Hokkaido, possibly as far north as southern Kuril Islands, Russia; southern California to Chile, including Gulf of California and Islas Galápagos. Rare in southern California; common in tropical waters. Length to 110 cm (43.3 in) TL. Pelagic; depth: surface to 135 m (443 ft). Most often attached to sharks, sometimes billfishes, occasionally free living. Dark gray to brown; black or brown stripe in midbody bordered by white; dark caudal fin partially bordered in white. D laminae 20–28, soft-rays 31–42; A 30–41; Pect. 21–24; GR 11–16 (lower limb).

## KEY TO THE REMORAS:
Edited by Julianne Kalman Passarelli
(Principal source: Miller & Lea, 1972)

NOTE: The disc is a modified 1st dorsal fin, the spines appearing as rough cross structures referred to as laminae.

1a Disc laminae 9–11:

**SLENDER SUCKERFISH**

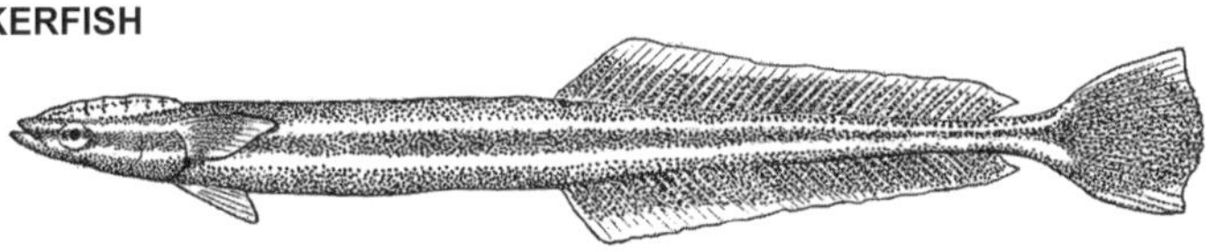

1b Disc laminae 12 or more….. 2

2a Sides with longitudinal black stripe in midbody bordered with white; anal fin soft-rays 30–41:

**SHARKSUCKER**

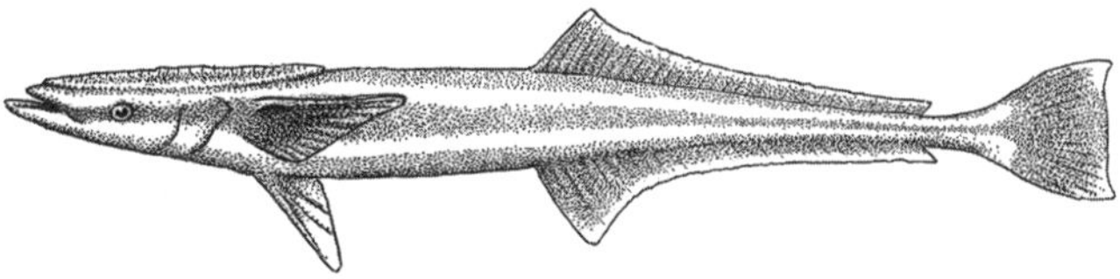

2b Sides without black stripe bordered with white; anal fin soft-rays fewer than 27
(except SPEARFISH REMORA has fewer than 35)….. 3 (next page)

## REMORAS (continued)

**WHALESUCKER, *Remora australis* (Bennett, 1840).** Circumglobal; British Columbia to Chile, including Islas Galápagos. Rare off west coast of North America; common in tropics. Length to 76.2 cm (30 in) TL. Pelagic; depth: surface to perhaps 200 m (656 ft). Light gray to blue, violet, brown, and nearly black; usually with white edging on fins. Often attaches to marine mammals. D laminae 24–28, soft-rays 20–27; A 20–26; Pect. 21–24; GR 1–3 + 13–19 = 14–21; Vert. 27. (Formerly *Remilegia australis* (Bennett, 1840): M&L).

**WHITE SUCKERFISH, *Remora albescens* (Temminck & Schlegel, 1850).** Circumglobal; San Francisco, northern California to Chile, including central and southern Gulf of California and Islas Galápagos. Rare off California; common in tropics. Length to 35 cm (13.8 in) TL. Pelagic; depth: surface to perhaps 50 m (164 ft). Attaches mostly to mantas, sharks, and sometimes billfishes. Uniform grayish to nearly white. D laminae 12–14, soft-rays 15–23; A 16–26; Pect. 16–21; GR 10 (lower limb); Vert. 26. (Formerly *Remorina albescens* (Temminck & Schlegel, 1850): M&L).

**MARLINSUCKER, *Remora osteochir* (Cuvier, 1829).** Circumglobal; Santa Catalina Island, southern California to northern Chile, including central and southern Gulf of California. Uncommon off southern California; more common southwards. Length to 40 cm (15.7 in) TL. Depth: surface to perhaps 200 m (656 ft). Most often attaches to billfishes. Uniform brown. D laminae 15–20, soft-rays 20–27; A 20–26; Pect. 20–24; Vert. 27. (Formerly HARDFIN MARLINSUCKER, *Rhombochirus osteochir* (Cuvier, 1829): M&L).

**SPEARFISH REMORA, *Remora brachyptera* (Lowe, 1839).** Circumglobal; in western Pacific as far north as southern Kuril Islands, Russia; San Diego County (32°50'N, 117°17'W), southern California (SIO 59-353) to Chile, including Gulf of California and Islas Galápagos. Length to 50 cm (19.7 in) TL. Pelagic; depth: surface to perhaps 200 m (656 ft). Commonly found attached to STRIPED MARLIN in southern California. Most often attaches to billfishes and OCEAN SUNFISH, occasionally sharks. Light brown to gray above, darker below. D laminae 14–18, soft-rays 26–34; GR at least 1–3 + 9–12; A 22–34; Pect. 23–28; Vert. 27. (Formerly GRAY MARLINSUCKER: M&L)

**REMORA, *Remora remora* (Linnaeus, 1758).** Circumglobal; in western Pacific as far north as southern Kuril Islands, Russia; in eastern Pacific from Washington to Chile, including central and southern Gulf of California and Islas Galápagos. Common from about central California southward into tropics. Length to 86.4 cm (34 in) TL. Pelagic; depth: surface to 100 m (328 ft) and perhaps to 200 m (656 ft). Attaches primarily to mantas and sharks. Uniform black or dark brown. D laminae 16–22, soft-rays 20–27; A 20–25; Pect. 25–32; GR 4–6 + 24–28 = 29–34; Vert. 27.

3a Disc laminae 24–28:

**WHALESUCKER**

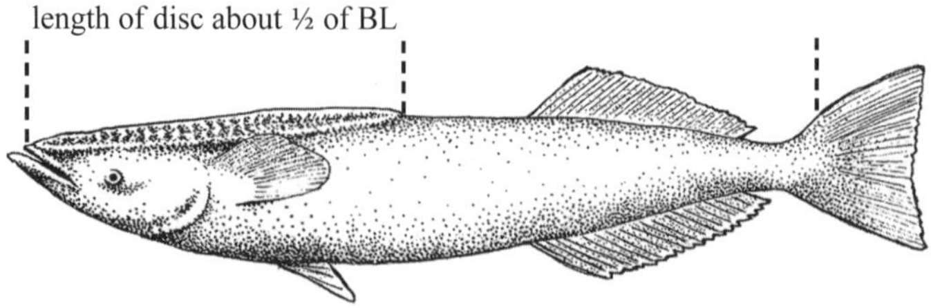


3b Disc laminae 22 or fewer….. 4 (next page)

4a Width of disc into length of disc less than 1.6; disc laminae 12–14:

**WHITE SUCKERFISH**

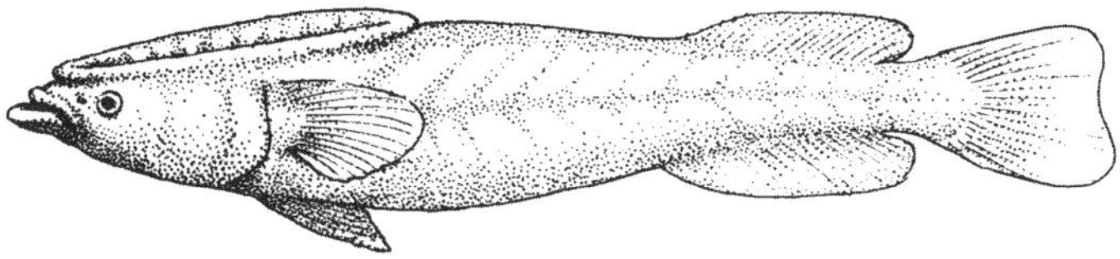

4b Width of disc into length of disc at least 1.8; disc laminae 14–22….. 5

5a Disc extending well beyond end of depressed pectoral fin:

**MARLINSUCKER**

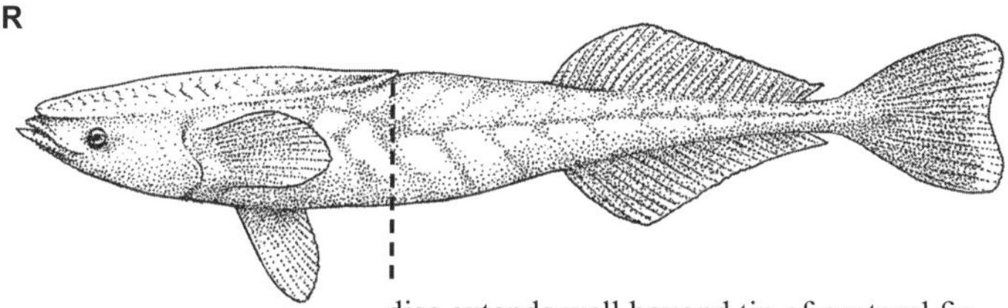


5b Disc not extending beyond end of depressed pectoral fin….. 6

6a Disc laminae 14–18; total gill rakers on 1st arch fewer than 21; dorsal fin soft-rays 26–34 (rarely under 28):

**SPEARFISH REMORA**

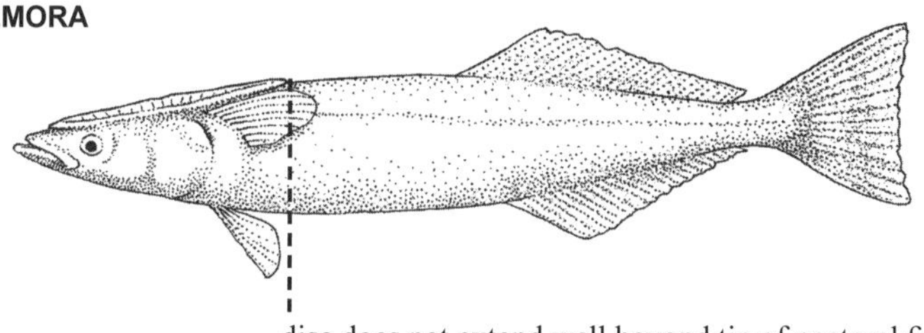


6b Disc laminae 16–22; total gill rakers on 1st arch 29–34; dorsal fin soft-rays 20–27:

**REMORA**

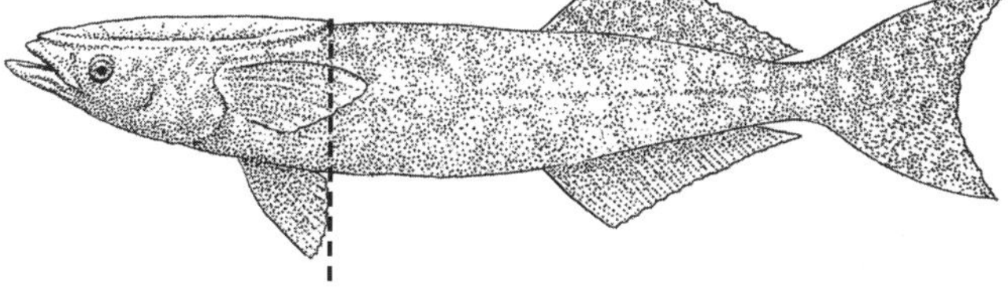

# CARDINALFISHES, Family Apogonidae

NOTE: With the exception of *Apogon guadalupensis*, cardinalfishes tend to be rare off southern California. However, some El Niños bring larvae into these waters, and juveniles and adults become temporarily common at specific locations.

**GUADALUPE CARDINALFISH, *Apogon guadalupensis* (Osburn & Nichols, 1916).** Anacapa Island and Santa Barbara Island, southern California to tip of Baja California and Islas Revillagigedo. Common in southern California during some years and common around Isla Guadalupe, Islas San Benito, and Rocas Alijos. Length to about 13 cm (5 in) TL. Depth: 10–30 m (33–98 ft). Body color somewhat variable: often red or orange, sometimes with yellow head, breast, and belly; posterior of body and median fins may be lavender or purplish. D V + I,9–10; A II,8; Pect. 11–12; Pelvic I,5; LLs 26; GR 5 + 13; Vert. 24. This species may be a synonym of *Apogon atricaudus* Jordan & McGregor, 1898.

**PLAIN CARDINALFISH, *Apogon atricaudus* Jordan & McGregor, 1898.** Anacapa and San Clemente Islands (SIO 96-93), southern California and Isla Guadalupe, central Baja California (SIO 50-40) to Gulf of California and central Mexico and islands of eastern Pacific. Usually rare in southern California; common in tropical waters. Length to 9 cm (3.5 in) TL. Depth: 3–50 m (10–165 ft). Head and belly yellow-orange or red-orange, rest of body lavender or bluish-red; dark streak on 1st dorsal fin. D VI + I,9; A II,8; Pect. 11–12; Pelvic I,5; GR 5 + 13; Vert. 24.

**BARSPOT CARDINALFISH, *Apogon retrosella* (Gill, 1862).** La Jolla, southern California; Islas San Benito, Isla Cedros, Isla Natividad, and Rocas Chester, central Baja California to Colombia, including Gulf of California. Rare in southern California; common from central Baja California into tropics. Length to 10.2 cm (4.1 in) TL. Depth: tide pools to 61 m (200 ft). Reddish-pink to red; black bar below 2nd dorsal fin; black spot on caudal fin base (diffuse in newly settled juveniles); black stripe bordered in white from snout through eye (absent in newly settled juveniles). D VI + I,9–10; A II,7–8; Pect. 11–12; GR 4–5 + 11–13; Vert. 24.

**PINK CARDINALFISH, *Apogon pacificus* (Herre, 1935).** San Clemente and Santa Catalina Islands, southern California and mainland off Arrecife Sacramento (29°40'N, 115°47'W), central Baja California to Cabo San Lucas, southern Baja California to Pucusana, Peru, including Gulf of California, Islas San Benito, and Islas Galápagos. Usually rare off southern California; common from about Islas San Benito into tropics. Length to 10 cm (3.9 in) TL. Depth: 1–96 m (3–315 ft). Pink to red; head, breast, and belly yellowish; black bar below 2nd dorsal fin; black stripe bordered in yellow from snout through eye. D VI + I,9; A II,8; Pect. 11–12; LLs 24–26; Vert. 24.

## KEY TO THE CARDINALFISHES:
Created by Milton S. Love

1a No bar and/or spot on body and no dark streak on 1st dorsal fin:

**GUADALUPE CARDINALFISH**

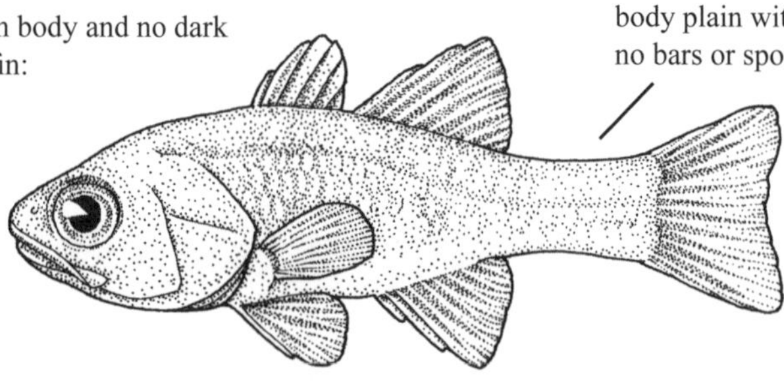


1b Either bar and/or spot on body or dark streak on 1st dorsal fin…. 2 (next page)

2a Dark streak on middle of 1st dorsal fin; no bar or spot on body:

**PLAIN CARDINALFISH**

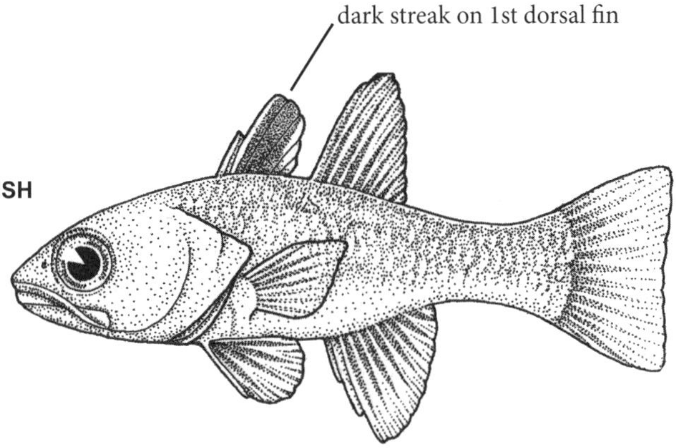


2b No dark streak on middle of 1st dorsal fin; bar and/or spot present on body…… 3

3a Large dark spot at base of caudal fin; black bar below 2nd dorsal fin:

**BARSPOT CARDINALFISH**

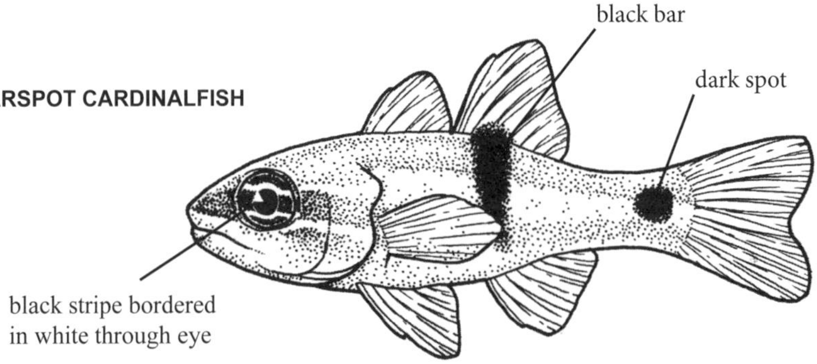


3b No large dark spot at base of caudal fin; black bar below 2nd dorsal fin:

**PINK CARDINALFISH**

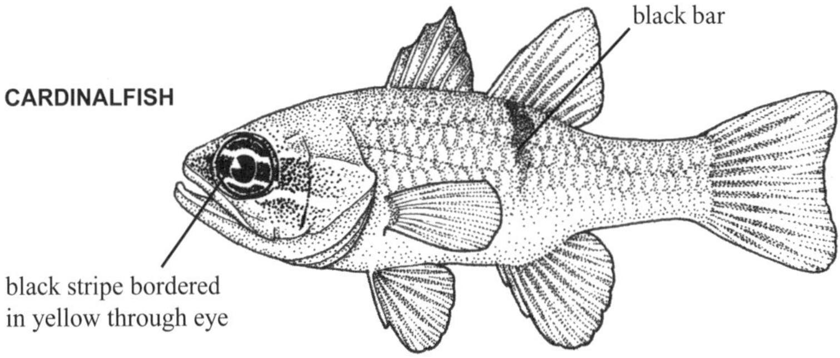

## JACKS, Family Carangidae

NOTE: A number of these jacks respond to El Niño conditions by moving northwards into California waters. The LEATHERJACKET (*Oligoplites saurus* Bloch & Schneider, 1801) has been removed because the southern California record in M&L was in error.

**PACIFIC MOONFISH, *Selene peruviana* (Guichenot, 1866).** Long Beach, southern California to Chile, including Gulf of California and Islas Galápagos. Rare in southern California; common in tropics. Length to 35 cm (13.8 in) TL. Inshore and shallow coastal waters; depth: near surface to 450 m (1,476 ft). Bluish or green above, sides silvery; often with black spot on upper angle of operculum. Juveniles with black spot mid-flank. D VIII + I,20–24; A II + I,16–19; LL scutes nearly obsolete; GR 8 + 28–32; Vert. 24. (Formerly *Vomer declivifrons* Meek & Hildebrand, 1925: M&L).

**MEXICAN LOOKDOWN, *Selene brevoortii* (Gill, 1863).** Seal Beach, southern California to northern Chile, including Gulf of California. Rare in southern California; common in tropics. Length to 42 cm (16.5 in) TL. Coastal waters, including bays and estuaries; depth: to 50 m (164 ft). Silvery, with bluish overtones; steeply angled head. First few dorsal fin spines long and filamentous in juveniles. D VII–VIII + I,20–24; A II + I,17–19; Pect. 18–19; GR 5–9 + 28–34; Vert. 24.

**PACIFIC BUMPER, *Chloroscombrus orqueta* Jordan & Gilbert, 1883.** San Pedro, southern California to Chilca, Peru, including Gulf of California and Isla Malpelo. Rare in southern California; common from southern Baja California into tropics. Length to 31 cm (12.2 in) SL. Shallow coastal waters and estuaries; depth: surface 2–53 m (5–174 ft). Dark blue, sometimes brownish above, silvery below; black spot on operculum, and black saddle on upper part of caudal fin base. D VII–VIII + I,26–30; A II + I,25–30; Pect. 19–21; Pelvic I,5; LL scutes nearly obsolete, fewer than 20; GR 8–10 + 30–37; Vert. 24.

**JACK MACKEREL, *Trachurus symmetricus* (Ayres, 1855).** Pacific Ocean south of Aleutian Islands and in Gulf of Alaska to Gulf of California and to Acapulco, Mexico. Common along the Pacific Coast between about Vancouver Island and southern Baja California. Length to 81.3 cm (32 in) TL. Primarily pelagic; depth: surf zone and surface to 403 m (1,320 ft). Metallic blue to olive-green above, silvery below; dark spot on upper gill cover. D VIII + I,28–38; A II + I,22–33; Pect. 21–24; Pelvic I,5; LLs 87–111, the latter 40–55 as enlarged scutes; GR 7–15 + 25–42 = 32–57; Vert. 23–25.

## KEY TO THE JACKS:
Revised by Dario W. Diehl
(Principal source: Fischer et al., 1995)

1a Head profile not strongly oblique; no embedded scales; body moderately compressed in adults….. 3 (next page)

1b Head profile strongly oblique; very small, embedded scales, leading to apparently naked body; body highly compressed in adults….. 2

2a Oblique head profile with slight concavity in front of eyes; juveniles with black spot above lateral line:

**PACIFIC MOONFISH**

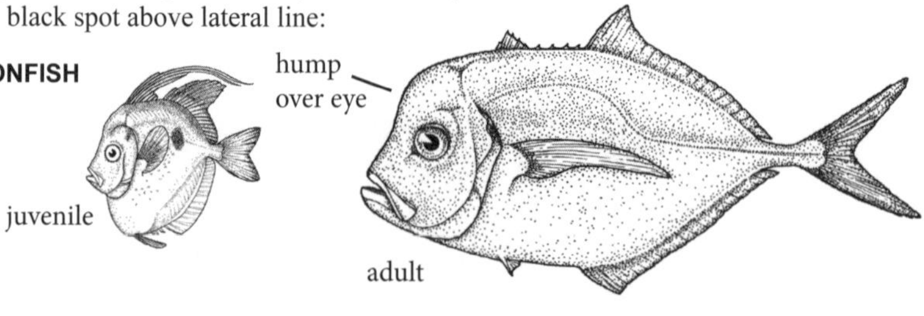


2b (next page)

2b Oblique head profile nearly straight in front of eyes;
juveniles with 4–5 interrupted dark bars on body:

**MEXICAN LOOKDOWN**

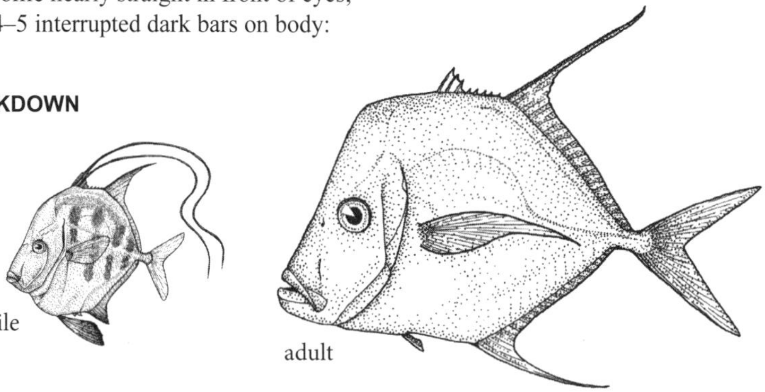


3a *From 1a: head profile not strongly oblique*
Posterior part of lateral line without scutes (pored scales only, not enlarged)….. 12 (page 240)

3b Posterior part of lateral line with hardened scutes or bony shields (may be poorly developed)….. 4

4a Lateral line with barely perceptible scutes; black saddle on upper region of caudal peduncle;
body moderately compressed:

**PACIFIC BUMPER**

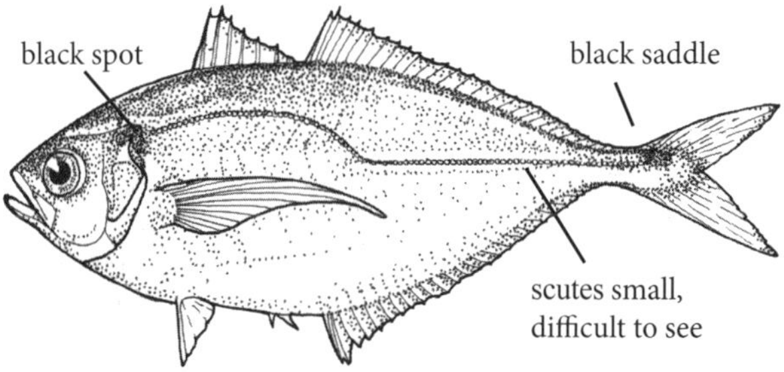


4b Lateral line with well-developed scutes; caudal peduncle without black saddle;
body not moderately compressed….. 5

5a Accessory dorsal branch (ADB) of lateral line extends beyond origin of 1st dorsal fin:

**JACK MACKEREL**

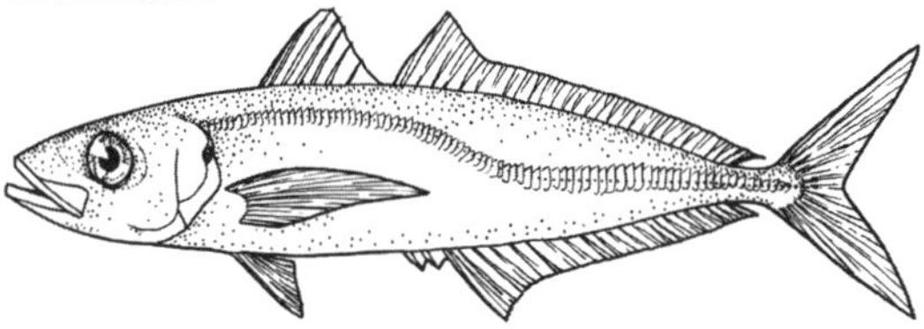

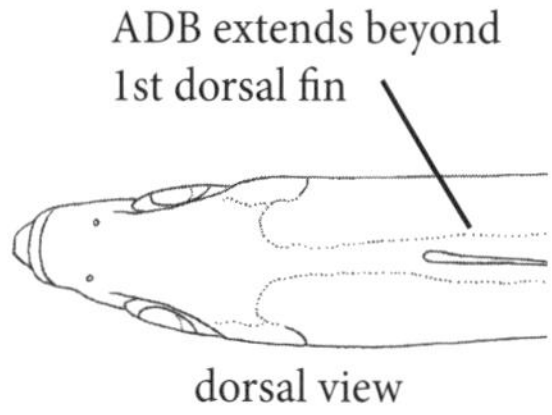


5b ADB terminating before origin of 1st dorsal fin….. 6 (next page)

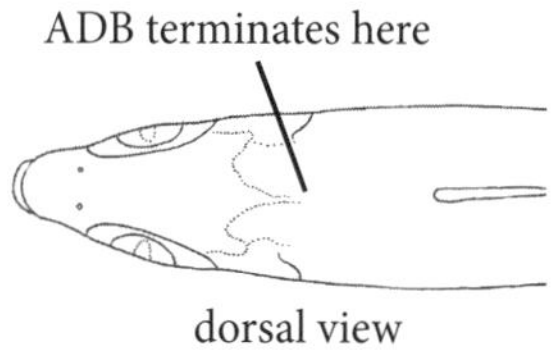

## JACKS (continued)

**AMBERSTRIPE SCAD, *Decapterus muroadsi* (Temminck & Schlegel, 1844).** Warm waters of Pacific; Japan to East China Sea; Pacific Grove, central California to Peru, Easter Island, and Islas Galápagos; apparently not in Gulf of California. Uncommon in California; common from Isla Guadalupe, central Baja California southward into tropics. Length to about 55 cm (21.7 in) TL. Depth: surface to 320 m (1,050 ft). Dark to light green or blue above, silvery below; often with yellow stripe along side; small black spot on upper angle of operculum. D VII–VIII + I,29–33 + finlet; A II + I,25–29 + finlet; Pect. 22–23; LL enlarged scutes about 30; GR 13–16 + 37–42; Vert. 24. (Formerly MEXICAN SCAD: M&L). (Includes *Decapterus hypodus* Gill, 1862 (M&L) and *Decapterus scombrinus* (Valenciennes, 1846) as junior synonyms.)

**BIGEYE SCAD, *Selar crumenophthalmus* (Bloch, 1793).** Circumglobal; Pacific coast of southern Japan and Sea of Japan; Palos Verdes Peninsula, southern California to Cabo Blanco, Peru, including Gulf of California, Islas Galápagos, and other offshore islands. Rare in southern California; common in tropics. Maximum length variously listed as 30 cm (11.8 in) or 70 cm (27.6 in) TL. Coastal waters; depth: surface to 170 m (558 ft). Metallic blue to bluish green above, shading to white below; yellow stripe sometimes present from margin of operculum to upper part of caudal fin base. D VIII + I,23–28; A II + I,20–23; Pect. 19–23; GR 9–12 + 24–37; Vert. 24.

**COTTONMOUTH JACK, *Uraspis helvola* (Forster, 1801).** Indo-Pacific; perhaps southern Kuril Islands, Russia and southern Japan; Santa Catalina Island, southern California to Ecuador, including Islas Galápagos. Rare in southern California; common in tropics. Length to 58 cm (22.8 in) TL. Benthopelagic; depth: 10–300 m (33–984 ft). Dusky, sometimes with 6 dark bars alternating with narrow spaces; tongue, roof, and floor of mouth bright white. D V–VIII + I,25–30; A II + I,19–22; Pect. I,22; LL with 32–38 keeled scutes; GR 6 + 16 = 22. (Formerly *Uraspis secunda* (Poey, 1860): M&L) (Alternative names WHITEMOUTH JACK, WHITETONGUE JACK). The Santa Catalina Island specimen was originally identified as *Uraspis secunda*, which is an Atlantic and Indo-Central Pacific species.

**PACIFIC CREVALLE JACK, *Caranx caninus* Günther, 1867.** Warm waters of eastern Pacific; Huntington Beach, southern California to Iquique, northern Chile, including Gulf of California, Islas Galápagos, and other offshore islands. Rare in southern California; common in tropics. Length to 100 cm (39.4 in) TL. Depth: surface, and less than 1 m (3 ft) (SIO 64-106) to 350 m (1,148 ft). Bluish, bluish-black, or greenish-blue on back, silvery or yellowish below; black spot on gill cover; black blotch on lower corner of pectoral fin; anal and caudal fins yellowish. Juveniles with dark bars on sides. D VII–VIII + I,18–23; A II+I,15–18; Pect. I,18–21; LL scutes 25–42; GR 15–19 (lower limb); Vert. 24. CREVALLE JACK, *Caranx hippos* (Linnaeus, 1766) (M&L) is considered a separate Atlantic and Caribbean species.

6a Finlets present:

**AMBERSTRIPE SCAD**

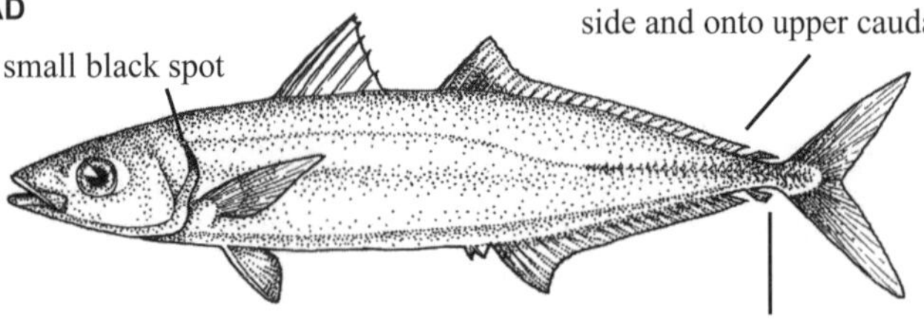


6b Finlets absent….. 7 (next page)

7a Cleithrum (under operculum) with large papilla-like structure; eye nearly covered by adipose eyelid, forming vertical slit on center of pupil:

**BIGEYE SCAD**

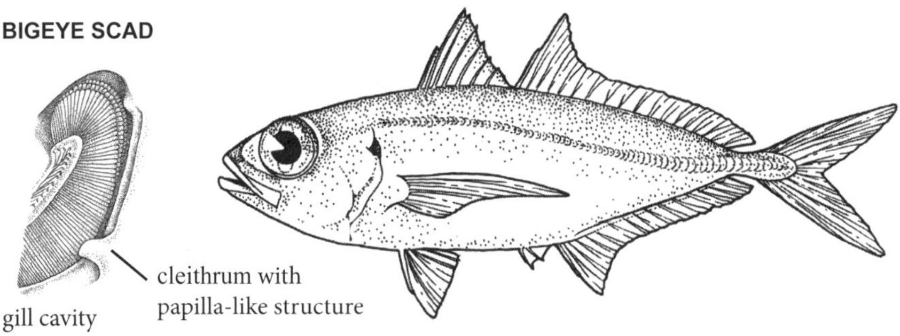


7b Cleithrum with smooth-edge; adipose eyelid marginally covering eye but not pupil….. 8

8a Inside of mouth mostly white; no teeth on vomer or palatines:

**COTTONMOUTH JACK**

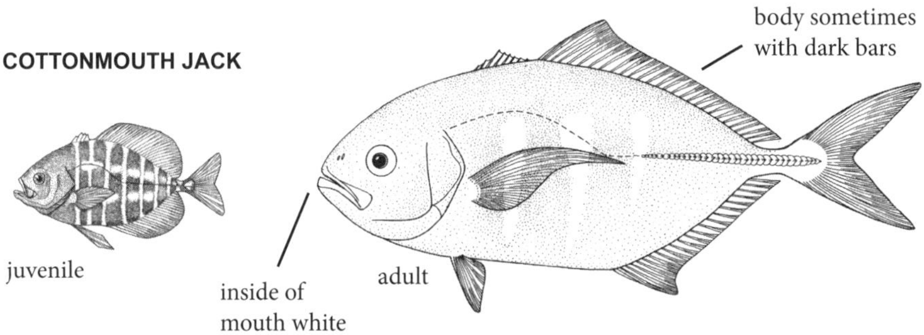


8b Mouth cavity not distinctly white; teeth present on vomer and palatines….. 9

9a Breast without scales except for small patch of scales at base of pelvic fins:

**PACIFIC CREVALLE JACK**

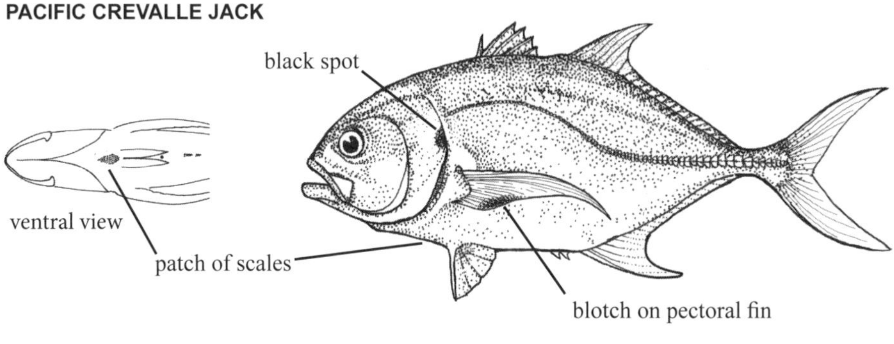


9b Breast completely scaled….. 10 (next page)

## JACKS (continued)

**BIGEYE TREVALLY, *Caranx sexfasciatus* Quoy & Gaimard, 1825.** Pacific and Indian Oceans; southern Japan; San Diego Bay, southern California to northern Peru, including lower Gulf of California and Islas Galápagos. Rare in southern California; common in tropics. Length to 120 cm (47.2 in) TL. Depth: 1–96 m (3–315 ft). Juveniles in estuaries and fresh water. Iridescent blue or blue-green on back, sides and belly silvery; black blotch on rear edge of gill cover; lateral line scutes yellowish to black. Juveniles brassy-yellow with 5–6 dark bars. D VII–VIII + I,19–22; A II + I,14–17; Pect. 18–21; Pelvic I,5; GR 4–8 + 15–19; Vert. 25. (Alternative name BIGEYE CREVALLE).

**GREEN JACK, *Caranx caballus* Günther, 1868.** Monterey Bay, central California to Chile, including Gulf of California, Islas Galápagos, and Hawai'i. Uncommon in California; common in tropics. Length to at least 70 cm (27.6 in) TL. Depth: surface, and surf zone to 100 m (328 ft). Olive to blue-green above, silvery below; black blotch on rear edge of gill cover. D VIII + I,21–25; A II + I,17–24; Pect. 20; LL scutes 45–56; GR 13–16 + 25–32; Vert. 25.

**COCINERO, *Caranx vinctus* Jordan & Gilbert, 1882.** San Diego Bay, southern California to Tumbes, Peru, including central and southern Gulf of California. Rare in California; common in tropics. Length to 41.2 cm (16.2 in) TL. Depth: surface 4–50 m (12–164 ft). Dusky-bluish or gray above, silvery, golden, or greenish on sides; 8–9 incomplete darkish bars; black blotch on rear edge of gill cover; anal and caudal fins yellow. D VII–VIII + I,22–24; A II + I,18–21; Pect. 19; GR 11–12 + 28–30; Vert. 25. (Recently as *Carangoides vinctus* (Jordan & Gilbert, 1882)) (Alternative name COCINERO JACK).

**PILOTFISH, *Naucrates ductor* (Linnaeus, 1758).** Circumglobal; in western Pacific as far north as Japan and southern Kuril Islands, Russia; Vancouver Island, British Columbia to Chile, including Gulf of California and such offshore islands as Islas Galápagos. Uncommon along U.S. Pacific Coast; common from southern Baja California into tropics. Length to 70 cm (27.6 in) TL. Depth: surface to 430 m (1,410 ft). Black, blue, or dark brown above, with 5–7 black bars; caudal fin white or white-tipped. D III–VI + I,24–29; A I–II + I,15–18; Pect. 18–20; Pelvic I,5; GR 5–8 + 12–19 = 18–26; Vert. 25.

10a Lateral line scutes 26–42; gill rakers on lower limb (including rudiments) 15–19; 2nd dorsal fin with white tip and height into FL 5.0–6.6 in adults:

**BIGEYE TREVALLY**

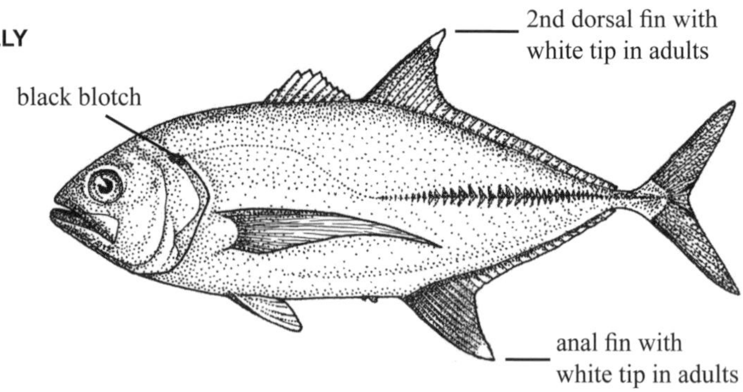


10b Lateral line scutes 42–56; gill rakers on lower limb (including rudiments) 25–32; 2nd dorsal fin without white tip and height into FL 6.0–8.0 in adults..... 11 (next page)

11a Body without dark bars in adults; scaly sheath along base of dorsal and anal fins with relatively small, narrow scales; fins almost entirely covered with small scales; adipose eyelid extends to edge of pupil:

**GREEN JACK**

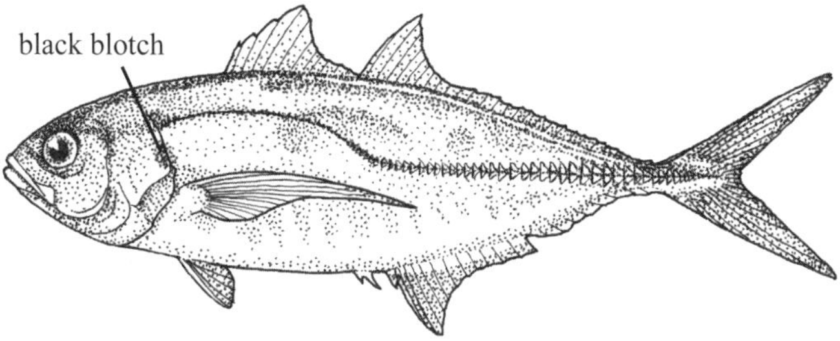


11b Body with 8–9 dark incomplete bars in adults; scaly sheath along base of dorsal and anal fins with relatively large, wide scales; fins lack small scales; adipose eyelid does not extend to edge of pupil:

**COCINERO**

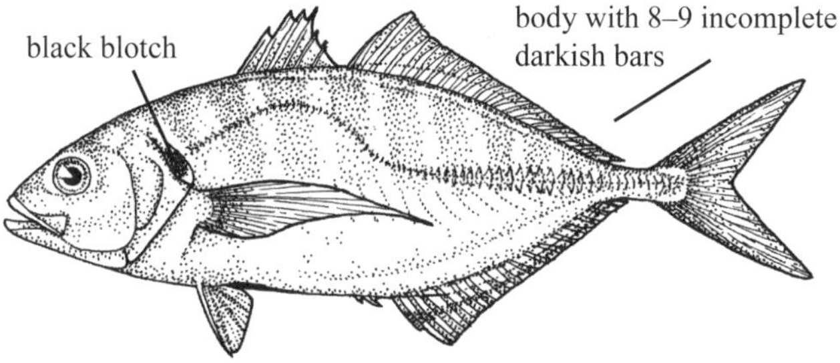


12a *From 3a: posterior part of lateral line without scutes*
Dorsal and ventral caudal peduncle grooves absent; soft anal fin base equal to or slightly shorter than dorsal fin base….. 15 (page 242)

12b Dorsal and ventral caudal peduncle grooves present; anal fin base noticeably shorter than dorsal fin base….. 13

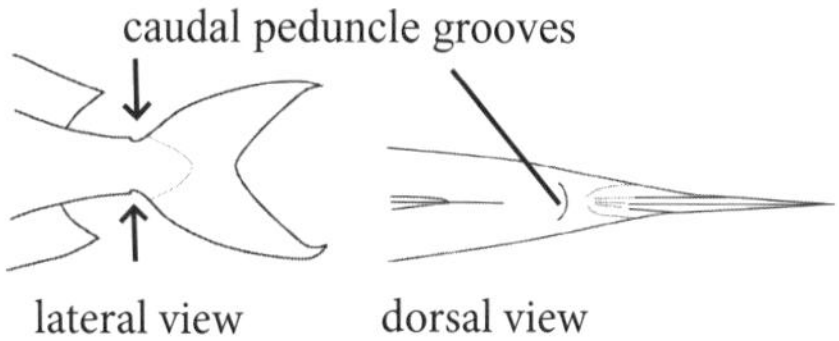


13a Fleshy keel on caudal peduncle well developed; anal fin soft-rays 15–18; body with 5–7 dark bars:

**PILOTFISH**

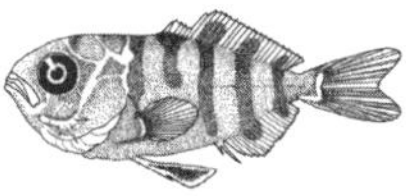
juvenile

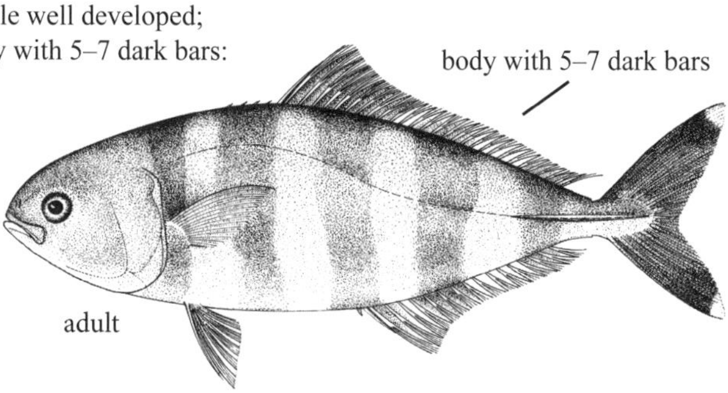

adult

13b Fleshy keel on caudal peduncle absent to moderately developed; anal fin soft-rays 18–25; body lacking obvious dark bars….. 14 (next page)

## JACKS (continued)

**YELLOWTAIL, *Seriola dorsalis* (Gill, 1863).** Northern British Columbia (54°35'N, 131°00'W) to central Mexico, including Gulf of California, Islas Galápagos, and Isla Malpelo. Unverified reports from Gulf of Alaska off Kodiak Island and Cordova. Common from southern California southward along Baja California coast and in Gulf of California. Length to 250 cm (98.4 in) TL. Primarily epipelagic; depth: surface to 312 m (1,023 ft). Blue-green, olive-brown, to brown above, with yellow stripe along midbody; fins yellowish; dark band through eye. Juveniles blue above, yellowish below with series of bars. Dorsoposterior corner of upper jaw rounded. D IV–VII + I,29–39; A 0–II + I,19–25; Pect. 19–20; Pelvic I,5; GR 5–10 + 15–22; Vert. 25. We follow Martinez-Takeshita et al. (2015) and consider there to be three species of "Yellowtail" worldwide: *Seriola dorsalis*, *S. aureovittata* Temminck & Schlegel (1845) (northwest Pacific), and *S. lalandi* Valenciennes, 1833 (Southern Hemisphere). (Alternative name YELLOWTAIL JACK).

**ALMACO JACK, *Seriola rivoliana* Valenciennes, 1833.** Circumglobal; Korea and southern Japan; Santa Catalina Island and Oceanside, southern California to Cabo Blanco, Peru, including Gulf of California and Islas Galápagos. Rare in southern California; common in tropics. Length to 160 cm (63 in) TL. Pelagic; depth: 3–250 m (10–820 ft). Color somewhat variable: green or blue above, silvery below; oblique dark band from snout to front of dorsal fin; often yellowish stripe along sides; edge of pelvic and anal fins white. Juveniles with 7 dark bars on sides. D VIII + I,26–33; A II + I,18–21; Pect. 19–22; LLs 167; GR 6–9 + 16–19 = 22–28; Vert. 24. (Formerly PACIFIC AMBERJACK, *Seriola colburni* Evermann & Clark, 1928: M&L).

**GAFFTOPSAIL POMPANO, *Trachinotus rhodopus* Gill, 1863.** Near Diablo Cove, central California to Callao, Peru, including southern and central Gulf of California and Islas Galápagos. Rare off California; common off southern Baja California and in tropics. Length to 61 cm (24 in) TL. Depth: surface to 30 m (98 ft). Body silvery, with 4–6 faint yellow to brown bars on sides; fins yellow to reddish. D V–VI + I,19–21; A II + I,17–21; Pect. 18–19; Pelvic I,5; GR 8–10 + 13–16 = 21–26; Vert. 24.

**PALOMA POMPANO, *Trachinotus paitensis* Cuvier, 1832.** Redondo Beach, southern California to Chile, including Gulf of California and Islas Galápagos. Rare in southern California; common at least as far northward as central Baja California and into tropics. Length to 50.8 cm (20 in) TL. Depth: shallow inshore areas to 100 m (328 ft). Greenish to bluish above, silver below; margin of dorsal and caudal fins dark. D VI–VIII + I,20–27; A II + I (occasionally A III),20–24; Pect. 16–18; Pelvic I,5; GR 9–11 + 11–17; Vert. 24.

14a Longest dorsal fin soft-ray about ½ length of head; supramaxilla relatively slender; caudal fin yellowish; horizontal dark band through eye; head longer than BD at origin of dorsal fin:

**YELLOWTAIL**

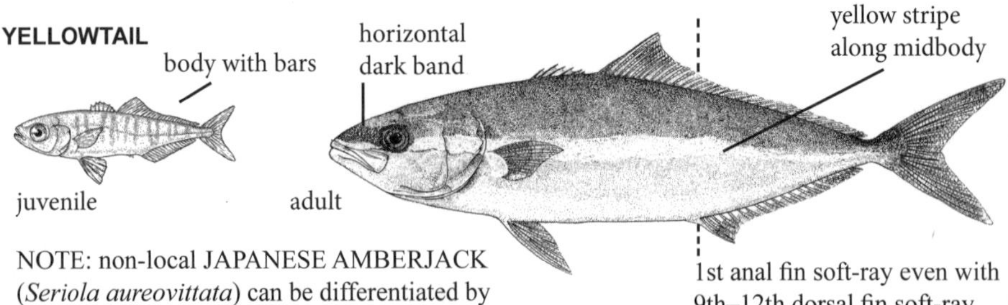


NOTE: non-local JAPANESE AMBERJACK (*Seriola aureovittata*) can be differentiated by more angular dorsoposterior corner of upper jaw and pectoral fin almost equal to pelvic fin. (Somtimes sold at fish markets in California.)

14b (next page)

14b Longest dorsal fin soft-ray about ⅔ length of head in fish over 18 cm FL; supramaxilla relatively broad; caudal fin dark to dusky; oblique dark band through eye to 1st dorsal fin spine; head shorter than BD at origin of dorsal fin:

**ALMACO JACK**

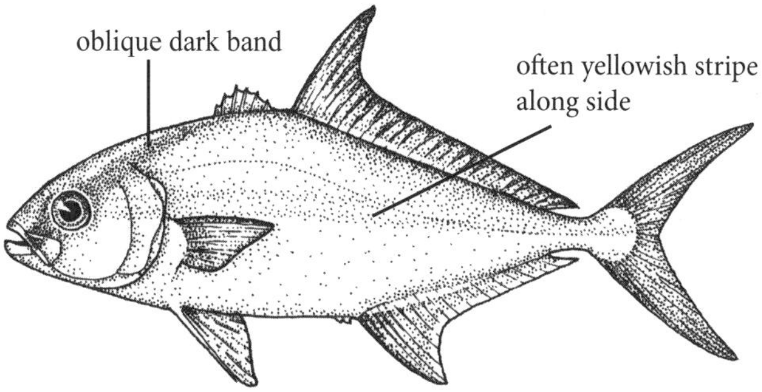


15a *From 12a: caudal peduncle grooves absent*
First 4–5 dorsal and anal fin soft-rays elongated, longer than HL in fish over 8 cm FL; 4–6 incomplete bars extending beyond lateral line in adults:

**GAFFTOPSAIL POMPANO**

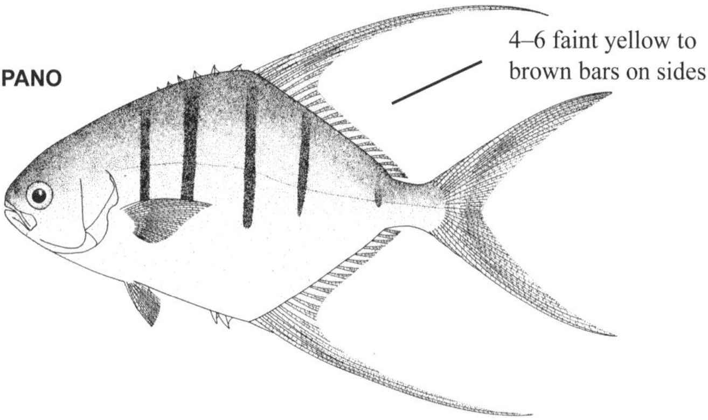


15b First 4–5 dorsal and anal fin soft-rays equal to or shorter than HL; no bars on body in adults:

**PALOMA POMPANO**

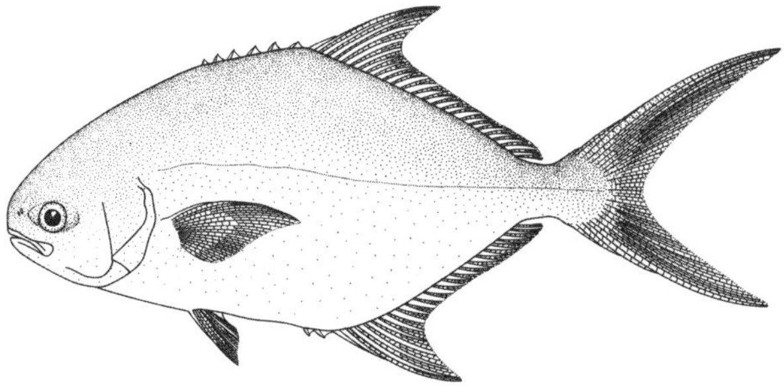

# DOLPHINFISH, Family Coryphaenidae and ROOSTERFISH, Family Nematistiidae

**DOLPHINFISH, *Coryphaena hippurus* Linnaeus, 1758.** Family Coryphaenidae

Circumglobal; Japan and as far north as southern Kuril Islands, Russia; Grays Harbor, Washington to Chile, including Islas Galápagos and Gulf of California. Common northwards into southern California during some years; common in tropics. Length to 210 cm (82.7 in) TL. Depth: surface to about 256 m (840 ft). Color variable and changing rapidly: blue to green above, sides yellowish with dark blue and green spots, white below. Juveniles with series of alternating light and dark bars. D 54–67; A 24–31; Pect. 17–21; Pelvic I,5; LLs 211–301; GR 4–7 + 11–12 = 15–16 (GRt 19–26 including rudiments); Vert. 30–31. (Alternative names DORADO, MAHIMAHI).

**ROOSTERFISH, *Nematistius pectoralis* Gill, 1862.** Family Nematistiidae

San Clemente, southern California to Sur de Taltal, northern Chile, including Gulf of California and Islas Galápagos. Rare in southern California; common in tropics. Length to at least 191 cm (75.2 in) TL. Nearshore; depth: surface and intertidal to 20 m (66 ft). Bluish-gray with yellowish tinges on back, silvery below, with 2 dark diagonal stripes along back and sides; outermost part of dorsal fin spines black, middle of spines yellow; base of dorsal fin dusky. D VIII–IX + I,26–28; A II–III,15–17; Pect. 16–17; Pelvic I,5 appearing as I,6 but last soft-ray divided in flesh and appearing as 2; LLs 119–130; GR 6–7 + 10–13 = 16–20; Vert. 24.

DOLPHINFISH

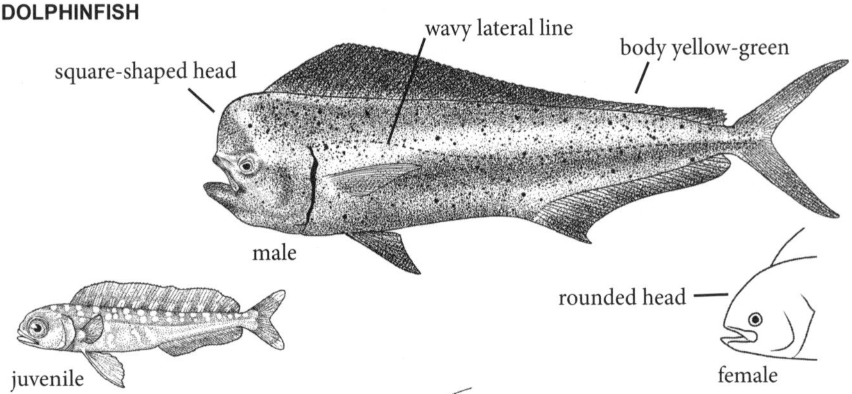


ROOSTERFISH

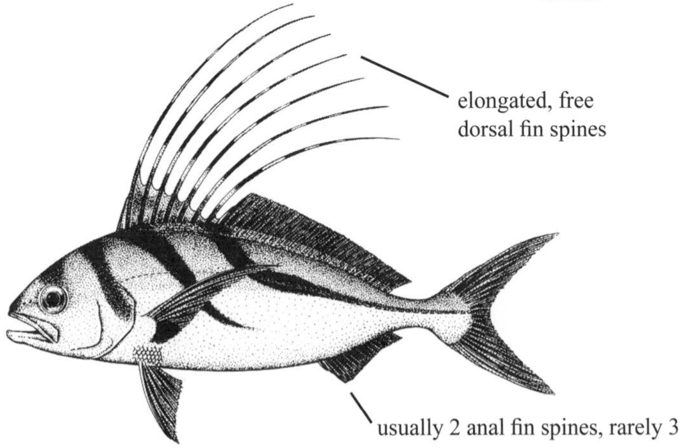

## MANEFISHES, Family Caristiidae

**DARK MANEFISH, *Paracaristius nudarcus* Stevenson & Kenaley, 2011.** Indian and Atlantic Oceans; Japan and central California to central Baja California. Rare off California. Larvae reported from as far south as San Ignacio, southern Baja California. Length to 22.3 cm (8.9 in) SL. Depth: 1–1,800 m (3–5,904 ft). Body dark; anal, pectoral, and pelvic fins elongate and black. D 27–31; A 17–20; Pect. 16–18; GR 5–8 + 14–16 = 20–24. Fish previously identified as *Caristius maderensis* Maul, 1949 from the eastern Pacific refer to this species.

**BLACKFIN MANEFISH, *Platyberyx andriashevi* (Kukuev, Parin & Trunov, 2012).** Circumglobal; Japan and San Pedro Basin, southern California. Rare. Length to 19.6 cm (7.7 in) SL. Mesopelagic; depth: 48–4,822 m (157–15,816 ft). Body brown; dorsal, pectoral, pelvic, and anal fins black. D 31–35; A 20–22; Pect. 17–18; GR 5–8 + 12–15 = 18–22; Vert. 36–39.

**BIGMOUTH MANEFISH, *Caristius macropus* (Bellotti, 1903).** Widespread in Pacific Ocean; Japan to southern Bering Sea and Aleutian Islands to central Baja California near Isla Cedros. Common at least off Japan and Alaska; apparently uncommon along California coast. Length to more than 39 cm (15.3 in) TL. Pelagic; depth: 100–1,660 m (320–5,449 ft) to more than 740 m (2,428 ft). Gray or brown; fins black. Juveniles pale with dark bars. D 33–35; A 20–23; Pect. 14–19; Pelvic I,5; GRt 17–23; Vert. 37–40. Also sometimes called *Platyberyx macropus* (Bellotti, 1903). (Alternative name VEILFIN).

### KEY TO THE MANEFISHES:
Created by Daniel J. Kamikawa
(Principal source: Kamikawa, 2017)

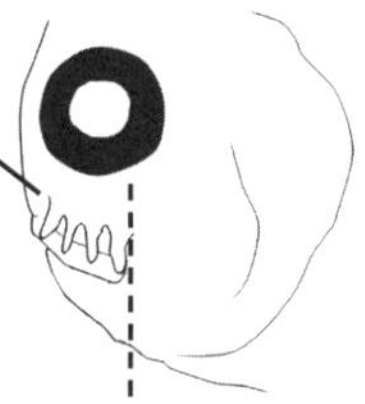


1a Suborbital series expanded over upper jaw; broad space between orbit and mouth; short upper jaw extending to about midorbit; interorbital space wide; lateral line absent:

**DARK MANEFISH**
(not illustrated; body shape as in 2b)

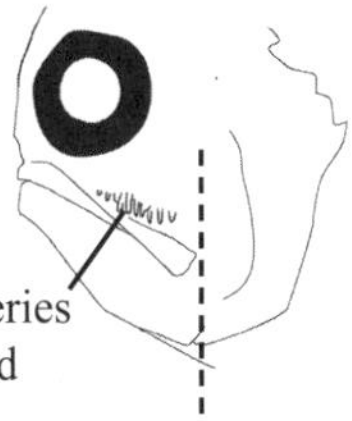


1b Suborbital series not expanded; space between orbit and mouth narrow; long upper jaw extending to or just beyond posterior margin of orbit; interorbital space narrow; lateral line present….. 2

2a Conspicuous lateral line with large scales:

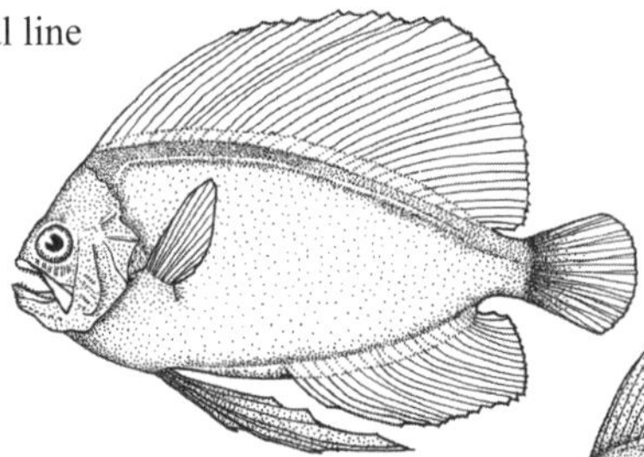

**BLACKFIN MANEFISH**

2b Inconspicuous lateral line with small scales:

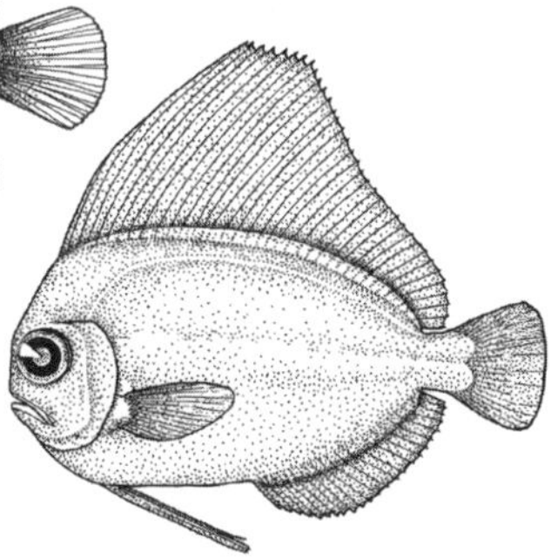

**BIGMOUTH MANEFISH**

## POMFRETS, Family Bramidae

**PACIFIC FANFISH, *Pteraclis aesticola* (Jordan & Snyder, 1901).** Cosmopolitan; Japan; northern California (37°50'N, 125°00'W) (SIO 90-73) to Chile. Rare off California. Length to 61 cm (24 in) TL. Pelagic; depth: surface to 100 m (328 ft). Silver; fins jet-black to blue. D 46–55; A 40–43; Pect. 15–20; Pelvic I,5; LLs 55–56; GR 1–2 + 7–8; Vert. 44–45. (Formerly FANFISH: M&L).

**ROUGH POMFRET, *Taractes asper* Lowe, 1843.** Circumglobal; Japan to Gulf of Alaska off Kodiak Island to southern California (31°20'N, 121°10'W) to Chile. Rare off California. Length to more than 50 cm (19.7 in) TL. Oceanic, primarily pelagic; depth: surface to about 1,000 m (3,280 ft). Uniform dark brown. D 26–34; A 20–30; Pect. 16–20; Pelvic I,5; LLs 40–47; GRt 8–15; Vert. 41–43. (Alternative name FLATHEAD POMFRET).

**SICKLE POMFRET, *Taractichthys steindachneri* (Döderlein, 1883).** Warmer waters of Pacific and Indian Oceans; Japan; southern California and central Baja California (27°15'N, 118°16'W) (SIO 89-101) and southwestern Gulf of California. Rare off California. Length to 91.4 cm (36 in) TL. Depth: at least to 360 m (1,181 ft). Uniform blackish. D 33–37; A 26–28; Pect. 19–22; Midlateral scales 34–38; GR 2–3 + 7–9 = 9–17; Vert. 44–46. Date of publication of the species description is sometimes seen as 1884, but the correct date is 1883. (Formerly BIGSCALE POMFRET: M&L).

**BIGTOOTH POMFRET, *Brama orcini* Cuvier, 1831.** Mid-Pacific and Indian Oceans to Imperial Beach, southern California. The sole California record was a beached specimen at Imperial Beach. Length to 35 cm (13.8 in) TL. Depth: surface to 100 m (328 ft). D 33–36; A 28–30; Pect. 20–22; Midlateral scales 52–56; Vert. 38–40. (Alternative name BIGBELLY POMFRET).

**PACIFIC POMFRET, *Brama japonica* Hilgendorf, 1878.** Southern Sea of Japan and off southern coast of Korean Peninsula to Pacific Ocean south of Aleutian Islands and southern Bering Sea to Chile; absent from tropics. Common at least off Japan and Kuril Islands and from the Gulf of Alaska to well off California or perhaps northern Baja California. Length to 61.4 cm (24.2 in) FL. Oceanic, primarily epipelagic; depth: surface to 620 m (2,034 ft). Dark on back and silvery below, becoming black after death. D 33–36; A 27–30; Pect. 20–23; Pelvic I,5; Midlateral scales 57–75; GR 5–6 + 11–15 = 16–21; Vert. 37–42. (Alternative name SMALL-SCALED POMFRET).

## KEY TO THE POMFRETS:

Created by Milton S. Love
(Principal source: Hatooka, 2002)

1a Dorsal and anal fins broadly expanded; origin of dorsal fin anterior to operculum:

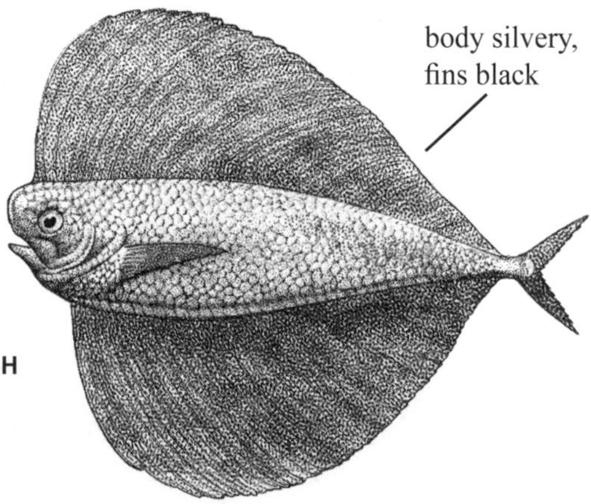


**PACIFIC FANFISH**

1b Dorsal and anal fins not broadly expanded; origin of dorsal fin posterior to operculum….. 2 (next page)

2a Dorsal contour of head almost flattened:

**ROUGH POMFRET**

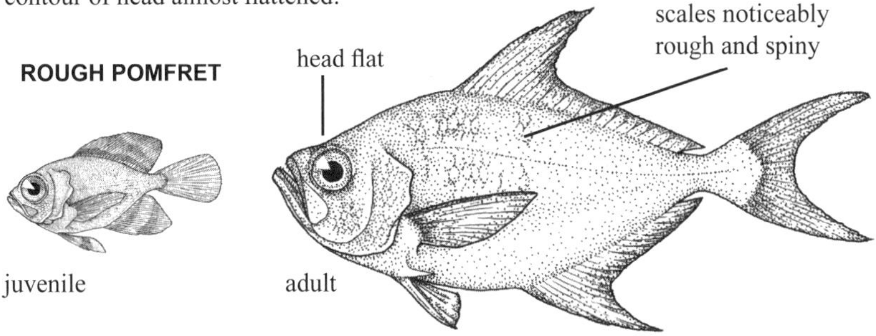


2b Dorsal contour of head distinctly rounded….. 3

3a Anal and dorsal fins sickle-shaped; scales rapidly decreasing in size from caudal peduncle to caudal fin base; pelvic fins relatively separated from each other:

**SICKLE POMFRET**

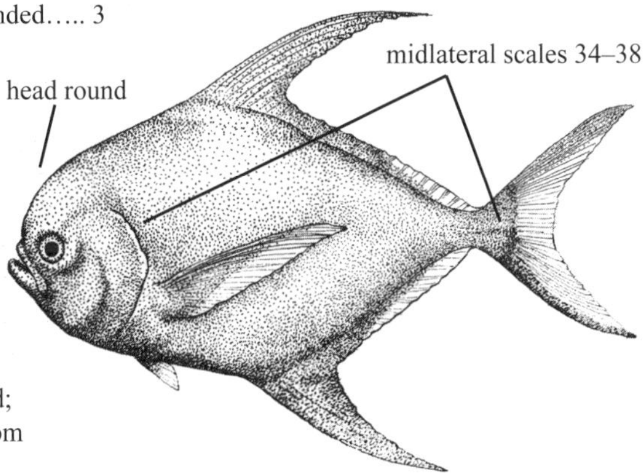


3b Anal and dorsal fins not sickle-shaped; scales gradually decreasing in size from caudal peduncle to caudal fin base; pelvic fins close to each other….. 4

4a Distance between insertion of pectoral fin and origin of pelvic fin less than 8 times SL; midlateral scales 52–56:

**BIGTOOTH POMFRET**

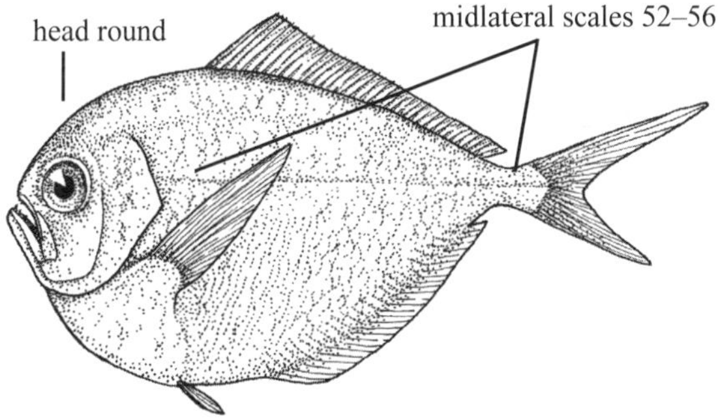


4b Distance between insertion of pectoral fin and origin of pelvic fin greater than 8 times SL; midlateral scales 65–75:

**PACIFIC POMFRET**

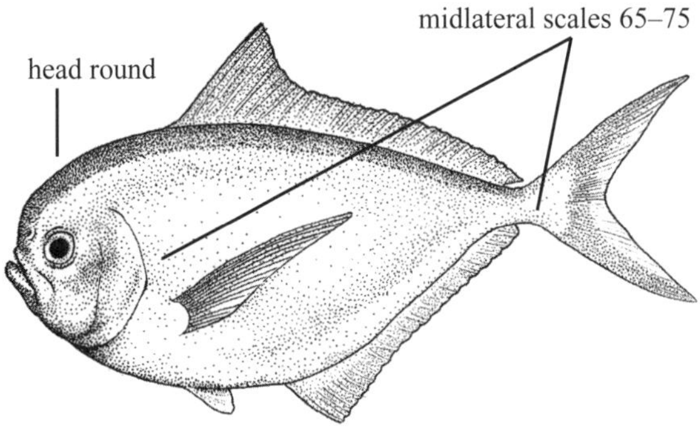

## SNAPPERS, Family Lutjanidae

**SPOTTED ROSE SNAPPER, *Lutjanus guttatus* (Steindachner, 1869).** Bahía Magdalena, southern Baja California to Huacho, Peru and perhaps to northern Baja California, including Gulf of California. Common in tropics. Length to 80 cm (31.5 in) TL. Brackish and marine waters; depth: surface to 120 m (394 ft). Silvery yellowish or pinkish with narrow brown, yellow, or yellow-brown stripes; black blotch under middle of dorsal fin; ventral area, pelvic and anal fins sometimes yellow. D X–XI,11–13; A III,8–9; Pect. 15–17; Pelvic I,5; LLs 47–50; GR 6–8 + 13–17; Vert. 24.

**PACIFIC DOG SNAPPER, *Lutjanus novemfasciatus* Gill, 1862.** Morro Bay, central California to Puerto Pizarro, Peru, including throughout Gulf of California and Islas Galápagos. Rare in California; common from Bahía Magdalena, southern Baja California into tropics. Length to 170 cm (67 in) TL. Depth: intertidal to 60 m (197 ft); also in estuaries and freshwater streams. Dark olive-brown, copper, and reddish on back and sides, silvery below; 8–9 dusky-brown bars on upper half, sometimes absent in large fish. D X–XI,13–15; A III,7–8; Pect. 15–17; Pelvic I,5; LLs 47–49; GR 6–7 + 9–13; Vert. 24. (Alternative name DOG SNAPPER).

**AMARILLO SNAPPER, *Lutjanus argentiventris* (Peters, 1869).** Oceanside, southern California to Islas Lobos de Afuera, Peru, including Gulf of California and Islas Galápagos. Rare in southern California; common from Bahía Magdalena, southern Baja California into tropics. Length to 76 cm (29.9 in). Depth: intertidal (juveniles) to 94 m (308 ft); also in estuaries and fresh water. Pink, rosy-red, or silvery anteriorly merging into yellow posteriorly; fins often yellow or orange; blue horizontal streak (sometimes formed by series of spots and sometimes quite faint) below eye. Juveniles yellowish with dark bar running from snout, through eye, to near dorsal fin. D X–XI,13–14; A III,7–9; Pect. 16–18; Pelvic I,5; LLs 45–48; GR 6–7 + 10–15; Vert. 24. (Alternative name YELLOW SNAPPER).

**PACIFIC RED SNAPPER, *Lutjanus peru* (Nichols & Murphy, 1922).** La Jolla, southern California and Bahía Santa Maria, southern Baja California to Huermey, Peru, including Isla Galápagos, and throughout Gulf of California. Rare in southern California; common in tropics. Length to 99.2 cm (39 in) TL. Depth: surface to at least 91 m (300 ft). Uniform red or pink; juveniles frequently with dark spot under dorsal fin soft-rays. D X,12–14; A III,8–9; Pect. 17–18; Pelvic I,5; LLs 48–49; GR 5–7 + 10–15; Vert. 24.

**COLORADO SNAPPER, *Lutjanus colorado* Jordan & Gilbert, 1882.** Morro Bay, central California to northern Peru, including Gulf of California. Rare in California; common perhaps as far northward as Bahía Magdalena and into tropics. Length to 107 cm (42.1 in) TL. Depth: surface to 90 m (295 ft); sometimes in estuaries. Mostly dark red, but back can be dark; belly pink or whitish. Juveniles sometimes with dusky bars on sides. D X,13–15; A III,7–8; Pect. 15–18; Pelvic I,5; LLs 44–47; GR 6–7 + 11–14.

## KEY TO THE SNAPPERS:

Created by Bruno Passarelli and Julianne Kalman Passarelli
(Principal source: Fischer et al., 1995)

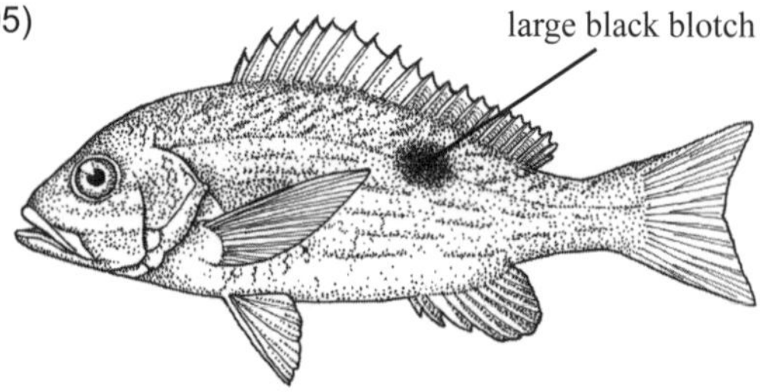


1a Large black spot below dorsal fin soft-rays:

**SPOTTED ROSE SNAPPER**

1b No large spot on below dorsal fin soft-rays….. 2 (next page)

2a Body with 8–9 dusky bars (sometimes absent in large fish):

**PACIFIC DOG SNAPPER**

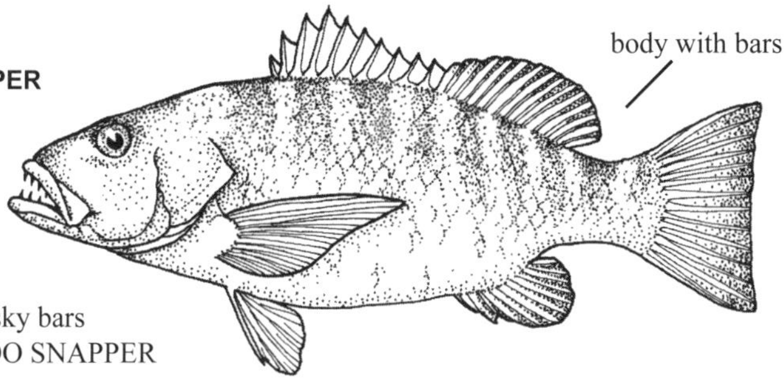


2b Body without 8–9 dusky bars (juvenile COLORADO SNAPPER may have bars)….. 3

3a Body predominantly yellow; anal fin rounded:

**AMARILLO SNAPPER**

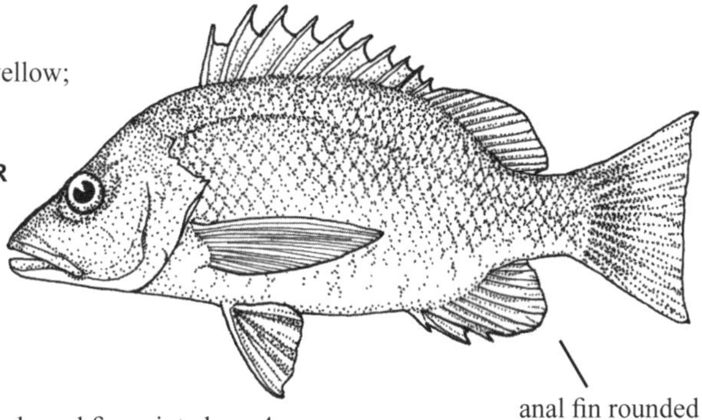


3b Body predominantly red; anal fin pointed….. 4

4a Vomerine teeth with medial posterior extension; lateral line scales 48–49:

**PACIFIC RED SNAPPER**

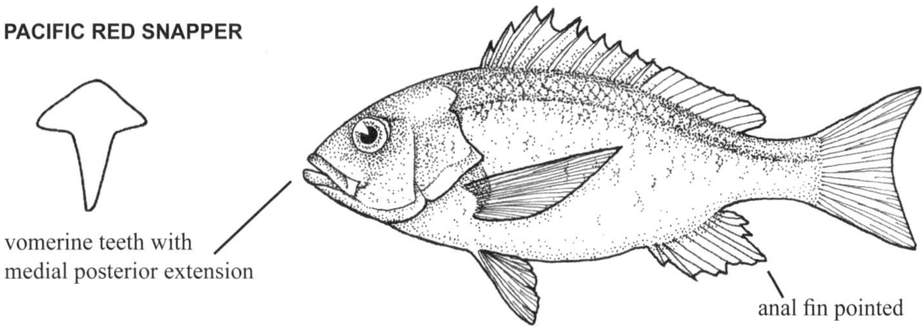


4b Vomerine teeth without medial posterior extension; lateral line scales 44–47:

**COLORADO SNAPPER**

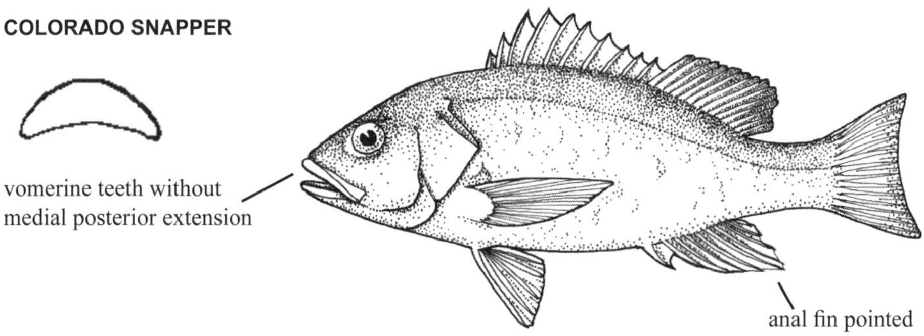

## GRUNTS, Family Haemulidae

**ARMED GRUNT, *Conodon serrifer* Jordan & Gilbert, 1882.** San Onofre, southern California to Paita, Peru, including Gulf of California. Rare in southern California; common from about Bahía San Juanico, southern Baja California into tropics. Length to 30 cm (11.8 in) TL. Nearshore waters; depth: 1–72 m (3–236 ft). Dusky or brownish on back, silvery or silvery blue-gray below; 6–8 black bars on upper sides; all fins yellowish in freshly caught specimens. D XII,12–13; A III,6–8; Pect. 15–17; GR 7 + 14. (Alternative name SERRATED GRUNT).

**CORTEZ GRUNT, *Haemulon flaviguttatum* Gill, 1862.** Newport Bay, southern California to throughout Gulf of California to Peru. Rare in southern California; common from Bahía Magdalena, southern Baja California into tropics. Length to 47.9 cm (18.9 in) TL. Depth: 1–107 m (3–351 ft). Back dusky, sides silvery-gray; small white spots on back and sides in oblique rows; all fins, except caudal, yellow; caudal fin gray or dark with yellow margin. Juveniles with yellow fins and dark spot at base of caudal fin. D X–XII,15–18; A III,9–11; Pect. 16–19; LLs 50–53; GRt 26–32. (Alternative name YELLOWSPOTTED GRUNT).

**SARGO, *Anisotremus davidsonii* (Steindachner, 1876).** Santa Cruz, central California to Todos Santos (23°25'N, 110°14'W), southern Baja California, Gulf of California, and Chiapas, Mexico. Common from about Santa Monica Bay, southern California southward to southern Baja California. Length to 60 cm (23.6 in) TL. Depth: surf zone to 61 m (201 ft). Brassy, gray, or silvery above, sides and belly silver; dark bar from dorsal fin to pectoral area; upper gill cover and part of pectoral fin base edged in black. Juveniles with several dark stripes and bars; individuals less than about 5 cm (2 in) lack bars. D XI–XII,14–17; A III,8–11; Pect. 17–19; Pelvic I,5; LLs 60–62; GR 9–12 + 13–16 = 22–27; Vert. 26. Sometimes seen, incorrectly, as *Anisotremus davidsoni.* (Formerly Pristipomatidae: M&L).

**SALEMA, *Haemulon californiensis* (Steindachner, 1876).** Monterey Bay, central California to northern Peru, including Gulf of California. Common from about Santa Monica Bay, southern California southward into tropics. Length to 30.3 cm (11.8 in) TL. Depth: 1–40 m (4–131 ft). Silvery with 6–8 orange-brown stripes on sides; fins yellow. Juveniles with fewer, and thicker, stripes. D XI–XIII,11–14; A II–III,9–12; Pect. 17–19; Pelvic I,5; LLs 52; GR 11–13 + 15–24; Vert. 26. (Formerly *Xenistius californiensis* (Steindachner, 1876), Pristipomatidae: M&L).

## KEY TO THE GRUNTS:

Translated and revised by Bruno Passarelli, Julianne Kalman Passarelli, and Bill Power (Principal sources: Miller & Lea, 1972; Fischer et al., 1995)

1a Preopercle with single large spine:

**ARMED GRUNT**

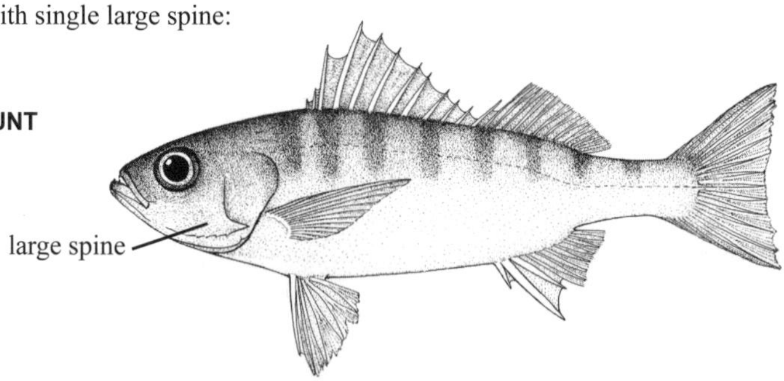


1b Preopercle lacking large spine….. 2 (next page)

2a Body without stripes or bars:

**CORTEZ GRUNT**

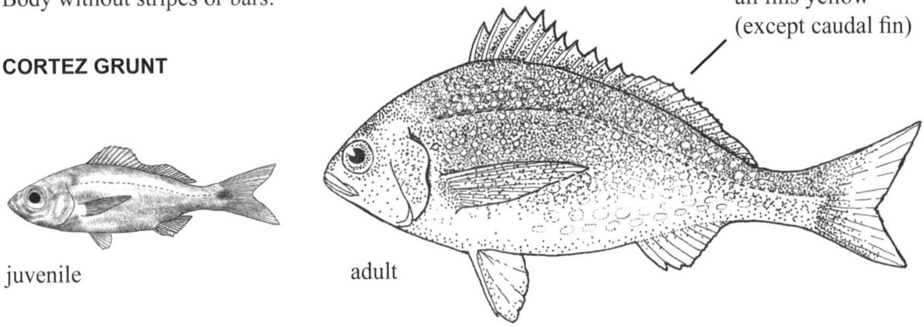


2b Body with stripes or bars (may be lacking in preserved specimens)….. 3

3a Body with single prominent black bar (juveniles may have several bars and may occasionally have stripes):

**SARGO**

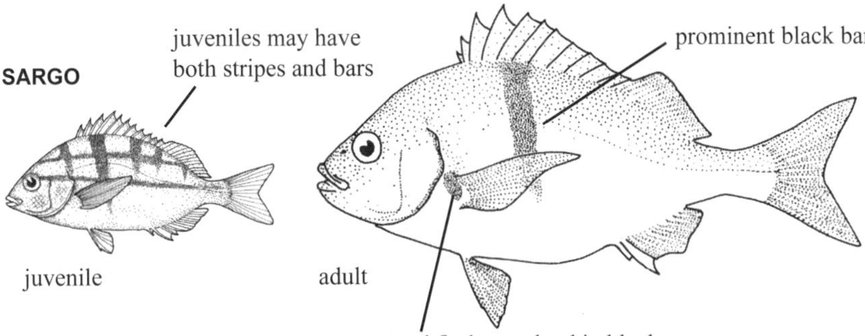


3b Body with stripes….. 4

4a Mouth strongly upturned:

**SALEMA**

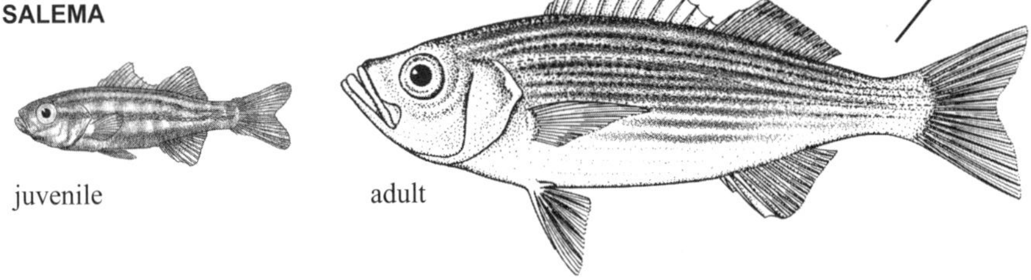


4b Mouth not strongly upturned….. 5 (next page)

## GRUNTS (continued)

**WAVYLINE GRUNT, *Microlepidotus inornatus* Gill, 1862.** Newport Bay, southern California into Gulf of California and at least as far south as Manzanillo, Mexico. Rare in southern California; common in tropics. Length to 45 cm (17.7 in) TL. Depth: 1–30 m (3–98 ft). Grayish or bluish back, silvery-gray flanks; 7–9 narrow orange stripes on back and sides (stripes on back slightly broken); dorsal and anal fins yellowish, caudal fin dusky. D XIII–XIV,15–17; A III,12–14; Pect. 18–21; LLs 78–80; GR 8 + 16–17.

**YELLOWSTRIPE GRUNT, *Haemulopsis axillaris* (Steindachner, 1869).** San Diego Bay, southern California and north of Boca de Soledad (25°18'N, 112°11'W), southern Baja California (SIO 64-79) to Ecuador, including Gulf of California. Rare in southern California; common in tropics. Length to 30 cm (11.8 in) TL. Near shorewaters; depth: surface to 113 m (371 ft). Silvery with narrow black upper edge of gill opening; triangular black spot on pectoral axilla; narrow brown stripes often on sides; 3–4 dark bars sometimes on sides. D XI,14–15; A III,8; GR 14–17 (lower limb); LLs 49–54. (Formerly *Pomadasys axillaris* (Steindachner, 1869)).

5a Dorsal fin spines 13–14; anal fin soft-rays 12–14:

**WAVYLINE GRUNT**

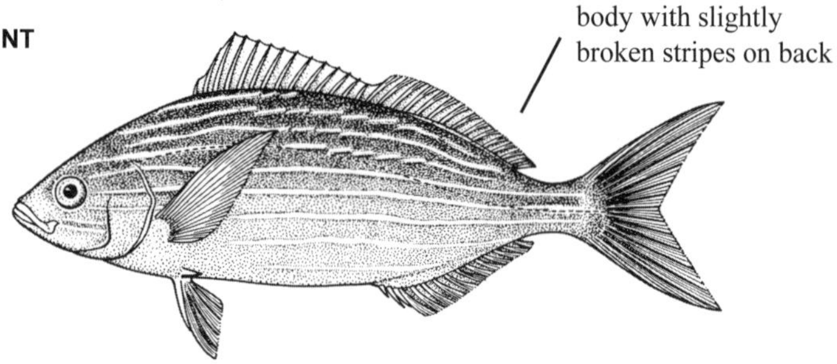


5b Dorsal fin spines 11; anal fin soft-rays 8:

**YELLOWSTRIPE GRUNT**

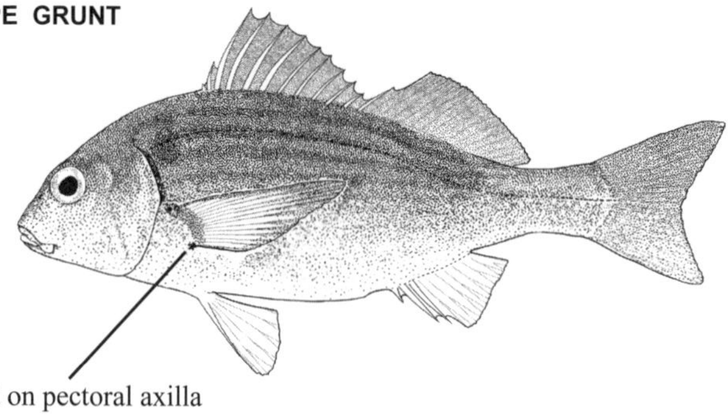

## MOJARRAS, Family Gerreidae

**PACIFIC FLAGFIN MOJARRA, *Eucinostomus currani* Zahuranec, 1980.** Anaheim Bay, southern California to Huacho, Peru, including Gulf of California, Islas Galápagos, and Isla Cocos. Rare in California; common at least from central Baja California and into tropics. Length to at least 21 cm (8.3 in) TL. Depth: intertidal to 100 m (328 ft); also in freshwater streams. Dusky, purplish, or greenish on back, silver below; dorsal fin tricolored: black on tip, silver in middle, and dusky along base. D IX,10; A III,7–8; Pect. 15–17; GR 5 + 8; Vert. 24. (Formerly *Eucinostomus* sp.: M&L) (Alternative names BLACKSPOT MOJARRA, FLAGFIN MOJARRA, SPOTTED-FIN MOJARRA).

**PACIFIC SPOTFIN MOJARRA, *Eucinostomus dowii* (Gill, 1863).** Camp Pendleton Harbor, southern California (SIO 76-191) to Gulf of California to northern Chile. Rare in southern California; common from Bahía de Sebastián Vizcaíno, central Baja California into tropics. Length to 20 cm (7.9 in) TL. Shallow bays and estuaries; depth: shallow water to 114 m (374 ft). Silvery; dorsal fin uniformly dusky. D IX,9–10; A II–III,7–8; Pect. 13–16; LLs 42; GR 4–7 + 7–9 = 12–15; Vert. 24. (Formerly SILVER MOJARRA, *Eucinostomus argenteus* Baird & Girard in Baird, 1855: M&L).

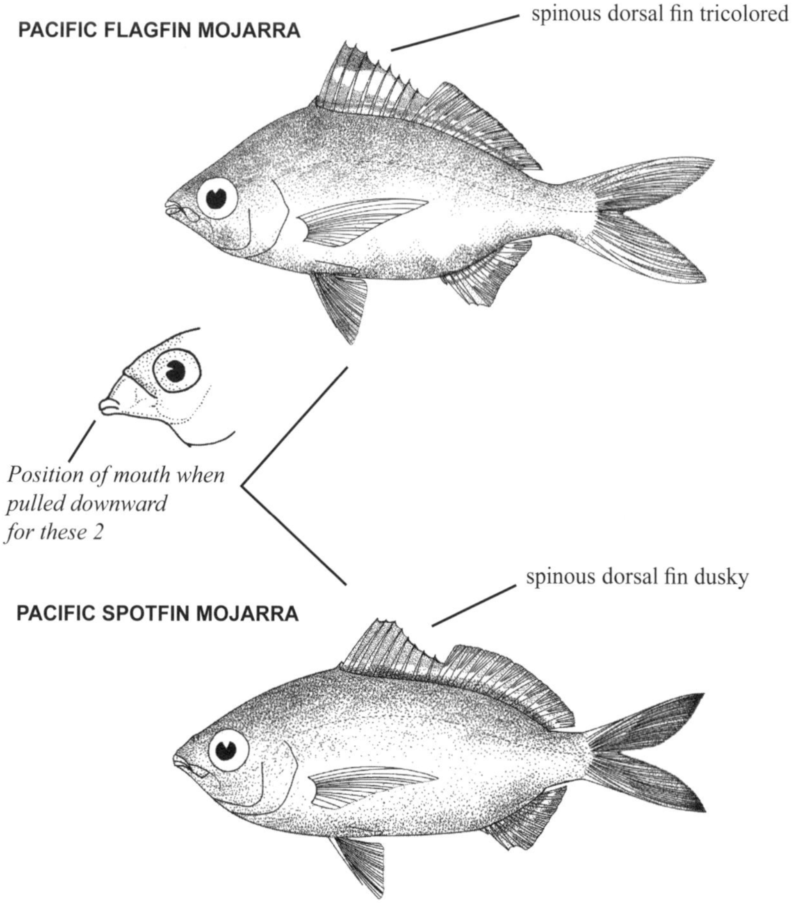

## PORGY, Family Sparidae, KNIFEJAW, Family Oplegnathidae, SPADEFISH, Family Ephippidae, and BOBOS, Family Polynemidae

**PACIFIC PORGY, *Calamus brachysomus* (Lockington, 1880).** Family SPARIDAE
Oceanside, southern California to northern Chile, including Islas Galápagos, Gulf of California, and Isla Malpelo. Rare in southern California; common from central Baja California southward into tropics. Length to about 61 cm (24 in) TL. Depth: surface 1–80 m (4–262 ft). Silver, with bluish, pinkish, greenish, or brassy overtones; snout to eye region often dark; back and sides with dusky bars and mottling on body and fins; black patch at base of pectoral fin. D XII–XIII,11–13; A II–III,9–11; Pect. 13–16; Pelvic I,5; LLs 48; GR 4–6 + 5–6 = 10–11; Vert. 24.

**BARRED KNIFEJAW, *Oplegnathus fasciatus* (Temminck & Schlegel, 1844).** Family OPLEGNATHIDAE
Primarily Japan, Korea, Taiwan, and Hawai'i; entering the eastern Pacific associated with debris from the 2011 Great Japan Earthquake and Tsunami, with scattered records off Washington, Oregon, and California as far south as Monterey Bay, central California. Length to 80 cm (31.5 in) TL. Depth: 1–10 m (3–33 ft). Body white or gray with 7 black bars (anteriormost through eye, posteriormost through base of caudal fin); adult males lack bars. D XI–XII,16–18; A III,12–13; Pect. 18; Pelvic I,5.

**PACIFIC SPADEFISH, *Chaetodipterus zonatus* (Girard, 1858).** Family EPHIPPIDAE
San Diego, southern California to Bahía de Sechura, Peru, including Gulf of California. Rare in southern California; common at least as far northward as central Baja California. Length to 66 cm (26 in) TL. Depth: 1–107 m (3–351 ft). Dusky on back, whitish below; 6 black bars on head, body, and caudal peduncle; fringe of dorsal, anal, and caudal fins often dark. D VIII + I,18–23; A II–III,16–20; Pect. 16–18; Pelvic I,5; LLp 48–50; LLs 70–90; GR 5–6 + 9–10 = 15–16; Vert. 24.

**BLUE BOBO, *Polydactylus approximans* (Lay & Bennett, 1839).** Family POLYNEMIDAE
Monterey Bay, central California (CAS 35305) to Chile, including Gulf of California and Islas Galápagos. Rare in California; common in tropics. Length to 40 cm (15.7 in) TL. Inshore brackish and marine waters; depth: intertidal to 107 m (351 ft). Silvery, silvery-blue, or silvery-yellow above, yellowish below; pectoral fin mostly black. D VIII + I,12–14; A III,13–15; Pect. 15 upper soft-rays, 5–6 free lower soft-rays; Pelvic I,5; LLs 56–63; GR 11–16 + 15–19 = 28–35; Vert. 24.

**YELLOW BOBO, *Polydactylus opercularis* (Gill, 1863).** Family POLYNEMIDAE
Los Angeles Harbor, southern California (SIO 15-1444) to Chile, including Gulf of California. Rare in California; common in tropics. Length to 50 cm (19.7 in) TL. Inshore; depth: intertidal to 107 m (351 ft). Greenish-brown, brown, or bronze above, yellowish below; fins yellow. D VIII + I,11–13; A III,12–14; Pect. 15 upper soft-rays, 8–9 free lower soft-rays; Pelvic I,5; LLs 68–75; GR 16–17 + 18–24; Vert. 24.

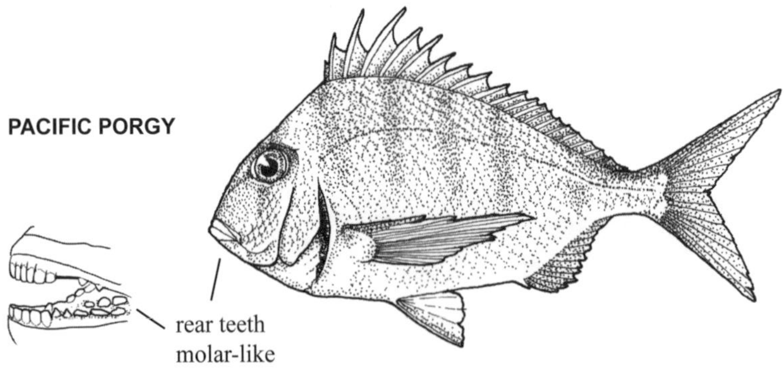

### BARRED KNIFEJAW

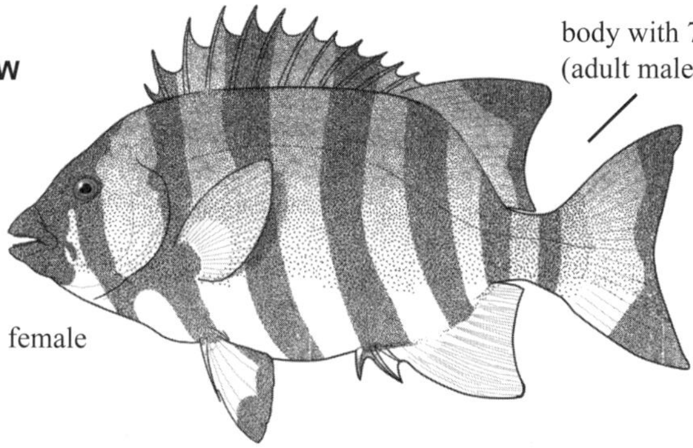


### PACIFIC SPADEFISH

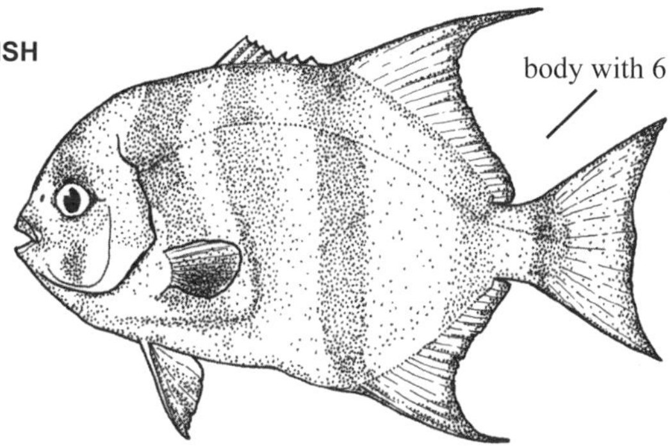


### BLUE BOBO

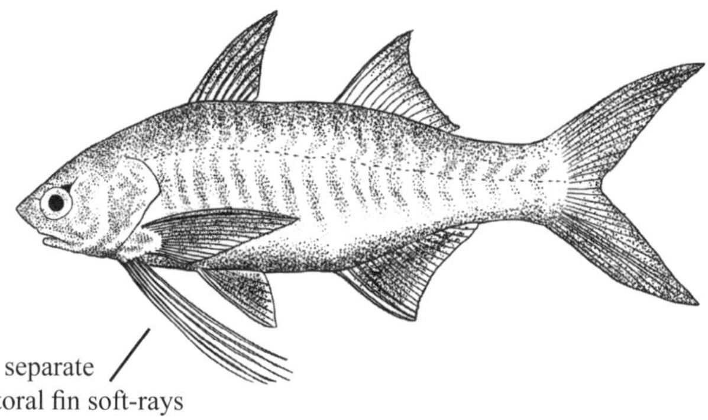


### YELLOW BOBO

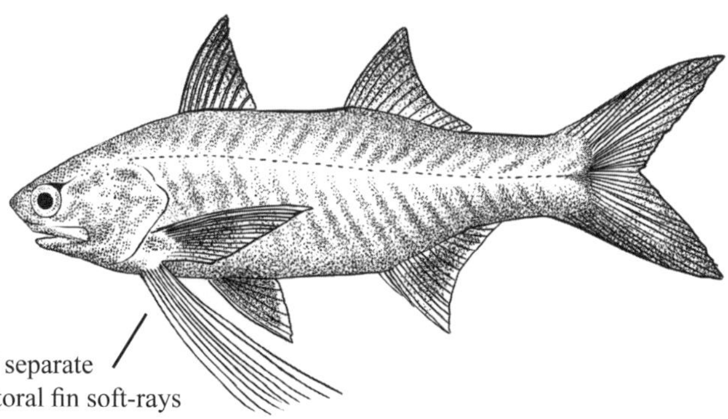

## CROAKERS, Family Sciaenidae

**QUEENFISH, *Seriphus politus* Ayres, 1860.** Burrard Inlet, Vancouver Island, British Columbia to southern Gulf of California. Common from southern California to at least Bahía Tortugas, southern Baja California. Length to 30.5 cm (12 in) TL. Depth: surf zone to 181 m (594 ft). Bluish or brownish on back, silvery below; fins yellowish. D VII–IX + I,18–21; A II,21–23; Pect. 16–18; Pelvic I,5; LLs 65; GR 7–10 + 15–17; Vert. 24–25.

**WHITE SEABASS, *Atractoscion nobilis* (Ayres, 1860).** Juneau, southeastern Alaska to Todos Santos (23°25'N, 110°14'W), southern Baja California and Gulf of California. Common as far northward as Monterey Bay during some periods, common from southern California into tropics. Length to 166 cm (65.4 in) TL. Depth: surf zone to 245 m (804 ft). Gray-blue, bronze, or yellowish above, sometimes with dark speckling, silvery below. Newly settled juveniles with large brown midline stripes and heavy dark bars; older juveniles silvery, brown, golden, or reddish, with dark bars, but without stripe. D IX–X + I,19–23; A I–II,8–10; Pect. 15–18; Pelvic I,5; LLp 70–80; LLs 88; GR 5 + 11–13 = 16–18; Vert. 25. (Formerly *Cynoscion nobilis* (Ayres, 1860): M&L).

**ORANGEMOUTH CORVINA, *Cynoscion xanthulus* Jordan & Gilbert, 1882.** Central Baja California to Acapulco, Mexico, including Gulf of California. Introduced into Salton Sea (but likely extirpated there); not found in marine waters of California. Length to 90 cm (35.4 in) TL. Coastal waters; depth: 1–50 m (3–164 ft). Bluish above, silver below; tail yellow; inside of mouth bright yellow-orange. D VIII–X + I,19–21; A I–II,8–9; LLp 66; LLs 86; GR 3–4 + 9–10 = 12–14; Vert. 22.

**SHORTFIN CORVINA, *Cynoscion parvipinnis* Ayres, 1861.** Huntington Beach, southern California to Mazatlán, Mexico, including Gulf of California. Rare in much of southern California, but apparently a small population in San Diego Bay. Somewhat more common from about Bahía San Quintin, northern Baja California southward and common from Bahía Magdalena, southern Baja California into tropics. Length to 60 cm (23.6 in) TL. Depth: 1–101 m (3–331 ft). Bright blue-gray above, silvery below. D VII–X + I,20–24; A II,9–11; Pect. 16–18; LLp 75; GR 2–4 + 7–9; Vert. 23.

### KEY TO THE CROAKERS:
Edited by Julianne Kalman Passarelli
(Principal source: Miller & Lea, 1972)

1a Snout projecting beyond mouth (with mouth closed); lower jaw usually shorter than upper….. 5 (next page)

1b Snout not projecting beyond mouth (with mouth closed); lower jaw extends beyond upper….. 2

2a Dorsal fins distinctly separated (by more than eye diameter); anal fin soft-rays 21–23:

**QUEENFISH**

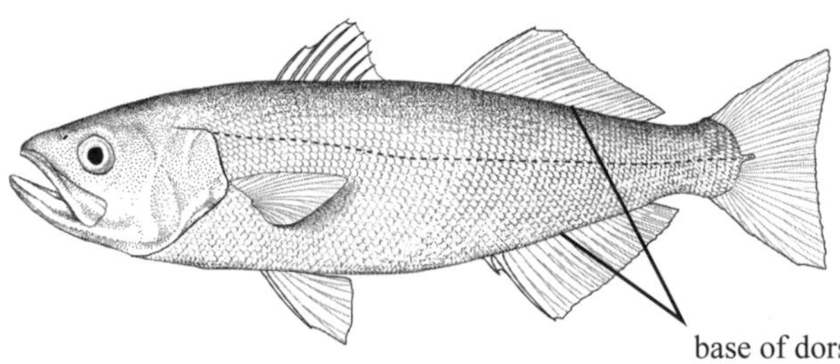


2b Dorsal fins contiguous or slightly joined by membrane (less than eye diameter); anal fin soft-rays 11 or fewer….. 3 (next page)

3a No large canine teeth on roof of mouth, teeth all about same size:

**WHITE SEABASS**

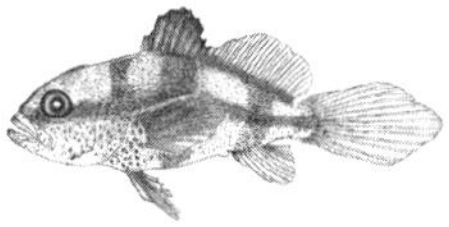

juvenile I

juvenile II

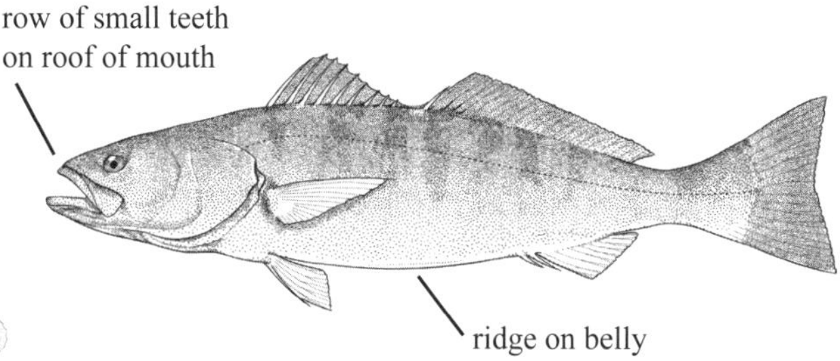


3b One or 2 large canine teeth on roof of mouth….. 4

4a Tail pointed (middle rays longest); pectoral fin long, even with or extending beyond tip of pelvic fin when depressed:

**ORANGEMOUTH CORVINA**

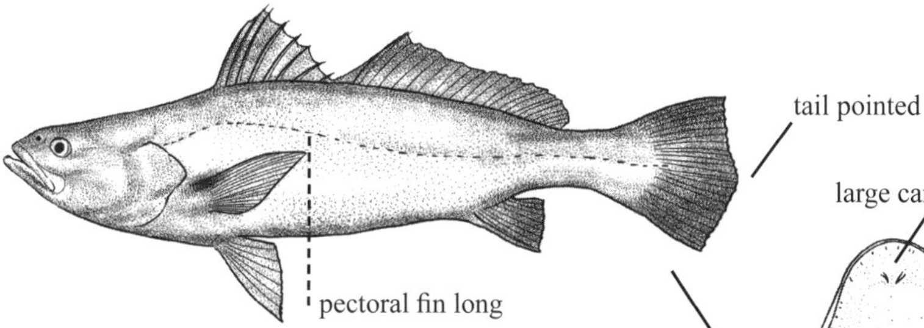


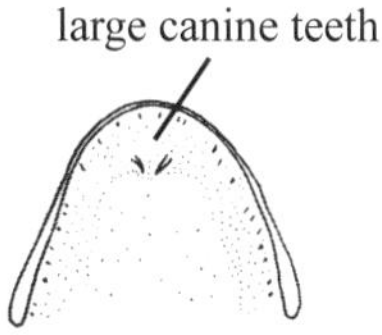


roof of mouth

*Large canine teeth on roof of mouth on these 2*

4b Tail slightly indented (middle rays shortest); pectoral fin short, not extending to tip of pelvic fin when depressed:

**SHORTFIN CORVINA**

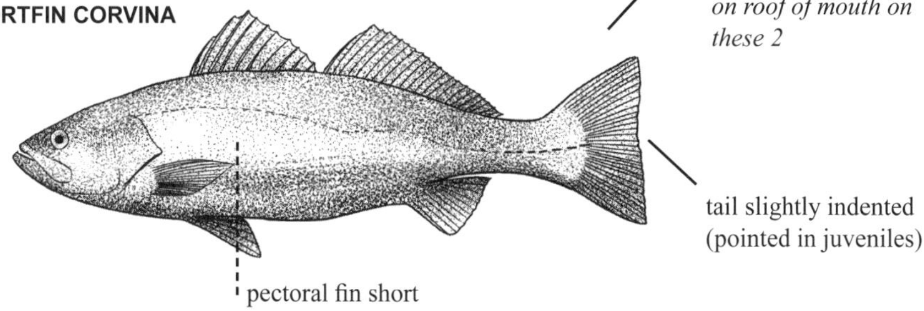


5a *From 1a: snout projecting*
Lower jaw without large, single barbel (WHITE CROAKER may have cluster of minute barbels on chin, but longest is shorter than width of lower lip)….. 7 (page 258)

5b Lower jaw with large, single barbel (barbel longer or equal to width of center of lower lip)….. 6 (next page)

## CROAKERS (continued)

**YELLOWFIN CROAKER, *Umbrina roncador* Jordan & Gilbert, 1882.** Point Conception, central California to Bahía Magdalena, southern Baja California and in Gulf of California; old records to San Francisco. Common from southern California southward along Baja California coast and in Gulf of California. Length to 55.6 cm (21.9 in) TL. Depth: surf zone to 46 m (150 ft). Back iridescent blue to gray, sides silver overlaid with dark wavy yellow-brown lines; fins yellowish; inner lining of gill cover blackish. D X–XI + I,24–31; A II,6–7; Pect. 15–20; Pelvic I,5; LLs 54–58; GR 7–9 + 10–14; Vert. 24–25.

**CALIFORNIA CORBINA, *Menticirrhus undulatus* (Girard, 1854).** Off Morro Rock, central California (CAS 58470) to Gulf of California; also reported from Ecuador to Arica, northern Chile. Common from southern California to at least Bahía Magdalena, southern Baja California and into tropics. Length to 83.6 cm (32.6 in) TL. Depth: surf zone to 20 m (66 ft). Brown or bluish with incandescent reflections; wavy diagonal lines on sides. D X–XI + I–II,23–27; A I–II,7–9; Pect. 17–20; Pelvic I,5; LLs 60; GR 5–8 + 4–10; Vert. 25.

**WHITE CROAKER, *Genyonemus lineatus* (Ayres, 1855).** Barkley Sound, British Columbia to Bahía Magdalena, southern Baja California. Patchily common at least as far north as San Francisco Bay and southward to central Baja California. Mostly in marine waters, but some ascend to lower saline waters and fresh water of San Pablo Bay, Napa River, and other waters of the San Francisco region. Length to 41 cm (16.3 in) TL. Depth: surf zone to 238 m (781 ft). Incandescent brownish to yellowish on back, silver below; black spot usually at base of pectoral fin; fins yellow to white. D XII–XV + I,18–25; A II,10–12; Pect. 17–18; Pelvic I,5; LLs 52–54; GR 9–12 + 17–21 = 27–33; Vert. 26.

**BAIRDIELLA, *Bairdiella icistia* (Jordan & Gilbert, 1882).** Laguna San Ignacio, southern Baja California to Chiapas, Mexico, including Gulf of California. Common at least from Laguna San Ignacio, southern Baja California, southwards. Introduced into the Salton Sea (but likely extirpated there); not present in marine waters of California. Length to 30 cm (11.8 in) TL. Inshore including estuaries; depth: to at least 18 m (59 ft). Grayish to silvery-yellow on back, silver below; dark spot at base of pectoral fin. D IX–XI + I,24–29; A II,7–8; Pect. 15–17; LLp 52; LLs 51– 62; GR 6–8 + 17 = 23–25; Vert. 25.

6a Pectoral fins yellowish; preopercle with bony teeth or spines on posterior margin; anal fin with 2 spines:

**YELLOWFIN CROAKER**

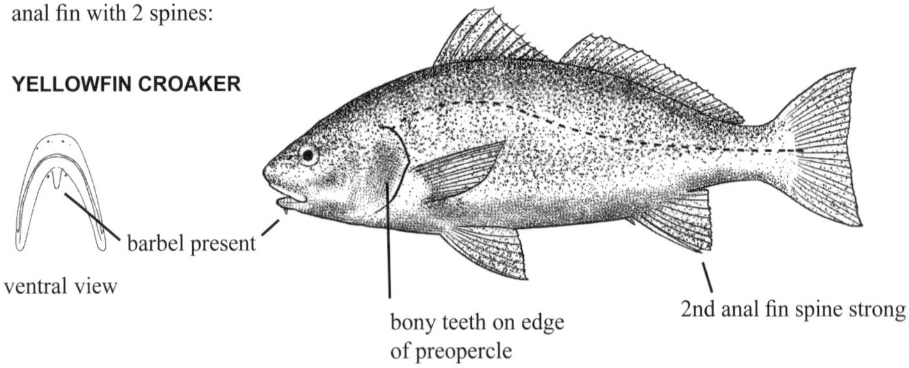


6b (next page)

6b Pectoral fins dark; posterior edge of preopercle serrated but not bony;
anal fin with 1–2 weak spines:

**CALIFORNIA CORBINA**

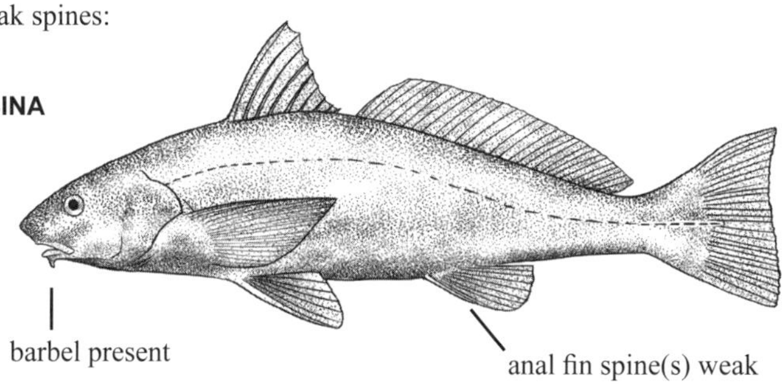


7a *From 5a: lower jaw without large, single barbel*
Dorsal fins with 12–16 spines; anal fin soft-rays 10–12; lower jaw often with cluster of minute barbels:

**WHITE CROAKER**

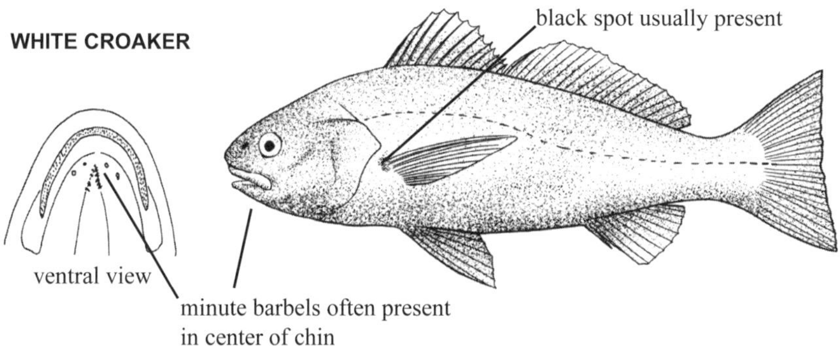


7b Dorsal fins with 12 or fewer spines; anal fin soft-rays 6–9; no chin barbels….. 8

8a Second anal fin spine extends past tip of last soft-ray when fin is depressed;
pelvic and anal fins yellowish:

**BAIRDIELLA**

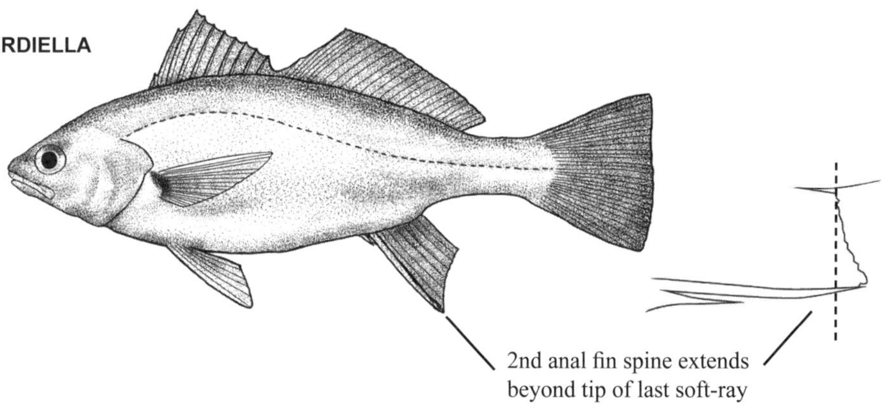


8b Second anal fin spine does not reach tip of last soft-ray when fin is depressed;
pelvic and anal fins not yellow….. 9 (next page)

## CROAKERS (continued)

**SPOTFIN CROAKER, *Roncador stearnsii* (Steindachner, 1876).** Point Conception, central California to tip of Baja California and eastern Gulf of California. One individual reported from south San Francisco Bay. Common from southern California southward to about Bahía Magdalena, southern Baja California. Length to 68.6 cm (27 in) TL. Depth: surf zone to 22 m (73 ft). Silvery-gray, bluish-gray, to bright brassy-orange (spawning-season males) above, white below; dark wavy lines on sides; black blotch at base of pectoral fin; spawning-season females with blackish streaks on belly. D IX–X + I,21–25; A II,7–9; Pect. 16–18; Pelvic I,5; LLs 60; GR 10–14 + 15–19; Vert. 25.

**BLACK CROAKER, *Cheilotrema saturnum* (Girard, 1858).** Point Conception, California to southern Baja California (23°23'N, 110°12'W) (SIO 07-89) and Gulf of California. Common from southern California southward to Bahía Magdalena, southern Baja California and in Gulf of California. Length to 45 cm (17.7 in) TL. Depth: surface and surf zone to 100 m (328 ft) or more. Blackish, brown, and purple with coppery reflections on back, silver below; pelvic fins black; dark mark on upper gill cover. Juveniles silvery-gray with 3 black stripes. D IX–XI + I–II,25–28; A II,6–9; Pect. 17–19; Pelvic I,5; LLs 55–60; GR 6–9 + 8–14; Vert. 24–25.

9a Black blotch at base of pectoral fin; edge of preopercle with bony teeth; length of pectoral fin into head less than 1.2:

**SPOTFIN CROAKER**

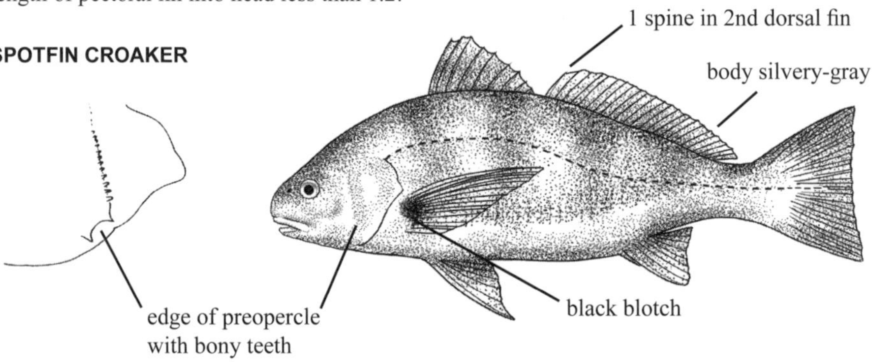


9b No black blotch at base of pectoral fin; edge of preopercle without bony teeth; pectoral fin into head 1.4–1.6:

**BLACK CROAKER**

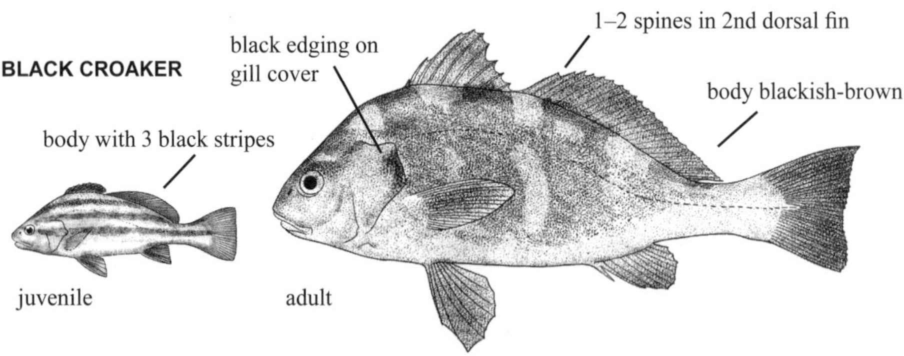

## BUTTERFLYFISHES, Family Chaetodontidae

**THREEBANDED BUTTERFLYFISH, *Chaetodon humeralis* Günther, 1860.** King Harbor, Redondo Beach, southern California (SIO 98-23) to Chile, including Islas Galápagos and Gulf of California. Rare in southern California; common from Bahía Magdalena, southern Baja California into tropics. Length to 26.4 cm (10.6 in) TL. Depth: intertidal to 107 m (351 ft). Brownish-yellow; 6 dark vertical bands, 1 on head, 2 on body, 1 on caudal peduncle, 2 on caudal fin. D XI–XIII,18–21; A III,14–17; Pect. 15–17; Pelvic I,5; LLs 30–40; GR obsolete; Vert. 24.

**SCYTHE BUTTERFLYFISH, *Prognathodes falcifer* (Hubbs & Rechnitzer, 1958).** Santa Cruz Island, southern California, along the outer Baja California Coast, eastern Gulf of California, and Islas Revillagigeos. A record from the Islas Galápagos (Eschmeyer and Herald 1983) is currently considered *Prognathodes carlhubbsi* Nalbant, 1995. While generally rare in southern California, for at least a short period of time in the early 2000s, several groups resided at Santa Catalina Island. Common around Isla Guadalupe and Islas San Benito and in tropics. Length to 17 cm (6.8 in) TL. Depth: 3–270 m (10–886 ft). Black on back, yellow or light on sides; large black inverted "V" marking on side; black diagonal band from snout to dorsal fin origin. D XIII,19–21; A III,14–16; Pect. 17–20; Pelvic I,5; LLp 42–46; GR 5 + 11 = 16; Vert. 24. (Formerly SCYTHE-MARKED BUTTERFLYFISH, *Chaetodon falcifer* Hubbs & Rechnitzer, 1958: M&L).

**THREEBANDED BUTTERFLYFISH**

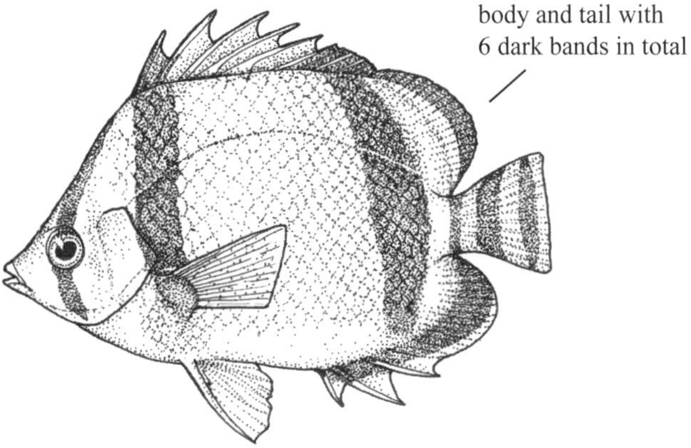


**SCYTHE BUTTERFLYFISH**

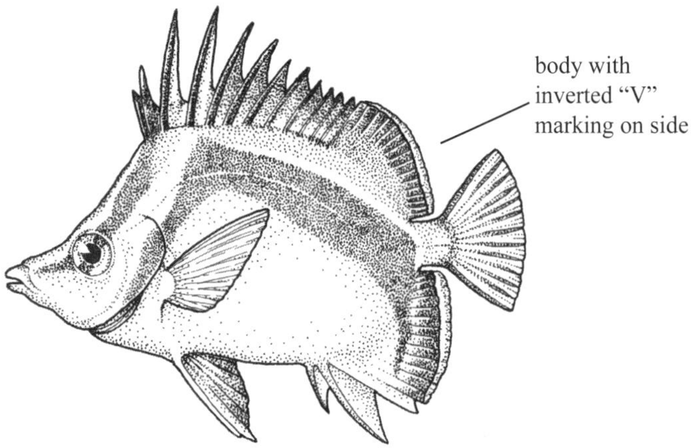

## SEA CHUBS, Family Kyphosidae

**OPALEYE, *Girella nigricans* (Ayres, 1860).** Otter Rock, Oregon to Cabo San Lucas, southern Baja California, with an isolated population in the Gulf of California. Common from central California to at least Bahía Magdalena, southern Baja California and in Gulf of California. Length to 66 cm (26 in) TL. Depth: intertidal (juveniles) to about 32 m (105 ft); pelagic juveniles near surface, often associated with floating material. Occasionally found in estuaries. Dark gray-green or olive-green; 1–3 yellow or white spots at base of dorsal fin; eye brilliant opal blue-green. D XII–XIV,12–15; A III,10–13; Pect. 18–20; Pelvic I,5; LLs 50; GR 11–14 + 16–21 = 28–24; Vert. 27. (Formerly Girellidae: M&L).

**HALFMOON, *Medialuna californiensis* (Steindachner, 1876).** Vancouver Island, British Columbia to southwestern corner of Gulf of California. Usually common from southern California to southern Baja California, but may be abundant at least as far northward as central California during El Niños and similar oceanographic anomalies. Length to 48.3 cm (19 in) TL. Depth: surface and intertidal to 44 m (144 ft). Dark blue or gray-blue above, light blue below; occasional dark bars on sides; usually dark spot above operculum. D IX–X,22–27; A III,17–21; Pect. 17–20; Pelvic I,5; LLs 58; GR 6–8 + 14–17; Vert. 25. (Formerly Scorpididae: M&L).

**ZEBRAPERCH, *Kyphosus azureus* (Jenkins & Evermann, 1889).** Klamath River estuary, northern California to Gulf of California. Common off southern California and southward along Baja California into Gulf of California. Length to 45 cm (17.7 in) TL. Depth: intertidal to 15 m (49 ft). Green, dusky-brown, to black above, whitish below; caudal fin often yellowish; about 12 dark bars on sides; bright blue or dark spot on operculum and black spot below pectoral fin. D X–XI,10–11; A III,9–10; Pect. 15–16; Pelvic I,5; LLs 49–55; GR 4–7 + 11–14; Vert. 25. (Formerly *Hermosilla azurea* Jordan & Evermann, 1889: M&L) (Alternative name RAINBOW SEA CHUB).

**BLUE-BRONZE CHUB, *Kyphosus vaigiensis* (Quoy & Gaimard, 1825).** Circumglobal; Monterey Bay, central California to Antofagasta, northern Chile, including Islas Galápagos and Gulf of California. Generally rare in southern California; common in tropics. Length to 49.7 cm (19.6 in) FL. Depth: surface to 20 m (65 ft). Adults bluish-gray; fine brassy stripes along sides; yellowish stripe often from mouth to gill cover; fins white or gray. Small juveniles dark with elongated silvery spots on flanks. D X–XI,13–15; A III,12–14; Pect. 17–20; Pelvic I,5; LLs 63–80; GR 5–10 + 16–23; Vert. 26. Knudsen and Clements (2013) placed the eastern Pacific species *Kyphosus analogus* (Gill, 1862) in the synonymy of this species and gave LOWFIN CHUB as the common name; we retain the name given in Page et al. (2013).

**BLUESTRIPED CHUB, *Kyphosus ocyurus* (Jordan & Gilbert, 1882).** Tropical, mostly eastern Pacific; one record from Japan; off Diablo Canyon, central California to Peru, apparently just into Gulf of California (23°06'N, 109°12'W), but including Islas Galápagos. Rare in southern California; common in tropics. Length to 70 cm (27.6 in) TL. Inshore and pelagic around floating material; depth: on bottom at 0–30 m (98 ft). Back blue, belly silvery; blue and yellow horizontal bands on back and sides (yellow fading in dead individuals); yellowish stripe often from mouth to gill cover; fins yellow. D XI,14–16; A III,13–14; Pect. 19–20; Pelvic I,5; LLs 80–85; GR 7–10 + 16–21; Vert. 26. (Formerly *Sectator ocyurus* (Jordan & Gilbert, 1882)).

# KEY TO THE SEA CHUBS:

Created by Bruno Passarelli and Julianne Kalman Passarelli

(Principal sources: Miller & Lea, 1972; Fischer et al., 1995; Knudsen & Clements, 2013)

1a One to 3 yellow or white spot(s) at base of dorsal fin; dorsal fin spines 12–14:

**OPALEYE**

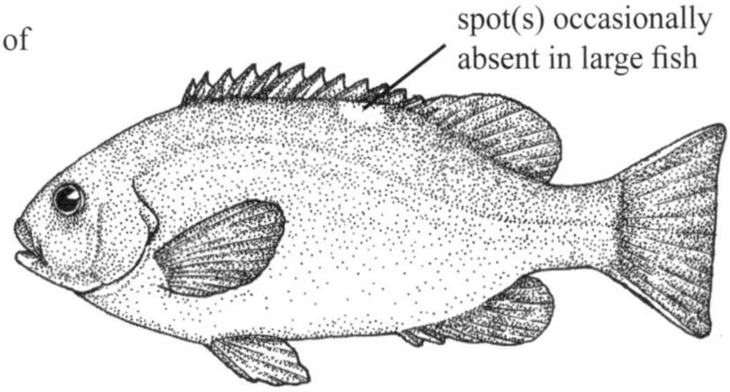


1b No yellow or white spot(s) at base of dorsal fin; dorsal fin spines 11 or fewer….. 2

2a No spot on or above operculum….. 4

2b Blue or black spot on or above operculum….. 3

3a Body typically without bars (occasionally present); black spot below pectoral fin lacking; dorsal fin soft-rays 22–27; anal fin soft-rays 17–21:

**HALFMOON**

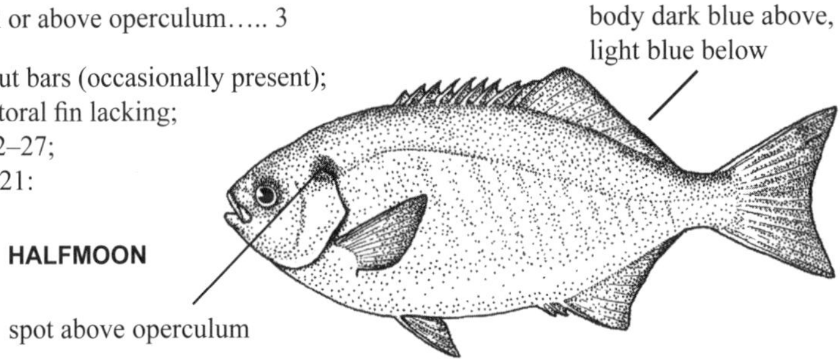


3b Body with about 12 dark bars; black spot below pectoral fin; dorsal fin soft-rays 10–11; anal fin soft-rays 9–10:

**ZEBRAPERCH**

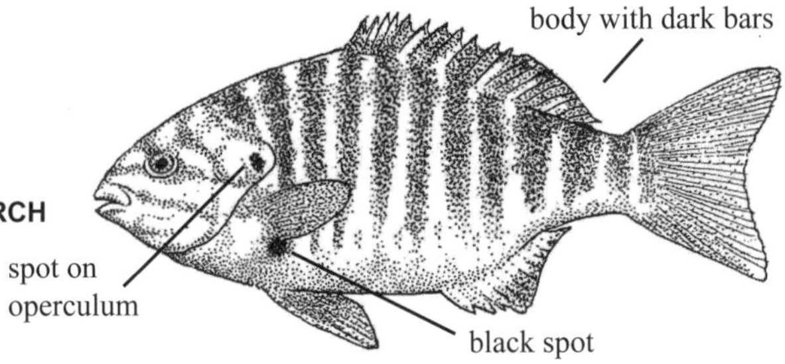


4a *From 2a: no spot on or above operculum*
Body with fine brassy stripes; body deep:

**BLUE-BRONZE CHUB**

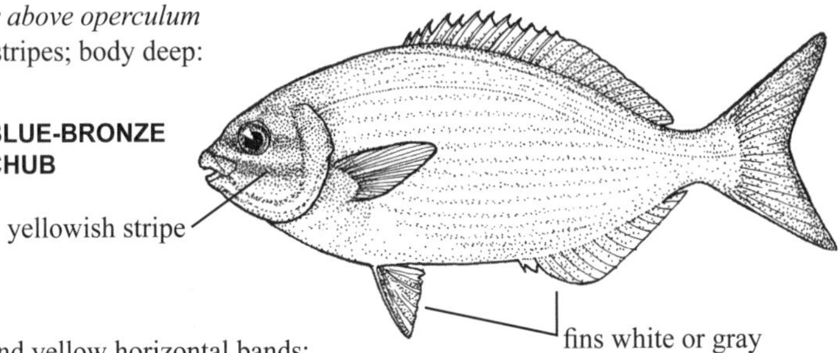


4b Body with thick blue and yellow horizontal bands; body slender and elongated:

**BLUESTRIPED CHUB**

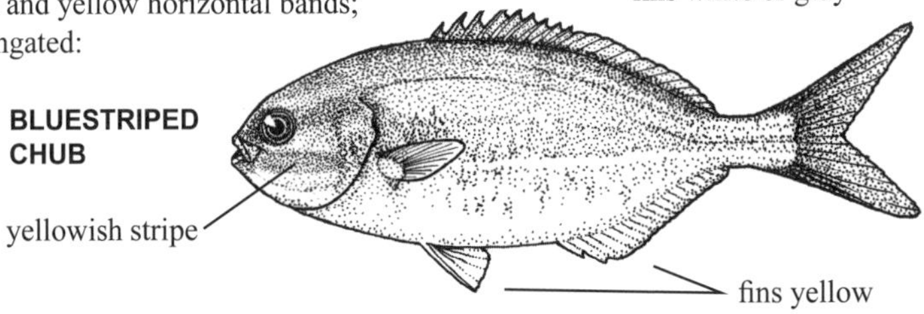

## ANGELFISH, Family Pomacanthidae, ARMORHEAD, Family Pentacerotidae, and TILAPIA, Family Cichlidae

**CORTEZ ANGELFISH, *Pomacanthus zonipectus* (Gill, 1862).** Family POMACANTHIDAE
Redondo Beach, southern California to northern Gulf of California to Máncora, Peru and Islas Galápagos. Rare off southern California; common from Bahía Magdalena into tropics. Length to about 50 cm (19.7 in) TL. Depth: intertidal to 50 m (164 ft). Adult gray and charcoal with orange or yellow bar on back of head, lighter yellow or cream bar midbody, and lighter caudal fin; edge of dorsal fin often blue. Juvenile black with 6 curved yellow bars, alternating with black and blue bars on head, body, and caudal fin. D XI,24–25; A III,20–22.

**NORTH PACIFIC ARMORHEAD, *Pentaceros wheeleri* (Hardy, 1983).** Family PENTACEROTIDAE
Japan to Hawai'i and Gulf of Alaska to central California. Bering Sea report is an error. Apparently rare off California. Length to 53 cm (21 in) TL. Pelagic and benthic; depth: surface to 1,060 m (3,478 ft). Pelagic juveniles and adults heavily mottled and vermiculated black interspersed with blue and silver. Adults living over western North Pacific seamounts uniform gray. D XIII–XV,8–10; A III–V,6–8; Pect. 17–19; Pelvic I,5; LLs 64–87; GR 6–9 + 16–21 = 22–29; Vert. 24–26. Includes North Pacific records of *Pentaceros richardsoni* Smith, 1844 (M&L) and *Pseudopentaceros richardsoni* (Smith, 1844). (Formerly PELAGIC ARMORHEAD: M&L).

**REDBELLY TILAPIA, *Tilapia zillii* (Gervais, 1848).** Family CICHLIDAE
Native to West and North Africa and Middle East. Length to 40 cm (15.7 in) SL. Body color somewhat variable: brown to olive, with blue sheen; lips may be green; anterior ventral area may be pinkish; dorsal, caudal, and anal fins with yellow spots, dorsal and anal fins outlined by narrow orange band; dorsal fin with large spot extending from last spine to 4th soft-ray, bordered by yellow band. D XIV–XVI,10–13; A III–IV,7–10; Pect. 14–15; GR 8–12 (lower limb).

**MOZAMBIQUE TILAPIA, *Oreochromis mossambicus* (Peters, 1852).** Family CICHLIDAE
Native to Africa. Length to 39 cm (15.4 in) SL. Female and non-breeding males silvery with 2–5 midlateral blotches; breeding males black with white lower part of head and red margin on dorsal and caudal fins. D XIV–XVIII,7–13; A II–V,6–13; Pect. 14–15; GR 14–20 (lower limb).

NOTE: Both REDBELLY and MOZAMBIQUE TILAPIA are non-natives that have been widely introduced worldwide. At least 2 species have been taken in the Long Beach–Newport Beach area. Primarily freshwater, they probably were washed down rivers or creeks. They hybridize freely and identification of cichlids to species in California is problematic (Moyle, 2002). Descriptions refer primarily to fish outside of California.

CORTEZ ANGELFISH

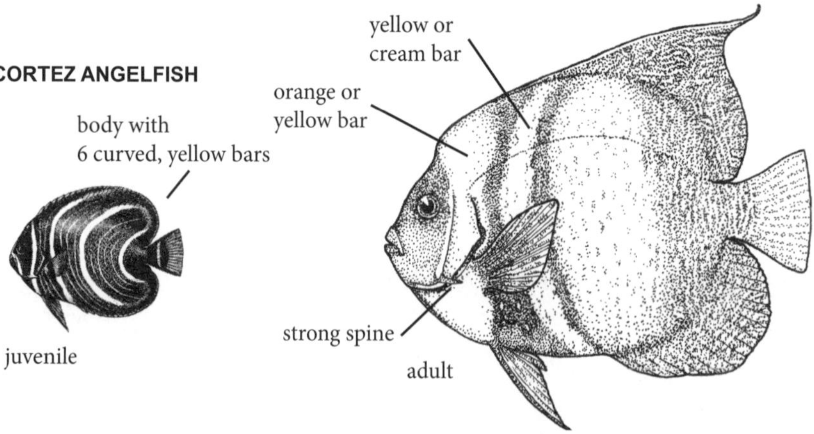

### NORTH PACIFIC ARMORHEAD

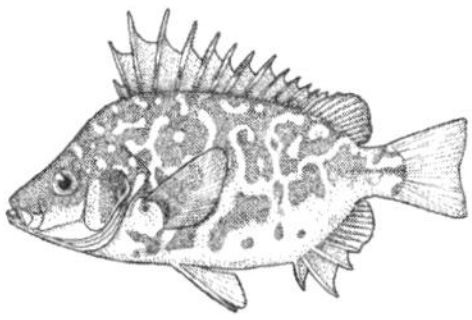

juvenile

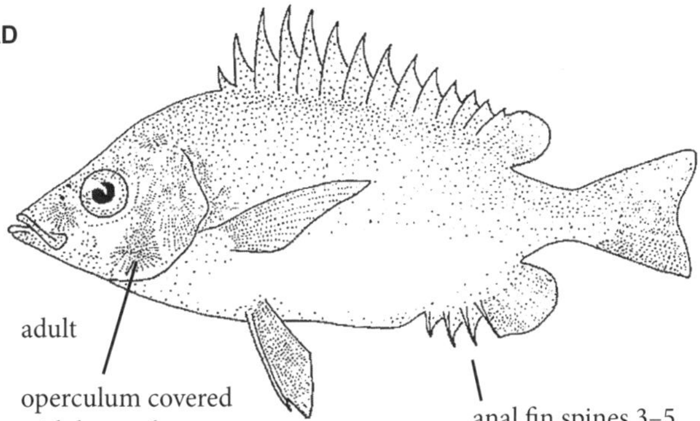


adult

### REDBELLY TILAPIA

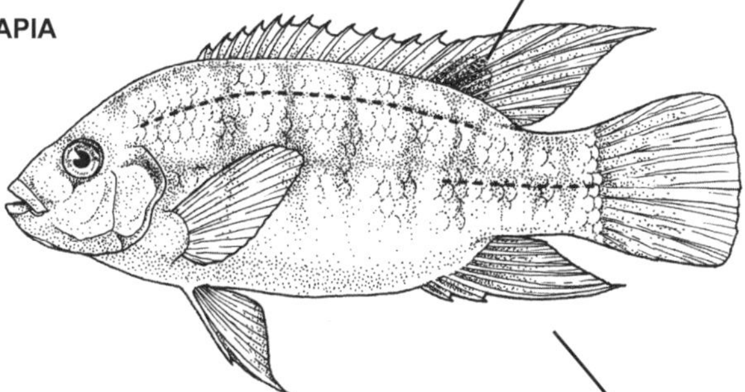


*Lateral line interrupted on these 2*

### MOZAMBIQUE TILAPIA

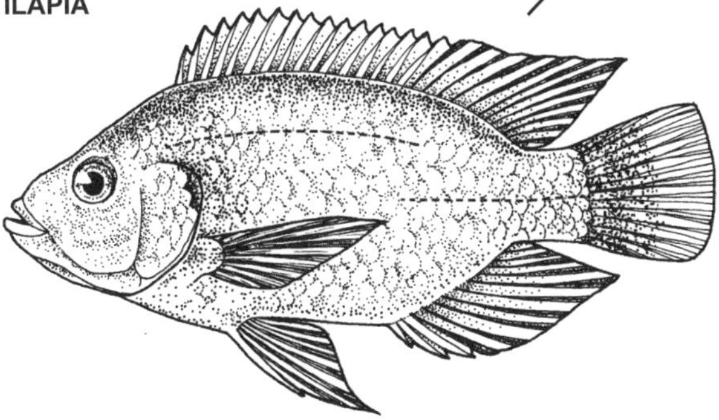

# SURFPERCHES, Family Embiotocidae

NOTE: We follow the proposed species reassignments within this family in Longo et al. (2018). Among other changes, we have placed the PILE PERCH (*Damalichthys vacca*) in the genus *Phanerodon*. However, we also note that Longo and Bernardi (2015) stated that both PINK SEAPERCH (*Zalembius rosaceus*) and RUBBERLIP SEAPERCH (*Rhacochilus toxotes*) are closely related to members of the genus *Phanerodon* and might also be more appropriately placed within that genus.

**RUBBERLIP SEAPERCH, *Rhacochilus toxotes* Agassiz, 1854.** Mendocino County, northern California to Cabo Thurloe, southern Baja California, including Isla Guadalupe, central Baja California. Common at least from San Francisco area southward to at least Bahía San Carlos, central Baja California. Length to 47 cm (18.5 in) TL. Depth: surf zone to 80 m (262 ft). Brown with brassy overtones above, tan below; often with dark bar. D IX–XI,20–25; A III,27–30; Pect. 21–24; Pelvic I,5; LLs 69–76 + 6–9 on tail; GR 8–9 + 17–19 = 26–28; Vert. 35–38. (Formerly RUBBERLIP SURFPERCH: M&L).

**BLACK PERCH, *Embiotoca jacksoni* Agassiz, 1853.** Fort Bragg, northern California to Bahía Magdalena, southern Baja California (SIO 62-113), including Isla Guadalupe. Common from at least Bolinas, northern California to about Punta Abreojos, southern Baja California. Length to 39 cm (15.4 in) TL. Depth: surface and intertidal to 73 m (239 ft). Various shades of brown, red, orange, gray, and green; scales often flecked with blue; sometimes blue and gold markings on anal fin; lips orange, yellow, or reddish-brown. D IX–XI,18–23; A III,23–27; Pect. 20–22; Pelvic I,5; LLs 52–59 + 6–10 on tail; GR 7–10 + 13–14 = 20–23; Vert. 32–36. (Formerly BLACK SURFPERCH: M&L).

**PINK SEAPERCH, *Zalembius rosaceus* (Jordan & Gilbert, 1880).** Point Delgada, northern California to Bahía de San Cristobal, southern Baja California; isolated population in Gulf of California. Common at least from Mendocino, northern California to Bahía de Sebastián Vizcaíno, central Baja California. Length to 20.3 cm (8 in) TL. Depth: surf zone to 276 m (905 ft). Brownish-pink; 2 chocolate-brown spots under dorsal fin. D IX–XI,16–20; A III,18–22; Pect. 17–19; Pelvic I,5; LLs 47–56 + 4–6 on tail; GR 5–7 + 10–12; Vert. 33–37. (Formerly PINK SURFPERCH: M&L).

**REEF PERCH, *Micrometrus aurora* (Jordan & Gilbert, 1880).** Tomales Bay, northern California to Punta Baja, central Baja California. Common from central California to Punta Baja. Length to 18 cm (7.1 in) TL. Depth: intertidal to 6.1 m (20 ft). Silvery with blue, green, and black on back, orange sides; crescent-shaped black mark on scales posterior to pectoral fins. D VII–IX,15–19; A III,17–21; Pect. 17–20; Pelvic I,5; LLs 43–52 + 4–5 on tail; GR 5–7 + 13–14 = 18–21; Vert. 34–37. (Formerly REEF SURFPERCH: M&L).

## KEY TO THE SURFPERCHES:

Revised by Fred Stern and Terra Petry
(Principal source: Miller & Lea, 1972)

1a Center of lower lip with 2 ventral lobes:

**RUBBERLIP SEAPERCH**

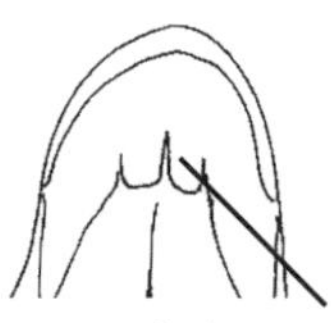


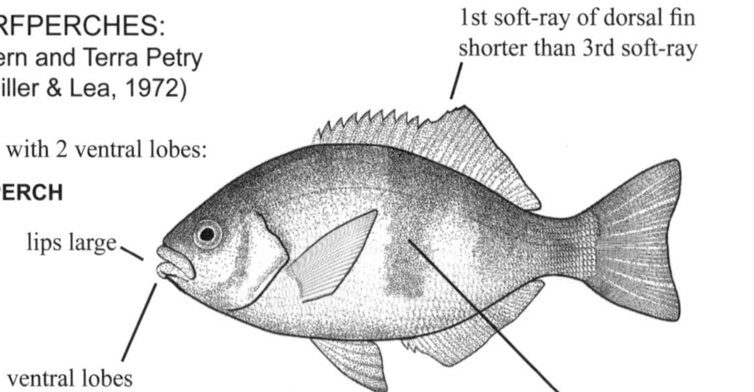


1b Center of lower lip without ventral lobes….. 2 (next page)

2a Patch of enlarged scales between pectoral and pelvic fins; dark to light blue band along base of anal fin:

**BLACK PERCH**

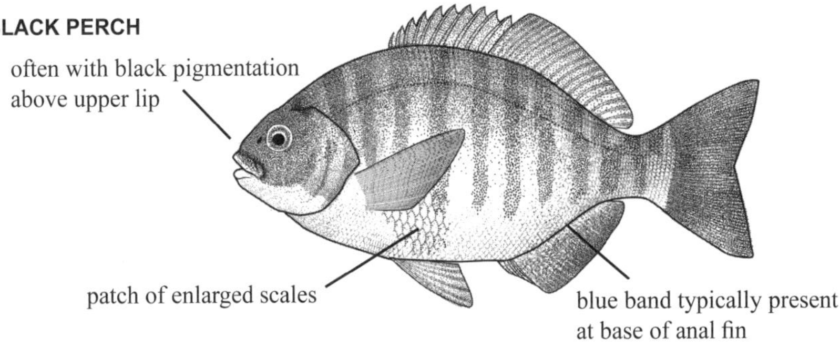


2b No patch of enlarged scales between pectoral and pelvic fins; no band along base of anal fin….. 3

3a Body brownish-pink with 2 chocolate-brown spots at base of dorsal fin; last anal fin soft-ray extended, thread-like:

**PINK SEAPERCH**

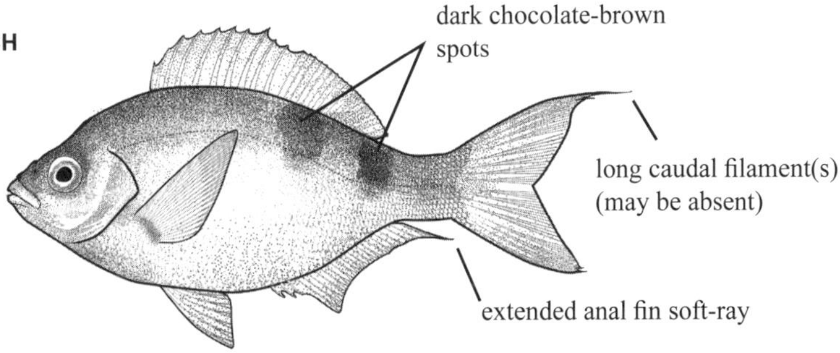


3b Body not as above; last anal fin soft-ray not extended….. 4

4a Scales between base of pectoral fin and vent with crescent-shaped black mark:

**REEF PERCH**

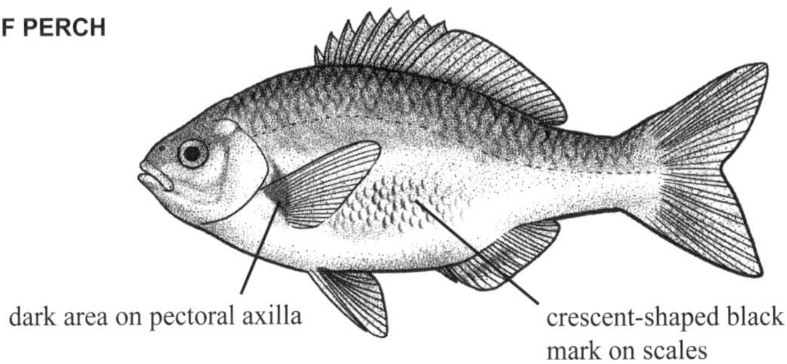


4b Scales not as above….. 5 (next page)

## SURFPERCHES (continued)

**PILE PERCH, *Phanerodon vacca* (Girard, 1855).** Southern British Columbia to Bahía Playa Maria (28°52'N, 114°30'W) (SIO 52-166) on mainland and Isla Guadalupe, Isla Cedros, and Isla Natividad, central Baja California. A reported occurrence from Wrangell, southeastern Alaska lacks documentation. Common from Vancouver Island southward to at least Bahía San Carlos, central Baja California. Mostly marine but will enter brackish waters. Length to 44.2 cm (17.4 in) TL. Depth: intertidal to 100 m (328 ft), possibly to 210 m (690 ft). Blackish or gray on back, silvery to dusky on sides; dark bar on midbody. D IX–XI,21–25; A III,25–31; Pect. 19–22; Pelvic I,5; LLs 56–69 + 5–8 on tail; GR 6–8 + 11–14 = 18–22; Vert. 34–39. (Formerly PILE SURFPERCH, *Damalichthys vacca* Girard, 1855: M&L) (Alternative name PORGY).

**SHINER PERCH, *Cymatogaster aggregata* Gibbons, 1854.** Saint John Baptist Bay (about 57°17'N, 135°34'W), southeastern Alaska to at least Punta Baja, northern Baja California. Common along much of their known geographic range. Length to 21 cm (8.3 in) TL. Mostly marine, but enter brackish waters. Depth: surf zone to 146 m (480 ft), possibly to 303 m (994 ft). Gray to greenish above, silver below, with 2–3 yellow bars on sides interspersed with black; orange pigment sometimes present on anal fin. Breeding males nearly black with yellow bars mostly covered with black speckles. D VIII–XI,18–23; A III,22–26; Pect. 19–21; Pelvic I,5; LLs 36–44 + 4–6 on tail; GR 9–11 + 19–22 = 28–33; Vert. 34–38. The ISLAND PERCH, *Cymatogaster gracilis* Tarp, 1952 (M&L), is a junior synonym. (Formerly SHINER SURFPERCH: M&L).

**RAINBOW SEAPERCH, *Embiotoca caryi* Agassiz, 1853.** Cape Mendocino, northern California to Bahía San Carlos (29°36'N, 115°12'W), central Baja California (SIO 52-214). Common from San Francisco Bay to at least northern Baja California. Length to 30.5 cm (12 in) TL. Depth: surf zone to 50 m (165 ft). Orange or red stripes on sides and head; blue markings on head; orange to dark reddish-brown bars; pelvic fins bright blue and red-orange; dark blotches on anal and soft dorsal fins. D IX–XI,20–24; A III,20–24; Pect. 21–23; Pelvic I,5; LLs 63–71 + 0–8 on tail; GR 7–8 + 13–14 = 20–22; Vert. 36–38. (Formerly RAINBOW SURFPERCH, *Hypsurus caryi* (Agassiz, 1853): M&L).

**KELP PERCH, *Brachyistius frenatus* Gill, 1862.** Near Sitka, southeastern Alaska to Bahía Tortugas, central Baja California, including Isla Guadalupe. Common from southeastern Alaska to at least Punta Banda, northern Baja California and at Islas San Benito, central Baja California. Length to 21.6 cm (8.5 in) TL. Depth: intertidal to 76 m (249 ft). Golden-brown to reddish above, tan below. D VII–X,13–16; A III–IV,20–25; Pect. 17–18; Pelvic I,5; LLs 37–44 + 4–6 on tail; GR 7–9 + 17–20 = 24–29; Vert. 32–35. (Formerly KELP SURFPERCH: M&L).

5a Longest dorsal fin soft-ray 1.6–3.0 times as long as longest dorsal fin spine; dark bar on midbody:

**PILE PERCH**

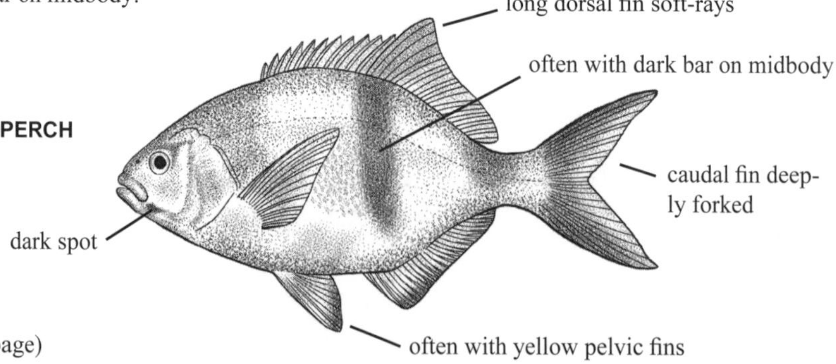


5b (next page)

5b Longest dorsal fin soft-ray less than 1.6 times as long as longest dorsal fin spine; no dark bar on midbody….. 6

6a TL less than 3 times BD….. 11 (page 270)

6b TL equal to or more than 3 times BD (except in some pregnant females)….. 7

7a Body without bars….. 9

7b Body with bars (may be faint or lacking in some SHINER PERCH)….. 8

8a Body with 2–3 yellow bars interspersed with black pigmentation:

**SHINER PERCH**

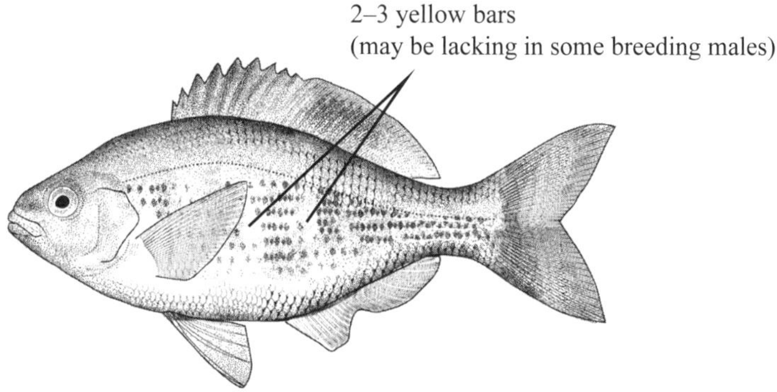


8b Body with numerous orange to dark reddish-brown bars:

**RAINBOW SEAPERCH**

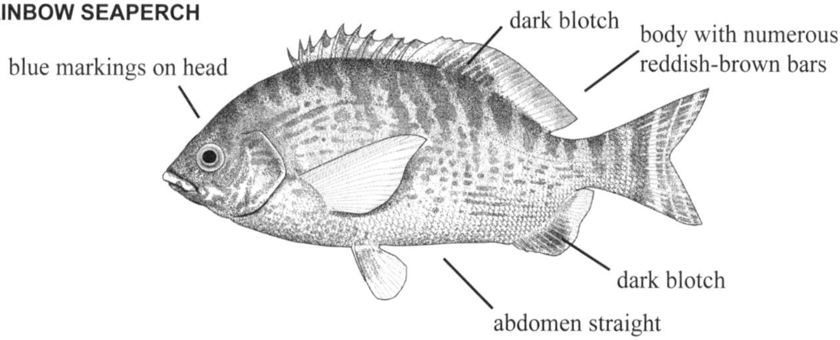


9a *From 7a: body without bars*
Dorsal fin soft-rays 13–16; anal fin soft-rays 20–25; body golden-brown:

**KELP PERCH**

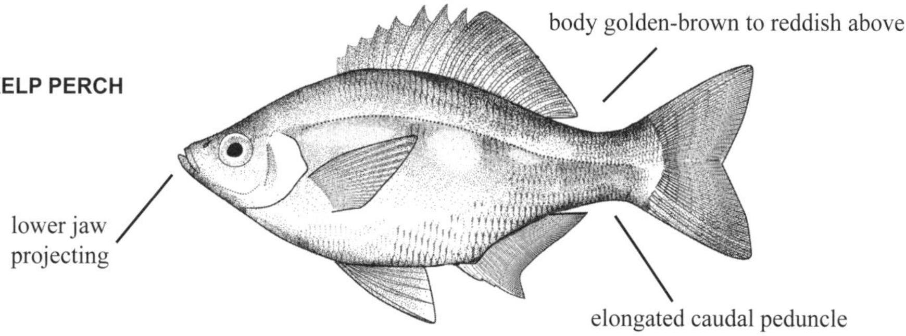


9b Dorsal fin soft-rays 20–26; anal fin soft-rays 27–34; body silvery….. 10 (next page)

## SURFPERCHES (continued)

**WHITE SEAPERCH, *Phanerodon furcatus* Girard, 1854.** Vancouver Island, British Columbia to Bahía San Carlos (29°36'N, 115°12'W) (SIO 52-209), and Isla Cedros and Islas San Benito, central Baja California. Common from at least California southward to at least Bahía San Quintin, northern Baja California. Mostly marine but occasionally enter brackish waters. Length to 37.5 cm (14.8 in) TL. Depth: surf zone to 86 m (282 ft). Silvery with dusky speckling on back; thin black line at base of soft dorsal fin; pelvic fins white or yellowish. D IX–XI,20–26; A III,29–34; Pect. 20–21; Pelvic I,5; LLs 56–67 + 5–7 on tail; GR 7–9 + 12–13 = 20–21; Vert. 37–41. (Formerly WHITE SURFPERCH: M&L).

**SHARPNOSE SEAPERCH, *Phanerodon atripes* (Jordan & Gilbert, 1880).** Yaquina Bay, Oregon to Islas San Benito, central Baja California. Common at least from central California to Punta Baja, northern Baja California. Length to 29 cm (11.5 in) TL. Depth: surface to 229 m (750 ft). Silvery with reddish-brown marks on back; pelvic fins dusky, black-tipped. D X–XI,22–24; A III,27–30; Pect. 20–22; Pelvic I,5; LLs 63–68 + 5–6 on tail. (Formerly SHARPNOSE SURFPERCH: M&L).

**DWARF PERCH, *Micrometrus minimus* (Gibbons, 1854).** Salt Point, northern California (CAS 28309) to Punta Baja, central Baja California and Isla Cedros, central Baja California. Common from Sonoma County, northern California to Bahía Playa Maria, central Baja California. Length to 16 cm (6.3 in) TL. Depth: intertidal to 9.1 m (30 ft). One individual collected from the mouth of a coastal creek at a salinity of 1.1 ppt. Silvery with greenish-blue reflections; yellow on sides, sometimes with dark stripes on belly. D VIII–IX,12–16; A III,13–23; Pect. 18–22; Pelvic I,5; LLs 37–45 + 3–6 on tail; GR 5–7 + 11–16 = 17–22; Vert. 31–36. (Formerly DWARF SURFPERCH: M&L).

**STRIPED SEAPERCH, *Embiotoca lateralis* Agassiz, 1854.** Southeastern Alaska at Klakas Inlet to Arrecife Sacramento, central Baja California (SIO 61-369). Reported but without documentation as far north as Wrangell, Alaska. Reyes-Bonilla et al. (2010) report a California Academy of Science (CAS) record from Isla Guadalupe. However, a search of the CAS database did not yield this record. Common from at least Haida Gwaii, British Columbia southward to northern Channel Islands, southern California, uncommon in much of southern California, and common again off northern Baja California. Mostly marine but will enter brackish waters. Length to 41.1 cm (16.4 in) FL. Depth: surface and intertidal to 96 m (312 ft). Body brown to golden and silvery below, with blue to whitish stripes; pelvic fins dusky. D X–XII,23–26; A III,29–33; Pect. 21–24; Pelvic I,5; LLs 59–65 + 6–8 on tail; GR 7–10 + 14–17 = 22–27; Vert. 33–35. (Formerly STRIPED SURFPERCH: M&L) (Alternative name BLUE SEAPERCH).

10a Pelvic fin margin not dusky to black; thin black line at base of soft-dorsal fin:

WHITE SEAPERCH

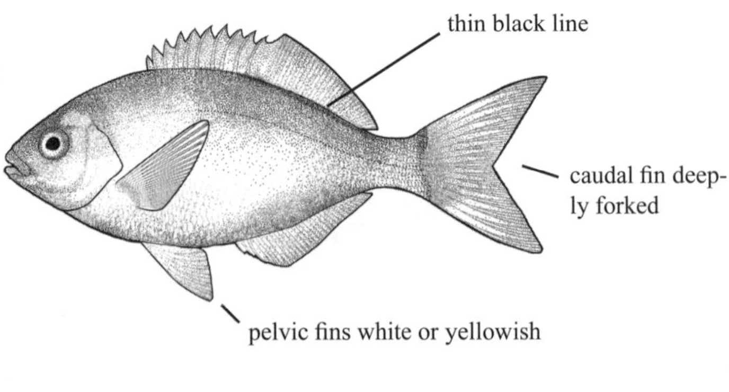


10b (next page)

10b Pelvic fin margin dusky to black; no thin black line at base of soft-dorsal fin:

**SHARPNOSE SEAPERCH**

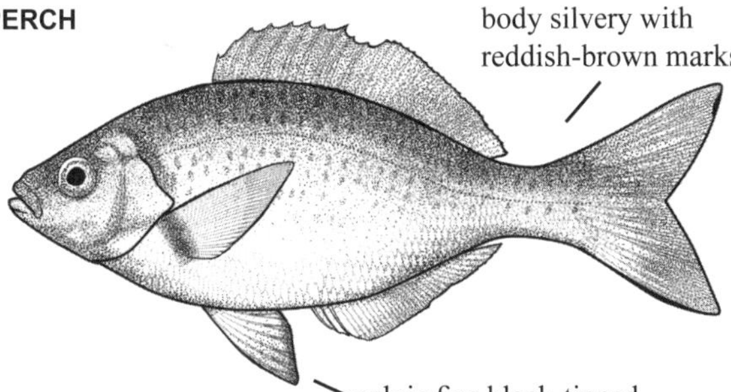


11a *From 6a: TL less than 3 times BD*
Lower lip without frenum….. 14 (page 272)

11b Lower lip with frenum….. 12

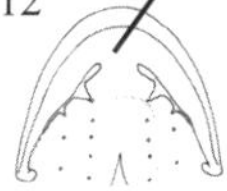


12a Pectoral axilla with black area;
dorsal fin base with black blotch;
dorsal fin soft-rays 12–16:

**DWARF PERCH**

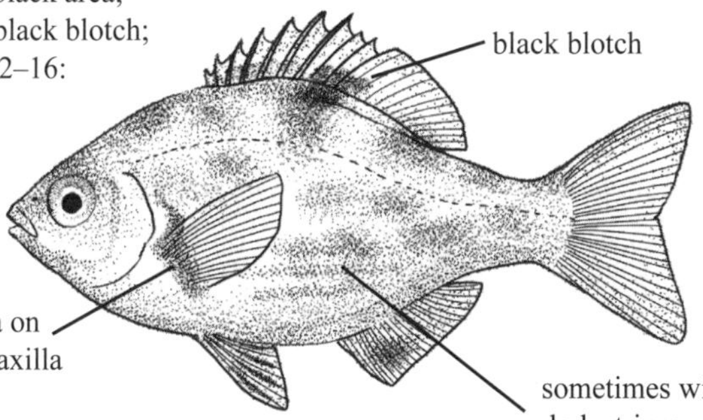


12b Pectoral axilla without black area;
dorsal fin base without black blotch;
dorsal fin soft-rays 21 or more….. 13

13a Body with distinct stripes; anal fin soft-rays 29–33:

**STRIPED SEAPERCH**

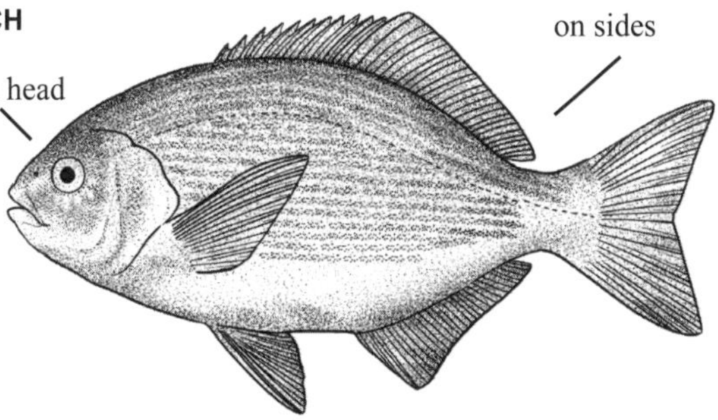


13b (next page)

## SURFPERCHES (continued)

**BARRED SURFPERCH, *Amphistichus argenteus* Agassiz, 1854.** Bodega Bay, northern California to Bahía Santa Rosalia (28°25'N, 114°15'W), central Baja California (SIO 52-154). Common from San Francisco area to at least Punta Blanca, central Baja California. Length to 43.2 cm (17 in) TL. Depth: surf zone to 80 m (262 ft); occasionally found in relatively low-salinity conditions (down to 24.6 ppt) in estuaries. Olive-green to yellow-green on back, silver below; often with bars on sides (some individuals in northern California lack bars). D IX–XII,21–27; A III–IV,24–29; Pect. 25–28; Pelvic I,5; LLs 59–67 + 5–7 on tail; GR 5–7 + 11–14 = 17–21; Vert. 29–33.

**SPOTFIN SURFPERCH, *Hypocritichthys analis* (Agassiz, 1861).** Seal Rock, Oregon to Bahía Blanca, central Baja California. Common from northern California as far southward as the Santa Barbara Channel, southern California. Length to 20 cm (8 in) TL. Depth: surface and intertidal to 101 m (331 ft). Silver with dusky on back; large black blotch on dorsal fin and black spot on anal fin. D VII–IX,20–25; A III,21–26; Pect. 23–27; Pelvic I,5; LLs 57–66 + 4–6 on tail; GR 7–9 + 17–21; Vert. 32–35. (Formerly *Hyperprosopon anale* Agassiz, 1861: M&L).

**WALLEYE SURFPERCH, *Hyperprosopon argenteum* Gibbons, 1854.** Willapa Bay, Washington to Punta San Rosarito and Isla Cedros, central Baja California (SIO 64-856), including Isla Guadalupe. A record from Vancouver Island, British Columbia (M&L) is in error. Common from Oregon southward to at least Bahía Playa Maria, central Baja California. Length to 30.5 cm (12 in) TL. Depth: surface and intertidal to 182 m (597 ft). One taken inside the mouth of a stream (24.6 ppt) during tidal inflow. Purplish or bluish back, silvery sides; tip of pelvic fins black; scales near pectoral fins have yellow spots; pelvic fins of males may be bright yellow. D VII–XI,25–29; A III,30–35; Pect. 25–28; Pelvic I,5; LLs 68–73 + 5–7 on tail; GR 7–10 + 20–23 = 28–32; Vert. 33–38.

**REDTAIL SURFPERCH, *Amphistichus rhodoterus* (Agassiz, 1854).** Kyuquot Channel, northwest Vancouver Island, British Columbia to Punta Baja, northern Baja California. Common from Vancouver Island to northern California and in northern Baja California. Length to 40.6 cm (16 in) TL. Depth: surf zone to 7.3 m (24 ft). Silver, olive-green mottling and bars on sides; caudal fin pink to deep purple. D VIII–X,25–29; A III,26–32; Pect. 27–28; Pelvic I,5; LLs 60–70 + 4–6 on tail; GR 6–8 + 10–14 = 16–22; Vert. 30–33.

13b Body without distinct stripes; anal fin soft-rays 24–29:

BARRED SURFPERCH

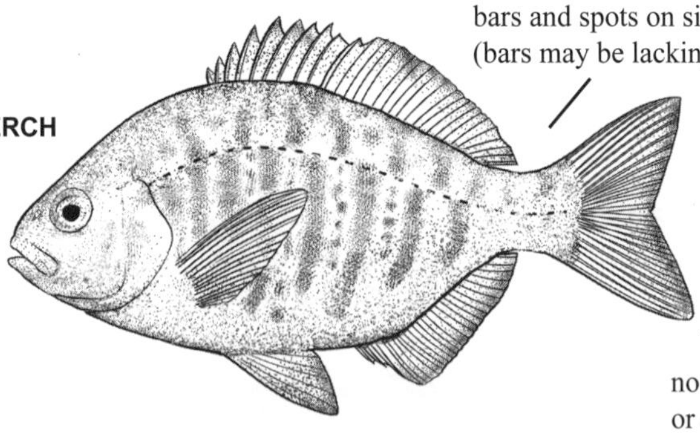


14a (next page)

14a *From 11a: lower lip without frenum*
Body without bars; black blotch on dorsal fin and black spot on anal fin:

SPOTFIN SURFPERCH

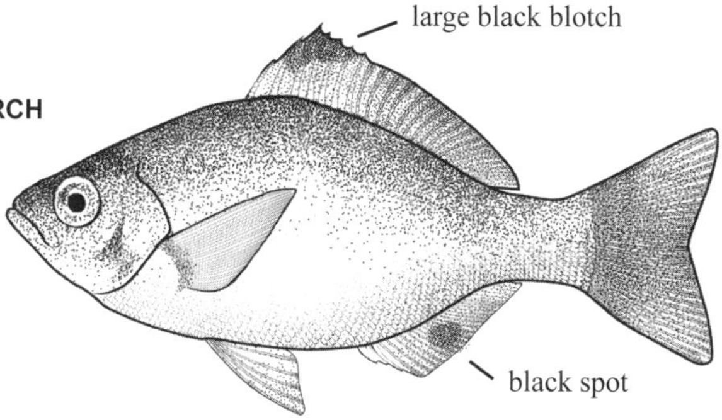


14b Body with bars or broken bars; no black blotch on dorsal fin and no black spot on anal fin….. 15

15a Pelvic fins with black tip; 20–23 rakers on lower limb of 1st gill arch:

WALLEYE SURFPERCH

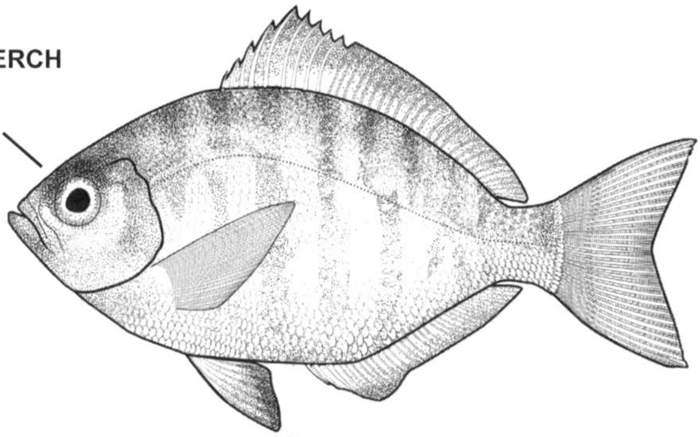


15b Pelvic fins without black tip; 10–19 rakers on lower limb of 1st gill arch….. 16

16a Last dorsal fin spine equal to or longer than 1st dorsal fin soft-ray; caudal fin indented:

REDTAIL SURFPERCH

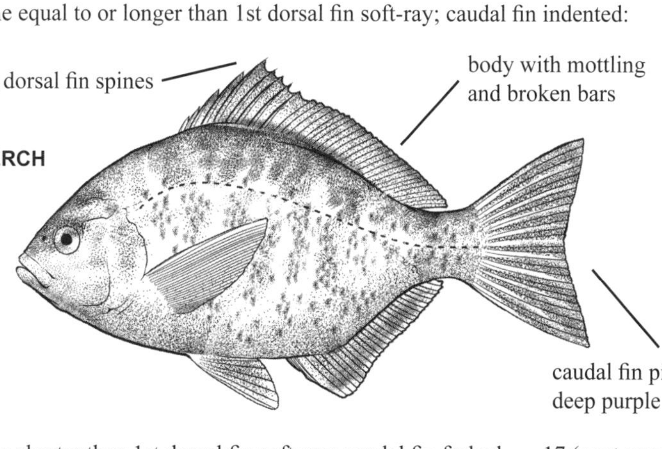


16b Last dorsal fin spine shorter than 1st dorsal fin soft-ray; caudal fin forked….. 17 (next page)

## SURFPERCHES (continued)

**CALICO SURFPERCH, *Amphistichus koelzi* (Hubbs, 1933).** Cape Flattery, Washington to Los Ojitos, central Baja California. Common from about southern Oregon to northern Santa Barbara Channel, southern California and perhaps off northern Baja California to Los Ojitos (about 29'N). Length to 32.5 cm(12.8 in) TL. Depth: surf zone to 9.1 m (30 ft). Body silver, may be tinged with red, with olive-green mottling, and bars on sides; caudal fin pinkish-red. D IX–XI,24–28; A III,25–32; Pect. 25–29; Pelvic I,5; LLs 61–68 + 4–6 on tail; GR 6–8 + 14–18 = 21–26; Vert. 32–35.

**SILVER SURFPERCH, *Hyperprosopon ellipticum* (Gibbons, 1854).** Brooks Peninsula, British Columbia to Rio San Vicente, northern Baja California. Common from at least as far north as Oregon southward to at least central California and Santa Rosa Island, southern California, and perhaps in northern Baja California; uncommon along southern California mainland. Length to 26.7 cm (10.5 in) TL. Depth: intertidal to 110 m (360 ft); one report from a brackish lagoon. Silver with duskiness on back and dusky bars on sides; caudal fin usually pink with black edging. Females with gray to black area on anal fin; males may have black or orange blotch on anal fin. D VIII–X,25–29; A III,29–35; Pect. 26–28; Pelvic I,5; LLs 59–67 + 4–6 on tail; GR 7–8 + 15–19 = 22–27; Vert. 32–35.

17a Bars or broken bars above and below lateral line; caudal fin without black posterior margin:

CALICO SURFPERCH

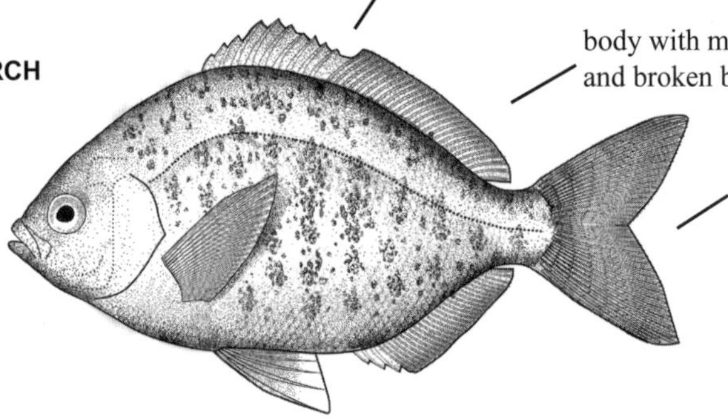


17b Bars or broken bars not extending above lateral line; caudal fin with black posterior margin:

SILVER SURFPERCH

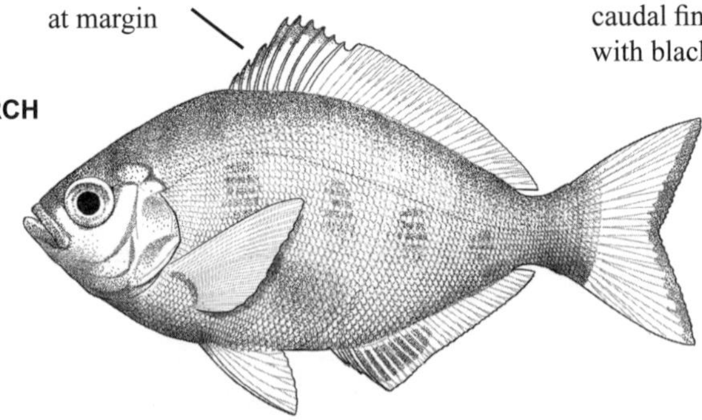

# GOATFISH, Family Mullidae and TRIPLETAIL, Family Lobotidae

**BIGSCALE GOATFISH, *Pseudupeneus grandisquamis* (Gill, 1863).** Family MULLIDAE

San Onofre, southern California (LACM 31847-1) to Chile, including Gulf of California and Islas Galápagos. Usually rare off southern California, but a few may appear in these waters during El Niños; common from Laguna San Ignacio, southern Baja California into tropics. Length to about 30 cm (12 in) TL. Depth: 1–67 m (3–220 ft). Back bright pink to violet, reddish, or pink on sides with dark red lateral stripe; pearly spots or streaks run from head through caudal peduncle. D VII–VIII + I,8; A I–II,6; Pect. 13–16; LLs 28–32. (Alternative name RED GOATFISH). *Mulloidichthys dentatus* (Gill, 1862) (MEXICAN GOATFISH) noted from southern California in M&L was based on a misidentification of *P. grandisquamis* (Lea and Rosenblatt, 2000).

**PACIFIC TRIPLETAIL, *Lobotes pacificus* Gilbert, 1898.** Family LOBOTIDAE

Circumglobal; Japan, Sea of Japan, and southern Kuril Islands; San Pedro Breakwater, southern California (LACM 45684-1) to Chimbote, Peru, including Gulf of California. Usually rare in southern California (although occasionally present during some warm-water years); common in tropics. Length to 110 cm (43.3 in) TL. Bays, brackish estuaries, coastal fresh waters, and sometimes well out to sea around floating objects. Usually brown or green, sometimes light and dark blotched. One California specimen chocolate brown on head, dorsal, anal, and caudal fins with silvery-bronze sides and operculum; juveniles yellowish with dark spots. D XI–XIII,15–16; A III,10–12; Pect. 15–17; Pelvic I,5; GR 5–7 + 13–15; Vert. 24. (Considered by some authors a junior synonym of *Lobotes surinamensis* (Bloch, 1790)).

BIGSCALE GOATFISH

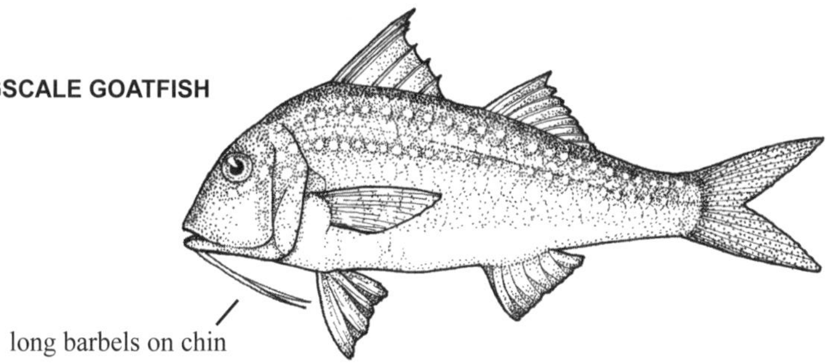


PACIFIC TRIPLETAIL

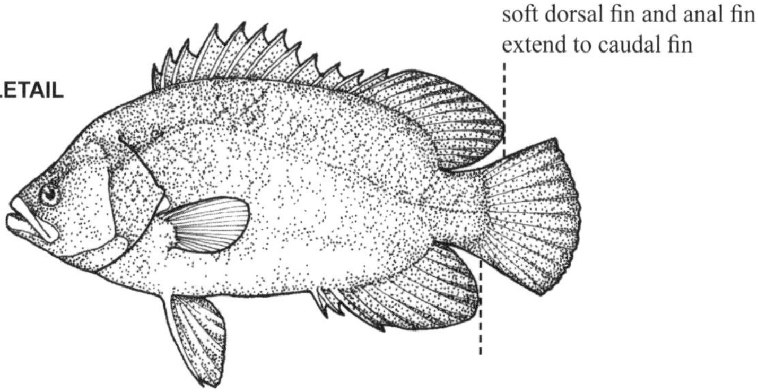

## DAMSELFISHES, Family Pomacentridae

**PANAMIC SERGEANT MAJOR, *Abudefduf troschelii* (Gill, 1862).** King Harbor, Redondo Beach, southern California to Pucusana, Peru, including Gulf of California and Islas Galápagos and other offshore islands. Rare in southern California; common at least as far northward as Bahía Magdalena, southern Baja California and into tropics. Length to 22.9 cm (9 in) TL. Depth: intertidal to 15 m (50 ft). Blue or silvery-green all over (except back often yellow); 5 dark bars on sides, partial or faint bar on caudal peduncle. D XII–XIII,12–13; A II,11–12; Pect. 16–20; GRt 23–33.

**WHITETAIL DAMSELFISH, *Stegastes leucorus* (Gilbert, 1892).** Santa Catalina and San Clemente Islands, southern California; Islas Coronados, northern Baja California; Isla Guadalupe and Islas San Benito, central Baja California (SIO 77-396); Bahía Magdalena, southern Baja California; southwestern Gulf of California; Mazatlán, Mexico. Rare in southern California. Length to 17 cm (6.7 in) TL. Depth: intertidal to 18 m (59 ft). Adults dark brown with dark scale margin; white band on caudal peduncle; soft dorsal, soft anal, and pelvic fins may be edged in blue; outer edge of pectoral fin light or yellow; iris blue. Juveniles blue or blue-brown with yellowish or greenish nape, upper back, and spinous dorsal fin; dark ocellus at rear of dorsal fin; caudal peduncle sometimes white. D XII,14–16; A II,12–14; Pect. 20–22; GRt 10–20.

**GARIBALDI, *Hypsypops rubicundus* (Girard, 1854).** Monterey Bay, central California to southwest corner of Gulf of California, southern Baja California and Islas Revillagigedos and Tres Marias. Common from San Miguel Island, southern California to Bahía Magdalena, southern Baja California. Length to 35.6 cm (14 in) TL. Depth: intertidal to 39 m (128 ft). Adult uniform golden-orange. Juveniles reddish-orange with bright blue spots; very young benthic juveniles with dark blue head and back. D XI–XIII,15–17; A II,12–15; Pect. 23–24; Pelvic I,5; LLp 21; LLs 30; GR 3 + 12; Vert. 26.

**BLACKSMITH, *Chromis punctipinnis* (Cooper, 1863).** Monterey Bay, central California to Punta San Pablo, southern Baja California. Historically, common from southern California to at least Isla Asuncion, southern Baja California; common into central California during some warm-water intrusions. Length to 30.5 cm (12 in) TL. Depth: 2–62 m (7–203 ft). Adults dark blue to black on back, gray-blue on sides; black spots on posterior half of body. Juveniles bicolored with blue-gray anterior and brassy-orange posterior. D XII–XIII,10–13; A II,10–12; Pect. 20–22; Pelvic I,5; LLp 18; LLs 29; GRt 20–22; Vert. 26.

## KEY TO THE DAMSELFISHES:
Created by Bill Power
(Principal sources: Miller & Lea, 1972; Allen, 1991)

1a Body with 5 dark bars and 1 on caudal peduncle (1st and last bars can fade in adults):

**PANAMIC SERGEANT MAJOR**

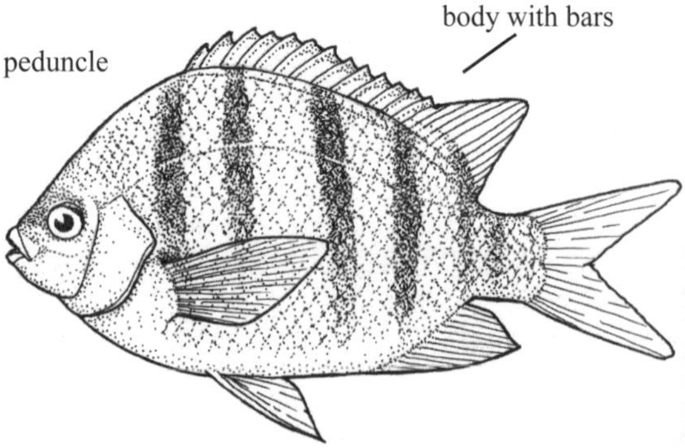


1b No bars on body….. 2 (next page)

2a Body dark with white band on caudal peduncle and yellow or light edge on pectoral fins (juveniles orange to yellow over purple to blue):

**WHITETAIL DAMSELFISH**

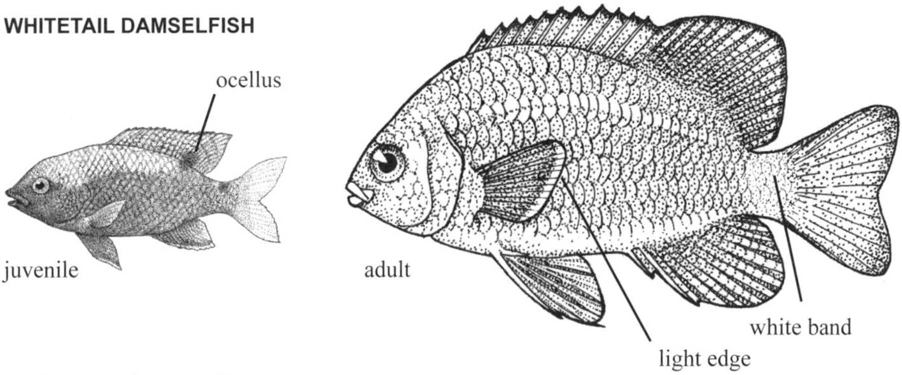


2b Body not as above….. 3

3a Body orange (juveniles with blue spots); dorsal fin soft-rays 15 or more:

**GARIBALDI**

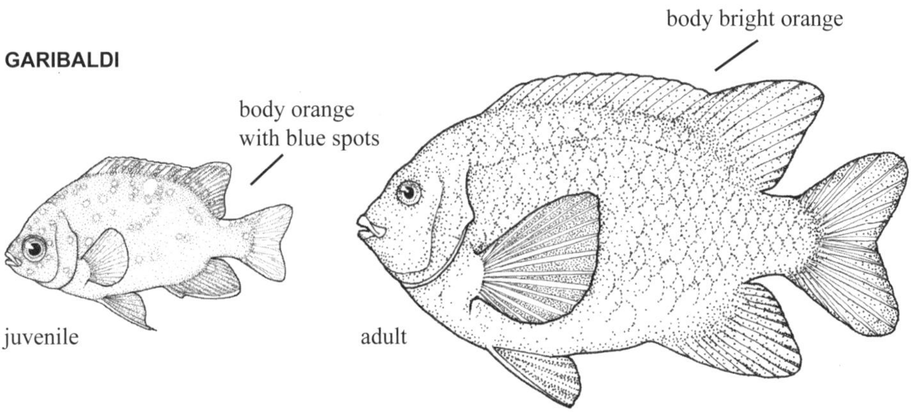


3b Body not orange; dorsal fin soft-rays fewer than 15….. 4

4a Body dark blue-black with black spots on posterior half (juveniles bicolored with brassy-orange tail):

**BLACKSMITH**

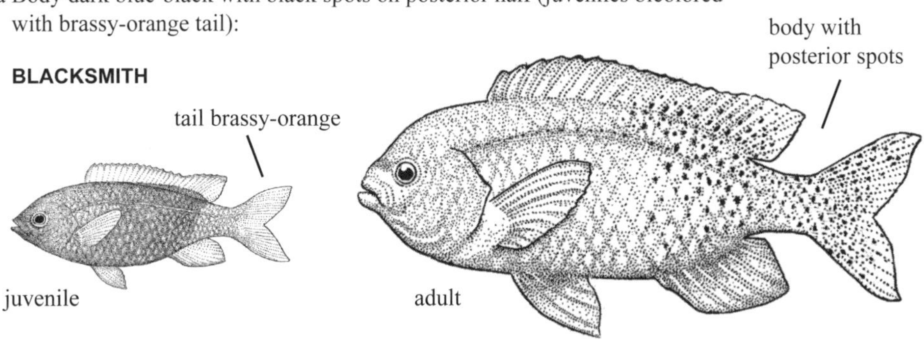


4b Body without spots….. 5 (next page)

## DAMSELFISHES (continued)

**SWALLOW DAMSELFISH, *Azurina hirundo* Jordan & McGregor, 1898.** Anacapa, Santa Catalina, and San Clemente Islands, southern California and Isla Guadalupe, Islas San Benito, Rocas Alijos, and Islas Revillagigedo. Rare in southern California. Length to 17 cm (6.8 in) TL. Depth: shallow waters to perhaps 30 m (98 ft). Blue to olive on back, silvery below; sometimes with light fin margin. D XII,10–12; A II,11–12; Pect. 20–21; LLp 27–31; GRt 25–27.

**SILVERSTRIPE CHROMIS, *Chromis alta* Greenfield & Woods, 1980.** Santa Catalina Island, southern California; Islas San Benito, central Baja California (SIO 85-199), and (mainland) Arrecife Sacramento (29°40'N, 115°47'W), central Baja California to Pucusana, Peru, including Gulf of California, Islas Galápagos, and many other offshore islands. Rare off southern California; common from Islas San Benito into tropics. Length to 17.3 cm (6.8 in) TL. Depth: 1–200 m (4–656 ft). Adults brown. Juveniles dark blue with light stripe running from anterior dorsal fin along back to caudal peduncle. D XIII,12–14; A II,12–13; Pect. 19–21; LLp 16–17; GR 7–9 + 20–24. (Alternative names OVAL CHROMIS, OVAL DAMSELFISH).

5a Body long, BD into TL more than 3; body silvery-blue; dorsal fin spines 12; lateral line pores 27–31:

**SWALLOW DAMSELFISH**

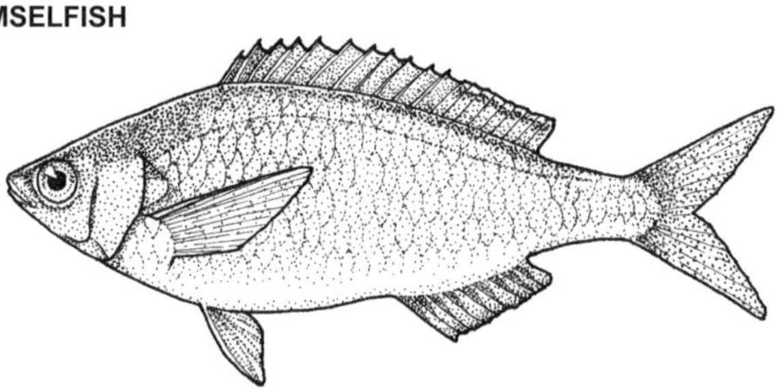

5b Body oval, BD into TL less than 3; body blue, black, or brown (juveniles with silver or white stripe along base of dorsal fin); dorsal fin spines 13; lateral line pores 16–19:

**SILVERSTRIPE CHROMIS**

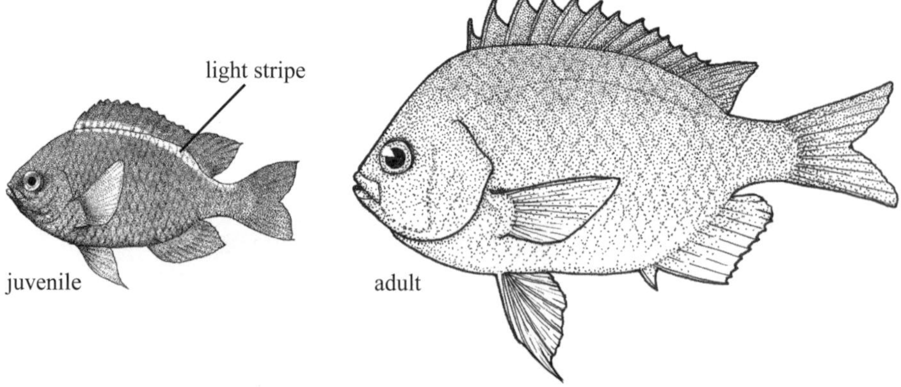

## RONQUILS, Family Bathymasteridae

**STRIPEFIN RONQUIL, *Rathbunella alleni* Gilbert, 1904.** Perhaps as far north as Barkley Sound, Vancouver Island; Marin County, north of San Francisco Bay, northern California to Bahía San Carlos, northern Baja California. Common at least from central to southern California. Length to 16.1 cm (6.3 in) SL. Depth: 2–146 m (6–479 ft). Color and pattern variable: head and body brown, gray, or pink, often with series of dark and light blotches and spots; anterior dorsal fin with dark blotch; anal fin with blue stripe; edge of anal fin dark in males and light in females. D 43–45; A 32–34; Pect. 15–18; GR 3–4 + 10–11; Vert. 46–50. (Formerly ROUGH RONQUIL: M&L).

**BLUEBANDED RONQUIL, *Rathbunella hypoplecta* (Gilbert, 1890).** Point Conception, southern California to San Tomás anchorage (31°33'N, 116°24'W), northern Baja California. Previous reports from San Francisco and farther north are probably due to confusion with STRIPEFIN RONQUIL and perhaps NORTHERN RONQUIL. Common at least in southern California. Length to 27.7 cm (10.9 in) TL. Depth: 3–119 m (9–390 ft), possibly to 136 m (446 ft). Color and pattern variable: gray, brown, or pink (males often dark brown or purple on back); regularly spaced white blotches below lateral line and dark and white blotches on back; anal fin with bright blue bands running parallel to soft-rays and with short oblique yellow band anteriorly; edge of anal fin dark in males and light in females. D 43–46; A 32–35; Pect. 16–19; GR 3–4 + 10–11; Vert. 49–51. Evidently this is the "DEEPWATER RONQUIL" of Eschmeyer and Herald (1983). (Formerly SMOOTH RONQUIL: M&L).

**NORTHERN RONQUIL, *Ronquilus jordani* (Gilbert, 1889).** Southeastern Bering Sea and Amchitka Island, Aleutian Islands to La Jolla, southern California. Common from about Alaska Peninsula to Oregon; uncommon in northern California, rare further southward. Length to 20 cm (8 in) TL. Depth: 3–275 m (10–902 ft), usually shallower than 150 m (492 ft). Head brownish-gray with 2 distinct yellow bands on cheek; body pale gray with dark mottling, belly light; dorsal and caudal fins light gray and yellow; anal fin with yellow stripe near base, distal portion dark in males, light in females; pectoral fin yellow, lower soft-rays and distal margin dark in males, dusky in females; pelvic fin black in males, white in females. D 40–47; A 31–36; Pect. 16–19; GR 3–4 + 10–11 = 13–15; Vert. 49–51.

**STRIPEFIN RONQUIL**

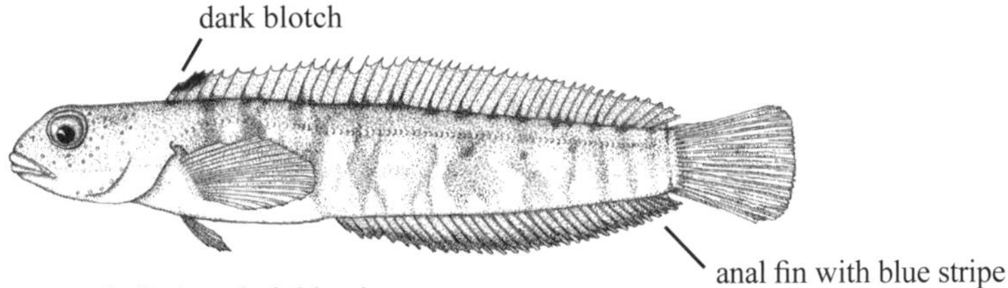


**BLUEBANDED RONQUIL**

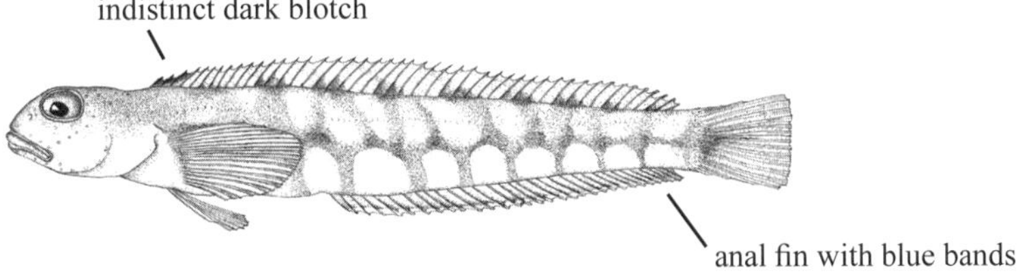


**NORTHERN RONQUIL**

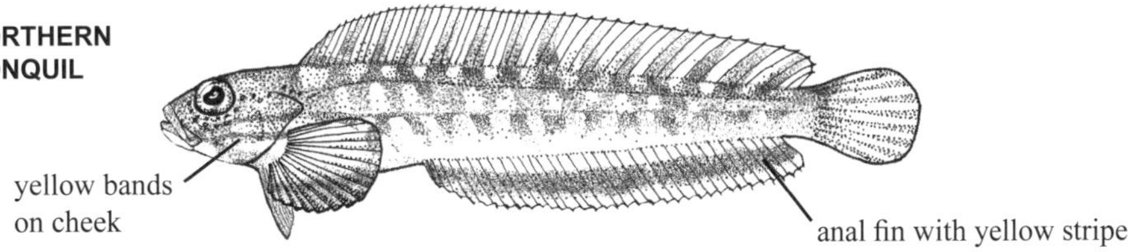

# WRASSES and PARROTFISH, Family Labridae

NOTE: Most labrids are protogynous hermaphrodites, whereby sex change is generally female to male. The terminal phase refers to adult males and the initial phase refers to females and/or juveniles.

**BLACKSPOT WRASSE, *Decodon melasma* Gomon, 1974.** Laguna Beach, southern California; Gulf of California to Banco de Máncora, Peru, including vicinity of Cabo San Lucas, southern Baja California and Islas Galápagos. Rare in southern California; common in tropics. Length to 32.3 cm (12.7 in) TL. Depth: 18–220 m (60–722 ft). Red or pink above, white abdomen; 3 bright yellow curved stripes on head (stripes may fade after death); dark blotch on side. Juveniles pink with 5–6 dusky bars on sides. D XI–XII,9–10; A III,9–10; Pect. 14–18; GR 5–7 + 9–12; Vert. 28–29.

**CALIFORNIA SHEEPHEAD, *Bodianus pulcher* (Ayres, 1854).** Monterey Bay, central California to Cabo San Lucas, southern Baja California, including Gulf of California and Isla Guadalupe, central Baja California. Common from southern California southward to southern Baja California and in Gulf of California. Length to 91.4 cm (36 in) TL. Depth: intertidal to 150 m (492 ft). Terminal phase with black head, red band in middle, and black in posterior portion of body. Adult female uniform brownish-red to rose. Chin white on both sexes. Juveniles red-orange, gold, salmon, or lemon-yellow with at least 1 white stripe along side; 2 black spots on dorsal fin, 1 each on pelvic, anal, and caudal fins. D XI–XII,10–11; A III,10–12; Pect. 17–19; Pelvic I,5; LLs 60; Vert. 28. (Formerly *Pimelometopon pulchrum* Ayres, 1854: M&L). We follow Baliga and Law (2016) and Santini et al. (2016) and remove this species from the genus *Semicossyphus*.

## KEY TO THE WRASSES and PARROTFISH:
Revised by Julianne Kalman Passarelli
(Principal source: Allen & Groce, 2001)

1a Dorsal fin spines 9–10….. 3 (page 281)

1b Dorsal fin spines 11–12….. 2

2a Scales large (about 30 in lateral line); lower limb of preopercle scaly; yellow stripes on head:

i. Single dark blotch on side; BD 25–30% of SL; body red; typically 13 cm SL or longer:

**BLACKSPOT WRASSE**
adult

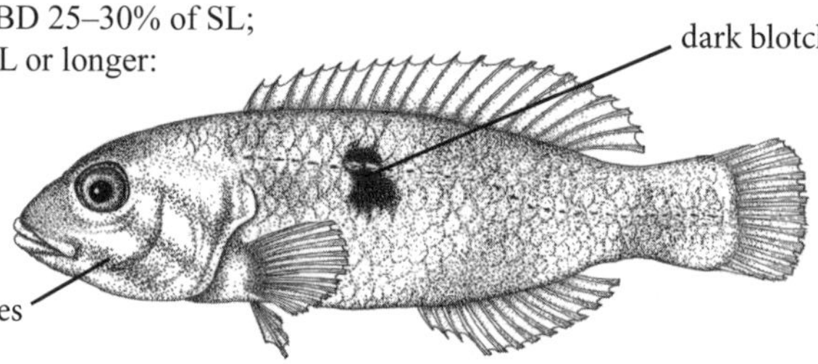


ii. Five to 6 dark bars on side (1 on caudal peduncle); BD about 20–25% of SL; body pink; typically less than 13 cm SL:

**BLACKSPOT WRASSE**
juvenile

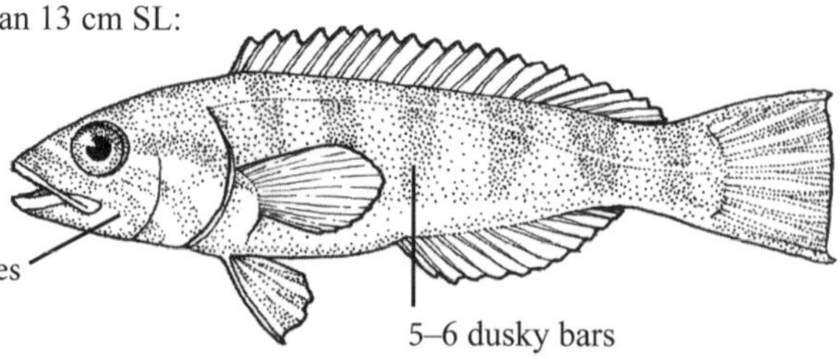


2b (next page)

2b Scales small (about 60 in lateral line); lower limb of preopercle naked; no yellow stripes on head:

i. Head and tail black, midbody red; fins without spots; typically 30 cm SL or longer:

**CALIFORNIA SHEEPHEAD**
male

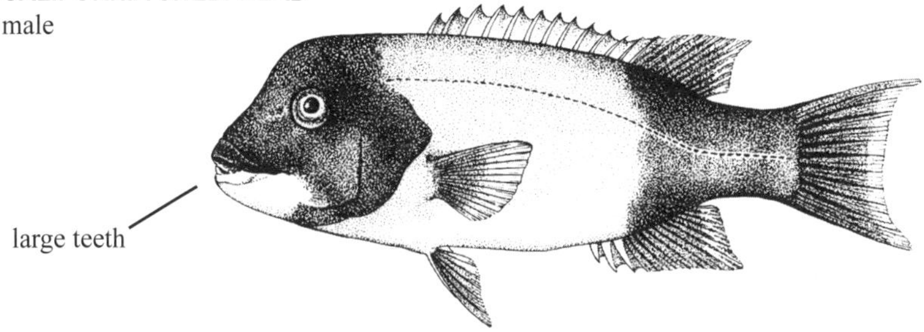


ii. Body pinkish; fins without spots; typically 15–30 cm SL:

**CALIFORNIA SHEEPHEAD**
female

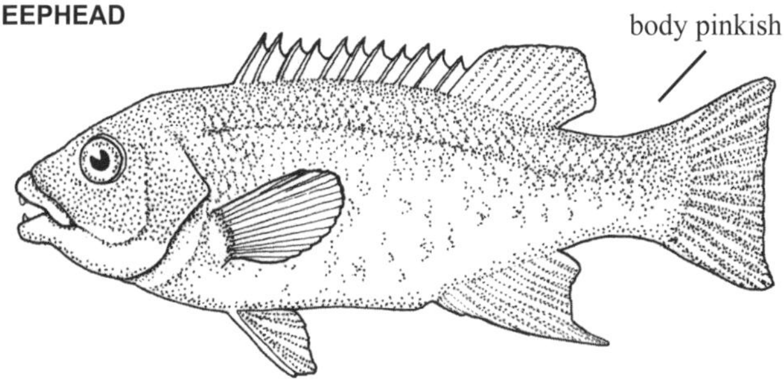


iii. Body reddish or gold with single white stripe on side; black spot(s) on dorsal fin, caudal base, anal fin, and pelvic fins; typically shorter than 15 cm SL:

**CALIFORNIA SHEEPHEAD**
juvenile

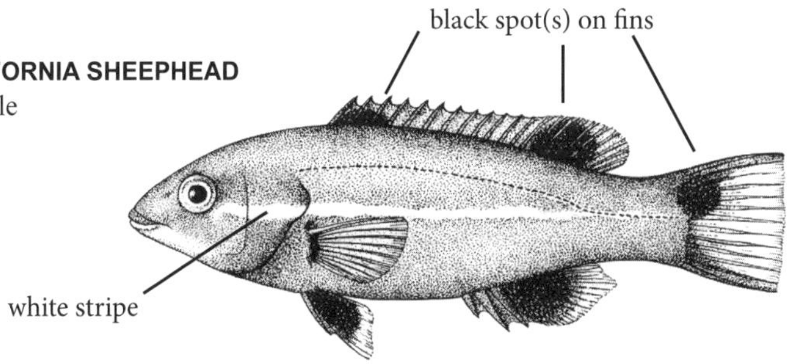


3a (next page)

## WRASSES and PARROTFISH (continued)

**LOOSETOOTH PARROTFISH, *Nicholsina denticulata* (Evermann & Radcliffe, 1917).** Santa Catalina Island, southern California; also Islas San Benito and Isla Cedros, and (mainland) Rocas Chester (27°53'N, 115°04'W), central Baja California to Iquique, northern Chile, including Gulf of California and Islas Galápagos. Rare in southern California; common from southern Baja California and into tropics. Length to 32 cm (12.6 in) TL. Depth: 1–30 m (4–98 ft). Terminal phase green, greenish-brown, or greenish-gray; bright red caudal fin (sometimes with lighter spots) and pectoral fin base; red or pink lower jaw and throat; black spot on anterior dorsal fin. Two initial phase patterns: 1) drab brown, gray, or reddish, with dark back and lateral stripe and 2) reddish with dark mottling. D IX,10; A III,9; Pect. 13–14; Pelvic I,5; GRt 11–13; Vert. 25. (Recently in the family Scaridae).

**SEÑORITA, *Oxyjulis californica* (Günther, 1861).** Salt Point, northern California to Bahía Magdalena, southern Baja California; also reported, although without attribution, from Bahía Concepcion, Gulf of California. Larvae taken south of Bahía Magdalena at about 23°30'N. Common from central California to about Bahía San Juanico, southern Baja California. Length to 25.4 cm (10 in) TL. Depth: intertidal to 101 m (331 ft). Reddish-orange above, yellow below; black area on caudal fin base. D IX–X,13; A III,13; Pect. 12–15; Pelvic I,5; LLs 28; GR 6–7 + 12–16; Vert. 26–27. This species and ROCK WRASSE may be in the same genus (Baliga and Law, 2016).

**ROCK WRASSE, *Halichoeres semicinctus* (Ayres, 1859).** Monterey Breakwater, central California to Gulf of California and Isla Guadalupe, central Baja California. Common from southern California southwards. Length to 38 cm (15 in) TL. Depth: surface and intertidal to 79 m (259 ft). Terminal phase green or orangish, dark bar behind pectoral fin; yellow pectoral fins; pink eyes. Initial phase (females and immature males) brownish, yellowish, reddish, or orangish, with series of dark scales on back. Mid-phase (males with female coloration) with dark bar behind pectoral fin. Juveniles orange-yellow with broad cream-white horizontal midline. D IX,11–12; A III,12–13; Pect. 12–13; Pelvic I,5; LLs 26; GR 5–7 + 11–13; Vert. 26. This species and SEÑORITA may be in the same genus (Baliga and Law, 2016).

3a *From 1a: dorsal fin spines 9–10*
Scales present on sides of head; anal fin soft-rays 9:

**LOOSETOOTH PARROTFISH**

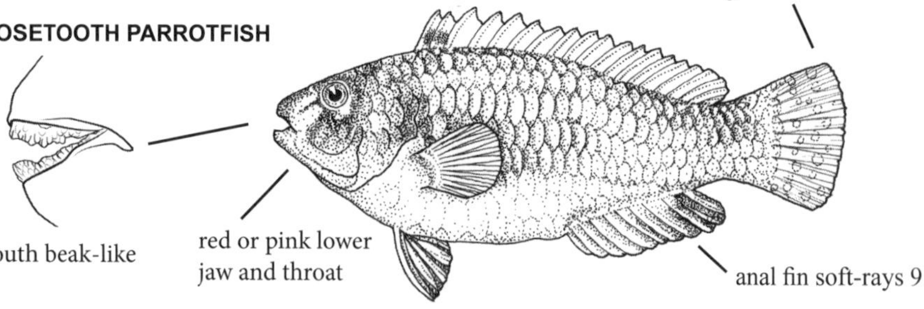


3b Scales few or absent on head; anal fin soft-rays 12–13….. 4

4a Body with broad black spot or band on base of caudal fin; posterior canines rudimentary:

**SEÑORITA**

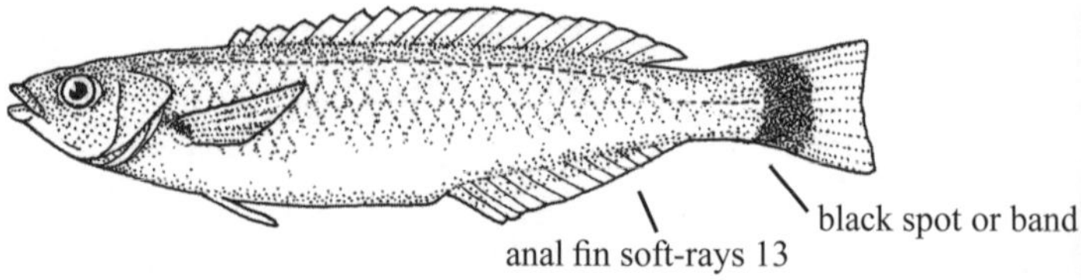


4b (next page)

4b Broad black spot or band lacking on base of caudal fin; posterior canines well developed:

i. Dark bar behind pectoral fin; back unmarked or with multiple light bars; typically 30 cm SL or longer:

**ROCK WRASSE**
male

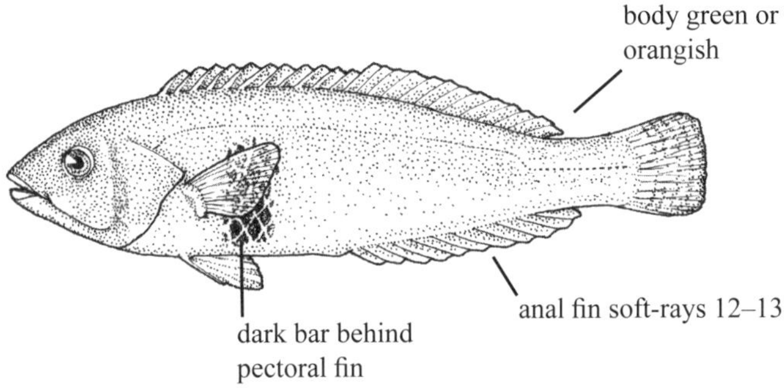


ii. Dark bar behind pectoral fin lacking; black flecks generally present on body; typically 12–30 cm SL:

**ROCK WRASSE**
female

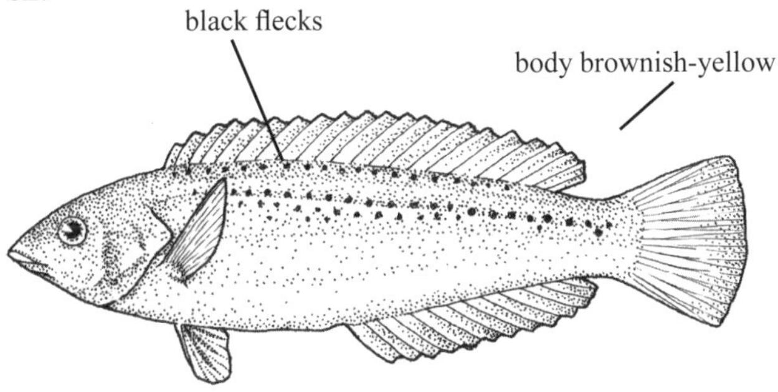


iii. Dark bar behind pectoral fin lacking; body with broad, cream-white stripe near midline and 2 black spots on dorsal fin; typically shorter than 12 cm SL:

**ROCK WRASSE**
juvenile

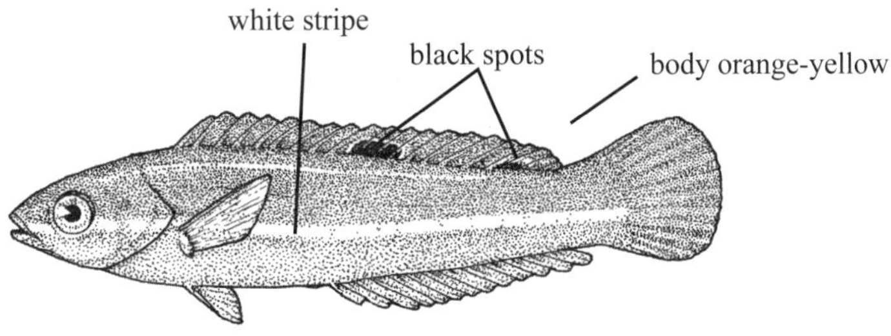

## EELPOUTS, Family Zoarcidae

**BEARDED EELPOUT, *Lyconema barbatum* Gilbert, 1896.** Northern Oregon (45°46'N, 124°40'W) to between Islas San Benito and Isla Cedros (28°17'N, 115°28'W), central Baja California (SIO 71-121). Published reports of occurrence in the Bering Sea are mistaken. Common at least from northern California to southern California. Length to 22 cm (8.7 in) TL. Depth: 45–472 m (148–1,548 ft). Light-colored with dark brown or dusky spots on sides and dorsal and anal fins. D 99–105; A 90–94; Pect. 15–17; Vert. 104–114.

**SNAKEHEAD EELPOUT, *Lycenchelys crotalinus* (Gilbert, 1890).** Western Bering Sea across Shirshov Ridge and Commander Plateau; eastern Bering Sea and Gulf of Alaska to central Baja California (27°12'N). Common at least from Bering Sea and Gulf of Alaska to southern California. Length to 46.8 cm (18.4 in) TL. Depth: 200–2,816 m (656–9,239 ft). Dark olive-brown to brown-black with light-colored, non-overlapping scale pockets (giving spotted appearance); head (and sometimes pectoral fins) mottled with blue and sometimes white. D 118–125; A 103–113; Pect. 15–18; Pelvic 3; GRt 15–18; Vert. 121–131. (Formerly FLATCHEEK EELPOUT, *Embryx crotalina* (Gilbert, 1890): M&L).

**BLACKBELLY EELPOUT, *Lycodes pacificus* Collett, 1879.** Aleutian Islands and Gulf of Alaska to Ensenada, northern Baja California. Common at least from Gulf of Alaska southward to at least southern California. Length to 46 cm (18 in) TL. Depth: 7–1,036 m (23–3,399 ft). Gray to reddish-brown; dorsal fin and rear of anal fin sometimes edged in black; pectoral fin light; juveniles with black blotch in anterior part of dorsal fin and white bands on body, both fading with age. D 90–107; A 70–90; Pect. 16–19; Pelvic 3; GR 0–3 + 8–17 = 8–19; Vert. 102–104. (Formerly *Lycodopsis pacifica* (Collett, 1879): M&L).

**BIGFIN EELPOUT, *Lycodes cortezianus* (Gilbert, 1890).** Southeastern Alaska (55°30'N, 134°53'W) to San Diego, southern California. Common at least from British Columbia to off San Diego. Length to 49.3 cm (19.4 in) TL. Depth: 20–1,190 m (66–3,903 ft). Light brown to blue-black dorsally, lighter ventrally; black blotch on anterior edge of dorsal fin, fading or absent in large adults; black on posterior portion of dorsal, anal, and caudal fins. D 105–109; A 89–92; Pect. 18–21; Pelvic 3; GR 2 + 11–15 = 13–19; Vert. 112–115. (Formerly *Aprodon cortezianus* Gilbert, 1890: M&L).

**KAMCHATKA EELPOUT, *Lycenchelys camchatica* (Gilbert & Burke, 1912).** Sea of Okhotsk and southeastern Kamchatka, and Commander Islands; Bering Sea south of Cape Navarin to near Unalaska Island to northern Baja California. Common at least from Kamchatka, Russia to Bering Sea to southern California. Length to 43 cm (16.9 in) TL. Depth: about 256–2,100 m (840–6,890 ft). Bluish-purple or olive-brown; bluish or greenish on head and pectoral fins; pectoral fin greenish or yellowish. D 112–117; A 100–105; Pect. 12–15; Pelvic 3; GRt 14–18; Vert. 118–125.

## KEY TO THE EELPOUTS:

Revised by Eric Anderson

(Principal sources: Miller & Lea, 1972; Anderson, 1994, 1995; Anderson et al., 2009)

1a Pelvic fins absent….. 8 (page 286)

1b Pelvic fins present (small or minute), with 2 or 3 soft-rays….. 2 (next page)

2a Two rows of cirri under each mandible; large brown spots on sides of body and median fins:

**BEARDED EELPOUT**

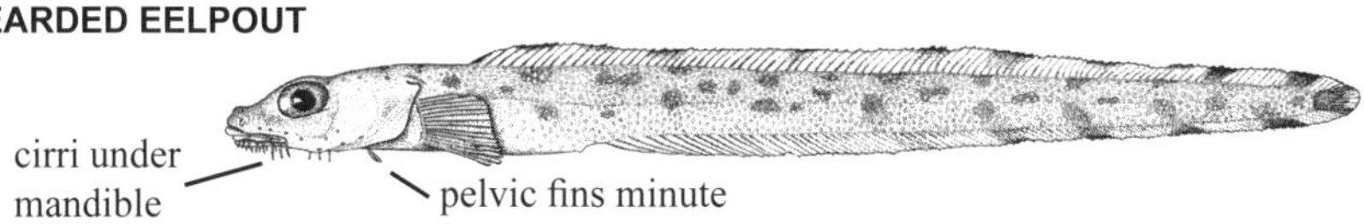


2b No cirri under each mandible; no brown spots on sides or median fins….. 3

3a Palatine and vomerine teeth present….. 6

3b Palatine and/or vomerine teeth absent….. 4

4a Body dark brown; BD at anal fin origin about 5−8% TL; sensory pores under eyes and mandible conspicuous:

**SNAKEHEAD EELPOUT**

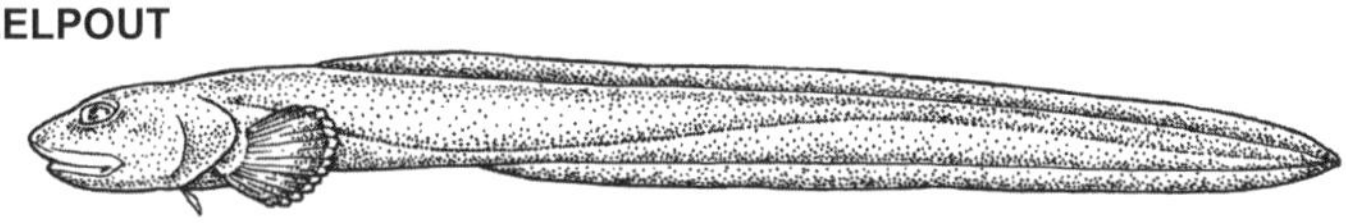

4b Body tan to reddish-gray; BD at anal fin origin 8% or greater than TL; sensory pores under eyes minute and mandible small….. 5

5a Vomerine and palatine teeth absent:

**BLACKBELLY EELPOUT**

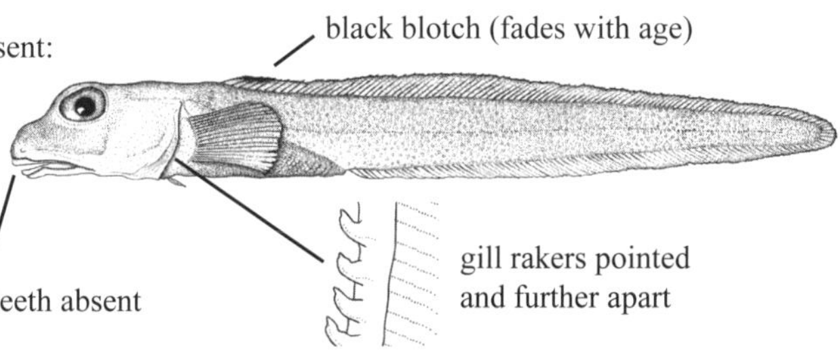


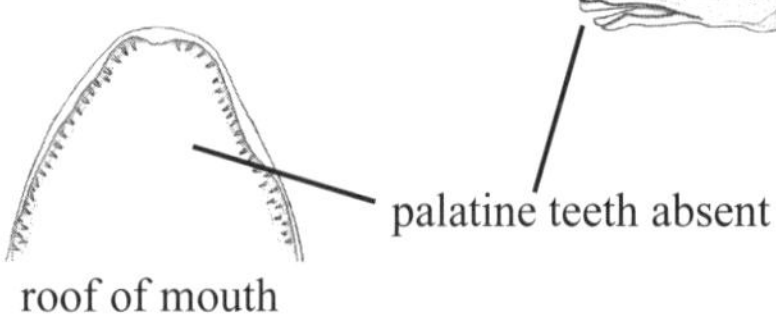


5b Vomerine teeth absent, palatine teeth present:

**BIGFIN EELPOUT**

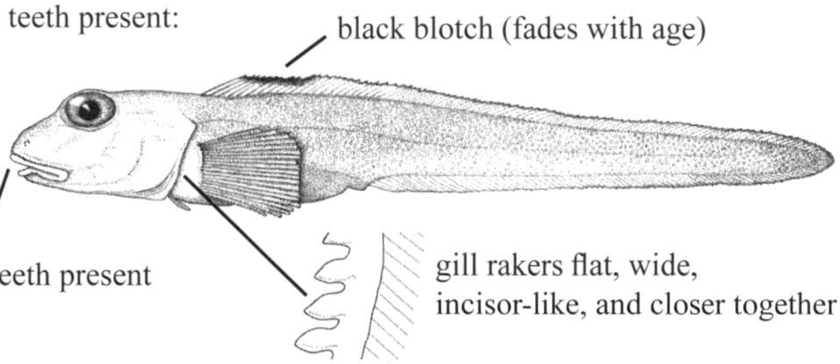


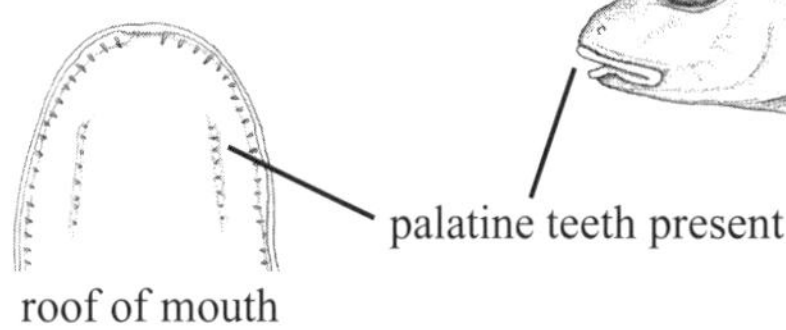


6a *From 3a: palatine and vomerine teeth present*
Pectoral fin soft-rays 12–15; head pores conspicuous; scales present on cheeks (readily seen under a microscope and most apparent in specimens over 10 cm):

**KAMCHATKA EELPOUT**

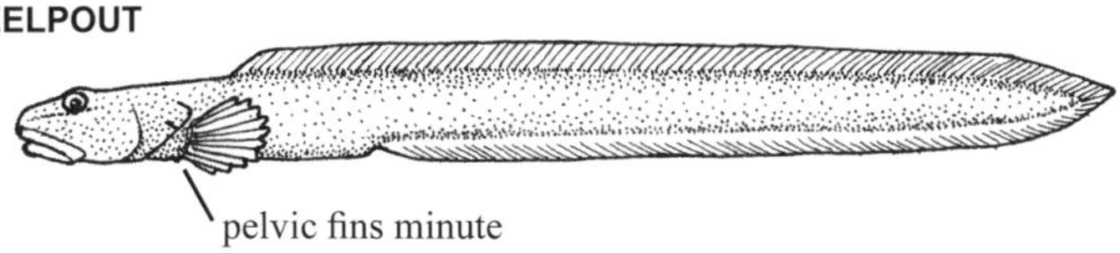


6b Pectoral fin soft-rays 17–21; head pores minute; no scales on cheeks….. 7 (next page)

## EELPOUTS (continued)

**BLACK EELPOUT, *Lycodes diapterus* Gilbert, 1892.** Sea of Japan to western Bering Sea; Vancouver Island, British Columbia to off San Diego, southern California (SIO 95-2). Apparently common along much of its geographic range. Length to 39 cm (15.4 in) TL. Depth: 13–1,300 m (43–4,264 ft). Dusky brown to black, somewhat lighter on sides; commonly 3–9 lighter bars on sides (faint or disappearing in adults); pelvic, pectoral, and anal fins blue-black; dorsal fin dark, commonly with dark blotch anteriorly; mouth and gill cavity dark. D 104–117; A 92–107; Pect. 17–21; Pelvic 3; GRt 14; Vert. 111–125.

**SHORTFIN EELPOUT, *Lycodes brevipes* Bean, 1890.** Western and eastern Bering Sea and eastern Aleutian Islands to central California (34°34'N). Common from Aleutian Islands and Bering Sea to Washington; apparently rare in California. Length to 39 cm (15.4 in) TL. Depth: 2–973 m (7–3,192 ft). Brown or gray-brown above, pale belly; underside of head cream or tan; 9–13 narrow light bands on dorsal fin and body (sometimes absent); dorsal and anal fins with dark margin. D 93–99; A 78–81; Pect. 18–21; Pelvic 3; GR 1–3 + 10–12 = 11–15; Vert. 99–103.

**PERSIMMON EELPOUT, *Eucryphycus californicus* (Starks & Mann, 1911).** Ascension Canyon, central California (SIO 07-183) to San Diego, southern California. Common at least in Monterey Bay in bottom drift algae; abundance in other areas unknown. Length to 22 cm (8.8 in) TL. Depth: 60–545 m (197–1,787 ft), primarily in 201 m (659 ft) and shallower. Dark orange or rose; pectoral fins bright orange. D 97–108; A 82–89; Pect. 13–15; Pelvic absent; Vert. 106–115. (Sometimes seen as *Maynea californicus* (Starks & Mann, 1911)).

**SOFT EELPOUT, *Bothrocara molle* Bean, 1890.** Southern Kamchatka Peninsula to Bering Sea to Chile, also reported from Gulf of California and western south Atlantic. Common from Vancouver Island, British Columbia to at least southern California. Length to 58.7 cm (23.2 in) TL. Depth: 60–2,688 m (197–8,819 ft). Brown, darker ventrally and posteriorly; dorsal and anal fins edged with black; mouth and gill chambers dark; peritoneum black. D 99–113; A 84–99; Pect. 13–16; Pelvic absent; GR 5–7 + 13–20 = 18–26; Vert. 104–119.

**TWOLINE EELPOUT, *Bothrocara brunneum* (Bean, 1890).** Sea of Okhotsk and Pacific Ocean off Kuril Islands to Commander-Aleutian Islands Chain and Bering Sea to southern Baja California (27°12'N); also Gulf of California and Gulf of Panama. Common from Sea of Okhotsk and Kamchatka-Kuril Islands and Bering Sea southward to at least southern California. Length to 74 cm (29.1 in) TL. Depth: 129–2,570 m (423–8,430 ft). Uniformly light gray, white, or tan; lips dark brown anteriorly; dorsal and anal fins black or blue. D 106–112; A 90–96; Pect. 14–18; Pelvic absent; GR 5–7 + 12–18; Vert. 111–116.

**MIDWATER EELPOUT, *Melanostigma pammelas* Gilbert, 1896.** Western Gulf of Alaska (53°25'N, 168°10'W) to Gulf of Tehuantepec, Mexico. Common at least from central California to southern California. Length to 13.3 cm (5.2 in) TL. Meso- and possibly bathypelagic; depth: 91–2,012 m (298–6,601 ft). Dark brown or black, particularly head and belly; juveniles with silver-blue hue. D 73–88; A 64–75; Pect. 6–8; Pelvic absent; GRt 11–13; Vert. 86–90.

7a Pectoral fins deeply notched; body bluish-brown with irregular, pale bars or blotches:

**BLACK EELPOUT**

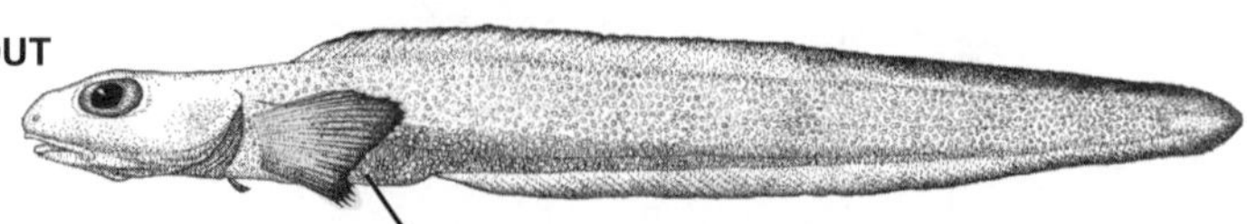


7b (next page)

7b Pectoral fins rounded; body brown with white bands extending from dorsal fin onto body and tail:

**SHORTFIN EELPOUT**

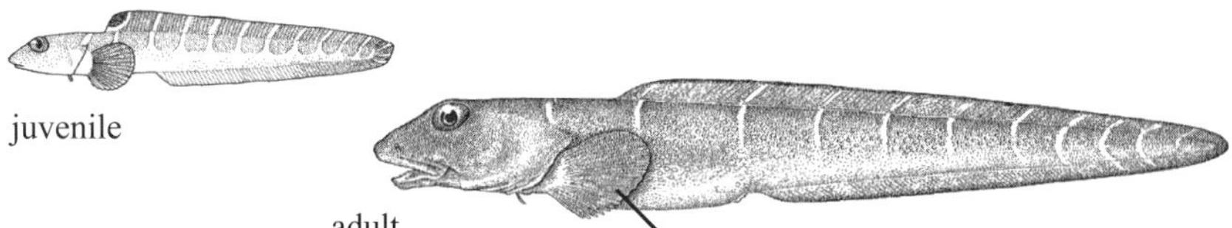


8a *From 1a: pelvic fins absent*
Scales absent….. 11

8b Scales small, cycloid….. 9

9a Three sensory pores across nape; head and body dark orange, abdomen light orange in life:

**PERSIMMON EELPOUT**

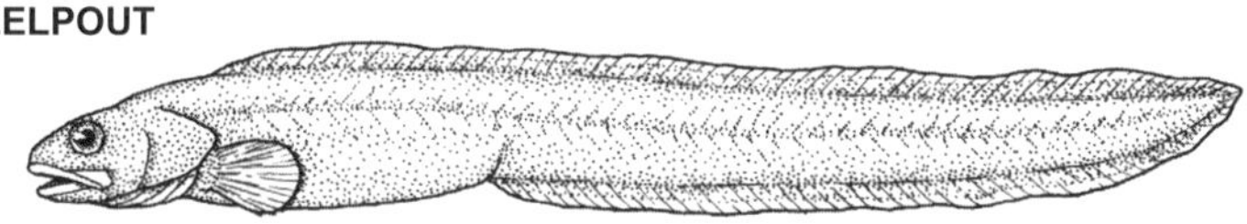

9b No pores across nape; head and body shades of gray, brown, black, silvery-blue or whitish in life….. 10

10a Gill rakers long and slender, with dorsal rakers on lower limb overlapping base of adjacent raker when pressed down; pectoral fin in adults reaching to or behind anus:

**SOFT EELPOUT**

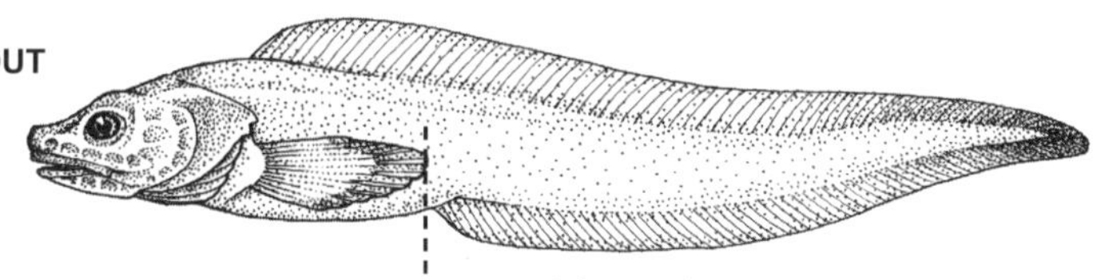


10b Gill rakers short and stout, with dorsal rakers on lower limb just reaching base of adjacent raker when pressed down; pectoral fin in adults not reaching anus:

**TWOLINE EELPOUT**

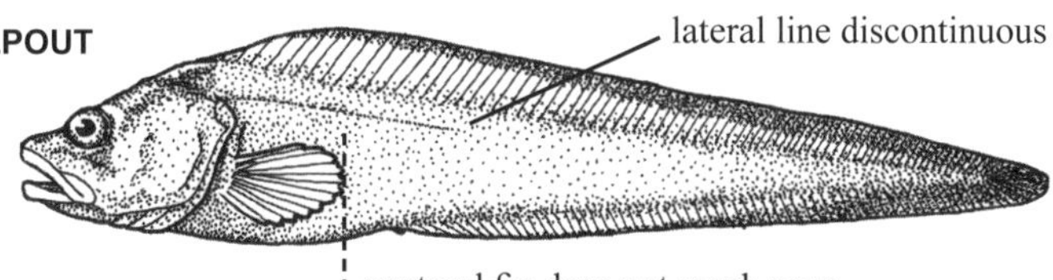


11a *From 8a: scales absent*
Body dark brown, head black; gill opening small, pore-like above pectoral fin; no interorbital pore:

**MIDWATER EELPOUT**

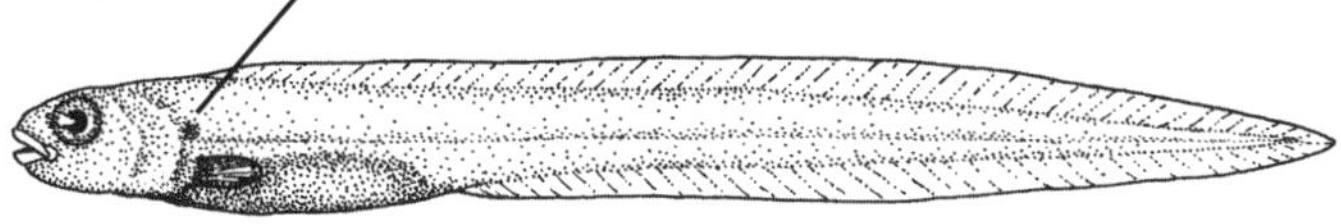


11b (next page)

# EELPOUTS (continued)

**PALLID EELPOUT, *Lycodapus mandibularis* Gilbert, 1915.** Prince William Sound, Gulf of Alaska to La Jolla Canyon, southern California. A reported occurrence off Peru is a mistake. Common from Gulf of Alaska to central California. Length to 20.6 cm (8.1 in) TL. Mesopelagic; depth: 96–1,237 m (315–4,057 ft). Translucent cream to silvery-white; faint black speckling on dorsal surface; back of mouth, gill cavity, and peritoneum dark. Some populations more darkly pigmented than others. D 76–90; A 65–79; Pect. 6–9; Pelvic absent; GR 1–2 + 9–13 = 10–15; Vert. 82–97.

**SPECKLEMOUTH EELPOUT, *Lycodapus psarostomatus* Peden & Anderson, 1981.** Eastern Bering Sea; British Columbia; Monterey Bay, central California. Length to 15.5 cm (6.1 in) SL. Mesopelagic; depth: 466–590 m (1,528–1,936 ft). The one record from California was a 9.8 cm (3.9 in) SL specimen collected by midwater trawl at 0–15 m (0–49 ft). Color in life unknown; mouth and gill cavity with dark speckles. D 89–98; A 86; Pect. 8; Pelvic absent; GRt 10; Vert. 96–100.

**DEEPWATER EELPOUT, *Lycodapus endemoscotus* Peden & Anderzson, 1978.** Sea of Okhotsk and Bering Sea as far northward as 59°43'N, 178°39'W and off central Aleutian Islands to Gulf of California and off Peru. Common at least from Sea of Okhotsk and Bering Sea and perhaps to central California. Length to 13.2 cm (5.2 in) SL. Meso- and bathypelagic; depth: 226–2,225 m (741–7,300 ft). Translucent whitish; very fine black speckles on back, head, and ventral surface, most dense posteriorly. D 84–91; A 74–81; Pect. 6–9; Pelvic absent; Vert. 87–95.

**LOOSESKIN EELPOUT, *Lycodapus dermatinus* Gilbert, 1896.** Welker Seamount, Gulf of Alaska to Gulf of California; Peru. Bering Sea and western Gulf of Alaska reports not verifiable. Common at least from Oregon to southern California. Length to 12.2 cm (4.8 in) SL. Meso- and bathypelagic; depth: 198–1,370 m (650–4,495 ft). Translucent white; rear of upper jaw, mouth, and gill cavity black. D 70–77; A 62–68; Pect. 6–8; Pelvic absent; GRt 14; Vert. 76–82.

**BLACKMOUTH EELPOUT, *Lycodapus fierasfer* Gilbert, 1890.** Western Bering Sea on Shirshov Ridge; eastern Bering Sea to Peru. Common at least from Bering Sea to northern Baja California. Length to 15.6 cm (6.1 in) TL. Meso-, bathy-, and benthopelagic; depth: 102–2,189 m (335–7,180 ft). Pearly with fine black speckling; mouth, gill cavity, and peritoneum black. D 82–85; A 70–74; Pect. 6–8; Pelvic absent.

11b Body whitish to beige, head pale with some silvery areas; gill opening broad, membranes free of isthmus posteriorly; interorbital pores 1 or 2 (may be slightly posterior of interorbit), rarely absent….. 12

12a Gill rakers long and slender; dorsal rakers on lower limb overlap base of 2 or 3 lower rakers when pressed down….. 15 (next page)

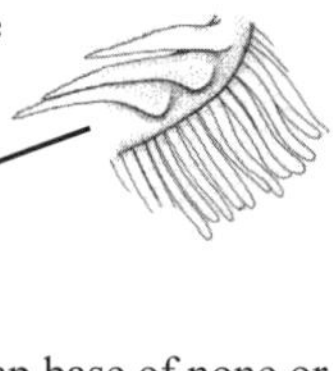

gill rakers long and slender

12b Gill rakers either short or nub-like; dorsal rakers on lower limb overlap base of none or 1 lower raker when pressed down….. 13 (next page)

gill rakers nub-like

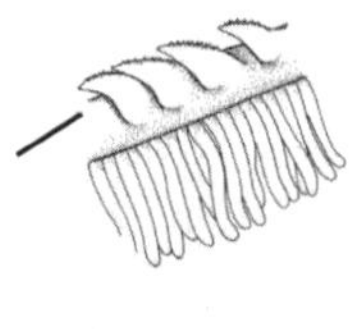

gill rakers short

13a Gill rakers short, with dorsal lower limb reaching almost to or just overlapping adjacent rakers when pressed down; vomerine teeth 1–5 (rarely absent):

**PALLID EELPOUT**

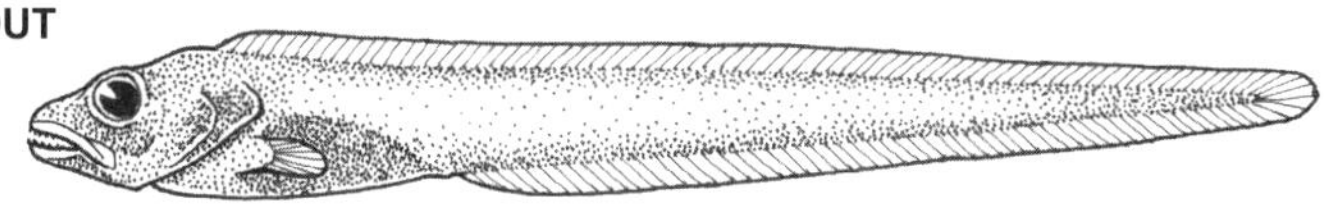

13b Gill rakers nub-like, with dorsal lower limb not overlapping adjacent rakers when pressed down; vomerine teeth 4–21 (fewest in large males)….. 14

14a Mouth cavity speckled with large melanophores; vertebrae 96–100:

**SPECKLEMOUTH EELPOUT**

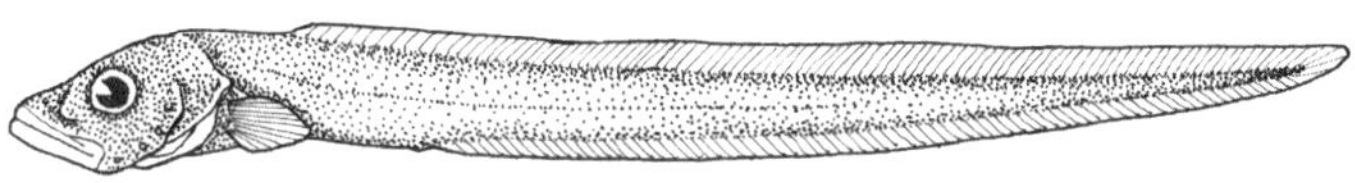

14b Mouth cavity black; vertebrae 87–95:

**DEEPWATER EELPOUT**

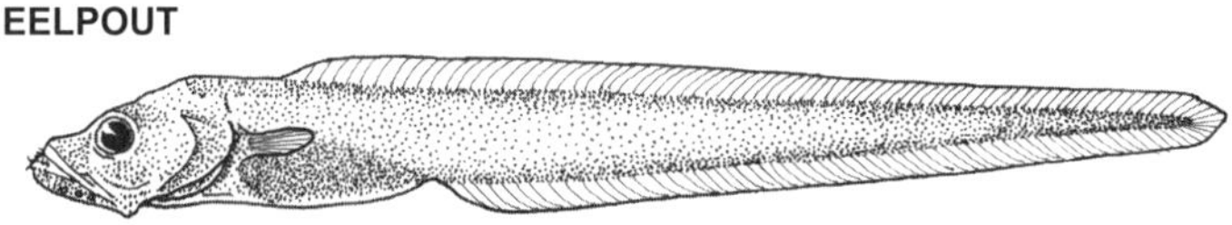

15a *From 12a: gill rakers long and slender*
Interorbital pore usually 1; jaws pale (except some black on rear portion of upper jaw):

**LOOSESKIN EELPOUT**

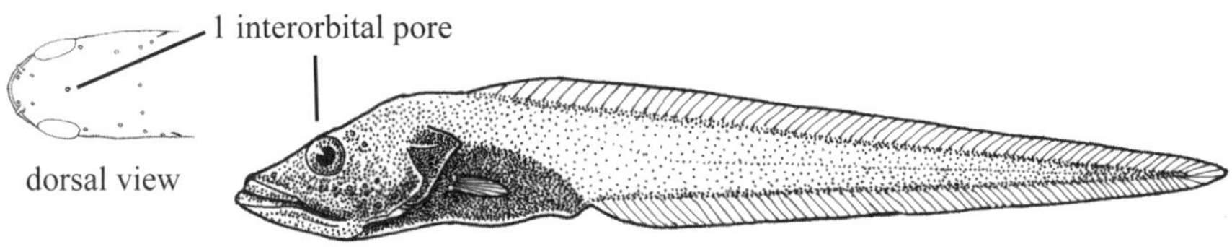


15b Interorbital pores usually 2; jaws black:

**BLACKMOUTH EELPOUT**

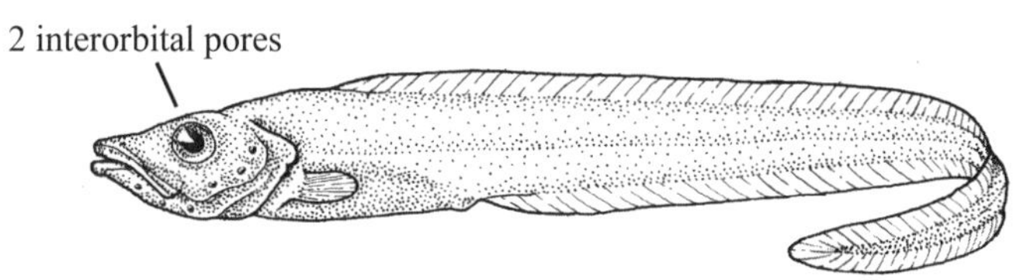

## PRICKLEBACKS, Family Stichaeidae

**MONKEYFACE PRICKLEBACK, *Cebidichthys violaceus* (Girard, 1854).** Netarts-Cape Mears area, Oregon to Bahia San Quintin, northern Baja California. Common off northern and central California and eastern-most northern Channel Islands, southern California. Length to 76.2 cm (30 in) TL. Depth: intertidal to 24 m (80 ft), possibly to 91 m (300 ft). Uniform black, gray, or olive; 2 dark bars below eye; few fish with orange spots on sides and orange-tipped fins. D XXII–XXV,40–43; A I–II,39–42; Pect. 10–11; Pelvic absent; GR 3–4 + 6–10 = 9–14; Vert. 65–71. (Formerly MONKEYFACE-EEL: M&L).

**THREELINE PRICKLEBACK, *Esselenichthys carli* (Follett & Anderson, 1990).** Pacific Grove, northern California to Bahia San Quintin, northern Baja California. Common at least in southern California. Length to 27 cm (10.6 in) SL. Depth: 1–29 m (4–95 ft). Color extremely variable, although generally olive mixed with brown, purplish-brown, or pinkish-cream flecking or reticulations, and shading to greenish-gray ventrally; cherry-brown, almost entirely white, and those with blue and pinkish markings also known; dark patch above gill opening. Fin colors also extremely varied, including based colors of cream, red-brown, pink, yellow, black and may be heavily streaked, spotted, and barred. D XXXVIII–XLIII,19–23; A II,44–49; Pect. 11–12; Pelvic absent; Vert. 65–70.

**TWOLINE PRICKLEBACK, *Esselenichthys laurae* (Follett & Anderson, 1990).** Farallon Islands, northern California to Punta Banda, northern Baja California. Common at least in southern California. Length to 9.8 cm (3.9 in) SL. Depth: 11–46 m (35–151 ft). Color in life unknown. D XXXVIII–XLIII,14–18; A II,41–44; Pect. 12; Pelvic 1; Vert. 60–62.

**SLENDER COCKSCOMB, *Anoplarchus insignis* Gilbert & Burke, 1912.** Attu Island, Aleutian Islands to Pribilof Islands and Bristol Bay, Bering Sea, Alaska to Arena Cove, northern California. Common from Aleutian Islands to perhaps northern California, although confusion with HIGH COCKSCOMB makes abundance estimates uncertain. Length to 11.8 cm (4.6 in) TL. Depth: intertidal to 84 m (276 ft). Gray or dark, often variegated with light and dark patterns; line of light dots may occur below dorsal fin; dorsal fin, particularly margin, may be reddish or orangish; short white diagonal bar below eye; numerous stripes on jaws; light bar at base of caudal fin. An occasional individual completely or partially brilliant red. D LVII–LXIV; A I,40–46; Pect. 9–10; GR 3 + 8–11 = 11–14; Vert. 60–69.

## KEY TO THE PRICKLEBACKS:

Revised by Donald G. Buth
(Principal sources: Miller & Lea, 1972; Eschmeyer & Herald, 1983; Follett & Anderson, 1990; Hastings & Walker, 2003)

1a Dorsal fin composed of only spines, no soft-rays….. 4 (next page)

1b Dorsal fin composed of anterior section of spines and posterior section of soft-rays….. 2

2a Dorsal fin spines 22–25 and soft-rays 40–43:

**MONKEYFACE PRICKLEBACK**

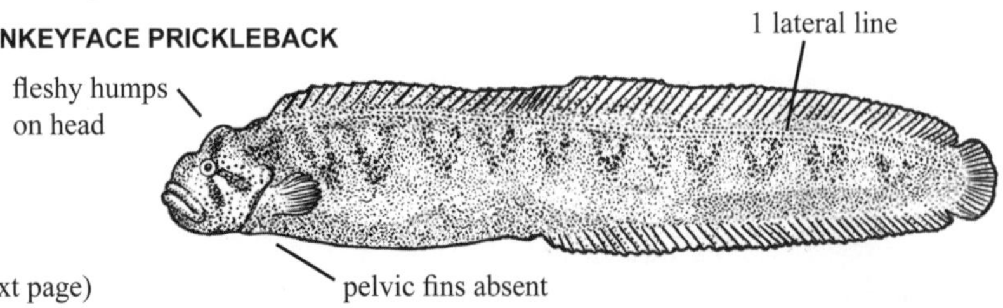


2b (next page)

2b Dorsal fin spines 38–43 and soft-rays 14–23….. 3

3a Pelvic fins absent; dorsal fin soft-rays 19–23; double row of pores on ventral surface:

**THREELINE PRICKLEBACK**

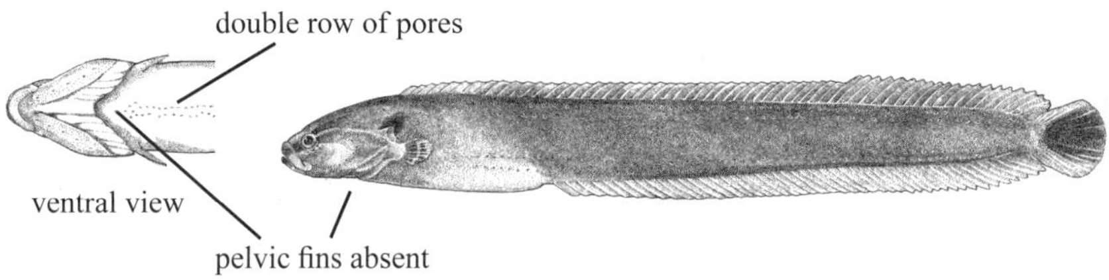


3b Minute pelvic fins present; dorsal fin soft-rays 14–18; no double row of pores on ventral surface:

**TWOLINE PRICKLEBACK**

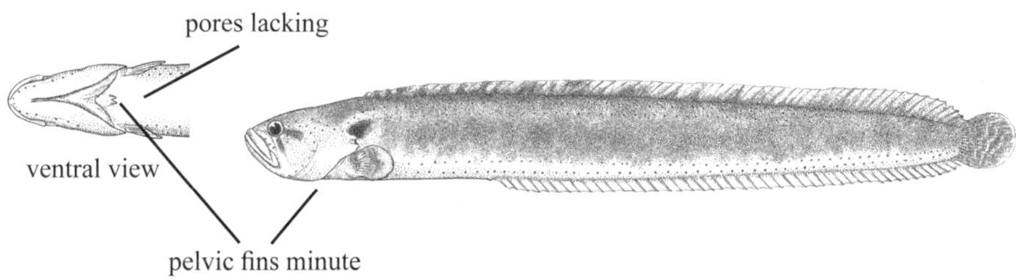


4a *From 1a: dorsal fin composed of only spines*
Pelvic fins present, equal to or longer than eye diameter….. 10 (page 293)

4b Pelvic fins absent, or represented by minute spines less than ½ eye diameter….. 5

5a No fleshy crest on head; gill membranes free from isthmus….. 7 (page 292)

5b Fleshy crest on head; gill membranes attached to isthmus….. 6

6a Width of gap between gill slits under head about ½ eye diameter or less; anal fin soft-rays 40–46; back usually with saddles:

**SLENDER COCKSCOMB**

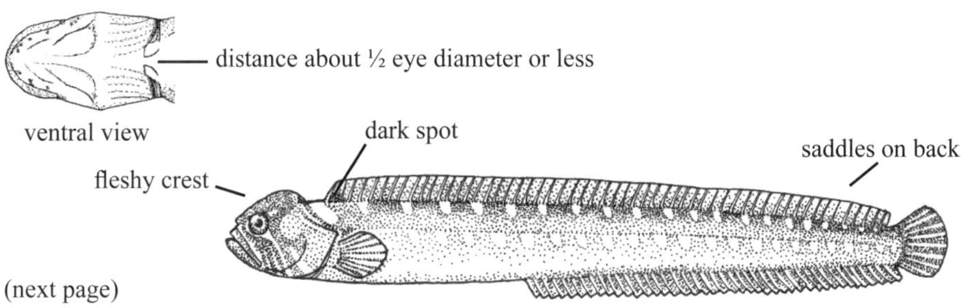


6b (next page)

# PRICKLEBACKS (continued)

**HIGH COCKSCOMB, *Anoplarchus purpurescens* Gill, 1861.** Attu Island, Aleutian Islands and Pribilof Islands, Bering Sea to Newport Beach, southern California (SBMNH 1185) and to Santa Rosa Island, southern California. Common at least from Amchitka Island, Aleutian Islands to central California and at least San Miguel Island, southern California. Length to 20 cm (7.8 in) TL. Depth: intertidal to 35 m (114 ft). Black, gray, or purplish, occasionally reddish. Some individuals with gray, pinkish, or olive-green dorsal fin and back. Males seasonally red-orange on dorsal, pectoral, and anal fins. D LIV–LX; A I–II,35–42; Pect. 9–10; Pelvic absent; GR 3–5 + 5–10 = 8–14; Vert. 58–64.

**SIXSPOT PRICKLEBACK, *Kasatkia seigeli* Posner & Lavenberg, 1999.** Mendocino County, northern California to Diablo Cove, central California. Length to 14 cm (5.5 in) TL. Depth: inshore to 26 m (85 ft). Brownish tan with greenish-cream splotches; belly cream-colored; 6 black ocelli, bordered with yellow, on dorsal fin membrane; anterior tip of jaw black; white band from beneath eye to pectoral fin. D LXI–LXIV; A II–III,39–41; Pect. 18–20; Pelvic may or may not be present; Vert. 66–69. (Formerly *Askoldia*? sp.: M&L).

**BLACK PRICKLEBACK, *Xiphister atropurpureus* (Kittlitz, 1858).** Kodiak Island, western Gulf of Alaska to Rio Santo Tomas, northern Baja California. Common at least from southeastern Alaska to central California and in the Punta Clara area of northern Baja California. Length to 32.3 cm (12.7 in) TL. Depth: intertidal to 27 m (90 ft). Reddish-brown to black; prominent white band across base of caudal fin. D LXV–LXXIII; A I,49–55; Pect. minute, 11–12; Pelvic absent; GR 2–3 + 6–10 = 8–13; Vert. 73–80.

**ROCK PRICKLEBACK, *Xiphister mucosus* (Girard, 1858).** Kodiak Island, western Gulf of Alaska to Santa Cruz Island, southern California. Common at least from British Columbia to central California; apparently not found along southern California mainland. Length to 58.6 cm (23.1 in) TL. Depth: intertidal to 18 m (60 ft). Greenish-black, gray, or brownish; smaller individuals with lighter marbling posteriorly. Prominent white band across base of caudal fin. D LXXI–LXXVIII; A I,46–50; Pect. minute, 12–13; Pelvic absent; GR 3 + 10–14 = 13–17; Vert. 73–83.

**RIBBON PRICKLEBACK, *Phytichthys chirus* (Jordan & Gilbert, 1880).** Amchitka Island, Aleutian Islands (UW 27080) and Gulf of Alaska to southern California. Common at least from Amchitka Island, Aleutian Islands to northern California. Length to 21.1 cm (8.3 in) TL. Depth: intertidal to 12 m (39 ft). Olive-green to brownish above, yellow to green below; small dark spots along sides. D LXIX–LXXVIII; A II–III,40–50; Pect. 14–15; Pelvic absent; GR 4 + 12 = 16; Vert. 75–76.

6b Width of gap between gill slits under head about ¾ eye diameter; anal fin soft-rays 42 or fewer; no saddles on back:

**HIGH COCKSCOMB**

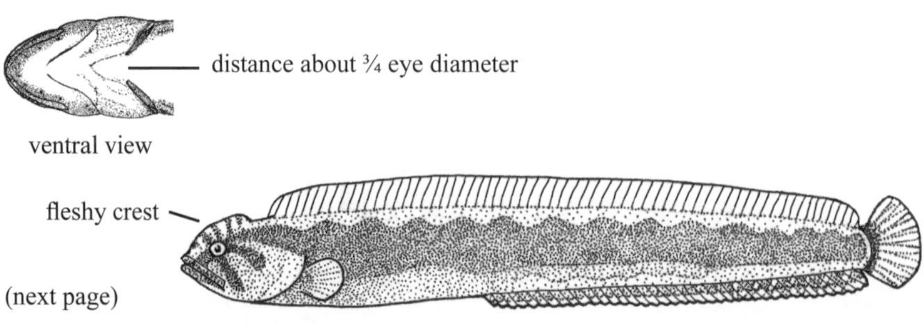


7a (next page)

7a *From 5a: no fleshy crest on head*
Pectoral fins large, longest soft-ray into head less than 2; dorsal fin with 6 equally spaced ocelli:

**SIXSPOT PRICKLEBACK**

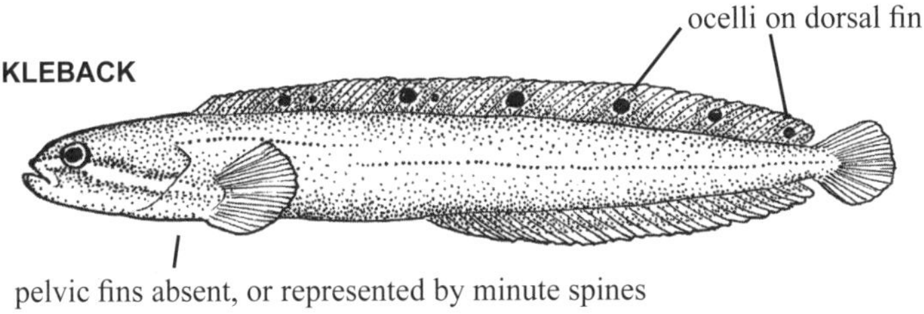


7b Pectoral fins small, longest soft-ray into head more than 2; no ocelli on dorsal fin….. 8

8a Origin of dorsal fin about ½ distance from snout to origin of anal fin, and about ½ HL (at least 2 eye diameters) behind tip of pectoral fin; 2–3 dark bars with white edging radiate from eye:

**BLACK PRICKLEBACK**

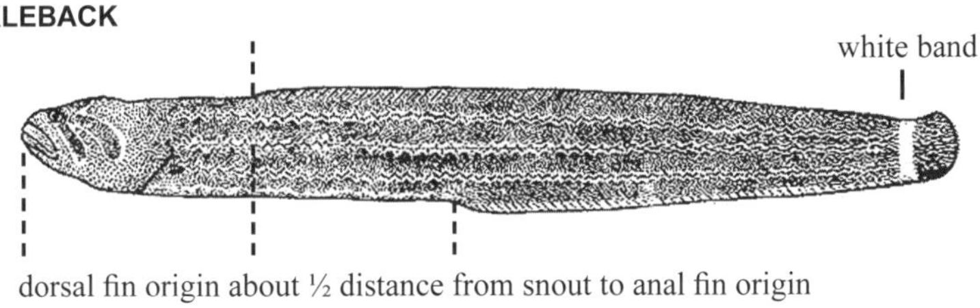


8b Origin of dorsal fin about ⅓ distance from snout to origin of anal fin, and over or slightly posterior to tip of pectoral fin; bars or streaks radiating from eye not edged in white….. 9

9a Pectoral fin length less than 1½ times eye diameter; anal fin spine 1; 2–3 black-edged bars radiate from eye:

**ROCK PRICKLEBACK**

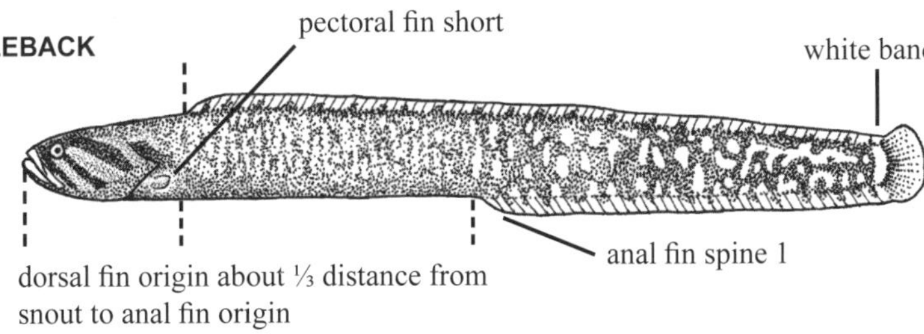


9b Pectoral fin length at least 1½ times eye diameter; anal fin spines 2–3; alternating light and dark streaks radiate back from eye:

**RIBBON PRICKLEBACK**

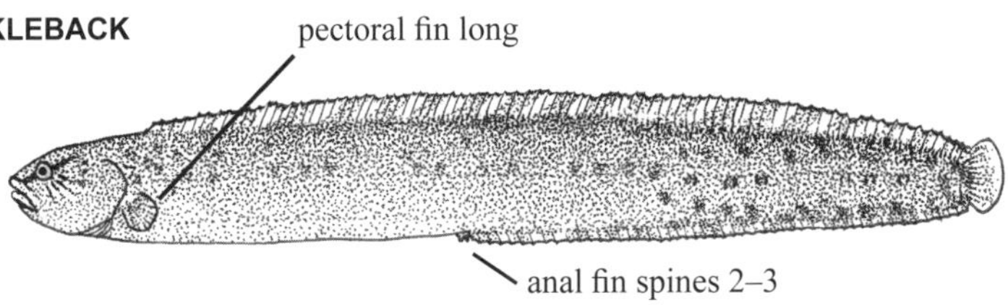


10a (next page)

## PRICKLEBACKS (continued)

**MOSSHEAD WARBONNET, *Chirolophis nugator* (Jordan & Williams, 1895).** Western Aleutian Islands, Alaska to San Nicolas Island, southern California. Common from about Kodiak Island, Gulf of Alaska southward to central California, and at San Miguel Island, southern California; apparently not found along southern California mainland. Length to more than 14.6 cm (5.8 in) TL. Depth: intertidal to 80 m (262 ft). Reddish-brown, red-orange, or cream; dorsal fin with 12–13 dark spots or bars. D LII–LV; A I,37–42; Pect. 13–14; Pelvic I,4; GR 3 + 10 = 13; Vert. 55–59.

**DECORATED WARBONNET, *Chirolophis decoratus* (Jordan & Snyder, 1902).** Norton Sound, eastern Bering Sea and Aleutian Islands, Alaska to Rittenburg Bank (37°53'N, 123°18'W), central California. Common from at least Kodiak Island region, Gulf of Alaska to Puget Sound; apparently rare in California. Length to 41.9 cm (16.5 in) TL. Depth: shallow subtidal to 91 m (298 ft). Body and fins heavily spotted and barred with shades of brown, orange, and white. D LXI–LXIII; A I,44–51; Pect. 14–15; Pelvic I,4; GR 6 + 14 = 20; Vert. 65–67.

**SADDLED PRICKLEBACK, *Lumpenopsis clitella* Hastings & Walker, 2003.** Collected in southern California off San Diego and Santa Catalina Island. Observed from a manned submersible at a number of offshore banks in southern California. Length to 5.5 cm (2.2 in) SL. Depth: 54–130 m (177–429 ft). Body light with 8 dark dorsal saddles. D XLVII–XLVIII; A I,30–31; Pect. 12–13; Vert. 53–54. Hastings and Walker (2003) note that specimens of *Lumpenopsis* collected off southern California and identified as *Lumpenopsis hypochroma* (Hubbs & Schultz, 1932) are *L. clitella.*

**WHITEBARRED PRICKLEBACK, *Poroclinus rothrocki* Bean, 1890.** Southeastern Bering Sea (57°00'N, 172°00'W) (UW 48670) and Aleutian Islands, Alaska to San Diego, southern California. Common from Bering Sea and Gulf of Alaska to Washington or perhaps Oregon; uncommon off California. Length to 25.4 cm (10 in) TL. Depth: 35–160 m (115–525 ft) or perhaps as deep as 449 m (1,473 ft). Light brown or tan above, white below; 10–12 white bars on sides. D LVII–LXVII; A III,40–44; Pect. 13–15; Pelvic I,3; GR 2 + 6–7 = 8–10; Vert. 65–68.

**SNAKE PRICKLEBACK, *Lumpenus sagitta* Wilimovsky, 1956.** Seas of Japan and Okhotsk, Pacific Ocean off Japan, to Commander-Aleutian Islands Chain to at least Saint Matthew Island and Norton Sound, northern Bering Sea to Monterey Bay, central California. Common from Sea of Japan to Bering Sea to Oregon; rare in northern California. Mostly marine but will enter brackish waters. Length to 51 cm (20.1 in) TL. Depth: intertidal to an unconfirmed depth of 425 m (1,394 ft), but almost always shallower than 200 m (656 ft), occasionally in surface waters. Light brown, gray, or green dorsally, cream below; numerous dark green to brown streaks on sides. D LXIV–LXXIV; A I,44–52; Pect. 13–17; Pelvic I,3–4; GR 4–7 + 12 = 16–19; Vert. 75–82.

10a *From 4a: pelvic fins present*
Top of head without cirri; none or few dark spots or bars on dorsal fin..... 12 (next page)

10b Cirri on top of head; many dark spots or bars on dorsal fin..... 11

11a Top of head covered with short cirri of similar length; dorsal fin with 12–13 dark spots or bars; first few dorsal fin spines without cirri at apex:

**MOSSHEAD WARBONNET**

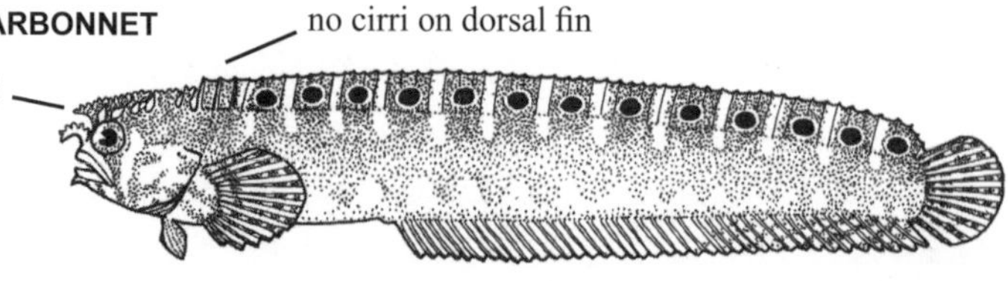


11b (next page)

11b Large cirrus in front of eye with dense patch of smaller cirri on top of head; dark bars on most fins; first few dorsal fin spines with cirri at apex:

**DECORATED WARBONNET**

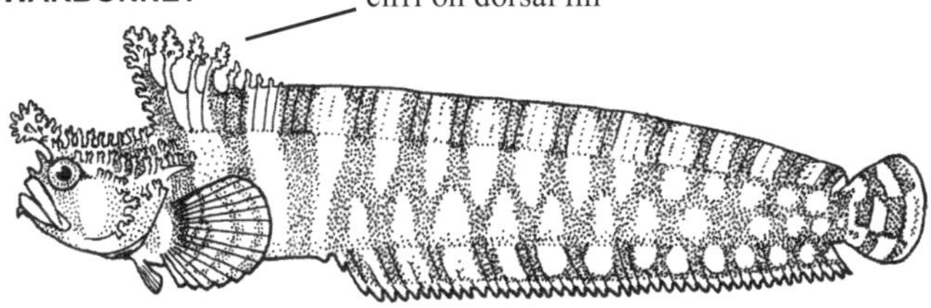


12a *From 10a: top of head without cirri*
Gill membranes either free from isthmus or at least with free fold across isthmus….. 15 (next page)

12b Gill membranes attached to isthmus and without free fold….. 13

13a Five or 6 spots along dorsal fin; anal fin soft-rays 30–31:

**SADDLED PRICKLEBACK**

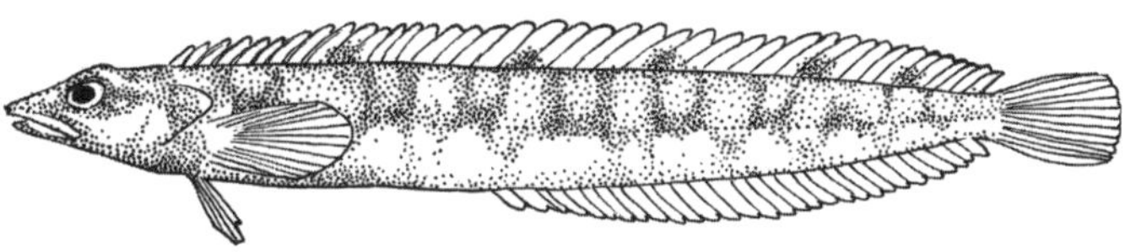

13b No spots along dorsal fin; anal fin soft-rays 40 or more….. 14

14a Series of white bars between dark saddles along sides; caudal fin not barred; anal fin spines 3; dorsal fin membrane attached to upper caudal fin ray:

**WHITEBARRED PRICKLEBACK**

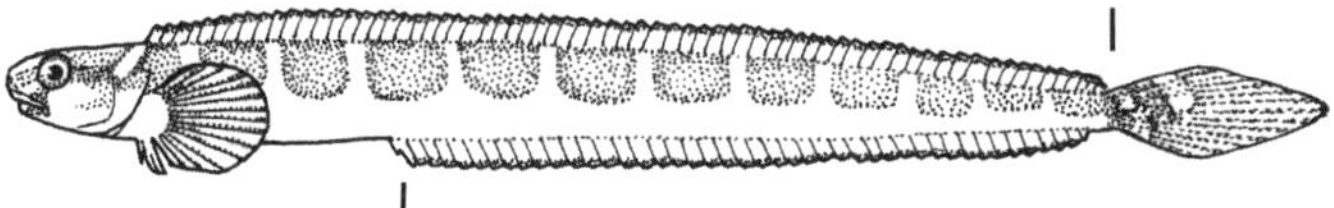


14b No white bars on sides; caudal fin barred; anal fin spine 1; dorsal and caudal fins not joined:

**SNAKE PRICKLEBACK**

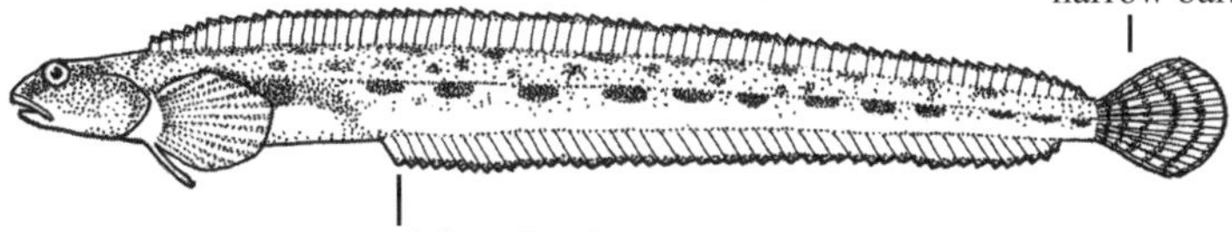


15a (next page)

## PRICKLEBACKS (continued)

**BLUEBARRED PRICKLEBACK, *Plectobranchus evides* Gilbert, 1890.** Central British Columbia to San Diego, southern California. Common from British Columbia to southern California. Length to 13.7 cm (5.4 in) TL. Depth: 57–368 m (186–1,206 ft). Dusky-olive; about 25 bars on sides; dorsal fin with dark oblique bars anteriorly becoming blotches posteriorly. D LIV–LVII; A II–III,33–36; Pect. 14–15; Pelvic I,3; GR 1–3 + 7–9 = 8–12; Vert. 59–60.

**CRISSCROSS PRICKLEBACK, *Plagiogrammus hopkinsii* Bean, 1894.** Pacific Grove, central California (CAS 21199) to San Nicolas Island, southern California (SIO 15-1211). Common in central California and western part of northern Channel Islands. Length to 19.7 cm (7.8 in) TL. Depth: intertidal to 21 m (70 ft). Black to dusky-brown; dark stripe through eye; fins black. D XXXVII–XLI; A II,26–29; Pect. 14; Pelvic I,4 (appearing as I,5, last soft-ray divided close to base); Vert. 43–45. (Formerly *Plagiogrammus hopkinsi*: M&L).

**MASKED PRICKLEBACK, *Ernogrammus walkeri* Follett & Powell, 1988.** Monterey Bay, central California to San Miguel Island, southern California. Common at least in central California. Length to 28.8 cm (11.3 in) SL. Depth: intertidal to 21.3 m (70 ft). Top of head and back pale tan; brown mask beginning at snout, running through eye, and then becoming series of irregular brown blotches along back to tail; lower sides pale tan; dorsal and anal fins heavily and darkly blotched. D XLVII–LII; A II,31–34; Pect. 15–17; Pelvic I,3; GR 1–3 + 5–10; Vert. 53–55. (Formerly *Stichaeopsis*? sp.: M&L).

15a *From 12a: gill membranes free from isthmus*

Two black spots on posterior half of dorsal fin; pelvic fins long, nearly as long as pectoral fins:

**BLUEBARRED PRICKLEBACK**

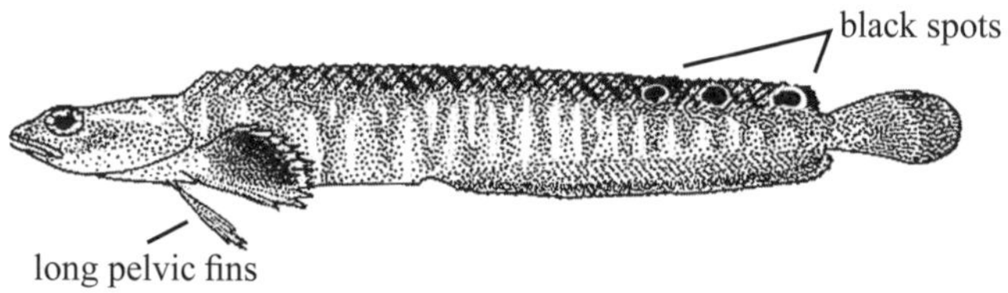


15b No black spots on dorsal fin; pelvic fins short, less than ½ length of pectoral fins….. 16

16a Cheek area dark brown to black; sides with lateral lines branching vertically forming plate-like divisions; pelvic fin soft-rays 4:

**CRISSCROSS PRICKLEBACK**

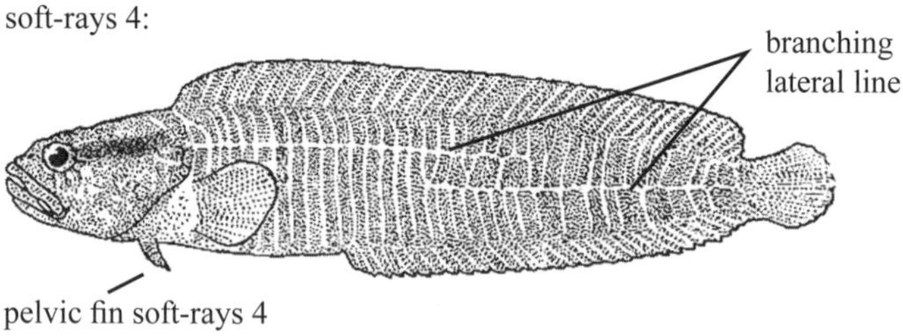


16b Cheek area cream-colored; lateral lines not as in 16a; pelvic fin soft-rays 3:

**MASKED PRICKLEBACK**

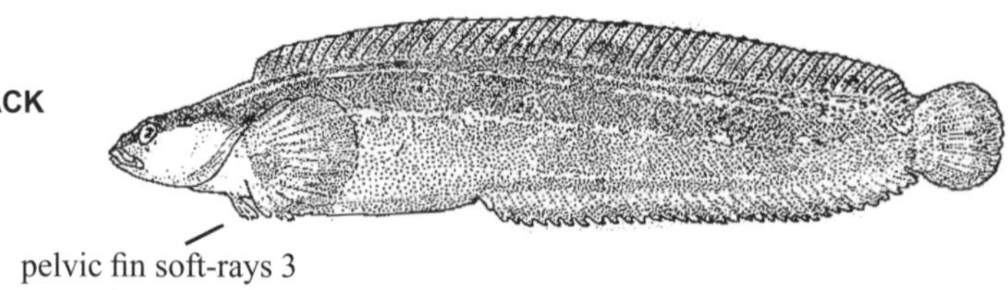

# GUNNELS, Family Pholidae

**KELP GUNNEL, *Ulvicola sanctaerosae* Gilbert & Starks, 1897.** Pacific Grove, central California to Punta Baja, northern Baja California and also Isla Guadalupe, central Baja California. Common at least from central California to northern Baja California and Isla Guadalupe, central Baja California. Length to 28.6 cm (11.3 in) TL. Depth: intertidal to 12 m (40 ft). Uniform yellow-tan to brown, and red-brown. D XCII–XCVIII; A I,40–48; Pect. absent; Pelvic absent; Vert. 99–108.

**PENPOINT GUNNEL, *Apodichthys flavidus* Girard, 1854.** Kodiak Island, western Gulf of Alaska to Santa Barbara Island and Palos Verdes, southern California (LACM 20542). Common from at least Prince William Sound, Gulf of Alaska to central California. Mostly marine, but occasionally enters brackish water. Length to 46 cm (18 in) TL. Depth: intertidal to 11 m (36 ft). Body color highly variable: solid orange, red, magenta, green, or bronze or mottled with dark and light spots along midline; adults with dark bar through eye. Young juveniles with horizontal silver stripe through and to rear of eye and small dark spots along sides. D LXXXVI–XCVI; A I,29–43; Pect. 12–15; Pelvic absent; GR 1–3 + 6–13 = 8–11; Vert. 96–101.

**ROCKWEED GUNNEL, *Apodichthys fucorum* Jordan & Gilbert, 1880.** Banks Island, British Columbia to Punta Escarpada (29°34'N, 119°10'W), central Baja California. Common from at least Puget Sound to northern Baja California. Mostly marine, but will enter brackish waters. Length to 22.9 cm (9 in) TL. Depth: intertidal to 9 m (30 ft). Greenish, yellow-brown, to red. D LXXXII–LXXXVII; A I–II,29–38; Pect. 12; Pelvic absent; GR 1–2 + 6–9 = 8–11; Vert. 84–93. (Formerly *Xererpes fucorum* (Jordan & Gilbert, 1880): M&L).

## KEY TO THE GUNNELS:
Revised by Donald G. Buth
(Principal sources: Rosenblatt, 1964; Miller & Lea, 1972; Kline et al., 2013)

1a Pectoral fins absent:

**KELP GUNNEL**

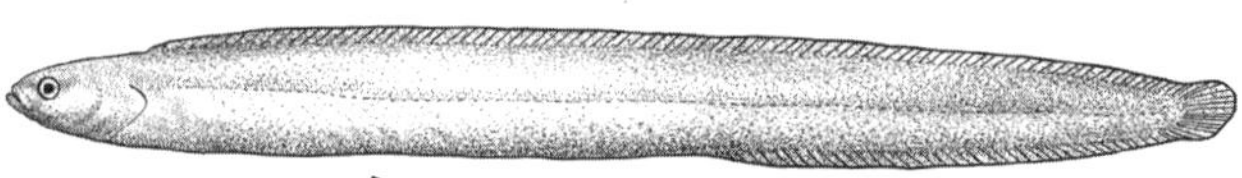


1b Pectoral fins present….. 2

2a Pelvic fins present….. 4 (next page)

2b Pelvic fins absent….. 3

3a Pectoral fins large, about 2 times eye diameter; anal fin spine strong and deeply grooved, about 2 times longer than snout length:

**PENPOINT GUNNEL**

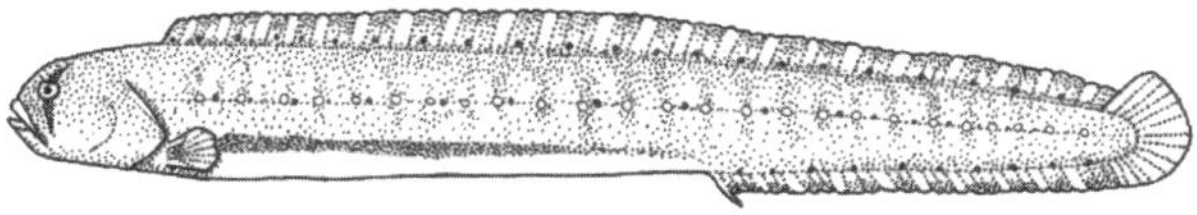


3b Pectoral fins small, about equal to eye diameter; anal fin spine weak and not grooved, about same length as snout:

**ROCKWEED GUNNEL**

4a (next page)

## GUNNELS (continued)

**SADDLEBACK GUNNEL, *Pholis ornata* (Girard, 1854).** Perhaps Honshu, Japan; Olga Bay, Russia; and Kodiak Island, Alaska; Vancouver Island, southern British Columbia to Point Loma, southern California. Uncommonly encountered throughout its range. Marine and brackish waters. Length to 30.5 cm (12 in) TL. Depth: intertidal to 60 m (198 ft). Olive-green to brown above, yellow to red below. D LXXIV–LXXX; A II,34–38; Pect. 11–12; Pelvic I,1; GR 3 + 7–10 = 10–13; Vert. 80–87. Reports of this species from the western Pacific may be misidentified *Pholis nea* Peden and Hughes, 1984 (or *P. nea* may be a junior synonym of *P. ornata*). Records of this species from Alaska are likely misidentified *Pholis laeta* (Peden and Hughes, 1984).

**CRESCENT GUNNEL, *Pholis laeta* (Cope, 1873).** Southeastern Kamchatka, Commander-Aleutian Islands Chain to Port Heiden, southeastern Bering Sea to Abalone Point, Humboldt County, northern California (LACM 35980-8). Common at least from Aleutian Islands and Bering Sea to Oregon. Length to 25.4 cm (10 in) TL. Depth: intertidal to 99 m (324 ft). Body color variable: red, yellowish, greenish-brown, or gray and solid or mottled; 13–15 concentric markings (resembling parentheses) along back (visible in juveniles as small as 7 cm (2.8 in) TL); during winter, mature males orange or reddish along cheeks, throat, pectoral fins, and ventral region anterior to vent. D LXXIV–LXXXI; A II,32–39; Pect. 10–13; Pelvic I,1; GR 3 + 10 = 13; Vert. 84–85.

**RED GUNNEL, *Pholis schultzi* Schultz, 1931.** Haida Gwaii (53°20'N, 131°38'W), British Columbia to Diablo Cove, central California. Common from at least Washington to central California. Length to 12.7 cm (5 in) TL. Depth: intertidal to 29 m (95 ft). Usually pinkish-red but occasionally light brown; vague bars and mottling on sides; 16–22 marks on dorsal fin. D LXXX–LXXXIX; A II,40–44; Pect. 10–13; Pelvic I,1–2; GR 1–2 + 7–10 = 8–12; Vert. 89–93.

**LONGFIN GUNNEL, *Pholis clemensi* Rosenblatt, 1964.** Prince William Sound, Gulf of Alaska to Point Lobos, central California. One unverifiable record from Kodiak Island, western Gulf of Alaska. Common at least as far southward as Bodega Bay, northern California and perhaps central California. Length to 13.4 cm (5.3 in) TL. Depth: 7–64 m (24–210 ft). Red, orangish-brown, reddish-brown; back and dorsal fin with about 15 white saddles with interior dark spots; lower sides light and dark mottled, or red or orange with white spots. D LXXVII–XCII; A II,48–53; Pect. 11–14; Pelvic I,1; GR 1 + 10 = 11; Vert. 95–98.

4a *From 2a: pelvic fins present*
Dorsal fin base and sides with series of marks without dark borders;
dorsal fin spines 77–92….. 6 (next page)

4b Dorsal fin base and sides with series of marks surrounded by dark borders;
dorsal fin spines 74–81…. 5 (next page)

5a Dorsal fin base with wedge- or V-shaped markings; pectoral fins large, into HL 1.8–2.3:

**SADDLEBACK GUNNEL**

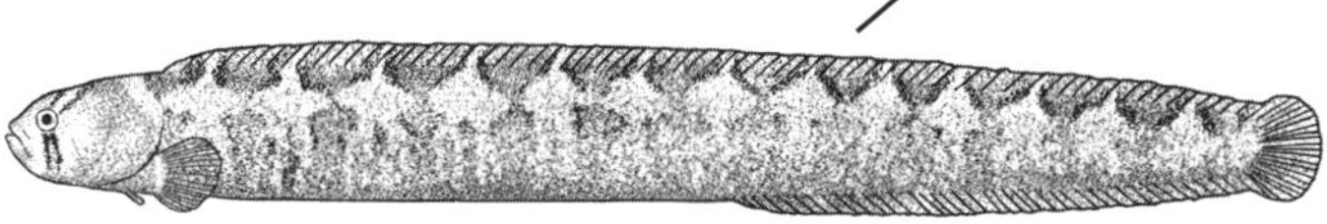


5b Dorsal fin base with borders of light oval-shaped (parentheses-shaped) markings, but often becoming indistinct posteriorly; pectoral fins slightly smaller, into HL 2.4–3.0:

**CRESCENT GUNNEL**

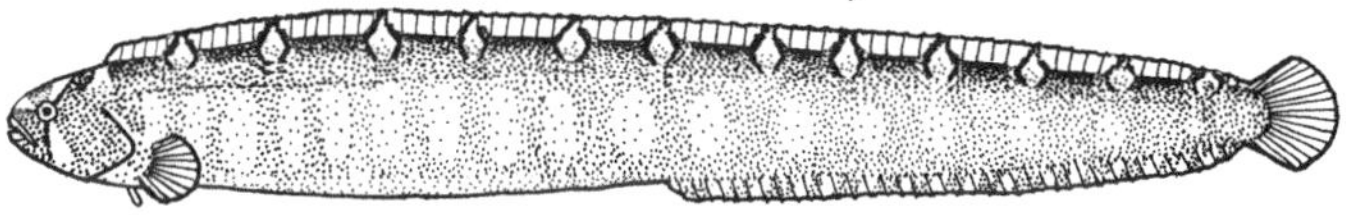


6a *From 4a: dorsal fin base and sides with series of dark spots without dark borders*
Anal fin shorter, less than ½ of BL; anal fin soft-rays 40–44; anal fin with numerous narrow white bars (bars rarely absent); 16–22 bars or V-shaped marks on dorsal fin; white bar below eye:

**RED GUNNEL**

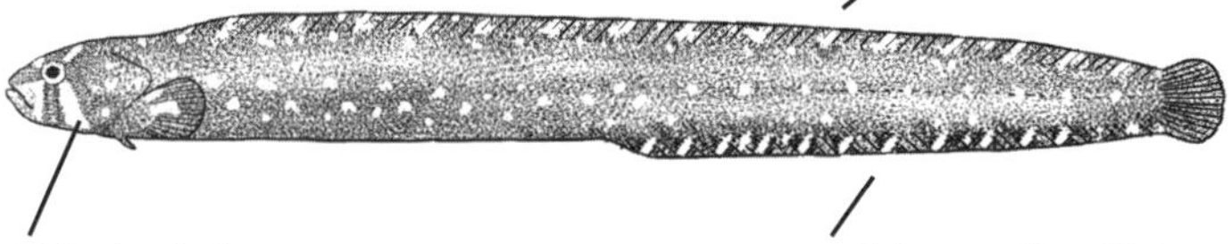


6b Anal fin longer, exceeds ½ of BL; anal fin soft-rays 48–53; anal fin plain or rarely with few faint bars; about 15 white saddles with interior dark spots at base of dorsal fin; no white bar below eye:

**LONGFIN GUNNEL**

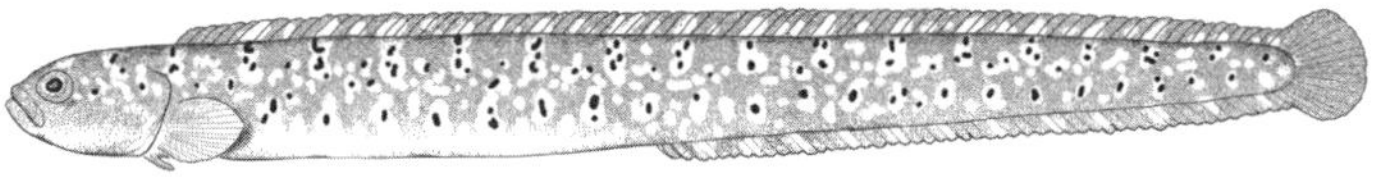

# WRYMOUTHS, Family Cryptacanthodidae and WOLF-EEL, Family Anarhichadidae

**DWARF WRYMOUTH, *Cryptacanthodes aleutensis* (Gilbert, 1896).** Family Cryptacanthodidae
Central Bering Sea (UW 66154) and eastern Aleutian Islands from Unalaska Island to Eureka, northern California. Common from Bering Sea to Oregon; rare in northern California. Length to 31 cm (12.2 in) TL. Depth: 21–750 m (70–2,460 ft). Uniform pink or red to gray. D LX–LXX; A II–III,45–49, confluent with caudal fin; Pect. 12–13; Pelvic absent; Scales absent; GR 3 + 7–9 = 10–12; Vert. 71–77. (Formerly *Lyconectes aleutensis* Gilbert, 1896: M&L).

**GIANT WRYMOUTH, *Cryptacanthodes giganteus* (Kittlitz, 1858).** Family Cryptacanthodidae
Southeastern Bering Sea and eastern Aleutian Islands from Unalaska Island to Humboldt Bay, northern California. Apparently common from about Alaska Peninsula to perhaps Washington; rare in northern California. Length to 123 cm (48.2 in) TL. Depth: 6–331 m (20–1,086 ft). Pale brown tinged with yellow and violet, lighter below; dark spots on head and sides; dark brown stripe along upper portion of back near dorsal fin (sometimes absent) and along lateral line. D LXXIII–LXXIX; A II,43–49, confluent with caudal fin; Pect. 11–14; Pelvic absent; Scales present on posterior portion of body and anteriorly on lateral line; GR 2 + 7–10 = 9–12; Vert. 81–85. (Formerly *Delolepis gigantea* (Kittlitz, 1858): M&L).

**WOLF-EEL, *Anarrhichthys ocellatus* Ayres, 1855.** Family Anarhichadidae
Southeastern Bering Sea east to Cape Menshikof, west along Aleutian Islands to Krenitzin Islands, and Gulf of Alaska to northern Baja California (31°41'N, 116°42'W). Also reported around Isla Guadalupe, central Baja California, but without documentation. Common from at least Gulf of Alaska southward to central California; uncommon, although not rare, in southern California. Length to at least 203 cm (79.9 in) TL or perhaps to 240 cm (94.5 in) TL. Depth: intertidal to 316 m (1,036 ft) and perhaps to 416 m (1,365 ft); juveniles pelagic. Adults blue-gray, gray, red-brown to almost white, darkly stippled and spotted. Pelagic juveniles brownish with many large dark spots on dorsal fin and series of alternating light and dark blotches on sides. D (all spines) 218–250; A 0–I,180–233; Pect. 19–20; Pelvic absent; LL absent; Scales minute, embedded; GR 3–5 + 11–17 = 15–20; Vert. 221–251.

**DWARF WRYMOUTH**

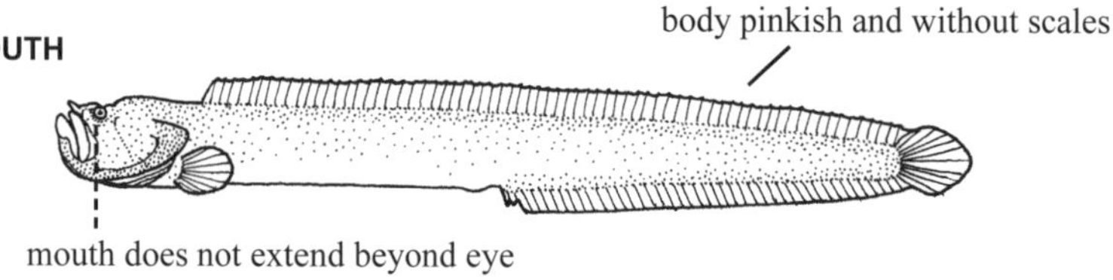


**GIANT WRYMOUTH**

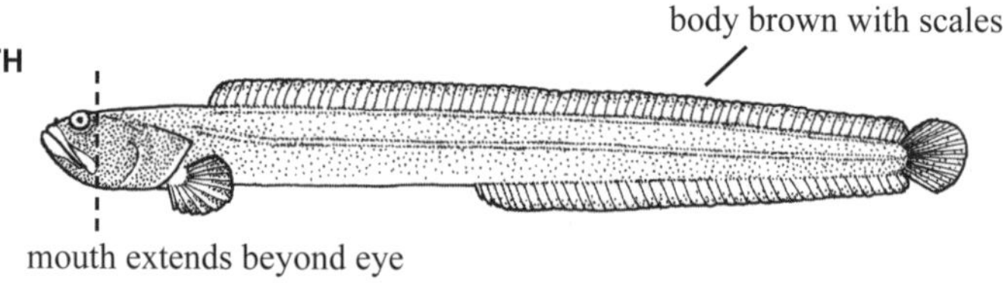


**WOLF-EEL**

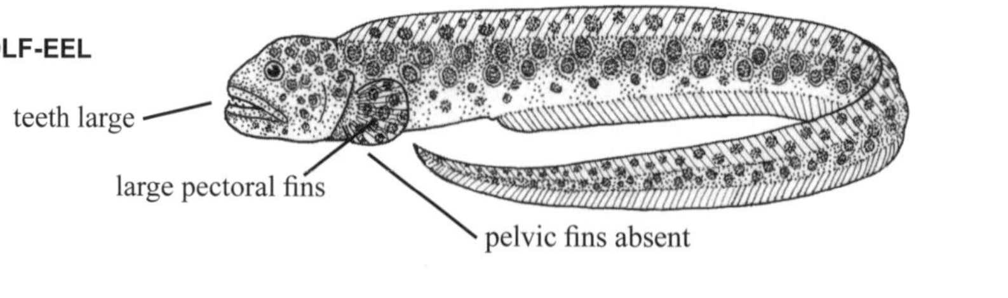

# SURGEONFISH, Family Acanthuridae and SANDFISH, Family Trichodontidae

**YELLOWFIN SURGEONFISH, *Acanthurus xanthopterus* Valenciennes, 1835.** FAMILY ACANTHURIDAE
Pacific and Indian Oceans; southern Japan; Palos Verdes Peninsula, southern California; Gulf of California to Ecuador, including tip of Baja California and Islas Galápagos. Rare off California; common in the Gulf of California and southward into tropics. Length to 70 cm (27.6 in) TL. Depth: surface (SIO 15-1276) and 1–120 m (3–394 ft). Body gray, purplish-gray, or brown; outer ⅓ of pectoral fin yellowish; yellow bar across eye; white bar often at base of caudal fin; depressible sharp spine at base of caudal fin. D IX,25–27; A III,23–25; Pect. 16–17; Pelvic I,5; GRt 16–24.

**PACIFIC SANDFISH, *Trichodon trichodon* (Tilesius, 1813).** FAMILY TRICHODONTIDAE
Japan to Kuril Islands, southeastern Kamchatka, and Commander-Aleutian Chain to southeastern Bering Sea, including Pribilof Islands to San Francisco, northern California. Common from eastern Kamchatka to Bering Sea and at least Washington; rare off northern California. Length to 30.5 cm (12 in) TL. Depth: intertidal, where it is often found buried in the sand after a receding tide, and surface waters to 375 m (1,230 ft). Adults light brown or greenish above, silvery below; dark stripe and spots on and above lateral line. Juveniles greenish-brown above, no markings along sides. D XIII–XVI + I,12–20; A 28–32; Pect. 21–24; Scales absent; GR 4–5 + 11–16 = 16–21; Vert. 44–47.

**YELLOWFIN SURGEONFISH**

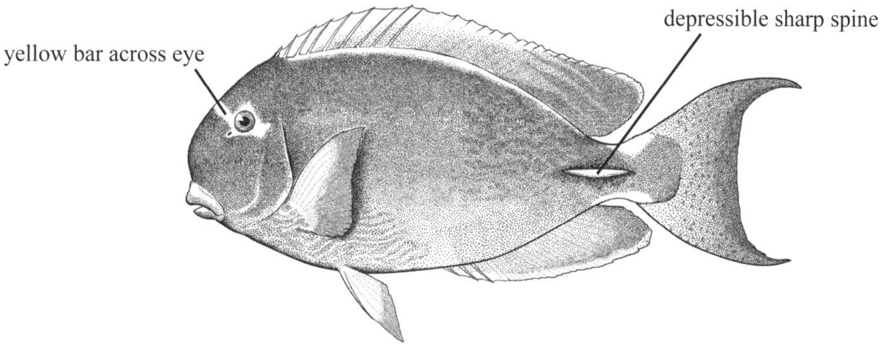


**PACIFIC SANDFISH**

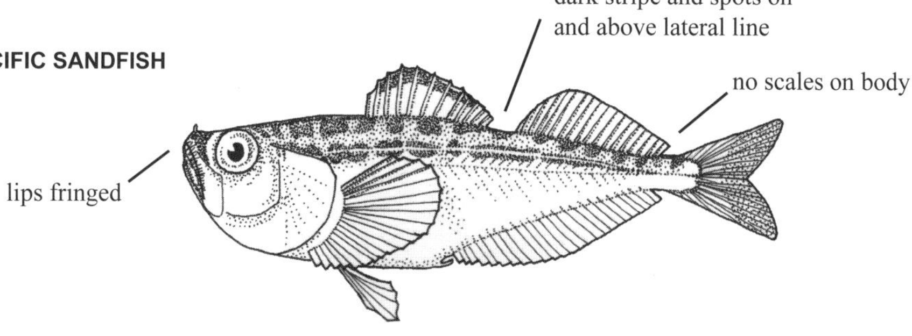

# GRAVELDIVER, Family Scytalinidae, SAND LANCE, Family Ammodytidae, QUILLFISH, Family Ptilichthyidae, PROWFISH, Family Zaproridae, and SLEEPER, Family Eleotridae

**GRAVELDIVER, *Scytalina cerdale* Jordan & Gilbert, 1880.** Family Scytalinidae

Western Aleutian Islands to Diablo Cove, central California. Common from perhaps Kenai Peninsula, Alaska to at least northern California. Length to 15.2 cm (6 in) TL. Depth: intertidal to 7.6 m (25 ft). Pink, purple, yellowish, or brown, sometimes with dark mottling and red or orange caudal fin margin. D 41–51; A 36–48; Pect. 7–8; Pelvic absent; LL absent; GR minute if present; Vert. 71–72.

**PACIFIC SAND LANCE, *Ammodytes personatus* Girard, 1856.** Family Ammodytidae

Norton Sound, eastern Bering Sea to Attu Island, Aleutian Islands, and to Balboa Island, southern California. May also range to Sea of Okhotsk. Common from Aleutian Islands to Bering Sea to northern California. Length to 27.4 cm (10.9 in) SL. Buries in substrate; depth: intertidal to at least 172 m (564 ft). Metallic blue or green on back, silvery below; dark blotch often at base of caudal fin. D 56–66; A 25–33; Pect. 13–16; Pelvic absent; GR 4–6 + 18–26 = 21–30; Vert. 65–73. (Formerly *Ammodytes hexapterus* Pallas, 1814: M&L).

**QUILLFISH, *Ptilichthys goodei* Bean, 1881.** Family Ptilichthyidae

Seas of Japan and Okhotsk to Aleutian Islands and Bering Sea (as far northward as 57°54'N, 169°40'W) to central Oregon. Length to 39 cm (15.3 in) SL. Possibly buries in substrate during day; depth: surface to 360 m (1,181 ft). Yellow or greenish on back, pale below; light and dark stripesalong body. D LXXXI–XC, 135–157; A 179–196; Pect. 12–14; Pelvic absent; GR 2–3 + 11–14 = 14–16; Vert. 227–240.

**PROWFISH, *Zaprora silenus* Jordan, 1896.** Family Zaproridae

Hokkaido, Japan and Sea of Okhotsk to eastern Chukchi Sea west of Kivalina, (67°32'N, 165°54'W) and Aleutian Islands to San Miguel Island, southern California. Common from Kuril Islands to Bering Sea to about Vancouver Island; rare off California. Length to at least 1 m (3.3 ft) TL. Depth: 10–801 m (33–2,628 ft); adults near bottom, young fish often near surface. Adults cobalt blue to greenish; sides sometimes with dark or light spotting or yellow blotches; head often profusely spotted with blue, silvery, or yellow. Juveniles brown; sometimes dark bars on dorsal and anal fins; sometimes lighter spots on sides. D LIV–LVIII; A 0–IV,24–30 (few spines weak and often counted as rays); Pect. 20–25; Pelvic absent; LLs about 200; GRt 24–29; Vert. 61–64.

**PACIFIC FAT SLEEPER, *Dormitator latifrons* (Richardson, 1844).** Family Eleotridae

Palos Verdes Peninsula, southern California to Peru, including Islas Galápagos; also Lake Merritt, San Francisco Bay area. Rare both in California and also apparently along Baja California coast. Length to 61 cm (24 in) TL. Usually in fresh waters, but also shallow inshore marine areas; depth: to 2 m (7 ft) or more. Red-brown, orange-brown, or dark olive, sometimes with dark brown bars or blotches. D VII–VIII + I,8–9; A I,8–9; Pect. 13–15; Pelvic I,5; LLs 30–35; Vert. 27–28.

**GRAVELDIVER**

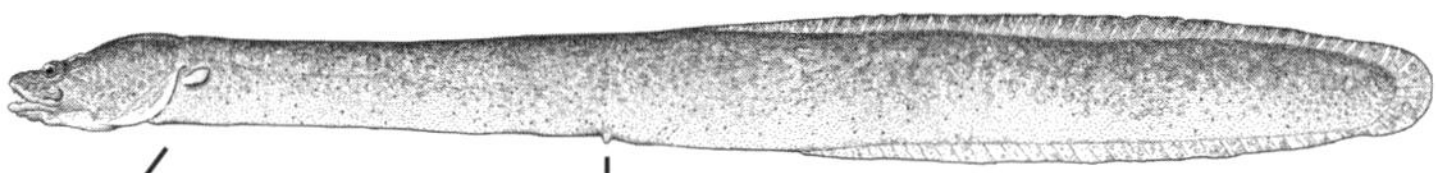


**PACIFIC SAND LANCE**

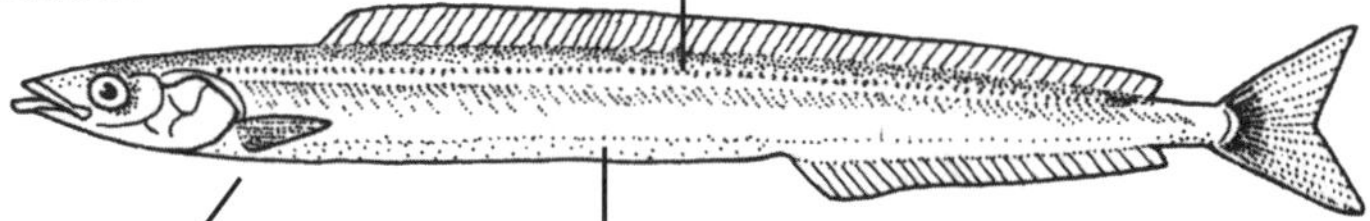


**QUILLFISH**

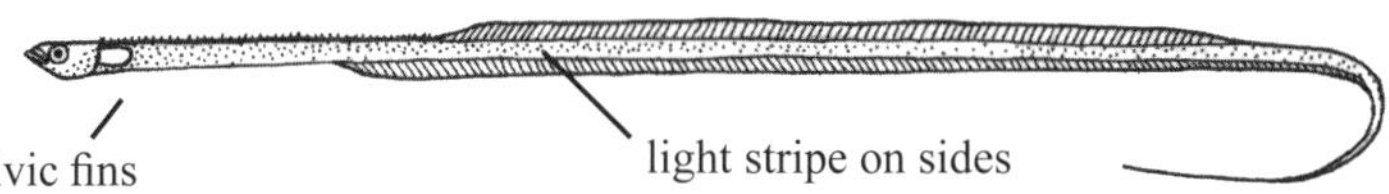


**PROWFISH**

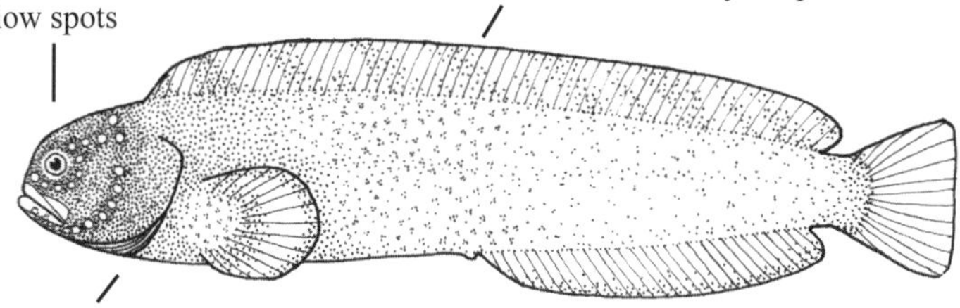


**PACIFIC FAT SLEEPER**

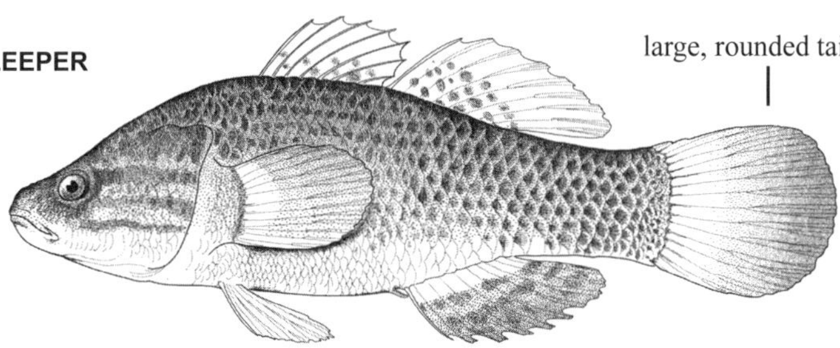

# RAGFISH, Family Icosteidae, DRAGONET, Family Callionymidae, and STARGAZERS, Family Uranoscopidae

**RAGFISH, *Icosteus aenigmaticus* Lockington, 1880.** Family ICOSTEIDAE

Sea of Okhotsk and Pacific coast of southern Honshu, Japan to Bering Sea and Gulf of Alaska to Point Loma, southern California. Larvae have been taken off northernmost Baja California. Common from at least the Aleutian Islands and southeastern Bering Sea to southern California. Length to at least 2.13 m (7 ft) TL. Depth: surf zone to 1,420 m (4,658 ft). RAGFISH under about 30 cm (12 in) TL in shallow water or offshore near surface; adults near bottom and deep. Adult dark chocolate brown to purple-brown; young light brown or gray with yellow and purple spotting and mottling. Adults with forked tail, juveniles with rounded tail. D 50–58; A 34–44; Pect. 18–22; Pelvic I,5 (occasionally I,4, absent in adult); Scales absent in adult; GR 1–7 + 5–10 = 7–17; Vert. 65–70.

**BLACKLIP DRAGONET, *Synchiropus atrilabiatus* (Garman, 1899).** Family CALLIONYMIDAE

Santa Catalina Island (SIO 00-79) and Point Loma, southern California and Bahia Magdalena, southern Baja California to Talara, Peru, including Gulf of California and Islas Galápagos and Isla Cocos. Rare in southern California and along much of Baja California coast. Length to at least 19.5 cm (7.8 in) TL. Depth: 3–235 m (10–771 ft). Head and back reddish, light brown, or yellowish with small dark blotches; belly and underside of head white; dark oval blotch between 3rd and 4th dorsal fin spines; dorsal, pelvic, and caudal fins with small dark spots; anal fin white near body, followed by dark outer band and white margin; upper jaw black. D IV + 9–10; A 8–9; Pect. 19–24; Pelvic I,5; Vert. 21.

**PACIFIC STARGAZER, *Astroscopus zephyreus* Gilbert & Starks, 1897.** Family URANOSCOPIDAE

Huntington Beach, southern California (CMA 1991.52.0001) to Chimbote, Peru, including Gulf of California. Rare in southern California; common at least from southern Baja California into tropics. Length to 52 cm (20.5 in) TL. Depth: surface and 1–385 m (4–1,263 ft). Dark brown to gray-brown on back and upper part of head with many small white spots; white on lower sides and ventral area; fins black to dusky; white stripes on caudal fin; 2 dark blotches on 2nd dorsal fin. D V + 13; A 13–14; Pect. 20–22; Pelvic I,5; Vert. 25.

**SMOOTH STARGAZER, *Kathetostoma averruncus* Jordan & Bollman, 1890.** Family URANOSCOPIDAE

Northern Monterey Bay (CAS 56960), central California to Isla Lobos de Tierra, Peru, including mouth of Gulf of California and Islas Galápagos. Often uncommon in southern California, but apparently more common during certain periods; common from southern Baja California into tropics. Length to 32 cm (12.6 in) TL. Depth: 13–600 m (42–1,968 ft). Dark gray to black above; light oval and round spots on back and dorsal, caudal, and pectoral fins; caudal fin with white margin. D 13–16; A 13–14; Pect. 20–21; Pelvic I,5; Scales absent; Vert. 28–30.

**RAGFISH**

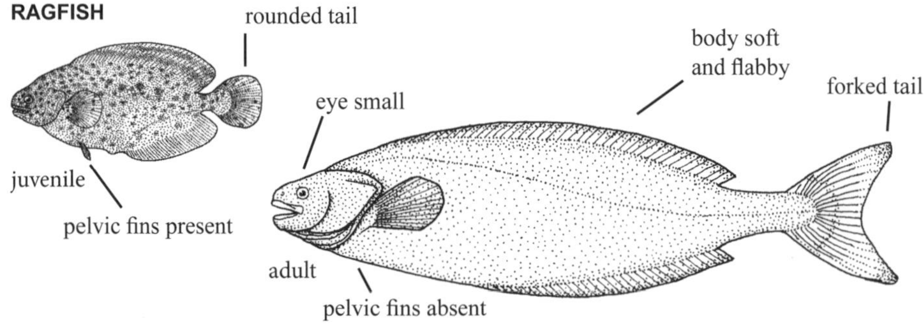

**BLACKLIP DRAGONET**

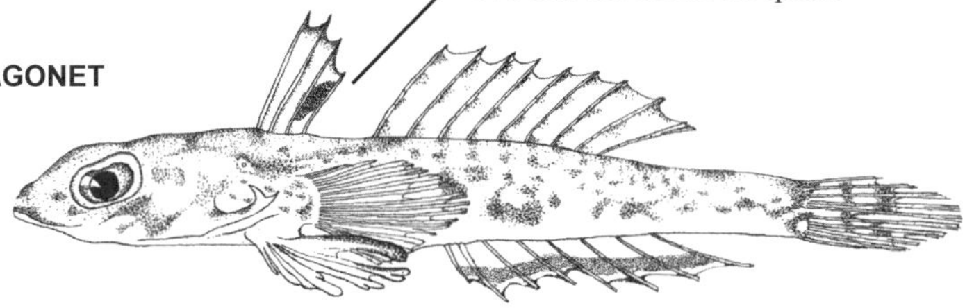


**PACIFIC STARGAZER**

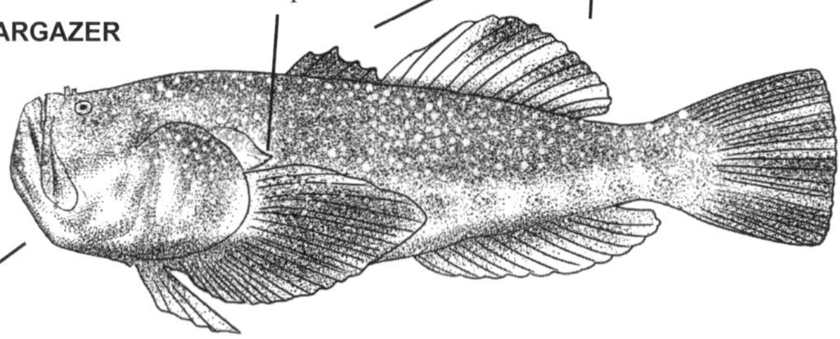


**SMOOTH STARGAZER**

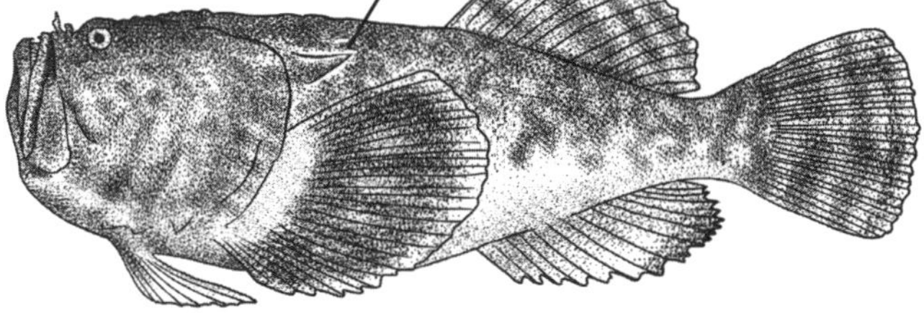

## COMBTOOTH BLENNIES, Family Blenniidae

**SABERTOOTH BLENNY, *Plagiotremus azaleus* (Jordan & Bollman, 1890).** King Harbor, Redondo Beach, southern California; Rocas Chester (27°53'N, 115°04'W); Isla Cedros, central Baja California to Puerto Pizarro, Peru, including Gulf of California and many other offshore islands. Rare in southern California; common beginning in Bahía Magdalena, southern Baja California and southwards. Length to 10.2 cm (4 in) TL. Depth: 2–25 m (7–83 ft). Brown or black band from snout, across eye, to caudal fin; narrow yellow or white stripes above, dark band below; dorsal fin black with blue margin; lower part of head and body white. After death, lower sides and belly may turn reddish. D VII–IX,31–36; A II,26–30; Pect. 12–13; Pelvic I,3; GR 0 + 10; Vert. 47–50.

**PANAMIC FANGED BLENNY, *Ophioblennius steindachneri* Jordan & Evermann, 1898.** Catalina Island, southern California; Isla Guadalupe, central Baja California, Isla Cedros and (mainland) Arricefe Sacramento (29°40'N, 115°47'W), central Baja California (SIO 57-184) into northern Gulf of California to at least Isla Angel de la Guarda and to Islas Lobos de Afuera, Peru, including Islas Galápagos. Rare in southern California. Length to 18 cm (7.1 in) TL. Depth: intertidal to at least 12 m (40 ft) and perhaps to 20 m (66 ft). Head and body dark brown, sometimes with yellowish or whitish bars on head and anterior part of body; head sometimes reddish; dark spot behind eyes; some fins occasionally with blue rim. Juveniles with black bar across base of caudal fin and red pectoral and caudal fins. D XI–XIII,21–23; A II,22–24; Pect. 15.

**BAY BLENNY, *Hypsoblennius gentilis* (Girard, 1854).** Monterey Bay, central California to Gulf of California. Common from Santa Barbara Channel, southern California southward into Gulf of California. Length to 14.7 cm (5.8 in) TL. Depth: intertidal to 24 m (80 ft). Colors variable, red and brown mottling predominating; females often with blackish or bluish spot on 1st–3rd dorsal fin spines, sometimes followed by red streak. D XI–XIII,16–18; A II,16–19; Pect. 11–12; Pelvic I,3; Vert. 34–35.

**ROCKPOOL BLENNY, *Hypsoblennius gilberti* (Jordan, 1882).** San Francisco Bay, northern California (CAS 58489) to Puerto Los Cabos, just inside the Gulf of California (SIO 76-284). Common from southern California to southern Baja California and into the Gulf of California to Cabo Pulmo. Length to 17 cm (6.8 in) TL. Depth: intertidal to 18 m (60 ft). Brown or olive-gray with red marks; males velvety black and females golden during spawning season. D XII–XIII,18–19; A II,19–21; Pect. 13–15; Pelvic I,3; Vert. 37–38.

**MUSSEL BLENNY, *Hypsoblennius jenkinsi* (Jordan & Evermann, 1896).** Morro Bay, central California to Punta Marquez, southern Baja California and Gulf of California. Common from Santa Monica Bay, southern California southward to Gulf of California. Length to 13 cm (5 in) TL. Depth: intertidal to 21 m (70 ft). Mostly heavily mottled brownish or gray. D XI–XIII,15–19; A II,15–20; Pect. 12–15; Pelvic I,3; Vert. 34–35.

## KEY TO THE COMBTOOTH BLENNIES:

Revised by Bill Power

(Principal source: Miller & Lea, 1972; Thompson et al., 2000)

1a No cirrus over eye; body slender with dark band from snout through eye to caudal fin; mouth subterminal; fewer than 10 dorsal fin spines, more than 30 dorsal fin soft-rays:

**SABERTOOTH BLENNY**

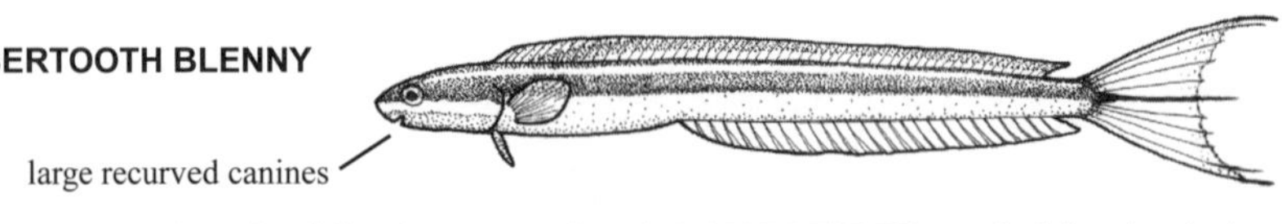


1b Cirrus over eye (may be difficult to see on female BAY BLENNY); no dark band as in 1a; mouth terminal; more than 10 dorsal fin spines, fewer than 24 dorsal fin soft-rays..... 2 (next page)

2a Lateral line divided into 2 independent segments; dark spot behind eye:

**PANAMIC FANGED BLENNY**

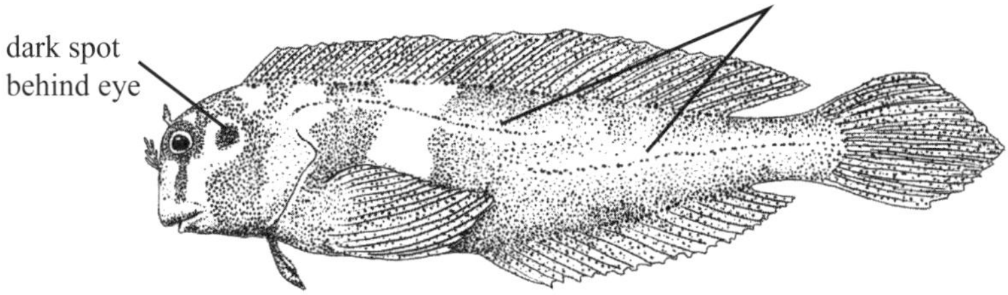


2b Lateral line not divided into 2 independent segments; no spot behind eye..... 3

3a Orbital cirrus serrated on posterior margin (cirrus about 1 mm on female, difficult to see without lens); female with blue or orange spot between 1st and 3rd dorsal fin spines (may be blue and partially ringed with orange); pectoral fin soft-rays 11–12:

**BAY BLENNY**

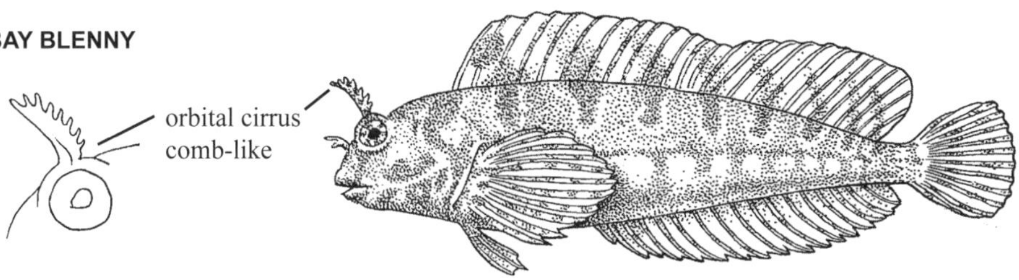


3b Orbital cirrus divided into long filaments; spot between 2nd and 3rd dorsal fin spines lacking; pectoral fin soft-rays typically 13–15 (MUSSEL BLENNY may have 12)….. 4

4a Orbital cirrus without stalk and divided into 7 or more filaments; lateral line arched and extending to at least midpoint of anal fin:

**ROCKPOOL BLENNY**

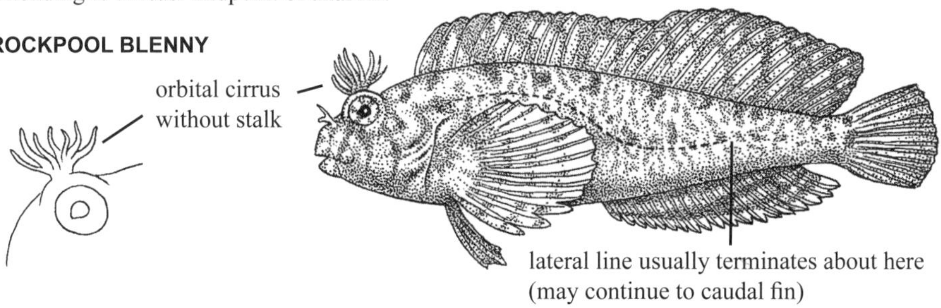


4b Orbital cirrus with stalk and divided on distal half with fewer than 7 filaments; lateral line not arched and terminating near origin of anal fin:

**MUSSEL BLENNY**

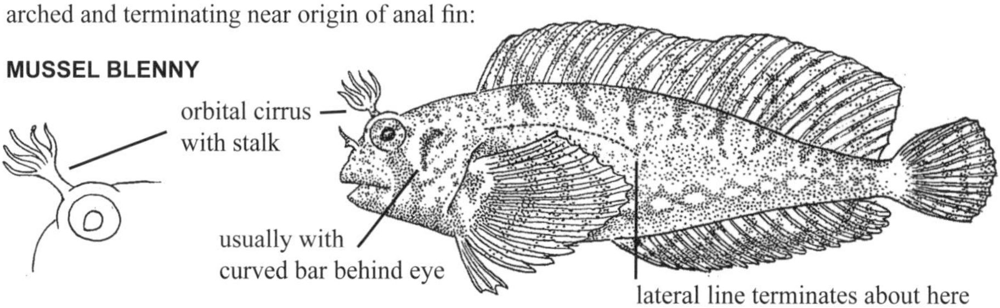

## KELP BLENNIES, Family Clinidae, LABRISOMID BLENNIES, Family Labrisomidae, and TUBE BLENNIES, Family Chaenopsidae

**REEF FINSPOT, *Paraclinus integripinnis* (Smith, 1880).** Family Labrisomidae
Santa Cruz Island, southern California and Naples, Santa Barbara County, southern California to Bahía Almejas, southern Baja California. Common from Santa Monica Bay, southern California to Bahía Magdalena complex, southern Baja California. Length to 7.8 cm (3.1 in) TL. Depth: intertidal to 15 m (50 ft). Dark brown, varying at times to white, mottled with reddish to cream; jet-black ocellus between 22nd and 27th dorsal fin spines. D XXVII–XXXIII; A II,18–21; Pect. 12–14; Pelvic 0–I,3; LLs 34–39; GR 2 + 4 = 6; Vert. 37–39. (Formerly Clinidae: M&L).

**ORANGETHROAT PIKEBLENNY, *Chaenopsis alepidota* (Gilbert, 1890).** Family Chaenopsidae
Point Sur, central California to Gulf of California. The California and Gulf of California populations are perhaps disjunct (Stephens et al., 1989). The only known mainland population in southern California is in King Harbor, southern California. Common along some islands in southern California and in Gulf of California; abundance along outer coast of Baja California unknown. Length to 15.2 cm (6 in) TL. Depth: intertidal to at least 27 m (90 ft). Body brown and green, with series of dark bars on sides; dark patch at rear of gill cover; pearly dots on sides and at base of dorsal and anal fins. Males in breeding condition have bright orange or red slash mark running backwards from mouth and dark ocellus on anterior dorsal fin. D XVIII–XXI,32–38; A II,34–38; Pect. 12–14; Pelvic I,3; GRt 11–12; Vert. 56–60. (Formerly Clinidae: M&L).

**YELLOWFIN FRINGEHEAD, *Neoclinus stephensae* Hubbs, 1953.** Family Chaenopsidae
San Francisco, northern California to Punta San Hipolito, central Baja California. Common from about Monterey Bay southward to northern Baja California. Length to 10 cm (4 in) TL. Depth: intertidal to 27 m (90 ft). Color variable: scarlet, orange, brown; and olive with variably colored body spots and fin striping; pelvic fins often yellow. D XIV–XXVII,15–18; A II,29–31; Pect. 15; Pelvic I,3; LLs 19–20; GR 6–8 + 12–14 = 18–22; Vert. 47–50. (Formerly Clinidae: M&L).

**ONESPOT FRINGEHEAD, *Neoclinus uninotatus* Hubbs, 1953.** Family Chaenopsidae
Bodega Bay, northern California to northern Baja California. Common from at least Monterey Bay to southern California. Length to 25 cm (9.8 in) TL. Depth: surf zone to 55 m (180 ft). Dark brown to red, with black speckling; 1 ocellus on anterior dorsal fin. D XXIII–XXVII,14–17; A II,26–31; Pect. 14–16; LLs 17–26; GR 3–5 + 8–11 = 11–16; Vert. 47–49. (Formerly Clinidae: M&L).

**SARCASTIC FRINGEHEAD, *Neoclinus blanchardi* Girard, 1858.** Family Chaenopsidae
Bodega Bay, northern California to Isla Cedros, central Baja California. Common from southern California southward to at least northern Baja California. Length to 30.5 cm (12 in) TL. Depth: 3–73 m (10–239 ft). Color variable: black, brown, gray, purple, green, and red, highly marked with red and green; 2 (rarely 1) blue, brown, or dark ocelli on dorsal fin. D XXIII–XXVII,15–18; A II,26–30; Pect. 14–15; Pelvic I,3; LLs 20–27; GR 4–6 + 8 = 12–14; Vert. 46–49. (Formerly Clinidae: M&L).

## KEY TO THE KELP BLENNIES, LABRISOMID BLENNIES, and TUBE BLENNIES:

### Revised by Julianne Kalman Passarelli (Principal source: Miller & Lea, 1972)

1a Large ocellus present on posterior portion of dorsal fin; dorsal fin wholly of spines:

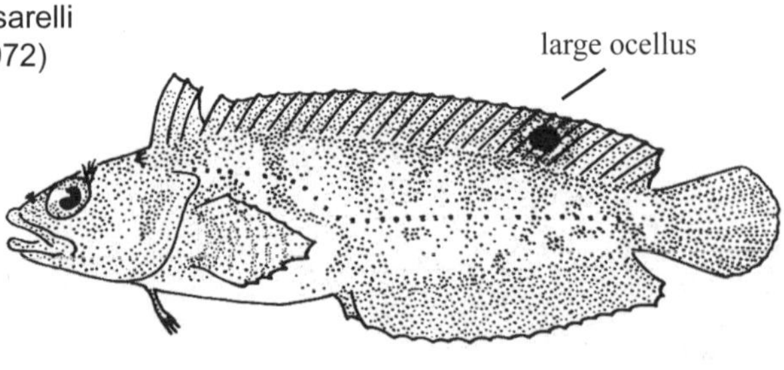


**REEF FINSPOT**

1b (next page)

1b No ocellus on posterior portion of dorsal fin; dorsal fin with spines and soft-rays….. 2

2a BD into TL more than 10; more soft-rays than spines in dorsal fin:

**ORANGETHROAT PIKEBLENNY**

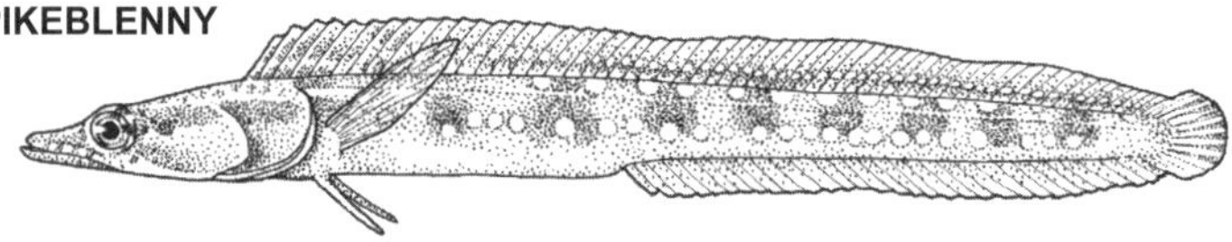

2b BD into TL less than 8; more spines than soft-rays in dorsal fin….. 3

3a Maxilla not extending behind eye….. 6 (next page)

3b Maxilla extending well behind eye….. 4

4a Orbital cirrus without stalk, divided at base; dorsal fin with no ocellus; total gill rakers 18–22; HL into SL 4.2–5.3:

**YELLOWFIN FRINGEHEAD**

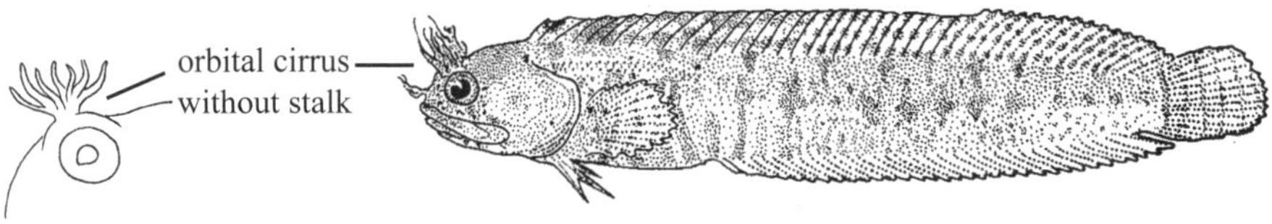


4b Orbital cirrus with stalk, simple or divided only on distal half; dorsal fin with 1 or 2 ocelli; total gill rakers 11–16; HL into SL 3.5–3.8….. 5

5a Dorsal fin with 1 ocellus between 1st and 2nd spines; orbital cirrus longer than eye and divided at tip:

**ONESPOT FRINGEHEAD**

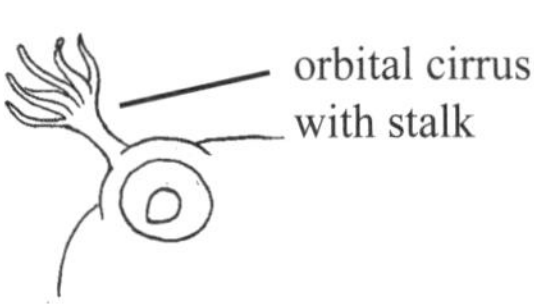


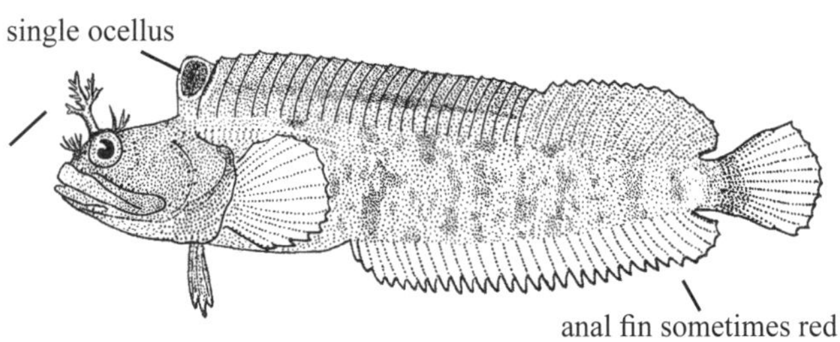


5b Dorsal fin with 2 ocelli, 1 between 1st and 2nd spines and other between 5th and 9th spines (posterior ocellus rarely absent); orbital cirrus usually shorter than eye diameter and simple:

**SARCASTIC FRINGEHEAD**

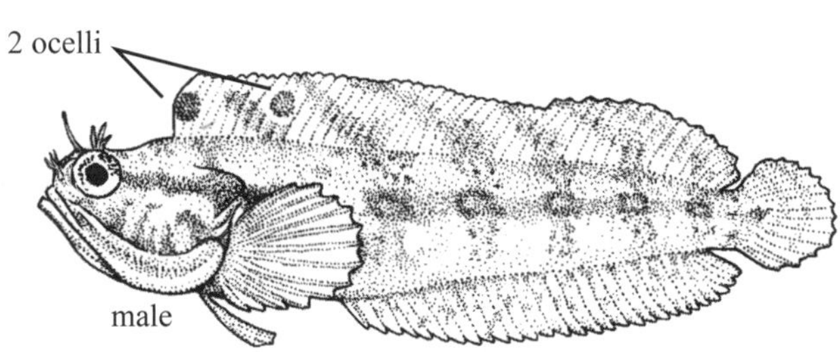


6a (next page)

# KELP BLENNIES, LABRISOMID BLENNIES, and TUBE BLENNIES (continued)

**GIANT KELPFISH, *Heterostichus rostratus* Girard, 1854.** Family CLINIDAE
British Columbia to Cabo San Lucas, southern Baja California, including Isla Guadalupe, central Baja California. Common from southern California to at least Bahía Magdalena, southern Baja California. Length to 61 cm (24 in) TL. Depth: intertidal to 40 m (132 ft). Color variable (changes with habitat): base color green, red, brown, and olive-brown; patterns include plain, striped, barred, and mottled with light and dark and occasional red spots on sides; some fish with white stripe from tip of snout to between eyes. D XXXIII–XXXVIII,11–13; A II,31–35; Pect. 12–14; Pelvic I,3; LLs 73–83; GR 5–8 + 12–13 = 18–20; Vert. 56–58.

**LARGEMOUTH BLENNY, *Labrisomus xanti* Gill, 1860.** Family LABRISOMIDAE
As far north as near Potato Harbor, Santa Cruz Island and King Harbor, Redondo Beach, southern California into Gulf of California and to northern Chile. Patchily common in southern California. Length to 17.8 cm (7 in) TL. Depth: tide pools to 11 m (36 ft). Color and pattern variable: body shades of browns to gray, lower half often covered in white spots; often 8 dark bars on body (sometimes very faint or missing); ocellus often between 2nd and 3rd dorsal fin spines; reproductive males red with blue spots on head. D XVII–XIX,10–13; A II,17–19; Pect. 13–15; LLs 64–69; GR 3 + 6–7; Vert. 34.

**ISLAND KELPFISH, *Alloclinus holderi* (Lauderbach, 1907).** Family LABRISOMIDAE
San Miguel Island, southern California to Punta San Pablo (27°12'N, 114°29'W), southern Baja California and in Gulf of California. Common from Santa Cruz Island, southern California southward to at least Isla Asuncion (27°06'N, 114°18'W), southern Baja California, Rocas Alijos (24°57.5'N, 115°45'W) (SIO 70-371), and into the Gulf of California. Length to 15 cm (5.9 in) TL. Depth: intertidal to 91 m (298 ft). Able to change color to match red, purple, or brown background; dark saddles on back, blotches along sides, lighter patch on each cheek; striping of various colors, spots of red, white, or blue, and bright orange fins. D XXIV–XXVI,9–13; A II,21–23; Pect. 13–14; Pelvic I,3; LLs 47–54; GR 4 + 9; Vert. 41–42. (Formerly Clinidae: M&L).

**DEEPWATER BLENNY, *Cryptotrema corallinum* Gilbert, 1890.** Family LABRISOMIDAE
Off Cook Point, San Miguel Island, southern California to Isla Asuncion, southern Baja California. Common from San Miguel Island, southern California southward to Isla Asuncion. Length to 12.7 cm (5 in) TL. Depth: 15–195 m (48–639 ft). Dusky-olive above with streaks of red below; dark blotches on sides. D XXVI–XXVIII,11–13; A I–II,24–27; Pect. 13–15; Pelvic I,3; LLs 65–75; GR 4–5 + 8–12. (Formerly Clinidae: M&L).

6a *From 3a: maxilla not extending behind eye*
Tail forked; head elongated and pointed; anal fin soft-rays 31 or more:

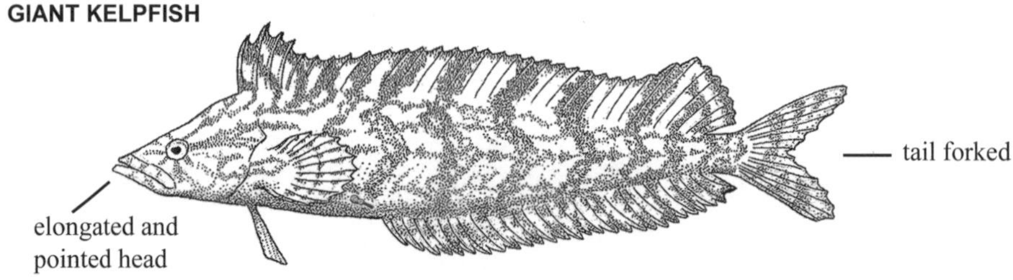


6b (next page)

6b Tail rounded (in adults); head not elongated, more stout; anal fin soft-rays fewer than 30….. 7

7a Pectoral fins short, not extending to anal fin origin;
maxilla into head more than 2.5….. 10 (next page)

7b Pectoral fins long, extending beyond anal fin origin; maxilla into head less than 2.5….. 8

8a Ocellus often between 2nd and 3rd dorsal fin spines; numerous cirri on head;
anal fin soft-rays 17–19:

**LARGEMOUTH BLENNY**

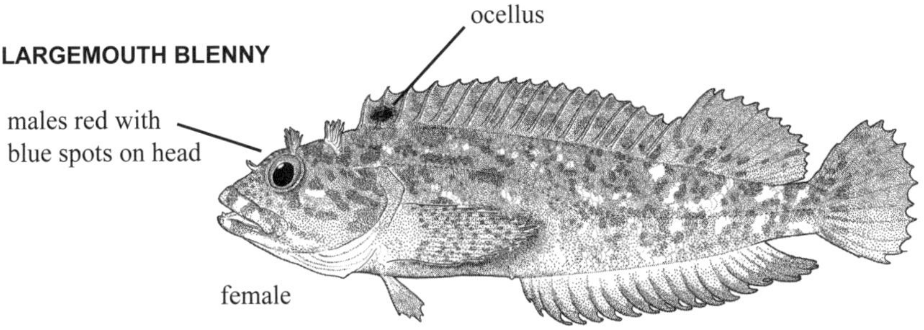


8b No ocellus on dorsal fin (ISLAND KELPFISH may have dark patch between 1st and 2nd dorsal fin spines); few cirri on head; anal fin soft-rays 21 or more….. 9

9a Lateral line descends to midbody immediately posterior to tip of pectoral fin;
anal fin soft-rays 21–23:

**ISLAND KELPFISH**

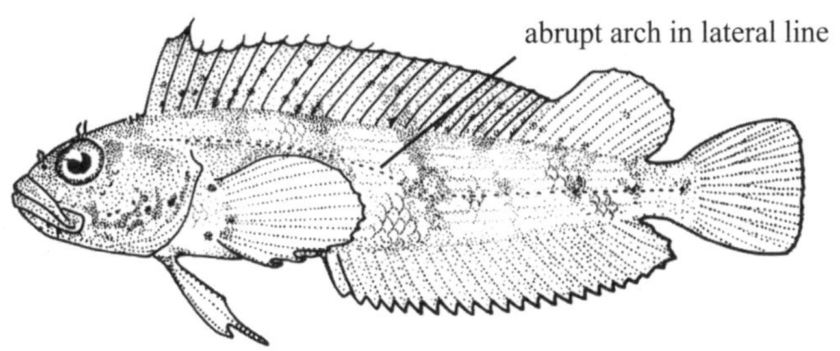


9b Lateral line remains in upper portion of body for at least ⅔ of distance to caudal fin;
anal fin soft-rays 24–27:

**DEEPWATER BLENNY**

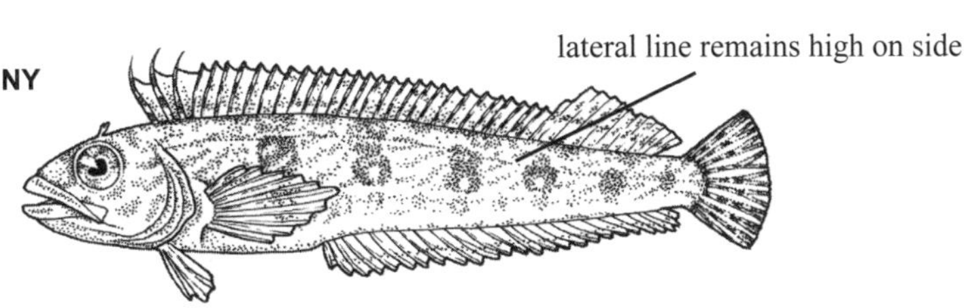


10a (next page)

## KELP BLENNIES, LABRISOMID BLENNIES, and TUBE BLENNIES (continued)

**STRIPED KELPFISH, *Gibbonsia metzi* Hubbs, 1927.** Family CLINIDAE
Vancouver Island, British Columbia to Punta Rompiente, southern Baja California. Common from about Mendocino County, northern California southward to Punta San Antonio, northern Baja California. Length to 23.5 cm (9.3 in) TL. Depth: intertidal to 18 m (59 ft). Reddish to light brown, usually with dark stripes on sides. D XXXIV–XXXVII,7–10; A II,24–29; Pect. 11–13; Pelvic I,3; Scale rows above LL 180–235; LLp 64–71; GR 3–4 + 7–8 = 11; Vert. 50–53.

**SPOTTED KELPFISH, *Gibbonsia elegans* (Cooper, 1864).** Family CLINIDAE
San Francisco Bay, northern California (CAS 215456) to Bahía Magdalena, southern Baja California, including Isla Guadalupe. Common from central California to Bahía Magdalena. Length to 16 cm (6.3 in) TL. Depth: intertidal to 56 m (185 ft). Base color red, green, and brown; 1–3 dark eyespots on back. Females usually have yellow or tan belly; males and immature fish with white belly. D XXXI–XXXV,5–8; A I–III,21–25; Pect. 11–13; Pelvic I,2–3; Scale rows above LL 125–170; LLp 62–71; GR 4–5 + 8–12 = 12–16; Vert. 47–49. The SPOTTED KELPFISH was mistakenly given the name *Gibbonsia evides* (Jordan & Gilbert, 1883) by Eschmeyer (1998).

**CREVICE KELPFISH, *Gibbonsia montereyensis* Hubbs, 1927.** Family CLINIDAE
British Columbia to Isla Guadalupe (SIO 60-15), Isla Cedros area, and Bahía San Carlos, central Baja California (SIO 52-215). Historically common from about Mendocino County, northern California to many southern California islands, and northern and central Baja California; not common along southern California mainland. Now also reported as common at least on the west coast of Vancouver Island. Length to 18.4 cm (7.2 in) SL. Depth: intertidal to 49 m (162 ft). Variously colored reds, purples, browns, and pinks; plain, blotched, spotted, and striped. D XXXIV–XXXVI,5–8; A II,23–28; Pect. 11–13; Pelvic I,3; Scale rows above LL 130–175; LLp 61–70; GR 2–5 + 7–10; Vert. 49–51. (Formerly *Gibbonsia erythra* Hubbs, 1952: M&L).

10a *From 7a: pectoral fins short*
Dorsal fin soft-rays 7–10, equally spaced; TL may be 16 cm or longer:

**STRIPED KELPFISH**

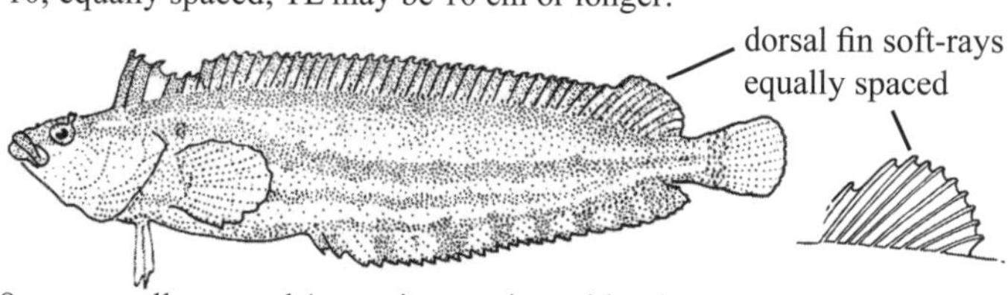


10b Dorsal fin soft-rays 5–8, not equally spaced (posterior spacing wider than anterior); TL 16 cm or shorter….. 11

11a Scales present on caudal fin; ocellus with ring:

**SPOTTED KELPFISH**

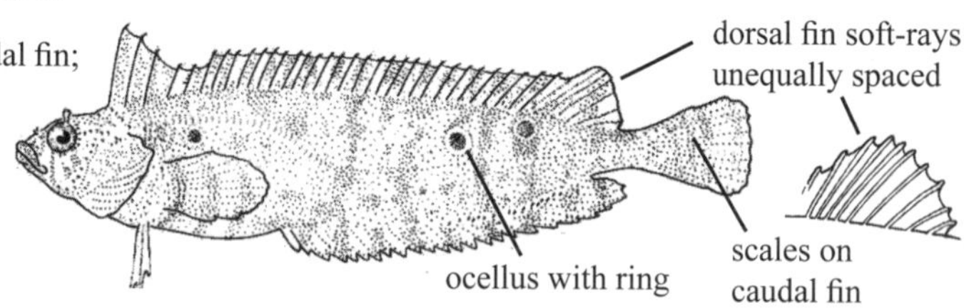


11b Scales absent on caudal fin; ocellus without ring:

**CREVICE KELPFISH**

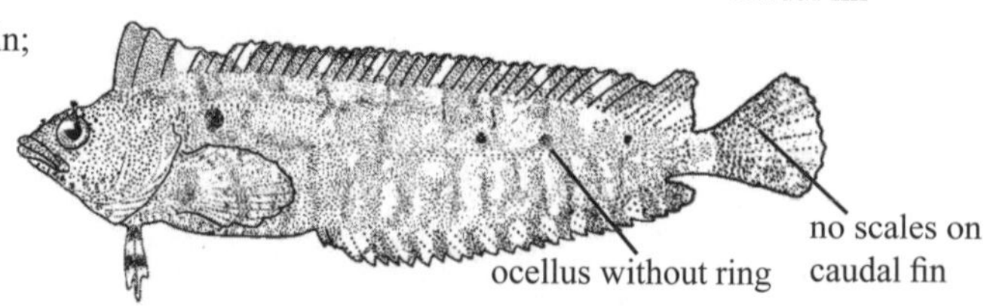

## CLINGFISHES, Family Gobiesocidae

**BEARDED CLINGFISH, *Gobiesox papillifer* Gilbert, 1890.** San Pedro, southern California to Panama Bay, including Gulf of California. Rare in southern California; common beginning in Bahía Magdalena and in other tropical waters. Length to 8 cm (3.2 in) TL. Depth: intertidal to 5 m (17 ft). Light brown to gray, often with dark spotting. D 14–15 (12–13)*; A 9–11 (7–9)*; Pect. 23–25.

**CALIFORNIA CLINGFISH, *Gobiesox rhessodon* Smith, 1881.** Pismo Beach, central California to Bahía Magdalena, southern Baja California (SIO 64-10). Common from southern California southward to at least Punta Abreojos, southern Baja California and perhaps Bahía Magdalena. Length to 6.4 cm (2.5 in) TL. Depth: intertidal to 11 m (35 ft). Gray to brown, with dark brown spotting. D 12–14 (10–12)*; A 11–12 (9–10)*; Pect. 18–21.

NOTE: *Dorsal and anal fin counts in ( ) do not include hidden soft-rays.

## KEY TO THE CLINGFISHES:
Revised by Bill Power and Julianne Kalman Passarelli
(Principal sources: Miller & Lea, 1972; Briggs, 2002)

1a Visible dorsal fin soft-rays 5–8 and widely separated from caudal fin; disc small, length into SL 5.4–6.6; upper lip about same width at front as at sides..... 5 (page 314)

1b Visible dorsal fin soft-rays 10–14 and slightly separated from caudal fin; disc large, length into SL 2.6–3.9; upper lip broad, wider at front than at sides..... 2

2a Rim of snout with numerous barbel-like papillae:

**BEARDED CLINGFISH**

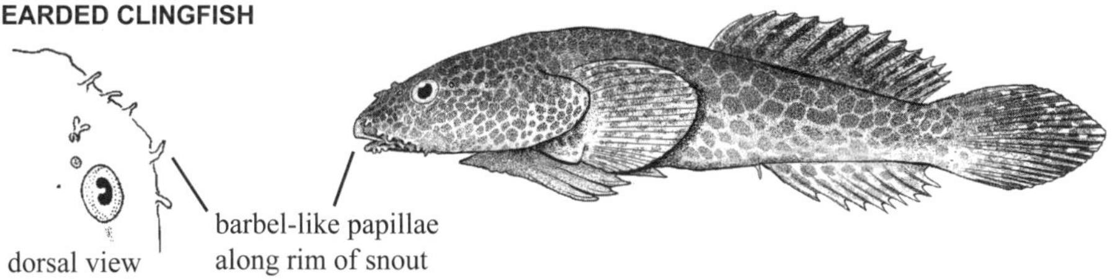


2b Rim of snout without barbel-like papillae..... 3

3a Lower incisors trifid; free posterior margin of fleshy pectoral pad complete, extending to upper edge of operculum:

**CALIFORNIA CLINGFISH**

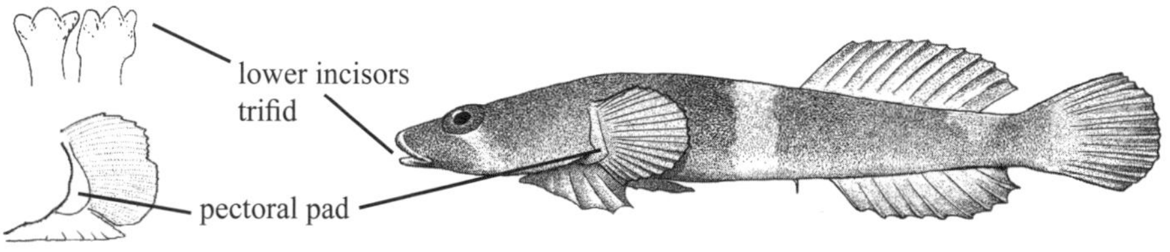


3b Lower incisors rounded with single cusp; free posterior margin of fleshy pectoral pad incomplete, not extending to upper edge of operculum..... 4 (next page)

## CLINGFISHES (continued)

**NORTHERN CLINGFISH, *Gobiesox maeandricus* (Girard, 1858).** Noyes Island, southeastern Alaska to central Baja California (between Isla Guadalupe and mainland on drifting kelp). Common from Prince of Wales Island, southeastern Alaska to central California. Length to 16.5 cm (6.5 in) TL. Depth: intertidal to 18 m (59 ft), along with several trawl records in the depth range of 140 m (459 ft). Dark or brown, translucent belly. D 12–16 (12–14)*; A 13–15 (11–13)*; Pect. 19–23; GRt 5; Vert. 31–35.

**LINED CLINGFISH, *Gobiesox eugrammus* Briggs, 1955.** Avalon Dive Park, Santa Catalina Island and Bird Rock, San Diego County, southern California to Islas San Benito (SIO 90-74) and Isla Guadalupe, central Baja California. Uncommon in southern California; common from northern Baja California and Isla Guadalupe. Length to 5.7 cm (2.3 in) TL. Depth: 9–82 m (30–270 ft). Translucent cream; orange to red markings on upper part of body and head; dorsal and caudal fins black with white margin; eye with red outer and yellow inner rings around black pupil. D 14–15 (11–13)*; A 11–13 (8–10)*; Pect. 21–26; Pelvic I,4; Vert. 26–29.

**KELP CLINGFISH, *Rimicola muscarum* (Meek & Pierson, 1895).** Glacier Bay, southeastern Alaska to Punta Baja, northern Baja California. Also reported from Kachemak Bay, northern Gulf of Alaska, but not verifiable. Common from at least Haida Gwaii, British Columbia to southern California. Length to 7 cm (2.8 in) TL. Depth: intertidal and in kelp beds to 5 m (16 ft). Variable in color, from green to various shades of brown. D 5–8; A 6–8; Pect. 14–17; LL absent; Vert. 34–36.

**SOUTHERN CLINGFISH, *Rimicola dimorpha* Briggs, 1955.** Gaviota, southern California to Islas San Benito, central Baja California. Rare in southern California; common in northern Baja California. Length to 3.4 cm (1.4 in) TL. Depth: kelp beds, occasionally in tide pools. Color in life unknown. D 6–7; A 6–8; Pect. 15–16.

**SLENDER CLINGFISH, *Rimicola eigenmanni* (Gilbert, 1890).** San Miguel Island, southern California (SIO 47-96) to Bahía Magdalena, southern Baja California (LACM 32088-24). Common from about San Diego, southern California to Bahía Magdalena. Length to 5.7 cm (2.3 in) TL. Depth: intertidal to 15 m (48 ft). Uniform tan, but variable with surroundings including bright green to red, brown, olive, or yellow. D 5–8; A 5–8; Pect. 17–19; Pelvic I,4; GRt 5; Vert. 33–35.

**CHANNEL ISLANDS CLINGFISH, *Rimicola cabrilloi* Briggs, 2002.** Islands off southern California (Santa Rosa, Santa Cruz, Santa Catalina, and San Nicolas). Apparently common around these islands. Length to 3.5 cm (1.4 in) SL. Depth: intertidal and shallow subtidal. Color in life unknown. In alcohol, no evidence of pigmentation. D 7–8; A 7–8; Pect. 17–19.

NOTE: *Dorsal and anal fin counts in ( ) do not include hidden soft-rays.

4a Eye small, diameter into HL 5.5–8.3 and into interorbital width 1.2–1.9; posterior nostril separated from anterior edge of eye:

**NORTHERN CLINGFISH**

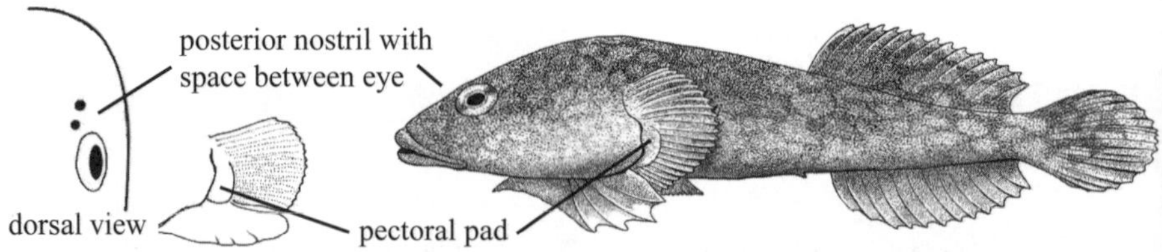


4b (next page)

4b Eye large, diameter into HL 3.7–5.1 and into interorbital width 0.8–1.4; posterior nostril touching anterior edge of eye:

**LINED CLINGFISH**

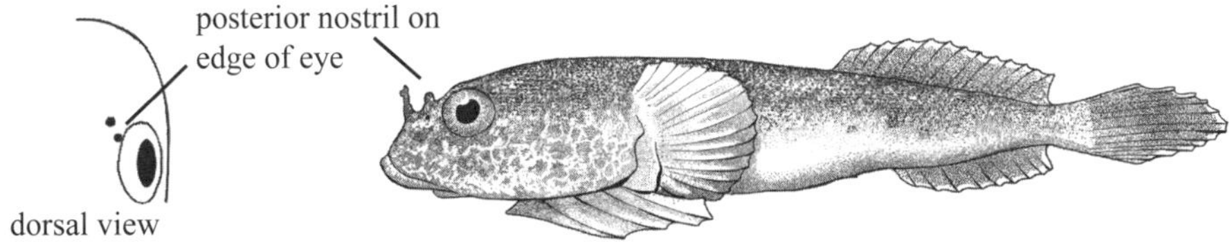


5a *From 1a: dorsal fin widely separated from caudal fin*
Pectoral fin soft-rays usually 18 (17–19)….. 7

5b Pectoral fin soft-rays 14–17….. 6
(KELP and SOUTHERN CLINGFISH difficult to identify in the field)

6a Eye diameter into interorbital width 1.2–1.8; males without incisors in lower jaw; males with small genital papilla:

**KELP CLINGFISH**

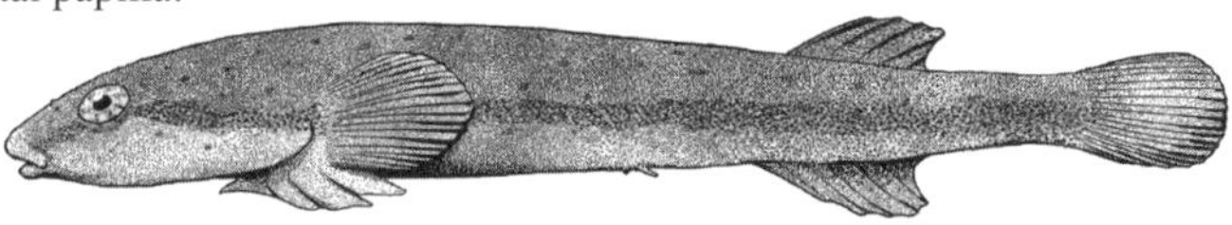

6b Eye diameter into interorbital width 1.0–1.2; males with broad incisors in lower jaw; males with large genital papilla:

**SOUTHERN CLINGFISH**

7a *From 5a: pectoral fin soft-rays 17–19*
Pores near tip of snout arranged approximately parallel; caudal peduncle comparatively deep, minimum depth into length 1.7–2.6:

**SLENDER CLINGFISH**

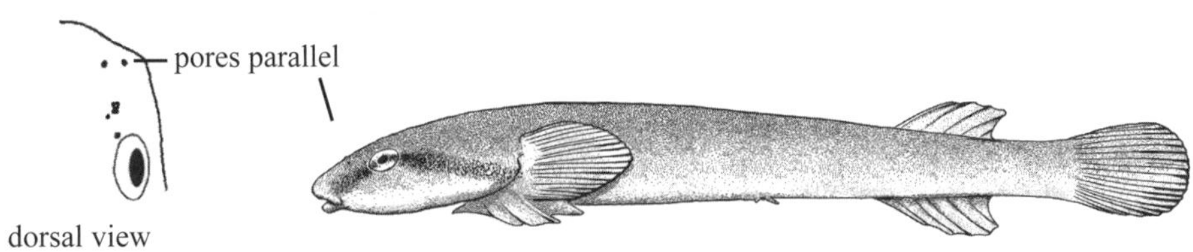


7b Inner pore near tip of snout posterior to outer pore; caudal peduncle comparatively narrow, minimum depth into length 2.8–4.2:

**CHANNEL ISLANDS CLINGFISH**

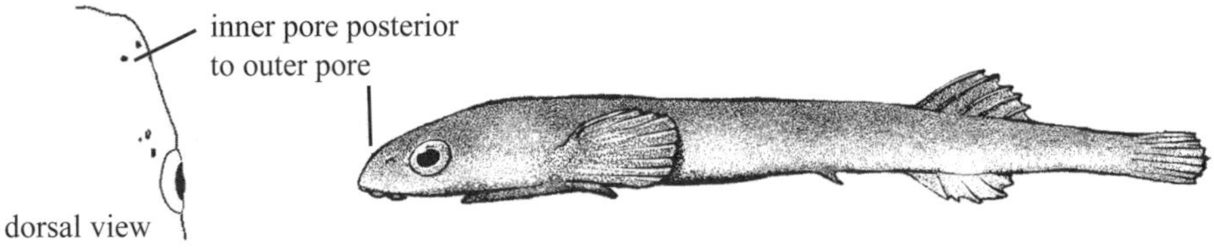

## GOBIES, Family Gobiidae

NOTE: Some authors place some of these species in the family Gobionellidae (Thacker, 2009) or Oxudercidae (Nelson et al., 2016).

**AMUR GOBY, *Rhinogobius brunneus* (Temminck & Schlegel, 1845).** Many parts of eastern Asia; introduced into western United States, currently in Columbia River Estuary, and associated waters. Length to 10 cm (3.9 in) TL. Shallow waters; depth: not reported. Dark, often red, stripe running from anterior part of eye to end of snout; body color variable, generally brownish with light and dark mottling; breeding males red and blue with white margin on dorsal and anal fins. D VI + I,8–10; A I,8–9; Pect. 19–22; Midlateral scales 29–32; GR 2 + 9; Vert. 25–26. Sometimes described as a complex of species.

**YELLOWFIN GOBY, *Acanthogobius flavimanus* (Temminck & Schlegel, 1845).** Native to Japan, Sea of Japan, China, and Korea; introduced to Estero Americano, Sonoma County, northern California,Tomales Bay, San Francisco Bay, and other central and southern California bays and estuaries to Ensenada, northern Baja California and perhaps to Isla Cedros, central Baja California. Common from San Francisco Bay to at least as far south as Tijuana Estuary, southern California. Length to 25 cm (9.8 in) TL in eastern Pacific, 30 cm (12 in) TL in Japan. Bays and estuaries, ascends rivers; depth: intertidal to 14 m (45 ft). Light gray with black speckling and bars. D VIII–IX + 0–I,12–14; A 0–I,11–12; Pect. 20–22; Pelvic I,5; Midlateral scales 42–55; GR 2 + 9; Vert. 33–35.

**LONGJAW MUDSUCKER, *Gillichthys mirabilis* Cooper, 1864.** Tomales Bay, northern California to Gulf of California. Common from Tomales Bay southward to southern Baja California and in upper Gulf of California. Length to 21 cm (8.3 in) TL. Marine to estuarine (will also live in hypersaline conditions). Shallow waters of bays and mudflats; depth: to at least 5 m (15 ft). Adults brown, black, or olive on back, belly lighter or yellowish; some mottling and faint bars on back and sides. Juveniles have about 8 bars on sides and dark blotch on posterior of 1st dorsal fin. Small juveniles, less than about 3 cm SL, with distinctly depigmented band at base of tail. D IV–VIII + I–III,9–14; A I–III,8–14; Pect. 18–23; Pelvic I,5; GR 1–4 + 9–12; Vert. 31–33.

**BLACKEYE GOBY, *Rhinogobiops nicholsii* (Bean, 1882).** Yakutat, eastern Gulf of Alaska to south of Punta Rompiente and Isla Guadalupe (SIO 54-215) and Isla Cedros, central Baja California. Common from northern British Columbia to northern Baja California. Length to 15 cm (6 in) TL. Open coast and bays; depth: intertidal to at least 195 m (640 ft). Tan, olive, and yellow with brownish and green speckling; black on outer edge of 1st dorsal fin. D IV–VI + I–II,9–15; A 0–I,11–13; Pect. 16–24; Pelvic I,5; Midlateral scales 24–28; GR 1–3 + 8–11 = 10–14; Vert. 26. (Formerly *Coryphopterus nicholsii* Bean, 1882): M&L).

**TAILSPOT GOBY, *Bollmannia stigmatura* Gilbert, 1892.** Oceanside (33°09'N, 117°23'W), southern California (LACM 57801-3) to Gulf of California and to northern Peru. Length to 12 cm (4.7 in) TL. Depth: 20–150 m (66–492 ft). Gray-brown body; head and body with orange spots; 2nd dorsal fin with 2 rows of orange spots; dark spot at base of caudal fin; black line on top lip. D VII + 13; Anal I,13; Pect. 22–25; Midlateral scales 26–30.

## KEY TO THE GOBIES:

Revised by Camm C. Swift and Kathy Hieb
(Principal sources: Miller & Lea, 1972; Fischer et al., 1995; Swift et al., 2016)

1a Dark stripe, often red, running from anterior part of eye to end of snout:

**AMUR GOBY**

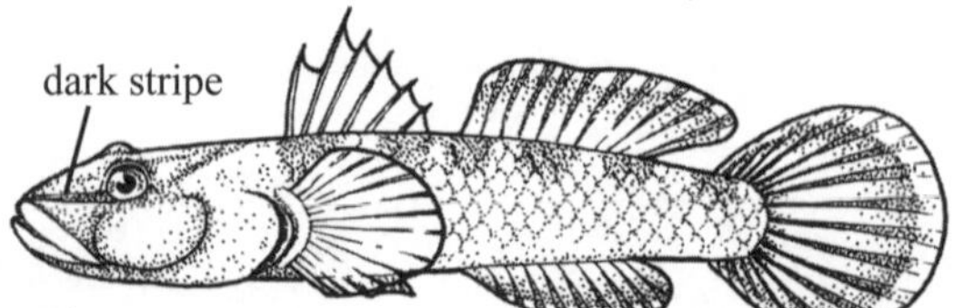


1b Dark stripe on head lacking….. 2 (next page)

2a TL shorter than 13 cm (includes juveniles of 2b)….. 7 (next page)

2b TL 13 cm or longer….. 3

3a Ventral 2–4 caudal fin soft-rays pale, appearing as white or yellow lower margin:

**YELLOWFIN GOBY**

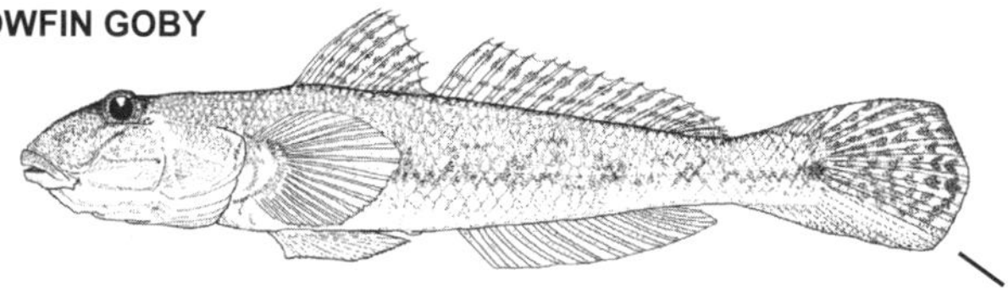


3b Caudal fin lacking lower pale margin….. 4

4a Upper jaw elongated, extending well beyond eye; scales small and irregular, imbedded in thick skin, barely visible:

**LONGJAW MUDSUCKER**

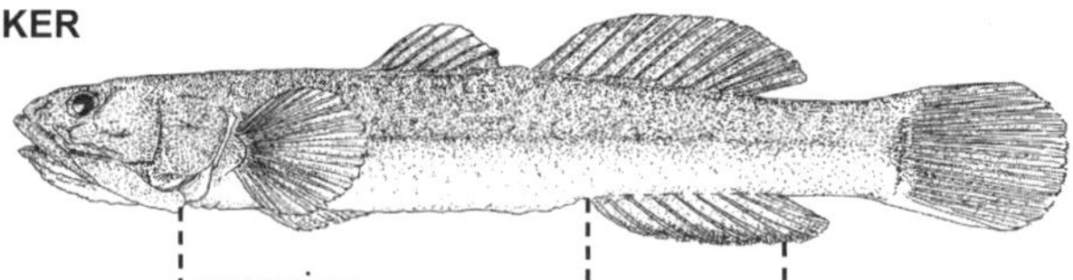


4b Upper jaw not elongated, or only slightly elongated, not extending beyond eye; scales regularly overlapping and scales or scale pockets visible on body….. 5

5a Outer edge on 1st dorsal fin black; body light or only slightly mottled with gray; midlateral scales 24–28:

**BLACKEYE GOBY**

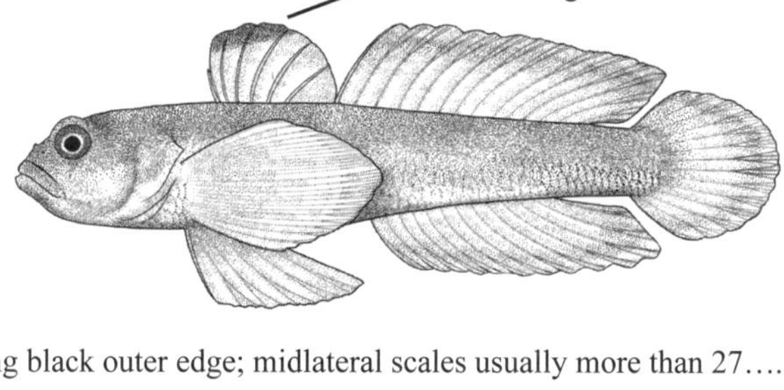


5b First dorsal fin lacking black outer edge; midlateral scales usually more than 27….. 6

6a Mouth distinctly upturned; middle spines of 1st dorsal fin elongated; midlateral scales 26–30; body moderately elongated, BD into SL 5 or less:

**TAILSPOT GOBY**

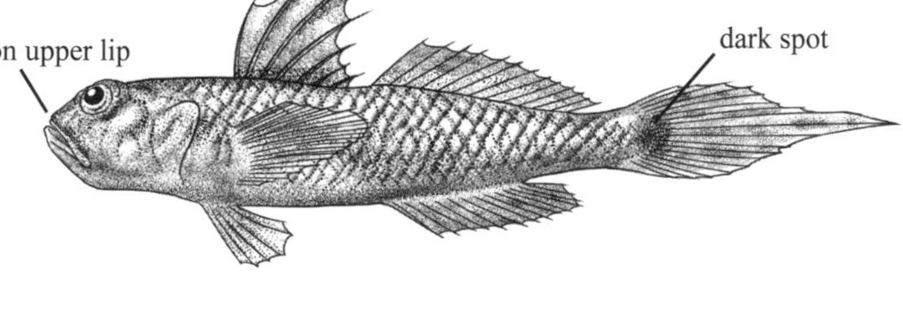


6b (next page)

## GOBIES (continued)

**LONGTAIL GOBY, *Ctenogobius sagittula* (Günther, 1861).** Marina del Rey, southern California (LACM 47551-1) to Puerto Pizarro, Peru. Periodically common in San Diego Bay and Tijuana Estuary and other southern California estuaries, but perhaps uncommon along much of Baja California coast, and common in Gulf of California. Length to about 30 cm (12 in) TL. Depth: intertidal to 5 m (17 ft). Light yellow-brown; black blotches on sides. D VI + I,12–14; A I,13–14; Pect. 16–17; Midlateral scales 55–65; GR 1 + 4–5; Vert. 26. (Formerly *Gobionellus longicaudus* (Jenkins & Evermann, 1889): M&L) (Alternative name LANCETAIL GOBY).

**BAY GOBY, *Lepidogobius lepidus* (Girard, 1858).** Kegan Cove, southeastern Alaska to Isla Cedros and Bahía de Sebastián Vizcaíno, central Baja California (SIO 84-90). Common from at least Vancouver Island to Bahía de Sebastián Vizcaíno, central Baja California. Length to 15.5 cm (6.1 in) TL. Open coast, bays, and estuaries; depth: intertidal to 305 m (1,000 ft). Brown, olive, or reddish-brown on sides, sometimes with small blotches or saddles. D VI–IX + 0–I,14–18; A 0–I,12–16; Pect. 20–24; Pelvic I,5; Midlateral scales about 86; GR 2–4 + 8–12 = 10–14; Vert. 37–38.

**HALFBLIND GOBY, *Lethops connectens* Hubbs, 1926.** Carmel, central California to Punta Colnett, northern Baja California. Common in southern California. Length to 8.9 cm (3.5 in) TL. Depth: intertidal to 18 m (60 ft). Uniform tan. D VI–VII + 0–I,12–14; A 0–I,12–13; Pect. 20–21; Pelvic I,5; GR 1–2 + 9–11; Vert. 34–36. (Formerly KELP GOBY: M&L).

**BLIND GOBY, *Typhlogobius californiensis* Steindachner, 1879.** San Simeon Point, central California to Bahía Magdalena, southern Baja California. Common from southern California to perhaps Bahía Tortugas, southern Baja California. Length to 8.3 cm (3.3 in) TL. Depth: intertidal to 15 m (50 ft). Uniform pink. D II–III + 0–I,10–12; A I,7–10; Pect. 15–16; Pelvic I,5; GR 2 + 8–11; Vert. 30–32.

**BLUEBANDED GOBY, *Lythrypnus dalli* (Gilbert, 1890).** Monterey Bay, central California (CAS 54911) to Islas Lobos de Afuera, Peru, including Gulf of California and Islas Galápagos. Common from southern California southward into tropics. Length to 6.4 cm (2.5 in) TL. Depth: intertidal to 76 m (250 ft). Red with 2–9 bright blue bars. D VI–VII + 0–I,15–19; A 0–I,12–14; Pect. 16–20; Pelvic I,5; Midlateral scales 39–45; GR 0–1 + 7–10; Vert. 26–27. (Alternative name CATALINA GOBY).

6b Mouth low, horizontal or subterminal; no elongated spines in 1st dorsal fin; midlateral scales 55–65; body elongated, BD into SL more than 5:

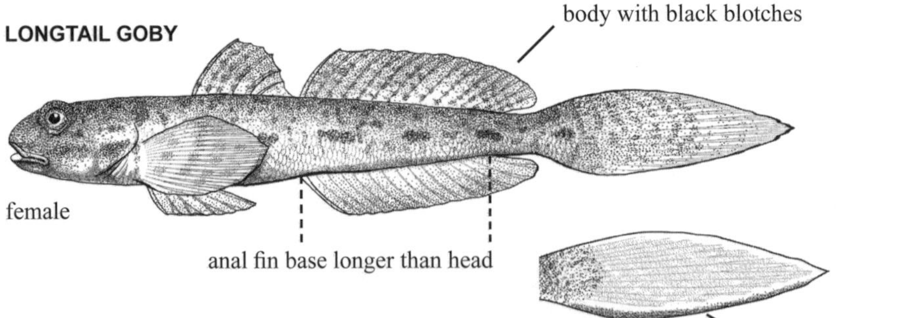


7a *From 2a: TL shorter than 13 cm*
First dorsal fin lacking black outer edge..... 9 (next page)

7b Outer edge on 1st dorsal fin black..... 8 (next page)

8a Scales large, midlateral scales 24–28; body pale or with gray areas; shoulder girdle (cleithrum) under operculum smooth; 1st dorsal fin spines 4–6; anal fin soft-rays 11–13:

**BLACKEYE GOBY**
(not illustrated here, see 5a)

8b Scales small, indistinct, midlateral scales more than 50; body with 3–5 distinct horizontally elongate dark blotches along midline; shoulder girdle (cleithrum) under operculum with 1–3 fleshy papillae; 1st dorsal fin spines 6–9; anal fin soft-rays 12–16:

**BAY GOBY**

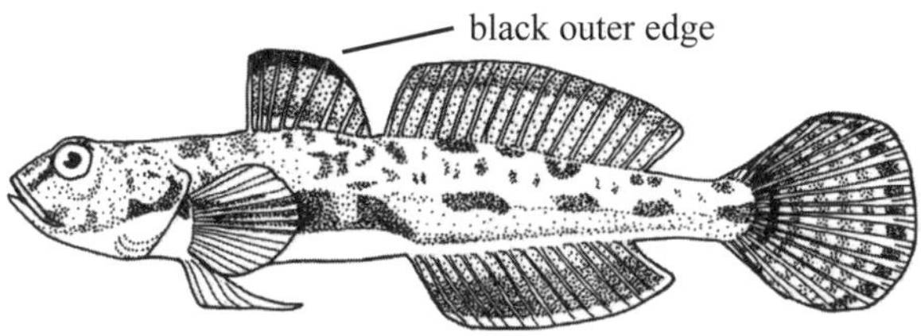


9a *From 7a: first dorsal fin lacking black outer edge*
Fleshy folds lacking on head; eyes large, distinct, functional; distinct pigment pattern present on head and body; scales present, small and imbedded to large and obvious….. 11

9b Head with fleshy longitudinal folds; eyes very small or absent; head and body very pale, lacking any pigment pattern; scales lacking….. 10

10a Body uniform tan; 1st dorsal fin spines 6–7; eyes small:

**HALFBLIND GOBY**

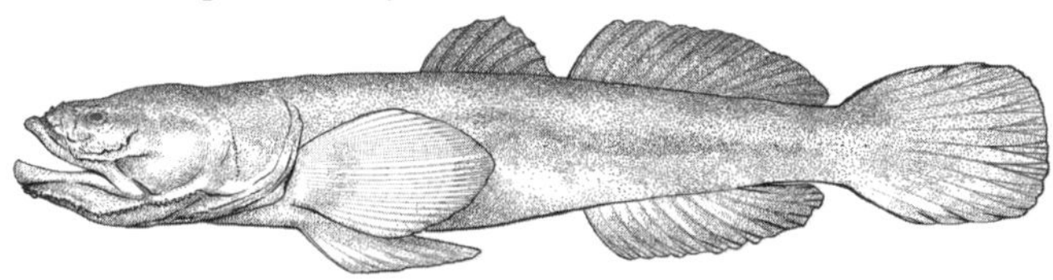

10b Body uniform pink; 1st dorsal fin spines 2–3; eyes absent (small in juveniles):

**BLIND GOBY**

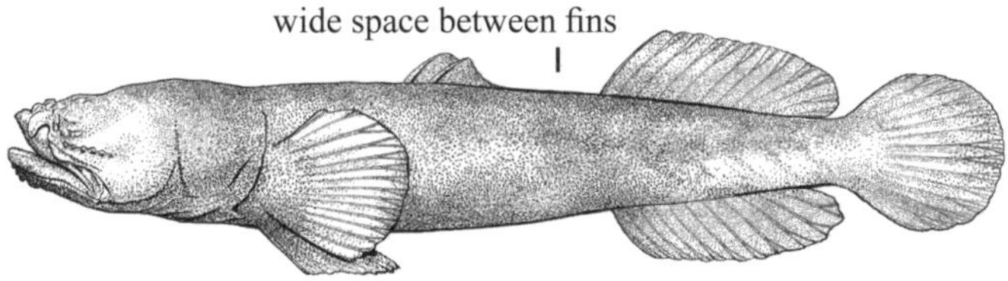


11a *From 9a: fleshy folds lacking on head*
Body pale cream, tan, yellow or orange, without blue bars; mouth not sharply upturned….. 13 (next page)

11b Body red or orange, with blue bars; mouth sharply upturned….. 12

12a Head and body with 2–9 blue bars:

**BLUEBANDED GOBY**

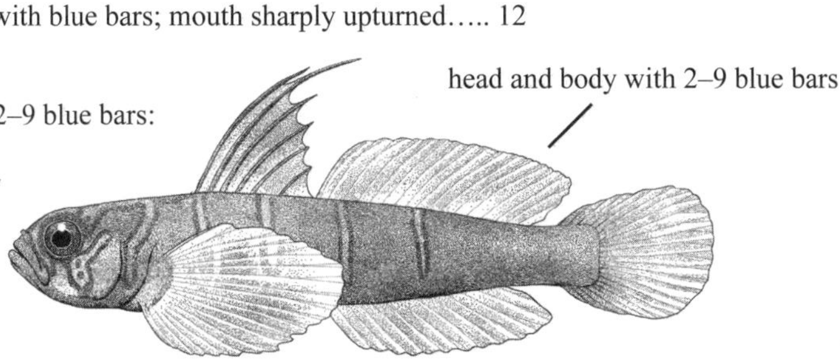


12b (next page)

## GOBIES (continued)

**ZEBRA GOBY, *Lythrypnus zebra* (Gilbert, 1890).** Carmel Bay, central California to barely into Gulf of California (SIO 59-225), Isla Clarión, and Islas Revillagigedo. Common from southern California to at least central Baja California. Length to 5.7 cm (2.3 in) TL. Depth: intertidal to 97 m (318 ft). Dull red with 18–21 bright blue bars. D VI + 0–I,11–14; A 0–I,8–10; Pect. 18–21; PelvicI,5; Midlateral scales 32–36; GR 0–2 + 9; Vert. 26.

**ARROW GOBY, *Clevelandia ios* (Jordan & Gilbert, 1882).** Rivers Inlet, British Columbia to Bahía Magdalena, southern Baja California (LACM 32093-1). Gulf of California record in M&L is likely in error. Common from southern British Columbia to Punta Abreojos, southern Baja California. Length to 6.7 cm (2.6 in) TL. Bays, estuaries, lagoons, and tidal sloughs; depth: 0.3 m or less to 45 m (1–148 ft). Light olive with dark mottling. D IV–VI + 0–I,14–17; A 0–I,13–17; Pect. 18–21; Pelvic I,5; Midlateral scales about 70; GR 1–3 + 5–9 = 7–10; Vert. 36–37.

**SHADOW GOBY, *Quietula y-cauda* (Jenkins & Evermann, 1889).** Morro Bay, central California to Gulf of California. Common from southern California southward to Gulf of California. Length to 7 cm (2.8 in) TL. Depth: intertidal to 6 m (20 ft). Dark to light brown with dark blotches; Y-shaped mark on caudal peduncle. D IV–V + I,13–15; A 0–I,12–15; Pect. 19–22; Pelvic I,5; Midlateral scales about 50; GR 2–4 + 8–10 = 11–13; Vert. 33–34.

**SHOKIHAZE GOBY, *Tridentiger barbatus* (Günther, 1861).** Native to western Pacific, Japan and Korea as far south as Taiwan; introduced to San Francisco Bay and estuaries and rivers associated with bays. Length to 10.9 cm (4.4 in) TL. Brackish and marine waters; depth: 2–26 m (6–85 ft). Tan; 6 dusky bands (fading ventrally) on body, first at nape of neck; 2 dark spots on upper and lower caudal fin base; dark pigmentation on much of dorsal fins. In juveniles, 2 dark caudal spots may merge forming large blotch on caudal peduncle. D VI + I,10; A I,9–10; Pect. 21–23; Midlateral scales 37–39; Vert. 26.

**CHAMELEON GOBY, *Tridentiger trigonocephalus* (Gill, 1859).** Native to China, Japan, and Siberia; introduced to San Francisco Bay, Los Angeles-Long Beach Harbors, and San Diego Bay. Primarily marine, but occasionally in somewhat brackish waters; depth: surf zone to more than 15 m (49 ft). Brownish-gray with dark mottling and stripes; white speckles on head; dorsal and anal fins edged in white. D VI + I,11–12; A I,10–11; Pect. 20–22; Pelvic I,5; Midlateral scales 54–60; GR 2–3 + 7–8; Vert. 26–27.

12b Head and body with 18–21 blue bars:

**ZEBRA GOBY**

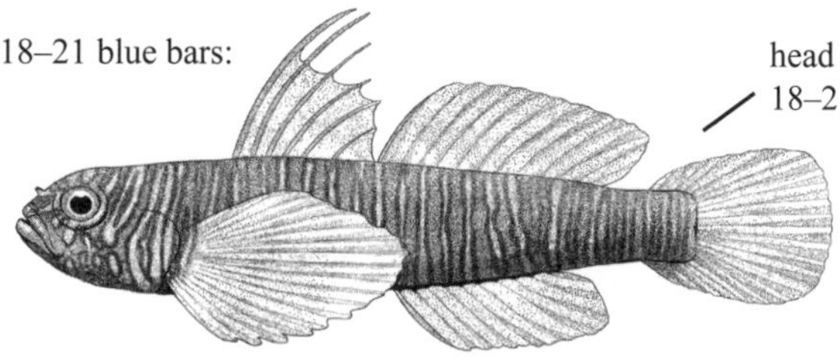

head and body with 18–21 blue bars

13a *From 11a: body pale cream, tan, yellow or orange, without blue bars*
Upper jaw does not extend beyond eye….. 16 (next page)

13b Upper jaw extends beyond eye (includes LONGJAW MUDSUCKER less than 4 cm TL)….. 14

14a Surface of cleithrum with low transparent cartilaginous ridge; BD into SL less than 5: **LONGJAW MUDSUCKER** (not illustrated here, see 4a)

14b Surface of cleithrum with 1–3 fleshy papillae; BD into SL 5 or more….. 15 (next page)

15a Head and body uniformly slender; BD into SL 6–7; 1st dorsal fin lower than 2nd dorsal fin; body pale and flecked with fine black dots; total gill rakers 7–9:

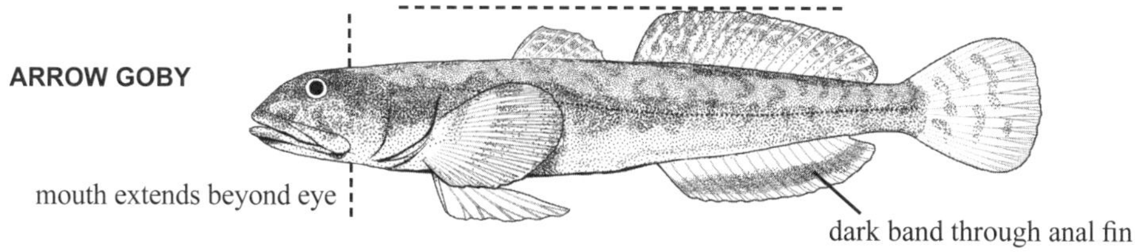


15b Head larger than body, body narrowing posteriorly; BD into SL about 5–6; dorsal fins about equal height; body distinctly bicolored, upper dark, lower light; total gill rakers 11–13:

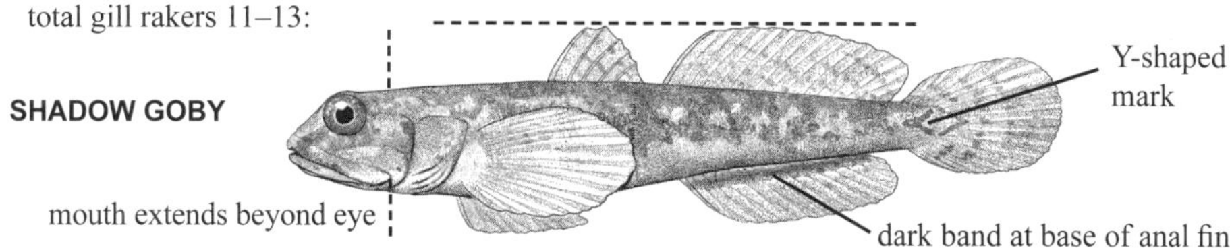


16a *From 13a: upper jaw does not extend beyond eye*
Upper and lower teeth with single point; head and body circular or only slightly compressed or depressed….. 19 (next page)

16b Upper and lower teeth forked or trifid; head often depressed, wider than body….. 17

17a Fleshy, hair-like papillae on lower jaw, preopercle, and under eye; body mostly dark with 3–4 large light blotches and saddles:

17b Papillae, if present, small, low and rounded; body with 3 distinct color patterns: 1) overall very dark, black or blue-black with vertical white band on pectoral base, 2) lighter with 10–14 dark bars, or 3) lighter with strong narrow, dark midlateral stripe on head and body….. 18

18a Pale speckles on sides of head and operculum, lacking on underside of head; anal fin edged in white; supraorbital lateral line canal pore large (about ⅔ to ¾ size of posterior nostril); upper pectoral fin soft-rays deeply incised and covered with fine papillae:

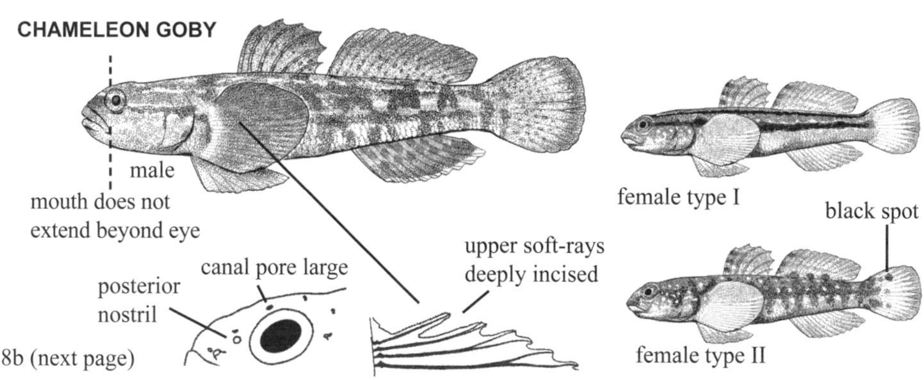


18b (next page)

## GOBIES (continued)

**SHIMOFURI GOBY, *Tridentiger bifasciatus* Steindachner, 1881.** Native to China, Korea, Japan, and Russian Sea of Japan; introduced to Sacramento–San Joaquin Delta and various freshwater systems in California as far south as the Santa Clara River drainage. Length to 10.4 cm (4.1 in) TL. Shallow waters; depth: not reported. Color variable; tiny white speckles on underside of head; 2nd dorsal and anal fins fringed with orange and lacking banding; white band at base of pectoral fin; rows of spots covering caudal fin; dark stripe running along top of each side from head to caudal fin; usually dark stripe along side. D VI–VII + I,11–14; A I,9–12; Pect. 19–23; Midlateral scales 54–60.

**CHEEKSPOT GOBY, *Ilypnus gilberti* (Eigenmann & Eigenmann, 1889).** Estero Americano, northern California to Bahía Magdalena, southern Baja California and Gulf of California. Common from Tomales Bay, northern California to Bahía Magdalena. Length to 6.8 cm (2.7 in) TL. Marine to almost fresh water. Mudflats and shallow bays and estuaries; depth: intertidal to 24 m (79 ft). Tan to light gray; blue-black spot on operculum. D V + 0–I,13–17; A 0–I,12–16; Pect. 21–22; Pelvic I,5; GR 3–5 + 10–11; Vert. 32–34.

**SOUTHERN TIDEWATER GOBY, *Eucyclogobius kristinae* Swift, Spies, Ellingson & Jacobs, 2016.** Aliso Creek, Orange County, southern California to Agua Hedionda Lagoon, San Diego County, southern California. Currently apparently found in only a handful of lagoons. Length to about 5.5 cm (2.2 in) TL. Coastal lagoons; depth: not reported. Body gray, greenish, or light tan, older fish becoming darker; upper edge of anterior part of 1st dorsal fin unpigmented, cream, or orange. Breeding females brighter tan or brown on head and tail, black between; dorsal and anal fins black. D IV–VIII + 9–13 (usually 10–11); A 8–13; Pect. 17–19 (usually 18–19); GRt 9–11; Vert. 33–35.

**NORTHERN TIDEWATER GOBY, *Eucyclogobius newberryi* (Girard, 1856).** Tillas Slough, mouth of Smith River, northern California to Santa Monica Artesian Springs, Los Angeles County, southern California. Historically extirpated from many sites and declining at many others. Length to about 5.5 cm (2.2 in) TL. Coastal lagoons and brackish bays at mouths of freshwater streams; depth: to 15 m (49 ft). Body gray, greenish, or light tan, older fish becoming darker; upper edge of anterior part of 1st dorsal fin unpigmented, cream, or orange. Breeding females brighter tan or brown on head and tail, black between; dorsal and anal fins black. D V–VIII + 10–13 (usually 11–12); A I,9–13; Pect. 17–21 (usually 19–21); Pelvic I,5; GRt 8–12; Vert. 32–35.

18b Pale speckles only on underside of head; anal fin with 1 pale stripe on ventral edge; supraorbital lateral line canal pore small (less than ½ the size of posterior nostril); upper pectoral fin soft-rays only slightly incised, lacking papillae:

**SHIMOFURI GOBY**
(body shape as in 18a)

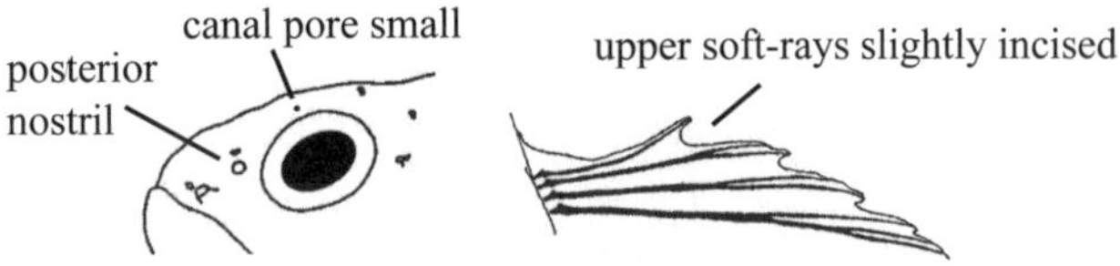


19a *From 16a: upper and lower teeth with single point*
Dorsal ¼ –⅓ of 1st dorsal fin unpigmented or pale, cream, yellow, or orange, remainder dusky or black; upper gill opening ends below upper edge of pectoral fin base..... 23 (next page)

19b First dorsal fin dusky, spotted, mottled, or pale, may have narrow pale margin; upper gill opening reaching or extending above pectoral fin..... 20 (next page)

20a Dark, well-defined oval spot on operculum; shoulder girdle under operculum with 1–3 fleshy papillae:

**CHEEKSPOT GOBY**

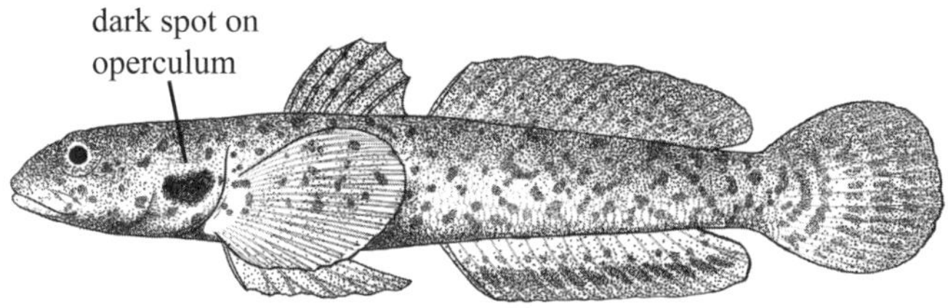


20b Operculum with some pigment, but not concentrated into well-defined oval spot; shoulder girdle under operculum smooth….. 21

21a Scales obvious and large, midlateral scales 26–30; eyes large, equal to or longer than snout length; middle 1st dorsal fin spines elongated:

**TAILSPOT GOBY** (not illustrated here, see 6a)

21b Scales small, midlateral scales more than 40; eyes small, shorter than snout length; middle 1st dorsal fin spines not elongated….. 22

22a Caudal fin not elongated, into SL more than 3; ventral 2–4 caudal fin soft-rays with distinct white or yellow lower edge; midlateral scales 42–55:

**YELLOWFIN GOBY** (not illustrated here, see 3a)

22b Caudal fin elongated, into SL less than 3; ventral caudal fin soft-rays pigmented or black; midlateral scales 55–65:

**LONGTAIL GOBY** (not illustrated here, see 6b)

23a *From 19a: dorsal ¼ –⅓ of dorsal fin colorless or pale, cream, yellow, or orange*
Anterior supraorbital canal lacking anterior extension, ending over middle of eye dorsally (in fish over about 2.5 cm SL); south of Palos Verdes Peninsula:

**SOUTHERN TIDEWATER GOBY**

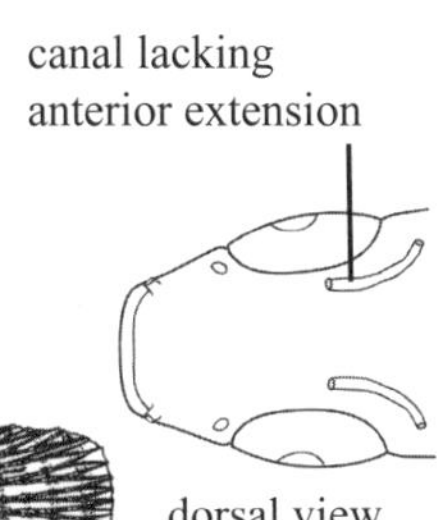


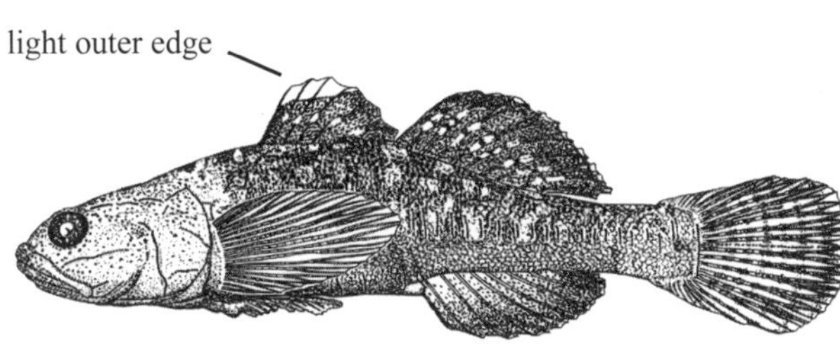


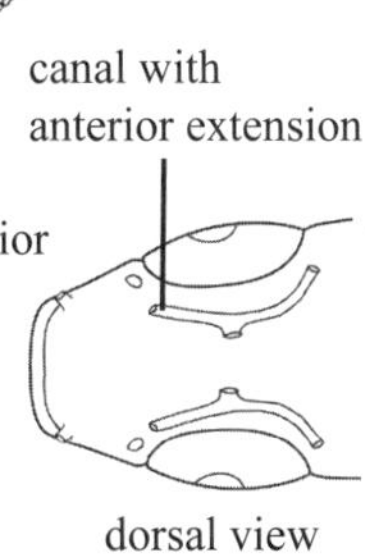


23b Anterior supraorbital canal with anterior extension, extending to near posterior nostril (in fish over about 2.5 cm SL); north of Palos Verdes Peninsula:

**NORTHERN TIDEWATER GOBY**
(body shape as in 23a)

## SNAKE MACKERELS, Family Gempylidae and CUTLASSFISHES, Family Trichiuridae

NOTE: Most studies conclude that the cutlassfishes evolved from a group of snake mackerels. Thus, some consider Gempylidae to be an invalid (paraphyletic) taxon.

**PACIFIC CUTLASSFISH, *Trichiurus nitens* Garman, 1899.** Family TRICHIURIDAE
Monterey County, central California (SIO 00-56) to Callao, Peru, including Gulf of California and Islas Galápagos. Common in southern California. Length to 82 cm (32.3 in) TL. Depth: surface to 384 m (1,260 ft). Silvery-blue in life, silvery-brown after death. D III,121–124 (spines are flexible and difficult to differentiate from unsegmented soft-rays); A I,98–103 (all anal soft-rays extremely reduced, spine-like, and barely penetrating skin); Pect. 11–12 (1st soft-ray spine-like and unsegmented); Pelvic and caudal fins absent; GR 11–14 + 11–18 = 25–31; Vert. 153–156. (Alternative name EASTERN PACIFIC HAIRTAIL, LARGEHEAD HAIRTAIL) (Perhaps a synonym of the ATLANTIC CUTLASSFISH, *Trichiurus lepturus* Linnaeus, 1758).

**STRIPED ESCOLAR, *Diplospinus multistriatus* Maul, 1948.** Family GEMPYLIDAE
Circumglobal in temperate and tropical waters; in western Pacific as far north as southern Japan and east of Kuril Islands; central California (35°00'N) to Chile. Rare off California. Length to about 33 cm (13 in) SL. Oceanic mesopelagic; depth: 50–1,000 m (164–3,280 ft). Silvery; narrow dark dotted lines along body; gill membranes black. D XXX–XXXVI + 35–44; A II,28–35; Pect. 11–13; Pelvic I (scale-like, rudimentary); GR 6–11 (1 large at angle) + 9–17; Vert. 57–64. (Alternative name LINED CUTLASSFISH).

**SNAKE MACKEREL, *Gempylus serpens* Cuvier, 1829.** Family GEMPYLIDAE
Circumglobal; in western Pacific as far north as southern Japan; San Pedro, southern California to central Chile, including lowermost Gulf of California and Islas Galápagos. Apparently rare in southern California. Length to 140.5 cm (55.3 in) TL. Oceanic epi- and mesopelagic; depth: surface to 1,000 m (3,280 ft). Uniformly dark brown or blackish. D XXVI–XXXII + I,11–14 + 5–6 finlets; A II + I,10–12 + 6–7 finlets; Pect. 12–15; Pelvic I,3–4; GR 1 at angle + 5–6 emerging from tooth patch; Vert. 48–55.

## KEY TO THE SNAKE MACKERELS and CUTLASSFISHES:
Created by F. Javier Gago
(Principal sources: Maul, 1948; Nakamura, 1982; Parin, 1983; Nakamura & Parin, 1993; Burhanuddin & Parin, 2008)

1a Caudal fin absent; anal fin soft-rays extremely reduced, spine-like, and barely penetrating through skin; anal fin membrane absent; lower posterior margin of gill cover concave:

PACIFIC CUTLASSFISH

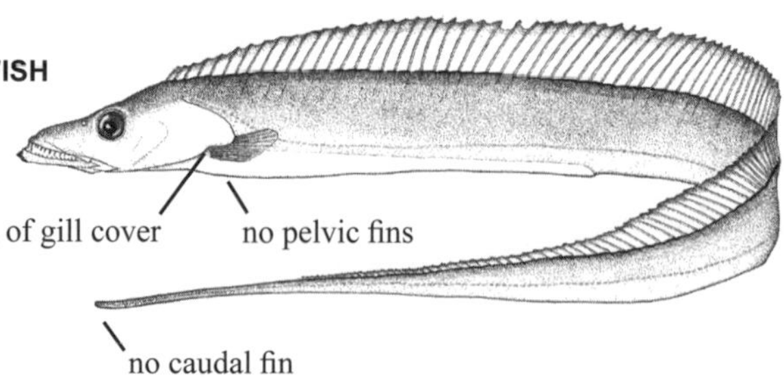


1b (next page)

1b Caudal fin present; anal fin soft-rays normal; anal fin membrane present throughout entire fin or at least on posterior portion; lower posterior margin of gill cover convex….. 2

2a One nostril on each side of snout; dorsal fins continuous or barely separated from each other by small notch on fin membrane….. 6 (page 326)

2b Two nostrils on each side of snout; dorsal fins contiguous and clearly separated from each other….. 3

3a Finlets absent; dorsal fin soft-rays 35 or more:

**STRIPED ESCOLAR**

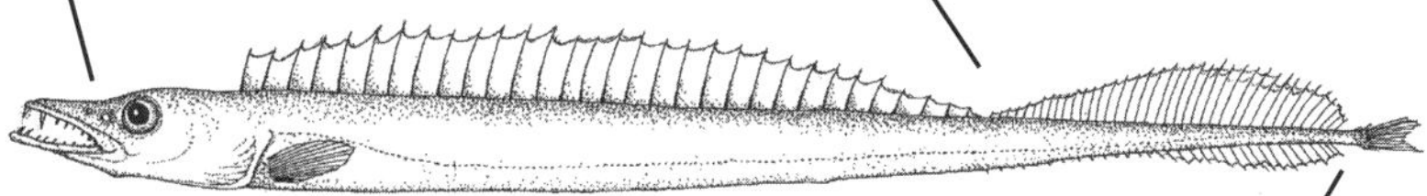


3b Finlets present; dorsal fin soft-rays 18 or fewer (not including finlets)..... 4

4a Body laterally compressed, moderately elongated; BD into SL 15–18; HL into SL 5.5–6; lateral line with 2 branches; scales absent except on posterior portion of body:

**SNAKE MACKEREL**

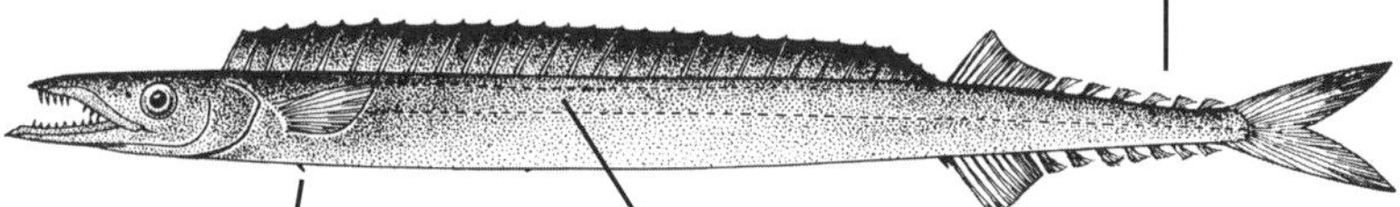


4b Body fusiform; BD into SL 4–5; HL into SL 3–4; lateral line single; scales present throughout body….. 5 (next page)

## SNAKE MACKERELS and CUTLASSFISHES (continued)

**ESCOLAR, *Lepidocybium flavobrunneum* (Smith, 1843).** Family Gempylidae

Circumglobal; in western Pacific as far north as Japan and southern Kuril Islands; Point Vicente, southern California to Cabo Blanco, Peru; apparently not in the Gulf of California. Rare off California. Length to 220 cm (86.6 in) TL. Oceanic pelagic; depth: 25–885 m (82–2,903 ft). Uniformly dark brown, larger fish almost black. D VIII–XI + 16–18 + 4–6 finlets; A I–II,12–17 + 4–5 finlets (small specimens have 3 anal spines, the first rudimentary); Pect. 15–17; Pelvic I,5; GR 0 + 6–9 or absent, 1 sharp spine at angle; Vert. 31–32. M&L give Washington State as northernmost record – a record without documentation according to Fitch and Schultz (1978). (Formerly Scombridae: M&L).

**OILFISH, *Ruvettus pretiosus* Cocco, 1833.** Family Gempylidae

Circumglobal in temperate and tropical waters; southern Japan and southern Kuril Islands; well off Bodega Bay, northern California (SIO 96-8) to southern Baja California and Costa Rica to Chile. Occasional off California. Length to 203 cm (80 in) TL, possibly to 305 cm (120 in) TL. Oceanic benthopelagic; depth: 60 m (197 ft), and probably shallower, to 1,160 m (3,806 ft). Blackish to dark brown; tip of pectoral and pelvic fins black; margin of 2nd dorsal and anal fins white in young fish. D XIII–XV + 15–18 + 2 finlets; A II–III,12–18 + 1–3 finlets; Pect. 13–15; Pelvic I,5; GR 1 large spine at angle, 6–8 emerging from tooth patch; Vert. 32.

**PACIFIC BLACK SCABBARDFISH, *Aphanopus arigato* Parin, 1994.** Family Trichiuridae

Hokkaido, Japan, Kuril Islands, and southeastern Kamchatka; British Columbia to near Punta Eugenia (27°33'N, 115°53'W), southern Baja California (SIO 74-40). Occasional off California. Length to 120 cm (47.2 in) TL. Benthopelagic; depth: adults 494–1,350 m (1,620–4,429 ft); juveniles mesopelagic; 146–1,100 m (479–3,608 ft). Dark copper-black at capture, black after death. D XXXIX–XLII,54–58; A II,47–50; Pect. 12; Pelvic, absent in adults (present as rudimentary, scale-like spine in juveniles); Vert. 103–105.

5a Keels on caudal peduncle; greatly undulating lateral line (maybe difficult to see in preserved specimens); scales surrounded by network of tubules with pores; no abdominal keel of large spiny tubercles between pelvic and anal fins:

**ESCOLAR**

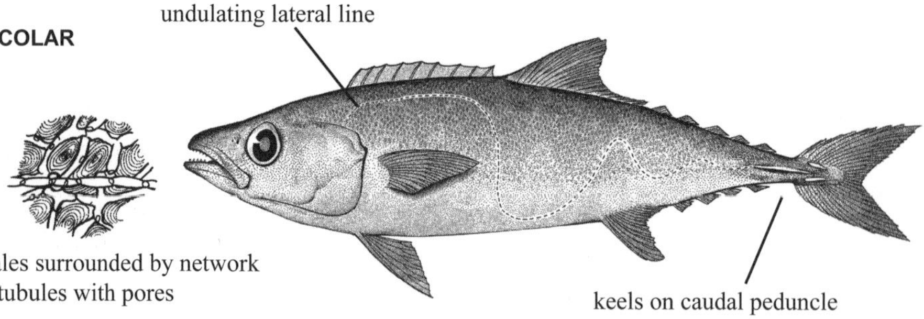


5b (next page)

5b No keels on caudal peduncle; lateral line straight, only curving above pectoral fin; skin rough with scales surrounded by spiny tubercles; abdominal keel of large spiny tubercles between pelvic and anal fins:

**OILFISH**

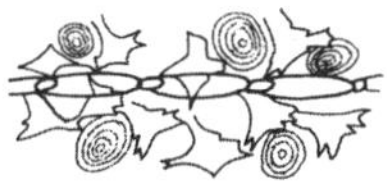


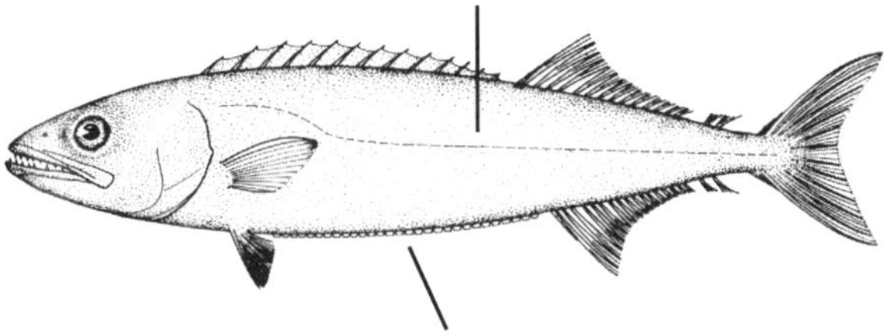


6a *From 2a: one nostril on each side of snout*
Dorsal profile of head convex, frontal ridges confluent postorbitally or fused and forming sagittal crest; dorsal fins continuous, no notch separating them….. 8 (page 328)

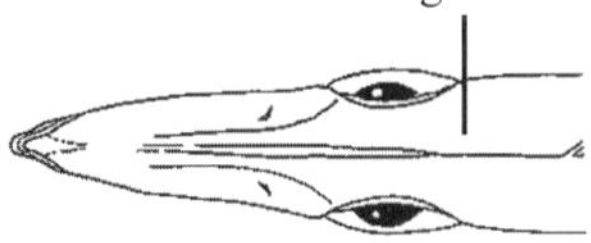


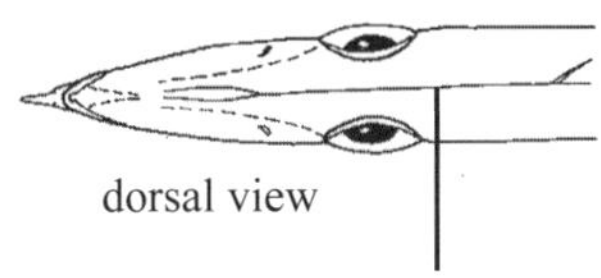


6b Dorsal profile of head flat or gently rising from snout to dorsal fin origin, frontal ridges parallel to each other, not confluent postorbitally or forming sagittal crest; dorsal fins continuous but slightly separated by small notch on fin membrane….. 7

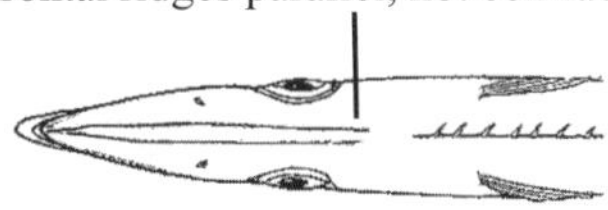


7a Pelvic fins absent in adults (present as rudimentary, scale-like spine in juveniles); total dorsal fin spines and soft-rays 100 or fewer; body moderately elongated; BD into SL 9–15.5; HL into SL 5–5.5:

**PACIFIC BLACK SCABBARDFISH**

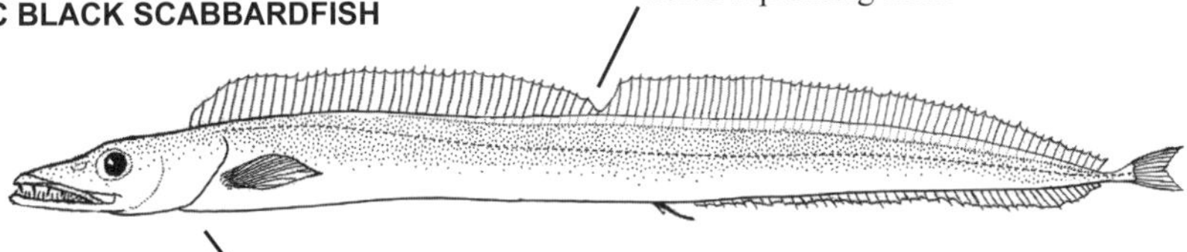


7b (next page)

# SNAKE MACKERELS and CUTLASSFISHES (continued)

**NORTH PACIFIC FROSTFISH, *Benthodesmus pacificus* Parin & Becker, 1970.** Family TRICHIURIDAE
Kyushu-Palau Ridge and Ryukyu Islands, Japan; British Columbia and Puget Sound, Washington to Monterey Bay, central California. Rare in California. Length to 112 cm (44.1 in) SL. Benthopelagic; depth: 380 m (1,246 ft) and perhaps deeper, sometimes migrating to surface; juveniles mesopelagic. Silvery; jaws, operculum, gill cavity, and inside of mouth dark. D XLIV–XLVII,98–106 (spines are flexible and difficult to differentiate from soft-rays); A II,90–94 (first spine rudimentary, second spine small and scale-like); Pect. 12; Pelvic I,1 (rudimentary scale-like spine, minute soft-ray); GR 5 (upper limb) + 1 (angle) + 8 (lower limb) = 14; Vert. 149–153.

**RAZORBACK SCABBARDFISH, *Assurger anzac* (Alexander, 1917).** Family TRICHIURIDAE
Circumglobal in temperate and tropical waters; southern Japan; Point Dume, southern California to Chile. Rare in southern California. Length to 250 cm (98.4 in) SL. Adults probably benthopelagic; depth: 15–400 m (50–1,312 ft). Uniformly silver; dorsal fin membrane black before 3rd–4th soft-ray. D XXXIV–XXXV,82–88 (spines are flexible and difficult to differentiate from soft-rays); A II,72–86 (1st spine rudimentary, 2nd spine small and scale-like, only posteriormost portion of fin with visible, external soft-rays); Pect. 12; Pelvic I,2 (rudimentary scale-like spine, minute soft-rays); GRt 13–14; Vert. 125–129.

**PACIFIC SCABBARDFISH, *Lepidopus fitchi* Rosenblatt & Wilson, 1987.** Family TRICHIURIDAE
Newport, Oregon to southern Peru, including Gulf of California. No collections appear to have been made between 20°00'N and 5°00'N. Common in southern California. Length to 210 cm (82.7 in) SL. Benthopelagic; depth: adults 150–500 m (492–1,640 ft) and perhaps to 1,080 m (3,542 ft). Adults black or brown with silvery shine along abdomen; juveniles silvery-white. D IX–XII,68–78 (spines are flexible and difficult to differentiate from soft-rays); A II,41–50 (first spine rudimentary, 2nd spine small and scale-like); Pect. 12; Pelvic I,2 (rudimentary scale-like spine, minute soft-rays); GRt 12–17; Vert. 84–93. (Formerly *Lepidopus xantusi* Goode & Bean, 1896: M&L) (Alternative name BLACK SCABBARDFISH). *Lepidopus manis* Rosenblatt & Wilson, 1987 may be a synonym.

7b Pelvic fins present, but extremely reduced to 1 scale-like spine and 1 minute soft-ray; total dorsal fin spines and soft-rays 142 or more; body elongated; BD into SL 22–26.5; HL into SL 7–9:

**NORTH PACIFIC FROSTFISH**

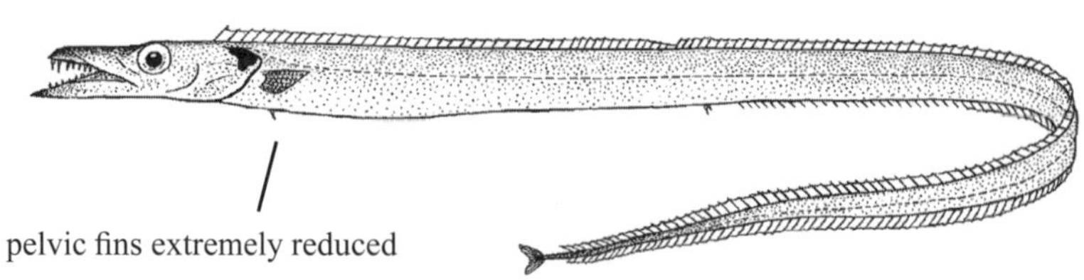


8a (next page)

8a *From 6a: dorsal profile of head convex*
Body greatly elongated; BD into SL 25–28; HL into SL 12–13.5; frontal ridges fused and forming highly elevated sagittal crest above orbital area; dorsal fin spines and soft-rays short and totaling 116 or more:

**RAZORBACK SCABBARDFISH**

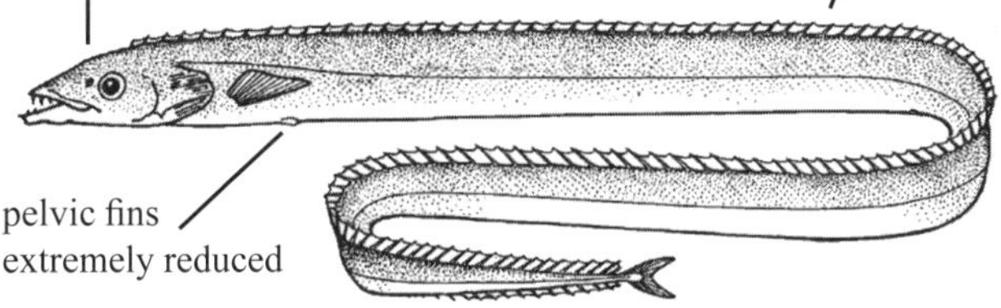


8b Body moderately elongated; BD into SL 9–13.5; HL into SL 4–5.5; frontal ridges confluent postorbitally but not forming sagittal crest above orbital area; dorsal fin spines and soft-rays high and totaling 90 or fewer:

**PACIFIC SCABBARDFISH**

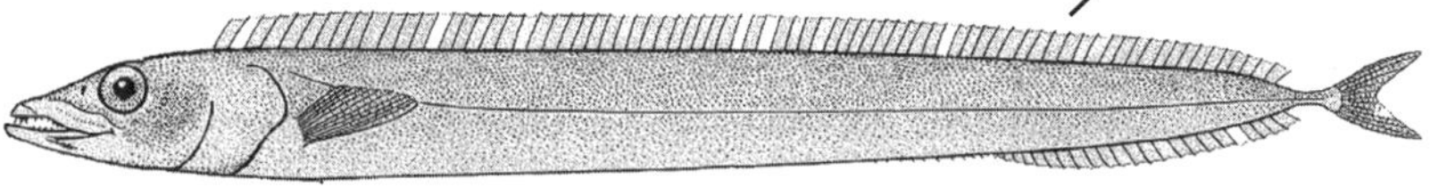

## MACKEREL and TUNAS, Family Scombridae

**WAHOO, *Acanthocybium solandri* (Cuvier, 1832).** Circumglobal; in western Pacific as far north as Japan and southern Kuril Islands; Santa Barbara and San Clemente Islands and off Oxnard, southern California to Paita, Peru and Easter Island, including mouth of Gulf of California and Islas Galápagos. Usually common from about southern Baja California southwards; however, common into southern California during some warm-water periods. Length to 2.5 m (8.2 ft) TL. Oceanic epipelagic; depth: surface to 296 m (971 ft). Back blue-green, sides silvery; 24–30 cobalt-blue bars – becoming gray after death. D XXIII–XXVII + 11–16 + 7–10 finlets; A 11–14 + 7–10 finlets; Pect. 22–26; GR none; Vert. 62–66. (Recently and commonly misspelled as *A. solanderi*).

**PACIFIC CHUB MACKEREL, *Scomber japonicus* Houttuyn, 1782.** Pacific and Indian Oceans; in western Pacific as far north as Japan, southern Kuril Islands, and southeastern Kamchatka; western Gulf of Alaska to Gulf of California and to Chile, including Islas Galápagos. In western Pacific common from northern Japan to at least Kuril Islands and to the east common as far northward as Vancouver Island (periodically) and common southward into Gulf of California. Length to nearly 63.5 cm (25 in) TL. Coastal pelagic to epi- or mesopelagic; depth: surface and surf zone to about 300 m (984 ft). Head dark blue or green, back green with dark wavy lines, silver-green below. D VIII–XIII + 10–15 + 4–6 finlets; A I–II,10–15 + 4–6 finlets; Pect. 19–22; GR 10–14 + 26–34; Vert. 30–32. (Formerly PACIFIC MACKEREL: M&L) (Alternative name CHUB MACKEREL).

**FRIGATE TUNA, *Auxis thazard* (Lacepède, 1800).** Circumglobal in tropical and warm-temperate waters; in eastern Pacific from Santa Catalina Island and Huntington Beach, southern California (LACM 6711-2) to Chile, including Gulf of California and Islas Galápagos. Rare off southern California. Length to 61 cm (24 in) TL. Neritic and oceanic epipelagic; depth: surface to perhaps 200 m (656 ft). Dark blue above, silvery below; fine wavy oblique to nearly horizontal lines on back. D X–XII + 10–12 + 8 finlets; A 9–15 + 7 finlets; Pect. 22–25; GR 8–12 + 29–37; Vert. 39. The eastern Pacific form is recognized as a subspecies *Auxis thazard brachydorax*. (Formerly FRIGATE MACKEREL: M&L).

**BULLET TUNA, *Auxis rochei* (Risso, 1810).** Circumglobal in tropical and warm-temperate waters; in western Pacific as far north as southern Kuril Islands; between Halfmoon Bay and San Francisco, central California (CAS 56944) to northern Chile, including Gulf of California and Islas Galápagos. Rare off California. Length to 55 cm (21.6 in) TL. Neritic and oceanic epipelagic; depth: surface to perhaps 200 m (656 ft). Dark blue on back anteriorly, silvery below; 15+ nearly vertical dark bars on back. D X–XII + 10–12 + 8 finlets; A 9–15 + 7 finlets; Pect. 22–23; GR 8–12 + 29–37; Vert. 39. The eastern Pacific form is recognized as a subspecies *Auxis rochei eudorax*. (Formerly BULLET MACKEREL: M&L).

## KEY TO THE MACKEREL and TUNAS:

Revised by Kurt Schaefer
(Principal sources: Miller & Lea, 1972; Collette & Nauen, 1983; Schaefer, 1999)

1a Dorsal fin spines 23–27; bars on sides 24–30; snout long, almost as long as rest of head:

**WAHOO**

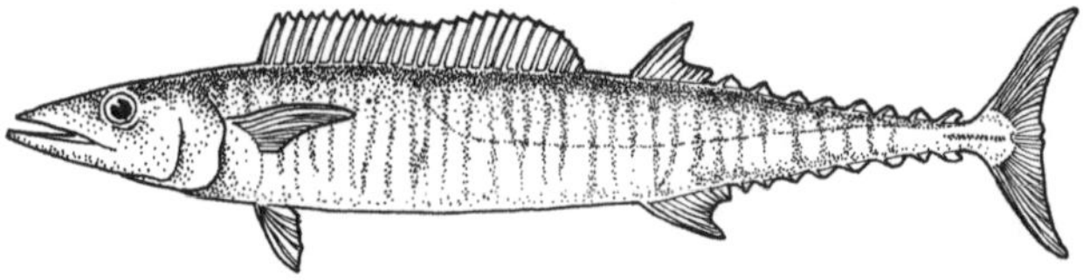

1b (next page)

1b Dorsal fin spines fewer than 21; bars absent or fewer than 24; snout short, 21–37% of HL….. 2

2a Space between dorsal fins shorter than snout length….. 5 (next page)

2b Space between dorsal fins longer than snout length….. 3

3a Vermiculations on back extend anteriorly beyond 1st dorsal fin; dorsal finlets 4–6; anal finlets 4–6:

**PACIFIC CHUB MACKEREL**

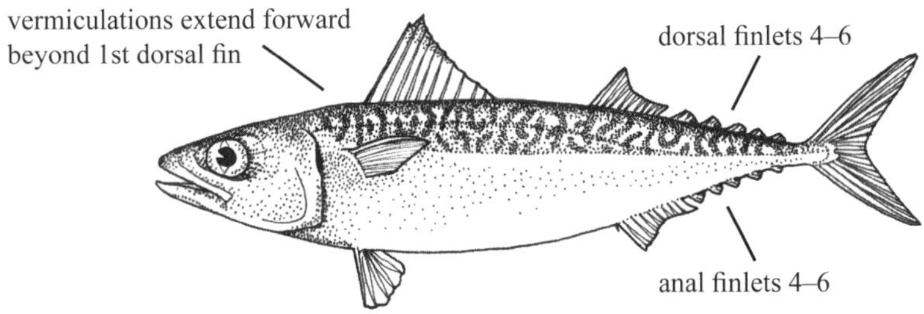


3b Vermiculations on back not extending anteriorly beyond 1st dorsal fin; dorsal finlets 8; anal finlets 7….. 4

4a Posterior extension of corselet only 1–5 scales wide under origin of 2nd dorsal fin; fine, wavy, oblique to nearly horizontal lines on back:

**FRIGATE TUNA**

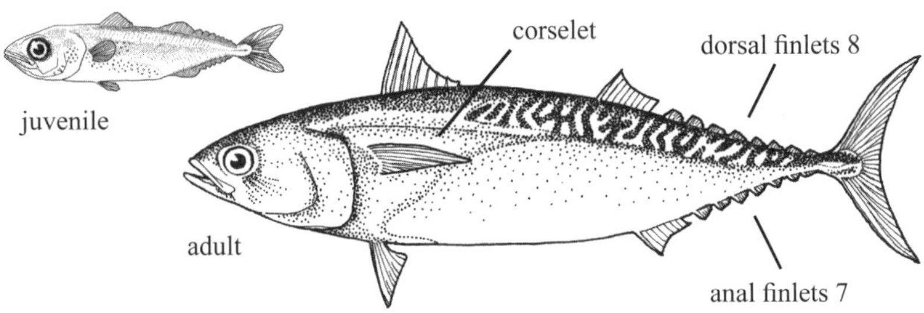


4b Posterior extension of corselet much wider, 13–30 scales wide under origin of 2nd dorsal fin; 15 or more nearly vertical dark bars on back:

**BULLET TUNA**

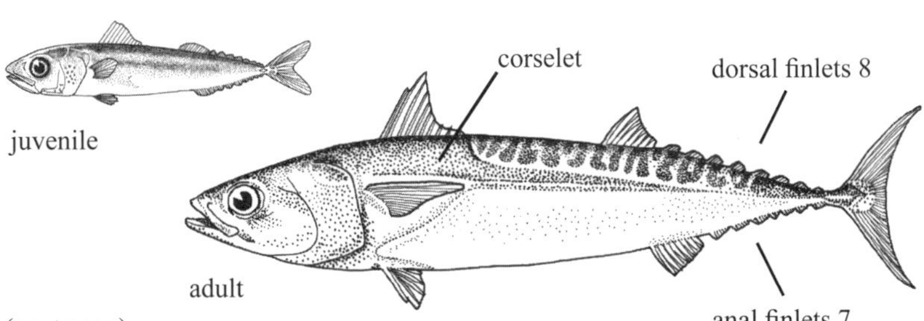


5a (next page)

## MACKEREL and TUNAS (continued)

**PACIFIC SIERRA, *Scomberomorus sierra* Jordan & Starks, 1895.** Marina del Rey, southern California (LACM 57166-1) to central Chile (33°35'S), including Gulf of California and Islas Galápagos. Unverified report as far north as Santa Cruz Island, southern California. Usually rare off southern California, although some may migrate northward during warm water periods; common from southern Baja California throughout tropics. Length to 112 cm (44.1 in) TL. Neritic epipelagic; depth: surface to at least 15 m (49 ft). Dark blue above (occasionally yellow), silvery below; yellowish spots on sides (not in series). D XV–XVIII + 16–19 + 7–10 finlets; A 16–21 + 7–10 finlets; Pect. 20–24; Pelvic I,5; LLp 165; GR 2–5 + 9–14 = 12–17; Vert. 46–49. (Formerly SIERRA: M&L).

**GULF SIERRA, *Scomberomorus concolor* (Lockington, 1879).** Soquel, Monterey Bay, central California to Gulf of California to central Mexico. Rare or absent off California; historically may have been more abundant here. Entire population may now exist only in the northern Gulf of California. Length to 87 cm (34.2 in) TL. Nearshore epipelagic; depth: surface to at least 15 m (49 ft). Males reported with metallic blue back, silvery sides and belly; females darker, with 2 series of alternating gold spots on sides. D XV–XVIII + 16–20 + 6–10 finlets; A 19–23 + 6–8 finlets; Pect. 19–22; GR 4–9 + 15–21 = 21–27; Vert. 46–48. (Formerly MONTEREY SPANISH MACKEREL: M&L).

**SKIPJACK TUNA, *Katsuwonus pelamis* (Linnaeus, 1758).** Circumglobal in tropical and warm-temperate waters; in western Pacific as far north as Japan and southern Kuril Islands; near Cordova (60°21'N, 146°05'W), Gulf of Alaska to Chile, including southern Gulf of California and Islas Galápagos. Common from southern California southward. Length to 108 cm (42.5 in) FL. Oceanic epipelagic; depth: surface to 596 m (1,955 ft). Blue or blue-purple on back, silver below, 4–6 stripes on ventral surface. D XIV–XVII + 12–16 + 7–10 finlets; A 13–18 + 6–8 finlets; Pect. 24–32; GR 16–22 + 33–43 = 53–65; Vert. 41. (Formerly SKIPJACK, *Euthynnus pelamis* (Linnaeus, 1758): M&L).

**KAWAKAWA, *Euthynnus affinis* (Cantor, 1849).** Primarily tropical waters of Indian Ocean and western and central Pacific; southern Japan; near Diablo Cove, central California and off southern Baja California. Rare off California. Length to 110 cm (43.3 in) TL. Neritic epipelagic; depth: surface to perhaps 50 m (164 ft). Blue or blue-green above, silvery below; usually black spots below pectoral base; oblique lines on back broken. D XIV–XVII + 11–14 + 7–10 finlets; A 12–15 + 6–8 finlets; Pect. 24–29; GR 7–10 + 22–26 = 29–33; Vert. 39. (Formerly WAVYBACK SKIPJACK: M&L).

5a *From 2a: space between dorsal fins less than snout length*
Corselet present; HL into TL about 4 or less….. 7 (next page)

5b Corselet absent; HL into TL at least 5….. 6 (next page)

6a Gill rakers 9–14 on lower limb of 1st gill arch:

**PACIFIC SIERRA**

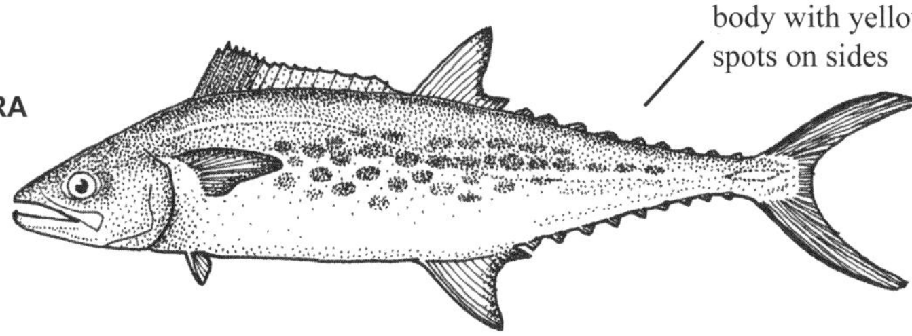


6b Gill rakers 15–21 on lower limb of 1st gill arch:

**GULF SIERRA**

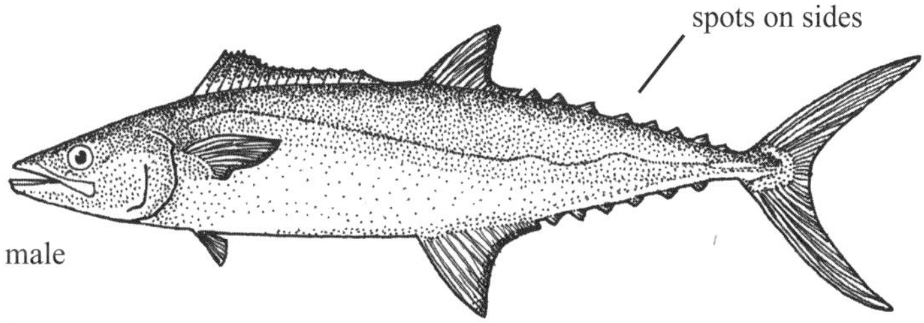


7a *From 5a: corselet present*
Body fully scaled, with enlarged scales in corselet area and along lateral line….. 10 (page 334)

7b Body not fully scaled, scales present in corselet area and on lateral line only….. 8

8a Back without stripes or oblique lines; no black spots between pectoral and pelvic fins; prominent black stripes on ventral surface:

**SKIPJACK TUNA**

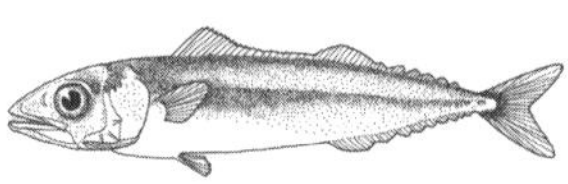


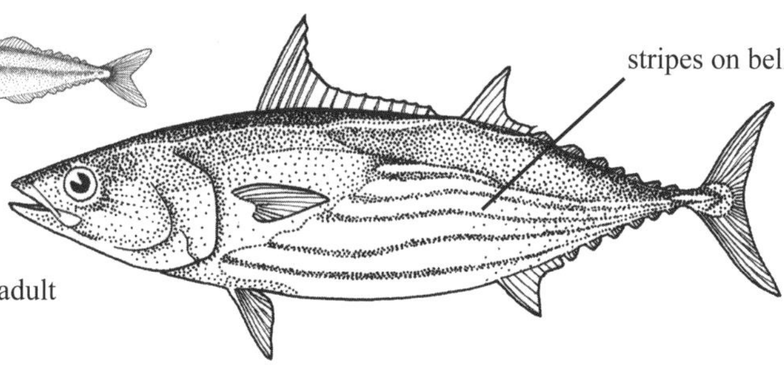


8b Back with stripes or oblique lines; black spots present between pectoral and pelvic fins; prominent black stripes on ventral surface lacking….. 9

9a Wavy oblique lines on back:

**KAWAKAWA**

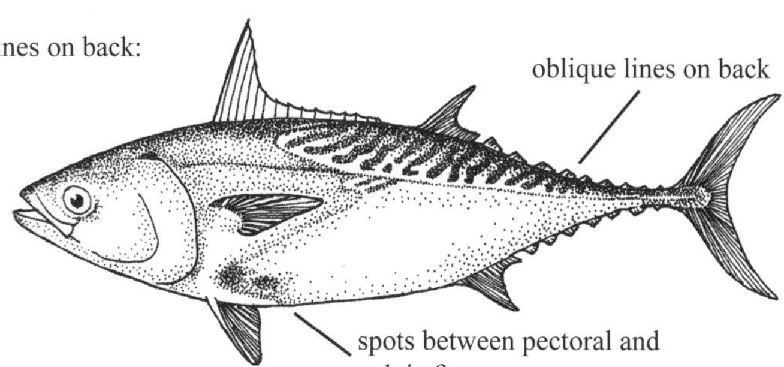


9b (next page)

## MACKEREL and TUNAS (continued)

**BLACK SKIPJACK, *Euthynnus lineatus* Kishinouye, 1920.** San Simeon, central California to northern Peru, including Gulf of California and Islas Galápagos. Rare off California; common beginning in southern Baja California. Length to 92 cm (36.2 in) TL. Neritic and oceanic epipelagic; depth: surface to about 73 m (240 ft). Blue or blue-green above, silver below; 3–5 continuous markings on back; black or gray spots above pelvic fin; light gray stripes on belly may be present. D XIII–XVII + 11–13 + 8–9 finlets; A 11–13 + 6–8 finlets; Pect. 24–29; GR 7–11 + 24–30 = 32–41; Vert. 36–38.

**PACIFIC BONITO, *Sarda chiliensis* (Cuvier, 1832).** Hawai'i; Eastern Pacific, with 2 populations: northern and eastern Gulf of Alaska to southern Baja California, just into Gulf of California on Baja California side, and Islas Revillagigedo; and Máncora, Peru to Talcahuano, Chile. In most years, common from southern California southward. In some years, common as far northwards as west coast of Vancouver Island and Washington. Length to 122 cm (48 in) TL. Nearshore epipelagic; depth: surface to 110 m (361 ft). Dark blue or green above, silvery below. D XVII–XX + 13–17 + 6–9 finlets; A 11–15 + 6–8 finlets; Pect. 22–27; Pelvic I,5; GR 7–10 + 11–19 = 23–27; Vert. 42–46.

**SLENDER TUNA, *Allothunnus fallai* Serventy, 1948.** Temperate and warm-temperate waters of Southern Hemisphere to 50°00'S; one report from North Pacific Subarctic Gyre (44°01'N, 151°13'W) and one from Los Angeles-Long Beach Harbor, southern California. Length to 106 cm (41.7 in) TL. Epipelagic; depth: surface to about 200 m (656 ft). Dark blue back, silvery sides and belly. D XV–XVIII + 12–13 + 6–8 finlets; A 12–14 + 6–7 finlets; Pect. 24–26; GR 21–25 + 48–53 = 70–80; Vert. 39–41.

**PACIFIC BLUEFIN TUNA, *Thunnus orientalis* (Temminck & Schlegel, 1844).** Japan to southern Kuril Islands and southern Sea of Okhotsk; Shelikof Strait, Gulf of Alaska to just inside southwest corner of the Gulf of California. Common from Washington southward to off Baja California. Length to 271 cm (107 in) FL, 458 kg (1,010 lb). Oceanic epipelagic; depth: surface to 1,426 m (4,677 ft). Dark blue or black on back, silvery below; 1st dorsal fin yellowish or bluish, 2nd dorsal fin red-brown. D XII–XV + 13–15 + 7–10 finlets; A 13–16 + 7–9 finlets; Pect. 30–38; GR 9–16 + 21–28; Vert. 39. (Formerly BLUEFIN TUNA, *Thunnus thynnus* (Linnaeus, 1758): M&L).

9b Stripes on back:

**BLACK SKIPJACK**

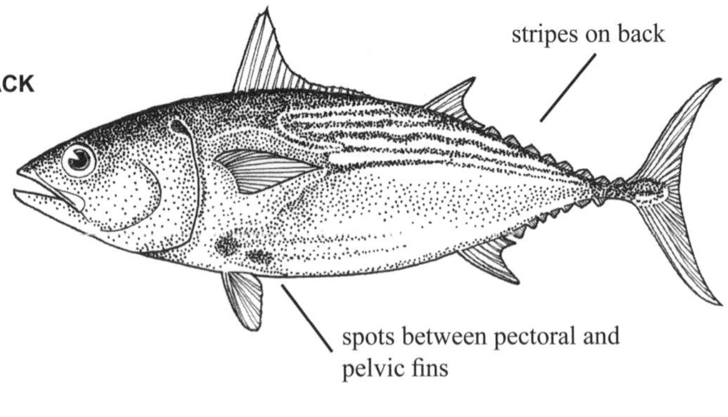


10a (next page)

10a *From 7a: body fully scaled*
Dark oblique lines on back; teeth large, usually widely spaced:

**PACIFIC BONITO**

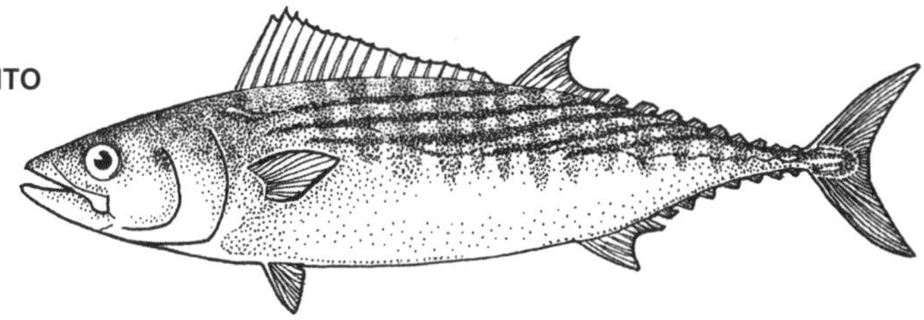

10b No dark lines on back (faint lines present on juveniles of some species); teeth minute, forming tight continuous band on jaws….. 11

11a Gill rakers fine and numerous with 70–80 on 1st gill arch:

**SLENDER TUNA**

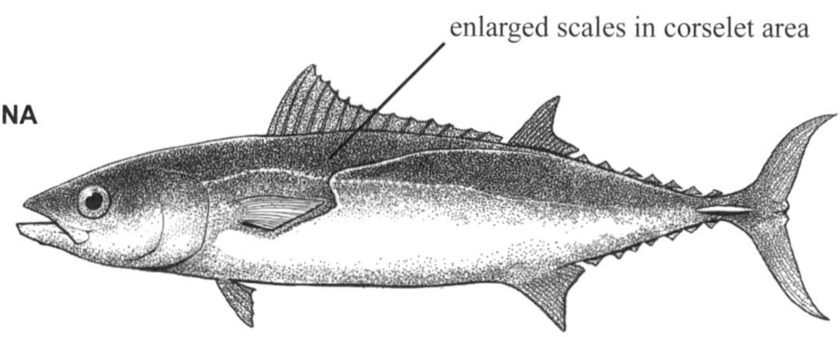


11b Gill rakers 34 or fewer on 1st gill arch….. 12

12a Pectoral fin short, less than 80% HL:

**PACIFIC BLUEFIN TUNA**

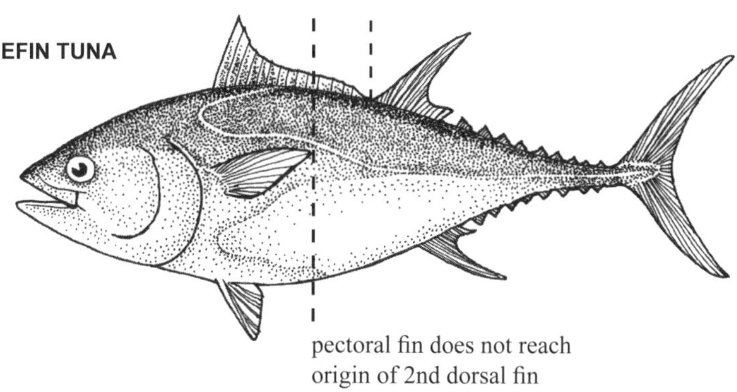


12b Pectoral fin long, more than 80% HL….. 13 (next page)

## MACKEREL and TUNAS (continued)

**ALBACORE, *Thunnus alalunga* (Bonnaterre, 1788).** Circumglobal in tropical to temperate waters; in western Pacific north to Japan and southern Kuril Islands; northern and eastern Gulf of Alaska to Chile, including Islas Galápagos and Gulf of California. Common from Vancouver Island to central Baja California. Length to 152 cm (60 in) TL. Oceanic epi- and mesopelagic; depth: surface to 1,185 m (3,887 ft). Dark blue back (almost black), silvery belly; iridescent stripe along sides may be present; posterior margin of caudal fin sometimes white. D IX–XIV + 12–16 + 7–10 finlets; A 11–16 + 7–10 finlets; Pect. 30–36; GR 7–11 + 18–24 = 25–31; Vert. 39.

**BIGEYE TUNA, *Thunnus obesus* (Lowe, 1839).** Circumglobal in tropical and subtropical waters; in western Pacific north to Japan and southern Kuril Islands; Iron Springs, central Washington to Chile, including Islas Galápagos; apparently not in Gulf of California. Occasionally common off southern California, but more predictably from central Baja California southward. Length to 236 cm (93 in) FL, 197.3 kg (435 lb). Oceanic epi- and mesopelagic; depth: surface to 1,902 m (6,239 ft). Back dark; lateral iridescent blue stripe in newly caught individuals; dorsal and anal fins often yellow; finlets yellow with black margin. D XI–XIV + 12–16 + 7–10 finlets; A 11–16 + 7–10 finlets; Pect. 30–36; GR 7–13 + 18–25 = 23–31; Vert. 39.

**YELLOWFIN TUNA, *Thunnus albacares* (Bonnaterre, 1788).** Circumglobal in tropical and subtropical waters; in western Pacific north to Japan and southern Kuril Islands; dead specimen found on beach near Tsiu River, Gulf of Alaska; also eastern North Pacific at 50°00'N, 150°02'W, and Morro Bay, central California to Chile, including Gulf of California and Islas Galápagos. In some years, common as far northward as southern California. Length to 206 cm (81 in) FL, 202 kg (445 lb). Oceanic epipelagic; depth: surface to 1,602 m (5,255 ft). Dark blue above, yellowish on sides; ventral region often with white lines and spots. In adults, dorsal and anal fins yellow; finlets yellow with black margin. D XI–XIV + 12–16 + 7–10 finlets; A 11–16 + 7–10; GR 8–11 + 18–25 = 26–34; Vert. 39.

13a Pectoral fin extends beyond anal fin base; caudal fin with narrow white margin:

**ALBACORE**

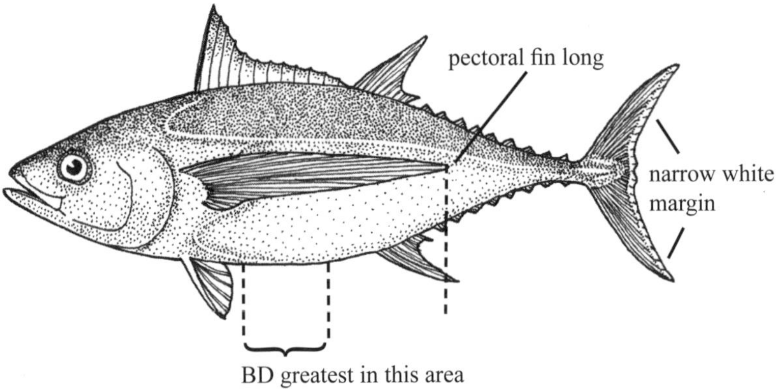


13b Pectoral fin does not extend beyond anal fin base (except for BIGEYE TUNA about 80 cm FL); caudal fin without white margin….. 14 (next page)

14a No broken vertical lines on ventral area; 2nd dorsal fin and anal fin not elongated in large adults:

**BIGEYE TUNA**
(pectoral fin length and shape varies with size)

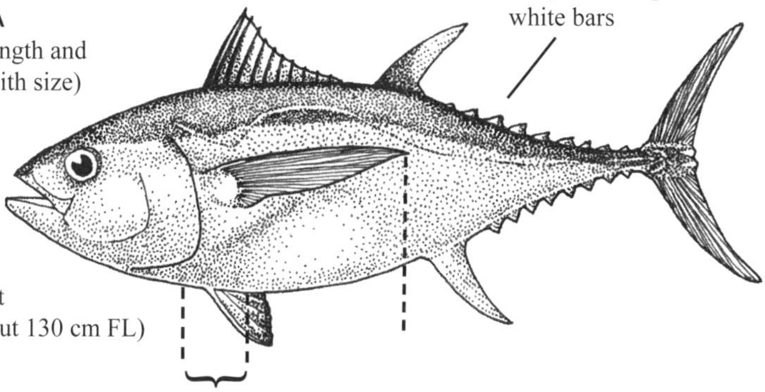


adult
(about 130 cm FL)

juvenile I
(about 40 cm FL)

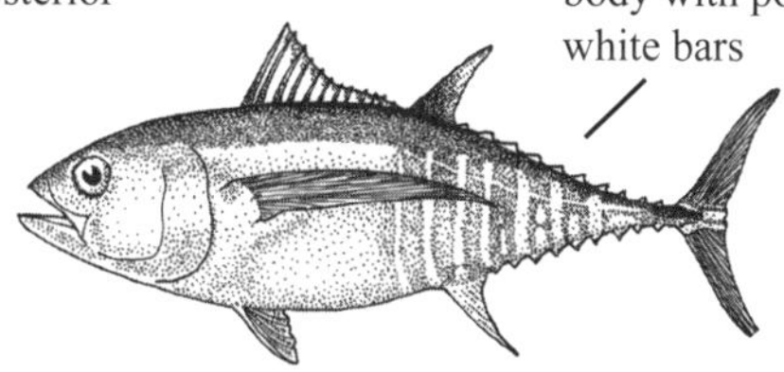


juvenile II
(about 80 cm FL)

14b Series of broken, nearly vertical lines on ventral area; 2nd dorsal fin and anal fin elongated in large adults:

**YELLOWFIN TUNA**
(pectoral fin length and shape varies with size)

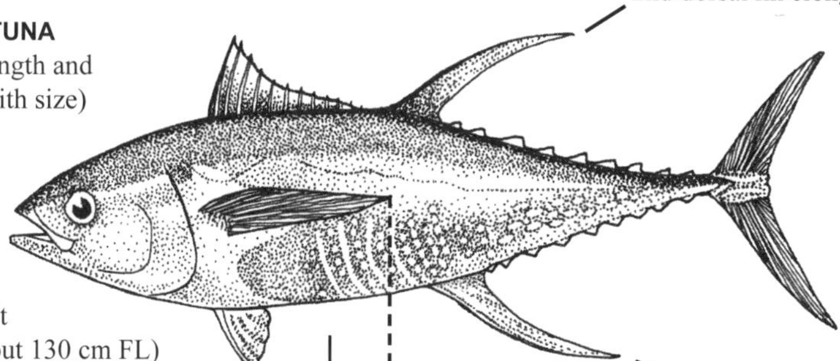


adult
(about 130 cm FL)

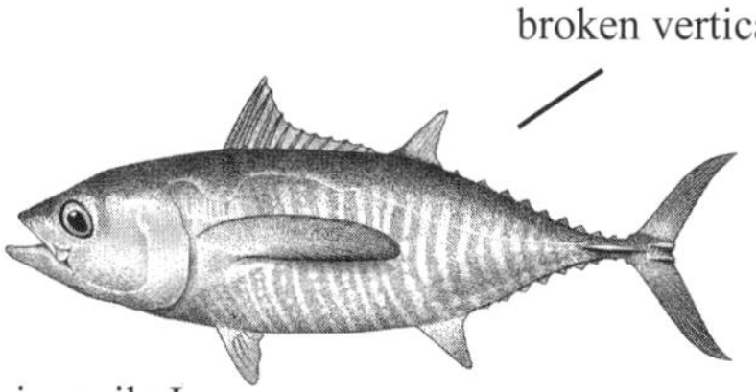

juvenile I
(about 40 cm FL)

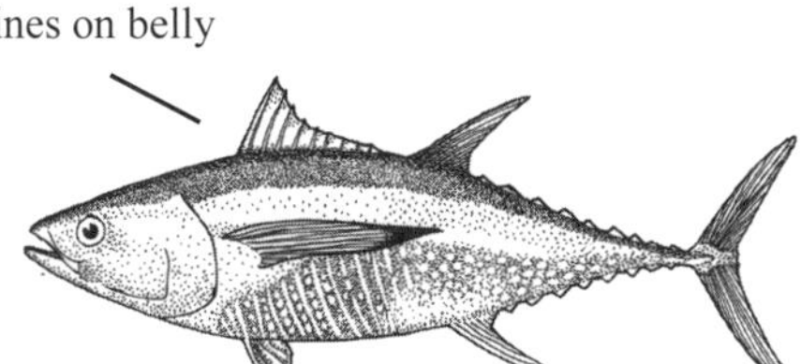

juvenile II
(about 80 cm FL)

# SWORDFISH, Family Xiphiidae and BILLFISHES, Family Istiophoridae

**SWORDFISH, *Xiphias gladius* Linnaeus, 1758.** Family Xiphiidae
Circumglobal; in western Pacific as far north as southern Kuril Islands, Russia; northern Vancouver Island (49°53'N, 128°10'W), British Columbia to Valdivia, Chile, including Gulf of California and Islas Galápagos. Common from northern California southward. Length to 4.57 m (15 ft) TL. Depth: surface to 2,878 m (9,442 ft). Dark gray to black above, gray to yellowish below. D XXXVIII–XLV,4–5; A XII–XVI,3–4; Pect. 17–19; Pelvic absent; GR none; Vert. 26.

**SHORTBILL SPEARFISH, *Tetrapturus angustirostris* Tanaka, 1915.** Family Istiophoridae
Circumglobal; Cape Mendocino, central California to Mejillones, Chile, including Islas Galápagos. Apparently not in Gulf of California. Occasionally found off southern California during some warm-water years; rare rest of time. Length to at least 2.4 m (8 ft) TL. Oceanic; depth: near surface to 1,830 m (6,004 ft). Bluish above, white below. D XLVII–L,4–7; A III–XV,6–7; Pect. 18–19; Pelvic I,2; Vert. 24.

**SAILFISH, *Istiophorus platypterus* (Shaw, 1792).** Family Istiophoridae
Circumglobal; in western Pacific as far north as southern Kuril Islands, Russia; Dana Point, southern California to Chile, including Gulf of California and Islas Galápagos. Rare off southern California; common from the southern tip of Baja California throughout tropics. Length to 3.6 m (11.7 ft) TL. Oceanic; depth: surface to 340 m (1,115 ft). Dark blue above, silver below. D XLI–XLVIII,6–7; A XII–XVI, 6–7; Pect. 17–20; Pelvic I,2; GR none; Vert. 24

**BLACK MARLIN, *Istiompax indica* (Cuvier, 1832).** Family Istiophoridae
Circumglobal; in western Pacific as far north as southern Kuril Islands, Russia; at least San Clemente and Santa Catalina islands, southern California to northern Chile, including Gulf of California and Islas Galápagos. Rare off southern California. Length to 5 m (16.4 ft) TL. Oceanic; depth: near surface to 258 m (846 ft). Dark blue above, silvery white below; sometimes with light blue bars; dorsal fin blackish to dark blue; other fins dark brown, sometimes tinged with dark blue. D XXXIV–XLIII,5–7; A X–XIV; Pect. 12–20; GR none; Vert. 24. (Formerly *Makaira indica* (Cuvier, 1832): M&L).

## KEY TO THE SWORDFISH and BILLFISHES:
Edited by Julianne Kalman Passarelli
(Principal sources: Miller & Lea, 1972; Nakamura, 1985; Nakabo, 2002)

1a Pelvic fins absent; single keel; scales on body lacking:

SWORDFISH

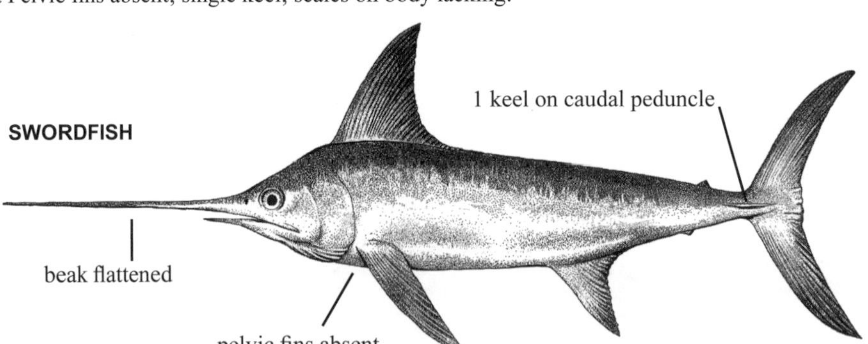


1b Pelvic fins present; paired keel; bony scales on body….. 2 (next page)

2a Distance from nostril to posterior edge of operculum greater than length of pectoral fin or sword (measured from nostril to tip); anus far from origin of anterior anal fin:

**SHORTBILL SPEARFISH**

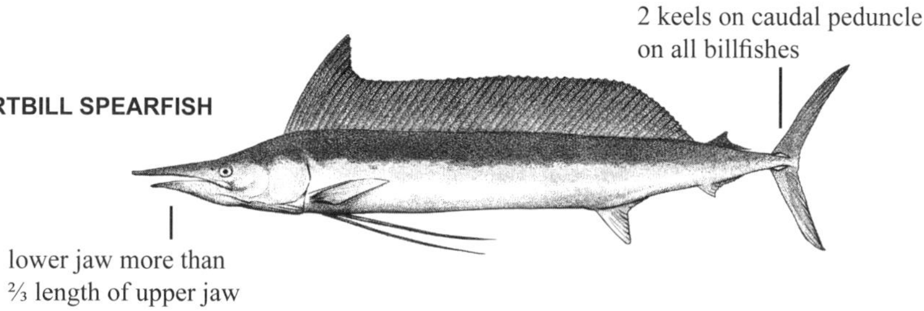


2b Distance from nostril to posterior edge of operculum less than length of pectoral fin or sword (measured from nostril to tip); anus close to origin of anterior anal fin….. 3

3a Dorsal fin sail-like, with middle spines longer than BD and longer than anterior spines; pelvic fins long, nearly reaching anal fin:

**SAILFISH**

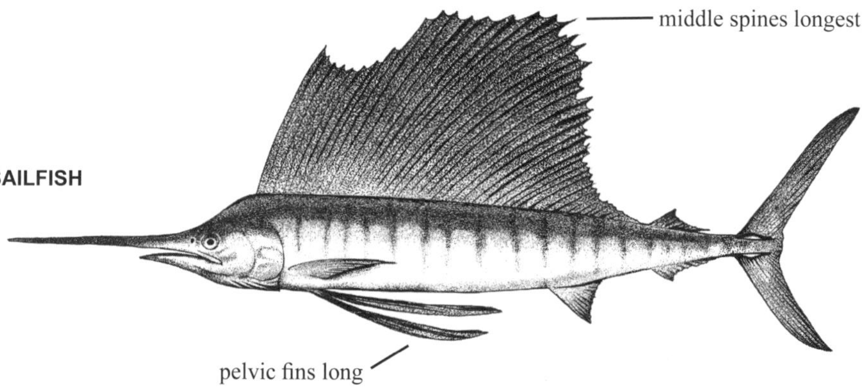


3b Dorsal fin elevated anteriorly only, with middle spines shorter than BD and shorter than anterior spines; pelvic fins short, not reaching anal fin….. 4

4a Pectoral fins rigid, not moveable; body without bars:

**BLACK MARLIN**

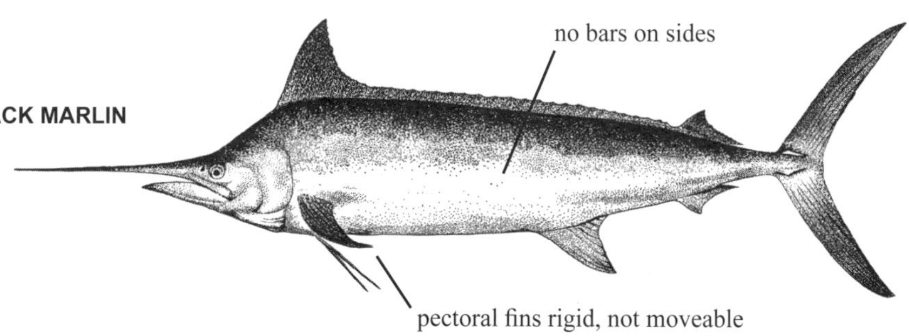


4b Pectoral fins not rigid, capable of being folded back along sides; body with bars….. 5 (next page)

## SWORDFISH and BILLFISHES (continued)

**BLUE MARLIN, *Makaira nigricans* Lacepède, 1802.** Family ISTIOPHORIDAE
Circumglobal; Sea of Japan and off southern Kuril Islands, Russia; southern California to Mejillones, Chile, including southernmost Gulf of California and Islas Galápagos. Uncommon off southern California. Length to 5 m (16.4 ft) TL. Oceanic; depth: surface to 600 m (1,968 ft). D XL–XLV,6–7; A XII–XVII,6–7; Pect. 20–23; GR none; Vert. 24. (Recently as *Makaira mazara* (Jordan & Snyder, 1901)).

**STRIPED MARLIN, *Kajikia audax* (Philippi, 1887).** Family ISTIOPHORIDAE
Pacific and Indian Oceans; in western Pacific as far north as southern Kuril Islands, Russia; near Westport, Washington to Chile (35°00'S), including southern Gulf of California and Islas Galápagos. Common as far north as southern California. Length to 4.2 m (13.8 ft) TL. Oceanic; depth: surface to 532 m (1,745 ft). Dark blue above, silvery below; dark blue bars on sides. D XXXVII–XLII,5–6; A XIII–XVIII,5–6; Pect. 18–22; Pelvic I,2; Vert. 24. (Recently as *Makaira audax* (Phillippi, 1887)) (Formerly *Tetrapterus audax* (Phillippi, 1887): M&L).

5a Length of longest dorsal fin spines less than BD; lateral line complex or chain-like; body not laterally compressed at origin of anal fin; body with approximately 15 bars:

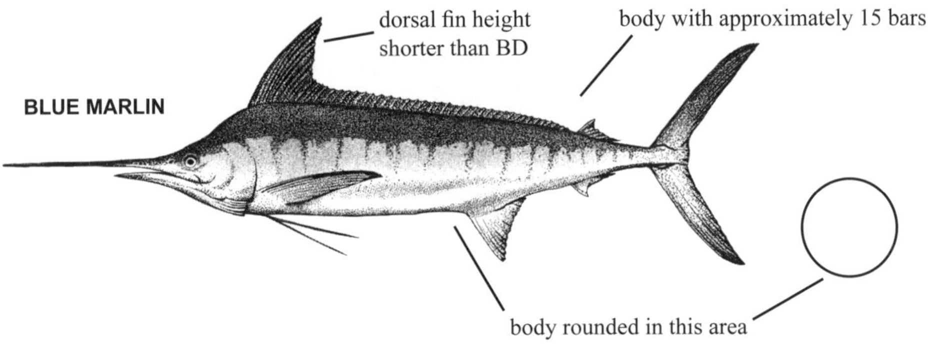


5b Length of longest dorsal fin spines equal to or greater than BD; lateral line straight; body laterally compressed at origin of anal fin; body with 15–25 bars:

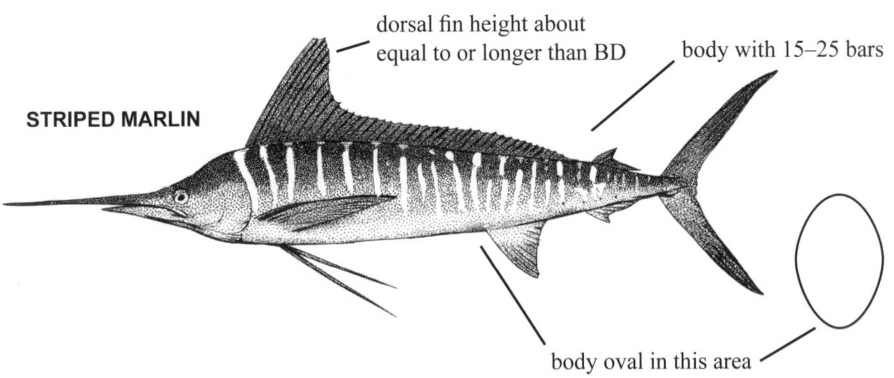

# BARRACUDAS, Family Sphyraenidae and LOUVAR, Family Luvaridae

**PACIFIC BARRACUDA, *Sphyraena argentea* Girard, 1854.** Family SPHYRAENIDAE
Kodiak Island, Gulf of Alaska to Gulf of California and Islas Revillagigedo. In most years, common from southern California southward to at least Bahía Tortugas, southern Baja California; common into central California during some warm-water years. Length to 122 cm (48 in) TL, possibly to 152 cm (60 in) TL. Nearshore epipelagic; depth: surface and surf zone to 38 m (125 ft). Dark brown above with bluish reflections, silvery below. D V + I,8–10; A I–II,8–10; Pect. 13–16; Pelvic I,5; LLs 166; GR none; Vert. 24. (Formerly CALIFORNIA BARRACUDA: M&L).

**MEXICAN BARRACUDA, *Sphyraena ensis* Jordan & Gilbert, 1882.** Family SPHYRAENIDAE
Oceanside, southern California (SIO 98-36) to Chile, including lower Gulf of California. Usually rare in southern California, although a number of these fish entered California waters during the 1997–1998 El Niño; apparently rare or uncommon along much or all of Baja California coast; common in Gulf of California. Length to 137 cm (53.9 in) TL. Depth: coastal water to 25 m (82 ft). Silvery, with series of dark chevron-shaped bars on upper ⅔ of body; caudal fin gray. D V + I,9; A II,7–8; Pect. 13; Pelvic I,5; GR none; Vert. 24.

**LOUVAR, *Luvarus imperialis* Rafinesque, 1810.** Family LUVARIDAE
Circumglobal; Graham Island, Haida Gwaii, British Columbia to Chile and into the Gulf of California as far northward as Loreto. Common from about central California southward; worldwide, generally found between 40°00'N and 40°00'S. Length to 200 cm (78.7 in) TL. Depth: epipelagic to 200 m (656 ft). Pink (silver when dead); fins red. D I,11–13 (juveniles I,21); A I,12–14 (juveniles I,16–18); Pect. 14–18 (juveniles 17–20); Pelvic I (juveniles I,3–4); Vert. 22.

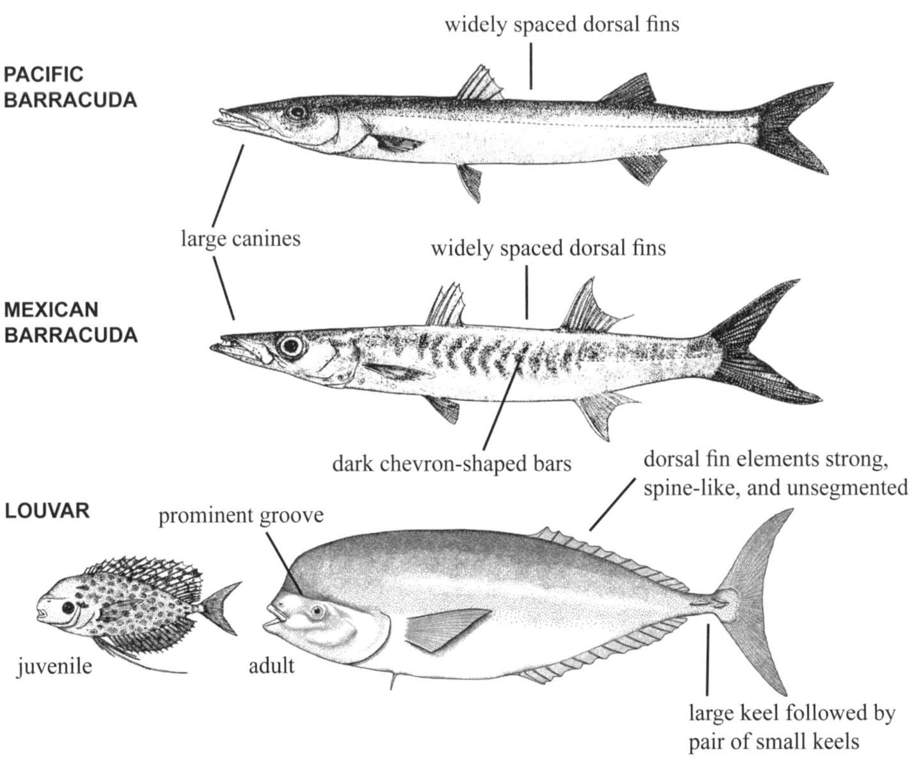

# BUTTERFISH, Family Stromateidae, MEDUSAFISH, Family Centrolophidae, and SQUARETAIL, Family Tetragonuridae

**PACIFIC BUTTERFISH, *Peprilus simillimus* (Ayres, 1860).** Family STROMATEIDAE

Eastern North Pacific; Haida Gwaii, British Columbia to southern Baja California (23°38'N, 110°28'W) and Gulf of California. Common from Vancouver Island to southern Baja California. Length to about 36 cm (14.2 in) TL. Pelagic nearshore; depth: surf zone to about 302 m (991 ft). Bright metallic silver or golden on sides, with greenish, blue, or purplish overtones. D II–IV,41–48; A II–III,35–44; Pect. 19–23; Pelvic absent; GR 5 + 18–21 = 23–26; Vert. 29–31. (Alternative name PACIFIC POMPANO).

**MEDUSAFISH, *Icichthys lockingtoni* Jordan & Gilbert, 1880.** Family CENTROLOPHIDAE

Japan and Kuril Islands, Russia to Pacific side of Aleutian Islands to central Baja California (26°39'N, 114°58'W) (LACM 30077-5). Larvae have been taken southward to Punta Abreojos, central Baja California. In western Pacific, common as far northward as southern Kuril Islands; in eastern Pacific, common as far northward as Washington and southward to at least central Baja California. Length to about 46 cm (18.4 in) TL. Oceanic pelagic; depth: juveniles near surface (commonly associated with medusae), adults to 1,010 m (3,314 ft) and perhaps to 1,257 m (4,124 ft); also reported as intertidal. Adults blue, gray, or brown; fine dark speckling on head; juveniles silvery, tan, pink, or blue. D III,34–46; A III,20–32; Pect. 18–21; Pelvic I,5; LLs 115–121; GR 4–6 + 8–15 = 18–21; Vert. 50–62.

**SMALLEYE SQUARETAIL, *Tetragonurus cuvieri* Risso, 1810.** Family TETRAGONURIDAE

Circumglobal; Japan to south of Aleutian Islands to Chile. Common at least off Japan and from Oregon to at least central Baja California. Length to 70 cm (27.6 in) SL. Oceanic pelagic; depth: young fish near surface, adults to 1,400 m (4,592 ft). Uniform dark brown to black often tinted with purple or yellow. D XV–XXI + 10–17; A 0–II,9–15; Pect. 14–21; Pelvic I,5; LLs 93–126; GR 5–6 + 7–14; Vert. 51–58.

PACIFIC BUTTERFISH

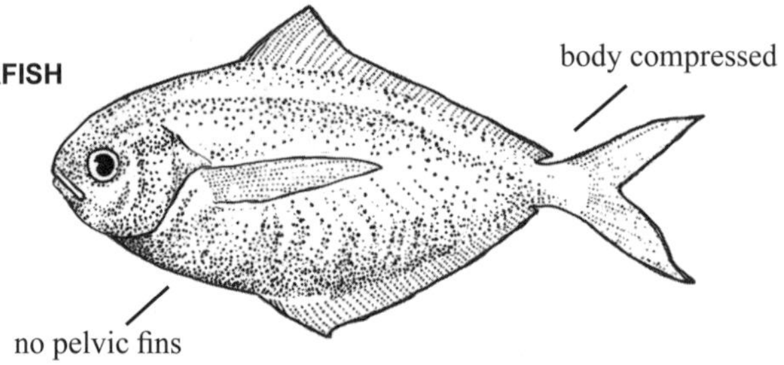


MEDUSAFISH

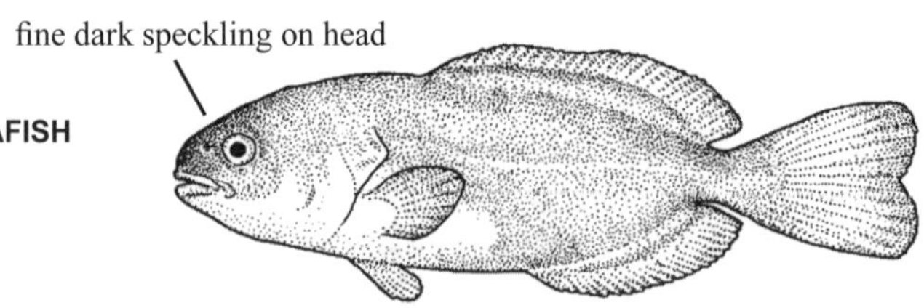


SMALLEYE SQUARETAIL

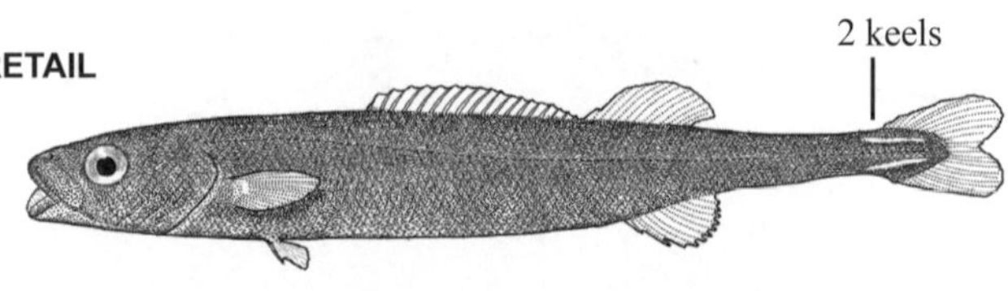

## DRIFTFISHES, Family Nomeidae

**BLUEFIN DRIFTFISH, *Psenes pellucidus* Lütken, 1880.** Circumglobal; Japan and southern Kuril Islands, Russia; Santa Catalina Island, southern California to southern end of Baja California and Chile, including Islas Galápagos. Rare off southern California. Length to 80 cm (31.5 in) TL. Depth: juveniles epipelagic, adults meso- and possibly bathypelagic to depths of 1,500 m (4,920 ft). Adults dark brown to deep purple; eye dark blue. Young translucent with brown spots; 1st dorsal fin dark. D IX–XII + I–II,26–32; A II–III,26–35; Pect. 18–20; Pelvic I,5; GR 8–9 + 15–17; Vert. 40–42.

**LONGFIN CIGARFISH, *Cubiceps paradoxus* Butler, 1979.** Off Mauritania, eastern Atlantic; North Pacific; in western Pacific as far north as southern Kuril Islands, Russia; Port Hueneme and Palos Verdes Peninsula, southern California (LACM 37048-1). Rare off southern California. Length to 123 cm (48.4 in) TL. Epi- and mesopelagic. Dark grayish or purplish back and silvery sides and belly. D XII + I,19–20; A III,20–21; Pect. 21–22; GR 10 + 19 = 29; Vert. 31.

**BLACK FATHEAD, *Cubiceps baxteri* McCulloch, 1923.** Circumglobal; Japan; southern California (32°00'N) to Chile, including Islas Galápagos. Rare off southern California. Maximum length unclear, but at least to 93 cm (36.6 in) SL. Epi- and mesopelagic; depth: near surface to 1,378 m (4,520 ft). Uniform dark-brown to black. D XI–XIII,20–24; A III,19–22; Pect. 20–23; Pelvic I,5; GR 6–10 + 16–18; Vert. 31.

**CAPE CIGARFISH, *Cubiceps capensis* (Smith, 1845).** Apparently circumglobal in subtropical and temperate waters; one specimen taken 145 km (90 mi) west-southwest of Morro Bay (35°08'N, 122°24'W), central California (CAS 218171). Length to 100 cm (39.3 in) TL. Epi- and mesopelagic; depth: to at least 800 m (2,624 ft). California specimen was grayish-brown to black, in other regions dark brown to deep purple. D XI–XII + I,20–23; A III,20–22; Pect. 21; Vert. 31.

### KEY TO THE DRIFTFISHES:

Created by Milton S. Love and Dario W. Diehl
(Principal sources: Butler, 1979; McCosker et al., 2004)

1a Anal fin soft-rays 26–35; dorsal fin soft-rays 26–32; pectoral fin shorter than HL:

**BLUEFIN DRIFTFISH**

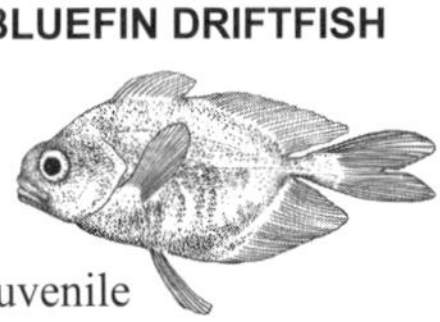

juvenile

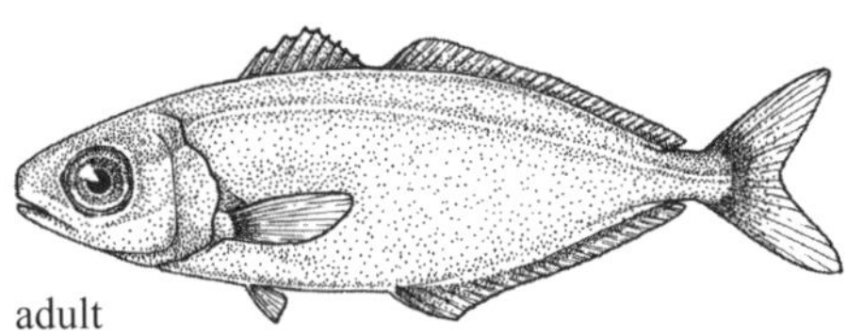

adult

1b Anal fin soft-rays 22 or fewer; dorsal fin soft-rays 24 or fewer; pectoral fin as long or longer than HL (may vary with juveniles)….. 2

2a Teeth on vomer and tongue lacking:

**LONGFIN CIGARFISH**

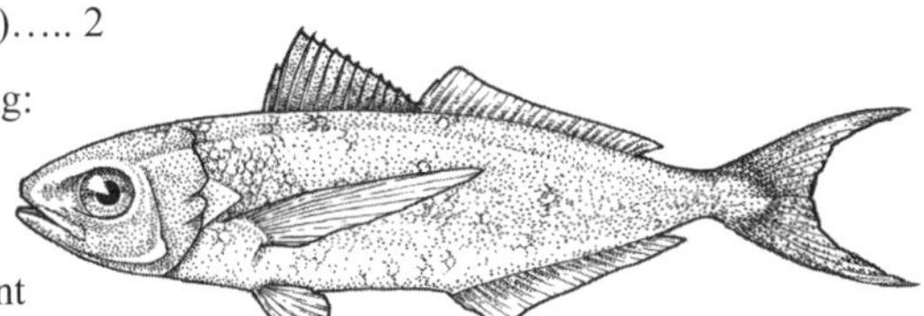

2b Teeth on vomer and tongue present (see FIGURE 11, page xxv)….. 3

3a Snout covered with large scales similar in size to those between eyes; upper procurrent caudal rays 8–10 (reliable only with x-ray):

**BLACK FATHEAD** (not illustrated; body shape as in 2a)

3b Snout naked or with few scales distinctly smaller than those between eyes; upper procurrent caudal rays 11–12 (reliable only with x-ray):

**CAPE CIGARFISH** (not illustrated; body shape as in 2a)

# FLATFISHES,
## Families Achiridae, Bothidae, Cynoglossidae, Paralichthyidae, and Pleuronectidae*

**PACIFIC LINED SOLE, *Achirus mazatlanus* (Steindachner, 1869).** Family Achiridae
Islas Coronados, northern Baja California to Puerto Pizarro, Peru, including Gulf of California. Common at least as far north as Laguna San Ignacio, southern Baja California and into tropics. Length to 24 cm (9.4 in) TL. Fresh, brackish, and marine waters; depth: 1–55 m (3–180 ft). Eyed side gray, brownish-gray, or tan; about 8 thin dark lines across eyed side; scattered clumps of dark hair-like filaments. D 55–60; A 41–46; Pect. 1–5; Pelvic 4–5; GR 0–5 + 7–11; Vert. 28–30.

**WHITETAIL TONGUEFISH, *Symphurus oligomerus* Mahadeva & Munroe, 1990.** Family Cynoglossidae
Off Point Mugu (34°02'N, 119°08'W), southern California and southern tip of Baja California to northern Peru, including Gulf of California. Rare in southern California; common in Gulf of California. Length to 16 cm (6.3 in) TL. Depth: 80–1,008 m (262–3,306 ft). Eyed side yellow-tan to dark brown; 3–7 mostly incomplete crossbands (or 8–13 black, irregular blotches). D 87–98; A 72–83; Pect. absent; Pelvic 4; Vert. 48–52. (Alternative name SPOTFIN TONGUEFISH).

**CALIFORNIA TONGUEFISH, *Symphurus atricaudus* (Jordan & Gilbert, 1880).** Family Cynoglossidae
Barkley Sound, Vancouver Island and Washington to Gulf of California, Chiapas, Mexico; also reported in northern Peru. Common from at least Gulf of Farallones and San Francisco Bay, northern California southward to at least Bahía Magdalena, southern Baja California and in Gulf of California. Length to 21 cm (8.3 in) TL. Mostly marine, but occasionally in estuarine waters; depth: surf zone to 470 m (1,542 ft). Eyed side gray to light brown, finely mottled. D 94–106; A 77–90; Pect. absent; Pelvic 4; Midlateral scales 100–110; GRt 3–4; Vert. 49–53. A right-eyed individual was taken near Long Beach, southern California. (Formerly *Symphurus atricauda*: M&L).

**SPECKLEDTAIL FLOUNDER, *Engyophrys sanctilaurentii* Jordan & Bollman, 1890.** Family Bothidae
North of La Jolla Submarine Canyon, southern California (SIO 00-81) to Bahía Salinas, Huacho, Peru, including Gulf of California. Rare in southern California; common from about Bahía Magdalena, southern Baja California through tropics. Length to 20 cm (7.9 in) TL. Depth: 20–232 m (66–761 ft). Eyed side olive-tan; dark spots on body and median fins (including 3 along lateral line and approximately 5 along each margin of body near dorsal and anal fins); curved dusky bands on blind side (absent or faint in small individuals). D 78–89; A 66–72; Pect. 10–13; Pelvic 6; GR 3–4 + 6; LLp eyed side 64–68 (absent from blind side); LLs 59–68.

NOTE: *Fin ray counts for paired fins are for eyed side.

## KEY TO THE FLATFISHES:
Revised by H. J. Walker, Jr.
(Principal source: Miller & Lea, 1972)

1a Pectoral fin normal or large; eyes normal or large….. 4 (next page)

1b Pectoral fin minute or lacking; eyes small….. 2 (next page)

2a Dorsal and anal fins separate from caudal fin; eyes on right side:

**PACIFIC LINED SOLE**

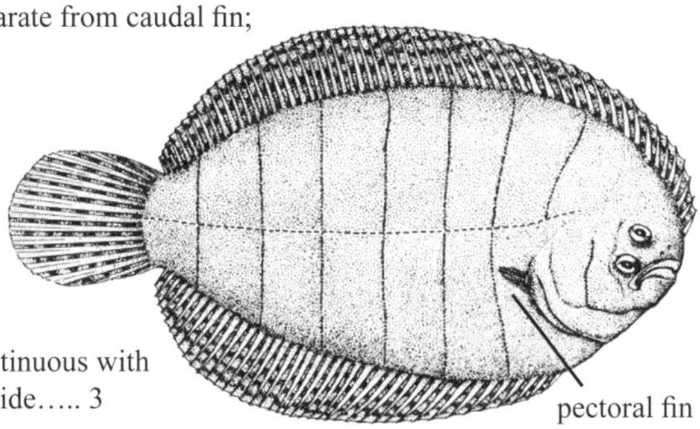


2b Dorsal and anal fins continuous with caudal fin; eyes on left side….. 3

3a Dorsal and anal fins with 8–13 black, irregular blotches; peritoneum black, visible externally:

**WHITETAIL TONGUEFISH**

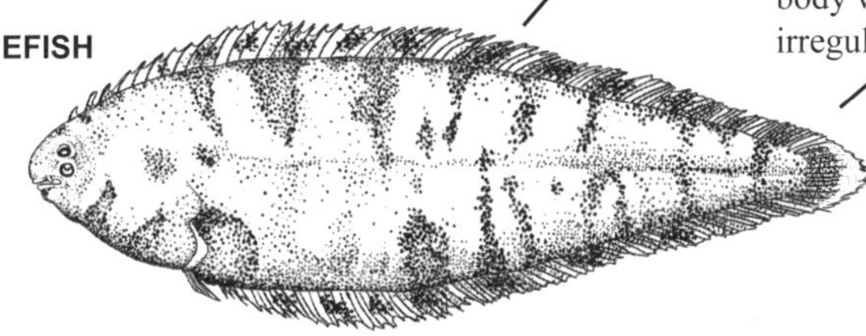


3b Dorsal and anal fins without blotches, generally uniformly pigmented, frequently darker posteriorly; peritoneum unpigmented:

**CALIFORNIA TONGUEFISH**

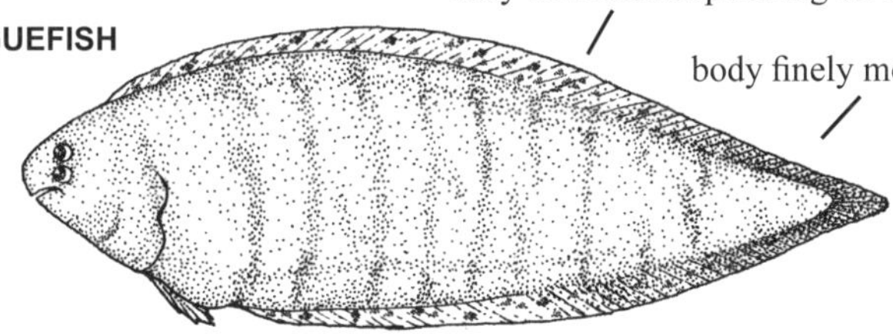


4a *From 1a: pectoral fin normal or large*
Lateral line without abrupt arch over pectoral fin….. 10 (page 348)

4b Lateral line with abrupt arch over pectoral fin….. 5

5a Pelvic fin of eyed side on or near ventral midline and anterior to pelvic fin of blind side; blind side (adults) usually with 5–6 dark, curved bands, 2–3 on head:

**SPECKLEDTAIL FLOUNDER**

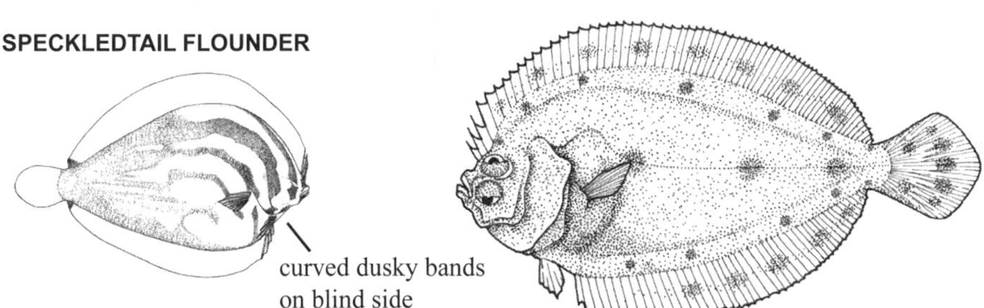


5b Pelvic fins nearly symmetrical; blind side without curved bands….. 6 (next page)

## FLATFISHES (continued)

**ROCK SOLE, *Lepidopsetta bilineata* (Ayres, 1855).** Family Pleuronectidae
Bering Sea as far northward as 56°58'N 173°40'W (transforming larva captured further northward at 57°54'N, 169°40'W) and western Aleutian Islands near Buldir Island (51°58'N, 176°05'E) to Cortes Bank and La Jolla, southern California (SIO 48-22). Common from eastern Bering Sea to central California. Length to 59.5 cm (23.4 in) TL. Depth: 11–339 m (36–1,112 ft), and likely in intertidal. Eyed side light to dark brown, gray, olive, or black, mottled with light and dark brown and sometimes red or yellow spots. D 67–89; A 54–66; Pect. 9–13; Pelvic 6; LLp 70–91; GR 1–4 + 4–7 = 6–11; Vert. 38–41. (Alternative name SOUTHERN ROCK SOLE).

**FANTAIL SOLE, *Xystreurys liolepis* Jordan & Gilbert, 1880.** Family Paralichthyidae
Monterey Bay, central California to Gulf of California. Common from southern California southward into Gulf of California. Length to 63.5 cm (25 in) TL. Depth: surf zone to 136 m (446 ft). Eyed side brown, often with blue and white markings; commonly 2 (sometimes more) dark eyespots, 1 behind head, 2nd near rear of body. D 73–80; A 57–62; Pect. 11–13; Pelvic 6; LLs 120–123; GR 2–4 + 6–7; Vert. 36–39. Both right-eye and left-eye individuals are common.

**BIGMOUTH SOLE, *Hippoglossina stomata* Eigenmann & Eigenmann, 1890.** Family Paralichthyidae
Gulf of Farallones, northern California (CAS 34726) to Gulf of California, including Isla Guadalupe, central Baja California. Common from southern California to southern Baja California. Length to 39.9 cm (15.7 in) TL. Depth: 10–478 m (33–1,568 ft). One estuarine record. Eyed side brown with blue speckling and dark blotches. D 63–70; A 47–55; Pect. 11–12; Pelvic 6; LLs about 80; GR 4–6 + 11–15 = 15–21; Vert. 37–39.

**CALIFORNIA HALIBUT, *Paralichthys californicus* (Ayres, 1859).** Family Paralichthyidae
Quillayute River, northern Washington to Cabo Falsa (22°50'N), southern Baja California; also reported from upper Gulf of California near Sonora, but not verifiable. Common from about Tomales Bay, northern California to southern Baja California and in Gulf of California. Length to 152 cm (60 in) TL. Brackish and marine waters; depth: surf zone to 317 m (1,040 ft). Eyed side greenish, brownish, or blackish, often with light and dark orange-brown eyespots and light or dark mottling. D 66–76; A 49–59; Pect. 10–13; Pelvic 6; LLs about 100; GR 7–11 + 18–23 = 25–32; Vert. 33–36. Both right-eye and left-eye individuals are common.

6a Caudal fin truncate or slightly indented….. 9 (next page)

6b Caudal fin rounded or pointed….. 7

7a Lateral line with accessory dorsal branch (ADB) extending from head onto trunk along base of dorsal fin:

**ROCK SOLE**

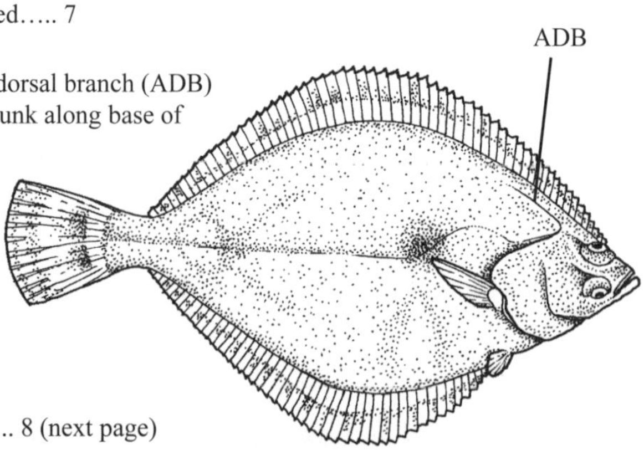


7b Lateral line without ADB….. 8 (next page)

8a Pectoral fin longer than head; 2 large eyespots on lateral line; upper jaw extends to midorbit:

**FANTAIL SOLE**

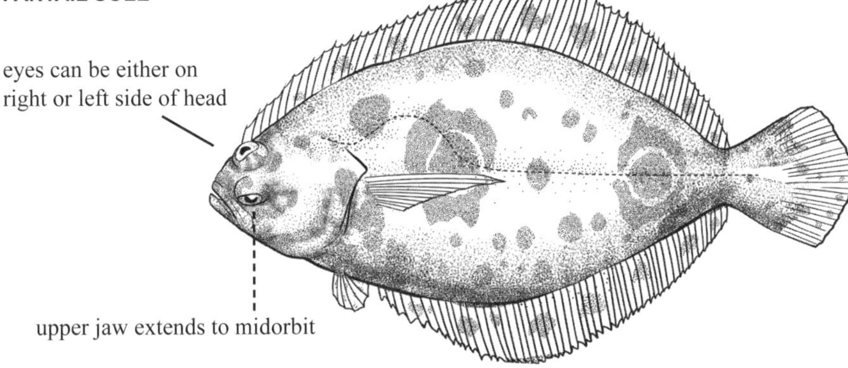


8b Pectoral fin shorter than head; no large eyespots on lateral line; upper jaw extends at least to posterior edge of orbit:

**BIGMOUTH SOLE**

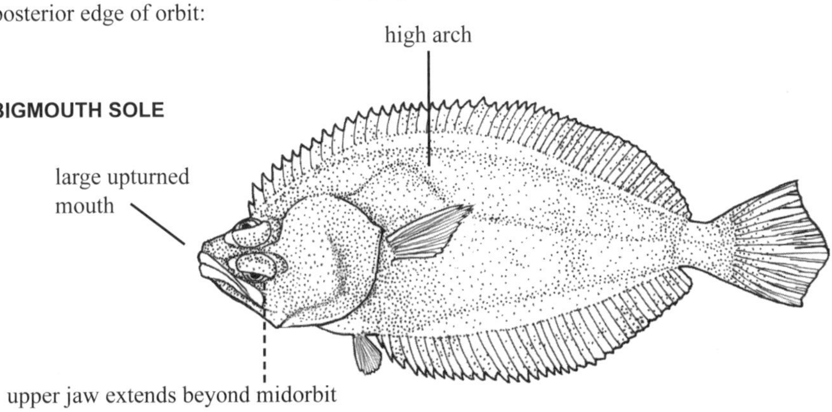


9a *From 6a: caudal fin truncate or slightly indented*
Upper jaw usually extends beyond posterior edge of orbit; pectoral fin soft-rays 10–13, usually 10–11:

**CALIFORNIA HALIBUT**

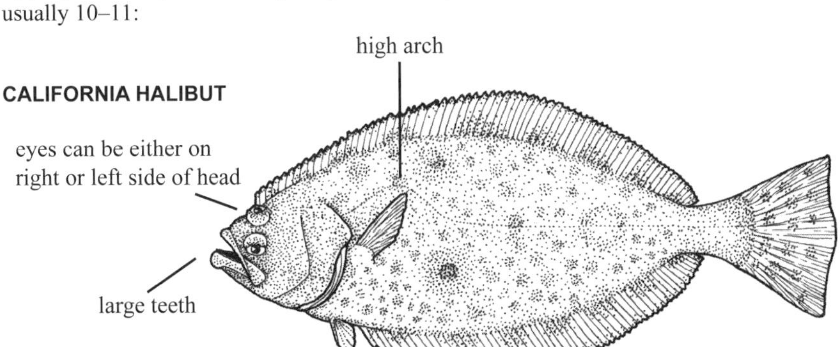


9b (next page)

## FLATFISHES (continued)

**PACIFIC HALIBUT, *Hippoglossus stenolepis* Schmidt, 1904.** Family PLEURONECTIDAE
Northern Japan and Seas of Japan and Okhotsk to Kuril Islands, Russia, Commander-Aleutian Islands Chain through Bering Sea to northeastern Chukchi Sea and to Punta Camalu, Baja California. Common from Sea of Japan and Sea of Okhotsk to throughout much of Bering Sea and southward to northern California. Length to 267 cm (105 in) TL. Depth: 2–2,000 m (7–6,560 ft). Eyed side dark brown, greenish-brown, to black above, with fine mottling. D 89–109; A 64–81; Pect. 14–19; Pelvic 6; LLs 150+; GR 1–4 + 7–10 = 9–13; Vert. 49–51.

**STARRY FLOUNDER, *Platichthys stellatus* (Pallas, 1787).** Family PLEURONECTIDAE
Seas of Japan and Okhotsk to Arctic Ocean in East Siberian Sea, Chukchi Sea, Beaufort Sea, and eastwards to at least Bathhurst Inlet, Nunavut and northeast to Count Melville Sound, Canada and Bering Sea and Commander-Aleutian Islands Chain to Los Angeles Harbor, southern California. Common from Sea of Japan to Bering Sea and in some locations in the Beaufort Sea and southward to central California. Length to 91 cm (36 in) TL. Depth: intertidal to about 600 m (1,968 ft), occasionally in surface waters; enters lower reaches of rivers. Eyed side dark brown; alternating dark and white-yellow or orange bands on dorsal, anal, and caudal fins. D 51–68; A 35–51; Pect. 9–12; Pelvic 5–6; LLp 63–78; GR 0–6 + 6–10 = 6–14; Vert. 34–38. Both right- and left-eye forms are common.

**ROUGHSCALE SOLE, *Clidoderma asperrimum* (Temminck & Schlegel, 1846).** Family PLEURONECTIDAE
Yellow Sea off Korean Peninsula, Japan and Okhotsk Seas to Commander Islands, Bering Sea, and Aleutian Islands to off Port San Luis (36°14'N, 126°29'W), central California (SIO 04-76). Common from Sea of Japan and Sea of Okhotsk to off Alaska; rare off California. Length to 62 cm (24.4 in) TL. Depth: 6–1,900 m (20–6,233 ft). Eyed side uniform brown, blind side gray to gray-brown. D 75–96; A 61–77; Pect. 12–15; Pelvic 6; GR 3–6 + 8–14; Vert. 45–46.

**LONGFIN SANDDAB, *Citharichthys xanthostigma* Gilbert, 1890.** Family PARALICHTHYIDAE
Monterey Bay, central California to Costa Rica, including Gulf of California. Common from southern California to southern Baja California. Length to 29 cm (11.4 in) TL. Depth: 2–250 m (7–820 ft). Eyed side dark brown; white, red, or orange speckling sometimes present. D 79–89; A 61–69; Pect. 10; LLs 50; GR 6–8 + 10–12 = 17–18; Vert. 36–38.

9b Upper jaw extends to anterior edge or middle of orbit; pectoral fin soft-rays 14–19, usually 16 or more:

PACIFIC HALIBUT

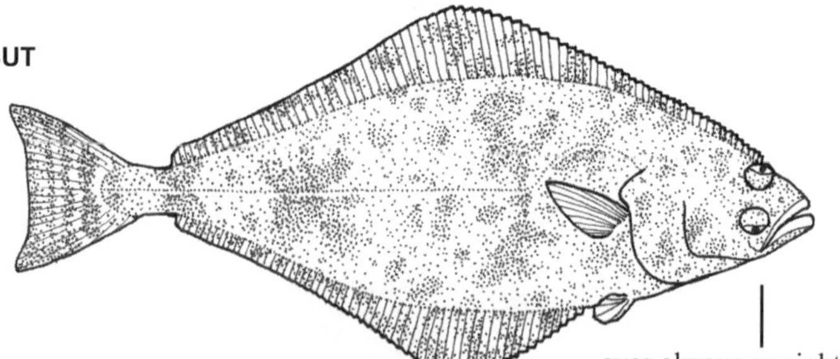


10a (next page)

10a *From 4a: lateral line without an abrupt arch*
Eyed side without areas of large modified scales….. 12

10b Areas of eyed side with large modified scales, either embedded with cluster of bumps or round with bony knobs….. 11

11a Dorsal, anal, and caudal fins with black and yellow, orange, or white bands; eyed and blind sides with enlarged, star-shaped scales:

**STARRY FLOUNDER**

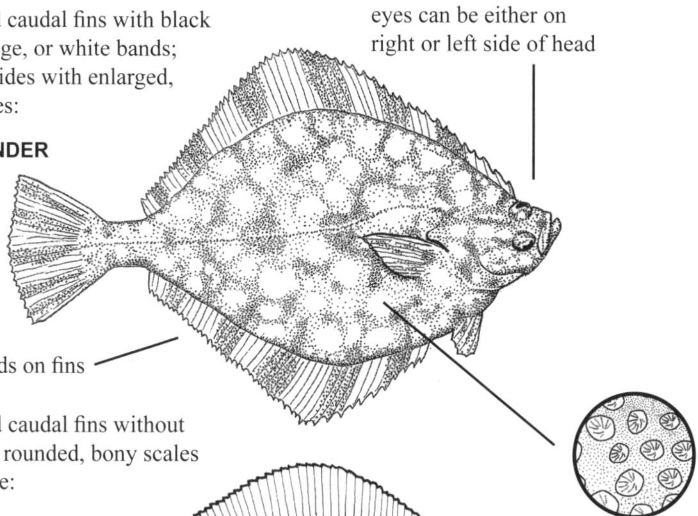


11b Dorsal, anal, and caudal fins without bands; enlarged, rounded, bony scales only on eyed side:

**ROUGHSCALE SOLE**

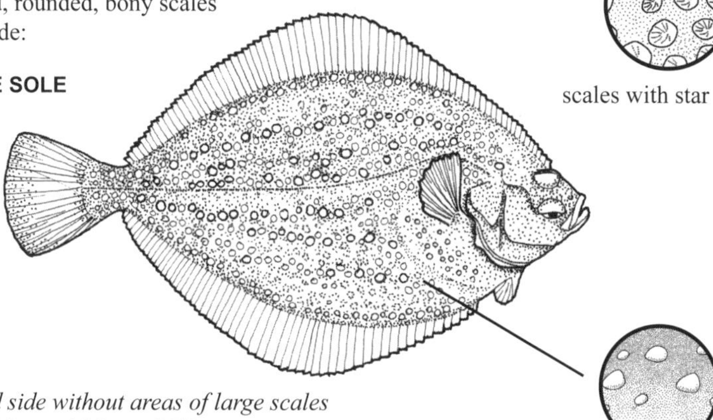


12a *From 10a: eyed side without areas of large scales*
Eyes on right side….. 16 (page 350)

12b Eyes on left side….. 13

13a Pectoral fin longer than HL:

**LONGFIN SANDDAB**

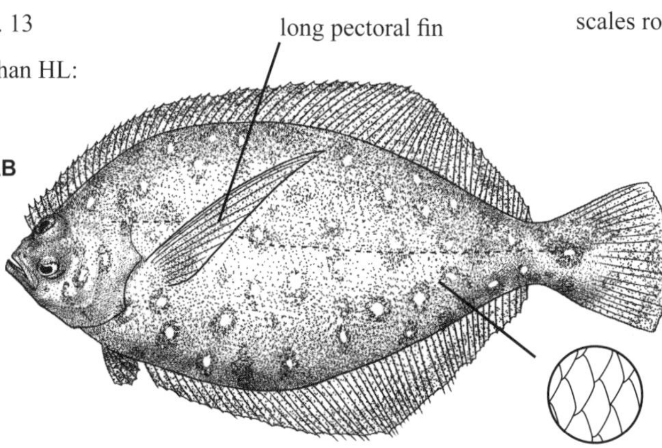


13b Pectoral fin shorter than HL….. 14 (next page)

## FLATFISHES (continued)

**GULF SANDDAB, *Citharichthys fragilis* Gilbert, 1890.** Family Paralichthyidae
Santa Cruz Island, southern California (LACM 57731-1) to Gulf of California; Peru. Often uncommon in southern California, but apparently population increases during some El Niños; common from northern Baja California southward. Length to 25 cm (9.8 in) TL. Depth: 18–347 m (60–1,138 ft). Eyed side brown. D 76–88; A 59–71; Pect. 10–12; Pelvic 6; GR 7–9 + 16–21; Vert. 36–38.

**SPECKLED SANDDAB, *Citharichthys stigmaeus* Jordan & Gilbert, 1882.** Family Paralichthyidae
Seward, northern Gulf of Alaska to Bahía Magdalena, southern Baja California and in Bahía Concepcion, Gulf of California. Larvae have been collected as far west in the Gulf of Alaska as near Kodiak Island. Also reported from Ecuador to Puerto Pizarro, Peru. Common from Gulf of Alaska to southern Baja California and in Gulf of California. Length to 19.2 cm (7.6 in) TL. Mostly marine, occasionally enters brackish waters; depth: intertidal to 366 m (1,200 ft). Eyed side brown or tan with black speckling and occasionally mottling. D 75–97; A 58–77; Pect. 10–12; LLs 52–58; GR 3–6 + 7–11 = 11–16; Vert. 34–39.

**PACIFIC SANDDAB, *Citharichthys sordidus* (Girard, 1854).** Family Paralichthyidae
Holiday Beach, Kodiak Island (57°42'N, 152°28'W), western Gulf of Alaska to Cabo San Lucas, southern Baja California. Records from southeastern Bering Sea and Aleutian Islands are not verifiable. Also reported off Peru. Common from British Columbia southward to at least Bahía de Sebastián Vizcaíno. Length to at least 41 cm (16 in) TL, possibly to 48 cm (18.9 in) TL. Mostly marine, but juveniles enter brackish waters; depth: intertidal to about 549 m (1,800 ft). Eyed side light brown, mottled with yellow, blue, and orange; dorsal and anal fin margin of males sooty; juveniles with black speckling on body and fins. D 86–102; A 67–81; Pect. 11–13; Pelvic 6; LLs 61–70; GR 6–9 + 11–16 = 18–23; Vert. 38–40.

**DIAMOND TURBOT, *Pleuronichthys guttulatus* Girard, 1856.** Family Pleuronectidae
Cape Mendocino, northern California to Gulf of California. Common from Tomales Bay, northern California to about Bahía Magdalena, southern Baja California and in Gulf of California. Length to 45.7 cm (18 in) TL. Depth: surf zone to 46 m (150 ft). Eyed side dark gray, green, or brown with bright blue round spots. D 65–75; A 47–55; Pect. 11–13; LLs 83–95; GR 1–2 + 5–6 = 6–8; Vert. 34–36. (Formerly *Hypsopsetta guttulata* (Girard, 1856): M&L).

14a Gill rakers on lower limb of 1st arch 16–21, usually 17–19:

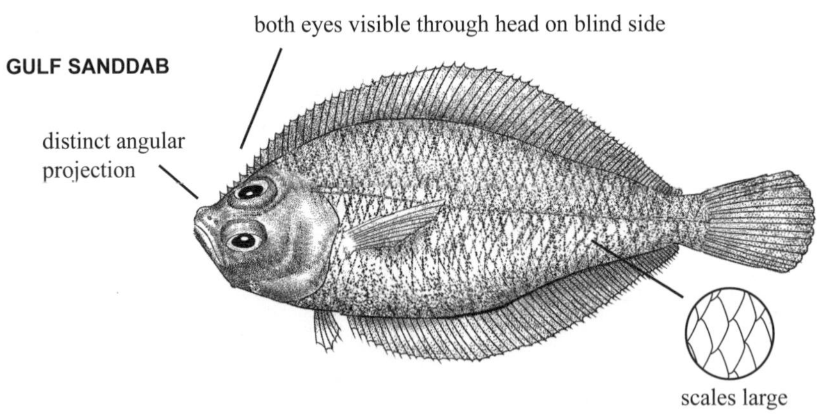


14b Gill rakers on lower limb of 1st arch 8–16, usually 8–15..... 15 (next page)

15a Lower eye shorter than snout length; gill rakers on lower limb of 1st arch usually 8–10:

**SPECKLED SANDDAB**

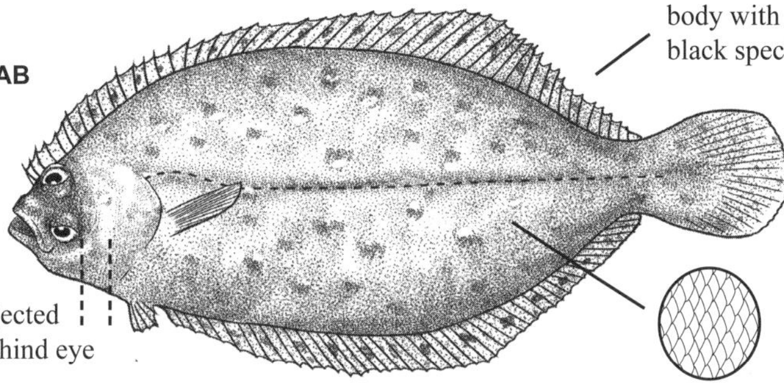


15b Lower eye longer than snout length; gill rakers on lower limb of 1st arch usually 12–15:

**PACIFIC SANDDAB**

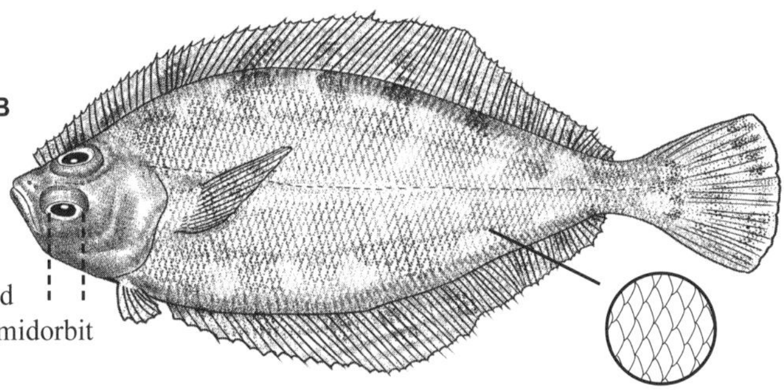


16a *From 12a: eyes on right side*
Lateral line without accessory dorsal branch (ADB)….. 25 (page 354)

16b Lateral line with ADB extending from head onto trunk, located along base of dorsal fin….. 17

17a ADB does not extend beyond pectoral fin….. 22 (page 353)

17b ADB extends well beyond pectoral fin….. 18

18a First 1 or 2 dorsal fin soft-rays inserted on blind side; eyed side with light blue spots:

**DIAMOND TURBOT**

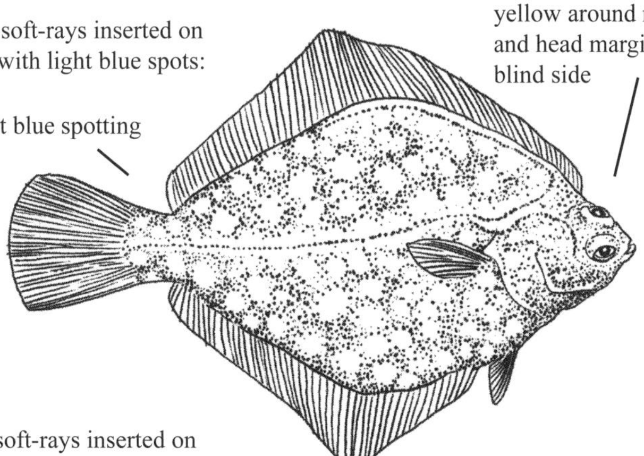


18b First 4–12 dorsal fin soft-rays inserted on blind side….. 19 (next page)

## FLATFISHES (continued)

**CURLFIN SOLE, *Pleuronichthys decurrens* Jordan & Gilbert, 1881.** Family PLEURONECTIDAE
Aleutian Islands off northwest coast of Unimak Island and Gulf of Alaska to just south of Punta San Juanico (25°59'N, 112°35'W), southern Baja California. Common from Hecate Strait, British Columbia to at least Bahía San Quintin, northern Baja California. Length to 44 cm (17.3 in) TL. Depth: surf zone to 440 m (1,443 ft). Maximum depth is sometimes given, incorrectly, as 532 m (1,746 ft or 291 fathoms). Eyed side greenish, yellowish, or reddish-brown with dark brown or gray mottling. D 67–81; A 45–55; Pect. 9–14; Pelvic 4–7; LLp 82–96; GR 2–4 + 5–9 = 9–13; Vert. 37–41. (Formerly CURLFIN TURBOT: M&L).

**HORNYHEAD TURBOT, *Pleuronichthys verticalis* Jordan & Gilbert, 1880.** Family PLEURONECTIDAE
Oregon to Bahía Magdalena, southern Baja California; isolated population in Gulf of California. Common at least from San Francisco Bay to Punta Abreojos, southern Baja California and in Gulf of California. Length to 36.8 cm (14.5 in) TL. Depth: 5–496 m (16–1,627 ft). Eyed side yellowish-brown to dark brown with gray, dark brown, or pale blotches and sometimes yellow spots. D 65–79; A 44–51; Pect. 10–12; Pelvic 6; LLp 88–103; GR 2–5 + 6–9 = 9–11; Vert. 36–38.

**C-O SOLE, *Pleuronichthys coenosus* Girard, 1854.** Family PLEURONECTIDAE
Prince William Sound, Alaska to Punta Abreojos, southern Baja California. Common from perhaps Vancouver Island or Hecate Strait, British Columbia to central Baja California. Length to 36 cm (14 in) TL. Depth: surf zone to 350 m (1,146 ft). Eyed side light to dark brown, variously splotched with white, purple, or black; dark spot in center of body and dark crescent and spot on tail (forming "C-O"). D 65–78; A 46–56; Pect. 9–13; Pelvic 6; LLp 77–92; GR 3–4 + 8–11 = 11–15; Vert. 36–39. (Formerly C-O TURBOT: M&L).

**SPOTTED TURBOT, *Pleuronichthys ritteri* Starks & Morris, 1907.** Family PLEURONECTIDAE
Morro Bay, central California (LACM 33703-1) to southern Baja California (24°12'N, 111°21'W) and upper Gulf of California. Common from southern California to at least Bahía Magdalena, southern Baja California and perhaps in the upper Gulf of California. Length to 29 cm (11 in) TL, possibly to 33 cm (13 in) TL. Depth: 1–219 m (3–718 ft). Eyed side brown to gray with light speckling; usually with 3 dark spots. D 61–72; A 43–52; Pect. 9–11; LLp 83–98; GR 3–5 + 8–12 = 12–17; Vert. 34–36.

19a First 9–12 dorsal fin soft-rays inserted on blind side, with 1st soft-ray extending to or beyond corner of mouth:

CURLFIN SOLE

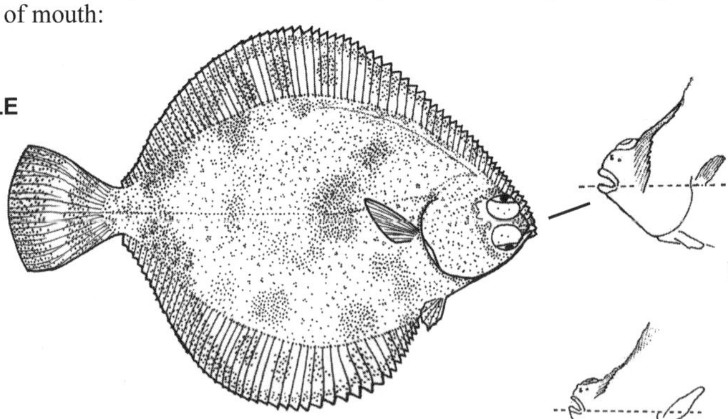

blind side

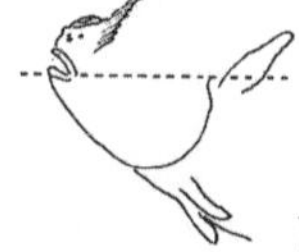

19b Only first 4–6 dorsal fin soft-rays inserted on blind side, with 1st soft-ray not extending to corner of mouth..... 20 (next page)

blind side

20a Posterior tip of interorbital ridge sharp, spine-like; no teeth on jaws:

**HORNYHEAD TURBOT**

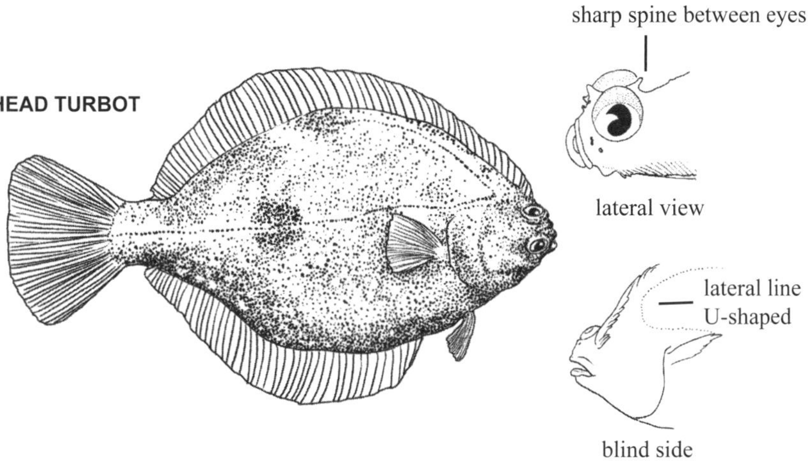


20b Posterior tip of interorbital ridge blunt; small teeth on eyed side of jaws….. 21

21a Dark pigment on base of caudal fin usually reverse “C” followed by large, dark spot;
depth of caudal peduncle into BD 3.8–4.4:

**C-O SOLE**

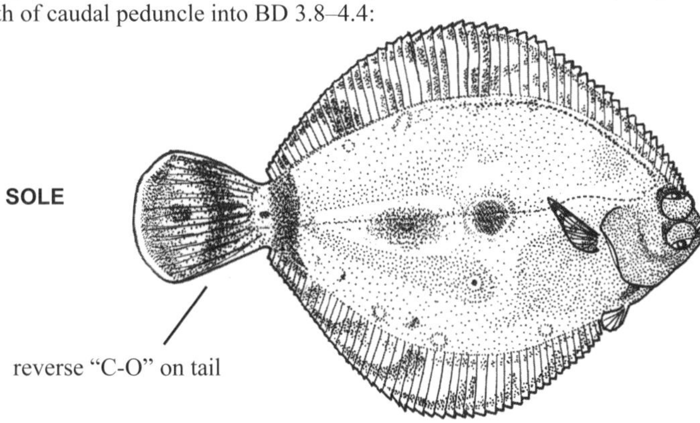


21b Two distinct spots near caudal peduncle, lateral line with 1 or 2 dark spots;
depth of caudal peduncle into BD 4.4–5.6:

**SPOTTED TURBOT**

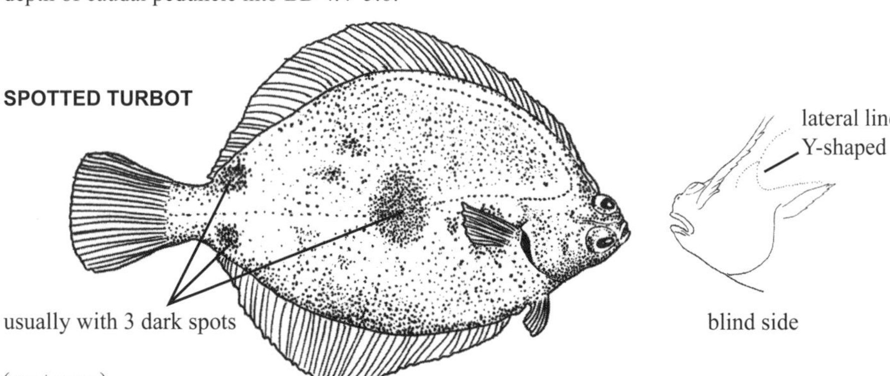


22a (next page)

## FLATFISHES (continued)

**SAND SOLE, *Psettichthys melanostictus* Girard, 1854.** Family PLEURONECTIDAE
Southeastern Bering Sea and Aleutian Islands from Unalaska Island to Port Heiden and Gulf of Alaska to La Jolla, southern California. Common from Alaska Peninsula southward to about Morro Bay, central California. Length to 63 cm (24.8 in) TL. Marine and brackish waters; depth: intertidal to 325 m (1,066 ft). Eyed side dark gray, gray-green, or brown with black speckling. D 72–90; A 53–66; Pect. 10–12; Pelvic 6; LLs 98–112; GR 5–7 + 13–18 = 18–27; Vert. 37–41.

**ENGLISH SOLE, *Parophrys vetulus* Girard, 1854.** Family PLEURONECTIDAE
Nunivak Island, Bering Sea and Agattu Island, Aleutian Islands to Bahía San Cristobal (27°22'N, 114°38'W), central Baja California. Common from at least Umnak Island, Aleutian Islands to Bahía de Sebastián Vizcaíno, southern Baja California. Length to 61 cm (24 in) TL. Adults offshore marine; juveniles often in estuaries and bays; depth: intertidal zone (juveniles) to about 550 m (1,800 ft). Eyed side uniform brown to light brown, sometimes with white spots; dorsal and anal fins sometimes dark-edged; blind side white, light yellow, or pinkish. D 71–93; A 52–70; Pect. 10–13; Pelvic 6; LLs 89–105; GR 4–6 + 10–13 = 14–18; Vert. 41–47. (Recently as *Pleuronectes vetulus* (Girard, 1854)).

**BUTTER SOLE, *Isopsetta isolepis* (Lockington, 1880).** Family PLEURONECTIDAE
Southeastern Bering Sea and Aleutian Islands (west to Amchitka Island) to San Pedro, southern California (VRG C39-2727). Common from eastern Aleutian Islands to northern California. Length to 55.2 cm (21.8 in) TL. Depth: 2 m (7 ft) or less to 425 m (1,394 ft). Eyed side dark to light brown with yellow or green mottling; fins sometimes edged with yellow. D 78–92; A 58–69; Pect. 10–13; Pelvic 6; LLs 78–90; GR 4–6 + 7–9 = 11–14; Vert. 39–42. A reversed individual (right eye migrated) was taken off the Klamath River, northern California. A hybrid of BUTTER SOLE and ENGLISH SOLE has been described from the Puget Sound region; it has meristic and other characters intermediate between the two species (Garrett, 2005). Whether this hybrid occurs in California waters is unknown. (Recently as *Pleuronectes isolepis* (Lockington, 1880)).

**HYBRID SOLE, *Inopsetta ischyra* (Jordan & Gilbert, 1880).** Family PLEURONECTIDAE
Southern British Columbia to San Francisco, northern California. Common in the Puget Sound area; uncommon off California. Length to 46 cm (18.1 in) TL. Nearshore waters; depth: perhaps 5–50 m (15–164 ft). Eyed side brown to olive-brown with light and dark mottling; dorsal and anal fins with faint dusky bars. D 65–77; A 49–58; Pelvic 6; LLs 76–86; GR 4–6 + 9–10; Vert. 41. (Alternative name FORKLINE SOLE). This "species" is a hybrid of STARRY FLOUNDER and ENGLISH SOLE (Garrett and Pietsch, 2007).

22a *From 17a: ADB does not extend beyond pectoral fin*
First 4–8 dorsal fin soft-rays mostly free from membranes:

**SAND SOLE**

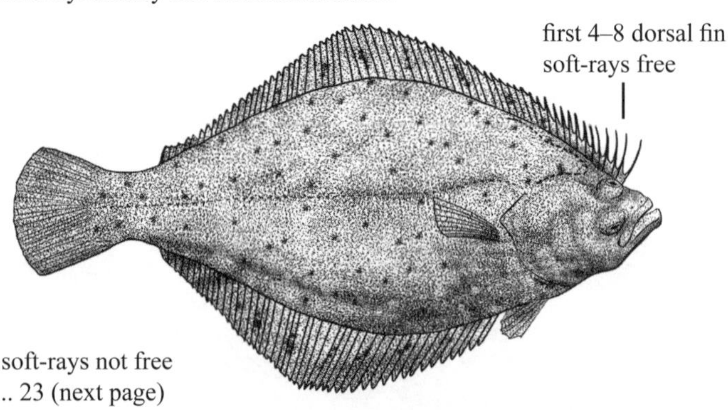


22b First 4–8 dorsal fin soft-rays not free from membranes….. 23 (next page)

23a Upper eye visible from blind side; dorsal and anal fins without scales; caudal fin not rounded:

**ENGLISH SOLE**

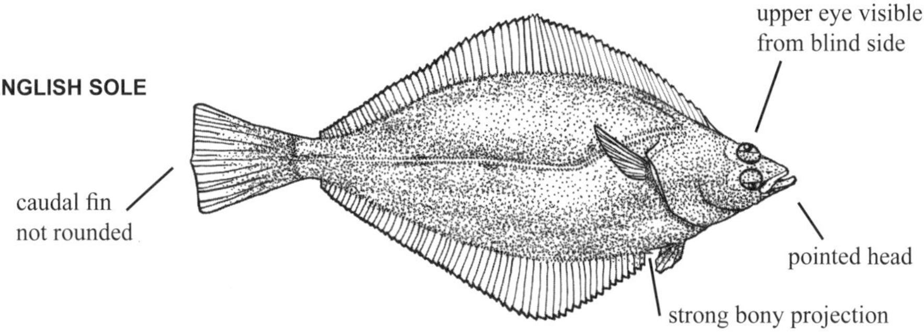


23b Upper eye not visible from blind side; dorsal and anal fins with scales; caudal fin rounded….. 24

24a Accessory dorsal branch (ADB) of lateral line extending beyond preopercle:

**BUTTER SOLE**

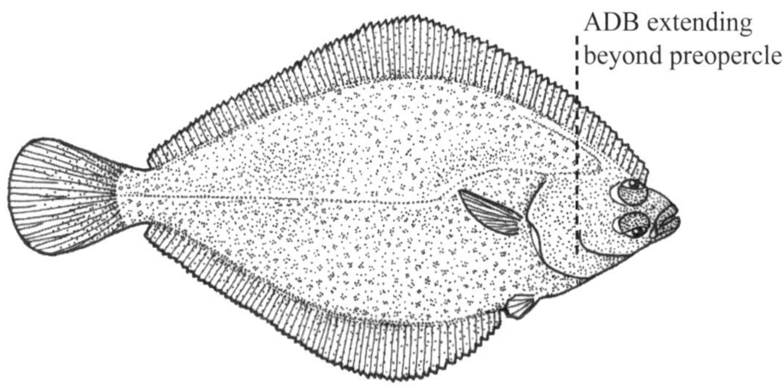


24b ADB forked, not extending beyond preopercle:

**HYBRID SOLE**

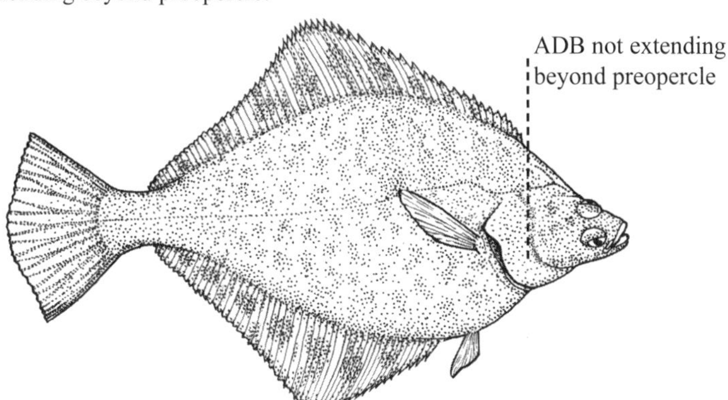


25a *From 16a: lateral line without ADB*
Caudal fin not indented; teeth relatively small….. 28 (page 356)

25b Caudal fin usually indented; teeth large….. 26 (next page)

# FLATFISHES (continued)

**GREENLAND HALIBUT, *Reinhardtius hippoglossoides* (Walbaum, 1792).** Family PLEURONECTIDAE
Nearly circumpolar; North Atlantic, Arctic, and North Pacific; Seas of Japan and Okhotsk to Bering, Chukchi, and Beaufort Seas, and Aleutian Islands and Gulf of Alaska to just south of U.S.–Mexico border. Common from Sea of Okhotsk to Bering Sea and Aleutian Islands; rare south of Alaska. Length to 130 cm (51.2 in) TL. Depth: 14–2,000 m (46–6,562 ft). Eyed side uniform dark brown to purplish-black; pigment also on blind side. D 83–109; A 62–84; Pect. 11–15; Pelvic 5–7; LLs 105–119; GR 2–6 + 10–16; Vert. 60–64. (Alternative name GREENLAND TURBOT).

**ARROWTOOTH FLOUNDER, *Atheresthes stomias* (Jordan & Gilbert, 1880).** Family PLEURONECTIDAE
Commander Islands and east coast of Kamchatka to Cape Navarin, eastern Bering Sea (northward to south of Saint Lawrence Island, 62°08'N, 170°18'W) to Aleutian Islands and Gulf of Alaska to Todos Santos (23°25'N, 110°19'W), southern Baja California. Common from Aleutian Islands, southern and eastern Bering Sea, and southward to about northern California. Length to 86 cm (34 in) TL. Depth: 9–1,176 m (29–3,857 ft). Eyed side mostly uniform dark grayish-brown to olive-brown, occasionally with faint mottling; blind side dirty white. D 92–115; A 72–99; Pect. 14–15; Pelvic 6; LLs about 135; GR 3–5 + 10–16 = 14–19; Vert. 47–50.

**KAMCHATKA FLOUNDER, *Atheresthes evermanni* Jordan & Starks, 1904.** Family PLEURONECTIDAE
Sea of Okhotsk and northern Sea of Japan to Gulf of Anadyr, western Bering Sea to eastern Bering Sea, Aleutian Islands, and southwestern Gulf of Alaska and off Davenport (about 37°01'N, 122°12'W), central California. Common from Sea of Okhotsk and Bering Sea to about Kodiak Island, Gulf of Alaska; rare in California. Length to 110 cm (44 in) TL. Depth: 25–1,200 m (83–3,936 ft). Eyed side uniform dark brown, blind side ranges from off-white to dark brown. D 97–117; A 73–95; Pect. 11–16; Pelvic 6; LLs 86–118; GR 2–3 + 9–12; Vert. 47–53.

**DEEPSEA SOLE, *Microstomus bathybius* (Gilbert, 1890).** Family PLEURONECTIDAE
Hokkaido, Japan to Bering Sea and Aleutian Islands to southern California (32°38'N, 119°24'W) (LACM 37464-1). Common at least from Kuril Islands, Russia and Bering Sea to southern California. Length to 52 cm (20.5 in) TL. Depth: 41–1,498 m (134–4,913 ft); individuals taken at shallower depths typically juveniles. Eyed side black or blue-black with white and blue mottling (older individuals often brown or brown-red). D 109–117; A 94–98; Pect. 10–13; Pelvic 5–6; LLs 165–247; GR 6–9 + 14–16; Vert. 57–65. (Formerly *Embassichthys bathybius* (Gilbert, 1890): M&L).

26a Origin of dorsal fin posterior to orbit; blind side with speckling; angle of preopercle sharp, approximately 90°:

**GREENLAND HALIBUT**

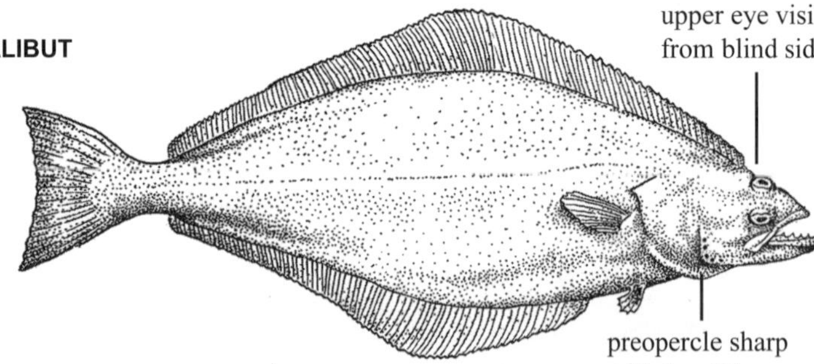


26b Origin of dorsal fin anterior to orbit or near midorbit; blind side without speckling; angle of preopercle rounded….. 27 (next page)

27a Upper eye visible from blind side; total gill rakers on 1st arch more than 14;
2 gill rakers on upper limb of 2nd arch:

**ARROWTOOTH FLOUNDER**

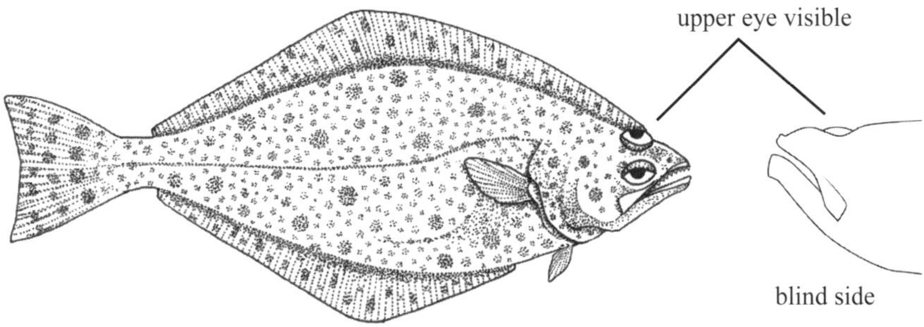


27b Upper eye not visible from blind side; total gill rakers on 1st arch fewer than 14;
1 gill raker on upper limb of 2nd arch:

**KAMCHATKA FLOUNDER**

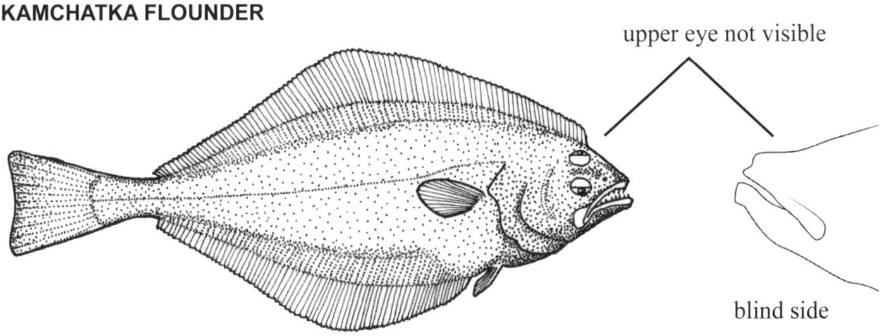


28a *From 25a: caudal fin not indented*
Length of caudal peduncle less than eye diameter; eyed side with bluish mottling:

**DEEPSEA SOLE**

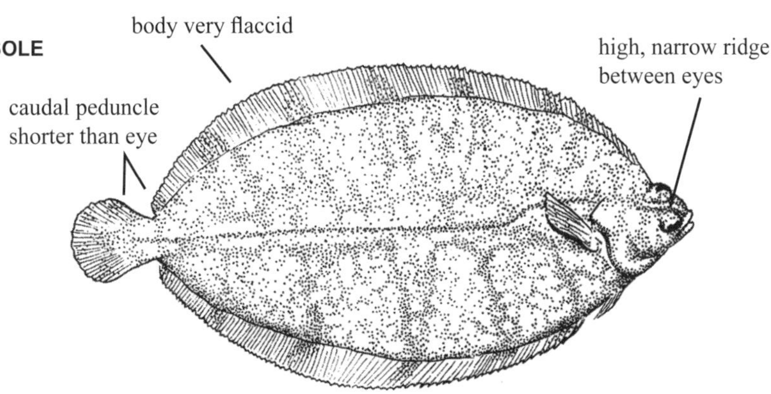


28b Length of caudal peduncle greater than eye diameter;
eyed side without bluish mottling….. 29 (next page)

# FLATFISHES (continued)

**DOVER SOLE, *Microstomus pacificus* (Lockington, 1879).** Family Pleuronectidae
Northwestern and southeastern Bering Sea, and Aleutian Islands from Stalemate Bank to just south of Punta San Juanico (25°59'N, 113°17'W), southern Baja California. Common from about the Alaska Peninsula to northern Baja California. Length to 76 cm (30 in) TL. Depth: 2 m (7 ft) or less to 1,400 m (4,592 ft). Eyed side brown or grayish-brown with some dark mottling; blind side dirty gray to brown-gray; fins blackish towards margin. D 88–116; A 75–96; Pect. 8–12; Pelvic 5–6; LLs 137–149; GR 4–8 + 8–11 = 13–17; Vert. 50–55.

**REX SOLE, *Glyptocephalus zachirus* Lockington, 1879.** Family Pleuronectidae
Northern Kuril Islands, Russia to Commander Islands and western Bering Sea to Navarin Canyon, and Aleutian Islands, eastern Bering Sea, and Gulf of Alaska to Todos Santos (23°25'N, 110°14'W), southern Baja California. Common from northwestern and eastern Bering Sea and Aleutian Islands southward to southern California. Length to 61 cm (24 in) TL. Depth: shallow water to 1,237 m (4,057 ft). Eyed side uniform brown or gray; pectoral fins black; dorsal, caudal, and anal fins often black-edged. D 87–110; A 78–93; Pect. 11–13; Pelvic 6; LLs 132–138; GR 0–4 + 5–8 = 9–12; Vert. 62–66.

**SLENDER SOLE, *Lyopsetta exilis* (Jordan & Gilbert, 1880).** Family Pleuronectidae
Eastern Bering Sea (55°19'N, 166°58'W) and Unalaska Island to Pacific off Boca de Santa Domingo (about 25°30'N), southern Baja California. Common from about Kodiak Island, Gulf of Alaska to central Baja California. Length to 40 cm (15.7 in) TL. Depth: 9–1,145 m (30–3,756 ft). Eyed side uniform light olive-brown to reddish-brown; fins with dark speckling on margin. D 72–88; A 57–66; Pect. 10; Pelvic 6; LLs 65–73; GR 2–3 + 9–11 = 11–14; Vert. 42–47. (Recently as *Eopsetta exilis* (Jordan & Gilbert, 1880)).

**PETRALE SOLE, *Eopsetta jordani* (Lockington, 1879).** Family Pleuronectidae
Aleutian Islands west at least as far as Unalaska Island, and Gulf of Alaska to Islas Coronados, northern Baja California. Common from the Yakutat region, Gulf of Alaska to southern California. Length to 75 cm (29.5 in) TL. Depth: shallow water to 550 m (1,800 ft). Eyed side uniform dark to light brown; dark mottling on dorsal and anal fins. D 82–103; A 62–80; Pect. 13; Pelvic 6; LLs 88–100; GR 2–6 + 15–17 = 17–22; Vert. 41–45.

**FLATHEAD SOLE, *Hippoglossoides elassodon* Jordan & Gilbert, 1880.** Family Pleuronectidae
Southwestern Kamchatka and northern Kuril Islands, Russia to Gulf of Anadyr and Bering Sea (northward to at least about Saint Lawrence Island) and Commander-Aleutian chain to Monterey, central California. Common from Sea of Okhotsk to Beaufort Sea and Gulf of Alaska to Oregon. Length to 56 cm (22 in) TL. Depth: intertidal to 1,050 m (3,445 ft). Eyed side dark brown, greenish-brown, reddish-brown, or black with light and dark blotches; dorsal and anal fins with dark blotches. D 66–94; A 51–73; Pect. 8–14; Pelvic 6; LLs 84–120; GR 1–5 + 8–25 = 17–30; Vert. 42–47. (*Hippoglossoides robustus* Gill & Townsend, 1897 is a junior synonym.)

29a Upper eye visible from blind side; opercular opening small, not extending above pectoral fin:

**DOVER SOLE**

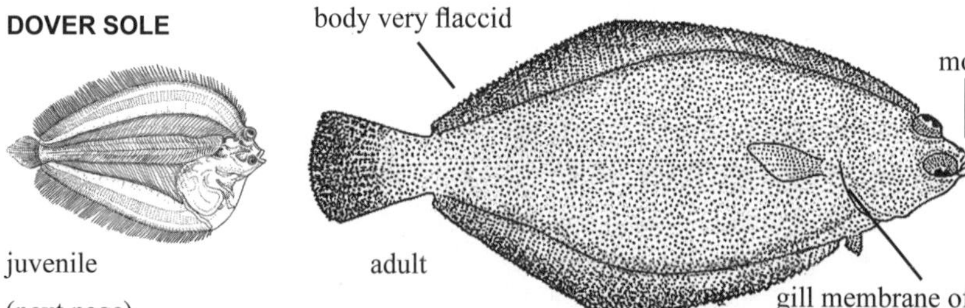


29b (next page)

29b Upper eye not visible from blind side; opercular opening large, extending dorsally above pectoral fin….. 30

30a BD into TL less than 3….. 32

30b BD into TL greater than 3….. 31

31a Pectoral fin black, longer than head:

**REX SOLE**

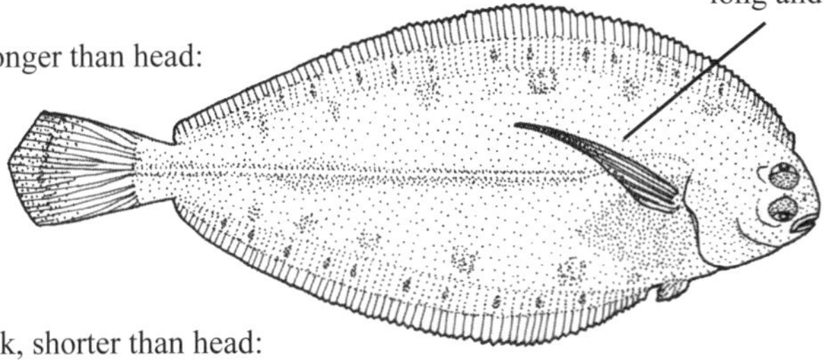


31b Pectoral fin not black, shorter than head:

**SLENDER SOLE**

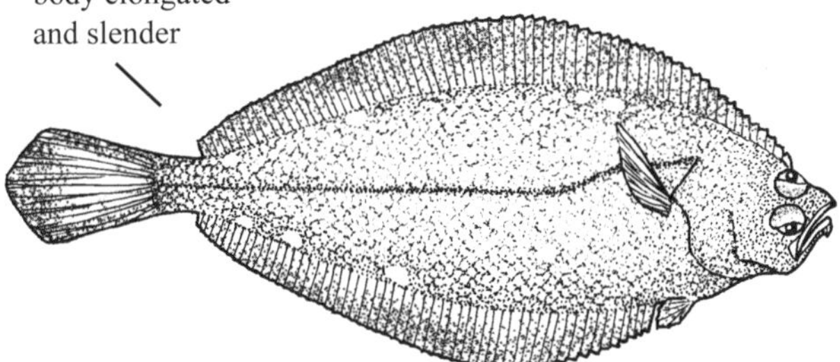


32a *From 30a: BD into TL less than 3*
Two rows of teeth on upper jaw; interorbital space with 4–5 scale rows; membranes of caudal fin pigmented:

**PETRALE SOLE**

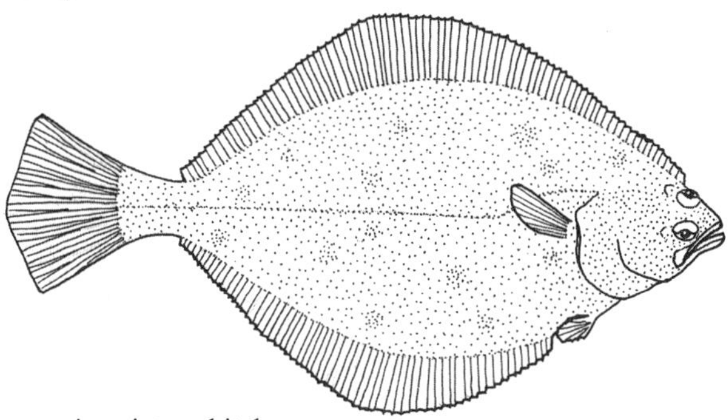

32b One row of teeth on upper jaw; interorbital space with 0–3 scale rows; membranes of caudal fin generally unpigmented:

**FLATHEAD SOLE**

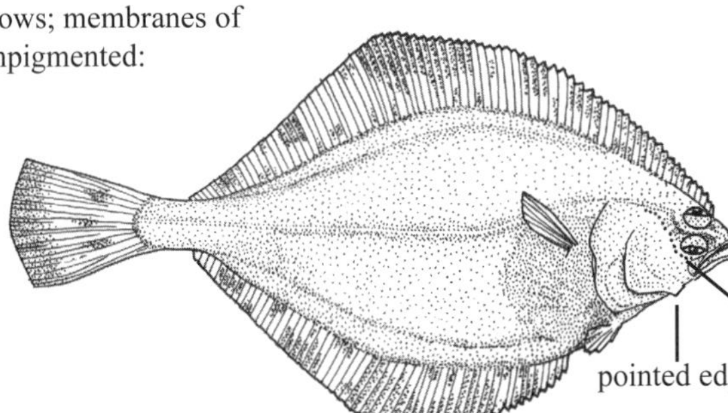

# OCEAN SUNFISHES, Family Molidae, BOXFISH, Family Ostraciidae, TRIGGERFISHES, Family Balistidae, PUFFERS, Family Tetraodontidae, and PORCUPINEFISHES, Family Diodontidae

**SLENDER MOLA, *Ranzania laevis* (Pennant, 1776).** Family Molidae
Circumglobal; Oceano, central California to Chile, including southern Gulf of California. Length to 90 cm (35.4 in) TL. Usually rare off California, although common offshore (for instance off San Clemente Island) during some warm-water periods (e.g., 2014). Depth: surface to 257 m (843 ft). Dusky or dark on back, silver on sides and belly; often blue or bluish-white streaks or dark spots with dark margin on body. D 17–19; A 18–19; Pect. 13; Pelvic absent; Vert. 18–19.

**OCEAN SUNFISH, *Mola mola* (Linnaeus, 1758).** Family Molidae
Circumglobal in temperate and tropical waters; Japan and southern Kuril Islands, Russia to Gulf of Alaska to Las Cruces (33°29'S), central Chile, including Gulf of California and Islas Galápagos. Common (at least in warm-water years) all along Pacific Coast as far northward as about southeast Alaska. Length confirmed to 2.7 m (8.9 ft) TL; possibly to 4 m (13.1 ft) TL. Depth: surface to 844 m (2,768 ft). Deepest known occurrence in eastern Pacific is 556 m (1,824 ft). Gray-blue on back, metallic silver on sides. D 16–18; A 14–18; Pect. 12–13; Pelvic absent; Scales absent; GR concealed; Vert. 16–18. (Formerly COMMON MOLA: M&L).

**HOODWINKER OCEAN SUNFISH, *Mola tecta* Nyegaard, Sawai, Gemmell, Gillum, Loneragan, Yamanoue & Stewart, 2018.** Family Molidae
Southern Hemisphere from Chile to Australia to South Africa and perhaps one record from the North Sea; 2 underwater records from Monterey Bay, central California and 1 record of a beached specimen at Coal Oil Point, Santa Barbara County, southern California. Length to at least 242 cm (95.3 in) TL. Depth range unknown, but may resemble that of OCEAN SUNFISH. Uniform gray or dark-brown with whitish spots and patterns. D 17–18; A 16–18; Pect. 11–13; Pelvic absent.

## KEY TO THE OCEAN SUNFISHES, BOXFISHES, TRIGGERFISHES, PUFFERS, and PORCUPINEFISHES:

Created by Bill Power
(Principal sources: Leis, 2001; Matsuura, 2001; Sawai et al., 2017; Nyegaard et al., 2018)

1a Caudal fin "normal"..... 4 (next page)

1b Caudal fin modified (clavus)..... 2

2a Body elongated, at least 2 times as long as tall; clavus margin straight:

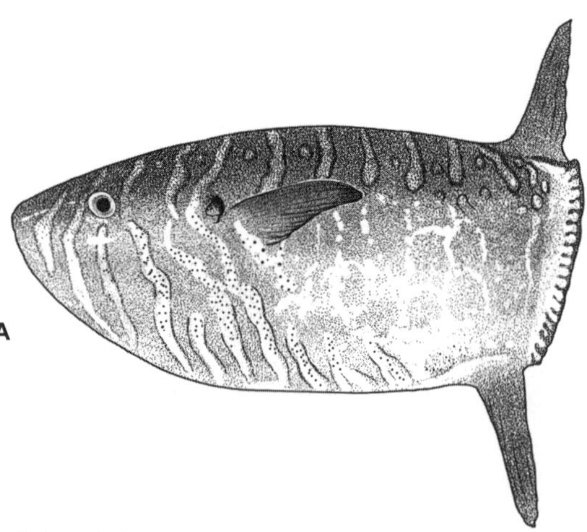

SLENDER MOLA

2b Body oval to round; clavus margin rounded..... 3 (next page)

3a Clavus scalloped; HW greatest below mouth:

**OCEAN SUNFISH**

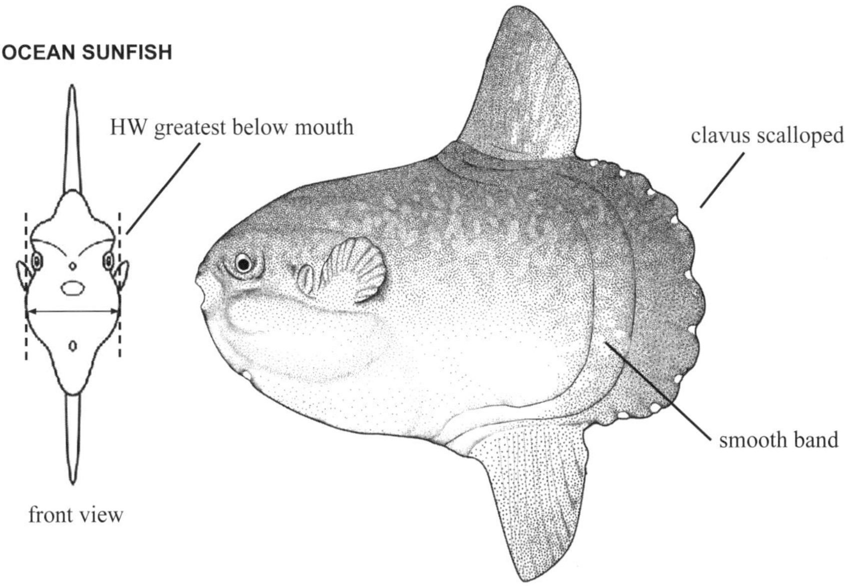


3b Clavus smooth with single indentation at midpoint; HW greatest above eyes:

**HOODWINKER OCEAN SUNFISH**

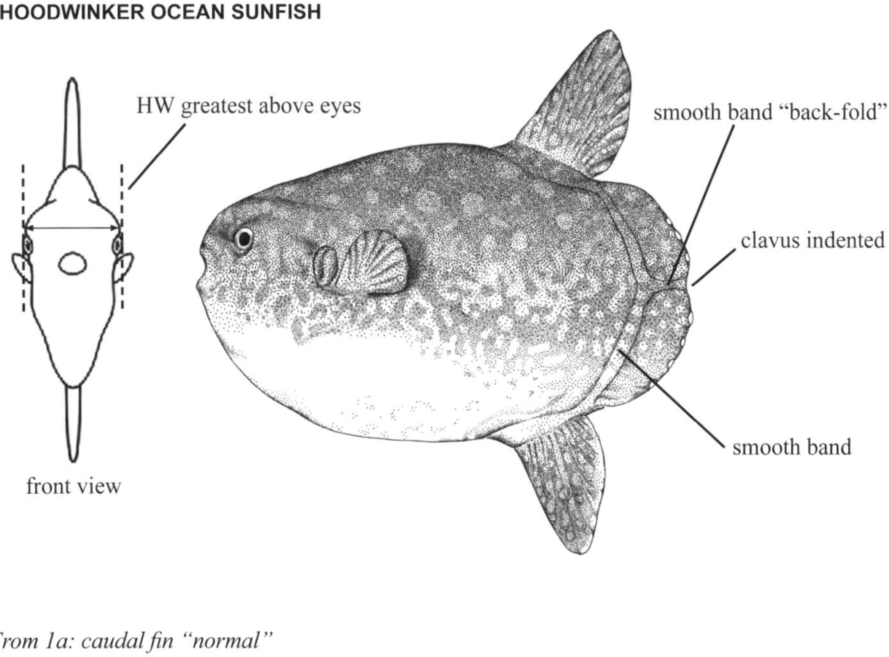


4a *From 1a: caudal fin "normal"*
Body capable of inflation; 1–2 modified teeth in each jaw….. 8 (page 363)

4b Body not capable of inflation; more than 2 teeth in each jaw….. 5 (next page)

## OCEAN SUNFISHES, BOXFISH, TRIGGERFISHES, PUFFERS, and PORCUPINEFISHES (continued)

**SPINY BOXFISH, *Lactoria diaphana* (Bloch & Schneider, 1801).** Family Ostraciidae
Pacific and Indian Oceans; Piedras Blancas, central California (CAS 56961) to Chile. Uncommon off California. Length to 34 cm (13.4 in) TL. Depth: surface to 171 m (561 ft). Body variously marked with black, tan, greenish-gray, or light brown blotches and small black spots. D 9; A 9–10; Pect. 10–11; Pelvic absent; Vert. 15. (Formerly *Ostracion diaphanum* Bloch & Schneider, 1801: M&L).

**FINESCALE TRIGGERFISH, *Balistes polylepis* Steindachner, 1876.** Family Balistidae
Metlakatla, southeastern Alaska to San Antonio (about 33°32'S), central Chile, including Gulf of California, Islas Galápagos, and Hawai'i. Common in southern California; common from Bahía Magdalena into tropics. Length to 80 cm (31.5 in) TL. Depth: 2–512 m (6–1,680 ft). Brownish to bluish-gray; blue speckling on head; scales dark. D III + 26–28; A 24–26; Pect. 13–15; GRt 29–37; Vert. 18.

**BLACK DURGON, *Melichthys niger* (Bloch, 1786).** Family Balistidae
Circumglobal; San Diego, southern California to southern Gulf of California, Costa Rica to Colombia, and Islas Galápagos. Not confirmed north of Mexico since it was reported off San Diego in the 1800s. A report of this fish from Metlatkatla, Alaska, represents a misidentified FINESCALE TRIGGERFISH. Length to 51 cm (20 in) TL. Depth: surface to 75 m (246 ft). Black to dark greenish-gray; white to bluish lines along base of dorsal and anal fins. D III + 23–25; A 23–25; Pect. 13–15; Midlateral scales 52–54; GRt 33–39; Vert. 18–19. (Formerly BLACK TRIGGERFISH: M&L).

**REDTAIL TRIGGERFISH, *Xanthichthys mento* (Jordan & Gilbert, 1882).** Family Balistidae
Tropical Pacific; in eastern Pacific taken in scattered locations including Ventura, southern California, Isla Guadalupe, Rocas Alijos, tip of Baja California, and Colombia. Rare off southern California. Length to 30 cm (11.7 in) TL. Depth: surface to 131 m (430 ft). Body yellow; dark scale outlines; blue stripes under eyes. Males with red caudal fin; dorsal and anal fins edged in gold. Females with yellow caudal fin; dorsal and anal fins edged in red. D III + 28–33; A 25–29; Pect. 12–16; Midlateral scales 42–43; GRt 40–47; Vert. 18. This species is occasionally released in southern California waters by commercial passenger fishing vessels returning from Baja California.

5a Body not compressed, rectangular-shaped in cross section; 1 dorsal fin; forward protruding spines over eyes:

**SPINY BOXFISH**

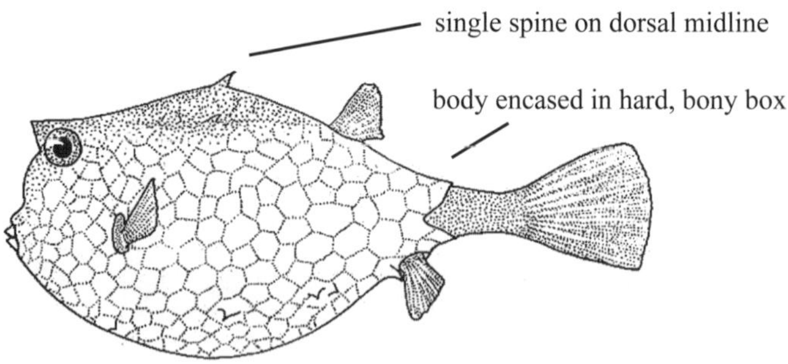


5b Body compressed; 2 dorsal fins; forward protruding spines over eyes lacking..... 6 (next page)

6a Three spines in 1st dorsal fin (3rd spine may be between dorsal fins):

**FINESCALE TRIGGERFISH**

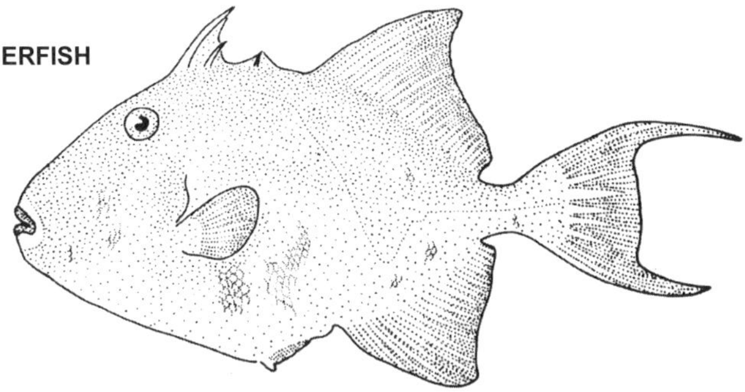

6b Two spines in 1st dorsal fin….. 7

7a Body black with white to blue stripe along base of dorsal and anal fins:

**BLACK DURGON**

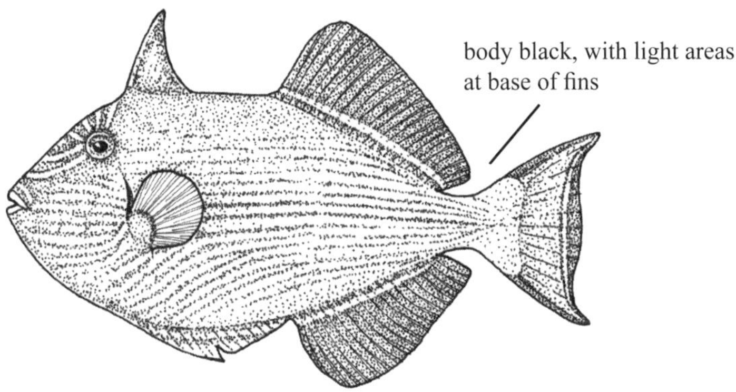


7b Body yellowish to blue-gray with blue stripes (and grooves) under eye and either red tail (male) or red along 1st dorsal and anal fins (female):

**REDTAIL TRIGGERFISH**

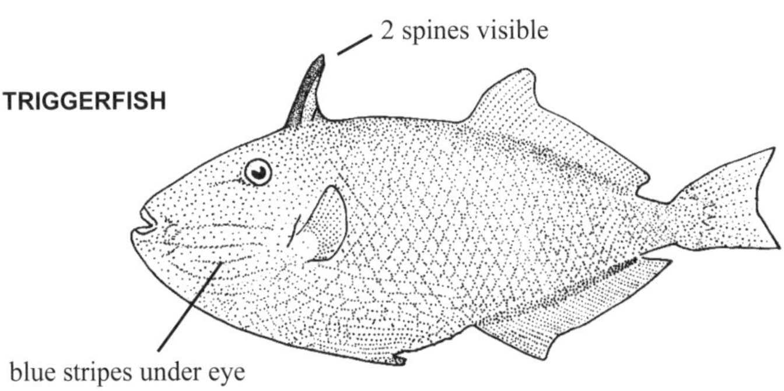


8a (next page)

## OCEAN SUNFISHES, BOXFISH, TRIGGERFISHES, PUFFERS, and PORCUPINEFISHES (continued)

**OCEANIC PUFFER, *Lagocephalus lagocephalus* (Linnaeus, 1758).** Family TETRAODONTIDAE
Circumglobal; Japan and southern Kuril Islands, Russia; Alder Creek Beach, Mendocino County, northern California to Peru, including Islas Galápagos. Rare in California. Length to 61 cm (24 in). Oceanic; depth: near surface to at least 1,000 m (3,280 ft). Back brown, sides and belly silvery; black spotting and bars; fins mostly gray, except white tip of caudal fin and white lower part of pectoral fin. Juveniles often with dark spots on head and body. D 0–I,11–16; A 0–I,11–14; Pect. 13–16; Pelvic absent; Vert. 18–19.

**BULLSEYE PUFFER, *Sphoeroides annulatus* (Jenyns, 1842).** Family TETRAODONTIDAE
Redondo Beach, southern California (LACM 22694) to Pisco, Peru, including Gulf of California and Islas Galápagos. Rare in southern California; common from Bahía de Sebastián Vizcaíno southward into tropics. Length to 48 cm (18.9 in) TL. Adults marine, juveniles in estuaries; depth: 1–105 m (3–344 ft). Dark brown above, white below; dark spots on back and sides; when viewed from above, series of concentric circles on back. D 0–I,7–9; A 0–I,6–9; Pect. 14–17; Pelvic absent; GR 8 (upper limb); Vert. 18–19.

**LONGNOSE PUFFER, *Sphoeroides lobatus* (Steindachner, 1870).** Family TETRAODONTIDAE
Redondo Beach, southern California to Salinas (33°57'S), central Chile, including southern and central Gulf of California and Islas Galápagos. Rare in southern California; common from Bahía Magdalena into tropics. Length to at least 30 cm (11.8 in) TL. Depth: surface, 1–107 m (3–351 ft). Brown or olive; body covered in small white spots; lower sides with larger, dark spots. D 7–8; A 6–7; Pect. 14; Pelvic absent; Vert. 17–18.

8a *From 4a: body capable of inflation*
Body with erect spines; 1 modified tooth (similar to parrot beak) in each jaw..... 11 (page 365)

8b Body without erect spines, but may have denticles; 2 modified teeth in each jaw..... 9

9a Lower eye margin at or below pectoral fin origin; BD less than 25% of SL (when uninflated):

**OCEANIC PUFFER**

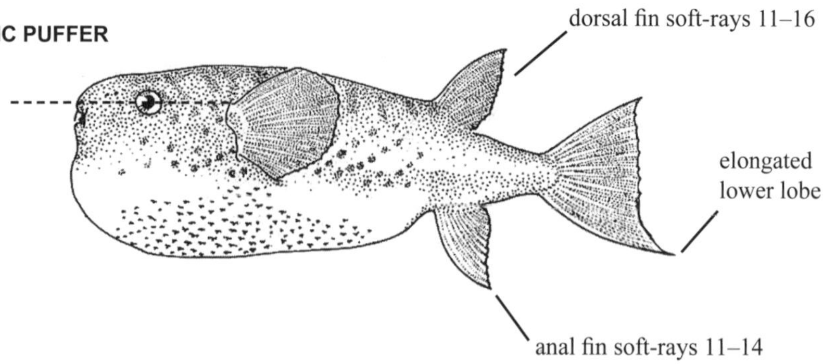


9b (next page)

9b Lower eye margin above pectoral fin origin; BD 25% or more of SL (when uninflated)….. 10

10a Bullseye pattern on dorsal surface with small dark spots on side; convex between eyes:

**BULLSEYE PUFFER**

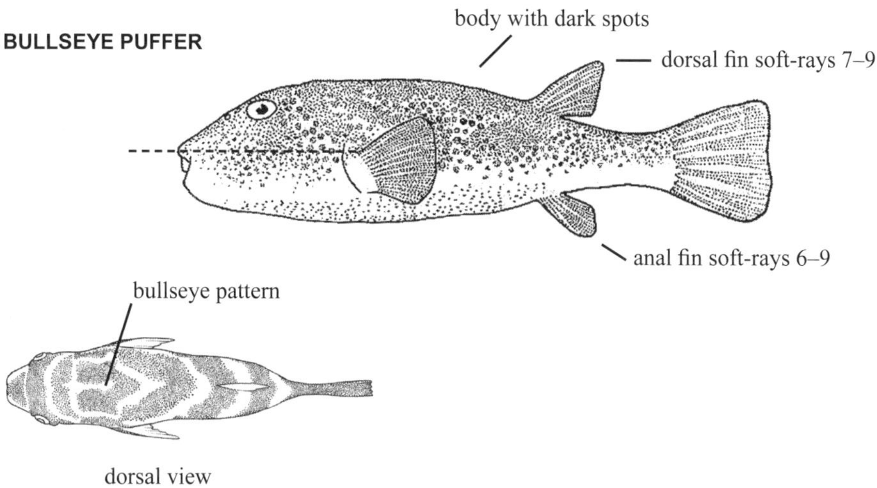


10b Bullseye pattern lacking, but with large dark spots on side to underside of body; concave between eyes:

**LONGNOSE PUFFER**

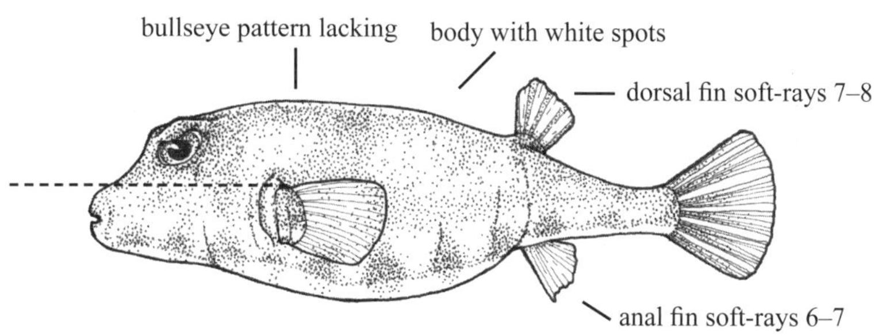


11a (next page)

## OCEAN SUNFISHES, BOXFISH, TRIGGERFISHES, PUFFERS, and PORCUPINEFISHES (continued)

**SPOTFIN BURRFISH, *Chilomycterus reticulatus* (Linnaeus, 1758).** Family DIODONTIDAE
Circumtropical; Japan and as far north as southern Kuril Islands, Russia; Long Beach Harbor, southern California to Chile, including Gulf of California and Islas Galápagos. Rare off southern California. Length to about 75 cm (29.5 in) TL. Depth: 1–141 m (3–462 ft). Gray to light-brown above, whitish below; dark spots on upper part of body and fins. D 12–14; A 11–14; Pect. 19–22; Pelvic absent; Vert. 22–23. (Formerly PACIFIC BURRFISH, *Chilomycterus affinis* Günther, 1870: M&L).

**BALLOONFISH, *Diodon holocanthus* Linnaeus, 1758.** Family DIODONTIDAE
Circumglobal; Japan; Bolinas, northern California (CAS 202295) to Easter Island, including Gulf of California and Islas Galápagos. Rare off California; common from Bahía Magdalena into tropics. Length to 50 cm (19.7 in) TL. Depth: 1 m (3 ft) to at least 100 m (328 ft). Light olive to brown on back, shading to white ventrally; scattered small black dots on upper ⅔ of head and body; variable number of brown bars from above to below eye, across top of head, and across portions of back; large oval brown blotch above pectoral fin; fins generally without spots. D 13–15; A 13–14; Pect. 22–25; Pelvic absent.

**PORCUPINEFISH, *Diodon hystrix* Linnaeus, 1758.** Family DIODONTIDAE
Circumglobal in warm waters; Japan and southeast of Kuril Islands, Russia; Santa Barbara (34°24'N, 119°45'W), southern California (SBMNH OS 5018) to Chile, including Gulf of California and Islas Galápagos. Rare off southern California. Length to 91 cm (36 in) TL. Depth: 1–135 m (3–443 ft). Light brown to olive on back, becoming white ventrally; upper body, dorsal, anal, and caudal fins profusely covered in small black dots. D 12–17; A 14–16; Pect. 21–25; Pelvic absent; GRt 6 (rudiments); Vert. 20. (Formerly SPOTTED PORCUPINEFISH: M&L).

**PELAGIC PORCUPINEFISH, *Diodon eydouxii* Brisout de Barneville, 1846.** Family DIODONTIDAE
Circumtropical; Los Angeles Harbor to tropics. Rare off southern California. Length to 30 cm (11.8 in) TL. Pelagic; depth: not reported. Medium to dark blue on back; body covered in large dark spots. D 16–18; A 16–18; Pect. 19–22; Pelvic absent.

11a *From 8a: body with erect spines*
Spines on head and belly fixed in erect position (not moveable) and with 3 roots:

**SPOTFIN BURRFISH**

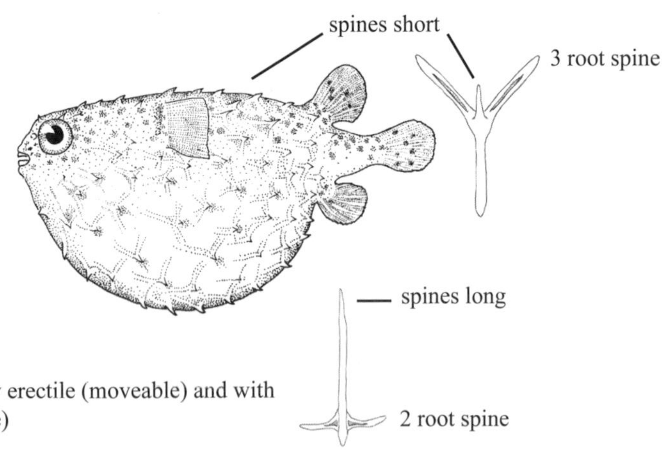


11b Spines on head and belly erectile (moveable) and with 2 roots….. 12 (next page)

12a No spines on caudal peduncle (although tip of spine(s) may extend into this area); several dark bars on back; no spots on fins:

**BALLOONFISH**

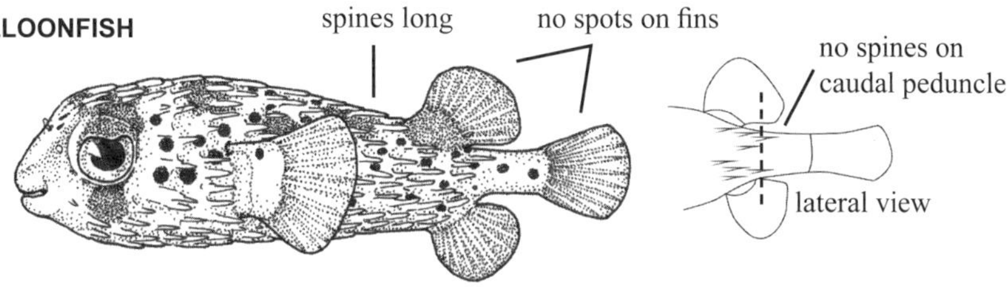


12b One or more spine(s) (including base of spine) on caudal peduncle; no dark bars on body; spots on fins….. 13

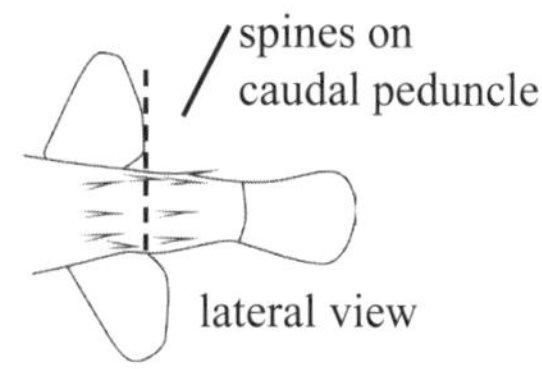


13a Small spots on body, including many on anal fin; lower margin of eye above mouth; dorsal and anal fins rounded:

**PORCUPINEFISH**

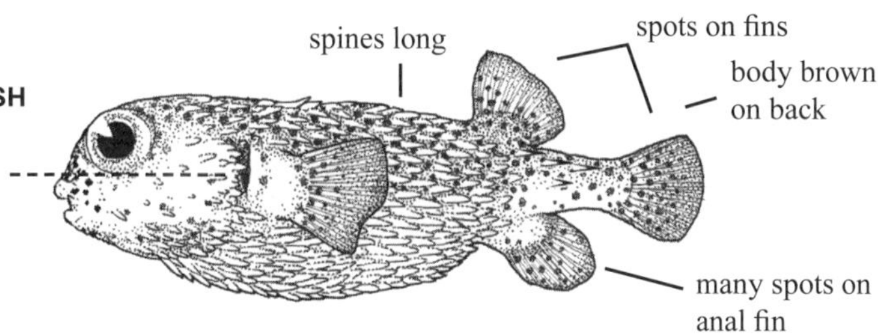


13b Elongate spots or blotches on body with few to none on anal fin; lower margin of eye equal to mouth; dorsal and anal fins pointed:

**PELAGIC PORCUPINEFISH**

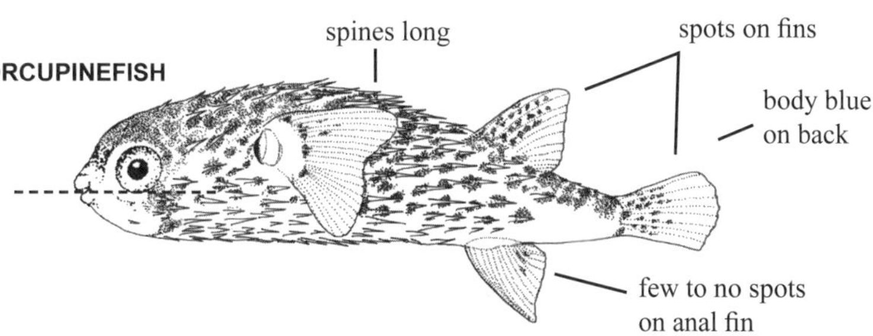

# REFERENCES

Allen, G. R. 1991. Damselfishes of the world. Mergus Press, Melle, Germany.

Allen, L. G., D. J. Pondella II, and M. H. Horn (eds.). 2006. The ecology of marine fishes: California and adjacent waters. University of California Press, Berkeley.

Allen, M. J. and A. K. Groce. 2001. First occurrence of blackspot wrasse, *Decodon melasma* Goman 1974 (Pisces: Labridae) in California. Bulletin of the Southern California Academy of Sciences 100:131–136.

Anderson, M. E. 1994. Systematics and osteology of the Zoarcidae (Teleostei: Perciformes). J. L. B. Smith Institute of Ichthyology, Ichthyological Bulletin 60:1–120.

Anderson, M. E. 1995. The eelpout genera *Lycenchelys* Gill and *Taranetzella* Andriashev (Teleostei: Zoarcidae) in the eastern Pacific, with descriptions of nine new species. Proceedings of the California Academy of Sciences 49:55–113.

Anderson, M. E., G. M. Cailliet, and B. S. Antrim. 1979. Note on some uncommon deep-sea fishes from the Monterey Bay area, California. California Fish and Game 65:256–264.

Anderson, M. E., D. E. Stevenson, and G. Shinohara. 2009. Systematic review of the genus *Bothrocara* Bean 1890 (Teleostei: Zoarcidae). Ichthyological Research 56:172–194.

Badcock, J. and R. C. Baird. 1980. Remarks on systematics, development, and distribution of the hatchetfish genus *Sternoptyx* (Pisces, Stomiatoidei). Fishery Bulletin 77:803–820.

Baird, R. C. 1971. The systematics, distribution, and zoogeography of the marine hatchetfishes (family Sternoptychidae). Bulletin of Museum of Comparative Zoology 142:1–128.

Baliga, V. B. and C. J. Law. 2016. Cleaners among wrasses: phylogenetics and evolutionary patterns of cleaning behavior within Labridae. Molecular Phylogenetics and Evolution 94:424–435.

Barnhart, P. S. 1936. Marine fishes of Southern California. University of California Press, Berkeley.

Barsukov, V. V. 1964. Key to the fishes of the family Scorpaenidae. Soviet Fisheries Investigation in the Northeast Pacific 53:226–262.

Berg, L. S. 1940. Classification of fishes, both recent and fossil. Russian and English texts. Trudy Zoologicheskogo Instituta AN SSSR 5:87–517.

Bolin, R. L. 1944. A review of the marine cottid fishes of California. Stanford Ichthyological Bulletin 3:1–135.

Bolin, R. L. 1950. Remarks on cottid fishes occasioned by the capture of two species new to California. Copeia 1950:195–202.

Boschung, H. T. and R. L. Mayden. 2004. Fishes of Alabama. Smithsonian Books, Washington, D. C.

Briggs, J. C. 2002. New species of *Rimicola* from California. Copeia 2002:441–444.

Britzke, R., N. A. Menezes, and M. Nirchio. 2019. Redescription of *Mugil setosus* Gilbert 1892 with comments on the occurrence of *Mugil curema* Valenciennes 1836 in the Pacific Ocean (Teleostei: Perciformes: Mugilidae). Zootaxa 4671: 396-406.

Burge, R. T. and S. A. Schultz. 1973. The marine environment in the vicinity of Diablo Cove with special reference to abalones and bony fishes. California Department of Fish and Game Marine Resources Technical Report 19.

Burhanuddin, A. I. and N. V. Parin. 2008. Redescription of the trichiurid fish, *Trichiurus nitens* Garman, 1899, being a valid of species distinct from *T. lepturus* Linnaeus, 1758 (Perciformes: Trichiuridae). Journal of Ichthyology 48:825–830.

Busby, M. S. and J. W. Orr. 1999. A pelagic basslet *Howella sherborni* (Family Acropomatidae) off the Aleutian Islands. Alaska Fishery Research Bulletin 6:49–53.

Butler, J. L. 1979. The nomeid genus *Cubiceps* (Pisces) with a description of a new species. Bulletin of Marine Science 29:226–241.

Butler, J. L., M. S. Love, and T. E. Laidig. 2012. A guide to the rockfishes, thornyheads, and scorpionfishes of the Northeast Pacific. University of California Press, Berkeley.

Chabot, C. L. and L. G. Allen. 2009. Global population structure of the tope (*Galeorhinus galeus*) inferred by mitochondrial control region sequence data. Molecular Ecology 18:545–552.

Chen, L.-C. 1971. Systematics, variation, distribution, and biology of rockfishes of the subgenus *Sebastomus* (Pisces, Scorpaenidae, *Sebastes*). Bulletin of the Scripps Institution of Oceanography 18:1–115.

Clemens, W. A. and G. V. Wilby. 1961. Fishes of the Pacific Coast of Canada. 2nd Edition. Bulletin of the Fisheries Research Board of Canada, Number 68.

Cohen, D. M. 1964. Suborder Argentinoidea, p. 1–70. *In* H. B. Bigelow et al. (eds.). Fishes of the Western North Atlantic. Memoir Sears Foundation for Marine Research, Number 1, Part 4.

# REFERENCES (continued)

Collette, B. B. and C. B. Nauen. 1983. Scombrids of the world. An annotated and illustrated catalogue of tunas, mackerels, bonitos, and related species known to date. FAO Fisheries Synopsis Number 125, Volume 2.

Craig, M. T. and P. A. Hastings. 2007. A molecular phylogeny of the groupers of the subfamily Epinephelinae (Serranidae) with a revised classification of the Epinephelinii. Ichthyological Research 54:1–17.

Craig, M. T., P. A. Hastings, and D. J. Pondella II. 2004. Notes on the systematics of the crestfish genus *Lophotus* (Lampridiformes: Lophotidae), with a new record from California. Bulletin of the Southern California Academy of Sciences 103:57–65.

DeMartini, E. E. 1985. Social behavior and coloration changes in painted greenling, *Oxylebius pictus* (Pisces: Hexagrammidae). Copeia 1985:966–975.

DeMartini, E. E. 1986. Reproductive colorations, paternal behavior and egg masses of kelp greenling, *Hexagrammos decagrammus*, and whitespotted greenling, *H. stelleri*. Northwest Science 60:32–35.

Ebert, D. A. 2003. Sharks, rays, and chimaeras of California. University of California Press, Berkeley.

Ebert, D. A., S. Fowler, and L. Compagno. 2013. Sharks of the world. Wild Nature Press, Plymouth, England.

Eschmeyer, W. N. (ed.). 1998. Catalog of fishes. Spec. Publ. No. 1, Center for Biodiversity Research and Information. California Academy of Sciences, San Francisco. Volumes 1 and 2.

Eschmeyer, W. N. and E. S. Herald. 1983. A field guide to Pacific Coast fishes of North America from the Gulf of Alaska to Baja California. Houghton Mifflin, Boston, Massachusetts.

Fischer, W., F. Krupp, W. Schneider, C. Sommer, K. E. Carpenter, and V. H. Niem (eds.). 1995. Guía FAO para la identificación de especies para los fines de la pesca. Pacífico centro-oriental. Vertebrados. Volume II:647–1200, Volume III:1201–1813. FAO, Rome.

Fitch, J. E. and S. A. Schultz. 1978. Some rare and unusual occurrences of fishes off California and Baja California. California Fish and Game 64:74–92.

Follett, W. I. and M. E. Anderson. 1990. *Esselinia*, a new genus of prickleback (Teleostei: Stichaeidae), with two new species from California and Baja California Norte. Copeia 1990:147–163.

Fritsche, R. 1980. Revision of the eastern Pacific Syngnathidae (Pisces: Syngnathiformes), including both recent and fossil forms. Proceedings of the California Academy of Sciences 42:181–227.

Garrett, D. L. 2005. A new intergeneric hybrid flatfish (Pleuronectiformes: Pleuronectidae) from Puget Sound and adjacent waters. Copeia 2005:673–677.

Garrett, D. L. and T. W. Pietsch. 2007. The hybrid sole *Inopsetta ischyra* (Teleostei: Pleuronectiformes: Pleuronectidae): hybrid or biological species? Transactions of the American Fisheries Society 136:460–468.

Grey, M. 1964. Family Gonostomatidae, p. 78–240. *In* H. B. Bigelow et al. (eds.). Fishes of the Western North Atlantic. Memoir Sears Foundation for Marine Research, Number 1, Part 4.

Hart, J. L. 1973. Pacific fishes of Canada. Fisheries Research Board of Canada, Bulletin 180.

Hastings, P. A. and H. J. Walker Jr. 2003. *Lumpenopsis clitella*: a new species of prickleback (Teleostei: Stichaeidae) from southern California, with comments on *Lumpenopsis* Soldatov. Copeia 2003:803–809.

Hatooka, K. 2002. Bramidae, p. 1–4. *In* T. Nakabo (ed.). Fishes of Japan. Tokai University Press, Tokyo, Japan.

Hedgpeth, J. W. 1957. Classification of marine environments, p. 17–28. *In* Treatise on marine ecology and paleoecology, Volume 1. Geological Society of America, Memoirs 67.

Heemstra, P. C. and J. E. Randall. 1993. Groupers of the world (family Serranidae, subfamily Epinephelinae). An annotated and illustrated catalogue of the grouper, rockcod, hind coral grouper and lyretail species known to date. FAO Species Catalogue. Fishery Synopsis 125(16).

Hyde, J. R., C. A. Kimbrell, J. E. Budrick, E. A. Lynn, and R. D. Vetter. 2008. Cryptic speciation in the vermilion rockfish (*Sebastes miniatus*) and the role of bathymetry in the speciation process. Molecular Ecology 17:1122–1136.

Ichthyoplankton Information System. http://access.afsc.noaa.gov/ichthyo/

Iwamoto, T. 1979. Eastern Pacific macrourine grenadiers with seven branchiostegal rays (Pisces: Macrouridae). Proceedings of the California Academy of Sciences 43:135–179.

Iwamoto, T. and D. L. Stein. 1974. A systematic review of the rattail fishes (Macrouridae: Gadiformes) from Oregon and adjacent waters. Occasional Papers of the California Academy of Sciences 111:1–79.

Jordan, D. S. and B. W. Evermann. 1896–1900. The fishes of North and Middle America. United States National Museum Bulletin Number 47, Volumes 1–4.

# REFERENCES (continued)


Kamikawa, D. J. 2017. Survey fishes: an illustrated list of the fishes captured during the Northwest Fisheries Science Center's fishery resource analysis and monitoring division's West Coast surveys. NOAA Technical Memorandum NMFS-NWFSC-138.

Kells, V., L. A. Rocha, and L. G. Allen. 2016. A field guide to coastal fishes from Alaska to California. John Hopkins University Press, Baltimore, Maryland.

Kline, D. E., N. E. Donlou, R. N. Lea, J. B. Lindholm, and G. G. Shester. 2013. Records of the longfin gunnel, *Pholis clemensi*, from California with a southern range extension to Point Lobos, California. Marine Biodiversity Records 6:1–4.

Knope, M. L. 2012. Phylogenetics of the marine sculpins (Teleostei: Cottidae) of the North American Pacific Coast. Molecular Phylogenetics and Evolution 66:341–349.

Knudsen, S. W. and K. D. Clements. 2013. Revision of the fish family Kyphosidae (Teleostei: Perciformes). Zootaxa 3751:1–101.

Kotlyar, A. N. 2009. Revision of the genus *Poromitra* (Melamphaidae): Part 4. Species of *P. cristiceps* Group: *P. atlantica*, *P. oscitans*, and *P. agofonovae* Kotlyar, species nova. Journal of Ichthyology 49:563–574.

Lamb, A. and P. Edgell. 2010. Coastal fishes of the Pacific Northwest. Harbour Publishing, Madeira Park, British Columbia.

Laroche, W. 1987. Guide to larval and juvenile rockfishes (*Sebastes*) of North America. Unpublished Manuscript.

Last, P., W. T. White, M. R. De Carvalho, B. Séret, M. F. W. Stehmann, and G. J. P. Naylor (eds.). 2016. Rays of the world. CSIRO Publishing, Australia.

Lea, R. N. 1988. Family Himantolophidae added to the ichthyofauna of the temperate Eastern North Pacific. California Fish Game 74:180–182.

Lea, R. N. and R. H. Rosenblatt. 2000. Observations on fishes associated with the 1997–98 El Niño off California. CalCOFI Rep. 41:117–129.

Leet, W. S. 2001. California's living marine resources: a status report. University of California, Division of Agriculture and Natural Resources.

Leis, J. M. 2001. Diodontidae. Porcupine fishes (burrfishes), p. 3958–3965. *In* K. E. Carpenter and V. Niem (eds.). FAO species identification guide for fishery purposes. The living marine resources of the Western Central Pacific. Vol. 6. Bony fishes part 4 (Labridae to Latimeriidae), estuarine crocodiles. FAO, Rome.

Lissner, A. L. and J. H. Dorsey. 1986. Deep-water biological assemblages of a hard-bottom bank-ridge complex of the southern California continental borderland. Bulletin of the Southern California Academy of Science 85:87–101.

Longo, G. and G. Bernardi. 2015. The evolutionary history of the embiotocid surfperch radiation based on genome-wide RAD sequence data. Molecular Phylogenetics and Evolution 88:55–63.

Longo, G. C., G. Bernardi, and R. N. Lea. 2018. Taxonomic revisions within Embiotocidae (Teleostei, Perciformes) based on molecular phylogenetics. Zootaxa 4482:591–596.

Love, M. 2012. Certainly more than you want to know about the fishes of the Pacific Coast. Really Big Press, Santa Barbara, California.

Love, M. S., M. Yoklavich, and L. Thorsteinson. 2002. The rockfishes of the Northeast Pacific. University of California Press, Berkeley.

MacGinitie, G. E. 1947. Notes on the devilfish, *Mobula lucasana*, and its parasites. Copeia 1947:276–278.

Martinez-Takeshita, N., C. M. Purcell, C. L. Chabot, M. T. Craig, C. N. Paterson, J. R. Hyde, and L. G. Allen. 2015. A tale of three tails: cryptic speciation in a globally distributed marine fish of the genus *Seriola*. Copeia 103:357–369.

Matarese, A. C., A. W. Kendall Jr., D. M. Blood, and B. M. Vinter. 1989. Laboratory guide to the early life history stages of northeast Pacific fishes. U. S. Department of Commerce, NOAA Technical Report MFS 80.

Matsuura, K. 2001. Balistidae. Triggerfishes, p. 3911–3928. *In* K. E. Carpenter and V. Niem (eds.) FAO species identification guide for fishery purposes. The living marine resources of the Western Central Pacific. Vol. 6. Bony fishes part 4 (Labridae to Latimeriidae), estuarine crocodiles. FAO, Rome.

Maul, G. E. 1948. Monografia dos peixes do Museu Municipal do Funchal. Ordem Isospondyli. Boletim do Museu Municipal do Funchal 3:5–41.

McCosker, J. A., S. Anderson, J. Richards, and M. Love. 2004. First record of the cape cigarfish, *Cubiceps capensis* (Family Nomeidae) from California waters. California Fish and Game 90:157–159.

## REFERENCES (continued)

Mecklenburg, C. W. and W. N. Eschmeyer. 2003. Family Hexagrammidae Gill 1889 — greenlings. California Academy of Sciences Annotated Checklists of Fishes 3.

Mecklenburg, C. W., T. A. Mecklenburg, and L. K. Thorsteinson. 2002. Fishes of Alaska. American Fisheries Society, Bethesda, Maryland.

Menezes, N. A., M. Nirchio, C. D. Oliveira, and R. Siccha-Ramirez. 2015. Taxonomic review of the species of *Mugil* (Teleostei: Perciformes: Mugilidae) from the Atlantic South Caribbean and South America, with integration of morphological, cytogenetic and molecular data. Zootaxa 3918: 1-38.

Miller, D. J and D. Gotshall. 1965. Ocean sportfish catch and effort from Oregon to Point Arguello, California July 1, 1957 – June 30, 1961. California Department of Fish and Game, Fish Bulletin 130.

Miller, D. J and R. N. Lea. 1972. Guide to the coastal marine fishes of California. California Department of Fish and Game, Fish Bulletin 157.

Moore, R. H. 1991. First record of the leather bass (*Epinephelus dermatolepis* Boulenger) in southern California. California Fish and Game 77:145–147.

Morrow, J. E. Jr. 1964. General discussion and key to families, p. 71–76. *In* H. B. Bigelow and W. C. Schroeder (eds.). Fishes of the Western North Atlantic. Sears Foundation for Marine Research, New Haven.

Morrow, J. E. Jr. and R. H. Gibbs Jr. 1964. Family Melanostomiatidae, p. 351–522. *In* H. B. Bigelow and W. C. Schroeder (eds.). Fishes of the Western North Atlantic. Sears Foundation for Marine Research, New Haven.

Moser, H. G. (ed.). 1996. The early stages of fishes in the California Current region. California Cooperative Oceanic Fisheries Investigations Atlas 33.

Moser, H. G. and J. L. Butler. 1996. Microstomatidae: argentines and pencilfishes, p. 208–215. *In* H. G. Moser (ed.). The early stages of fishes in the California Current Region. California Cooperative Oceanic Fisheries Investigations Atlas 33.

Moyle, P. B. 2002. Inland fishes of California. Revised and expanded. University of California Press, Berkeley.

Nakabo, T. (ed.). 2002. Fishes of Japan with pictorial keys to the species, English Edition. Tokai University Press, Tokyo.

Nakamura, I. 1982. Lateral line of *Diplospinus multistriatus* (Teleostei: Gempylidae). Proceedings of the Biological Society of Washington 95:408-411.

Nakamura, I. 1985. Billfishes of the world. An annotated and illustrated catalogue of marlins, sailfishes, spearfishes and swordfishes known to date. FAO Fisheries Synopsis 125, Volume 5.

Nakamura, I. and N. V. Parin. 1993. Snake mackerels and cutlassfishes of the world (Families Gempylidae and Trichiuridae). An annotated and illustrated catalogue of the snake mackerels, snoeks, escolars, gemfishes, sackfishes, domine, oilfish, cutlassfishes, scabbardfishes, hairtails and frostfishes known to date. FAO Fisheries Synopsis 125, Volume 15.

Naylor, G. J. P., J. N. Caira, K. Jensen, K. A. M. Rosana, W. T. White, and P. R. Last. 2012. A DNA sequence-based approach to the identification of shark and ray species and its implications for global elasmobranch diversity and parasitology. Bulletin of the American Museum of Natural History 367:1–262.

Nelson, J. S. 2006. Fishes of the world. 4th Edition. John Wiley and Sons, Hoboken, New Jersey.

Nelson, J. S., T. C. Grande, and M. V. H. Wilson. 2016. Fishes of the world. 5th Edition. John Wiley and Sons, Hoboken, New Jersey.

Nielsen, J. G. and D. G. Smith. 1978. The eel family Nemichthyidae (Pisces, Anguilliformes). Dana-Reports Carlsberg Foundation 88.

Nielsen, J. G., D. M. Cohen, D. F. Markle, and C. R. Robins. 1999. Ophidiiform fishes of the world (Order Ophidiiformes). An annotated and illustrated catalogue of pearlfishes, cusk-eels, brotulas and other ophidiiform fishes known to date. FAO Fisheries Synopsis 125, Volume 18.

Nyegaard, M., E. Sawai, N. Gemmell, J. Gillum, N. R. Loneragan, Y. Yamanoue, and A. L. Stewart. 2018. Hiding in broad daylight: molecular and morphological data reveal a new ocean sunfish species (Tetraodontiformes: Molidae) that has eluded recognition. Zoological Journal of the Linnean Society 182:631–658.

Page, L. M., H. Espinosa-Pérez, L. T. Findley, C. R. Gilbert, R. N. Lea, N. E. Mandrak, R. L. Mayden, and J. S. Nelson. 2013. Common and scientific names of fishes from the United States, Canada, and Mexico. 7th Edition. American Fisheries Society, Special Publications 34, Bethesda, Maryland.

## REFERENCES (continued)


Parin, N. V. 1983. *Aphanopus mikhailini* sp. n. and *A. intermedius* sp. n. (Trichiuridae, Perciformes) two new scabbardfishes from the temperate waters of the Southern Hemisphere and the tropical Atlantic. Voprosy Ikhtiologii 23:355–365. [In Russian].

Partridge, J. C., R. H. Douglas, N. J. Marshall, W.-S. Chung, T. M. Jordan, and H. J. Wagner. 2014. Reflecting optics in the diverticular eye of a deep-sea barreleye fish (*Rhynchohyalus natalensis*). Proceedings of the Royal Society B 281:2013–3223.

Peden, A. E. 1966. Reexamination of two species in the stichaeid genus, *Anoplarchus*. Copeia 1966:340–345.

Peden, A. E. 1978. A systematic revision of the hemilepidotine fishes (Cottidae). Syesis 11:11–49.

Peden, A. E. and M. E. Anderson. 1978. A systematic review of the fish genus *Lycodapus* (Zoarcidae) with descriptions of two new species. Canadian Journal of Zoology 56:1925–1961.

Peden, A. E. and G. W. Hughes. 1984. Distribution, morphological variation, and systematic relationship of *Pholis laeta* and *P. ornata* (Pisces: Pholididae) with a description of the related form *P. nea* n. sp. Canadian Journal of Zoology 62:291–305.

Phillips, J. B. 1957. A review of the rockfishes of California. California Department of Fish and Game, Fish Bulletin 104.

Pietsch, T. W. 1986. Systematics and distribution of bathypelagic anglerfishes of the family Ceratiidae (Order: Lophiiformes). Copeia 1986:479–493.

Pietsch, T. W. 2009. Oceanic anglerfishes. University of California Press, Berkeley.

Pondella, D. J. II. 1999. First record of deepwater bass, *Serranus aequidens* (Serranidae), from California. California Fish and Game 85:130–134.

Pondella, D. J. II. 2001. The phylogeny of *Paralabrax* Girard (Perciformes: Serranidae). PhD Dissertation. University of California, Los Angeles.

Prokofiev, A. M. 2007. Osteology and some other morphological characters of *Howella sherborni*, with a discussion of the systematic position of the genus (Perciformes, Percoidei). Journal of Ichthyology 47:413–426.

Reyes-Bonilla, H., A. Ayala-Bocos, S. González-Romero, I. Sánchez-Alcántara, M. W. Mendoza, Y. R. Bedolla-Guzmán, A. Ramirez-Valdez, L. E. Calderon-Aguilera, and N. C. Olivares-Bañuelos. 2010. Checklist and biogeography of fishes from Guadalupe Island, western Mexico. California Cooperative Oceanic Fisheries Investigations Reports 51:195–209.

Roberts, T. R. 2012. Systematics, biology and distribution of the species of the oceanic oarfish genus *Regalecus* (Teleostei, Lampridiformes, Regalecidae). Memoirs Museum National Histoire Naturelle 202:1–266.i

Robison, B. H. and K. R. Reisenbichler. 2008. *Macropinna microstoma* and the paradox of its tubular eyes. Copeia 2008:780–784.

Roedel, P. M. 1953. Common ocean fishes of the California coast. California Department of Fish and Game, Fish Bulletin Number 91.

Rosenblatt, R. H. 1964. A new gunnel, *Pholis clemensi*, from the coast of western North America. Journal of the Fisheries Research Board of Canada 21:933–939.

Rosenblatt, R. H. and L.-C. Chen. 1972. The identity of *Sebastes babcocki* and *Sebastes rubrivinctus*. California Fish and Game 58:32–36.

Rosenblatt, R. H. and G. D. Johnson. 1974. Two new species of sea basses of the genus *Diplectrum*, with a key to the Pacific species. California Fish and Game 60:178–191.

Rosenblatt, R. H. and W. L. Smith. 2004. *Icelinus limbaughi*: a new species of sculpin (Teleostei: Cottidae) from southern California. Copeia 2004:556–561.

Sakamoto, A. and K. Sakamoto. 1989. Reexamination of the status of the striped goby. Japanese Journal of Icthyology 36:100–112.

Santini, F., L. Sorenson, and M. E. Alfaro. 2016. Phylogeny and biogeography of hogfishes and allies (*Bodianus*, Labridae). Molecular Phylogenetics and Evolution 99:1–6.

Sawai, E., Y. Yamanoue, M. Nyegaard, and Y. Sakai. 2018. Rediscription of the bump-head sunfish *Mola alexandrini* (Ranzani 1839), senior synonym of *Mola ramsayi* (Giglioli 1883), with designation of a neotype for *Mola mola* (Linnaeus 1758) (Tetraodontiformers: Molidae). Ichthyological Research 65:142–160.

## REFERENCES (continued)

Schaefer, K. M. 1999. Comparative study of some morphological features of yellowfin (*Thunnus albacares*) and bigeye (*Thunnus obesus*) tunas. Inter-American Tropical Tuna Comission 21:491–525.

Schultz, L. P. 1936. Keys to the fishes of Washington, Oregon and closely adjoining regions. University of Washington Publication in Biology 2:103–228.

Sheiko, B. A. 1993. A catalogue of fishes of the family Agonidae sensu lato (Scorpaeniformes: Cottoidei). Proceedings of the Zoological Institute of the Academy of Sciences USSR 235:65–95 [In Russian].

Sheiko, B. A. and C. W. Mecklenburg. 2004. Family Agonidae Swainson 1839-poachers. California Academy of Sciences Annotated Checklists of Fishes No. 30.

Smith, W. L. and M. S. Busby. 2014. Phylogeny and taxonomy of sculpins, sandfishes, and snailfishes (Perciformes: Cottoidei) with comments on the phylogenetic significance of their early-life-history specializations. Molecular Phylogenetics and Evolution 79:332–352.

Smith, W. L. and M. T. Craig. 2007. Casting the percomorph net widely: the importance of broad taxonomic sampling in the search for the placement of serranid and percid fishes. Copeia 2007:35–55.

Smith, W. L., E. Everman, and C. Richardson. 2018. Phylogeny and taxonomy of flatheads, scorpionfishes, sea robins, and stonefishes (Percomorpha: Scorpaeniformes) and the evolution of the lachrymal saber. Copeia 106:94–119.

Snytko, V. A. 1986. New distribution records of rockfishes of the subfamily Sebastinae in the northern Pacific Ocean. Journal of Ichthyology 26:124–130.

Stein, D. L. 1978. A review of the deepwater Liparidae (Pisces) from the coast of Oregon and adjacent waters. Occasional Papers of the California Academy of Sciences 127:1–55.

Stephens, J. S. Jr., M. Singer, and L. Targgart. 1989. Notes on the first record of the orangethroat pikeblenny, *Chaenopsis alepidota* (Gilbert), in mainland California. California Fish and Game 75:180–183.

Swift, C. C., S. Howard, J. Mulder, and T. P. Keegan. 2014. Expansion of the non-native Mississippi silverside, *Menidia audens* (Pisces, Atherinopsidae), into fresh and marine waters of coastal southern California. Bulletin of the Southern California Academy of Sciences 113:153–164.

Swift, C. C., B. Spies, R. A. Ellingson, and D. K. Jacobs. 2016. A new species of the bay goby genus *Eucyclogobius*, endemic to southern California: evolution, conservation, and decline. PLoS ONE 11:1–33.

Thacker, C. E. 2009. Phylogeny of Gobioidei and placement within Acanthomorpha, with a new classification and investigation of diversification and character evolution. Copeia 2009:93–104.

Thompson, D. A., L. T. Findley, and A. N. Kerstitch. 2000. Reef fishes of the Sea of Cortez. Revised Edition. University of Texas Press, Austin.

Underkoffler, K. E., M. A. Luers, J. R. Hyde, and M. T. Craig. 2018. A taxonomic review of *Lampris guttatus* (Brünnich 1788) (Lampridiformes; Lampridae) with descriptions of three new species. Zootaxa 4413:551–565.

Walford, L. A. 1937. Marine game fishes of the Pacific coast from Alaska to the equator. University of California Press, Berkeley.

Walker, H. J. Jr., P. A. Hastings, and R. H. Steele. 2002. The Pacific golden-eyed tilefish, *Caulolatilus affinis* Gill (Teleostei:Malacanthidae), first occurrence in California. California Fish and Game 88:139–141.

Wang, J. C. S. 2010. Fishes of the Sacramento-San Joaquin River Delta and adjacent waters, California: a guide to early life histories. Tracy Fish Facility Studies California, Volume 44—Special Publication.

Whitehead, P. J. P., G. J. Nelson, and T. Wongratana. 1988. Clupeoid fishes of the world (suborder Clupeoidei). An annotated and illustrated catalogue of the herrings, sardines, pilchards, sprats, shads, anchovies and wolf-herrings. Part 2 – Engraulididae. FAO Fisheries Synopsis 125, Volume 7.

Wilimovsky, N. J. 1958. Provisional keys to the fishes of Alaska. United States Fish and Wildlife Service, Juneau Fisheries Research Laboratory (mimeographed copy).

Wisner, R. L. 1974. The taxonomy and distribution of lanternfishes (Family Myctophidae) of the eastern Pacific Ocean. NORDA Report-3.

Wisner, R. L. and C. B. McMillan. 1990. Three new species of hagfishes, genus *Eptatretus* (Cyclostomata, Myxinidae), from the Pacific Coast of North America, with new data on *E. deani* and *E. stoutii*. Fishery Bulletin 88:787–804.

# DRAWING CITATIONS

Composite drawings and key to the families drawings from Leonardo Alannis, Roberta Bloom, Laurel Mundy, Miller and Lea (1972), Iwamoto (1979), after Nakabo (2002), and Ebert (2003).

## SPECIES PRESENTATION

All drawings sourced from Miller and Lea (1972) except the following:

| SCIENTIFIC NAME | COMMON NAME | DRAWING | ILLUSTRATOR |
|---|---|---|---|
| *Abudefduf troschelii* | Panamic Sergeant Major | adult | after Laurel Mundy |
| *Acanthocybium solandri* | Wahoo | adult | Laurel Mundy |
| *Acanthogobius flavimanus* | Yellowfin Goby | adult | after Alan Marciochi |
| *Acanthurus xanthopterus* | Yellowfin Surgeonfish | adult | Leonardo Alannis |
| *Achirus mazatlanus* | Pacific Lined Sole | adult | after Fischer et al. (1995) |
| *Acipenser medirostris* | Green Sturgeon | adult | Leonardo Alannis |
| *Acipenser transmontanus* | White Sturgeon | adult | Leonardo Alannis |
| *Agonomalus mozinoi* | Kelp Poacher | adult | Laurel Mundy |
| *Agonopsis sterletus* | Southern Spearnose Poacher | adult | after Atsuhiro Kubo |
| *Agonopsis sterletus* | Southern Spearnose Poacher | head | after Atsuhiro Kubo |
| *Agonopsis vulsa* | Northern Spearnose Poacher | adult | Atsuhiro Kubo |
| *Albula gilberti* | Cortez Bonefish | adult | after Laurel Mundy |
| *Albula gilberti* | Cortez Bonefish | juvenile | after Atsuhiro Kubo |
| *Albula gilberti* | Cortez Bonefish | larvae | Atsuhiro Kubo |
| *Alepisaurus ferox* | Longnose Lancetfish | adult | Laurel Mundy |
| *Alepocephalus tenebrosus* | California Slickhead | adult | Leonardo Alannis |
| *Allosmerus elongatus* | Whitebait Smelt | adult | Leonardo Alannis |
| *Allothunnus fallai* | Slender Tuna | adult | Leonardo Alannis |
| *Alopias pelagicus* | Pelagic Thresher | adult | Laurel Mundy |
| *Alopias pelagicus* | Pelagic Thresher | teeth | Ebert et al. (2013) |
| *Alopias superciliosus* | Bigeye Thresher | adult | Laurel Mundy |
| *Alopias superciliosus* | Bigeye Thresher | head, dorsal | after Ebert et al. (2013) |
| *Alopias superciliosus* | Bigeye Thresher | teeth | Ebert et al. (2013) |
| *Alopias vulpinus* | Common Thresher Shark | adult | Atsuhiro Kubo |
| *Alopias vulpinus* | Common Thresher Shark | teeth | Ebert et al. (2013) |
| *Alopias vulpinus* | Common Thresher Shark | head, dorsal | Leonardo Alannis |
| *Alopias vulpinus* | Common Thresher Shark | head, ventral | Leonardo Alannis |
| *Alosa sapidissima* | American Shad | adult | Leonardo Alannis |
| *Ammodytes personatus* | Pacific Sand Lance | adult | Laurel Mundy |
| *Amphistichus argenteus* | Barred Surfperch | adult | Leonardo Alannis |
| *Amphistichus koelzi* | Calico Surfperch | adult | Leonardo Alannis |
| *Amphistichus rhodoterus* | Redtail Surfperch | adult | Leonardo Alannis |
| *Anarrhichthys ocellatus* | Wolf-eel | adult | after Laurel Mundy |
| *Anchoa compressa* | Deepbody Anchovy | adult | Fischer et al. (1995) |
| *Anchoa delicatissima* | Slough Anchovy | adult | Fischer et al. (1995) |
| *Anisotremus davidsonii* | Sargo | juvenile | after Laurel Mundy |

# DRAWING CITATIONS

## SPECIES PRESENTATION (continued)

| SCIENTIFIC NAME | COMMON NAME | DRAWING | ILLUSTRATOR |
|---|---|---|---|
| *Anoplagonus inermis* | Smooth Alligatorfish | adult | Laurel Mundy |
| *Anoplarchus insignis* | Slender Cockscomb | adult | after Laurel Mundy |
| *Anoplarchus insignis* | Slender Cockscomb | head, ventral | after Peden (1966) |
| *Anoplarchus purpurescens* | High Cockscomb | adult | after Laurel Mundy |
| *Anoplarchus purpurescens* | High Cockscomb | head, ventral | after Peden (1966) |
| *Anoplogaster cornuta* | Longhorn Fangtooth | adult | Laurel Mundy |
| *Anotopterus nikparini* | North Pacific Daggertooth | adult | after Mecklenburg et al. (2002) |
| *Antimora microlepis* | Pacific Flatnose | adult | Leonardo Alannis |
| *Aphanopus arigato* | Pacific Black Scabbardfish | adult | Leonardo Alannis |
| *Aphanopus arigato* | Pacific Black Scabbardfish | head | after Nakamura & Parin (1993) |
| *Apodichthys flavidus* | Penpoint Gunnel | adult | Laurel Mundy |
| *Apodichthys fucorum* | Rockweed Gunnel | adult | Laurel Mundy |
| *Apogon atricaudus* | Plain Cardinalfish | adult | after Laurel Mundy |
| *Apogon guadalupensis* | Guadalupe Cardinalfish | adult | Laurel Mundy |
| *Apogon pacificus* | Pink Cardinalfish | adult | Laurel Mundy |
| *Apogon retrosella* | Barspot Cardinalfish | adult | Laurel Mundy |
| *Apristurus brunneus* | Brown Cat Shark | adult | Atsuhiro Kubo |
| *Apristurus brunneus* | Brown Cat Shark | head, ventral | Ebert et al. (2013) |
| *Apristurus kampae* | Longnose Cat Shark | adult | Leonardo Alannis |
| *Apristurus kampae* | Longnose Cat Shark | head, ventral | Ebert et al. (2013) |
| *Arctozenus risso* | Ribbon Barracudina | adult | after Laurel Mundy |
| *Argentina sialis* | Pacific Argentine | adult | Leonardo Alannis |
| *Argyropelecus hemigymnus* | Spurred Hatchetfish | adult | Laurel Mundy |
| *Argyropelecus lychnus* | Tropical Hatchetfish | tail | Leonardo Alannis |
| *Argyropelecus sladeni* | Lowcrest Hatchetfish | adult | after Laurel Mundy |
| *Aristostomias scintillans* | Shining Loosejaw | adult | Laurel Mundy |
| *Artedius corallinus* | Coralline Sculpin | adult | Bolin (1944) |
| *Artedius corallinus* | Coralline Sculpin | spine | Leonardo Alannis |
| *Artedius corallinus* | Coralline Sculpin | body, lateral | Leonardo Alannis |
| *Artedius corallinus* | Coralline Sculpin | scales | Leonardo Alannis |
| *Artedius fenestralis* | Padded Sculpin | adult | Bolin (1944) |
| *Artedius harringtoni* | Scalyhead Sculpin | adult | Bolin (1944) |
| *Artedius lateralis* | Smoothhead Sculpin | adult | Bolin (1944) |
| *Artedius lateralis* | Smoothhead Sculpin | body, lateral | Leonardo Alannis |
| *Artedius lateralis* | Smoothhead Sculpin | scales | Leonardo Alannis |
| *Artedius notospilotus* | Bonyhead Sculpin | adult | Bolin (1944) |
| *Ascelichthys rhodorus* | Rosylip Sculpin | adult | Bolin (1944) |
| *Asemichthys taylori* | Spinynose Sculpin | male | after Hart (1973) |
| *Assurger anzac* | Razorback Scabbardfish | adult | Nakamura & Parin (1993) |
| *Assurger anzac* | Razorback Scabbardfish | head | after Nakamura & Parin (1993) |

# DRAWING CITATIONS

## SPECIES PRESENTATION (continued)

| SCIENTIFIC NAME | COMMON NAME | DRAWING | ILLUSTRATOR |
|---|---|---|---|
| *Astroscopus zephyreus* | Pacific Stargazer | adult | Leonardo Alannis |
| *Atheresthes evermanni* | Kamchatka flounder | adult | Laurel Mundy |
| *Atheresthes evermanni* | Kamchatka Flounder | head, blind side | Leonardo Alannis |
| *Atheresthes stomias* | Arrowtooth Flounder | adult | after Laurel Mundy |
| *Atheresthes stomias* | Arrowtooth Flounder | head, blind side | Leonardo Alannis |
| *Atherinops affinis* | Topsmelt | adult | Atsuhiro Kubo |
| *Atherinops affinis* | Topsmelt | head | Atsuhiro Kubo |
| *Atherinopsis californiensis* | Jacksmelt | adult | Atsuhiro Kubo |
| *Atractoscion nobilis* | White Seabass | adult | Leonardo Alannis |
| *Atractoscion nobilis* | White Seabass | juvenile I | after Atsuhiro Kubo |
| *Atractoscion nobilis* | White Seabass | juvenile II | Atsuhiro Kubo |
| *Aulorhynchus flavidus* | Tubesnout | adult | Leonardo Alannis |
| *Auxis rochei* | Bullet Tuna | adult | Laurel Mundy |
| *Auxis rochei* | Bullet Tuna | juvenile | Laurel Mundy |
| *Auxis thazard* | Frigate Tuna | adult | Laurel Mundy |
| *Auxis thazard* | Frigate Tuna | juvenile | Laurel Mundy |
| *Avocettina bowersii* | Smalleye Snipe Eel | head, lateral | after Atsuhiro Kubo |
| *Avocettina infans* | Blackline Snipe Eel | adult | after Atsuhiro Kubo |
| *Avocettina infans* | Blackline Snipe Eel | head, male | after Nielsen & Smith (1978) |
| *Azurina hirundo* | Swallow Damselfish | adult | Laurel Mundy |
| *Bagre panamensis* | Chihuil | adult | Leonardo Alannis |
| *Bairdiella icistia* | Bairdiella | adult | Leonardo Alannis |
| *Bairdiella icistia* | Bairdiella | anal fin | Leonardo Alannis |
| *Barbourisia rufa* | Red Whalefish | adult | Laurel Mundy |
| *Bathophilus flemingi* | Highfin Dragonfish | adult | Leonardo Alannis |
| *Bathyagonus alascanus* | Gray Starsnout | adult | Laurel Mundy |
| *Bathyagonus alascanus* | Gray Starsnout | head, ventral | after Mecklenburg et al. (2002) |
| *Bathyagonus infraspinatus* | Spinycheek Starnout | adult | Laurel Mundy |
| *Bathyagonus nigripinnis* | Blackfin Poacher | adult | after Laurel Mundy |
| *Bathyagonus pentacanthus* | Bigeye Poacher | adult | after Atsuhiro Kubo |
| *Bathyagonus pentacanthus* | Bigeye Poacher | head, ventral | after Mecklenburg et al. (2002) |
| *Bathylagoides wesethi* | Snubnose Blacksmelt | adult | Leonardo Alannis |
| *Bathylagus pacificus* | Pacific Blacksmelt | adult | Leonardo Alannis |
| *Bathylychnops exilis* | Javelin Spookfish | adult | Leonardo Alannis |
| *Bathyraja abyssicola* | Deepsea Skate | adult | after Laurel Mundy |
| *Bathyraja aleutica* | Aleutian Skate | adult | after Laurel Mundy |
| *Bathyraja kincaidii* | Sandpaper Skate | adult | after Laurel Mundy |
| *Bathyraja spinosissima* | Pacific White Skate | adult | after Laurel Mundy |
| *Bathyraja trachura* | Roughtail Skate | adult | after Laurel Mundy |
| *Benthalbella dentata* | Northern Pearleye | adult | Leonardo Alannis |
| *Benthodesmus pacificus* | North Pacific Frostfish | adult | Nakamura & Parin (1993) |

# DRAWING CITATIONS
## SPECIES PRESENTATION (continued)

| SCIENTIFIC NAME | COMMON NAME | DRAWING | ILLUSTRATOR |
|---|---|---|---|
| *Beringraja binoculata* | Big Skate | adult | after Laurel Mundy |
| *Beringraja inornata* | California Skate | adult | after Laurel Mundy |
| *Beringraja inornata* | California Skate | ventral | Leonardo Alannis |
| *Beringraja rhina* | Longnose Skate | adult | after Laurel Mundy |
| *Beringraja stellulata* | Starry Skate | adult | after Laurel Mundy |
| *Blepsias cirrhosus* | Silverspotted Sculpin | adult | Bolin (1944) |
| *Bodianus pulcher* | California Sheephead | female | after Laurel Mundy |
| *Bodianus pulcher* | California Sheephead | male | after Fischer et al. (1995) |
| *Bodianus pulcher* | California Sheephead | juvenile | after Fischer et al. (1995) |
| *Bolinichthys longipes* | Popeye Lampfish | adult | Leonardo Alannis |
| *Bothragonus swanii* | Rockhead | adult | Laurel Mundy |
| *Bothrocara brunneum* | Twoline Eelpout | adult | Laurel Mundy |
| *Bothrocara molle* | Soft Eelpout | adult | Laurel Mundy |
| *Brachyistius frenatus* | Kelp Perch | adult | Leonardo Alannis |
| *Brama japonica* | Pacific Pomfret | adult | Leonardo Alannis |
| *Brama orcini* | Bigtooth Pomfret | adult | Laurel Mundy |
| *Brosmophycis marginata* | Red Brotula | adult | Leonardo Alannis |
| *Brotula clarkae* | Pacific Bearded Brotula | adult | Atsuhiro Kubo |
| *Caelorinchus scaphopsis* | Shoulderspot Grenadier | adult | Laurel Mundy |
| *Calamus brachysomus* | Pacific Porgy | adult | after Laurel Mundy |
| *Caranx caballus* | Green Jack | adult | Laurel Mundy |
| *Caranx caninus* | Pacific Crevalle Jack | adult | after Laurel Mundy |
| *Caranx sexfasciatus* | Bigeye Trevally | adult | after Laurel Mundy |
| *Caranx vinctus* | Cocinero | adult | Laurel Mundy |
| *Carcharhinus brachyurus* | Narrowtooth Shark | adult | Fischer et al. (1995) |
| *Carcharhinus brachyurus* | Narrowtooth Shark | head | Ebert et al. (2013) |
| *Carcharhinus brachyurus* | Narrowtooth Shark | teeth | Ebert et al. (2013) |
| *Carcharhinus leucas* | Bull Shark | adult | Atsuhiro Kubo |
| *Carcharhinus leucas* | Bull Shark | head | Ebert et al. (2013) |
| *Carcharhinus leucas* | Bull Shark | teeth | Ebert et al. (2013) |
| *Carcharhinus longimanus* | Oceanic Whitetip Shark | adult | Atsuhiro Kubo |
| *Carcharhinus longimanus* | Oceanic Whitetip Shark | interdorsal ridge | Leonardo Alannis |
| *Carcharhinus longimanus* | Oceanic Whitetip Shark | teeth | Ebert et al. (2013) |
| *Carcharhinus obscurus* | Dusky Shark | adult | Atsuhiro Kubo |
| *Carcharhinus obscurus* | Dusky Shark | teeth | Ebert et al. (2013) |
| *Carcharodon carcharias* | White Shark | adult | Atsuhiro Kubo |
| *Carcharodon carcharias* | White Shark | teeth | Ebert et al. (2013) |
| *Carcharodon carcharias* | White Shark | teeth, juvenile | Leonardo Alannis |
| *Careproctus colletti* | Alaska Snailfish | adult | Leonardo Alannis |
| *Careproctus cypselurus* | Falcate Snailfish | adult | Leonardo Alannis |
| *Careproctus gilberti* | Smalldisk Snailfish | adult | after Laurel Mundy |

# DRAWING CITATIONS

## SPECIES PRESENTATION (continued)

| SCIENTIFIC NAME | COMMON NAME | DRAWING | ILLUSTRATOR |
|---|---|---|---|
| *Careproctus melanurus* | Blacktail Snailfish | adult | Leonardo Alannis |
| *Caristius macropus* | Bigmouth Manefish | adult | Laurel Mundy |
| *Caristius macropus* | Bigmouth Manefish | head | Leonardo Alannis |
| *Cataetyx rubrirostris* | Rubynose Brotula | adult | after Atsuhiro Kubo |
| *Caulolatilus affinis* | Pacific Golden-Eyed Tilefish | adult | Leonardo Alannis |
| *Caulolatilus princeps* | Ocean Whitefish | adult | Leonardo Alannis |
| *Cebidichthys violaceus* | Monkeyface Prickleback | adult | Leonardo Alannis |
| *Centroscyllium nigrum* | Combtooth Dogfish | adult | Leonardo Alannis |
| *Cephalopholis colonus* | Pacific Creolefish | adult | Laurel Mundy |
| *Cephaloscyllium ventriosum* | Swell Shark | adult | Atsuhiro Kubo |
| *Ceratias holboelli* | Northern Seadevil | female | Leonardo Alannis |
| *Ceratias holboelli* | Northern Seadevil | male | after Moser (1996) |
| *Ceratoscopelus townsendi* | Dogtooth Lampfish | adult | Leonardo Alannis |
| *Ceratoscopelus townsendi* | Dogtooth Lampfish | head, dorsal | Leonardo Alannis |
| *Cetengraulis mysticetus* | Anchoveta | adult | Leonardo Alannis |
| *Cetengraulis mysticetus* | Anchoveta | gill membrane | Atsuhiro Kubo |
| *Cetorhinus maximus* | Basking Shark | adult | Fischer et al. (1995) |
| *Chaenopsis alepidota* | Orangethroat Pikeblenny | female | Laurel Mundy |
| *Chaetodipterus zonatus* | Pacific Spadefish | adult | Laurel Mundy |
| *Chaetodon humeralis* | Threebanded Butterflyfish | adult | after Laurel Mundy |
| *Chanos chanos* | Milkfish | adult | after Fischer et al. (1995) |
| *Chauliodus macouni* | Pacific Viperfish | adult | Leonardo Alannis |
| *Cheilopogon pinnatibarbatus* | Smallhead Flyingfish | pectoral fin | Leonardo Alannis |
| *Cheilotrema saturnum* | Black Croaker | adult | Leonardo Alannis |
| *Cheilotrema saturnum* | Black Croaker | juvenile | Leonardo Alannis |
| *Chesnonia verrucosa* | Warty Poacher | female | after Laurel Mundy |
| *Chilara taylori* | Spotted Cusk-Eel | adult | Atsuhiro Kubo |
| *Chilomycterus reticulatus* | Spotfin Burrfish | spine | Leonardo Alannis |
| *Chirolophis decoratus* | Decorated Warbonnet | adult | Laurel Mundy |
| *Chirolophis nugator* | Mosshead Warbonnet | adult | Laurel Mundy |
| *Chitonotus pugetensis* | Roughback Sculpin | male | Bolin (1944) |
| *Chitonotus pugetensis* | Roughback Sculpin | spine | Leonardo Alannis |
| *Chlamydoselachus anguineus* | Frill Shark | adult | Fischer et al. (1995) |
| *Chloroscombrus orqueta* | Pacific Bumper | adult | Laurel Mundy |
| *Chromis alta* | Silverstripe Chromis | adult | after Laurel Mundy |
| *Chromis alta* | Silverstripe Chromis | juvenile | Leonardo Alannis |
| *Chromis punctipinnis* | Blacksmith | adult | Leonardo Alannis |
| *Chromis punctipinnis* | Blacksmith | juvenile | Leonardo Alannis |
| *Citharichthys fragilis* | Gulf Sanddab | adult | Leonardo Alannis |
| *Citharichthys fragilis* | Gulf Sanddab | scales | Leonardo Alannis |
| *Citharichthys sordidus* | Pacific Sanddab | adult | Leonardo Alannis |

# DRAWING CITATIONS

## SPECIES PRESENTATION (continued)

| SCIENTIFIC NAME | COMMON NAME | DRAWING | ILLUSTRATOR |
|---|---|---|---|
| *Citharichthys stigmaeus* | Speckled Sanddab | adult | Leonardo Alannis |
| *Citharichthys stigmaeus* | Speckled Sanddab | scales | Leonardo Alannis |
| *Citharichthys stigmaeus* | Pacific Sanddab | scales | Leonardo Alannis |
| *Citharichthys xanthostigma* | Longfin Sanddab | adult | Leonardo Alannis |
| *Citharichthys xanthostigma* | Longfin Sanddab | scales | Leonardo Alannis |
| *Clevelandia ios* | Arrow Goby | adult | Leonardo Alannis |
| *Clidoderma asperrimum* | Roughscale Sole | adult | Laurel Mundy |
| *Clidoderma asperrimum* | Roughscale Sole | scales | Leonardo Alannis |
| *Clinocottus acuticeps* | Sharpnose Sculpin | male | Bolin (1944) |
| *Clinocottus analis* | Woolly Sculpin | male | Bolin (1944) |
| *Clinocottus embryum* | Calico Sculpin | female | Bolin (1944) |
| *Clinocottus globiceps* | Mosshead Sculpin | male | Bolin (1944) |
| *Clinocottus recalvus* | Bald Sculpin | male | Bolin (1944) |
| *Clupea pallasii* | Pacific Herring | adult | after Laurel Mundy |
| *Cololabis saira* | Pacific Saury | adult | Fischer et al. (1995) |
| *Conodon serrifer* | Armed Grunt | adult | after Fischer et al. (1995) |
| *Coryphaena hippurus* | Dolphinfish | male | Leonardo Alannis |
| *Coryphaena hippurus* | Dolphinfish | head, female | Leonardo Alannis |
| *Coryphaena hippurus* | Dolphinfish | juvenile | Laurel Mundy |
| *Coryphaenoides acrolepis* | Pacific Grenadier | adult | Laurel Mundy |
| *Coryphaenoides cinereus* | Popeye Grenadier | adult | Laurel Mundy |
| *Coryphaenoides filifer* | Threadfin Grenadier | adult | after Laurel Mundy |
| *Coryphaenoides leptolepis* | Ghostly Grenadier | adult | Laurel Mundy |
| *Coryphaenoides pectoralis* | Giant Grenadier | adult | Laurel Mundy |
| *Cosmocampus arctus* | Snubnose Pipefish | adult | after Atsuhiro Kubo |
| *Cottus aleuticus* | Coastrange Sculpin | adult | Chris Van Dyck |
| *Cottus asper* | Prickly Sculpin | adult | after Chris Van Dyck |
| *Cryptacanthodes aleutensis* | Dwarf Wrymouth | adult | Laurel Mundy |
| *Cryptacanthodes giganteus* | Giant Wrymouth | adult | Laurel Mundy |
| *Cryptopsaras couesii* | Triplewart Seadevil | female | Leonardo Alannis |
| *Cryptopsaras couesii* | Triplewart Seadevil | male | after Moser (1996) |
| *Cryptotrema corallinum* | Deepwater Blenny | adult | Laurel Mundy |
| *Ctenogobius sagittula* | Longtail Goby | female | Leonardo Alannis |
| *Ctenogobius sagittula* | Longtail Goby | tail, male | Leonardo Alannis |
| *Cubiceps paradoxus* | Longfin Cigarfish | adult | after Laurel Mundy |
| *Cyclothone pallida* | Tan Bristlemouth | adult | after Laurel Mundy |
| *Cymatogaster aggregata* | Shiner Perch | adult | Leonardo Alannis |
| *Cynoscion parvipinnis* | Shortfin Corvina | adult | Leonardo Alannis |
| *Cynoscion xanthulus* | Orangemouth Corvina | adult | Leonardo Alannis |
| *Danaphos oculatus* | Bottlelight | adult | Leonardo Alannis |
| *Decapterus muroadsi* | Amberstripe Scad | adult | Laurel Mundy |

# DRAWING CITATIONS
## SPECIES PRESENTATION (continued)

| SCIENTIFIC NAME | COMMON NAME | DRAWING | ILLUSTRATOR |
|---|---|---|---|
| *Decapterus muroadsi* | Amberstripe Scad | lateral line | Leonardo Alannis |
| *Decodon melasma* | Blackspot Wrasse | adult | after Atsuhiro Kubo |
| *Decodon melasma* | Blackspot Wrasse | juvenile | after Laurel Mundy |
| *Dermatolepis dermatolepis* | Leather Bass | adult | Fischer et al. (1995) |
| *Dermatolepis dermatolepis* | Leather Bass | juvenile | Fischer et al. (1995) |
| *Desmodema lorum* | Whiptail Ribbonfish | adult | Leonardo Alannis |
| *Diaphus theta* | California Headlightfish | adult | Leonardo Alannis |
| *Diodon eydouxii* | Pelagic Porcupinefish | adult | after Rick Feeney |
| *Diodon eydouxii* | Pelagic Porcupinefish | spines | Leonardo Alannis |
| *Diodon holocanthus* | Balloonfish | adult | after Laurel Mundy |
| *Diodon holocanthus* | Balloonfish | spine | Leonardo Alannis |
| *Diodon holocanthus* | Balloonfish | spines | Leonardo Alannis |
| *Diodon hystrix* | Porcupinefish | adult | after Laurel Mundy |
| *Diogenichthys atlanticus* | Longfin Lanternfish | adult | Leonardo Alannis |
| *Diplectrum maximum* | Greater Sand Perch | adult | Fischer et al. (1995) |
| *Diplectrum maximum* | Greater Sand Perch | operculum | Leonardo Alannis |
| *Diplospinus multistriatus* | Striped Escolar | adult | Atsuhiro Kubo |
| *Dolichopteryx longipes* | Brownsnout Spookfish | adult | after Laurel Mundy |
| *Dormitator latifrons* | Pacific Fat Sleeper | adult | Leonardo Alannis |
| *Dorosoma petenense* | Threadfin Shad | adult | Leonardo Alannis |
| *Echeneis naucrates* | Sharksucker | adult | Leonardo Alannis |
| *Echinorhinus cookei* | Prickly Shark | adult | Fischer et al. (1995) |
| *Elassodiscus caudatus* | Humpback Snailfish | adult | Leonardo Alannis |
| *Electrona risso* | Chubby Flashlightfish | adult | Leonardo Alannis |
| *Elops affinis* | Machete | adult | after Fischer et al. (1995) |
| *Embiotoca caryi* | Rainbow Seaperch | adult | Leonardo Alannis |
| *Embiotoca jacksoni* | Black Perch | adult | Leonardo Alannis |
| *Embiotoca lateralis* | Striped Seaperch | adult | Leonardo Alannis |
| *Engraulis mordax* | Northern Anchovy | adult | Fischer et al. (1995) |
| *Engraulis mordax* | Northern Anchovy | gill membrane | Leonardo Alannis |
| *Engyophrys sanctilaurentii* | Speckledtail Flounder | adult, eyed side | after Laurel Mundy |
| *Engyophrys sanctilaurentii* | Speckledtail Flounder | adult, blind side | Atsuhiro Kubo |
| *Enophrys bison* | Buffalo Sculpin | adult | after Bolin (1944) |
| *Enophrys taurina* | Bull Sculpin | adult | after Bolin (1944) |
| *Entosphenus tridentatus* | Pacific Lamprey | adult | Leonardo Alannis |
| *Entosphenus tridentatus* | Pacific Lamprey | mouth | Leonardo Alannis |
| *Eopsetta jordani* | Petrale Sole | adult | after Laurel Mundy |
| *Epinephelus analogus* | Spotted Cabrilla | adult | after Fischer et al. (1995) |
| *Epinephelus labriformis* | Flag Cabrilla | adult | Laurel Mundy |
| *Esselenichthys carli* | Threeline Prickleback | adult | Follett & Anderson (1990) |
| *Esselenichthys carli* | Threeline Prickleback | head, ventral | after Follett & Anderson (1990) |

# DRAWING CITATIONS

## SPECIES PRESENTATION (continued)

| SCIENTIFIC NAME | COMMON NAME | DRAWING | ILLUSTRATOR |
|---|---|---|---|
| *Esselenichthys laurae* | Twoline Prickleback | adult | Follett & Anderson (1990) |
| *Esselenichthys laurae* | Twoline Prickleback | head, ventral | after Follett & Anderson (1990) |
| *Etrumeus acuminatus* | Round Herring | adult | after Laurel Mundy |
| *Eucinostomus currani* | Pacific Flagfin Mojarra | adult | Leonardo Alannis |
| *Eucinostomus dowii* | Pacific Spotfin Mojarra | adult | Leonardo Alannis |
| *Eucryphycus californicus* | Persimmon Eelpout | adult | Laurel Mundy |
| *Eucyclogobius kristinae* | Southern Tidewater Goby | adult | Camm Swift |
| *Eucyclogobius kristinae* | Southern Tidewater Goby | head | Leonardo Alannis |
| *Eucyclogobius newberryi* | Northern Tidewater Goby | head | Leonardo Alannis |
| *Euleptorhamphus viridis* | Ribbon Halfbeak | adult | Leonardo Alannis |
| *Euprotomicrus bispinatus* | Pygmy Shark | adult | Atsuhiro Kubo |
| *Euthynnus affinis* | Kawakawa | adult | after Laurel Mundy |
| *Euthynnus lineatus* | Black Skipjack | adult | after Laurel Mundy |
| *Facciolella equatorialis* | Dogface Witch Eel | adult | Atsuhiro Kubo |
| *Fistularia commersonii* | Reef Cornetfish | adult | Leonardo Alannis |
| *Fistularia corneta* | Deepwater Cornetfish | adult | Leonardo Alannis |
| *Fodiator acutus* | Sharpchin Flyingfish | adult | Laurel Mundy |
| *Fundulus parvipinnis* | California Killifish | adult | Laurel Mundy |
| *Gadus chalcogrammus* | Walleye Pollock | adult | Leonardo Alannis |
| *Gadus macrocephalus* | Pacific Cod | adult | Leonardo Alannis |
| *Galeocerdo cuvier* | Tiger Shark | adult | Atsuhiro Kubo |
| *Galeocerdo cuvier* | Tiger Shark | teeth | Ebert et al. (2013) |
| *Galeocerdo cuvier* | Tiger Shark | nictitating membrane | Leonardo Alannis |
| *Galeorhinus galeus* | Soupfin Shark | adult | Fischer et al. (1995) |
| *Galeorhinus galeus* | Soupfin Shark | teeth | Ebert et al. (2013) |
| *Gambusia affinis* | Western Mosquitofish | female | Chris Van Dyck |
| *Gambusia affinis* | Western Mosquitofish | male | Chris Van Dyck |
| *Gasterosteus aculeatus* | Threespine Stickleback | adult | Leonardo Alannis |
| *Gempylus serpens* | Snake Mackerel | adult | Nakamura & Parin (1993) |
| *Genyonemus lineatus* | White Croaker | adult | Leonardo Alannis |
| *Gibbonsia elegans* | Spotted Kelpfish | dorsal fin soft-rays | Laurel Mundy |
| *Gibbonsia metzi* | Striped Kelpfish | dorsal fin soft-rays | Laurel Mundy |
| *Gillichthys mirabilis* | Longjaw Mudsucker | adult | Alan Marciochi |
| *Girella nigricans* | Opaleye | adult | after Laurel Mundy |
| *Glyptocephalus zachirus* | Rex Sole | adult | Laurel Mundy |
| *Gnathophis cinctus* | Hardtail Conger | adult | Laurel Mundy |
| *Gobiesox eugrammus* | Lined Clingfish | adult | Leonardo Alannis |
| *Gobiesox eugrammus* | Lined Clingfish | head | Leonardo Alannis |
| *Gobiesox maendricus* | Northern Clingfish | adult | Leonardo Alannis |
| *Gobiesox maendricus* | Northern Clingfish | head | Leonardo Alannis |
| *Gobiesox papillifer* | Bearded Clingfish | adult | Leonardo Alannis |

# DRAWING CITATIONS
## SPECIES PRESENTATION (continued)

| SCIENTIFIC NAME | COMMON NAME | DRAWING | ILLUSTRATOR |
|---|---|---|---|
| *Gobiesox rhessodon* | California Clingfish | adult | Leonardo Alannis |
| *Gonostoma atlanticum* | Atlantic Fangjaw | adult | after Laurel Mundy |
| *Grammonus diagrammus* | Purple Brotula | adult | Leonardo Alannis |
| *Gymnothorax mordax* | California Moray | adult | Leonardo Alannis |
| *Haemulon californiensis* | Salema | adult | after Fischer et al. (1995) |
| *Haemulon californiensis* | Salema | juvenile | Leonardo Alannis |
| *Haemulon flaviguttatum* | Cortez Grunt | adult | after Laurel Mundy |
| *Haemulon flaviguttatum* | Cortez Grunt | juvenile | Leonardo Alannis |
| *Haemulopsis axillaris* | Yellowstripe Grunt | adult | Leonardo Alannis |
| *Halichoeres semicinctus* | Rock Wrasse | female | after Laurel Mundy |
| *Halichoeres semicinctus* | Rock Wrasse | male | after Laurel Mundy |
| *Halichoeres semicinctus* | Rock Wrasse | juvenile | after Laurel Mundy |
| *Harengula thrissina* | Flatiron Herring | adult | after Fischer et al. (1995) |
| *Harriotta raleighana* | Longnose Chimaera | adult | Leonardo Alannis |
| *Hemanthias signifer* | Hookthroat Bass | adult | Leonardo Alannis |
| *Hemilepidotus spinosus* | Brown Irish Lord | adult | Bolin (1944) |
| *Hemiramphus saltator* | Longfin Halfbeak | adult | Leonardo Alannis |
| *Hemitripterus bolini* | Bigmouth Sculpin | adult | Laurel Mundy |
| *Heterodontus francisci* | Horn Shark | adult | Leonardo Alannis |
| *Heterostichus rostratus* | Giant Kelpfish | adult | Leonardo Alannis |
| *Hexagrammos lagocephalus* | Rock Greenling | adult | Laurel Mundy |
| *Hexagrammos stelleri* | Whitespotted Greenling | adult | Laurel Mundy |
| *Hexanchus griseus* | Bluntnose Sixgill Shark | adult | Fischer et al. (1995) |
| *Heteropriacanthus carolinus* | Pacific Glasseye | adult | Leonardo Alannis |
| *Himantolophus nigricornis* | Black Horned Footballfish | esca | after Laurel Mundy |
| *Himantolophus sagamius* | Pacific Footballfish | adult | after Laurel Mundy |
| *Himantolophus sagamius* | Pacific Footballfish | esca | Laurel Mundy |
| *Hippocampus ingens* | Pacific Seahorse | adult | Atsuhiro Kubo |
| *Hippoglossina stomata* | Bigmouth Sole | adult | after Laurel Mundy |
| *Hippoglossoides elassodon* | Flathead Sole | adult | after Laurel Mundy |
| *Hippoglossus stenolepis* | Pacific Halibut | adult | Laurel Mundy |
| *Hirundichthys rondeletii* | Blackwing Flyingfish | pectoral fin | Leonardo Alannis |
| *Holtbyrnia latifrons* | Streaklight Tubeshoulder | adult | Leonardo Alannis |
| *Howella sherborni* | Shortspine Basslet | adult | Laurel Mundy |
| *Hydrolagus colliei* | Spotted Ratfish | adult | Laurel Mundy |
| *Hydrolagus melanophasma* | Eastern Pacific Black Ghostshark | adult | Laurel Mundy |
| *Hygophum reinhardtii* | Broadhead Lanternfish | adult | Leonardo Alannis |
| *Hyperprosopon argenteum* | Walleye Surfperch | adult | Leonardo Alannis |
| *Hyperprosopon ellipticum* | Silver Surfperch | adult | Leonardo Alannis |
| *Hypocritichthys analis* | Spotfin Surfperch | adult | Leonardo Alannis |
| *Hypomesus nipponensis* | Wakasagi | adult | after Chris Van Dyck |

# DRAWING CITATIONS
## SPECIES PRESENTATION (continued)

| SCIENTIFIC NAME | COMMON NAME | DRAWING | ILLUSTRATOR |
|---|---|---|---|
| *Hypomesus pretiosus* | Surf Smelt | adult | Leonardo Alannis |
| *Hypomesus transpacificus* | Delta Smelt | adult | after Chris Van Dyck |
| *Hyporhamphus naos* | Pacific Silverstripe Halfbeak | adult | Leonardo Alannis |
| *Hyporhamphus rosae* | California Halfbeak | adult | Leonardo Alannis |
| *Hyporthodus acanthistius* | Gulf Coney | adult | after Fischer et al. (1995) |
| *Hyporthodus acanthistius* | Gulf Coney | juvenile | after Fischer et al. (1995) |
| *Hyporthodus niphobles* | Star-Studded Grouper | adult | Leonardo Alannis |
| *Hyporthodus niphobles* | Star-Studded Grouper | juvenile | after Laurel Mundy |
| *Hypsoblennius gentilis* | Bay Blenny | adult | Leonardo Alannis |
| *Hypsoblennius gentilis* | Bay Blenny | cirrus | Leonardo Alannis |
| *Hypsoblennius gilberti* | Rockpool Blenny | adult | Leonardo Alannis |
| *Hypsoblennius gilberti* | Rockpool Blenny | cirrus | Leonardo Alannis |
| *Hypsoblennius jenkinsi* | Mussel Blenny | adult | Leonardo Alannis |
| *Hypsoblennius jenkinsi* | Mussel Blenny | cirrus | Leonardo Alannis |
| *Hypsypops rubicundus* | Garibaldi | adult | Laurel Mundy |
| *Hypsypops rubicundus* | Garibaldi | juvenile | Laurel Mundy |
| *Icelinus burchami* | Dusky Sculpin | adult | Bolin (1944) |
| *Icelinus cavifrons* | Pit-Head Sculpin | female | Bolin (1944) |
| *Icelinus filamentosus* | Threadfin Sculpin | adult | after Bolin (1944) |
| *Icelinus fimbriatus* | Fringed Sculpin | male | Bolin (1944) |
| *Icelinus fimbriatus* | Fringed Sculpin | dorsal scale band | Leonardo Alannis |
| *Icelinus limbaughi* | Canyon Sculpin | adult | Rosenblatt & Smith (2004) |
| *Icelinus oculatus* | Frogmouth Sculpin | male | Bolin (1944) |
| *Icelinus quadriseriatus* | Yellowchin Sculpin | adult | after Bolin (1944) |
| *Icelinus tenuis* | Spotfin Sculpin | male | Bolin (1944) |
| *Ichthyococcus irregularis* | Bulldog Lightfish | adult | after Atsuhiro Kubo |
| *Icichthys lockingtoni* | Medusafish | adult | Leonardo Alannis |
| *Icosteus aenigmaticus* | Ragfish | adult | after Laurel Mundy |
| *Idiacanthus antrostomus* | Pacific Blackdragon | adult | Leonardo Alannis |
| *Ilypnus gilberti* | Cheekspot Goby | adult | Leonardo Alannis |
| *Inopsetta ischyra* | Hybrid Sole | adult | after Laurel Mundy |
| *Isistius brasiliensis* | Cookiecutter Shark | adult | after Laurel Mundy |
| *Isopsetta isolepis* | Butter Sole | adult | after Laurel Mundy |
| *Istiophorus platypterus* | Sailfish | adult | Leonardo Alannis |
| *Isurus oxyrinchus* | Shortfin Mako | adult | Laurel Mundy |
| *Isurus oxyrinchus* | Shortfin Mako | teeth | Ebert et al. (2013) |
| *Isurus oxyrinchus* | Shortfin Mako | lateral tooth | Leonardo Alannis |
| *Isurus paucus* | Longfin Mako | adult | Fischer et al. (1995) |
| *Isurus paucus* | Longfin Mako | teeth | Ebert et al. (2013) |
| *Jordania zonope* | Longfin Sculpin | adult | after Bolin (1944) |
| *Kajikia audax* | Striped Marlin | adult | Leonardo Alannis |

# DRAWING CITATIONS
## SPECIES PRESENTATION (continued)

| SCIENTIFIC NAME | COMMON NAME | DRAWING | ILLUSTRATOR |
|---|---|---|---|
| *Kasatkia seigeli* | Sixspot Prickleback | adult | Leonardo Alannis |
| *Kathetostoma averruncus* | Smooth Stargazer | adult | Leonardo Alannis |
| *Katsuwonus pelamis* | Skipjack Tuna | adult | Laurel Mundy |
| *Katsuwonus pelamis* | Skipjack Tuna | juvenile | Laurel Mundy |
| *Kyphosus azureus* | Zebraperch | adult | Leonardo Alannis |
| *Kyphosus ocyurus* | Bluestriped Chub | adult | after Laurel Mundy |
| *Kyphosus vaigiensis* | Blue-bronze Chub | adult | after Laurel Mundy |
| *Labrisomus xanti* | Largemouth Blenny | female | Leonardo Alannis |
| *Lamna ditropis* | Salmon Shark | adult | after Atsuhiro Kubo |
| *Lamna ditropis* | Salmon Shark | teeth | Ebert et al. (2013) |
| *Lamna ditropis* | Salmon Shark | tail | Leonardo Alannis |
| *Lampadena urophaos* | Sunbeam Lampfish | adult | Leonardo Alannis |
| *Lampanyctus tenuiformis* | Slender Lanternfish | adult | Leonardo Alannis |
| *Lampetra ayresii* | Western River Lamprey | adult | Leonardo Alannis |
| *Lampetra ayresii* | Western River Lamprey | mouth | Leonardo Alannis |
| *Lampris incognitus* | Smalleye Pacific Opah | adult | Leonardo Alannis |
| *Lampris incognitus* | Smalleye Pacific Opah | head | Leonardo Alannis |
| *Lampris incognitus* | Smalleye Pacific Opah | spotting | Leonardo Alannis |
| *Lampris megalopsis* | Bigeye Pacific Opah | head | Leonardo Alannis |
| *Lampris megalopsis* | Bigeye Pacific Opah | spotting | Leonardo Alannis |
| *Lamprogrammus niger* | Paperbone Cusk-Eel | adult | Atsuhiro Kubo |
| *Leiocottus hirundo* | Lavender Sculpin | adult | Bolin (1944) |
| *Lepidocybium flavobrunneum* | Escolar | adult | Leonardo Alannis |
| *Lepidocybium flavobrunneum* | Escolar | scales | Nakamura & Parin (1993) |
| *Lepidogobius lepidus* | Bay Goby | adult | Laurel Mundy |
| *Lepidopsetta bilineata* | Rock Sole | adult | Laurel Mundy |
| *Lepidopus fitchi* | Pacific Scabbardfish | adult | after Nakamura & Parin (1993) |
| *Lepidopus fitchi* | Pacific Scabbardfish | head | after Nakamura & Parin (1993) |
| *Leptocottus armatus* | Pacific Staghorn Sculpin | adult | Bolin (1944) |
| *Lestidiops ringens* | Slender Barracudina | adult | after Laurel Mundy |
| *Lethops connectens* | Halfblind Goby | adult | Leonardo Alannis |
| *Leuresthes tenuis* | California Grunion | adult | Atsuhiro Kubo |
| *Leuroglossus stilbius* | California Smoothtongue | adult | Leonardo Alannis |
| *Liparis adiastolus* | Rosybrown Snailfish | adult | Leonardo Alannis |
| *Liparis florae* | Tidepool Snailfish | adult | Leonardo Alannis |
| *Liparis fucensis* | Slipskin Snailfish | adult | Leonardo Alannis |
| *Liparis mucosus* | Slimy Snailfish | adult | Leonardo Alannis |
| *Liparis pulchellus* | Showy Snailfish | adult | Leonardo Alannis |
| *Liparis pulchellus* | Showy Snailfish | tail | Leonardo Alannis |
| *Liparis* spp. | Snailfish | head | Leonardo Alannis |
| *Lipolagus ochotensis* | Popeye Blacksmelt | adult | Leonardo Alannis |

# DRAWING CITATIONS

## SPECIES PRESENTATION (continued)

| SCIENTIFIC NAME | COMMON NAME | DRAWING | ILLUSTRATOR |
|---|---|---|---|
| *Lobotes pacificus* | Pacific Tripletail | adult | Laurel Mundy |
| *Lophiodes caulinaris* | Spottedtail Goosefish | adult | Laurel Mundy |
| *Lophotus capellei* | North Pacific Crestfish | adult | Leonardo Alannis |
| *Lucania goodei* | Bluefin Killifish | adult | after Laurel Mundy |
| *Lucania parva* | Rainwater Killifish | adult | Chris Van Dyck |
| *Lumpenopsis clitella* | Saddled Prickleback | adult | Leonardo Alannis |
| *Lumpenus sagitta* | Snake Prickleback | adult | after Laurel Mundy |
| *Lutjanus argentiventris* | Amarillo Snapper | adult | after Laurel Mundy |
| *Lutjanus colorado* | Colorado Snapper | adult | after Laurel Mundy |
| *Lutjanus colorado* | Colorado Snapper | teeth | Leonardo Alannis |
| *Lutjanus guttatus* | Spotted Rose Snapper | adult | Laurel Mundy |
| *Lutjanus novemfasciatus* | Pacific Dog Snapper | adult | after Laurel Mundy |
| *Lutjanus peru* | Pacific Red Snapper | adult | Laurel Mundy |
| *Lutjanus peru* | Pacific Red Snapper | teeth | Fischer et al. (1995) |
| *Luvarus imperialis* | Louvar | adult | Leonardo Alannis |
| *Luvarus imperialis* | Louvar | juvenile | Fischer et al. (1995) |
| *Lycenchelys camchatica* | Kamchatka Eelpout | adult | Laurel Mundy |
| *Lycenchelys crotalinus* | Snakehead Eelpout | adult | Laurel Mundy |
| *Lycodapus dermatinus* | Looseskin Eelpout | adult | Laurel Mundy |
| *Lycodapus dermatinus* | Looseskin Eelpout | head | Leonardo Alannis |
| *Lycodapus endemoscotus* | Deepwater Eelpout | adult | Laurel Mundy |
| *Lycodapus endemoscotus* | Deepwater Eelpout | gill rakers | Peden & Anderson (1978) |
| *Lycodapus fierasfer* | Blackmouth Eelpout | adult | Laurel Mundy |
| *Lycodapus fierasfer* | Blackmouth Eelpout | gill rakers | Peden & Anderson (1978) |
| *Lycodapus mandibularis* | Pallid Eelpout | adult | Laurel Mundy |
| *Lycodapus mandibularis* | Pallid Eelpout | gill rakers | Peden & Anderson (1978) |
| *Lycodapus psarostomatus* | Specklemouth Eelpout | adult | Laurel Mundy |
| *Lycodes brevipes* | Shortfin Eelpout | adult | after Mecklenburg et al. (2002) |
| *Lycodes brevipes* | Shortfin Eelpout | juvenile | Laurel Mundy |
| *Lycodes cortezianus* | Bigfin Eelpout | adult | Atsuhiro Kubo |
| *Lycodes cortezianus* | Bigfin Eelpout | mouth | Atsuhiro Kubo |
| *Lycodes cortezianus* | Bigfin Eelpout | gill rakers | Leonardo Alannis |
| *Lycodes diapterus* | Black Eelpout | adult | after Atsuhiro Kubo |
| *Lycodes pacificus* | Blackbelly Eelpout | adult | Atsuhiro Kubo |
| *Lycodes pacificus* | Blackbelly Eelpout | mouth | Atsuhiro Kubo |
| *Lycodes pacificus* | Blackbelly Eelpout | gill rakers | Leonardo Alannis |
| *Lyconema barbatum* | Bearded Eelpout | adult | Atsuhiro Kubo |
| *Lyopsetta exilis* | Slender Sole | adult | after Laurel Mundy |
| *Lythrypnus dalli* | Bluebanded Goby | adult | Leonardo Alannis |
| *Lythrypnus zebra* | Zebra Goby | adult | Leonardo Alannis |
| *Macropinna microstoma* | Barreleye | adult | Leonardo Alannis |

# DRAWING CITATIONS
## SPECIES PRESENTATION (continued)

| SCIENTIFIC NAME | COMMON NAME | DRAWING | ILLUSTRATOR |
|---|---|---|---|
| *Macroramphosus scolopax* | Longspine Snipefish | adult | Leonardo Alannis |
| *Magnisudis atlantica* | Duckbill Barracudina | adult | after Laurel Mundy |
| *Makaira indica* | Black Marlin | adult | Leonardo Alannis |
| *Makaira nigricans* | Blue Marlin | adult | Leonardo Alannis |
| *Malacocephalus laevis* | Softhead Grenadier | adult | Laurel Mundy |
| *Medialuna californiensis* | Halfmoon | adult | after Laurel Mundy |
| *Megachasma pelagios* | Megamouth Shark | adult | Fischer et al. (1995) |
| *Melamphaes lugubris* | Highsnout Bigscale | adult | Laurel Mundy |
| *Melanocetus johnsonii* | Blackdevil | female | after Laurel Mundy |
| *Melanocetus johnsonii* | Blackdevil | male | Moser (1996) |
| *Melanolagus bericoides* | Bigscale Deepsea Smelt | adult | Leonardo Alannis |
| *Melanonus zugmayeri* | Arrowtail | adult | after Laurel Mundy |
| *Melanostigma pammelas* | Midwater Eelpout | adult | after Laurel Mundy |
| *Melichthys niger* | Black Durgon | adult | Laurel Mundy |
| *Menidia audens* | Mississippi Silverside | adult | Moyle (2002) |
| *Menticirrhus undulatus* | California Corbina | adult | Leonardo Alannis |
| *Merluccius productus* | Pacific Hake | adult | Leonardo Alannis |
| *Mesobius berryi* | Midwater Grenadier | adult | Laurel Mundy |
| *Microgadus proximus* | Pacific Tomcod | adult | Leonardo Alannis |
| *Microlepidotus inornatus* | Wavyline Grunt | adult | Fischer et al. (1995) |
| *Micrometrus aurora* | Reef Perch | adult | Leonardo Alannis |
| *Micrometrus minimus* | Dwarf Perch | adult | Leonardo Alannis |
| *Microstoma microstoma* | Dusky Pencilsmelt | adult | after Laurel Mundy |
| *Microstoma microstoma* | Dusky Pencilsmelt | lateral line | Leonardo Alannis |
| *Microstomus bathybius* | Deepsea Sole | adult | Leonardo Alannis |
| *Microstomus pacificus* | Dover Sole | juvenile | Laurel Mundy |
| *Mitsukurina owstoni* | Goblin Shark | adult | Laurel Mundy |
| *Mobula birostris* | Manta | adult | Laurel Mundy |
| *Mobula birostris* | Manta | mouth | Leonardo Alannis |
| *Mobula mobular* | Giant Devilray | adult | after Laurel Mundy |
| *Mobula mobular* | Giant Devilray | mouth | Leonardo Alannis |
| *Mola mola* | Ocean Sunfish | adult | Leonardo Alannis |
| *Mola mola* | Ocean Sunfish | front view | Sawai et al. (2017) |
| *Mola tecta* | Hoodwinker Sunfish | adult | Leonardo Alannis |
| *Mola tecta* | Hoodwinker Sunfish | front view | Sawai et al. (2017) |
| *Morone saxatilis* | Striped Bass | adult | after Moyle (2002) |
| *Mugil cephalus* | Striped Mullet | adult | after Laurel Mundy |
| *Mugil curema* | White Mullet | adult | after Laurel Mundy |
| *Muraena argus* | Argus Moray | adult | Laurel Mundy |
| *Mustelus californicus* | Gray Smoothhound | adult | after Atsuhiro Kubo |
| *Mustelus californicus* | Gray Smoothhound | teeth | Ebert et al. (2013) |

# DRAWING CITATIONS
## SPECIES PRESENTATION (continued)

| SCIENTIFIC NAME | COMMON NAME | DRAWING | ILLUSTRATOR |
|---|---|---|---|
| *Mustelus henlei* | Brown Smoothhound | adult | Atsuhiro Kubo |
| *Mustelus henlei* | Brown Smoothhound | teeth | Ebert et al. (2013) |
| *Mustelus lunulatus* | Sicklefin Smoothhound | adult | after Atsuhiro Kubo |
| *Mustelus lunulatus* | Sicklefin Smoothhound | teeth | Ebert et al. (2013) |
| *Mycteroperca jordani* | Gulf Grouper | adult | Leonardo Alannis |
| *Mycteroperca rosacea* | Leopard Grouper | adult | Leonardo Alannis |
| *Mycteroperca xenarcha* | Broomtail Grouper | adult | Leonardo Alannis |
| *Myliobatis californica* | Bat Ray | adult | Leonardo Alannis |
| *Myrophis vafer* | Pacific Worm Eel | adult | after Fischer et al. (1995) |
| *Nannobrachium ritteri* | Broadfin Lampfish | adult | Leonardo Alannis |
| *Nansenia candida* | Bluethroat Argentine | adult | Laurel Mundy |
| *Naucrates ductor* | Pilotfish | adult | Fischer et al. (1995) |
| *Naucrates ductor* | Pilotfish | juvenile | Laurel Mundy |
| *Naucrates ductor* | Pilotfish | tail, lateral | Leonardo Alannis |
| *Naucrates ductor* | Pilotfish | tail, dorsal | Leonardo Alannis |
| *Nautichthys oculofasciatus* | Sailfin Sculpin | adult | after Bolin (1944) |
| *Nectoliparis pelagicus* | Tadpole Snailfish | adult | Leonardo Alannis |
| *Nematistius pectoralis* | Roosterfish | adult | Fischer et al. (1995) |
| *Nemichthys larseni* | Pale Snipe Eel | adult | after Atsuhiro Kubo |
| *Nemichthys larseni* | Pale Snipe Eel | lateral line | Leonardo Alannis |
| *Nemichthys scolopaceus* | Slender Snipe Eel | head, lateral | Atsuhiro Kubo |
| *Nemichthys scolopaceus* | Slender Snipe Eel | lateral line | Leonardo Alannis |
| *Neoclinus blanchardi* | Sarcastic Fringehead | head, female | Leonardo Alannis |
| *Neoclinus blanchardi* | Sarcastic Fringehead | male | Leonardo Alannis |
| *Nezumia liolepis* | Smooth Grenadier | adult | Laurel Mundy |
| *Nezumia stelgidolepis* | California Grenadier | adult | Laurel Mundy |
| *Nicholsina denticulata* | Loosetooth Parrotfish | adult | after Laurel Mundy |
| *Nicholsina denticulata* | Loosetooth Parrotfish | mouth | Leonardo Alannis |
| *Notacanthus chemnitzii* | Snubnosed Spiny Eel | adult | Laurel Mundy |
| *Notorynchus cepedianus* | Broadnose Sevengill Shark | adult | Fischer et al. (1995) |
| *Odontaspis ferox* | Ragged-Tooth Shark | adult | Fischer et al. (1995) |
| *Odontaspis ferox* | Ragged-Tooth Shark | teeth | Ebert et al. (2013) |
| *Odontopyxis trispinosa* | Pygmy Poacher | adult | Atsuhiro Kubo |
| *Oligocottus maculosus* | Tidepool Sculpin | male | Bolin (1944) |
| *Oligocottus rimensis* | Saddleback Sculpin | male | Bolin (1944) |
| *Oligocottus rubellio* | Rosy Sculpin | male | Bolin (1944) |
| *Oligocottus snyderi* | Fluffy Sculpin | male | Bolin (1944) |
| *Oncorhynchus clarkii* | Cutthroat Trout | teeth | Leonardo Alannis |
| *Oncorhynchus gorbuscha* | Pink Salmon | head, female | Chris Van Dyck |
| *Oncorhynchus gorbuscha* | Pink Salmon | male | after Chris Van Dyck |
| *Oncorhynchus gorbuscha* | Pink Salmon | juvenile | Chris Van Dyck |

# DRAWING CITATIONS

## SPECIES PRESENTATION (continued)

| SCIENTIFIC NAME | COMMON NAME | DRAWING | ILLUSTRATOR |
|---|---|---|---|
| *Oncorhynchus keta* | Chum Salmon | head, female | Chris Van Dyck |
| *Oncorhynchus keta* | Chum Salmon | male | Chris Van Dyck |
| *Oncorhynchus keta* | Chum Salmon | juvenile | Chris Van Dyck |
| *Oncorhynchus keta* | Chum Salmon | gill raker | Leonardo Alannis |
| *Oncorhynchus kisutch* | Coho Salmon | head, female | Chris Van Dyck |
| *Oncorhynchus kisutch* | Coho Salmon | male | Chris Van Dyck |
| *Oncorhynchus kisutch* | Coho Salmon | juvenile | Chris Van Dyck |
| *Oncorhynchus mykiss* | Steelhead | adult | after Chris Van Dyck |
| *Oncorhynchus mykiss* | Steelhead | juvenile | Laurel Mundy |
| *Oncorhynchus nerka* | Sockeye Salmon | head, female | Chris Van Dyck |
| *Oncorhynchus nerka* | Sockeye Salmon | male | Chris Van Dyck |
| *Oncorhynchus nerka* | Sockeye Salmon | juvenile | Chris Van Dyck |
| *Oncorhynchus nerka* | Sockeye Salmon | gill raker | Leonardo Alannis |
| *Oncorhynchus tshawytscha* | Chinook Salmon | head, female | Chris Van Dyck |
| *Oncorhynchus tshawytscha* | Chinook Salmon | male | Chris Van Dyck |
| *Oncorhynchus tshawytscha* | Chinook Salmon | juvenile | Chris Van Dyck |
| *Oneirodes eschrichtii* | Cosmopolitan Dreamer | adult | after Laurel Mundy |
| *Ophichthus triserialis* | Pacific Snake Eel | adult | after Fischer et al. (1995) |
| *Ophichthus zophochir* | Yellow Snake Eel | adult | Fischer et al. (1995) |
| *Ophidion scrippsae* | Basketweave Cusk-Eel | adult | Atsuhiro Kubo |
| *Ophioblennius steindachneri* | Panamic Fanged Blenny | adult | Leonardo Alannis |
| *Ophiodon elongatus* | Lingcod | juvenile | Laurel Mundy |
| *Opisthonema libertate* | Deepbody Thread Herring | adult | after Laurel Mundy |
| *Opisthonema medirastre* | Middling Thread Herring | adult | after Laurel Mundy |
| *Oplegnathus fasciatus* | Barred Knifejaw | female | Leonardo Alannis |
| *Oreochromis mossambicus* | Mozambique Tilapia | adult | after Laurel Mundy |
| *Orthonopias triacis* | Snubnose Sculpin | adult | Bolin (1944) |
| *Orthonopias triacis* | Snubnose Sculpin | spine | Leonardo Alannis |
| *Oxyjulis californica* | Señorita | adult | after Laurel Mundy |
| *Oxylebius pictus* | Painted Greenling | adult | Laurel Mundy |
| *Pallasina barbata* | Tubenose Poacher | adult | Laurel Mundy |
| *Paracaristius nudarcus* | Dark Manefish | head | Leonardo Alannis |
| *Paralabrax auroguttatus* | Goldspotted Sand Bass | adult | Leonardo Alannis |
| *Paralabrax auroguttatus* | Goldspotted Sand Bass | juvenile | Leonardo Alannis |
| *Paralabrax clathratus* | Kelp Bass | adult | after Laurel Mundy |
| *Paralabrax clathratus* | Kelp Bass | juvenile | Leonardo Alannis |
| *Paralabrax maculatofasciatus* | Spotted Sand Bass | adult | after Laurel Mundy |
| *Paralabrax maculatofasciatus* | Spotted Sand Bass | juvenile | Leonardo Alannis |
| *Paralabrax nebulifer* | Barred Sand Bass | adult | after Laurel Mundy |
| *Paralabrax nebulifer* | Barred Sand Bass | juvenile | Leonardo Alannis |
| *Paralichthys californicus* | California Halibut | adult | Laurel Mundy |

# DRAWING CITATIONS
## SPECIES PRESENTATION (continued)

| SCIENTIFIC NAME | COMMON NAME | DRAWING | ILLUSTRATOR |
|---|---|---|---|
| *Paraliparis albescens* | Phantom Snailfish | adult | Leonardo Alannis |
| *Paraliparis cephalus* | Swellhead Snailfish | adult | Leonardo Alannis |
| *Paraliparis dactylosus* | Red Snailfish | adult | Leonardo Alannis |
| *Paraliparis deani* | Prickly Snailfish | adult | after Laurel Mundy |
| *Paricelinus hopliticus* | Thornback Sculpin | adult | Bolin (1944) |
| *Parmaturus xaniurus* | Filetail Cat Shark | adult | after Atsuhiro Kubo |
| *Parophrys vetulus* | English Sole | adult | after Laurel Mundy |
| *Pentaceros wheeleri* | North Pacific Armorhead | juvenile | Laurel Mundy |
| *Peprilus simillimus* | Pacific Butterfish | adult | Leonardo Alannis |
| *Phanerodon atripes* | Sharpnose Seaperch | adult | Leonardo Alannis |
| *Phanerodon furcatus* | White Seaperch | adult | Leonardo Alannis |
| *Phanerodon vacca* | Pile Perch | adult | Leonardo Alannis |
| *Pholis clemensi* | Longfin Gunnel | adult | Leonardo Alannis |
| *Pholis laeta* | Crescent Gunnel | adult | after Laurel Mundy |
| *Pholis ornata* | Saddleback Gunnel | adult | Leonardo Alannis |
| *Pholis schultzi* | Red Gunnel | adult | Leonardo Alannis |
| *Photonectes margarita* | Sooty Dragonfish | adult | Laurel Mundy |
| *Phtheirichthys lineatus* | Slender Suckerfish | adult | Leonardo Alannis |
| *Physiculus rastrelliger* | Hundred-Fathom Codling | adult | Leonardo Alannis |
| *Phytichthys chirus* | Ribbon Prickleback | adult | after Laurel Mundy |
| *Plagiotremus azaleus* | Sabertooth Blenny | adult | after Laurel Mundy |
| *Platichthys stellatus* | Starry Flounder | adult | Leonardo Alannis |
| *Platichthys stellatus* | Starry Flounder | scales | Leonardo Alannis |
| *Platyberyx andriashevi* | Blackfin Manefish | adult | Laurel Mundy |
| *Platyrhinoidis triseriata* | Thornback | adult | Leonardo Alannis |
| *Pleurogrammus monopterygius* | Atka Mackerel | adult | Laurel Mundy |
| *Pleurogrammus monopterygius* | Atka Mackerel | eye | Laurel Mundy |
| *Pleuronichthys coenosus* | C-O Sole | adult | after Laurel Mundy |
| *Pleuronichthys decurrens* | Curlfin Sole | adult | after Laurel Mundy |
| *Pleuronichthys guttulatus* | Diamond Turbot | adult | Leonardo Alannis |
| *Pleuronichthys ritteri* | Spotted Turbot | adult | Leonardo Alannis |
| *Pleuronichthys ritteri* | Spotted Turbot | head, blind side | Leonardo Alannis |
| *Pleuronichthys verticalis* | Hornyhead Turbot | adult | Leonardo Alannis |
| *Pleuronichthys verticalis* | Hornyhead Turbot | head, blind side | Leonardo Alannis |
| *Podothecus accipenserinus* | Sturgeon Poacher | adult | Laurel Mundy |
| *Poecilia latipinna* | Sailfin Molly | female | after Laurel Mundy |
| *Poecilia latipinna* | Sailfin Molly | male | Leonardo Alannis |
| *Polydactylus approximans* | Blue Bobo | adult | Leonardo Alannis |
| *Polydactylus opercularis* | Yellow Bobo | adult | Leonardo Alannis |
| *Pomacanthus zonipectus* | Cortez Angelfish | adult | Laurel Mundy |
| *Pomacanthus zonipectus* | Cortez Angelfish | juvenile | Fischer et al. (1995) |

# DRAWING CITATIONS
## SPECIES PRESENTATION (continued)

| SCIENTIFIC NAME | COMMON NAME | DRAWING | ILLUSTRATOR |
|---|---|---|---|
| *Poroclinus rothrocki* | Whitebarred Prickleback | adult | after Laurel Mundy |
| *Poromitra crassiceps* | Crested Bigscale | adult | Leonardo Alannis |
| *Prionace glauca* | Blue Shark | adult | Atsuhiro Kubo |
| *Prionace glauca* | Blue Shark | teeth | Ebert et al. (2013) |
| *Prionotus stephanophrys* | Lumptail Searobin | adult | Leonardo Alannis |
| *Pristigenys serrula* | Popeye Catalufa | adult | Laurel Mundy |
| *Prognathodes falcifer* | Scythe Butterflyfish | adult | Laurel Mundy |
| *Pronotogrammus multifasciatus* | Threadfin Bass | adult | Laurel Mundy |
| *Protomyctophum crockeri* | California Flashlightfish | adult | Leonardo Alannis |
| *Psenes pellucidus* | Bluefin Driftfish | adult | Laurel Mundy |
| *Psenes pellucidus* | Bluefin Driftfish | juvenile | Leonardo Alannis |
| *Psettichthys melanostictus* | Sand Sole | adult | Leonardo Alannis |
| *Pseudobathylagus milleri* | Stout Blacksmelt | adult | Leonardo Alannis |
| *Pseudobatos productus* | Shovelnose Guitarfish | adult | Leonardo Alannis |
| *Pseudupeneus grandisquamis* | Bigscale Goatfish | adult | Laurel Mundy |
| *Psychrolutes phrictus* | Giant Blob Sculpin | adult | Leonardo Alannis |
| *Pteraclis aesticola* | Pacific Fanfish | adult | Leonardo Alannis |
| *Ptilichthys goodei* | Quillfish | adult | Laurel Mundy |
| *Quietula y-cauda* | Shadow Goby | adult | Leonardo Alannis |
| *Radulinus asprellus* | Slim Sculpin | male | Bolin (1944) |
| *Radulinus boleoides* | Darter Sculpin | male | Bolin (1944) |
| *Ranzania laevis* | Slender Mola | adult | Leonardo Alannis |
| *Rathbunella alleni* | Stripefin Ronquil | adult | Atsuhiro Kubo |
| *Rathbunella hypoplecta* | Bluebanded Ronquil | male | Atsuhiro Kubo |
| *Regalecus russelii* | Oarfish | adult | Leonardo Alannis |
| *Reinhardtius hippoglossoides* | Greenland Halibut | adult | Leonardo Alannis |
| *Remora albescens* | White Suckerfish | adult | Leonardo Alannis |
| *Remora australis* | Whalesucker | adult | Leonardo Alannis |
| *Remora brachyptera* | Spearfish Remora | adult | Leonardo Alannis |
| *Remora osteochir* | Marlinsucker | adult | Leonardo Alannis |
| *Remora remora* | Remora | adult | Leonardo Alannis |
| *Rhacochilus toxotes* | Rubberlip Seaperch | adult | Leonardo Alannis |
| *Rhamphocottus richardsonii* | Grunt Sculpin | adult | Leonardo Alannis |
| *Rhincodon typus* | Whale Shark | adult | Leonardo Alannis |
| *Rhinogobiops nicholsii* | Blackeye Goby | adult | Leonardo Alannis |
| *Rhinogobius brunneus* | Amur Goby | adult | Laurel Mundy |
| *Rhinoliparis attenuatus* | Slim Snailfish | adult | Leonardo Alannis |
| *Rhinoliparis barbulifer* | Longnose Snailfish | adult | Leonardo Alannis |
| *Rhizoprionodon longurio* | Pacific Sharpnose Shark | adult | Atsuhiro Kubo |
| *Rhizoprionodon longurio* | Pacific Sharpnose Shark | teeth | Ebert et al. (2013) |
| *Rhynchohyalus natalensis* | Glasshead Barreleye | adult | Leonardo Alannis |

# DRAWING CITATIONS
## SPECIES PRESENTATION (continued)

| SCIENTIFIC NAME | COMMON NAME | DRAWING | ILLUSTRATOR |
|---|---|---|---|
| *Rimicola cabrilloi* | Channel Islands Clingfish | adult | Leonardo Alannis |
| *Rimicola dimorpha* | Southern Clingfish | adult | Leonardo Alannis |
| *Rimicola eigenmanni* | Slender Clingfish | adult | Leonardo Alannis |
| *Rimicola eigenmanni* | Slender Clingfish | head | Leonardo Alannis |
| *Rimicola muscarum* | Kelp Clingfish | adult | Leonardo Alannis |
| *Rimicola muscarum* | Kelp Clingfish | head | Leonardo Alannis |
| *Roncador stearnsii* | Spotfin Croaker | adult | Leonardo Alannis |
| *Ronquilus jordani* | Northern Ronquil | adult | after Laurel Mundy |
| *Ruscarius creaseri* | Roughcheek Sculpin | adult | after Bolin (1944) |
| *Ruscarius meanyi* | Puget Sound Sculpin | adult | Rick Feeney |
| *Ruvettus pretiosus* | Oilfish | adult | Nakamura & Parin (1993) |
| *Ruvettus pretiosus* | Oilfish | scales | Nakamura & Parin (1993) |
| *Sagamichthys abei* | Shining Tubeshoulder | adult | Leonardo Alannis |
| *Sarda chiliensis* | Pacific Bonito | adult | Laurel Mundy |
| *Sardinops sagax* | Pacific Sardine | adult | after Fischer et al. (1995) |
| *Scomber japonicus* | Pacific Chub Mackerel | adult | Laurel Mundy |
| *Scomberomorus concolor* | Gulf Sierra | adult | Laurel Mundy |
| *Scomberomorus sierra* | Pacific Sierra | adult | Laurel Mundy |
| *Scopelogadus bispinosus* | Twospine Bigscale | adult | Leonardo Alannis |
| *Scopelosaurus harryi* | Scaly Waryfish | adult | Laurel Mundy |
| *Scorpaena guttata* | California Scorpionfish | adult | Leonardo Alannis |
| *Scorpaena mystes* | Stone Scorpionfish | adult | Fischer et al. (1995) |
| *Scorpaena mystes* | Stone Scorpionfish | pectoral fin | Laurel Mundy |
| *Scorpaenichthys marmoratus* | Cabezon | adult | after Bolin (1944) |
| *Scorpaenodes xyris* | Rainbow Scorpionfish | adult | Fischer et al. (1995) |
| *Scytalina cerdale* | Graveldiver | adult | Leonardo Alannis |
| *Sebastes* sp. | Rockfish | mandible | Laurel Mundy |
| *Sebastes aleutianus* | Rougheye Rockfish | adult | Laurel Mundy |
| *Sebastes alutus* | Pacific Ocean Perch | adult | after Laurel Mundy |
| *Sebastes aurora* | Aurora Rockfish | adult | Laurel Mundy |
| *Sebastes borealis* | Shortraker Rockfish | adult | Love et al. (2002) |
| *Sebastes carnatus* | Gopher Rockfish | adult | Laurel Mundy |
| *Sebastes caurinus* | Copper Rockfish | adult | after Love et al. (2002) |
| *Sebastes ciliatus* | Dark Rockfish | adult | after Love et al. (2002) |
| *Sebastes constellatus* | Starry Rockfish | adult | after Laurel Mundy |
| *Sebastes crameri* | Darkblotched Rockfish | adult | Laurel Mundy |
| *Sebastes dallii* | Calico Rockfish | adult | after Laurel Mundy |
| *Sebastes diaconus* | Deacon Rockfish | adult | Laurel Mundy |
| *Sebastes diploproa* | Splitnose Rockfish | juvenile | Laurel Mundy |
| *Sebastes elongatus* | Greenstriped Rockfish | adult | after Laurel Mundy |
| *Sebastes emphaeus* | Puget Sound Rockfish | adult | Love et al. (2002) |

# DRAWING CITATIONS
## SPECIES PRESENTATION (continued)

| SCIENTIFIC NAME | COMMON NAME | DRAWING | ILLUSTRATOR |
|---|---|---|---|
| *Sebastes ensifer* | Swordspine Rockfish | adult | Love et al. (2002) |
| *Sebastes goodei* | Chilipepper | adult | Leonardo Alannis |
| *Sebastes jordani* | Shortbelly Rockfish | adult | Love et al. (2002) |
| *Sebastes levis* | Cowcod | adult | Love et al. (2002) |
| *Sebastes levis* | Cowcod | juvenile | Laurel Mundy |
| *Sebastes macdonaldi* | Mexican Rockfish | adult | after Laurel Mundy |
| *Sebastes macdonaldi* | Mexican Rockfish | juvenile | after Laroche (1987) |
| *Sebastes melanosema* | Semaphore Rockfish | adult | after Love et al. (2002) |
| *Sebastes melanostictus* | Blackspotted Rockfish | adult | Laurel Mundy |
| *Sebastes melanostomus* | Blackgill Rockfish | adult | Laurel Mundy |
| *Sebastes melanostomus* | Blackgill Rockfish | juvenile | Laurel Mundy |
| *Sebastes miniatus* | Vermilion Rockfish | juvenile | after Laurel Mundy |
| *Sebastes moseri* | Whitespotted Rockfish | adult | Love et al. (2002) |
| *Sebastes mystinus* | Blue Rockfish | adult | Laurel Mundy |
| *Sebastes mystinus* | Blue Rockfish | head | Laurel Mundy |
| *Sebastes nigrocinctus* | Tiger Rockfish | adult | after Laurel Mundy |
| *Sebastes ovalis* | Speckled Rockfish | juvenile | Laurel Mundy |
| *Sebastes paucispinis* | Bocaccio | adult | Leonardo Alannis |
| *Sebastes pinniger* | Canary Rockfish | juvenile | Laurel Mundy |
| *Sebastes proriger* | Redstripe Rockfish | adult | Love et al. (2002) |
| *Sebastes reedi* | Yellowmouth Rockfish | adult | after Laurel Mundy |
| *Sebastes rosaceus* | Rosy Rockfish | adult | Leonardo Alannis |
| *Sebastes ruberrimus* | Yelloweye Rockfish | adult | Laurel Mundy |
| *Sebastes ruberrimus* | Yelloweye Rockfish | juvenile | Love et al. (2002) |
| *Sebastes rubrivinctus* | Flag Rockfish | adult | Laurel Mundy |
| *Sebastes saxicola* | Stripetail Rockfish | adult | after Laurel Mundy |
| *Sebastes serranoides* | Olive Rockfish | adult | Laurel Mundy |
| *Sebastes serranoides* | Olive Rockfish | juvenile | Laurel Mundy |
| *Sebastes serriceps* | Treefish | adult | Laurel Mundy |
| *Sebastes variabilis* | Dusky Rockfish | adult | Laurel Mundy |
| *Sebastes variegatus* | Harlequin Rockfish | adult | Love et al. (2002) |
| *Sebastolobus altivelis* | Longspine Thornyhead | adult | after Atsuhiro Kubo |
| *Selar crumenophthalmus* | Bigeye Scad | adult | after Laurel Mundy |
| *Selar crumenophthalmus* | Bigeye Scad | papilla | Leonardo Alannis |
| *Selene brevoortii* | Mexican Lookdown | adult | Laurel Mundy |
| *Selene brevoortii* | Mexican Lookdown | juvenile | after Laurel Mundy |
| *Selene peruviana* | Pacific Moonfish | adult | Laurel Mundy |
| *Selene peruviana* | Pacific Moonfish | juvenile | after Laurel Mundy |
| *Seriola aureovittata* | Japanese Amberjack | supramaxilla | after Laurel Mundy |
| *Seriola dorsalis* | Yellowtail | adult | after Fischer et al. (1995) |
| *Seriola dorsalis* | Yellowtail | juvenile | after Laurel Mundy |

# DRAWING CITATIONS

## SPECIES PRESENTATION (continued)

| SCIENTIFIC NAME | COMMON NAME | DRAWING | ILLUSTRATOR |
|---|---|---|---|
| *Seriola rivoliana* | Almaco Jack | adult | Laurel Mundy |
| *Seriphus politus* | Queenfish | adult | Leonardo Alannis |
| *Serranus aequidens* | Deepwater Serrano | adult | after Laurel Mundy |
| *Serrivomer sector* | Sawtooth Eel | adult | Leonardo Alannis |
| *Somniosus pacificus* | Pacific Sleeper Shark | adult | Leonardo Alannis |
| *Sphoeroides annulatus* | Bullseye Puffer | body, dorsal | Leonardo Alannis |
| *Sphoeroides lobatus* | Longnose Puffer | adult | Laurel Mundy |
| *Sphyraena argentea* | Pacific Barracuda | adult | Fischer et al. (1995) |
| *Sphyraena ensis* | Mexican Barracuda | adult | after Fischer et al. (1995) |
| *Sphyrna lewini* | Scalloped Hammerhead | adult | Fischer et al. (1995) |
| *Sphyrna lewini* | Scalloped Hammerhead | head | Fischer et al. (1995) |
| *Sphyrna tiburo* | Bonnethead | adult | after Fischer et al. (1995) |
| *Sphyrna tiburo* | Bonnethead | head | Fischer et al. (1995) |
| *Sphyrna zygaena* | Smooth Hammerhead | adult | Fischer et al. (1995) |
| *Sphyrna zygaena* | Smooth Hammerhead | head | Fischer et al. (1995) |
| *Spirinchus starksi* | Night Smelt | adult | Leonardo Alannis |
| *Spirinchus thaleichthys* | Longfin Smelt | male | after Chris Van Dyck |
| *Squalus suckleyi* | Pacific Spiny Dogfish | adult | Atsuhiro Kubo |
| *Squatina californica* | Pacific Angel Shark | adult | Leonardo Alannis |
| *Stegastes leucorus* | Whitetail Damselfish | adult | after Laurel Mundy |
| *Stegastes leucorus* | Whitetail Damselfish | juvenile | Leonardo Alannis |
| *Stellerina xyosterna* | Pricklebreast Poacher | adult | Atsuhiro Kubo |
| *Stenobrachius leucopsarus* | Northern Lampfish | adult | Leonardo Alannis |
| *Stereolepis gigas* | Giant Sea Bass | adult | Fischer et al. (1995) |
| *Stereolepis gigas* | Giant Sea Bass | juvenile | after Atsuhiro Kubo |
| *Sternoptyx diaphana* | Longspine Hatchetfish | adult | after Laurel Mundy |
| *Sternoptyx obscura* | Dusky Hatchetfish | adult | after Laurel Mundy |
| *Sternoptyx pseudobscura* | Highlight Hatchetfish | adult | after Laurel Mundy |
| *Stomias atriventer* | Blackbelly Dragonfish | adult | after Laurel Mundy |
| *Strongylura exilis* | California Needlefish | adult | Laurel Mundy |
| *Strongylura exilis* | California Needlefish | head, juvenile | Leonardo Alannis |
| *Symbolophorus californiensis* | Bigfin Lanternfish | adult | Leonardo Alannis |
| *Symphurus atricaudus* | California Tonguefish | adult | after Laurel Mundy |
| *Symphurus oligomerus* | Whitetail Tonguefish | adult | Leonardo Alannis |
| *Synchiropus atrilabiatus* | Blacklip Dragonet | adult | after Atsuhiro Kubo |
| *Synchirus gilli* | Manacled Sculpin | adult | Laurel Mundy |
| *Syngnathus auliscus* | Barred Pipefish | adult | Atsuhiro Kubo |
| *Syngnathus auliscus* | Barred Pipefish | body rings | Atsuhiro Kubo |
| *Syngnathus californiensis* | Kelp Pipefish | adult | after Atsuhiro Kubo |
| *Syngnathus euchrous* | Chocolate Pipefish | adult | after Atsuhiro Kubo |
| *Syngnathus exilis* | Barcheek Pipefish | adult | after Atsuhiro Kubo |

# DRAWING CITATIONS
## SPECIES PRESENTATION (continued)

| SCIENTIFIC NAME | COMMON NAME | DRAWING | ILLUSTRATOR |
|---|---|---|---|
| *Syngnathus exilis* | Barcheek Pipefish | head | after Atsuhiro Kubo |
| *Syngnathus leptorhynchus* | Bay Pipefish | adult | after Atsuhiro Kubo |
| *Syngnathus leptorhynchus* | Bay Pipefish | dorsal fin | Leonardo Alannis |
| *Synodus lacertinus* | Calico Lizardfish | adult | after Fischer et al. (1995) |
| *Synodus lucioceps* | California Lizardfish | adult | Atsuhiro Kubo |
| *Tactostoma macropus* | Longfin Dragonfish | adult | Laurel Mundy |
| *Taractes asper* | Rough Pomfret | adult | Laurel Mundy |
| *Taractes asper* | Rough Pomfret | juvenile | Laurel Mundy |
| *Taractichthys steindachneri* | Sickle Pomfret | adult | Leonardo Alannis |
| *Tarletonbeania crenularis* | Blue Lanternfish | adult | Leonardo Alannis |
| *Tetragonurus cuvieri* | Smalleye Squaretail | adult | Leonardo Alannis |
| *Tetrapturus angustirostris* | Shortbill Spearfish | adult | Leonardo Alannis |
| *Tetronarce californica* | Pacific Electric Ray | adult | Leonardo Alannis |
| *Thaleichthys pacificus* | Eulachon | adult | Laurel Mundy |
| *Thunnus alalunga* | Albacore | adult | Laurel Mundy |
| *Thunnus albacares* | Yellowfin Tuna | adult | after Laurel Mundy |
| *Thunnus albacares* | Yellowfin Tuna | juvenile I | Leonardo Alannis |
| *Thunnus albacares* | Yellowfin Tuna | juvenile II | Laurel Mundy |
| *Thunnus obesus* | Bigeye Tuna | adult | Laurel Mundy |
| *Thunnus obesus* | Bigeye Tuna | juvenile I | Leonardo Alannis |
| *Thunnus obesus* | Bigeye Tuna | juvenile II | Laurel Mundy |
| *Thunnus orientalis* | Pacific Bluefin Tuna | adult | Laurel Mundy |
| *Tilapia zillii* | Redbelly Tilapia | adult | after Laurel Mundy |
| *Trachinotus paitensis* | Paloma Pompano | adult | Fischer et al. (1995) |
| *Trachinotus rhodopus* | Gafftosail Pompano | adult | Fischer et al. (1995) |
| *Trachipterus altivelis* | King-Of-The-Salmon | adult | Leonardo Alannis |
| *Trachipterus altivelis* | King-Of-The-Salmon | juvenile | after Atsuhiro Kubo |
| *Trachipterus fukuzakii* | Tapertail Ribbonfish | adult | Leonardo Alannis |
| *Trachurus symmetricus* | Jack Mackerel | adult | Laurel Mundy |
| *Trachurus symmetricus* | Jack Mackerel | lateral line | Leonardo Alannis |
| *Triakis semifasciata* | Leopard Shark | adult | after Atsuhiro Kubo |
| *Trichiurus nitens* | Pacific Cutlassfish | adult | Atsuhiro Kubo |
| *Trichodon trichodon* | Pacific Sandfish | adult | Laurel Mundy |
| *Tridentiger barbatus* | Shokihaze Goby | adult | Leonardo Alannis |
| *Tridentiger bifasciatus* | Shimofuri Goby | head | after Sakamoto & Sakamoto (1989) |
| *Tridentiger bifasciatus* | Shimofuri Goby | pectoral fin | after Sakamoto & Sakamoto (1989) |
| *Tridentiger trigonocephalus* | Chameleon Goby | female I | Leonardo Alannis |
| *Tridentiger trigonocephalus* | Chameleon Goby | female II | Leonardo Alannis |
| *Tridentiger trigonocephalus* | Chameleon Goby | male | Leonardo Alannis |
| *Tridentiger trigonocephalus* | Chameleon Goby | head | after Sakamoto & Sakamoto (1989) |
| *Tridentiger trigonocephalus* | Chameleon Goby | pectoral fin | after Sakamoto & Sakamoto (1989) |

# DRAWING CITATIONS
## SPECIES PRESENTATION (continued)

| SCIENTIFIC NAME | COMMON NAME | DRAWING | ILLUSTRATOR |
|---|---|---|---|
| *Triphoturus mexicanus* | Mexican Lampfish | adult | Leonardo Alannis |
| *Typhlogobius californiensis* | Blind Goby | adult | Leonardo Alannis |
| *Ulvicola sanctaerosae* | Kelp Gunnel | adult | Leonardo Alannis |
| *Umbrina roncador* | Yellowfin Croaker | adult | Leonardo Alannis |
| *Uraspis helvola* | Cottonmouth Jack | adult | Fischer et al. (1995) |
| *Uraspis helvola* | Cottonmouth Jack | juvenile | Laurel Mundy |
| *Urobatis halleri* | Round Stingray | adult | Fischer et al. (1995) |
| *Vinciguerria lucetia* | Panama Lightfish | adult | Leonardo Alannis |
| *Vinciguerria nimbaria* | Oceanic Lightfish | adult | Leonardo Alannis |
| *Xeneretmus latifrons* | Blacktip Poacher | adult | Atsuhiro Kubo |
| *Xeneretmus leiops* | Smootheye Poacher | adult | Atsuhiro Kubo |
| *Xeneretmus ritteri* | Stripefin Poacher | adult | after Atsuhiro Kubo |
| *Xeneretmus ritteri* | Stripefin Poacher | spine | Leonardo Alannis |
| *Xeneretmus triacanthus* | Bluespotted Poacher | adult | after Atsuhiro Kubo |
| *Xenomystax atrarius* | Deepwater Conger | adult | Fischer et al. (1995) |
| *Xenomystax atrarius* | Deepwater Conger | head | Leonardo Alannis |
| *Xiphias gladius* | Swordfish | adult | Leonardo Alannis |
| *Xiphister mucosus* | Rock Prickleback | adult | after Laurel Mundy |
| *Xystreurys liolepis* | Fantail Sole | adult | Leonardo Alannis |
| *Zalembius rosaceus* | Pink Seaperch | adult | Leonardo Alannis |
| *Zameus squamulosus* | Velvet Dogfish | adult | after Laurel Mundy |
| *Zaniolepis frenata* | Shortspine Combfish | adult | after Laurel Mundy |
| *Zaniolepis latipinnis* | Longspine Combfish | adult | Laurel Mundy |
| *Zaprora silenus* | Prowfish | adult | Laurel Mundy |
| *Zapteryx exasperata* | Banded Guitarfish | adult | Leonardo Alannis |
| *Zesticelus profundorum* | Flabby Sculpin | adult | Bolin (1944) |
| *Zu cristatus* | Scalloped Ribbonfish | adult | Leonardo Alannis |
| N/A | Unidentified Jawfish | adult | Laurel Mundy |

# INDEX TO SCIENTIFIC AND COMMON NAMES

## A

## INDEX TO SCIENTIFIC AND COMMON NAMES (continued)

# INDEX TO SCIENTIFIC AND COMMON NAMES
(continued)



## C

# INDEX TO SCIENTIFIC AND COMMON NAMES
(continued)

# INDEX TO SCIENTIFIC AND COMMON NAMES
(continued)



## D

## INDEX TO SCIENTIFIC AND COMMON NAMES (continued)



## E

# INDEX TO SCIENTIFIC AND COMMON NAMES (continued)



## F

# INDEX TO SCIENTIFIC AND COMMON NAMES
(continued)

## G

## INDEX TO SCIENTIFIC AND COMMON NAMES (continued)

# INDEX TO SCIENTIFIC AND COMMON NAMES (continued)

## INDEX TO SCIENTIFIC AND COMMON NAMES
(continued)

## INDEX TO SCIENTIFIC AND COMMON NAMES (continued)

## INDEX TO SCIENTIFIC AND COMMON NAMES (continued)



## N

## INDEX TO SCIENTIFIC AND COMMON NAMES
(continued)

# INDEX TO SCIENTIFIC AND COMMON NAMES (continued)

## INDEX TO SCIENTIFIC AND COMMON NAMES (continued)



### Q



### R

## INDEX TO SCIENTIFIC AND COMMON NAMES
(continued)

## INDEX TO SCIENTIFIC AND COMMON NAMES (continued)

## INDEX TO SCIENTIFIC AND COMMON NAMES
(continued)

## INDEX TO SCIENTIFIC AND COMMON NAMES (continued)

# INDEX TO SCIENTIFIC AND COMMON NAMES
(continued)

# INDEX TO SCIENTIFIC AND COMMON NAMES
(continued)

## INDEX TO SCIENTIFIC AND COMMON NAMES
(continued)

## INDEX TO SCIENTIFIC AND COMMON NAMES (continued)

PARK PROUD LA

With its spectacular natural setting adjacent to the Cabrillo Beach Coastal Park in San Pedro, California, Cabrillo Marine Aquarium (CMA) is uniquely suited to its leadership role in marine science education, community engagement, and field research. Since 1935, CMA has provided visitors with both a natural and interactive approach to learning about the marine environment of southern California. The historic Frank Gehry-designed aquarium displays the largest collection of southern California marine life in the world. The mission of the aquarium is to be a trusted resource that inspires exploration, respect, and conservation of southern California marine life.

Cabrillo Marine Aquarium is owned and operated by the City of Los Angeles, Department of Recreation and Parks with support from Friends of CMA (FCMA) 501(c)(3).

Cabrillo Marine Aquarium

Cabrillo Marine Aquarium
3720 Stephen M. White Drive
San Pedro, CA 90731
(310) 548-7562
www.cabrillomarineaquarium.org